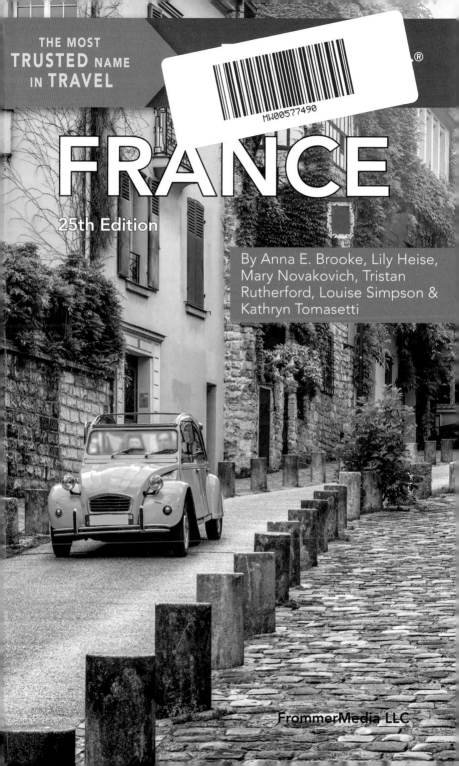

THE MOST
TRUSTED NAME
IN **TRAVEL**

FRANCE

25th Edition

By Anna E. Brooke, Lily Heise,
Mary Novakovich, Tristan
Rutherford, Louise Simpson &
Kathryn Tomasetti

FrommerMedia LLC

Published by:
Frommer Media LLC

Copyright © 2024 by Frommer Media LLC, New York City, New York. All rights reserved. No part of this publication may be reproduced, stored in a retrieval system, or transmitted in any form or by any means, electronic, mechanical, photocopying, recording, scanning or otherwise, except as permitted under Sections 107 or 108 of the 1976 United States Copyright Act, without the prior written permission of the Publisher. Requests to the Publisher for permission should be addressed to Support@FrommerMedia.com.

Frommer's is a registered trademark of Arthur Frommer. Frommer Media LLC is not associated with any product or vendor mentioned in this book.

ISBN 978-1-62887-591-1 (paper), 978-1-62887-592-8 (e-book)

Editorial Director: Pauline Frommer   Cartographer: Andrew Dolan
Editor: Pauline Frommer   Page Compositor: Lissa Auciello-Brogan
Production Editor: Heather Wilcox   Photo Editor: George Olson

For information on our other products or services, see www.frommers.com.

Frommer Media LLC also publishes its books in a variety of electronic formats. Some content that appears in print may not be available in electronic formats.

Manufactured in Malaysia

5 4 3 2 1

HOW TO CONTACT US

In researching this book, we discovered many wonderful places—hotels, restaurants, shops, and more. We're sure you'll find others. Please tell us about them, so we can share the information with your fellow travelers in upcoming editions. If you were disappointed with a recommendation, we'd love to know that, too. Please write to us: Support@FrommerMedia.com

FROMMER'S STAR RATINGS SYSTEM

Every hotel, restaurant and attraction listed in this guide has been ranked for quality and value. Here's what the stars mean:

★ Recommended
★★ Highly Recommended
★★★ A must! Don't miss!

AN IMPORTANT NOTE

The world is a dynamic place. Hotels change ownership, restaurants hike their prices, museums alter their opening hours, and buses and trains change their routings. And all of this can occur in the several months after our authors have visited, inspected, and written about these hotels, restaurants, museums, and transportation services. Though we have made valiant efforts to keep all our information fresh and up-to-date, some few changes can inevitably occur in the periods before a revised edition of this guidebook is published. So please bear with us if a tiny number of the details in this book have changed. Please also note that we have no responsibility or liability for any inaccuracy or errors or omissions, or for inconvenience, loss, damage, or expenses suffered by anyone as a result of assertions in this guide.

CONTENTS

LIST OF MAPS

ABOUT THE AUTHORS

British-born **Anna E. Brooke** moved to Paris in 2000 and hasn't looked back since. She is now a full-fledged bohemian, juggling life between freelance travel writing, songwriting, and authoring children's books. She has written several books for Frommer's and is a France travel expert for the UK's *Times and Sunday Times.*

Lily Heise went to Paris as an exchange student in 2000 and fell in love with the country. She has extensive experience in the travel and culture sectors and contributes to various international and local publications, both in print and online. She lives in Montmartre and spends her free time exploring off-beat Paris, in addition to villages and vineyards around the country.

Mary Novakovich is an award-winning travel writer and journalist based in Hertfordshire, UK. She shares her love of France in publications including the *Times, Telegraph, Guardian, Independent,* and CNN Travel. Her Croatia travelogue, *My Family and Other Enemies,* won the 2023 British Guild of Travel Writers Best Travel Narrative Book Award.

Tristan Rutherford is a seven-time award-winning travel journalist. He contributes to the *Times* in London and the *Wall Street Journal* in New York. His first travel commission took him to Nice, France, where he's been based ever since. His favorite destination is the car-free Lérins islands, a short ferry hop from the Cannes coast.

Louise Simpson fell in love with all things French as a teenager on holidays to her family home in Dordogne and as a French student at Cambridge University. Since moving to Southern France in 2003, she has authored more than 10 print and online travel guides to Southern and Central France and written for the *Daily Telegraph, Financial Times Weekend,* the *Spectator, Independent on Sunday,* and *TimesOnline.* She is also interviewed regularly on TV and radio about life in Southern France. Louise lives in Grasse, France.

Kathryn Tomasetti is an award-winning food and travel writer whose work appears in *Delicious* and the *Guardian.* Picking her favorite French city would be like choosing between her three bilingual children, but she loves Arles for chilled sightseeing, Avignon for historic elegance, and Marseille for its melting-pot cuisine.

ABOUT THE FROMMER TRAVEL GUIDES

For most of the past 65 years, Frommer's has been the leading series of travel guides in North America, accounting for as many as 24% of all guidebooks sold. I think I know why.

Though we hope our books are entertaining, we nevertheless deal with travel in a serious fashion. Our guidebooks have never looked on such journeys as a mere recreation, but as a far more important human function, a time of learning and introspection, an essential part of a civilized life. We stress the culture, lifestyle, history, and beliefs of the destinations we cover, and urge our readers to seek out people and new ideas as the chief rewards of travel.

We have never shied from controversy. We have, from the beginning, encouraged our authors to be intensely judgmental, critical—both pro and con—in their comments, and wholly independent. Our only clients are our readers, and we have triggered the ire of countless prominent sorts, from a tourist newspaper we called "practically worthless" (it unsuccessfully sued us) to the many rip-offs we've condemned.

And because we believe that travel should be available to everyone regardless of their incomes, we have always been cost-conscious at every level of expenditure. Though we have broadened our recommendations beyond the budget category, we insist that every lodging we include be sensibly priced. We use every form of media to assist our readers, and are particularly proud of our feisty daily website, the award-winning Frommers.com.

I have high hopes for the future of Frommer's. May these guidebooks, in all the years ahead, continue to reflect the joy of travel and the freedom that travel represents. May they always pursue a cost-conscious path, so that people of all incomes can enjoy the rewards of travel. And may they create, for both the traveler and the persons among whom we travel, a community of friends, where all human beings live in harmony and peace.

Arthur Frommer

THE BEST OF FRANCE

By Tristan Rutherford & Kathryn Tomasetti

F rance presents visitors with an embarrassment of riches—
you may find yourself overwhelmed by all the choices.
We've tried to make the task easier by compiling a list
of our favorite experiences and discoveries. In the following pages, you'll find the kind of candid travel advice
we'd give our closest friends.

FRANCE'S best AUTHENTIC EXPERIENCES

○ **Buying Your Daily Bread:** That cute little boulangerie just down the street? Depending on where you are, there's likely to be another—or several—a short stroll away. The daily baguette run is a ritual for many French people. Get your coins ready (1€, give or take 10 cen-times) and join the queue. To really fit in, ask for your baguette chewy (*pas trop cuite*) or crusty (*bien cuite*).

○ **Wine Tasting at a Vineyard:** Where better to taste a top French wine than in the vineyard where it was made? Many wineries today offer the opportunity to sample their nectar on site. Either take a trip with a wine expert, or pre-book tastings and tours online. See chapter 20.

○ **Whiling Away an Afternoon in a Parisian Cafe:** There is something quintessentially Parisian about doing nothing in a public space, especially when that space is a cafe. You can read a book, look out the window, chat with a friend, sip some wine, or simply ponder the mysteries of life. Better still, no one will attempt to dislodge you from your cafe chair, even if you sit there for hours. See chapter 4.

○ **Taking a Trip on a *Gabarre* down the Dordogne River** (Dordogne): *Gabarres* are traditional flat-bottomed boats that used to ply the shallow Dordogne, taking goods from one

A *gabarre* floats on the Dordogne River.

town to the next. Today they are used for guided river cruises, offering a unique way to experience this unspoiled waterway. See p. 800.

o **Breaking the Bank at Monte-Carlo:** The **Casino de Monte-Carlo** has been the most opulent place to have a flutter for over 150 years. Its creation by architect Charles Garnier (of Paris Opera House fame) in 1863 transformed Monaco from a provincial port into a world-class destination. See p. 664.

o **Eating *Boeuf Bourgignon:*** Burgundy is as well known for its gastronomy as its wine. One of its most famous dishes is *boeuf bourgignon,* ideally made with Charolais beef (from the famous white cows that originated in the Charolais area near Mâcon) slow cooked with onions and mushrooms in a regional red wine. See chapter 11.

o **Shopping at a Market:** Markets are one of the best ways to explore French towns like a local. We recommend the open-air market in **Arles,** where a colorful line of vendors sells olives, fresh bread, cheese, and local ham underneath the city ramparts, a few blocks from the town's Roman amphitheater. Alternatively, Bordeaux's vast **Marché des Capucins,** a covered market, offers not just good things to take home, but great things to eat on site from various stands, including oysters straight out of nearby Arcachon Bay. See p. 758. And in the Rhône Valley, local gourmands crowd the covered market of Lyon's **Les Halles** to stock up on high-quality Lyonnaise specialties, from creamed fish *quenelles* to sweet *bugnes*—either round and doughnut-like, or flat and crunchy. See p. 470.

o **Strolling along the Seine:** The lifeblood of the City of Light, the Seine is at the center of Paris's history, which becomes obvious when you stroll along its banks. Just about every major monument can be seen from here, including the **Eiffel Tower, Notre-Dame,** and the **Louvre.** And now that many of Seine's embankments have become car-free, promenading along them is a delight. See chapter 4.

undiscovered **FRANCE**

o **Meandering through *Traboules* in Vieux Lyon** (Rhône Valley): Hidden behind brown-painted doorways lie flower-ringed courtyards and vaulted masonry ceilings. You'll discover many architectural gems when you duck into Vieux Lyon's medieval *traboules*—corridors connecting two streets through a building or courtyard. See p. 457.

o **Going Underground at Touraine's Troglodyte Caves:** Admire art, sample regional wine, and even stay the night underground in the Loire's Touraine region, home to France's largest concentration of inhabited Troglodyte caves. See p. 266.

An outdoor antiques market in Nice.

o **Reveling in St-Etienne-du-Mont:** One of the prettiest in Paris, this stunning church that sits atop the highest point in Paris's Latin Quarter is often left off the tourist itinerary. A delightful mix of late-Gothic and Renaissance styles, the church has a 16th-century chancel boasting the city's only rood screen, a magnificent work with decorations inspired by the Italian Renaissance. See p. 121.

o **Peeking at Crypt Murals,** Auxerre (Burgundy): The overused term *hidden gems* is appropriate to describe Auxerre's two crypt murals because that is exactly what they are. Underneath the remains of the **Abbaye Saint-Germain** are a series of religious wall murals dating from the 9th century, the oldest so far found in France. Those at the nearby **Cathédrale Saint-Etienne** go back to the 11th century and are famous for depicting a rare image of Christ on a horse. See p. 428.

o **Hunting for Antiques:** The 18th- and 19th-century French aesthetic was gloriously different from that of England and North America. Many objects bear designs with mythological references to the French experience. France has some 13,000-plus antiques shops and open markets throughout the country. Stop where you see the sign ANTIQUAIRE or BROCANTE.

o **Discovering Secret Beaches between Monaco and Roquebrune-Cap-Martin** (Riviera): The Riviera's rippling coastal path turns up plenty of hidden surprises. Head east out of Monaco, passing the Monte-Carlo Beach Hotel. The trail then meanders along the

Mediterranean shoreline. Aleppo pines and fig trees part to reveal the tiniest turquoise coves. Pack your swimming suit. See p. 672.

o **Exploring the Glamorous Château des Milandes** (Dordogne): This splendid Renaissance castle was the former home of singer/dancer Josephine Baker. Learn about her fascinating life and visit rooms furnished as they were when she lived there, then take a stroll in the gardens. See p. 800.

o **Rambling the Sentier des Ocres de Roussillon** (Provence): Located in the heart of the Luberon, Roussillon once possessed some of the world's most important ochre quarries. Today this landscape is just as brilliantly hued and can be explored via a picturesque hiking trail. See p. 537.

FRANCE'S best FREE THINGS TO DO

o **Visiting a Municipal Museum:** Paris has 14 municipal museums and you won't pay a cent to get into their permanent collections. This includes the **Musée d'Art Moderne (MAM),** the **Petit Palais,** the **Maison de Victor Hugo,** and the **Musée Zadkine.** Head to the city of Dijon and almost all of the museums are owned by the city and thus free to enter.

One of the treasures at the Dijon's spectacular Musée des Beaux Arts.

o **Reveling in the Tour de France:** Join the party in one of the 150 or so municipalities along the route. Each town puts on festivities, and sponsors hand out lots of free swag to the crowds. See p. 65.

o **Getting Festive at Medieval Fairs** (Normandy): The Middle Ages come to life in the summer as many of Normandy's picturesque towns put on lively medieval festivals. The biggest and most spectacular of the region's medieval fairs is in Bayeux every July. Costumed performers fill the streets alongside market stalls, medieval games for kids, and colorful jousters. See p. 305.

A jester entertains the festival crowd in Bayeux.

o **Ogling the Orchids in Lyon** (Rhône Valley): Housed within the grounds of France's largest city-based public park, Lyon's Botanical Garden is completely free. One may explore over 6,000 plants ranging from orchids to cacti and carnivorous flowers. You'll also find deer wandering freely around the surrounding Parc de la Tête d'Or with its broad tree-lined avenues and lakeside setting. See p. 461.

o **Photographing Provence's Fields of Lavender:** Sure, we've all seen those shots of iridescent Provençal hills cloaked with purple lavender. But it's another thing entirely to get out and experience these stunning—and fragrant—fields in person. Lavender's peak blooming season is usually between mid-June and mid-July; the area around Plateau de Valensole is particularly vibrant. See chapter 14.

FRANCE'S best MUSEUMS

o **The Louvre** (Paris): Set in the whopper former royal palace, the most famous museum in the world has no less than 400 rooms and 35,000 artworks. Not sure where to start? Hit the Denon wing and you'll see three of its most iconic works—the *Mona Lisa,* the *Raft of the Medusa,* and the *Victory of Samothrace*—then everything else will be a happy bonus. See p. 85.

o **Picasso-Paris:** In a glorious 17th-century mansion, this is the place to see many of Picasso's most famous works—from the 1911 Cubist *Man with a Guitar* to his 1930 *Crucifixion* masterpiece. The museum's rooftop café is a lovely spot for a quick coffee. See p. 96.

- **Musée de Grenoble** (the French Alps): Founded in 1796, this is one of the country's oldest art museums. It was the first French museum outside of Paris to focus on modern art, and features an extensive collection of Impressionist and post-Impressionist paintings by Monet, Gauguin, Bonnard, among others. See p. 504.

- **Musée National de Porcelaine Adrien-Dubouché,** Limoges: There's nothing niche about this glorious porcelain museum—the largest in the world (in a city renowned for its arts and crafts), with wonderful displays following the history of ceramics through the ages. The shop is a great spot for a classy souvenir. See p. 812.

- **Cité du Vin** (Bordeaux): The designers of this cleverly constructed museum would say it's more a cross between a cultural space, a gallery, and a theme park, with interactive exhibits showcasing the entire world of wine. Cafes, a restaurant, and a panoramic bar (where wine tastings are held) complete the picture. See p. 754.

- **Musée Fabre,** Montpellier (Occitanie): Trace the evolution of art from the Renaissance to the 20th century, including works by Rubens, Delacroix, Courbet and Maillol, while touring the vast galleries of this elegant 18th-century mansion. See p. 690.

- **Musée des Confluences,** Lyon (Rhône Valley): Designed by Austrian architects Coop Himmelb(l)au, this ethnology museum charts

Visitors view the exhibits at the highly interactive Cité du Vin.

the universe and our place in it, from the Big Bang and various species on earth—now and in the past—to the meaning of life. See p. 461.

o **Chapelle du Rosaire,** Vence (Riviera): A three-dimensional artwork in its own right, this bright and sunny chapel, with its colorful stained-glass windows, was designed by Henri Matisse and completed in 1951. See p. 627.

FRANCE'S best HISTORIC SIGHTS & ATTRACTIONS

o **France's "Stonehenge"** (Brittany): The seaside resort of Carnac is home to the largest megalithic site in the world. A visit might not answer how these massive stones got turned upright, but it will certainly leave you pondering the mysteries and theories surrounding this curious site. See p. 342.

o **Go underground above ground in Marseille** (Provence): Opened in 2022, **Cosquer Méditerranée** is a near exact replica of a 20,000-year-old cave, complete with ancient drawings and handprints. This spellbinding site was discovered 30 years ago in nearby Cassis. See p. 563.

o **Ancient Rome in Nîmes** (Occitanie): After visiting the spectacular ancient Roman sites in and around Nîmes, dig deep into the era at the sleek contemporary **Musée de la Romanité,** which displays archeological finds, artwork and interactive displays. See p. 684.

Nîmes is home to one of the best-preserved Roman amphitheaters in Europe.

○ **Crusades in Carcassonne** (Occitanie): Carcassonne was built for war with its fortifications, imposing citadel, and double ring of defensive walls. But even its massive towers didn't keep it safe from conquest and re-conquest during the endless feuds of catholic vs heretics and medieval power politics. Its inevitable decline was reversed in the 19th century with a massive restoration, and today Carcassonne is one of the great sites of Europe. See p. 704.

○ **Tracing the Trenches:** While Normandy usually attracts most visitors interested in war history, the western front of World War I carved its way through Eastern France. Many moving battlefield sites and memorials are located near Verdun. See p. 411.

○ **Normandy's D-Day Beaches:** On June 6, 1944, the largest armada ever assembled departed on rough seas and in dense fog from southern England. For about a week, the future of the civilized world teetered between the Nazi and Allied armies. It's easy to immerse oneself in the past with superb interactive exhibits, such as the personal tales detailed at the **Normandy American Cemetery.** Also a highlight: **Le Mémorial de Caen,** which gives a thorough (and heart-wrenching) account of 20th-century history, from WWI to the Cold War and beyond. See chapter 7.

○ **All of France's History at Musée d'Unterlinden,** Colmar (Alsace): Traverse France's 7,000 years of history at Alsace's most visited museum, housed in a Medieval convent, a former public bathhouse, and new structures designed by renowned contemporary architects Herzog and de Meuron. See p. 397.

FRANCE'S best ARCHITECTURAL LANDMARKS

○ **Eiffel Tower** (Paris): When the tower opened in 1889 for the World Fair, it was the tallest building in the world at 311m (1,024 ft.). Today, it's just the tallest building in Paris, but its statistics are still impressive: 1,665 stairs, 18,000 pieces of iron bolted by 2.5 million rivets, and 20,000 lightbulbs. Make sure you book an advance ticket to avoid never-ending lines. See p. 125.

○ **Palace of Versailles,** Versailles: "Baroque grandeur" sums up Louis XIV's beautiful behemoth—a sprawling 2,300-room palace, dripping in sculpture, and frescos, and enough shiny gilding to give the sun a run for its money. You'll easily need a whole day to visit the palace and its equally as impressive gardens. See p. 191.

○ **Hôtel-Dieu des Hospices Civil de Beaune** (Burgundy): This hospital is a must-see for its 15th-century, flamboyant Gothic architecture, which includes one of France's finest examples of Burgundian polychrome roof tiling. See p. 442.

Interior of the Royal Monastery of Brou.

- **Notre-Dame de Paris** (Paris): The history of Paris is inseparable from the iconic Gothic cathedral (consecrated in 1189). Kings were crowned here, Napoleon was coroneted emperor here; not even the Revolution, or a humongous blaze in 2019, could bring it down. See p. 81.

- **Royal Monastery of Brou,** Bourg-en-Bresse (Rhône Valley): A Gothic mausoleum of gargantuan proportions, this monastery was constructed during the 16th century. Don't miss the secret passageway between the monastery and the nearby chapel. See p. 473.

- **Rocher de la Vierge,** Biarritz (the Basque Country): From the Port des Pêcheurs, cross the Eiffel-designed footbridge to reach Rocher de la Vierge a rocky islet that offers the most dramatic walk in Biarritz. As the surf crashes on both sides, take in the views of the city as well as the Spanish Basque mountains. See p. 737.

- **La Rochelle's towers** (the Atlantic Coast): Dating from the 14th and 15th centuries, the three stone towers that were built to guard La Rochelle's harbor—Tour de la Chaîne, Tour St-Nicolas and Tour de la Lanterne—are a vital part of the city's long history. All three offer fantastic views as well as fascinating exhibits. See p. 776.

- **Palais de l'Île,** Annecy (the French Alps): This is the town's most potent and most frequently photographed symbol. Built before the 18th century and connected to the "mainland" of Annecy via a bridge, it resembles a miniature château, surrounded by water, despite its long-term use as a prison. See p. 498.

o **Château de Chambord,** near Blois (Loire): Designed as the not-so-modest hunting lodge of King François I, this Renaissance masterpiece is France's second most visited castle after Versailles. See p. 238.

o **Pont du Gard,** near Nîmes (Occitanie): Marvel at ancient Roman engineering while gazing up at this incredibly well-preserved aqueduct bridge. It was built during the 1st century and crosses the Gardon River. See p. 684.

o **Cathédrale Notre-Dame de Strasbourg** (Alsace): One of France's finest Gothic churches, this unmissable site in the Alsatian capital boasts an ornately decorated facade, delicate stained glass and the tallest tower from Medieval times. See p. 382.

o **Trophée des Alps,** La Turbie (Riviera): Still partially intact and an imposing hilltop sight, this monument was created in a celebration of local Roman victories. It was installed by Emperor Augustus in 6 B.C. See p. 658.

o **Palais des Papes,** Avignon (Provence): Those medieval popes knew a thing or two about interior design. Avignon's **Palais des Papes,** or Pope's Palace, is a moneyed medley of Gothic architecture and vast banqueting halls. Another reason to go: Châteauneuf-du-Pape papal vineyards, just north of Avignon, still produce some of the most luscious wine in France. See p. 523.

o **Hôtels Particuliers,** Dijon (Burgundy): Dijon has more than 100 town houses built for wealthy families between the 15th and 18th centuries. Some of the finest examples can be seen on rue des Forges, including **Hôtel Chambellan** (no. 34) and the ornately decorated **Maison Maillard** (no. 38), both of whose courtyards can be visited for free (enter via the open passageways). See chapter 11.

FRANCE'S best ROAD TRIPS

o **The Routes Touristiques du Champagne** (Champagne Country): Wind your way through the back roads and villages of Champagne along this 70km (45-mile) drive. In addition to hillside vineyards, woods, and Marne River views, you'll pass dozens of independent Champagne houses, some—like **Champagne Telmont** in Damery (p. 365)—open for drop-in tastings. In addition, the south of the Champagne region has some little-known gems that will delight art lovers. The **Musée d'Art Moderne** in Troyes, housed in an atmospheric former bishops' palace, has an exquisite collection of modern art from 1850–1960. In this area, art lovers should also seek out **Auguste Renoir's family home** in Essoyes, and the **Musée Camille Claudel** in Nogent-sur-Seine, which celebrates the talent of Auguste Rodin's student and lover. See p. 375.

- **Touring the Villages along France's Oldest "Wine Road"** (Alsace-Lorraine): More than 60 villages line the famous Alsatian wine road. Enjoy their medieval town squares and half-timbered houses while stopping in at the local vineyards. If you've done the wine road, head uphill along la Route des Crêtes for the best panoramic views of the valley and the Vosges mountains beyond. See chapter 10.

- **Chateau-Hopping through the Loire Valley:** Road trips to the chateaux dotting the valley's rich fields and forests are an enjoyable crash course in French Renaissance architectural aesthetics and the intrigues of the kings and their courts. The Loire isn't just palaces, you'll also enjoy winery tours, strolls through magnificent churches and one of the largest monasteries in Europe (Abbey of Fontevraud, also the final resting place of most of the Plantagenets), and more. See chapter 6.

Ruf de Crêtes.

- **A Water Path: Cruising France's rivers:** Floating slowly down one of France's major rivers is a superb way to see hidden corners of the countryside. Most luxury barge cruises offer daily excursions, elegant dinners on deck, and bicycles for solitary exploration. See chapter 20.

FRANCE'S best ACTIVE ADVENTURES

- **Cycling in the Countryside:** The country that hosts the Tour de France offers thousands of options for bike trips, all of them ideal for leaving the crowds behind. You're even welcome to take your bike aboard most trains in France, free of charge. For cycling through Provence's vineyards and past pretty hilltop villages, Vélo Loisir Provence has marked hundreds of kilometers of bike routes throughout the region's vineyards and lavender fields. In Bordeaux, over 200km (125 miles) of cycling routes around Arcachon Bay take you through beaches, oyster villages, and pine forests, with over 35 places to rent bikes along the way. There are also spectacular cycling trails in the Loire Valley, Occitanie, and a number of other regions.

- **A surf lesson in Anglet, St-Jean-de-Luz, or Biarritz:** The beaches as you head down towards the Spanish border offer brilliant surfing opportunities. Be careful: The waves and currents of the Atlantic can be strong. See p. 738.

- **Skiing Chamonix** (the French Alps): The place where skiing came to the masses—and French skiing came to the world, during the 1924 Winter Olympics. More affordable than nearby Megève or Courchevel, this is the people's ski resort and a party town. See p. 513.

- **Kayaking to Calanque d'En Vau** (Provence): In the heart of Parc National des Calanques, Calanque d'En Vau wouldn't look out of place in the tropics, thanks to its ice-white pebbly sands and transparent turquoise waters. Set at the base of limestone cliffs, it's accessible by kayak, boat or a very treacherous hike. See p. 575.

- **Joining the Cowboys in the Camargue** (Provence): Riding a sturdy Camarguais horse and with a local cowboy to guide you, make your way through the marshes of these beautiful, remote wetlands. Spot pink flamingos and watch the *gardians* with their large felt hats rounding up black bulls bred for the bullrings of the south. See p. 548.

- **Self-Drive a Barge on a Canal** (Burgundy): Burgundy has France's largest network of waterways. As well as the navigable rivers of the Yonne, Saône, and Seille, seven canals were built between the 17th and 19th centuries to link the rivers Seine, Loire, and Rhône. Hire your own boat for an adventure that will take you to and past châteaux and vineyards, going through tunnels, over aqueducts, and up or down staircase locks. See chapter 11. (We're also big fans of the historic Canal du Midi in Occitanie for barging; see p. 703.)

- **Hiking the Caps** (Riviera): The Riviera's *sentier du littoral* is an almost continuous coastal footpath that winds its way along the country's seductive southern shores. Leave the coastal hubbub behind and spend a day—or longer—wandering between the wealthy private mansions and the sparkling sea on Cap Ferrat or Cap d'Antibes. See chapter 15.

- **Beachcombing in Brittany:** The whole of the Breton coastline makes for phenomenal touring. Hike or bike from the northern Emerald coast with its sparkling waters to the

A skier glides through the powder of Chamonix.

wilder western seaboard with its rocky bays and Atlantic waves. See chapter 8.

FRANCE'S best FOR FAMILIES

o **Getting Medieval in the Hilltop Town of Les Baux** (Provence): The age-old fortified hill town of **Les Baux** includes the hilltop ruins of a "ghost village." Kids will love its car-free medieval streets and awesome views, not to mention the daily display of a siege engine catapult. See p. 541.

o **Visiting Lascaux IV** (Dordogne): This replica of France's famous caves, with their prehistoric drawings (no longer open to the public) uses a range of digital technology (including a very clever tablet guide) to take visitors back 20,000 years. It is particularly good for children—and afterwards you can take them to nearby Le Thot Zoo to see live animals like those on the Lascaux walls. See p. 792.

o **Climbing the Heights of Mont-St-Michel** (Normandy): Straddling the tidal flats between Normandy and Brittany, this Gothic marvel is the most spectacular fortified island in northern Europe. Crowned by its abbey and said to be protected by the archangel Michael, much of it stands as it did during the 1200s—though with the addition of many more tourists. A beach is below. See chapter 7.

o **Kid-Friendly Modern Art in Antibes** (Riviera): The **Musée Picasso** (Picasso Museum) in Antibes highlights some of the most accessible art in France. The Spanish painter set up shop in the atmospheric Château Grimaldi and in such relaxed surroundings, children can appreciate the color, vibrancy, and playfulness that made Picasso incomparable. The far-out sculptures and sunny views of the surrounding coastline will please non-art fans, too. See p. 616.

o **Getting a Chocolate Education** (Rhône Valley): All five senses are used in the interactive exhibits that entertain little ones with the rich experience of chocolate making and tasting at **La Cité du Chocolat.** See p. 483.

o **Walking through a Real Fairy Tale** (Loire): The whole region of the Loire offers kids the chance to live out their fairy-tale fantasies, but it was **Château d'Ussé** that served as the inspiration for "Sleeping Beauty." See p. 271.

o **Playing in the Jardin des Plantes** (Paris): This historic botanical garden is a quiet oasis in the Latin Quarter, where families can relax and tiny travelers can enjoy the playground, hothouses, and green spaces. It also has a small zoo and natural-history museum. See p. 118.

o **Getting Nerdy at Cité des Sciences et de l'Industrie** (Paris): This huge museum of science and industry includes a planetarium, an

Children run on the beach in front of Mont-St-Michel.

Imax theater, and even an authentic 1950s submarine that kids can climb into. But the biggest draw is the Cité des Enfants, a supremely kid-friendly collection of hands-on exhibits and displays. See p. 116.

o **Hameau Duboeuf,** Romanèche-Thorins (Burgundy): A "wine hamlet," created by wine merchant Georges Duboeuf in the Beaujolais wine area, teaches the history of this particular drink in a very child friendly way (no samples for tots, don't worry). Kids will love "flying" over the Mâconnais countryside and playing crazy golf, while adults can enjoy a tasting or two. See p. 478.

o **Pioneering à la Francaise,** Ungersheim (Alsace): Enter a rebuilt historic Alsatian hamlet at the **Ecomuseum** near Colmar. Kids will adore the horse-and-cart ride and observing the costumed "villagers" at work. See p. 402.

FRANCE'S best RESTAURANTS

o **Tour d'Argent** (Paris): There aren't many restaurants where you can both savor an exquisite meal and eat it in a place where Henri III and IV are said to have dined. Set atop a Seine-side "tower," with sweeping views over the Seine onto Notre-Dame, the Tour d'Argent has been open since the 16th century and has fed everyone from Czars to aristocrats and the literati. Now it's your turn. See p. 162.

- **Les Beaux Mets,** Marseille (Provence): Shock your friends by sharing that you dined in France's toughest prison—and that its menu is prepared under the guidance of a Michelin-trained chef. This brand-new gourmet outpost (yes, inside a maximum-security jail) rehabilitates prisoners while offering Marseille's best value lunch. See p. 569.

- **La Couronne,** Rouen (Normandy): Julia Child enjoyed her first-ever French meal at this traditional Norman restaurant. A bustling *auberge* in business for more than 6 centuries—and pulling in plenty of celebrity diners along the way—La Couronne makes the most of this region's hearty produce, from *côte de boeuf* (rib steak) to aged Camembert cheeses. See p. 286.

- **Le Louis XV,** Monaco (Riviera): Superchef Alain Ducasse oversees this iconic restaurant—regularly rated as one of the finest in the world—located in Monte-Carlo's Hôtel de Paris. See p. 670.

- **Café de la Table Ronde,** Grenoble (the French Alps): Founded in 1739, this is the second oldest cafe in France; only the well-touted Procope in Paris is older. The delicious fondue Savoyarde is the epitome of French alpine cuisine. See p. 506.

- **Fleur de Loire,** Blois (Loire): Hay transforms the best ingredients of the Loire, including some from his own garden, into exquisite creations. This new restaurant has a superb location, overlooking the Château de Blois, in a 17th-century hospice. See p. 237.

- **Auberge de l'Ill,** north of Colmar (Alsace): For over 100 years the Haeberlin family have tempted gastronomes to their exceptional restaurant. The menu shines with dishes like fillet of venison coated with grilled buckwheat and herb Kasknepfla. See p. 400.

- **Chez Yvonne,** Strasbourg (Alsace): Sink your teeth into some of the region's best sausage and choucroute at this charming *winstub,* a favorite with the locals since 1873. See p. 386.

- **Michel Sarran,** Toulouse (Occitanie): For almost 30 years chef Michel Sarran has been concocting some of France's best fusion cuisine. Pushing boundaries, or rather borders, his salmon is served with curry and his saddle of rabbit is paired with regional Lucques olives, and Provencal *pissaladière.* See p. 722.

- **Pressoir d'Argent,** Bordeaux (Bordeaux): One of the best restaurants in a city that is increasingly packed full of great places to eat, the Pressoir d'Argent is overseen by Gordon Ramsay and has a brilliant wine list that goes way beyond simply Bordeaux. See p. 757.

- **Auberge du Père-Bise,** Talloires (the French Alps): Helmed by Jean Sulpice, who received two Michelin stars at his Val Thorens restaurant, here diners enjoy their meals from the picturesque shore of Lake Annecy. See p. 501.

Rouen's La Couronne.

- **L'Assiette Champenoise,** Reims (Champagne Country): This restaurant was voted 2nd best restaurant in the world by La Liste. 'Nuf said. See p. 363.

- **Maison Lameloise,** Chagny (Burgundy): Burgundian cuisine with a Modern French touch, plus you're dining in a restaurant set in the heart of the vineyards. See p. 446.

- **Régis et Jacques Marcon** (Rhône Valley): On a plateau overlooking the Mézenc hills, this restaurant abounds in local flavors such as Puy lentils, chestnuts, and mushrooms grown in the nearby pinewoods. Along with the restaurant is a village empire that now includes a cooking school, bakery, hotel and spa. See p. 489.

- **Oustau de Baumanière,** Les Baux (Provence): The cinematic setting of the ancient fortress of Les Baux had troubadours singing in its streets during the Middle Ages. Today it is no less romantic. Several picturesque hideaways are tucked into the hills surrounding the village, including this gem housed in a 16th-century farmhouse. See p. 543.

FRANCE'S best HOTELS

- **Relais St-Germain** (Paris): A luxurious mix of past and present makes this hotel a romantic and modern haven, just steps from the bustle of Boulevard St-Germain. Run by the same management as the famous restaurant Le Comptoir du Relais (downstairs), this beautiful spot makes the perfect gourmet getaway. See p. 145.

- **Le Manoir Les Minimes,** Amboise (Loire): Regional charm and character shine through at this reasonably priced manor, a perfect base for exploring the château country. Some rooms offer glimpses of the royal château of Amboise. See p. 246.

- **Le Grand Hôtel des Thermes,** St-Malo (Brittany): Relive the era of grand Victorian seaside resorts at one of the period's finest hotels. This luxurious hotel-spa features an innovative thalassotherapy center, gourmet dining facilities, and sweeping views of the sea and St-Malo's rooftops and ramparts. See p. 324.

o **Cour du Corbeau,** Strasbourg (Alsace): One of the oldest hotels in France, this 17th-century inn combines the historic character of thick wooden beams and sainted-glass windows with stylish contemporary furnishings and amenities. See p. 385.

o **Hôtel de la Cité,** Carcassonne (Languedoc-Roussillon): Wood paneling, friezes, and four-poster beds take you back to this hotel's origins as the bishop's palace. But there's also a heated pool, a top restaurant, and every 21st-century mod con. See p. 706.

o **Clos 1906,** St-Emilion (Bordeaux): Choose one of four beautiful guest rooms or a fully equipped apartment in this 18th-century manor house. When you're not relaxing in the pool in the landscaped gardens, you can browse the hotel's own antiques shop. See p. 761.

o **Hotel de Bouilhac,** Montignac (Dordogne): Not just lovely, but a great value too. This hotel is located near the new Lascaux caves exhibition. See p. 793.

o **Hôtel Parc Beaumont,** Pau (the Basque Country): Some of Pau's best accommodation, with good-sized beds, balconies, and beautiful views over the park. The hotel's Jeu de Paume restaurant is particularly recommended. See p. 729.

o **Hotel Le Normandy,** Deauville (Normandy): This legendary hotel, built in 1912, is a giant fairy-tale concoction that overlooks the seafront. See p. 295.

Hotel Le Normandy in Deauville.

- **Le Strato,** Courchevel (the French Alps): It's not rare for guests to arrive by private helicopter at this uber-luxurious hotel, right beside the ski slopes and part of Courchevel 1850. See p. 509.

- **Le Champ des Oiseaux,** Troyes (Champagne Country): Step back into the middle ages at this half-timbered hotel which has been elegantly renovated by master craftsmen. See p. 373.

- **Château de Bagnols** (Rhône Valley): Surrounded by Beaujolais vineyards, this fairy-tale Renaissance castle comes complete with a drawbridge, moat, fortifications, extensive formal gardens, and a spa. See p. 477.

- **Maisons du Mondes,** Marseille (Provence): Forget chain hotels. Here 16 apartment-suites are stuffed with funky objets d'arts and are totally individual. It's also slap bang on the Vieux Port. See p. 567.

- **Anantara Plaza,** Nice (Riviera): Nice's newest and hippest hotel looks like a spaceship has landed on top of a historic town house. The rooftop (awesome bar, epic dining) has a fabulous sea view. Achingly cool yet incredibly friendly. See p. 640.

FRANCE'S best BEACHES

- **Plage de Deauville** (Normandy): Coco Chanel used the chic resort of Deauville to propel herself to stardom and then added greatly to the town's sense of glamour. Revel in the sun-kissed sense of style and nostalgia with a stroll along the elegant Les Planches boardwalk, which skirts the edge of Deauville's silky, sandy, parasol-dotted *plage* for 2km (1¼ miles). See p. 294.

- **Plage de Pampelonne** (St-Tropez, Riviera): Anyone can feel like Brigitte Bardot in sunny St-Tropez. And the scantily clad satyrs and nymphs splashing in the surf at Plage de Pampelonne can perk up the most sluggish libido. The real miracle here is that the charm of this 5km (3-mile) crescent of white sand still manages to impress, despite the hype. See p. 586.

- **Paloma Plage** (Cap Ferrat, Riviera): Tucked into one of Cap Ferrat's sheltered bays, petite Paloma Plage is part chic beach club and part family-friendly stretch of pebbly shoreline. In the afternoon, fragrant Aleppo pines shade much of the beach. See p. 650.

- **Plage de Arromanches-les-Bains** (Normandy): This immense beach is dotted with the mammoth, otherworldly remains of Winston, a prefabricated port essential for the D-day landings. At low tide, the sandy expanse is firm (you can push a stroller or cycle along it!) and truly vast, rendering it ever-popular with families. See p. 312.

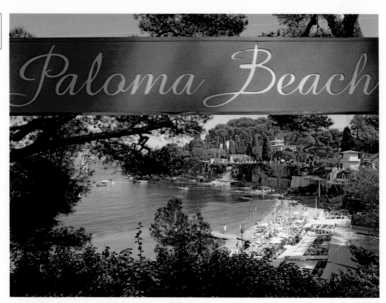

Paloma Beach in Cap Ferrat.

○ **Plages de Dinard** (Brittany): The poshest *plage* along Brittany's Emerald coast, this historic seaside resort features 10 easy-access beaches, the best being la plage du Prieuré. See p. 328.

○ **Plage des Grand-Sables** (Brittany): Gorgeous beaches line the wild coast of Quiberon peninsula near Carnac. Take the ferry out to Belle-Ile and set your towel down on the nice sandy beach of Grand-Sables. The tropical waters will make you doubt you're in France. See p. 343.

SUGGESTED ITINERARIES

By Tristan Rutherford & Kathryn Tomasetti

2

W hen the Frommer's guidebooks were first launched, founder Arthur Frommer cautioned his readers, "You can get lost in France." It's still an apt warning—and promise—today. For those with unlimited time, one of the world's great pleasures is getting "lost" in France, wandering at random, making new discoveries off the beaten path. Few of us have this luxury, however, and so here we present 1- and 2-week itineraries to help you make the most of your time.

France is so treasure-filled that you could barely do more than skim the surface in a week. So relax and savor Paris, Mont-St-Michel, Chardonnay, or Cannes—among other alluring destinations—saving the rest for another day. You might also review chapter 1, "The Best of France," to find out what experiences or sights have special appeal and then adjust your itineraries to suit your particular travel plans.

The itineraries that follow take you to some major attractions and some charming off-the-beaten-track towns. The pace may be a bit breathless for some visitors, so feel free to skip a town or sight if you'd like to give yourself some chill-out time. You're on vacation, after all. Of course, you might also use these itineraries merely as a jumping-off point to develop your own custom-made trip.

THE REGIONS IN BRIEF

Although France's 547,030 sq. km (211,209 sq. miles) make it slightly smaller than the American state of Texas, no other country has such a diversity of sights and scenery in such a compact area. A visitor can travel through the north's flat, fertile lands; the Loire Valley's green hills; the east's Alpine ranges; the Pyrénées; and the southeast's Mediterranean coast. Even more noteworthy are the cultural and historical differences of each region.

Destinations in France are within easy reach from Paris and each other. **French National Railroads (SNCF)** offers fast service to and from Paris. For example, the highlights of Normandy and the Loire Valley (the château country) are just 1 or 2 hours from Paris by train. You can travel from Paris to Cannes on the Riviera in 5 hours—or fly down in 45 minutes.

You can motor along nearly 71,000km (about 44,020 miles) of French roads, including a good number of well-maintained superhighways. But do your best to drive the secondary roads too: Nearly all of France's scenic splendors are along these routes.

A "grand tour" of France is nearly impossible for the visitor who doesn't have a lifetime to explore. If you want to get to know a province, try to devote at least a week to a specific region. Note that you'll probably have a more rewarding trip if you concentrate on getting to know two or three areas at a leisurely pace rather than racing around trying to see everything! To help you decide where to spend your time, we've summarized the highlights of each region for you.

PARIS & ILE DE FRANCE   The Ile de France is an island only in the sense that rivers—with odd-sounding names such as Essonne, Epte, Aisne, Eure, and Ourcq—and a handful of canals delineate its boundaries (about an 81km/50-mile radius from the center of Paris). France was born in this temperate basin, where the attractions include **Paris, Versailles, Fontainebleau, Notre-Dame de Chartres,** and **Giverny.** Despite industrialization (and Disneyland Paris), many pockets of charm remain, including the forests of Rambouillet and Fontainebleau, and the artists' hamlet of Barbizon. For more information, see chapters 4 and 5.

THE LOIRE VALLEY   This area includes two ancient provinces, Touraine (centered on **Tours**) and Anjou (centered on **Angers**). It was beloved by

Château de Sully-sur-Loire, Loire Valley.

royalty and nobility, flourishing during the Renaissance until Henry IV moved his court to Paris. Head here to see the most magnificent castles in France. Irrigated by the Loire River and its many tributaries, the valley produces many superb wines. For more information, see chapter 6.

NORMANDY   This region will forever be linked to the 1944 D-day invasion. Some readers consider a visit to the D-day beaches the most emotionally worthwhile part of their trip. Normandy boasts 599km (371 miles) of coastline and a maritime tradition. It's a popular weekend getaway from Paris, and many hotels and restaurants thrive here, especially around the casino town of **Deauville.** Normandy's great attractions include **Rouen**'s cathedral, medieval **Bayeux,** the fishing village of **Honfleur,** and the abbey at **Mont St-Michel.** For more information, see chapter 7.

BRITTANY   Jutting into the Atlantic, the westernmost region of France is known for its rocky coastlines, Celtic roots, frequent rain, and ancient dialect, akin to the Gaelic tongues of Wales and Ireland. Many French vacationers love the seacoast (rivaled only by the Côte d'Azur) for its sandy beaches, cliffs, and relatively modest—by French standards—prices. **Quimper** is Brittany's cultural capital, whereas **Carnac** is home to ancient Celtic dolmens and burial mounds. For more information, see chapter 8.

CHAMPAGNE COUNTRY   Every French monarch since A.D. 496 was crowned at **Reims,** and much of French history is linked with this holy site. In the path of any invader wishing to occupy Paris, Reims and the Champagne district have seen much bloodshed, including the World War I battles of the Somme and the Marne. Industrial sites sit among patches of forest, and vineyards sheath the steep sides of valleys. The 126km (78-mile) road from Reims to Vertus, one of the **Routes du Champagne,** takes in a trio of winegrowing regions that produce 80% of the world's bubbly. For more information, see chapter 9.

BURGUNDY   Few trips will prove as rewarding as several leisurely days spent exploring Burgundy, with its splendid old cities such as **Dijon.** Besides its famous cuisine (*boeuf* and *escargots à la bourguignonne*), the district contains, along its Côte d'Or, hamlets whose names (Mercurey, Beaune, Puligny-Montrachet, Vougeot, and Nuits-St-Georges) are synonymous with great wine. For more information, see chapter 11.

ALSACE-LORRAINE   Between Germany and the forests of the Vosges is the most Teutonic of France's provinces: Alsace, with cosmopolitan **Strasbourg** as its capital. Celebrated for its cuisine, particularly its *foie gras* and *choucroute,* this area is home to villages with half-timbered designs and the oldest wine road in France. Lorraine, birthplace of Joan of Arc, witnessed many battles during the world wars, though its capital

Village of Vergisson surrounded by vineyards, Burgundy.

Nancy, remains elegant and holds the beautiful place Stanislas. The much-eroded peaks of the Vosges forest, the closest thing to a wilderness in France, offer lovely hiking. For more information, see chapter 10.

THE FRENCH ALPS   This area's resorts rival those of neighboring Switzerland and contain incredible scenery: snowcapped peaks, glaciers, and Alpine lakes. **Chamonix** is a famous ski resort facing **Mont Blanc,** western Europe's highest mountain. **Courchevel** and **Megève** are chicer. During the summer, you can enjoy such spa resorts as **Evian** and the restful 19th-century resorts ringing **Lake Geneva.** For more information, see chapter 13.

THE RHÔNE VALLEY   This fertile area in eastern France follows the curves of the River Rhône from Beaujolais wine country in the north towards the borders of Provence in the south. The district is thoroughly French, unflinchingly bourgeois, and dedicated to preserving the gastronomic and cultural traditions that have produced some of the most celebrated chefs in France. Only 2 hours by train from Paris, the region's cultural centerpiece, **Lyon,** is France's "second city." Wine lovers will enjoy contrasting the aromatic red wines of **Beaujolais** with the robust red wines of the Northern Rhône or mythical appellations such as Côte

Mont Blanc reflected in Cheserys Lake, French Alps.

Rôtie and Hermitage. Gourmands should travel to **Valence** to dine with France's only three-Michelin-starred female chef or to Bresse's ancient capital, **Bourg-en-Bresse,** which produces the world's finest poultry. Try to visit the medieval villages of **Pérouges** and **Vienne,** 27km (17 miles) south of Lyon; the latter is known for its Roman ruins. For more information, see chapter 12.

OCCITANIE Occitanie is the new name given to the region known before 2016 as Languedoc and Roussillon. It may not be as chic as Provence, but it's less frenetic and more affordable. We'd also say it's the rock-strewn French answer to Catalonia, just across the Spanish border. Also appealing are **Toulouse,** the bustling pink capital of the region; and the "red city" of **Albi,** birthplace of Toulouse-Lautrec. **Carcassonne,** a magnificent walled city with fortifications, begun around A.D. 500, is Occitanie's highlight. For more information, see chapter 16.

PROVENCE One of France's most popular destinations stretches from the southern Rhône River to the French Riviera. Long frequented by starving artists, *la bourgeoisie,* and the downright rich and famous, its premier cities are **Aix-en-Provence,** associated with Cézanne; **Arles,** famous for bullfighting and Van Gogh; **Avignon,** the 14th-century capital of Christendom; and **Marseille,** a port city established by the Phoenicians that today is the melting pot of France. Quieter and more romantic are villages such as **St-Rémy-de-Provence, Les Baux,** and **Gordes.** To the west, the **Camargue** is the marshy delta formed by two arms of the Rhône River. Rich in bird life, it's famous for its grassy flats and such fortified medieval sites as **Aigues-Mortes.** For more information, see chapter 14.

THE FRENCH RIVIERA (CÔTE D'AZUR)   The resorts of the fabled Côte d'Azur (Azure Coast) still evoke glamour: **Cannes, St-Tropez, Cap d'Antibes,** and **Juan-les-Pins.** July and August are the most buzzing months, while spring and fall are still sunny but way more laid-back. **Nice** is the biggest city and most convenient base for exploring the area. The Principality of **Monaco** only occupies about 2 sq. km (¾ sq. mile) but has enough sights, restaurants, and opulence to go around. Along the coast are some sandy beaches, but many are pebbly. Topless bathing is common, especially in St-Tropez, and some of the restaurants are citadels of conspicuous consumption. Dozens of artists and their patrons have littered the landscape with world-class galleries and art museums. For more information, see chapter 15.

THE BASQUE COUNTRY   Since prehistoric times, the rugged Pyrénées have formed a natural boundary between France and Spain. The Basques, one of Europe's most unusual cultures, flourished in the valleys here. In the 19th century, resorts such as **Biarritz** and **St-Jean-de-Luz** attracted the French aristocracy; the empress Eugénie's palace at Biarritz is now a hotel. Four million Catholics make annual pilgrimages to the city of Lourdes. In the villages and towns of the Pyrénées, the old folkloric traditions, permeated with Spanish influences, continue to thrive. For more information, see chapter 17.

BORDEAUX & THE ATLANTIC COAST   Flat, fertile, and frequently ignored by North Americans, this region includes towns pivotal in French history (**Poitiers, Angoulême,** and **La Rochelle**), as well as wine- and liquor-producing villages (**Cognac, St-Emilion,** and **Sauternes**) whose names are celebrated around the world. **Bordeaux,** the district's largest city, has an economy based on wine merchandising and showcases grand 18th-century architecture. For more information, see chapter 18.

THE DORDOGNE & THE LOT   The splendid Dordogne River valley has been a favorite vacation spot since Cro-Magnon peoples were painting bison on cave walls in **Lascaux.** Today visitors flock to the valley to marvel at prehistoric sites near **Les Eyzies-de-Tayac** and to ramble through exquisite villages like **Sarlat-le-Canéda** and **Beynac-et-Cazenac.** The land of truffles and foie gras, Périgord has long been famed as a gastronomic Mecca, while nearby **Cahors** is celebrated for its rich red wine. For more information, see chapter 19.

FRANCE ITINERARIES
1 WEEK IN PARIS & NORMANDY

If you budget your days carefully, 1 week provides enough time to visit the major attractions of Paris, such as the **Musée du Louvre** (the world's greatest art gallery), the **Eiffel Tower,** and **Notre-Dame.** After 2 days in Paris, head for the former royal stamping grounds of **Versailles,** followed by Normandy (an easy commute from Paris), visiting such highlights as the **D-day beaches,** the cathedral city of **Rouen** (where Joan of Arc was burned at the stake), the tapestry of **Bayeux,** and the incredible monastery of **Mont-St-Michel.**

DAYS 1 & 2: arrive in Paris

Take a flight that arrives in Paris as early as possible on **DAY 1.** Check into your hotel and hit the nearest cafe for a pick-me-up café au lait and a croissant. Since you are probably still groggy with jet lag, limit intellectual activity and head to the **Eiffel Tower** for a literal over-view of the city (you'll need a prebooked time slot; p. 125). After coming back to Earth, take the RER Line C to **place St-Michel** and find lunch in the **Latin Quarter** (avoiding tourist-trap eateries around rue de la Huchette). If jet lag is a problem, now is the time to return

The famed Neptune Fountain at Versailles.

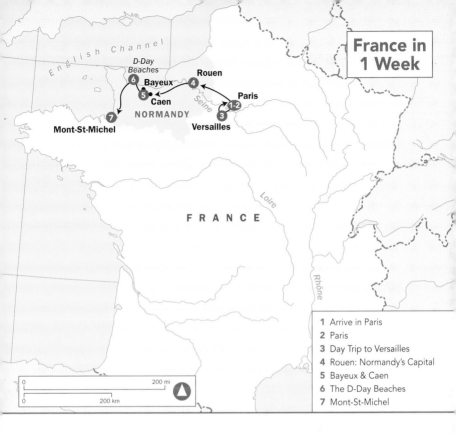

English Channel

D-Day Beaches

6 Bayeux **4** Rouen

5 Caen

Paris **1-2**

Caen

NORMANDY

3

7

Versailles

Mont-St-Michel

Seine

Loire

F R A N C E

Rhône

0   200 mi

0   200 km

1   Arrive in Paris
2   Paris
3   Day Trip to Versailles
4   Rouen: Normandy's Capital
5   Bayeux & Caen
6   The D-Day Beaches
7   Mont-St-Michel

to the hotel and take a nap. Continue, refreshed, to the **Ile de la Cité** and marvel at the stained glass of the **Ste-Chapelle** and the final restoration work of the Cathedral of **Notre-Dame** (set to fully reopen in Dec 2024 after 2019's fire; p. 81). Now take a break from cultural icons and enjoy some shopping or sit in a cafe and enjoy the sunset in the trendy—and beautiful—**Marais** neighborhood, before scouting out a restaurant for dinner (if you have the wherewithal, you can visit one of the many smallish museums in this area). Walk off your meal with a romantic stroll along the **quays of the Seine** and enjoy the magical nighttime lighting of the iconic monuments along the river's banks.

On **DAY 2,** get an early start and head for the **Louvre** (remember, you'll need to purchase a timed ticket online before your visit; p. 88). Spend at least a couple hours soaking in its many artistic wonders (and don't forget to see the *Mona Lisa*). Recover with a stroll and a sit in the **Tuileries Garden,** and perhaps a picnic. Continue strolling to the **place de la Concorde** and admire the Egyptian obelisk, then peer down the **Champs-Elysées** and see the **Arc de Triomphe** in the distance. End the day poking around the delightful **St-Germain** neighborhood, where you can visit a church (St-Germain-des-Près or St-Sulpice), check out famous cafes (Les Deux Magots, Café de Flore), or shop until you drop. Enjoy one of the many nearby restaurants and then scope out Parisian nightlife.

DAY 3: a day trip to Versailles

Bid *adieu* to Paris (for the day; you'll return to your hotel at night) and take the RER Line C to the Versailles/Rive Gauche station. You can spend a full day at **Versailles** (p. 191) and see the château (with its Grands and Petits Appartements and glittering Hall of Mirrors), meander in the gardens, and visit Marie Antoinette's domain. Grab an audio guide for extra tidbits of information, or opt for one of the many excellent guided tours, some of which allow you to see some areas off-limits on a self-guided visit, like the Queen's Theater.

DAY 4: Normandy's capital of Rouen

Take an early train to Rouen and check in to one of the city's great hotels. Spend at least 2 hours exploring the city's ancient core, especially its **Cathédrale Notre-Dame** (p. 283), immortalized in paintings by Monet. Stand at the **place du Vieux-Marché** (p. 282), where Joan of Arc was executed for heresy in 1431, and visit the **Église St-Maclou** (p. 284), a 1432 church in the Flamboyant Gothic style. After lunch, rent a car for the rest of your trip and drive to **Giverny**— it's only 60km (37 miles) southeast of Rouen. At Giverny, visit the **Fondation Claude Monet** (p. 213), returning to your hotel in Rouen for the night.

DAY 5: Bayeux & Caen

Even after a leisurely breakfast, you can easily be in the city of Caen by late morning, with plenty of time to visit **Abbaye aux Hommes** (p. 301), founded by William the Conqueror. After a hearty Norman lunch in Caen, continue west to the city of **Bayeux** to view the celebrated **Musée de la Tapisserie de Bayeux** (p. 306). Stay overnight in Bayeux.

DAY 6: the D-day beaches

Reserve this day for exploring the D-day beaches where Allied forces launched "the Longest Day," the mammoth invasion of Normandy in June 1944 that signaled the beginning of the end of Hitler's Third Reich.

Your voyage of discovery can begin at the seaside resort of Arromanches-les-Bains, where you can visit the **Musée du Débarquement** (p. 311) before heading to **Omaha Beach** (p. 310), the moving

Normandy American Cemetery (p. 310), and the **Overlord Museum** (p. 311), with an easy roadside lunch en route.

That evening, drive to **Mont-St-Michel** (less than 2 hr. away) and overnight in the pedestrianized village on "the Rock," giving you plenty of time for an early-morning visit to this popular UNESCO-protected attraction.

DAY 7: Mont-St-Michel

Allow around 3 hours to explore **Mont-St-Michel** (p. 314). Taking an English-language tour is one of the best ways to enjoy its great abbey, founded in 966. After lunch, return your car to Rouen, where you'll find frequent train service back to Paris and your flight home the following day.

A 1-WEEK EXTENSION TO THE LOIRE VALLEY & THE CÔTE D'AZUR

If you have 2 weeks to explore France, you'll have time to visit several regions—not only Paris, but also the best of the Loire Valley châteaux, the most history-rich town of Provence (Avignon), and several resorts on the Riviera, taking in the beaches, art galleries, and even the Principality of Monaco.

For **days 1 through 7,** follow the "1 Week in Paris & Normandy" itinerary, above.

DAY 8: Orléans, gateway to the Loire Valley

Leave Paris on an early train to **Orléans** (trip time: 1 hr., 10 min.; p. 226). Rent a car here and drive west to the **Château de Chambord** (p. 238), the largest château in the Loire Valley, representing the apogee of the French Renaissance architectural style. Allow 2 hours for a visit. Back on the road again, continue southwest to the **Château de Blois** (p. 236), called "the Versailles of the Renaissance" and a virtual illustrated storybook of French architecture. Stay overnight in Blois.

DAY 9: Amboise & Chenonceau

In the morning, continue southeast from Blois to **Amboise,** where you can check into a hotel for the night. Visit the 15th-century **Château d'Amboise** (p. 243), in the Italian Renaissance style, and also **Clos-Lucé** (p. 245), last residence of Leonardo da Vinci. In the afternoon, drive southeast to the **Château de Chenonceau** (p. 247), famous for the French dames who have occupied its precincts, including Diane de Poitiers (mistress of the king) and Catherine de Médicis (the jealous queen). You can spend a couple of hours at the château before driving back to Amboise for the night.

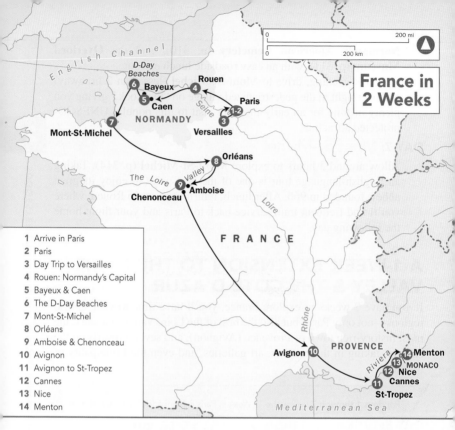

France in 2 Weeks

1 Arrive in Paris
2 Paris
3 Day Trip to Versailles
4 Rouen: Normandy's Capital
5 Bayeux & Caen
6 The D-Day Beaches
7 Mont-St-Michel
8 Orléans
9 Amboise & Chenonceau
10 Avignon
11 Avignon to St-Tropez
12 Cannes
13 Nice
14 Menton

DAY 10: Avignon, gateway to Provence

From Amboise, get an early start and drive east to Orléans to return
your rental car. Then take an early train from Orléans to Paris's Gare
d'Austerlitz, then the Métro or a taxi to the Gare de Lyon, and hop on
a TGV bound for Avignon (2½ hr.).

Check into a hotel in **Avignon** (p. 518), one of Europe's most
beautiful medieval cities. Before the day fades, you should have time
to wander through the old city to get your bearings, shop for Provençal souvenirs, and see one of the smaller sights, such as the **Pont St-
Bénézet.** See p. 522.

DAY 11: Avignon to St-Tropez

In the morning, spend 2 hours touring the **Palais des Papes** (p. 523),
the capital of Christendom during the 14th century. After lunch in
one of Avignon's cozy bistros or cobblestoned outdoor cafes, rent a
car and drive to **St-Tropez** (p. 583). Spend a good part of the early
evening in one of the cafes along the harbor, indulging in that favorite
French pastime of people-watching.

DAY 12: chic Cannes

Before leaving St-Tropez in the morning, check out the Impressionist paintings at **Musée de l'Annonciade** (p. 586). Drive 50km (31 miles) east along the coast until you reach Cannes.

Assuming it's summer, get in some time at the beach, notably at **Plage de la Croisette** (p. 597), and feel free to wear your most revealing swimwear. In the afternoon, take the ferry to **Ile Ste-Marguerite** (p. 603), where the *Man in the Iron Mask* was imprisoned. You can visit his cell. That evening, you may want to flirt with Lady Luck at one of the plush **casinos** (p. 602).

DAY 13: Nice, capital of the Riviera

It's only a 32km (20-mile) drive east from Cannes to **Nice,** the Riviera's largest city. After checking in to a hotel (the most affordable options along the Riviera), stroll through **Vieille Ville** (p. 633), the Old Town. Enjoy a snack of *socca,* a round crepe made with chickpea flour that vendors sell steaming hot in the **cours Saleya market.** Then head for the **promenade des Anglais** (p. 633), the wide boulevard along the waterfront. In the afternoon, head for the famed hill town of **St-Paul-de-Vence,** only 20km (12 miles; p. 621) to the north. You can wander its ramparts in about 30 minutes before descending

The Mediterranean Sea at Nice, French Riviera.

to the greatest modern-art museum in the Riviera, the newly renovated **Fondation Maeght** (p. 623).

Continue on to **Vence** (p. 626) for a visit to the great Henri Matisse's artistic masterpiece, **Chapelle du Rosaire** (p. 627). From there, it's just 24km (15 miles) southeast back to Nice, where you can enjoy dinner at a typical Niçois bistro.

DAY 14: Nice to Menton

While still overnighting in Nice, head east for the most thrilling drive in all of France, a trip along the **Grande Corniche** highway, which stretches 31km (19 miles) east from Nice to the little resort of **Menton** (p. 673) near the Italian border. Allow 3 hours for this trip. Highlights along this road include **Roquebrune-Cap Martin** and **La Turbie** (p. 657). The greatest view along the Riviera is at the **Eze Belvedere,** at 1,200m (3,936 ft.). Return to Nice by dinnertime and prepare for your flight home in the morning.

FRANCE FOR FAMILIES

France offers many attractions for kids. Our suggestion is to limit the bustle of **Paris** to 2 days, and then spend a day wandering the spectacular grounds and glittering interiors of **Versailles,** 2 days in **Disneyland Paris,** and 2 days on the **Riviera.**

DAYS 1 & 2: Paris

On **DAY 1**, spend the morning at the **Luxembourg Gardens** (p. 121), where your offspring can go wild at the huge playground, sail toy boats in the fountain, ride a pony, or just run around and have fun. Parents can take turns sneaking off to visit nearby attractions like the **Panthéon** (p. 120), **Musée Zadkine** (p. 122), and **St-Etienne-du-Mont** (p. 121), or just find peace and quiet in a **Latin Quarter** cafe. Then walk down to **St-Germain-des-Prés** (p. 124) and visit the church before lunch. For a post-prandial visit, try 17th-century **St-Sulpice** church (p. 125), which contains paintings by Delacroix, and then hop on the no. 86 bus to the **Champs de Mars** and visit the **Eiffel Tower** (p. 125). After that, everyone will probably be pooped and ready to relax with **a boat ride on the Seine,** which departs near the tower.

On **DAY 2,** start the day at the **Jardin des Plantes**, botanical gardens, where you can choose between the **Muséum National d'Histoire Naturelle** (p. 120), the **Ménagerie** (a small zoo; p. 118), and a playground. Lunch at the nearby **Jardin des Pâtes** (p. 163). Once stomachs are filled, head over to **Nôtre-Dame** (p. 81), and the

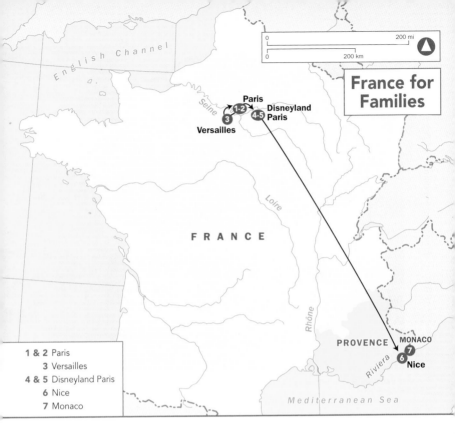

France for Families

Paris
Disneyland
Paris

Versailles

Seine

Loire

F R A N C E

Rhône

PROVENCE   MONACO

Riviera   Nice

Mediterranean Sea

English Channel

200 mi
200 km

1 & 2 Paris
3 Versailles
4 & 5 Disneyland Paris
6 Nice
7 Monaco

nearby **Conciergerie,** a former palace turned Revolutionary jail, where Histopads (augmented reality smart devices) let you see what the building would have looked like in medieval times and during the Revolution. Now meander the streets to Sèvres-Babylone metro to take line 12 to Abbesses station on the **Butte Montmartre,** for a fabulous sunset from the esplanade in front of the **Basilique du Sacré-Coeur** (p. 110). Even if your kids don't appreciate the view, they will enjoy the ride in the **funicular** that you take to get there. Up on the esplanade, you'll find plenty of room to run around, and lots of buskers for entertainment. If that doesn't work, there is always the merry-go-round at **place des Abbesses** (p. 110) when you head back down towards your hotel.

DAY 3: Versailles

Tear yourself away from the glories of Paris for a day at the **Château de Versailles** (p. 191). Take the RER Line C to the Versailles/Rive Gauche station. Hopefully, your kids will be old enough to appreciate that they are wandering around a royal palace and seeing where the

In Paris, there's almost always a carousel nearby. If the kids start melting down, head to the nearest one!

king and queen slept. If not, they might enjoy running around or riding a bike through the park or rowing a boat on the Grand Canal. You can buy a picnic lunch in Paris and enjoy it on the grounds, or else purchase a sandwich at one of the stands placed in discreet corners of the garden.

DAYS 4 & 5: Disneyland Paris

Do you have a choice here? Do **Disneyland Paris** (p. 216), allowing a full 2 days for the main park (with all its classic areas—Main Street, Fantasyland, etc.) and the recently vamped **Walt Disney Studios** (p. 218), home to the new Avengers Campus (hotel packages range from ridiculously expensive to only slightly so; the RER commuter express train A takes you from Etoile in Paris to Marne-la-Vallée/ Chessy in 45 min.). Or—because this is France after all—opt for the very French (and less expensive) **Parc Astérix** (p. 219), based on France's famous and beloved Astérix the Gaul comic-strips (by René Goscinny and Albert Uderzo). Not only are the hotels and their restaurants excellent, but you don't feel the same "hard sell" as at Disney, and the park has France's tallest and faster coaster, the Toutatis, which reaches a top speed of 110kmph (68 mph).

DAY 6: Nice

Fly to Nice, capital of the French Riviera. If you flew Air France transatlantic, Nice can often be attached as a low-cost extension of your round-trip fare.

In Nice, you can check into your hotel for 2 nights, as the city has the most affordable hotels on the coast. Set out to explore this old city. There's always a lot of free entertainment in summer along Nice's seafront boardwalk, the **promenade des Anglais** (p. 633), and the people-watching on the Riviera—particularly on the beach—is likely to leave your kids wide-eyed.

In the afternoon, journey to the evocative hill town of **St-Paul-de-Vence** (p. 621). Children delight in touring the ramparts, strolling along the pedestrian-only rue Grande, or exploring the sculpture garden at the newly renovated **Fondation Maeght** (p. 623), one of France's greatest modern-art museums.

Return to Nice for the evening and take your kids for a stroll through the Old Town, dining as the sun dips over the Mediterranean.

DAY 7: Monaco

While still based in Nice, head for the tiny Principality of Monaco, which lies only 18km (11 miles) east of Nice.

Children will enjoy the changing-of-the-guard ceremony at **Les Grands Appartements du Palais** (p. 665), official residence of the royal family, including twins Princess Gabriella and Prince Jacques. But the best part of Monaco for kids is the **Musée Océanographique de Monaco** (p. 666), home to sharks and other exotic sea creatures.

Return to Nice that night and prepare for your flight home in the morning.

AN ART LOVER'S TOUR OF FRANCE

From contemporary art in Paris to modern masters along the southern coast, France is a country infused with art. Aficionados can experience an unforgettable trip taking in Paris (2 days), Aix-en-Provence (1 day), and then the Riviera between St-Tropez and Nice (4 days). Museum visits can be interspersed with wonderful meals, sunbathing, and stops at the area's architectural and artistic highlights.

DAYS 1 & 2: Paris

Start **DAY 1** of your art tour of Paris with a quick check of what's currently on in the city: The **Musée Jacquemart André** (p. 104) and the **Musée du Luxembourg** both host excellent temporary exhibitions.

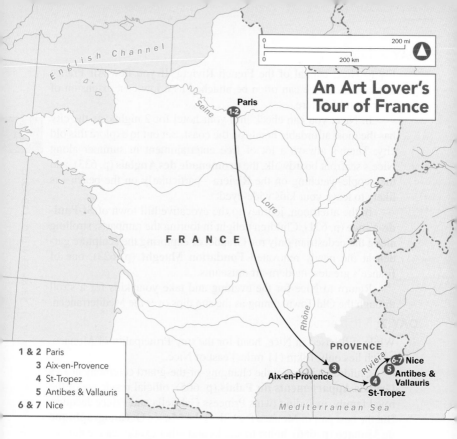

An Art Lover's
Tour of France

1 & 2 Paris
3 Aix-en-Provence
4 St-Tropez
5 Antibes & Vallauris
6 & 7 Nice

You can attend a show at any of these venues or begin your day at the newly renovated **Musée de Montmartre** (p. 110), formerly home to both Renoir and Utrillo. Then hop onto the Métro and head south to the **Jardin du Luxembourg.** After a leisurely stroll in the gardens, head over to tiny **Musée Zadkine** dedicated to sculptor Ossip Zadkine and located in the artist's former house and atelier. Take a minute to rest in the pretty little garden. Enjoy a leisurely lunch at one of the neighborhood's many bistros. Round out the afternoon by taking in a cutting-edge contemporary exhibition at the wacky **Palais de Tokyo** (p. 107), overlooking the Seine and Eiffel Tower.

On **DAY 2,** spend the morning admiring the world's most iconic Impressionist paintings at the **Musée d'Orsay** (p. 130). After walking to the **Marais** (p. 91) and dining in one of its many restaurants, either cruise the art galleries, or visit the **Picasso-Paris** (p. 96), set in the sumptuous 17th-century mansion, L'Hôtel Salé.

Mid-afternoon, jump aboard one of the many TGV trains heading south to Aix-en-Provence. The journey takes around 3 hours, leaving you plenty of time to enjoy a typical Provençal dinner upon arrival.

DAY 3: Aix-en-Provence

Paul Cézanne is Aix's most celebrated son. Begin your day at his **Atelier** (p. 553), almost perfectly preserved as it was when the great artist worked here more than a century ago. There are regularly scheduled English-language tours of the site. Afterward, a visit to the city's famed **Musée Granet** (p. 553)—one of the region's most superb modern-art museums—is a must. Aix's plane-tree-shaded **cours Mirabeau,** where Cézanne used to drink and debate with the famous French writer Emile Zola, is almost a work of art in itself.

Clock tower in Aix-en-Provence.

After lunch, rent a car and drive to **St-Tropez** (p. 583). Warm evenings are best enjoyed strolling the port's pretty quays or taking in the million-dollar panoramas from the hilltop **Citadelle** (p. 586).

DAY 4: St-Tropez

Since the 1890s, when painters Signac and Bonnard discovered St-Tropez, artists and their patrons have been drawn to the French Riviera. Spend the morning appreciating the **Musée de l'Annonciade**'s (p. 586) Impressionist paintings, many of them depicting St-Tropez and the surrounding coast.

After lunch in one of the town's sidewalk cafes, drive around 100km (62 miles) east along the coast until you reach Nice, where you'll base yourself for the next 3 nights. Return your rental car—traffic-heavy roads, combined with excellent public transportation, render your own vehicle unnecessary here.

DAY 5: Antibes & Vallauris

Today you'll spend the day following in the footsteps of one of the 20th century's modern masters: Pablo Picasso. Take one of the frequent trains from Nice to Antibes (20 min.). On the edge of the picturesque, pedestrian-friendly Old Town sits the 14th-century Grimaldi Château, now home to the **Musée Picasso** (p. 616). The Spanish artist lived and worked in this castle in 1946.

Stroll through Antibes' covered market, then—appetite piqued—stop into a small bistro for a light lunch. Next, make your way to Antibes' bus station, where frequent buses depart for Vallauris (35 min.). Picasso moved to this hilltop village during the 1950s, reviving the local ceramic-making industry and personally pro-

Ocean views and art at Antibe's Musée Picasso.

ducing thousands of pieces of pottery. Visit Picasso's mammoth paintings in the **Musée National Picasso La Guerre et La Paix** (p. 608), the artist's tribute to pacifism.

Make your way back to Nice (it's quickest to simply reverse your route). Spend the evening strolling the promenade des Anglais or wandering the city's atmospheric Old Town.

DAYS 6 & 7: Nice

Outside of Paris, Nice is home to more museums than any other city in France. Begin your **DAY 6** citywide explorations in the neighborhood of Cimiez, where both the famed **Musée Matisse** (p. 636) and the **Musée National Marc Chagall** (p. 637) are located. It's possible to walk between the two (around 15 min.) but be sure to hit the Matisse Museum first—then it's downhill all the way to see Chagall's ethereal artworks.

If it's summertime, spend a couple of hours picnicking on the beach or relaxing with a glass of wine in one of the city's many sidewalk cafes. Mid-afternoon, make your way over the **Musée Masséna** (p. 635), where a combination of local art and history gives visitors a peek at the ritzy French Riviera of the past.

Use your final day to make a day trip to the hilltop village of **St-Paul-de-Vence** (p. 621), 20km (12 miles) to the north. Wander the St-Paul-de-Vence's ramparts for 30 minutes, before descending to

Art isn't just inside museums in Nice. Keep your eyes peeled for the city's sculptural public library.

the world-class modern art on display at the newly renovated **Fondation Maeght** (p. 623). En route back to Nice, stop into the **Musée Renoir** (p. 648) in Cagnes-sur-Mer, which comprises the artist's former home and gardens. Note that you can either rent a car for the day or access both St-Paul-de-Vence and Cagnes-sur-Mer via frequent buses from Nice.

Spend your final night in Nice savoring a hearty Niçois dinner, paired with plenty of local wine.

3

FRANCE IN CONTEXT

By Tristan Rutherford & Kathryn Tomasetti

The civilization and culture of France—not to mention the French way of life—makes the country easily the most visited in the world. The savoir-faire of its people lures travelers from across the globe to a country that covers an area smaller than Texas. Yet despite France's size, each region is so intriguing and varied that you may immerse yourself in one province so deeply that you'll never have time to see other regions. You'd be surprised how many people do just that. Perhaps more than any other country in the world, France is a land to be savored. Ideally, France is discovered slowly by car or along the country's magnificent rail network, which lets you stop whenever and wherever you wish.

No European country, not even Britain, Italy, or Spain, can beat France in its pageantry of personalities. Its colorful characters range from Madame de Pompadour to Charles de Gaulle, from Jean-Luc Godard to Gustave Flaubert, from Catherine de Médici to Joan of Arc, from Emperor Napoleon to soccer star Kylian Mbappé. You'll be introduced to some of these figures in the pages ahead. Seeing where they lived, worked, loved, and became legends is part of the experience of visiting France.

This guide is meant to help you decide where to go in France, but ultimately the most gratifying experience will be your own serendipitous discoveries—sunflowers, a picnic in a poppy field, an hour spent chatting with a small winemaker—whatever it is that stays in your memory for years to come.

FRANCE TODAY

France remains one of the world's most hyped and written-about destinations. It can inspire a masterpiece—and has on countless occasions. Even the cantankerous James McNeill Whistler would allow his masterpiece, a portrait of his mother, to hang in no other city save Paris.

Although not large by North American standards (about the size of Britain and Germany combined), France is densely packed with attractions, both cultural and recreational. Even better, it's permeated with cool and known for its *joie de vivre.*

As for style, it has always been foolhardy to try to compete with the French on their terms. The Gallic monarchs ranked among the richest people in the world and were given to conspicuous displays of wealth. (Just tour any chateau!) Make a list of the 21st century's most fashion

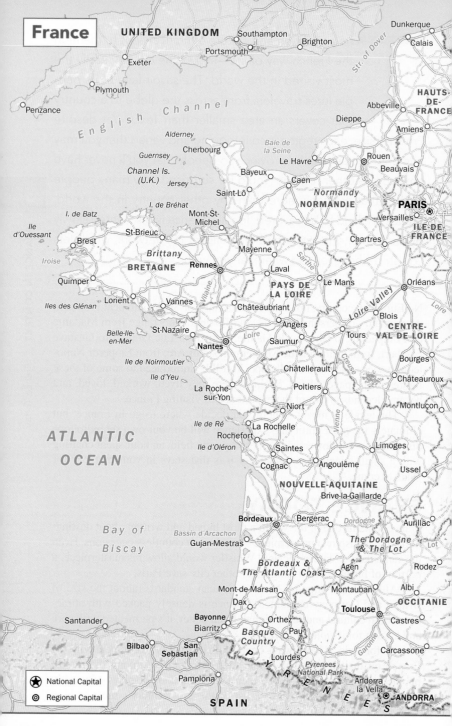

France

UNITED KINGDOM

Southampton
Brighton
Portsmouth
Exeter
Plymouth
Penzance

Dunkerque
Calais
Str. of Dover

English Channel

Alderney
Guernsey
Channel Is.
(U.K.)
Jersey

Cherbourg
Baie de
la Seine
Le Havre
Bayeux
Caen
Saint-Lô

Abbeville
Dieppe
Rouen
Beauvais

HAUTS-
DE-
FRANCE
Amiens

Seine

Normandy
NORMANDIE

PARIS
Versailles

ILE-DE-
FRANCE

Chartres

I. de Batz
I. de Bréhat
Ile
d'Ouessant
Brest
Iroise
St-Brieuc
Mont-St-
Michel

Mayenne
Sarthe
Laval
Rennes

Brittany
BRETAGNE

Le Mans
Orléans
Loire

Quimper
Iles des Glénan
Lorient
Vannes
Châteaubriant

PAYS DE
LA LOIRE

Loire Valley
Blois
Tours

CENTRE-
VAL DE LOIRE

Belle-Ile-
en-Mer
St-Nazaire
Nantes
Ile de Noirmoutier
Ile d'Yeu

Loire
Angers
Saumur

Bourges
Châteauroux

La Roche-
sur-Yon

Châtellerault
Poitiers
Niort

Creuse

Montluçon

ATLANTIC
OCEAN

Ile de Ré
Rochefort
Ile d'Oléron

La Rochelle
Saintes
Cognac

Vienne

Limoges
Angoulême

Ussel

NOUVELLE-AQUITAINE

Brive-la-Gaillarde

Bay of
Biscay

Bassin d'Arcachon
Gujan-Mestras

Bordeaux
Bergerac
Dordogne

The Dordogne
& The Lot

Aurillac
Lot

Bordeaux &
The Atlantic Coast

Mont-de-Marsan
Dax

Agen
Montauban

Rodez
Albi

OCCITANIE

Santander
Bayonne
Biarritz
Bilbao
San
Sebastian

Orthez
Basque
Country
Pau

Lourdes
Pyrenees
National Park

Toulouse
Castres
Castres

Garonne

Carcassone

Pamplona

PYRENEES

Andorra
la Vella
ANDORRA

SPAIN

National Capital

Regional Capital

44

45

designers and style icons, and you'll find that half the names on it are French.

In politics and ideology, France has long been a leader and remains so today. Fueled by Enlightenment writings, whose most articulate voices were French, the 1789 Revolution toppled Europe's most deeply entrenched regime and cracked the foundations of dozens of other governments. In 1968 the revolutionaries were on the streets again: the original political spring. As they were in 2023, one of the biggest recent years for protest, when older strikers challenged the reform of France's generous pension system, and urban youth challenged racism.

Newcomers have commented (often adversely) on the cultural arrogance of the French. But despite its linguistic and cultural rigidity, France has received more immigrants and political exiles than any other European country. Part of this derives from France's status as one of Europe's least densely populated nations per square mile, and part of it from the tendency of the French to let others be until their actions become dangerous or obnoxious, not necessarily in that order.

If you're a first-timer, everything in France, of course, is new. But if you've been away for a long time, expect changes. Taxi drivers in Paris may no longer correct your fractured French but address you in English— and that's tantamount to a revolution. Part of this derives from the country's interest in music, culture, and films from foreign countries, and part from France's growing awareness of its role as a leader of a united Europe.

Yet France has never been more concerned about the loss of its unique identity within a landscape that has attracted an increasing number of immigrants from its former colonies. Today some seven million immigrants (foreign-born people) represent more than 10% of the total population. Many worry that France will continue to lose the battle to keep its language strong, distinct, and unadulterated by foreign slang or catchwords (and good luck with banning such terms as *l'email* and *le weekend*). But as the country moves deeper into the roaring twenties, foreign tourists spending much-needed cash are no longer perceived as foes or antagonists. *Au contraire:* France welcomes the world to its palaces, parks, beaches, and UNESCO World Heritage sites. And if those tens of millions of guests spend a few euros—and soak up a little local culture while they're here—that's all to the good.

THE HISTORY OF FRANCE

EARLY GAUL   When the ancient Romans considered France part of their empire, their boundaries extended deep into the forests of the Paris basin and up to the edges of the Rhine. Part of Julius Caesar's early reputation came from his defeat of King Vercingetorix at Alésia in 52 B.C., a victory he was quick to publicize in one of the ancient world's literary masterpieces, *The Gallic Wars.* In that year, the Roman colony of Lutetia (Paris) was established on an island in the Seine (Ile de la Cité).

The Roman Arena in Arles, Provence.

As the Roman Empire declined, its armies retreated to the flourishing colonies that had been established along a strip of the Mediterranean coast—among others, these included Orange, Arles, Antibes, and Marseille, which today retain some of the best Roman monuments in Europe.

As one of their legacies, the Roman armies left behind the Catholic Church, which, for all its abuses, was the only real guardian of civilization during the anarchy following the Roman decline. A form of low Latin was the common language. This slowly evolved into the archaic French that the more refined language is based upon today.

THE CAROLINGIANS From the wreckage of the fall of the Roman Empire emerged a new dynasty: the Carolingians. One of their leaders, Charles Martel, halted a Muslim invasion of northern Europe at Tours in 743 and left a much-expanded kingdom to his son, Pepin. The Carolingian empire eventually stretched from the Pyrénées to a point deep in the German forests, encompassing much of modern France, Germany, and northern Italy. The heir to this vast land was Charlemagne. Crowned emperor in Rome on Christmas Day in 800, he returned to his capital at Aix-la-Chapelle (Aachen) and created the Holy Roman Empire. Charlemagne's rule saw a revived interest in scholarship, art, and classical texts, defined by scholars as the Carolingian Renaissance.

THE MIDDLE AGES   When the Carolingian dynasty died out in 987, the hectic, migratory Middle Ages officially began. Invasion by Hungarians, Vikings, and the English (who ruled half the country) fractured Gallic society. Politically driven marriages among the ruling families more than doubled the size of the territory controlled from Paris, a city that was increasingly recognized as the country's capital. Philippe II (reigned 1179–1223) infiltrated more prominent families with his genes than anyone else in France, successfully marrying members of his family into the Valois, Artois, and Vermandois. He also managed to win Normandy and Anjou back from the English. Louis IX (St. Louis) emerged as the 13th century's most memorable king, though he ceded most of the hard-earned military conquests of his predecessors back to the English.

The 14th century saw an increase in the wealth and power of the French kings, an increase in general prosperity, and a decrease in the power of the feudal lords. The death of Louis X without an heir in 1316 prompted more than a decade of scheming and plotting before the eventual emergence of the Valois dynasty.

France's burgeoning wealth and power was checked by the Black Death, which began in the summer of 1348. The rat-borne plague killed an estimated 33% of Europe's population, decimating the population of Paris and setting the stage for the exodus of the French monarchs to safer climes in such places as the Loire Valley. A financial crisis, coupled with a series of ruinous harvests, almost bankrupted the nation.

During the Hundred Years' War, the English made sweeping inroads into France in an attempt to grab the throne. At their most powerful, they controlled almost all of the north (Picardy and Normandy), Champagne, and parts of the Loire Valley. The peasant-born charismatic visionary Joan of Arc rallied the dispirited French troops as well as the timid *dauphin* (crown prince), whom she managed to have crowned as Charles VII. As threatening to the Catholic Church as she was to the English, she was declared a heretic and burned at the stake in Rouen in 1431. The place of her demise is now sited in the city's marketplace.

THE RISING POWER   By the early 17th century, France was a modern state. Few vestiges of feudalism remained. In 1624, Louis XIII appointed a Catholic cardinal, the duc de Richelieu, as his chief minister. Amassing enormous power, Richelieu virtually ruled the country until his death in 1642. His sole objective was investing the monarchy with total power, and in trying to attain this goal he committed a series of truly horrible acts, paving the way for the eventual absolutism of a dynasty of future despotic rulers.

Although he ascended the throne when he was only 9, Louis XIV was the most powerful monarch Europe had seen since the Roman emperors. The estimated population of France at this time was 20 million, as opposed to 8 million in England and 6 million in Spain. French colonies in Canada, the West Indies, and America (Louisiana) were stronger than ever. The mercantilism that Louis's brilliant finance minister, Colbert, implemented was one of the era's most important fiscal policies, hugely increasing France's power and wealth. The arts flourished, as did a sense of aristocratic style that's remembered with a bittersweet nostalgia today. Louis's palace of Versailles is the perfect monument to the most flamboyantly consumptive era in French history.

Louis's territorial ambitions so deeply threatened the other nations of Europe that they united to hold him in check. France entered a series of expensive and demoralizing wars that, coupled with high taxes and bad harvests, stirred up much civil discontent. England was viewed as a threat both within Europe and in the global rush for lucrative colonies. The rise of Prussia as a militaristic neighbor posed an additional problem. Fresh political ideas from abroad unsteadied the status quo.

THE REVOLUTION & THE RISE OF NAPOLEON Meanwhile, the Enlightenment was training a new generation of thinkers for the struggle against absolutism, religious fanaticism, and superstition. On August 10, 1792, troops from Marseille, aided by a Parisian mob, threw the dimwitted Louis XVI and his tactless Austrian-born queen, Marie Antoinette, into prison. After months of bloodshed and bickering among violently competing factions, the two thoroughly humiliated monarchs were executed.

France's problems got worse before they got better. In the ensuing bloodbaths, both moderates and radicals were guillotined in full view of a bloodthirsty crowd that included voyeurs like Dickens's Mme. Defarge, who brought her knitting every day to place de la Révolution (later renamed place de la Concorde) to watch the beheadings. Only the militaristic fervor of Napoleon Bonaparte could reunite France and bring an end to the revolutionary chaos. A political and military genius who appeared on the landscape at a time when the French were thoroughly sickened by the anarchy following their revolution, he restored a national pride that had been severely tarnished.

Chapel of Saint Louis des Invalides, Paris, site of Napoleon's tomb.

He also established a bureaucracy and a code of law that has been emulated in other legal systems around the world. In 1799, at the age of 30, he entered Paris and was crowned first consul and master of France. Soon after, a decisive victory in his northern Italian campaign solidified his power at home.

Alas, Napoleon's victories made him overconfident—and made the rest of Europe clamor for his demise. Just as he was poised on the verge of conquering the entire continent, Napoleon's famous retreat from Moscow during the winter of 1812 reduced his formerly invincible army to tatters. As a plaque in the Lithuanian town of Vilnius once told the tale: "NAPOLEON BONAPARTE PASSED THIS WAY IN 1812 WITH 400,000 MEN"—and on the other side are the words "NAPOLEON BONAPARTE PASSED THIS WAY IN 1812 WITH 9,000 MEN." Napoleon was then decisively beaten at Waterloo by the combined armies of the English, Dutch, and Prussians. Exiled to the British-held island of St. Helena in the South Atlantic, he died in 1821, probably the victim of a prison poisoner.

THE BOURBONS & THE SECOND EMPIRE In 1814, following the destruction of Napoleon and his dream of Empire, the Congress of Vienna redefined the map of Europe. The Bourbon monarchy was reestablished, with reduced powers for Louis XVIII, an archconservative. After a few stable decades, Napoleon I's nephew, Napoleon III, was elected president in 1848. Appealing to the property-protecting instinct of a nation that hadn't forgotten the violent upheavals of less than a century before, he initiated a repressive right-wing government in which he was awarded the totalitarian status of emperor in 1851. Steel production was begun, and a railway system and Indochinese colonies were established. New technologies fostered new kinds of industry, and the bourgeoisie flourished. The baron Georges-Eugène Haussmann radically altered Paris by laying out the grand boulevards the world knows today.

As ever, intra-European conflict knocked France off its pedestal once again. In 1870, the Prussians—a rising power in the German east—defeated Napoleon III at Sedan and held him prisoner with 100,000 of his soldiers. Paris was besieged and occupied, an inglorious state for the world's greatest city. After the Prussians withdrew, a violent revolt ushered in the Third Republic and its elected president, Marshal MacMahon, in 1873. Peace and prosperity slowly returned, France regained its glamour, a mania of building occurred, the Impressionists made their visual statements, and writers like Flaubert redefined the French novel into what today is regarded as the most evocative in the world. As if as a symbol of this period, the Eiffel Tower was built as part of the 1889 Universal Exposition.

THE WORLD WARS International rivalries, lost colonial ambitions, and conflicting alliances led to World War I, which, after decisive German victories for 2 years, degenerated into the mud-slogged horror of trench warfare. Mourning between 4 and 5 million casualties, Europe was inflicted with psychological scars that never healed. In 1917, the United States broke the European deadlock by entering the war.

After the Allied victory, grave economic problems, plus the demoralization stemming from years of fighting, encouraged the growth of socialism and communism. The French government demanded every centime of reparations it could wring from a crushed Germany, humiliating the country into a vengeful spiral that would have repercussions 2 decades later.

The worldwide Great Depression of 1929 devastated France. Poverty and widespread bankruptcies weakened the Third Republic to the point where successive coalition governments rose and fell (although a number of expatriate writers, among them Ernest Hemingway and F. Scott Fitzgerald, enjoyed the dollar exchange rate and relative freedoms while they could). The crises reached a crescendo on June 14, 1940, when Hitler's armies arrogantly marched down the Champs-Elysées, and newsreel cameras recorded French people openly weeping. Under the terms of the armistice, the north of France was occupied by the Nazis, and a puppet French government was established at Vichy under the authority of Marshal Pétain. The immediate collapse of the French army is viewed as one of the most significant humiliations in modern French history. In Europe, Britain was left to counter the Nazi threat alone.

Pétain and his regime cooperated with the Nazis in unbearably shameful ways. Not the least of their errors included the deportation of more than 75,000 French Jews to German work camps. Pockets of resistance fighters (*le maquis*) waged small-scale guerrilla attacks against the Nazis throughout the course of the war. Charles de Gaulle, the irascible giant who is forever associated with the politics of his era, established himself as the head of the French government-in-exile.

The scene was radically altered on June 6, 1944, when the largest armada in history—a combination of American, British, and Canadian troops—successfully established a beachhead on the shores of Normandy. Paris rose in rebellion before the Allies arrived. On August 26, 1944, de Gaulle entered the capital as head of the government. The Fourth Republic was declared even as pockets of Nazi snipers continued to shoot from scattered rooftops throughout the city.

THE POSTWAR YEARS Plagued by the bitter residue of colonial policies that France had established during the 18th and 19th centuries, the Fourth Republic witnessed the rise and fall of 22 governments and 17 premiers. Many French soldiers died on foreign battlefields as once-profitable colonies in North Africa and Indochina rebelled. After suffering a bitter defeat in 1954, France ended its occupation of Vietnam and freed its former colony. It also granted internal self-rule to Tunisia and Morocco.

Algeria was to remain a greater problem. The advent of the 1958 Algerian revolution signaled the end of the much-maligned Fourth

Republic. De Gaulle was called back from retirement to initiate a new constitution, the Fifth Republic, with a stronger set of executive controls. To nearly everyone's dissatisfaction, de Gaulle ended the Algerian war in 1962 by granting the country full independence. The sun had finally set on most of France's far-flung empire.

In 1968, major social unrest and a violent coalition hastily formed between the nation's students and blue-collar workers eventually led to the collapse of the government. De Gaulle resigned when his attempts to placate some of the marchers were defeated. The reins of power passed to his second-in-command, Georges Pompidou, and his successor, Valérie Giscard d'Estaing, both of whom continued de Gaulle's policies emphasizing economic development and protection of France as a cultural resource to the world.

THE 1980S, 1990S & THE NEW MILLENNIUM   In 1981, François Mitterrand was elected the first Socialist president of France since World War II (with a close vote of 51%). In almost immediate response, many wealthy French decided to transfer their assets out of the country, much to the delight of banks in Geneva, Monaco, and the Cayman Islands. Though reviled by the rich and ridiculed for personal mannerisms that often seemed inspired by Louis XIV, Mitterrand was reelected in 1988. During his two terms, he spent billions of francs on his *grands projets* (like the Louvre pyramid, Opéra Bastille, Cité de la Musique, and Grande Arche de La Défense), although unemployment and endemic corruption remained.

On his third try in 1995, Jacques Chirac won the presidency with 52% of the vote and immediately declared war on unemployment. But his popularity soon faded in the wake of unrest caused by an 11.5% unemployment rate and a stressed economy struggling to meet entry requirements for the European Union that France had signed up for 3 years before.

Financial crisis or not, in May 1996 thousands (about 3½ weeks) of Parisian workers took to the streets, disrupting passenger train service to demand a workweek shorter than the usual 39 hours. Most French now work a 35-hour week and retire at 60 years old.

In 1999, France joined with other European countries in adopting the euro as its standard of currency. The new currency accelerated the creation of a single economy comprising over 500 million Europeans, although the ability of several fiscally wayward states to borrow at preferential rates has led to a sovereign debt crisis that remains today. Nonetheless, the European Union now boasts a combined gross national product approaching 16€ trillion ($17 trillion), a fifth smaller than that of the United States.

Although Chirac steadied the ship—and most French today think he ran a decent presidency—in 2005 a rotten core was exposed. Decades of pent-up resentment felt by the children of African immigrants exploded into an orgy of violence and vandalism. Riots began in the suburbs of Paris and spread around the country. Throughout France, gangs of youths battled the French police, torching schools, cars, and businesses. Rioting followed in such cities as Dijon, Marseille, and Rouen. Most of the rioters were the sons of Arab and Black African immigrants, Muslims living in a mostly Catholic country. The reason for the protests? Leaders of the riots claimed they live "like second-class citizens," even though they are French citizens. Unemployment is 30% higher in the ethnic ghettos of France.

Against a backdrop of discontent regarding issues of unemployment, immigration, and healthcare, the charismatic Nicolas Sarkozy swept into the presidential office in 2007. Sarkozy, the combative son of a Hungarian immigrant, promised to reinvigorate ties with France's traditional ally, the United States.

In the ensuing years, Sarkozy found time to divorce a wife and take a beautiful new bride. A glamorous model-turned-singer, Carla Bruni, became first lady of France in 2008. The tabloids had a field day with Bruni, whose former lovers include Mick Jagger and Donald Trump.

Outside of politics, the French looked at Sarkozy's personal life with ridicule. His marriage to Bruni and his holidays with the rich and famous earned him the title of the "bling bling president." In a show of how divided France was over his administration, he lost the 2012 presidential election by a whisker to Socialist challenger François Hollande.

Hollande promised a government of hard-working technocrats. Alas, "Monsieur Normal" proved anything but. A series of gaffes—including employing a minister with a secret Swiss bank account to superintend France's endemic tax evasion—made him the least popular president since polling began, with a disapproval rating of 75%. Soaring unemployment didn't help either. Nor did his decision to raise taxes (in particular, his infamous 75% tax rate for those who earn more than a million) in order to boost the economy. That said, Hollande's handling of the atrocities that rocked Paris and Nice in 2015 and 2016, where hundreds of civilians were killed in France's worst terrorist attacks, was broadly praised.

In 2017, Emmanuel Macron was voted in next as a generational change from the geriatric, often corrupt, leadership of old. At the tender age of 39, he was some 24 years younger than his glamorous wife, Brigitte.

Far from appearing a political lightweight, Macron has led a charge to reinvent France's ailing economy. Fights have been picked with the powerful unions, who insist on maintaining the country's prized 35-hour week. The president's next task is to trim the French state, a Herculean task, given that some 50% of taxpayers work for the government. With the UK spiraling from Brexit, and Germany in political disarray, Macron increasingly counts himself as the de facto leader of Europe with a mandate to rule until the next Presidential election in 2027.

Better still, Macron aims to avoid the scandals that have tarnished every French leader since the 1960s. He seems ever-besotted with his school sweetheart, Brigitte. The fact the couple fell in love when she was his teacher has only recently ceased to raise eyebrows across the land.

Politics aside, France still leads the world in tourism and culture. New museum and transport openings abound, and annual visitor numbers could top 100 million during the 2020s. The country continues to bask under a spotlight in terms of wine, food, fashion (Chanel and Louis Vuitton, among others) and television (anyone miss *Emily in Paris*?). The annual Tour de France cycle race is essentially a month-long marketing campaign for rural France. In 2024, the Paris Olympics—with its nationwide roster of events—placed a crown upon the world's most visited nation.

ART

France's manifold art treasures range from Rodin's *The Thinker* to Monet's Impressionist *Water Lilies;* its architecture encompasses Roman ruins and Gothic cathedrals as well as Renaissance châteaux and postmodern buildings like the Centre Pompidou. This brief overview is designed to help you make sense of it all.

A fine place to start is Paris's **Louvre** (p. 85). The world's greatest museum abounds with Renaissance works by Italian, Flemish, and German masters, including **Michelangelo** (1475–1564) and **Leonardo da Vinci** (1452–1519). Da Vinci's *Mona Lisa* (1503–05), the most famous painting on the planet, hangs here.

Back in the early 19th century, the **romantics** felt that both the ancients and the Renaissance had gotten it wrong and that the Middle Ages was the place to be. They idealized romantic tales of chivalry and the nobility of peasantry. Some great artists and movements of the era, all with examples in the **Louvre,** include **Theodore Géricault** (1791–1824), who painted *The Raft of the Medusa* (1819), which served as a model for the movement; and **Eugène Delacroix** (1798–1863), whose *Liberty Leading the People* (1830) was painted in the romantic style.

Decades later, the **Impressionists** adopted a free, open style, seeking to capture the *impression* light made as it reflected off objects. They painted deceptively loose compositions, using swift, visible brushwork and often light colors. For subject matter, they turned to landscapes and scenes of modern life. You'll find some of the best examples of their works in the **Musée d'Orsay** (p. 130).

Impressionist greats include **Edouard Manet** (1832–83), whose groundbreaking *Luncheon on the Grass* (1863) and *Olympia* (1863) helped inspire the movement with their harsh realism, visible brush strokes, and thick outlines; **Claude Monet** (1840–1926), who launched the movement officially in an 1874 exhibition in which he exhibited his Turner-inspired *Impression, Sunrise* (1874), now in the **Musée Marmottan Monet** (p. 105); **Pierre-Auguste Renoir** (1841–1919), known for his figures' ivory skin and chubby pink cheeks; **Edgar Degas** (1834–1917), an accomplished painter, sculptor, and draftsman—his pastels of dancers and bathers are particularly memorable; and **Auguste Rodin** (1840–1917), the greatest Impressionist-era sculptor, who crafted remarkably expressive bronzes. The **Musée Rodin** (p. 132), Rodin's former Paris studio, contains, among other works, his *Burghers of Calais* (1886), *The Kiss* (1886–98), and *The Thinker* (1880).

The smaller movements or styles of Impressionism are usually lumped together as "post-Impressionism." Again, the best examples of these turn-of-the-20th-century works are exhibited at the **Musée d'Orsay,** though you'll find pieces by Matisse, Chagall, and the cubists, including Picasso, in the **Centre Pompidou** (p. 91) and the key museums of Nice, Rouen, Avignon, and Marseille. Important post-Impressionists include

Edouard Manet's *Le Dejeuner sur L'Herbe* at the Musee d'Orsay.

Paul Cézanne (1839–1906), who adopted the short brush strokes, love of landscape, and light color palette of his Impressionist friends; **Henri de Toulouse-Lautrec** (1864–1901), who created paintings and posters of wispy, fluid lines anticipating Art Nouveau and often depicting the bohemian life of Paris's dance halls and cafes; **Vincent van Gogh** (1853–90), who combined a touch of crazy Japanese influence with thick, short strokes; **Henri Matisse** (1869–1954), who created **fauvism** (a critic described those who used the style as *fauves,* meaning "wild beasts"); and **Pablo Picasso** (1881–1973), a Málaga-born artist who painted objects from all points of view at once, rather than using such optical tricks as perspective to fool viewers into seeing "cubist" three dimensions.

FRANCE IN POPULAR CULTURE
Books

For a taste of French culture before you travel, we recommend you load a half-dozen titles on your iPad or Kindle. Simon Schama's *Citizens* is the pick of the bunch for a history of the French Revolution. Moving into the 20th century, *Paris Was Yesterday, 1925–1939* is a fascinating collection of excerpts from Janet Flanner's "Letters from Paris" column in the *New Yorker,* while *On Paris* comprises a newly bound series of essays by Ernest Hemingway, written for the *Toronto Star* between 1920 and 1924. Two unusual approaches to French history are Rudolph Chleminski's *The French at Table,* a funny and honest history of why the French know how to eat better than anyone and how they go about it; and *Parisians: An Adventure History of Paris* by Graham Robb, entertaining historical snippets that range from the French Revolution through the 1968 riots. More recently, *Chocolat* by Joanne Harris illustrates the tension between tradition and modernity in rural France by way of the nation's favorite treat.

And travel? Well, since 1323, some 10,000 books have been devoted to exploring Paris. One of the best is *Paris: Capital of the World,* by Patrice Higonnet. This book takes a fresh social, cultural, and political look at the City of Light, exploring Paris as "the capital of sex" and, in contrast, the "capital of art." In *The Flâneur: A Stroll Through the Paradoxes of Paris,* Edmund White wants the reader to experience Paris as Parisians do. Hard to translate exactly, a *flâneur* is someone who wanders, loafs, or idles. And for the frequent visitor, Jean-Christophe Napais's *Quiet Corners of Paris: Unexpected Hideaways, Secret Courtyards, Hidden Gardens* is sure to turn up plenty of undiscovered gems.

Representing the city's most fabulous era are *A Moveable Feast,* Ernest Hemingway's recollections of Paris during the 1920s, and Morley Callaghan's *That Summer in Paris: Memories of Tangled Friendships with Hemingway, Fitzgerald and Some Others,* an anecdotal account of the same period. Another great read is *The Autobiography of Alice B. Toklas,* by Gertrude Stein.

For a fictional tour of the 19th century, pick up *Madame Bovary,* by Gustave Flaubert. The carefully wrought characters, setting, and plot attest to Flaubert's genius in presenting the tragedy of Emma Bovary; Victor Hugo's *Les Misérables,* a classic tale of social oppression and human courage set in the era of Napoleon I; and *Selected Stories,* by the master of the genre, Guy de Maupassant.

Films

The world's first movie was shown in Paris on December 28, 1895. Its makers were the Lumière brothers, who scared an audience to death with images of a train moving towards the audience seats. Later, Charles Pathé and Léon Gaumont were the first to exploit filmmaking on a grand scale.

The golden age of the French silent screen on both sides of the Atlantic was 1927 to 1929. Actors were directed with more sophistication, and technical abilities reached an all-time high. The film *Hugo* (2011), directed by Martin Scorsese, is a heart-warming tale set against the film industry's transformation during this period. And despite its mind-numbing length, Abel Gance's masterpiece *Napoleon* (1927) is also sweepingly evocative. Its grisly battle scenes are easily as chilling as any war film made today.

In 1936, the Cinémathèque Française was established to find and preserve old (usually silent) French films. By that time, an average of 130 films a year was made in France, by (among others) Jean Renoir, Charles Spaak, and Marcel Carne. This era also brought such French luminaries as Claudette Colbert and Maurice Chevalier to Hollywood.

After World War II, two strong traditions—*film noir* and French comedy—offered viewers new kinds of genre, like Jacques Tati's sidesplitting *Les Vacances du Monsieur Hulot* (*Mr. Hulot's Holiday*). By the mid-1950s, French filmmaking ushered in the era of enormous budgets and the creation of such frothy potboilers as director Roger Vadim's *And God Created Woman,* which helped make Brigitte Bardot a celebrity around the world, contributing greatly to the image in America of France as a kingdom of sexual liberation.

By the late 1950s, counterculture was flourishing on both sides of the Atlantic. François Truffaut, widely publicizing his auteur theories, rebelled with a series of short films (like *The 400 Blows* in 1959). Other contemporary directors included Jean-Luc Godard (*A Bout de Soufflé*),

Alain Resnais (*Muriel*), Agnès Varda (*Le Bonheur*), Jacques Demy (*Les Parapluies de Cherbourg*), and Marguerite Duras (*Detruire, Dit-elle*).

Many American films were filmed in Paris (or else used sets to simulate Paris). Notable ones have included the classic *An American in Paris,* starring Gene Kelly, and *Moulin Rouge,* starring Ewan McGregor as a Parisian artist. Woody Allen's acclaimed *Midnight in Paris* celebrated the City of Light. The film features beautiful shots of the city and includes cameos of iconic figures who lived in Paris in the 1920s. In 2022, *Downton Abbey: A New Era* shone a similar spotlight on the sun-kissed French Riviera.

One French film that continues to enchant is Jean-Pierre Jeunet's *Amélie,* with its beautiful scenes shot in Montmartre. More recently, *La Vie en Rose* earned Marion Cotillard an Oscar in 2008 for her performance as "the Little Sparrow," Edith Piaf.

In recent years, television has encapsulated the grit and glamor of France and offers a swift introduction to the nuances of the modern state. *Lupin* describes the adventures of a Senegal-born adventurer with a mixed-race child. *Call My Agent!* epitomizes the celebrity scramble inside a Parisian talent agency. *Emily in Paris*—which follows the madcap antics of an unsophisticated American in the city—was declared soppy and silly by Parisians, although in private, most concede the clichés of amorous, wine-imbibing locals hold some truth, and many adore the show.

Music

Music and France have gone together since the monks in the 12th century sang Gregorian chants in Notre-Dame. Troubadours with their ballads traveled all over France in the Middle Ages. In the Renaissance era, **Josquin des Prez** (c. 1440–1521) was the first master of the High Renaissance style of polyphonic vocal music. He became the greatest composer of his age, a magnificent virtuoso. **Jean-Baptise Lully** (1632–87) entertained the decadent court of Versailles with his operas. During the reign of Robespierre, **Claude-Joseph Rouget de Lisle** (1760–1836) immortalized himself in 1792 when he wrote "La Marseillaise," the French national anthem. Regrettably, he died in poverty.

The rise of the middle class in the 1800s gave birth to both grand opera and opéra comique. Both styles merged into a kind of lyric opera, mixing soaring arias and tragedy in such widely popular hits as Bizet's *Carmen* in 1875 and St-Saën's *Samson et Dalila* in 1877.

During the romantic period of the 19th century, foreign composers moving to Paris often dominated the musical scene. **Frédéric Chopin** (1810–49) was half French, half Polish. He became the most influential composer for piano and even invented new musical forms such as the ballade. **Félix Mendelssohn** (1809–47) had to fight against anti-Semitism to establish himself with his symphonies, concerti, and chamber music.

At the dawn of the 20th century, music became more impressionistic, as evoked by **Claude Débussy** (1862–1918). In many ways, he helped launch modernist music. His "Prélude à L'Après-midi d'un Faune" in 1894 and "La Mer" in 1905 were performed all over Europe. From Russia came **Igor Stravinsky** (1882–1971), who made *Time* magazine's list of the 100 most influential people of the 20th century. He achieved fame as a pianist, conductor, and composer. His *Le Sacre du Printemps* (*The Rite of Spring*), with its pagan rituals, provoked a riot in Paris when it was first performed in 1913.

A revolutionary artist, **Yves Klein** (1928–62) was called a "neo-Dada." His 1960 *The Monotone Symphony* with three naked models became a notorious performance. For 20 minutes, he conducted an orchestra on one note. Dying of a heart attack at the age of 34, Klein is considered today an enigmatic postmodernist. **Pierre Boulez** (1925–2016) developed a technique known as integral serialism using a 12-tone system pioneered in the 1920s. As director of the IRCAM institute at the Centre Pompidou from 1970 to 1992, he influenced young musicians around the world.

France took to American jazz like no other country. Louis Armstrong practically became a national hero to Parisians in the 1930s, and in 1949 Paris welcomed the arrival of Miles Davis. **Stéphane Grappelli** (1908–97), a French jazz violinist, founded the Quintette du Hot Club de France, the most famous of all-string jazz bands. **Django Reinhardt** (1910–53) became one of the most prominent jazz musicians of Europe, known for such works as "Belleville" and "My Sweet."

Some French singers went on to achieve world renown, notably **Edith Piaf** (1915–63), "the Little Sparrow" and France's greatest pop singer. Wherever you go in France, you will hear her "La Vie en Rose," which she first recorded in 1946. Born in 1924, **Charles Aznavour** remains an eternal favorite. He's known for his unique tenor voice with its gravelly and soulful low notes. **Jacques Brel** (1929–78), a singer-songwriter, saw his songs interpreted by everybody from Frank Sinatra to David Bowie.

Among rock stars, the French consider **Johnny Halladay** (1943–2017) their equivalent of Elvis Presley. He scored 18 platinum albums, selling more than 100 million records, and a million Frenchmen took to the streets to mourn his passing in 2017. Another pop icon is **Serge Gainsbourg** (1928–91). He was a master of everything from sexy rock to jazz and reggae. Upon his death, President François Mitterrand called him "our Baudelaire, our Apollinaire." In the late 1990s, a dreamy French house music secured international notoriety with bands such as **Air** and **Daft Punk.** More recently, chart-topping indie band **The Dø** performed another first—headlining the French album charts with songs sung entirely in English. Superstar DJ **David Guetta** continues to rock the party from New York to Ibiza.

Artists with immigrant backgrounds often are the major names in the vibrant French music scene of today, with influences from French Africa, the French Caribbean, and the Middle East. Along with rap and hip-hop, these sounds rule the nights in the boîtes of France's biggest cities. **Khaled** (b. 1960), from Algeria, has become known as the "King of Raï." Among the most influential French rappers today is **MC Solaar** (b. 1969); born in Senegal, he explores racism and ethnic identity in his wordplays. Younger rapper **Kekra** (who hides both his real identity and age) smashed the music mold by releasing his tracks on the Internet for free before garnering up to a million monthly views on Spotify.

EATING & DRINKING IN FRANCE

As any French person will attest, French food is the best in the world. That's as true today as it was during the 19th-century heyday of the master

Vineyards outside of Bergerac in the South of France.

chef Escoffier. A demanding patriarch who codified the rules of French cooking, he ruled the kitchens of the Ritz in Paris, standardizing the complicated preparation and presentation of *haute cuisine.*

However, at the foundation of virtually every culinary theory ever developed in France is a deep-seated respect for the *cuisine des provinces* (also known as *cuisine campagnarde*). Ingredients usually included only what was produced locally, and the rich and hearty result was gradually developed over several generations of *mères cuisinières.* Springing from an agrarian society with a vivid sense of nature's cycles, the cuisine provided appropriate nourishment for bodies that had toiled through a day in the open air. The movement is alive and well today with a tradition for eating locally produced—or *zero km*—foods.

Despite the availability of top-quality ingredients across the country, regional cuisine is more sought after than ever before. Try salmon, lark pâté, goat's milk cheese, partridge, rillettes, herb-flavored black pudding, and fine white wines from the Loire Valley. Not forgetting sole, brill, mackerel, turbot, mussels, and big fat lobsters from the Normandy coast, often bathed in the region's rich butter sauce. Just don't forget the Camembert for dessert.

Gourmets, not just beach lovers, should go to the Riviera. Bouillabaisse, an exquisite fish soup said to have been invented by Venus, is Marseille's best-known dish. Riviera specialties include *daube* (slow-cooked beef stew), *soupe au pistou* (vegetable soup with basil), and *salade Niçoise* (traditionally made with tomatoes, olives, radishes, scallions, peppers, and tuna or anchovies). All are best served with a glass of ice-cold *rosé* in the afternoon sun.

And Paris? At the center of the country's gastronomic crossroads, it tops the lot. The city literally has thousands of restaurants to choose from. The best of them are listed in this book or discussed on websites like **Le Fooding** (www.lefooding.com) and **Time Out** (www.timeout.fr). Beef from Lyon, lamb from the Auvergne, crêpes from Brittany, and *cassoulet* from southwest France are served up in abundance. This city of 10 million gastronomes has also become a mecca for creative foreign fare. Until you've eaten sashimi, bibimbap, ceviche, and gourmet burgers in Paris, you haven't lived.

To accompany such cuisine, let your own good taste—and your wallet—determine your choice of wine. Most wine stewards, called *sommeliers,* are there to help you in your choice, and only in the most dishonest of restaurants will they push you toward the most expensive selections. Of course, if you prefer only water, or perhaps a beer, or even a cider in Normandy, then be firm and order your choice without embarrassment. Some restaurants include a beverage in their menu rates (*boisson compris*), either as part of a set tasting menu in ritzy restaurants or as part of a fixed-price formula in cheaper establishments. Some of the most satisfying wines we've drunk in France came from unlabeled house bottles or carafes, called *vin de la maison.* In general, unless you're a real connoisseur, don't worry about labels and vintages. When in doubt, you can rarely go wrong with a good Burgundy or Bordeaux. As a rule of thumb, expect to spend about one-third of the restaurant tab on wine.

WHEN TO GO

The best time to visit France is in the spring (Apr–June) or fall (Sept–Nov), when things are easier to come by, from Métro seats to good-tempered waiters. The weather is temperate year-round. July and August are the worst for crowds but best for beaches. That's when Parisians desert their city, leaving it to tourists, especially as climate change has rendered France hotter than ever. Note that some visitors might be surprised at the

A Bastille Day (July 14) parade, Paris.

lack of air-conditioning, which is hard and often illegal to fit on centuries-old buildings.

France's weather varies from region to region. Despite its latitude, Paris never gets very cold. Normandy is a little fresher—and foggier—but the Mediterranean boasts one long summer, with the French Riviera soaking up 300 days of sun per year. Provence dreads *le mistral* (an unrelenting wind), which most often blows in the winter for bouts of a few days at a time but can also last up to 2 weeks.

Paris's Average Daytime Temperature & Rainfall

	JAN	FEB	MAR	APR	MAY	JUNE	JULY	AUG	SEPT	OCT	NOV	DEC
TEMP. °F	38	39	46	51	58	64	66	66	61	53	45	40
TEMP. °C	3	4	8	11	14	18	19	19	16	12	7	4
RAINFALL (IN.)	3.2	2.9	2.4	2.7	3.2	3.5	3.3	3.7	3.3	3.0	3.5	3.1
RAINFALL (CM)	8.1	7.4	6	6.9	8.1	8.9	8.4	9.4	8.4	7.6	8.9	7.9

France Calendar of Events

JANUARY

Monte Carlo Motor Rally (Le Rallye de Monte Carlo). The world's most venerable car race. Mid-January. www.acm.mc

FEBRUARY

Carnival of Nice. Parades, music, fireworks, and "Les Batailles des Fleurs" (Battles of the Flowers) are all part of this celebration. The climax is the burning of the Carnival king effigy. Late February to early March. www.nicecarnaval.com

APRIL

Foire du Trône, on the Reuilly Lawn of the Bois de Vincennes, 12e, Paris. This mammoth fun fair operates daily from noon to midnight. Early April to late May. www.foiredutrone.com

International Garden Festival, Château de Chaumont, Amboise (Loire). An international competition showcasing the best in garden design. Mid-April to mid-October. www.domaine-chaumont.fr

Côte d'Azur Garden Festival, French Riviera. Biannual contest between avant-garde outdoor designers in six prime Riviera spots, with the next editions in 2025 and 2027. April. www. www.cote dazurfrance.fr

International Marathon of Paris. Runners from around the world compete along the Champs-Elysées. Early April. www. parismarathon.com

MAY

Cannes Film Festival (Festival International du Film). Movie madness transforms this Mediterranean town into a media circus. Admission to films and parties is by invitation. Other films play 24 hours a day. Mid-May. www.festival-cannes.com

Normandy Impressionist Festival. Region-wide event that showcases the area's favorite painters (Monet, Manet, Signac) in museums across Normandy, held every 2 to 3 years; most recent edition in 2024. April to September. normandie-tourisme.fr

Monaco Formula 1 Grand Prix. The world's most high-tech cars race through Monaco's narrow streets in a blizzard of hot metal and ritzy architecture. Late May. www.formula1.com

Coupes Moto Légende, Dijon. Thousands of motorcyclists, including well-known names, descend upon Dijon to race their vintage bikes around the Prenois track. Late May. www.coupes-moto-legende.fr

Festival de St-Denis. A celebration of music in the burial place of the French kings, a grim early Gothic monument in Paris's northern suburb of St-Denis. Late May to late June. www.festival-saint-denis.com

French Open Tennis Championship, Stade Roland-Garros, 16e, Paris. The French Open features 2 weeks of men's, women's, and doubles tennis on hot, red, dusty clay courts. Late May to early June. www.rolandgarros.com

JUNE

Prix du Jockey Club and Prix Diane-Longines, Hippodrome de Chantilly. Thoroughbreds from as far away as Kentucky and Dubai compete in this race. On race days, dozens of trains depart from Paris's Gare du Nord for Chantilly, where racegoers take free shuttle buses to the track. Early to mid-June. www.france-galop.com

Paris Air Show. France's military-industrial complex shows off its high-tech hardware. Fans, competitors, and industrial spies mob Le Bourget Airport. Next event mid-June 2025. www.paris-air-show.com

Catalpa Festival, Auxerre. This 3-night world music festival takes place in various venues around town including the atmospheric surrounds of the cloister of the Abbaye Saint-Germain. www.lesilex.fr

Les 24 Heures du Mans Voitures. Racing cars blast around the clock at this venerable circuit. Also hosts the huge September motorcycle rally. Mid-June. www.24h-lemans.com

Festival de Cornouaille in Quimper.

Getting Tickets

Visitors can purchase tickets for almost every music festival, soccer game, or cultural event in France online. Try the official website first, or log onto **Fnac** (www.fnactickets.com), France's largest music chain, which offers both a digital reservation service as well as in-store ticket booths.

Festival Chopin, Paris. Everything you've ever wanted to hear by the Polish exile, who lived most of his life in Paris. Piano recitals take place in the Orangerie du Parc de Bagatelle, 16e. Mid-June to mid-July. www.frederic-chopin.com

Gay Pride Parade, place du 18 Juin 1940 to place de la Bastille, Paris. A week of expositions and parties climaxes in a parade patterned after those in New York and San Francisco, with smaller festivities outside Paris in cities like Nice and Lyon. Late June. www.gaypride.fr

JULY

Fêtes Médiévales, Bayeaux. The Middle Ages come to life as many of Normandy's picturesque towns put on lively medieval festivals. The biggest and most spectacular is in Bayeux. Costumed performers fill the streets alongside market stalls, medieval games for kids, and colorful jousters. First weekend of July. www.bayeux.fr

Les Chorégies d'Orange, Orange. One of southern France's most important lyric festivals presents oratorios, operas, and choral works in France's best-preserved Roman amphitheater. Early July to early August. www.choregies.fr

Les Nocturnes du Mont-St-Michel. This sound-and-light tour meanders through the stairways and corridors of one of Europe's most impressive medieval monuments. Early July to late August. www.ot-montsaintmichel.com

Colmar International Festival, Colmar. Classical concerts are held in public buildings of one of the most folkloric towns in Alsace. Early July. www.festival-colmar.com

Tour de France. The world's most hotly contested bicycle race sends crews of wind-tunnel–tested athletes along an itinerary that detours deep into the Pyrenees, Alps, Provence, and Normandy. The finish line is on the Champs-Elysées. First 3 weeks of July. www.letour.fr

Festival d'Avignon. This world-class festival has a reputation for exposing new talent to critical scrutiny and acclaim. The focus is usually on avant-garde works in theater, dance, and music. Last 3 weeks of July. www.festival-avignon.com

Bastille Day. Celebrating the birth of modern-day France, the nation's festivities reach their peak with country-wide street fairs, fireworks, and feasts. In Paris, the day begins with a parade down the Champs-Elysées and ends with fireworks at Montmartre. July 14.

Paris Quartier d'Eté. For 4 weeks, music rules around the city. Two dozen French and international performances take place at unusual venues like the Musée de Cluny, the Gare du Nord, and the Parc de Belleville. Mid-July to mid-August. www.parislete.fr

Nice Jazz Festival. Concerts begin in the afternoon and go on until late at night (sometimes all night) in place Masséna and the Jardin Albert 1er, overlooking Nice's promenade des Anglais. Big names including Herbie Hancock and Sir Tom Jones headlined the 2023 event. Mid-July. www.nicejazzfestival.fr

Festival d'Aix-en-Provence. A musical event *par excellence,* with everything from Gregorian chants to operas composed on synthesizers. Recitals are in the medieval cloister of the Cathédrale St-Sauveur. Expect heat, crowds, and loud sounds. July. www.festival-aix.com

Réncontre d'Arles. The prettiest town in Provence hosts a city-wide photography festival. Prepare to be wowed. July to September. www.rencontres-arles.com

Festival de Cornouaille, Quimper. An annual weeklong celebration of Breton culture. The festivities include parades in traditional costume and Celtic and Breton concerts throughout the city. Late July. www.quimper.bzh

AUGUST

Festival Interceltique de Lorient, Brittany. Celtic verse and lore are celebrated in the Celtic heart of France. The 150 concerts include classical and folkloric musicians, dancers, singers, and painters. Traditional Breton *pardons* (religious processions) take place in the once-independent maritime duchy. Mid August. www.festival-interceltique.bzh

Musical Gatherings (Les Rencontres Musicales), Vézelay. Four days of classical music concerts held in several venues including the magnificent basilica. www.lacitedelavoix.net

SEPTEMBER

Deauville American Film Festival. The likes of Clooney, Pitt, and Travolta jet in for a yearly celebration of movies, glitz, and glamour. First week September. www.festival-deauville.com

La Villette Jazz Festival. Some 50 concerts are held in churches, auditoriums, and concert halls in the Paris suburb of La Villette. Past festivals have included Kenny Garrett, Jamie Callum, and other international artists. Early to mid-September. www.jazzalavillette.com

Festival d'Automne, Paris. One of France's most famous festivals is also one of its most eclectic, focusing mainly on modern music, ballet, theater, and art. Mid-September to mid-January. www.festival-automne.com

Festival de la Loire, Orléans (Loire). The Loire River and its banks come alive with sails, music, and food during the largest boat festival in Europe. Late September, every other year; next in 2025 and 2027. www.orleans.fr

OCTOBER

Paris Auto Show, Parc des Expositions, Porte de Versailles, 15e, Paris. This biennial showcase for European car design comes complete with glitzy attendees, lots of hype, and the latest models. Mid-October; next in 2024 and 2026. www.mondial.paris

Prix de l'Arc de Triomphe, Hippodrome de Longchamp, 16e, Paris. France's answer to England's Ascot is the country's most prestigious horse race, culminating the equine season in Europe. Early October. www.prixarcdetriomphe.com

NOVEMBER

Armistice Day, nationwide. In Paris, the signing of the document that ended World War I is celebrated with a military parade from the Arc de Triomphe to the Hôtel des Invalides. November 11.

Dijon Gastronomy Fair (Foire Gastronomique de Dijon). One of France's biggest food fairs attracts around 600 exhibitors and 200,000 visitors each year. www.foirededijon.com

Hospices de Beaune Wine Auction (Vente des Vins des Hospices de Beaune). Three days of wine tastings, street entertainment and a half marathon culminating in the world-famous charity wine auction. www.beaune-tourisme.fr

DECEMBER

Boat Fair (Le Salon Nautique de Paris). Europe's major exposition of what's afloat, at Porte de Versailles. One week in early December. www.salonnautique paris.com

Fête de Lumières, Lyon. In honor of the Virgin Mary, lights are placed in windows throughout the city. Early December. www.fetedeslumieres.lyon.fr

Fête de St-Sylvestre (New Year's Eve), nationwide. In Paris, this holiday is most boisterously celebrated in the Latin Quarter. At midnight, the city explodes. Strangers kiss, and boulevard St-Michel and the Champs-Elysées become virtual pedestrian malls. December 31.

RESPONSIBLE TRAVEL

From pioneering eco-friendly *autopartage* (car-sharing) programs to an unabashed enthusiasm for *biodynamique* wines, the French have embraced sustainability. In an age when environmental, ethical, and social concerns are becoming ever more important, France's focus on green principles— whether through traditional markets, carbon-neutral public transport, or all-natural outdoor adventure—offers visitors and residents alike plenty in the way of sustainable tourism.

Nearly 2 decades ago, Paris mayor Bertrand Delanoë introduced the **Vélib'** scheme (www.velib-metropole.fr), a public bicycle "sharing" program. With tens of thousands of bicycles and bike-rental stations spread throughout the city, it is a fast and inexpensive way to get around. Similar schemes have been joined by eScooter "sharing" programs in many other major French cities, including Nice, Avignon, Aix-en-Provence, Rouen, Lyon, Bordeaux, and Marseille.

In order to crisscross France's vast countryside, many French ditch their cars and opt instead for travel on a **TGV** (www.sncf-connect.com). This network of high-speed trains is powered by SNCF, France's government-owned rail company, which is dedicated to becoming completely carbon-neutral. TGVs run from Paris's hub to cities throughout the country, including Nantes, Rouen, Lyon, Dijon, Rennes, Avignon, Aix-en-Provence, Nice, and Marseille. The ride is more comfortable and often far quicker than taking a car.

Many hotels in France have undertaken measures to preserve the environment, and those that have are awarded with a green label. Look for hotels with the title of *La Clef Verte* (Green Key; www.laclefverte.org). The label rewards hotels that take a more environmental approach to water, energy, and waste, and help raise the awareness of their guests. Even if you don't stay at a green hotel, you can still do your bit: Turn off the air-conditioning when you leave the room, request that your sheets aren't changed every day, and use your towels more than once. Laundry makes up around 40% of an average hotel's energy use.

When planning your travels, it's equally important to consider the impact your visit will have on the environment. France's rippling vineyards, Grande Randonnée (GR) hiking trails, and pristine coastline all make for enchanting (and eco-friendly) escapes.

Responsible tourism also means leaving a place in the same condition you found it. You can do this by not dropping litter and respecting the color-coded garbage bin system. Support the local economy and culture by shopping in small neighborhood stores and at open-air markets that showcase the seasonal harvest of local, often organic (*bio*) producers. Look out for organic and *biodynamique* (biodynamic) wines, frequently sold at wine shops and farmers' markets, too. And given the myriad of tiny, family-run restaurants scattered throughout France's cities, towns, and countryside, it's all too easy to dig into a home-cooked meal.

PARIS

By Anna E. Brooke

4

The name "Paris" conjures up such a potent brew of images and ideas that it's sometimes hard to find the meeting point between myth and reality. But the city's graceful streets, soaked in history, really are as elegant as they say, its monuments and museums as extraordinary; and a slightly world-weary, *fin-de-siècle* grandeur really is part of day-to-day existence. Paris is much more than a beautiful assemblage of buildings, however; it is the pulsing heart of the French nation.

Where to begin? With so many wonderful things to see, it's easy to get overwhelmed in the City of Light. If you are here for only a few days, you'll probably be spending most of your time in the city center, the nucleus of which is the Ile de la Cité. The **top neighborhoods** on most short-term visitors' hit parade are the 1st through 8th arrondissements (see "City Layout," below), which includes the Ile de la Cité, the Louvre area, the Champs Elysées, the Eiffel Tower, the Latin Quarter, the Marais, and St-Germain. **If you have a bit more time,** you should explore some of the outlying neighborhoods, like Montmartre in the 18th arrondissement, and the funky, eastern areas of Menilmontant, Belleville, Canal St-Martin, and Bastille, as well as the elegant, museum-rich depths of the 16th arrondissement. Whether you're here for a few days or longer, this chapter is designed to give you the essential information you need to create a Paris itinerary that's just right for you.

ESSENTIALS & ORIENTATION
Arriving
BY PLANE

Paris has two international airports: **Aéroport d'Orly (ORY),** 18km (11 miles) south of the city (for both airports: www.parisaeroport.fr; © **00-33-1-70-36-39-50** from abroad, or **39-50** from France), and **Aéroport Roissy-Charles-de-Gaulle (CDG),** 30km (19 miles) northeast. If you are taking Ryanair or another discount airline that arrives at **Beauvais** (BVA; www.aeroportparisbeauvais.com; © **08-92-68-20-66**), be advised that this airport is located about 70km (40 miles) from Paris.

CHARLES DE GAULLE AIRPORT (ROISSY) By commuter train: The quickest way into central Paris is the **RER B** (www.ratp.fr), suburban trains that leave every 10 to 15 minutes between 4:50am and 1am (midnight on weekends). It takes about 40 minutes to get to Paris, and RER B stops at several Métro stations including Châtelet-Les-Halles, Saint-Michel-Notre-Dame, and Luxembourg. A single ticket costs 11.45€ (7.40€ children ages 4–10, free for children 3 and under), and you can buy it from the machines in the stations at both terminals.

By bus: The **Roissybus** (www.ratp.fr; ✆ **34-24**) departs every 20 minutes from the airport daily from 6am to 12:30am and costs 16.20€ for the 70-minute ride. The bus leaves you in the center of Paris, at the corner of rue Scribe and rue Auber, near the Opéra.

By taxi: The flat rate for a **taxi** from CDG into the city is 55€ for the Right Bank and 62€ for the Left Bank, not including supplements (4€ for immediate reservation, 7€ for advance reservation). Taxi stands can be found outside each of the airport's terminals. Alternatively, Uber functions in France, and costs around 45€ to 50€ in an UberX car (www.uber.com), depending on traffic and distance.

ORLY AIRPORT   Orly has two terminals: Orly Sud (south) and Orly Ouest (west). To get to the center of Paris, take the 8-minute monorail **OrlyVal** to the RER station "Antony" to get **RER B** into the center. Combined travel time is about 40 minutes. Trains usually run between 5am and 1am, and the one-way fare for the OrlyVal plus the RER B is 13.25€ (6.60€ children ages 4–10, free for children 3 and under).

The **Orlybus** (www.ratp.fr), which leaves every 15 minutes between 5am and 12:30am, links the airport with place Denfert-Rochereau, a 30-minute trip that costs 11.20€ for both adults and children.

The flat rate for a **taxi** from Orly to central Paris is 35€ to the Left Bank and 41€ to the Right Bank, not including supplements (4€ for immediate reservation, 7€ for advance reservation). Uber costs around 32€ for the Left Bank and 37€ for the Right Bank in an UberX car (www.uber.com; see p. 76).

BEAUVAIS AIRPORT   Buses leave about 20 minutes after each flight has landed, and, depending on the traffic, take about 1 hour and 15 minutes to get to Paris. The bus drops you at Porte Maillot (Métro: Porte Maillot). To return to Beauvais, you need to be at the bus station at least 3 hours before the departure of your flight. A one-way ticket costs 17€ (29.90€ return). For information call ✆ **08-92-68-20-64.**

BY TRAIN

Paris has seven major train stations: **Gare d'Austerlitz** (13th arrond.), **Gare de Lyon** (12th arrond.), **Gare de Bercy** (12th arrond.), **Gare Montparnasse** (14th arrond.), **Gare St-Lazare** (8th arrond.), **Gare de l'Est** (10th arrond.), and **Gare du Nord** (10th arrond.). Each station can be reached by bus or Métro. *Warning:* I have never had trouble, but as in most major cities, the stations and surrounding areas can be seedy and frequented by pickpockets. Be alert, especially at night. To buy train

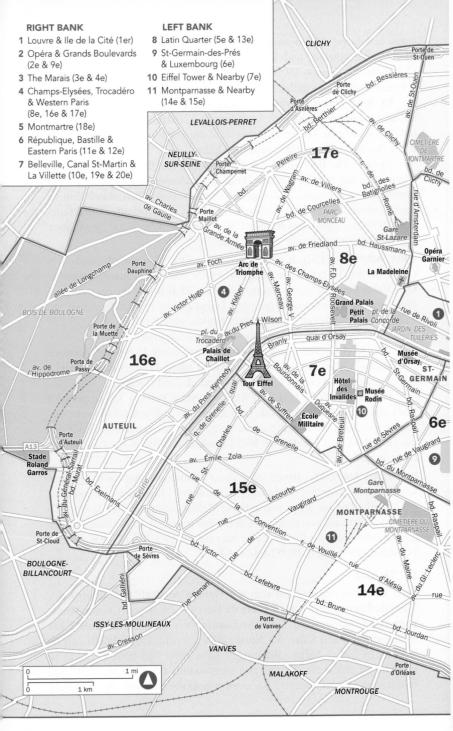

RIGHT BANK
1 Louvre & Ile de la Cité (1er)
2 Opéra & Grands Boulevards
  (2e & 9e)
3 The Marais (3e & 4e)
4 Champs-Elysées, Trocadéro
  & Western Paris
  (8e, 16e & 17e)
5 Montmartre (18e)
6 République, Bastille &
  Eastern Paris (11e & 12e)
7 Belleville, Canal St-Martin &
  La Villette (10e, 19e & 20e)

LEFT BANK
8 Latin Quarter (5e & 13e)
9 St-Germain-des-Prés
  & Luxembourg (6e)
10 Eiffel Tower & Nearby (7e)
11 Montparnasse & Nearby
   (14e & 15e)

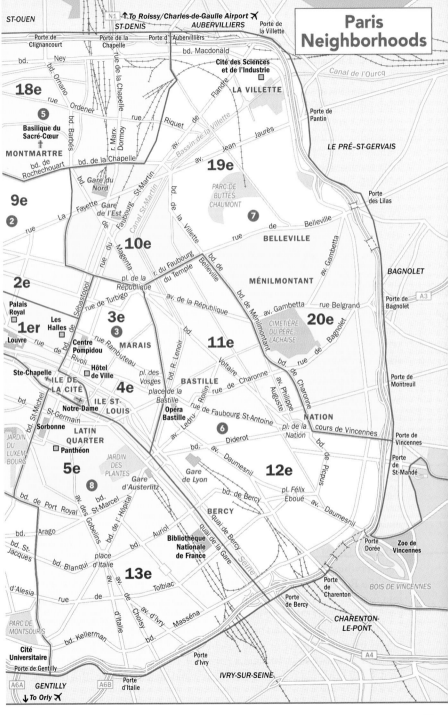

tickets, visit www.sncf-connect.com, call ✆ **36-35,** or go to a desk in one of the stations.

The **Eurostar** (www.eurostar.com), which passes under the channel for 20 minutes, will get you from Paris' Gare du Nord to St. Pancras Station, London (or vice versa), in just 2¼ hours. Regular ticket prices can be high (around 200€ one-way!), but scads of discounts are available (from as little as around 40€ one-way) on the website, especially if you purchase in advance and/or are flexible about times. Brussels is only 1 hour and 15 minutes away on the high-speed **Thalys** (www.thalys.com) train, and tickets range anywhere from 25€ to 145€ depending on what deal you get. Visit the site for high-speed trains to Brussels, Amsterdam, and Cologne. For rail passes that you can use throughout Europe, visit **Rail Europe** (www.raileurope.com).

BY BUS

You can travel to and from Paris from other European countries by bus via two main companies: **Flixbus** (https://global.flixbus.com), which has more than 1,000 routes, and tickets starting for as little as 5€ (buy online, via the app, or in Paris go to the FlixShop at Gare-Bercy, 208 quai de Bercy, 12th arrond.); and **BlaBlaCar Bus** (www.thetrainline.com/bus-companies/blablabus; reserve online or via the app), offering 400 routes with even cheaper tickets starting at 2.99€. The main bus stop for both of these companies is Bercy-Seine (210 quai de Bercy, 12th arrond.).

BY CAR

While I wouldn't recommend driving in Paris, renting a car and driving around France before or after your Paris trip can be a lovely way to see France. All the major car-rental companies have offices here, but you'll often get better deals if you reserve before you leave home. **AutoEurope** (www.autoeurope.com) is an excellent source for discounted rentals. Even better, however, may be **AutoSlash.com,** which applies discount codes to rentals from all of the major multinational firms, which can mean savings. It also monitors prices, so if a rate drops, it re-books you automatically. You pay for the rental at the counter, not in advance.

Getting Around Town

For everything you ever wanted to know about the city's public transport, visit the **RATP** (www.ratp.fr; ✆ **34-24**). Paris and its suburbs are divided into five travel zones, but you'll probably only be concerned with zones 1 and 2, which cover the city itself.

RATP tickets are valid on the Métro, bus, tram and RER. You can buy tickets over the counter or from machines at most Métro/RER entrances. A **single ticket** costs 2.10€ and a *carnet* of 10 tickets costs 16.90€. Children 4 to 9 years old pay half price; kids 3 and under ride free. But bear in mind that the RATP is gradually phasing out paper tickets, replacing them with plastic passes, so you may no longer be able to buy a paper *carnet*. You will only be able to buy one with the **Navigo Easy card,** sold at ticket booths for 2€. Once you have your card, you charge it, either on your phone with the app Bonjour RATP (www.ratp.fr/apps/bonjour-ratp) or at a machine. The downside to this is that you can no longer share your *carnet* with fellow travelers. Each individual will need a card.

Tourists can benefit from a **Paris Visite** pass, which offers unlimited travel in zones on bus, Métro, and RER, and discounts on some attractions. Think hard about how much you are going to use your pass however, as you'll probably end up walking a lot, and in the end a cheaper *carnet* of 10 tickets might do the trick. A 1-day Paris Visite adult pass for zones 1 to 3 costs 13.55€, a 2-day pass 22.05€, a 3-day pass 30.10€, and a 5-day pass 43.30€. It is also possible to buy more expensive passes for zones 1 to 5, which will also get you to the airport.

For a slightly cheaper 1-day pass, try a **Mobilis** ticket, which offers unlimited travel in zones 1 up to 5; a pass for zones 1 and 2 costs 8.45€. If you're staying for a week or longer, it may be worth getting the **Navigo weekly pass,** a swipe card, which like the Navigo Easy, above) can be bought at the ticket booth for 2€, then charged on the RATP app (www.ratp.fr/apps/bonjour-ratp) and at certain Métro or train stations. The weekly tariff (which runs Fri–Thurs) for zones 1 to 5 is 30€. That includes going to and from the airports (except OrlyVal) and transport for day trips such as Versailles or Fontainebleau, so it could quickly pay off. If your trip fits into a Friday-to-Thursday schedule, this 7-day card is substantially cheaper than a 5-day Paris Visite card.

The historic Abbesses metro entrance.

BY MÉTRO OR RER (SUBWAY)

The city's first Métro, or subway, was the apex of high tech when it was inaugurated on July 19, 1900. Today, more than a century later, it still functions very well. The lack of wheelchair/stroller access are its greatest downfalls and somewhat embarrassing for the city hosting the 2024 Paralympics. A big push to render the city more accessible is underway, however, so don't be surprised to find some stations closed between certain hours. Aside from the occasional strike, the Métro is usually efficient and civilized, especially if you avoid rush hour (7:30–9:30am and 6–8pm). It's generally safe at night (although you might want to think twice about using it to get to more isolated parts of the city); the service shuts down between midnight and 1am weekdays, and at 2am on Friday, Saturday, and pre-holiday evenings.

The **RER** (pronounced "ehr-euh-ehr") is the suburban train network that dashes through the city making limited stops; it closes down around the same time at the Métro (without the weekend bonus hour). The downsides to the RER trains are (a) they don't run as often as the Métro, and (b) they're hard to figure out since they run on a different track system, and the same lines can have multiple final destinations. To check your destinations, check the departure boards (or screens) on the quays: The stops served by the next train are either listed or lit up

Important: Make sure to hold on to your ticket; you'll need it to get *out* of the turnstile on the way out.

BY BUS

Buses can be an efficient way to get around town, and you'll get a scenic tour to boot. The majority run from 6am to 9:30pm (a few operate until 12:30am), with reduced service on Sundays and holidays. After the bus and Métro services stop running, head for the **Noctilien** night bus (www.transilien.com/static/noctilien). The 52 lines crisscross the city and head out to the suburbs every half-hour or so from 12:30 to 5:30am. Tickets cost the same as for the regular bus. You can use Métro tickets and passes on the buses or you can buy an onboard SMS ticket for 2.50€ directly from your mobile phone. All you have to do, when you see your bus approaching, is send an SMS to ℂ **93100** with the word "BUS," followed by the number of the route (with no gaps between the two). For instance, if you're on route 86, type BUS86; if you're on route 2 of the Noctilien night bus, write BUSN02. You'll immediately receive an SMS in return, with your ticket. Alas, you can't reuse a ticket you've used on the Métro on the bus. You can, however, reuse the same ticket you've used on the bus on a tram (and vice versa) within a 90-minute limit. Tickets and passes need to be validated in the machine next to the driver's cabin (except bus tickets on your phone).

BY TRAM

Over the past few years, Paris has added twelve new tramway lines, with extensions and new lines in progress. They connect Paris with its suburbs; within Paris they run along the outer circle of boulevards that trace the city limits. Tickets are the same price as the Métro.

BY TAXI

Changing the taxi landscape in France (much to the disdain of regular taxi drivers) are ride sharing services, of which the most well-known is **Uber** (www.uber.com). For central Paris, you rarely have to wait more than 5 minutes for an Uber to arrive. You will be charged more for your ride, when demand is high, but usually Uber is cheaper than standard taxis. Other Apps offering the similar services in Paris are **Bolt** (https://bolt.eu/en-fr/cities/paris) and **Heech** (www.heetch.com).

Paris's main taxi company is **G7** (www.g7-france.fr; ☏ **01-89-61-42-92**). They, too, have an app, allowing users to track drivers and reserve cars. Or you can hail taxis in the street, but not all will stop (only hail those with a full green or white light). Or look for a taxi stand, which resembles a bus stop and usually sports a blue TAXI sign. Once inside, you'll have to pray that your driver is skilled in dodging Parisian traffic, which is horrendous.

Calculating fares is a complicated business. When you get in, the most the meter should read is 4.18€. Then, the maximum basic rate for central Paris (arrond. 1–20) is 1.21€ (depending on the day of the week and the hour, this may be lower). The minimum fare is 7.30€; if you have more than four people in your party, you'll be charged an extra 4.50€ for the fifth person. If you reserve a taxi for immediate pick-up, the extra charge is 4€; to reserve in advance costs 7€. The saving grace here is that the distances are usually not huge, and barring excessive traffic, your average crosstown fare should fall between 15€ and 25€ for two without baggage. Tipping is not obligatory but rounding up or a .50€ to 1€ tip is customary.

Important: Avoid unlicensed taxis, which you'll recognize from the lack of a regular taxi light on the roof.

BY BICYCLE

Cycling in Paris has been revolutionized by the hugely successful **Vélib'** bike rental scheme (the name comes from *vélo,* meaning "bicycle," and *liberté,* meaning "freedom") launched in 2007; see box below. Alternatively, you can rent a bike from **Paris à vélo, c'est sympa!,** 22 rue Alphonse Baudin, 11th arrond. (https://parisavelo.fr; ☏ **01-48-87-60-01;** Métro: St-Sébastien-Froissart or Richard Lenoir). Rentals cost 17€ for half a day and 20€ for a full day, but they do require 250€ as a deposit. If you're feeling extra lazy, electric bikes are available from 35€ for half a day and 42€ for a full day.

ON FOOT

If you have the time and the energy, the best mode of transport in this small and walkable city is your own two feet. You can cross the center of town (say, from the place St-Michel to Les Halles) in about 20 minutes. This is the finest way to see and experience the city and take in all the little details that make it all so wonderful.

vélib': A GREAT WAY TO CYCLE AROUND PARIS

Since July 2007, when the mayor's office inaugurated the **Vélib'** (vel-LEEB) system of low-cost bike rentals, Parisians have been pedaling up a storm. Traffic be dammed: It's fun to ride around town, drop off your bike near your destination, and not have to worry about locking it up. And with more than 1,000 km (620 miles) of bike lanes, it's safe to say Paris has become a cyclists' city. Vélib now also includes electric bikes (colored blue, around 40% of the 20,000-strong fleet; the pedal bikes are green), so you can get around even faster.

Visitors have several subscription options (online or from the machine at more than 1,400 bike stands): Buy a single journey ticket for 3€, for a 45-minute journey on either a pedal bike or an electric bike; get a 1-day pass for 5€ (pedal bike) or 10€ (electric), which gives you the right to as many 30-minute (45-min. for electric) rides as you'd like for 24 hours; and purchase the 3-day pass for 20€ (pedal or electric). If you want to go over 30 minutes, you pay 1€ for your extra 30 minutes on a pedal bike, and 2€ for the 45 minutes on an electric bike.

The bikes are fitted with a V-Box, a computer system set between the handlebars, which enables you to lock and unlock the bikes. It also lets you leave your bike in an otherwise full station; follow the instructions and park it top-to-tail with another bike. The English version of the website (www.velib-metropole.fr/en) explains how everything works; the assistance number is ℂ **01-76-49-12-34.**

The one big catch is that to use the machines you must have a credit or debit card with a chip in it (at time of writing, you couldn't use phone pay apps like Apple Pay). This can be a problem for North American tourists, so I advise either getting a TravelEx "cash passport" with money on it (www.travelex.com), or even easier, buy your subscription ahead of time online (make sure you have your secret code to punch in on the stand).

Helmets are not provided, so if you're feeling queasy about launching into traffic, bring one along. The city has an ever-increasing number of bike lanes, and success has been such that new ones are being added. **Note:** Cyclists no longer always have the right to ride in the bus lanes; check for road signs. One more **tip:** Before you ride, download the app on your phone, so you don't waste precious time looking for a place to check in or check out.

BY E-SCOOTER

Driving is *not* recommended in Paris, but the auto-adventurous may want to try tooling around on an e-scooter (self-serve, two-wheeled, moped-style electric scooters). They're all the rage right now, and people 18 and over can use them on the road (not in bike lanes or on the sidewalk). The main company is **Cityscoot** (www.cityscoot.eu), costing .46€/min (that's 13.80€ for 30 min.). If you were born before 1988, you don't need a driver's license to use an e-scooter; if you were born after 1988, you must have either a valid E.U. driving license or a license that was issued in your own country and translated into French by an accredited translator (plan well ahead and check with your embassy; the translation process can be costly and time-consuming). *Note:* Helmets are provided (with disposable helmet liners), but bring your own motocycle gloves, which French law requires you to wear.

Visitor Information

The **Paris Tourist Office** is at 29 rue de Rivoli, 1st arrond., inside the Hôtel de Ville City Hall (https://parisjetaime.com/Métro: Hôtel-de-Ville). The Tourist Office has two other offices in the city, at Gare du Nord and inside th Carousel du Louvre, the shopping mall, below the Louvre Museum; check the website for addresses and hours.

City Layout

One of the nice things about Paris is that it's relatively small. It's not a sprawling megalopolis like Tokyo or London; in fact, Paris *intramuros,* or inside the long-gone city walls, numbers a mere 2.15 million habitants, and, excluding the large exterior parks of Bois de Vincinnes and the Bois de Boulogne, measures about 87 sq. km (34 sq. miles). (The suburbs, on the other hand, are sprawling, but chances are you won't be spending much, if any, time there.) Getting around is not difficult, provided you have a general sense of where things are.

The city is vaguely egg shaped, with the Seine cutting a wide upside-down U-shaped arc through the middle. The northern half is known as the **Right Bank,** and the southern, the **Left Bank.** To the uninitiated, the only way to remember is to face west, or downstream, so that the Right Bank will be to your right, and the Left to your left.

If you can't get your banks straight, don't worry, because most Parisians don't talk in terms of Right or Left Bank, but in terms of ***arrondissements,*** or districts. The city is neatly split up into 20 official arrondissements, which spiral out from the center of the city. The lower the number, the closer you'll be to the center, and as the numbers go up, you'll head toward the outer limits. Though their borders don't always correspond to historical neighborhoods, they do chop up the city into easily digestible chunks, so if you know what arrondissement your destination is in, your chances of finding it easily go way up.

[Fast FACTS] PARIS

ATMs/Banks   ATMs can be found all over the city, and they tend to give a better exchange rate than currency exchange agencies.

Dentists & Doctors
To download a list of English-speaking dentists and doctors in Paris, visit the U.S. Citizens Services page on the U.S. Embassy

website (https://fr.us embassy.gov) and click on "Medical Assistance." You can also reach U.S. Citizens Services by phone at ☎ **01-43-12-22-22.**

Hospitals   Paris has excellent public hospitals; visit www.aphp.fr for locations and details on specialties. Private hospitals with English-speaking staff: **American Hospital of Paris,** 55 bd. du Château, 92200 Neuilly-sur-Seine (www.american-hospital.org; ℰ **01-46-41-25-25**), and **Hôpital Franco-Britannique,** 3 rue Barbès or 4 rue Kleber, Levallois (www.hopitalfrancobritannique.org/en; ℰ **01-47-59-59-59**).

Emergencies   For an ambulance, call ℰ **15.** For the police, call ℰ **17.** Emergency services: ℰ **112.** You can also call the fire brigade (S*apeurs-Pompiers*; ℰ **18**), who are trained to deal with all kinds of medical emergencies, not just fires.

Lost & Found   Lost property in Paris makes its way to the **Service des Objets Trouvés** (https://objetstrouvesprefecturede police.franceobjetstrouves.fr). Fill in an online form, then you will be informed if they find your item. You will receive a time, date, and address to collect it. If you lose something in the Métro or on a train, contact the station on the line where you lost the object.

Mail & Postage   Every arrondissement has a post office (**La Poste;** www.laposte.fr; ℰ **36-31**). Most are open Monday to Friday 8:30am to 8pm, Saturday 8am to 1pm; the main post office (50 rue du Louvre; Métro: Louvre-Rivoli) is open Monday to Saturday 8am to midnight and Sunday 10am to midnight. Stamps are also sold in *tabacs* (tobacconists).

Pharmacies   Pharmacies are all over the city; look for the green neon cross above the door. Some are closed Sundays; both the **Pharmacie du 13ème,** 5 bis. avenue de l'Italir (ℰ **01-45-82-86-60**), and the **Pharmacie Européene,** 6 pl. de Clichy (ℰ **01-48-74-65-18**), are open daily 24 hours.

Safety   In general, Paris is a safe city and it is safe to use the Métro at any time, though it's best to avoid the RER late at night. **Beware of pickpockets,** especially in tourist areas and the Louvre; organized gangs will even use children as decoys. Avoid walking around the less safe neighborhoods (Barbès-Rochechouart, Strasbourg St-Denis, Châtelet-Les-Halles) alone at night and never get into an unmarked taxi.

Toilets   Paris is full of gray-colored, street toilet kiosks, which are a little daunting to the uninitiated, but free, and are automatically washed and disinfected after each use.

EXPLORING PARIS

With more than 130 world-class museums to visit, scores of attractions to discover, extraordinary architecture to gape at, and wonderful neighborhoods to wander, Paris is an endless series of delights. Fortunately, you can have a terrific time even if you don't see everything. In fact, some of your best moments may be simply roaming around the city without a plan. Lolling on a park bench, dreaming over a drink at a sidewalk cafe, or noodling around an unknown neighborhood can be the stuff of some of your best travel memories.

The following pages highlight the best that Paris has to offer, from iconic sights known the world over to quirky museums and hidden gardens, from medieval castles to galleries celebrating the most challenging contemporary art.

The Right Bank

LOUVRE & ILE DE LA CITÉ (1ST ARROND.)

This is where it all started. Back in the city's misty and uncertain beginnings, the Parisii tribe set up camp on the right bank of the Seine and started hunting on the **Ile de la Cité.** Many centuries later, the **Louvre** popped up, first as a fortress, then a royal palace and now one of the world's mightiest museums. The city's epicenter packs in a high density of must-see monuments and museums, but don't miss the opportunity for aimless strolling, in the magnificent **Tuileries Gardens,** say, or over the **Pont Neuf.** *Note:* For simplicity's sake, the entire Ile de la Cité has been included in this section, though technically half of it lies in the 4th arrondissement.

Cathédrale de Notre-Dame ★★★ CATHEDRAL   This remarkably harmonious ensemble of carved portals, huge towers, and flying buttresses has survived close to a millennium's worth of French history and served as a setting for some of the country's most solemn moments. Even the vast fire that consumed its spire and gutted the entire roof in 2019 didn't bring it down (thanks to 400 firefighters). And the good news is, it's expected to re-open at the end on 2024—too late for the 2024 summer Olympics, but in keeping with the deadline set by President Emmanuel Macron. Until it reopens, if you'd like to see the cathedral in all its former glory, head to the cathedral's **Crypte Archéologique** (7 place Jean-Paul II, 4th arrond., www. crypte.paris.fr; ✆ **01-55-42-50-10;** admission 9€ adults, free for children 17 and under; Tues–Sun 10am–6pm; Métro: Cité, Châtelet, or St-Michel; RER: St-Michel), where you can put on a VR headset to see the cathedral as recreated for the Ubisoft game Assassin's Creed. Or take the virtual reality flight at **FlyView** (p. 98), which jetpacks you over the Seine to Notre-Dame (and other monuments) using 360-degree film footage shot by drone several years before the tragedy. You could also opt of a **free guided tour** in English around the outskirts of the building works. For schedules, check www. acck.fr/GuidesCasa-calendrierCasa.

Cathédrale de Notre-Dame.

About Notre Dame: Napoléon crowned himself Emperor here, Napoléon III was married here, and the funerals of some of France's greatest generals (Foch, Joffre, Leclerc) were held here. In August 1944, the liberation of Paris from the Nazis was commemorated in the cathedral, as was the death of General de Gaulle in 1970.

Construction on the cathedral began in 1163 and lasted more than 200 years. The building was relatively untouched up until the end of the 17th century, when monarchs started meddling with its windows and architecture. By the time the Revolutionaries decided to convert it into a "Temple of Reason," the cathedral was in sorry condition—and the pillaging that ensued didn't help. The interior was ravaged, statues were smashed, and the cathedral became a shadow of its former glorious self.

We can thank the famous Hunchback himself for saving Notre-Dame. Victor Hugo's novel *The Hunchback of Notre-Dame* drew attention to the state of disrepair, and other artists and writers began to call for restoration of the edifice. In 1844 Louis-Phillipe hired Jean-Baptiste Lassus and Viollet-le-Duc to restore Notre Dame. They finished in 1864.

Over 1 billion euros were donated to the cathedral in the first week following the fire, so money for repairs haven't—for once—been lacking. Though some treasures were lost, the organ, Quasimodo's bell (the Bourdon), and relics such as the **Crown of Thorns** (brought back from Constantinople by Saint Louis in the 13th c.) are safe and will soon be back on display.

Place du Parvis Notre-Dame. www.notredamedeparis.fr.

Conciergerie ★ HISTORIC SITE   Despite looking like a turreted, fairy-tale castle, the Conciergerie is in fact a dark relic of the Revolution—a famous prison that commemorates the Reign of Terror, when murderous infighting between the various revolutionary factions engendered panic and paranoia that led to tens of thousands of people being arrested and executed. Many of the Revolution's pivotal characters spent their final days here before making their way to the guillotine, including Marie Antoinette.

Though it's been a prison since the 15th century, the building itself is actually what remains of a 14th-century royal palace built by Philippe le Bel. The enormous **Salle des Gens d'Armes,** with its 8.4m-high (28-ft.) vaulted ceiling, is an impressive reminder of the building's palatial past, and is where you begin your self-guided tour, courtesy of a Histropad, a smart tablet with augmented reality functions that lets you see parts of the building as it would have looked in the 14th century and during the Revolution. Stand out areas include the **Cours des Femmes** (the women's courtyard), which virtually hasn't changed since the days when female prisoners did their washing in the fountain. **Marie Antoinette's cell** was converted into a memorial chapel during the Bourbon Restoration; a recreation of her cell, containing some original objects, is on display. The

Conciergerie can be visited in conjunction with the **Sainte-Chapelle,** which lies along the same road (p. 90; joint tickets with time slots 18.50€ adults, free for children 17 and under, also free for ages 18–25 from E.U. countries).

2 bd. du Palais, 1st arrond. www. paris-conciergerie.fr. © **01-53-40-60-80.** Admission 11.50€ adults, free for children 17 and under. Daily 9:30–5pm (until 7pm Apr–Sept). Métro: Cité, Châtelet, or St-Michel. RER: St-Michel.

Jardin des Tuileries ★★★ GARDENS   This exquisite park spreads from the Louvre to the place de la Concorde. What you see today is based on the design by 17th-century master landscape artist André Le Nôtre—the man behind the gardens of Versailles. Le Nôtre's elegant geometry of flowerbeds, parterres, and groves of trees made the Tuileries Gardens the ultimate stroll for the era's well-to-do Parisians. It continues to delight both tourists and locals in the 21st century.

During World War II, the furious fighting that went on here damaged many statues. Little by little in the postwar years, the garden put itself back together. Seventeenth- and 18th-century representations of various gods and goddesses were repaired, and the city added new works by modern masters such as Alberto Giocometti, Jean Dubuffet, and Henry Moore.

The Pont au Change, in front of the Orangerie, is the bridge Inspector Javert throws himself off of in the novel *Les Misérables.*

Rodin's *The Kiss* and *Eve* are here, as well as a series of 18 of Maillol's curvaceous women, peeking out of the green **labyrinth** of hedges in the Carousel Gardens near the museum.

Pulling up a metal chair and sunning yourself on the edge of the large **fountain** in the center of the gardens (the **Grande Carrée**) is a delightful respite for tired tourists after a day in the Louvre.

Near pl. de la Concorde, 1st arrond. Free admission. Daily 7:30am–dusk. Métro: Tuileries or Concorde.

MAD (Musée des Arts Décoratifs) ★★ MUSEUM   Possessing some 150,000 items in its rich collection, the MAD (standing for Musée des Arts Décoratifs) is a fascinating museum that offers a glimpse of history through the prism of decorative objects, with a spectrum that ranges from medieval traveling trunks to Philippe Starck stools. The collection is organized by period and style, so on your journey you will pass by paintings from the First Italian Renaissance, through a room filled with exquisite 15th-century intarsia ("paintings" made out of intricately inlaid wood), before gaping at huge, intricately carved 17th-century German armoires. Other highlights include a tiny room covered in gilded woodwork from an 18th-century mansion in Avignon, a stunning Art Nouveau dining room, and fashion designer Jeanne Lanvin's decadent, purple Art Deco boudoir. While the objects themselves are beautiful, the link between style and historic context is illuminating; the endless curlicues of the rococo style, which perfectly reflected the excesses of Louis XV's court, for example, gives way to more puritanical neoclassicism, which developed during the Enlightenment, when unrestrained frivolity began to look degenerate.

Two other collections worthy of your time are the Publicité/Graphisme collection, which takes on the history of advertising, and the Mode/Textile fashion displays. While the former will mostly be of interest to those who are in the biz, the latter hosts a terrific range of works from famous couture houses like Jean-Paul Gaultier and Dior. Another intriguing addition is a collection of wallpaper through the ages—the earliest of which dates from 1864 and depicts a bucolic hunting scene. *Note:* Tickets can be combined with the **Musée Nissim de Camondo** (20€; p. 106).

Palais du Louvre, 107 rue de Rivoli, 1st arrond. http://madparis.fr. © **01-44-55-57-50.** Admission 14€ adults (audio guide included), free for ages 25 and under. Tues–Sun 11am–6pm (until 9pm Thurs for some temporary exhibitions). Métro: Louvre–Palais-Royal or Tuileries.

Musée de l'Orangerie ★★ MUSEUM   Since 1927, this former royal greenhouse has been the home of Monet's *Nymphéas,* or **water lilies,** which he conceived as a "haven of peaceful meditation." Two large oval rooms are dedicated to these masterpieces, in which Monet tried to replicate the feeling and atmosphere of his garden at Giverny. He worked on these enormous canvases for 12 years, with the idea of creating an environment that would soothe the "overworked nerves" of modern men and women.

The other highlight here is the Walter-Guillaume collection, an impressive assortment of late-19th- and early-20th-century paintings. The first light-filled gallery displays works by Renoir and Cezanne. The rest of the collection includes slightly sinister landscapes by Rousseau, enigmatic portraits by Modigliani and distorted figures by Soutine.

Jardin des Tuileries, 1st arrond. www.musee-orangerie.fr. ✆ **01-44-77-80-07.** Admission 12.50€ adults, 10€ ages 18–25, free for children 17 and under. Wed–Mon 9am–6pm (until 9pm Fri). Métro: Concorde.

Musée du Louvre ★★★ MUSEUM   The best way to thoroughly visit the Louvre would be to move in for a month. Not only is it one of the largest museums in the world, with more than 35,000 works of art displayed over 60,000 sq. m (645,835 sq. ft.), but it's packed with enough masterpieces to make the Mona Lisa weep. Rembrandt, Reubens, Botticelli, Ingres, and Michelangelo are all represented here; subjects range from the grandiose (Antoine-Jean Gros's gigantic *Napoleon Bonaparte Visiting the Plague-Stricken in Jaffa*) to the petite (Vermeer's tiny,

The Louvre with I. M. Pei's famous pyramid.

exquisite *Lacemaker*). You can gape at a diamond the size of a golf ball in the royal treasury, or marvel over exquisite bronze figurines in the vast Egyptian section.

Today, the building is divided into three wings, Sully, Denon, and Richelieu, each one with its own clearly marked entrance, found under I. M. Pei's glass pyramid. Get your hands on a museum map (the museum's website has an excellent interactive map), choose your personal "must-sees," and plan ahead. There's no way to see it all, but mercifully, the museum is well organized and has been very reasonably arranged into color-coded sections. If you're really in a rush or you just want to get an overall sense of the place, you can take the introductory "Welcome to the Louvre" guided tour in English (17€; 1½ hr.; usually at 11am (and 2pm Sat–Sun), but check the website or call © **01-40-20-52-63**), as times sometimes change.

The museum's three biggest stars are all located in the Denon wing. La Joconde, otherwise known as the *Mona Lisa,* now has an entire wall to herself, making it easier to contemplate her enigmatic smile. Another inscrutable female in this wing is the *Venus de Milo,* who was found on a Greek island in 1820. The *Winged Victory of Samothrace,* another magnificent Greek sculpture, stands at the top of a majestic flight of stairs, her powerful body pushing forward as if about to take flight. This headless deity originally overlooked the Sanctuary of the Great Gods on the island of Samothrace.

Because a complete listing of the Louvre's highlights would fill a book, below is a decidedly biased selection of my favorite areas:

13TH- TO 18TH-CENTURY ITALIAN PAINTING   A few standouts in the immense Italian collection include the delicate fresco by Botticelli called *Venus and the Three Graces Presenting Gifts to a Young Woman,* Veronese's enormous *Wedding Feast at Cana,* and of course, the *Mona Lisa.* The Divine Miss M is in a room packed with wonders, including Titians and Tintorettos. Once you've digested this rich meal, stroll the endless Grande Galerie, past more da Vincis (*Saint John the Baptist, The Virgin of the Rock*), as well as works by Raphael, Caravaggio, and Gentileschi.

GREEK & ROMAN SCULPTURE   While the *Venus de Milo* and the *Winged Victory of Samothrace* are not to be missed, the Salle des Caryatides (the room itself is a work of art) boasts marble masterworks like *Artemis* hunting with her stag and the troubling *Sleeping Hermaphrodite,* an alluring female figure from behind—and something entirely different from the front.

THE GALERIE D'APOLLON   The gold-encrusted room is an excellent example of the excesses of 17th-century French royalty. Commissioned by Louis XIV, aka "the Sun King," every inch of this gallery is covered with gilt stucco sculptures and flamboyant murals invoking the journey of

Winged Victory of Samothrace.

the Roman sun god Apollo (ceiling paintings are by Charles Le Brun). The main draw here is the collection of crown jewels. Among necklaces bedecked with quarter-sized sapphires and tiaras dripping with diamonds and rubies is the jewel-studded crown of Louis XV and the **Regent,** a 140-carat diamond that decorated his hat.

THE EGYPTIANS   This is the largest collection outside of Cairo, due in large part to Jean-François Champollion, the 19th-century French scientist and scholar who first decoded Egyptian hieroglyphs. Sculptures, figurines, papyrus documents, steles, musical instruments, and of course, mummies, fill numerous rooms in the Sully Wing, including the colossal statue of Ramses II and the strangely moving Seated Scribe. He gazes intently out of intricately crafted inlaid eyes: A combination of copper, magnesite, and polished rock crystal create a startlingly lifelike stare.

LARGE-FORMAT FRENCH PAINTINGS   Enormous floor-to-ceiling (and these are high ceilings!) paintings of monumental moments in history cover the walls in these three rooms. The *Coronation of Napoléon* by Jacques-Louis David depicts the newly minted Emperor crowning Josephine, while the disconcerted pope and a host of notables look on. Farther on are several tumultuous canvases by Eugène Delacroix, including *Liberty Guiding the People,* which might just be the ultimate expression of French patriotism.

Note: When visiting the museum, **watch your wallets and purses**—there has been an unfortunate increase in pickpockets; organized groups even use children to prey on unsuspecting art lovers. On a more positive note, the Louvre has made great strides in improving **accessibility for travelers with disabilities,** including special programs, ramps, free wheelchairs, and folding chairs. For more info, click "visit" and then "accessibility" at the top of the museum's website.

1st arrond. Main entrance in the glass pyramid, cour Napoléon. www.louvre.fr. ℂ **01-40-20-50-50.** Admission 15€ adults, free for children 17 and under. Sat–Mon and Thurs 9am–6pm; Wed and Fri 9am–9:45pm. Métro: Palais-Royal–Musée du Louvre.

The Louvre is so popular that even before Covid, buying a time-stamped ticket ahead of time was the only way to guarantee entry to the museum. Get yours at **www.ticketlouvre.fr** and print it out or store it in your phone; your waiting time in line should not exceed 30 minutes.

If you are of an improvisational bent and prefer to try your luck, head down to the ticket machines below the glass pyramid in the Carousel du Louvre. Now for the leaping the lines part:

○ If you have a ticket, try the little-known Porte des Lions entrance (look right when facing the Pyramid; you should see an arched entrance flanked by lions). When lines are long elsewhere, you can usually waltz in here.

○ Go for late-night opening (after 6pm Wed and Fri when the museum closes at 9:45pm), usually a quiet time to visit.

Palais Royal ★★ HISTORIC SITE/GARDEN   The gardens and long arcades of the Palais Royal are not only a delight to stroll through, they were also witness to one of the most important moments in French history. Built by Cardinal Richelieu, the lavish palace eventually came into the hands of a certain Duke Louis Philippe d'Orleans at the end of the 18th century. An inveterate spendthrift, the young lord soon found himself up to his ears in debt. To earn enough money to pay off his creditors, he came up with the shockingly modern idea of opening the palace gardens to development, building apartments on the grounds. The bottom floor of the galleries, which make up three sides of the enclosure you see today, were let out as shops, cafes, and boutiques. Gambling houses and bordellos sprang up between the shops and cafes, and the gardens became the central meeting place for revolutionaries. Things came to a head on July 12, 1789, when Camille Desmoulins stood up on a table in front of the Café de Foy and called the people to arms—2 days later, the mob would storm the Bastille, igniting the French Revolution. In more recent times, the palace was taken over by various government ministries, and the apartments were rented to artists and writers, including Colette and Jean Cocteau.

Today the shops in the arcades are very subdued, and very expensive—mostly high-end designer clothes, and pricey restaurants. The *cour d'honneur* on the south end is filled with black-and-white-striped columns by Daniel Buren; though most Parisians have now gotten used to this unusual installation, when it was unveiled in 1987 it caused almost as much of a stir as Camille Desmoulins did on that fateful day.

Rue St-Honoré, 1st arrond. Free admission to gardens and arcades; buildings closed to public. Daily 7:30am–dusk. Métro: Palais Royal–Musée du Louvre.

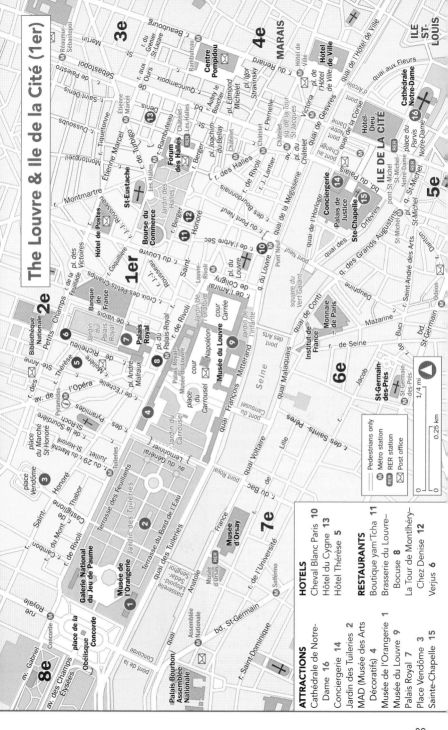

The Louvre & Ile de la Cité (1er)

3e

4e MARAIS

ILE ST-LOUIS

ILE DE LA CITÉ

5e

1er

2e

6e

7e

8e

St-Germain-des-Prés

Seine

- Pedestrians only
- Ⓜ Métro station
- RER RER station
- ☒ Post office

1/4 mi
0.25 km

89

Place Vendôme ★★ SQUARE   In 1686, Louis XIV decided the time had come to design a magnificent square, at the center of which would stand a statue of His Royal Highness. Though the statue is long gone, this is still one of the classiest squares in the city. The work of Jules Hardouin-Mansart, this über-elegant octagonal ensemble of 17th-century buildings today is the home of the original Ritz Hôtel, as well as the world's most glitzy jewelry makers. When Napoléon took over, he erected a huge Roman-style column honoring his glorious army (yes, once again), this time documenting its victory at Austerlitz. A long spiral of bas-reliefs recounting the campaign of 1805 march up the Colonne de la Grande Armée, crowned by a statue of the Emperor himself.

Enter by rue de Castiglione, 1st arrond. Métro: Tuileries or Concorde.

Sainte-Chapelle ★★★ CHURCH   A wall of color greets visitors who enter this magnificent chapel. Stained-glass windows make up a large part of the upper level of the church, giving worshippers the impression of standing inside a jewel-encrusted crystal goblet. What isn't glass is elaborately carved and painted in gold leaf and rich colors: vaulting arches, delicate window casings, and an almost Oriental wainscoting of arches and medallions. The 15 windows recount the story of the Bible, from Genesis to the Apocalypse, as well as the story of St-Louis, who was responsible for the chapel's construction. During the Crusades, Louis IX (who was later canonized) brought home some of the holiest relics in Christendom from Constantinople: the crown of thorns and a piece of the Holy Cross. Such a treasure required an appropriately splendid chapel in the royal palace, and thus the chapel was built (the relics are now in the treasury of Notre-Dame). The record is not clear, but the architect may have been the illustrious Pierre de Montreuil, who worked on the cathedrals of St-Denis and Notre-Dame. What is sure is that the mysterious architect was brilliant: He managed to support the structure with arches and buttresses in such a way that the walls of the upper chapel are almost entirely glass.

Sainte-Chapelle.

The **lower chapel,** which was meant for the servants, has a low, vaulted ceiling painted in blue, red, and gold and covered with fleur-de-lys motifs. Up a small staircase is the **upper chapel,** clearly meant for the royals. This masterpiece suffered both fire and floods in the 17th century and was pillaged by zealous Revolutionaries in the 18th. By the mid–19th century, the chapel was being used to store archives—2m (6½ ft.) of the bottom of each window was removed to install shelves. Fortunately, renewed interest in medieval art eventually led to a conscientious restoration by a team advised by master restorer Viollet-le-Duc. The quality of the work on the windows is such that it is almost impossible to detect the difference between the original and the reconstructed stained glass (which makes up about one-third of what you see).

Palais de Justice, 4 bd. du Palais, 1st arrond. www.sainte-chapelle.fr. ℂ **01-53-40-60-80.** Admission 11.50€ adults, free for children 17 and under. Apr–Sept daily 9:30am–7pm; Oct–Mar daily 9am–5pm. Métro: Cité, St-Michel, or Châtelet–Les Halles. RER: St-Michel.

LE MARAIS (3RD & 4TH ARROND.)

Home to royalty and aristocracy between the 14th and 17th centuries, the Marais still boasts remarkable architecture, some of it dating back to the Middle Ages. One of the few neighborhoods that was not knocked down during Baron Haussmann's urban overhaul, the Marais has narrow streets still lined with magnificent *hôtels particuliers* (that is, mansions) as well as humbler homes from centuries past. The **Pompidou Center** and **Picasso-Paris** are probably the biggest and most well-known attractions, but the Marais also harbors a wealth of terrific smaller museums, as well as the delightful **place des Vosges.** The remnants of the city's **historic Jewish quarter** are found on rue des Rosiers, which has been invaded by chic clothing shops in recent years. Nowadays, a larger Jewish neighborhood is in the 19th arrondissement.

Centre Pompidou ★★ MUSEUM   The bizarre architecture of this building provokes such strong emotions, it's easy to forget that there is something inside. It was designed in 1971 by Italo-British architects Renzo Piano and Richard Rogers, whose concept was to put the support structure on the outside of the building, thereby liberating space on the inside for a museum and cultural center. The result was a gridlike exoskeleton with a tubular escalator inching up one side and huge multicolored pipes and shafts covering the other. To some, it's a milestone in contemporary architecture; to others, it's simply a horror. Either way, it's one of the most visited structures in France. For the Pompidou is much more than an art museum. Its some 100,000 sq. m (1,076,390 sq. ft.) of floor space includes a vast **reference library,** a **cinema archive,** bookshops, and a **music institute,** as well as a performance hall, a **children's gallery,**

Centre Pompidou.

and areas for educational activities. The actual museum, the **Musée National d'Art Moderne,** is on the fourth and fifth floors.

Because the museum collection is in constant rotation, it's impossible to say what you're likely to see on your visit, but the emphasis is generally on works from the second half of the 20th century, with a good dose of surrealism, Dada, and other modern movements from the first half. It includes relatively tame abstracts by **Picasso** and **Kandinsky** to **Andy Warhol**'s multiheaded portrait of Elizabeth Taylor to a felt-wrapped piano by **Joseph Beuys.** Just outside of the front of the center is the **Atelier Brancusi,** where the sculptor's workshop has been reconstituted in its entirety.

The Pont Neuf

Despite its name (*neuf* means "new"), this is, in fact, the oldest bridge in Paris. The bridge was an instant hit when it was inaugurated by Henri IV in 1607: Ample sidewalks, and the fact that it was the first bridge sans houses, made it a delight for pedestrians. It still is, especially if you ignore the cars and just take in the lovely views.

Don't miss the view from the top floor—a wonderful opportunity to gaze at the city's rooftops. Even if you don't visit the museum, you can buy a ticket to the top for 5€. Or you can admire it from within **Georges** (http://restaurantgeorgesparis.com), the museum's rooftop cafe/restaurant. The

Le Marais (3e & 4e)

Pedestrians only
Ⓜ Métro station
RER RER station
✉ Post office

2e
10e
11e
3e
MARAIS
1er
4e
ILE DE LA CITÉ
ILE ST-LOUIS

ATTRACTIONS
Centre Pompidou **7**
Hôtel de Ville **9**
Maison de Victor Hugo **17**
Musée Carnavalet **12**
Musée d'Art et Histoire
   du Judaïsme **6**
Musée de la Chasse et
   de la Nature **5**

Picasso Paris **4**
Place des Vosges **16**

HOTELS
Pavillon de la Reine **15**
Hôtel Caron de
   Beaumarchais **10**
Hôtel Jeanne d'Arc
   le Marais **14**

RESTAURANTS
Benoit **8**
BigLove **3**
Café des Musées **13**
ELMER **1**
L'As du Fallafel **11**
Le Potager du Marais **18**
Marché des Enfants
   Rouge **2**

93

staff are a little snooty, however. ***Note:*** Even behemoths require make-overs. At time of writing, the Centre Pompidou was set to close for renovations towards the end of 2024 until 2030, so many of its 120,000 works will go on show in multiple exhibitions all across France.

pl. Georges-Pompidou, 4th arrond. www.centrepompidou.fr. ℂ **01-44-78-12-33.** Admission 15€ adults, 12€ students ages 18–25, free for children 17 and under; admission varies, depending on exhibits. Wed–Mon 11am–9pm (Thurs until 11pm during temporary exhibitions). Métro: Rambuteau, Hôtel de Ville, or Châtelet–Les Halles.

Hôtel de Ville ★ HISTORIC SITE   No, it's not a hotel. This enormous Neo-Renaissance wedding cake is Paris's city hall, and you can't go inside the official parts of the building, though it does host regular art exhibits on subjects linked to Paris's history, usually for free (access is through the back entrance on rue Lobau). But even if you can't get in to see the sumptuous halls and chandeliers, you will be able to feast on the lavish exterior, which includes 136 statues representing historic VIPs of Parisian history. Since the 14th century, this spot has been an administrative seat for the municipality; the building you see before you dates from 1873, but it is a copy of an earlier Renaissance version that stood in its place up until 1870, when it was burned down during the Paris Commune. The vast square in front of the building, which used to be called the place du Grève, was used for municipal festivals and executions, and it was also the stage for several important moments in the city's history, particularly during the Revolution: Louis XVI was forced to kiss the new French flag here, and Robespierre was shot in the jaw and arrested here during an attempted coup. Today the square is host to more peaceful activities: There's a merry-go-round to captivate the little ones, and a winter **ice-skating rink** is sometimes set up.

29 rue de Rivoli, 4th arrond. www.paris.fr. ℂ **01-42-76-43-43.** Free admission. Métro: Hôtel-de-Ville.

Maison de Victor Hugo ★ MUSEUM   The life of Victor Hugo was as turbulent as some of his novels. Regularly visited by both tragedy and triumph, the author of *The Hunchback of Notre-Dame* lived in several apartments in Paris, including this one on the second floor of a corner house on the sumptuous place des Vosges. From 1832 to 1848, he lived here with his wife and four children. When Napoleon III seized power in 1851, this passionate advocate of free speech declared the new king a traitor of France. Fearing for his life, Hugo left the country and lived in exile until 1870 when he triumphantly returned and was elected to the senate. By the time he died in 1885 he was a national hero; his funeral cortege through the streets of Paris is the stuff of legend, and his body was one of the first to be buried in the Panthéon. The small museum's collection charts this dramatic existence through the author's drawings, manuscripts, notes, furniture, and personal objects, which are displayed in rooms that recreate the ambiance of the original lodgings. The museum's latest addition is a space for temporary contemporary art exhibitions and a charming cafe set in a leafy courtyard.

6 pl. des Vosges, 4th arrond. www.maisonsvictorhugo.paris.fr. © **01-42-72-10-16.** Free admission to the permanent collections. Tues–Sun 10am–6pm. Métro: St-Paul, Bastille, or Chemin-Vert.

Musée d'Art et Histoire du Judaïsme ★★ MUSEUM   Housed in the magnificent Hôtel de Saint Aignan, this museum chronicles the art and history of the Jewish people in France and Europe. It features a superb collection of objects of both artistic and cultural significance (a splendid Italian Renaissance torah ark, a German gold-and-silver Hanukkah menorah, a 17th-c. Dutch illustrated torah scroll, documents from the Dreyfus trial), which is interspersed with texts, drawings, and photos telling the story of the Jews and explaining the basics of both Ashkenazi and Sephardic traditions.

You'll do a lot of reading here; documentation is translated in English, but there's a very informative audio guide too. The final rooms include a collection of works by Jewish artists, including Modigliani, Soutine, Lipchitz, and Chagall. Be prepared for airportlike security at the entrance.

71 rue du Temple, 3rd arrond. www.mahj.org. © **01-53-01-86-53.** Admission 10€ adults, 7€ ages 18–25, free for children 17 and under. Tues–Fri 11am–6pm; Sat–Sun 10am–6pm. Métro: Rambuteau or Hôtel de Ville.

Musée Carnavalet ★★★ MUSEUM   Paris has served as a backdrop to centuries' worth of dramatic events, from Roman takeovers to barbarian invasions, from coronations to decapitations to the birth of the modern French republic. These stories and others are told at this fascinating museum through objects, paintings, and interiors. These include Gallo-Roman figurines, Napoleon's toiletry kit, and an 18th-century portrait of

Benjamin Franklin painted when he was the U.S. ambassador to France, and even a prehistoric canoe from 4600 B.C. The collection is displayed in two extraordinary 17th-century mansions—works of art in their own right. It's a fascinating place, with an outdoor summer cafe in its stunning landscaped garden, where you can sip tea amongst the pretty parterres before or after your visit.

16 rue des Francs-Bourgeois, 3rd arrond. www.carnavalet.paris.fr. © **01-44-59-58-58.** Free admission for permanent collection except during certain temporary exhibits. Tues–Sun 10am–6pm. Métro: St-Paul or Chemin Vert.

The courtyard of the Musée Carnavalet.

Musée de la Chasse et de la Nature ★★ MUSEUM   If you can get over the fact that it's a museum dedicated to hunting, this small, freshly renovated museum makes for a pleasant outing. You'll find the expected taxidermied animals, but they are discreetly presented among an elegant collection of paintings, tapestries, sculptures, and even contemporary art. Each room has a theme, exploring ideas like the relationship between Man and animals, or mythical beasts like unicorns The emphasis is not so much on the kill as the symbolism behind each piece, and it's all rather intriguing. It reminds you that the relationship between humans and animals dates to well before there were naturalists and environmentalists, and if that relationship was filled with animosity and fear, it was also tinged with a sort of mystical respect.

62 rue des Archives, 3rd arrond. www.chassenature.org. ⓒ **01-53-01-92-40.** Admission 12€ adults, 10€, free for children 17 and under. Tues–Sun 11am–6pm (until 9:45pm Wed). Métro: Rambuteau.

Musée des Arts et Métiers ★ MUSEUM   Here's a museum for the techies in your crowd. With a collection that runs from astrolabes to supercomputers, this place is a goldmine for geeks of all ages. The goodies are organized into seven categories: scientific instruments, materials, construction, communication, energy, mechanics, and transportation. Learn how the metric system was born, what the first waterwheels looked like, and how the machine age got up to speed. Probably the most famous item on display is Foucault's original pendulum, which still gracefully demonstrates the rotation of the Earth, just like it does in Umberto Eco's eponymous novel. The museum is housed in the ancient abbey of St-Martin-des-Champs.

60 rue Réaumur, 3rd arrond. www.arts-et-metiers.net. ⓒ **01-53-01-82-00.** Admission 8€ adults, 5.50€ students, free for children 17 and under. Tues–Wed and Fri–Sun 10am–6pm; Thurs 10am–9:30pm. Métro: Arts et Métiers.

Musée Picasso-Paris ★★★ MUSEUM   This shrine to all things Picasso is housed in the stunning Hôtel Salé, a 17th-century mansion built by salt-tax farmer Pierre Aubert, whose position gave the mansion its name—*salé* means "salty." This unique institution valiantly strives to make sense of the incredibly diverse output of this prolific genius: Some 400 carefully selected paintings, sculptures, collages, and drawings are presented in a more or less chronological and thematic order, no small task when dealing with an artist who experimented with every style, from neoclassicism to surrealism to his own flamboyantly abstract inventions. Impressionist portraits (*Portrait of Gustave Coquiot,* 1901), Cubist explorations (*Man with Guitar,* 1911), mannerist allegories (*The Race,* 1922), and deconstructionist forms (*Reclining Nude,* 1932) make up only part of his oeuvre, which has been estimated to include some 50,000 works. Not only that, Picasso often worked in wildly different styles during the same period, sometimes treating the same subjects. For example, the rounded yet realistic lovers dancing in *La Danse des Villageois* painted in 1922, hang next to two forms in a blaze of color representing *The Kiss* painted in 1925. There's also a sampling of the somewhat disturbing portraits of the many women in his life, including portraits of Dora Maar and Marie-Thérèse, both painted in 1937. On the top floor is Picasso's private collection, which includes works by artists he admired like Courbet and Cézanne, as well as paintings by his friends, who included masters like Braque and Matisse.

All in all, what you see on the walls is less than 10% of the 5,000 works in the museum's collection; the presentation rotates every couple of years. Unless you enjoy waiting in long lines exposed to the elements, **buy your ticket in advance online;** you'll usually walk right in with your e-ticket. The museum's rooftop cafe is a pleasant spot for a snack.

5 rue de Thorigny, 3rd arrond. www.museepicassoparis.fr. ℰ **01-85-56-00-36.** Admission 14€ adults, free for children 17 and under. Tues–Fri 10:30am–6pm; Sat–Sun 9:30am–6pm. Métro: St-Paul or Chemin Vert.

Place des Vosges ★★★ PLAZA   Possibly the prettiest square in the city, this beautiful spot combines elegance, greenery, and quiet. Nowhere in Paris will you find such a unity of Renaissance-style architecture; the entire square is bordered by 17th-century brick town houses, each

Place des Vosges.

conforming to rules set down by Henri IV himself, under which runs arched arcades. The square's history dates back to a mishap in 1559, when the site was occupied by a royal palace. During a tournament, feisty King Henri II decided to fight Montgomery, the captain of his guard. A badly aimed lance resulted in Henri's untimely death; his wife, Catherine de Medicis, was so distraught she had the palace demolished. His descendant, Henri IV, took advantage of the free space to construct a royal square. Over the centuries, a number of celebrities lived in the 36 houses, including Mme de Sévigny and Victor Hugo (now the **Maison de Victor Hugo;** p. 94). Today the homes are for the rich, as are the chic boutiques under the arcades, but the lawns, trees, fountains, and playground are for everyone.

4th arrond. Métro: St-Paul.

OPÉRA & GRANDS BOULEVARDS (2ND & 9TH ARROND.)

The grandiose **Opéra Garnier** reigns over this bustling neighborhood, which teems with office workers, tourists, and shoppers scuttling in and around the Grands Magasins (the big department stores) on boulevard Haussmann. So yes, there are more opportunities for outstanding retail experiences here than for cultural ones, but the hip 9th has a two small museums worthy of your time: Symbolist painter Gustave Moreau's period house, **Musée Gustave Moreau** (www.musee-moreau.fr) and **Musée de la Vie Romantque** (https://museevieromantique.paris.fr), the villa where Romantic painter Ary Scheffer (1795–1858) once entertained such illustrious guests as Baronne Aurore Dupin (George Sand), Eugène Delacroix, Chopin, and Charles Dickens.

FlyView ★★ VIRTUAL REALITY EXPERIENCE   This virtual reality tour presents itself as a futuristic mini-airport, with flight times displayed on screens and flight attendants in quaint turquoise uniforms. Once in the departure room, depending on your choice of "flight," you'll either by seated in a chair or strapped into a jetpack, then you put on the headset and hold on (white-knuckled) for roughly 13 minutes of virtual sightseeing. There are several "flights" to choose from, but for sweeping city vistas, I recommend "The Fly Over Paris," where you take off from a Paris rooftop before whooshing through the air to Concorde's needle, then float under the Arc de Triomphe, dash between the Eiffel Tower's filigree girders, and zip over the Seine to Notre-Dame. FlyView uses impressively detailed 360-degree images taken by drone. By filming Notre-Dame before its roof burned down (and after, for the "Rebuilding Notre-Dame" ride), FlyView has become the only way you can see the edifice close up—reason alone to book. Minimum height is 1.2m (4 ft.).

30 rue du Quatre Septembre, 2nd arrond. www.flyview360.com. ℰ **01-83-62-12-36.** Admission 19.50€, 16.50€ children ages 11 and under. Wed 2:30–7pm; Sat–Sun and daily during French school holidays 10:30am–7pm. Métro: Opéra, Chaussée d'Antin-Lafayette or Quatre Septembre. RER: Auber.

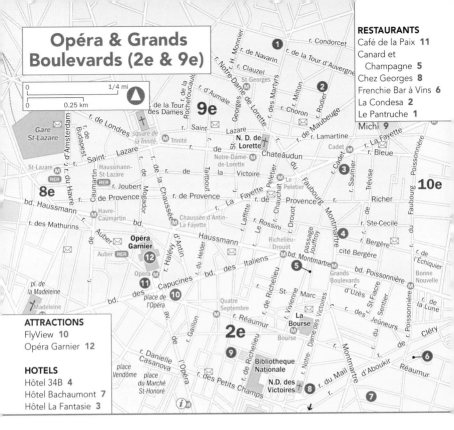

Opéra & Grands Boulevards (2e & 9e)

9e

8e

10e

2e

Opéra Garnier ★★ OPERA HOUSE   Flamboyant, extravagant, and baroque, this opulent opera house is a splendid example of Second Empire architectural excess. Corinthian columns, loggias, busts, and friezes cover the **facade** of the building, all topped by a gold dome. The interior is no less dramatic. The vast **lobby,** built in a spectrum of different-colored marble, holds a spectacular double staircase that sweeps up to the different levels of the auditorium, as well as an array of glamorous antechambers, galleries, and ballrooms that make you wonder how the opera scenery could possibly compete. Mosaics, mirrors, gilt, and marble line these grand spaces, whose painted ceilings dance with fauns, gods, and nymphs. The main event, of course, is the **auditorium,** which might seem a bit small, considering the size of the building. In fact, it holds not even 2,000 seats. The beautiful **ceiling** was painted with colorful images from various operas and ballets by Marc Chagall in 1964.

All of this (with the exception of the Chagall ceiling) sprang from the mind of a young, unknown architect named Charles Garnier, who won a competition launched by Napoléon III. Though the first stone was laid in 1862, work was held up by war, civil unrest, and a change in regime; the

Palais Garnier was not inaugurated until 1875. Some contemporary critics found it a bit much (one called it "an overloaded sideboard"), but today it is generally acknowledged as a masterpiece of the architecture of the epoch.

And what about that phantom? Gaston Leroux's 1911 novel, *The Phantom of the Opera,* clearly was inspired by the building's **underground lake,** which was constructed to help stabilize the building and is used today by Paris' firebrigade for underwater training.

You can visit the building on your own (for a fee), but with so much history and so many good stories, you might want to take advantage of the **guided visits in English** (18.50€ adults, 13€ children 9 and under; check website for times; 22€ for all tickets for the 5pm tour), or simply **buy tickets to a show.** *Note:* At time of writing, the opera's facade was undergoing renovations (until the end of 2024).

Corner of rue Scribe and rue Auber, 9th arrond. www.operadeparis.fr. © **08-25-05-44-05** (.35€/min.). Admission 14€ adults, 9€ students and ages 12–25, free for children 11 and under. Oct to mid-July daily 10am–5pm; mid-July to Sept 10am–6pm. Métro: Opéra.

CHAMPS-ELYSÉES, TROCADÉRO & WESTERN PARIS (8TH, 16TH & 17TH ARROND.)

Decidedly posh, this is one of the wealthiest parts of the city in both per-capita earnings and cultural institutions. While the **Champs-Elysées ★★** is more glitz than glory, the surrounding neighborhoods offer high-end shops and restaurants as well as some terrific museums and concert halls. This is also where you will find grandiose architectural gestures, like the **Arc de Triomphe** and the **place de la Concorde,** which book-end the Champs, and the **Grand Palais** and **Petit Palais,** leftovers from the legendary 1900 Universal Exposition.

Arc de Triomphe ★★★ MONUMENT   If there is one monument that symbolizes "La Gloire," or the glory of France, it is this giant triumphal arch. Crowning the Champs-Elysées, this mighty archway both celebrates the military victories of the French army and memorializes the sacrifices of its soldiers. Over time, it has become an icon of the Republic and a setting for some if its most emotional moments: the laying in state of the coffin of Victor Hugo in 1885, the burial in 1921 of the ashes of an unknown soldier who fought in World War I, and General de Gaulle's pregnant pause under the arch before striding down the Champs-Elysées to the cheering crowds after the Liberation in 1944.

It took a certain amount of chutzpah to come up with the idea to build such a shrine, and sure enough, it was Napoléon who instigated it. In 1806, still glowing after his stunning victory at Austerlitz, the Emperor decided to erect a monument to the Imperial Army along the lines of a Roman triumphal arch. Unfortunately, the Empire came to an end before the arch was finished, and construction dragged on until 1836 when it was completed by Louis-Philippe.

Champs-Élysées, Trocadéro & Western Paris (8e, 16e & 17e)

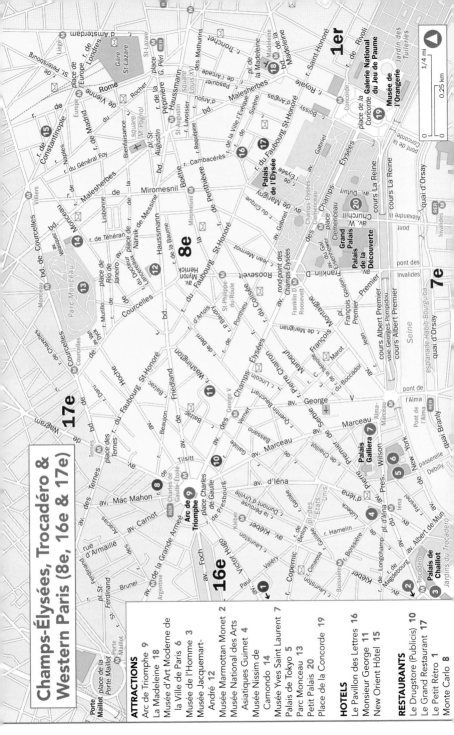

Aerial view of the Arc de Triomphe.

The arch is covered with bas-reliefs and sculptures, the most famous of which is the massive *Depart of the Volunteers* of 1792, better known as the Marseillaise, by François Rude. Just above is one of the many smaller panels detailing Napoleonic battles—in this case, Aboukir—wherein the Emperor trods victoriously over the Ottomans. At the base of the arch is the Tomb of the Unknown Soldier, over which a flame is relit every evening. The inscription reads ICI REPOSE UN SOLDAT FRANÇAIS MORT POUR LA PATRIE, 1914–1918 ("Here lies a French soldier who died for his country").

Don't try crossing the vast traffic circle to get to the arch; take the underpass near the Métro entrances. The panorama from the rooftop terrace is quite impressive; you will see the 12 boulevards that radiate from the star-shaped intersection (hence the moniker "Etoile"), most of which are named after Napoleonic battles. Out front is the long sweep of the Champs-Elysées, ending at place de la Concorde, behind which lurks the pyramid of the Louvre. In the other direction you will get a good gander at the modern Grande Arche de la Défense, a huge, hollow cubelike building that could fit Notre-Dame under its arch.

pl. Charles de Gaulle–Etoile, 8th arrond. www.paris-arc-de-triomphe.fr. ✆ **01-55-37-73-77.** Admission 13€ adults, free for children 17 and under. Apr–Sept daily 10am–11pm; Oct–Mar daily 10am–10:30pm. Métro: Charles-de-Gaulle–Etoile.

La Madeleine ★★ CHURCH   As you peer up rue Royale from the place de la Concorde, you'll see something that very closely resembles a Roman temple. When the first stone was laid in 1763, it was destined to be a church with a neoclassical facade. But then the architect died, and the Revolution broke out, and construction ground to a halt. No one knew what to do with the site until Napoléon strode onto the scene and declared that it would become the Temple de La Gloire, to honor the glorious victories of his army. He wanted something "solid" because he was sure that the monument would last "thousands of years." Unfortunately for him, military defeats and mounting debt would again delay construction until Napoléon decided that maybe it wouldn't be such a bad idea to make it a church after all—that way Rome would foot the bill. Once Napoléon was out of the picture, inertia sunk in again. It wasn't until 1842, under the Restoration, that La Madeleine was finally consecrated.

The inside of the church is pretty dark, due to a lack of windows, but there are some interesting works of art here, if you can make them out in the gloom. On the left as you enter is François Rude's *Baptism of Christ;* farther on is James Pradier's sculpture *La Marriage de la Vierge.*

pl. de la Madeleine, 8th arrond. https://lamadeleineparis.fr. ✆ **01-44-51-69-00.** Free admission. Daily 9:30am–7pm. Métro: Madeleine.

Musée d'Art Moderne de la Ville de Paris ★ MUSEUM   Housed in a wing of the massive Palais de Tokyo, this municipal modern-art museum covers ground similar to that of the Pompidou Center but on a smaller scale. Though several big names are represented (Picasso, Rouault, and Picaba, to name a few), in general these are not their best-known works; highlights include a room dedicated to surrealism (the personal collection of André Breton) and a series of paintings by Delaunay and Léger. There's also a huge room covered with brilliant wall murals by Raoul Dufy (*La Fée Electricité*), as well as another vast room with two enormous versions of *La Danse* by Matisse. The contemporary section, from 1960 on, covers seriously abstract movements like Fluxus and Figuration. In recent years, the collection has acquired several new works from the 1980s on, but for the most recent cutting-edge ideas,

Grande Arche de la Défense.

you are better off at the Palais de Tokyo museum (see below) in the wing next door.

11 av. du Président-Wilson, 16th arrond. www.mam.paris.fr. © **01-53-67-40-00.** Free admission to permanent collections. Tues–Sun 10am–6pm (Thurs during exhibitions until 9:30pm). Métro: Iéna or Alma-Marceau.

Musée de l'Homme ★★ MUSEUM The primitive art housed in this museum once inspired Picasso. Today, it is a state-of-the-art anthropology museum showcasing the richness of human culture and the evolution of mankind. In true existential Sartre fashion, this is where you come to reflect on the hard questions: What does it mean to be human? Where do we come from? And where are we headed—especially in the light of climatic change? The answer is there's no one answer, but it's great thinking about it as you work your way around the exhibits—everything from a Cro-Magnon skull to André Pierre Pinson's anatomical waxworks (fabulous, intricate examples of anatomy from the French Enlightenment and a gallery of 19th-c. busts designed to illustrate the diversity of human beings). The building itself is a showpiece. Set in the Passy wing of the Palais de Chaillot—built for the 1937 World Fair on the site of the former 1878 Trocadéro Palace—it is an Art Deco treasure filled with natural light, thanks to rows of floor-to-ceiling windows that look out onto the most famous icon of all, the Eiffel Tower. For the best views, head to **Café Lucy x Mozza&Co,** an ultra-modern cafeteria on the 2nd floor and the **Café de l'Homme,** a chic brasserie with a terrace.

17 pl. du Trocadéro, 16th arrond. www.museedelhomme.fr. © **01-44-05-72-72.** Admission 10€ adults, free for ages 25 and under. Wed–Mon 11am–7pm. Métro: Trocadéro.

Musée Jacquemart-André ★★★ MUSEUM *Note: As we went to press, the museum was closed for renovations until at least September 2024.* The love-child of a couple of passionate art collectors, this terrific museum takes the form of a 19th-century mansion filled with fine art and decorative objects. Not only is the collection superb, but it is also of a blissfully reasonable size—you can see a wide range of beautiful things here without wearing yourself to a frazzle.

Nélie Jacquemart and Edouard André devoted their lives to filling this splendid dwelling with primarily 18th-century French art and furniture. The paintings of Fragonard, Boucher, and Chardin are in evidence, as is an impressive assortment of Louis XV– and Louis XVI–era decorative objects. The many superb portraits include *Comte Français de Nantes* by David. The couple also amassed a number of 17th-century Dutch paintings, including a jaunty *Portrait of a Man* by Frans Hals, and Rembrandt's evocative *Pilgrims at Emmaus.*

The peripatetic couple, who traveled frequently in search of new items for their collection, also took an interest in Renaissance Italian art;

though at the time considered "primitive" by most art fans, that didn't stop them from snapping up Quattrocento masterpieces like Botticelli's *Virgin and Child.* The Italian collection (on the second floor) is the most awe-inspiring part of the museum; not only are there works by masters like Bellini, Uccello, and Mantegna, they are presented in an intimate space with excellent lighting. You feel like you are walking into a jewel box. Enjoy a light lunch or tea in the lovely tea room.

158 bd. Haussmann, 8th arrond. www.musee-jacquemart-andre.com. © **01-45-62-11-59.** Métro: Miromesnil or St-Philippe-du-Roule.

Musée Marmottan Monet ★★ MUSEUM   Boasting the world's largest collection of Monets, this museum offers an in-depth look at this prolific genius and some of his talented contemporaries. Among the dozens of Monet canvases is the one that provided the name of an entire artistic movement. Pressed to give a name to this misty play of light on the water for the catalog for an 1874 exposition that included Cézanne, Pissarro, Renoir, and Degas, Monet apparently said, "put 'impression.'" The painting, *Impression, Sunrise,* certainly made one, as did the show— thereafter the group was referred to as the Impressionists. Monet never stopped being fascinated with the interaction of light and water, be it in a relatively traditional portrait of his wife and daughter against the stormy sea in *On the Beach at Trouville,* or in an almost abstract blend of blues and grays in *Charing Cross Bridge.* Monet often painted the same subject at different times of the day, as in his famous series on the Cathedral of Rouen, one of which is here: *Effect of the Sun at the End of the Day.* Fans of the artist's endless water lily series will not be disappointed; the collection includes dozens of paintings of his beloved garden in Giverny.

Paintings by Renoir, Sisley, Degas, Gauguin, and other contemporaries can be seen in the light-filled rooms on the upper floor, as well as works by one of the only female members of the group, Berthe Morisot, who gets an entire room devoted to her intimate portraits and interiors.

2 rue Louis-Boilly, 16th arrond. www.marmottan.com. © **01-44-96-50-33.** Admission 14€ adults, 9€ students 25 and under and ages 8–18, free for children 7 and under. Tues–Wed and Fri–Sun 10am–6pm; Thurs 10am–9pm. Métro: La Muette. RER: Bouilainvilliers.

Musée National des Arts Asiatiques Guimet ★★ MUSEUM   Founded in 1889 by collector and industrialist Emile Guimet, today this vast collection of Asian art is one of the largest and most complete in Europe. Here you'll find room after room of exquisite works from Afghanistan, India, Tibet, Nepal, China, Vietnam, Korea, Japan, and other Asian nations. You could spend an entire day here, or you could pick and choose regions of interest (displays are arranged geographically). Highlights include a Tibetan bronze sculpture (*Hevajra and Nairâtmya*) of a multi-headed god embracing a ferocious goddess with eight faces and 16 arms;

a blissfully serene stone figure of a 12th-century Cambodian king (*Jayavarman VII*) and superb Chinese scroll paintings, including a magnificent 17th-century view of the Jingting mountains in autumn. A few minutes' walk from the museum is the **Panthéon Bouddhique,** also known as the Hôtel d'Heidelbach, 19 av. d'Iéna (✆ **01-40-73-88-00;** free admission; Wed–Mon 10am–5:30pm), an old mansion and tea ceremony venue (18€ for the tea; reserve on the museum website: https://billetterie.guimet.fr).

6 pl. d'Iéna, 16th arrond. www.guimet.fr. ✆ **01-56-52-53-00.** Admission to permanent collection 11.50€ adults, 8.50€ ages 18–25, free for children 17 and under. Wed–Mon 10am–6pm. Métro: Iéna.

14th-century Buddha at Musée National des Arts Asiatiques Guimet.

Musée Nissim de Camondo ★★ MUSEUM   In 1914 Count Moïse de Camondo built a mansion in the style of the Petit Trianon at Versailles and furnished it with rare examples of 18th-century furniture, paintings, and art objects. After the count's death in 1935, the house and everything in it was left to the state as a museum. This little-visited museum is a delight—the count's will stipulated that the house be left exactly "as is" when it was transformed into a museum, as a result you can wander through salons filled with gilded mirrors, inlaid tables, and Beauvais tapestries; a fully equipped kitchen; and a gigantic tiled bathroom—all in the same configuration as when Camondo and his family lived there. A special room displays the Buffon service, a remarkable set of Sèvres china decorated with a myriad of bird species, reproductions of drawings by the renowned naturalist, the Count of Buffon. Be sure to pick up a free English audio guide. Tickets can be combined with the **Musée des Arts Décoratifs** (p. 84; 20€). The museum's hip restaurant/bar, **Le Camondo** (http://lecamondo.fr), is a handy spot for lunch, set in the mansion's former garage with tables that spill out onto an umbrella-shaded courtyard.

63 rue de Monceau, 8th arrond. http://madparis.fr. ✆ **01-53-89-06-40.** Admission 12€ adults, free for ages 25 and under. Wed–Sun 10am–5:30pm. Métro: Villiers.

Musée Yves Saint Laurent ★★ MUSEUM   This museum for fashion lovers is set in the sumptuous 19th-century mansion Yves Saint Laurent used as his HQ from 1974 to 2002. The king of couture planned for a museum from the 1980s onward, marking important items with an "M" (for Musée). There are some 5,000 in all, plus over 15,000 accessories. Though Saint Laurent died in 2008 and didn't see the opening of the museum (in 2017), he would undoubtedly have been happy with the result: Room after room show temporary retrospectives that highlight both his career and his creative genius, resulting in rich and fascinating displays of game-changing outfits—like his Mondrian dress and the "smoking" tuxedo—as well as lesser-known pieces designed for the ballet and the theater. The spaces are beautiful, especially Saint Laurent's studio, filled with his books and sketches, unchanged, as if the great designer is about to come home.

5 av. Marceau, 16th arrond. https://museeyslparis.com. ✆ **01-44-31-64-00.** Admission 10€ adults, 7€ ages 10–18, free for children 9 and under. Tues–Sun 11am–6pm (until 9pm Thurs). Métro: Alma Marceau.

Palais de Tokyo ★★ MUSEUM/PERFORMANCE SPACE   If you're traveling with cranky teenagers who've had enough of La Vieille France, or if you're also sick of endless rendezvous with history, this is the place to come for a blast of contemporary madness. This vast art space not only offers a rotating bundle of expositions, events, and other happenings, but it's also one of the only museums in Paris that stays open until 10pm (even

until midnight on Thurs). While some might quibble over whether or not the works on display are really art, there's no denying that this place is a lot of fun. Without a permanent collection, the Palais de Tokyo hosts continuous temporary exhibits, installations, and events, which include live performances and film screenings. The center is now one of the largest sites devoted to contemporary creativity in Europe. In warm weather, you can eat on the splendid terrace of its chic, neo–Art Deco brasserie, **Monsieur Bleu,** which has Eiffel Tower views, or sip cocktails in its restaurant/bar **Bambini.** Both stay open until 2am.

13 av. du Président-Wilson, 16th arrond. www.palaisdetokyo.com. ✆ **01-81-97-35-88.** Admission 12€ adults, 9€ ages 18–25, free for children 17 and under. Wed–Mon 10am–10pm (until midnight Thurs). Métro: Iéna.

Video art at Palais de Tokyo.

Parc Monceau ★★ PARK/GARDENS   Marcel Proust used to laze under the trees in this beautiful park, and who could blame him? The lush lawns and leafy trees of this verdant haven would brighten the spirits of even the melancholiest writer. Located in a posh residential neighborhood and ringed by stately mansions, this small park, commissioned by the duke of Chartres in 1769, is filled with *folies,* faux romantic ruins, temples, and antiquities inspired by exotic faraway places. Don't be surprised to stumble upon a minaret, a windmill, or a mini-Egyptian pyramid here. The most famous *folie* is the **Naumachie,** a large oval pond surrounded in part by Corinthian columns. You'll find a sizeable **playground** in the southwest corner, as well as a **merry-go-round** near the north entrance.
35 bd. de Courcelles, 8th arrond. Free admission. Daily 8am–sundown. Métro: Monceau or Villiers.

Petit Palais ★★ MUSEUM   The collection may not be exhaustive, and you may not see any world-famous works, but you will enjoy a wonderful mix of periods and artists at this small-ish municipal fine arts museum, whose chronology stretches from the ancient Greeks to World War I. The paintings of masters like Monet, Ingres, and Rubens are displayed here, as well as the Art Nouveau dining room of Hector Guimard, and the exquisite multilayered glass vases of Emile Gallé. Those interested in earlier works will find Greek vases, Italian Renaissance majolica, and a small collection of 16th-century astrolabes and gold-and-crystal traveling clocks. Intricately carved ivory panels and delicately sculpted wood sculptures stand out in the small Medieval section, and a series of rooms dedicated to 17th-century Dutch painters like Steen and Van Ostade is considered one of the best collections of its kind in France (after the Louvre). Refresh yourself after your visit at the cafe in the gorgeous inner courtyard.
av. Winston Churchill, 8th arrond. www.petitpalais.paris.fr. ✆ **01-53-43-40-00.** Free admission to permanent collection. Tues–Sun 10am–6pm (Fri until 9pm during temporary exhibitions). Métro: Champs-Elysées Clémenceau.

Place de la Concorde ★★★ PLAZA   Like an exclamation point at the end of the Champs-Elysées, the place de la Concorde is a magnificent arrangement of fountains and statues, with a 3,000-year-old Egyptian obelisk (a gift to France from Egypt in 1829) at its center. Looking at it today, it is hard to believe that this magnificent square was once bathed in blood, but during the Revolution, it was a grisly stage for public executions. King Louis XVI and his wife, Marie-Antoinette, both bowed down to the guillotine here, as did many prominent figures of the Revolution, including Danton, Camille Desmoulins, and Robespierre. Once the monarchy was back in place, the plaza hosted less lethal public events like festivals and trade expositions.

Fontaines de la Concorde and Luxor Obelisk.

In 1835 the *place* was given its current look: Two immense fountains, copies of those in St. Peter's Square in Rome, play on either side of the obelisk; 18 sumptuous columns decorated with shells, mermaids, and sea creatures each hold two lamps; and eight statues representing the country's largest cities survey the scene from the edges of the action. On the west side are the famous **Marly Horses,** actually copies of the originals, which were suffering from erosion and have since been restored and housed in the Louvre. On the north side of the square are two palatial buildings that date from the 18th century: On the east side is the **Hôtel de la Marine** (which opened in 2021 as a vast art museum to house the Qatarian Al Thani Collection; www.hotel-de-la-marine.paris), and on the west side is the **Hôtel Crillon,** where in 1778, a treaty was signed by Louis XVI and Benjamin Franklin, wherein France officially recognized the United States and became its ally.

Note: Cars tend to hurtle around the obelisk like racers in the Grand Prix; if you feel compelled to cross to the obelisk and you value your life, find the stoplight and cross there.

8th arrond. Métro: Concorde.

MONTMARTRE (18TH ARROND.)

Few places in this city fill you with the urge to belt out sappy show tunes like the *butte* (hill) of Montmartre. Admiring the view from the esplanade in front of the oddly Byzantine **Basilique du Sacré-Coeur,** you'll feel as if you've finally arrived in Paris. Ignore the tour buses and crowds mobbing the church and the hideously touristy **place du Tertre** and wander off into the warren of streets towards the **place des Abbesses** ★ or up **rue Lepic,** where you'll eventually stumble across the **Moulin de la Galette** and **Moulin du Radet,** the two surviving windmills of the 30 that were once on this hill.

Basilique du Sacré-Coeur ★★ CHURCH   Poised at the apex of the hill like a *grande dame* in crinolines, this odd-looking 19th-century basilica has become one of the city's most famous landmarks. After France's defeat in the Franco-Prussian War, prominent Catholics vowed to build a church consecrated to the Sacred Heart of Christ as a way of making up for whatever sins the French may have committed that had made God so angry at them. Since 1885, prayers for humanity have been continually chanted here (the church is a pilgrimage site, so dress and behave accordingly). Inspired by the Byzantine churches of Turkey and Italy, this multidomed confection was begun in 1875 and completed in 1914, though it wasn't consecrated until 1919 because of World War I. The white stone was chosen for its self-cleaning capabilities: When it rains, it secretes a chalky substance that acts as a fresh coat of paint. Most visitors climb the 300 stairs to the **dome,** where the splendid city views extend over 48km (30 miles).

Parvis de la Basilique, 18th arrond. www.sacre-coeur-montmartre.com. ℭ **01-53-41-89-00.** Free admission to basilica; ticket to dome 7€ adults, 4€ ages 4–16, free for children 3 and under (though with 300 steps, it's not advisable). Basilica daily 6:30am–10:30pm; dome Mar–Oct daily 10am–7pm. Métro: Abbesses; take elevator to surface and follow signs to funicular.

Musée de Montmartre ★ MUSEUM   The main reason to visit this small museum is to get an inkling of what Montmartre really was like back in the days when Picasso, Toulouse-Lautrec, Van Gogh, and so on were painting and cavorting up here on the *butte.* While there are few examples of the artists' works here, plenty of photos, posters, and even films document the neighborhood's famous history, from the days when its importance was mainly religious, to the gory days of the Paris Commune, and finally to the artistic boom in the 19th and 20th centuries. The 17th-century house that shelters the museum was at various times the studio and home of Auguste Renoir, Raoul Dufy, Susan Valadon, and Maurice Utrillo. Surrounded by gardens it offers a lovely view of the last scrap of the Montmartre vineyard. There's a great cafe too, **Café Renoir,** set in

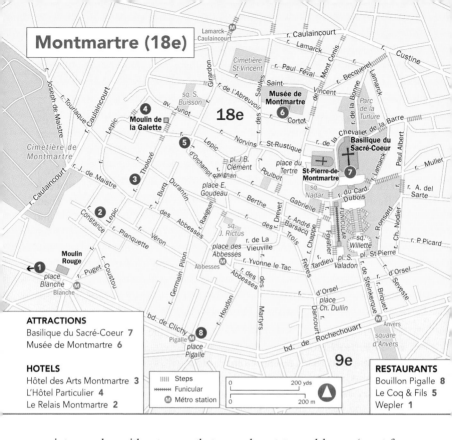

Montmartre (18e)

18e

9e

ATTRACTIONS
Basilique du Sacré-Coeur **7**
Musée de Montmartre **6**

HOTELS
Hôtel des Arts Montmartre **3**
L'Hôtel Particulier **4**
Le Relais Montmartre **2**

RESTAURANTS
Bouillon Pigalle **8**
Le Coq & Fils **5**
Wepler **1**

IIII Steps
++++++ Funicular
Ⓜ Métro station

0   200 yds
0   200 m

a winter garden with a terrace that sprawls out toward lawns (great for small kids to run around without your having to worry about traffic).

12 rue Cortot, 18th arrond. www.museedemontmartre.fr. ⓒ **01-49-25-89-37.** Admission to garden only 5€; museum 15€ adults, 7.50€ ages 18–25, 7€ ages 10–17, free for children 9 and under. Daily 10am–6pm. Métro: Lamarck-Caulaincourt.

RÉPUBLIQUE, BASTILLE & EASTERN PARIS (11TH & 12TH ARROND.)

While you can't really point to any major tourist attractions in this area, this is a nice part of town for eating (thanks to a plethora of neo-bistros), and aimless wandering, especially if you are (a) in search of youth-oriented nightlife, (b) in search of youth-oriented clothing shops, or (c) a history buff. The French Revolution was brewed in the workshops of the **Faubourg St-Antoine** and ignited at the **place de la Bastille.**

Atelier des Lumières ★★ IMMERSIVE MUSEUM   Set in a converted foundry, the entire indoor space here—floors, walls, and ceilings—is one monumental, moving canvas. Around 140 projectors and a high-tech sound system transport you smack-dab into famous paintings, as if you've shrunk and become part of the work. The main space covers the history of art, a second, smaller in size one is for today's emerging digital artists. Because of flashing lights, people with epilepsy and kids ages 2 and under should not visit.

38 rue St-Maur, 11th arrond. www.atelier-lumieres.com. ☏ **01-80-98-46-00.** Admission 16€ adults, 13€ students 12–25, 11€ ages 5–25. Times may vary, according to the exhibition, but it's mostly daily 10am–6pm (until 10pm Fri–Sat). Métro: St-Ambroise or Rue St-Maur.

La Promenade Plantée ★★ WALKING TRAIL

Transformed from an unused train viaduct, this aerial garden walkway runs from the place de la Bastille to the Bois de Vincennes. The 4.5km (2.8-mile) pedestrian path runs along flower gardens, tree bowers, rose trellises, and fountains and takes you over the 12th arrondissement, past the Gare de Lyon, and through the Reuilly Gardens. At ground level along av. Daumesnil, the brick archways now shelter the **Viaduct des Arts,** galleries and workshops that show off the work of highly skilled artisans.

Enter by the staircase on av. Daumesnil, just past the Opéra Bastille, 12th arrond.

Parc Zoologique de Paris ★★ ZOO

This lush, ecologically correct animal reserve invites visitors to five regions of the world, from the plains of Sudan to Europe, via Guyana, Patagonia, and Madagascar. Going for quality instead of quantity, the zoo may not have room for elephants and bears, but it does introduce visitors to animals they might not be familiar with, like the fossa, a catlike carnivore from Madagascar, or the capybara, a giant South American rodent. There is also a good sampling of zoo favorites like lions, baboons, penguins, and giraffes—if you are lucky you can get an up-close look while the latter lunch in the giraffe house. The enclosures are well adapted to their inhabitants, so much so that at times it's hard to see them. But if you are patient you'll spy wolves peeking out of the foliage, or a bright red tomato frog gripping a vine. There are more than 1,000 animals in all, yet the zoo is human-sized—you can see it in a couple of

Colonne de Juillet monument at place de la Bastille.

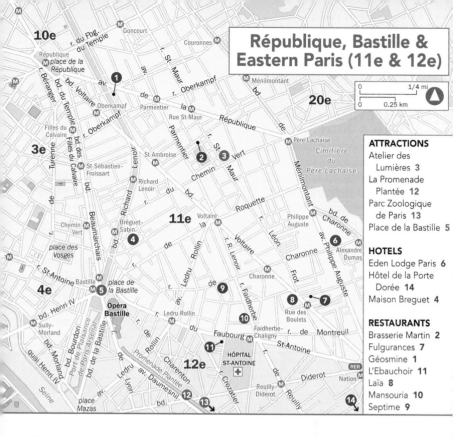

République, Bastille &
Eastern Paris (11e & 12e)

10e

r. du Fbg.
du Temple

Goncourt

République
place de la
République

Couronnes

bd. Béranger

bd. du Temple

bd. Voltaire

av.

r. St-Maur

r. Oberkampf

Ménilmontant

20e

0   1/4 mi

0   0.25 km

Oberkampf

de

Parmentier

la

Rue St-Maur

République

Filles du
Calvaire

3e

r. Oberkampf

bd. des Filles du Calvaire

r. Turenne

bd. Beaumarchais

St-Ambroise

St-Sébastien-
Froissart

Richard
Lenoir

Parmentier

r. St-Maur

St-Maur

Chemin

Vert

du

bd.

2

3

Richard
Lenoir

bd.

Père Lachaise

Cimitière
du
Père-Lachaise

Roquette

ATTRACTIONS
Atelier des
Lumières **3**
La Promenade
Plantée **12**
Parc Zoologique
de Paris **13**
Place de la Bastille **5**

Chemin
Vert

Bréguet-
Sabin

11e

Voltaire

la

Ménilmontant

Philippe
Auguste

bd. de Charonne

av. Philippe Auguste

Alexandre
Dumas

6

place des
Vosges

4

de

r. Rollin

Voltaire

r. R. Lenoir

Léon

Charonne

Frot

HOTELS
Eden Lodge Paris **6**
Hôtel de la Porte
Dorée **14**
Maison Breguet **4**

r. St-Antoine

Bastille

place de
la Bastille

Charonne

r. Ledru

r. de la Roquette

r. de Faidherbe

9

8

7

4e

5

bd. Henri IV

Sully-
Morland

Opéra
Bastille

Port de Plaisance
bd. Bourdon

bd. de Plaisance
de Paris Arsenal

r. Ledru Rollin

du

de

Rollin

Faubourg

Rue des
Boulets

Faidherbe-
Chaligny

St-Antoine

r. de Montreuil

RESTAURANTS
Brasserie Martin **2**
Fulgurances **7**
Géosmine **1**
L'Ebauchoir **11**
Laïa **8**
Mansouria **10**
Septime **9**

10

quai Henri IV

quai Morland

av. Ledru

Charenton

Promenade Plantée

av. Daumesnil

12e

11

HÔPITAL
ST-ANTOINE

r. Crozatier

Diderot

Reuilly-
Diderot

Reuilly

Nation

RER

Seine

place
Mazas

av. Lyon

bd.

12

13

14

hours. Don't miss the huge aviaries, one of which is home to a large flock of flamingos.

Parc de Vincennes, 12th arrond. www.parczoologiquedeparis.fr. ⓒ **01-44-75-20-10.** Admission 20€ adults, 17€ students 12–25, 15€ children ages 3–11, free for children 2 and under. Mid-Oct to mid-Mar Wed–Mon 10am–5pm; mid-Mar to mid-May and Sept to mid-Oct Mon–Fri 10am–6pm, Sat–Sun and school holidays 9:30am–7:30pm; mid-May to late Aug daily 9:30am–8:30pm and night hours Thurs 7–11:30pm. Métro: Porte Dorée.

Place de la Bastille ★   The most notable thing about this giant plaza is the building that's no longer here: the Bastille prison. Now an enormous traffic circle where cars careen around at warp speed, this was once the site of an ancient stone fortress that became a symbol for all that was wrong with the French monarchy. Over the centuries, kings and queens condemned rebellious citizens to stay inside these cold walls, sometimes with good reason, other times on a mere whim. By the time the Revolution started to boil, though, the prison was barely in use; when the angry mobs stormed its walls on July 14, 1789, there were only seven prisoners to set free. Still, the destruction of the Bastille came to be seen as the ultimate revolutionary moment; July 14 is still celebrated as the birth of the Republic. Surprisingly, the giant bronze column in the center honors the victims of a different revolution, that of 1830.

12th arrond. Métro: Bastille.

BELLEVILLE, CANAL ST-MARTIN & LA VILLETTE (10TH, 19TH & 20TH ARROND.)

One of the most picturesque attractions in this area is the **Canal St-Martin** itself, which crosses a formerly working-class neighborhood that is now inhabited by an arty mix of regular folk and *bobos* (bourgeois bohemians). The Belleville neighborhood is home to one of the city's bustling **Chinatowns,** as well as many artists' studios.

Cimetière du Père-Lachaise ★★★ CEMETERY This hillside resting place is green and romantic, with huge leafy trees and narrow paths winding around the graves, which include just about every French literary or artistic giant you can imagine, plus several international stars. Proust, Moliére, La Fontaine, Colette, Delacroix, Seurat, Modigliani, Bizet, Rossini are all here, as well as Sarah Bernhardt, Isadora Duncan, Simone Signoret, and Yves Montand (buried side-by-side, of course), not

Père-Lachaise Cemetery.

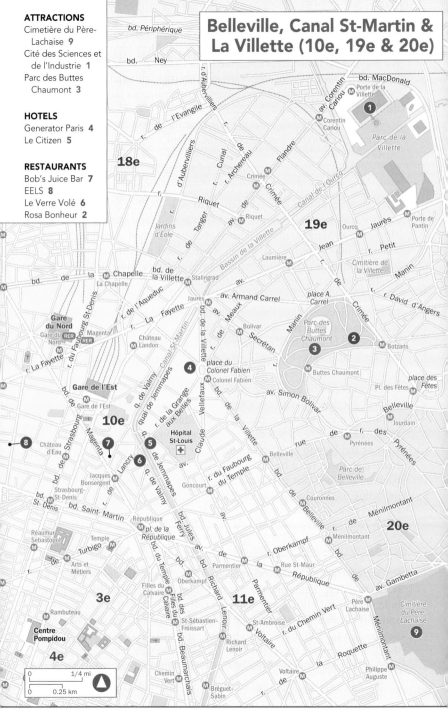

ATTRACTIONS
Cimetière du Père-
  Lachaise **9**
Cité des Sciences et
  de l'Industrie **1**
Parc des Buttes
  Chaumont **3**

HOTELS
Generator Paris **4**
Le Citizen **5**

RESTAURANTS
Bob's Juice Bar **7**
EELS **8**
Le Verre Volé **6**
Rosa Bonheur **2**

Belleville, Canal St-Martin & La Villette (10e, 19e & 20e)

to mention Oscar Wilde, whose huge stone monument is usually covered with lipstick kisses. Even the Lizard King, Jim Morrison, is here. Though the grave itself is unexceptional, the tomb of the '60s rock star is possibly the most visited in the cemetery. In 1971, battling drug, alcohol, and legal problems, the singer/musician came to Paris; 4 months later, he was found dead in a Parisian bathtub, at age 27.

A map is essential. You can find one at the newsstand across from the main entrance, on the website, or at the visitor's booth.

16 rue de Repos, 20th arrond. www.paris.fr/dossiers/bienvenue-au-cimetiere-du-pere-lachaise-47. Free admission. Mon–Fri 8am–6pm; Sat–Sun 8:30am–6pm (Nov to early Mar until 5pm). Métro: Père-Lachaise or Philippe Auguste.

Cité des Sciences et de l'Industrie ★★ MUSEUM   This gigantic science and industry museum was built upon the site of the city's former 19th-century slaughterhouse auction room, which had closed in 1974 due to competition from the suburban Rungis food market, leaving the city with derelict land to fill. Today it includes a planetarium, and a 3D movie theater (closed for renovations until further notice), not to mention a real submarine and an entertainment mall. The heart of the museum is its permanent collection: huge floors of interactive exhibits and displays on subjects like sound, mathematics, and human genes. On the ground floor, parents will be delighted to find the **Cité des Enfants** (separate admission 12€ for a 90-minute session, or 16€ for a combined ticket; see website for hours; reservations essential), which has separate programs for 2- to 7-year-olds and 5- to 12-year-olds. Kids get to explore the world around them in a series of hands-on activities and displays. If all this isn't enough, outside you can clamber into the **Argonaut** (access included with your ticket; must be over age 3 to enter), a real submarine that was one of the stars of the French navy in the 1950s, or if the kids still have energy to burn, take them for a run around the adjacent **Parc de la Villette,** a vast park with a brilliant play area, concert halls, and cultural institutions, including the **Philharmonie de Paris** (https://philharmoniedeparis.fr/en). Parc de La Villette, 30 av. Corentine-Cariou, 19th arrond. www.cite-sciences.fr. ✆ **01-40-05-70-00.** Varied ticket packages from 12€ adults, 9€ ages under 25, free for children 2 and under. Tues–Sat 10am–6pm; Sun 10am–7pm. Métro: Porte de La Villette.

Parc des Buttes Chaumont ★★ PARK   Up until 1860, this area was home to a deep limestone quarry, but thanks to Napoléon III, the gaping hole was turned into an unusual park, full of hills and dales, rocky bluffs, and cliffs. It took 3 years to make this romantic garden; more than a 1,000 workers and a 100 horses dug, heaped, and blasted through the walls of the quarry to create green lawns, a cooling grotto, cascades, streams, and a small lake. By the opening of the 1867 World's Fair, the garden was ready for visitors. The surrounding area was, and still is, working-class; the Emperor built it to give this industrious neighborhood a green haven. There are **pony rides** for the kids on weekends and Wednesdays, plus a **puppet theater,** a **carousel,** and **two playgrounds.** The *guinguette*-style (open-air) bar/cafe—**Rosa Bonheur** (www. rosabonheur.fr), named after the 19th-century feminist artist—is a bucolic spot, staying open even after the park has closed.

Rue Botzaris, 19th arrond. Daily 7am–dusk. Métro: Botzaris or Buttes Chaumont.

The Left Bank

LATIN QUARTER (5TH & 13TH ARROND.)

What's so Latin about this quarter? Well, for several hundred years, the students that flocked here spoke Latin in their classes at the **Sorbonne** (founded in the 13th c.) and other nearby schools. The students still flock and the Sorbonne is still in biz, and though classes are now taught in French, the name stuck. This youth-filled neighborhood is a lively one, packed with art-house cinemas and cafes. History is readily visible here, dating back to the Roman occupation: The **rue St-Jacques** and **boulevard Saint-Michel** mark the former Roman cardo, and you can explore the remains of the **Roman baths** at the **Cluny Museum** (p. 118).

Institut du Monde Arabe ★★ MUSEUM   In an age when Arab culture is all over the headlines, this is a good place to come to find out what the phrase actually means. The airy museum space presents a collection that emphasizes the diversity of peoples and cultures in the Middle East, reminding us, among other things, that it was the birthplace of all three major Western religions. While the collection is intellectually stimulating, if art is what you are after, the Islamic Art section of the Louvre will be more satisfying. Still, the building itself, designed by architect Jean Nouvel in 1987, is worth the price of admission. The south facade, which has a metallic latticework echoing traditional Arab designs, includes 30,000 light-sensitive diaphragms that regulate the penetration of light by opening and closing according to how bright it is outside. There's a terrific view of the Seine and Notre-Dame from the panoramic terrace (open 10am–6pm), plus an interesting cycle of concerts (12€–26€; tickets available online).

1 rue des Fossés St-Bernard, 5th arrond. www.imarabe.org. © **01-40-51-38-38.** Admission to permanent collections 8€, free for ages 25 and under. Tues–Fri 10am–6pm; Sat–Sun 10am–7pm. Métro: Jussieu, Cardinal Lemoine, Sully-Morland.

4

Jardin des Plantes ★★★ GARDENS   This delightful botanical garden, tucked between the Muséum National d'Histoire Naturelle (see below) and the Seine, is one of my favorite picnic spots. Created in 1626 as a medicinal plant garden for King Louis XIII, in the 18th century it became an internationally famed scientific institution thanks to naturalist, mathematician, and biologist Georges-Louis Leclerc, Count of Buffon, with the help of fellow-naturalist Louis-Jean-Marie Daubenton. Today the museums are still part academic institutions, but you certainly don't need to be a student to appreciate the lush grounds.

The garden also harbors a small, but well-kempt zoo, the **Ménagerie, le Zoo du Jardin des Plantes** ★ (www.mnhn.fr; ☎ 01-40-79-56-01; 13€ adults, free for children 3 and under; daily 9am–6pm). Created in 1794, this is the second oldest zoo in the world (after the Tiergarten Schönbrunn in Vienna). Because of its size, the zoo showcases mostly smaller species, in particular birds and reptiles, but it also has a healthy selection of mammals, including rare species like red pandas, Przewalski horses, and even Florida pumas.

rue Geoffroy-St-Hilaire, 5th arrond. www.jardindesplantesdeparis.fr. ☎ **01-40-79-56-01.** Free admission to gardens. Daily 8am–dusk. Métro: Gare d'Austerlitz.

Musée de Cluny (Le Monde Médiéval) ★★ MUSEUM   Ancient Roman baths and a 15th-century mansion set the stage for a terrific collection of Medieval art and objects at this museum. Built somewhere between the 1st and 3rd centuries, the baths (visible from bd. St-Michel) are some of the best existing examples of Gallo-Roman architecture. They are attached to what was once the palatial home of a 15th-century abbot, whose last owner, a certain Alexandre du Sommerard, amassed a vast array of Medieval masterworks. When he died in 1842, his home was turned into a museum and his collection put on display. Sculptures, textiles, furniture, and ceramics are on display, as well as gold, ivory, and enamel work. Of the several magnificent tapestries the biggest draw is the late-15th-century *Lady and the Unicorn* series, one of only two sets of complete unicorn tapestries in the world (the other is in New York City).

Lady and the Unicorn tapestry, Musée de Cluny.

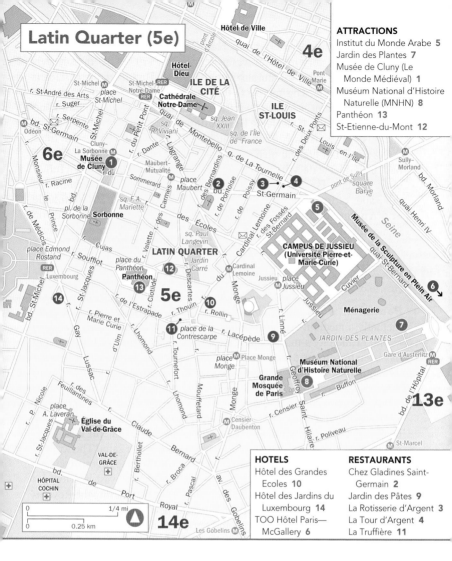

Latin Quarter (5e)

Among the many sculptures displayed are the famous severed heads from the facade of Notre-Dame. Knocked off their bodies during the furor of the Revolution, 21 of the heads of the Kings of Judah were found by chance in 1977 during repair work in the basement of a bank. Other treasures include Flemish retables, Visigoth crowns, bejeweled chalices, wood carvings, stained-glass windows, and beautiful objects from daily life, like hair combs and game boards.

6 pl. Paul Painlevé, 5th arrond. www.musee-moyenage.fr. ℰ **01-53-73-78-00.** Admission 12€ adults, 10€ ages 18–24, free for children 17 and under. Tues–Sun 9:30am–6:15pm. Métro/RER: Cluny–La Sorbonne or St-Michel.

Muséum National d'Histoire Naturelle (MNHN) ★★ MUSEUM
This natural-history museum was established in 1793 under the supervision of two celebrated naturalists, the Count of Buffon and Louis Jean-Marie Daubenton. This temple to the natural sciences contains a series of separate museums, each with a different specialty. The biggest draw is no doubt the **Grande Galerie de l'Evolution,** where a sort of Noah's ark of animals snakes its way around a huge hall filled with displays that trace the evolution of life and man's relationship to nature. Another interesting hall, the **Galerie de Minérologie et de Geologies,** includes a room full of giant crystals. For dinosaurs, saber-toothed tigers, ancient humans, and thousands of fossilized skeletons, repair to the **Galeries de Paléontologie et d'Anatomie Comparée.** A recent **Galerie des Enfants** has hands-on interactive displays for the little tykes. You'll have to pay for each *galerie* separately, but a ticket to one gives you a reduced rate at the other.

36 rue Geoffrey, 5th arrond. www.mnhn.fr. ☎ **01-40-79-54-79.** Admission to each gallery 10€–13€ adults, free for ages 26 and under. Wed–Mon 10am–6pm. Métro: Jussieu or Gare d'Austerlitz.

Panthéon ★★ CHURCH/MAUSOLEUM High atop the *montagne* (actually a medium-size hill) of St-Geneviève, the dome of the Panthéon is one of the city's most visible landmarks. This erstwhile royal church has been transformed into a national mausoleum—the final resting place of luminaries such as Voltaire, Rousseau, Hugo, and Zola, as well as Marie and Pierre Curie, World War II heroes of the Résistance, and (since 2021) the American-born entertainer and activist Josephine Baker, the first Black woman to be given a place in the monument. Initially dedicated to St-Geneviève, the church was commissioned by a grateful Louis XV, who attributed his recovery from a serious illness to the saint. The work of architect Jacques-Germain Soufflot, who took his inspiration from the Pantheon in Rome, it must have been magnificent—the vast interior was clearly created with a higher power in mind. However, during the Revolution its sacred mission was diverted toward a new god—the Nation—and it was converted into a memorial and burial ground for Great Men of the Republic. This meant taking down the bells, walling up most of the windows, doing away with religious statuary and replacing it with works promoting patriotic virtues. The desired effect was achieved—the enormous empty space, lined with huge paintings of great moments in French history, resembles a cavernous tomb. The star attraction in the nave is **Foucault's Pendulum** (named after the French physicist Léon Foucault, who invented it in 1851), a simple device—a heavy ball suspended on a long wire above markers—that proves the rotation of the Earth. Visitors can climb the Panthéon's lofty dome between April and October (it was the highest spot in Paris until the Eiffel Tower was erected in 1889) to see the city unfurl in a higgledy-piggledy sprawl of gray rooftops. It's a breathtaking sight, spreading all the way out past the Eiffel Tower to the high-rises of Paris's out-of-town business district, La Defense.

pl. du Panthéon, 5th arrond. www.paris-pantheon.fr. ℂ **01-44-32-18-00.** Admission 11.50€ adults, free for children 17 and under. Dome 3.50€ extra. Apr–Sept daily 10am–6:30pm; Oct–Mar daily 10am–6pm. Dome Apr–Oct only. Métro: Cardinal Lemoine. RER: Luxembourg.

St-Etienne-du-Mont ★★ CHURCH One of the city's prettiest churches, this ecclesiastical gem is a joyous mix of late Gothic and Renaissance styles. The 17th-century facade combines Gothic tradition with a dash of classical Rome; inside, the 16th-century chancel sports a magnificent **rood screen** (an intricately carved partition separating the nave from the chancel) with decorations inspired by the Italian Renaissance. Book-ended by twin spiraling marble staircases, this rood screen is the only one left in the city. A pilgrimage site, this church was once part of an abbey dedicated to St-Geneviève (the city's patron saint), and stones from her original sarcophagus lie in an ornate shrine here. That's about all that is left of her—the saint's bones were burned during the Revolution and their ashes thrown in the Seine. The remains of two other great minds, Racine and Pascal, are buried here.

1 pl. St-Geneviève, 5th arrond. www.saintetiennedumont.fr. ℂ **01-43-54-11-79.** Free admission. Tues–Fri 10am–1pm and 2–7:30pm; Sat–Sun 8:30am–1pm and 2–8pm; Mon 2:30–7:30pm (times vary during school holidays). Métro: Cardinal Lemoine or Luxembourg.

ST-GERMAIN-DES-PRÉS & LUXEMBOURG (6TH ARROND.)

In the 20th century, the St-Germain-des-Prés neighborhood became associated with writers like Jean-Paul Sartre, Simone de Beauvoir, Albert Camus, and the rest of the intellectual bohemian crowd that gathered at **Café de Flore** or **Les Deux Magots** (p. 165). But back in the 6th century, a mighty abbey founded here ruled over a big chunk of the Left Bank for 1,000 years. The French Revolution put a stop to that, and most of the original buildings were pulled down. Remains of both epochs can still be found in this chic and artsy neighborhood, notably at the 10th-century church **St-Germain-des-Prés,** and the surviving bookstores and publishing houses that surround it.

Jardin du Luxembourg ★★★ GARDENS Rolling out like an exotic Oriental carpet before the Italianate Palais du Luxembourg, this vast expanse of fountains, flowers, lush lawns, and shaded glens is the perfect setting for a leisurely stroll, a relaxed picnic, or a serious make-out session, depending on who you're with. At the center of everything is a fountain with a huge basin, where kids can sail toy wooden sailboats (4€/30 min.) and adults can sun themselves in the green metal chairs at the pond's edge. Sculptures abound: At every turn, there is a god, goddess, artist, or monarch peering down at you from their pedestal. The most splendid

Fontaine de Observatoire, Luxembourg Gardens.

waterworks is probably the Medici Fountain (reached via the entrance at place Paul Claudel behind the Odéon), draped with lithe Roman gods and topped with the Medici coat of arms, in honor of the palace's first resident, Marie de Medicis.

In 1621, the Italian-born French queen, homesick for the Pitti Palace of her youth, bought up the grounds and existing buildings and had a Pitti-inspired palace built for herself as well as a smaller version of the sumptuous gardens. During the Revolution, it was turned into a prison. American writer Thomas Paine was incarcerated there in 1793 after he fell out of favor with Robespierre; he narrowly escaped execution. On the plus side, the Revolutionaries increased the size of the garden and made it a public institution. Visitors can visit a horticulture school where pear trees have been trained into formal, geometric shapes, as well as beehives (yes, beehives) maintained by a local apiculture association.

Entry at pl. Edmond Rostand, pl. André Honnorat, rue Guynemer, or rue de Vaugirard, 6th arrond. www.senat.fr/visite/jardin. Daily 7:30am–dusk (from 8:15am in winter). Métro: Odéon. RER: Luxembourg.

Musée Zadkine ★★ MUSEUM You could easily miss the alleyway that leads to this tiny museum in the small but luminous house where

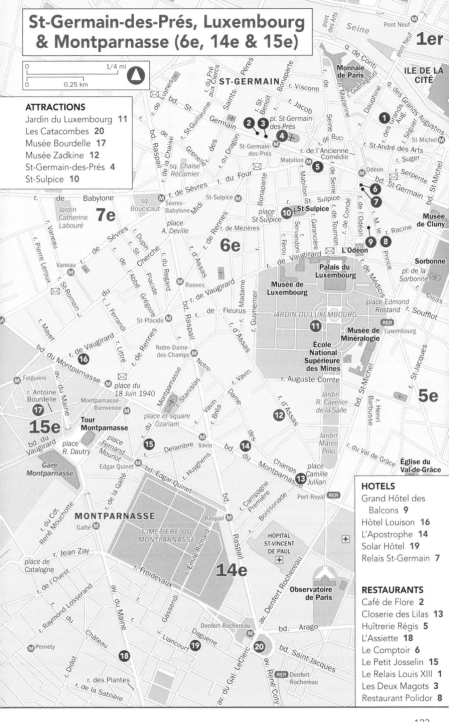

St-Germain-des-Prés, Luxembourg & Montparnasse (6e, 14e & 15e)

1er

ILE DE LA CITÉ

7e

6e

15e

5e

14e

Attention Bored Kids & Tired Parents

Frazzled parents take note: The Jardin du Luxembourg has lots of activities for kids who need to blow off steam. First off, there is the extra-large **playground** (2€ adults, 2.50€ children 11 and under) filled with all kinds of things to climb on and play in. Then there are the wonderful wooden **sailboats** (4€/30 min.) to float in the main fountain, as well as an ancient **carousel** (2.50€, next to the playground) and **pony rides** (8€–10€). At the **marionette theater** (7.20€ each for parents and children; Wed, Sat, Sun, and school vacation days; shows usually start after 3:15pm and 4:30pm, Sat–Sun additional show at 11am), you can see Guignol himself (the French version of Punch) in a variety of French-language puppet shows aimed at ages 2 to 6.

Ossip Zadkine lived and worked from 1928 to his death in 1967. A contemporary and neighbor of artists such as Brancusi, Lipchitz, Modigliani, and Picasso, this Russian-born sculptor is closely associated with the Cubist movement; his sober, elegant, "primitive" sculptures combine abstract geometry with deep humanity. Be sure to visit the artist's workshop, tucked behind the tranquil garden. *Note:* Due to the museum's small size, during temporary exhibits you'll have to pay to enter the permanent collection (check the website for prices).

100 bis rue d'Assas, 6th arrond. www.zadkine.paris.fr. ✆ **01-55-42-77-20.** Free admission to permanent collections. Tues–Sun 10am–6pm. Métro: Notre-Dame des Champs or Vavin.

St-Germain-des-Prés ★★★ CHURCH   The origins of this church stretch back over a millennium. First established by King Childebert in 543, who constructed a basilica and monastery on the site, it was built, destroyed, and rebuilt several times over the centuries. Nothing remains of the original buildings, but the bell tower dates from the 10th century and is one of the oldest in France. The church and its abbey became a major center of learning and power during the Middle Ages, remaining a force to be reckoned with up until the French Revolution, when all hell broke loose: The abbey was destroyed, the famous library burned, and the church vandalized. Restored in the 19th century, the buildings have regained some of their former glory, though the complex is a fraction of its original size.

Much of the interior is painted in a range of greens and golds—one of the few Parisian churches to retain a sense of its original decor. The heart of King Jean Casimir of Poland is buried here, as are the ashes of the body of René Descartes (his skull is in the collections of the **Musée de l'Homme;** p. 104). On the left as you exit you can peek inside the **chapel of St-Symphorien,** where during the Revolution over 100 clergymen were imprisoned before being executed on the square in front of the church. The chapel was restored in the 1970s and decorated by contemporary artist Pierre Buraglio in 1992.

Classical music concerts are regularly held in the church. (Tickets and info at www.fnactickets.com.) On the last Sunday of the month, afternoon organ recitals are free.

3 pl. St-Germain-des-Prés, 6th arrond. www.eglise-saintgermaindespres.fr. ✆ **01-55-42-81-10.** Free admission. Daily 8am–7:45pm. Métro: St-Germain-des-Prés.

St-Sulpice ★★ CHURCH   The majestic facade of this enormous edifice looms over an entire neighborhood. Construction started in the 17th century over the remains of a medieval church; it took over a hundred years to build, and one of the towers was never finished. Inside, the cavernous interior seems to command you to be silent. Tucked into the chapels that line the church are several important works of art. The most famous of them are **three masterpieces by Eugène Delacroix,** *Jacob Wrestling with the Angel, Heliodorus Driven from the Temple,* and *St-Michael Vanquishing the Devil* (on the right just after you enter the church). Jean-Baptiste Pigalle's statue of the *Virgin and Child* lights up the Chapelle de la Vierge at the farthest most point from the entrance. A bronze line runs north–south along the floor; this is part of a **gnomon,** an astronomical device set up in the 17th century to calculate the position of the sun in the sky. A small hole in one of the stained-glass windows creates a spot of light on the floor; every day at noon it hits the line in a different spot, climbing to the top of an obelisk and lighting a gold disk at winter equinox.

pl. St-Sulpice, 6th arrond. www.paroissesaintsulpice.paris ✆ **01-42-34-59-98.** Free admission. Daily 8am–7:45pm. Métro: St-Sulpice.

EIFFEL TOWER & LES INVALIDES (7TH ARROND.)

The Iron Lady towers above this stately neighborhood, where the very buildings seem to insist that you stand up straight and pay attention. Stuffed with embassies and ministries, you'll see lots of elegant black cars with smoked glass cruising the streets, as well as many a tourist eyeing the **Eiffel Tower** or the golden dome of **Les Invalides** and scurrying in and out of some of the city's best museums, like the **Musée du Quai Branly, Musée d'Orsay,** and **Musée Rodin.**

Eiffel Tower ★★★ MONUMENT   In his wildest dreams, Gustave Eiffel probably never imagined that the tower he built for the 1889 World's Fair would become the ultimate symbol of Paris and, for many, of France. Originally slated for demolition after its first 20 years, the Eiffel Tower has survived more than a century and is one of the most visited sites in the nation. No less than 50 engineers and designers worked on the plans, which resulted in a remarkably solid structure that despite its height (324m/1,063 ft., including the antenna) does not sway in the wind.

But while the engineers rejoiced, others howled. When the project for the tower was announced, a group of artists and writers, including Guy de Maupassant and Alexandre Dumas, published a manifesto that referred to it as an "odious column of bolted metal." Others were less diplomatic: Novelist Joris-Karl Huysmans called it a "hole-riddled suppository." Despite the objections, the tower was built—over 18,000 pieces of iron, held together with some 2.5 million rivets. In this low-tech era, building techniques involved a lot of elbow grease: The foundations, for example, were dug entirely by shovel, and the debris was hauled away in horse-drawn carts. Construction dragged on for 2 years, but finally, on March 31, 1889, Gustave Eiffel proudly led a group of dignitaries up the 1,710 steps to the top, where he unfurled the French flag for the inauguration.

Over 100 years later, the tower has become such an integral piece of the Parisian landscape that it's impossible to think of the city without it. Over time, even the artists came around—the tower's silhouette can be found in the paintings of Seurat, Bonnard, Duffy, Chagall, and especially those of Robert Delaunay, who devoted an entire series of canvases to the subject. It has also inspired a whole range of stunts, from Pierre Labric riding a bicycle down the stairs from the first level in 1923 to Philippe Petit walking a 700m-long (2,296-ft.) tightrope from the Palais de Chaillot to the tower during the centennial celebration in 1989. Eiffel performed his own "stunts" towards the end of his career, using the tower as a laboratory for scientific experiments. By convincing the authorities of the tower's usefulness in studying meteorology, aerodynamics, and other subjects, Eiffel saved it from being torn down.

The most dramatic view of the tower itself is from the wide esplanade at the Palais de Chaillot (Métro: Trocadéro) across the Seine. From there it's a short walk down through the gardens and across the Pont d'Iena to the base of the tower.

A Workout & a Bargain at the Eiffel Tower

No need to go to the gym after marching up the 704 steps that lead you to the second floor of the Eiffel Tower. Not only will you burn calories, but you'll save money: At 10€ adults, 5€ ages 12 to 24, and 2.50€ ages 4 to 11, this is the least expensive way to visit. Extra perks include an up-close view of the amazing metal structure and avoiding long lines for the elevator.

The first floor has a restaurant and displays and a bit of glass floor, so you can pretend you are walking on air. Personally, I think the view from the second level is the best; you're far enough up to see the entire city, yet close enough to clearly pick out the monuments. But if you are aching to get to the top, an airplanelike view awaits. The third level is, mercifully, enclosed, but thrill-seekers can climb up a few more stairs to the outside balcony (entirely protected with a grill). The base of the tower is surrounded by bulletproof glass walls as part of a plan to protect visitors from terror

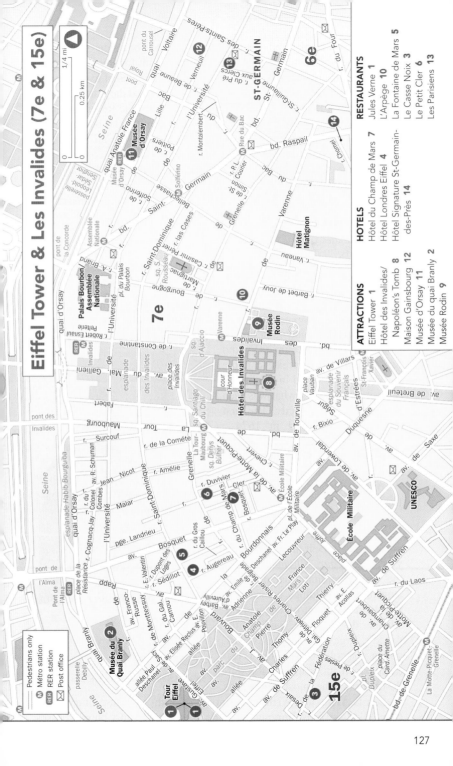

Eiffel Tower & Les Invalides (7e & 15e)

ST-GERMAIN

6e

7e

15e

UNESCO

École Militaire

Hôtel des Invalides

cour d'Honneur

Musée du Quai Branly

Tour Eiffel

Musée d'Orsay

Palais Bourbon/ Assemblée Nationale

Musée Rodin

Hôtel Matignon

Seine

0   0.25 km
0   1/4 mi

Pedestrians only
Métro station
RER station
Post office

ATTRACTIONS
Eiffel Tower 1
Hôtel des Invalides/
Napoléon's Tomb 8
Maison Gainsbourg 12
Musée d'Orsay 11
Musée du quai Branly 2
Musée Rodin 9

HOTELS
Hôtel du Champ de Mars 7
Hôtel Londres Eiffel 4
Hôtel Signature St-Germain-
des-Prés 14

RESTAURANTS
Jules Verne 1
L'Arpège 10
La Fontaine de Mars 5
Le Casse Noix 3
Le Petit Cler 6
Les Parisiens 13

127

attacks. Don't be alarmed: It's precautionary and not a sign of imminent danger, and you'll still be able to walk underneath for free once you've passed the security checks. Build in at least 20 minutes of extra time for the check points. The construction of the wall marked the start of a major modernization plan that aims to improve access to the tower in general and provide shelter for visitors in bad weather (until 2031, but the monument will remain open throughout the work). *Note:* For all access, you should book a time-stamped e-ticket in advance online so you can spend as little time as possible in lines. The line time without a slot can easily climb to 4 hours or more.

Champ de Mars, 7th arrond. www.toureiffel.paris. ℂ **01-44-11-23-23.** Elevator to 2nd floor 18.10€ adults, 9€ ages 12–24, 4.50€ ages 4–11; elevator to 2nd and 3rd floors 28.30€ adults, 14.10€ ages 12–24, 7.10€ ages 4–11; stairs to 2nd floor 11.30€ adults, 5.60€ ages 12–24, 2.80€ ages 4–11; stairs to 2nd floor and elevator to the top 21.50€ adults, 10.70€ ages 12–24, 5.40€ ages 4–11. Free for children ages 3 and under. Daily 9:15am–10:45pm (but times may vary with the season, so check the website). Métro: Trocadéro or Bir Hakeim. RER: Champ de Mars–Tour Eiffel.

Hôtel des Invalides/Napoléon's Tomb ★★ MUSEUM This gran-
diose complex houses a military museum, church, tomb, hospital, and military ministries, among other things. Commissioned by Louis XIV, who was determined to create a home for soldiers wounded in the line of duty, it was built on what was then the outskirts of the city. The first war veterans arrived in 1674—between 4,000 and 5,000 soldiers would eventually move in, creating a mini-city with its own governor. An on-site hospital was constructed for the severely wounded, which is still in service today.

As you cross the main gate, you'll find yourself in a huge courtyard, the *cour d'honneur,* once the site of military parades. The surrounding buildings house military administration offices and the **Musée de l'Armée,** one of the world's largest military museums, with a vast collection of objects testifying to man's capacity for self-destruction. The most impressive

Statue of Napoleon in the Hôtel des Invalides.

section is **Arms and Armor,** a panoply of 13th- to 17th-century weaponry. Viking swords, Burgundian battle axes, 14th-century blunderbusses,

Balkan *khandjars,* Browning machine guns, engraved Renaissance serpentines, musketoons, grenadiers—if it can kill, it's enshrined here. There is also a huge wing covering the exploits of everyone from **Louis XIV** to **Napoléon III;** another is on the two **World Wars.** Also onsite is the **Musée des Plans et Reliefs,** a somewhat dusty collection of scale models of fortresses and battlefields and the and the **Musée de l'Ordre de la Libération,** which retraces the history of the Liberation (1940–45).

The **Eglise du Dôme** is split in two, the front half being the light-filled Soldier's Church, decorated with magnificent chandeliers and a collection of flags of defeated enemies. On the other side of the glass partition the **Tomb of Napoléon** lies under one of the most splendid domes in France. Designed by Hardouin-Mansart, it took over 2 decades to build. The interior soars 107m (351 ft.) up to a skylight, which illuminates a brilliantly colored cupola. Ethereal light filters down to an opening where you can look down on the huge porphyry sarcophagus, which holds the emperor's remains, encased in five successive coffins (one tin, one mahogany, two lead, and one ebony). Surrounding the sarcophagus are the tombs of two of Napoléon's brothers, his son, and several French military heroes. Don't blame the over-the-top setting on Napoléon; the decision to transfer his remains to Paris was made in 1840, almost 20 years after his death. Tens of thousands crowded the streets to pay their respects as the coffin was carried under the Arc de Triomphe and down the Champs-Elysées to Les Invalides, where it waited another 20 years until the tomb was finished. *Please note that the museum will be undergoing renovations until 2030, but will remain open.*

pl. des Invalides, 7th arrond. www.musee-armee.fr. ⓒ **01-44-42-37-72.** Admission to all the museums, the church, and Napoléon's Tomb 14€ adults (10€ from 6pm on late-night opening), free for children 17 and under. Daily 10am–6pm (1st Fri of the month until 10pm). Métro: Latour-Maubourg, Varenne, or Invalides. RER: Invalides.

Maison de Gainsbourg ★★ MUSEUM   Paris's newest museum is the former home of Chanson legend, Serge Gainsbourg (already a historical landmark, smothered in fan graffiti), now open to the public as a hybrid cultural spot called Maison de Gainsbourg—part museum, part period home (looking pretty much as Gainsbourg left it when he died in 1991), part shop and part cafe. If you're a music fan, this is the only place dedicated entirely to the songwriting icon and so may well be worth your time (though you'll need to book ahead; at time of writing, there was a month's wait for museum tickets and more than 3 months for the house). Serge's house takes about 30 minutes to get around, thanks to an immersive audio guide (performed by actress Charlotte Gainsbourg, Serge's daughter), while the museum will take you through his works and life, showing lots of hitherto unseen material.

14 rue de Verneil, 7th arrond. www.maisongainsbourg.fr. No phone. Admission to museum only 12€ adults, 6€ ages 7–24, free for children 6 and under. Admission to house and museum 25€ adults, 16€ ages 7–24, free for children 6 and under. Tues–Sat 10am–6pm. Métro: Saint-Germain-des-Près.

Musée d'Orsay.

Musée d'Orsay ★★★ MUSEUM What better setting for a world-class museum of 19th-century art than a beautiful example of Belle Epoque architecture? In 1986, the magnificent Gare d'Orsay train station, built to coincide with the 1900 World's Fair, was transformed into an exposition space. The huge, airy central hall lets in lots of natural light, which is artfully combined with artificial lighting to illuminate a collection of treasures.

The collection spans the years 1848 to 1914, a period that saw the birth of many artistic movements, but today it is best known for the emergence of Impressionism. All the superstars of the epoch are here, including Monet, Manet, Degas, Renoir, Cézanne and Van Gogh.

The top floor is the home of the most famous Impressionist paintings, like Edouard Manet's masterpiece, *Le Déjeuner sur l'Herbe.* Though Manet's composition of bathers and friends picnicking on the grass draws freely from those of Italian Renaissance masters, the painting shocked its 19th-century audience, which was horrified to see a naked lady lunching with two fully clothed men. Manet got into trouble again with his magnificent *Olympia,* a seductive odalisque stretched out on a divan. There was nothing new about the subject; viewers were rattled by the unapologetic look in her eye—this is not an idealized nude, but a real woman, and a tough cookie to boot.

The middle level is devoted to the post-Impressionists, with works by artists like Gauguin, Seurat, Rousseau, and Van Gogh, like the latter's *Church at Auvers-sur-Oise,* an ominous version of the church in a small town north of Paris where he moved after spending time in an asylum in Provence. This was one of some 70 paintings he produced in the 2 months leading up to his suicide.

1 rue de la Légion d'Honneur, 7th arrond. www.musee-orsay.fr. ℂ **01-40-49-48-14.** Admission 16€ adults, 13€ ages 18–25, free for children 17 and under. Tues–Wed and Fri–Sun 9:30am–6pm; Thurs 9:30am–9:45pm. Métro: Solférino. RER: Musée d'Orsay.

Musée du quai Branly ★★★ MUSEUM   It's just a few blocks from the Eiffel Tower, but this museum's wildly contemporary design has forever changed the architectural landscape of this rigidly elegant neighborhood. Its enormous central structure floats on a series of pillars, under which lies a lush garden, separated from the noisy boulevard by a huge glass wall. However you feel about the outside, you cannot help but be impressed by the inside: The vast space is filled with exquisite examples of the traditional arts of Africa, the Pacific Islands, Asia, and the Americas. Designed by veteran museum-maker Jean Nouvel, this intriguing space makes an ideal showcase for a category of artwork that too often has been relegated to the sidelines of the museum world.

This magnificent collection is displayed in a way that invites you to admire the skill and artistry that went into the creation of these diverse objects. Delicately carved headrests from Papua New Guinea in the form of birds and crocodiles and intricately painted masks from Indonesia vie for your attention. Look at and listen to giant wooden flutes from Papua New Guinea (there's an ongoing recording). A selection of "magic stones" from the island nation of Vanuatu includes smooth abstract busts reminiscent of Brancusi sculptures. A fascinating collection of Australian aboriginal paintings segues into the Asian art section, and the journey continues into Africa, starting with embroidered silks from Morocco and heading south through magnificent geometric marriage cloths from Mali and wooden masks from the Ivory Coast. The Americas collection includes rare Nazca pottery and Inca textiles, as well as an intriguing assortment of North American works, like Haitian voodoo objects and Sioux beaded tunics. Though some documentation is translated in English, **audio guides** (5€) are a big help for non-French speakers.

37 quai Branly and 206 and 218 rue de Université, 7th arrond. www.quaibranly.fr. ℂ **01-56-61-70-00.** Admission to permanent exhibitions 12€ adults, free for children 17 and under. Tues–Wed and Fri–Sun 10:30am–7pm; Thurs 10:30am–10pm. Métro: Alma-Marceau. RER: Pont d'Alma.

Musée Rodin ★★★ MUSEUM   There aren't many museums that can draw thousands of visitors who never even go inside. But the grounds of this splendid place are so lovely that many are willing to pay 4€ just to stroll around. Behind the Hôtel Biron, the mansion that houses the museum, is a formal garden with benches, fountains, and even a little cafe. Of course, it would be foolish *not* to go inside and drink in the some of the 6,600 sculptures in this excellent collection (don't worry, not all are on display), but it would be equally silly not to take the time to admire the large bronzes in the garden, which include some of Rodin's most famous works. Take, for example, *The Thinker.* Erected in front of the Panthéon in 1906 during a political crisis, Rodin's first public sculpture soon became a Socialist symbol and was quickly transferred here by the authorities, under the pretense that it blocked pedestrian traffic. Other important outdoor sculptures include the *Burghers of Calais, Balzac,* and the *Gates of Hell,* a monumental composition that the sculptor worked on throughout his career.

Sculpture of the Three Shades at the Musée Rodin.

Indoors, marble works prevail, although there are also works in terracotta, plaster, and bronze, as well as sketches and paintings on display. The most famous of the marbles is *The Kiss,* which was originally meant to appear in the *Gates of Hell.* In time, Rodin decided that the lovers were too happy for this grim composition, and he explored it as an independent work. As usual with Rodin's works, the critics were shocked by the couple's overt sensuality, but not as shocked as they were by the large, impressionistic rendition of *Balzac,* exhibited at the same salon, which critic Georges Rodenbach described as "less a statue than a strange monolith, a thousand-year-old menhir." The museum holds hundreds of works, many of them legendary, so don't be surprised if after a while your vision starts to blur. That'll be your cue to head outside and enjoy the garden.

79 rue de Varenne, 7th arrond. www.musee-rodin.fr. ℂ **01-44-18-61-10.** Admission 14€ adults, 9€ ages 18–25, free for children 17 and under. Tues–Sun 10am–6:30pm. Métro: Varenne or St-Francois-Xavier.

MONTPARNASSE (14TH & 15TH ARROND.)

Even though it had its heart ripped out in the 1970s when the original 19th-century train station was torn down and the ugly Tour Montparnasse was erected, this neighborhood still retains a redolent whiff of its artistic past. Back in the day, artists like Picasso, Modigliani, and Man Ray hung out in cafes like **Le Dôme, La Coupole, La Rotonde,** and **Le Sélect,** as did a "Lost Generation" of English-speaking writers like Hemingway, Fitzgerald, Faulkner, and Joyce. Today the famous cafes are mostly filled with tourists, but you can still find quiet corners. Amazingly, **La Ruche,** the legendary artists' studio from the Golden Years, is still standing (http://laruche-artistes.fr).

Les Catacombes ★ CEMETERY/HISTORIC SITE   Definitely not for the faint of heart, the city's catacombs are filled with the remains of millions of ex-Parisians, whose bones line the narrow passages of this mazelike series of tunnels. In the 18th century, the Cimetière des Innocents, a centuries-old, overpacked cemetery near Les Halles, had become so foul and disease-ridden that it was finally declared a health hazard and closed. The bones of its occupants were transferred to this former quarry, which were later joined by those of other similarly pestilential Parisian cemeteries.

In 1814, the quarry stopped accepting new lodgers. Rather than leaving just a hodge-podge of random bones, they organized them in neat stacks and geometric designs, punctuating the 2km (1¼ miles) with sculptures and epigrammatic sayings carved into the rock. The one at the entrance sets the tone: STOP—HERE IS THE EMPIRE OF DEATH. The visit

Les Catacombes.

will be fascinating for some, terrifying for others; definitely not a good idea for claustrophobics or small children. Wear comfortable shoes and bring a sweater of some sort, as it's cool down here (around 57°F/14°C). For security reasons, only a limited number are allowed to visit at a time. Buy an e-ticket with a time slot online in advance; you'll still have to wait in line, but hopefully not for more than 10 minutes.

1 av. du Colonel Henri Rol-Tanguy, 14th arrond. www.catacombes.paris.fr. ✆ **01-43-22-47-63.** Admission 29€ adults, 23€ ages 18–26, 10€ ages 5–17, free for children 4 and under. Tues–Sun 9:45am–8:30pm (last entry 7:30pm). Métro and RER: Denfert-Rochereau.

Musée Bourdelle ★ MUSEUM   Recently renovated and expanded (to include a lovely cafe), this quaint museum is a testament to the sculptor Antoine Bourdelle, whose work went far beyond the 10 years he spent as Rodin's assistant. A renowned teacher who influenced an entire generation of sculptors, including Alberto Giacometti and Aristide Maillol, Bourdelle was one of the pioneers of 20th-century monumental sculpture. Proud, muscular centaurs, gods, and goddesses stride across these rooms, as well as monuments to famous people. You can also visit the sculptor's studio. **Audio guides** in English (5€) are a big help here.

18 rue Antoine-Bourdelle, 15th arrond. www.bourdelle.paris.fr. ✆ **01-49-54-73-73.** Free admission to the permanent collection. Tues–Sun 10am–6pm. Métro: Montparnasse-Bienvenüe.

WHERE TO STAY

Paris has more than 1,500 hotels, from palaces fit for a pasha to tiny family-run operations whose best features are their warm welcome and personal touch. Over the last few years, a plethora of new establishments have opened too, many with exquisite, modern decor. In theory, you should be able to find something in line with your budget, timeframe, and personal tastes. But even if you can't find the hotel of your dreams in the list below, don't despair—at the end of this section I list alternative lodging options, including B&Bs and short-term apartment rentals.

The Right Bank

LOUVRE & ILE DE LA CITÉ (1ST ARROND.)

The area surrounding the Louvre is littered with hotels, some of which are dreadfully overpriced. Yes, if you only are in town for 1 day or 2, a central locale is key, since time is of the essence. But if you have a little more time, you'll find much more comfortable lodgings, at the same or lower prices, a 10-minute walk away.

Expensive

Cheval Blanc Paris ★★   Set within the iconic **La Samaritaine** department store (p. 176) along the Seine, this ultra-refined spot is one of the only hotels in Paris to overlook the Seine—and not just any stretch of the river: the historic part, where the water flows gracefully around the islands, past Notre-Dame and the city's glorious tree-lined quays. If that's not enough for you, romance oozes inside the hotel's Dior spa (home to a 30m/98-ft. pool and a hammam) and in the chic rooftop brasserie, which morphs into an all-day cocktail bar with 360° skyline views—perfect for a panoramic tête-à-tête. Rooms are an elegant mix of Art Deco and contemporary details, and many offer views over the Seine, the rooftops, and/or monuments like the Pompidou Center, the Eiffel Tower, and Montmartre. It's a mega-splurge to stay here, but even if you can't afford a night, stop by for the rooftop or a refined afternoon tea.

8 quai du Louvre, 1st arrond. www.chevalblanc.com. ℂ **01-40-28-00-00.** 72 units. 1,350€–1,750€ double; 1,850€ and up suite. Métro: Louvre-Rivoli or Châtelet. **Amenities:** Restaurant; bar; gym; spa; children's playroom; concierge; room service; free Wi-Fi.

Moderate

Hôtel Thérèse ★★   Just a few steps from the Palais Royal and the Louvre, these warm, cozy lodgings combine old-fashioned Parisian charm with modern Parisian chic. Soft grey/teal blues highlight a creative decor that complements the building's age instead of fighting it. Comfy sofas invite you to relax in the lobby, whose stylish look includes mirrors, bookcases, and unique lighting fixtures. The comfort factor extends to the rooms, many of which have very high ceilings, interesting drapery fabrics, and upholstered headboards.

5–7 rue Thérèse, 1st arrond. www.hoteltherese.com. ℂ **01-42-96-10-01.** 40 units. 180€–370€ double; 315€–420€ family room (up to 4). Métro: Palais-Royal or Pyramides. **Amenities:** Concierge; library/bar; free Wi-Fi.

Inexpensive

Hôtel du Cygne ★★   Chock-full of exposed beams and stone walls, this 17th-century building has been carefully restored, and the simple lodgings receive ongoing tender-loving care. Most rooms are predictably small but cheerfully decorated, with fresh white walls, thick bedspreads, and quality mattresses. Because the hotel is near Les Halles and the Montorgueil neighborhood (very hip at night), staying on a Sunday is much cheaper than other nights. If you're noise sensitive, ask for a room that overlooks the back of the hotel, not the street. Some single rooms have bathrooms down the corridor. *Warning:* There is no elevator (all rooms are upstairs) or air-conditioning.

3–5 rue du Cygne, 1st arrond. www.hotelducygne.fr. ℂ **01-42-60-14-16.** 18 units. 90€–135€ double; 155€–185€ suite up to 3 people, less for singles. Métro: Etienne Marcel. RER: Les Halles. **Amenities:** Free Wi-Fi.

LE MARAIS (3RD & 4TH ARROND.)

Centuries ago, this neighborhood was a swamp (*marais*), but now it's merely swamped with stylish boutiques, restaurants, and people who seem to have just stepped out of a hair salon. Stunning 16th- and 17th-century mansions house terrific museums; the narrow streets harbor clothing stores, cool bars, clubs, and the remnants of the city's historic Jewish quarter. The 4th arrondissement is the city's main LGBTQ district and draws the most tourists thanks to picturesque spots like **place des Vosges** (p. 97), while the 3rd arrondissement has a fashionista vibe, and a great set of restaurants and coffee shops.

Expensive

Pavillon de la Reine ★★★ Just off place des Vosges, the "Queen's Pavilion" harkens back to the days when the magnificent square was home to royalty. Set back from the hustle and bustle of the Marais, this heavenly hideaway feels intimate, like a lord's private hunting lodge in the country. The decor is a suave combination of subtle modern and antique: The dark period furniture blends with rich colors on the walls and beds; choice objects and historic details abound. Several deluxe duplexes have staircases leading to cozy sleeping lofts. Guests have access to a full spa, offering sauna and fitness room, as well as massages and treatments. There's also a chic French restaurant, **Anne,** with a 150€ tasting menu that's worth staying in for (Wed–Sat lunch and dinner, Sun lunch only; lunch menu 59€–69€).

28 pl. des Vosges, 3rd arrond. www.pavillon-de-la-reine.com. ✆ **01-40-29-19-19.** 56 units. 400€–755€ double; 1,100€ and up suite. Métro: Bastille. **Amenities:** Bar; concierge; fitness room; laundry service; room service; sauna; spa; free Wi-Fi.

Moderate

Hôtel Caron de Beaumarchais ★★★ In the 18th century, Pierre Auguste Caron de Beaumarchais—author of *The Barber of Seville*—lived near here, and this small hotel celebrates both the playwright and the magnificent century he lived in. Delightful details give you a taste of what life was like back in the day: Walls are covered in high-quality reproductions of period fabrics; rooms are furnished with authentic antique writing tables; and period paintings and first-edition pages of *The Barber of Seville* hang on the walls. You half expect Pierre Auguste himself to come waltzing through the door. The rooms are smallish, but the high ceilings (with exposed beams) and tall windows let in lots of light, making them feel spacious. Unlike other parts of the Marais, food stores, buses, and Métro stops are

A guest room at Hôtel Caron de Beaumarchais.

close by, and it's a short walk to the Seine. *Note:* Some beds are smaller than standard sizes.

12 rue Vieille-du-Temple, 4th arrond. www.carondebeaumarchais.com. ℂ **01-42-72-34-12.** 19 units. 145€–300€ double. Métro: St-Paul or Hôtel de Ville. **Amenities:** Free Wi-Fi.

Inexpensive

Hôtel Jeanne d'Arc le Marais ★★   With a prime location, comfortable rooms, and great prices, it's no wonder this hotel books up months in advance. It's located in the lower Marais, right next to the leafy place du Marché St-Catherine. While definitely not luxurious, the rooms are in excellent shape, decked out in warm colors and (in some cases) vintage-style prints; several have been given a more modern makeover and new bathrooms. For groups there are reasonably priced quads as well as two adjoined rooms on the sixth floor.

3 rue de Jarente, 4th arrond. www.hoteljeannedarc.com. ℂ **01-48-87-62-11.** 34 units. 135€–320€ double; 195€–400€ quad. Métro: St-Paul. **Amenities:** Free Wi-Fi.

CHAMPS-ELYSÉES, TROCADÉRO & WESTERN PARIS (8TH, 16TH & 17TH ARROND.)

Affordable lodgings are scarce in this opulent environment, especially near the Champs and the Arc de Triomphe, where high prices often have more to do with location than the quality of the lodging. But here are a few that are worth checking out.

Expensive

Monsieur George ★★★   Steps from the Champs-Élysées, this hotel (named, like the street it sits on, after George Washington) is as refined as its surroundings and has a lovely young staff. Chic rooms in blacks, grays, and blues have a distinct Art Deco feel that continues in the bathrooms, where the marble sinks and gold taps wouldn't look amiss on a luxury 1920s ocean liner. Several rooms have small balconies, and a few even overlook the Sacré-Coeur or the Eiffel Tower. The garden suite is a duplex with its own garden courtyard. Guests have access to the hotel's spa and fitness space, set under vaulted ceilings. There's also a hip bar and a gourmet restaurant, **Galanga.**

17 rue Washington, 8th arrond. www.monsieurgeorge.com. ℂ **01-87-89-48-48.** 46 units. 385€–650€ double; 670€ and up suite. Métro: Georges V. **Amenities:** Restaurant; bar; fitness center; spa; concierge; loaner smart devices; room service; laundry service; free Wi-Fi.

Moderate

Le Pavillon des Lettres ★★★   Tastefully chic, this hotel is in the navel of the French political universe, being just across the street from the powerful Ministry of the Interior. The theme here, however, is literature. Each of the 26 exquisite rooms is designated by a different letter and linked to a famous author. If you are in room Z, for example, you might find a copy of Zola's *Nana* on the bedside table and some of the author's text on the wall. The room design is serenely hip, with handsome shades of gray, olive green, beige, and mauve. While the rooms are a little small, the ceilings are mostly high and bathrooms are spacious. Tapas are served at cocktail hour.

12 rue des Saussaies, 8th arrond. www.pavillondeslettres.com. ℂ **01-49-24-26-26.** 26 units. 225€–430€ double; 330€–590€ junior suite. Métro: Madeleine. **Amenities:** Bar; bicycles; concierge; library; laundry service; room service; loaner iPads; free Wi-Fi.

Inexpensive

New Orient Hôtel ★★★   This lovely hotel, which offers comfortable rooms with high ceilings, 19th-century moldings, and antique headboards and armoires, may not be on top of the Champs Elysées, but it's not far, and it is close to stately Parc Monceau and a quick trot to the Saint Lazare train station. The friendly owners, inveterate flea market browsers, have refinished and restored the antique furniture themselves. Rooms (many of which have small balconies) are in tip-top shape, and bathrooms sparkle. Though there's an elevator, you'll have to negotiate stairs to get to it.

16 rue de Constantinople, 8th arrond. www.hotelneworient.com. ℂ **01-45-22-21-64.** 30 units. 95€–230€ double; 130€–250€ family room for 4. Métro: Villiers, Europe, or St-Lazare. **Amenities:** Computer in lobby; concierge; free Wi-Fi.

OPÉRA & GRANDS BOULEVARDS (2ND & 9TH ARROND.)

Grands Boulevards (those wide throughways that Baron Haussmann plowed through Paris in the 19th c.) and the area just below Montmartre is a lovely mix of hip bars and restaurants and old-time Paris, with a good sprinkling of small museums. While you won't find too many big monuments around here, the area's upsides include lower room rates and a more neighborhood-y feel, at least away from the boulevards.

Expensive

Hôtel La Fantaisie ★★★   This spanking new hotel has a lot going for it. Its location on villagelike rue Cadet lined with boutiques, cafes and delis in a non-touristy part of the 9th makes you feels like you're in "real" Paris. The decor—a savvy, retro-inspired mix of wicker, velvet and kitschy knickknacks—wouldn't look amiss in a Wes Anderson movie. And the restaurant, **Golden Poppy,** is run by chef Dominique Crenn, the first woman to receive 3 Michelin stars. As if that weren't enough, there's a lush garden, a rooftop bar and a spa.

24 rue Cadet, 9th arrond. www.lafantaisie.com. ℂ **01-55-07-85-07.** 73 units. 525€–650€ double; from 750€ suite. Métro: Cadet. **Amenities:** Restaurant; bar; rooftop bar; spa; concierge; room service; free Wi-Fi.

Moderate

Hôtel Bachaumont ★★   Art Deco design gets a colorful, modern twist in this trendy little spot in the Montorgeuil district that draws

Parisians as much as travelers, thanks to an excellent brasserie and a cock-tail bar. Sit below the beautiful glass ceiling and tuck into delights like juicy steak in wine-rich Bordelaise sauce, and langoustines with sage potatoes. Then sleep it off in sleek, blue-toned rooms set with dark-wood retro furnishings. Standard rooms are larger than most (if you're a light sleeper, ask for a courtyard room overlooking the brasserie's atrium), while suites are downright big for Paris, with a loftlike vibe. One even has a balcony for extra romance and rooftop views.

18 rue Bachaumont, 2nd arrond. www.hotelbachaumont.com. © **01-81-66-47-00.** 49 units. 202€–300€ double; 405€–550€ suite. Métro: Sentier or Etienne-Marcel. **Amenities:** Restaurant; bar; room service; free Wi-Fi.

Inexpensive

Hôtel 34B ★★   In a restaurant-rich part of town, this quirky, France-themed hotel offers offers comfortable lodgings at great prices. Rooms have modern decor, with cool headboards made to look like stripy French t-shirts or clusters of berets, and glass-topped desks filled with fake turf and miniature French cars or bikes. Wallpaper in the corridors is a bold recreation of the French flag (blue, white, and red stripes), a design mir-rored on the facades overlooking the lobby atrium (which doubles as the breakfast room). Freebies include breakfast for under 12s, non-alchoholic minibar drinks and afternoon soft drinks. There's also a fitness room and a sauna.

34 rue Bergère, 9th arrond. https://en.astotel.com/hotel/34b-en/overview. © **01-47-70-34-34.** 128 units. 120€–160€. Métro: Grands Boulevards. **Amenities:** Sauna; gym; free Wi-Fi.

MONTMARTRE (18TH ARROND.)

Once you leave behind the tourist hordes that invade the Sacré-Coeur and place du Tertre, you'll find a neighborhood of lovely little lanes and small houses, harkening back to the days when Picasso and the boys were at the Bateau Lavoir. Unfortunately, the pickings are a bit slim if you want to actually sleep here. If you are determined to stay up on the Butte, book early, as the few quality lodgings are generally in high demand.

Expensive

L'Hôtel Particulier ★★   If your vision of Montmartre involves secret little cobbled lanes and old town houses with tree-filled gardens, this chic, arty hotel is for you. To get to it, you must buzz in from the street, then take a narrow, private path—Passage de la Sorcière (aka the "witch's alley")—to an elegant former mansion. Each of the five suites was designed by a different artist: One evokes a fancy bordello, with a riot of leopard print on all the walls; another has psychedelic floral wallpaper and stunning views over the garden; all are sumptuous. The loftlike, top-floor suite is awash in natural light and flaunts a glass roof with views over the city and the Eiffel Tower. Into food? You may want to consider dining in: The hotel's on-site restaurant, **Le Grand Salon,** offers exquisite French

L'Hôtel Particulier.

dishes with a modern twist, and serves afternoon tea (Wed–Sun) in an *olde-worlde* courtyard—a treat on a sunny day.

23 av. Junot (Pavillon D), 18th arrond. https://hotelparticulier.com. © **01-53-41-81-40.** 5 units. 790€–890€ suite. Métro: Lamarck Caulincourt. **Amenities:** Restaurant; bar; garden; laundry service; room service; free Wi-Fi.

Moderate

Hôtel des Arts Montmartre ★★   On a narrow street just off lively rue des Abbesses, this unassuming hotel once hosted artists and even a few dancers from the Moulin Rouge. It's currently run by the third generation of the Lameyre family. Today's guests are generally tourists, who enjoy the great rates, comfortable lodgings, and welcoming atmosphere. Rooms are small yet spotless, with funky decor, reminiscent of the '80s. A few have distant views of the Eiffel Tower over Parisian rooftops; the "Romantic" room comes with a bottle of champagne and has a small balcony. Montmartre's two remaining windmills, Moulin de la Galette and Moulin du Radet, are just up the street.

5 rue Tholozé, 18th arrond. www.arts-hotel-paris.com. © **01-46-06-30-52.** 50 units. 200€–280€ double. Parking 20€. Métro: Blanche or Abbesses. **Amenities:** Concierge; room service; free Wi-Fi.

Inexpensive

Le Relais Montmartre ★★   These comfortable lodgings include small but impeccable rooms decked out in light, warm colors and a stylish, classic decor of tasteful floral prints. The hotel is on a peaceful little side street, right around the corner from a delicious stretch of food shops on rue Lepic. Families can book into adjoining rooms. In good weather, breakfast is served on a lovely little patio; speaking of breakfast, this is one of the few hotels around to serve a really decent one, thanks to products brought in from the aforementioned gourmet shops. If you're in a hurry, the *lève tôt* (early bird) option, served before 7am in reception, is a very good value at just 6€.

6 rue Constance, 18th arrond. www.hotel-relais-montmartre.com. (℡ **01-70-64-25-25.** 26 units. 150€–191€ double. Métro: Blanche. **Amenities:** Concierge; laundry service; loaner iPad; free Wi-Fi.

RÉPUBLIQUE, BASTILLE & EASTERN PARIS (11TH & 12TH ARROND.)

Encompassing the recently overhauled place de la République, as well as the historic place de la Bastille, this area is a good choice for both budget travelers and creatures of the night—it includes the bars and clubs of the Oberkampf and Charonne neighborhoods and is close to the Marais. It's also one of the most exciting areas for restaurants, housing a plethora of small, chef-driven neo-bistros that draw foodies from across town.

Expensive

Maison Breguet ★★★   With its slick glass-roofed cocktail bar and a neo-bistro (a bistro serving modern versions of traditional French dishes) offering beautifully executed dishes like langoustines poached with mandarin oranges and roasted apples with pecans, this hip hotel embodies the up-and-coming vibe of the 11th arrondissmement. You can dine in the peaceful courtyard on sunny days, and the rooms are as cool as can be, with a classy retro-Scandinavian vibe and an earthy color palette. The other draw here (aside from the price, which is lower than most other properties of the same class) is the wellness area, with a lovely indoor pool, sauna, hammam, and gym.

8 rue Breguet, 11th arrond. www.maisonbreguet.com. (℡ **01-58-30-32-31.** 53 units. 304€–368€ double; from 450€ suite. Métro: Breguet Sabin or Chemin Vert. **Amenities:** Restaurant; bar; indoor pool; sauna; fitness rooms; hammam; free Wi-Fi.

Moderate

Eden Lodge Paris ★★★   Hidden from the street in the back of a beautiful garden, this modern wooden structure combines environmental awareness with extremely comfortable lodgings. With only five rooms and a free breakfast, some might call this a B&B not a hotel. The warm smell of larch wood (the construction material) hits your nose when you enter the lobby, a glassed-in atrium with a staircase leading up to the rooms. Quality insulation, LED lighting, solar panels, and zero-carbon output give these lodgings its ecological creds, as well as self-cleaning tiles that absorb air-pollution. There's no skimping on comfort though: Rooms are chic, warm, and minimalist, with vintage-look furniture and high-tech Japanese toilets. A microwave and refrigerator are available for guests in the breakfast room, which is open all day. Bicycles on hand, as well as a 500-sq.-m (5,381-sq.-ft.) garden for communing with nature.

175 rue de Charonne, 11th arrond. www.edenlodgeparis.net. (C) **01-43-56-73-24.** 5 units. 235€ double; 365€ suite. Breakfast included. Métro: Alexandre Dumas. **Amenities:** Bicycles; garden; free Wi-Fi.

Inexpensive

Hôtel de la Porte Dorée ★★   True, it's a little out of the way, but these lovely lodgings are well worth the Métro fare. Soothing neutral tones, antique headboards, high ceilings, wood floors, and original curlicue moldings are all part of the package at this hotel, owned by a friendly Franco-American couple. The hotel goes the extra mile for both the environment (ecologically correct policies) and babies (toys, playpens, and even potty seats available). And you'll pay less for all this than you will for something utterly basic in the center of town. What's more, it is right next to the verdant Bois de Vincennes, where you can rent bikes, picnic, or visit the Paris zoo. The nearby Métro will get you to the city center in about 15 minutes.

273 av. Daumesnil, 12th arrond. www.hoteldelaportedoree.com. (C) **01-43-07-56-97.** 43 units. 104€–155€ double; 160€ triple. Métro: Porte Dorée. **Amenities:** Babysitting; bicycles; free Wi-Fi.

BELLEVILLE, CANAL ST-MARTIN & LA VILLETTE (10TH, 19TH & 20TH ARROND.)

When historic arty neighborhoods like Saint-Germain and Montmartre became too expensive for up-and-coming artists, many immigrated to these more proletarian neighborhoods, giving the area a funky, bohemian feel. Even though it's gentrifying, Belleville is still known for artists' studios, while dozens of hip cafes and restaurants have popped up along the Canal St-Martin and the Bassin de la Villette. The young and adventurous will appreciate this part of town, but others may find it too much of a commute to the main sights.

Moderate

Le Citizen ★★   Maybe it's the smiling young staff in jeans, or the ecological ethos, but there's something alternative in the air at this adorable boutique hotel on the Canal St-Martin. While the rooms are on the small side, they are light and airy, with lots of blonde wood and clean lines; all look out on the tree-lined canal. When you check in, you'll be handed an iPad loaded with information and apps on Paris. The minibar and a delicious buffet breakfast are included in your room rate.

96 quai de Jemmapes, 10th arrond. www.lecitizenhotel.com. ℂ **01-83-62-55-50.** 12 units. 167€–220€ double; 240€–300€ suite; 405€–540€ apartment. Breakfast included. Métro: Jacques Bonsergent. **Amenities:** Free minibar; iPad; room service; free Wi-Fi.

Inexpensive

Generator Paris ★★   A 20-minute walk from Gare du Nord (the Eurostar terminal) and 5 minutes from the picturesque quays and bars of Canal St-Martin, this trendy establishment (opposite Oscar Niemeyer's iconic French Communist party's HQ) blurs the lines between hotel and hostel by offering both private rooms and dormitories (for up to 10 people). It also offers perks that many of the city's standard hotels can't provide—namely, a roof-top bar with views onto the Sacré Coeur and a Métro-themed basement "club" with a fab cocktail happy hour. The bright dorms are filled with young, mostly English-speaking travelers, but the more expensive private rooms attract a more demanding set of mature clients with extras like terraces. Female-only dorms are available.

9-11 pl. du Colonel Fabien, 10th arrond. https://staygenerator.com/hostels/paris. ℂ **01-70-98-84-00.** 199 units. 23€–31€ per person in dormitories; 78€–98€ double. Métro: Colonel Fabien. **Amenities:** Cafe; bar; in-room lockers; laundromat; towel rental; free Wi-Fi.

Rooftop bar at Generator Paris.

The Left Bank

LATIN QUARTER (5TH & 13TH ARROND.)

Central and reasonably priced, the Latin Quarter is a long-time favorite for travelers in search of affordable accommodations. As a consequence, a few corners of this famously academic neighborhood are overrun with tourists and trinket shops. The streets immediately surrounding the place St-Michel (especially around rue de la Huchette) are where you'll find the worst tourist traps, both hotel and restaurant-wise; better prices and quality are to be had in the quieter, more authentic areas around the universities, a little farther from Notre-Dame but still within easy walking distance. Further south, the 13th arrondissement includes the Chinese Quarter and the ultra-modern Avenue de France area, where contemporary buildings rub shoulders with revamped factories—a largely unknown side to Paris.

Expensive

TOO Hôtel Paris—McGallery ★★★   Fancy going to sleep with the Eiffel Tower twinkling beyond your toes? It's possible in this slick new hotel, set between the 17th and 25th floors of architect Jean Nouvel's 120m-tall (393 ft.) Tours Duo (two contempory skyscrapers with tilted "heads" on the edge of the modern Avenue de France district). The views are, hands down, the best I've ever seen from a hotel bed, largely thanks to the rooms' picture windows and carefully calculated bed height. On the upper floors you'll find the **TacTac,** a rooftop cocktail spot with yet more of those views, and just below it, the **TOO Restaurant,** a glass-enclosed cube where chef Benjamin Six serves fantastic Asia-inspired dishes (from 40€). Book for about an hour before dusk, then watch the sun set over Paris's steely gray rooftops as you tuck in. It's easily one of the most exciting places to stay or eat in Paris right now. 65 rue Bruneseau, 13th arrond. https://toohotel.com. ℰ **01-47-07-41-92.** 139 units. 205€–500€ double; 450€ and up suite. Métro: Bibliothèque François-Mitterand. **Amenities:** Rooftop bar; restaurant; massages; sauna; hot tub; free Wi-Fi.

Moderate

Hôtel des Grandes Ecoles ★★★   Tucked into a private garden on the slope of the Montagne St-Geneviève, this hotel makes you feel as if you have just walked out of Paris and into the countryside. A path leads to a flower-bedecked interior courtyard, where birds chirp in the trees; the reception area adjoins an inviting breakfast room. The spotless rooms are filled with country-style furniture, with crocheted bedspreads and framed etchings of flowers. The calm is such that the hotel has nixed TVs. What's more, this unique ambience comes at a reasonable price. Rooms in the "Garden Building" are more modern, with newer bathrooms; families will appreciate the six large suites that can sleep four. 75 rue de Cardinal-Lemoine, 5th arrond. https://en.hoteldesgrandesecoles.com. ℰ **01-43-26-79-23.** 51 units. 185€–260€ double; 300€ family room. Parking 25€. Métro: Cardinal Lemoine or pl. Monge. **Amenities:** Free Wi-Fi.

Inexpensive

Hôtel des Jardins du Luxembourg ★★   Just around the corner from its glorious namesake and down the street from the university, these intimate lodgings are tucked away on a quiet cul-de-sac, making it a favorite with the professorial crowd. The building's claim to fame is that Sigmund Freud stayed here on his first visit to Paris. Today it exudes elegance, from the nature-themed wallpaper behind the beds to the glossy white tiles in the bathrooms. While the standard rooms are pretty, the superior rooms, which cost only a few euros more, have nicer views and small balconies.

5 impasse Royer-Collard, 5th arrond. www.hoteljardinsluxembourg.com. ✆ **01-40-46-08-88.** 26 units. 189€–290€ double; 380€ suite. Métro: Cluny–La Sorbonne. RER: Luxembourg. **Amenities:** Bar; free Wi-Fi.

ST-GERMAIN-DES-PRÉS & LUXEMBOURG (6TH ARROND.)

Sleek boutiques and restaurants abound in this legendary neighborhood; historic cafes and monuments lend plenty of atmosphere. Unlike some other Parisian neighborhoods, this one is lively even late at night; it is also centrally located and within walking distance of many top sights.

Expensive

Relais St-Germain ★★★   Fashioned from three adjoining 17th-century town houses, this intimate hotel mixes old-world charm and jazzy modernity. Rooms are spacious, and even the smallest are equipped with a comfortable sitting area. The decor blends period furniture with modern prints, like the Louis XV armchair covered in zigzagged leather, or the 18th-century painting hung on a wall of mirrors. The effect is both stylish and deeply comforting. There are some extra stairs between floors, so if you have mobility issues, be sure to make that clear when you reserve. Guests have priority at the hotel restaurant, **Le Comptoir** (p. 164), where you might otherwise have a 6-month wait for a reservation.

9 carrefour de l'Odéon, 6th arrond. www.hotel-paris-relais-saint-germain.com. ✆ **01-44-27-07-97.** 22 units. 295€–385€ double; 415€–460€ suite. Breakfast included if you reserve on the hotel's website. Métro: Odéon. **Amenities:** Restaurant; babysitting; concierge; laundry service; free Wi-Fi.

Moderate

Hôtel Louison ★★   Hovering on the invisible border between the Montparnasse and Saint-Germain neighborhoods, this adorable hotel is a quick walk to the Luxembourg Gardens and the delights of the Bon Marché department store. While maintaining the original detailing and mood of this 19th-century building, the period decor is spiced up with contemporary colors and textures, like a gold and purple version of traditional *toile de jouy* wallpaper, or lush velvet pillows and contemporary headboards. Off the lobby, a cozy reading room is available for quiet pursuits; nearby, the yoga room (equipped with mats, bricks, and a big mirror) is open 24/7. Connecting rooms are available for families, as well as a furnished apartment for rent by the week.

105 rue de Vaugirard, 6th arrond. www.louison-hotel.com. © **01-53-63-25-50.** 42 units. 177€–250€ double; 275€–435€ triple (enquire for the apartment). Métro: Duroc or Falguière. Parking 38€. **Amenities:** Concierge; guest iPad; laundry service; yoga room; free Wi-Fi.

Inexpensive

Grand Hôtel des Balcons ★★   For the neighborhood, the rooms in this simple hotel are remarkably spacious. Most have small balconies, and if you look up the street you'll see the columns of the 18th-century Odéon theater. Decor is simple, with plain walls and furnishings, jazzed up with plush drapes and curtains. The roomy triples and quads are a good bet for families, and a wheelchair-accessible room is on the ground floor. The lobby has an Art Nouveau feel, and the well-kept rooms are impeccably clean, if not particularly stylish.

3 rue Casimir Delavigne, 6th arrond. www.balcons.com. © **01-46-34-78-50.** 49 units. 140€–200€ double; 230€ triple; 280€ quad. Métro: Odéon. **Amenities:** Free Wi-Fi.

EIFFEL TOWER & NEARBY (7TH ARROND.)

For some reason, many visitors to Paris clamor for hotels that are right near the Eiffel Tower, perhaps under the mistaken impression that this is a central location. It isn't. Still, there's no denying that this extremely posh area is beautiful, and there is something magical about wandering out of your hotel in the morning and seeing the Eiffel Tower looming in the background.

Expensive

Hôtel Signature St-Germain-des-Près ★★★   Run by the friendly Prigent family (also of the Hôtel de Londres Eiffel; see below), this delightful boutique hotel has a homey retro charm. Bright colors on the walls blend harmoniously with subdued bedsteads and linens; mid-century reproduction furniture and faux antique phones take the edge off sleek modern lines. The "Prestige" rooms cost more but are especially roomy (30 sq. m/323 sq. ft.). In addition to particularly attentive service, this hotel is also blessed with an excellent location for shopping addicts: It's just down the street from Bon Marché.

5 rue Chomel, 7th arrond. www.signature-saintgermain.com. © **01-45-48-35-53.** 26 units. 280€–490€ double; 360€–490€ triple; 440€–650€ 2-room connecting family suite. Métro: Sèvres-Bablylone or St-Sulpice. **Amenities:** Concierge; free Wi-Fi.

Moderate

Hôtel du Champ de Mars ★★   An adorable and affordable little inn right around the corner from the food shops of rue Cler—what more could you ask for? Owners Françoise and Stéphane Gourdal have given their hotel the kind of care people generally reserve for their own homes: The impeccably maintained rooms are decorated with thick cotton bedspreads, framed etchings, toile de jouy wallpaper, and warm colors. The concierge service is a real plus.

7 rue du Champ de Mars, 7th arrond. www.hotelduchampdemars.com. © **01-45-51-52-30.** 25 units. 215€–350€double. Métro: Ecole Militaire. **Amenities:** Laptop; free Wi-Fi.

Hôtel Londres Eiffel ★★★   From the moment you enter, you feel like you are in a private home. In fact, you may very well be welcomed by Samba, the hospitable owners' lovely golden retriever. Polished wood banisters lead up spiral staircases to narrow hallways and cozy rooms decorated with a personal touch; walls are covered with fabrics printed with tasteful 19th-century kitsch; and the comfort level is terrific. A few rooms have views of the Eiffel Tower. They book up early. Connecting rooms are available for families.

1 rue Augereau, 7th arrond. www.hotel-paris-londres-eiffel.com. © **01-45-51-63-02.** 30 units. 220€–390€ double; 330€–390€ triple; 350€–680€ quad. Métro: Ecole Militaire. **Amenities:** Free Wi-Fi.

MONTPARNASSE & NEARBY (14TH & 15TH ARROND.)

Montparnasse is more centrally located than it might seem—it's right on the border of St-Germain and close to the Luxembourg gardens. Also, the train station is a major transit hub for a bundle of Métro lines and bus routes. Though the utterly unaesthetic Tour Montparnasse now casts a shadow over this ancient artists' haunt (Henry Miller, Man Ray, Chagall, Picasso), the little streets in the surrounding area are full of personality.

Inexpensive

L'Apostrophe ★   Honoring the area's literary history (nearby writers' haunts include La Coupole and the Closerie des Lilas), this "poem hotel" is dedicated to the beauty and mystery of writing. The decor is a little off the wall, but very tastefully so, starting with an impressive silhouette of a tree on the hotel's facade. Rooms are themed: "Calligraphy" has Chinese characters set on royal blue walls; "Musique" features stenciled sheet music and instruments. Larger rooms include a Jacuzzi bathtub right in the room.

3 rue de Chevreuse, 6th arrond. www.apostrophe-hotel.com. © **01-56-54-31-31.** 16 units. 130€–250€ double; 180€–290€ double with a Jacuzzi. Métro: Vavin. **Amenities:** Bar; free Wi-Fi.

Solar Hôtel ★★   Declaring itself "the first ecological, economical, and activist hotel," this basic lodging feature energy-efficient lighting, water-saving measures, and composting and recycling. Breakfast, included in the low rate, is organic; bicycles are available for guests; and there is a nice garden for sipping your fair-trade tea. The bright rooms have a hostel-like feel (although they are private), but the mattresses are firm, and everything is clean and tidy. Just around the corner from rue Daguerre, a cute pedestrian market street, the hotel has two buildings.

22 rue Boulard, 14th arrond. www.solarhotel.fr. ✆ **01-43-21-08-20.** 34 units. 99€ double. Rates include breakfast. Métro: Denfert-Rochereau. **Amenities:** Bicycles; free Wi-Fi.

Alternative Accommodations

Hotels are all very well and good, but for some, nothing beats staying in a private home or apartment, particularly if you are a family on a budget. Fortunately for travelers with an independent streak, several Parisian options are available including short-term rentals, bed-and-breakfasts, and "aparthotels," that is, short-term apartments with some hotel services.

SHORT-TERM RENTALS

Dozens of agencies offer hundreds of apartments smack in the center of the City of Light. Though the rates for two people are sometimes (but not always) significantly less than what you'd pay at a hotel, the advantages are many, not the least of which is the fact that you can cook some of your meals at home and save yourself a ton of time and money. Other benefits are privacy, independence, and a chance to see what it's like to live like a Parisian, even if it's just for a week.

If you are more than two, and especially if you are traveling *en famille,* the benefits can be huge. Family suites and/or adjoining rooms are rare in Parisian hotels, so you'll often end up paying for two doubles—somewhere around 350€ to 600€ per night—whereas you could rent a one-bedroom apartment with a foldout couch and/or extra bed in the living room for anywhere from 180€ to 300€ per night.

So how should you book? While established agencies like the ones listed below come with more services and guarantees, rates also tend to be more expensive than Internet rental platforms like **Airbnb.com, Flipkey. com,** and **VRBO.com,** as many of the rentals listed on these sites are done by the owners directly, so there's no middle man to pay. Agencies justify their costs by having cleaning staff, all-inclusive rates, and an office you can call when something goes wrong. They also vet all of their apartments to make sure they are legal and pleasant. There is no denying that thousands of people happily use Airbnb and similar sites and find great accommodations for reasonable rates. The problem is that these sites cannot check up on every owner, so you cannot be entirely sure that your rental is legal or indeed as good or clean as it looks in the photos.

Bottom line: If you want to minimize risk and are willing to pay more for it, go with a well-established agency like **Parisian Home** (www. parisianhome.com; ✆ **01-45-08-03-37**), **Paris Attitude** (www.paris attitude.com; ✆ 01-42-96-31-46), or **Paris Appartements Services** (www. paris-appartements-services.com; ✆ **01-40-28-01-28**). **Apartments Actually** (http://apartmentsactually.com) also has two stunning properties in the Marais. And if you're looking for a place with a wow-factor, try **High-stay** (www.highstay.com; 🕐 **01-76-40-25-25**), which has upscale, full-service apartments in truly breathtaking locations, like opposite the Louvre in rue de Rivoli. In most cases, you will deal directly with the agency (not the owners), and the minimum stay is usually 4 days to 1 week.

BED & BREAKFASTS

Though bed-and-breakfasts (*chambres d'hôtes*) are common in the French countryside, in the big city, where privacy and anonymity are treasured, they are still relatively rare. Three B&Bs I wholeheartedly recommend are:

- **52 Clichy** (www.52clichy.com) in the new foodie quarter, the 9th arrondissement. Run by a British expat, Rosemary, there are two lovely spaces: one for two people (from 125€) and another (with a kitchen) for up to four people (from 200€). On sunny days breakfast is served on a balcony overlooking rooftops.

- **La Villa Paris** (www.la-villa-paris.com) in a 1920s villa in the residential 13th arrondissement. This place feels like a secret boutique hotel with five warmly decorated rooms and luxurious bathrooms, not to mention a leafy breakfast terrace (145€–185€).

- **Bonne Nuit Paris** (www.bonne-nuit-paris.com) in a 17th-century house in the hip end of the Marais (3rd arrond.). It's right by the Marché des Enfants Rouges food market, and the four rooms and an apartment all have a chic, old-world vibe (220€–275€).

APARTHOTELS

Mostly designed for business travelers, these utilitarian lodgings are a cross between a hotel and an apartment. Short on charm, *aparthotels* are decidedly practical, as each unit comes with a kitchenette as well as hotel services such as fresh towels, dry cleaning, and a reception desk. Rates are generally higher than short-term rentals, but you do have the comfort of knowing you are dealing with a large company (if that makes you comfortable), with standardized apartments, organized websites, and customer service.

The best-known *aparthotel* company is **Citadines** (www.citadines.com; 🕐 **01-41-05-79-05, 888/534-4965** from the US, **0808 145 3774** from the UK; 132€–350€), which offers clean, comfortable units in excellent locations around the city. Another good one to try is **Adagio** (www.adagio-city.com), which has several locations in central Paris and offers bright, modern, fully equipped spaces (150€–350€ a night).

WHERE TO EAT

Everywhere you look in Paris, someone is doing their best to ruin your waistline. *Boulangeries* (bakeries) with buttery croissants and decadent pastries lurk on every street corner; open-air markets tempt the senses; and restaurants with intriguing menus sprout up on every block.

Fortunately, you don't have to have a king-size budget to dine like royalty. Sure, there are those world-famous, multistarred restaurants that everyone has heard about. But today, a whole new crop of **"neo-bistros"** has emerged, offering high-quality eats for a fraction of what you would pay in a gourmet palace. One outgrowth of this movement is the obsession with "noble" ingredients—high-quality, regional products, often from a small-scale farm or artisan, often organic, and always in keeping with the oldest and best traditions.

Note: Restaurants tend to be small in Paris, and when it comes to reservations, size matters. To be sure to get a table, reserve ahead for the restaurants listed below under the "Expensive" or "Moderate" categories.

The Right Bank

LOUVRE & ILE DE LA CITÉ (1ST ARROND.)

Dining near the Louvre can be an expensive and frustrating affair; it's rife with overpriced, mediocre tourist restaurants (menus of at least five languages are a good way to spot them). If you poke around some of the smaller streets however, you'll discover plenty of little restaurants where you can eat well and affordably. That said, if you are ready to spend, gourmet opportunities abound.

Expensive

Verjus ★★★ MODERN FRENCH   Okay, the chef's American, but that doesn't stop this nosh nirvana from being utterly Parisian, from the setting (an all-white dining room, nestled at the top of a hidden staircase, with Art Deco–style furniture and views onto Théâtre du Palais Royal) to the food (contemporary takes on French classics). The dishes are served in tasting menus that list the ingredients in each dish—chicken, asparagus, and wild garlic or artichoke with caviar. But don't be fooled: On the plate, this simplicity translates to perfectly executed delicacies that may well be the highlight of your trip. Paris has few "gastronomique" restaurants where you can eat like a king for under 130€, and this, along with **Septime** (p. 159) and **Geosmine** (p. 158), is one of the best. The wine list is also a treat, filled with biodynamic and organic wines. The 62€ wine pairing option is worth the splurge.

52 rue Richelieu, 2nd arrond. www.verjusparis.com. ✆ **01-42-97-54-40.** Tasting menu 98€. Mon–Fri 7–11pm. Closed 2 weeks in Aug. Métro: Palais Royal–Musée du Louvre or Pyramides.

Moderate

Brasserie du Louvre–Bocuse ★★ MODERN BRASSERIE Lyonnais cooking legend Paul Bocuse (nicknamed the "Pope of Gastronomy") passed away in 2018, but his legacy lives on in this vintage-chic brasserie on the ground floor of the Hôtel du Louvre. Tuck into wonderfully executed versions of his signature regional dishes, like hot pistachio-studded sausage (rolled in a soft brioche), sole meunière, and pike quenelle with Nantua (lobster) sauce, while admiring the views of the Comédie Française and Louvre through the bay windows or arcaded terrace. All of the desserts are excellent, but I have a particular fondness for the crème brûlée—it's possibly the best in the city. *Note:* There are copious breakfast buffet options, too.

1 pl. du Palais Royal, 1st arrond. www.hyatt.com (then search for Hôtel du Louvre). ✆ **01-44-58-37-21.** Main courses 21€–65€; fixed-price breakfast 22€–32€. Wed–Sun noon–3pm and 6–11pm. Closed first 3 weeks of Aug. Métro: Palais-Royal–Musée du Louvre.

Inexpensive

Boutique yam'Tcha ★★★ FRENCH-ASIAN STREET FOOD Book a table at renowned chef Adeleine Grattard's Michelin-starred restaurant

---

Dining After Hours

There aren't many restaurants that stay open until the wee hours of the Parisian night, but a few stalwarts are around Les Halles. **Le Tambour,** 41 rue de Montmartre, 2nd arrond. (https://menuonline.fr/letambour/carte-restaurant; ✆ **01-42-33-06-90;** Métro: Les Halles), serves reliable dishes like steak-frites (main courses 14€–24€) from 7am to 2am every day in a dining room filled with kitschy Paris memorabilia. Nearby, **Au Pied de Cochon,** 6 rue Coquillière, 1st arrond. (www.pieddecochon.com; ✆ **01-40-13-77-00; Métro: Les Halles**), is a late-night brasserie (open 8am–5am) that specializes in pork and more pork (main courses 22€–50€). Au Pied du Cochon also has some good seafood dishes and a restorative onion soup is ideal at 4am after a night on the town. For a midnight beef fix, head to **La Tour de Montlhéry–Chez Denise,** 5 rue des Prouvaires, 1st arrond., where the steak is as juicy as it is huge and opening is usually until 12:30am.

yam'Tcha and you'll certainly have a fabulous meal (121 rue St. Honore, 1st arrond.; ✆ **01-40-26-08-07;** from 170€ tasting menu; reserve 2 months in advance). Grattard works miracles with ingredients such as lobster, seabass, truffles, and pork. But her second place near the Louvre—a duel take-out *bao* bar (steamed Taiwanese buns) and tearoom—lets you taste her cooking for a fraction of the price. The bar section is a window open to the street, where foodies queue for buns filled with delectables such as smoked tofu or crab with vegetables, plus unexpected mixes like stilton and cherries. The tearoom is run by Grattard's Hong Kong-born husband Chi Wah Chan, a veritable tea guru who pairs teas with dishes in the same way sommeliers pair wines.

4 rue Sauval, 1st arrond. www.yamtcha.com. ✆ **01-40-26-06-06.** Bao buns 4.50€ each or 20€ for 5. Wed–Sat noon–7pm. Métro: Louvre-Rivoli.

OPÉRA & GRANDS BOULEVARDS (2ND & 9TH ARROND.)

Buzzing with cafes and theaters back in the 19th century, the long-overlooked Grand Boulevards have come back to life, especially near the Opéra and the hip part of the 9th arrondissement that borders Montmartre. Less trendy, but also less expensive, the little streets around the Bourse (the French stock exchange) have a wide range of restaurant options, especially at lunch. The covered passages that crisscross parts of the 2nd arrondissement also harbor some excellent dining options.

Expensive

La Condesa ★★★ MODERN BISTRO   On an up-and-coming street in SoPi, this joint is emblematic of Paris' cosmopolitan dining scene: At the helm is a Mexican chef who trained at Lyon's legendary Institut Paul Bocuse, worked in three-star restaurants in Paris, whizzed off to learn

---

Japantown, Paris-Style

You are wandering around the streets near the Opéra, when you take a sharp turn onto the rue Ste-Anne. Suddenly, everything is in Japanese, and there are noodle shops everywhere! Plunge into a bowl at one of these restaurants (all a short walk from Métro Pyramides):

○ **Udon Jubey,** 39 rue Ste-Anne, 1 arrond. (https://kintarogroup.com/udon-jubey); sit at the counter or grab one of the limited number of tables.

○ **Higuma,** 32 bis rue Ste-Anne, 1 arrond. (www.higuma.fr; ✆ **01-47-03-38-59**),

features an open kitchen, ramen soups, and a long line out the front door.

○ **Aki,** 11 bis rue Sainte Anne, 1st arrond. (https://akiparis.fr; ✆ **01-42-97-54-27**), specializes in *okonomiyaki*, a delicious sort of grilled omelet topped with meat or seafood and a yummy sauce. Watch the cooks create yours on a griddle in the open kitchen. Just down the road at no. 16 is their bakery-tearoom, **Aki Boulangerie,** an excellent spot for white bread and savory goodies, and at no. 75 is their **Aki Café,** the place to go for Katsu curry.

more in Japan, then came back to launch his own restaurant. And what a restaurant it is: Green tones and natural wood provide a slick backdrop for beautifully executed dishes like celery granita, kombu-marinated veal, and yellow pollock with spiced pineapple. Take it all in with wines from France and Italy, Mexican mezcal, or Japanese whisky.

17 rue Rodier, 9th arrond. https://lacondesa-paris.com. ℰ **01-53-20-94-90.** Fixed-price lunch 65€ or dinner 150€–180€. Tues–Thurs 6:30–10:30pm; Fri 12:15–1:30pm and 6–11pm; Sat 6–11pm Closed 2 weeks in Aug. Métro: Anvers or Notre-Dame de Lorette.

Moderate

Canard et Champagne ★★ MODERN BISTRO   Tucked away in the old-world Passage des Panoramas, this delightful spot attracts the eye with a giant wall mural of French actor Louis de Funès (in his iconic role as Mr. Septime in the 1966 movie *Le Grand Restaurant*), then reels patrons in with fabulous duck dishes—foie gras, *confit de canard,* and *magret*—all washed down with hand-picked champagne from the region's best small producers. The concept is fabulous, especially since it won't break the bank: The set menus, which include two or three courses and up to three glasses of champagne, start at 30€. Reserve in advance or arrive early (noon for lunch, 7pm for dinner).

57 passage des Panoramas, 2nd arrond. http://frenchparadox.paris. ℰ **09-81-83-95-69.** Fixed-price lunch 18.50€–22€ or dinner 30€, including champagne 37€–61€. Daily noon–2:30pm and 7–10:30pm. Closed 2 weeks in Aug. Métro: Bonne Nouvelle.

Le Pantruche ★★ TRADITIONAL FRENCH/BISTRO   The name is old-fashioned slang for Paris, but this little bistro has a decidedly modern feel to it. Another case of a runaway chef from Michelin-starred restaurants, Le Pantruche offers deliciously updated bistro fare like braised sweetbreads with carrots in a licorice glaze, or suckling pig with pears, celery root, and chestnuts. It's hard to resist dessert when chocolate ganache or Grand Marnier soufflé are on the menu. Definitely reserve ahead, as the fixed-price menus are a terrific value and the tiny dining room fills quickly.

3 rue Victor Massé, 9th arrond. www.lapantruchoise.com/lepantruche. ℰ **01-48-78-55-60.** Main courses 21€–26€; fixed-price lunch 22€ or dinner 40€. Mon–Fri 12:30–2pm and 7:30–9:30pm. Closed first 3 weeks of Aug. Métro: Pigalle.

Inexpensive

Michi ★★ JAPANESE   So discreet is Michi's facade (on rue Ste-Anne, the hub of Paris's "Little Tokyo") that you'd be forgiven for walking past without so much as batting an eyelid. But miss it and you'll miss one of the best sushi joints in town, a tiny spot where fish is as fresh as it gets, and the chef works tirelessly to prepare every dish in front of a seven-seater counter, the best seat in the house if you can get it (there's also a basement). It regularly serves delicacies like sea urchin, and a wide ranges of sake and Japanese beer.

58 bis rue Ste-Anne, 2nd arrond. © **01-40-20-49-93.** Main courses 13€–19€; fixed-price menu 13€–23€. Tues–Sat noon–2pm and 7–10pm. Métro: Quatre-Septembre or Bourse.

LE MARAIS (3RD & 4TH ARROND.)

You should have no trouble finding good things to eat in the Marais. Between its working-class roots and its more recent makeover, it offers a wide range of choices, from humble falafel joints to trendy brasseries.

Expensive

Benoit ★★ TRADITIONAL FRENCH   This historic bistro had already hosted a century's worth of Parisian notables when Alain Ducasse took the helm in 2005. The dining room is still lined with mirrors, zinc, and tiles, while the classic menu has been given an extra dash of pizzazz. Dishes like escargots in garlic butter and brill braised with Jura wine share the stage with roasted milk-fed lamb from the Pyrenées and sautéed scallops *grenobloise.* The sommelier will help you navigate the huge wine list.

20 rue St-Martin, 4th arrond. www.benoit-paris.com. © **01-42-72-25-76.** Main course 18€–48€; fixed-price lunch 32€–42€. Daily noon–2pm and 7:30–10pm. Closed first 3 weeks of Aug. Métro: Hôtel-de-Ville.

Moderate

Café des Musées ★★ TRADITIONAL FRENCH/BISTRO   Weary culture vultures who've just finished the Picasso Museum will appreciate this bustling corner cafe with its appealing sidewalk tables. This is not just any old corner cafe, mind you, but one where the inventive chef works wonders with bistro classics like steak frîtes and *andouillette* (tripe sausage) as well as lighter fare like fresh vegetable casserole with basil oil, or shrimp with Thai curry. If you're here early enough (8–11:30am), it's a top spot for breakfast too: Think hot drink, pastry, and fruit juice for 8€.

49 rue de Turenne, 3rd arrond. www.lecafedesmusees.fr © **01-42-72-96-17.** Main course 23€–37€, fixed-price lunch 21€ and 24€. Mon–Thurs noon–2:30pm and 7–10:30pm, Fri–Sun noon–4pm and 7–11pm. Closed mid-Aug to early Sept. Métro: St. Paul or Chemin Vert.

Inexpensive

L'As du Fallafel ★ FALAFEL/ISRAELI   This Marais institution offers, without a doubt, one of the best falafels in Paris. True, falafel joints are scarce in this city, but that doesn't take away from the excellence of these overstuffed beauties, brimming with cucumbers, pickled turnips, shredded cabbage, tahini, fried eggplant, and those crispy balls of fried chickpeas and spices. Wash it down with an Israeli beer. Service is fast and furious, but basically friendly—be prepared to deal with hordes at lunch. Closed Friday afternoon and all day Saturday.

34 rue des Rosiers, 4th arrond. © **01-48-87-63-60.** Main course 8€–20€. Sun–Thurs noon–11pm; Fri noon–4pm. Métro: St. Paul.

Le Potager du Marais ★★ VEGAN   The shoebox-size dining room fills up quickly, as Paris doesn't have many vegan eateries, so make sure you reserve in advance. But even omnivores enjoy the delicious veggie offerings here, which might include seitan *bourguignon,* mushroom pâté, and pumpkin Parmentier. Many items are gluten-free. Finish off with a simple but scrumptious apple compote or crème brûlée.

26 rue Saint-Paul, 4th arrond. www.lepotagerdumarais.fr. 🕐 **01-57-40-98-57.** Main courses 14€–18€. Wed–Sun noon–3pm and 7–10:30pm. Métro: St-Paul.

Marché des Enfants Rouge ★★ STREET FOOD   On rue de Bretagne, this quaint, 400-year-old food market (the oldest in Paris) is a bustling, fragrant labyrinth of ready-to-eat food stalls hawking everything from Caribbean curries to couscous, sushi, and pasta. Alain Miam Miam's organic crêpe stand gets queues every day for its made-to-order paninis and pancakes dripping in tasty cheese and ham. (If the lines are too long, try his shop around the corner, at 26 rue Charlot.) This is also where you'll find some of the best burgers in town: Burger Fermier (https://leburger fermier.fr) makes the bread on-site; slathers the burgers in French cheese, such as cider-infused Tomme; and only uses hand-picked beef from a

Marché des Enfants Rouge.

farm in northern France. Come late afternoon and you can join the post-shopping crowd over a glass of wine.

39 rue de Bretagne, 3rd arrond. www.paris.fr/lieux/marche-couvert-des-enfants-rouges-5461. No phone. Main courses 7.50€–20€. Tues–Sat 8:30am–8:30pm; Sun 8:30am–5pm. Métro: Saint Sébastien-Froissart.

CHAMPS-ELYSÉES, TROCADÉRO & WESTERN PARIS (8TH, 16TH & 17TH ARROND.)

Mobbed with tourists, oozing with opulence, the Champs-Elysées is a difficult place to find a good meal, unless you are willing to spend a lot of money. Mediocre chain restaurants abound on the grand avenue itself, and tacky joints mingle with frighteningly expensive gourmet palaces on the surrounding side streets.

Expensive

Le Grand Restaurant ★★★ MODERN FRENCH   Chef Jean-François Piège is—in my humble opinion—the most exciting chef in France right now. His ultra-modern take on traditional "bourgeois" cuisine is playful, delicious, and wholly unlike anything you'll taste anywhere else. Book ahead for a table in his swish, grey dining room (decked in concrete walls and geometric ceiling panels that wouldn't look amiss in Kubrick's *2001: A Space Odyssey*), then sit back for a rollercoaster ride of haute cuisine: shellfish-stuffed potato with caviar, Parmesan-infused spaghetti with truffles and fall-off-your-fork pork, and a delightful bergamot-flavored custard cream to finish. Don't be fooled by the simplicity of the descriptions; Piège's cooking is as complex as it is satisfying.

7 rue d'Aguesseau, 8th arrond. www.jeanfrancoispiege.com. ℰ **01-53-05-00-00.** Main course 72€–155€; fixed-price lunch 166€ and 246€ or dinner 326€ to 466€. Thurs–Fri 12:30–2pm and 7:30–9pm, Mon–Wed 12:30–1:30pm. Closed 3 weeks in Aug and last week in Dec. Métro: Concorde or Madeleine.

Moderate

Le Drugstore (Publicis) ★★ MODERN BRASSERIE   You won't find toothpaste at this "drugstore," whose name comes from a former 1950s incarnation that consisted of a warren of shops, restaurants, and services "à l'americaine." This ultra-modern, oh-so-chic complex has replaced the funky original but kept the multi-use concept intact with shops, restaurants, and a cinema. The Brasserie is a gourmet delight—a light-filled expanse with an incredible view of the Champs and the Arc de Triomphe from its terrace, and high-end versions of hamburgers, grilled fish, steak tartare, and fillet of sole delivered by a young and beautiful wait staff. Meals are served non-stop until 1am (Thurs–Sat), a good bet for a late-night meal. Up early? A long daily breakfast menu is available from 8 to 11:30am too.

133 av. des Champs Elysées, 8th arrond. www.publicisdrugstore.com. ℰ **01-44-43-77-64.** Main courses 27€–42€. Mon–Wed 8am–11pm, Thurs–Sat 10am–11pm. Métro: Charles de Gaulle–Etoile.

Inexpensive

Monte Carlo ★ SELF-SERVICE/FRENCH   Hitting a self-serve canteen might not be your idea of Parisian dining, but if you're on a budget, don't dismiss this handy spot by the Arc de Triomphe. Monte Carlo has been a favorite with local police officers, office workers, and tourist bus drivers alike since the 1970s—largely because it serves food all day, but also because it's one of the cheapest spots around the Champs-Élysées. A mere 10.80€ gets you a main course like chicken in mushroom sauce or smoked sausage and lentils and there are cheap menus (that include dessert) too. This won't be the culinary highlight of your stay, but the food is well prepared and tasty, and I honestly cannot name anywhere else in the area with such a good quality/price ratio.

9 av. de Wagram, 17th arrond. www.monte-carlo.fr. ✆ **01-43-80-02-20.** Fixed-price menus 14.30€–19.50€. Daily 11am–10pm (until 11pm Fri–Sat). Closed 2 weeks in mid-Aug. Métro: Charles de Gaulle–Étoile.

MONTMARTRE (18TH ARROND.)

When you get away from the tourist traps of place du Tertre, you start to understand why this neighborhood is a favorite with the artsy-hipster set. And where there's art, you are bound to find an artist in the kitchen.

Moderate

Le Coq & Fils ★★★ ROTISSERIE   At the top of the Butte de Montmartre, this popular rotisserie is where renowned chef Antoine Westerman proves that poultry can go way beyond the nugget. When raised in the right conditions (in the open air, with space and nutritious food), poultry can be just as delicious as the finest cut of beef. On the menu are such delicacies as guinea fowl in a hazelnut crumb, succulent whole duck from the Dombes region (to share) and tantalizingly juicy Challans chicken—the lot accompanied by crispy, hand-cut fries or macaroni and cheese. The desserts are worth leaving space for, too: Île Flottante (an island of soft meringue in a sea of custard cream), caramelized brioche with marmelade, and one of the best chocolate mousses in town.

98 rue Lepic, 18th arrond. https://lecoq-fils.com. ✆ **01-42-59-82-89.** Main courses 19€–52€; whole birds to share for 4 people 132€–150€. Daily noon–2:30pm and 7–11:30pm. Métro: Abbesses or Lamarck-Caulincourt.

Wepler ★★ FRENCH BRASSERIE   Picasso and Modigliani used to hang out at this venerable brasserie on place de Clichy, as did writer Henry Miller, who made it his headquarters. "I knew it like a book," he wrote. "The faces of the waiters, the managers, the cashiers, the whores, the clientele, even the attendants in the lavatory, are engraved in my memory as if they were illustrations in a book which I read every day." Today the atmosphere is quite sedate, but it's still a wonderful place to sit and watch the world go by, and the prices are accessible enough that it is still frequented by artists and writers. The menu is classic brasserie (steak tartare, shellfish platters, poached haddock in *beurre blanc*), but with a light, gourmet touch. If you don't want a big meal, ask for the less expensive cafe menu, which features delicate omelets, a *plat du jour,* and meal-size salads served on the covered terrace.

14 pl. de Clichy, 18th arrond. www.wepler.com. ℭ **01-45-22-53-24.** Main courses 13€–32€; seafood platters 38€–63€. Daily 7:30am–midnight. Métro: Place de Clichy.

Inexpensive

Bouillon Pigalle ★★ TRADITIONAL FRENCH The word *bouillon* refers to the workers' restaurants, found all over Paris back in the 19th century. The idea was to offer good food at modest prices, a concept that still speaks to working Parisians some 100 years later, if the line out the door of this 300-seater joint is any indication (reserve, however, and you'll waltz straight in). You come here to tuck into classics like leeks in vinaigrette, beef bourguignon, and chocolate eclairs at prices so low (think 2.50€ for a starter, 9.40€ for a main, and less than 4€ for dessert), you wonder how they make a profit. The menu covers a wide variety of traditional dishes like steak with fries or rum baba. Service is fast and furious, but it's all part of the atmosphere, which is something that belongs to another time and place. Be prepared to get to know your neighbors; tables are crammed into every inch of space.

22 boulevard de Clichy, 18th arrond. https://bouillonlesite.com/bouillon-pigalle. ℭ **01-42-59-69-31.** Main courses 9.40€–12.40€. Daily noon–midnight Métro: Pigalle.

RÉPUBLIQUE, BASTILLE & EASTERN PARIS (11TH & 12TH ARROND.)

Home to a mix of working-class families, hipsters, and *bobos* (bourgeois bohemians), the area between République and Nation is diverse, young, and fun. It's also one of the most exciting places for food right now, with a plethora of young chefs opening restaurants.

Expensive

Geosmine ★★★ MODERN FRENCH The bathrooms at this restaurant contain the coolest toilets in Paris. Water cascades into the tank from through a long, glass tube, making each flush an event. That might seem like a strange way to start a restaurant review, but it's indicative of the imaginativeness that's goes into every aspect of the dining experience at this young restaurant. The silverware looks like something the painter Gustave Klimt might have invented, and the food combinations read like impossibilities on the menu, but meld into new flavor profiles unlike any we've ever tasted before. These might include smoked eel tart, made even richer by a layer of pistachio cream; a starter of mozzarella and melon taken to another level by the addition of kalamata olives; and, on the more traditional side, perfectly cooked beef bathed in the most flavorsome bernaise sauce on earth. Also unusual: the kindliness of the waitstaff here,

Fish with tomato foam and oyster mushrooms at Geosmine.

who seem genuinely invested in making sure each diner has a meal to remember.

71 rue de la Folie Mericourt, 11th arrond. https://geosmine.com. ✆ **09-78-80-48-59.** Lunch a la carte 11€–42€; prix-fixe dinner 109€–139€. Thurs–Mon 12:30–2:30pm and 7:30–10pm. Metro: République or Parmentier.

Septime ★★★ MODERN FRENCH   With its seafood tapas bar next door **(Clamato)** and its tiny wine bar across the street **(Septime la Cave),** Septime has done more to gentrify this stretch of the 11th arrond. than years of town planning ever could. People cross the entire city for a table in Bertrand Grébaut's retro-chic neo-bistro, reserving at least a month in advance. Why? The progressive, seasonal dishes—anything from line-caught squid with mustard and leek sauce to pigeon with beetroot and Morello cherries—are consistently delicious, and the menus change daily according to what's freshest in the market. If you can't score a dinner reservation, try lunchtime. And if all else fails, nip next door to Clamato, where fabulous small plates of crab fritters, clams, or trout roe are washed down with lip-smacking wine that starts for as little as 5.50€ a glass. You won't be disappointed.

80 rue de Charonne, 11th arrond. www.septime-charonne.fr. ✆ **01-43-67-38-29.** Fixed-price lunch 70€ or dinner 120€. Mon–Fri 12:15–2pm and 7:30–11pm. Closed Aug. Métro: Charonne or Ledru-Rollin.

Moderate

Mansouria ★★ MOROCCAN   Generally accepted as the queen of Moroccan cooking (she's published half a dozen cookbooks), Fatéma Hal rules the kitchen of this elegant restaurant. Naturally, it offers a wide variety of delicious couscous dishes, garnished with fragrant broths and grilled meats, but the real treat here are the tagines, or stews, like the one with chicken and walnut-stuffed figs, or another with lamb, eggplant, and preserved lemons. One dish, La Mourouzia, is prepared from a 12th-century recipe featuring lamb seared in real *ras al hanout*—an intense mixture of 27 spices—and stewed in honey, raisins, and almonds.

11 rue Faidherbe, 11th arrond. www.mansouria.fr. ℰ **01-43-71-00-16.** Main courses 19€–26€, fixed-price dinner 36€. Tues–Sat noon–2pm and 7–9:45pm (until 10pm Fri–Sat). Métro: Faidherbe-Chaligny.

Laïa ★★★ MEDITERRANEAN   A team of alums from the George V palace hotel set up this wonderful Mediterranean restaurant, tucked away in a hidden garden along the tourist-free boulevard Voltaire, on the site of a former distillery. It's a slice of urban paradise—just you, the flowers, and not a peep from the traffic—not to mention that you get some of the most competitive menus on the block: 18€ for a two-course lunch and 55€ for the fixed-priced dinner. And boy, are the dishes delicious: marinated grilled chicken, beef with mint and blackberries, and barbecued octopus. In fact, much of the food is barbecued on a robata (a Japanese-Spanish grill), with herbs and vegetables from the restaurant's rooftop garden. Classic cocktails are given a Mediterranean spin (from 8€). Vegetarian and gluten-free options too. And the service? It's what you'd expect from an ex-palace team: relaxed yet ultra-attentive. Laïa is open for coffee from 10am.

226 bd. Voltaire, 11th arrond. https://laia-restaurant.com. ℰ **09-75-65-27-21.** Main courses 18€–65€, fixed-price lunch 18€, fixed-price dinner 55€. Mon–Sat 10am–midnight. Closed 2 weeks in Aug. Métro: Rue des Boulets or Voltaire.

Inexpensive

Brasserie Martin ★★ BISTRO   If you don't reserve a week ahead, you'll have to wait in line for a table at this excellent brasserie. The draw? Excellently executed bistro classics, served at low, low prices—like a delicious starter of egg and mayo for 2€, a main of sausage and mashed potato for 13€, and soul-satisfying desserts like chocolate mousse and Paris-Brest (coux pastry with praline cream) for 8€. The menu has other delectable meat and fish dishes, as well as sharing plates and terrines, and service is with a smile.

24 rue St-Amboise, 11th arrond. https://nouvellegardegroupe.com/en/brasserie-martin. ℰ **01-48-05-34-36.** Main courses 13€–21€. Daily 8:30pm–midnight. Métro: Saint-Amboise or Rue Saint-Maur.

BELLEVILLE, CANAL ST-MARTIN & LA VILLETTE (10TH, 19TH & 20TH ARROND.)

One of the last strongholds of Paris's bohemian set, here you can find both gourmet bistros and funky cheap eats, as well as a good number of wine bars that serve both nibbles and the fruit of the vine.

Moderate

EELS ★★★ BISTRO/SEAFOOD   Foodies have been flocking to this fabulous seafood-orientated bistro ever since it opened in 2017. And once you've tasted the namesake starter of smoked "eels" with apple, you'll understand why. Every single dish is a taste explosion, from the grilled sea trout with confit of fennel to the haunch of veal with caper leaves and the chocolate crisp with cardamom and pomegranate cream. At 39€, the three-course lunch menu is a steal. If you're up for an all-gourmet experience, the 79€, five-course tasting menu is a special experience.

27 rue d'Hauteville, 10th arrond. www.restaurant-eels.com ℰ **01-42-28-80-20.** Main courses 33€–44€, fixed-price lunch 32€–39€, fixed-price dinner 84€, wine pairing 49€. Tues–Sat 12:30–2pm and 7:30–10pm. Closed 2 weeks in Aug. Métro: Bonne-Nouvelle or Poissonnière.

Rosa Bonheur ★★ TAPAS   This unconventional space is named after an unconventional 19th-century painter/sculptress. It's a tapas bar, but it's also a sort of off-the-wall community center, hosting various expositions and events—it even has its own chorus and soccer team. Located in an old *buvette* (refreshment pavilion) inside the Parc des Buttes Chaumont, dating from the Universal Exposition of 1900, the restaurant boasts a sprawling terrace and one of the best panoramic views in town. A huge crowd gathers to drink and nibble tapas outside or sample dishes from the creative menu. A second location is on a docked barge on the Seine, **Rosa Bonheur Sur Seine** (right near the Pont des Invalides on the Left Bank; open year-round Wed–Fri 6pm–1:30am, Sat noon–1:30am, Sun noon–12:30am).

2 allée de la Cascade, 19th arrond. www.rosabonheur.fr. ℰ **01-42-00-00-45.** Tapas 6€–11€. Thurs–Sun noon–midnight. Closed first 2 weeks in Jan. Métro: Botzaris.

Le Verre Volé ★ WINE BAR/MODERN FRENCH   The sun is shining, the leafy trees are posing prettily along the Canal St-Martin, and you are walking over one of the pretty footbridges that curve over the water. All that's missing is a table and a glass of wine. Luckily, this wine bar/ restaurant is on hand to delight you with its vast selection. You could share a plate of sliced smoked meats and sausage, the usual accompaniment to a glass of red, or explore the menu, which might include a slice of milk-fed veal or mullet ceviche. Then select a bottle of wine from the shelves that line the walls and enjoy it (for a nominal corkage fee) in this informal, if crowded, setting.

67 rue de Lancry, 10th arrond. www.leverrevole.fr. ℰ **01-48-03-17-34.** Main courses 16€–23€, fixed-price lunch 19€–21€. Daily 12:30–2pm and 7:30pm–midnight. Métro: Jacques Bonsergent.

Inexpensive

Bob's Juice Bar ★ VEGETARIAN   Hip Parisians are tripping all over themselves to try "smoossies" (that is, smoothies) these days, and some of the best can be found at this terrific vegetarian restaurant, which has muffins, bagels, soups, and other goodies. The brainchild of Marc Grossman (alias "Bob"), an erstwhile New Yorker, this may not be the most authentically French experience, but it certainly is a tasty one. You can sit down or take out here, or try the **Bob's Bake Shop** in La Chapelle (Halle Pajol, 12 Espl. Nathalie Sarraute, 18th arrond.) or in the famous **Shakespeare and Company bookshop cafe** (p. 172).

15 rue Lucien Sampaix, 10th arrond. www.bobsjuicebar.com. ℂ **09-50-06-36-18.** Smoothies 6€–7.50€, main courses 5€–10.50€. Mon–Fri 8:30am–3pm. Métro: Jacques Bonsergent.

The Left Bank

LATIN QUARTER (5TH & 13TH ARROND.)

Steer clear of the unbearably touristy area around rue de la Huchette and the often mediocre restaurants on rue Mouffetard. Venture farther afield, where innovative restaurateurs have been cultivating a knowledgeable clientele of professors, professionals, and food savvy locals.

Expensive

La Tour d'Argent ★★★ CLASSIC FRENCH   Everyone from Queen Elizabeth II to Orson Welles has dined in this venerable restaurant, famed for its history (a restaurant has stood here since 1582); its impeccable service; and its sweeping view of the Seine and Notre-Dame. In 2023, the place was given a makeover, adding a 1930s-inspired bar: Bar des Maillets d'Argent on the ground floor and a rooftop for wine and cocktails. Inside the panoamamic 6th-floor dining room, where you gaze out over Paris though huge windows, chef Yannick Franques woos well-dressed crowds with inventive French cuisine and the establishment's coveted signature dish of pressed duck (each duck has been numbered since 1890). Five or six different waiters will visit your table at one time or another, accomplishing various tasks (opening wine bottles, pulling out your chair, and even leading you to the bathroom) with utmost professionalism and not a hint of snobbery. For something simpler and cheaper, check out the **Rotisserie d'Argent** (below), just across the street—the Tour's gingham-clad sister establishment with a terrace that sprawls out onto the Tournelles bridge just outside.

15–17 quai de la Tournelle, 5th arrond. www.latourdargent.com. ℂ **01-43-54-23-31.** Main courses 115€–185€, fixed-price lunch 150€ or dinner 360€ and 440€. Tues–Sat noon–2pm and 7–9pm. Closed Aug. Métro: St-Michel or Maubert-Mutualité.

Moderate

La Rotisserie d'Argent ★★ FRENCH/ROTISSERIE   This sister brasserie of the *gastronomique* Tour d'Argent serves some of the best half

Paris actually has two Chinatowns: the more established one, among the ugly apartment towers between avenues d'Ivry and Choisy in the 13th arrondissement (about a 5-min. walk from place d'Italie), and another newer one in Belleville in the 20th. Neither Chinatown is strictly Chinese—the population also includes communities from Vietnam, Cambodia, and other Asian countries. The 13th's Chinatown has dozens of good restaurants. A couple of my favorites for Chinese food are **Imperial Choisy,** 32 av. de Choisy, 13th arrond. (www.imperialchoisy.fr/menu; ℂ **01-45-86-42-40**), and across the street, **Likafo,** 39 av. de Choisy, 13th arrond. (ℂ **01-45-84-20-45**), for great shrimp ravioli soup.

chickens in town–juicy and garlicky with piles of mashed potato. There are other birds too, namely pigeon and duck, with sides ranging from spinach and candied onions to delicious, crispy fries. Dessert-wise, expect creamy Île flottante (meringue floating in custard cream) or a classic, vanilla-infused crème brûlée. The wine list is ample. A personal fave is the 2020 Morgon Tradition by Domaine des Améthystes in the Beaujolais region, a light, lively red with notes of red fruits (42€).

19 quai de la tournelle, 5th arrond. https://rotisseriedargent.com/en/. ℂ **01-43-54-62-53.** Main dishes 28€–48€. Daily noon–2:15pm and 6–7:30pm. Closed 2 weeks in Aug. Métro: Maubert Mutualité, Cardinal Lemoine or Jussieu.

Inexpensive

Jardin des Pâtes ★★ PASTA/VEGETARIAN   This light-filled restaurant specializes in pasta. But this is no ordinary pasta—not only are the rice, wheat, rye, and barley noodles made fresh every day, but the organic flour that goes into them is ground daily on the premises. The focus on wholesome ingredients is menu-wide; even the ice cream is 100% natural. While you won't find the usual Italian sauces, you will find original creations like rye pasta with ham, cream, sweet onions, white wine, and Comté cheese or barley pasta with fresh salmon, leeks, seaweed, and crème fraîche. Vegetarians have lots of choices here, and the relaxed atmosphere makes it a good place to bring (well-behaved) kids. Pastas are made to order, so don't be in a hurry.

4 rue Lacépède, 5th arrond. ℂ **01-43-31-50-71.** Main courses 13€–19€. Daily noon–2:30pm and 7–11pm. Métro: Place Monge.

ST-GERMAIN-DES-PRÉS (6TH ARROND.)

Saint Germain is a mix of expensive eateries that only the lucky few can afford and stalwart holdouts from the days when poverty-stricken intellectuals and artists frequented the Café de Flore. Though the Marché St-Germain has been transformed into a type of mall, the restaurants hugging its perimeter are still authentic and offer a wide range of possibilities.

Expensive

Le Relais Louis XIII ★★★ CLASSIC FRENCH   This acclaimed restaurant pays homage to traditional French cuisine at its most illustrious. No tonka beans or reduced licorice sauce here—Chef Manuel Martinez trains his formidable skills on classic sauces and time-honored dishes like sea-bass quenelles and roast duck, though he's not opposed to topping off the meal with a little lemon-basil sherbet. Signature dishes include lobster and foie gras ravioli, or braised sweetbreads with wild mushrooms. The atmospheric dining room, crisscrossed with exposed beams and ancient stonework, makes you wonder if the Three Musketeers might tumble through the doorway bearing your mille feuille with bourbon vanilla cream.

8 rue des Grands-Augustins, 6th arrond. https://relaislouis13.fr. ✆ **01-43-26-75-96.** Fixed-price lunch 80€ or dinner 145€–195€. Tues–Sat 12:15–2:30pm and 7:15–10:30pm. Closed 1st week Jan, 1st week May, and all of Aug. Métro: Odéon or St-Michel.

Moderate

Le Comptoir du Relais ★★★ TRADITIONAL FRENCH/BISTRO The brainchild of super-chef Yves de Camdeborde, this small and scrumptious bistro serves relatively traditional fare during the daytime—say, a slice of lamb with thyme sauce or maybe the *panier de cochonaille,* a basket of the Camdeborde family's own brand of smoked meats. On weeknights, however, it's a temple to haute cuisine, with a five-course tasting menu. You'll need to reserve 2 weeks in advance for this meal (or have a room in the adjoined **Relais St-Germain** hotel; p 145), which changes every night and is nonnegotiable—the chef decides what you are going to eat (though allergies are, of course, taken into account). If you can't get a seat, try **L'Avant Comptoir,** the restaurant's adjacent wine bar/counter serving small plates of charcuterie and seafood.

9 carrefour de l'Odéon, 6th arrond. www.hotel-paris-relais-saint-germain.com.✆**01-44-27-07-50.** Main courses 24€–39€, fixed-price dinner Mon–Fri 70€. Daily noon–11pm. Métro: Odéon.

Le Comptoir du Relais.

CAFE SOCIETY: PARIS'S top cafes

Cafe life is an integral part of the Parisian scene, and it simply won't do to visit the capital without joining in. Here are a few ideas for your own personal cafe tour. **Tip:** Coffee or other drinks at the bar often cost half of what they do at a table.

Café de Flore ★★ Every great French intellectual and artist seems to have had his moment here: Apollinaire, André Breton, Picasso, Giacometti, and of course, Simone de Beauvoir and Jean-Paul Sartre, who virtually lived here during World War II. The atmosphere today is less thoughtful and more showbiz, but it's still worth an overpriced cup of coffee just to come in and soak it up.

172 bd. St-Germain, 6th arrond. www.cafedeflore.fr. ℭ **01-45-48-55-26.** Daily 7:30am–1:30am. Métro: St-Germain-des-Prés.

Café de la Paix ★★★ A Parisian institution ever since it was inaugurated by Empress Eugenie in 1862, this is the home of one of the most expensive cups of coffee (7€). Everyone from Emile Zola to Yves Montand has done time in this Second Empire marvel, whose gold leaf and curlicues looks as perfect as the day it was built. Its outdoor terrace offers a magnificent view over the Palais Garnier opera house.

Corner of Pl. de l'Opéra and bd. des Capucines, 9th arrond. www.cafedelapaix.fr. ℭ **01-40-07-36-36.** Daily 8am–11pm. Métro: Opéra.

Le Bistrot du Peintre ★ Artists, hipsters, and other fauna from the bustling rue de Charonne area flock to this popular spot, which sports an authentic Art Nouveau interior with the original peeling paint.

116 av. Ledru-Rollin, 11th arrond. www.bistrotdupeintre.com. ℭ **01-47-00-34-39.** Daily 7am–midnight (Fri–Sat until 2am). Métro: Ledru-Rollin.

Les Deux Magots ★★ The literary pedigree here is impressive: Poets Verlaine and Rimbaud camped out here, as did André Gide and Albert Camus. Sartre and de Beauvoir moved in postwar and stayed for decades. The outdoor terrace is pleasant early in the morning before the crowds awake.

6 pl. St-Germain-des-Prés, 6th arrond. www.lesdeuxmagots.fr. ℭ **01-45-48-55-25.** Daily 7:30am–1am. Métro: St-Germain-des-Prés.

Le Nemours ★★ Cuddled up in a corner next to the Comedie Française, this beautiful cafe has a great terrace stretching out onto the place Colette. The ideal spot for taking a load off after a day at the nearby Louvre.

2 pl. Colette. www.lenemours.paris. ℭ **01-42-61-34-14.** Mon–Fri 8am–midnight, Sat 9am–midnight, Sun 9am–8:30pm. Métro: Palais Royal–Musée du Louvre.

Inexpensive

Restaurant Polidor ★ TRADITIONAL FRENCH/BISTRO An unofficial historic monument, Polidor is not so much a restaurant as a snapshot of a bygone era. The decor has not changed substantially for at least 100 years, when Verlaine and Rimbaud, the bad boys of poetry, would come here for a cheap meal. In the 1950s, it was dubbed "the College of Pataphysics" by a rowdy group of young upstarts that included Max Ernst, Boris Vian, and Eugene Ionesco; André Gide and Ernest Hemingway were reputed regulars. The menu features hefty bistro standbys like boeuf bourguignon and *blanquette de veau* (veal stew), but you'll also find lighter fare like salmon with basil. These days, the artsy set has moved elsewhere; you'll probably be sharing the long wooden tables with other tourists, along with a dose of locals. Though the food is not particularly memorable, the ambience is unique.

41 rue Monsieur-le-Prince, 6th arrond. www.polidor.com. ℂ **01-43-26-95-34.** Main courses 13.50€–22€, fixed-price lunch menu 15.50€ and dinner 25€. Daily noon–3pm and 7pm–midnight. Métro: Odéon.

EIFFEL TOWER & NEARBY (7TH ARROND.)

Crowded with ministries and important people, this neighborhood is so grand, you half expect to hear trumpets blowing each time you turn a corner. Though it's a rather staid neighborhood, a few streets are fairly lively, namely rue Cler, a pretty market street, and rue St-Dominique, home to some of the best restaurants on this side of the Seine.

Expensive

Jules Verne ★★★ MODERN FRENCH   Sometimes Paris is about embracing the clichés, and dining on the second floor of the Eiffel Tower is definitely a cliché worth embracing. Not only are the views magnificent, with the city's iconic rooftops undulating in graceful higgledy-piggledydom between Trocadéro, Les Invalides, and La Défense's sky-scrapers, but now that award-winning chef Frédéric Anton has taken over the kitchen, the food is worth writing home about, too. Try wonders like langoustine ravioli in tarragon sauce, vanilla-salted pigeon, and a bitter chocolate soufflé—all beautifully presented to evoke (in the words of the chef) "the cogs, the nuts, and bolts" of the Eiffel Tower. For an extra dose of romance, dine at night when the city sparkles at your feet. Reservations are required at least 2 months in advance.

2nd floor of the Eiffel Tower, av. Gustave Eiffel, 7th arrond. www.restaurants-tour eiffel.com. ℂ **01-83-77-34-34.** Fixed-price lunch 160€ (Mon–Fri only) to 275€, tasting menu (lunch and dinner) 255€ and 275€. Daily noon–1:30pm and 7–9pm. Métro: Bir-Hakeim or Trocadéro. RER: Champs de Mars Tour Eiffel. Closed 14 July dinner.

Beaupassage: The Left Bank Food Arcade

Though Paris is peppered with market streets and old-word *passages* (18th-c. precursors to today's shopping malls), Beaupassage in the chic 7th arrondisse-ment is the city's first ever arcade entirely dedicated to the glories of food. Opened in 2018 on the site of a former convent and a car showroom, it marries ultramodern design and contemporary art installations with restaurants and food shops run by the city's top chefs. Though the 7th is as chic as can be, and the chefs have multiple Michelin stars among them, you'll actually find food for all budgets—*breadmakis* (maki-style club sandwiches, rolled and cut into big slices) from 6.50€ in Thierry Marx's **Boulange-rie;** gourmet burgers at Père & Fils par **Alléno** (the joint award-winning chef Yannick Alleno runs with his son Antoine); and a 24.95€ fixed-price seafood menu at **Mersea** (famed for its fish and chips). Capping things off are a butcher, a cheese shop, an organic supermarket, and a gym. Beaupassage is at 53–57 rue du Grenelle, 7th arrond. (www.facebook. com/beaupassageparis; daily 7am–midnight).

Moderate

La Fontaine de Mars ★★ BISTRO/SOUTHWESTERN FRENCH
Red and white checks are everywhere at this old-school bistro: on the
tablecloths, the wicker chairs, and even the curtains. A venerable institution since it first opened in 1908, its low-key classy decor and traditional
menu attracted the attention of President Obama, who made a surprise
visit here with his wife Michele in 2009. The kitchen turns out reliable and
succulent southwestern French dishes like cassoulet, foie gras, and duck
breast with black cherry sauce. Starters include *escargots* (snails) and
oeufs au Madiran (eggs baked with red wine and bacon), and the dessert
list is full of classics, such as île flottante, crème brûlée, and dark chocolate mousse.
129 rue St-Dominique, 7th arrond. www.fontaine-de-mars.com. © **01-47-05-46-44.**
Main courses 21€–39€. Daily noon–3pm and 7–11pm. Métro: Ecole Militaire.

Les Parisiens ★★★ MODERN FRENCH/BISTRO   On the ground
floor of the Pavillon Faubourg St-Germain hotel (the building where
James Joyce once lived), this gorgeous new restaurant packs a flavorful
punch. Orange velvet chairs, wood panels and an Art Deco–style tile floor
provide a chic background for chef Thibault Sombardier's exceptional
brasserie dishes, like meunière-style frogs legs with ginger, a giant *Paris-
Deauville vol-au-vent* (a pastry cup filled with seafood, with mushroom
sauce) and sweetbreads with capers. Desserts—think almond and apricot
soufflé, chocolate mousse, peaches poached in champagne—are just as
satisfying. Wash everything down with a wine from their 22-page list and
you've got yourself a memorable meal.
5 rue du Pré-aux-Clercs, 6th arrond. www.pavillon-faubourg-saint-germain.com/
restaurant-les-parisiens. © **01-42-61-01-51.** Main courses 34€–45€, fixed-price
lunch 39€–45€. Daily noon–2:15pm and 7–10:15pm. Métro: Rue du Bac or Saint
Germain-des-Près.

Inexpensive

Le Petit Cler ★★ TRADITIONAL FRENCH/BISTRO   This cute little cafe tumbles out onto the rue Cler pedestrian market street and serves
high quality but simple food at very reasonable prices. While you won't
find many red and white checks, you will find classic cafe fare (steaks
with sautéed potatoes, omelets, and tartines—open-faced grilled sandwiches) as well as a daily special, which might be roast chicken (Sun) or
fresh fish (Fri). You can also get a good continental breakfast here (15€).
29 rue Cler, 7th arrond. https://menuonline.fr/lepetitcler. © **01-45-50-17-50.** Main
courses 16€–24€. Daily 8am–1am. Closed 2 weeks in Aug. Métro: Ecole Militaire.

MONTPARNASSE & NEARBY (14TH & 15TH ARROND.)

The famous cafes and brasseries (Le Dôme, Le Select, La Coupole, and
Closerie des Lilas; p. 168) where struggling writers and artists like
Picasso, Hemingway, and Chagall once hung out make for atmospheric
spots, but there are plenty of other good options, from Breton creperies

near the train station (along rue du Montparnasse) to a bundle of new gourmet bistros farther south. Check out rue Daguerre, a quaint street market by Denfert Rochereau Métro that's peppered with restaurants.

Expensive

Closerie des Lilas ★★ TRADITIONAL FRENCH/BRASSERIE   This restaurant, brasserie, and piano bar was a favorite of Picasso and Gertrude Stein, not to mention Ernest Hemingway, who downed whiskey here so often that both the bar and a signature dish (pan-fried steak in creamy whiskey sauce) bear his name. With such history, you'd expect this to be on every tourist's radar, but the Closerie has managed to remain resolutely Parisian, drawing in locals with the promise of indulgent dishes like fresh seafood platters, panfried sweetbreads, and even caviar with steamed potatoes and cream. Literary fans will be pleased to learn that every year, the Closerie awards female writers with prestigious literary prizes.

161 bd. du Montparnasse, 6th arrond. www.closeriedeslilas.fr. ✆ **01-40-51-34-50.** Mains 45€–58€, seafood platters 50€–115€. Daily noon–2:15pm and 7–10pm; piano bar noon–1:30am. Closed Aug. Métro: Raspail or Vavin. RER: Port-Royal.

Moderate

L'Assiette ★★ TRADITIONAL FRENCH   There's a whiff of the Belle Epoque in this old-fashioned dining room, which has its share of mirrors and ceiling ornaments. The menu appeals to culinary nostalgia as well, with dishes like homemade cassoulet, pike quenelles (long and delicate fish dumplings) with Nantua sauce, as well as escargots and homemade foie gras for starters. For dessert, indulge in crème caramel made with salted butter or profiteroles with chocolate sauce.

181 rue du Château, 14th arrond. https://restaurant-lassiette.paris. ✆ **01-43-22-64-86.** Main courses 29€–44€, fixed-price lunch 24€. Wed–Sun noon–2:30pm and 7:30–10:30pm. Closed Aug. Métro: Gaîté.

Inexpensive

Le Petit Josselin ★★ CRÊPERIE   Of the dozens of crêperies concentrated near the Montparnasse train station, this tiny dining room is one of the best. The *galettes* and crepes are perfectly cooked with lacy,

Le Petit Josselin is very kid-friendly.

crispy edges, and include fillings like bacon and egg, smoked salmon, and the can-do-no-wrong classic, ham and cheese. Try to save room for a sweet crepe after—the salted caramel butter crepe is a wonder. Tradition demands that this meal be accompanied by a bowl of "brut" cider (low alcohol content, for adults only).

59 rue du Montparnasse, 14th arrond. www.creperielepetitjosselin.fr. © **01-43-22-91-81.** Main courses 7€–15€. Mon–Sat noon–2:30pm and 6:30–11pm. Métro: Edgar Quinet.

SHOPPING

Vuitton, Chanel, Baccarat—the names of famous French luxury brands roll around the tongue like rich chocolate. But while it's fun to window-shop at Cartier, few of us can actually afford to buy anything there. Guess what? Neither can most Parisians. Thus, there's so much more shopping to explore than those big-box luxury stores on the Champs-Élysées. Seek out the small boutiques by up-and-coming designers, lesser-known but fab chocolate stores, and hip yet inexpensive French chain stores where you can throw together a look in minutes. Paris is shopaholic heaven, if you know where to go to find your *bonheur* (happiness).

Business Hours

In general, shops are open from 9 or 10am to 7pm; some are closed on Monday, and most are closed on Sunday (see box on p. 174 for Sun shopping). Unfortunately, that means that the stores are jam-packed on Saturday, so don't say I didn't warn you.

Some smaller, family-run operations still close between noon and 2pm for lunch, but most stores stay open all day. Many larger stores and most department stores stay open until 8pm. For food and toiletry emergencies, tiny minimarkets (called *alimentations*) stay open late into the night daily. *Note:* Many shops close down for 2 or 3 weeks in July or August, when the vacation exodus empties out major portions of the city.

Great Shopping Areas

STREETS FOR BARGAIN HUNTING

You can find clothes and knickknacks at significantly reduced prices at discount shops, which tend to conglomerate on certain streets. **Rue d'Alésia** (14th arrond.; Métro: Alésia) is lined with outlet stores (*déstock*) selling discounted wares, including designer labels like Sonia Rykiel; and **Rue St-Placide** (6th arrond.; Métro: Sèvres-Babylone) has both outlet stores and discount shops like **Mouton à Cinq Pattes** (p. 175).

MIDRANGE SHOPPING HUBS

Several areas have high concentrations of chain and midrange stores where you can get a lot of shopping done in a small area. They are **Rue de Rennes** (6th arrond., especially near the Tour Montparnasse); **Les Halles** (1st arrond., with its underground Forum des Halles mall); **Rue de Rivoli** (1st arrond., btw. rue du Pont Neuf and Hôtel de Ville); and **Grands Magasins** (9th arrond.)—be sure to look in the little streets that weave around the Printemps and Galeries Lafayette department stores.

CHIC BOUTIQUE-ING

Paris has an endless number of darling boutiques, ranging from funky to fantastic. A few of the best streets for boutique shopping or *lèche-vitrine* (window shopping) are **Rue des Abbesses** (18th arrond.; Métro: Abbesses), for affordable chic and the shops of hip, young startup designers; **Rue de Charonne** (11th arrond.; Métro: Bastille), a youth-oriented street that has recently taken a turn upscale with a dose of hip boutiques; **Rue des Francs Bourgeois** (4th arrond.; Métro: St-Paul), for a cornucopia of fashionable/cool stores, most of which are open on Sunday; and **Rue Etienne Marcel** (2nd arrond.; Métro: Etienne Marcel), next to the fab Montorgueil pedestrian zone, with stylish boutiques galore.

THE SKY'S THE LIMIT

If you don't look at price tags and are always searching for the ultimate everything, Paris does not disappoint. For centuries, Paris has been the capital of luxury goods, many of them for sale on **avenue Montaigne** (8th arrond.; Métro: Franklin D. Roosevelt), with breathtakingly expensive designer flagships like Dior and Chanel; the **place Vendôme** (1st arrond.; Métro: Concorde or Tuileries), with eye-popping jewelry shops (Cartier, Boucheron, and so on); and **Rue du Faubourg St-Honoré** (8th arrond.; Métro: St-Philippe du Roule), with deeply elegant boutiques filled with choice morsels of designer goods.

Markets: Food & Flea

Marchés (open-air or covered markets) are small universes unto themselves where nothing substantial has really changed for centuries. These markets are great local spots to hunt for fresh food or browse flea-market finds.

FOOD MARKETS

Paris's food markets are noisy, bustling, joyous places where you can buy fresh, honest food. Following is a short list of food *marchés;* you can find more on Paris' website (www.paris.fr/pages/les-marches-parisiens-2428). *Note:* Unless you see evidence to the contrary, don't pick up your own fruits and vegetables with your hands. Wait until the vendor serves you.

Marché Batignolles ★★ (bd. Batignolles, btw. rue de Rome and place Clichy, 17th arrond.; Sat 9am–2:30pm; Métro: Rome): A terrific, all-organic Saturday market with fresh regional produce and close proximity to pretty sidewalk cafes for an after-marché coffee.

Marché d'Aligre ★★★ (also called Marché Beauveau, place d'Aligre, 12th arrond.; outdoor market Tues–Fri 7:30am–1:30pm, Sat–Sun 7:30am–2pm, covered market Tues–Fri 8am–1pm and 4–7:30pm, Sat 8am–7:30pm, Sun 8am–1:30pm; Métro: Ledru Rollin or Gare de Lyon): One of the city's largest markets, this sprawling affair invades a whole neighborhood, with both outdoor stalls and a covered market.

Marché Raspail ★★ (bd. Raspail, btw. rue de Cherche-Midi and rue de Rennes, 6th arrond.; Tues and Fri 7am–1:30pm, organic Sun 9am–3pm; Métro: Rennes): Stretching several blocks down the center divider of a wide avenue, this outdoor market makes a delicious gourmet stroll.

FLEA MARKETS
Marché aux Puces de la Porte de Vanves ★★ (av. Georges-Lafenestre, 14th arrond.; www.pucesdevanves.fr; Sat–Sun 7am–2pm; Métro: Porte de Vanves): This weekend event sprawls along two streets and is the best flea market in Paris—dealers swear by it. Look for old linens, vintage Hermès scarves, toys, ephemera, costume jewelry, perfume bottles, and bad art. Get there early—the best stuff goes fast.

Marché aux Puces de Paris St-Ouen-Clignancourt ★ (Porte de Clignancourt, 18th arrond.; www.pucesdeparissaintouen.com. Fri 8am–noon, Sat–Sun 10am–6pm, Mon 11am–5pm; Métro: Porte de Clignancourt): At the northern edge of the city, this claims to be the world's largest antiques market. It was once a bargain-hunter's dream, but prices now often rival those of antiques dealers. Hard-core browsers will get a kick out of wandering the serpentine alleyways of this Parisian medina. *Note:* Beware of pickpockets.

Shopping A to Z
ANTIQUES & COLLECTIBLES
Drouot ★ This auction house sells a bit of everything, from fine art to vintage and reproduction decorative objects, jewelry, and housewares—many of them affordable. It has been an institution since it opened in 1852, with 15 rooms dedicated to art, collectibles and furniture. Artworks are usually displayed the day before the auction. Anyone can bid; just raise your hand and shout out a price. L'Hôtel Drouot, 9 rue du Drouot, 9th arrond. www.drouot.com. © **01-48-00-20-20.** Métro: Richelieu-Drouot.

Village St-Paul ★★ When you pass through an archway on rue St-Paul, you come upon a lovely villagelike enclosure, the remnant of a centuries-old hamlet that was swallowed up by the city. Today, it's a little village of antiques dealers and design shops, selling everything from old bistro chairs and vintage lingerie to Brazilian eco-furniture and Iranian kilim rugs. www.levillagesaintpaul.com. No phone. Métro: St-Paul.

BEAUTY & PERFUME

Editions de Parfums Frédéric Malle ★★
This chic temple to the nose offers a superb range of original fragrances. Sample M. Malle's wares in special "smelling columns," round, phone-booth-like tubes where you can experience aromas like Noir Epice and Lipstick Rose. The three other stores are at 140 av. Victor Hugo in the 16th arrondissement, 13 rue des Francs Bourgeois in the 4th, and 21 rue du Mont Thabor in the 1st. 37 rue de Grenelle, 7th arrond. www.fredericmalle.com. ✆ **01-42-22-76-40.** Métro: Rue du Bac.

Detaille 1905 ★★
Founded by the Countess of Presle in 1905, this handsome, old-fashioned store offers its own elegant line of *eau de toilette* and other beauty products for both men and women, such as its signature *Baume Automobile,* developed by the Countess when she realized (even back then) what pollution can do to your skin. These unique products can only be purchased at the wood-paneled boutique or online through the shop's website. 10 rue St-Lazare, 9th arrond. www.detaille.com. ✆ **01-48-78-68-50.** Métro: Notre-Dame-de-Lorette.

La Station by The Different Company ★★
Indeed, something *is* different about this perfume and cosmetics company. This independent operation, founded in 2000, not only makes its own unique fragrances, but it also showcases small French cosmetics and perfume brands like Avril (organic cosmetics made in Lille in Northern France) and Nolenca (fragrances made in Toulouse in the southeast). If you're looking for something quintessentially French, this is the place to get it. 10 rue Ferdinand Duval, 4th arrond. https://lastationtdc.fr. ✆ **01-42-78-19-34.** Métro: St-Paul.

BOOKS

The Abbey Bookshop ★
This cozy store specializes in Canadian authors, as well as other English-language literature. You'll have to squeeze in between the piles of books, but this is a welcoming place with good readings and events, including hikes in nearby forests. 29 rue de la Parcheminerie, 5th arrond. https://abbeybookshop.wordpress.com/about. ✆ **01-46-33-16-24.** Métro: St-Michel.

Shakespeare & Company ★★★
This venerable shrine is a must on any Parisian literary tour. Run by George Whitman for some 60 years before he passed away in 2011 at 98, today it is helmed by his daughter, Sylvia, who was named for Sylvia Beach (who founded the original

Sylvia Whitman, owner of Shakespeare & Company.

bookshop in 1919). Many a legendary writer has stopped in over the decades for tea; many an aspiring author has camped out in one of the back rooms (Whitman liked to think of this store as a "writer's sanctuary"). Today, Whitman's presence is still felt at this historic bookshop, which sells used and new books. Check the website for readings and other events. 37 rue de la Bûcherie, 5th arrond. www.shakespeareandcompany.com. ⓒ **01-43-25-40-93.** Métro/RER: St-Michel–Notre-Dame.

Smith & Son ★★★   A wide selection in a fabulous setting! Formerly the Paris branch of this English chain, WH Smith, this is now the biggest indie bookstore in the city, and has been around since 1870. Along with its huge range of English-language books and magazines, it hosts signings by famous authors, and harbors a lovely tearoom next to the children's' section. Look out for the shop's stunning fireplace and Domestic Revival-style reliefs, dating from the turn of the last century. There's even a period stained-glass window of George Washington's coat of arms, and no one really knows why it's there. 248 rue de Rivoli, 1st arrond. www.smithandson. com. ⓒ **01-53-45-84-40.** Métro: Concorde.

Don't shop on Saturday if you can avoid it; the crowds are annoying, to say the least. If you do want to shop on a Sunday, try the **Marais** (4th arrond.), **Abbesses** (18th arrond.) in Montmartre and the **Canal St Martin** (10th arrond.) areas, where multiple boutiques stay open. Or for larger shops, hit the **Carousel du Louvre,** a chic shopping mall below the Louvre museum and the **Champs Elysées.**

CLOTHING & ACCESSORIES

Balibaris ★★   Founded by a young fashion entrepreneur, this is where Parisian men go for cool, smart outfits that work just as well on a night out as in the office. You'll find classically cut pants and chinos, and denim and suede jackets, along with a spattering of cotton and leather bags. The city has multiple branches (including in **Galeries Lafayette,** p. 176, and **Printemps,** p. 177). 13 rue Vavin, 6th arrond. www.balibaris.com. ℭ **01-42-38-18-67.** Métro: Notre-Dame des Champs or Vavin.

French Trotters ★   Airy and spacious, this Marais emporium is the flagship store for this temple of urban chic. While the original store (which is still open; 30 rue de Charonne, 11th arrond.) featured both hot local French labels and the store's own brand of relaxed *branchitude* (hipness), this one sells all that plus housewares, books, and stationary. Terrific styles for both men and women. 128 rue Vieille du Temple, 3rd arrond. www.frenchtrotters.fr. ℭ **01-44-61-00-14.** Métro: Saint Sébastien–Froissart or Files du Calvaire.

Make My Lemonade ★★   Despite the English name, this independent, affordable women's fashion house is resolutely French. It feels like an urban boudoir and offers beautiful clothes cut to fit women with real curves (think velvet jackets and long flowing floral dresses). Regular sewing or nail art workshops are held in the front room. 61 Quai de Valmy, 10th arrond. www.makemylemonade.com. ℭ **09-67-42-23-97.** Métro: Jacques Bonsergent.

Children

Botoù ★★   If you're looking for something funky for your children's feet, this is where to head. These cool and colorful shoes will make your kids look like they live in this fun and hip neighborhood (SoPi), with everything from goldfish-print sneakers to chick-yellow ankle boots. 20 rue Milton, 9th arrond. http://botou.fr. ℭ **09-83-82-06-58.** Métro: Notre-Dame-de-Lorette.

Marie Puce ★★   A little softer and gentler, Marie offers easy elegance for tots who need to dress up (at least a little) but can't stand frills. Most of the clothing here is 100% made in France. 60 rue du Cherche Midi, 6th arrond. www.mariepuce.com. ✆ **01-45-48-30-09.** Métro: Sèvres-Babylone or St-Placide.

Designer Discount Outlets
Mouton à Cinq Pattes ★ Sift through the packed racks of designer markdowns and you just might find Moschino slacks or a Gaultier dress at a fabulous price. If you do, grab it fast—it might not be there tomorrow. The store at no. 8 is women's apparel only; no. 18 serves both sexes, and a third store at 138 bd. St-Germain is just for men. 8 and 18 rue St-Placide, 6th arrond. www.moutonacinqpattesparis.com. ✆ **01-45-48-86-26.** Métro: Sèvres-Babylone.

Lingerie
Fifi Chachnil ★★★ A boudoir-boutique tucked into a courtyard, this is where young French movie stars go to find retro-sexy-fun-posh underthings with a decidedly girly feel. Prices are steep, but the experience and the lingerie are unique. It has one other pink and fluffy boutique at 34 rue de Grenelle in the 7th. 68 rue Jean-Jacques Rousseau, in the courtyard, 1st arrond. www.fifichachnil.com. ✆ **01-42-21-19-93.** Métro/RER: Les Halles.

Saint Germain des Slips ★★ This is a Left Bank outpost of Le Slip Français, a quirky company (*slip* means "underpants") that makes every undergarment it sells—from men's boxer shorts to women's bras—in France. You can accessorize with bags and t-shirts to match your undies too. More locations on the website. 20 rue du Vieux Colombier, 6th arrond. www.leslipfrancais.fr. ✆ **01-45-38-90-56.** Métro: St-Sulpice.

CONCEPT STORES
Over the last few years, these hard-to-categorize stores with eclectic collections have popped up in several parts of the city. These are good places to hunt for that atypical gift you've been seeking.

Bü ★ A cross between Ikea, and an upscale hardware store, this Ali Baba's cave of treasures, his enigmatically named store (it's French, not Scandinavian) has shelves upon shelves of reasonably priced housewares, stationary, leather handbags, luggage, and toys, as well as regional edibles. 45 rue Jussieu, 5th arrond. www.bu-store.com. ✆ **01-40-56-33-22.** Métro: Jussieu or Cardinal-Lemoine.

Empreintes ★★ French art and crafts take center stage in this glorious, four-story space that showcases over a thousand pieces of handmade jewelry, tableware, furniture, lighting and *objets d'art*. Prices start under 75€ but can climb high. A projection room shows arts and crafts-themed movies too. 5 rue de Picardie, 3rd arrond. www.empreintes-paris.com. ✆ **01-40-09-53-80.** Métro: Filles du Calvaire or Temple.

La Tresorerie ★★★ *Architectural Digest* called this homewares store "the French Williams Sonoma" and that's somewhat right. It has all kinds of kitchen gadgets plus handsome plates and flatware. But prices are fairer at this French store, and the array of goods wider, ranging from glass vases that look like ancient Roman busts, to sleek modern couches, to cottagecore cute hand-painted salad bowls. The name comes from the setting in a former bank; another branch is across the street. 8 and 11 rue du château d'eau, 10th arrond. www.latresorerie.fr. No phone. Metro: Republique.

Landline ★★★ If you only have chance to go to one boutique in Paris, make it this gorgeous general supply store in the Boho 11th arrondissements. Created by Franco-American Caroline Morrison, it's the place to find equisite, built-to-last items from Europe to use at home (pans, knives, terracotta ceramics by Parisian artist Katherine Oh) and on your body (organic face creams, artisan wool vests, Venetian velvet slippers). There are toys too—glorious wooden one that will last a lifetime. And a whole section on brushes—including a special wooden-brush just for dusting bookcases. Who'd have thought? I can't stress how wonderful this place is! 107 ave Parmentier, 11th arrond. https://landlineparis.com. ℂ **01-43-55-83-61.** Métro: Parmentier or Goncourt.

Merci ★★ Set in a former factory on the edge of the Marais, Merci offers hand-picked designer brands mixed with vintage one-offs on the 2nd floor, while you'll find cool kitchenware in the basement. Jewelry, linen, and stationery are other favorites here. Sip coffee over a slice of cake in one of the cafes. 111 bd. de Beaumarchais, 3rd arrond. www.merci-merci.com. ℂ **01-42-77-00-33.** Métro: Filles du Calvaire.

DEPARTMENT STORES

Galeries Lafayette ★★ The biggest of the *grand magasins* (department stores) sports an over-the-top Art Nouveau dome under which oodles of fashionable goodies are displayed for style-conscious shoppers. A bit less expensive than its more glamorous rival next door (see **Printemps,** p. 177), it's also so huge that you can usually find just what you are looking for. It has everything from luxury labels to kids' stuff, not to mention books, stationary, wine, and a gourmet shop. 40 bd. Haussmann, 9th arrond. www.galerieslafayette.com. ℂ **01-42-82-34-56.** Métro: Chausée d'Antin–Lafayette.

La Samaritaine ★★ After almost 2 decades of renovations, the famous riverfront department store reopened in June 2021 to include a fashion concept store, the biggest beauty studio on the European continent (only Harrods in London has a bigger one), a spa, and even a luxury hotel (**Cheval Blanc Paris;** p. 134). To differentiate La Samaritaine from the city's other department stores, many brands by French creators are exclusive to the store—and if nothing else, its Art Nouveau and Art Deco interiors are more than worth checking out. 19 rue de la Monnaie, 1st arrond. www.dfs.com. ☏ **01-56-81-28-40.** Métro: Hôtel de Ville.

Le Bon Marché ★★★ Founded in the mid-1800s, this was one of the world's first department stores. Despite its name (*bon marché* means "affordable"), this is the most expensive of Paris' *grand magasins*. It is also the most stylish, with beautiful displays and fabulous clothes of every imaginable designer label, both upscale and midrange. Right next door is its humongous designer supermarket, **La Grande Epicerie Paris** (see "Specialty Groceries," p. 178). 24 rue de Sèvres, 7th arrond. www.24s. com. ☏ **01-44-39-80-00.** Métro: Sèvres–Babylone.

Galeries Lafayette.

Printemps ★★ The glistening domes of this 19th-century building bring to mind a grand hotel on the French Riviera. High fashion gets priority here; four of the seven floors of women's wear are devoted to designer labels. If you can't handle the crowds inside, you can always enjoy the famed *vitrines*, or **window displays,** outside. Better yet, ride to the top of Printemps Beauté/Maison and enjoy the splendid **panoramic view;** it even has a cafe at the top where you can lunch. 64 bd. Haussmann, 9th arrond. www.printemps.com. ☏ **01-42-82-50-00.** Métro: Havre-Caumartin or St-Lazare.

FOOD & DRINK

Chocolate

A La Mère de Famille ★ Founded in 1761, this piece of Parisian history (rumor has it the original owner hid the mother superior of the nearby convent from raging revolutionaries during the Terror) has committed its soul to candies and chocolates à l'ancienne. You'll find classic chocolates as well as old-fashioned bonbons like *berlingots*, lemon drops, caramels, and jellied fruits. There are nine other locations. 35 rue du Faubourg Montmartre, 9th arrond. www.lameredefamille.com. ☏ **01-47-70-83-69.** Métro: Grands Boulevards.

Patrick Roger ★★ This cutting-edge chocolate boutique could easily be mistaken for a jewelry shop. Here you can sample chocolates with names like "Insolence" (almond and chestnut) and "Zanzibar" (thyme and lemon), as well as candied fruits, nougat, and other delicacies. Five other stores in the city. 108 bd. St-Germain, 6th arrond. www.patrickroger.com. ℰ **01-43-29-38-42.** Métro: Odéon.

Specialty Groceries

La Grande Epicerie Paris ★★ This humongous gourmet grocery mecca, an outgrowth of Le Bon Marché department store (see above) stocks every gourmet substance you could possibly imagine, and many that you couldn't. Sculpted sugar cubes, designer mineral waters, truffled balsamic vinegar, pink salt from the Himalayas—need I go on? It also has an excellent (if expensive) takeout department for picnic items. A second address has opened at 80 rue de Passy, 16th arrond. 38 rue de Sèvres, 7th arrond. www.lagrandeepicerie.fr. ℰ **01-44-39-81-00.** Métro: Sèvres-Babylone.

Maille ★★ True, you can find Maille gourmet mustard all over the place, but you can only get it hand-pumped here in the official boutique (and in Dijon; see p. 424). Pumped fresh into a genuine stoneware pot and sealed with a cork, it has an altogether different taste, and it is delicious. Choose from mustard made with a dash of Chablis, Sauternes, or splurge on Chablis with truffle bits. 6 pl. de la Madeleine, 8th arrond. www.maille.com. ℰ **01-40-15-06-00.** Métro: Madeleine.

Wines

Before you start planning to stock your wine cellar back home, consider this sad truth: Most non–EU countries won't let you bring back much more than a bottle or two. Your best bet is to drink up while you're here.

Les Domaines Qui Montent ★ This association of some 150 wine producers offers a vast selection of wines that come from small, independent vineyards where the emphasis is on quality and *terroir*, not quantity. An on-site wine bar also serves meals. There are several other locations, including at 136 bd. Voltaire in the 11th arrondissement and on the corner of rue Ballu and rue Vintimille in the 9th. 22 rue Cardinet, 17th arrond. www.lesdomainesquimontent.com. ℰ **01-42-27-63-96.** Métro: Courcelles or Wagram.

Legrand Filles et Fils ★★ More than just a wine store, this is a place where you can learn everything there is to know about the sacred grape. Not only does this store have a dedicated, knowledgeable staff and a huge stock of wines, but it also hosts wine tastings and classes, and sells books and paraphernalia. Located in the glamorous Galerie Vivienne. 1 rue de la Banque, 2nd arrond. www.caves-legrand.com. ℰ **01-42-60-07-12.** Métro: Bourse.

JEWELRY

Monsieur ★★   Unique jewelry at reasonable prices handmade in an atelier in the Marais—who could ask for more? Nadia Azoug is known for her beautiful, delicate Art Deco-inspired pieces, made with gold, silver, semiprecious stones, and the occasional set of diamonds. The designs are very light and elegant, and many are unisex. Prices start at a very affordable 80€. 53 rue Charlot, 3rd arrond. www.monsieur-paris.com. ☏ **06-50-02-01-75.** Métro: Filles du Calvaire.

WHITEbIRD ★★   Need a unique engagement ring or present for your sweetheart? WHITEbIRD has a terrific selection of jewelry made by talented, independent craftspeople/designers. 38 rue du Mont Thabor, 1st arrond. www.whitebirdjewellery.com. ☏ **01-58-62-25-86.** Métro: Concorde.

KITCHENWARES

E. Dehillerin ★★★   Established in 1820, E. Dehillerin is Paris's most famous cookware shop. Set near Les Halles, this is where chefs come to buy their kitchen utensils. E. Dehillerin sells everything from copper pans and ergonomic zesters, to fish-bone tweezers, whipped cream siphons, and plenty of other things you never knew you needed. Keep track of what you want to buy on a piece of paper, then pay at the till, where you'll be handed your order. Prices are displayed without VAT, which is added when you pay. 18 and 20 rue Coquillère, 1st arrond. www.edehillerin.fr. ☏ **01-42-36-53-13.** Métro/RER: Les Halles.

ENTERTAINMENT & NIGHTLIFE

Paris blooms at night; its magnificent monuments and buildings become even more beautiful when they're cloaked in their evening illuminations. The already glowing Eiffel Tower bursts out in twinkling lights for the first 5 minutes of every hour after dark. While simply walking around town can be an excellent night out, the city is also a treasure trove of evening offerings: bars and clubs from chic to shaggy, sublime theater and dance performances, top-class orchestras, and scores of cinemas.

With few exceptions, the city's major concert halls and theaters are in action between September and June, taking off during the summer months during the annual vacation exodus. On the upside,

---

Finding Out What's On

Sortir à Paris (www.sortiraparis.com) lists everything from plays and festivals to concerts and movie screenings in English. If you can read French, two other websites to try are **l'Officiel des Spectacles** (www.offi.fr) and **Télérama** (www.telerama.fr). Or for the latest info about live music, try **Lylo** (www.lylo.fr), also in French. By the way, if you see a sign at a theater or on an events website that says *location*, that means "box office," not "location."

summer is the time for several wonderful music festivals, including **Solidays,** which receives an international line up of pop artists, and **Jazz à La Villette** (https://jazzalavillette.com), many of which take place in Paris's lovely parks and gardens.

GETTING TICKETS You can get tickets in person at **Fnac,** the giant bookstore/music chain that has one of the most comprehensive box offices in the city (a central location open daily is at Galerie du Claridge, 74 av. des Champs-Elysées; follow the signs to the "Billeterie"). You can also **order your tickets online in English** at www.fnactickets.com or by phone at ℂ **01-41-57-32-19. Ticketmaster.fr** offers a similar service.

Discount hunters can stand in line at one of the city's three **half-price ticket booths,** all run by **Le Kiosque Théâtre** (www.kiosque culture.com). One is in front of the Montparnasse train station (place Raoul Dautry; Tues–Sat 12:30–2:30pm and 3–7:30pm), another on the west side of the Madeleine (facing 15 pl. de la Madeleine, exit rue Tronchet from the Madeleine Métro stop; Tues–Sat 12:30–2:30pm and 3–7:30pm, Sun 12:30–3:45pm), and a third in Paris's main tourist office (29 rue de Rivoli, 4th arrond.; Tues–Sat 12:30–5:30pm, Sun 12:30–3:45pm). Plenty of ticket discounts can also be had at **BilletRéduc,** www.billetreduc.com (in French).

Theater

Paris has hundreds of theaters, many of which have nightly offerings. Although most of it is in French, you can find a few English-language shows (see "Entertainment in English," below). Of course, avant-garde shows combining dance, theater, and images really need no translation.

Entertainment in English

English-language performances are rare, but there are a few comedy nights that are worth a detour. One of the best stand-up performers is **Paul Taylor** (https://paultaylorcomedy.com), who plays at numerous theaters and even fills up big concert venue like the Zenith (https://le-zenith.com). Another good one is **Sebastien Marx** (https://sebmarx.com/en), who presents the **"New York Comedy Night,"** every Saturday at 10pm at the Petit Palais des Glaces (www.palaisdesglaces.com), where multiple local comics perform, along with the occasional international star. And look out for American **Sarah Donnelly** (www.sarahdcomedy.com), whose stand-up show is often at the Théâtre Bo (https://en.theatrebo.fr). For open-mic nights, check the **Comedy in Paris** website (www.comedyinparis.com). And if you're looking for "theater" proper, an excellent English-language box-office service is **Theatre in Paris** (www.theatreinparis.com), with tickets to multiple shows offering English supertitles.

Comédie-Française ★★ Established by Louis XVI in 1680, this legendary theater is the temple of classic French theater (Corneille, Racine, Molière), though in recent decades the troupe has branched out into more modern territory. In addition to the gorgeous main theater **(Salle Richelieu),** the company presents its offerings in its two other theaters: the medium-size **Théâtre du Vieux Colombier** (21 rue du Vieux Colombier, 6th arrond.; ✆ **01-44-39-87-00;** Métro: St-Sulpice or Sèvres–Babylone) and the smaller **Studio-Théâtre** (Galerie du Carrousel du Louvre, under the Pyramid, 99 rue de Rivoli, 1st arrond.; Métro: Palais Royal–Musée du Louvre). pl. Colette, 1st arrond. www.comedie-francaise.fr. ✆ **01-44-58-15-15.** Métro: Palais-Royal–Musée du Louvre.

Théâtre National de Chaillot ★★ Dance and theater are on equal footing at this beautiful Art Deco theater in the Palais de Chaillot, where contemporary choreographers and theater directors share a jam-packed program. There is a lot of blurring of lines here between the two disciplines; dance programs often include video and text, and theater productions often incorporate the abstract. 1 pl. du Trocadéro, 16th arrond. www.theatre-chaillot.fr. ✆ **01-53-65-30-00.** Métro: Trocadéro.

Opera, Dance & Classical Concerts

Opéra Comique/Salle Favart ★★ For a lighter take on opera, try this architectural puff pastry filled with operettas and (French) musicals. Created in 1714 for theatrical performances that included songs, the Opéra Comique endured several fires before finally settling down in a beautiful 19th-century theater complete with huge chandeliers. An excellent opportunity to enjoy both history and music in a splendid setting. 5 rue Favart, 2nd arrond. www.opera-comique.com. ✆ **01-70-23-01-31.** Métro: Richelieu–Drouot or Quatre-Septembre.

Opéra de Paris ★★★ This mighty operation includes both the **Palais Garnier** (pl. de l'Opéra, 9th arrond.; p. 99), an attraction in itself, and the **Opéra Bastille** (2 pl. de la Bastille, 12th arrond.) a slate-colored behemoth that has loomed over the place de la Bastille since 1989. The company splits its energies between the two venues. In theory, more operas are performed at the Bastille, which has more space and top-notch acoustics, and the Garnier, home of the **Ballet de l'Opéra de Paris,** focuses more on dance, but the reality is you can see either at both. Subtitles are often in English. www.operadeparis.fr. ✆ **08-92-89-90-90,** +33 (0)1-71-25-24-23 from outside France.

Philharmonie de Paris ★★★ Hovering over La Villette like a visiting spaceship, this mega venue seats 2,400 spectators and serves as the new home of the Orchestre de Paris. Yet another creation of über-architect

Jean Nouvel (this time in partnership with Harold Marshall and with input from Yasuhisa Toyota), this silvery apparition also encompasses a music museum and other performance spaces in the adjacent **Cité de la Musique,** as well as a nifty cafe and restaurant. The season includes symphonic and choral concerts, as well as a good dose of the offbeat and unexpected, like a silent film accompanied by the music of Philip Glass, or a weekend of dance and music dedicated to African women. 221 av. Jean-Jaurès, 19th arrond. https://philharmoniede paris.fr. ℂ **01-44-84-44-84.** Métro: Porte de Pantin.

The ultra-contemporary Philharmonie de Paris.

Cabaret

Some visitors feel they simply haven't had the true Paris experience without seeing a show at the Moulin Rouge. Today's audiences are more likely to arrive in tour buses than touring cars, and the shows are more Vegas than Paris. What you will see here is a lot of scenic razzmatazz and many sublime female bodies, mostly *torse nue* (topless).

The Crazy Horse ★   This temple to "The Art of the Nude" presents an erotic dance show with artistic aspirations. Be advised that unlike the other shows, this one is known for what the girls *aren't* wearing. The performers, who slither, swagger, and lip-synch with panache, have names like Zula Zazou and Nooka Karamel. ***Note:*** While it has no dining on site, it has fairly priced dinner-show packages with nearby Asian fusion restaurant Ginger. An average three-course meal at Ginger costs around 70€. The show alone is 115€. Separately, you'd pay 185€, whereas the dinner and show packages start at 180€. 12 av. George V, 8th arrond. www.lecrazy horseparis.com. ℂ **01-47-23-32-32.** 115€ show only, from 135€ show and champagne, show plus dinner packages 180€–250€. Métro: George V or Alma Marceau.

Moulin Rouge ★   When it opened in 1889, the Moulin Rouge was the talk of the town, and its huge dance floor, multiple mirrors, and floral garden inspired painters like Toulouse-Lautrec. Times have changed— today's Moulin Rouge relies heavily on lip-synching and pre-recorded music, backed up by dozens of befeathered Doriss Girls, long-legged ladies who prance about the stage. If kitsch is not your thing, go instead to the next-door nightclub, replete with a rooftop cocktail bar (**Machine du Moulin Rouge;** p. 185). 82 bd. Clichy, pl. Blanche, 18th arrond. www.moulin rouge.fr. ℂ **01-53-09-82-82.** 113€–198€ show alone, 235€–290€ show with dinner. Métro: Blanche.

Jazz Clubs

Paris has been a fan of jazz from its beginnings, and many legendary performers like Sidney Bechet and Kenny Clark made the city their home. Still a haven for jazz musicians and fans of all stripes, Paris offers dozens of places to duck in and listen to a good set or two. Here are a few of the best:

Baiser Salé ★★   On a street lined with famous jazz clubs, this one holds its own with a lineup that shows off jazz in all its diversity. Some of the biggest Franco-African jazz stars, like Richard Bona and Angelique Kidjo, got their start here, and the program still highlights the best in African, Caribbean, and Asian, as well as French jazz. Regular jam sessions are on Sundays and Mondays. 58 rue des Lombards, 1st arrond. www.lebaiser sale.com. ℂ **01-42-33-37-71.** Cover free–25€, depending on the act. Métro: Châtelet.

The Moulin Rouge.

Le Sunset/Le Sunside ★★   One of several famous jazz clubs on rue des Lombards (and it's a short street!), this one has a split personality. Le Sunset Jazz is dedicated to electric jazz and world music, whereas le Sunside hosts mainly acoustic jazz. The hottest names in French jazz appear here regularly (Jacky Terrasson, Pierre-Yves Plat) along with international stars. 60 rue des Lombards, 1st arrond. www.sunset-sunside.com. ✆ **01-40-26-46-60.** Tickets free–35€. Métro: Châtelet.

New Morning ★★★   If you are looking for big names and hot acts, look no further. This place has lineups of jazz giants, pop legends, and international superstars, as well as top-grade local talent. This relatively large club (the room holds about 300) fills up quickly, and no wonder: This truly is one of the best jazz venues in town, and the top ticket price is only around 30€. 7 rue des Petites-Ecuries, 10th arrond. www.newmorning.com. No phone. Cover from 30€. Métro: Château-d'Eau.

The Bar Scene

Paris may not be the 24-hour party city some other international capitals claim to be, but it has plenty of places to sip, flirt, and be merry. The bars in such hotels as **La Fantaisie** (p. 138) and **TOO Hotel** (p. 144) draw a very Parisian crowd. But no matter where you go, in general, bars stay open until around 2am.

Andy Wahloo ★★   North African kitsch meets 1970s glam at this ultra-cool bar, a stalwart with the hip crowd since 2004—no mean feat in Paris. It's secret? Friendly bartenders who outdo themselves working up clever cocktails. 69 rue des Gravilliers, 3rd arrond. www.andywahloo-bar.com. ✆ **01-42-71-20-38.** Métro: Arts et Métiers.

Café Charbon ★★   A turn-of-the-20th-century beauty, this cafe welcomes hordes of happy night owls under its arched ceilings. The door in the back leads to the nightclub, **Nouveau Casino** (p. 185), where live bands and DJs shake it up until the wee hours. You can come here any time of day for coffee, a drink, or a decent meal. 109 rue Oberkampf, 11th arrond. http://lecafecharbon.fr. ✆ **01-43-57-55-13.** Métro: Parmentier or Ménilmontant.

Le Bar du Plaza Athénée ★★   Knock yourself out and order a shockingly expensive drink at this classy, historic joint, which simply drips with glamour and fabulousness. The bar itself literally glows (it's lit from inside), fashioning an even more luminous aura around the sleek patrons. Hotel Plaza-Athénée, 25 av. Montaigne, 8th arrond. www.dorchestercollection.com/paris/hotel-plaza-athenee. ✆ **01-53-67-66-65.** Métro: Alma-Marceau.

WINE BARS

Le Baron Rouge ★★   This neighborhood institution spills out onto a corner that it shares with the sprawling Marché d'Aligre, a giant outdoor and covered market. It only has a few tables, but most people stand at the counter or outside, glass in hand, especially during market hours. It's a little rough-and-tumble getting your drink order in at the bar, but that's half the fun. 1 rue Théophile Roussel, 12th arrond. ✆ **01-43-43-14-32.** Métro: Ledru-Rollin.

Le Perchoir ★★★ Take in a fabulous view of eastern Paris from this rooftop bar, which has been so successful it has spawned a passel of other high-altitude nightspots on top of buildings in the Marais, Buttes Chaumont, and even (in summer) on the roof of the Gare de l'Est (check website for all locations). Sip a cocktail on an outdoor sofa and gaze at the Sacré-Coeur, or flirt at the tented bar. It's popular, so reserve at least a week ahead. 14 rue Crespin du Gast, 11th arrond. https://leperchoir.fr. ✆ **01-48-06-18-48.** Métro: Ménilmontant.

The Club Scene

If you want to go out to a *boîte de nuit* (nightclub), you'll have plenty to choose from in Paris. Keep in mind that the French love their fashion, so dressing to impress is obligatory—sneakers will rarely get you past the line outside. Most clubs don't get going until at least 11pm, if not later.

NIGHTCLUBS

Machine du Moulin Rouge ★★ A heck of a lot hipper than its historic next-door neighbor, this three-story club has dance floors, concert space, and bars—basically, everything you need for a rollicking night out. The music-savvy crowds come for electronic everything: rock, funk, pop, dubstep, glitch, drum'n'bass, house—not to mention live music by rising stars. There's also a seasonal rooftop and a champagne bar that serves copious platters and plonks you right below the famous windmill—a fab selfie spot. 90 bd. de Clichy, 18th arrond. www.lamachinedumoulinrouge.com. ✆ **01-53-41-88-89.** Métro: Blanche.

Nouveau Casino ★★ This former movie theater is now a giant dance club with live music, a huge bar that vaguely resembles an iceberg, hanging chandeliers, and a terrific program that includes all sorts of avant-garde dance music and bands with names like Moon Safari Club. 109 rue Oberkampf, 9th arrond. http://nouveaucasino.fr. ✆ **01-43-57-57-40.** Métro: St-Maur, Parmentier, or Ménilmontant.

LGBTQ BARS & CLUBS

Paris has a vibrant LGBTQ nightlife scene, primarily centered around the **Marais.** Pick up one of the magazines devoted to the subject—like *Qweek* (www.qweek.fr)—for free in gay bars and bookstores. Also look for *Têtu* magazine at newsstands—it has special nightlife sections. Both publications are in French.

4

PARIS

Entertainment & Nightlife

Bonjour Madame ★★   A new spot for dining, drinking "margayritas," debating, and attending concerts and exhibitions, this isn't a lesbian bar per se, but it has a feminist slant and a desire to welcome the LGBTQ community. To find out what's on, check out the Facebook page www.facebook.com/bonjourmadame.paris11. 40 rue de Montreuil, 11th arrond. ℰ **09-83-51-61-33.** Métro: Faidherbe-Chaligny or Rue des Boulets.

Le Cox ★★   You'll know it when you get here: A ginormous sausage protrudes out of the wall into the street, and a crowd spills out onto the sidewalk. Le Cox is popular despite its age; people come for the bar as well as the great DJs. The clientele is a pleasant mix of tourists and Parisians. 15 rue des Archives, 4th arrond. www.cox.fr. ℰ **01-42-72-08-00.** Métro: Hôtel de Ville.

Le Tango (aka La Boîte à Frissons) ★   This wacky hetero-friendly LGBT dance hall plays all sorts of cheesy pop and accordion music. Arrive early for foxtrot and tango lessons, or come later for the DJ who'll play everything except techno. 13 rue au Maire, 2nd arrond. ℰ **01-42-72-17-78.** https://tangoparis.com. Métro: Arts et Métiers.

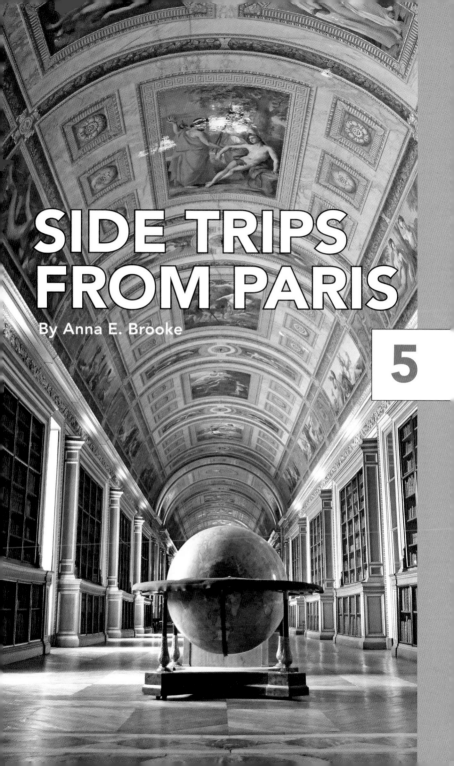

SIDE TRIPS
FROM PARIS

By Anna E. Brooke

5

Whether you are escaping Paris for the day or embarking on an adventure to another part of France, plenty of wonderful destinations are just 1 hour from the capital. Royal castles like **Versailles, Vaux-le-Vicomte,** and **Fontaine-bleau,** as well as the forest of **Rambouillet,** and even **Disneyland** and **Parc Astérix** are all within the borders of the Ile-de-France, which is not an island but a region encompassing Paris and its outer environs (also known as Greater Paris). Just outside its borders but still within easy reach are Monet's famous gardens at **Giverny,** the stained-glass windows of the cathedral of **Chartres** and the floating gardens of Amiens.

Your main problem will be deciding where to go. If you've never been there, your first choice should probably be the château and gardens of **Versailles.** They're close by, easily accessible by train, and truly mind-blowing. **Chartres** would be my second choice, for its breathtaking Gothic cathedral, winding streets, and half-timbered houses. After that, it's a toss-up. If you like cities, **Amiens** is fascinating, with its Gothic cathedral, floating gardens and Jules Verne's former home. If castles are your game, **Fontainebleau** and **Vaux-le-Vicomte** should be high on your list. Fans of Claude Monet will love exploring the gardens at **Giverny,** and families with kids in tow will appreciate **Parc Astérix,** a theme park dedicated to beloved French comic character, Asterix the Gaul, and (of course) **Disneyland Paris.**

VERSAILLES ★★★

21km (13 miles) SW of Paris; 71km (44 miles) NE of Chartres

The grandeur of the Château of Versailles is hard to imagine until you are standing in front of it. Immediately, you start to get an idea of the power (and ego) of the man who was behind it, King Louis XIV. One of the largest castles in Europe, it is also forever associated with another, less fortunate king, Louis XVI and his wife Queen Marie Antoinette, who were both forced to flee when the French Revolution arrived at their sumptuous doorstep. The palace's extraordinary gardens, designed by the legendary landscape architect André Le Nôtre, are almost worth the visit on their own.

PREVIOUS PAGE: **The library at Fontainebleau.**

Don't feel you have to see everything! For many, a visit to the palace is enough culture, and a nice relaxing stroll/picnic/nap in the park is a great way to finish off the day. If you can't handle crowds but you still want to get a taste of life during the Ancien Régime, you could just visit Marie Antoinette's Estate—you'll miss the palace, but you'll get to revel in a beautiful garden and see the pretty Trianons, hamlet, and other small buildings.

Essentials

ARRIVING   Take the **RER C** (www.transilien.fr; 30 min. from the Champs de Mars station) to **Versailles Rive Gauche–Château de Versailles.** Make sure the final destination for your train is Versailles Rive Gauche and *not* Versailles Chantier, which will leave you on the other end of town, a long walk from the Château. Even worse, the Versailles Chantier trains actually run in the opposite direction, touring all around Paris before arriving at Versailles, which will add 1 hour or so to your journey. Assuming you've taken the right train, it's about a 5-minute walk from the train station to the Château. For a little more (4.95€ adults one-way), you can also take the **SNCF** Transilien suburban train (www.transilien.fr; 36 min.) from the Gare St-Lazare station to **Versailles-Rive Droite,** and then walk about 10 minutes to the Château (around 45 min. total). This is a great option if you plan to picnic in the palace grounds, as you'll go down Rue du Maréchal Foch, past a U Express supermarket (no. 45) and **Marché Notre-Dame** (p. 198), the town's main market, where you can fill up on French delights. Glass is permitted in the park, so don't feel you have to skimp on wine!

Unless you have a **Paris Visite** (p. 75) or other pass that includes zones 1 to 5, you will need to buy a special ticket (one-way fare 4.05€ adults, 2€ children ages 4–10, free for 3 and under); a regular Métro ticket will not suffice. You can buy a ticket from any Métro or RER station; the fare includes a free transfer on the Métro.

TICKETS   If you are made of tough stuff and want to see everything, you can buy the all-inclusive, 1- or 2-day **Château Passeport,** which grants you access to the main château, the gardens, the Trianon Palaces, and the Marie Antoinette Estate (1 day Nov–Mar 21.50 € adults; Apr–Oct including *Les Grandes Eaux Musicales* 28.50€ adults; 2 days Nov–Mar 25€, Apr-Oct 30€; free for children 17 and under). If you'd like to make an overnight of it (and it's worth doing, as Versailles is such a lovely city), consider the **2-day Passeport.** If you have limited time and energy, you can buy a **ticket to just the Palace** (19.50€, free for children 17 and under) or **just the Trianons and Marie Antoinette's Estate** (12€).

VISITOR INFORMATION Château de Versailles, www.chateau versailles.fr; ℂ **01-30-83-78-00; Palace:** Apr–Oct Tues–Sun 9am–6:30pm; Nov–Mar Tues–Sun 9am–5:30pm. **Marie Antoinette's Estate:** Tues–Sun noon–5:30. **Garden and park:** Apr–Oct daily 7am–8:30pm; Nov–Mar daily 8am–6pm. **Versailles Tourist Office:** Place Lyautey (opposite the Versailles Rive-Gauche station; www.versailles-tourisme. com; ℂ **01-39-24-88-88**).

EVENING SHOWS   From mid-June to mid-September, there are spectacular **fountain night shows** (31€ adults, 27€ ages 6–17), where you stroll around the gardens and enjoy illuminated fountains, music, and fireworks.

And most of the year, the **Opéra Royal,** Louis XV's chef d'oeuvre, built in 1770, opens to the public for opera, theatre and ballet performances. Restored to its 18th-century glory, it's a magical place to take in a show (prices from 40€).

DAYTIME SHOWS   From April to October on weekends and Tuesdays, fountains play to Baroque music throughout the gardens closest to the castle, otherwise known as *Les Grandes Eaux Musicales* (depending on

Versailles is so popular you will not be alone, so grin and bear it. But there are two little-known ways to avoid the lines at the entrance and waltz straight in. **The first:** Reserve a 90-minute guided tour in English (10€ on top of your entry ticket, free for children 9 and under). You will be given a time slot and enter the château via a different door to the masses so you shouldn't have to wait. Once the tour is over, you're free to roam the rest of the palace and gardens. **The second:** Go for early lunch in world-famous chef Alain

Ducasse's new restaurant Ore, set inside the palace. Open from 11:30am, you can buy a lunch/passport ticket for 85€ (that's 56.50€ for a three-course meal, plus mineral water and a glass of wine. Excellent value, as the three-course lunch alone costs 55€!) then head straight into the palace without even seeing the snaking lines outside. And as a general rule, remember that **Versailles is busiest on weekends and on Tuesdays** (when many Parisian museums are closed), so the quietest days are Wednesday to Friday.

your ticket, this could be included; otherwise 10.50€, 9€ children ages 6–17). If your ticket does not offer entrance to this part of the gardens, the rest of the park is accessible from side entrances for free.

The **Académie Equestre de Versailles** (www.bartabas.fr) is housed in the **Les Grandes Ecuries** (royal stables), a palatial edifice immediately opposite the château. Both the school and its shows are directed by Bartabas, whose equestrian theater company, Zingaro, has garnered world fame. On weekend afternoons (Sat 6pm, Sun 5pm; 16€–28€), you can watch their "equestrian ballet" in full swing. You can also buy a combined 2-day passport with the show included for 44.50€ (and with the Grandes Eaux Musicales for 53.50€). After the shows, visitors can tour the stables. Buy tickets at www.chateauversailles.fr.

TICKETS   Unless otherwise stated, purchase tickets to the shows at the château, online at www.chateauversailles-spectacles.fr.

The Château of Versailles

Back in the 17th century, after having been badly burned by a nasty uprising called Le Fronde, Louis XIV decided to move his court from Paris to Versailles, a safe distance from the intrigues of the capital. He also decided to have the court move in with him, where he could keep a close eye on them and nip any new plots or conspiracies in the bud. This required a new abode that was not only big enough to house his court (anywhere from 3,000 to 10,000 people would be palace guests on any given day), but also one that would be grand enough to let the world know who was in charge.

A château was already on the site when Louis came to town; his father, Louis XIII, had built a small castle, "a hunting lodge," there in

Château of Versailles.

1623. Louis, aka the "Sun King," brought in architects, artists, and gardeners to enlarge the castle and give it a new look. In 1668, architect Louis Le Vau, began work on the enormous "envelope," which literally wrapped the old castle in a second building.

Meanwhile, legendary garden designer André Le Notre was carving out formal gardens and a huge park out of what had been marshy countryside. Thousands of trees were planted, and harmonious geometric designs were achieved with flower beds, hedges, canals, and pebbled pathways dotted with sculptures and fountains.

Construction involved as many as 36,000 workers and ground on for years; in 1682 the King and his court moved in, but work went on right through the rest of his reign and into that of Louis XV. Louis XVI and his wife, Marie Antoinette, made few changes, but history made a gigantic one for them: On October 6, 1789, an angry mob of Parisians marched on the palace and the royal couple was forced to return to Paris. Versailles would never again be a royal residence.

The palace was ransacked during the Revolution, and in the years after it fell far from its original state of grace. Napoleon and Louis XVIII did what they could to bring the sleeping giant back to life, but by the

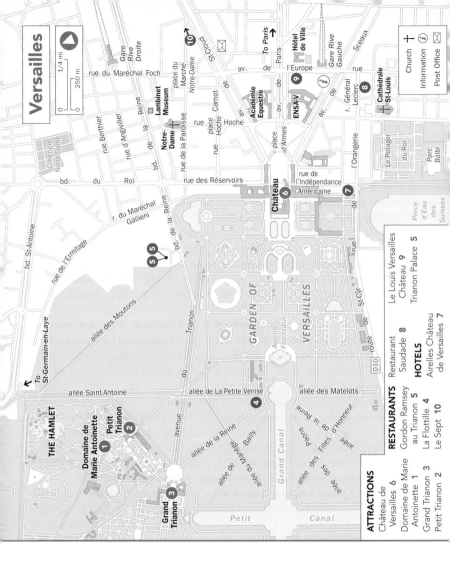

early 1800s, during the reign of Louis-Philippe, the castle was slated for demolition. Fortunately for us, this forward-thinking king decided to invest his own money to save Versailles for future generations, and in 1837 the vast structure was made into a national museum. Little by little, precious furniture and art objects were retrieved or re-created; paintings, wall decorations, and ceilings were restored. Not surprisingly, restoration is ongoing, so be prepared for the unexpected when you arrive. Even if a few areas are closed, the place is so huge that should you feel so inclined, you can still tour yourself into a 17th-century stupor.

TOURING THE PALACE

The "envelope," or the newer part of the building, includes a series of rooms called the **Grand Apartments,** used primarily for ceremonial events (a daily occurrence), the **Queen's Apartments,** and the **Galerie des Glaces.** These, along with the **King's Apartments,** and the **Chapel,** are the must-sees of the palace. If you have time and fortitude, you can take a **guided visit** to the royal family's private apartments (10€ on top of your ticket, some in English; schedule is online) to see a more intimate look at castle life and skip the lines at the entrance (p. 191).

Each room in the **Grand Apartments ★★★** is dedicated to a different planet, and each has a fabulous painting on the ceiling depicting the god or goddess associated with said heavenly sphere. The first and probably the most staggering paintings are in the **Salon d'Hercule ★★:** an enormous canvas by Paolo Veronese, *Christ at Supper with Simon,* and a splendid, divinity-bedecked ceiling portraying Hercules being welcomed by the gods of Olympus by Antoine Lemoyne. The **Salon d'Apollon ★★**, not surprisingly, was the throne room, where the Sun King would receive ambassadors and other heads of state.

The ornate **Salon de Guerre ★★** and **Salon de Paix ★★** bookend the most famous room in the place, the recently restored **Galerie des Glaces (the Hall of Mirrors) ★★★.** Louis XIV commanded his painter-in-chief, Charles Le Brun, to paint the 12m-high (40-ft.) ceiling of this 73m-long (240-ft.) gallery with representations of his accomplishments. This masterwork is illuminated by light from the 17 windows that overlook the garden, which are matched on the opposite wall by 17 mirrored panels. This splendid setting was the scene of a historic event in a more recent century: In 1919, World War I officially ended when the Treaty of Versailles was signed here. In 2023, President Macron threw a decadent banquet there for the UK's King Charles III and Queen Camilla.

The **Queen's Apartments ★★** include a gorgeous bedroom with silk hangings printed with lilacs and peacock feathers, which looks exactly as it did in 1789, when the Queen, Marie Antoinette, was forced to flee revolutionary mobs through a secret door (barely visible in the wall near her bed). The **King's Apartments ★★★** are even more splendiferous, though in a very different style: Here, the ceilings have been left blank white, which brings out the elaborate white and gold decoration on the walls. The **King's bedroom ★★★,** hung from top to bottom with gold brocade, is fitted with a banister that separated the King from the 100 or so people who would watch him wake up in the morning.

You should also make sure to see the **Chapel ★★★,** a masterpiece of light and harmony by Jules Hardouin Mansart, where the kings attended mass. This lofty space (the ceiling is more than 25m/82 ft. high) reflects both Gothic and Baroque styles, combining a vaulted roof, stained glass,

The Hall of Mirrors, Versailles.

and gargoyles with columns and balustrades typical of the early 18th century.

TOURING THE DOMAINE DE MARIE ANTOINETTE

Northwest of the fountain lies the **Domaine de Marie Antoinette ★★★** (if you don't have a Château passport or museum pass, you'll buy a separate ticket to get in). It was here that the young queen sought refuge from the strict protocol and infighting at the castle. Her husband gave her the **Petit Trianon ★★**, a small manor that Louis XV used for his trysts, which she transformed into a stylish haven. She created an entire world around it, including a splendid **English garden ★★**, several lovely pavilions, a jewel-like **theater ★★**, and even a small **hamlet ★★** with a working farm and a dairy, where she and her friends would play cards and gossip, or just stroll in the "country." Although the **Grand Trianon ★★** is not really linked to the story of Marie Antoinette, it is worth a brief visit. Built by Louis XIV as a retreat for himself and his family, this small marble palace consists of two large wings connected by an open columned terrace from which there is a delightful **view ★★** of the gardens. The furniture and decor dates from the Napoleonic era.

TOURING THE GARDENS & PARK

The entire 800-hectare (2,000-acre) park is laid out according to a precise, symmetrical plan. From the terrace behind the castle is an astounding **view ★★★** that runs past two parterres, down a central lawn (the Tapis Vert), down the **Grand Canal ★★** and seemingly on into infinity. Le Nôtre's masterpiece is the ultimate example of French-style gardens; geometric, logical, and in perfect harmony—a reflection of the divine order of the cosmos. A solar theme is reflected in the statues and fountains along the main axis of the perspective; the most magnificent of these is the **Apollo Fountain ★★★** where the sun god emerges from the waves at dawn on his chariot. On the sides of the main axis, near the castle, are a set of six groves, or **bosquets ★★**, leafy mini-gardens hidden by walls of shrubbery; some were used as small outdoor ballrooms for festivities, others for intimate rendezvous out of reach of the prying eyes of the court. Today, you

One of many fountains in the gardens at Versailles.

can **picnic, bike ride** (bikes can be rented next to the restaurant), or even **row a boat** on a sunny day.

Where to Stay

EXPENSIVE

Trianon Palace, a Waldorf Astoria Hotel ★★★ Versailles is close enough to Paris that you don't need to spend the night, but if you are celebrating something special or have bought the 2-day passport, this is one of the poshest hotels in the Ile de France. Elegant gardens and grounds, an indoor heated pool, 19th-century frills, luxurious rooms, and a one-star Michelin restaurant with a famous Scottish chef, **Gordon Ramsey au Trianon** (see below). A more low-key dining option is La Veranda, and if you need total relaxation, there's a Guerlain spa.

1 bd. de la Reine. www.waldorfastoriaversailles.fr/trianon-palace. ℂ **01-30-84-50-00.** 199 units. 260€–650€ double; 360€–900€ jr. suite; from 1,000€ suite. Parking 30€. **Amenities:** 2 restaurants; bar; concierge; indoor pool; spa; free Wi-Fi.

MODERATE

Le Louis Versailles Château ★★★ This hip hotel was built on the site of Napoleon III's former military barracks (the original 19th-c. arch

Fancy a night in the palace? You're in luck (if you have the budget). You can sleep like the Sun King at Versailles' new **Airelles Château de Versailles, Le Grand Contrôle** hotel, set in three palatial 17th-century buildings on the château's grounds. Each of the 14 rooms costs a pretty packet (from around 2,000€/night), but boy, are they special: busy French country–style decor with bold patterns, chandeliers, antique furniture, palatial bathrooms, and views over the Orangerie (the royal citrus grove).

Food-wise, expect French classics with a modern twist, courtesy of celebrated French chef Alain Ducasse. There's also a sumptuous spa by Valmont (famed for their cellular cosmetics). The most exciting part, perhaps, is that guests get daily private after-hours tours of the palace, so you can walk its endless gilded chambers and really get a feel for what royal life would have been like without the crowds. www.airelles.com/en; *℄* **01-85-36-05-50.**

still fronts the building), a 5-minute walk from the château's entrance. All bedrooms flaunt a chic contemporary style; some suites add a touch of pizazz with crystal chandeliers and painted ceilings. If you've still got energy after a day in the château, there's a gym with a sauna. Or you could opt for a cocktail at the bar, before dinner at Alcôve, the hotel's excellent restaurant, serving creative dishes like flambéed shrimp with saffron ratatouille and Thai-style beef tartare with fries for about 34€.

2 bis avenue de Paris. https://all.accor.com. *℄* **01-39-07-46-46.** 152 units. 170€–297€ double; 220€–600€ suite. **Amenities:** Restaurant; bar; gym, sauna, room service; free Wi-Fi.

Where to Eat

EXPENSIVE

Gordon Ramsay au Trianon ★★★ FRENCH/INTERNATIONAL The *enfant terrible* of chefs, Gordon Ramsay, invaded Versailles and is king of the roost at this stylish restaurant inside the swanky Trianon Palace Hotel. He is a master at traditional French cooking done in a modern style and changes his menu frequently to take advantage of the best and the freshest in any season. No one does filet of turbot like Ramsay. But the same could be said of his Brittany lobster with 100-year-old balsamic vinegar and signature duck with persimmon and Grand Marnier. He stuffs delectable ravioli with langoustines, and you can toss a pork belly his way, and he'll create a culinary masterpiece for you. The service, the setting, everything here is a delight. In summer, you can dine under the canopy on the front terrace. Reservations required.

In the Hotel Trianon Palace, 1 bd. de la Reine. www.trianonpalace.com. *℄* **01-30-84-55-55.** Fixed-price menu 160€–199€. Tues–Sat 7:30–9:30pm. Closed 1 week in Jan and 1 week in Mar.

MODERATE

Restaurant Saudade ★★ PORTUGUESE   This little bistro opened in 1966, and though just 7 minutes on foot from the palace, makes for an ideal lunch or dinner spot away from the maddening crowds. Sitting in a rustic-chic setting of tile walls, wood floors and Chesterfield-style chairs, you'll enjoy lip-smacking Portuguese dishes like suckling pig with orange and carrot puree, and hunky *polvo à lagareiro* (octopus and herby potatoes). Music with that? One or two Fridays a month, musicians play traditional Fado.

20 rue du Général Leclerc. https://restaurant-saudade-versailles.eatbu.com. *℘* **01-30-21-23-43.** Main courses 16€–26€. Tues–Sun 10am–3:30pm and 6–11:30pm.

INEXPENSIVE

La Flottille ★ FRENCH   One of the few restaurants inside the château's grounds (at the head of the Grand Canal), this Belle Époque-style bistro has a sweeping view over some of Europe's most famous landscaping. Both restaurant and snack-bar service are available. The traditional French cuisine is nothing special, but not bad, making this a handy place to have up your sleeve in such a touristy spot. In warm weather, meals are also served at outside tables. Reservations are recommended.

Parc du Château. https://laflottille.fr. *℘* **01-39-51-41-58.** Main courses 12€–24€. Daily 8am–7pm (5pm Nov–Mar).

Le Sept ★★ WINE RESTAURANT/BOUTIQUE   You'll want to reserve in advance for a table in this bistro-cum-wine-shop, where hearty homemade dishes like duck terrine, entrecote, and apple tart are served alongside a choice of 200 wines, most of them biodynamic, sold at 15€ above shop price, if you eat in (takeout is shop price). Le Sept's motto? Only serve quality, seasonal produce from traceable, hand-picked sources. And it shows: The beef (from an artisan farmer in Normandy) cuts like butter, and the small plates of cheese and cold meats are flavor explosions unto themselves. Reservations are required.

7 rue de Montreuil. lesept-versailles.com. *℘* **01-39-49-55-27.** Main courses 18€–22€; fixed-price lunch menus 24€. Tues–Sat noon–2pm and 7–9:30pm.

Shopping

Founded by the Sun King himself, Louis XIV, **Marché Notre-Dame,** pl. du Marché Notre-Dame, is the major public market in Versailles, housed in a series of red-brick buildings. The present look dates from the 19th century. Indoor shops selling local cheeses, meats, and fresh fruits are open Tuesday to Sunday 7am to 7:30pm (until 2pm Sun), but the outdoor stalls in the center of the square flourish only on Tuesday, Friday, and Sunday, from about 9am to 2pm. It's best to go before noon; some of the stalls start shutting down in the early afternoon.

Close to the mammoth market, **Passage de la Geôle** (www.antiques-versailles.com; ✆ **01-30-21-15-13**) is open Friday to Sunday 10am to 7pm, housing antiques shops of furniture and objets d'art at "all prices."

Versailles Nightlife

In addition to the bars in the afore-listed hotels, try **O'Paris Pub,** 15 rue Colbert, off place d'Armes (www.puboparis.com; ✆ **01-39-50-36-12**), an Irish pub where you can order the best brews in town and where, in warm weather, seating spills out into the street outside to offer views of the châ-teau. And the Basque country comes to Versailles at **L'Équilibre,** 8 rue des Deux Portes (https://equilibre-bar.com; ✆ **01-39-49-42-68**), a bar close to the market where a bottle of wine (there are 30 to choose from) and a good companion should get you through an evening, enhanced by tapas such as delicious Spanish hams and local cheeses.

CHARTRES ★★★

88km (58 miles) SW of Paris; 76km (47 miles) NW of Orléans

You'll see it long before you see the actual town: the spire of the cathedral of Chartres rising above a sea of wheat fields. About 1 hour from Paris, you can easily visit this stunning church and its inspiring stain-glassed windows and still have enough time to wander through the narrow streets of the old town.

Essentials

ARRIVING   Direct **trains** leave from Paris' Gare Montparnasse and take just over 1 hour (from 10€ one-way). For information visit www.sncf-connect.com or call ✆ **36-35.** If **driving** from Paris take A10/A11 south-west and follow signs to Le Mans and Chartres. The Chartres exit is marked.

VISITOR INFORMATION   The **Office de Tourisme** in the Maison du Saumon, 8 rue de la Poissonerie (www.chartres-tourisme.com; ✆ **02-37-18-26-26**).

Exploring the Cathedral

With its carved portals and three-tiered flying buttresses, this cathedral would be a stunning sight even without its legendary **stained-glass windows**—though the world would be a drearier place. For these ancient glass panels are truly glorious: a kaleidoscope of colors so deep, so rich, and so bright, it's hard to believe they are some 700 years old. Meant as teaching devices more than artwork, the windows functioned as a sort of enormous cartoon, telling the story of Christ through pictures to a mostly illiterate populace. From its beginnings, pilgrims came from far and near to see a piece of cloth that believers say was worn by the Virgin Mary dur-ing Christ's birth. The **relic** is still here, but these days it's primarily a different sort of pilgrim that is drawn to Chartres: More than 1.5 million tourists come here every year.

A Romanesque church stood on this spot until 1194, when a fire burnt it virtually to the ground. All that remained were the towers, the Royal Portal, and a few remnants of stained glass. The locals were so horrified that they sprung to action; in a matter of only 3 decades a new cathedral was erected, which accounts for its remarkably unified Gothic architecture. This was one of the first churches to use buttresses as a building support, allowing the architect (whose name has been lost) to build its walls at twice the height of the standard Romanesque cathedrals and make space

Stained-glass rose window at Chartres Cathedral.

for its famous windows. The new cathedral, dedicated 1260, has miraculously survived the centuries with relatively little damage. The French Revolution somehow spared the cathedral. During World War I and World War II, the precious windows were carefully dismounted piece by piece and stored in a safe place in the countryside.

The cathedral's **facade ★★★** is a remarkable assemblage of religious art and architecture. The tower to your right (the **Old Tower** or South Tower) is topped by its original sober Romanesque spire; that on your left (**New Tower** or North Tower) was blessed with an elaborate Gothic spire in the early 1500s, when the original burned down. Below is the **Royal Portal ★★★**, a masterpiece of Romanesque art. Swarming with kings, queens, prophets, and priests, this sculpted entryway tells the story of the life of Christ. You can **climb to the top of the New Tower** to

Tours, Guided & Otherwise

Public tours in English are offered by both Malcolm Miller, a scholar who has been studying the cathedral for more than 3 decades, and his collaborator of 7 years, the former Chicagoan Anne Marie Woods (noon Tues–Sat early May to late Sept; 18€ adults, 12€ ages 13–18, free for children 12 and under). Anne Marie also offers private guided tours on request (email Anne Marie Woods at annemariechartres@gmail.com for prices and information). You can also rent an **audio guide** at the cathedral bookshop (in English; usually 6.50€).

take in the **view** ★★★ and even visit the inside of the roof to admire the 19th-century metal framework (check the website for times); just remember to wear rubber-soled shoes, as the 300 steps are a little slippery after all these centuries.

As you enter the cathedral, the radiant colors of the **stained-glass windows** ★★★ pierce the dim light. Three windows on the west side of the building, as well as the beautiful rose window to the south called **Notre Dame de la Belle Verièrre** ★ date from the earlier 12th-century structure; the rest, with the exception of a few modern panels, are of 13th-century origins. The scenes depicted in glass, read from bottom to top, recount stories from the Bible as well as the lives of the saints. You will soon find yourself wondering how medieval artists, with low-tech materials, managed to create such vivid colors. The blues, in particular, seem to be divinely inspired. In fact, scientists have pierced at least part of the mystery: The blue was made with sodium and silica compounds that made the color stand up to the centuries better than other colors.

Another marvel is the **chancel enclosure** ★★★, which separates the chancel (the area behind the altar) from the ambulatory (the walkway that runs around the outer chapels). Started in 1514 by Jehan de Beauce, this intricately sculpted wall depicts dozens of saints in a recounting of the lives of the Virgin and Christ. Back in the ambulatory is the Chapel of the Martyrs, where the cathedral's cherished **relic** resides: a piece of cloth that the Virgin Mary apparently wore at the birth of Christ, which was a gift of Charles the Bald in 876.

Chartres also harbors a rare **labyrinth** ★★, traced on the floor of the cathedral near the nave. A large circle, divided into four parts, is entirely filled by a winding path that leads to the center. *Note:* The cathedral asks that visitors not talk or wander around during mass, which is generally held in the late morning and early evening. You are welcome to sit in on services, of course.

16 Cloître Notre-Dame. www.chartres-cathedrale.fr. ✆ **02-37-21-22-07.** General admission to the cathedral is free; admission to the towers and roof 6€ adults, 5€ adults 18–25, free for children 17 and under. Cathedral daily 10am–12:45 and 2–5pm (until 6pm May–Sept).

Exploring the Old Town

Give yourself a little time to explore the medieval cobbled streets of the **Vieux Quartier (Old Town)** ★★. The narrow lanes near the cathedral have several gabled houses, including the colorful facades of **rue Chantault,** one of which is 8 centuries old. Seek out rue du Bourg, where you'll find the famous **Salmon House** (which houses the tourist office) and some lovely sculptures (including a certain fish). In the lower town, you can stroll along the picturesque **Eure River** with its stone bridges and ancient wash-houses. If you go on a Saturday or Wednesday morning, a covered farmers market is in **place Billard** (until 1pm; also 4:30–7:30pm Wed), the perfect place to grab some lunch supplies for the park behind the cathedral or along the river.

Musée des Beaux-Arts de Chartres ★★ MUSEUM   Housed in an impressive former Episcopal palace, this museum of fine arts boasts a collection covering the 16th to 20th centuries, including the work of masters such as Zurbarán, Watteau, and Soutine.

29 Cloître Notre-Dame. ✆ **02-37-90-45-80.** May–Oct Thurs 10am–12:30pm and 2–8pm, Wed and Fri–Sat 10am–12:30pm and 2–6pm, Sun 2–5pm; the rest of the year, until 5pm. Free admission.

Where to Stay

Grand Monarque Best Western ★★   This appealing hotel occupies an imposing civic monument whose 600-year-old foundations and infrastructures were "gentrified" sometime in the 19th century with white stucco, neoclassical detailing, and touches of the baroque. Functioning as an inn since its original construction in the 15th century, it attracts guests who enjoy its mix of old-world and contemporary charm—such as Art Nouveau stained glass and vintage furniture in the wood-paneled bar— and those looking for a bit of pampering: Amenities include two excellent restaurants (see "Le Georges," below) and a spa with a pool and a sauna.

22 pl. des Epars. www.grand-monarque.com. ✆ **02-37-18-15-15.** 60 units. 125€–185€ double; 207€–280€ suite. Parking 10€. **Amenities:** 2 restaurants; bar; room service; spa; gym free Wi-Fi.

Jehan de Beauce Hostellerie ★★   Right by the train station, this grand old hotel has been revamped in an Art Deco style. Many of the comfortably chic rooms have bold black-and-white 1920s-inspired patterned carpets and drapes; others are subtler, with wood headboards and a gold theme. The hotel is famed for its bar, Le Fitzgerald, where you can sip champagne and cocktails to the rhythm of jazz. There's also a restaurant, and a wellness area with a sauna and a gym.

1 pl. Pierre Semard. www.jehandebeauce.fr. ✆ **02-37-21-01-41.** 35 units. 98€–175€ double; 165€–280€ suite. Parking 9€. **Amenities:** Bar; restaurant, 24-hr. room service; wellness area; free Wi-Fi.

Le Parvis ★★   Overlooking the cathedral, this restaurant with five rooms is in a great spot if you don't mind the high-season crowds. The cozy guest rooms are each individually decorated; for instance, the Pénélope room is kitschy-modern with a circular bed, while the Les Louis suite features antique-style furnishings, an old-world fireplace, and fab views of the cathedral. The brasserie-style restaurant serves French classics and has a sidewalk terrace. The wee tea salon that doubles as a boutique selling regional produce.

5 rue du Cheval Blanc (GPS); 13 pl. de la Cathédrale. www.le-parvis-chartres.fr. ✆ **02-37-21-12-12.** 5 units. 120€–180€ double. Breakfast included. **Amenities:** Restaurant; bar; tea room; free Wi-Fi.

Where to Eat

Le Georges ★★★ FRENCH   The most upscale and delicious dining experience in Chartres (with one Michelin star) is in the Grand Monarque, a hotel with roots that date from the 15th century, when the site served food and drink (not as elegant as what you'll find today) to weary travelers and postal workers. Today's diners feast in a formal, high-ceilinged dining room outfitted in soft grays and browns. Menu items change with the seasons but might include savory portions of catfish and caviar, freshly grilled scallops, or a superb Lièvre Royale (hare braised in red wine). Another specialty is Pâté de Chartres, the local meat pie. Desserts are sumptuous, and the chef Thomas Parnaud is known locally for his Grand-Marnier soufflé.

In the Grand Monarque Best Western, 22 pl. des Epars. ✆ **02-37-18-15-15.** Fixed-price menus 98€–155€. Wed–Sat noon–1:30pm; Tues–Sat 7–10pm.

Le 21 ★★ FRENCH   This quaint little bistro opposite the cathedral has a lot going for it: friendly owners and simple, honest French cuisine, like a starter of egg mayonnaise, a main course of steak in shallot sauce with baby potatoes, and roasted pear with biscuit and caramel crumble dessert. Sweet tooth? Opt for the café gourmand, a coffee served with a selection of little dessert portions that might include panna cotta, chocolate mousse, and mille-feuille. The dining room, outfitted in old wood paneling, is pleasantly low-key; ask for a spot by the window to admire the cathedral's façade as you dine.

21 Cloître Notre-Dame. ✆ **02-37-21-49-13.** Main courses 19€–23€; fixed-priced lunch 23.50€–26.50€. Tues–Sat noon–2pm; Fri–Sat 7–11pm.

Shopping

Your best shopping bet is place des Epars, a pedestrian area home to most of the apparel shops and even some haute couture boutiques. Many shops selling regional items line the narrow streets that fan southeast from the cathedral.

At **Galerie du Vitrail,** 17 Cloître Notre-Dame (www.galerie-du-vitrail.com; ✆ **02-37-36-10-03**), you'll find a huge selection of stained glass. **Lassaussois Antiquités,** 17 rue des Changes (www.antiquites lassaussois.com; ✆ **02-37-21-37-74**), specializes in antique objets d'art and contemporary furnishings.

Chartres Nightlife

For an evening of theatre (in French) or modern dance from September to June, try the **Théâtre de Chartres,** place de Ravennes (www. theatredechartres.fr; ✆ **02-37-23-42-79**). A wild night on the town probably isn't in the cards in Chartres, but the bar at the **Grand Monarch** is fun for wine or cocktails. **Le Serpente,** 2 Cloître Notre-Dame (https://leserpente.fr; ℭ **02-37-21-68-81**), by the cathedral, serves brasserie fare, stays open until midnight daily, and does an excellent Irish coffee (even decaffeinated).

RAMBOUILLET

55km (34 miles) SW of Paris; 42km (26 miles) NE of Chartres

Once known as La Forêt d'Yveline, the **Forest of Rambouillet** ★ is one of the loveliest forests in France. More than 19,000 hectares (46,930 acres) of greenery stretch from the valley of the Eure to the high valley of Chevreuse, the latter rich in medieval and royal abbeys. Lakes, copses of deer, and even wild boar are some of the attractions of this "green lung." Most people, however, come here to see the château, which you can visit when it's not in use as a "Camp David" for French presidents.

Essentials

GETTING THERE   **Trains** depart from Paris's Gare Montparnasse every 30 minutes throughout the day for a 35-minute ride. Information and train schedules can be obtained by contacting the Transilien suburban train service (www.transilien.com; 2.10€ one-way). By **car,** take N10 southwest from Paris, passing Versailles along the way.

VISITOR INFORMATION   The **tourist office** is at 1 rue du Général de Gaulle (www.rambouillet-tourisme.fr; ℭ **01-34-83-21-21**).

Touring the Château de Rambouillet ★

Stately, elegant, and surrounded by formal French gardens and a park, the château is located in one of the most famous forests in France. While its origins lie deep in the Middle Ages, most of the facades were reconstructed in the 19th century, and the interiors date from the 16th. Superb woodwork is used throughout, and the walls are adorned with tapestries, many from the era of Louis XV. François I, the Chevalier king, died of a fever here in 1547 at age 52. When the château was later occupied by the comte de Toulouse, Rambouillet was often visited by Louis XV, who was amused (in more ways than one) by the comte's high-spirited wife. Louis XVI eventually acquired the château, but Marie Antoinette found it boring and called it "the toad." In his surprisingly modest boudoir are four panels representing the continents.

After the Revolution, the Bonaparte family moved in, leaving behind the emperor's ornate bathroom, decorated with Pompeian frescos. Before his final exile to the remote island of St-Helena, Napoleon insisted on spending a final night at Rambouillet, where he secluded himself with his meditations and memories.

In 1830, the elderly Charles X, Louis XVI's brother, abdicated the throne at Rambouillet as a mob marched on the château and his troops began to desert him. From Rambouillet, he embarked for a safe but controversial haven in England. Afterward, Rambouillet fell into private hands. At one time, it was a fashionable restaurant attracting Parisians by offering gondola rides. Napoleon III returned it to the Crown. In 1896, it was designated a residence for the presidents of the republic. In 1944, Charles de Gaulle lived here briefly before giving the order for what was left of the French army to join the Americans in liberating Paris. In more recent years, major political figures like Boris Yeltsin, Nelson Mandela, and Hosni Mubarak have been château guests.

Two must-sees in the park include the **Queen's Dairy,** built for Marie Antoinette and sporting a romantic artificial grotto; and the **Shell Cottage,** a "humble" thatched cottage built for the Princess de Lamballe, whose interior is decorated with an astounding array of seashells, marble, and mother-of-pearl. Another fascinating place within the castle grounds (but requiring a separate ticket; 8.50€ adults, 3.50€ children 3–12) is the **Bergerie Nationale** (the national sheepfold; www.bergerie-nationale. educagri.fr), a small farm created by Louis XVI, famed for its rare breed of merino sheep (purebred on site since 1786). In addition to the animals, there are horse and cart rides through parts of the forest that are usually out of bounds to the public.

It takes about 2 hours to see the château at Rambouillet.

Parc du Château. www.chateau-rambouillet.fr. ℂ **01-34-83-00-25.** Admission 7.50€ adults; free for anyone 25 and under. Apr–Sept Wed–Mon 10am–noon and 1–6pm; Oct–Mar Wed–Mon 10am–noon and 1–5pm. Gardens 8am–9pm (or sundown).

Where to Eat

Orangerie des Trois Roys ★★ HAUTE FRENCH   Set in a former 17th-century girls' school, every corner of this chic restaurant oozes elegance—from the lounge's leather chesterfields and stained glass to the veranda's contemporary sculptures. On the plate expect equally refined delights like crab tartare with caviar, poached blue lobster, and Grand

---

Through an Enchanted Forest

Rambouillet and its forests can provide a verdant interlude. If you've exhausted the idea of a ramble through the gardens that surround the château (or if they're closed because of a visit from the president of France), consider a visit to the **Rochers d'Angennes,** rocky hillocks that remain as leftovers from the Ice Age. To reach them, park your car on the D107, where you'll see a sign pointing to the **Rochers et Etang d'Angennes,** about 4km (2½ miles) north of the hamlet of Epernon. Walk along a clearly marked trail through a pine forest before you eventually reach a rocky plateau overlooking the hills and a pond (*l'Etang d'Angennes*). Round-trip, from the site of your parked car to the plateau and back, your promenade should take between 30 and 45 minutes.

Marnier soufflé. Also popular are the wagu-style Charolais beef, and the traditional sole meunière.

4 rue Raymond Poincaré. www.lorangeriedestroisroys.fr. *C* **01-30-88-69-95.** Main courses 28€–59€. Mon–Fri noon–2pm and 7–10pm.

Ty Bilig ★★ CRÊPERIE   In the town's historic center, in an unlikely corner-building on the square opposite the entrance to the château's park, this no-frills crêperie is in a handy spot for a quick lunch or dinner. The interior is nothing to write home about with simple wooden furnishings and fake flowers on the tables, but the savory galettes and sweet crêpes are as tasty as they are cheap, and cider is served in classic Breton bowls. In summer a terrace sprawls out onto the cobbles in front.

13 pl. Félix Faure. *C* **01-30-46-23-11.** Main courses 9€–14€. Tues–Sat 11:45am–2pm and 6:45–10pm. Closed 1st week of Jan and 2 weeks in Aug.

FONTAINEBLEAU ★★★

60km (37 miles) S of Paris; 74km (46 miles) NE of Orléans

Napoleon called it "the house of the centuries; the true home of kings," and he had a point: Fontainebleau was a royal residence for more than 700 years. Elegant and dignified, this grand château carries the architectural imprint of many a monarch, in particular, Francis I, Henri IV, and Napoleon I. Surrounded by dense forest and verdant countryside, a trip out here is a relaxing green interlude to your Parisian trip.

Essentials

ARRIVING   **Trains** to Fontainebleau leave from the Gare de Lyon (www.transilien.fr). The 40-minute trip costs 5€ for adults and 2.50€ for children ages 4 to 10 one-way. From the Fontainebleau–Avon train station take the local bus (line 1), direction Lilas, to the Château stop; you should use a regular Métro ticket for this. Buses are timed to arrive with the train from Paris. If you're **driving** from Paris, take the A6 south, exit Fontainebleau.

VISITOR INFORMATION   The **Office de Tourisme** is at 4 bis place de la République (www.fontainebleau-tourisme.com; *C* **01-60-74-99-99**), opposite the main entrance to the château.

Exploring Fontainebleau

Though kings were already living here by the 12th century, it was during the Renaissance that Fontainebleau really took on its regal allure. In 1528, inveterate castle-builder King François I decided to completely rebuild Fontainebleau and make it into a palace that would rival the marvels of Rome. He tore down most of the medieval castle and hired an army of architects and artisans to construct a new one. He also imported a passel of Italian painters, including Il Rosso and Primaticcio, whose style of painting, featuring frescoes in bright colors with sensuous (often nude) figures in mythological landscapes, became known as the School of Fontainebleau.

After François' death, work continued, but it wasn't until Henri IV arrived on the scene in the 17th century that there were more major transformations. Henri added several wings and a courtyard (the **Cour des Offices**), and invited a new clutch of artists, who established a second School of Fontainebleau. This time, the artists were of French and Flemish origins (Ambrose Dubois, Martin Fréminet, and others), and used oil paint and canvas instead of frescos. Louis XIV, preferring Versailles, didn't bother much with Fontainebleau, but both Louis XV and Louis XVI left their mark. Napoleon also made a lasting imprint on the castle's interior. Fontainebleau made an imprint on the Emperor as well: On April 20, 1814, he abdicated here, before being sent off to exile on the island of Elba.

TOURING THE CHÂTEAU

The visit to the chateau allows access to the **Grands Appartements** and the Napoleon I museum (**Musée Napoleon 1er**).

Your first stop will be the **Cour du Cheval Blanc** ★★ at the entrance to the palace. It was in this grand square, which is surrounded by wings of

The Chapel of Fontainebleau.

the castle on three sides, that Napoleon said adieu to his faithful imperial guards. "Continue to serve France," he pleaded. "Her welfare was my only concern." The sumptuous **horseshoe staircase ★★** was contributed by Henri II. On the left, as you enter, is the **Chapelle de la Trinité ★★**. When he was 7, Louis XIII climbed up the scaffolding to watch Martin Fréminet, his art instructor, paint the glorious ceiling. Linking the chapel with the royal apartments is the **Gallery of François I ★★★**, a stunning example of Renaissance art, whose walls are covered with exceptional frescos, moldings, and boisseries (carved woodwork). Throughout the gallery (and elsewhere in the castle), you will see the salamander, François' official symbol.

The other major must-see is the **Salle de Bal ★★★**. This 30m (98-ft.) long ballroom is a feast of light and color; the frescos by Primaticcio and Nicolo dell'Abate have been completely restored, and their rich hues radiate like they were painted yesterday. The monumental fireplace at the far end was designed by 16th-century architect Philibert Delorme.

The **Royal Apartments ★★** were decorated and redecorated by successive monarchs. Louis XIII was born in the **Salon Louis XIII ★**, a fact that is symbolized in the ceiling mural showing Love riding a dolphin. Though several different queens slept in the **Chambre de l'Impératrice ★★**, its current set-up reflects the epoch of Empress Josephine (Napoleon's first wife). The sumptuous bed, crowned in gilded walnut and covered in embroidered silk, was made for Marie Antoinette in 1787. The queen would never see it; the Revolution exploded before she could arrange a royal visit to the château. Napoleon transformed the Kings' bedroom into the **Salle du Trône ★**, or Throne Room—the only one preserved as-it-was-made in France. It's easy to imagine the emperor receiving his subjects up there in blue velvet, bookended by two huge Napoleonic standards.

The **Musée Napoléon 1er ★**, in the Louis XV wing, celebrates the life of the emperor with historic memorabilia and artwork relating to his reign, like the tent he slept in during military campaigns, and a remarkable mechanical desk. On a guided tour (French only at time of writing), you can visit the **Salon Chinois de l'Impératrice,** which dates from 1863 and contains the Empress Eugénie's lavish collection of Oriental artefacts, some of which were given to her by the Embassy of Siam in 1861.

TOURING THE GARDENS

Though not as lavish as Versailles' gardens, the **Grand Parterre** at Fontainbleau (the formal gardens) that André Le Nôtre created in the 17th century, are the biggest in Europe at 14 hectares (35 acres). More lush, however, is the **Garden of Diane ★★**, a quiet spot of green on the north side of the castle created during the time of François I, which centers around a statue of the goddess surrounded by four dogs. The **English Garden ★**, complete with an artificial stream and lush groves of tall trees, was added by Napoleon. The vast **Carp Pond ★★**, which extends directly from the south side of the **Cour de la Fontaine,** has a small island with a pavilion where an afternoon snack would be served to royal residents. Surrounding the gardens and its park is the enormous **Fontainebleau Forest ★★★**, which, if you have the time, is definitely worth the visit (see box, below).

Pl. du Général-de-Gaulle. www.musee-chateau-fontainebleau.fr. © **01-60-71-50-70.** Grands appartements & Musée Napoléon 1er 14€ adults, 12€ students 18–25; free for children 17 and under. Apr–Sept Wed–Mon 9:30am–6pm; Oct–Mar Wed–Mon 9:30am–5pm.

The Hiking Trails of French Kings

The Forest of Fontainebleau is riddled with *sentiers* (hiking trails) made by French kings and their entourages who went hunting in the forest. A *Guide des Sentiers* is available at the tourist information center (p. 206; you can also download trail maps from their website). Bike paths cut through the forest too. You can rent bikes and helmets at **A La Petite Reine,** 14 rue de la Paroisse, a few blocks from the château (www.alapetite reine.com; © **01-60-74-57-57;** 8€/hr., 15€ for a full day; 3€ helmet.)

Where to Stay

Hôtel Aigle-Noir ★★   This 18th-century mansion, once the home of Cardinal de Retz, is just down the street from the château. You'll pass through mighty gates and a grand courtyard before you enter the hotel, which is one of Fontainebleau's most elegant. Rooms are either decked out with antiques and period prints or with art deco-style furnishings coupled with bold nature-themed frescos. The staff will make you feel that you are one of the cardinal's close friends. A hip cocktail bar completes the picture.

27 pl. Napoleon–Bonaparte. www.hotelaiglenoir.com. © **01-60-74-60-00.** 53 units. 145€–360€ double; 280€–520€ suite. Parking 15€. **Amenities:** Bar; concierge; laundry service; room service; free Wi-Fi.

Hôtel de Londres ★★   With a historic 1850s-era facade, this hotel enjoys one of the best locations in town for anyone fascinated by the architecture of the château of Fontainebleau. It's directly in front of the cour des Adieux, site of Napoleon's farewell to his troops before his exile to Elba. It's been owned and managed by the same family for three generations. The well-maintained rooms are tastefully and cozily outfitted with a mix of modern and period furniture and have extra-long beds. Other than breakfast, no meals are served.

1 pl. du Général-de-Gaulle. www.hoteldelondres.com. © **01-64-22-20-21.** 16 units. 178€–288€ double. Closed 1 week in Aug and Christmas through 1st week in Jan. **Amenities:** Bar; free Wi-Fi.

Where to Eat

Auberge de la Croix d'Augas ★★ SAVOYARD   This quirky wooden chalet is located 2.5km (1½ miles) from the château in the forest of Fontainebleau, making it a good pit-stop during a hike. The decor and the menu resemble that of an Alpine lodge; Savoyard specialties like fondue, raclette, and tartiflette figure prominently here. Don't worry, if you aren't up for these cheese, potato, and ham-laden dishes—there are also pasta, fish, and steak choices. The rustic setting has lots of wood beams and a lovely terrace for outdoor dining in good weather.

Exit Fontainebleau on bd. de Maréchal Foch (rte. D606) to rte. D116, about 1km (½ mile) into the forest. www.restaurant-fontainebleau.fr. © **01-64-23-49-25.** Main courses 17€–33€. Daily noon–2pm and 7–10:30pm.

In Casa ★★ CORSICAN/DELI   Off the beaten tourist track, but only 10-minute's walk from the chateau, this gourmet little spot is part shop, part deli, and part restaurant. Stop by for top-notch Corsican picnic delights like tuna and brocciu cheese paté, green olive tapenade, and saucisson. Or dine in (at a table in the middle of the shop) on light fare like Corsican hotdog (figatelli sausage, brocciu cheese cream, walnuts, and honey) or plates of Corsican cold meats and cheeses. Either way, you should wash it down with a Mattei, a citrussy, red-colored Corsican aperitif that makes Spritz cocktails soar.

28 rue de la Paroisse. © **06-51-48-74-77.** Main courses 14€–20€. Tues–Sat 11am–3pm and 5–9pm. Closed 2 weeks in Aug and 1 week in Dec.

L'Axel ★★★ MODERN FRENCH   If, after a few hours experiencing life in a castle you feel like treating yourself to a royal meal, this is the place. Acclaimed chef Kunihisa Goto creates exciting French dishes with a dash of Japanese *je ne sais quoi,* like Wagyu steak with minted peas, or lobster with miso, served in a classy dining room with contemporary art on the walls. Reservations are a must.

43 rue de France. www.laxel-restaurant.com. © **01-64-22-01-57.** Main courses 65€–120€; fixed-price lunch 70€ or dinner 90€–165€. Wed–Sun 12:15–2pm and 7:30–9:30pm.

VAUX-LE-VICOMTE ★★★

47km (29 miles) SE of Paris; 24km (15 miles) NE of Fontainebleau

This jewel of a castle comes with a story that reads like a Hollywood screenplay. Nicolas Fouquet, the château's original owner, was a brilliant finance minister and lover of arts and leisure. In the early 1700s he was the toast of Paris. His circle included France's top artists and intellectuals, drawn to his gorgeous home in the country. Unfortunately, Fouquet underestimated the jealousy of his superiors, in particular the young king, Louis XIV.

Château de Vaux-le-Vicomte.

Things came to a head one fateful night in the summer of 1661. As Voltaire put it, "On August 17, at 6 in the evening, Nicolas Fouquet was the King of France; at two in the morning, he was nobody." Oblivious to the fact that the king was already fed up with his penchant for stealing the spotlight, Fouquet organized a stupendous party in his honor. He pulled out all the stops: There was a sumptuous meal, a play written and performed by Molière, and a fireworks display—no one had seen anything like it. Three weeks later, Fouquet was arrested on trumped-up charges of embezzlement. The king seized the castle, confiscated its contents, and hired its artists and architects to work on Versailles. Though writers like Madame de Sévigné and La Fontaine pleaded with the king on Fouquet's behalf, the once untouchable financial minister spent the rest of his life in prison.

Essentials

ARRIVING   Though it's close to Paris, Vaux-le-Vicomte is hard to reach by mass transit. By **car,** take the A4 east to the N104 south to Vert Saint-Denis, then the D82 east to Vaux-le-Vicomte. **Trains** run from Gare de Lyon to Melun (25 min.; www.sncf-connect.com; ✆ **36-35;** 9€ adults, 4.50€ children 4–10). Then you'll need to take taxi (about 20€) or, if it's a weekend, a shuttle bus ("Châteaubus") from the Melun train station (6€ per person round-trip; free for children 11 and under).

Touring the Château

Though his reaction was extreme, Louis XIV's jealousy is not too hard to understand when you are standing in front of Vaux-le-Vicomte; the edifice is the epitome of 17th-century elegance. The castle was eventually released to Fouquet's widow, and has remained in private hands ever since. The ancestors of the current owners, Jean-Charles and Alexandre de Vogüé, bought the palace in 1875, when they started a much-needed program to restore Vaux to its original splendor. The restored château is now filled with splendid tapestries, carpets, and art objects.

One of its most impressive rooms was actually never finished: the oval **Grand Salon ★★**, which Fouquet never got a chance to paint or furnish. Here, you actually don't miss all the decorative trimmings; the bare white pilasters and detailed carvings have a classical beauty that stands on its own. For something more ornate, there is the **King's bedroom ★★**; this lavish ensemble of chandeliers, brocade, and painted ceiling (by Le Brun) was a model for the King's Apartments in Versailles. The **Salon des Muses ★** also gets a fabulous ceiling by Le Brun, as well as several fine tapestries covering its walls. To help imagine what Fouquet's dinner parties were like, take a stroll through the elaborately decorated **Salle à Manger ★** (dining room), where a table is set with stacks of rare fruits and gold candlesticks, and a sideboard displays a set of extraordinary majolica. You can see life on the other side of the banquet table downstairs in the **kitchen,** with its humbler servants' dining area.

The **gardens ★★★** are almost as spectacular as the château. The carefully calculated geometry of the flowerbeds and alleyways makes this a study in harmony, even if you couldn't call them exactly natural. Nature is lurking close by, however—the entire ensemble is surrounded by seemingly endless forest. Just behind the castle are two enormous beds of boxwood trimmed into elaborate designs; Le Nôtre took his inspiration from

---

Vaux by Candlelight

To give you just an inkling of what Vaux looked like on the evening of the famous party Fouquet threw for Louis XIV back in 1661, visit the castle when it's illuminated by candlelight. From May to September on Saturday nights, some 2,000 candles burn from 7pm to midnight, when you can visit the castle's interior, stroll in the gardens, and enjoy a fireworks display with classical music at 11pm (22€ adults, 17.50€ for children ages 6–16, free for children 5 and under). Top it off with a meal at the château's cafeteria, Le relais de l'Ecureuil (main course from 15€), or the gourmet garden restaurant, Les Charmilles (fixed-price menu from 30€), open during candlelit nights only.

the patterns in Turkish carpets. The far end of the gardens is crossed by a large **canal.** There you will also find a series of grottos, each sheltering a statue of a different river god. Finally, from the last basin, turn around and take in the lovely **view** ★★ of the gardens with the château rising in the background.

77950 Maincy. www.vaux-le-vicomte.com. ✆ **01-64-14-41-90.** Admission 17€ adults; 13.50€ students, seniors, and children ages 6–16; free for children 5 and under. Mid-Mar to mid-Nov 10am–6pm. Closed mid-Nov to mid-Mar, except for certain days during the Christmas holidays.

Where to Stay & Eat

Château de Courtry ★★   Unless you want to sleep in the uninspiring town of Melun, your best overnight bet is to find a bed-and-breakfast, like this lovely little château, with its classic stone frontage and sloping slate tile roof. While the inside might not be quite as impressive as its noble exterior, the three guest rooms are quite comfortable, and your hosts also offer various meal possibilities, from brunch to gourmet picnics to candlelight dinner (12€–40€).

12 rue du Château, Sivry-Courtry, 6km (3¾ miles) from the château on the D215 and the D126. www.facebook.com/lechateaudecourtry. ✆ **01-60-69-36-01** or 06-62-79-78-20. 3 units. 99€ double; 135€–167€ family room for up to 5 people. Breakfast included. **Amenities:** Meals for guests; free Wi-Fi (on ground floor only).

R.Mana ★★★ MODERN FRENCH   This elegant 17th-century farmhouse, whose oak beams and exposed stone walls were once associated with the nearby **Château de Vaux-le-Pénil,** is a real charmer. Menu items change with the seasons but are as appealing, though they're not always classicly French: tempura of shrimp with gazpacho; veal sweetbreads with mushroom ravioli; beef filet with truffles; and hazelnut and plum soufflé. Our top dining pick in this area.

11 rue de Libération, Ferme Saint Just, Vaux-le-Pénil. https://rmana.fr. ✆ **01-64-52-09-09.** Main course 35€–41€; fixed-price lunch menu 36€–39€; main courses 24€–35€. Wed–Sat noon–1:30pm and 7:30–9pm; Sun noon–1:30pm. Closed 3 weeks in Aug, 2 weeks at Christmas, and 1 week at Easter. From Vaux-le-Vicomte, drive 5.5km (3½ miles) west, following signs to Melun, then to Maincy, and then to Vaux-le-Pénil.

GIVERNY ★★★

74km (46 miles) NW of Paris

In 1883, Claude Monet and his family moved to a tiny town north of Paris, where they rented a house that came with almost 1 hectare (2½ acres) of land. He didn't know it then, but he would spend the rest of his life there, painting scenes from the fabulous garden that he would create out of the grassy slope behind his house. Today, the **Fondation Claude Monet** is open to the public, and for a fee, you too can wander in and out of the brilliant flower beds, lush bowers, and shady arbors that inspired this impressionist master. Because much of the visit takes place in the gardens, we recommend doing this trip only when the weather is good.

Essentials

ARRIVING **Trains** (SNCF; www.sncf-connect.com; ✆ **36-35**) leave roughly every hour from the Gare St-Lazare train station to Vernon, the closest stop to Giverny, which is about 7km (4½ miles) away. The trip takes around 45 minutes and costs 9€ to 24€ one-way. From Vernon, you can either take a shuttle bus (10€ round-trip) or rent a bike at the station (L'Arrivé de Giverny; ✆ **02-32-21-16-01;** 17€/day) and pedal there on the marked bike path.

If you're **driving,** take the Autoroute A14 to the A13 toward Rouen. Take exit 16 for Vernon and follow the D181 across the Seine into the town. From Vernon, take the D5 to Giverny. Expect it to take about an hour from Paris; try to avoid weekends.

VISITOR INFORMATION The **Office de Tourisme des Portes de l'Eure** is at 36 rue Carnot in Vernon (www.nouvelle-normandie-tourisme.com; ✆ **02-32-51-39-60**).

Exploring Giverny

When you enter this green haven, you'll quickly realize that Monet wasn't just a brilliant painter; he was also a gifted gardener. By the end of his life, the garden was just as much a work of art as the paintings, or perhaps they *were* the paintings. If you have already visited the Orangerie in Paris, and seen his magical Nympheas, or water lilies, spread across huge canvases in two oval-shaped rooms, in a way, you have already visited this garden; they were painted here, with the aim of faithfully recreating the feeling you would have if you were looking at the same flowers at Giverny.

There are actually two gardens here: The first and closest to the house is the **Clos Normand ★★**, a French-style garden that is resolutely orderly and geometric, despite the riot of colors. Gladioli, larkspur, phlox, daisies, and asters clamor for your attention; irises and oriental poppies brighten the western lawn. Monet painted here, but his famous water lily series was born in the **Water Garden ★★★**. Monet bought this piece of property in 1893 with the intention of building a garden that resembled those in the Japanese prints he collected; the ornate **Japanese bridge ★★** figures prominently in several of his canvases. Today the garden looks much as it did when Monet was immortalizing it. Willows weep quietly into the ponds, heather, ferns, azaleas, and rhododendrons carpet the banks. This garden was a sanctuary for the painter, who came here to contemplate and explore one of his favorite subjects: the complex interplay of water and light.

The bridge and pond made famous by Monet at Giverny.

At **Monet's house** ★★ you can see the artist's living spaces as well as his **Japanese print collection.** Unfortunately, none of his paintings are on display.

Be advised that it will be virtually impossible to experience the gardens as Monet did—more or less alone. This is an extremely popular outing for both individuals and tour groups, so your best bet is to come on a slow day like Monday or Wednesday, and/or to arrive after 3pm, when the groups have left.

84 rue Claude-Monet. www.fondation-monet.com. ℭ **02-32-51-28-21.** Admission 11€ adults, 6.50€ children ages 7–18 and students, free for children 6 and under. End of Mar to end of Oct daily 9:30am–6pm. Closed Nov to end of Mar.

Where to Stay & Eat

La Musardière ★★   A short walk from Monet's museum and gardens, this family-run hotel is in a former manor house. A scenic park filled with ancient trees surrounds the hotel and restaurant. The mansard-roofed building dates from 1880 and was around in Monet's time. Many of the antique features and architectural adornments are still in place, though the décor throughout is modern. *Musardière* is French for a place for "idling or dawdling along," and that is just what you do here. Each medium-size

After you've explored the gardens, take a stroll along the main street up the cemetery to visit the **Monet family tomb.** To dig deeper into Impressionism, visit the **Musée Giverny Impressionismes,** 99 rue Claude Monet (www.mdig.fr; ℂ **02-32-51-94-65;** 10€ adults, free for children 17 and under; Apr–Oct 10am–6pm; times may vary), which explores the high points of the movement, as well as what lead up to it and what came after.

guest room, attractively and comfortably furnished, has a small bathroom with tub or shower. The hotel also operates its own restaurant, where fixed-price menus of creative bistro fare cost 39€ and mains start at 24€.

123 rue Claude-Monet. www.la musardiere.fr. ℂ **02-32-21-03-18.** 10 units. 125€–160€ double. Free parking. Closed Nov to mid-Mar. **Amenities:** Restaurant; bar; free Wi-Fi.

Le Jardin des Plumes ★★★ Top chef David Gallienne's Anglo-Norman mansion is a chic yet comfy hotel and restaurant, offering colorful and fresh accommodations and excellent cuisine to Monet fans (and others). Half of the eight guest rooms are in the main house, the others are in a modern annex; some look out on a lovely garden. The restaurant shares the garden view; the exquisite fixed-price menus are a splurge (starting at 85€), but worth every centime. If you fancy yourself a chef, sign up for one of David's cooking lessons (Thurs–Sun 9:30–11:30am; 120€).

1 rue de Milieu, a short walk the gardens. www.lejardindesplumes.fr. ℂ **02-32-54-26-35.** 8 units. 180€–240€ double; 280€–340€ suite. Nov–Mar closed Mon–Tues; closed Jan. **Amenities:** Restaurant; free Wi-Fi.

DISNEYLAND PARIS

41km (25 miles) E of Paris

You have two parks here to choose from: **Disneyland Paris** and **Walt Disney Studios.** Depending on your stamina, you can do both in 1 day. Disneyland is in the throes of a 2€-billion makeover, with the addition of themed lands in Walt Disney Studios, based on Marvel (now open) and *Frozen* (coming in 2025). As a result, some rides might be closed during your visit. Also, bear in mind that the popular free line-jumping voucher known as the **FastPass** has been replaced with the **Disney Premier Access** scheme, a far less user-friendly system. Disney Premier Access gives park goers two options: the **Disney Premier Access Ultimate,** whose high price (from about 90€ to more than 140€ per person, depending on the season) allows for unlimited direct access to all rides without a long line. And the **Disney Premier Access One,** which allows the bearer to make use of fast-track lines only after they've paid for them, on a ride-by-ride basis (8€–13€, depending on the attraction's popularity). The app is supposed to show waiting times for each ride, in real time, so that visitors can decide whether to pay extra to jump the lines. In reality, though, the new system has proved notoriously unreliable; during our last visit it stopped working in the afternoon, and real waiting times were longer than suggested. All in all the new system is sapping some of the joy out of visiting. Here's hoping they improve it soon.

Essentials

ARRIVING From central Paris, by far the easiest way to get to the parks is to take the **RER A** (www.ratp.fr; 40 min.; 5€ adults, 2.50€ ages 4–10 one-way) all the way to its terminus at Marne-la-Vallée–Chessy-Parc Disney (just make sure that this is the terminus—the RER A has multiple destinations). When you get out, you'll be about a 5-minute walk from the entrance. By **car,** head east on the A4 and take the Parc's Disney exit. By train, from outside Paris, you could arrive by **TGV** (the French railway's high-speed train); see www.sncf-connect.com. From Paris' Roissy-Charles de Gaulle (CDG) and Orly airports, you could also catch the **Magic Shuttle** (http://magicalshuttle.co.uk; 24€ adults, 11€ children 3–10, free for children 2 and under), a direct shuttle to the parks and Disney hotels.

VISITOR INFORMATION The **Visitor Relations Office** is located in City Hall on Main Street, U.S.A. (www.disneylandparis.com; ✆ **03448-008-898**). For general regional tourist information, visit the **Point Information Tourisme** between the train station and Disney Village (www.visitparisregion.com).

ADMISSION Admission varies depending on the season whether you buy tickets online or at the gate, but here's a general price guide: In peak season, a 1-day park ticket (for either the main park or Walt Disney Studios) costs around 64€ for adults, 58€ for children ages 3 to 11, and is free for children 2 and under; a 2-day park-hopper ticket is around 152€ for adults, 142€ for kids; and a 3-day park-hopper ticket is around 216€ for adults, 200€ for kids. Special offers can include transportation to and from Paris; check the website.

HOURS Hours vary throughout the year, but often are 10am to 7pm with later closings in the summer. Check the website/app for exact hours.

Exploring Disney

The U.S. has Disneyland and Disney World; in France, you could call it Disney Universe. This giant resort has two parks: the classic **Disneyland,** complete with the Buzz Lightyear Laser Blast and Star Wars rides, like Hyperspace Mountain; and **Disney Studios,** which, in addition to the Marvel Avengers Campus (and the *Frozen* land under construction) has thrill rides and exhibits themed around Disney animation techniques and

5

SIDE TRIPS FROM PARIS

Disneyland Paris

films. Outside the parks, there's a golf course, a spa, tennis courts, and **Disney Village,** with its boutiques, restaurants, disco, and IMAX theatre.

However, unless you're a diehard Disney fan in search of the classics, don't expect your mind to be blown in or out of the parks: Only Marvel brings anything particularly new to the table; staff, though helpful, seem under pressure and barely smile; and without the FastPass system (discontinued), lines can be horrifically long (I'm talking 110 min., at one point during our visit, for Crush's Coaster; see p. 216 for more on the new system). And don't get me started on the noise: With hundreds crammed into snaking spaces, the decibel levels were so high there were times we couldn't hear the piped-in ambiance music on rides (like the haunted house) where sound is a big part of the experience. If you're a huge Disney fan, you may still find some enjoyment. But if you're not, see **Parc Astérix** (p. 219), where you get the theme park thrills in a much more pleasant environment—plus a bit of French culture for good measure.

DISNEYLAND PARK

When you enter the park, you'll step right into **Main Street USA,** that utopian rendition of early-20th-century America, complete with horse and buggies and barbershop quartets. Here you'll find the **information center** as well as a train, which leaves from Main Street Station. The train, which does a circuit around the park, will whisk you off to **Frontierland,** where you'll find a paddle-wheel steamboat, and the Lucky Nugget saloon, among other things. Next, you'll chug through **Adventureland,** with old favorites like the Swiss Family Robinson treehouse and the Pirates of the Caribbean. Onward towards **Fantasyland** with Sleeping Beauty's Castle (Le Château de Belle au Bois Dormant), whizzing teacups, flying Dumbos, and "It's a Small World." Last stop is **Discoveryland,** home of the Star Wars Hyperspace Mountain and Star Tours: The Adventure Continues. Main Street has parades virtually every afternoon, and around closing time there's a light and fountain show.

DISNEY STUDIOS

Walt Disney Studios is now the go-to park for Marvel fans, thanks to the spanking new **Marvel Avengers Campus,** replete with Iron Man and Spiderman-themed attractions, and an after-dark drone light show. Split into four worlds—Pixar, Marvel, Toon Studio and Production Courtyard—the Studios Park is also the place for films and parades and yet more musical shows. Fun rides here include **Avengers Flight Force,** a 91kmph (57 mph) ride where you whoosh off into the black of space to help Iron Man and Captain Marvel fight an intergalactic threat. And **Crush's Coaster,** which plunges you into the world of Finding Nemo. Smaller visitors can try the **Toy Soldiers Parachute Drop** or the **Cars ROAD TRIP** ride, where they can speed along Route 66 on the lookout for popular characters like Mater and Lightning McQueen.

Where to Stay & Eat

You can easily make Disney a day trip from Paris—the transportation links are excellent—or you can spend a night. Most overnight guests take a package that includes park entry, breakfast, and a couple of nights in one of the seven hotels (which now includes **Disney's Hotel New York – The Art of Marvel,** the world's first Marvel hotel). The per-night hotel prices can range wildly, depending on the package you book, the number of days you stay, the time of year, and so on. Your best bet is to study the website or call the reservations service shared by the resort's seven theme hotels. If you'd like to reserve by phone, call ✆ **01-60-30-60-53,** in France or adding +33 and taking off the first 0, from abroad.). Otherwise, you can always reserve online at www.disneylandparis.com.

Food wise you won't starve at Disneyland Paris, which offers a myriad of restaurants and snack bars. You can live on burgers and fries or try one their more upscale restaurants, like the **Bistrot Chez Remy** (French food), straight out of the Ratatouille movie in Walt Disney Studios Park or **Captain Jack's Restaurant des Pirates** (Caribbean fare) in Adventureland. One way or another, the bill will probably be higher than you bargained for. Many restaurants offer a click and collect service (accessible via the app). For all restaurant **reservations,** book online or call ✆ **01-60-30-40-50.**

PARC ASTÉRIX ★★★

41km (25 miles) E of Paris

While Disney is all about transposed Americana, **Parc Astérix** is all about France. Well, a comical vision of France, at least, as seen through the eyes of Roman Bashers, Astérix the Gaul and his best friend Obélix, comic-book/cartoon characters, created by the late Franco-Belge writer René Goscinny and illustrator Albert Uderzo, and beloved to the French. If you're not familiar with Asterix (created in 1959), what you need to know is this: Asterix, the main character, is a wily Gaul who lives in the last remaining Gaulish village of the Roman Empire. Thanks to a magical strength potion, prepared by the druid Panoramix (Getafix in English), he and Obelix (who fell in the potion as a baby and displays extra-human strength) defend their village from the Romans, and frequently go on adventures around the world.

Even if you don't speak French, the theme park (40km/25 miles north of Paris), is a fun place to visit, with some fifty attractions and shows, including France's fastest rollercoaster, the 51m-tall (167 ft.) Toutatis, which reaches a top speed of 110kmph (68 mph). You can easily make a night of it, with three themed hotels to choose between, all within walking distance of the park.

Essentials

ARRIVING   From Paris, the easiest option is to take the **RER B** (www. ratp.fr; 30 min.; 11.45€ adults, 7.70€ ages 4–10 one-way) to Aeroport Charles-de-Gaulle Terminal 3 (the first airport stop). Inside the RER building (upstairs), look for the Parc Astérix desk, where you will be directed to the shuttle bus to the park (10€ adults return, 9€ children 3–11). By **car,** head north on the A1 (direction Lille) and take the Parc Asterix exit (between exits 7 and 8).

VISITOR INFORMATION   Check www.parcasterix.fr (© **09-86-86-86-87**). There's an information point at the entrance to the park. You should also download the app for waiting times at the rides, show schedules and restaurant reservations.

ADMISSION   Admission varies upon the season and whether you buy tickets online or when you arrive, but generally, a 1-day ticket costs around 59€ for adults and 51€ for children ages 3 to 11 (free for children 2 and under). Seasonal offers can include nights in a hotel and the park's line-jumping **Filotomatix pass** (check the website). Filotomatix offers several options, from line-skipping at one attraction of your choice (5€–12€, depending on the ride) to having unlimited line jumping all day at all the big rides (125€ per person).

HOURS   Hours vary throughout the year, but are usually 10am to 7pm with later closings in the summer, Halloween and Christmas. Check the website for details.

Exploring Parx Astérix

Split into seven of the comics' worlds—**Gaul,** the **Vikings, Egypt, Ancient Greece,** the **Roman Empire, time-travel,** and the druid **Festival Toutatis**—there are big and small rides throughout the park, along with eating places and live performance spots, including the popular outdoor high-diving pool—**Les Plongeons d'Olympe**—in Ancient Greece. You can defy gravity on genuinely thrilling rollercoasters in most worlds, like on **Goudurix** (a play on words for *gout du risque,* as in "a taste for risk"), which has no less than 5 loops in the Viking zone; and on **Festival Toutatais** (in its same-named world), which aside from being fast, holds the world record for air times (the number of times your bottom leaves the seat), at 23. There are numerous water rides too, from **Le Grand Splatch** to the **Menhir Express** (both in Gaul; for the Menhir Express, wear a rain poncho. Seriously!), as well as meet-and-greets with the characters, and gentle rides and play areas for smaller ones.

Where to Stay & Eat

Parc Astérix is doable as a day trip from Paris, but for full immersion, think about spending the night. On-line packages usually combine park entry, breakfast, a Filotomatix pass and a night in one of the three themed hotels: the three-star **Trois Hiboux** (decked out like a wood cabin), three-star **La Cité Suspendue** (a cluster of quaint, stilted forest cabins linked by bridges), and four-star **Les Quais de Lutèce** (dressed up like a Roman town, complete with its own waterway). Staying in any of the hotels gets you 30 minutes of access to the park before opening. To reserve by phone, call ✆ **09-86-86-86-87,** in France (or add +33 and take off the first 0 from abroad). Or reserve online at www.parcasterix.fr.

Restaurant-wise, there are multiple options, hawking everything from croissants and burgers (ubiquitous now all over France) to pizza and fries. If you would like a sit-down meal with waiter service, reserve ahead (on the app, online at www.parcasterix.fr) for one of two restaurants. The **Restaurant du Lac** (which looks like a giant bowl of fruit) in Time Travel world serves Obélix's favorite: wild boar. Or pick the outdoor **Le Patio** in the Roman Empire, which offers Italian fare. The hotels also have buffet restaurants serving an array of classic French cuisine (around 35€–50€ per person).

AMIENS ★★★

130km (80 miles) N of Paris

Is it worth the journey from Paris to see yet another cathedral? If that cathedral is in Amiens, the answer is absolutely. **Amiens,** the capital of Picardy, has been a textile center since medieval days. Its old town is a warren of jumbled streets and canals, branching off from the south bank of the Somme River. It's also famed for its floating gardens and Saturday waterborne fruit and veg market, not to mention 19th-century writer Jules Verne's former home.

Essentials

ARRIVING   The quickest and easiest option is by train from Gare du Nord, which takes just over 1 hour (from 5€ one-way). For information visit www.sncf-connect or call ✆ **36-35**). If **driving** from Paris take the A16 north and follow signs to Amiens (journey time about 1 hr., 45 min.).

VISITOR INFORMATION   The **tourist office** (www.visit-amiens.com; ✆ **03-22-71-60-50**) is on the north side of the square in front of the cathedral at 23 place Notre-Dame.

Exploring Amiens

The city's centerpiece is boldly Gothic **Cathédrale Notre-Dame d'Amiens ★★★**, place Notre-Dame (www.cathedrale-amiens.fr; ✆ **03-22-80-03-41;** free admission; daily 8:30am–6:30pm), France's largest cathedral, and the only one with its medieval spire still standing. The

Amiens Cathedral.

dazzling, UNESCO-protected edifice was started in 1220 to house the head of St. John the Baptist (still visible today), brought back from the Crusades in 1206. One of the biggest Gothic cathedrals ever constructed, it's 113m (370 ft.) tall with a girth of 200,000 cubic meters (more than 7 million cubic feet). Its **labyrinth** (a black-paved trail that was believed to bring spiritual transformation to those who followed it) is 234m long (770 ft.).

The cathedral is the crowning example of French Gothic architecture. In John Ruskin's Bible of Amiens (1884), which Proust translated into French, he extolled the door arches. The **portals** of the west front are lavishly decorated, important examples of Gothic cathedral sculpture. Two **galleries** surmount the portals; the upper has 22 statues of kings. The large **rose window** is from the 16th century.

Inside are **carved stalls** and a Flamboyant Gothic **choir screen.** Local artisans made these stalls, with some 3,500 figures, in the early 16th century. Slender pillars—126 of them—hold up the interior of the church, the zenith of the High Gothic in the north of France. The cathedral escaped destruction in World War II. You can also visit the **towers,** which offer sweeping views over the city (6€ adults; free for ages 25 and under).

From the cathedral, head to the city's **Quartier St-Leu,** across the water and criss-crossed by narrow canals (giving Amiens the nickname Venice of the North). The quarter used to be a thriving medieval craft center, bustling with water mills. Today its narrow streets contain art galleries, bookshops, and antiques boutiques, making the area a wonderful place to wander.

During the Middle Ages, **Les Hortillonages,** an expanse of almost 242 hectares (598 acres) at the eastern edge of the core, was set aside for the cultivation of all kinds of herbs, fruits, and vegetables. Irrigated by a web of canals fed by the Somme, this marshy district is still producing foodstuffs. Not long ago, the harvest was floated on barges and in shallow-bottomed boats to be sold on the Quai Bélu, near the cathedral. Today only some of the produce comes from the Hortillonages (the rest is from the fields and enters the town center by truck), but the ritual retains its medieval name, the **Marché sur l'Eau** (though locals increasingly refer to it as Marché St-Leu). The tradition continues every Saturday from 8:30am to 1pm, when the river's quays are transformed into a huge outdoor vegetable market. And every year, on the third Sunday in June, a market festival takes place here, with sellers descending the River Somme in 19th-century costume to hawk their produce from their boats. You can visit the Hortillonages by traditional jon boat between April and October (reserve at www.leshortillonnages-amiens.com or ✆ **03-22-92-12-18;** 10€ adults, 9€ children 11–16, 6€ children 3–10, free for ages 2 and under).

Another fascinating place is the **Maison de Jules Verne,** 2 rue Charles Dubois (✆ **03-22-45-45-75;** 7.50€ adults, 4€ children ages 6–17, free for EU residents ages 25 and under; Wed–Mon 10am–12:30pm and 2–6pm), a stately town house where the author plunged himself into his imaginary worlds. Period rooms convey how the house would have looked in Verne's day, and a collection of more than 700 objects reveals the author's inspiration.

A final notable attraction: The **Musée de Picardie ★**, 48 rue de la République (www.amiens-tourisme.com/musee-de-picardie; 9€ admission; Tues–Fri 9:30am–6pm, Sat–Sun 11am–6pm). This art and archeology museum occupies a building constructed from 1855 to 1867 as a palace of the Napoleonic dynasty (it was inaugurated by Napoleon III himself). The sculpture and painting collection traces the European schools from the 16th to the 20th centuries, with works by El Greco, Maurice Quentin de La Tour, Guardi, and Tiepolo. Sol LeWitt painted the rotunda in the 1990's—it's quite a sight. Fragonard's Les Lavandières is a highlight, and one of his most beautiful works. On the archeology front are exhibits dealing with the Roman occupation of Gaul, the Merovingian era, and ancient Greece and Egypt.

Where to Stay & Eat

Ail des Ours ★★ MODERN FRENCH   A short walk from the cathedral, this deep turquoise-shaded foodie haunt is run by young chef Stéphane Bruyer, whose open kitchen churns out delicious dishes that bring out the best of the region's produce. A typical meal might start with white asparagus and cockles, followed by guineafowl with shitake mushrooms, then chocolate tart with blackberries—the lot beautifully presented and served with a smile. The wine list features plenty of organic wines.

11 rue Sire Firmin Leroux. www.aildesours-restaurant.fr. ℂ **03-22-48-35-40.** Fixed-priced lunch 23€–30€ and dinner 43€–55€. Wed–Sat noon–2pm and 7:30–9pm; Tues 7:30–9pm. Closed 2 weeks in Aug.

IBIS Styles Amiens Centre ★★   Yes, this is a chain. But Ibis has done a lot to revamp its style in recent years. Outside the façade is stripy pink; inside rooms are vintage-chic with boldly patterned green carpets that offset the slick grey furnishings. Upper-floor rooms have balconies with sweeping views over the rooftops to the cathedral. Some family rooms include a cool fury swing seat. Amiens has plenty of eateries, but if you did decide to eat in, you could do worse than at **Corso,** the hotel's Italian restaurant, dressed up like a funky loft, with a cocktail bar to boot (main courses around 17€; fixed-price menu 22€).

5 passage Auguste Perret. ℂ **03-75-14-05-00.** https://all.accor.com. 105 units. 106€–140€ double; 132€–160€ family room. Breakfast 12€. **Amenities:** Restaurant; free Wi-Fi; free parking.

THE LOIRE VALLEY

6

By Lily Heise

Just 2 hours south of Paris, the Loire Valley enchants visitors with a stunning landscape of castles and vineyards straight out of a fairy tale. King François I and his Renaissance court left a spectacular cultural legacy, earning the entire valley a place on the World Heritage Site list. History buffs follow Joan of Arc from Orléans to Chinon; romantics fall in love with the storybook châteaux of Chenonceau, Azay-le-Rideau, and Ussé; garden lovers revel in the verdant paradise of Chaumont and Villandry; gastronomes tantalize their palates at world-class restaurants and rustic *auberges;* and outdoor adventurers can see it all by bike.

As its name would imply, the region's rolling hills and forests hug the winding Loire River, encompassing 800 sq. km (308 sq. miles) of land south of Ile-de-France, from the city of Orléans and extending west to Nantes on the Atlantic coast. Most visitors use Tours or Orléans as their starting point; however, the towns of Blois, Amboise, or Saumur make excellent bases for exploring the region.

Most visitors to the Loire arrive via Paris; there are about six direct trains daily from the TGV station at Charles de Gaulle airport to the Tours TGV station Saint-Pierre (1 hr., 15 min.; 30€–70€ one-way). At least one high-speed train (TGV) an hour runs to both Orléans and Tours, smart starting points for anyone not renting a car directly in Paris.

You can also seek additional assistance planning your trip via the Loire Valley's **main regional tourist offices: Comité Régional de Tourisme du Centre-Val de Loire,** 3 bd. de Verdun, Orléans 45000 (www.valdeloire-france.com; ℰ **02-38-79-95-00**), or through the various local tourist offices listed throughout the chapter.

ORLÉANS ★

119km (74 miles) SW of Paris; 72km (45 miles) SE of Chartres

Ever since **Joan of Arc** relieved the besieged city from the Burgundians and the English in 1429, the city has honored the "Maid of Orléans." This deliverance is celebrated every year on May 8, the anniversary of her victory. But even if you aren't in town for the celebration, it's impossible to overlook the city's affection for the warrior; her name adorns everything from streets and cafes to chocolates and candies. Though it suffered damage in World War II, the city's downtown still remains quaint, though it

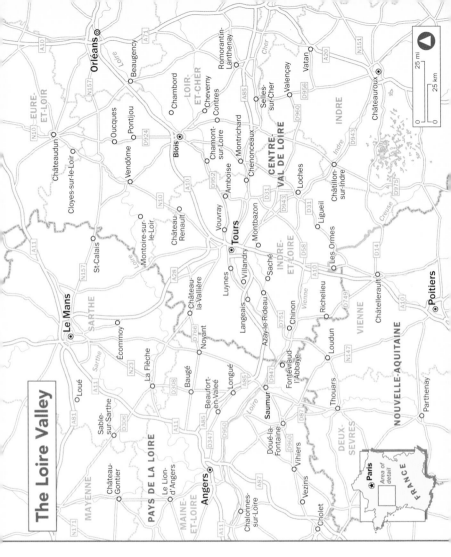

has gradually been losing its regional prominence to the more prosperous Tours to the southwest.

Essentials

ARRIVING   One **train** per hour arrives from Paris's Gare d'Austerlitz (1 hr., 10 min.; www.sncf-connect.com; © **36-35;** 10€–25€ one-way); there are also a dozen connections from Tours (50–70 min.). The one-way fare from Tours to Orléans is about 21€. Orléans lies on the road between Paris and Tours. If you're **driving** from Paris, take A10 south; from Tours, take A10 north.

VISITOR INFORMATION   The **Office de Tourisme** is at 23 place du Martroi (www.tourisme-orleansmetropole.com; © **02-38-24-05-05**).

BIKING YOUR WAY through THE LOIRE

Ten years and several million euros later, a vast program called **La Loire à Vélo ("The Loire on a Bike";** www.cycling-loire.com) has completed the 900km-long (496-mile) **Loire à Vélo trail,** so visitors can now safely pedal from Nevers to the sea on a dedicated bike path, past châteaux, villages, and natural areas. The path was designed for low-key cycling and is linked to cycling-friendly hotels and bike-rental outfits along the way (look for the ACCUEIL VÉLO signs). More paths are added every year, and the trail hooks up to an even more massive project called **EuroVelo 6,** a cycling path that leads all the way to the Black Sea, at the eastern edge of Europe.

La Loire à Vélo has partnered with various tourist offices and travel agencies to offer a range of bike-trip packages that include hotel, meals, bike rental, and baggage transport (very important if you don't want to haul extra weight). For more information, visit the "Organize your stay" tab on **www.cycling-loire.com.** The website also has detailed information on dozens of bike-rental outfits along the route, as well as brochures and links to guidebooks on various sections of the path.

One of the better-known outfitters is **Detours de Loire,** 35 rue Charles Gille, Tours (www.detoursdeloire.com; ✆ **02-47-61-22-23**), which has three other shops in Orléans, Blois, and Nantes. This means that you can pick up your bike in one town and leave it at another outlet along the way without backtracking. If you are arriving in the Loire Valley by train, its shops are all located close to the town station. The price for all-purpose bikes is 18€ per day, with discounts for multi-day rentals. E-bikes are also available at 40€ per, but since the Loire's bike trails are almost all flat, most cyclists won't need the electric pedaling assistance. A 300€ deposit (usually a credit card imprint) is required. Detours de Loire can also organize hotel-bike packages, deliver your bike to your hotel, and store your bags while you are pedaling. *Note:* Most outlets are open only from April/May to October, except for the outlet in Blois and Tours.

Getting Around

ON FOOT   Orléans's city center is small and many streets are pedestrianized. For short stays, it's easiest to explore the town on foot.

BY BICYCLE   **Détours de Loire,** 58 rue de la Charpenterie (www.detoursdeloire.com; ✆ **02-38-77-12-52**), rents bikes starting at 15€ for a half-day and 18€ for a full day.

BY CAR   All the sites in the city can be explored on foot. Underground parking is well sign-posted; convenient lots are beside the Hotel de Ville, the Cathedral, and near the river at place du Châtelet.

BY TAXI   **Taxis Orléans** (www.taxis-orleans.fr; ✆ **02-38-53-11-11**) can be found throughout the city. You can order one or grab one from the ranks in front of the train station and at the corner of rue Royal and place du Martroi.

BY PUBLIC TRANSPORT   Orléans has both buses and trams that snake through the city run by the **TAO** (www.reseau-tao.fr; ✆ **08-00-01-20-00**).

ATTRACTIONS
Cathédrale Ste-Croix **7**
Eglise St-Aignan **8**
Hôtel Groslot **5**
Musée des Beaux-Arts **6**

HOTELS
Empreinte Hôtel **3**
Hôtel de l'Abeille **1**

RESTAURANTS
Chez Dionysos **2**
La Parenthèse **4**

Church +
Information (i)
Post Office ✉

Orléans

Trams will serve your visit best; line A reaches the train station and line B goes by the cathedral. Tickets (1.60€) can be purchased from automatic kiosks at the Tram station, or for the bus (1.90€) directly from the driver and a 24-hour pass costs (4.10€).

[FastFACTS] ORLÉANS

ATMs/Banks The city center has plenty of banks, especially around shopping hub place du Châtelet.

Doctors & Hospitals **Centre Hospitalier**

Régionale d'Orléans, 1 rue Porte Madeleine (www.chr-orleans.fr; ℂ **02-33-51-44-44**).

Mail & Postage **La Poste,** 19 rue Royale (ℂ **36-31**).

Pharmacies **Pharmacie du Châtelet,** 38 Pl. du Châtelet (ℂ **02-38-53-34-50**).

Exploring Orléans

Orléans, pop. 114,000, is the chief town of Loiret, on the Loire, and benefi-ciary of many associations with the French aristocracy. It gave its name to the dukes and duchesses of Orléans. Wander the narrow lanes of the city center to get the feel for what the city might have been like during Joan of Arc's time. Note the equestrian statue of Jeanne d'Arc on place du Martroi. From the square, you can walk past the elegant arched galleries on rue Royal (rebuilt in 18th-c. style) across pont George-V (erected in 1760). A simple cross marks the site of the Fort des Tourelles, which Joan of Arc and her men captured.

Once the French capital of vinegar, this local tradition is maintained by 200-year-old producers **Martin-Pouret,** 11 Rue Jeanne d'Arc (https://martin-pouret.com; 🕻 **02-38-62-19-64**), whose boutique is filled with fine vinegars, mustards and other gourmet prod-

Street in Orléans.

ucts. If you're more into sweets, your cravings will be satisfied at the **Chocolaterie Royale,** 51 rue Royale (www.lachocolaterieroyale.com; 🕻 **02-38-53-93-43**), markers of regal chocolates since 1760.

Cathédrale Ste-Croix ★★ CATHEDRAL   Begun in 1287 after a Romanesque church here collapsed from old age, the cathedral was burned by the Huguenots in 1568. Henri IV laid the first stone of the present building in 1601; work continued until 1829. The cathedral boasts a 17th-century organ and woodwork from the early 18th century in its chancel, the masterpiece of Jules Hardouin-Mansart and other artists associated with Louis XIV.

Pl. Ste-Croix. 🕻 **02-38-77-87-50.** Free admission. May–Sept daily 9:15am–7pm; Oct–Apr daily 9:15am–6pm.

Eglise St-Aignan ★ CHURCH   One of the most frequently altered churches in the Loire Valley, St-Aignan was consecrated in 1509 in the form you see today. It possesses one of France's earliest vaulted hall crypts, complete with polychromed capitals. Scholars of pre-Romanesque art praise its rare 10th- and 11th-century aesthetics. Above ground, the church's Renaissance-era choir and transept remain, but the Protestants burned the nave during the Wars of Religion. In a wood-carved shrine are the remains of the church's patron saint.

Pl. St-Aignan. No phone. Crypt can be visited only on a guided tour 4€; sign up at the tourist office.

Hôtel Groslot ★★ HISTORIC HOME   This brick Renaissance mansion was begun in 1550 and embellished in the 19th century. François II (the first husband of Mary, Queen of Scots) lived here during the fall of 1560 and died on December 5. It was here that his brother and successor Charles IX met his lovely Marie Touchet. Between the Revolution and the mid-1970s, it functioned as the town hall. Marriage ceremonies, performed by the town's magistrates, are still held here. The statue of Joan of Arc praying was the work of Louis-Philippe's daughter, Princesse Marie d'Orléans. In the garden, you can see the remains of the 15th-century Chapelle St-Jacques.

Pl. de l'Etape (northwest of the cathedral). ✆ **02-38-79-22-30.** Free admission. July–Sept daily 9am–7pm; Oct–June Mon–Fri and Sun 10am–noon and 2–6pm, Sat 10am–7pm (occasionally closed Sat for weddings).

Musée des Beaux-Arts ★★★ MUSEUM   The best art museum in the region, the fairly large collection is made up of mostly French, but also Italian, Dutch, and Flemish works from the 15th to 20th centuries. It includes some impressive treasures by Tintoretto, Boucher, Van Dyke, and Vélasquez as well as a variety of portraits, including one of Mme. de Pompadour by Drouais. The museum also holds one of the country's best collections of pastels with works by Quentin de la Tour and Chardin.

1 Rue Fernand Rabier. https://mba rouen.fr/en. ✆ **02-38-79-21-83.** Ticket includes exhibits at other museums in town 6€ adults, 3€ students; free for children 18 and under and for all visitors on 1st Sun of the month. Tues–Sat 10am–6pm and Sun 1–6pm (Thurs until 8pm).

Sleep Like a King (or Queen)

As one of the most visited regions of France, it's not surprising to find a great variety of accommodation options. Enjoy a regal sleep in one of the Loire's many châteaux hotels such as the hidden **Hauts de Loire,** the sumptuous **Château d'Artigny** (p. 257) or the gastronomic **Fleur de Loire** (p. 237). The valley is also dotted with thousands of unique *gîtes* (B&Bs) including medieval towers, houseboats, and even troglodyte caves. For details and reservations, go to www.gites-de-france.com/en.

Where to Stay

Hôtel de l'Abeille ★★★   This is the city's most charming hotel. Stepping into the foyer, you will be instantly transported back to the turn of the 20th century. In fact, the hotel dates from 1903 and has been run for four generations by the same family. The cozy Belle Epoque feel flows into the guest rooms, each decorated with vintage prints and antiques. Throughout the building are ornamental nods to both Napoleon, whose symbol was the bee and the namesake of the hotel, and Joan of Arc, the liberator of Orléans. Take a late afternoon break or morning coffee on its peaceful rooftop terrace.

64 rue Alsace-Lorraine. http://hotel-abeille.com. ✆ **02-38-53-54-87.** 24 units. 105€–165€ double; 130€–235€ family suite. Parking 16.50€. **Amenities:** Bar; room service; free Wi-Fi.

Empreinte Hôtel ★★   Enjoy lovely views of the Loire and easy access to shops and restaurants at this stylish boutique hotel. Located on the site of the former Châtelet castle, the current building dates to the 19th century, although the interiors have been completely renovated. The inviting lounge, where you can get drinks and snacks, has oversized armchairs, a large lighting fixture of golden balls over the bar, and contemporary art on the walls. These design touches are found in the compact guest rooms, especially in the eclectic lighting fixtures, and bed frames. Bathrooms are a bit snug, with mostly showers, however you can relax in the spa's Jacuzzi before bed.

80 Quai du Châtelet. https://empreinte-hotel.com. ℰ **02-38-75-1-52.** 31 units. 146€–303€ double; 379€–473€. Public parking nearby. **Amenities:** Bar, room service; sauna; hammam; Jacuzzi; free Wi-Fi.

THE LOIRE VALLEY FOR kids

The Loire is a wonderful family holiday destination, and the highlights, of course, are the castles (**Valençay,** p. 241; **Langeais,** p. 260; **Clos Lucé,** p. 245; and **Loches,** p. 263, being the best to include for children). In addition to these larger castles, the **Château de la Ferté Saint-Aubin** (www.chateau-ferte.com; ℰ **02-38-76-5-72**), located 18km (11 miles) south of Orléans, has family-friendly activities, from baking demonstrations to scavenger hunts as well as vintage games kids can try out. It's open daily July and August 11am to 7pm; reduced hours the rest of the year. Admission varies, depending on current activities, from 9.50€ to 20€ adults, 12€ to 17.50€ for ages 12 to 17, 6.50€ to 15€ for ages 4 to 11, and free for ages 3 and under.

The two most frequently visited attractions for families are located at the same address: the **Aquarium du Val de Loire** (www.grandaquariumdetouraine.com; ℰ **02-47-23-44-44**) and the **Parc des Mini-Châteaux** (www.parcmini chateaux.com; ℰ **02-47-23-44-57**), 9.5km (6 miles) west of Amboise, near the village of Lussault-sur-Loire.

The **Parc des Mini-Châteaux** (daily early Apr–May 10:30am–7pm, June–Aug 10am to 7 or 8pm, Sept–Nov 14 10:30am–6pm; closed mid-Nov to early Apr) holds replicas of France's most famous castles, built at ¹⁄₃₀ the size of the originals. Chambord, for example, is less than 3.5m (11 ft.) tall. It's all very patri-otic—a sort of learning game that teaches French schoolchildren the glories of their *patrimoine* (heritage) and collects some of the most celebrated architecture in Europe. Admission is 14.50€ adults,

11.50€ students and children aged 4 to 14, and free for children 3 and under; for a full day of fun get a discounted joint ticket with the Aquarium 26€ and 20€. The **aquarium** is home to some 10,000 freshwater and saltwater fish. Admission is 14.50€ adults, 11.50€ children ages 4 to 14 (daily Jan–Mar and Sept–Dec 10:30am–6pm, Apr–May 10:30am–7pm, June to late July 10am–7pm, and late July to mid-Aug 10am–8pm; closed 2 weeks in Nov and Jan).

The area also offers plenty of activi-ties for outdoor adventures. Take a break from navigating the castles of the Loire by paddling it. **The Canoe Company** (www.canoe-company.fr; ℰ **06-37-01-89-92**) rents canoes daily on both the Loire River at Rochecorbon and on the Cher at the foot of the Château de Che-nonceau (rates are 11€–24€ per person for a 1- to 2-hr. ride near the castle).

Where to Eat

Chez Dionysos ★★ TRADITIONAL FRENCH   Don't worry that the facade and dining room of this restaurant are quite plain: The quality of the food more than makes up for that lack of style. And if choosing between menu items like scallops served with yogurt and zaatar, or steak with béarnaise and bergamot mousse, seems like a (sorry!) Herculean task, buttonhole owner Denis-Philippe Vaello. He'll also pair your dish with the right wine from his huge list of regional and international labels.
1 Rue du Tabour. www.chezdionysos.fr. © **02-38-53-71-12.** Main course 16€–22€; fixed-price lunch 25.50€ or dinner 31.50€. Tues–Sat noon–2pm and 7–10pm.

La Parenthèse ★★★ MODERN FRENCH   For excellent traditional French cuisine with a contemporary twist, seek out this discreet restaurant in the heart of Orléans. Located in a half-timbered house on picturesque place du Châtelet, the interiors feature minimalistic, modern decor. The juxtaposition of the old and new is further explored in chef David Sterne's regularly changing seasonal menu which might combine roasted cod with French saffron emulsion or pork confit with local Saint-Maure goat cheese and Chinon wine sauce.
26 Place du Châtelet. www.restaurant-la-parenthese.com. © **02-38-62-07-50.** Main course 18€–25€; fixed-price lunch 22€–25€ or dinner 32€-36€. Mon–Fri noon–1pm and 7:30–9pm. Closed last week of July to mid-Aug.

BEAUGENCY

150km (93 miles) SW of Paris; 85km (53 miles) NE of Tours

On the right bank of the Loire, the charming town of Beaugency boasts many medieval sites including a long 12th-century bridge with 23 arches, said to have been built by the Devil himself. The heart of town is an archaeological garden called the City of the Lords, named after the counts who enjoyed great power in the Middle Ages.

Essentials

ARRIVING   If you're **driving** from Blois to Beaugency, take N152 north-east. About 20 **trains** per day run between Beaugency and either Blois or Orléans; each trip takes about 20 minutes, and the one-way fare is 6€. For railway information, visit www.sncf-connect.com or call © **36-35.**

Exploring Beaugency

A major medieval event took place here: the 1152 annulment of the marriage of Eleanor of Aquitaine and her cousin, Louis VII. She then married Henry II of England, bringing southwestern France as her dowry, an act that set off the Hundred Years' War. This remarkable woman was the mother of Richard the Lion-Hearted. (The film *The Lion in Winter* dramatizes these events.)

Although the brooding and impressive **Château de Beaugency** (www.chateau-beaugency.com) has roots back to medieval times, today it's one of the most modern castles in the Loire. The current castle was built in the 15th century by Jean d'Orléans, who fought alongside Joan of Arc in the siege of Orléans, on the foundations of the earlier 10th-century fortress of the lords of Beaugency, whose feudal power extended throughout the region. Now owned by renowned digital artist Jérémie Bellot, its rooms display sensational digital art and immersive installations.

Astride the street (la rue du Pont) that leads to one of the château's secondary entrances, the **Voûte St-Georges (St. George's Vault)** is an arched gateway from the earlier château. More medieval moodiness is on hand at **La Tour César,** a 36m-tall (118-ft.) castle keep remaining from an 11th-century citadel. It's a fine example of Romanesque military architecture, but the interior is in ruins.

Eglise Notre-Dame, pl. Saint-Fermin, a 12th-century abbey, was rebuilt after it was burned during the Wars of Religion (1562–98). You can still see traces of its original Romanesque architecture in the chancel and transept. Nearby, the 16th-century **Tour St-Fermin,** a bell tower with a panoramic view of the valley, is famous for bells that ring out a traditional tune three times a day.

The 10th-century **Eglise St-Etienne,** pl. du Martroi, is one of the oldest churches in France. Now deconsecrated, it is owned by the municipality and is open only for temporary exhibitions of painting and sculpture.

Where to Stay & Eat Nearby

For lunch in the center of Beaugency, the **Château de Beaugency** has a café in the courtyard serving light lunch fare and snacks or **Le Relais du Château,** 8 rue du Pont (www.lerelaisduchateau-beaugency.com; ✆ 02-38-44-55-10), at the foot of the castle, serves up satisfying traditional dishes and a lunch menu from 18€.

La Tonnellerie ★★ Situated a short drive south of Beaugency, this 19th-century manor house makes for the perfect restful stay in the immediate area. Filled with antiques, vintage artwork, and tasteful pastel wallpaper, the hotel feels straight out of a novel by Balzac or Flaubert. Nevertheless, its philosophies are firmly from the 21st century having obtained the European Eco-label certification in 2016 for their efforts towards environmental sustainability. Soak up the supremely serene setting in the lush garden, copy of *La Comédie Humaine* or *Madame Bovary* in hand.

12 rue des Eaux-Bleues, Tavers, Beaugency 45190. www.latonnelleriehotel.com. ✆ **02-38-44-68-15.** 19 units. 95€–120€ double; 175€ suite; family rooms available. Closed mid-Nov–Jan. Take A10, exit at Beaugency, and then take N152 to Beaugency/Tavers. **Amenities:** Bar; bike rental; outdoor pool; free Wi-Fi.

BLOIS

180km (112 miles) SW of Paris; 60km (37 miles) NE of Tours

The star attraction in this town of 52,000 is unquestionably the **Château de Blois,** but if time remains after a château visit, you may want to wander around the quaint historic core to get a feel for a real Loire Valley town.

Château de Blois.

Essentials

ARRIVING Several direct **trains** run from Paris's Gare de Austerlitz every day (1 hr., 30 min.; from 15€-45€ one-way), and around a dozen depart from the Gare Montparnasse, which involves a change in Tours (around 1 hr., 50 min.; 22€–68€). From Tours, trains run almost every hour (trip time: 40 min.), at a cost of 12€ one-way. For information and schedules, visit www.sncf-connect. com or call ✆ **36-35.** From April to October, you can take a **bus** (www. remi-centrevaldeloire.fr/tourisme/ navette-chateaux; ✆ **02-54-58-55-55**) from the Blois train station to tour nearby châteaux, including Chambord, Cheverny, and Beauregard. If you're **driving** from Tours, take RN152 east to Blois, which runs along the Loire; if you want to get there fast, take the A10 autoroute. If you'd like to explore the area by **bike,** go to **Détours de Loire,** 39 Avenue du Dr Jean Laigret (www.detoursdeloire.com; ✆ **02-54-56-07-73**). Rentals are 15€ per half day, 18€ per day.

VISITOR INFORMATION The **Office de Tourisme** is at 5 Rue de la Voûte du Château (www.bloischambord.co.uk; ✆ **02-54-90-41-41**).

Exploring the Blois & the Château

Blois is a piece of living history, with cobblestone streets and restored white houses with slate roofs and redbrick chimneys. Some of its "streets" are mere alleyways originally laid out in the Middle Ages or lanes linked by a series of stairs. If you have time for **shopping,** head for the area around **rue St-Martin** and **rue du Commerce** for high-end clothing, perfume, shoes, and jewelry. On Saturday, a daylong **food market** is on place

235

Lights, Sound, Action!

Many of the Loire châteaux present evening *son-et-lumière* (sound and light) shows. The **Château de Blois** hosts one of the best, nightly from April to November (Apr–Sept 10–10:30pm, Oct–Nov 7:15pm; English audio guide available).

As a taped lecture plays, colored lights and readings evoke the age in which the château was built. Admission 11.50€ adults, 9.50€ students, 7€ children 6 to 17, and free for children 5 and under (www.chateaudeblois.fr).

Louis XII and place de la République, lining several blocks in the center of town at the foot of the château.

Château de Blois ★★★ CASTLE   On the misty morning of December 23, 1588, Henri I, the duc de Guise, had just left a warm bed of one of Catherine de Médicis' ladies-in-waiting. His archrival, King Henri III, had summoned him, but when the duke arrived, only the king's minions were about. The guards approached with daggers. Wounded, the duke made for the door, where more guards awaited him. Staggering, he fell to the floor in a pool of his own blood. Only then did Henri III emerge from behind the curtains. "Mon Dieu," he reputedly exclaimed, "he's taller dead than alive!" The body couldn't be shown: The duke was too popular. Quartered, it was burned in a fireplace. The murder of the duc de Guise is only one of the events associated with the Château de Blois, begun in the 13th century by the comte de Blois. Blois reached the apex of its power in 1515, when François I moved to the château. For that reason, Blois is often called the "Versailles of the Renaissance," the second capital of France, and the "City of Kings." But Blois soon became a palace of exile. Louis XIII banished his mother, Marie de Médicis, to the château, but she escaped by sliding into the moat down a mound of dirt left by the builders.

If you stand in the courtyard, you'll find that the château is like an illustrated storybook of French architecture. The Hall of the Estates-General is a beautiful 13th-century work; Louis XII built the Charles d'Orléans gallery and the Louis XII wing from 1498 to 1501. Mansart constructed the Gaston d'Orléans wing between 1635 and 1637. Most remarkable is the François I wing, a French Renaissance masterpiece containing a spiral staircase with ornamented balustrades and the king's symbol, the salamander.

Blois. www.chateaudeblois.fr. ✆ **02-54-90-33-33.** Admission 14€ adults; 10.50€ students; 7€ children 6–17; free for children 5 and under. Additional fees for light shows and special events; joint tickets available. July–Aug daily 9am–7pm; Apr–June and Sept–Oct daily 9am–6:30pm; Nov–Mar daily 10am–5pm; closed Jan 1 and Dec 25.

Where to Eat & Stay

In addition to the following places to dine, **Assa** ★★ (189 quai Ulysse Besnard; www.assarestaurant.com) is a fusion Japanese/French restaurant with stellar food, and river views.

Côté Loire–Auberge Ligérienne ★★   Only a 5-minute walk from the château, this lodging is a smart option for travelers touring the region without a car. And there's plenty of character at this B&B-like inn with a seafaring aesthetic, from the vintage maritime posters, pillows with sailboat motifs, and ancient building features from the 12th, 15th, and 16th centuries. Most rooms are large for the size of the establishment, though beware of the narrow staircase. A restaurant (main courses 23€, fixed-price lunch menu 25.50€ and dinner 38€; Tues–Sat noon–1:30pm and 7:30–9pm) on the ground floor, with outdoor seating in a pretty courtyard, is open to outside guests, with one of the owners doing double duty as chef. His love of the region shines in such culinary creations as savory blancmange with goat cheese and tomatoes confit or guinea fowl cooked in local Crémant de Loire sparkling wine.

2 pl. de la Grève. www.coteloire.com. ✆ **02-54-78-07-86.** 9 units. 74€–109€ double. Closed Jan to early Feb. **Amenities:** Restaurant; bar; free Wi-Fi.

Fleur de Loire ★★★   Star chef Christophe Hay pays homage to his native Loire Valley in his new (and quite stylish) hotel and gastronomic restaurant. Opened in 2022, every detail was carefully considered in this impressive transformation of a former 17th-century residence of Gaston d'Orléans, the brother of King Louis XIII. The banks and waters of the Loire River are cleverly represented through artwork by local artists, vegetal wall panels and mellow-toned textiles are used in common spaces and the spacious rooms. Guests can further absorb the Loire, and exquisite views of the city and castle, from the private terraces of suites, or while relaxing next to the outdoor pool. Hay's love of his region's terroir and his dedication to sustainability are also celebrated in his two-Michelin-starred restaurant and more casual bistro, with the bounty of the river and its surrounding lands—including from the hotel's own vegetable gardens—highlighted in each dish. The results are sublime.

26 Quai Villebois Mareuil. https://fleurdeloire.com. ✆ **02-46-68-01-20.** 44 units. 268€–544€ double; 362€–947€ suite. **Amenities:** 2 restaurants; bar; indoor pool; outdoor pool; spa; Jacuzzi; hammam; room service; free Wi-Fi.

Le Médicis ★★ TRADITIONAL FRENCH   It's worth the short 1km (.5 mile) trip from the center of town to dine at this gourmet restaurant and inn. It will be hard to choose from original dishes like lobster with Vouvray wine emulsion and seasonal vegetables, pigeon suprême with gnocchi of green peas and beans, or veal sweetbreads with spinach ravioli. Even more difficult will be selecting an accompanying bottle from an extensive wine list of over 250 labels. The inn also rents 10 elegant rooms; double rates start at 80€ and suites at 120€. Reservations are required.

2 allée François 1er. www.le-medicis.com. ✆ **02-54-43-94-04.** Main course 24€–45€; fixed-price menu 32€–80€. Tues–Sat noon–1:15pm and 7–9pm and Sun noon–1:15pm. Closed most of Jan and Nov–Mar Sun evening and Mon.

L'Oratoire ★ INTERNATIONAL   Located in a former outbuilding of the castle, this new restaurant is a convenient lunch spot after a morning inside the château. On sunny days, its large terrace facing the castle beckons, however, the interior, with a clever bird-themed decor, is equally appealing. Fuel up for more castle-hopping with dishes like croque-monsieur of mozzarella, mortadella and pesto, lamb chops with vegetable tajine and couscous or veal cutlet with Thai vegetables.

1 av. Jean-Laigret. www.loratoireblois.fr ✆ **02-54-78-05-36.** Main course 14€–24€. Daily noon–2pm and 6–10pm.

CHAMBORD ★★★

91km (118 miles) SW of Paris; 18km (11 miles) E of Blois

The Château de Chambord, the grandest of the region's castles, is the culmination of François I's two biggest obsessions: hunting and architecture. It's a must for any Loire castle itinerary.

Essentials

ARRIVING   It's best to **drive** to Chambord. Take D951 northeast from Blois to Saint Dyé, turning on to the rural road to Chambord. You can also rent a **bicycle** in Blois and ride the 18km (11 miles) to Chambord or take a **tour** to Chambord from Blois in summer. From April to October, **Rémi** (www.remi-centrevaldeloire.fr/tourisme/navette-chateaux; ✆ **02-54-58-55-55**) operates bus service to Chambord from Blois train station.

Exploring the Château

The Château de Chambord ★★★ CASTLE   Built as a hunting lodge, this colossal edifice is a masterpiece of architectural derring-do. Some say Leonardo da Vinci had something to do with it, and when you climb the amazing double spiral staircase, that's not too hard to believe. The staircase is superimposed upon itself so that one person may descend and a second ascend without ever meeting. While da Vinci died a few months before construction started in 1519, what emerged after 20 years was the pinnacle of the French Renaissance and the largest château in the Loire Valley. The castle's proportions are of exquisite geometric harmony, and its fantastic arrangement of turrets and chimneys makes it one of France's most recognizable châteaux.

Construction continued for decades; François I actually stayed at the château for only a few weeks during hunting season, though he ensured Chambord would forever carry his legacy by imprinting his "F" emblem and symbol, the Salamander, wherever he could. After he died, his successors, none too sure what to do with the vast, unfurnished, and unfinished castle, basically abandoned it. Finally, Louis XIII gave it to his brother, who saved it from ruin; Louis XIV stayed there on several occasions and saw to restorations, but not a single monarch ever really moved in. The state acquired Chambord in 1932, and restoration work has been ongoing ever since, which most recently involved the replanting of its 18th-century formal gardens.

Château de Chambord.

Four monumental towers dominate Chambord's facade. The three-story keep has a spectacular terrace from which the ladies of the court watched the return of their men from the hunt. Some of the vast rooms have been filled with period furniture and objects, giving an idea of what the castle looked like when it was occupied. Other areas host contemporary art and a new permanent exhibit illustrates the castle's role in protecting the Louvre's masterpieces during WWII. The château lies in a park of more than 5,260 hectares (12,992 acres), featuring miles of hiking trails and bike paths, as well as picnic tables and bird-watching posts.

www.chambord.org. ✆ **02-54-50-40-00.** Admission 16€ adults; free for children 17 and under accompanied by an adult (additional fee for horse show and Histopad rental). Daily Apr–Oct 9am–6pm and Nov–Mar 9am–5pm, closed Jan 1, Nov 27 and Dec 25.

CHEVERNY ★

192km (119 miles) SW of Paris; 19km (12 miles) SE of Blois

Unlike most of the Loire castles, Cheverny is the residence of the original owner's descendants, offering a rare glimpse into the normally very private life of French aristocrats.

Essentials

ARRIVING Cheverny is 19km (12 miles) south of Blois, along D765. It's best reached by **car** or on a **bus tour** (Apr–Aug only) from Blois with **TLC Transports du Loir et Cher** (www.tlcinfo.net; ✆ **02-54-58-55-44**). Bus no. 4 leaves from the railway station at Blois once or twice per day;

see the TLC website for the schedule. You can also take a **taxi (𝒞 02-54-78-07-65**) from the railway station at Blois.

Exploring the Château

Château de Cheverny ★ CASTLE   The family of the vicomte de Sigalas can trace its lineage from Henri Hurault, the son of the chancellor of Henri III and Henri IV, who built the château in 1634. Designed in classic Louis XIII style, it is resolutely symmetrical. Its elegant lines and sumptuous furnishings provoked the Grande Mademoiselle, otherwise known as the Duchess of Montpensier, to proclaim it an "enchanted castle." You, too, will be impressed by the antique furnishings, tapestries, and objets d'art. A 17th-century French artist, Jean Mosnier, decorated the fireplace with motifs from the legend of Adonis. The Guards' Room contains a collection of medieval armor; also on display are Gobelin tapestries depicting the abduction of Helen of Troy and the trials of Ulysses. Most impressive is the stone stairway of carved fruit and flowers. To complete the regal experience, your arrival or departure may be heralded by red-coated trumpeters accompanied by an enthusiastic pack of hunting hounds.

www.chateau-cheverny.fr. 𝒞 **02-54-79-96-29.** Admission 14€ adults; 10€ students 24 and under and children 7–18; free for children 6 and under; additional fee for exhibits; boat and golf cart rentals also available. Daily Apr–Oct 9:15am–6:30pm; Nov–Mar 10am–5pm.

The geometric gardens of Château de Cheverny.

Where to Stay & Eat

The **Orangerie** on the castle grounds makes a nice option for a quick bite, serving a variety of snacks, lunch, and teatime fare. The castle also rents six luxurious apartments in the restored outbuildings which have either a balcony or private garden.

St-Hubert ★ TRADITIONAL FRENCH This excellent-value inn offers fixed-price menus of regional specialties such as Muscadet-infused rabbit terrine with pear compote; local free-range Touraine Géline chicken with *pommes darphin* (thick potato pancake), topped with a tomato caviar; and for "dessert" Ste. Maure goat cheese or Sologne strawberry melba. While it's a far cry from the luxurious bedrooms of the castle, the St-Hubert offers economic **lodging** with 20 conservatively decorated rooms for 77€ to 89€ for a double.

122 rte. Nationale. www.hotel-sthubert.com. ℭ **02-54-79-96-60.** Main course 18€–26€; fixed-price menu 24€–36€; children's menu 12€. Daily noon–2pm and 7–9pm. Closed Sun night off-season.

VALENÇAY ★★

233km (144 miles) SW of Paris; 56km (35 miles) S of Blois

One of the Loire's most handsome Renaissance châteaux, Valençay has two additional lures for those getting castle-weary: family-friendly outdoor activities and a classic car museum.

Essentials

ARRIVING **Driving** from Tours, take A85 east, turning south on D956 (exit 13 to Selles-sur-Cher) to Valençay. From Blois, follow D956 south.

Exploring the Château & Park

Château de Valençay ★★ CASTLE Talleyrand acquired this château in 1803 on the orders of Napoleon, who wanted his minister of foreign affairs to receive dignitaries in style. The d'Estampes family built Valençay in 1520. The dungeon and west tower are of this period, as is the main body of the building, but other wings were added in the 17th and 18th centuries. The effect is grandiose, all domes and turrets. The apartments are sumptuously furnished, mostly in the Empire style, but with Louis XV and Louis XVI trappings as well. A star-footed table in the main drawing room is said to have been the one on which the final agreement of the Congress of Vienna was signed in June 1815 (Talleyrand represented France).

After your visit to the château, take a walk through the garden and deer park. Kids will enjoy plenty of activities here, including a giant labyrinth, a miniature farm, a playground, and a golf cart circuit through the forest. A few nights each summer the château and its grounds return to the

Château de Valençay.

Renaissance, decked out with thousands of candles, costumed perform-ers, and musical entertainment (see website for details).

Classic car enthusiasts' motors can get revved up at the **Musée de l'Automobile de Valençay,** situated a mere 200m (656 ft.) from the châ-teau. The exhibit shows the evolution of the automobile with over 60 antique vehicles, including a rare tandem style pulley-operated Bédélia (ca. 1914).

2 rue de Blois. www.chateau-valencay.fr. (✆ **02-54-00-10-66.** The Automobile Museum is located at 12 av. de la Résistance (www.musee-auto-valencay.fr; (✆**02-54-00-07-74**). Admission for castle 14.50€ adults; 11.50€ students; 5€ children ages 4–6; free for ages 3 and under (joint pass including automobile museum available). Daily mid-March to mid Sept 10am–6pm; Oct to mid-Nov 10:30am–5pm.

AMBOISE ★★
219km (136 miles) SW of Paris; 35km (22 miles) E of Tours

Amboise is on the banks of the Loire in the center of vineyards known as Touraine-Amboise. The good news: This is a real Renaissance town. The bad news: Because it is so beautiful, tour buses overrun it, especially in summer. Other than the myriad of notable royal residences, the town has also played host to Leonardo da Vinci, who spent his last years here, and more recently, royal rocker Mick Jagger, lord of a nearby château.

Essentials

ARRIVING   About a dozen **trains** per day leave from both Tours and Blois. The trip from Tours takes 20 minutes and costs 6€ one-way; from Blois, it takes 20 minutes and costs 7€ one-way. Several conventional trains a day leave from Paris's Gare d'Austerlitz (trip time: about 2 hr., 15 min.), and several TGVs depart from the Gare Montparnasse, with a change to a regular train at St-Pierre-des-Corps, next to Tours (trip time: 1 hr., 30 min.). Fares from Paris start at 30€. For information, visit www. sncf-connect.com or call ℂ **36-35.**

If you prefer to travel by bus, **Rémi** (www.remi-centrevaldeloire.fr), which operates out of Gare Routière in Tours, just across from the railway station, runs about six to eight **buses** every day between Tours and Amboise. The one-way trip takes about 45 minutes and costs 3€.

If you're **driving** from Tours, take the D751, following signs to Amboise.

VISITOR INFORMATION   The **Office de Tourisme** is on quai du Général-de-Gaulle (www.amboise-valdeloire.com; ℂ **02-47-57-09-28**).

Exploring Amboise

Château d'Amboise ★★ CASTLE   On a rocky spur above the town, this medieval château was rebuilt in 1492 by Charles VIII, the first in France to reflect the Italian Renaissance.

Kitchen in Château de Valençay.

Visitors enter on a ramp that opens onto a panoramic terrace fronting the river. At one time, buildings surrounded this terrace, and fêtes took place in the enclosed courtyard. The castle fell into decline during the Revolution, and today only about a quarter of the once-sprawling edifice remains. You first come to the Flamboyant Gothic **Chapelle de St-Hubert,** home to the **tomb of Leonardo da Vinci,** who died in Amboise. Tapestries cover the walls of what's left of the château's grandly furnished rooms, which include the **Logis du Roi (King's Apartment).** The vast **Salle du Conseil,** bookended by a Gothic and a Renaissance fireplace, was once the venue of the lavish fêtes, some planned by DaVinci himself in his last years. Exit via the **Tour des Minimes** (also known as the Tour des Cavaliers), noteworthy for its ramp that could accommodate horsemen and their mounts. The other notable tower is the Heurtault, which is broader than the Minimes, with thicker walls.

www.chateau-amboise.com. ℂ **02-47-57-00-98.** Admission 15€ adults; 12.20€ students; 9.30€ ages 7–14; free for children 6 and under. Daily Jan 10am–12:30pm and 2–4:30pm; Feb 9am–5pm; Mar 9am–5:30pm; Apr–June 9am–6:30pm; July–Aug 9am–7pm; Sept–Oct 9am–6pm; Nov–Dec 15 9am–12:30pm and 2–4:30pm, Dec 16–31 9am–5pm.

This statue commemorates Leonardo da Vinci's time in Amboise.

Château du Clos-Lucé ★ HISTORIC HOME/MUSEUM Within 3km (1¾ miles) of the base of Amboise's château, this brick-and-stone building was constructed in the 1470s. Bought by Charles VII in 1490, it became the summer residence of the royals and also served as a retreat for Anne de Bretagne, who, according to legend, spent a lot of time praying and meditating. Later, François I installed "the great master in all forms of art and science," Leonardo himself. Da Vinci lived here for 3 years, until his death in 1519. Today the site functions as a small museum, where you can step back into the life and imagination of da Vinci. The manor contains furniture from his era; examples of his sketches; models for his flying machines, bridges, and cannon; immersive exhibits; and a Renaissance musical festival in late September (a nod to da Vinci's musical talents).

2 rue de Clos-Lucé. https://vinci-closluce.com. ☏ **02-47-57-00-73.** Admission 18€ adults; 12.50€ students and ages 7–18; 49€ family ticket (2 adults, 2 children); free for children 6 and under. Daily Jan 10am–6pm; Feb–June 9am–7pm; July–Aug 9am–8pm; Sept–Oct 9am–7pm; Nov–Dec 9am–6pm.

Where to Stay & Eat

The best gastronomic restaurants in the area are those in the hotels listed below.

Le Choiseul ★★★ Composed of three mansions dating from the 15th through 18th centuries and nestled on the banks of the Loire River, Le Choiseul is the best hotel in Amboise and serves its best cuisine. Its rooms are opulent with traditional charm and all the modern comforts of a luxury hotel. Be sure to explore the grounds, where an outdoor pool is surrounded by Italian sculptures; ask the staff about visiting the impressive Greniers de César troglodyte caves nearby.

Enjoy creative cuisine and views of the Loire at the hotel's restaurant, **Le 36** (open to nonguests). Chef Hervé Lussault's seasonal menu includes the likes of roasted monkfish with saffron gnocchi and pan-fried veal quarter, with truffle and sparking Loire white wine sauce. Lunch ranges from 32€ to 40€, with dinner going for 58€ to 88€.

36 quai Charles-Guinot. www.le-choiseul.com. ☏ **02-47-30-45-45.** 30 units. 175€–269€ double; 346€ suite. **Amenities:** Restaurant; bar; bikes; outdoor pool; room service; free Wi-Fi.

L'Ecluse ★★ MODERN FRENCH Escape the castle crowds at this charming restaurant a few minutes' walk from all the action. Alongside the small Amasse River, this restaurant offers seating in the peaceful garden under the weeping willow or in the simple yet stylish dining room. Chef Mélanie Popineau has sourced the best local producers for her seasonal, creative dishes. You might find goat cheese panna cotta with cherry tomatoes, filet of roasted duck with potato rosettes, glazed melon and lemon confit or veal chop smoked eggplant and zucchini flower stuffed with feta. Splurge on the regional cheese plate or the apricot macaron with apricot and raspberry sorbet.

Rue Racine. www.ecluse-amboise.fr. ✆ **02-47-79-94-91.** Main course 6€–22€; fixed-price weekday lunch menu 22€ or evening 30€–50€; children's menu 19€. Tues–Sat noon–1pm and 7–9pm. Closed 1st Tues of the month; Dec 23–Feb 1.

Le Fleuray ★★   The welcome couldn't be warmer at this lovely ivy-covered manor house run by a family of English expats, a short drive from Amboise. With their cross-cultural approach, the Newingtons turned a rundown farmhouse into the perfect mélange of Anglo-Saxon comfort and French sophistication. This attention to detail is evident from the intimate foyer to the spacious guest rooms, several of which have private terraces. With peaceful surroundings and plenty to do on the extensive grounds, this is an excellent base for château touring and some family fun. The hotel also has a restaurant serving food infused with regional and international flavors. Items on the fixed-price menus (39€–59€) might include roasted cod, with squash purée topped with hazelnuts and hollandaise of local organic red Miso of Hirai Akiko, duck from Sologne with celeriac mousseline, kale and red cabbage dropped in kumquat sauce or wild mushroom risotto topped with baby glazed onions and mature parmesan shavings.

Route D74, near Amboise. www.lefleurayhotel.com. ✆ **02-47-56-09-25.** 22 units. 88€–270€ double. Free parking. From Amboise, take the D952 on the north side of the river, following signs to Blois; 12km (7½ miles) from Amboise, turn onto D74, in the direction of Cangey. **Amenities:** Restaurant; bar; free bikes; golf course; Jacuzzi; massage; outdoor pool; room service; tennis court; free Wi-Fi.

Le Manoir Les Minimes ★★   In the shadow of the looming castle is this welcoming and reasonably priced hotel, set in a magical restored 18th-century mansion. Built on the foundations of an ancient convent, the hotel is made up of the main building, draped in wisteria, and a small annexed cottage, centered by a tranquil garden. Once inside, you feel like you've entered a fine aristocratic home, with tasteful furnishings and decorations chosen with a careful eye to detail. The most charming rooms are in the main building, especially those in the attic with their beautiful exposed beams (though tall guests might have trouble with the slanted ceilings). The rooms in the annex aren't as quaint but are more spacious. Many second- and third-floor rooms open to views of the Loire or the château. A few rooms only have a bathtub (with a shower head), which may not appeal to all guests.

34 quai Charles Guinot. www.manoirlesminimes.com. ✆ **02-47-30-40-40.** 15 units. 149€–290€ double; 303€–535€ suite. Free parking. **Amenities:** Wheelchair accessible room; bar; free Wi-Fi.

CHENONCEAUX ★★★

224km (139 miles) SW of Paris; 26km (16 miles) E of Tours

Chenonceau is one of the most remarkable castles in France. Its impressive setting, spanning a whole river, along with an intriguing history and renowned residents, make it many visitors' favorite château in France. (*Note:* The village, whose year-round population is less than 300, is spelled with a final *x*, but the château isn't.)

Essentials

ARRIVING   About a dozen daily **trains** run from Tours to Chenonceaux (trip time: 30 min.), costing 7€ one-way. The train deposits you at the base of the château; from there, it's an easy walk. For information, visit www. sncf-connect.com or call ℂ **36-35.** If you're **driving,** from the center of Tours follow the signs to the D40 east, which will take you to the signposted turnoff for Chenonceaux.

Exploring the Château, Museum & Gardens

Château de Chenonceau ★★★ CASTLE   A Renaissance masterpiece, the château is best known for the dames de Chenonceau, who once occupied it. Built first for Katherine Briçonnet, the château was bought in 1547 by Henri II for his mistress, Diane de Poitiers. For a time, this

Château de Chenonceau.

remarkable woman was virtually queen of France, infuriating Henri's dour wife, Catherine de Médicis. Diane's critics accused her of using magic to preserve her celebrated beauty and keep Henri's attentions from waning. Apparently, Henri's love for Diane continued unabated, and she was in her 60s when he died in a jousting tournament in 1559.

When Henri died, Catherine became regent (her eldest son was still a child), and one of the first things she did was force Diane to return the jewelry Henri had given her and abandon her beloved home. Catherine then added her own touches, building a two-story gallery across the bridge—obviously inspired by her native Florence. The gallery, which was used for her opulent fêtes, doubled as a military hospital in World War I. The gallery also played a crucial role in World War II, serving as the demarcation line between Nazi-occupied France and the "free" zone.

Gobelin tapestries, including one depicting a woman pouring water over the back of an angry dragon, and several important paintings by Poussin, Rubens, and Tintoretto adorn the château's walls. The chapel contains a marble Virgin and Child by Murillo, as well as portraits of Catherine de Médicis in black and white. There's even a portrait of the stern Catherine in the former bedroom of her rival, Diane de Poitiers. In François I's Renaissance bedchamber, the most interesting portrait is that of Diane as the huntress Diana.

The château boasts some of the loveliest grounds of the whole Loire that include a maze, a vegetable garden, and a beautiful *jardin à la française.* At the end of your visit, stop in at the Cave des Dômes, located near the Former Royal Stables, to sample wines produced in the vineyards surrounding the castle (extra fee applies).

www.chenonceau.com. ℃ **02-47-23-90-07.** Admission 15.50€ adults; 12.50€ students and children 7–17; free for children 6 and under; admission for evening garden light show 5€ adults, free for children 6 and under. Daily July–Aug 9am–7pm; June and Sept 9am–6pm; Oct 9am–5:30pm; Nov–mid Dec 9:30am–4:30pm; mid-Dec to Jan 2 9:30am–5:30pm; Jan 3–April 7 9:30am–4:30pm; April 8–May 9am–5:30pm.

Where to Stay & Eat

From March to November, the grounds of the castle have a decent tea salon, a snack bar, and picnic areas.

Auberge du Bon-Laboureur ★★   This inn, within walking distance of the château, is your best bet in town for a comfortable night's sleep and exceptional Loire Valley cuisine. A former coach house opened in 1786, the hotel authentically evokes the era with its tiled, turreted tower, ivy-covered walls and antique furniture. Spread across various buildings, guest rooms are generally spacious and some have fireplaces or open out onto the garden with private terraces. Dine like a *reine* at its gourmet restaurant; its seasonal menu uses produce direct from the hotel's garden and may include green pea and langoustine *millefeuille,* with beetroot puree or preserved shoulder of lamb with garlic cream. The excellent value two-course menu at lunch is 37€; dinner menus run from 62€ to 96€ and a vegetarian menu is also available.

6 rue du Dr. Bretonneau. www.bonlaboureur.com. ✆ **02-47-23-90-02.** 27 units. 154€–296€ double; 296€–442€ suite. Closed mid-Nov to mid-Dec and Jan 7–Feb 14. **Amenities:** Restaurant; bar; spa; heated outdoor pool; room service; free Wi-Fi.

Au Gâteau Breton ★ TRADITIONAL FRENCH   A brief jaunt from the château, this restaurant is ideal for a casual lunch or tea. This pretty 18th-century inn was formerly a grocery store run by locals of neighboring Brittany. On a warm summer day, opt for a table on one of its shady terraces or in its pretty garden adorned with flowers and statues. Worthwhile dishes include homey favorites like local andouillette sausage, coq au vin, and their specialty poulet Tourangelle (sautéed chicken with mushroom and cream sauce).

16 rue du Dr. Bretonneau. https://au-gateau-breton-chenonceaux.metro.bar. ✆ **02-47-23-90-14.** Main course 9.90€–24€; fixed-price menus 28.50€–32.50€; kids' menu 10.90€. May–Aug daily noon–2:30pm and 7–8:30pm; Apr–Sept Thurs–Tues noon–2:30pm and 7–8:30pm, Wed 7–8:30pm; Nov–Mar daily noon–2:30pm.

CHAUMONT-SUR-LOIRE ★★

200km (124 miles) SW of Paris; 40km (25 miles) E of Tours

The connections of this lesser-visited castle to Diane de Poitiers make it an excellent château to pair with a visit to the Château de Chenonceau. It is also a wonderful stop for garden enthusiasts.

Essentials

ARRIVING   Several **trains** a day travel to Chaumont from Blois (trip time: 10–15 min.) and Tours (about 40 min.). The one-way fare is 3€ from Blois, 9€ from Tours. The railway station serving Chaumont is in Onzain, a nice 2.4km (1½-mile) walk north of the château. For train schedules and ticketing information, visit www.sncf-connect.com or call ✆ **36-35.** In high season, **Azalys** (https://bus.azalys.agglopolys.fr) operates a shuttle bus between the château and Onzain station which costs 1.25€.

Exploring the Château & Garden

Château de Chaumont ★★ CASTLE   On the morning when Diane de Poitiers first crossed the drawbridge, the Château de Chaumont looked grim. Henri II, her lover, had recently died. The king had given her Chenonceau, but his angry widow, Catherine de Médicis, forced her to trade her favorite château for Chaumont, a comparative dungeon for Diane, with its medieval battlements, pepper-pot turrets and perch high above the Loire.

The château belonged to the Amboise family for 5 centuries. In 1465, when one of them, a certain Pierre, rebelled against the rule of Louis XI, the king had the castle burned to the ground as a punishment. Pierre and

Château de Chaumont.

his descendants rebuilt for the next few decades. The castle's architecture spans the period between the Middle Ages and the Renaissance, and the vast rooms still evoke the 16th and 17th centuries. In the bedroom occupied by Catherine de Médicis, hangs a portrait of the Italian-born queen. The superstitious Catherine housed her astrologer, Cosimo Ruggieri, in one of the tower rooms (a portrait of him remains). He reportedly foretold the disasters awaiting her husband and sons.

The château passed through the hands of various owners and was eventually acquired and restored by the eccentric Marie Say and Amédée de Broglie in the late 18th century, who also added elaborate stables, a farm, and gardens. Since 1992, the latter has hosted the **International Garden Festival,** a world-renowned gathering of cutting-edge landscape designers that lasts from mid-April to October, included in your entrance ticket and well-worth viewing. Each year, a dozen different gardens are created, using thousands of different plants and innovative garden designs. More recently, the château has also been a site for contemporary art and photography exhibits; check the website for this year's program.

www.domaine-chaumont.fr. ℭ **02-54-51-26-26.** Admission to castle and festival Apr–Oct 20€ adults, 12€ children 12–18, 8€ children 6–11; rest of year castle admission 14€ adults, 8€ children 12–18, 4€ children 6–11; free for children 5 and under. Daily May–Sept 10am–7pm; Nov–Jan 10:30am–5:30pm; Feb–Mar from 10am–6pm; Apr and Oct 10am–6pm.

Where to Stay & Eat

From April to October, the château grounds are home to four places you can dine or snack, the best being the **Grand Velum** restaurant with refined dishes mainly using local or organic ingredients.

Le Bois des Chambres ★★   Chaumont-sur-Loire's focus on nature has been extended to this newly opened hotel on the castle's grounds. Occupying a restored farmhouse and two new buildings bordered by a frog pond and gardens of wildflowers, the hotel has been designed so that guests are enveloped by nature. Rooms are decorated in muted greens, beiges and pinks and light wood furnishings. Beds are snugly set within alcoves facing the gardens or in adjacent sleeping cabins, bringing guests even closer to the great outdoors.

This emphasis on the Loire's nature flows into the hotel's restaurant, **Le Grand Chaume,** where chef Guillaume Foucault finesses regional products into refined dishes of Loire Basin shrimp with endives and fig leaves and Noire du Berry chicken with cinnamon-infused beetroot. It's open in the evening only and also to non-guests. Menus range from 55€ to 110€.

Route de Queneau. https://leboisdeschambres.fr. ✆ **02-54-20-99-22.** 39 units. 148€–320€ double. Closed Dec–Jan. **Amenities:** Restaurant; bar; room service; free Wi-Fi.

Les Hauts de Loire ★★   A 3km (1¾-mile) drive from the Château de Chaumont, this is one of the finest château-hotels on the eastern Loire circuit. Perched on the north side of the Loire, this estate house was built by the owner of a Paris-based newspaper in 1840. He referred to it as his "hunting lodge," much in the lines of Louis XIII and his grand Versailles. Rooms have been recently refurbished and feature vintage print wallpaper and textiles, whitewashed wooden beams and plush armchairs and sofas. Most are quite large; though those in the half-timbered annex that was originally the stables are less coveted. After your busy day of castle-hopping, enjoy a tranquil sunset stroll through the estate's sprawling park or pamper yourself in the new Clarins spa.

Its one-Michelin-starred restaurant is definitely a highlight. The creative menu may offer white asparagus from Sologne baked in crispy pastry or lamb saddle with chickpea and wild garlic mousse. Main courses range from 44€ to 96€, with fixed-price menus ranging from 142€ to 182€ and a vegetarian menu at 99€. The hotel has recently added a new modern "Bistrot" for those looking for a more casual, though equally delicious, meal in the area.

Rte. d'Herbault. www.hautsdeloire.com. ✆ **02-54-20-72-57.** 31 units. 193€–441€ double; 427€–926€ suite. Closed Dec–Jan. **Amenities:** Restaurant; bar; spa; hammam; sauna; outdoor pool; room service; tennis court; free Wi-Fi.

TOURS

232km (144 miles) SW of Paris; 113km (70 miles) SW of Orléans

Located at the doorstep of some of the most magnificent châteaux in France, and with a high-speed train line to Paris, Tours (pop. 137,000) is the starting point for many visits to the Loire. Though it doesn't have a major château itself, Tours, at the junction of the Loire and Cher rivers, is known for its food, wine and its lively nightlife, thanks to a large student population. Sadly, many of its historic buildings were bombed in World War II and replaced with 20th-century apartment blocks. However its elegant pedestrian-only streets, and well-preserved Medieval square (in the downtown core), merit exploring—if you have the time.

Essentials

ARRIVING As many as 14 high-speed TGV **trains** per day depart from Paris's Gare Montparnasse and arrive at St-Pierre des Corps station, 6km (3¾ miles) east of the center of Tours, in 1 hour. Free *navettes,* or shuttle buses, await your arrival to take you to the center of town (the Tours Centre train station). A limited number of conventional trains also depart from Gare d'Austerlitz and arrive in the center of Tours, but these take twice as long (about 2¼ hr.). One-way fares range from 16€ to 70€. For information, visit www.sncf-connect.com or call ✆ **36-35.** If you're **driving,** take highway A10 to Tours.

VISITOR INFORMATION The **Office de Tourisme** is at 78–82 rue Bernard-Palissy (www.tours-tourisme.fr; ✆ **02-47-70-37-37**).

Getting Around

ON FOOT Besides the TGV train station, which is in the suburb of St-Pierre des Corps, most sites of interest in Tours are accessible on foot.

BY BICYCLE Tours has safe and extensive bike paths. You can rent a bike at **Detours de Loire,** 35 rue Charles Gilles (www.locationdevelos.com; ✆ **02-47-61-22-23**), at a cost of 15€ per half-day and 18€ per day.

BY CAR If you have a car for exploring the Loire, you can find a number of underground parking garages downtown. A convenient one is at the Tours Centre train station and another at rue Nationale and rue de la Préfecture. You can rent a car at **Avis** (www.avis.fr; ✆ **02-47-20-53-27**), located in the Tours Centre station, or **Europcar,** at the St-Pierre des Corps station (www.europcar.fr; ✆ **02-47-63-28-67**).

BY TAXI The most extensive taxi network is **Taxis Tours** (www.taxistours.fr; ✆ **02-47-20-30-40**). Their hotline has some English-speaking operators or you can usually find a taxi in front of the train station.

BY PUBLIC TRANSPORT Tours has both buses and a tram line, a network called **Le Fil Bleu,** 9 rue Michelet (www.filbleu.fr; ✆ **02-47-66-70-70**). Tickets (1.70€) can be purchased from automatic kiosks at a Tram station, from bus drivers or from their office.

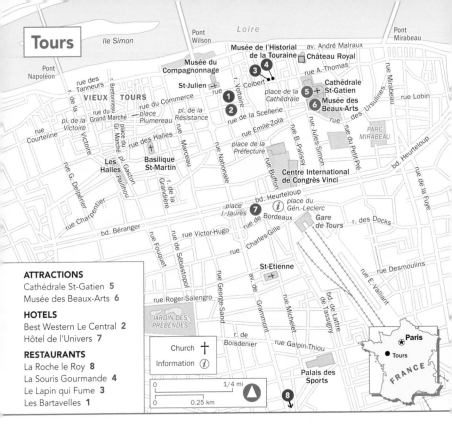

ATTRACTIONS
Cathédrale St-Gatien **5**
Musée des Beaux-Arts **6**

HOTELS
Best Western Le Central **2**
Hôtel de l'Univers **7**

RESTAURANTS
La Roche le Roy **8**
La Souris Gourmande **4**
Le Lapin qui Fume **3**
Les Bartavelles **1**

Church ✝
Information ⓘ

0   1/4 mi
0   0.25 km

[FastFACTS] TOURS

ATMs/Banks   The city
center has plenty of banks,
especially around place
Gaston Paillhou or along
rue Nationale.

Doctors & Hospitals
Centre Hospitalier Régionale de Tours, 2 bd.
Tonnellé (www.chu-tours.fr;
ⓒ **02-47-47-47-47**).

Mail & Postage   **La
Poste,** 1 Bd Béranger
(ⓒ **36-31**).

Pharmacies   **Pharmacie
du Centre,** 28 rue des
Halles (ⓒ **02-47-05-65-20**).

Exploring Tours

Pilgrims en route to Santiago de Compostela in northwest Spain once
stopped here to pay homage at the tomb of St-Martin, the "Apostle of
Gaul" and bishop of Tours in the 4th century. One of the most significant
conflicts in European history, the 732 Battle of Tours checked the Arab
advance into Gaul. In the 15th century, French kings set up shop here and
Tours became France's capital, a position it held for more than 100 years.

Most Loire Valley towns are rather sleepy, but Tours is where the
action is, where streets and cafes bustle with a large student population.
The heart of town is **place Jean-Jaurès.** The principal street is **rue**

Place Plumereau, Tours.

Nationale, running north to the Loire River. Head west along rue du Commerce and rue du Grand-Marché to Vieux Tours/Vieille Ville (old town). If you turn left on rue du Commerce toward the old town center, you can explore the streets and courtyards for regional specialties, books, toys, and crafts. A hotbed for antiques is east of rue Nationale (toward the cathedral), along **rue de la Scellerie.** Up rue Nationale toward the river are more shops and upscale boutiques and a small mall with chain stores.

    Place Plumereau (often shortened to "place Plume"), a square of medieval buildings, houses a concentration of restaurants and bars. In the warmer months, the square explodes with tables that fill with people who like to people-watch (and be watched themselves). This is a good place to start if you're going out in the evening; otherwise, venture to the trendy bars on **rue Colbert,** which lies in the heart of Tours, midway between the place Plumereau and the cathedral. Allow a morning, afternoon, or evening to see Tours.

Cathédrale St-Gatien ★ CATHEDRAL This cathedral honors a 3rd-century evangelist and has a Flamboyant Gothic facade flanked by towers with bases from the 12th century. The lanterns date from the Renaissance. The choir is from the 13th century, with new additions built in each century through the 16th. Sheltered inside is the handsome

16th-century tomb of Charles VIII and Anne de Bretagne's two children. Some of the glorious stained-glass windows are from the 13th century.

5 pl. de la Cathédrale. ℂ **02-47-70-21-00.** Free admission. Daily 9am–7pm.

Musée des Beaux-Arts ★ ART MUSEUM   For an art fix in Tours, stop by this provincial museum, worth visiting just to see the lovely rooms and gardens of the former Archbishop's palace, with parts dating to the 12th century. Hanging on the walls are works by Rubens, Delacroix, Rembrandt, and Boucher; the sculpture collection spans Roman busts to moody Rodin.

18 pl. François Sicard. https://mba.tours.fr. ℂ **02-42-88-05-90.** Admission 8.40€ adults; 4.20€ seniors; free for 26 and under. Mon 9:30am–6pm; Wed to Sun 9am–6pm. Bus: 3.

Where to Stay

Staying in a small town or the countryside, rather than in Tours, is the best way to do the Loire Valley, we think. But these hotels provide a comfortable overnight for those who must, for whatever reason, stay in the city center. Tours also has the best hostel in the region for those traveling on very low budgets. **The People—Tours,** 84 Av. de Grammont (thepeople hostel.com/en/destinations/tours; ℂ **02-36-43-50-74**), is part of a French chain of sustainable hostels. This outpost is set within a verdant garden and

has spiffy shared dorms, single, double and family rooms starting at 30€.

Best Western Le Central ★ This central hotel is a good value option. Despite being walking distance from the station and the cathedral, the surrounding greenery gives it an almost country feel. Parts of the building face a leafy garden, reducing street traffic noise, though it makes the hotel a little tricky to find. Rooms are forgettable looking, but their size is generous by French standards.

21 rue Berthelot. www.bestwestern.com. ℂ **800/528-1234** in the U.S. and Canada, or 02-47-05-46-44. 36 units. 85€–185€ double. Parking 11€. **Amenities:** Bar; babysitting; room service; free Wi-Fi.

Hôtel de l'Univers ★★ This grand old 19th-century hotel has been completely revamped in recent

Cathédrale St-Gatien.

years, returning it to its former grandeur as a top hotel in town. Its star-studded line of guests has included Rockefeller, Churchill, and Hemingway. Its midsize rooms are decorated in a stylish contemporary style in beiges and creams accented with splashes of vibrant color. The bathrooms have been renewed with shower/tubs, some with Jacuzzi functions. If you don't have one in your room, make your way to the hotel's wellness center with a Jacuzzi, heated pool and hammam. Its restaurant serves a good quality and value fixed menus at 25€ to 29€ if you don't venture out into the city. On weekdays, the hotel is popular with business travelers; on most weekends it offers greatly reduced rates.

5 bd. Heurteloup. www.oceaniahotels.com. ✆ **02-47-05-37-12.** 91 units. 122€–197€ double; 170€–209€ suite. Parking 20€. **Amenities:** Restaurant; bar; gym; hammam; heated indoor pool; room service; free Wi-Fi.

Where to Eat

Restaurants in Tours can be pricey, but you can keep costs low by dining at **La Souris Gourmande,** 100 rue Colbert (http://lasourisgourmande. com; ✆ 02-47-47-04-80), where the chef is respected for the diversity of his cheese selection. You may be asked to join a communal table. Main courses cost 13.50€ to 15.50€. At the raffish but cheerful bistro **Le Lapin qui Fume,** 90 rue Colbert (www.aulapinquifume.fr; ✆ **02-47-66-95-49**), a daily lunch special is 12€ and other standard bistro dishes including, as the name suggests, rabbit, range from 15€ to 21€.

La Roche le Roy ★★★ MODERN FRENCH   Serious gastronomes should head straight to this tasty and tasteful restaurant set in a picturesque 18th-century manor south of the center. Chef Maximilien Bridier adds a dash of modern elegance to traditional French dishes. His market-based menus could include sautéed frogs' legs served on a bed of artichokes and watercress, a *meunière* of local Saint Pierre fish with seasonal vegetables and shavings of Persian lime or quail with cherries, fresh marjoram and spelt. Save room for the restaurant's signature dessert, a soufflé that is adapted to the seasons.

55 rte. St-Avertin. www.rocheleroy.com. ✆ **02-47-27-22-00.** Main course 38€–52€; dinner menu 60€–95€. Tues–Sat noon–1:30pm and 7:30–9:30pm. Closed 2 weeks in Feb and 3 weeks in Aug. From the center of town, take av. Grammont south (follow signs to St-Avertin–Vierzon).

Les Bartavelles ★★ MODERN FRENCH   In the center of Tours, this delightful gastronomic restaurant is run by brother-sister team Gishlain and Véronique Damaye (the name is an homage to French novelist and filmmaker Marcel Pagnol). Véronique oversees the stylish dining room while Gishlain works culinary magic in the kitchen, creating photogenically presented and flavor-packed dishes. These might include smoked sturgeon with broccoli, pine nuts and watercress jus, rack of lamb with roasted butternut squash, pear and black olives or blood orange tart with meringue and bitter orange sorbet.

33 rue Colbert. www.bartavelles.fr. ✆ **02-47-61-14-07.** Main courses 30€–38€; fixed-price lunch 42€ or dinner 52€–78€. Tues, Thurs–Sat 12–1pm and 7:15–8:45pm.

Where to Eat & Stay Near Tours

Château d'Artigny ★★★   If you want to have the utmost castle experience, this is the glitziest château-hotel in the valley. Nestled in a forest 1.5km (1 mile) west of the hamlet of Montbazon and 15km (9¼ miles) south of Tours, the château is newer than it looks, built in 1912 for the perfume and cosmetics king François Coty, who spared no cost. Much of this character remains today, with fine antiques, Louis XV–style chairs, and various bronze and marble statuary. Only 31 units are in the main building; the others are in four annexes: a former chapel, gatehouse, mill, and staff dormitory. Complete your château experience at the Artigny's regal restaurant **L'Origan** (lunch menu from 32€, dinner from 42€, including a vegetarian option).

Rte. des Monts (D17). www.artigny.com. ✆ **02-47-34-30-30.** 56 units. 167€–387€ double; 317€–475€ junior suite; excellent special rates available online for advance bookings. From Tours, take N10 south for 11km (6¾ miles) to Montbazon, and then take D17 1.5km (1 mile) southeast. **Amenities:** Restaurant; bar; babysitting; bike rental; exercise room; outdoor heated pool; indoor pool; room service; sauna; Jacuzzi; spa; 2 tennis courts; free Wi-Fi.

Château de Beaulieu ★★   If you'd like the convenience of staying close to Tours while enjoying the Loire's countryside charm, book this lovely and reasonably priced 18th-century manor situated only 5km (3 miles) south of the city. The estate sits on a 3-hectare park complete with fountains and a manicured French garden. A gracious double-curving stairway takes you to the welcoming reception hall. Guest rooms have elegant wooden furniture, fireplaces, and refitted bathrooms. The nine best rooms are in the main château; the other 10 are in the nearby turn-of-the-20th-century pavilion. Before heading out on your castle touring, relax in the steam room or get a massage in their spa. The restaurant is appreciated around the area for its inventive cuisine and extensive wine list (lunch menu 35€, dinner menu 47€–60€).

67 rue de Beaulieu, Joué-les-Tours. www.chateaudebeaulieu37.com. ✆ **02-47-53-20-26.** 19 units. 115€–197€ double. From Tours, take av. de Grammont south, and turn right on bd. Winston Churchill and then left on av. de Pont Cher and right on rue de Beaulieu. **Amenities:** Restaurant; bar; bike rental; spa; free Wi-Fi.

Tours Nightlife

Long a student town, Tours has a lively young population. Much of the evening action centers around **place Plumereau** and **rue Colbert.** The twenty-something crowd gets early evening drinks and snacks at **Le**

Château-Hopping Made Easy

If you aren't renting a car, several tour companies in Tours arrange full- and half-day visits to nearby castles that leave daily from the tourist office. **Acco-Dispo** (www.accodispo-tours.com; 📞 06-82-00-64-51) offers good value small group tours visiting two to four châteaux and costing 40€ to 80€ per person. The price usually does not include meals or admission to the châteaux, but participation in the tour qualifies you for reduced group rates. **A La Francaise** (www.alafrancaise.fr/en/loire-valley; 📞 05-57-30-04-27) has half and full-day minibus and e-bike tours, some of which include food and wine tastings, from 89€ per person. Keep in mind that less is sometimes more when it comes to castle viewing; after two or three, you may not be able to remember which was which.

Baron, 11 rue des Ofèvres (www.facebook.com/lebaron.tours). You can keep the tempo of your night going with some live jazz at the friendly **Strapontin Café,** 23 rue de Châteauneuf (www.facebook.com/strapontin.cafe; 📞 02-47-47-02-74).

In summer, many locals camp out at **La Guinguette,** a vast open-air "bar" by the Pont Wilson along the Loire River, much in the spirit of Paris Plages. The daytime activities extend nightly with concerts, dancing, food, drink, and games. It's open early May to late September and note that some vendors only accept cash.

If you have the urge for more dancing, the hottest place in town is **L'Excalibur,** 35 rue Briçonnet (www.facebook.com/excalibur.tours; 📞 02-47-64-76-78), with an electro beat and video system. A clientele of all ages, many from the surrounding countryside, heads to **Le Pyms,** 170 av. de Grammont (www.lepyms.com; 📞 02-47-66-22-22), where one space plays '80s nostalgia and another contemporary electro.

VILLANDRY ★★★

253km (157 miles) SW of Paris; 32km (20 miles) NE of Chinon; 18km (11 miles) W of Tours; 8km (5 miles) E of Azay-le-Rideau

The Renaissance Château de Villandry should be at the top of the list for any garden lover. Its 16th-century-style *jardins* are celebrated throughout Touraine and amaze visitors from around the world with their beauty and faithful historic preservation.

Essentials

ARRIVING   Three daily **buses** operate from Tours from July to October only; the trip takes about 30 minutes and costs 1.70€. For bus information see **Le Fil Bleu** (www.filbleu.fr; 📞 02-47-66-70-70). Villandry has no train service. The nearest connection from Tours is in Savonnières; the trip takes 11 minutes and costs 3€ one-way. For information, see www.

sncf-connect.com or call 𝄐 **36-35.** From Savonnières, you can walk along the Loire for 4km (2½ miles) to reach Villandry or take a **taxi.** You can also **drive,** following D7 from Tours.

Exploring the Gardens & Château

Château de Villandry ★★★ CASTLE/GARDENS   Every square meter of the gardens is like a geometric mosaic. Designed on a trio of superimposed cloisters with a water garden on the highest level, the gardens were restored by the Spanish doctor and scientist Joachim Carvallo, great-grandfather of the present owner. The grounds contain 17km (11 miles) of boxwood sculpture, which the gardeners cut to style in only 2 weeks each September. The borders symbolize the faces of love: tender, tragic (represented by daggers), and crazy (with a labyrinth that doesn't go anywhere). The arbors, citrus hedges, and walks keep six men busy full-time. The vegetable garden is being reverted to all-organic.

A feudal castle once stood at Villandry. In 1536, Jean le Breton, François I's finance minister and former ambassador to Italy, acquired the property and built the present château with influences of the Italian Renaissance. The buildings form a U and are surrounded by a moat. Near the gardens is a terrace from which you can see the small village and its 12th-century church. A tearoom, **La Doulce Terrasse** (𝄐 **02-47-50-02-10;** closed

Château de Villandry.

mid-Nov to Mar), serves light dishes using vegetables from the garden and other local ingredients as well as fresh-baked bread and homemade ice cream. For a more gourmet meal, try **Le Cheval Rouge** (see below).

www.chateauvillandry.com. ✆ **02-47-50-02-09.** Gardens and château 13€ adults, 7.50€ children 8–18; gardens only 8€ adults, 5.50€ children 8–18; free for children 7 and under. Gardens daily 9am–5 or 7:30pm, depending on the hour of sunset; château daily Feb to mid-Nov and during the Christmas holidays 9am–4:30 or 6:30pm, according to a complicated seasonal schedule available online.

Where to Stay & Eat

Le Cheval Rouge ★★ MODERN FRENCH   Next to the château, this surprising country restaurant serves up sophisticated versions of French classics. You may dine in the bright and welcoming dining room or a large enclosed terrace. The chef highlights local specialties in dishes like pork belly *rillons* with chestnuts and chanterelle mushrooms, bass poached in sparkling Vouvray wine, and saddle of rabbit stuffed with goat cheese and thyme. On a hot day, finish off with the frozen soufflé with Cointreau. The inn also rents 31 rooms with contemporary appeal and furnishings. A double is 74€; the hotel also has several three to five bed family rooms renting for 87€ to 176€.

9 rue Principale. www.lecheval-rouge.com. ✆ **02-47-50-02-07.** Main course 18€– 20€; fixed-price menu 25€–30€. Daily noon–2:30pm and 7–9pm.

LANGEAIS ★

259km (161 miles) SW of Paris; 26km (16 miles) W of Tours

Dominating the town on a steep slope, this medieval fortress is one of the few châteaux actually on the Loire. Crossing over its drawbridge and through its massive towers takes you back 500 years to the start of the golden age of the Loire.

Essentials

ARRIVING   Several **trains** per day stop here en route from Tours or Saumur. One-way from Saumur is 9€; one-way from Tours is 6€. Transit time from both cities is around 20 minutes. For schedules and information, visit www.sncf-connect.com or call ✆ **36-35.** If you're **driving** from Tours, take D952 southwest to Langeais.

Exploring the Château

Château de Langeais ★★ CASTLE   On December 6, 1491, 15-year-old Anne de Bretagne was wed to Charles VIII at Langeais, permanently attaching Brittany to France. The original castle was built in the 10th century when Fulk III (972–1040), Count of Anjou, sometimes called the "Black Falcon," seized Langeais from the Count of Blois. He erected the first keep, the ruins of which can still be seen. The present structure was

built in 1465 in late medieval style. The interior is well preserved and furnished, thanks to Jacques Siegfried, who not only restored it over 20 years, but also bequeathed it to the Institut de France in 1904. The rooms recreate the ambience of a regal residence of the late Middle Ages, rich with ornamental fireplaces and tapestries. A remarkable 15th-century millefleurs tapestry decorates the Chambre de la Dame, and seven superb tapestries known as the "Valiant Knights" cover the walls of the Salle des Preux.

The Banquet Hall features a mantelpiece carved to resemble a fortress, complete with crenellated towers. The Wedding Hall includes a re-creation of the marriage of Anne de Bretagne and Charles VIII with lavishly costumed wax figures. In the Luini Room is a large 1522 fresco by that artist, removed from a chapel on Lake Maggiore, Italy. It depicts Saint Francis of Assisi and Saint Elizabeth of Hungary with Mary and Joseph. Kids can learn medieval castle construction with interactive displays, or have fun exploring the tree house and the two playgrounds.

Château d'Azay-le-Rideau in autumn.

www.chateau-de-langeais.com. © **02-47-96-72-60.** Admission 11.50€ adults; 9.50€ students and ages 18–25; 5.80€ children 10–17; free for children 9 and under. Daily Apr–June and Sept to mid-Nov 9:30am–6:30pm; mid-Nov to Jan 10am–5pm; Feb–Mar 9:30am–5:30pm; July–Aug 9am–7pm.

AZAY-LE-RIDEAU ★★

261km (162 miles) SW of Paris; 21km (13 miles) SW of Tours

With its idyllic location and fairy-tale turrets, the Renaissance Château d'Azay-le-Rideau was deemed by neighboring writer Honoré de Balzac to be "a facetted diamond set in the Indre."

Essentials

ARRIVING   To reach Azay-le-Rideau, take the **train** from Tours or Chinon. From either starting point, the trip time is about 30 minutes; the one-way fare is 6€ from Chinon or Tours. For the same fare, the SNCF railway also operates a bus between Tours and Azay; the trip takes 35 min and costs 3€. For schedules and information, visit www.sncf-connect.com or call ✆ **36-35.** If you're **driving** from Tours, take D751 southwest to Azay-le-Rideau.

Exploring the Château

Château d'Azay-le-Rideau ★★ CASTLE   Its machicolated towers and blue-slate roof pierced with dormers give it a medieval air; however, its defensive fortresslike appearance is all for show. The château was actually commissioned in the early 1500s for Gilles Berthelot, François I's finance minister, and his wife, Philippa, who supervised its construction. They didn't have long to enjoy their elegant creation: In 1527, Berthelot was accused of misappropriation of funds and forced to flee, and the château reverted to the king. He didn't live here, but granted it to Antoine Raffin, one of his high-ranking soldiers. It became the property of the state in 1905.

Before you enter, circle the château and note the perfect proportions of this crowning achievement of the Renaissance in the Touraine. Check out its most fancifully ornate feature, the bay enclosing a grand stairway with a straight flight of steps. From the second-floor Royal Chamber, look out at the gardens. This lavish bedroom housed Louis XIII when he came through in 1619. The private apartments are lined with rich tapestries dating from the 16th and 17th centuries and feature examples of rare period furniture.

www.azay-le-rideau.monuments-nationaux.fr. ✆ **02-47-45-42-04.** Admission 10.50€ adults; 8.50€ youth 18–25; free for children 17 and under. Daily July–Aug 9:30am–7pm; Apr–June and Sept 9:30am–6pm; Oct–Mar 10am–5:15pm, closed Jan 1, May 1 and Dec 25.

Where to Eat

L'Aigle d'Or ★★ MODERN FRENCH   It might not look very special from the outside, which helps keep away the masses; however, inside the Golden Eagle, you'll find one of the central Loire's best value gastronomic restaurants. After training under top chefs around France, Simon Desiles uses his culinary prowess on his own inventive dishes like trout with summer squash and earl grey tea jus and veal carpaccio with Crouzilles lentils and red pepper chutney. Guests can choose to enjoy these in the classy dining room with wooden-beamed ceilings or in the verdant terrace in the walled garden.

10 av. Adélaïde-Riché. https://laigle-dor.com. ✆ **02-47-45-24-58.** Main course 16€–27€; fixed-price lunch 22€–24€ or dinner 53€–75€. Weds 7:15–8:45pm Thurs–Sat 12:15–1:30pm and 7:15–8:45pm, Sun 12:15–1:30pm. Closed 21-30 Dec.

LOCHES ★★

258km (160 miles) SW of Paris; 40km (25 miles) SE of Tours

Forever linked to legendary beauty Agnès Sorel, Loches is an exquisite medieval village, situated on the banks of the Indre River. Known as the acropolis of the Loire, the château and its satellite buildings form a complex called the Cité Royale. The House of Anjou, from which the Plantagenets descended, owned the castle from 886 to 1205. The kings of France occupied it from the mid–13th century until Charles IX became king in 1560.

Essentials

ARRIVING   You can reach Loches by **train** or **bus,** both of which are operated by the SNCF railway. Six to 10 depart daily; the trip takes 50-to-70-min and costs 3€-9€ one-way. For schedules, visit www.sncf-connect.com or call ✆ **36-35.** If you're **driving** from Tours, take N143 southeast to Loches.

VISITOR INFORMATION   The **Office de Tourisme** is near the bus station on place de la Marne (www.loches-valdeloire.com; ✆ **02-47-91-82-82**).

Exploring Loches

Sitting high on a bluff overlooking the valley, the château and its satellite buildings form a complex called the **Cité Royale ★**.

Château de Loches ★★, 5 pl. Charles-VII (www.chateau-loches.fr; ✆ **02-47-59-01-32**), one of the region's best examples of medieval architecture, is remembered for the *belle des belles* (beauty of beauties) Agnès Sorel, who lived there in the 15th century. Maid of honor to Isabelle de Lorraine, Charles VII became so enamored by Agnès that he gifted his new mistress the château. She bore the king three daughters and wielded great influence over him until her mysterious death. She was immortalized on canvas posthumously by Fouquet as a nearly topless Virgin Mary—with a disgruntled Charles VII looking on. (The original is in Antwerp; the château has a copy.) The château also contains the oratory of Anne de Bretagne, decorated with ermine tails. One of its outstanding treasures is a triptych of *The Passion* (1485) from the Fouquet school.

The massive 36m-high (118 ft.) keep, or *donjon,* of the comtes d'Anjou was built in the 11th century and turned into a prison by Louis XI. The Round Tower contains rooms used for torture; a favorite method involved suspending the victim in an iron cage. In the 15th century, the duke of Milan, Ludovico Sforza, was imprisoned in the Martelet and painted frescoes on the walls to pass the time; he died here in 1508.

You can visit the château, the keep, and medieval garden without a guide daily. It's open May to August from 9am to 7pm, March-April and October-November from 9:30am to 6pm and November to March 9:30am to 5pm; in August, the castle usually holds a medieval festival.

Tickets to the château and the dungeon cost 10.50€ adults, 8.50€ for students and children 7 to 18. Children 6 and under enter free.

The tomb of Agnès Sorel rests nearby at the Romanesque **Collégiale St-Ours (Collegiate Church of St-Ours),** 1 rue Thomas-Pactius (✆ **02-47-59-02-36**), which was erected in the 11th and 12th centuries. Sculpted figures of saints and animals decorate the portal. Stone pyramids (*dubes*) surmount the nave; the carving on the west door is exceptional. The church recently underwent extensive renovations completed in 2022. It is open daily from 9am to 6pm, except during mass; admission is free.

Finally, you may want to walk the ramparts and enjoy the view of the town, including a 15th-century gate and Renaissance inns.

Where to Stay & Eat

Hotel de France ★★   Located in the medieval center of Loches, this charming hotel was a postal relay station until the mid–19th century. In 1932, three floors were added, converting it into an inn. Though the rooms have been upgraded and redecorated, the place keeps its classic provincial charm. The quietest rooms overlook the courtyard; however, the front rooms might be preferred for their balconies. This atmosphere is carried over into the excellent quality and value of the restaurant; guests and day-trippers can dine in the graceful dining room or in the peaceful paradise of the verdant courtyard (menus 18€–55€).

6 rue Picois. www.hoteldefrance-loches.com. ℂ **02-47-59-00-32.** 17 units. 58€–95€ double. Parking 5€. **Amenities:** Restaurant; bar; room service; free Wi-Fi.

Le Pet't Restau ★★ FRENCH   Don't be misled by its name, this restaurant might be "petit" in size, cost, and menu, however, it's "très grand" in flavor and finesse. Located in the historic center of Loches, you'll be greeted with *grand* friendliness as soon as you enter the bright and modern dining room. In the kitchen, chef Marie Bally applies her culinary prowess to the best locally sourced ingredients, while her partner Matthieu will help you decide which local Loire wine to sample with your meal. The menu may offer fish *rillettes* with homemade aioli, chicken risotto with shiitake mushrooms or exotic pork filet mignon with lemongrass and coconut milk. They will also happily adapt their dishes for vegetarians, celiacs, and those with other dietary concerns.

6 Grande Rue. www.leptitrestau.fr. ℂ **02-47-19-85-32.** Main course 15€; fixed-price lunch menu 15€ or dinner 25€. Fri–Tues noon–2:30pm and 7:30–10pm and Wed noon–2:30pm. Closed 1 week mid-Aug and 2 weeks mid–Feb.

SAUMUR

299km (185 miles) SW of Paris; 53km (33 miles) SE of Angers

Saumur lies in a region of vineyards, where the Loire separates to encircle an island. It makes one of the best bases for exploring the western Loire Valley. A small but thriving town, it doesn't entirely live off its past: Saumur produces some 100,000 tons per year of the mushrooms the French adore. Balzac left us this advice: "Taste a mushroom and delight in the essential strangeness of the place." The cool tunnels for the *champignons* also provide the ideal resting place for the region's celebrated sparkling wines. Enjoy both of these local favorites at a neighborhood cafe.

Rock-carved troglodyte home near Saumur.

Essentials

ARRIVING   **Trains** run frequently between Tours Centre and Saumur. Some 20 trains per day arrive from Tours (trip time: 30–40 min.); the one-way fare is 12€. From the station, take bus A into town. For schedules and information, visit www.sncf-connect.com or call ℰ **36-35.** If you're **driving** from Tours, follow D952 or the A85 autoroute southwest to Saumur.

VISITOR INFORMATION   The **Office de Tourisme** is found at 8 bis Quai Carnot (www.ot-saumur.fr; ℰ **02-41-40-20-60**).

Exploring the Area

Of all the Loire cities, Saumur remains the most bourgeois; perhaps that's why Balzac used it for his classic characterization of a smug little town in "Eugénie Grandet." Saumur is also famous as the birthplace of the *couturière* Coco Chanel.

The men of Saumur are among the best equestrians in the world. Founded in 1768, the city's riding school, **Cadre Noir de Saumur ★**, av. de l'Ecole Nationale d'Equitation (www.cadrenoir.fr; ℰ **02-41-53-50-60**), is one of the grandest in Europe, rivaling Vienna's, enough so to be deemed a UNESCO World Heritage Site in 2011. The stables house some

Going Underground

As you drive along the Loire, something other than castles may catch your eye along the riverbanks. The region of Anjou holds the largest concentration of troglodyte caves in all of France. The beige limestone of the area was put to good use building the many châteaux, and the empty caverns from the excavated stone were not left abandoned.

Not surprisingly, the caves were first used to store bottles of the region's bubbly wine; more recently, however, many have been converted into homes, art galleries, and even restaurants. For a true troglodyte experience, stop in at the bustling and mainly underground artist town of **Turquant,** 10km (6 miles) east of Saumur (www.turquant.fr).

350 horses. February to October, 1-hour tours (8€ adults, 6€ children) run from 2pm to 5:30pm Monday, 9am to 12:30pm and 2pm to 5:30pm Tuesday to Friday and 9am to 12:30pm Saturday. Tours depart about every 30 minutes with English on request (reservations by email or phone recommended). Some 48km (30 miles) of specialty tracks wind around the town—to see a rider carry out a curvet is a thrill. The performances peak during the **Carrousel de Saumur ★★** on the third weekend in July.

Predating many of the region's other castles, the 12th-century **Château de Saumur** (www.chateau-saumur.fr; ✆ **02-41-40-24-40**) was converted into the royal residence of Philippe II in the early 13th century. In 1410 it was immortalized in the September scene of the famous illuminated manuscript *Les Très Riches Heures* and, as you'll be able to see for yourself, it hasn't changed much since. The interior of the castle has displays recounting the history of the château as well as examples of tapestries, porcelain, furniture, and other decorative arts. Admission to the château museum is 8.50€ adults, 6.50€ children ages 7 to 16, free for children 6 and under (July–Aug daily 10am–7pm, Apr–June and Sept Tues–Sun 10am–6pm, Feb–Mar and Oct–Dec Tues–Sun 10am–1pm and 2–5:30pm; closed Jan).

The area surrounding the town has become famous for its delicate sparkling wines. In the center of Saumur, you can wander the many aisles of **La Maison du Vin,** 7 quai Carnot (www.vinsvaldeloire.fr; ✆ **02-41-38-45-83**), and choose from a large stock direct from the surrounding vineyards.

An alternative is to travel east of Saumur to the village of **St-Hilaire,** where you'll find a host of vineyards. One of the better ones is **Veuve Amiot,** 21 rue Jean-Ackerman (www.veuveamiot.fr; ✆ **02-41-83-14-14**), where you can tour the wine cellars, taste different vintages, and buy bottles right in the showroom (daily 10am–1pm and 2–6pm, closed Sun Jan–Feb; English tours at 11:45am and 4:45pm).

Mushroom enthusiasts can learn about the cultivation of the local fungi first-hand at the **Musée du Champignon** (www.musee-du-champignon. com; © **02-41-50-31-55**). Museum admission is 9€ adults, 7€ children under 18 (daily Feb–Nov 10am–6pm, until 7pm Apr–Sept).

Where to Stay

Hôtel St-Pierre ★★   Sophisticated Saumur style shines through at this reasonably priced hotel. In the shadows of the Eglise St-Pierre, this 500-year-old building has been brought up to 21st-century standards with creative care to every last detail. Guest rooms have been uniquely decorated with artistic touches and many showcase their architectural aspects such as stone fireplaces or thick wooden beams; the prestige rooms are the best and well worth the splurge. The small French town ambience is completed by listening to the tolling church bells while relaxing in the garden terrace.

Rue Haute-Saint-Pierre. www.saintpierresaumur.com. © **02-41-50-33-00.** 14 units. 95€–218€ double; 257€–283€ suite. Free parking. **Amenities:** Babysitting; room service; free Wi-Fi.

Where to Eat

If you're just breezing through town or looking for a casual bite, try **Les Tontons** (http://lestontonshugo.wixsite.com/bistrotlestontons; © **02-41-59-59-40**), a welcoming bistro with great-value lunch specials. Gaze up at the castle's towers while sampling dishes like filet mignon with Saumur Champigny wine sauce at the **L'Orangeraie** (https://orangeraie-saumur. com; © **02-41-67-12-88**), open from May to September in outbuildings of the château. If you're visiting the equestrian center, you can rub shoulders with the riders at nearby **Le Carrousel** (www.le-resto-du-carrousel.com; © **02-41-51-00-40**), showcasing a freshly renovated dining room and excellent regional cuisine available à la carte or in their reasonably priced menus of 15€ for lunch and from 22€ for dinner.

Le Boeuf Noisette ★★ MODERN FRENCH   Sample Saumur's finest seasonal cuisine at this reinvented historic bistro. A coach inn opened in the 18th century, the building was later converted into a restaurant, whose iron spiral staircase and large painted mirrors from the 1920s have been beautifully preserved. Talented young chef Delphine Ruggeri gains inspiration from her childhood for her revised French classics, including her signature dish and the restaurant's namesake, *le boeuf noisette,* rump steak with brown butter sauce. This, and the other daily specials, come with a changing roster of "all-you-can-eat" sides of from sauteed locally grown mushrooms to homemade *frites.*

29 rue Molière. www.leboeufnoisette.fr. © **09-81-73-73-10.** Main course 26€–31€; fixed-price menu 29€–34€. Tues–Sat noon–2pm and 7–9:30pm.

CHINON ★★

283km (175 miles) SW of Paris; 48km (30 miles) SW of Tours; 31km (19 miles) SW of Langeais

In the film *Joan of Arc*, Ingrid Bergman identified the dauphin as he tried to conceal himself among his courtiers. This took place in real life at the Château de Chinon, one of the oldest fortress-châteaux in France. Charles VII centered his government at Chinon from 1429 to 1450. In 1429, with the English besieging Orléans, the Maid of Orléans prevailed upon the dauphin to give her an army. The rest is history. The seat of French power stayed at Chinon until the end of the Hundred Years' War.

Essentials

ARRIVING   The SNCF runs about seven **trains** and four **buses** every day to Chinon from Tours (trip time: 45 min. by train; 1 hr., 15 min. by bus); the one-way fare is 9€. For schedules and information, www.sncf-connect. com or call ✆ **36-35.** Both buses and trains arrive at the train station, which lies at the edge of the very small town. If you're **driving** from Tours, take D751 southwest through Azay-le-Rideau to Chinon.

Chinon's turreted roofs.

VISITOR INFORMATION The **Office de Tourisme** is at 1 rue Rabelais (www.azay-chinon-valdeloire.com; © **02-47-93-17-85**).

Exploring Chinon & the Château

On the banks of the Vienne, the winding streets of Chinon are lined with many medieval turreted houses, built in the heyday of the court. The most typical street is **rue Voltaire,** lined with 15th- and 16th-century town houses. At no. 44, Richard the Lion-Hearted died on April 6, 1199, from a wound suffered during the siege of Chalus in Limousin. The Grand Carroi, in the heart of Chinon, was the crossroads of the Middle Ages. For the best view, drive across the river and turn right onto quai Danton. From this vantage point, you'll be able to see the castle in relation to the town and the river.

Chinon is known for its delightful red wines. After you visit the attractions, stop for a glass on one of Chinon's terraced cafes or visit a few local vineyards (see below).

Château de Chinon ★★ CASTLE   The château, which was more or less in ruins, underwent a massive restoration completed in 2010 which returned it (or mostly) to its former glory. After being roofless for 200 years, the apartments now have pitched and gabled slate roofs and wood floors, and the keep is once again fortified. The restoration, while not exact (due to the state of the original building), gives the overall impression of what the castle looked like around the time of Joan of Arc's visit. The buildings are separated by a series of moats, adding to its medieval look. A new building, constructed on the foundations of the Fort of St-George, serves as an entrance hall and museum, where you can view archeological finds discovered during the restoration, as well as objects and interactive displays that recount the story of Joan of Arc, Charles VII, and the castle's history.

Btw. rue St-Maurice and av. Francois Mitterrand. www.forteressechinon.fr. © **02-47-93-13-45.** Admission 8.50€ adults; 6.50€ students; free for children 6 and under. Daily May–Aug 9:30am–7pm; Mar–Apr and Sept–Oct 9:30am–6pm; Nov–Feb 9:30am–5pm.

Musée Rabelais–La Devinière ★ MUSEUM   The most famous son of Chinon, François Rabelais, the earthy humanist Renaissance writer, lived in town on rue de la Lamproie. (A plaque marks the spot where his father practiced law and maintained a home and office.) The museum in his honor, just outside the hamlet of Seuilly 5.5km (3½ miles) west of Chinon, was an isolated cottage at the time of his birth. Spending the early years of his life here profoundly affected the writer, and the area served as inspiration for parts of his most famous work, *Gargantua.* Exhibits are spread out on the three floors of the main building, in the dovecote and the

IN PURSUIT OF THE grape

Chinon is famous for its wines, which crop up on prestigious lists around the world. Supermarkets and wine shops throughout the region sell them; families who have been in the business longer than anyone can remember maintain the two most interesting stores. At **Caves Plouzeau,** 94 rue Haute-St-Maurice (www.plouzeau.com; *C* **02-47-93-32-11**), the 12th-century cellars were dug to provide building blocks for the foundations of the château. In the same family since 1929, it is currently being converted into a fully organic vineyard. You're welcome to climb down to the cellars (open for visits and wine sales Apr–Sept Tues–Sat 11am–1pm and 3–7pm; Oct–Mar Thurs–Fri 2–6pm, Sat 11am–1pm and 2–6pm).

The cellars at **Couly-Dutheil,** 12 rue Diderot (www.coulydutheil-chinon.com; *C* **02-47-97-20-20**), are suitably medieval; many were carved from rock. This company produces largely Chinon wines (mostly reds); the popularity of its Bourgueil and St-Nicolas de Bourgueil has grown in North America in recent years. Tours of the caves and a *dégustation des vins* (wine tasting) and cost 9€ per person. Tours held year-round Tuesday to Saturday 9am to noon and 2 to 5:30pm.

wine cellars, each area dedicated to an aspect of Rabelais, his times, and his role in Chinon. It is still an active vineyard, producing 4,000 bottles of excellent wine that would do the writer proud.

La Devinière, just outside of Seuilly off the N751. www.musee-rabelais.fr. *C* **02-47-95-91-18.** Admission 5.50€ adults, 4.50€ students, free for children 6 and under. Daily Apr–June and Sept–Oct 10am–1pm and 2–6pm; July–Aug 10am–7pm; Nov–Mar Wed–Mon 10am–12:30pm and 2–5pm. From Chinon, follow road signs pointing to Saumur and the D117.

Where to Stay & Eat

Hotel Diderot ★★ Within a 5-minute walk of the town's historic core, this is a comfortable hotel with strands of ivy climbing romantically up its stone front. Although the foundations date from the 14th century, the building was radically altered in the 1700s; today you'll see remnants of thick wall and ceiling beams throughout the public rooms and in some of the guest rooms. Rooms are midsize to spacious, outfitted in Henry II or Napoleon III style, usually with big windows letting in maximum sunlight. One of the architectural highlights is a magnificent 15th-century fireplace in the breakfast room, where you'll enjoy as many as 52 kinds of homemade jams and jellies as part of your breakfast. The congenial hosts' enthusiasm for the charms of their hometown is contagious.

4 rue du Buffon. www.hoteldiderot.com. *C* **02-47-93-18-87.** 27 units. 72€–112€ double. Parking 8€. **Amenities:** Bar; free Wi-Fi. Closed last 3 weeks of Nov and last week of Jan through 1st week of Feb.

Les Années 30 ★★ FRENCH   Tucked away on the oldest street in Chinon is the town's most cutting-edge cuisine. Set in an appealing 16th-century building the interior is decorated with paintings and photos from the 1930s, hence the restaurant's name. Its excellent-value menu could include such dishes as rabbit terrine with grapefruit mousse and ginger sorbet, or duck with cherry reduction and poached pear. The raspberry millefeuille with thyme ice cream is the perfect way to end a summertime lunch on the vine-draped terrace. Vegetarian menu available on request.

78 Rue Haute St Maurice. www.facebook.com/lesannees30. ✆ **02-47-93-37-18.** Main course 16€–28€; fixed-price lunch weekdays 19.50€ or dinner 27€–45€. Thurs-Mon 12:15–2pm; Tues 7:30–10pm Jul–Aug. Closed June 10–Jul 1 and 2 weeks mid-Nov to Dec.

USSÉ ★

295km (183 miles) SW of Paris; 14km (8¾ miles) NE of Chinon

The Château d'Ussé is truly a fairy-tale castle. At the edge of the dark forest of Chinon in Rigny-Ussé, it was the inspiration for Perrault's legend of "The Sleeping Beauty" ("La Belle au Bois Dormant").

Essentials

ARRIVING   The château is best visited by car or on an organized bus tour from Tours. If you're driving from Tours or Villandry, follow D7 to Ussé.

Exploring the Château

Château d'Ussé ★ CASTLE   Conceived as a fortress in 1424, this complex of steeples, turrets, towers, and dormers was erected at the dawn of the Renaissance on a hill overlooking the Indre River. The terraces, laden with orange and lemon trees, were laid out by the royal gardener Le Nôtre. When the need for a fortified château passed, the north wing was demolished to open up a greater view. The château was later owned by the duc de Duras and then by Mme. de la Rochejacquelin; its present owner, the duc de Blacas, has opened many rooms to the public, most recently the private dining room and the dungeon. The visit begins in the Renaissance chapel, with its sculptured portal and handsome stalls. You then proceed to the royal apartments, furnished with tapestries and antiques. One gallery displays an extensive collection of swords and rifles. A spiral stairway leads to a tower with a panoramic view of the river and a waxwork Sleeping Beauty waiting for her prince to come.

www.chateaudusse.fr. ✆ **02-47-95-54-05.** Admission 14€ adults; 7€ children 8–16; free for children 7 and under. Daily mid-Feb to Mar 10am–6pm; Apr–Sept 10am–7pm; and Oct–early Nov 10am–6pm; closed the rest of the year.

FONTEVRAUD-L'ABBAYE ★★

304km (188 miles) SW of Paris; 16km (10 miles) SE of Saumur

The Plantagenet dynasty is buried in the Abbaye Royale de Fontevraud. The kings, whose male line ended in 1485, were also the comtes d'Anjou, and they wanted to be buried in their native soil. This regal patronage led to the building of one of Europe's largest medieval monastery complexes.

Essentials

ARRIVING If you're **driving**, take D147 about 4km (2½ miles) from the village of Montsoreau. In season, you can take a **bus** (Line 1) from Saumur; schedules vary according to school holidays—visit the bus company's website, www.agglobus.fr, to download the schedule or call ℰ **02-41-51-11-87.** The one-way fare for the 30-minute trip is 1.50€.

Exploring the Abbey

Fontevraud-l'Abbaye ★★ ABBEY   In this 12th-century Roman-esque church—with four Byzantine domes—lie the remains of two Eng-lish kings and princes, including Henry II of England, the first Plantagenet king, and his wife, Eleanor of Aquitaine, the most famous woman of the Middle Ages. Her crusading son, Richard the Lion-Hearted, is also

Tomb of Henry II of England.

entombed here. The Plantagenet line ended with the death of Richard III at the 1485 Battle of Bosworth. The tombs fared badly during the Revolution, when mobs desecrated the sarcophagi and scattered their contents on the floor.

More intriguing than the tombs is the octagonal **Tour d'Evraud,** the last remaining Romanesque kitchen in France. Dating from the 12th century, the tower contains five of its original eight *apsides* (half-rounded indentations originally conceived as chapels), each crowned with a conically roofed turret. A pyramid tops the conglomeration, capped by an open-air lantern tower pierced with lancets. Robert d'Arbrissel, who spent much of his life as a recluse, founded the abbey in 1101. Aristocratic ladies occupied one part; many, including discarded mistresses of kings, had been banished from court. The four youngest daughters of Louis XV were educated here. Since 2018, the Abbey has also displayed the modern art collection of Martine and Léon Cligman, with hundreds of works by artists like Toulouse-Lautrec, Edgar Degas and André Derain.

www.fontevraud.fr. ℂ **02-41-51-73-52.** Admission 11€ adults; 7.50€ students; free for children 8 and under. Daily Apr–Oct 10am–7pm (until 8pm July–Aug); Jan–Mar and Nov–Dec Wed–Mon 10am–6pm.

Where to Eat

Casual meals are also offered at the Abbey's wine bar and its lunchtime terrace.

Fontevraud Le Restaurant ★★★ MODERN FRENCH   The Fontevraud Abbey's prestigious heritage is reflected in its renowned gastronomic restaurant. Overlooking the Abbey's cloisters, the vaulted dining room and its minimalistic décor evoke a Medieval refectory. A purist approach is also taken by chef Thibaut Ruggeri in his simple yet exquisite cuisine which allows top-quality, sustainable regional products to shine. In sync with nature, the restaurant's "lune" menu changes with the moon's cycle and includes the likes of Lorient blue lobster with blueberries and green beans or Anjou pigeon with eggplant and figs drizzled in the Abbey's own honey.

38 Rue Saint Jean de L'Habit. www.fontevraud.fr. ℂ **02-46-46-10-10.** Fixed-price menu 89€. Wed–Fri 7–9:30pm; Sat–Sun noon–1:30pm and 7–9:30pm. Closed Dec 24–25 and 31, Jan 1 and 2 weeks in Feb.

La Licorne ★★ MODERN FRENCH   Luckily the frugal monks' lifestyle of the Fontevraud Abbey isn't replicated at this nearby popular dining spot. Located on a walkway between the abbey and the parish church, this 18th-century bourgeois home exudes the grace of the *ancien régime.* However, the service isn't quite as regal and can be somewhat slow. So sit back and relax in its walled garden; the excellent-value menu is certainly worth the wait. It includes refined dishes such as poached sea bream stuffed with shellfish and quinoa grown in the region or royal Maine

D'Anjou filet of beef draped in Saumur-Champigny red wine reduction, and such delectable desserts as local Alienor pastries.

Allée Ste-Catherine. www.lalicorne-restaurant-fontevraud.fr. ☎ **02-41-51-72-49.** Main course 19€–39€; fixed-price lunch menu 19€ or dinner 26€–72€. Nov–Apr Tues–Sun noon–2pm and Tues and Thurs–Sat 7–9pm; May–Oct daily noon–2pm and 7–9pm. Closed last 2 weeks of Dec.

ANGERS ★★

288km (179 miles) SW of Paris; 89km (55 miles) E of Nantes

Once the capital of Anjou, Angers straddles the Maine River at the western end of the Loire Valley. Though it suffered extensive damage in World War II, it has been restored, blending provincial charm with a hint of sophistication. The bustling regional center is often used as a base for exploring the châteaux to the west. Young people, including some 30,000 college students, keep this vital city of 155,700 jumping until late at night.

Essentials

ARRIVING High-speed **trains** make the 1½-hour trip every hour from Paris's Gare Montparnasse; the cost is 19€ to 80€ one-way. From Tours, about 10 trains per day make the 1-hour trip; a one-way ticket is 8€ to 20€. The Angers train station is a convenient walk from the château. For schedules and information, visit www.sncf-connect.com or call ☎ **36-35.** From Saumur, there are direct **bus** connections (1½ hr.); visit https://aleop. paysdelaloire.fr or call ☎ **09-69-39-14-14** for schedules. If you're **driving** from Tours, take the A85 autoroute west and exit at Angers Centre.

VISITOR INFORMATION The **Office de Tourisme,** 7 pl. Kennedy (www. angersloiretourisme.com; ☎ **02-41-23-50-00**), is opposite the entrance to the château.

Exploring the Town

If you have time for shopping, wander to the pedestrian zone in the center of town. Its boutiques and small shops sell everything from clothes and shoes to jewelry and books. To satisfy your sweet-tooth stop in at **Benoit,** 2 rue Lices (www.chocolats-benoit.com; ☎ **02-41-88-94-52**). The best chocolate shop in Angers was passed from father to daughter and Anne-Francoise's new recipes have garnered her enough awards and renown to open a boutique in Paris.

Oenophiles will not be disappointed with the selection at the **Maison du Vin de l'Anjou,** 5 bis pl. Kennedy (www.vinsdeloire.fr; ☎ **02-41-17-68-20**), where you can learn about the area's vineyards and buy a bottle or two for gifts or a picnic.

Cathédrale St-Maurice ★★ CATHEDRAL The cathedral dates mostly from the 12th and 13th centuries; the main tower is from the 16th century. The statues on the portal represent everybody from the Queen of

Sheba to David at the harp. The tympanum depicts Christ Enthroned. The stained-glass windows from the 12th through 16th centuries have made the cathedral famous. The oldest one illustrates the martyrdom of St. Vincent; the most unusual is of St. Christopher with the head of a dog. The 12th-century nave, a landmark in cathedral architecture, is a work of harmonious beauty.

Pl. Freppel. ☏ **02-41-87-58-45.** Free admission; donations appreciated. Daily 8am–8pm.

Château d'Angers ★★★ CASTLE   The château, dating from the 9th century, was the base of the comtes d'Anjou. At the end of the 11th century, the notorious Black Falcon, Foulques III d'Anjou, who conquered much of the Western Loire, lived here, and in time, the Plantagenets took up residence. From 1230 to 1238, the outer walls and 17 enormous towers were built, creating a fortress. King René favored the château, and during his reign, a brilliant court life flourished until he was forced to surrender to Louis XI. Louis XIV turned the château into a prison. In World War II, the Nazis used it as a munitions depot, and the Allies bombed it in 1944.

Visit the castle to see the **Apocalypse Tapestries ★★★**. They weren't always so highly regarded—they once served as a canopy to protect orange trees and were also used to cover the damaged walls of a church. Woven in Paris by Nicolas Bataille from cartoons by Jean de Bruges around 1375 for Louis I of Anjou, they were purchased for a nominal sum in the 19th century. The series of 77 sections, illustrating the Book of St. John, stretches 100m (328 ft.).

A full visit should also include the ramparts, windmill tower, and 15th-century chapel. Once you've paid the entrance fee, you can take an hour-long guided tour focusing on the architecture and history of the

---

A Toast with the Home-Brew: Cointreau

In the early 19th century, two confectioner brothers set out to create a drink of "crystal-clear purity." The result was Cointreau, a twice-distilled alcohol from the peels of two types of oranges, bitter and sweet. The factory has turned out the drink since 1849. Cointreau is a key ingredient in such popular cocktails as the cosmopolitan and the sidecar. Recent marketing campaigns, including one featuring seductress Dita Von Teese, have helped modernize the brand and today some 13 million bottles of Cointreau are consumed annually.

La Carée Cointreau, 2 bd. des Bretonnières (www.carre-cointreau.fr; ☏ **02-41-31-50-50**), is in the suburb of St-Barthèlemy, a 10-minute drive east of the town center. If you call ahead to reserve, you can take a 1½-hour-long guided tour of the distillery and then visit the showroom, where you can sample and stock up on the fruity liqueur. Hours are variable; tours run on Saturdays only from October to mid-April, and Tuesday through Saturday the rest of the year (12€–20€ adults, depending on tastings; 4.50€ children 12–17; free for children 11 and under).

château, or a tour devoted to the Apocalypse Tapestries. Both are available only in French; a self-guided tour with audio guide is available in English.

2 promenade du Bout-du-Monde. www.chateau-angers.fr. ℘ **02-41-86-48-77.** Admission 9.50€ adults; free for children 17 and under and to all on 1st Sun of the month from Nov–March. Sept–Apr daily 10am–5:30pm; May–Aug daily 9:30am–6:30pm.

Musée Jean Lurçat ★★ MUSEUM   The town has four museums, but the most interesting is in the Ancien Hôpital St-Jean. Visitors to this hospital established in 1174 now come for its famous tapestry, *Le Chant du Monde* (*The Song of the World*), created by Jean Lurçat between 1957 and 1966. This monumental work of 10 panels is a symphony of the artist's interpretation of the destiny of the world, from awe-inspiring space travel to the horrible apocalypses of war. Be sure to view the more than 60 tapestries the museum has on view and its 17th-century dispensary, equipped with shelves of earthenware jars and trivets. Don't miss the Romanesque cloister with its secret garden on your way out.

4 bd. Arago. www.musees.angers.fr. ℘ **02-41-24-18-45.** Admission 6€ adults, 3€ students, free for visitors 25 and under; joint ticket with the Château d'Angers 10.50€ adults. Tues-Sun 10am–6pm.

Where to Stay & Eat

L'Hôtel d'Anjou ★★★   A 2022 makeover has converted the historic Hôtel d'Anjou into one of the most stylish hotels in the region. Originally opened in 1857, the graceful hotel is found in the heart of Angers and a short walk to the château. Entirely refurbished, the bright guest rooms have chic decorative touches in greys, pumpkin and peacock green. The new bathrooms have treated marble or light wood counters and tub/showers or rain showers.

The hotel's reinvented restaurant, **Odorico,** pays tribute to Isidore Odorico, the Italo-Breton mosaic artist behind its stunning Art-Deco dining room. After a cocktail in its swank bar, feast on caramelized black tomatoes with tomato foam and rocket sorbet, grilled sea bass with fennel confit and figs in balsamic vinegar and "bread of Genoa" almond cake with roasted apricots infused with lemon balm. Main courses are 23€ to 29€ and fixed-price menus 25€ for lunch and 50€ for dinner.

1 bd. du Maréchal Foch. www.hoteldanjou.fr. ℘ **02-41-21-12-11.** 53 units. 99€–170€ double. Parking 8€. **Amenities:** Restaurant; bar; room service; spa; sauna; hammam; free Wi-Fi.

L'Hôtel de France ★★   Situated across from the railway station, this comfortable 19th-century hotel is the best place for a quick overnight in Angers. It's been in the careful hands of the Bouyer family since 1893. The spacious rooms are decorated in mainly cream and beige tones with

A street in the historic core of Angers.

smart classic furnishings. It is a common stopover for business travelers and room rates go up 15€ to 25€ per night during trade shows.

8 pl. de la Gare, Angers. www.hoteldefrance-angers.com. ℂ **02-41-88-49-42.** 55 units. 110€–222€ double. Parking 8€. **Amenities:** Restaurant; bar; room service; free Wi-Fi.

Provence Caffè ★ PROVENÇAL   If you've had your fill of Loire specialties, come here for the flavors of Provence. From the outside, it doesn't look like much, but that helps keep it a good local secret. Recently revamped, the dining room is bright and modern, matching the fresh seasonal menu. The best tables are next to the windows, overlooking the pretty main town square. Chef Arnaud Le Calloch has a fondness for fish, covered in his red mullet salad with pistou or sea bream with ratatouille tart, yet carnivores fear not, you can sink your teeth into a succulent braised lamb shank with mashed potatoes topped with confit garlic and rosemary juice. To cleanse your palate, order a *Versinthe,* the lesser-known Provençal cousin to absinthe.

9 pl. du Ralliement. www.provence-caffe.com. ℂ **02-41-87-44-15.** Main course 17€; fixed-price menu 19€–35€. Tues–Sat noon–2pm and 7–10pm.

7

NORMANDY & MONT-ST-MICHEL

By Anna E. Brooke

T he gentleness in Normandy's rich rolling landscape gives little clue to the region's long and turbulent history. Look a little closer, however, and you see haunting reminders of some of the Second World War's most dramatic and decisive battles. The Allied landings on Normandy's beaches in June 1944 changed the course of the Second World War. Although the embarkation beaches teem with visitors in the summer, they remain living memorials to bravery, determination, and ingenuity.

But these sights don't exclusively define the region either. Fashionable Deauville and its family-friendly neighbor Trouville have been drawing sun-seekers since the 19th century. As the age of the railway expanded during the Victorian era, so too did genteel seaside resorts that dot this stretch of France's northern coast.

Bayeux attracts lovers of history and art, many to see the extraordinary tapestry that recounts another battle that altered the course of history: the Norman Conquest. Honfleur is a place of arty pilgrimage, and Rouen's history and bustling restaurant scene attract foodies hungry for culture. At the western border is Mont-St-Michel, which has stood guard for a millennium and is linked to the coastline via a pedestrian bridge.

Head inland to savor the cream of Normandy produce—namely, the pungent cheeses from Camembert, Pont l'Evêque, and Livarot. Instead of the vineyards that characterize the South of France, Normandy has apple orchards that produce the region's renowned cider and Calvados brandy.

ROUEN ★★

135km (84 miles) NW of Paris; 89km (55 miles) E of Le Havre

Normandy's capital buzzes from dawn 'til dusk, thanks to its busy port (fifth largest in France) and lively university. Its agreeable atmosphere invites leisurely strolls along medieval lanes, where some of Normandy's most delicious produce sits temptingly in shop windows. Former celebrated residents of Rouen include writer Gustave Flaubert (who grew up along the city's enchanting cobbled streets), Claude Monet (who endlessly painted Rouen's Cathédrale de Notre-Dame), and Joan of Arc, who met her tragic end in the place du Vieux Marché, the Old Marketplace, in 1431.

Victor Hugo called Rouen "the city of a hundred spires." Half of it was destroyed during World War II, mostly by Allied bombers, and many Rouennais were killed. During the reconstruction of the old quarters,

Rouen's famous clock tower.

some of the almost-forgotten crafts of the Middle Ages were revived. Today its metropolitan area is home to half a million people, with about 115,000 clustered in the large center.

Essentials

ARRIVING   From Paris's Gare St-Lazare, **trains** leave for Rouen about once an hour (trip time: 1½ hr.). The one-way fare is about 25€, but you can get fares online for as little as 9€. The main station is a 10-minute walk to the city center. For rail information and schedules, visit www.sncf-connect.com or call ✆ **36-35.** To **drive** from Paris, take A13 northwest to Rouen (trip time: 2 hr.).

VISITOR INFORMATION   The **Office de Tourisme** is at Esplanade Marcel Duchamp (en.rouentourisme.com; ✆ **02-32-08-32-40**).

CITY LAYOUT   As in Paris, the Seine splits Rouen into a **Rive Gauche** (Left Bank) and **Rive Droite** (Right Bank). The old city is on the Rive Droite.

Getting Around

ON FOOT   Rouen's old town is compact and best navigated on foot, as many of its medieval streets are pedestrianized. The Tourist Office offers free maps marked with walking tours around the city.

BY BICYCLE   To register for Rouen's bike-share program **Lovélo** (lovelo libreservice.fr/en) download the app to register, then grab a bike from one of Rouen's 64 bike stands; fees range from 1€ for a day to 5€ for a week, with the first 30-minutes free of charge.

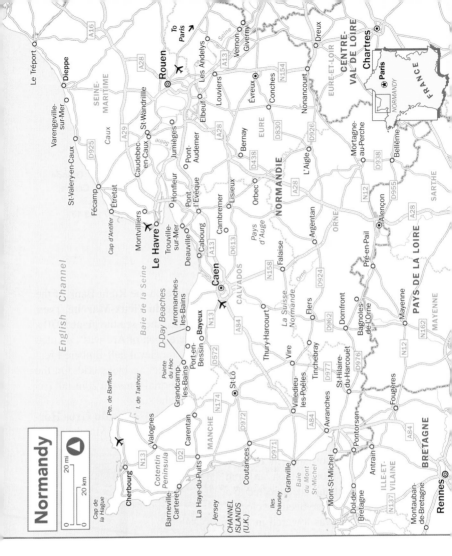

Normandy

20 mi
20 km

Cap de la Hague

English Channel

Baie de la Seine

D-Day Beaches

BY CAR **Rouen Normandie Stationnement** (rouen-normandie-stationnement.fr/en/home) details the city's five central public parking lots and their hourly prices. As prices average 16.50€ for 24 hours, having a car in Rouen can be expensive. Unless you plan to visit other areas, you won't be needing a car in Rouen itself.

BY TAXI **Les Taxi Blancs** (taxis-blancs-rouen.fr; ✆ 02-35-61-20-50). There should be a maximum of 2.60€ on the clock when you get in, then it should cost roughly 1.92€ per kilometer for your ride. Prices increase to 2.47€/km between 7pm and 7am.

BY PUBLIC TRANSPORT Rouen's **Métro** (reseau-astuce.fr) has two lines running north-south through the city, underground on Rive Droite and at street level on Rive Gauche. The most central stations in Rive Droite are Théâtre des Arts, Palais de Justice, and the train station, Gare-Rue Verte. Tickets cost 1.70€ (or 14.50€ for a carnet of 10) and are on sale at automatic kiosks at each station.

[FastFACTS] ROUEN

ATMs/Banks Dozens of banks are all around the city center, with 10 along rue Jeanne d'Arc.

Doctors & Hospitals Centre Hospitalier

Universitaire de Rouen (www.chu-rouen.fr; ✆ **02-32-88-89-90**).

Mail & Postage **La Poste,** 45 bis rue Jeanne d'Arc (✆ **36-31**).

Pharmacies **Grande Pharmacie du Centre,** 29 pl. Cathédrale (✆ **02-35-71-33-17**).

Exploring Rouen

The city's main sights—and the old town—are on the Right Bank of the Seine. Visitors usually make a beeline for **place du Vieux-Marché.** Their first impression is often one of bafflement when they see the giant 1970s-era **Church of Ste-Jeanne** in the place where Joan of Arc was executed for heresy on May 30, 1431. Surrounded by medieval half-timbered restaurants and shops, the church's modern architecture looks odd. On the west side of the church is the Joan of Arc Memorial Cross, a 20m-tall (65 ft.) cross on the spot where she was burned at the stake.

The pedestrianized "Street of the Great Clock"—**rue du Gros Horloge**—runs between Rouen's cathedral and place du Vieux Marché and is one of the hubs of the city. It's named for an ornate gilt Renaissance clock mounted on an arch over the street and is connected to a bell tower; this had been the clock's home until it was lowered in 1529 so that the Rouennais could get a closer look at it. You can climb the **bell tower** (Apr–Oct Tues–Sun 10am–1pm and 2–7pm, Nov–Mar daily 2–6pm; 7.50€ adults, 3.80€ ages 6–18, free for children under 6; fee includes audio guide at rouen.fr/gros-horloge), stopping at the exhibition rooms along the way to learn about the structure's history and watch the bells in action. At the top are lovely views of the old town and cathedral.

Cathédrale Notre-Dame de Rouen.

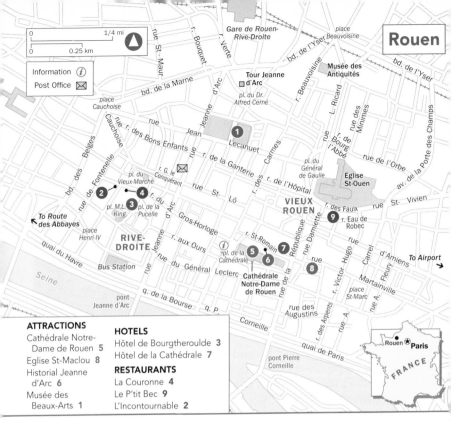

ATTRACTIONS

Cathédrale Notre-Dame de Rouen **5**

Eglise St-Maclou **8**

Historial Jeanne d'Arc **6**

Musée des Beaux-Arts **1**

HOTELS

Hôtel de Bourgtheroulde **3**

Hôtel de la Cathédrale **7**

RESTAURANTS

La Couronne **4**

Le P'tit Bec **9**

L'Incontournable **2**

In addition to the attractions below are several museums that will appeal to those with interest in the decorative arts and ancient France. All are free to enter. They are the **Musée de la Céramique ★★** (94 rue Jeanne d'Arc; https://museedelaceramique.fr/en), known for its 17th- and 18th-century Rouen faïence (opaquely glazed earthenware), which has a distinctive red hue because of the color of the local clay; **Musée Le Secq des Tournelles ★** (Rue Jacques-Villon; https://museelesecqdestournelles.fr/en), which houses handsome Norman wrought iron works in a 15th-century church; and **Musée des Antiquités ★** (198 Rue Beauvoisine; https://museedesantiquites.fr/en) set in a 17th-century monastery, with a notable collection of 1st- and 2nd-century BC weapons, jewelry, and mosaics.

Cathédrale Notre-Dame de Rouen ★★★ CATHEDRAL   Monet immortalized Rouen's cathedral (particularly the facade, with its galaxy of statues) in his paintings. The main door, Porte Central, is embellished with sculptures (some decapitated) depicting the Tree of Jesus. The 12th-century Porte St-Jean and Porte St-Etienne flank it. Consecrated in 1063, the cathedral, a symphony of lacy stonework, was reconstructed after suffering damage in World War II. Two towers distinguish it: **Tour de Beurre**

was financed by the faithful who were willing to pay for the privilege of eating butter during Lent. Containing a carillon of 56 bells, the **Tour Lanterne** (Lantern Tower)—built in 1877 and using 740 tons of iron and bronze—rises to almost 150m (492 ft.).

The cathedral's interior is fairly uniform. The **choir** is a masterpiece, with 14 soaring pillars. The **Booksellers' Stairway**, in the north wing of the transept, is adorned with a stained-glass rose window that dates, in part, from the 1500s. The 13th-century **chancel** is beautiful, with simple lines. Especially interesting is the **Chapelle de la Vierge,** adorned with Renaissance tombs of the cardinals d'Amboise. Also

Interior, Cathédrale Notre-Dame de Rouen.

entombed is the heart of Richard the Lion-Hearted, a token of his affection for the people of Rouen. Along the south-facing side of the cathedral is an entrancing collection of statues of saints that had previously adorned the exterior.

Pl. de la Cathédrale. www.cathedrale-rouen.net. ✆ **02-35-71-51-23.** Free admission. Apr–Oct Mon 2–7pm, Tues–Sat 9am–7pm, Sun 9am–6pm; Nov–Mar Mon 2–6pm, Tues–Sat 9am–noon and 2–6pm, Sun 2–6pm. Closed during Mass and some holidays. Metro: Palais de Justice.

Église St-Maclou ★★ CHURCH

St-Maclou was built in the Flamboyant Gothic style with a crenelated porch and cloisters. It's known for the 16th-century panels on its doors; the Portail des Fontaines on the left is especially exquisite. The church was built in 1200, rebuilt in 1432, and consecrated in 1521. Its lantern tower is from the 19th century.

Well worth a peek is the nearby **Aître Saint-Maclou,** 184 rue Martainville (aitresaintmaclou.fr/en; ✆ **02-35-52-48-21;** Apr–Oct daily 9am–7pm, Nov–Mar Sat–Sun 9am–5pm; free admission). Half-timbered buildings, decorated with creepy skull motifs, mark the site of a cemetery for victims of the 1348 Great Plague. The site offers guided visits and audio-guided visits (from 5€), and hosts regular art exhibitions.

3 pl. Barthélémy. rouen.fr/eglise-saint-maclou. ✆ **02-35-08-69-00.** Free admission. Apr–Oct Mon, Sat–Sun 10am–noon and 2–6pm; Nov–Mar Sat–Mon 10am–noon and 2–5:30pm.

Historial Jeanne d'Arc ★★ MUSEUM

Set within the Archbishop's Palace behind the cathedral is France's largest site devoted to Joan of Arc. The palace's elaborate interior is an impressive setting for the story of the

Maid of Orléans, told in multimedia and interactive displays, with English-language audio guides (included in your ticket price). These compelling exhibits do an excellent job in telling Joan's tragic story and subsequent trial. You'll also see the room where she was condemned to death in 1431.
7 rue Saint-Romain. www.historial-jeannedarc.fr. ℂ **02-35-52-48-00.** Admission 11€ adults; 8€ for children 6–17; free for 5 and under. Tues–Sun 10am–7pm.

Musée des Beaux-Arts ★★★ MUSEUM   Featuring the second-largest collection of Impressionist paintings in France, this splendid fine arts museum displays more than 8,000 artworks ranging from medieval primitives to contemporary paintings. Within this handsome 19th-century building are works by Renaissance masters, including Veronese, Velázquez, Caravaggio, and Rubens. You'll find portraits by David and works by Delacroix and Ingres (seek out his *La Belle Zélie*). A Gérard David retable (altarpiece), *La Vierge et les saints* (*The Virgin and the Saints*), is a masterpiece. Fans of Impressionism can marvel at paintings by Monet, Renoir, Sisley, and Pissarro, including several of Monet's paintings of Rouen's cathedral.
Esplanade Marcel Duchamp. http://mbarouen.fr. ℂ **02-35-71-28-40.** Free admission. Wed–Mon 10am–6pm.

Where to Stay

Hotel de Bourgtheroulde ★★★   Ancient meets modern in dazzling style at Rouen's only truly high-end hotel. Step inside this 15th-century mansion by the place du Vieux Marché and you're immediately in one of the most modern and chicest hotel interiors in the region. The galleried Atrium Bar makes a bold statement with its soaring red ceiling and glass floor exposing the spa's enormous indoor pool below. No two rooms are alike: Some have sleek, minimalist decor, while others go for the full traditional look, with antique-style furnishings, exposed ceiling beams, and wood-paneled walls. In addition to an indoor pool, the **Spa du Drap d'Or** features a steam bath, sauna, and fitness room.
15 pl. de la Pucelle. www.hotelsparouen.com. ℂ **02-35-14-50-50.** 78 units. 280€– 350€ double; 320€–430€ suite. Parking 28€. **Amenities:** 2 bars; 2 restaurants; indoor pool; spa; free Wi-Fi.

Hôtel de la Cathédrale ★★   It's hard to beat the location of this simple yet charming hotel: It's just off a pedestrian street midway between the cathedral and the Église St-Maclou. Some rooms have more dash than others, with pretty *toile de jouy* wallpaper, deep leather armchairs and exposed beams. The courtyard garden is a haven in summer. When it's too chilly to eat outside, the cozy breakfast room—with its beamed ceiling and inglenook fireplace—is a delightful alternative. Some of the public areas could do with sprucing up, though, and the hotel might not suit people with limited mobility.
12 rue St-Romain. www.hotel-de-la-cathedrale.fr. ℂ **02-35-71-57-95.** 26 units. 115€– 155€ double; 155€ triple; 175€ quadruple. **Amenities:** Free Wi-Fi.

Where to Eat

Don't be surprised to find plenty of fresh, succulent seafood in France's fourth largest port. Rouen lives up to its status as Normandy's capital in offering a superb selection of restaurants serving fantastic Norman cuisine. Restaurants are dotted all around the city, with many found in the antiques quarter near Église St-Maclou and, inevitably, in the old market square. Key local ingredients include fresh fish, rich cream, butter, and apples, which are on tantalizing display in the **daily market,** place du Vieux Marché (Tues–Sat 7am–7pm, Sun 7am–1pm). A much larger **food market** is in the place St-Marc east of the cathedral (Tues and Fri–Sat 6am–6pm, Sun 6am–1:30pm).

La Couronne ★★★ TRADITIONAL FRENCH   It calls itself France's oldest *auberge* and has been keeping travelers well fed since 1345 in its superb location on the place du Vieux Marché. Step upstairs and you'll see the photos of those who passed through this cocoonlike half-timbered house—everyone from Salvador Dalí to Patti Smith. Julia Child had her first-ever lunch in France here in 1948, and swooned over the supremely buttery *sole meunière,* which you can have with oysters on the 68€ menu named after her. The Gourmet Harmony menu (59€) includes pigeon roasted with honey, but save room for the cheese trolley and its 21 mouthwatering choices.

31 pl. du Vieux Marché. www.lacouronne.com.fr. ℂ **02-35-71-40-90.** Main course 35€–58€; fixed-price lunch menu 29€–68€ or dinner 42€–83€. Daily noon–2:30pm and 7–10:30pm.

Le P'tit Bec ★★ FRENCH   Gratin dishes are the specialty of this cheerful, friendly bistro. It's pure comfort food, like the Paysan: potatoes, ham, eggs, bacon, cream, and Emmental, all baked to crispy goodness. Or an all-cheese extravaganza of camembert, goats' cheese, Emmentaler, and Neufchâtel. The menu also has French classics such as confit de canard.

182 rue Eau de Robec. www.leptitbec.com. ℂ **02-35-07-63-33.** Main course 14.50€–19.50€; fixed-price lunch 15.70€-18.80€. Mon noon–2:30pm; Tues–Sat noon–2:30pm and 7–10:30pm.

L'Incontournable ★★★ FRENCH   In an interior as bright and cheery as the cuisine, chef Eric Autin serves his wonderful, contemporary takes on French and Normand dishes. This might mean local BBQ beef, served with watercress sauce and purée of Jerusalem artichokes, or pollock with oyster cream and citrusy carrots, followed by a ginormous Mont Blanc (meringue with chestnut cream and whipped cream) to share. You can even stop by for tea and cake in the afternoon.

1 rue de la Pie. lincontournable-rouen.fr ℂ **02-35-88-21-68.** Fixed-price lunch menu 22€–27€; fixed-price dinner menu 65€; main courses 32€-40€. Mon–Sat noon–9am-9pm.

Normandy might not have the vineyards of other parts of France, but it does have endless apple orchards that produce the acclaimed Calvados brandy, refreshing alcoholic cider, and *pommeau,* a mixture of Calvados and apple juice. In the lush rolling hills of the Pays d'Auge east of Caen, producers open their half-timbered farms (mostly by appointment) to thirsty tourists eager to try the different varieties of apple nectar. Some of the region's most delightful villages lie on this 40km (25-mile) **Route du Cidre** (route ducidre.com), notably Cambremer and **Beuvron-en-Auge,** the latter being one of the designated Most Beautiful Villages of France (normandie-cabourg-pays-dauge-tourisme.fr/destinations/beuvron-en-auge). In Pont-l'Evêque, **Calvados Père Magloire L'Experience** is an entertaining museum that uses multisensory displays to show how apple brandy is made, and also offers tastings (www.calvados-experience.com; ☎ **02-31-64-30-31;** 14.50€ adults, 6€ children 12–17, free for children 11 and under; Mar–Dec daily 10am–7pm, Jan–Mar daily 10am–6pm).

Shopping

Rouen was once one of France's major producers of the fine decorative ceramic ware known as *faïence de Rouen.* For traditional faïence, your best bet is **Faïences Saint-Romain,** 47 place du Vieux Marché (☎ **06-28-22-68-21**). Rouen is also an antiques capital, with dozens of vendors in the Old Town. The best hunting ground is along **rue Damiette,** and **rue St-Romain.** Other antiques shops worth visiting are **Galerie Bertran,** 108 rue Molière (galeriebertran.com; ☎ **02-35-98-24-06**), with a good selection of 18th- and 19th-century paintings, especially by School of Rouen Impressionists; and **Librairie Bertran,** 112 rue Molière (librairie-bertran-rouen.fr; ☎ **02-35-70-79-96**), with its collection of antique books. A **flea market** joins the food stalls in place St-Marc on Tuesdays, and Fridays to Sundays.

Chocolate lovers are spoiled for choice, with delectable treats at **Le Cacaotier,** 116 rue du Gros Horloge (www.lecacaotier.com; ☎ **02-35-62-71-06**), and **Auzou,** 163 rue du Gros Horloge (www.auzouchocolatier.fr; ☎ **02-35-70-59-31**).

Nightlife

In the desacralized Saint-Nicaise church (with foundations dating back to the 7th c.), **L'Église Brasserie,** 12 rue Saint-Nicaise (brasserieragnar.com), claims to be the world's biggest church-set brewery—and boy is it impressive, with barrels lined up where pews once stood below billowing arches. By 2027 there will be a Scandinavian restaurant in the organ area; until then you can make do with hearty platters of cheese and charcuterie as you sip pints of local Ragnar beer, inspired (fittingly for the medieval setting) from 11th-century recipes.

Le Vicomté, rue de la Vicomté (facebook.com/Levicomtebar; ✆ 02-35-71-24-11), is another popular night spot, attracting everyone from the after-work crowd to clubbers, with five levels devoted to fun and food. The space has a club with live bands and DJs, classy fireside cocktail bar, restaurant, patio, and even a billiard room.

Opéra de Rouen, 7 rue du Docteur Rambert (www.operaderouen.fr; ✆ 02-35-98-74-78), schedules year-round ballet, opera, and classical music performances. The former hangar Le 106, quai Jean de Béthancourt (www.le106.com; ✆ 02-32-10-88-60), offers a jam-packed lineup of French and international pop and rock shows. Also check the Tourist Office's website for the latest events.

HONFLEUR ★★

201km (125 miles) NW of Paris; 63km (39 miles) NE of Caen

This exquisite fishing port dating from the 11th century has been the focus of artists for hundreds of years—native son Eugène Boudin, Gustave Courbet, and Claude Monet, to name but three. Stroll along the Vieux Bassin (old harbor) and you can still see art students with their sketchbooks trying to capture the enchanting light that dances off the white boats and glistening water. Impossibly tall 18th-century town houses tower over the harbor, where cafes and restaurants crowd around the pleasure boats.

It's busy and, yes, full of tourists from all over the world. But it's such a beguiling place that it's worth putting up with the throngs. Time your visit so that you have lunch a bit early, about noon. Then you'll have the streets to yourself while everyone else is still eating.

The approach from the east is along the impressive Pont de Normandie bridge that spans the Seine River from Le Havre. And the Côte de Grace—the start of the alluring Côte Fleurie—meanders westwards from here, passing half-timbered Norman homes and ancient chapels en route to Trouville.

Essentials

ARRIVING   There's no direct **train** service into Honfleur, but you can book combined train and bus tickets from Paris via www.sncf-connect. com: Roughly half a dozen trains leave Gare St-Lazare for Trouville-Deauville each day, where you can catch a Car Nomad (bus) to Honfleur; the one-way fares start at 37€ and the combined train and bus trip takes about 3 hours.

To **drive** from Paris (trip time: 2–2½ hr.; around 20€ in tolls), take A13 west, then the A29 north in the direction of Le Havre. From Pont l'Evêque or other points southwest, D579 leads to Honfleur's major boulevard, rue de la République.

VISITOR INFORMATION   The **Office de Tourisme** is on quai Lepaulmier (www.ot-honfleur.fr; ✆ 02-31-89-23-30).

Sailboats in Honfleur harbor.

Getting Around

ON FOOT   Honfleur is small enough to get around on foot.

BY CAR   During high season, it can be difficult to find a place to park. The tourist board's website has a handy map detailing which areas are free and which car parks charge and their fees.

BY TAXI   **Benoit Taxi** (✆ **06-21-73-32-70**).

[FastFACTS] HONFLEUR

ATMs/Banks   Half a dozen banks are along rue de la Foulerie, pl. Pierre Berthelot and rue des Longettes.

Mail & Postage   **La Poste,** 7 cours Albert Manuel (✆ **36-31**).

Pharmacies   **Pharmacie du Dauphin,** 5 rue Dauphin (pharmacie-du-dauphin-honfleur.fr; ✆ **02-31-89-10-80**).

Exploring Honfleur

Begin your tour of Honfleur by picking up a map from the Tourist Office (or downloading it from the website) to follow four well-curated, themed walking routes, each detailing points of interest around town. The "Footsteps of the Painters" map leads you to 14 panels of paintings by

19th-century artists around town. There's also a self-guided tour with an audio guide (5€). Stroll along the scenic quays, past the fishing boats and narrow, slate-roofed houses that line the **Vieux Bassin.** On the north side of the harbor, the former governor's house, the imposing **Lieutenance,** dates from the 16th century. Nearby is France's largest wooden church, **Église Ste-Catherine,** pl. Ste-Catherine (✆ **02-31-89-11-83**), which was built by 15th-century shipbuilders. The church is open daily from 9am–7pm except during services and ceremonies.

See the village from a different perspective on one of the regular **boat trips** (www.promenade-en-bateau-honfleur.fr; 45–90 min.; 10€–16€) that depart from jetties east of the Vieux Bassin. The 45-minute ride on *La Calypso* explores the harbors that make up the port of Honfleur, while the 90-minute journey on *Ville d'Honfleur* takes you out into the Seine estuary.

Les Maisons Satie ★★ MUSEUM   It helps if you know even a little of the background to Erik Satie before you visit the wonderfully whimsical museum in the house where he was born in 1866. The composer, perhaps best known for his *Gymnopédies* piano compositions, was also part of the Surrealist and Dadaist crowd and was great friends with Picasso and Cocteau. So don't be surprised by the giant bizarre pear sculpture at the start of the tour, which is enhanced by the equally eccentric audio guide.

67 bd. Charles V. www.musees-honfleur.fr. ✆ **02-31-89-11-11.** Admission 6.30€ adults; 4.80€ students 16–25; free for children 15 and under. Wed–Mon 10am–6pm. Closed 3 weeks Jan.

Musée Eugène Boudin ★★ MUSEUM   Many Impressionists and other painters flocked to Honfleur in the 19th century, captivated by its light and water. You can see their works, including some by Monet, Courbet, Dufy, and Dubourg, in this handsome museum set in the former chapel of an Augustinian convent. But the star of the museum is Honfleur's native son, Eugène Boudin, whose pastels and paintings form part of an extensive permanent collection. In addition to local photographs (snapped between 1880–1920), Norman tourism posters, and antiques, the museum features a regularly changing roster of temporary exhibitions.

Rue de l'Homme de Bois. www.musees-honfleur.fr. ✆ **02-31-89-54-00.** Admission 8€ adults; 6.50€ ages 16 to 25; free for children 15 and under. Apr–Jul 6 and Sept Wed–Mon 10am–noon and 2–6pm; Jul–Aug 31 Wed–Mon 10am–6pm; Oct–Mar Wed–Mon 10am-noon and 2:30–5:30pm. Closed Jan 1–20.

NaturoSpace ★★ MUSEUM   You'll feel as if you've landed in the tropics in this captivating "equatorial zoo." In this luxuriant space, you'll be surrounded by countless butterflies, birds, and exotic plants. More than 50 species from South America, Asia, Africa, and Oceania flutter through an indoor rainforest that is kept at steady temperature of 25°C (77°F).

Visit in the morning to watch chrysalises crack open and butterflies make their first flight.

bd. Charles V. www.naturospace.com. ✆ **02-31-81-77-00.** Admission 10€ adults, 7.50€ students and children 3–13; family package 37.50€. Daily Apr–June and Sept 9:30am–6:30pm; July–Aug 9:30am–7pm; Oct–Mar 9:30am–4:30pm. Closed Jan–Feb.

Where to Stay

Hotel l'Ecrin ★★★   Step into the 18th century in this quietly grand three-star Norman manor house just a 5-minute walk from the Vieux Bassin. Cozy rooms, some with four-poster beds, have antique-style furnishings and plenty of chintz that hark back to the days of Louis XIV. The gardens are a wonderful place to relax and have breakfast, and it's unusual to find an outdoor pool so close to the center. The free parking is another bonus.

19 rue Eugène Boudin. www.hotel-ecrin-honfleur.com. ✆ **02-31-14-43-45.** 30 units. 120€–150€ double; 250€ suite. Free parking. **Amenities:** Outdoor pool; spa; free Wi-Fi.

La Maison de Lucie ★★   This 18th-century town house is only about a 5-minute walk from the main port, but you really get a sense of being in a peaceful private house. The fact that it only has 12 rooms helps. There are open fires in the lounges and a friendly, warm welcome. Elegant, traditionally furnished rooms ring the internal courtyard while some rooms open directly into the garden; one has its own little terrace. The suite is in its own pavilion, with a fireplace and parquet floors adding to the luxurious feel. Check out an atmospheric vaulted cellar of the main house for a relaxing session in the hot tub.

44 rue des Capucins. www.lamaisondelucie.com. ✆ **02-31-14-40-40.** 12 units. 190€–260€ double; 380€ suite. Parking 20€. **Amenities:** Spa 45€ for two; free Wi-Fi.

Les Maisons de Léa Hotel & Spa ★★★   Covered in ivy, this collection of 16th-century buildings in place Sainte-Catherine is one of the most romantic spots in Honfleur. You won't find two identical rooms within this converted salt warehouse, adjoining houses, and former school. Themes range from marine decor to soft floral fabrics and plump leather armchairs. Indulge in afternoon tea in the library or unwind in the spa's steam room. The intimate **Tourbillon** restaurant has refined, inventive dishes, including lobster in vanilla sauce. Main courses range from 24€ to 55€.

Pl. Sainte-Catherine. www.lesmaisonsdelea.com. ✆ **02-31-14-49-49.** 30 units. 147€–290€ double; 210€–390€ suite. **Amenities:** Restaurant; bar; spa; free Wi-Fi.

Where to Eat

Honfleur has its fair share of mediocre restaurants, especially along the Vieux Bassin. Too many cater to large tour groups, knowing that these patrons are unlikely to come back. If you want better quality food, then check out the back streets.

Monet's Garden at Giverny

Claude Monet spent the last 43 years of his life in creative contentment in his house and sprawling gardens in the Normandy village of Giverny, 75km (47 miles) northwest of Paris. It's just as enchanting as when he lived there with his wife and eight children surrounded by colorful gardens and ponds decked with the water lilies and green Japanese bridge seen in so many of his paintings. Most people make the visit from Paris. However, direct trains from Rouen to Vernon (the nearest station) take about 40 minutes and can cost as little as 9€ one-way when booked online in advance. From Vernon, you take a shuttle bus or bike to Giverny. See p. 214 for more information.

La Fleur de Sel ★★ FRENCH   Chef Vincent Guyon helms this classy restaurant in a handsome half-timbered town house. He has a very individual take on French cuisine. The menus change but could include a lighter-than-air mousseline of reblochon cheese and Iberico ham. Carnivores can feast on bone marrow with pigs' trotters, cèpes, and a mustard hollandaise. It's a small space, so book ahead.

17 rue Haute. www.lafleurdesel-honfleur.com. ✆ **02-31-89-01-92.** Fixed-price menu 30€–79€. Wed-Sun 10am–9pm.

L'Envie ★★ FRENCH   This cheerful bistro opposite the tourist office offers no-nonsense, good-value, homemade French food in convivial surroundings. Start with local oysters or a creamy risotto made with celery and Spanish ham, before continuing with veal cooked Normandy style with a wonderfully rich sauce of Calvados, cream, and lots of butter.

14 pl. de la Porte de Rouen. facebook.com/lenviehonfleur. ✆ **02-14-63-13-64.** Main course 15.50€–20.50€; fixed-price lunch menu 18.50€; fixed-price dinner 25.50€–50€. Wed–Mon 11:45am–2:30pm and 6:30–9:30pm.

SaQuaNa ★★★ CONTEMPORARY FRENCH   Alexandre Bourdas serves clever, exquisite cuisine that trades on his parentage (father from Normandy, mother from Aveyron) and a deep love of Japan. In a minimalist interior lined with exposed brick walls, Bourdas is open all day from breakfast (14€) through to dinner. Menus are fish focused (though there is always a meat dish too) and might include a John Dory filet with tempura kale, pumpkin purée, and a sharp Japanese ponzu sauce. Save room for the massive desserts.

22 pl. Hamelin. www.alexandre-bourdas.com. ✆ **02-31-89-40-80.** Fixed-price menu 22€–38€. Wed–Sun 7:30am–midnight.

DEAUVILLE ★★★

206km (128 miles) NW of Paris; 47km (29 miles) NE of Caen

Deauville (attached at the hip to Trouville below) has been associated with the rich and famous since the Duc de Morny, Napoleon III's half-brother, founded it as an upscale resort in 1859. In 1913, it entered sartorial history when Coco Chanel launched her career here, opening a boutique selling tiny hats that challenged the fashion of huge-brimmed hats loaded with flowers and fruit. Chanel cultivated a tradition of elegance that dominates Deauville. It's classy, restrained, and understated—precisely the qualities that have been attracting well-heeled Parisians in overwhelming numbers since the early 20th century. They're the ones who unselfconsciously call Deauville the 21st arrondissement of Paris.

Essentials

ARRIVING Four to nine daily **trains** run from Paris's Gare St-Lazare (trip time: 2–2½ hr.); prices start at 16€ one-way (sncf-connect.com; *©* **36-35**). The rail depot is midway between Trouville and Deauville, within walking distance

Colored parasols on the beach at Deauville.

of both. The **Nomad** bus company (nomadcar14.fr; *©* **08-70-83-00-14**) serves the Normandy coast from Caen to Le Havre. To **drive** from Paris (trip time: 2½ hr.), take A13 west to Pont L'Evêque, and then follow D677 north to Deauville.

VISITOR INFORMATION The **Office de Tourisme** is at Quai de l'Impératrice Eugénie (www.deauville.fr; *©* **02-31-14-40-00**).

[FastFACTS] DEAUVILLE

ATMs/Banks   A half-dozen banks are clustered on and around rue Eugène-Colas.

Mail & Postage   **La Poste,** 20 rue Robert Fossorier (*©* **36-31**).

Pharmacies   **Pharmacie de l'Horloge,** 14 pl. de Morny (*©* **02-31-88-20-47**).

Getting Around

ON FOOT Deauville is compact enough to get around on foot.

BY CAR Streets in the town center can get busy, but free parking can be found: Try Rue du Général Leclerc and Avenue du Général de Gaulle behind the casino.

BY TAXI **Central Taxis** (gie-central-taxis.fr; *©* **02-31-87-11-11**).

Exploring Deauville

Some of the architecture looks as if it had stepped out of a gothic fairy tale. The style is ostensibly Norman—lots of half-timbered buildings mostly in suitably muted shades. But then you see turrets sprouting here and there, with gables and balconies wedged into every nook and cranny. It's as if a French version of the Addams Family had a hand in designing some of these glorious confections. The overall effect is delightful, enhanced by the profusion of flowers in the public spaces. With its golf courses, casinos, deluxe hotels, La Touques and Clairefontaine racetracks, regattas, yacht harbor, polo grounds, and tennis courts, Deauville hums with moneyed patronage. Soak up the exclusive vibe with an afternoon spent people-watching, particularly along boutique-lined **rue Eugène-Colas, place Morny** (named for the resort's founder), and **place du Casino.**

Outdoor Activities

BEACHES Deauville's boardwalk, **Les Planches,** is an impossibly pretty promenade running parallel to the town's 2km (1-mile) beach, **Plage de Deauville.** Beaux Arts and half-timbered Norman-inspired buildings line its edges. Deauville's distinctively primary-colored parasols dot the sands—even out of season. Visitors parade along the boardwalk past private bathing cabins, each one's entrance stenciled with the names of Hollywood film stars who have attended the Deauville American Film Festival, which takes place in September. It's hard not to smile at some of the misspellings.

Access to every beach in Normandy is free, although beach clubs cover some stretches of sand. You can rent a beach umbrella for 17€ a day or an umbrella and two sun-loungers for 28€. Rent two sun-loungers and an umbrella for 20€ per half-day. A bathing cabin costs from 17€ a day. Parking costs from 2€ per hour in the public lots beside the sea; sometimes the first hour is free.

The **Piscine Olympique,** bd. de la Mer (indeauville.fr/loisirs/piscine-olympique; ☎ **02-31-14-02-17**), is a large indoor, heated seawater pool. Bathers pay from 5€ per person. You can buy the obligatory caps and trunks from machines if you don't have your own.

HORSE RACES/POLO You can watch horses—either racing or competing at polo—most days from late June to early September. The grounds have a very festive, family-friendly atmosphere, with plenty of activities for children. The venues are the **Hippodrome de Deauville-La Touques,** 45 av. Hocquart de Turtot (www.france-galop.com; ☎ **02-31-14-20-00**), in the heart of town near the Mairie de Deauville (town hall); and the **Hippodrome de Deauville Clairefontaine,** route de Clairefontaine (www.hippodrome-deauville-clairefontaine.com; ☎ **02-31-14-69-00**), within the city limits, 2km (1 mile) west of the center. Entrance costs from 5€ for adults and is free for those 17 and under.

Where to Stay

Hotel Le Normandy ★★★   Sprawling over an entire block, this legendary hotel (built in 1912) is belle époque Norman-style half-timbering at its most grandiose. It's a giant concoction of pale green and cream gables clustering around a courtyard and overlooking the seafront. Its spacious rooms are a riot of *toile de jouy* fabrics and wallpaper, giving it a French country style but with city comforts. Moneyed film buffs can stay in the voluptuous "Un Homme et Une Femme Suite," where Anouk Aimée and Jean-Louis Trintignant stayed while making the cult 1966 film *A Man and a Woman.* Smart Parisian families relax in the glass-ceilinged indoor pool; the spa features a yoga studio.

38 rue Jean Mermoz. www.hotelsbarriere.com. ✆ **02-31-98-66-22.** 271 units. 275€–700€ double; from 455€ suite. Parking 40€; 20€ per charge for electric vehicles. **Amenities:** Restaurant; bar; babysitting; spa; exercise room; heated indoor pool; room service; children's club; free bike rental; free Wi-Fi.

Villa Augeval Hotel & Spa ★★   A flower-filled garden, a swimming pool, and two Norman-style villas greet you when you walk through the gate of the Villa Augeval. This tranquil three-star hotel is barely a 10-minute walk from the center, and it's also very close to the Hippodrome. The style is elegantly French, with furnishings recalling the 18th and 19th centuries, and a few of the rooms have whirlpool baths for an extra touch of luxury. The newer annex, the Trait de l'Union, has more spacious rooms, but most of the rooms will have balconies and the suite has a gorgeous loggia, lovely for relaxing and hearing the sounds of the horses in the nearby stables.

15 av. Hocquart-de-Turtot. www.augeval.com. ✆ **02-31-81-13-18.** 42 units. 85€–345€ double; 160€–395€ suite. **Amenities:** Bar; babysitting; exercise room; outdoor pool; table tennis; room service; spa (private sauna and steam room access from 79€ for 1 hr.); free Wi-Fi.

Where to Eat

Deauville has its share of fine-dining restaurants, and those that simply are touristy and overpriced, particularly along rue Eugène Colas. You also pay a premium to sit at one of the restaurants along the beachfront promenade Les Planches—the sea views don't come cheap.

Étoile des Mers ★★★ SEAFOOD   On one side of this hybrid restaurant-cum-market, a stall hawks fish and shellfish fresh off the morning boats; on the other, hungry patrons sit at tables tucking into hearty platters of *fruits de mer* and fish like sea bass, tuna, sardines, and mackerel grilled à la plancha. The signature dishes are French-style surf-and-turf and lobster rolls. Wash it down with a crisp glass of chardonnay and you've got yourself a typical Deauville-style meal.

74 rue Gambetta. etoile-des-mers-deauville.com ✆ **02-14-63-10-18.** Main course 19€–32€. Tue–Wed 9am–5pm, Thu–Fri 9am–7pm, Sat 9am–9:30pm, Sun 9am–2pm.

La Cantine de Deauville ★★ FRENCH   This bustling brasserie stands out from the touristy restaurants along Eugène Colas. Inside its industrial-chic interior are generous plates of hearty food, ranging from enormous burgers and steaks to hefty salads of chicken, foie gras, and poached eggs.

90 rue Eugène Colas. facebook.com/lacantinededeauville. ℂ **02-31-87-47-47.** Main course 17€–35€; fixed-price menus 35€-55€. Daily 9:30am–9pm.

L'Essentiel ★★★ FRENCH/ASIAN   South Korea meets northern France—with the odd Spanish touch—in this innovative restaurant run by a husband-and-wife chef team who won their first Michelin star in 2018. While the limited menu changes regularly, it could include veal loin jazzed up with pungent shiso leaves and spicy kosho juice. There aren't many tables, so book ahead.

29 rue Mirabeau. lessentieldeauville.com. ℂ **02-31-87-22-11.** Main course 28€–34€; fixed-price lunch 41€; fixed-price dinner 75€-120€. Thu–Mon noon–1:30pm and 7:30–8:30pm (Sat until 9pm).

Shopping

Luxury boutiques such as Hermès, Ralph Lauren, and Louis Vuitton cluster around the **place du Casino.** If you're looking for more inclusive and slightly more affordable shops, including a lovely Norman-style Printemps department store, take a stroll along **rue Eugène-Colas** and **place de Morny.**

To see Norman produce in all its glory, head for the **Marché de Deauville** (open-air market) in place du Marché beside place de Morny. In July, August, Easter, Christmas, and French school holidays, it's open daily 7am to 1:30pm. The rest of the year, market days are Tuesday, Friday, and Saturday, as well as Sunday from February to November. In addition to fruits, vegetables, poultry, cider, wine, and cheese, you'll find cookware, porcelain tableware, and cutlery (mairie-deauville.fr/ville/marches). An organic market occupies Place de l'église Saint-Augustin every Thursday morning too (8am–1pm).

Nightlife

The **Casino de Deauville,** rue Edmond Blanc (www.casinobarriere.com; ℂ **02-31-14-31-14**), has been one of France's foremost casinos since it opened in 1912. Over the years, the original Belle Epoque has expanded to include a theater, Le Brummel nightclub, three restaurants, two bars, and a huge collection of slot machines (*machines à sous*). The casino distinguishes areas for slot machines from more formal zones containing such games as roulette, baccarat, blackjack, and poker. The slots are open daily 10am to 2am (to 3am Fri and 4am Sat) and have no dress code, although shorts are not allowed. The areas containing *les jeux de table* (table games) are open Monday to Thursday 7pm to 2am, Friday 7pm to 3am, and Saturday and Sunday 4pm to 4am. Entrance is free, and you must present a passport or ID to gain admission.

For drinks and a boogie, you could stay on at the casino, at posh Club 13, 2 rue Edmond Blanc (casinosbarriere.com/fr/deauville/club13-deauville.html), open until 5am. Polo players frequent the perennially hip and popular **Brok Café,** 14 av. du Général-de-Gaulle (facebook.com/BrokCafeDeauville; ✆ **02-31-81-30-81**), for cocktails and small plates. Or for a more chilled-out vibe, check out **La Plancha,** 57 av. de la République (http://laplancha-deauville.com; ✆ **02-31-89-98-19**), known for live music and delicious tapas.

TROUVILLE-SUR-MER ★★★

206km (128 miles) NW of Paris; 47km (29 miles) NE of Caen

Hugging the eastern bank of the Touques River is Deauville's less fashionable—but no less fascinating—neighbor Trouville-sur-Mer. Deauville might have the chic boutiques, but Trouville has the soul of a working fishing port. Cross the Touques at the Pont des Belges (a short 10- to 15-min. walk), and you immediately see the change in atmosphere. The large fish market, **Marché aux Poissons,** is a hive of activity and teems with small cafes selling the freshest seafood. More restaurants line the quayside, which becomes even livelier every Wednesday and Sunday when the open-air food market sets up its stalls (8am–1pm).

Essentials

ARRIVING **Trains** connect Trouville with Gare St-Lazare in Paris (see the "Deauville" section, earlier in this chapter). **Nomad buses** (nomadcar14.fr) link Trouville, Deauville, and the surrounding region with the rest of Normandy. Trouville and Deauville are also connected by ferry and footbridge. See "Exploring Trouville," below.

VISITOR INFORMATION The **Office de Tourisme** is at 32 bd. Fernand-Moureaux (www.trouvillesurmer.org; ✆ **02-31-14-60-70**).

[Fast FACTS]
TROUVILLE-SUR-MER

ATMs/Banks Banks are along bd. Fernand Moureaux, rue Victor Hugo and Pl. Foch.

Mail & Postage **La Poste,** 5 place Fernand Moureaux (✆ **36-31**).

Pharmacies **Pharmacie Centrale du Port,** 138 bd. Fernand Moureaux (pharmacieduport14.fr; ✆ **02-31-88-10-59**).

Exploring Trouville

The bustle of Trouville's quayside carries on into the narrow alleyways that wind behind the port. It's a pleasure to get lost here among the many restaurants and little shops that somehow squeeze into the haphazard collection

BYO Speedo

France's municipal swimming pools require all bathers wear swimming caps. Men have to wear Speedo-style trunks. No baggy shorts allowed. Many pools sell these items on-site, but when in doubt, pack your own.

of lanes. Eventually you'll come to the grand Victorian villas along **Les Planches,** the first seaside boardwalk on the Normandy coast, which dates back to 1867. In those days, artists and writers including Gustave Flaubert, Marguerite Duras, Claude Monet, and Eugène Boudin flocked to Trouville's beach, **Plage de Trouville,** captivated by the light and fresh air. Nowadays it's a firm favorite with families, with a giant children's play area, donkey rides, tennis courts, and the **Complexe Nautique** (trouvillesurmer.org; ℂ **02-31-14-48-10**), an indoor freshwater pool that gets very crowded in summer. The heated outdoor pool is open May to August. Depending on the season, bathers pay 2.20€ to 5.60€ per person. Hours July to August are Monday to Friday 10am to 7pm and from 1pm to 7pm on Saturday and Sunday; other times vary according to the French school holiday schedule.

If you want to cross over to Deauville, you can take the little foot ferry at Quai Albert 1er—Le Bac de Trouville Deauville—that trundles back and forth at high tide (daily Mar–Sept; weekends and holidays only Oct–Feb; 1.50€) or the pedestrian walkway (same charge). Or just walk south to the permanent bridge, the Pont des Belges, which spans the Touques. It's only a 10- to 15-minute walk between Deauville and Trouville. On the Trouville quayside, you can rent bikes of all shapes and sizes by the hour at **Les Trouvillaises** (www.lestrouvillaises.com; ℂ **02-31-98-54-11**).

Where to Stay

Hotel Flaubert ★★ Step out of this 1930s Norman-style three-star hotel and you're right on the beach. The friendly Flaubert is old-fashioned seaside charm at its best, with traditionally furnished rooms, some with exposed ceiling beams and New England-style wood paneling. Many of the rooms have balconies overlooking the beach, and it's worth the extra few euros to get a sea view. If you're a light sleeper, you might not want a room facing the street as it can get noisy in high season.

Rue Gustave Flaubert. www.flaubert.fr. ℂ **02-31-88-37-23.** 31 units. 139€–209€ double; 220€–445€ suite. Closed mid-Nov to mid-Feb. Parking 35€. **Amenities:** Bar; free Wi-Fi.

Les Cures Marines Trouville Hotel Thalasso & Spa ★★★ Trouville's first five-star hotel occupies a palatial wing of the very grand belle époque casino built in 1912 in a prime seafront location. Its minimalist rooms and suites are cool and calming, many with views of the sea and some with terraces. The original thermal baths were replaced with a state-of-the-art thalassotherapy spa with two indoor seawater pools. Seafood is the star at the elegant 1912 restaurant, and the warm ambience of the Eugène bar is irresistible.

bd. de la Cahotte. www.lescuresmarines.com. ☏ **02-31-14-26-00.** 103 units. 309€–490€ double; 450€–857€ suite. Closed Jan. Parking 25€. **Amenities:** Restaurant; bar; spa; exercise room; babysitting; free Wi-Fi.

Where to Eat

Trouville's restaurants are well served by the constant supply of seafood that comes into the port. It doesn't have the fine-dining scene of Deauville—nor, for the most part, its high prices. That doesn't mean it's particularly cheap, but you can find a delicious lunch in one of the many quayside bistros and cafes. A visit to the **Marché aux Poissons** is a must: Browse its stalls and take your pick of whatever seafood is on offer—from oysters and tiny shrimps to whelks and scallops. Then get the stallholder to cook it for you. Grab a glass of chilled muscadet and perch on one of the high tables surrounding the market. One of the best stalls is **Poissonnerie Pillet-Saiter** (maisonsaiter.com; ☏ **02-31-88-02-10**).

La Régence ★★ FRENCH   Don't let the wonderfully ornate Napoleon III interior distract you from one of Trouville's most elegant dining experiences. Seafood, not surprisingly, is the star—the lobster tanks give a clue. Highlights include the *pot au feu de la mer,* which puts together the most succulent and freshest fish to have come from the market, as well as the lobster gratin with a saffron sauce.

132 bd. Fernand Moureaux. www.restaurant-laregence.fr. ☏ **02-31-88-10-71.** Main courses 28€-50€; fixed-price menu 27€–60€. Daily noon–2pm and 7–9pm (10pm Sat).

Les Mouettes ★★ SEAFOOD/NORMAN   The writer Marguerite Duras counted Les Mouettes among her favorite Trouville restaurants. Set just behind the quayside, this former fishermen's hangout serves good-quality seafood and meat dishes. Specialties include a champagne and seafood *choucroute* (sauerkraut)—poached cod, haddock, cockles and mussels stewed in champagne—as well as the full range of fantastically fresh seafood and shellfish.

11 rue des Bains. facebook.com/lesmouettestrouville. ☏ **02-31-98-06-97.** Main courses 20€–55€. Daily 8am–midnight.

Maison Marcel ★★ FRENCH/NORMAN   In a quaint half-timbered building, this hybrid bar and grocery store (in a handy spot across the water from the train station) is the place to soak up Normandy beer, cider and wine, with plates of locally produced cold meats, pâtés, and cheeses. It's also a good place to shop for artisanal, French-made picnic goods like tapenade, pâté, chocolate, and chips. Fill your basket, then tuck in on the beach just a 10-minute walk away.

2 place Fernand Moreaux. maisonmarceltrouville.com. ☏ **02-31-87-48-04.** Fixed-price lunch 15€, main courses 14€–20€. Tues–Fri 10am–10pm; Sun 8am–6pm.

Trouville Nightlife

Trouville's casino, **Casino Barrière de Trouville,** pl. du Maréchal-Foch (www.casinosbarriere.com; ℂ **02-31-87-75-00**), is smaller and less stuffy than Deauville's, and features two restaurants and a bar. Entrance is free. You must present a passport or ID card to gain admission and be 18 or over. The formal area is open Sunday through Friday 9:30pm to 3am and Saturday to 4am. Though the casino does not have a formal dress code as such, but you should dress smartly.

CAEN ★★

238km (148 miles) NW of Paris; 119km (74 miles) SE of Cherbourg

Situated on the banks of the Orne, the port of Caen suffered great damage in the 1944 invasion of Normandy. Mercifully, though, the twin abbeys founded by William the Conqueror and his wife, Mathilda, were spared. Today much of Caen is both cosmopolitan and commercial, with a vibrant, welcoming vibe. The capital of Lower Normandy, it's home to a student population of 34,000 and several great museums; it also serves as a convenient base for exploring the surrounding coast.

Essentials

ARRIVING   From Paris's Gare St-Lazare, between 18 and 21 **trains** a day arrive in Caen (trip time: 2–2½ hr.). Online fares start at 16€ one-way (www.sncf-connect.com; ℂ **36-35**). To **drive** from Paris, travel west along A13 to Caen (drive time: 2½–3 hr.).

VISITOR INFORMATION   The **Office de Tourisme** is at 12 place St-Pierre in the 16th-century Hôtel d'Escoville (www.caen-tourisme.fr; ℂ **02-31-27-14-14**).

CITY LAYOUT   Downtown Caen stretches from Abbaye aux Dames in the east to Abbaye aux Hommes in the west. The pedestrianized rue St-Pierre bisects the town's main shopping district. The train station is southeast of the city center. The towering ramparts of the hilltop Château de Caen make an ideal spot to get your bearings.

Getting Around

ON FOOT   Caen's city center is small and much of it is pedestrianized. For short stays, it's easiest to explore the town on foot.

BY BICYCLE   Caen has its own bike-sharing scheme, **Twisto Vélo** (www. twisto.fr). You can register online or directly at one of Caen's 23 bike stands; access costs at 1€ per hour.

BY CAR   It's best to park your wheels and explore the city center on foot. The handiest parking lots are on place de République (smack bang in the center, just south of the Château; about 10€/day).

BY TAXI **Taxis Abbeilles,** 54 pl. de la Gare (www.taxis-abbeilles-caen.com; ✆ **02-31-52-17-89**).

BY PUBLIC TRANSPORT The **Twisto bus and tram network** (www.twisto.fr; ✆ **02-31-15-55-55**) crisscrosses the city. Its three tram lines all pass via the Château, making it very easy to get around (lines 2 and 3 link the station to the center). Tickets (1.60€) can be purchased from automatic kiosks at each station and are valid for an hour. A free electric shuttle bus goes through the center from Monday to Saturday 7:30am to 8pm.

[FastFACTS] CAEN

ATMs/Banks The city center has plenty of banks, including several on rue Jean Eudes.

Doctors & Hospitals **Centre Hospitalier Universitaire de Caen,** av. De la Côte de Nacre (www.chu-caen.fr; ✆ **02-31-06-31-06**).

Mail & Postage **La Poste,** 2 rue Georges Lebret (✆ **36-31**).

Pharmacies **Pharmacie du Château,** 27 av. De la Libération (pharmacie duchateau-caen.fr; ✆ **02-31-93-64-78**).

Exploring Caen

A fun way to visit Caen's major sites, including both Abbayes and the Château, is to follow the self-guided **William the Conqueror Circuit.** Maps can be picked up at the Tourist Office, which is the convenient start of the walking tour. Along the way, there are flash codes, which get you a free audio guide of the tour.

Abbaye aux Dames ★★ RELIGIOUS SITE William the Conqueror's wife Mathilda founded this abbey around 1060, which embraces Église de la Trinité and its Romanesque towers. Its spires were destroyed in the Hundred Years' War. The 12th-century choir houses the tomb of Queen Mathilda. Around it, the vast Parc d'Ornano has tree-lined alleys and sweeping city views.
Pl. Reine Mathilde. ✆ **02-31-06-98-45.** Free admission. Daily 2–6pm. Guided 1-hr. tour of choir, transept, and crypt (in French) daily 2:30 and 4pm; tickets 5€, free for children 17 and under.

Abbaye aux Hommes ★★ RELIGIOUS SITE Founded by William the Conqueror in 1066 to ensure a papal pardon for marrying his distant cousin Mathilda, this abbey is next to the Église St-Etienne. During the Allied invasion, residents of Caen fled to St-Etienne for protection. Twin Romanesque towers 84m (276 ft.) tall dominate the church. A marble slab inside the high altar marks the site of William's tomb. The Huguenots destroyed the tomb in 1562—only a hipbone was recovered. During the French Revolution, the last of William's dust was scattered to the wind.

The hand-carved wooden doors and elaborate wrought-iron staircase are exceptional. From the cloisters, you get a good view of the two towers of St-Etienne.

Esplanade Jean-Marie Louvel. ℂ **02-31-30-42-81.** Oct–Mar 6€ adults; Apr–Sept 8€ adults; free for children 17 and under. Oct–Mar Mon–Thurs 8am–6pm, Fri 8am–5pm, Sat (and Sun during school holidays) 9am–1pm and 2–5:30pm; Apr–June and Sept Mon–Fri 8am–6pm, Sat–Sun 9am–1pm and 2–6pm; July–Aug Mon–Fri 8am–6.30pm, Sat–Sun 9:30am–6:30pm.

Le Château de Caen ★★ CASTLE This castle complex was built on the ruins of a fortress erected by William the Conqueror in 1060. As soon as the weather warms up, much of the population picnics in the surrounding grounds. The castle is undergoing major renovations until 2025, but you can still climb to the top of the extensive ramparts for sublime views over Caen, visit its two museums and admire its multiple contemporary sculptures—the most impressive of which is a statue of Willian and Mathilde on horseback (opposite rue St-Piere) by local artist Claude Quiesse. The **Musée de Normandie** (www.musee-de-normandie.caen.fr; ℂ **02-31-30-47-60**) displays local archaeological finds, along with a collection of regional sculpture, paintings, and ceramics. Admission is 3.50€ to 5.50€ depending on the exhibitions (free for visitors 25 and under), and it's open Monday to Friday 9:30am to 12:30pm and 2 to 6pm, Saturday 11am to 6pm (closed Sept–June Mon). Also within the walls is the **Musée**

Abbaye Aux Hommes.

des Beaux-Arts (www.mba.caen.fr; ☎ **02-31-30-47-70**), a collection of Old Masters including Veronese, Tintoretto, and Rubens. Admission is 3.50€ to 5.50€, depending on the exhibition (free for visitors 25 and under). It's open Monday to Friday 9:30am to 12:30pm and 1:30 to 6pm and Saturday and Sunday 11am–6pm (closed Sept–June and Mon).

Esplanade de la Paix, rue de Geôle, av. De la Libération. musee-de-normandie.caen.fr.

Le Mémorial de Caen (Caen Memorial) ★★★ MONUMENT/MEMORIAL

This is not a museum to be rushed through, as it explores history from 1918 to the present day in engrossing and thought-provoking exhibits. It puts the 20th century in context by starting with the end of the First World War, leading to the horrors of the Second World War and beyond to the Cold War and the Berlin Wall. Civilian stories are told in heartbreaking detail, along with tales of courage and ingenuity of Allied soldiers. Not surprisingly, a large exhibition is dedicated to the D-day landings and the headquarters used by German General Richter during the war. The museum's cafe is reasonably priced and a good spot to relax in between exhibitions.

Esplanade Général Eisenhower. www.memorial-caen.fr. ☎ **02-31-06-06-45.** Admission 19.80€ adults, 17.50€ students and children 10–18; free to children 9 and under. Feb–Mar 9am–6pm; Apr–Sept 9am–7pm; Oct–Dec 9:30am–6pm (closed Mon Nov–Dec). Closed Jan. Times may change so check online before you go.

Where to Stay

Hotel le Dauphin ★★

You can't beat the location of this hotel—it's just a few steps from the Château as well as Caen's pedestrianized center. It's made up of three separate buildings, one of which was built on the site of a 15th-century priory. It's a bit of a hodge podge, with some rooms featuring more contemporary furnishings while others have traditional 19th-century-style decor tucked into alcoves. The spa (20€ for 90 min.) is a welcome place to relax, especially under the pulsating jets of the hydrotherapy pools. The restaurant is renowned for its Normandy-inspired menus (think local fish in a dill crust and lamb from the Cotentin peninsula; main courses around 35€, fixed-price lunch menus 25€–36€).

29 rue Gémare. le-dauphin-normandie.com. ☎ **02-31-86-22-26.** 37 units. 170€–230€ double. Breakfast 16€. Parking free but limited. **Amenities:** Restaurant; bar; room service; spa; free Wi-Fi.

Le Clos St-Martin ★★★

This stylish and cozy *chambres d'hôtes,* or bed-and-breakfast, has a mere six rooms set in a town house dating from the 16th and 17th centuries, so it's worth booking well ahead. All feel very romantic, with a mix of antique-style and modern furnishings, and some have atmospheric exposed ceiling beams. There's also a 4-person cottage from 130€ with a kitchen.

18 bis pl. Saint Martin. clossaintmartin.com. ☎ **07-81-39-23-67.** 6 units. 90€–170€ double; 120€–230€ family rooms or suites, including breakfast. Public parking nearby. **Amenities:** Free Wi-Fi.

Where to Eat

A large student population helps make Caen's dining scene one of the most dynamic in Normandy. Sidewalk cafes and restaurants line rue du Vaugueux and the surrounding neighborhood, east of the Château.

A Contre Sens ★★★ FRENCH/NORMAN   On a street filled with booksellers and art galleries, Anthony Caillot's Asian-inflected restaurant is among the best in the city. And he gets more creative every year. Take your pick from the fixed-price menus, which change all the time, but might include locally sourced frog legs, oysters, langoustines or pork, pimped with yuzu, kimchi or ginger. His Intuition menu (the only menu served on Sat) features seven courses that Caillot chooses for you. Reservations are highly recommended.

8 rue des Croisiers. acontresens.fr. ✆ **02-31-97-44-48.** Fixed-price lunch 48€–78€ or dinner 68€–78€. Wed–Sat 10:30am–3:30pm and 7:30–9:15pm.

Le Bouchon du Vaugueux ★★ FRENCH   The husband-and-wife team that runs this warm little bistro has come up with a winning formula. The food is beautifully prepared with little fuss and a great deal of skill. The seasonal menu changes but could include a tasty fricassee of snails with smoked pepper, or pork that's been slow-cooked for 24 hours served with creamy puréed potatoes. Book ahead for a table in this small space.

12 rue Graindorge. www.bouchonduvaugueux.com. ✆ **02-31-44-26-26.** Fixed-price lunch 26€ or dinner 30€; main courses 30€–32€. Wed–Sat noon–1:30pm and 7–9:30pm; Tues 7–9:30pm.

A Proustian Remembrance of "Balbec"

If you read Marcel Proust's *Remembrance of Things Past,* you'll discover that the resort of "Balbec" was really Cabourg, 24km (15 miles) northeast of Caen. Guests can check into the **Le Grand Hôtel Cabourg—MGallery,** Les Jardins du Casino, promenade Marcel Proust, 14390 Cabourg (www.grand-hotel-cabourg.com; ✆ **02-31-91-01-79;** doubles from 230€–750€; suites 850€–1,150€), a holdover from the opulent days when it was first built in 1855. What used to be Marcel Proust's favorite room has been restored from a description in his novel. Film buffs will also recognize the Grand Hotel's dining room from the 2011 French hit comedy-drama *The Untouchables,* with its majestic floor-length windows overlooking the sea.

The town of Cabourg (www.cabourg.net) is just as charming, its Victorian streets fanning out from the grand circle where the hotel stands. Beneath the hotel is the indoor municipal swimming pool, where locals flock when it's too cold to take to the huge stretch of sands in front of Promenade Marcel Proust. Every June, the beach becomes the setting for the Romantic Film Festival (festival-cabourg.com), when a giant screen shows dozens of romance-themed films over 5 days. The large covered market is worth a visit, too, on Wednesdays, Fridays, and weekends (daily July–Aug), when farmers bring their fresh Normandy produce.

Shopping

Caen has some excellent boutique-lined shopping streets, including **boulevard du Maréchal-Leclerc, rue St-Pierre,** and **rue de Strasbourg. Antiques** hunters should check out the shops along **rue Ecuyère.** The **market** at place Courtonne on Sunday morning sells secondhand goods.

For foodie souvenirs, **Chocolaterie Charlotte Corday,** 114 rue St-Jean (✆ **02-31-86-33-25**), has an irresistible collection of chocolate and other sweet goodies. Cheese-lovers can taste before they buy at the *bar à fromages* and boutique at **Fromagerie Conquérant,** 27 rue Guillaume le Conquérant (http://fromagerie-conquerant.com; ✆ **02-50-65-47-33**).

Nightlife

Take a walk down rue de Bras, rue St-Pierre, and rue Vaugueux to size up the action. **Au Verre Dit Vin,** quai Vendeuvre (www.auverreditvincaen.fr; ✆ **02-31-91-38-03**), is a cozy wine bar that offers good food along with a piano bar on Thursdays and live music on Fridays and Saturdays. For offbeat international gigs, head to **Le Cargö,** 9 cours Caffarelli, Port de Caen (www.lecargo.fr; ✆ **02-31-86-79-31**).

BAYEUX ★★

267km (166 miles) NW of Paris; 25km (16 miles) NW of Caen

Bayeux's alluring medieval heart was spared bombardment in 1944 and was the first town to be liberated—the day after D-day, in fact. Its half-timbered houses, stone mansions, cobblestoned streets, and ancient water-mills have remained more or less intact, making this immensely pleasant town a joy to explore. It does get busy in summer—with the double whammy of the nearby D-day beaches and the extraordinary historical document that is the Bayeux Tapestry—but it retains its agreeable Norman atmosphere and the sense that it exists beyond the tourist crowds.

Essentials

ARRIVING   Eleven direct **trains** depart daily from Paris's Gare St-Lazare. The 2- to 2½-hour trip to Bayeux costs from 16€ if booked in advance (www.sncf-connect.com; ✆ **36-35**). To **drive** to Bayeux from Paris (trip time: 3 hr.), take A13 to Caen and N13 west to Bayeux.

VISITOR INFORMATION   The **Office de Tourisme** is on Rue Saint Jean (www.bayeux-bessin-tourisme.com; ✆ **02-31-51-28-28**).

SPECIAL EVENTS   The town goes wild on the first weekend in July during **Fêtes Médiévales** (lesmedievales.bayeux.fr; ✆ **02-31-92-03-30**); the streets fill with market stalls, medieval dress, and themed treats during 2 days of medieval revelry. In mid-June, Bayeux is usually the finishing point for the annual **Tour de Normandie** (www.tourdenormandie.com; ✆ **06-28-33-00-75**), a classic car race that winds through the Normandy countryside in elegant style.

[FastFACTS] BAYEUX

ATMs/Banks Many
banks are along rue
Saint-Malo.

Mail & Postage **La
Poste** rue Larcher
(🕐 **36-31**).

Pharmacies **Pharmacie
St Martin,** 20 rue St Martin
(🕐 **02-31-92-00-22**).

Exploring Bayeux

This compact town is best explored on foot. At its heart in rue du Général de Dais is **Cathédrale Notre-Dame de Bayeux,** a Norman medieval structure consecrated in 1077 in the presence of William the Conqueror. It was partially destroyed in 1105 but Romanesque towers from the original church still rise on the western side. The central tower is from the 15th century. The nave is a fine example of Norman Romanesque style. The 13th-century choir, in Norman Gothic style, is rich in sculpture and has Renaissance stalls. It's open daily 9am to 7pm (until 6pm Oct–Dec and from 8:30am June–Aug). Entrance is free, although guided visits are available for 6€. Check with the tourist office for dates and times.

Musée d'Art et d'Histoire Baron Gérard (MAHB) ★★ MUSEUM
Five thousand years of art history are on display in this well-designed museum in the ancient bishop's palace, which dates from the 11th to the 18th centuries. About 600 local archaeological finds mingle with 1,000 pieces of lacework and delicate porcelain, as well as more than 600 regional artworks created between the 15th and 20th centuries.

37 rue du Bienvenu. www.bayeuxmuseum.com. 🕐 **02-31-51-25-50.** Admission 7.50€ adults; 5.50€ students and children; free for children 9 and under. May–Sept daily 9:30am–6:30pm; Feb–Apr and Oct–Dec daily 10am–12:30pm and 2–6pm. Closed Jan.

Musée de la Tapisserie de Bayeux ★★★ MUSEUM   This extraordinary tapestry—actually an elaborate embroidery on linen—is one of the sights of Bayeux that really shouldn't be missed, even if historians believe it was created in Kent, not France (between 1066–1077). Measuring 69m (226 ft.) long and 50cm (20 in.) wide, this masterpiece is displayed in a 270-degree glass case that curves along a tunnel-like room. Throughout its 58 scenes, you discover the story of the conquest of England by William the Conqueror. The free audio guide is definitely worth following, as it provides fascinating details that you are likely to overlook. The devil is in the detail—in more ways than one—so look out for surprising depictions at the top and bottom of the cloth. *Important:* The museum is set to close for renovations at the end of 2024 until at least 2027.

Centre Guillaume le Conquérant, 13 bis rue de Nesmond. bayeuxmuseum.com. 🕐 **02-31-51-25-50.** Admission 12€ adults, 7.50€ students, free for children 9 and under. Mar–Nov daily 9am–6:30pm (May–Aug until 7pm); Feb and Nov–Dec daily 9:30am–12:30pm and 2–6pm. Closed Jan.

7

Fast Facts: Bayeux

NORMANDY & MONT-ST-MICHEL

306

Detail of the Bayeux Tapestry.

Musée Memorial de la Bataille de Normandie ★★ MUSEUM
The Battle of Normandy (June 6–Aug 29, 1944) is told in compelling
detail in this bunkerlike building. Displays of beach landings, maps, tanks,
and weapons recall the battle, during which Bayeux was among the first
towns to be liberated. A 25-minute film shows news clips from the period.
The **Commonwealth Cemetery** across the street contains 4,144 graves of
British soldiers who were killed during the battle.

bd. Fabian Ware. www.bayeuxmuseum.com. ℂ **02-31-51-25-50.** Admission 7.50€
adults, 5.50€ students and children, free for children 9 and under. May–Sept daily
9:30am–6:30pm; Oct–Apr daily 10am–12:30pm and 2–6pm. Closed Jan.

Where to Stay

Hôtel d'Argouges ★★ You step into a tranquil little world once you
go through the hidden stone archway of this 18th-century mansion. Elegant rooms hark back to the 19th century with their antique-style furnishings, wood paneling, gilt mirrors, polished parquet floors, and period
fireplaces. The garden is a delight, and a relaxing place for breakfast under
the shade of the trees.

21 rue St-Patrice. www.hotel-dargouges.com. ℂ **02-31-92-88-86.** 28 units. 85€–171€
double; 130€–205€ triple and family rooms; 170€–295€ suite. Free parking. **Amenities:** Breakfast room; bar; room service; free Wi-Fi.

Villa Lara ★★★   Five-star luxury meets intimate boutique hotel in Villa Lara, where they've found the right balance between refinement and relaxation. Some of its spacious rooms come with balconies and views of Bayeux's cathedral, but they all have elegant antique-style furnishings with plenty of brocade and velvet. A second villa, Villa Augustine, on the hotel grounds is home to four plush presidential suites that sleep up to eight people. The wood-paneled lounge is a cozy spot, complete with library and fireplace.

6 pl. du Québec. www.hotel-villalara.com. ℂ **02-31-92-00-55.** 32 units. 300€–380€ double; 380€–1,600€ suite. Breakfast 25€. Free parking. **Amenities:** Breakfast room; gym; bar; free Wi-Fi. Closed Dec–Feb.

Where to Eat

Bayeux has plenty of informal cafes offering quick snacks for visitors touring the D-day beaches or just popping in to visit the tapestry. There are, however, a couple of special places worth checking out.

L'Alcôve ★★ NORMAN   Typical Norman dishes with a touch of pizazz is what you get in this cozy bistro by the cathedral. The menu changes with the seasons, but it might include delights like lobster ravioli in a coconut and granny smith apple broth, fall-off-your-fork rabbit with celeriac and tonka beans, and peaches poached in verbena—and don't get me started on the cheese! It's a small restaurant, and has a faithful following, so you might want to book ahead.

31 ter Rue Larcher. https://sites.google.com/view/lalcovebayeux/accueil. ℂ **02-31-92-30-08.** Fixed-price lunch 17.50€–25€ and dinner 36€–42€; main courses 20€–23€. Tues noon–1:30pm, Wed–Sat noon–1:30pm and 7–9pm.

Le Volet qui Penche ★★ NORMAN   Everything on chef Jerôme Alix's menu is made with locally sourced ingredients—cheese from Caen, bread from the Maison Moisson bakery in Bayeux (17 rue St Martin), meat from the Orne region, oysters from Asnelles and eggs from a farm in Castillon just up the road—the lot, lovingly concocted into delicious dishes like *millefeuille* (layers) of beet and goat's cheese, tartare of beef, and sweet, vanilla crème brûlée. Live music is sometimes performed too.

3 impasse de l'Islet. levoletquipenche.com. ℂ **02-31-21-98-54.** Main courses 14€–19€. Tues–Fri noon–2pm and 6:30–9pm, Sat 6:30–9pm.

THE D-DAY BEACHES ★★★

Arromanches-les-Bains: 272km (169 miles) NW of Paris, 11km (6¾ miles) NW of Bayeux; Grandcamp-Maisy (near Omaha Beach): 299km (185 miles) NW of Paris, 56km (35 miles) NW of Caen

A visit to the beaches, where the greatest invasion force of all time landed, is a must for anyone visiting Normandy's north coast.

It was a rainy week in early June 1944 when the greatest armada ever was assembled along the southern coast of England. A full moon and cooperative tides were needed for the cross-Channel invasion. Britain's top meteorologist for the USAAF and RAF—Sir James Stagg—forecast a small window in the inclement weather. Over in France, Normandy's German occupiers lacked such a detailed weather forecast, so many Nazi officers drifted home for the weekend in the belief that no landing could take place soon.

Supreme Allied Commander Dwight D. Eisenhower believed Stagg's reports—and knew that further delays would hinder his element of surprise. With the British invasion commander, Field Marshal Montgomery, at his side, Eisenhower made the ultimate call.

At 9:15pm on June 5, the BBC announced to Normandy's French Resistance that the invasion was imminent by way of coded messages. The underground movement started dynamiting the region's railways to hinder German troop movement.

Before midnight, Allied planes began bombing the Norman coast. By 1:30am on June 6 ("the Longest Day," and what the French call *Jour-J*), members of the 101st Airborne were parachuting to the ground on German-occupied French soil. At 6:30am, the Americans began landing on the beaches, code-named Utah and Omaha. An hour later, British and Canadian forces made beachheads at Juno, Gold, and Sword, swelling the number of Allied troops in Normandy to a massive 135,000. That evening a joint beachhead had been formed and yet more troops, tanks, trucks, and other *matériel* poured into Normandy. The push to Paris—and Berlin— had begun.

Essentials

ARRIVING A **car** is practically essential to explore the D-day Beaches at leisure. Each monument, museum, and beach has plenty of parking.

Nomad buses (nomad.normandie.fr; © **02-22-55-00-10**) runs buses from Bayeux to Arromanches (no. 121) and from Bayeux to Omaha Beach and the American Cemetery (no. 120) every few hours for 3.90€ per trip.

Several group tours also cover the D-day Beaches. From Bayeux, **Normandy Tours,** Hotel de la Gare (www.normandy-landing-tours.com; © **02-31-92-10-70**), runs a 4- to 5-hour tour (in English) to Arromanches, Omaha Beach, the American Military Cemetery, and Pointe du Hoc for 75€ to 87€ adults and 65€ to 77€ students from April to October.

VISITOR INFORMATION The **Office de Tourisme,** 2 rue Maréchal-Joffre, Arromanches-les-Bains (www.bayeux-bessin-tourisme.com; © **02-31-22-36-45**), is open daily year-round, but from January to February and November to December it's open only on Saturday and Sunday.

The beach at Arromanches, with the remains of Mulberry Harbour in the distance.

Reliving the Longest Day

Few places in the world have a more concentrated—or more moving—selection of sights than Normandy's D-day beaches. More than 30 memorials, cemeteries, and museums, which range from coastal batteries to museums dedicated to underwater military finds, are spread out along this 50km (31-mile) stretch of coast—all with information in English. The most spellbinding site for all nationalities is the **Normandy American Cemetery** and its **visitor's center ★★★**, behind **Omaha Beach** at Colleville-sur-Mer (www.abmc.gov; © **02-31-51-62-00**). The graves of 10,000 Allies who liberated mainland France lie within 70 hectares (173 acres) of manicured grounds above the cliffs. The visitor center retells the dramatic story of the American landings—and those of British, Canadian, Polish, Free French, and other allies—on the morning of June 6, 1944. Most dramatic are the personal tales, often told via video and interactive displays. Make certain you leave enough time for a good look at the exhibitions—they really are captivating. Admission is free. The cemetery is open daily 9am to 6pm from April 14 to September 15, and until 5pm the rest of the year. Public access to Omaha Beach itself is no longer available from the memorial, but other public paths are nearby.

At the **Overlord Museum,** Colleville-sur-Mer (www.overlordmuseum. com; ✆ **02-31-22-00-55**), half a mile uphill from the Normandy American Cemetery, more than 10,000 pieces of *matériel* and 35 military vehicles are showcased in D-day dioramas around a great hall. Admission is 9.50€ adults and 7€ students and children ages 7 to 15; free for children 6 and under. Open daily 10am to 5:30pm February to March, November, and December; 10am to 6:30pm April, May, and September; 9:30am to 7pm June to August; closed January.

Farther west along the coast, you'll see the jagged lime cliffs of the **Pointe du Hoc.** A cross honors a group of American Rangers who scaled the cliffs using hooks to get at the gun emplacements. The pockmarked landscape has a lunar look, with giant craters showing where the bombs fell. Farther along the Cotentin Peninsula is the first beach to be stormed, **Utah Beach,** where the 4th U.S. Infantry Division landed at 6:30am. A U.S. monument commemorates their heroism and the **Utah Beach Musée du Débarquement** (utah-beach.com; ✆ **02-33-71-53-35**) offers moving, chronological displays of the D-day landings. Open daily 10am to 5pm February to March; 10am to 6pm April and October to January; May to September 9:30am to 7pm; closed first 2 weeks December.

Normandy American Visitor Center and Cemetery, Omaha Beach.

Eastward along the coast in the British invasion sector is the seaside resort of **Arromanches-les-Bains.** A deep-water port was deemed essential to Allied success, so in June 1944, two mammoth prefabricated ports known as Mulberry Harbours were towed across the Channel. The one that landed in Arromanches was nicknamed Port Winston. "Victory could not have been achieved without it," Eisenhower later said. Indeed, in 10 months this "temporary" artificial harbor delivered 2.5 million men and countless vehicles into northern France. The wreckage is still visible just off the beach. The **Musée d'Arromanches,** pl. du 6-Juin (https://musee-arromanches.fr; ✆ 02-31-22-34-31), opened in 2023 to replace the former D-day landing museum. Within its fittingly austere glass and concrete frame are collections that illuminate the scale of the D-day landings through maps, models, films, photos, and information about the technology used in the battle. Admission is 12.50€ adults and 8.20€ students and children ages 6 to 18; free for children ages 5 and under. Open May to August daily 9am to 7pm (until 6pm in Sept); February, November, and December 10am to 5pm; March and October 9:30am to 5:30pm; April 9am to 6pm (closed Jan).

Eastward again through the British and Canadian invasion sectors is **Musée Gold Beach,** 2 pl. Amiral Byrd, Ver-sur-Mer (www.goldbeach musee.fr; ✆ 02-31-22-58-58). The museum focuses on the heroism of Britain's RAF and Royal Navy and the meticulous Allied coordination that went into the D-day landings. Admission is 4.50€ adults, 2.50€ students, 2€ children ages 5 to 15; free for children ages 4 and under. From April to October, hours are daily 10am to 1pm and 2 to 6pm.

Just eastward along the coast in Courseulles-sur-Mer is the **Centre Juno Beach ★★**, voie des Français Libres (www.junobeach.org; ✆ 02-31-37-32-17). This gem of a museum details Canada's entire war effort, with particular focus on the Battle of the Atlantic and the march through Germany. Outside the museum is a stark memorial to the Canadian dead of D-day, their names inscribed simply on blue towers. Walk towards the beach and pause in front of the sculpture with the words to Paul Verlaine's poem "Chanson d'Automne": This was the code the BBC used to alert the French Resistance on June 5. Admission is 7.50€ adults and 6€ students and children, with reduced rates for visits only to the park or temporary exhibits. Hours are daily February to March and November to December 10am-5pm; April and May 10am-6:30pm; June to August 9:30am to 7pm; September to October 10am-6pm. Closed January.

Where to Stay & Eat near the D-Day Beaches

Château le Chenevière ★★★   Smack bang between Bayeux and Omaha Beach, this gorgeous 18th-century castle is a plush and convenient place to base yourself for the D-day beaches. "Understated grandeur" best describes the rooms, which are peppered with a savvy mix of antique and modern furniture and fabrics. The outdoor pool and spa are perfect places for unwinding after a day's sightseeing—as are the hotel's two **restaurants:** one serving bistro fare in a winter garden; the other serving fine-dining dishes in a botanical-themed dining room; both using fruits and vegetables from the château's garden. Main courses in the bistro start at 19€; fine-dining fixed-price menus start at 72€.

Escures-Commes, Port-en-Bessin. lacheneviere.com. ✆ **02-31-51-25-25.** 29 units. 330€–452€ double; 550€–800€ suites. Free parking. **Amenities:** Restaurant; bar; breakfast room; outdoor pool; spa; free Wi-Fi.

Ferme de la Rançonnière ★★★ Everything about this baronial manor house is awe inspiring, but the prices and immensely warm welcome are anything but intimidating. Four stone mansions dating from the 13th to the 15th centuries and clustering around a large courtyard combine to form a wonderfully romantic, charming country hotel only a few miles south of the coast near Asnelles. The restaurant, with its exposed stone walls and beamed ceiling, is just as charming. Traditional Norman cuisine gets a modern twist, with dishes that might include beet-marinated salmon with pineapple tartare or confit of pork with creamed corn and tandoori popcorn. Fixed-price menus run between 37€ and 49€, with a popular weekend brunch at 39€.

Route de Creully, Crépon. www.ranconniere.fr. ✆ **02-31-22-21-73.** 35 units. 102€–187€ double; 200€–246€ suite. Free parking. **Amenities:** Restaurant; bar; breakfast room; playground; helipad; massage services; free Wi-Fi.

Hôtel de la Marine ★★ Endless sea views! That's what you get at this friendly 19th-century hotel, right on Gold Beach, where the British landed on D-day. Individually decorated bedrooms have a simple, breezy style, but some have balconies with those fabulous vistas. The restaurant, which also has a sea-facing terrace, focuses on fresh seafood—including big platters of *fruits de mer*—as well as hearty meat dishes, and vegetarian and vegan options. Main courses from 15€, and half-board options are offered.

1 quai du Canada, Arromanches-les-Bains. www.hotel-de-la-marine.fr. ✆ **02-31-22-34-19.** 33 units. 135€–163€ double. Free parking. Closed Nov 12–Feb 10. **Amenities:** Restaurant; bar; free Wi-Fi.

La Marée ★ NORMAN Half way between Omaha and Utah beaches, this cozy waterfront restaurant has a superb selection of local shellfish including oysters, whelks and langoustines as well as beautifully cooked fish dishes including *sole meunière.* Meat-eaters can enjoy tender creamy, Normandy chicken supreme. When it's warm, you can eat by the water's edge.

5 quai Henri Chéron, Grandcamp Maisy. www.restolamaree.com. ✆ **02-31-21-41-00.** Fixed-price menus 20€–35€. Daily noon–2pm and 7–9pm; closed Sun evenings out of season. Closed Jan 1–Feb 3.

MONT-ST-MICHEL ★★★

324km (201 miles) W of Paris; 129km (80 miles) SW of Caen; 48km (30 miles) E of St-Malo

A UNESCO World Heritage Site, Mont-St-Michel is one of the most alluring spots on France's northern coast. The fortified island seems to float on a shifting bed of sand and sea. Once a bastion marking the border between Normandy and Brittany, then a place of monastic retreat, this Disney-like town now attracts 3 million visitors every year. In high summer it's exceptionally busy, but enthralling nevertheless.

Essentials

ARRIVING   The most efficient way to reach Mont-St-Michel is to **drive.** From Caen, follow A84 southwest towards Avranches, eventually taking the D43 and following signs to its end at Mont-St-Michel. Total driving time from Paris is just under 4 hours.

There are no direct **trains** between Paris and Mont-St-Michel. One option is to take a local TER train from Paris's Gare St-Lazare to Caen, then another local TER train to Pontorson, where a 3.10€ shuttle bus ferries passengers directly to the visitor center. Another is to take a TGV (fast

Exploring Mont-St-Michel means a lot of ups and downs.

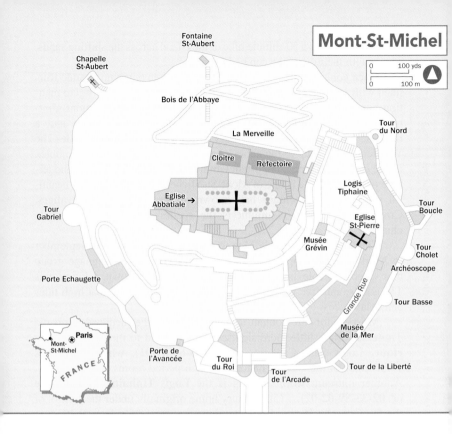

Mont-St-Michel

train) from Paris Montparnasse to Rennes in Brittany, from where a coach (keolis-armor.com or destination-montsaintmichel.com) takes you to Mont-St-Michel for 15€ each way. For train information, visit www.sncf-connect.com or call ℰ **36-35.**

VISITOR INFORMATION   The **Tourist Information Center** is at Grande Rue, Le Mont-Saint-Michel (ot-montsaintmichel.com; ℰ **02-33-60-14-30**).

Exploring Mont-St-Michel

France's biggest tourist attraction outside of Paris has been undergoing major changes over the past 2 decades. Before 2012, the causeway linking the island with the mainland was rammed with parked cars, and the bay was in danger of silting up. To restore Mont-St-Michel to its island status, the authorities built a **new approach** and banished cars to a parking lot by a visitor center. Free shuttle buses take visitors to the island 2.5km (1½ miles) away. Parking costs 12€ to 25€ for 24 hours (depending on the season), but is free if you stay less than 30 minutes.

Otherwise it's a 50-minute hike to the island across the shifting sands. Those with their own bike can pedal over.

Once you reach the island, you'll have a steep climb up Grande Rue, lined with 15th- and 16th-century houses and souvenir shops (not to mention hordes of tourists), to reach its famous **abbey** (abbaye-mont-saint-michel.fr; ✆ **02-33-89-80-00**). Ramparts encircle the church and a three-tiered ensemble of 13th-century buildings called **La Merveille** (The Wonder) that rise up to the abbey's pointed spire. This terraced complex is one of Europe's most important Gothic monuments. On the second terrace of La Merveille is one of Mont-St-Michel's largest and most beautiful spaces, a 13th-century hall known as the **Salle des Chevaliers.** Crowning the mount's summit is the spellbinding **Eglise Abbatiale** church.

The abbey is open daily May to August 9am to 7pm, and September to April 9:30am to 6pm. Entrance includes an English-language group tour when available, but you can also explore on your own. Admission is 11€ adults, and free for children 17 and under. Be aware that high tides can delay access to Mont-St-Michel.

Most visitors are content to wander around the medieval ramparts. Those seeking a little more sightseeing may head to the **Musée Historique,** Logis Saint-Catherine (✆ **02-33-60-07-01**), which showcases 1,300 years of the island's history, through period rooms and waxworks. Another museum worth visiting is the **Logis Tiphaine,** Grande Rue (✆ **02-33-89-02-02**), a 15th-century home originally under the control of the Du Guesclin family. Both museums are open daily from 9:30am to 5pm (closed Wed–Thurs in Feb), and cost 9€ for adults, free for children 18 and under. You can buy a pass for 18€ that covers the cost of three museums.

To admire Mont-St-Michel from across the mudflats—there's something invigorating about gazing at the island with your toes in the brackish mud—join one of the English guided, barefoot walks from the island to the mainland with **Chemins de la Baie** (www.cheminsdelabaie.com; ✆ **02-33-89-80-88**). The crossing costs 15€ and lasts 2 hours, 30 minutes. Places should be reserved in advance.

Where to Stay & Eat

If you plan to stay overnight on the island, be prepared to pay a premium. It is, however, an unforgettable experience, as you can explore the island in the evening in peace after the crowds have left. But **travel light:** The hotels are a long, mostly uphill walk from where the shuttle bus drops you off, and the cobblestoned streets don't make it easy to transport your luggage. And don't expect to have a late supper; most restaurants close soon after the day-trippers leave, apart from hotel restaurants. But there are advantages to staying overnight—particularly in the summer, when evening concerts are staged in the abbey and sound-and-light shows illuminate the island.

Auberge Saint-Pierre ★★ You'll be sleeping in an official historic monument in this 15th-century half-timbered inn. While the rooms are on the small side, their exposed ceiling beams and half-timbered walls make them immensely comfortable and cozy. Rooms are divided between the Chapeau Blanc Logis, a secluded former fisherman's cottage a few minutes' (uphill) walk from the hotel, and the Logis, which has small terraces with gorgeous views. The restaurant is an impossibly romantic place, with an enormous fireplace and a little courtyard garden (where breakfast is served). Fixed-price menus cost from 26.80€ to 68€, which include lobster from neighboring Brittany, and the famously fluffy Mont-St-Michel omelet.

Grande Rue. www.auberge-saint-pierre.fr. © **02-33-60-14-03.** 23 units. 230€–295€ double; 320€–380€ suite. **Amenities:** Restaurant; bar; free Wi-Fi.

Crêperie La Sirène ★★ NORMAN Set in a 15th-century building, this cheerful crêperie is a good choice for lunch. It specializes in savory buckwheat crepes known as galettes, which come stuffed with everything from mushrooms, eggs, and ham to gooey goat's cheese and potatoes. The butter galette (just a crepe with butter) is a steal at 2.90€. A sweet crepe makes a fine dessert, accompanied by Normandy cider. *Tip:* With throngs of tourists and a no-reservations policy, miss the lines by arriving just before opening time or after 2:30pm.

Grande Rue. © **02-33-60-08-60.** Main course 2.90€–11€. Daily 11:45am–4pm; closed Jan.

BRITTANY

By Lily Heise

"**L**ittle Britain," as it was called by the 4th- and 5th-century Celts who came to settle this northwestern peninsula, always seems apart from the rest of France. While this was once politically true (the region resisted conquer and incorporation into Charlemagne's Frankish empire, remaining an independent duchy until 1532), even today's Bretons hold fast to their traditions, and their independent spirit is undeniable. The original Breton language, with its roots in Welsh and Cornish, though once suppressed, has experienced a revival. The *Gwenn-ha-du*—the black-and-white Breton flag—still flies proudly in every town. This unique cultural identity, along with its wild coast, succulent seafood, rustic hamlets, and medieval fortresses make it one of the most evocative areas of France.

Brittany is home to some of the most alluring towns in the country. You can't help but be charmed strolling the streets of the former fortress town of St-Malo or medieval Dinan. Quimper is the bastion of Breton culture and Nantes is becoming a cool outpost for Parisians. Traditionally, the province is divided into Haute-Bretagne and Basse-Bretagne. Promontories, coves, traffic-free islands and beaches stud the rocky coastline, some 1,207km (748 miles) long. The interior is a land of hamlets, farmhouses, and moors covered with yellow broom and purple heather.

The British, just a channel-hop away, think of Brittany as a resort region. They tend to frequent Dinard, although the water can be choppy and cold, with high waves But the French typically go south to chase their sun. Therefore, you'll never run into huge tourist masses, though popular beaches can get a bit crowded in summer.

We suggest first-time visitors stick to the coast, where you can see salt-meadow sheep grazing. If you're coming from Mont-St-Michel, you can use St-Malo, Dinan, or Dinard as a base. Visitors from the château country of the Loire can explore the coastline of southern Brittany (and get there in under 3 hr.).

ST-MALO ★★★

414km (257 miles) W of Paris; 69km (43 miles) N of Rennes; 13km (8 miles) E of Dinard

Built on a granite rock in the Channel, St-Malo is joined to the mainland by a causeway. It's popular with the English, especially Channel Islanders, and its warm brown sands give it a modest claim to being a beach

PREVIOUS PAGE: **The Petit Minou Lighthouse near Finistere.**

resort. The peninsula curves around a natural harbor that comprises several smaller basins. The walled city radiates outward from the town's château and its spiritual centerpiece, the Cathédrale St-Vincent, both of which lie near the peninsula's tip.

Despite past lives as a fortress and the site of a monastery, St-Malo is best known for the *corsaires* who used it as a base during the 17th and 18th centuries. During wartime, a decree from the French king sanctioned the seafaring mercenaries to intercept British ships and requisition their cargo. During peacetime, they acted as intrepid merchant marines, returning from Asia and the Americas with gold, coffee, and spices. Indeed, the sea is in the hearts of all *Malouins,* as natives of St-Malo are called—especially during the city's famous transatlantic sailing race, the *Route du Rhum,* which is held every 4 years and finishes in Guadeloupe.

Walking the ramparts and cobblestone streets, it's hard to imagine that 80 % of St-Malo was destroyed in World War II. What you see today is thanks to a meticulous, decades-long restoration.

St-Malo encompasses the communities of St. Servan and Paramé, but most tourists head for the walled city, or *Intra-muros.* In summer, the Grande Plage du Sillon towards Paramé is dotted with sun-seekers; year-round it's sought after for its deluxe seawater spa. St. Servan's marina is adjacent to a large terminal where ferries depart for and arrive from the Channel Islands and England.

Essentials

ARRIVING From Paris's Gare Montparnasse, about 12 TGV **trains** per day make the journey; a one-way ticket ranges from 32€ to 112€. Four of these trains are direct, making the journey in 2¼ to 2½ hours; transferring at Rennes takes 2½ to 3¼ hours. For information, visit www.sncf-connect.com or call ✆ **36-35.** If you're **driving** from Paris, take A13 west to Caen and continue southwest along N175 to the town of Miniac Morvan. From there, travel north on N137 directly to St-Malo. Driving time is 4 hours from Paris.

VISITOR INFORMATION The **Office de Tourisme** is on esplanade St-Vincent (www.saint-malo-tourisme.com; ✆ **02-99-56-66-99**).

SPECIAL EVENTS The **Festival de la Musique Sacrée** (www.festival demusiquesacree-stmalo.com), from mid-July to mid-August, stages evening concerts twice a week in various churches. The famous transatlantic yacht race, the **Route du Rhum** (www.routedurhum.com), departs from St-Malo every 4 years in November.

Getting Around

ON FOOT With its layout and tiny one-way streets, it's best to tour the city on foot.

BY BICYCLE Many of the city's streets have bike lanes. You can rent bikes in St-Malo, Dinard, and Dinan and even have them delivered to your

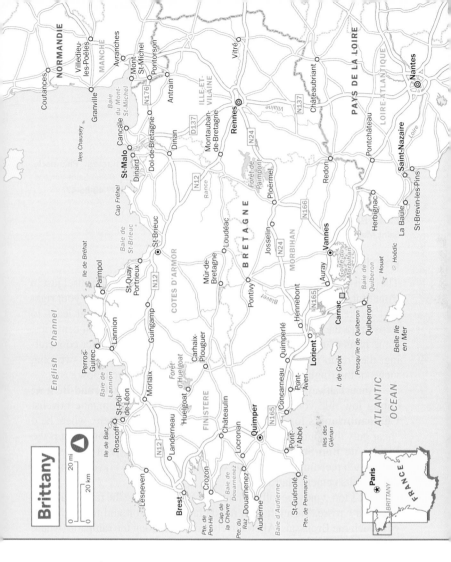

hotel from **Vélo Emeraulde** (www.velo-corsaire.fr; ☏ **06-58-02-24-61**). Rentals are 16€ daily for adults and 13.50€ for children (multi-day rates and e-bikes also available).

BY CAR   Several parking lots are along Quai Saint-Vincent, but they fill up quickly in summer months. You can rent a car at the TGV train station from **Europcar** (www.europcar.fr; ☏ **02-99-56-75-17**) or **Avis** (www. avis.fr; ☏ **02-99-40-18-54**).

BY TAXI   Taxis are usually in front of the station or call **Saint Malo Taxi** (www.taxi-st-malo.com; ☏ **02-99-81-30-30**).

BY PUBLIC TRANSPORT   The local bus service does not go into the old city but you can get a bus (line C1 or C2) from the station to the city walls;

the network is run by **MAT** (www.reseau-mat.fr; ✆ **02-99-40-19-22**). Buy your one-way tickets from ticket machines (1.35€) or directly from the bus driver (2€).

[FastFACTS] ST-MALO

ATMs/Banks Several ATMs are around the cathedral or along rue Broussais.

Doctors & Hospitals
Centre Hospitalier de Saint Malo, 1 rue de la Marne (www.gh-re.fr; ✆ **02-99-21-21-21**).

Mail & Postage **La Poste,** 6 pl. du Prieuré (✆ **36-31**).

Pharmacies **Pharmacie Lecoq,** 8 Rue Saint-Vincent (✆ **02-99-40-86-47**).

Exploring St-Malo

The 15th-century **Porte St-Vincent,** with a Belle Epoque carrousel just in front of it, is the main entrance to St-Malo Intra-muros. Walk to your right past the restaurant terraces on place Chateaubriand—a portal leads to steps up to the **ramparts ★★★**. Built and rebuilt over several centuries, some parts of these walls date from the 14th century. Weather cooperating, they're an ideal place to start a walking tour and take in sweeping views of the English Channel and the **Fort National** (see below).

About halfway round, you'll see an islet called the **Ile du Grand-Bé ★★**; during low tide you can walk to it and visit French Romantic novelist **Chateaubriand's tomb.** His last wish was to be buried here, where he'd "hear only the sounds of the wind and the ocean." Also within sight is the **Piscine de Bon-Secours,** a 1930s outdoor swimming pool whose three walls catch receding seawater. On warm days you'll see brave divers leaping from its cement platform.

If it's too windy, get off the ramparts by descending the ramp that joins rue de la Crosse. Turn left onto rue de la Pie Qui Boit and follow it until you reach rue Broussais. Alternatively, continue along the ramparts (where the view just keeps getting better) until you reach the **Porte de Dinan.** The street below it, rue de Dinan, becomes rue Broussais. Both routes lead to the **place de Pilori** back in the center. Head back toward the Porte St-Vincent for the greatest concentration of shopping and dining options.

Cathédrale St-Vincent ★★★ CATHEDRAL   Transformation of a monastic church into this cathedral began in 1146. Over the centuries, various architects added Romanesque, Gothic, and Neoclassical elements— only to have the steeple knocked off and the transept destroyed during fierce fighting in 1944. It took nearly 30 years to restore the structure and its magnificent stained glass. A floor mosaic commemorates the 1535 blessing of St-Malo native Jacques Cartier before he set off to discover Canada. Cartier's tomb is here, along with that of René Duguay-Trouin, a

Fort National has seen a lot of action over the years, including during World War II, when Germany used it briefly as a prison.

legendary privateer so successful he was made a commander in the French navy.

12 rue St-Benoît. ℭ **02-99-40-82-31.** Free admission. Daily 9:30am–6:30pm.

Fort National ★ HISTORIC SITE   Designed by famed military architect Sébastien de Vauban, construction of this fortress began in 1689. You can access it by walking 300m (984 ft.) over sand at low tide (heed the tidal information, or you may find yourself wading back). Thirty-five-minute guided tours (in French, English info sheet provided) take you into the dungeon and explain the fort's history; it's equally rewarding to wander on your own and enjoy the views of the bay.

Grande Plage de Sillon. www.fortnational.com. ℭ **06-72-46-66-26.** Tours: 5€ adults; 3€ ages 6–16; free for children 5 and under. Jun–Sept; hours depend on the tide. Call in advance or look to the fort itself (when the French flag is flying, it's open to visitors).

Beaches

Along the coast, stretches of sand intersperse with rugged outcroppings that suggest fortresses protect Brittany from Atlantic storms. Both the **Grande Plage du Sillon** and the **Plage de Bon Secours,** west of the city walls, are very popular. Situated between the two, the **Plage de l'Eventail** is small and especially rocky. Beach amenities are scarce, but Sillon does have lifeguards on duty in the summertime.

Where to Stay

While some hotels inside the city walls are up to snuff, others are a bit run down. An alternative is to stay along the Plage du Sillon and walk the 10 minutes into the historic center.

Hotel Alba ★★   Facing the shimmering sea, this is the perfect beach-based hotel in St-Malo. You almost have the impression of staying on a boat, due to its proximity to the water; the smallish rooms gain in size thanks to their expansive views. Each is tastefully decorated in earthy tones, with modern, comfortable furnishings. The best rooms feature balconies and you can also choose from several family rooms. If you're not strolling on the beach at sunset, enjoy a drink on its terrace or its scenic bar.
17 rue des Dunes. www.hotelalba.com. ✆ **02-99-40-37-18.** 22 units. 99€–171€ double; 200€ family room. Free parking. **Amenities:** Bar; room service; free Wi-Fi.

Hôtel France et Chateaubriand ★★   Experience the 19th-century heyday of the Emerald coast by staying at the birthplace of one of its heroes: writer Chateaubriand. Located inside the walls of old St-Malo, the flowering courtyard feels as though you've stepped into the Romantic era. Common areas still have this bygone feeling; however, guest rooms have been brought into the 21st century with modern sea-inspired prints and colors. Request a room with views of the ramparts or the sea. The sweeping sea views can also be enjoyed from **Le 5,** the hotel's rooftop restaurant which serves gourmet seafood dishes. More well-prepared surf and turf, including the famed Chateaubriand steak, can be sampled in the swank ground-floor **Brasserie.**
12 pl. Chateaubriand. www.hotel-chateaubriand-st-malo.com. ✆ **02-99-56-66-52.** 80 units. 96€–232€ double; 153€–319€ family room. Parking 15€. **Amenities:** Restaurant; cafe; bar; babysitting; room service; free Wi-Fi.

Le Grand Hôtel des Thermes ★★★   Pamper yourself with a night or two at one of Brittany's top historic hotels and premier thalassotherapy centers. Located on the Plage du Sillon, the glamorous hotel was originally built in 1883 and was expanded to a second building in 1990. A calming aura prevails throughout thanks to large windows and a serene color scheme reflecting the emerald waters beyond. *Tip:* Because this is an older hotel, a handful of its rooms are very small and so are sold at a great discount to solo travelers. They have private facilities, just not much floor space, and single beds.

The hotel is home to an innovative thalassotherapy spa, which pumps in purified seawater for its treatments and pools, as well as three dining facilities: **Le Cap-Horn,** a gastronomic seafront restaurant; **La Verrière,** a stylish eatery beneath a glass atrium with both health-focused and traditional options; and **La Terrasse,** a summertime patio serving dainty lunch fare. Mains range from 15€ to 42€ and menus from 38€ to 76€.
100 Boulevard Hébert. www.le-grand-hotel-des-thermes.fr. ✆ **02-99-40-75-75.** 177 units. 202€–732€ double; 886€–1076€ suites. Parking 19€. **Amenities:** 3 Restaurants; bar; indoor pool; spa; hammam; sauna; room service; beauty salon; boutique; free Wi-Fi.

Quic en Grogne ★★   Ideally positioned on a quiet street close to shops and the beach, this is the perfect budget hotel within the historic center of St-Malo. Located in a former home, the hotel retains a friendly, welcoming feel. The small guest rooms have a subtle nautical theme while steering clear of kitsch. All bathrooms have been refitted; the more expensive ones have bathtubs. The best rooms look over a flowery courtyard. Breakfast is served in a glass-covered sunroom, and the hotel's convenient private parking allows guests to avoid the hassle of parking outside the ramparts.

8 rue d'Estrées. www.quic-en-groigne.com. © **02-99-20-22-20.** 15 units. 82€–120€ double; 126€–138€ family room. Parking 20€. Closed end of Dec–Jan. **Amenities:** Free Wi-Fi.

Where to Eat

Satisfy your summer taste buds with the best ice cream in St-Malo at **Sanchez,** 9 rue Vieille Boucherie (www.sanchez-artisanglacier.fr; © **02-99-56-67-17**). With over 120 flavors, it'll be hard to choose, but we love their signature flavor "Le péché Malouin" (salted butter caramel with a twist). For breakfast, a light lunch or quality coffee, seek out **Cavoua,** 3 rue des Orbettes (www.cavoua.fr; © **02-56-52-00-32**), a cozy cafe in the heart of the old town that also does take-away. For full meals, in addition to the suggestions below, consider dining at the excellent restaurants located at Le Grand Hôtel des Thermes and Hôtel France et Chateaubriand (see above for both).

La Brasserie du Sillon ★★ SEAFOOD/FRENCH   Outside the city walls you'll find St-Malo's most innovative restaurant. Set in a lovely stone building facing the Sillon beach, the interior is refined and the best tables overlook the sea. Dishes are beautifully presented, though on the pricey side *à la carte;* savings can be made with their great value fixed-priced menus. Savor specialties such as fisherman's *choucroute* (fish and fermented cabbage in cream sauce), scallops in butter sauce, roasted Mont-St-Michel lamb with garlic and thyme jus, or you might be easily tempted by 13 different *plateaux de fruit de mer,* overflowing with freshly caught shrimp, crab, and lobster.

3 Chaussée du Sillon. www.brasseriedusillon.com. © **02-99-56-10-74.** Main course 23€–62€; fixed-price menus 28€–82€. Daily noon–2:30pm; Sun–Thurs 7–10pm; Fri–Sat 7–10:30pm.

Méson-Chalut ★★ SEAFOOD/FRENCH   Meaning "fish-net home" in the local Gallo dialect, here's where you can reel in the freshest—and most sustainable—catches in town. Chef Jean-Philippe Foucat has earned a "Green Food" label thanks to his numerous environmentally conscious initiatives, from waste and energy reduction to using only locally sourced fish, seafood and other ingredients, some from his own organic garden. Within a modern, nature-inspired dining room, try delicately prepared line-caught pollack with artichokes and French caviar, abalones with cauliflower and Paimpol beans or blue lobster served with green beans and peas.

8 rue de la Corne-de-Cerf. www.meson-chalut.bzh. © **02-99-56-71-58.** Main course 25€–30€; fixed-price lunch 52€–85€ or dinner 79€–99€. Mon 7–8:30pm, Wed–Sun noon–1:30pm and 7:15–8:30pm.

LUNCH ON THE half-shell

If you're driving east from St-Malo to Mont-St-Michel (or don't mind hopping on a local bus), consider a stop in **Cancale** ★★★—a harbor town famous for its oysters since the 17th century, when Louis XIV had them delivered regularly to Versailles.

Head to the northernmost end of the Port de la Houle, just beyond the jetty, where you'll see a handful of stalls selling shellfish out of crates. Come armed with a baguette and half-bottle of muscadet (sold at a nearby kiosk or on the port's main street) and order a dozen oysters to go. The sellers will shuck them immediately and hand them to you on a plastic plate. Find a spot on a bench or the rocks, slurp down your mollusks and toss the shells onto the sun-bleached pile below.

For a second course, pop in to the **Crêperie du port,** 1 pl. du Calvaire, 7 quai Thomas (✆ **02-99-89-60-66**), for inventive buckwheat *galettes* and dessert crepes.

Oysters at Cancale.

Shopping

If you're in St-Malo on Tuesday or Friday between 8am and 1pm and want to experience a great Breton market, head for the **Halle au Blé,** in the heart of the old city. You can't miss the bustle and the hawking of seafood, fresh produce, local dairy products, and baked goods.

Check out **Marin-Marine,** 5 Grand Rue (✆ **02-99-40-90-32**), for men's and women's fashions including mariner's shirts and Breton wool sweaters. **Gauthier Marines,** 2 rue Porcon de la Barbinais (www.gauthier marines.com; ✆ **02-99-40-91-81**), is a walk-in treasure chest of model ships, wooden sculpture, and marine-themed gift items.

Brittany's most revered chef and modern-day spice hunter, Olivier **Roellinger,** has an eponymous shop at 12 rue Saint-Vincent (www.epices-roellinger.com; ✆ **06-18-80-44-10**). His beautifully presented blends, made from spices found all over the world, are worth collecting. And just try leaving **Maison Larnicol,** 6 rue St Saint-Vincent (www.chocolaterielarnicol.fr; ✆ **02-99-40-57-62**), empty-handed. It specializes in Breton sweets including baked goods, chocolates, and a variety of flavored caramels.

St-Malo Nightlife

For an evening of gambling, head to **Le Casino Barrière,** 2 chaussée du Sillon (www.casinosbarriere.com/en/saint-malo.html; ✆ **02-99-40-64-00**). You can also order dinner, sometimes accompanied by live music. You must present your passport.

For dancing, consider **L'Escalier,** La Buzardière (www.escalier.fr; ✆ **02-99-81-65-56**), open Thursday to Saturday midnight to 7am. The cover never exceeds 15€. You'll need wheels, as the club is in the countryside 5km (3 miles) east of town. It does have a free shuttle, however; for information and reservations call ✆ **06-85-31-27-64.**

Popular pubs include **L'Aviso,** 12 rue du Point du Jour (www.facebook.com/BarLAVISO; ✆ **07-68-15-01-07**), offering 300 types of beer and Breton beer on tap, and **Pub Saint Patrick,** 24 rue Sainte-Barbe (✆ **02-99-56-66-90**), serving 50 different Irish whiskeys, along with Breton beer. Concerts are regularly scheduled at the latter.

DINARD ★★

417km (259 miles) W of Paris; 23km (14 miles) N of Dinan

Dinard (not to be confused with its inland neighbor, Dinan) sits on a rocky promontory at the top of the Rance River, opposite St-Malo. Once a small fishing community, by the late 19th century, it was a favorite of the European jet set, thanks largely to wealthy British families who built grand Victorian villas along the coast.

Though its golden age has tarnished somewhat, Dinard is still one of France's best-loved resorts. It's also a destination for cinephiles, who flock to the British film festival here at the end of September.

Essentials

ARRIVING   If you're **driving,** take D186 west from St-Malo to Dinard. SNCF **trains** go only as far as St-Malo; from there, take bus no. 16, which departs from the St-Malo rail station daily for the 30-minute ride to Dinard. The one-way fare is 2.50€. **Buses** arrive from many towns and cities in Brittany, including Rennes. Schedule and fare information is available via **BreizhGo** (www.breizhgo.bzh; ☎ **02-99-30-03-00**). Between April and October, **Compagnie Corsaire,** Gare Maritime de la Bourse, St-Malo (www.compagniecorsaire.com; ☎ **02-23-18-15-15**), operates ferryboats from St-Malo to Dinard. The trip takes 10 minutes and costs 5.90€ one-way. A **taxi** to Dinard from St-Malo is another option; it costs around 30€. For information, call ☎ **02-99-81-30-30.**

VISITOR INFORMATION The **Office de Tourisme** is at 2 bd. Féart (www.ot-dinard.com; ☎ **08-21-23-55-00**).

[FastFACTS] DINARD

ATMs/Banks Easy-access ATMs are on avenue Edouard VII and pl. Rochaid.

Doctors & Hospitals **Centre Hopital Arthur Gardiner,** 1 rue Henri Dunant (www.ch-dinard.org; ☎ **02-99-16-88-88**).

Mail & Postage **La Poste,** 8 pl. Rochaid (☎ **36-31**).

Pharmacies **Pharmacie Centrale Française Anglaise,** 15 bd. Féart (☎ **02-99-46-88-04**).

Enjoying the Town

Most visitors come to Dinard for the beach. It's a 10-minute walk from the town's historic core to the Pointe du Moulinet and encircles most of the old town with its haunting 19th-century villas and encompasses views as far away as St-Malo.

BEACHES & SWIMMING Dinard's main beach is the **Plage de l'Ecluse** (La Grande Plage), the strip of sand between the peninsulas that defines the edges of the old town. Favored by families and vacationers, it's crowded on hot days. Smaller and more isolated is the **Plage de St-Enogat** (you pass through the village of St-Enogat on the 20-min. hike east from Dinard). The **Plage du Prieuré,** a 10-minute walk from the center, has a few trees that shade the sand. The beaches have a few restaurants, toilets, showers, changing cabins, rental boats, and lifeguards (in summer). Because of the big difference between high and low tides, the municipality has built swimming pool–style basins along the Plage de L'Ecluse and the Plage du Prieuré to catch the seawater.

The **Piscine Olympique,** boulevard du Président-Wilson, next to the casino (☎ **02-99-46-22-77**), is a covered, heated seawater pool open year-round. Entrance is 5€ for adults, 4€ for ages 5 to 17, and free for children 4 and under. From July to mid-September, it's open Monday to Friday 10am to 12:30pm and 3 to 7:30pm, weekends 10am to 12:30pm and 3 to 6:30pm. Hours vary the rest of the year according to the needs of school groups and swim teams (inquire at the tourist office). A swim cap (for everyone) and a speedo (for men) are required and available for purchase on site.

Where to Stay

Didier Méril (see "Where to Eat," below) also rents rooms.

Grand Hôtel Barrière de Dinard ★★★   The glory of the Victorian era lives on at one of the Emerald coast's grandest hotels. First opened in 1858, the majestic two-winged building overlooks the Vicomté bay. Luxury knows no bounds, from the glamorous foyer to the deluxe indoor pool and spa. Guest rooms feature a light color palette, with touches of blue or orange, and are decorated in tasteful modern furnishings paired with seaside-themed artwork. Bathrooms are sumptuously fitted and it's well worth splurging on rooms with balconies. In the evening you can savor succulent seafood in the regal restaurant or a cocktail in the posh bar.

46 av. George V. www.hotelsbarriere.com/fr/dinard/le-grand-hotel.html. ℂ **02-99-88-26-26.** 89 units. 240€–744€ double; from 900€ suite. Closed mid-Nov to Dec 26 and Jan 2 to early Feb. **Amenities:** Restaurant; bar; babysitting; kids' club; fitness center; indoor pool; room service; rooms for those w/limited mobility; sauna; hammam, spa; free bike rental; free Wi-Fi.

Hôtel Printania ★★   The keys to Breton hospitality are handed to you at this quaint hotel. Considered by its family-run management as a *musée-hôtel*, you're definitely in for a cultural experience, right down to the staff dressed in folkloric costumes. Although recently upgraded, the hotel has retained its traditional charm and features solid wooden furniture, traditional floral wallpaper, and grandmother-style nautical antiques and artwork dating back to when it opened in 1920. Your room might even feature *lits clos*—Breton-style beds akin to ships' bunks. Don't worry, there are also modern flat-screen TVs and wireless Internet. It's only 5 minutes from the beach, which you can appreciate from the glassed-in terraces or great restaurant that, not surprisingly, serves up tasty local classics.

5 av. George-V. www.printaniahotel.com. ℂ **02-99-46-13-07.** 56 units. 72€–214€ double; 277€–352€ suite. Closed mid-Nov to mid-Mar (except 2 weeks over Christmas). Parking 16€. **Amenities:** 2 restaurants; bar; free Wi-Fi.

Where to Eat

The **Grand Hôtel Barrière de Dinard** (see above) offers fine dining.

Didier Méril ★★★ MODERN FRENCH/BRETON   The best meal in Dinard comes with the best views. Located right on the Bay of Prieuré, this historic stone building has been refurbished with designer furniture. This new-meets-old is carried over on Chef Didier Méril's refined menu with such dishes as Breton octopus with naval orange extract, Timut pepper and wasabi and veal chop with creamed white sweet potato and honey-roasted celery. The wine list is equally impressive, with over 450 labels, and the cheese trolly is hard to pass up. If those aren't enough, the view of the bay from its terrace will certainly leave you awestruck.

8

BRITTANY

Dinard

Above the restaurant are six recently renovated bedrooms and two suites for rent, some with sea views; rates range from 65€ to 320€.

1 pl. du Gen. de Gaulle. www.restaurant-didier-meril.com. 🕐 **02-99-46-95-74.** Main course 36€–43€; fixed-price menu lunch 47€ and dinner 70€–115€. Daily 12:15–1:30pm and 7:15–8:30pm.

La Passerelle du Clair de Lune ★★ MODERN FRENCH   As its name indicates, this restaurant is located at one end of the Promenade du Claire de Lune, a perfect spot to enjoy the views of the sea and its excellent catches. Since taking over the reins in 2022, chef Enzo Polini has retained the restaurant's local clientele thanks to his creative bistronomic cuisine. The seasonally driven menu includes the likes of tuna tartare with fresh cherries and tarragon, spare ribs with polenta and smoked garlic and their signature dessert, *tiramisu breton* made with local shortbread cookies and salted butter caramel.

3 av. George-V. www.la-passerelle-restaurant.com. 🕐 **02-99-16-96-37.** Main course 20€–23€. Tues 7–10pm; Wed–Sat noon–2pm and 7–10pm, Sun noon–2pm.

Shopping

For shops and boutiques, concentrate on rue du Maréchal-Leclerc, rue Levavasseur, and boulevard Féart. You'll find unique gift items at **Esperluette,** 45 rue Maréchal Leclerc (https://esperluettedinard.fr; 🕐 **09-52-36-21-09**), a boutique and gallery featuring eco-responsible art, homeware and jewelry. Stop in at **Ma Kibell,** 53 rue Levavasseur (https://makibell.com; 🕐 **09-54-37-18-56**), for locally made cosmetics, soaps and creams using all-natural ingredients.

Nightlife

Like many French beach resorts, Dinard has a casino. **Le Casino Barrière,** 4 bd. Du Président-Wilson (www.casinosbarriere.com/fr/dinard.html; 🕐 **02-99-16-30-30**), is liveliest from Easter to late October with games including roulette, blackjack, and slot machines and a bar and restaurant in-house. Hours are Sunday through Thursday from 10am to 2am, Friday and Saturday from 10am to 3am. Admission is free though you must present your passport; dress code is smart casual. An alternative is **La Suite,** 2 rue la Ville Biais, off of route du Barrage (www.facebook.com/lasuitedinard; 🕐 **02-99-46-46-46**), a nightclub and dance club on the outskirts with a loyal following thanks to a good wine selection and amiable ambience. It's open Thursdays through Saturdays, with varying cover charges and free shuttle-bus service to Dinard and St-Malo. According to its club rules, "Homosexuality is not a problem—but homophobia is."

In the evenings from July to September, tourists stroll the **Promenade du Clair de Lune** to admire specially illuminated buildings and gardens and enjoy open-air concerts and film screenings.

DINAN ★★★

396km (246 miles) W of Paris; 52km (32 miles) NW of Rennes

Once a fortified stronghold of the Dukes of Brittany, Dinan is one of the prettiest and best-preserved towns in the region. It's noted for its *maisons à piliers,* medieval half-timbered houses built on stilts over the sidewalks. For centuries, the town has served as a hub of cultural and commercial activity, from the original merchants and traders to today's artists and craftspeople. The tourist bustle can detract, but it's hard not to be moved by a walk atop the ramparts or a visit to the basilica.

Essentials

ARRIVING   Dinan has an SNCF **train** station, but service is infrequent. The trip from Rennes, with one stop, takes about 1 hour and costs 11€ to 15€. From St-Malo it takes about as long and costs 11€. Most rail passengers just transfer to one of the **buses** from the train stations for connection to Dinan. The trip time is almost the same, but tickets are 2.50€. For information on bus schedules visit www.breizhgo.bzh or call ℂ 02-99-30-03-00. If you're **driving** from Dinard, take highway D166 south to Dinan.

VISITOR INFORMATION   The **Office de Tourisme** is at 9 rue du Château (www.dinan-tourisme.com; ℂ **02-96-87-69-76**).

SPECIAL EVENTS   One of the biggest medieval festivals in the world, the **Fêtes des Remparts** (www.fete-remparts-dinan.com), is held the third

An aerial view of the lovely medieval town of Dinan.

weekend of July in odd-numbered years. Mingle amongst the knights and maidens and enjoy authentic street entertainment, food, and crafts. Take in an archery competition or even a jousting match (see festival website for tickets).

[FastFACTS] DINAN

ATMs/Banks Several ATMs are in pl. Duclos or on rue Thiers.

Doctors & Hospitals **Centre Hospitalier Dinan/ St Brieuc,** av. Saint-Jean de Dieu (www.chdinanstbrieuc. fsjd.fr; ℰ **02-96-87-18-00**).

Mail & Postage **La Poste,** 7 pl. Duclos (ℰ **36-31**).

Pharmacies **Pharmacie Centrale Gildas Morvan,** 8 pl. Duclos (ℰ **02-96-39-07-10**).

Exploring Dinan

Dinan's ramparts, which include 14 watchtowers and four gates, extend for almost 3.5km (2 miles) around the town. The tourist office provides a printed walking guide, and it's a lovely ramble.

The sloping rue du Jerzual, flanked with 15th-century dwellings and shops with craftspeople selling their wares, also rewards exploration. In the middle is the **Porte du Jerzual,** a 13th- and 14th-century gate—you can still see traces of its drawbridge in the stone. In the direction of the river the street becomes **rue du Petit-Fort,** which has a number of photo-worthy 15th-century *maisons;* it leads to the town's small port and its Gothic style bridge.

Basilique St-Sauveur ★★ CHURCH   Built between the 12th and 16th centuries, this church has Romanesque, Gothic, Baroque, and Classical elements. A monument holds the heart of Bertrand du Guesclin, the beloved Breton knight who defended Dinard during the Hundred Years' War. Just behind the basilica, the terraced **Jardin Anglais (English Garden)** provides a panoramic view of the Rance Valley and direct access to the ramparts.
pl. St-Sauveur. ℰ **02-96-39-06-67.** Free admission. Daily 9am–7pm.

Château Musée de Dinan ★★ MUSEUM   Three medieval structures, united in the 16th century, form this surprisingly fun municipal museum. Renovations completed in 2019 have modernized its displays on Dinan's history dating back to prehistory, and now there are a number of entertaining interactive elements and lots of wall text in English. The chapel contains holy artifacts, furniture, and silver. The dungeon of the colossal 14th-century fortress was a residence for the Duke of Brittany before being converted into a jail.
rue du Château. www.chateaudedinan.fr. ℰ **02-96-39-45-20.** Admission 7€ adults; 3.50€ ages 6–18 and students; free for children 5 and under. Apr–Sept daily 10:30am–7pm; Oct–Dec Tues–Sun 1:30–6:30pm. Closed Jan to late Mar.

Tour de l'Horloge ★ HISTORIC SITE   This structure boasts a clock made in 1498 and a bell donated by Anne de Bretagne in 1507. After the 158 steps you'll be rewarded with a view of Dinan from the 23m (75-ft.) belfry—one of only two intact belfries in all of Brittany. Its main bell is named after Anne—three smaller ones are engraved with the names Jacqueline, Françoise, and Noguette.

rue de l'Horloge. (*) **02-96-87-58-72.** Admission 4€ adults; 2.50€ ages 8–18 and students; free for children 7 and under. Apr–Sept Mon 10:30am–1pm and 2–6:30pm, Tues–Sun 10:30am–6:30pm; Feb–Mar daily 1:30–6:30pm.

Where to Stay

Hôtel Arvor ★★   The entrance to this former 14th-century Jacobin convent ushers you into the most romantic hotel in town. The building was first refurbished in the 18th century in a Renaissance style, and thankfully, again in more recent years, bringing it up to 21st-century standards.

AN idyll ON AN ILE

The **Ile de Bréhat** is home to some 350 hearty folk who live most of the year in isolation—until the summer crowds arrive. The tiny island (actually two islands, Ile Nord and Ile Sud, linked by a bridge, Le Pont Vauban) is in the Gulf of St-Malo, north of Paimpol. A visit to Bréhat is an adventure, even to the French. The only settlement on the islands is Le Bourg, in the south. The only bona fide beach is a strip of sand at Guerzido.

Walking is the primary activity, and it's possible to stroll the footpaths around the island in a day. Cars, other than police and fire vehicles, aren't allowed. Tractor-driven carts carry visitors on an 8km (5-mile) circuit of Bréhat's two islands, charging 9€ for the 45-minute jaunt (it's 4€ for children 4–11, free for children 3 and under). A number of places rent bikes, but they aren't necessary.

The rich flora here astonishes many visitors, who arrive expecting a wind-swept island only to discover a more Mediterranean clime. Flowers abound in summer, though both the gardens and houses appear tiny because of the scarcity of land. At the highest point, Chapelle St-Michel, you'll be rewarded with a panoramic view.

The tourist office, pl. du Bourg, Le Bourg (www.brehat-infos.fr; (*) **02-96-20-04-15**), is open Monday to Saturday mid-June to mid-September.

To reach Paimpol, **drive** west on D768 from Dinard to Lamballe, then take E50 west to Plérin and D786 north to Paimpol. To reach the island, take D789 4km (2½ miles) north of Paimpol, where the peninsula ends at the Pointe de l'Arcouest. From Paimpol, **BreizhGo** (www.breizhgo.bzh; (*) **02-99-30-03-00**) bus line 24 make the 10-minute run to the point for a one-way fare of 1€. Then, catch one of the **ferries** operated by **Les Vedettes de Bréhat** (www.vedettesde brehat.com; (*) **02-96-55-79-50**). Ferries depart about every 30 minutes in summer, around seven times per day in the off-season; the round-trip costs 17.50€ for adults, 12€ for ages 4 to 11, free for children 3 and under. Visitors in April, May, June, and September will find the island much less crowded than in July and August. Cars are not allowed on the ferry.

Guest rooms carry on in an amorous ambiance with colorful drapery, plush armchairs and even some heart-shaped throw pillows, with six entirely renovated in 2023. The rooms are spacious, especially in contrast to the small, though well-equipped bathrooms. Families will be able to spread out in their spacious duplex suite that sleeps six.

5 rue Pavie. www.hotelarvordinan.com. © **02-96-39-21-22.** 22 units. 82€–181€ double; 276€–329€ suite. Parking 10€. Closed Jan. **Amenities:** Free Wi-Fi.

Hôtel d'Avaugour ★★　Set in a stone house just inside the ramparts, this is a perfect and comfortable base for exploring Dinan. The entire hotel is tastefully decorated in a contemporary style with hints of Brittany in the decor. The guest rooms have simple yet plush furnishings in tones of grays and reds. The views either showcase the surrounding historic buildings or the large and lovely backyard garden, where you can take tea in the afternoon.

1 pl. du Champs. www.avaugourhotel.com. © **02-96-39-07-49.** 24 units. 110€–175€ double; 290€–320€ suite. Closed Nov–Mar. **Amenities:** Free Wi-Fi.

Where to Eat

For a less formal meal, lighter eateries are on rue de la Poissonnerie. Stop in at busy **Creperie Ahna,** no. 7 (© **02-96-39-09-13**), which has been run by the same family for four generations.

Fleur de Sel ★★ MODERN FRENCH/BRETON　Enjoy surf and turf with a nice dash of creativity at this friendly local favorite in the heart of the old city. You'll find the likes of fennel pannacotta with smoked eel and rocket pesto, sea bream with seaweed gnocchi and shellfish juice or soft black noodles with crispy vegetables—all certainly served with a healthy dash of Brittany *fleur de sel.*

7 rue Sainte Claire. www.restaurantlafleurdesel.com. © **02-96-85-15-14.** Main course 21€–28€; fixed-price menu 37€–47€; children's menu 14€–20€. Tues–Sat noon–2:30pm and 7–10pm, Sun noon–2:30pm.

QUIMPER ★★

570km (353 miles) W of Paris; 205km (127 miles) NW of Rennes

Quimper, the town that pottery built, is the historic capital of Brittany's most traditional region, La Cornouaille. It takes its name from the Breton word *kemper,* the meeting of two rivers—in this case the Odet and the Steir. There's no better place to get a feel for southern Breton culture, whether during its annual festival or just trolling the *vieux centre* for Quimperware, the hand-painted *faïence* that's symbolized Brittany for centuries. Modern-day Quimper is somewhat bourgeois, home to some 67,000 *Quimperois* who walk narrow streets spared from World War II damage.

Essentials

ARRIVING　Speedy **TGV trains** take only 3½ to 4 hours from the Montparnasse station in Paris. The one-way fare ranges from 25€ to 88€. For information, visit www.sncf-connect.com or call ☏ **36-35.** If you're **driving,** the best route is from Rennes: Take E50/N12 west to just outside the town of Montauban, continue west along N164 to Châteaulin, and head south along N165 to Quimper.

VISITOR INFORMATION The **Office de Tourisme** is at 8 rue Elie Fréron (www.quimper-tourisme.com; ☏ **02-98-53-04-05**).

SPECIAL EVENTS For 6 days around the third week of every July, the **Festival de Cornouaille** celebrates Breton culture. The festivities include parades in traditional costume and Celtic and Breton concerts throughout the city. For information, contact the tourist office.

[Fast FACTS] QUIMPER

ATMs/Banks Several ATMs can be found on rue du Parc and rue René Medec.

Doctors & Hospitals **Centre Hospitalier de Cornouaille,** av.

Yves Thépot (www.ch-cornouaille.fr; ☏ **02-98-52-60-60**).

Mail & Postage **La Poste,** 37 bd. Amiral de Kerguélen (☏ **36-31**).

Pharmacies **Pharmacie de la Cathédrale,** 24 pl. Saint-Corentin (☏ **02-98-95-00-20**).

Exploring Quimper

In some quarters, Quimper maintains its old-world atmosphere, with narrow medieval streets and footbridges spanning the rivers.

Cathédrale St-Corentin ★★ CATHEDRAL Characterized by two towers that climb 75m (246 ft.), this cathedral was built between the 13th and 15th centuries. The twin steeples were added in the 19th. Inside, note the 15th-century stained glass—windows on the north side were funded by religious donors, those on the south by secular ones.

pl. St-Corentin. ☏ **02-98-95-06-19.** Free admission. Sept–June daily 9:45am–noon and 1:30–6:30pm; July–Aug daily 9:45am–6:30pm; closed during Sun morning services.

Musée Departemental Breton ★★★ MUSEUM Located in the medieval Palais des Eveques de Cornouaille (Palace of the Bishops of Cornwall), next to the cathedral, this is a highlight of any visit to Quimper. Recent renovations have revamped its displays of the archaeological and decorative history of the region. It is one of the best ways to learn about the customs and traditions of Brittany, illustrated in items of stained glass, sculpture, furniture, painting, and *faience,* in addition to four rooms showcasing quotidian and ceremonial Breton costumes.

1–3 rue Roi Gradlon. www.museedepartementalbreton.fr. ☏ **02-98-95-21-60.** Admission 5€ adults; 3€ ages 18–25; free for children 17 and under; free on weekends Oct to mid-June. Mid-June to Sept daily 9am–6pm; Oct to mid-June Tues–Sat 9am–12:30pm and 1:30–5pm, Sun 2–5pm.

A sunny day in Quimper.

Musée des Beaux-Arts ★★ MUSEUM This museum is a nice cultural surprise along the mostly outdoorsy Brittany coast. First opened in 1872, the collection features some impressive names including Rubens, Boucher, Fragonard, and Corot, in addition to a strong collection of the Pont-Aven school (Gaugin, Sérusier, Bernard, Lacombe, Maufra, Denis). A special tribute is also paid to Quimper native Mac Jacob, a Surrealist poet and painter.

40 pl. St-Corentin. www.mbaq.fr. © **02-98-95-45-20.** Admission 5€ adults; 3€ ages 12–26; free for children 11 and under. July–Aug daily from 10am–6pm; Apr–June Wed–Mon 9:30am–noon and 2–6pm; Nov–Mar Mon and Wed–Sat 9:30am–noon and 2–5:30pm, Tues and Sun 2–5:30pm.

Where to Stay

Hôtel Kregenn ★★ For a solid sleep in the center, this is your best option. Located on a quiet street a block from the river, this hotel is an excellent value for the money. Though a Best Western, the hotel is still family-run, with an exceptionally friendly staff. Guest rooms are relatively spacious and have recently been revamped with stylish touches like designer lamps and velour armchairs juxtaposed by exposed stone walls and black and white photos of Quimper. The interior garden-terrace is the place to retire for a relaxing break. A coffee or glass of wine can be had at the bar; however, breakfast, for 15€, is the only meal served.

11–15 rue des Réguaires. www.hotel-kregenn.fr. © **02-98-95-08-70.** 32 units. 92€–380€ double; 112€–478€ suite. Parking 7€. Pets 15€. **Amenities:** Bar; limited room service; free Wi-Fi.

Manoir du Stang ★★ Hidden away in the Fouesnant Forest is one of Brittany's loveliest manor-hotels. Only 13km (8 miles) from Quimper, this refined 16th-century estate has changed hands only once in its 400-year history. The imposing stone walls and impeccably maintained grounds are proof of this test of time. The 10 hectares (25 acres) of natural woodland are perfect for idyll strolls, and golfers delight in teeing off at the neighboring 18-hole course. The lounge is cozy with a toasty fireplace and is furnished with antiques and patterned armchairs. Guest room decor is a little old fashioned, but this adds to its homey Breton feel. There's no restaurant, but breakfast can be brought to your bed.

La Forêt-Fouesnant. www.manoirdustang.com. © **02-98-56-96-38.** 16 units. 104€–150€ double; 165€–195€ family room. Free parking. Closed early Nov to late Apr. Drive 1.5km (1 mile) north of the village center and follow signs from N783; access is by private road. **Amenities:** Bar; free Wi-Fi.

Where to Eat

For a drink or meal at any time of the day, sit down at the stylish **Café de l'Epée,** 14 rue du Parc (© **02-98-95-28-97**). The oldest "brasserie" in Brittany, it dates back to 1830 and serves elegant bistro fare, and, of course, copious seafood options.

L'identité ★ MODERN FRENCH/BRETON   It didn't take long for this new bistronomic restaurant to build a faithful clientele of local *Quimpérois* since opening in 2023. After running a restaurant in Nantes for 10 years, Manu and Audrey Le Gouil have returned to their Quimper area roots—and to their "identity." Within the restaurant's attractive dining room, or on the small terrace with views towards the cathedral, enjoy chilled pea soup topped with mussels, sea bass with creamed zucchini and grey shrimp sauce or veal quarter with artichoke mousse.

9 Rue Sainte-Catherine. www.lidentiterestaurant.fr. © **02-98-90-06-15.** Fixed-price lunch 20€–25€ or dinner 36€; vegetarian menu 29€; children's menu 15€. Tues–Sat noon–1:30pm and 7:30–9:30pm (Fri–Sat until 10pm).

Shopping

Quimper's proximity to the rivers gave it plenty of access to clay; it's been known as a pottery town since the late 1600s. *Faience,* the French term for glazed earthenware (as opposed to porcelain, manufactured to be more delicate) is your go-to souvenir here. Quimperware is recognized for its bright, hand-painted motifs, often Breton figures, fruits, and flowers. One of the most popular designs is a male *Breton* or female *Bretonne,* both in profile and in traditional costume. Today, this 19th-century motif is copyrighted and fiercely protected.

The best shopping streets are **rue Kéréon** and **rue du Parc,** where you'll find Breton products including pottery, dolls and puppets, clothing made from regional cloth and wool, jewelry, lace, and beautiful Breton costumes. See what contemporary artisans of Quimper are creating at **L'Atelier Corail,** 4 rue du Lycée (www.lateliercorail.com), which showcases locally made pottery, jewelry, and home decor items.

One site that produces stoneware is open for tours. Tuesday to Friday in April and Monday to Friday from May to September, two to seven tours per day depart from the visitor information center of **La Faïencerie Henriot-Quimper,** rue Haute, Quartier Locmaria (www.henriot-quimper. com; ✆ **02-98-90-09-36**). Tours in English, French, or both last 40 to 45 minutes and cost 5€ for adults, 2.50€ for children 8 to 14, and are free for children 7 and under. On site, a store sells the most complete inventory of Quimper porcelain in the world. You can invest in first-run (nearly perfect) pieces or slightly discounted "seconds," with almost imperceptible flaws. Everything can be shipped.

CONCARNEAU ★★

539km (334 miles) W of Paris; 93km (58 miles) SE of Brest

This port is a favorite of painters, who never tire of capturing the subtleties of the fishing fleet. It's also unique among the larger coastal communities because fishing, not tourism, is its main industry (Concarneau's canneries produce most of the tuna in France). Walk along the quays, especially in the evening, and watch the Breton fishers unload their catch; later, join them for a pint of cider in the taverns.

Essentials

ARRIVING   Concarneau does not have rail service. If you're driving, the town is 21km (13 miles) southeast of Quimper along D783. **BreizhGo bus** 43 runs from Quimper to Concarneau (trip time: 40 min.); the one-way fare is 2.50€ (www.breizhgo.bzh; ✆ **02-99-30-03-00**). The bus from Rosporden, site of another SNCF railway station, runs about eight times per day (trip time: 20 min.) for a fare of 1€ (www.coralie-cca.fr; ✆ **02-98-60-55-55**).

VISITOR INFORMATION   The **Office de Tourisme** is on quai d'Aiguillon (www.tourismeconcarneau.fr; ✆ **02-98-97-01-44**).

Exploring the Area

The town is built on three sides of a natural harbor whose innermost, sheltered section is the **Nouveau Port.** In the center of this is the heavily fortified **Ville Close ★★**, an ancient hamlet surrounded by ramparts, some from the 14th century. From the quay, cross the bridge and descend into the town. Souvenir shops have taken over, but don't let that spoil it. You can spend an hour wandering the alleys, gazing up at the towers, peering at the stone houses, and stopping in secluded squares.

For a splendid view of the port, walk the **ramparts ★**. They're open to pedestrians daily 10am to 7:30pm, with seasonal variations.

Also in the old town is a fishing museum, **Musée de la Pêche ★**, 3 rue Vauban (www.musee-peche.fr; ✆ **02-98-97-10-20**). The 17th-century building displays ship models and exhibits chronicling the development of the fishing industry. Be sure to also tour the *Hemerica,* a restored fishing boat docked in the port and included in your entrance ticket. Admission is 5€ for adults, 3€ for students and free for children 18 and under. It's open July and August 10am to 7pm and September to December and February to June from Tuesday to Sunday 10am to 6pm. Closed January.

BEACHES Concarneau's largest, most beautiful beach, popular with families, is the **Plage des Sables Blancs,** near the historic core. Within a 10-minute walk are the **Plage de Cornouaille** and two small beaches, the **Plage des Dames** and **Plage de Rodel,** where you'll find fewer families with children. The wide-open **Plage du Cabellou,** 5km (3 miles) west of town, is less crowded than the others.

SEA EXCURSIONS Boat rides are usually fine between June and September but can be treacherous the rest of the year. The dazzling Glenans archipelago, 16km (10 miles) off the coast, is a must if you have the time and sea legs. It can be visited on excursions through **Vedettes de l'Odet** (www.vedettes-odet.com; ☏ **02-98-57-00-58**), which runs several times per day from April to September and cost 49€ for adults, 42€ for children ages 13 to 17, 25€ for children 4 to 12 and 7€ for children 3 and under. In midsummer, you can arrange deep-sea fishing with the captain of the *Santa Maria* (www.santamariapeche.com; ☏ **06-62-88-00-87**).

Where to Stay & Eat

La Coquille ★★ SEAFOOD/TRADITIONAL FRENCH   Located right on the port, you can practically see your dinner being reeled in at the freshest venue in town. While it might not look sophisticated from the outside, the sleek dining room features light wood walls and tables, designer lighting, nautical paintings and a spectacular view of the harbor. Not surprisingly, you'll find a lot of seafood on the menu at La Coquille (the shell). The menu varies according to the latest catches. It could include scallops with algae butter, grilled lobster with Kari Gosse sauce or, to please the carnivores, filet of beef with red wine reduction sauce. Reservations are a must in season.

1 quai du Moros, at Nouveau Port. www.lacoquille-concarneau.fr. ☏ **02-98-97-08-52.** Main course 25€–31€; fixed-price lunch 18€–25€ or dinner 35€–50€. Tues–Sun noon–2pm, Thurs–Sat 7–9pm. Closed 3 weeks late Oct to mid-Nov.

Les Sables Blancs ★★   Overlooking Concarneau's loveliest beach, you can't have a better seaside stay than at this boutique hotel. Recent renovations made to this 1930s building transformed it into a glass paradise. Each of the spacious rooms has large windows facing the sea in addition to small private terraces. Marine colors in the pillows, artwork and some painted wall sections contrast nicely with the clean white used elsewhere. Bathrooms are sparkling, fully refitted in 2023. For some sophisticated surf and turf grab a table on the terrace or in the stylish dining room of the hotel's restaurant, with reasonably priced menus from 30€ to 36€.

Plage des Sables Blancs. www.hotel-les-sables-blancs.com. ☏ **02-98-50-10-12.** 21 units. 147€–318€ double; 289€–527€ suite. **Amenities:** Restaurant; free Wi-Fi.

PONT-AVEN ★★

522km (324 miles) W of Paris; 32km (20 miles) SE of Quimper; 16km (10 miles) S of
Concarneau

Paul Gauguin loved this inland village, with its white houses flanking the
River Aven on its gentle course to the Atlantic. It's also known for 15
moulins, or water mills, that once operated along the waterways. Only one
of them is still functional, but the rest have been restored for historical and
aesthetic purposes. With such picturesque surroundings, one might sus-
pect Pont-Aven of being a tourist trap, but its modest, pleasant atmosphere
endures.

Essentials

ARRIVING If you're **driving** from Quimper, go southeast on N165 and
follow signs into Pont-Aven. From Quimperlé, head west along D783
until N165 and follow signs. SNCF **trains** (www.sncf-connect.com;
✆ **36-35**) stop at Quimper, where you can transfer to between two to four
daily **buses** to Pont Aven. The trip, via Concarneau, takes an hour, and a
one-way fare is 2.50€ (www.breizhgo.bzh; ✆ **02-99-30-03-00**).

VISITOR INFORMATION The **Office de Tourisme** is at 5 pl. de l'Hôtel-
de-Ville (www.pontaven.com; ✆ **02-98-06-87-90**).

Exploring the Area

Themed walking tours are available in the village, such as the artists' trail
or the *promenade des moulins*—the tourist office can provide maps. You
can also visit one of the shops that produce the famous *galette de Pont-
Aven,* a round, butter-rich cookie that Bretons like to dunk in their coffee.
Two of the oldest are **Traou Mad,** 28 rue du Port (✆ **02-98-06-18-18**),
and **Penven-Délices de Pont-Aven,** 1 quai Théodore Botrel (https://
galettes-penven.com; ✆ **02-98-06-02-75**).

In the Footsteps of Gauguin

In the summer of 1886, Paul Gauguin
arrived in the Breton village of Pont-
Aven. Lesser-known artists, including
Maurice Denis, Paul Sérusier, and Emile
Bernard, soon followed. Breaking from
mainstream Impressionism, the Pont
Aven School—as the style of Gauguin
and his 20 or so followers came to be
known—emphasized pure colors,
shunned perspective and shadowing,
and simplified human figures. Both *The
Yellow Christ* and *The Green Christ,* two
of Gauguin's most memorable works,

exemplify this method, also known as
Synthetism.

The **Musée des Beaux-Arts de Pont-
Aven,** pl. de l'Hôtel de Ville (www.
museepontaven.fr; ✆ **02-98-06-14-43**),
underwent extensive renovations in 2016
which provided a fresh look and doubled
the exhibition space. The exhibits display
key works of 19th-century painters that
put this town on the map. Admission to
the museum and exhibits is 8€ for adults,
6€ for students and free for children 17
and under. It's open daily 10am to 6pm
(until 7pm July–Aug). Closed January.

The 16th-century **Chapelle de Trémalo,** lieu-dit Trémalo (✆ **02-98-06-01-68**), is 1.2km (¾ mile) north of the town center. It contains the wooden crucifix that inspired two of Gauguin's best-known paintings, *The Yellow Christ* (displayed today in a museum in Buffalo, New York) and his *Self-Portrait with the Yellow Christ* (displayed at the Musée d'Orsay in Paris). On private lands which still belong to descendants of the family who originally built and consecrated it in 1532, the chapel is unlocked every morning at 10am and closed at 6pm (July–Aug 7pm). It's still a place of worship, so masses are conducted from time to time. Plunk a coin or two into a machine to briefly illuminate the interior—otherwise, mid-day sunlight from the windows is sufficient.

Where to Stay & Eat

Hotel Les Mimosas ★★   Wake up to views from a Gauguin painting at this friendly excellent value inn. Facing the river with its bobbing sail-boats, the hotel has been recently redone in a smart contemporary look achieved with attractive flower print wallpaper and contemporary furnishings. Spend a little extra and you can have a room with a large terrace. The hotel also has a popular local restaurant serving mainly fish and seafood available in good-value menus ranging from 30€ to 39€. Or stop in after your day of sightseeing for their "apéro" special of a glass of white wine and small seafood platter for 11€ per person.

22 square Théodore Botrel. www.lesmimosas-pontaven.com. ✆ **02-98-06-00-30.** 10 units. 85€–135€ double. Amenities: Restaurant; free Wi-Fi. Restaurant: July to mid-Sept daily 12–2:30pm and 7–10pm; mid-Sept to June Tues–Sun noon–2pm and 7–9pm.

La Taupinière ★★ SEAFOOD/TRADITIONAL FRENCH   Skip the casual crèperies in town and make your way to this excellent gastronomic restaurant. Located in a lovely thatched cottage nestled in the woods on the outskirts of town, you'll be warmly received in the elegant yet homey dining room. After 54 years in the kitchen, its renowned chef, Guy Guilloux, passed his apron on to Éric Stéphan in 2023. The new chef is maintaining the storied restaurant's dedicated to Breton traditions while adding a dash of contemporary flare with such dishes as scallop *crème brulée;* crab crepes with truffles; and Challons duck Peking-style.

Route de Concarneau-Croissant Saint-André. www.lataupiniere.fr. ✆ **02-98-06-03-12.** Main course 30€–55€; fixed-price menu 60€–110€. Wed–Sat 12:30–2pm and 7:30–9pm, Sun 12:30–2pm.

CARNAC ★★

486km (301 miles) W of Paris; 37km (23 miles) SE of Lorient; 100km (62 miles) SE of Quimper

Aside from being a popular beach resort, Carnac is home to the largest megalithic site in the world. Spread out over 4km (2½ miles), **Les**

Alignements, as three fields of huge, upright stones are known, date back more than 6,000 years to Neolithic times. Scholars have debated their purpose for centuries, though most suggest they had astronomical or religious significance. One theory is that the stones marked burial sites. Another legend claims they are Roman soldiers turned to stone by the wizard Merlin. In all, the town contains 2,732 *menhirs,* some rising to heights of 20m (66 ft.).

Carnac's five beaches stretch over nearly 3km (1¾ miles). Protected by the Quiberon Peninsula, they back up onto sand dunes and shady forests. **Carnac-Plage** is a family resort and camping hotspot beside the ocean and along the waterfront boulevard de la Plage. The area is packed in July and August.

The prehistoric megaliths of Carnac.

Essentials

ARRIVING   **Driving** is the most convenient way to get to Carnac. From Pont-Aven, travel southeast along N165, passing through Hennebont. At the intersection with D768, continue south along the signposted road to Carnac. From Nantes, take N165 northwest to Auray and then D768.

Links to Carnac by public transport are inconvenient, as there's no railway station. **Train** travelers leave the SNCF network at either Quiberon or Auray and take a bus into town. An additional option, available between June and August only, is to get off the train at Plouharnel-Carnac station, 3km (1¾ miles) from Carnac. For more information about bus transit from any of these hamlets, see www.breizhgo.bzh or call ℭ **02-99-30-03-00.**

VISITOR INFORMATION   The **Office de Tourisme** is at 74 av. des Druides (www.ot-carnac.fr; ℭ **02-97-52-13-52**). It also offers free Wi-Fi.

Exploring the Area

Out of fear of vandalism, the local tourist authorities have fenced in the megaliths and allow visitors to wander freely among the *menhirs* only between October and March, when the park is open daily from 10am to 5pm, and when entrance is free. From April to September, the park can be visited only as part of a 1-hour guided tour, priced at 11€ for adults (6€ for students or anyone ages 18–24; free for visitors under 18). Tours are usually in French but, depending on the perceived need, may include some additional commentary in English. The only way to be sure is to call the **visitor center, La Maison des Mégalithes** (✆ **02-97-52-29-81**) for a rundown on the tours arranged for the day of your intended visit. For more information, visit www.menhirs-carnac.fr.

At Carnac Ville, **Musée de Préhistoire,** 10 pl. de la Chapelle (www.museedecarnac.com; ✆ **02-97-52-22-04**), displays collections from 450,000 b.c. to the 8th century. Admission is 7€ for adults, 3€ for ages 6 to 18, and free for children 5 and under. Hours are as follows: July and

THE WILD, WILD coast

Follow the D768 south from Carnac over the isthmus connecting the mainland to **Quiberon,** with its crescent of white sand. You'll probably see weathered Breton fishers hauling in their sardine catch.

The entire **Côte Sauvage,** or Wild Coast, is rugged and dramatic, with waves breaking ferociously against the reefs. Winds, especially in winter, lash the dunes, shaving the short pines that grow here. On the landward side, the beach is calm and relatively protected.

A 45-minute ferry ride from Quiberon is **Belle-Ile-en-Mer,** an 83-sq.-km (32-sq.-mile) outpost of sand, rock, and vegetation. It feels blissfully isolated, despite a scattering of hotels and seasonal restaurants. Depending on the season, 7 to 12 **ferries** depart daily from Port Maria in Quiberon (www.compagnie-oceane.fr; ✆ **02-97-31-34-45**). A round-trip ticket costs 35€ for adults, 27€ for students 18 to 26, 22€ for ages 4 to 17, and free for children 3 and under. In summer, you must reserve space for your car, as well as for passengers. The ferry docks at **Le Palais,** a fortified 16th-century port that is the island's window to mainland

France. The **Office de Tourisme** is here, on Quai Bonnelle Le Palais (✆ **02-97-31-81-93**).

Excellent accommodation and dining can be found in **Port de Goulphar,** an inlet on the southern shore framed by cliffs. The standout is the 66-unit Relais & Châteaux property **Castel Clara** (www.castel-clara.com; ✆ **02-97-31-84-21**), with restful rooms, two heated swimming pools (one seawater), and extensive spa services. Ideal service and first-class cuisine add to the sense of peace. Depending on the season, and on the view from the room (sea or garden), rates range from 165€ to 385€ double, 300€ to 525€ suite. The hotel is closed from mid-November to mid-December.

A fitting souvenir are sardines from **La Belle-Iloise boutique** on the place de la République (www.labelleiloise.fr; ✆ **02-97-31-29-14**). Even if you don't like sardines, the attractive tins make unusual *objets*. The last cannery in Belle-Ile-en-Mer closed in 1975, but production continues in Quiberon, and Belle-Iloise boutiques can be found in most Breton towns.

August Wednesday to Monday 10am to 6:30pm; April to June and September 10am to 12:30pm and 2 to 6pm; October 10am to 12:30pm and 2 to 5:30pm; and November to March 2 to 5:30pm.

Where to Stay & Eat

Auberge le Ratelier ★★ BRETON A true taste of Brittany is savored at this converted farmhouse, situated a short stroll from the center of Carnac. The stone building is draped in vines and the interior is equally charming with rustic decor, a fireplace, and wooden beams. Due to its seaside location the menu showcases local seafood, particularly celebrated in its "trip around lobster" set menu. You can also enjoy non-fish dishes like smoked duck with Breton artichokes and Camembert toasts, or filet of beef with scallop potatoes and Porto sauce.

Upstairs, the inn has eight small, slightly old-fashioned but comfortable guest rooms with showers. They are a steal at 62€ to 80€.

4 chemin du Douët. www.le-ratelier.com. ✆ **02-97-52-05-04.** Main course 25€–40€; fixed-price menu 22€–68€. Thurs–Mon noon–2pm and 7–9pm. Closed mid-Nov to Jan.

Camping La Grande Métairie ★ A 5-minute drive from the center of Carnac is this family fun paradise. The large complex next to the Megaliths is surrounded by trees and is a short drive to the beach. Multiple activities onsite include a large pool complex, water slides, a tree adventure park, mini-golf, tennis, and more. They even have a little farm and a circus school. You can either pitch your own tent or rent a variety of equipped mobile homes or for something different, opt for one of their tree-houses perched safely in the branches.

Route des Alignements de Kermario–Kerlescan. www.lagrandemetairie.com. ✆ **02-30-26-02-29.** From 25€ tent lots; 60€–170€ mobile homes; discounts on weekly rates. Closed early Nov to Apr. **Amenities:** Restaurant; babysitting; bar; disco; grocery; Jacuzzi; outdoor pool; Wi-Fi (paid).

Château de Locguénolé ★★★ Crowning a small bay enveloped by a 120-hectare (297-acre) forest, the grandest hotel in southern Brittany has just become grander, thanks to a complete makeover. Located near the town of **Hennebont,** 29km (18 miles) northwest of Carnac, the château reopened in late 2023 after extensive renovations which doubled its rooms and transformed it into a stylish modern retreat. The new decor discreetly pays tribute to Brittany's past of seafaring and trade with the East Indies through vintage-style prints, textiles and furnishings. Spread over the main castle and three annexes, guest rooms don a palette of soft greens and blues paired with dark wood and marble. Some rooms have canopy beds, others have views over the elegant grounds and the most original is found inside a 1920s boat that is seemingly beached against the side of the château.

Guests can choose to dine in **L'Inattendu,** a gastronomic restaurant under the helm of Meilleur Ouvrier de France chef Yann Maget and situated beneath a vast glass atrium with leafy plants, or at **La Maison Alyette,** a more casual bistro which opens onto a lovely terrace.

Rte. De Port-Louis en Kervignac. www.chateau-de-locguenole.com. © **02-97-76-76-76.** 47 units. 180€–650€ double; 400€–1,000€ suite. Closed Jan to mid-Feb. **Amenities:** 2 restaurants; babysitting; outdoor pool; room service; spa; sauna; hammam; tennis; free bike rental; free Wi-Fi.

NANTES ★★★

385km (239 miles) W of Paris; 325km (202 miles) N of Bordeaux

Technically, Nantes (pop. 303,000) is outside of Brittany. In 1941, the Vichy Government transferred it from the region into a newly created one, the Pays de la Loire. This administrative action did nothing to change Nantes' deeply Breton soul, however, and no guide to Brittany would be complete without its inclusion.

The capital of Brittany is Rennes (pop. 215,000), but when comparing the two cities, many agree that Nantes is more vibrant. It's best known for its busy port, which suffered great damage in World War II, and for the 1598 Edict of Nantes, which guaranteed religious freedom to Protestants (this was later revoked). During the Middle Ages, Nantes expanded from

The Erdre River in Nantes.

an island in the Loire to the northern edge of the river, where its center lies today. Many famous people, from Molière to Stendhal, have lived here.

In more recent years, Nantes has become a kind of Atlantic Coast Parisian annex for young *bobos* and families tired of the capital's rat race. Impressive revitalization is changing the city, as once-dreary industrial suburbs are being transformed into places you'd actually like to visit.

Essentials

ARRIVING   The **TGV train** from Paris's Gare Montparnasse takes about 2 to 2¼ hours to get to Nantes, and costs range from 29€ to 77€. For information, visit www.sncf-connect.com or call ✆ **36-35.** Nantes's **Gare SNCF,** 27 bd. de Stalingrad, is a 5-minute walk from the town center. If you're **driving,** take A11 for 385km (239 miles) west of Paris. The trip takes about 4 hours. **Aéroport Nantes-Atlantique** (✆ **02-40-84-80-00**) is 12km (7½ miles) southeast of town. **Air France** (www.airfrance.fr; ✆ **36-54** within France only) offers daily flights from Paris. A shuttle bus between the airport and the Nantes train station takes 25 minutes and costs 10€. A taxi from the airport costs 30€ to 35€ and takes about 20 minutes.

VISITOR INFORMATION   The **Office de Tourisme** is at 9 rue des Etats (www.nantes-tourisme.com; ✆ **08-92-46-40-44**).

Getting Around

ON FOOT   The downtown, cathedral, castle, and the island are accessible on foot, and the central train station helps visitors without wheels.

BY BICYCLE   Nantes has a Paris-style bike-sharing program called **Bicloo** (www.bicloo.nantesmetropole.fr; ✆ **01-30-79-33-44**). With 123 stations it's a great way to get around. You can register online at machines at most stations or at the tourist office. Fees are 2€ for a day pass or 5€ for a 3-day pass.

BY CAR   As the downtown core is highly pedestrianized, it's best to park your car; around the station are ideal official lots. Otherwise, another is at the cathedral. You can rent a car near the train station through **Europcar,** 325 rue Marcel Paul (www.europcar-atlantique.fr; ✆ **02-40-47-19-38**), or **Hertz,** rue Cornulier (www.hertz.fr; ✆ **02-40-35-78-00**).

BY TAXI   For an English-speaking service call **Taxis Nantes** or reserve online (www.taxisnantes.fr; ✆ **06-88-28-16-29**).

BY PUBLIC TRANSPORT   Nantes has an extensive transit system of trams, buses, and ferries run by the **TAN** (www.tan.fr; ✆ **02-40-44-44-44**). A one-way ticket costs 1.70€ and can be purchased from a machine at tram stations or 2€ from the bus driver or an unlimited day pass is 6€. On weekends all public transit is free throughout the city.

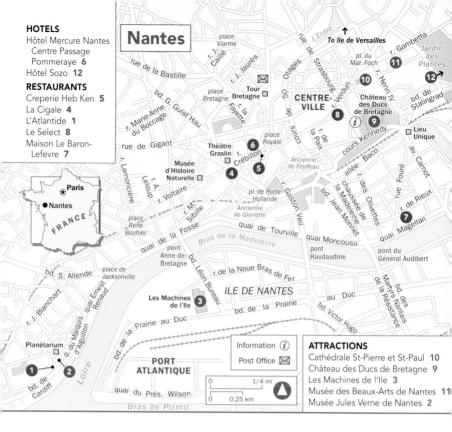

HOTELS
Hôtel Mercure Nantes
Centre Passage
Pommeraye **6**
Hôtel Sozo **12**

RESTAURANTS
Creperie Heb Ken **5**
La Cigale **4**
L'Atlantide **1**
Le Select **8**
Maison Le Baron-
Lefevre **7**

ATTRACTIONS
Cathédrale St-Pierre et St-Paul **10**
Château des Ducs de Bretagne **9**
Les Machines de l'Île **3**
Musée des Beaux-Arts de Nantes **11**
Musée Jules Verne de Nantes **2**

[FastFACTS] NANTES

ATMs/Banks Easy-access ATMs are in front of the cathedral or around place Royale.

Doctors & Hospitals **Centre Hospitalier Universitaire de Nantes,** 85 rue Saint-Jacques (www.chu-nantes.fr; ℂ 02-40-08-33-33).

Internet Access Free Wi-Fi is available at the tourist office or at many cafes in the downtown core like the hip cafe-bookshop **Les Bien-Aimés,** 2 Rue de la Paix (www.les-bien-aimes. fr; ℂ 02-85-37-36-01).

Mail & Postage **La Poste,** 2 pl. de Bretagne (ℂ 36-31).

Pharmacies **Grand Pharmacie de Paris,** 17 rue Orléans (ℂ 02-40-48-64-48).

Exploring Nantes

Cathédrale St-Pierre et St-Paul ★★ CATHEDRAL   Begun in 1434, this cathedral wasn't finished until the late 19th century. Still, it managed to remain architecturally harmonious—a rare feat. Two square towers dominate the facade; more impressive is the 100m-long (328-ft.) interior. Its *pièce de résistance* is the Renaissance tomb of François II, duc de Bretagne, and his second wife, Marguerite de Foix. The couple were the parents of Anne de Bretagne, who commissioned sculptor Michel Colombe to create their final resting place. White walls and pillars contrast with the rich colors of the stained-glass windows; helpful signs explain the significance of most objects. ***Important:*** Because of a fire, the cathedral interior is closed for renovations until early 2025.

pl. St-Pierre. 🕐 **02-40-47-84-64.** Free admission. Daily 8:30am–6:15pm. Crypt: Sat–Sun 3–6pm.

Château des Ducs de Bretagne ★★ CASTLE/MUSEUM   This enormous complex, seat of the Dukes of Brittany, was constructed in the 9th or 10th century, enlarged in the 13th century, destroyed, then rebuilt into its present shape by François II in 1466. The Duchesse du Berry, royal courtesan, was imprisoned here, as was Gilles de Retz (aka "Bluebeard"), one of France's most notorious mass murderers. The castle's rich inventory has been presented as a museum since the 17th century. About 30 rooms are devoted to the history of the port, displaying evocative objects such as scale models of the city during different eras. The museum charges admission, but you can visit the courtyard, freshly restored in 2023, and stroll along the ramparts for free.

4 pl. Marc-Elder. www.chateau-nantes.fr. 🕐 **08-11-46-46-44.** Ramparts free daily 8:30am–7pm (July–Aug until 8pm). Museum 9€ adults; 5€ students 25 and under; free for children 17 and under. Sept–June Tues–Sun 10am–6pm; July–Aug daily 10am–7pm. Closed public holidays.

Musée d'Arts de Nantes ★ MUSEUM   Refreshed displays completed in 2023 have given new life to this notable fine arts museum. The vast body of its collection was amassed in the late 18th century by the Cacault brothers and features a fine array of paintings from the 12th to the late 19th centuries. The strong Italian representation (Perugino, Tintoretto, Gentileschi) is due to François Cacault's travels as a diplomat. The municipality added to this foundation with purchases of 19th-century works by Delacroix, Rousseau, Renoir, and Gauguin, in addition to modern and contemporary artists, whose works are displayed in a 21st-century annex called The Cube.

10 rue Georges Clemenceau. https://museedartsdenantes.nantesmetropole.fr. 🕐 **02-51-17-45-00.** Admission 9€ adults; 4€ students ages 18–26; free for children 17 and under and all visitors on the 1st Sun Sept–June. Wed–Mon 11am–7pm (Thurs until 9pm). Closed public holidays.

Musée Jules Verne de Nantes ★ MUSEUM   Nantes's most renowned historic figure is the novelist Jules Verne (*Journey to the Center of the Earth, Around the World in Eighty Days*). Born in Nantes in 1828, he sat for hours on end, looking out his window at the busy port, imagining the exotic destinations the ships had traveled from. His adventures best come to life not at the museum, but at **Les Machines de L'Ile** (see "Brittany for Kids" box at the end of the chapter). However, fans of the author and young explorers will enjoy the museum's displays of memorabilia and artifacts inspired by his writings, from ink spots to a "magic" lantern with glass slides. Die-hard fans can seek out his former residence at 4 rue de Clisson in the Ile-Feydeau, though it is privately owned and not open to the public.

3 rue de l'Hermitage. https://julesverne.nantesmetropole.fr. ℂ **02-40-69-72-52.** Admission 4€ adults; 1.50€ students; free children ages 17 and under and all visitors on the 1st Sun Sept–June. July–Aug daily 10am–7pm; Sept–June Mon, Wed–Fri, and Sun 2–6pm, Sat 10am–noon and 2–6pm.

Where to Stay

Hôtel Mercure Nantes Centre Passage Pommeraye ★★   Situated in the heart of town, this is a convenient option for a reasonably priced overnight in Nantes. It's surrounded by a multitude of shops, restaurants, and the historic Passage Pommeraye. Acquired by Accor Hotels,

The Jules Verne Museum, Nantes.

On the Rivers

Nantes might not be on the sea, but it's still highly connected to water with its two rivers: the Loire and the Erdre. You can hop on the Loire's **Navibus** public watertaxi and in 15 minutes, you disembark at the charming former fishing village of **Trentemoult.** You wouldn't know you were in the Nantes suburbs while strolling its narrow lanes lined with colorful three-story houses, artist studios, and secret gardens. On your way back, grab a coffee at one of the cafes by the ferry dock. The small ferries depart regularly from the Nantes Gare Maritime on the Quai de la Fosse; the journey goes for a regular bus/tram ticket.

The Erdre River, deemed by King François I as "the most beautiful river of France," empties into the Loire, hidden

underground through downtown, but it pops above not far from la Tour de Bretagne. A visit to its **Ile de Versailles** offers various pleasures, namely its tranquil Japanese garden. In summer, you can rent small boats from its tip. Or better yet, take a leisure cruise along the Erdre to admire its beautiful plush landscape and graceful castles; **Bateaux Nantais** (http://bateaux-nantais.fr; ℰ **02-40-14-51-14**) arranges these trips which depart twice daily in summer (and several times weekly the rest of the year) just north of Ile de Versailles on the Quai de la Motte. The cruise lasts 1 hour, 45 minutes and costs 15.50€ adults and teens, 8.50€ children ages 4 to 12, free 3 and under; they also run lunch and dinner options.

in 2018 the compact rooms were redone in stylish sea green and coral tones, and brass light fixtures and some sections of floral wallpaper were added (sounds odd, but it's very appealing). Rooms also feature high-quality beds, linen and newly refitted bathrooms. Those on the street side have lovely views of town, yet can be noisy, so for a peaceful sleep request a room facing the courtyard.

2 rue Boileau. https://all.accor.com/hotel/B094/index.fr.shtml. ℰ **02-40-48-78-79.** 60 units. 91€–165€ double; 144€–195€ suite. Small pets 5€. **Amenities:** Restaurant; bar; room service; free Wi-Fi.

Hôtel Sozo ★★★   Located in a renovated 19th-century chapel across from the Jardin des Plantes, this exceptional boutique hotel is more than just a place to lay your head, it's a philosophy. *Sozo* means "creation and imagination" in Japanese, the driving force behind the hotel's inception and its ongoing spirit. Guest rooms are small though extremely well appointed; each one features characteristics of the chapel from stained glass to pillars and arches. The room size matters less since the monumental foyer is the place to be. Enjoy a cocktail or take your turn at the grand piano, that is, unless it's already occupied by a famous musician—the hotel is a favorite for visiting artists and performers.

16 Rue Frédéric Cailliaud. http://sozohotel.fr. ℰ **02-51-82-40-00.** 24 units. 128€–234€ double; 310€–340€ suite. Parking 15€. **Amenities:** Room service; bar; spa with hammam, sensory shower, and ice room (private time slot 50€ per couple); free Wi-Fi.

Where to Eat

You can't beat a traditional Breton crepe to satisfy hunger and the best in town have been flipped for the last 40 years at **Creperie Heb Ken,** 5 rue de Guérande (www.creperie-hebken.fr; ✆ **02-40-48-79-03**). Adventurous eaters should try the scallops with saffron sauce. Or for brunch, a light lunch, or afternoon tea surrounded by crystal chandeliers and stuffed animal heads with sunglasses, pop into the hip **Le Select,** 14 rue du Château (www.leselect-nantes.com; ✆ **02-40-89-04-49**).

For a fancier *chocolat chaud* or *confit de canard,* settle in at the glitzy Belle Epoque brasserie **La Cigale,** 4 pl. Gralin (www.lacigale.com; ✆ **02-51-84-94-94**).

L'Atlantide 1874 ★★★ MODERN FRENCH   The panoramic view rivals the amazing culinary creativity at the best restaurant in Nantes. Situated on the 4th floor of the city's chamber of commerce building, the Jean-Pierre Wilmotte designed dining room has a wall of windows looking out onto the city and Loire River. Chef Jean-Yves Guého took his knives around the world before returning to his native Brittany, and earning a Michelin star. His travels have influenced his innovative menu, which may include lobster glazed with spicy tomato tartare, lime and ginger, roasted squab with hibiscus-candied rhubarb or apricot, rosemary and honey soufflé. These are best enjoyed with some muscadet or anjou from the excellent cellar stocked mostly with Loire Valley wines.

5 rue de l'Hermitage. www.atlantide1874.fr. ✆ **02-40-73-23-23.** Main course 44€–75€; fixed-price lunch 50€ or dinner 80€–120€. Mon–Sat noon–1:15pm and 7:30–9pm. Closed 1st 3 weeks in Aug and Dec 24–26 and 1st week of Jan.

Maison Le Baron-Lefevre ★ TRADITIONAL FRENCH   Located in a former wholesale market building, excellent food traditions are carried on at this locavore restaurant—so local that all the vegetables come from their own garden. Chef Jean Charles Baron sticks to classic dishes to focus on the flavor of the products. His seasonal menu may feature creamy squash soup, sole meunière with *pot à feu* vegetables, or supreme of chicken with new potatoes. Service is very attentive, with personal touches like seasonal fruit or nuts with your coffee. They also sell a range of their preserves and products.

33 rue de Rieux. www.baron-lefevre.fr. ✆ **02-40-89-20-20.** Main course 24€–35€; weekday lunch menu 17€; dinner 32€–38€. Tues–Sat noon–2pm and 7–11pm.

Shopping

As the bustling regional capital, Nantes overflows with shops and boutiques. The principal shopping streets are rue du Calvaire, rue Crébillon, rue Boileau, rue d'Orléans, rue de la Marne, and rue de Verdun. Most of these encompass the shopping districts around place Graslin, place

Royale, the château, and the cathedral. The Passage Pommeraye, a historic gallery that dates back to 1843, houses upscale shops that continue in a modern extension, le passage Cœur de Nantes.

A handful of antiques shops can be perused on rue Jean Jaures such as **Antiquités Dubois,** at no. 29 (© **02-40-47-78-18**), offering 18th- and 19th-century furniture and decorative pieces such as historic mantels. Further historic knickknacks can be picked through every Saturday morning at the flea market in **place Viarme.**

For some local gastronomic specialties, start filling your basket at **La Fraiseraie,** 13 rue de la Marne (www.lafraiseraie.com; © **02-51-72-13-18**), which sells a variety of jams, juices, and candies made from famous Pornic strawberries. More tasty treats can be picked up at **Gautier Debotte,** 9 rue de la Fosse (© **02-40-48-23-19**), a historic *chocolatier* established in 1823, and makers of "Le Muscadet Nantais"—a chocolate-covered white grape macerated in local muscadet wine. Other Debotte boutiques are at 2 rue des Hauts Pavé, 3 rue de Budapest, and 15 rue Crébillon (the latter two have tea salons). Finish off your food shopping with some actual bottles of muscadet and a range of other wines and specialty food items at the **Maison Maitre,** 12 rue de la Paix (www.maisonle maitre.fr; © **02-40-47-04-12**).

Duck into the Passage Pommeraye to see it, even if you don't intend to shop.

BRITTANY FOR kids

St-Malo is a great destination for families. Not only is there the beach, but kids will also love exploring the ramparts, the château, and the fort (p. 314). For some additional family fun nearby, head to the side-by-side **Cobac Parc & Aqua'Fun Park** (www.cobac-parc.com; ☎ **02-99-73-80-16**). A day's worth of fun is had zooming down its waterslides, swinging clubs at the mini-golf, and twirling around on its small amusement park rides. Cobac Parc is open daily 10:30am to 6:30pm in July and August and sporadic hours, usually including weekends, April to June and September (consult website calendar); Aqua'Fun is open the same days, but from 1pm. A joint ticket for both parks is 24€ for ages 12 and up and 20.50€ for children 11 and under.

Breton history and culture come to life at the **Village de Poul-Fetan** (www.poul-fetan.bzh; ☎ **02-97-39-51-74**), a restored hamlet in Quistinic, a 35-minute drive northeast of Lorient. As you amble through the set of stone houses, historical interpreters demonstrate traditional tasks of daily life and arts and crafts. Children can try their hand at spinning wool, test out some rustic games, and even learn a few words of Breton.

Admission is 14€ for adults, 8€ for children ages 4 to 12, and free for ages 3 and under; passes for families of 4 are 37.50€. It's open daily April, May, June and September 10:30am to 6:45pm, and July and August 10:15am to 7:15pm.

One of the regional highlights for families is Nantes's **Les Machines de l'Ile,** 3 rue de l'Hermitage (www.les machines-nantes.fr; ☎ **02-51-17-49-89**), a fantastical workshop based on home-town writer Jules Verne's imagined creatures and the mechanical drawings of Leonardo da Vinci. A 12m (147-ft.) elephant, made from 45 tons of wood and steel, takes 50 passengers at a time for a stroll around the premises. Don't leave without a ride on the massive Carrousel des Mondes Marins, with three levels representing the ocean, seabed, and abyss. One ticket gives access to the rides, another admits you to the Galerie, where you can see future creations taking shape. Admission is 9.50€ adults, 7.50€ ages 4 to 18, free for children 3 and under. Because the site is a functioning workshop, its opening hours change weekly; check the English pages of their website for details

Nantes Nightlife

When the sun goes down, the town turns into one big party. On **place du Bouffay, place du Pilori,** and the pedestrian streets in between, you'll find lots of cafes and pubs, many with live music and fun people. A younger crowd rules **rue Scribe.**

Live music fans can catch blues, jazz, or rock concerts at the speak-easy style **L'Univers Café,** 16 rue Jean-Jacques-Rousseau (☎ **02-40-73-49-55**), while oenophiles won't be disappointed with the wine lists at the modern **Comédie des Vins,** 4 rue Suffren (www.bistrotdelacomedie.fr; ☎ **02-40-73-11-68**), or the rustic **Café de Provence,** 2 rue Vauban (www.baravinslaprovencenantes.com; ☎ **02-40-48-78-71**). On warm summer nights, amble along the **Ile de Nantes** to the **Le Hangar des Bananes** (www.hangarabananes.com). These former storage buildings for exotic fruit from the colonies have been converted into a line of bars and restaurants with large terraces.

The hippest location in Nantes, and the town's leading cultural center, is **Le Lieu Unique,** 2 rue de la Biscuiterie (www.lelieuunique.com; © **02-51-82-15-00**). Converted from a 19th-century biscuit factory, the venue offers presentations ranging from plays (in French) to art exhibitions. Admission is free to the dimly lit, concrete-floored bar at ground level, frequented by students and artists who pack the dance floor. The restaurant here also has the same vibe. The bar is open Monday 11am to 8pm, Tuesday and Wednesday 11am to midnight, Thursday 11am to 2am, Friday and Saturday 11am to 3am, and Sunday 3 to 8pm.

For dancing, head to the stylish **Le Royal Club Privé,** 7 rue des Salorges (www.leroyal.fr; © **02-40-69-11-10**). Be sure to dress up, avoid jeans and sneakers, and be prepared to pay 15€ to 20€.

THE CHAMPAGNE REGION

by Anna E. Brooke

9

Geographical luck—both good and bad—has played a large part in the history of Champagne. Warm enough to grow grapes in, but cold enough for snow in winter, the climate frustrated early winemakers by causing an uneven fermentation that resulted in bubbles—a "fault" that led to one of France's most famous luxury products. In 2015, Champagne Hillsides, Houses and Cellars were inscribed onto UNESCO's World Heritage List. On the less-good side, the region's position between the Western Front and Paris meant that the 20th century saw many of its buildings destroyed, especially during the First World War.

Champagne's major tourist towns, Reims and Epernay, are easily reached by train from Paris in under 90 minutes. Travelers with their own wheels, however, will get the most out of the winding roads, vineyard-draped hills, deciduous forests, and farmland that lend themselves to this area's natural beauty.

REIMS ★★

143km (89 miles) E of Paris; 29km (18 miles) N of Epernay

Blessed with a gorgeous cathedral, site of royal coronations for a thousand years, Reims (pronounced "rahns") is the largest city in the region and the unofficial capital of that deliciously fizzy nectar known as champagne. While it was almost obliterated by bombing during World War I, parts of the historic center have survived, including the above-mentioned cathedral, which, as well as the Basilique St-Rémi, Palais du Tau and St-Nicaise hill (vineyards), is a UNESCO World Heritage Site. While not as quaint as other French cities, Reims is still an enjoyable place to visit, with a large pedestrian-only shopping district, important historic sights, and some attractive Art Deco architecture. The Christmas market is considered one of the best in France.

The main draw though, aside from the cathedral, is bubbly. Some of the most famous names in champagne are found here, notably Lanson, Mumm, Pommery, Ruinart, Taittinger, and Veuve Clicquot; all offer tours and tastings. Reims makes a good base for exploring the Champagne region and is just a short hop from Epernay.

PREVIOUS PAGE: Champagne vineyards.

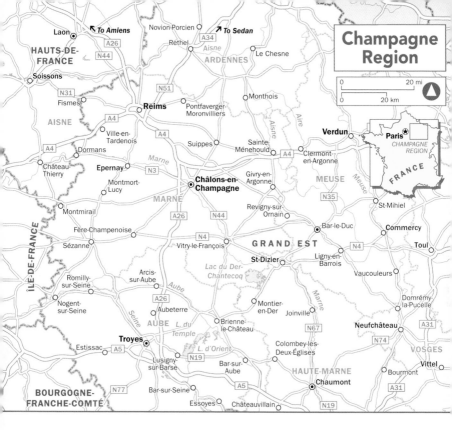

Essentials

ARRIVING High-speed, direct **TGV trains** leave for Reims from Paris's Gare de l'Est several times per day (trip time: 45 min.). For information, visit www.sncf-connect.com or call ☎ **36-35.** It's about a 15-minute walk southeast of the station to the cathedral. Alternatively, you'll find taxis and trams (see www.citura.fr for public transport; a day travel pass *ticket journée* is available for 4.60€ from ticket machines) in front of the station. If you are **driving** from Paris, take the A4 east (2 hr.).

VISITOR INFORMATION The **Tourist Office** is by the cathedral, 6 rue Rockefeller (www.reims-tourisme.com; ☎ **03-26-77-45-00;** daily 10am–6pm).

Exploring Reims

Basilique St-Rémi ★★ CHURCH AND MUSEUM This 11th-century church, about a 20-minute walk south of the cathedral, is one of the best examples of Romanesque religious architecture in Northern France.

Within the complex is a museum set in the former royal abbey of St-Rémi—the Bishop of Reims who converted Clovis, King of the Franks, to Christianity around A.D. 496; it now houses an extensive collection covering the city's history, military history, and regional archaeology including some fine Roman mosaics. The church contains St. Rémi's tomb and a collection of 12th-century stained-glass windows. Audio guides (6€) are useful here, as not everything is in English.

Basilique: pl. Chanoine Ladame. reims-tourisme.com/en/activite/basilique-saint-remi. ℭ **03-26-85-31-20.** Free admission. Mon–Sat 9am–noon and 2–7pm; Sun 2–7pm (or nightfall in winter). Musée: 53 rue Simon. musees-reims.fr/fr/musees/musee-saint-remi. ℭ **03-26-35-36-90.** Admission 5.50€ adults; free for students 25 and under and children 18 and under. Tues–Sun 10am–6pm.

Cathédrale Notre-Dame de Reims ★★★ CATHEDRAL   This mighty cathedral has survived the centuries (it was damaged but left standing when the city was bombed to smithereens in World War I) and today draws tourists (and the faithful) from far and wide who come to admire its magnificent Gothic architecture and elaborate statuary, not to mention stunning **stained-glass windows,** including **three by Marc Chagall** in the axial chapel. The official setting for royal coronations for

Cathédrale Notre-Dame de Reims.

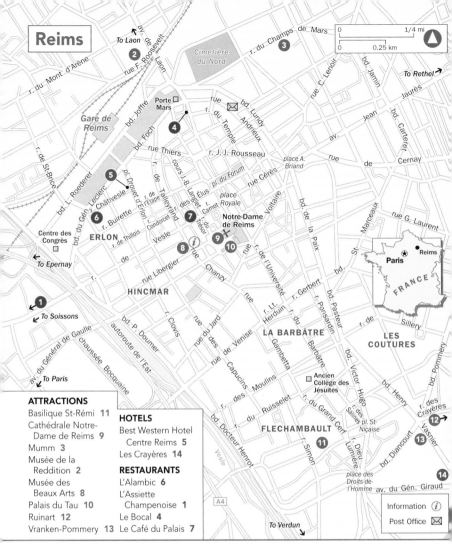

Reims

To Laon

Cimetière du Nord

r. du Champs de Mars

To Rethel →

Gare de Reims

Porte Mars

Centre des Congrès

To Epernay ←

To Soissons ←

ERLON

Notre-Dame de Reims

HINCMAR

To Paris ←

Paris

FRANCE

Reims

LA BARBÂTRE

LES COUTURES

Ancien Collège des Jésuites

FLECHAMBAULT

place des Droits-de-l'Homme

av. du Gén. Giraud

To Verdun ↘

Information ⓘ
Post Office ✉

ATTRACTIONS

Basilique St-Rémi 11
Cathédrale Notre-
 Dame de Reims 9
Mumm 3
Musée de la
 Reddition 2
Musée des
 Beaux Arts 8
Palais du Tau 10
Ruinart 12
Vranken-Pommery 13

HOTELS

Best Western Hotel
 Centre Reims 5
Les Crayères 14

RESTAURANTS

L'Alambic 6
L'Assiette
 Champenoise 1
Le Bocal 4
Le Café du Palais 7

a thousand years, perhaps its most dramatic moment was the one engineered by Joan of Arc. Instructed by voices, the teenage shepherdess made it her mission to get Charles VII back on the throne, and to get the English out of France. Though she accomplished the first here at Reims in 1429 (the maiden personally led Charles to the ceremony here), she was unfortunately burned at the stake before she could complete the second.

Back in the 5th century, France's first king, Clovis I, was baptized by St-Rémi in a small church on this site, giving the sit a royal reputation that would follow it through the centuries. The current cathedral dates from the 13th century and harbors 2,303 statues carved into its facades and decorating its interior. Its western and northern facades are graced with elaborate portals carved with hundreds of saints and angels. Inside, the narrow nave reaches 38m (125 ft.), giving the impression that the soaring arches reach all the way to heaven.

pl. Cardinal Luçon. www.cathedrale-reims.com. ℰ **03-26-47-55-34.** Free admission. Daily 7:30am–7:30pm (until 7:15 Sun).

Musée de la Reddition ★★ HISTORIC SITE/MUSEUM This humble site, a former technical school north of the train station, was the setting for one of the 20th century's turning points: the surrender of the Germans to the Allies, which ended World War II. General Eisenhower himself was on hand on the fateful day, May 7, 1945, and the room hasn't changed since the papers were signed. The exhibit includes an extensive collection of military uniforms, original US newspaper cuttings, German streets signs from Reims, and a short film in French, German, and English.

12 rue Franklin Roosevelt. www.musees-reims.fr. ℰ **03-26-47-84-19.** Admission 5.50€ adults; free for students 25 and under and children 18 and under. Wed–Mon 10am–6pm. Tram stop: Schneiter.

Musée des Beaux-Arts ★★ MUSEUM This fine arts museum has a remarkable collection that stretches from the 15th to 20th centuries. On the ground floor are decorative arts from Art Nouveau to Art Deco, while upstairs highlights include a charming collection of animal portraits by Jacques-Raymond Brascassat (1804–67), some fine works by well-known artists from the beginnings of modern art, and the largest collection in Europe of Franco-Japanese painter and printmaker Léonard Foujita (1886–1968); the museum ticket also gives entry to the chapel Foujita built in 1966 in the gardens of Mumm champagne house. *Important:* The museum is closed for renovations until 2025.

8 rue Chanzy. musees-reims.fr. ℰ **03-26-35-36-00.**

Palais du Tau ★★ MUSEUM On the southern side of the cathedral lies the former Archbishop's Palace which now houses a museum dedicated to the royal coronations that took place next door. The collection includes eerie statuary and items from the cathedral's treasury, including St. Rémi's 12th-century coronation chalice and the Sainte-Ampoule, a holy flask that held the oil used to anoint new kings. *Important:* Closed for renovations until 2025.

2 pl. Cardinal Luçon. palais-du-tau.fr. ℰ **03-26-47-81-79.**

Exploring the Champagne Cellars ★★★

Underneath Reims is a vast network of tunnels left over from centuries of chalk extraction. The former quarries turned out to be perfect for storing

Champagne house of Mumm.

champagne, and today some 200km (124 miles) of champagne cellars lie 20 to 40m (65–131 ft.) under the city, holding millions of bottles of bubbly in various stages of fermentation. Most of the top champagne *maisons* (houses) offer daily tours of their operations; many insist you reserve in advance. Below are three different experiences; for a complete listing of available tours in both **Reims** and **Epernay** (a 30-min. drive south on the D951), visit the official site of the **Union des Maisons de Champagne** (maisons-champagne.com).

Mumm ★★ WINERY   One of the most venerable names in champagne, the Mumm family started this enterprise in 1827. There are three visits of 1 hour, 30 minutes to choose between: All include a descent into the tunnels (the whole lot is 25km/15½ miles long) and a tour of the museum, accompanied by an introduction to champagne basics and a glass of bubbly. The main difference is the type of champagne you'll taste, from the famed Cordon Rouge to the house's prestige wines. Reservations required.

34 rue du Champ-de-Mars. www.mumm.com. ✆ **03-26-49-59-70.** Tours (in English) 28€, 35€, and 50€ adults; 14€ ages 11–17; free for children 10 and under. Opening times and tour times vary so check the website.

TINY bubbles

The difference between champagne and other wines is in-the-bottle fermentation. Once the wine has completed its first fermentation in tanks, it is blended, bottled, sugar and yeast are added, and the bottles sealed with metal caps. Placed horizontally, the bottles are then inverted and turned at regular intervals, allowing the yeast to settle in the neck. This process (called *remuage*, or "riddling") is mostly done by machines now, but some houses still employ *remueurs*, professionals who can hand-turn up to 40,000 bottles per day. Next, the bottles are dipped neck-first into a freezing agent to create an easily removed plug containing the sediment (*dégorgement*). Finally, they are topped up with a mixture of wine and sugar syrup (the *dosage*), the classic corks are inserted, and the finished product goes to the caves, where it ages anywhere from 2 to 10 years.

Ruinart ★★ WINERY Founded in 1729, the oldest and most prestigious champagne house is the perfect option for those looking for something special. The small-group 2-hour tours explore the listed, cathedral-like chalk cellars and end with a tasting of two prestigious *cuvées*. Art is also a passion here and the house regularly collaborates with internationally renowned artists to create works for the site. Reservations required.

4 rue des Crayères. www.ruinart.com. ✆ **03-26-77-51-51.** Admission 75€ adults; free for children 17 and under. Opening times and tour times vary, so check the website.

Vranken-Pommery ★★★ WINERY A 2-hour tour, "La Rêve d'Henry Vasnier" (a local artist and philanthropist), combines a visit to the well-known Pommery cellars with a scout around the stunning Art Nouveau/Art Deco Villa Damoiselle. Bought and restored by Pommery's owner Paul-François Vranken in the 2000s, the villa's own cellars now house rare vintages. The visit ends with a glass of the specially created Champagne Demoiselle and a glass of Pommery Brut Royal. Reservations required (inquire about villa tours in English). Other options include separate visits to the cellars and the Villa (both 26€–32€ adults and 15€ children ages 10–18).

56 bd. Henry Vasnier. vrankenpommery.com/visites/en. ✆ **03-26-35-80-50.** Admission 48€ adults (self-guided); 56€ adults (guided); 20€ children ages 10–18 (self-guided); 25€ children ages 10–18 guided; free for children 9 and under. Fri–Sat 10am–1pm and 2–6pm, Sun until 5pm.

Where to Stay

Best Western Hotel Centre Reims ★★ Much of Reims was destroyed during World War I and rebuilt in the years thereafter. This chic hotel, just off the pedestrianized Place Drouet d'Erlon, has been around for over a century and includes part of an old-world stone chapel. Rooms are elegant and modern, in tones of brown, blue or gold. The hotel has a popular bar-brasserie, the Café de la Paix, with a large range of champagnes, and a menu full of steak, salads and seafood—a great place to eat, even if you don't stay in the hotel. There's also an indoor pool.

9 rue Buirette. bestwestern.fr. ☏ **03-26-40-04-08.** 50 units. 150€–195€ double; 200€–300€ family suite. Breakfast 13€. **Amenities:** Bar; restaurant, gym; indoor pool; free Wi-Fi.

Les Crayères ★★★ This palatial neoclassic château is one of the region's most desirable accommodations. Located in a 7-hectare (17-acre) park, think lush, classically French decor, rich fabrics, ornate paneling and opulent details. The guest rooms range from the "Premium" category to two splendid "Prestige" suites; some rooms are located in a cottage in the grounds. The restaurant, **Le Parc,** is equally exquisite, complete with two Michelin stars (lunch menu 115€; dinner menus 260€–390€). **Le Jardin,** the onsite brasserie, is a more casual option (fixed-price menu for lunch and dinner 35€–50€; main courses 28€–45€). The elegant bar **La Rotonde** has 600 champagnes and over 1000 wines on offer. At night it hosts live jazz.

64 bd. Henri-Vasnier. www.lescrayeres.com. ☏ **03-26-24-90-00.** 20 units. 490€–1,400€ double. Breakfast 35€. Free parking. Closed last week in Dec through first 2 weeks of Jan. **Amenities:** 2 restaurants; bar; babysitting; concierge; laundry service; room service; tennis court; free Wi-Fi.

Where to Eat

L'Alambic ★★ FRENCH This restaurant, set in a low-ceilinged, window-free champagne cellar, might not appeal if you're claustrophobic. But you'd be missing out on a unique experience setting and delicious French food, like smoked guinea fowl in pinot noir sauce and cod with coriander infused leek. The desserts, such as the homemade lemon tart, are particularly good and the *menu* is excellent value at 37€.

63 bis rue de Chativesle. www.restaurant-lalambic.fr. ☏ **03-26-35-64-93.** Main course 19€–35€; fixed-price menu 37€. Mon–Thurs 7–8:30pm, Fri–Sat noon–1:15pm and 6:30–9:15pm.

L'Assiette Champenoise ★★★ MODERN FRENCH With three Michelin stars, this ultra-stylish restaurant in a 19th-century half-timbered manor house in a suburb of Reims, is guaranteed to knock your culinary socks off. Chef Arnaud Lallement cooks up creative dishes using the finest French seasonal ingredients, such as scallops from Brittany with Périgord truffles. Make a night of it by booking a room or suite (266€–950€) in the attached five-star hotel.

40 av. Paul Vaillant-Couturier, Tinqueux. www.assiettechampenoise.com. ☏ **03-26-84-64-64.** Fixed-price lunch 155€ or dinner 285€–385€; main courses 105€-135€. Thurs–Mon noon–1:30pm and 7:30–9:30pm. Closed mid-Feb to mid-Mar and first 2 weeks of Aug. 2km (1¼ miles) west of the cathedral via the D980.

Le Bocal ★★ SEAFOOD Hidden in the back of a fish store (it's right across from the city's fab covered market), Le Bocal is a surprisingly genteel place to take a meal. Once you head past the display cases, with fresh catches proudly laid on piles of ice, you'll find yourself in a light-flooded, dove-grey tea room. Though there's no English-language menu, and the choices are usually extensive (raw bar items, seafood pâtés, grilled dishes, bouillabaisse, paellas), at least one of the staff speaks excellent English and will walk you through all the choices. Le Bocal is known, especially, for its oysters, both in the raw and the cooked preparations. Follow the bivalves with one of the excellent seafood pâtés and then a grilled cut of fish, done very simply, but with just the right amount of char and lemon.

27 rue de Mars. www.restaurantlebocal.fr. ℰ **03-26-47-02-51.** Meals 20€–40€. Tues–Sat noon–1:30pm and 7–11pm.

Le Café du Palais ★★ FRENCH Reims has some lovely examples of Art Deco architecture, not least this attractive cafe run by the same family since 1930. The *grandes assiettes* are a popular choice: "La Champenoise" consists of *jambon de Reims* (coarsely cut ham terrine) and local Chaource cheese accompanied by boiled potatoes and salad. Snacks and cakes are served outside mealtimes.

14 pl. Myron Herrick, www.cafedupalais.fr. ℰ **03-26-4752-54.** Main course 19€–29€; fixed-price menus 35€–39€. Tues–Fri 9am–9pm, Sat 9am–11pm.

Shopping

To purchase some bubbly, head to **Trésors de Champagne,** 2 rue Olivier Métra (clubtresorsdechampagne.com; ℰ **03-26-48-28-42**), where you can also enjoy a tasting. *Biscuits roses* (pink biscuits) are traditionally eaten with champagne; you can get them from **Fossier,** 25 cours Jean-Baptiste Langlet (www.fossier.fr; ℰ **03-26-47-59-84**). For a good selection of gourmet products from Champagne and all over France, including mustard, **Les Saveurs de l'Hexagone,** 51 rue de Tallyrand (essaveursdelhexagone. fr; ℰ **06-24-54-06-16**), is your best bet.

Nightlife

Reims has the most vibrant nightlife in the region. For lively bars and clubs head to **place Drouet-d'Erlon.** Locals call it simply "place d'Erlon." A 10-minute walk from the Cathedral, **Le Clos,** 25 rue du Temple (facebook.com/LeClos.Reims; ℰ **03-26-07-74-69;** Tues–Thurs 6:30pm–12:30am, Fri 6pm–2am, Sat noon–2am), is a hip, shabby-chic wine bar with a boudoirlike interior and a vast Art Deco–era courtyard decorated with umbrellas. Wine bar **Le Vintage,** 16 pl. du Forum (winebar-reims.com; ℰ **03-26-05-89-94;** Mon 6:30–10pm, Tues–Fri 6–11:30pm, Sat 6pm–midnight), offers a similar experience. If you're

9

THE CHAMPAGNE REGION | Reims

around in summer, head up to the rooftop bar of the **Holiday Inn,** 46 rue Buirette (ihg.com; ☎ **03-26-78-99-99;** Mon–Sat 4–11pm), for panoramic views across the cathedral and city. If you speak French and enjoy theater, the **Comédie de Reims,** chaussée Bocquaine (www.lacomediedereims.fr; ☎ **03-26-48-49-10**), has a varied schedule.

Day Trips from Reims

PROVINS

117km (72 miles) SW of Reims

If Disney's re-created medieval towns were real, they would undoubtedly look like Provins. Bridging the Greater Paris and Champagne regions, this quaint, fairy tale–like settlement of half-timbered houses, medieval ramparts, spooky underground passages, and cobbled streets was once the Count of Champagne's capital, famed across medieval France for its *foires,* or fairs. Today, it's just over a 1½-hour drive from Reims (take the

---

The Champagne Trail

The **Routes Touristiques du Champagne** are six itineraries developed by tourist offices to show motorists and cyclists the best their region has to offer. From 70km up to 220km (45–136 miles), they wind their way through vineyards, villages, and sites of interest, clearly marked by black and white signs. One of the shortest, and prettiest, is the route dedicated to the Montagne de Reims, which is not really a mountain at all but a forested plateau between Reims and Epernay.

Along this route, as with the others, you'll pass dozens of small champagne producers. One of the loveliest villages to stop in is hilltop **Hautvilliers** (off the D951, along D386), where Benedictine monk, Dom Pérignon, perfected the champagne-making technique in the 17th century. See his epitaph in the village church, then toast his memory at **G. Tribaut** champagne house (champagne-tribaut-hautvillers.com; ☎ **03-26-59-40-57;** bottles from 20€), which offers breathtaking views over the valley.

Then head west along the D1 to **Champagne Telmont** in Damery (champagne-telmont.com; ☎ **03-26-58-40-33;** bottles from 48.50€), which, hands down, makes some of the finest bubbly around. It even caught the eye—or taste buds—of movie star Leonardo Di Caprio, who is now an investor.

If you're with kids, don't miss **Champagne Charlier & Fils,** farther west (off the D1, then D24; champagne-charlier.com; ☎ **03-26-58-35-18;** bottles from 19.30€). It's one of the only wineries to still ferment their champagnes inside *foudres* (huge oak barrels that can hold the equivalent of 50,000 bottles of wine), with a showpiece foudre to climb inside.

Tourist offices can give you a list of other wineries open to tastings; sometimes you'll happen along one with a drop-in policy; others require reservations. Or for more information about the routes, visit tourisme-en-champagne.com/route-touristique-du-champagne.

A4, then the D980, D18, D11, and D403) and is a great place for a family-friendly day out, with falconry and jousting shows, and pleasant strolls along age-old streets lined with UNESCO-protected medieval buildings like the vaulted Grange aux Dîmes and the Tour César, a 12th-century dungeon. For more information, visit the tourist website provins.net (② **01-64-60-26-26**).

SEDAN
106km (65 miles) NE of Reims

In the French Ardennes, the 16th-century **Château Fort de Sedan** (www.chateau-fort-sedan.fr; ② **03-24-29-98-80;** daily) is said to be the largest castle in Europe. Set over seven floors and with an area of 35,000 sq. m (376,736 sq. ft.), the castle took over 150 years to build and, in its heyday, housed more than 4,000 men. You can take a tour and even stay here in the onsite four-star **hotel,** which has a very nice **restaurant.** The castle also hosts a medieval festival on the last weekend in May.

Several trains a day leave from Reims (trip time: 1 hr., 20 min.), or you can drive there in about 1 hour, 10 minutes via the A34.

EPERNAY ★★
140km (87 miles) E of Paris; 26km (16 miles) S of Reims

Although it has one-sixth the population of Reims, Epernay produces nearly as much champagne, with an estimated 322km (200 miles) or more of cellars and tunnels. Day-trippers also find it more doable, as the town center and major champagne houses are within walking distance of the train station. Unlike urban Reims, it has a quieter, yet monied, atmosphere.

Invading armies have destroyed or burned Epernay nearly two dozen times—this explains a somewhat disappointing lack of architectural character. The stately 1km-long avenue de Champagne, a UNESCO World Heritage Site, helps make up for it though, with neoclassical villas housing the headquarters of Mercier, Moët et Chandon, Perrier-Jouet, and Pol Roger, among others.

Essentials

ARRIVING If you're **driving** to Epernay from Reims, head south on the D951. From Paris, take the A4. By **train,** leave from Paris Gare de l'Est (just over 1 hr.). From Reims, there are approximately two trains per hour (trip time: 30 min.) on weekdays, fewer on weekends. For information, visit sncf-connect.com or call ② **36-35.** For information on bus services linking Epernay to other towns in Champagne, visit citura.fr.

VISITOR INFORMATION The **Office de Tourisme** is at 7 av. De Champagne (epernay-tourisme.com; ✆ **03-26-53-33-00;** closed Sun mid-Oct to mid-Apr).

Exploring Epernay

The center of town and shopping district radiate out from the **place Hugues Plomb** and its fountain. Gourmet foodstuffs can be found in and around the iron-and-glass **Halle Saint-Thibault** near the place d'Europe (a very seductive food market is held inside Wed 7am–12:30pm and Sat 7am–2pm).

For champagne, you can go to the individual houses along the avenue de Champagne or one of the shops representing a variety. Both **La Cave Salvatori,** 11 rue Flodoard (✆ **03-26-55-32-32;** Tues–Fri 10am–noon and 2–7pm, Sat 10am–7pm), and **Les Grands Vins de France,** just a few doors down the road (6 rue Flodoard; les-grands-vins.fr; ✆ **03-26-54-23-11;** daily 10am–7:30pm, until 8pm Fri–Sat), stocks a wide array of labels and vintages.

For wine-themed items such as champagne buckets and flutes, try **Home,** 12 rue du Professeur Langevin (www.home-boutique.fr; ✆ **03-26-51-83-83;** Tues–Sat 10am–noon and 3–6pm).

Champagne de Castellane ★★ WINERY   De Castellane gives you a comprehensive view of how champagne is produced, with several tours on offer, from a simple cellar tour to the Heritage Tour, which gives an insight into the corking and labeling processes. All include tastings and access to the on-site museum. If you're with kids, the Cellar Tour and Tower visit is a good option as you can climb the tower (237 steps) for a panoramic view of the area. The tower is from 1904 and has become an Epernay landmark. Reservations recommended.

57 rue de Verdun. www.castellane.com. ✆ **03-26-51-19-11.** Admission 20€–50€; free for children ages 12 and under. Mid-Mar to mid-Dec daily 10–11am and 2–5pm.

Mercier ★★★ WINERY   Mercier is near Moët et Chandon (below), and you can visit them both on the same day. Mercier conducts tours in English of its 18km (11 miles) of tunnels from laser-guided trains—reached by an elevator that descends past rudimentary champagne-themed dioramas. The caves contain one of the world's largest wooden barrels, with a capacity of more than 200,000 bottles. The best tour to choose here is the 2-hour Exploring the Vineyard tour, which does what it says on the label: takes you through the cellar and into the vineyards. Reservations recommended.

70 av. de Champagne. www.champagnemercier.fr. ✆ **03-26-51-22-22.** Admission 40€; 10€ children ages 10–17; free for children 9 and under. Mid-Mar to mid-Nov daily 9:30–11:30am and 2–4:30pm.

Old Moët et Chandon signs and vineyards.

Moët et Chandon Champagne Cellars ★★ WINERY   One of the most prestigious champagne houses runs an informative tour, describing the champagne-making process and filling you in on champagne lore: Napoleon, a friend of Jean-Rémy Moët, used to stop by for thousands of bottles on his way to battle. The only time he didn't take a supply was at Waterloo—and look what happened there. All tours include two glasses of champagne; more expensive tickets entitle you to more expensive champagne. Reservations required.

20 av. de Champagne. www.moet.com. ✆ **03-26-51-20-20.** Admission 40€–75€; 13€ children ages 10–17; free for children 9 and under. Apr–Dec with varying days and times so check on-line.

Where to Stay

La Villa Eugene ★★★   This charming 19th-century mansion once belonged to the Mercier family. It's just a short walk west to the major champagne houses. The rooms are light and spacious and elegantly decorated in a variety of styles, from colonial to Louis XVI. Breakfast is served in a grand glass conservatory, complete with cherub-painted ceiling, overlooking the garden.

82-84 av. de Champagne. www.villa-eugene.com. ✆ **03-26-32-44-76.** 15 units. 190€–400€ double. Breakfast 21€. Free parking. **Amenities:** Outdoor pool; bar; free Wi-Fi.

Le Clos Raymi ★★ This 19th-century mansion was formerly owned by Monsieur Chandon (of "Moët et" fame). The decor, however, harks back to the 1930s and contemporary artworks adorn the walls. Rooms, with original fireplaces, are individually furnished and possess some nice luxury touches for a three-star hotel, such as dressing gowns and organic toiletries. It's a short (10-min.) walk west of the town center.

30 rue Joseph de Venoge. closraymi-hotel.com. ☎ **03-26-51-00-58.** 7 units. 152€–210€ double. Breakfast 18€. Free parking. **Amenities:** Free Wi-Fi.

Where to Eat

Bistrot Le 7 ★★ FRENCH Within the hotel Les Berceaux, acclaimed chef Patrick Michelon creates delicious, beautifully presented dishes made from seasonal ingredients, often with international flavors—for instance the guinea-fowl comes with a deliciously sticky honey and citronella sauce. Unsurprisingly, the wine list is excellent and the decor—burnt orange walls, white tablecloths and plenty of knickknacks—pleasantly relaxing. Upstairs are 28 pleasant guest rooms, where a double with a tub/shower costs from 105€.

13 rue des Berceaux. www.lesberceaux.com. ☎ **03-26-55-28-84.** Fixed-price menus 38€–45€. Fri–Tues noon–2pm and 7–10pm. Closed 2 weeks in Aug.

La Cave à Champagne ★★ FRENCH This traditional, family-run restaurant with typical dark-wood furniture, will give you a real taste of Epernay, thanks to its excellent list of champagnes. Try baked pan-fried foie-gras and grapes for starters followed by *potée champenoise* (thick bean stew with sausages, ham, and cabbage). At 25.50€, the three-course menu served at lunch and dinner is a steal.

16 rue Léon Gambetta. www.cave-champagne.fr. ☎ **03-26-55-50-70.** Main courses 20€–29€; fixed-price menus 25.50€. Thurs–Mon noon–1:30pm and 7–10pm. Closed Tues–Wed.

La Table Kobus ★★★ FRENCH Just behind the church of Notre Dame, this stylish Belle Époque brasserie is noted for its *bistronomique* cuisine: refined dishes made with high-quality seasonal products. The menu offers a seasonal selection of creative dishes such as lamb with asparagus in aniseed jus or veal roasted with bay leaves on crushed potatoes with preserved lemons. The wine list features several dozen local champagnes as well as top-notch French AOCs.

3 rue Docteur Rousseau. www.la-table-kobus.fr. ☎ **03-26-51-53-53.** Main course 33€; fixed-price lunch menus 27€ to 32€; fixed-price dinner menus 41€–46€. Tues–Sun noon–1:30pm and 7–8:30pm. Closed Thurs and Sun eve.

Nightlife

As you'd imagine, Epernay has its fair share of champagne bars. The smartest is undoubtedly **Chez Georges** (www.georgescartier.com;

Battles of the Marne

World War I history buffs automatically think of Verdun and its trenches (see chapter 10), but the Marne Valley saw more than its share of bloody conflict. The German offensive got no further west than **Château-Thierry** (87km/54 miles NE of Paris, 51km/32 miles SW of Reims via A4) thanks to a ferocious standoff with U.S. forces in early June 1918. Today an imposing hilltop monument commemorates the battle. Two days later, fighting began at the Bois de Belleau **(Belleau Wood).** Control of the area switched sides six times before the Americans triumphed, having suffered more than 9,000 casualties. The American cemetery, also known as **Le Cimetière de Belleau,** contains 2,288 graves and a chapel damaged in World War II. You can learn more at the **Musée de la Mémoire de Belleau** (museede belleau.com; ✆ **03-23-82-03-63**), in place du Général Pershing, which also offers guided tours. In a peaceful park in **Dormans,** the **Mémorial des Batailles de la Marne,** Parc du Château (www. memorialdormans14-18.com; ✆ **03-26-53-35-86**), honors all soldiers killed in the summers of 1914 and 1918. The site houses a chapel and ossuary containing the bones of a thousand soldiers from the U.S. and Europe.

✆ **03-26-32-06-22;** Wed–Sat 6pm–2am, Sun 4pm–midnight) at **Champagne Georges Cartier,** 9 rue Jean Chandon Moët. A DJ spins on Friday and Saturday evenings and you can enjoy the outside terrace in summer. For a change of scenery along the Marne River, **Le C Nautique,** 1 quai de l'Île Belon (le-c-lanautique.fr; ✆ **09-74-97-27-16**), is open daily until 8pm (until 9pm Fri–Sat). Sit outside and soak up the riverside views, as you sip excellent but little-known champagnes by the glass (a four-glass sampler costs 31€; you can also order cheese and charcuterie, or plates of smoked salmon for 13€).

TROYES ★★★

143km (89 miles) SE of Paris; 108km (67 miles) S of Reims

In the southwestern part of Champagne bordering Burgundy, the old center of Troyes is an architectural delight. The underwhelming approach past outlet malls and apartment-filled suburbs might tempt you to turn around and leave—but don't. In store is a walk-through history lesson, thanks to one of the largest remaining medieval residential quarters in France.

Troyes was known in Roman times as Augustobona and served as a meeting point between major roads. What's left of the Agrippa Way, linking Milan and Boulogne-sur-Mer on the northern coast, is buried 3m (10 ft.) under the current rue de la Cité. Stone from the ancient ramparts, long since destroyed, serves as foundations for some of the city's buildings, including the former Bishop's palace, now the Museum of Modern Art.

Gorgeously restored, half-timbered 16th-century houses are the real showstopper here. A project to bring them back to life, using antique engravings as a guide, began fifty years ago; today the jewel-colored dwellings are well on their way to earning UNESCO World Heritage status.

Essentials

ARRIVING   Troyes is a 2½-hour **drive** southeast from Paris via the A5 autoroute. It's most easily reached by **train,** with departures out of Paris's Gare de l'Est roughly every 2 hours (trip time: 1½ hr.). Unfortunately, from Reims and Epernay you must go back through Paris. For information, visit sncf-connect.com or call ℂ **36-35.** For information on **bus** service linking Troyes to other towns in Champagne, visit fluo.eu. A direct bus to Reims several times a day (trip time: 2 hr.) is much quicker than getting the train.

VISITOR INFORMATION   The **Maison de Tourisme** is situated in a beautiful half-timbered building at 16 rue Aristide-Briand (troyeslachampagne.com; ℂ **03-25-82-62-70;** closed Sun Nov–Easter).

Exploring Troyes

Keep your head up and camera ready: Wandering the ancient streets, you'll find surprises around every corner, such as the **Ruelle des Chats** (Cats' Alley) between 30 and 32 rue Champeaux. The buildings on either

Old town of Troyes.

side lean so close that a cat can easily jump from one roof to the other. Inside Église Saint-Pantaléon, Rue de Vauluisant (troyeslachampagne. com/patrimoine-culturel/eglise-saint-pantaleon), take a pew to gaze up at breathtaking Renaissance stained glass and religious sculptures, many of which were saved from other buildings after the Revolution.

Cathédrale St-Pierre et St-Paul ★★ CATHEDRAL   The spectacular stained-glass windows in this cathedral—180 of them—helped Troyes earn its nickname, the "Holy City of Stained Glass." Arguably the building's main claim to fame is that the Order of the Knights Templar was founded here in 1128/9 by St. Bernard of Clairvaux, whose remains are kept here in an exquisite reliquary casket. On Friday evenings in July and August, the cathedral stays open until 10pm to give visitors the chance to see the sumptuous patterns of colored light cast onto the cathedral's stone through the stained-glass windows at sunset–a lovely sight, set to music.

pl. St. Pierre. www.cathedraledetroyes.com. No phone. Free admission. Mon–Sat 9:30am–12:30pm and 2–5pm; Sun 2–5pm.

Maison de l'Outil et de la Pensée Ouvrière (Museum of the Tool and Workers' Thought) ★ MUSEUM   This unusual museum contains 12,000 hand tools, which, although fascinating to some, will have limited appeal to most. Save your money and just enter the leafy courtyard of the 16th-century Renaissance-style building, Hôtel de Mauroy, to admire the 1560s architecture.

7 rue de la Trinité. www.mopo3.com. ✆ **03-25-73-28-26.** Admission 8€; 4€ ages 12–18; free for children 11 and under. Apr–Sept daily 9am–noon and 2–6pm; Oct–Mar Wed–Mon 9am–noon and 2–6pm. Closed Dec 25 and Jan 1.

Musée d'Art Moderne ★★★ MUSEUM   Housed in the former Bishop's Palace, the collection of textile magnates Pierre et Denise Lévy is one of the most interesting regional art exhibitions we've come across, aided by its atmospheric 16th-century surrounds. Among the works, from the mid–19th century to the 1960s, are paintings by Picasso, Modigliani, Matisse, Derain, and Cézanne; and sculptures by Degas and Maillol. Of particular interest is the Art Deco glasswork of Maurice Marinot (1882–1960), as well as some African artworks, whose style inspired many of the modern artists.

pl. St. Pierre. www.musees-troyes.com/art-moderne. ✆ **03-25-76-26-80.** Admission 7€; free for children ages 18 and under (free for all Nov–Mar). Apr–Oct Tues–Sun 10am–1pm and 2–6pm; Mar–Nov Tues–Sun until 5pm. Closed Jan 1, May 1, Nov 1, Nov 11, and Dec 25.

Where to Stay

Best Western Hôtel De La Poste & Spa ★★   In keeping with its origins as a coaching inn, this four-star hotel has been renovated with an equestrian theme. Standard rooms are decorated in contemporary style, but the two "senior suites" under the roof have added character thanks to exposed beams and skylights (they are accessed by a short staircase, as the elevator stops one floor below). The Nuxe Spa is where guests and the public can enjoy face and body treatments as well as a sauna and hammam.

35 rue Emile Zola. www.hotel-de-la-poste.com. © **03-25-73-05-05.** 32 units. 145€–380€ double. Breakfast 18.50€. Parking 12€. **Amenities:** Bar; spa; free Wi-Fi.

Le Champ des Oiseaux ★★★

Walking down the medieval street south of the cathedral to this four-star hotel feels like you're stepping back in time. The 14 rooms are set around a quiet courtyard in three buildings from the 15th and 16th centuries, which have been carefully restored by master craftsmen. Decor is rustic and cozy, and the "suite Loft," under the eaves, is the stuff of fairytales. The small restaurant is open on Tuesday to Saturday evenings (main courses 29€).

20 rue Linard Gonthier. www.champdesoiseaux.com. © **03-25-80-58-50.** 14 units. 200€–430€ double. Breakfast 31€. Parking 30€. **Amenities:** Bar; restaurant; spa; outdoor pool; free Wi-Fi.

Les Comtes de Champagne ★★

This budget hotel in a half-timbered house oozes character. The en-suite rooms, most with exposed bricks and beams, range from the basic "comfort" option to "charm," which feature the likes of a four-poster bed. The vast beam across the bar ceiling "holds up the whole house," according to the receptionist—something you can't help thinking about as you tipple (it's right above the table). Breakfast can be taken in the courtyard in summer.

54–56 rue de la Monnaie. hotel-troyes.brithotel.fr. © **03-25-73-11-70.** 35 units. 70€–105€ double. Breakfast 11€. Parking 10€. **Amenities:** Bar; free Wi-Fi.

Where to Eat

Chez Félix ★★ FRENCH In the quaintest street in town, this quirky, vintage-style bistro with young staff is a good choice for lunch or dinner. Try the lamb coated with local honey for a main course and leave room for vanilla ice cream doused in *prunelle de Troyes* (see "Shopping," below). Champagnes from the *département* and *vins* from nearby Burgundy dominate the wine list. The outdoor terrace is in an attractive leafy courtyard bordered by half-timbered houses.

5 ruelle des Chats. www.chez-felix.fr. © **03-10-94-03-03.** Main courses 19€–25€. Daily noon–1:30pm and 7–9:30pm.

Le Jardin ★★★ FRENCH Troyes is famous for its *andouillette* (chitterling sausage), and this is a very good place to try one—if you're an adventurous eater—especially in Chablis sauce (there are lots of sauces to choose between, from mustard to champagne and foie-gras). Menu favorites include vanilla-scented salmon and chicken with dark chocolate and coffee. The interior is a bit cramped, so ask for a table in the pretty court-yard in summer.

31 rue Paillot de Montabert. facebook.com/lejardin.troyes. ℂ **03-25-73-36-13.** Main course 19€–28€; fixed-price menu 24€–45€. Tues–Sat noon–1:30pm and 7:30–9pm (until 9:30pm Fri–Sat). Closed 2 weeks in Mar and 3 weeks in Sept.

L'Illustré ★★ FRENCH Housed in a former newspaper office (hence the name), this buzzy restaurant, with a gorgeous wooden ceiling and staircase, has a wide selection of dishes—from snacks like omelets to hefty steaks—as well as an excellent choice of local wines and cham-pagnes. Try a *champagne gourmand* (glass of champagne with a selection of small desserts) to finish.

8 rue Champeaux. lillustre.com. ℂ **03-25-40-00-88.** Main courses 10€–35€; fixed-price menu 34€–41€; fixed-price kids' menu 9€. Daily 10am–10pm (until 10:30pm Fri–Sat).

Shopping

Troyes is home to one of the most renowned *pâtissier-chocolatiers* in the world. **Pascal Caffet ★★★** has taken first place in a half dozen interna-tional pastry and chocolate competitions—he's even been decorated by the French government for his cultural contribution. Caffet's sleek, epon-ymous shop, 2 rue de la Monnaie (www.maison-caffet.com; ℂ **03-25-73-35-73**), captivates the eyes and anyone with a sweet tooth in equal measure.

Opposite the cathedral, **Le Cellier St. Pierre,** 1 pl. St. Pierre (www.celliersaintpierre.fr; ℂ **03-25-80-59-25**), has been open since 1840 and is the oldest continuously run-ning shop in Troyes. It's also a distillery, where *prunelle de Troyes,* a prune-based liqueur, is still made and for sale along with dozens of wines in every price category.

> ### Did You Know?
>
> The biggest export market for champagne is the United States (34 million bottles per year), followed by the United Kingdom (30 million bottles).

Nightlife

The best option for a few drinks is **Chez Philippe** (chez-philippe.fr; ℂ **06-61-02-71-69;** daily 4pm–1:30am), at 11 rue Champeaux. This styl-ish champagne bar specializes in single origin bubbles from the commune of Celles-sur-Ource in the Côte des Bar; you can also get snacks here.

Day Trips from Troyes
ESSOYES
60km (37 miles) SE of Troyes

This small village on the border with Burgundy is on the map thanks to its artistic connections: Essoyes was the birthplace of Aline Charigot who went on the become Mme. Auguste Renoir. The couple bought a house here in 1896 and in 2017 it opened to the public as **Maison des Renoir,** now part of a Renoir-themed cultural village that include a trail and the artist's light-filled studio. You buy a ticket in the Espace Renoir, 9 pl. de la Mairie (www.renoir-essoyes.fr; ℂ **03-25-29-10-94;** 12€ adults, free for children 17 and under; Feb–Apr and Nov Wed and Fri–Sun 10–10:30am and 2–2:30pm; May–Oct daily [except Tues May–June and Sept] 10am–12:30pm and 1:30–6pm), where you can browse an exhibition and watch a film on the artist's life before going on to visit the whole center. A nice spot for lunch, notably grilled meat, is **La Guinguette des Arts,** 4 bis quai de l'Ource (ℂ **03-25-29-70-59;** Wed–Mon noon–2pm and 7–10pm), next to the river. The easiest and cheapest way to get to Essoyes is by car, which takes around 50 minutes on the A5.

NOGENT-SUR-SEINE
52km (32 miles) NW of Troyes

Most famous for being the lover and student of Auguste Rodin, Camille Claudel (1864–1943) was one of the unsung artists of the 19th century until recent years. Finally, today (as well as having works on show at the Musée Rodin in Paris; see p. 132) her birthplace is open to the public with an attached museum, **Musée Camille Claudel,** 10 rue Gustave Flaubert (museecamilleclaudel.fr; ℂ **03-25-24-76-34;** 8€, free for ages 26 and under, free to all first Sun of month; Apr–Oct Tues–Sun 10am–6pm, Nov–Mar Tues–Sun 10am–6pm). Here, dozens of her works are exhibited alongside some of her contemporaries, including Rodin and Bourdelle, to celebrate this rich period of French sculpture. A short walk south is wine bar **Au Numéro Vins,** 5 rue de l'Étape au Vin (facebook.com/aunumero vins; ℂ **03-25-25-73-47;** daily), where you can savor traditional French dishes or platters of cheese and charcuterie.

From Troyes, several direct TER trains a day run (trip time: 30 min.), or by car it's about 50 minutes along the D442.

ALSACE-LORRAINE

By Lily Heise

10

T he easternmost regions of France, Alsace and Lorraine, with ancient capitals at Strasbourg and Nancy,
were the object of a centuries-old dispute between
Germany and France. In fact, they were annexed by
Germany between 1870 until after World War I and
from 1940 to 1944. Though they've remained part of France since
the end of World War II, Alsace is reminiscent of Germany's Black
Forest, with its flower-laden half-timbered houses and traditional
winstub taverns serving *choucroute* and sausage.

With this cultural mélange, it's not surprising Strasbourg became the base
of the European parliament. In contrast, Lorraine, with its rolling landscape and regal architecture, appears and feels more distinctly French in
character and is even the homeland of one of the country's greatest hero-
ines: Joan of Arc. Ponder these local traits while wandering through the
quaint towns of the Alsatian Wine Road or through the natural splendor of
the Vosges Mountains.

STRASBOURG ★★★

483km (300 miles) SE of Paris; 217km (135 miles) SW of Frankfurt

Situated about 483km (300 miles) southeast of Paris and tucked in the
elbow of northeast France, Strasbourg ping-ponged between Germany
and France for centuries. Today this capital of wine-growing Alsace
blends Teutonic might with a cosmopolitan flair. With the majestic gothic
Cathédrale Notre-Dame and its astronomical clock, the maze of cobbled
streets, half-timbered houses and the poetic canals of La Petite France,
this UNESCO World Heritage Site on the River Ill weaves fairy-tale
charm with the European Parliament's political clout.

Essentials

ARRIVING   The **Strasbourg-Entzheim Airport** (Aéroport International
Strasbourg; www.strasbourg.aeroport.fr; ✆ **03-88-64-67-67**), 15km (9¼
miles) southwest of the city center, receives daily flights from many European cities, including Paris, London, Rome, Amsterdam, and Moscow.
The **shuttle train** (look for the signs to pedestrian footbridge connecting
the airport to the station platform) whisks you to Strasbourg main station
in 9 minutes. The shuttles run every 15 minutes from 5:30am until 10pm
Monday through Friday, once or twice an hour on Saturday between
6:30am and 10pm, and Sundays between 7am and 10:30pm. The one-way
cost is 4.70€ and includes connection to the municipal tram system. For

PREVIOUS PAGE: **A boat tour through the historic core of Colmar.**

La Petite France, Strasbourg.

information, see the "Access" tab on the airport website or call ☎ **08-05 41-54-15.**

The superfast TGV **train** makes round-trips from Paris to Strasbourg, cutting travel time nearly in half, to 1 hour, 45 minutes. At least 15 **trains** a day arrive from Paris's Gare de l'Est; the one-way fare is 45€ to 110€. For information and schedules, visit www.sncf-connect.com or call ☎ **36-35.**

By **car,** the giant A35 crosses the plain of Alsace, with occasional references to its original name, the N83. It links Strasbourg with Colmar and Mulhouse.

VISITOR INFORMATION   The **Office de Tourisme** is on 17 pl. de la Cathédrale (www.visitstrasbourg.fr; ☎ **03-88-52-28-28**). A second branch is inside the main train station (same telephone number).

STRASBOURG CITY CARD   If you plan to do several tourist activities or museums, you can save with the Strasbourg City Card. Valid for 7 days, it grants discounted entrance to the cathedral towers, museums, guided tours, Batorama boat cruise, bike rentals and more; 5€ for adults and 3.50€ for children 17 and under. It's only available at the tourist office.

SPECIAL EVENTS   Jazz fans descend on the city every June for **Wolfi Jazz** (https://wolfijazz.com) and every November for **Jazzdor** (https://jazzdor. com), both of which feature top international musicians. Ticket prices range from 25€ to 75€. **Musica** (www.festivalmusica.fr), a festival held the

last 2 weeks of September, combines contemporary concerts with movies and modern opera performances. Tickets (11€–24€) go on sale in late June.

In late November and December, the place de Cathédrale erupts with the city's world-famous **Marché de Noël** (Christmas Market), where you can purchase handmade ornaments and gifts and warm up with hot *vin chaud* (mulled wine).

CITY LAYOUT   The center of Strasbourg is mainly located on **Grand Ile,** a large island hugged by two branches of the Ill River. **Petit France** is the area between these two branches; with its crooked streets and half-timbered houses, it's a major visitor destination.

Getting Around

ON FOOT   Most of the main sites are accessible on foot and the city center is highly pedestrianized.

BY BICYCLE   Like a growing number of French cities, Strasbourg has a bike-sharing program called **Vélhop** (www.velhop.strasbourg.eu; ✆ **03-67-70-70-70**). You can register in their boutiques at 3 rue d'Or or in the Strasbourg station; fees are 1€ per hour or 5€ per half day. A deposit is required.

BY CAR Strasbourg can be easily visited on foot. However, if you have a car for exploring Alsace, convenient underground parking lots are in place Gutenberg, place Kléber, and near the train station. You can rent a car at **Avis** (www.avis.fr; ✆ **08-20-61-16-98**), located at the train station or in the Kléber parking garage, or **Europcar,** at the station (www.europ car.fr; ✆ **09-77-40-32-42**).

BY TAXI A good number of taxis circulate around the city to serve the many business travelers. You can either hail one on the street or order one from **Strasbourg Taxi** (www.strasbourg-taxi.fr; ✆ **03-88-12-21-22**).

BY PUBLIC TRANSPORT Strasbourg has an extensive transit network of trams and buses run by the **CTS** (www.cts-strasbourg.eu; ✆ **02-47-66-70-70**). A one-way ticket costs 2.10€ or an unlimited day pass is 4.60€ (reduced rates with a loadable BADGEO card). Tickets can be purchased from automatic kiosks at a tram station or single tickets from a bus driver for 2.50€.

[FastFACTS] STRASBOURG

ATMs/Banks The city center has plenty of banks; you'll definitely find one around place Kléber.

Doctors & Hospitals **Hopitaux Universitaires de Strasbourg,** 1 pl. de l'Hopital (www.chru-strasbourg.fr; ✆ **03-88-11-67-68**).

Mail & Postage **La Poste,** 3A rue du 22 Novembre (✆ **36-31**).

Pharmacies **Pharmacie de l'Homme de Fer,** 2 pl. de l'Homme de Fer (✆ **03-88-32-55-55**).

Exploring Strasbourg

Despite World War I and World War II damage, much remains of Old Strasbourg, including covered bridges and towers from its former fortifications, plus many 15th- and 17th-century dwellings with painted wooden fronts and carved beams.

The city's traffic hub is **place Kléber** ★, dating from the 15th century. Sit here with a tankard of Alsatian beer and get to know Strasbourg. The bronze statue in the center is J. B. Kléber, born in Strasbourg in 1753; he became one of Napoleon's most noted generals and was buried under the monument. Apparently, his presence offended the Nazis, who removed the statue in 1940. This Alsatian bronze was restored to its proper place in 1945.

From here, take rue des Grandes-Arcades southeast to **place Gutenberg,** one of the city's oldest squares. The central statue (1840), by David d'Angers, is of Gutenberg, who perfected his printing press in Strasbourg in the winter of 1436 and 1437. The former town hall, now the **Hôtel du Commerce,** was built in 1582 and is one of the most significant Renaissance buildings in Alsace. The neighborhoods within a few blocks of the city's **Notre Dame Cathedral** are loaded with medieval references and historical charm.

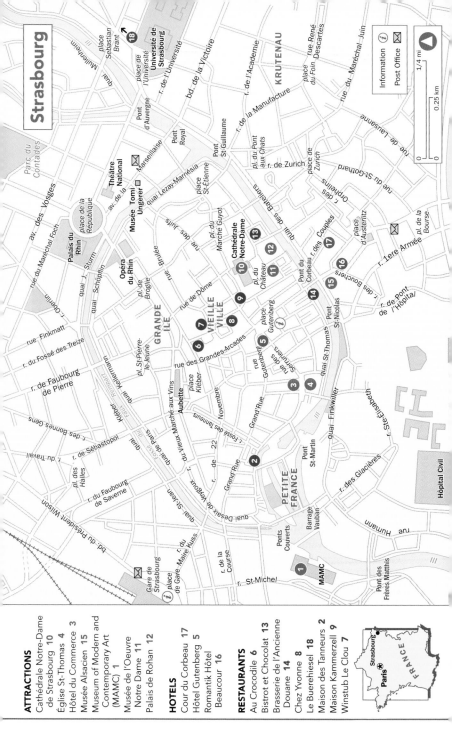

Strasbourg

Parc du Contades

KRUTENAU

VIEILLE VILLE

GRANDE ILE

PETITE FRANCE

Hôpital Civil

Information ⓘ
Post Office ☒

0   0.25 km
0   1/4 mi

FRANCE
Strasbourg
Paris

381

La Petite France ★★ is Strasbourg's most interesting quarter. A virtual island, it's surrounded by scenic canals on four sides, and its 16th-century houses reflect in the waters of the Ill River. In "Little France," old roofs with gray tiles have sheltered families for ages, and the cross-beamed facades with roughly carved rafters are in typical Alsatian style. For a good view, walk along rue des Moulins, branching off from rue du Bain-aux-Plantes.

Cathédrale Notre-Dame de Strasbourg ★★★ CATHEDRAL
The city's crowning glory is an outstanding example of Gothic architecture, representing a transition from the Romanesque. Construction began in 1176. The pyramidal tower in rose-colored stone was completed in 1439; at 141m (462 ft.), it's the tallest one from medieval times. This cathedral is still in use; religious ceremonies, particularly on feast days,

meld perfectly with the architectural majesty. Individual tourists can visit the tower only in the summer (you may have to wait to climb it). The Office de Tourisme (see above) organizes tours for groups; call for the schedule.

Four large counterforts divide the **main facade** ★★★ into three vertical parts and two horizontal galleries. Note the **rose window,** which looks like stone lace. The facade is rich in decoration: On the portal of the south transept, the *Coronation and Death of the Virgin* in one of the two tympanums is the finest such medieval work. In the north transept, see also the facade of the **Chapelle St-Laurence,** a stunning achievement of the late Gothic German style.

Stained-glass rose window, Cathédrale Notre-Dame de Strasbourg.

A Romanesque **crypt** lies under the chancel, which is covered with square stonework. The stained-glass window is the work of Max Ingrand. The **nave** is majestic, with windows depicting emperors and kings on the north Strasbourg aisle. Five chapels cluster around the transept, including one built in 1500 in the Flamboyant Gothic style. In the south transept stands the **Angel Pillar** ★★, illustrating the Last Judgment, with angels lowering their trumpets.

The **astronomical clock** ★ was built between 1547 and 1574. It stopped during the Revolution, and from 1838 to 1842, the mechanism was replaced. Each day at 12:30pm, crowds gather to see its show of allegorical figures. On Sunday, Apollo drives his sun horses; on Thursday, you see Jupiter and his eagle. The body of the clock has a planetarium based on the theories of Copernicus. Close-up views of the clock are available Monday to Saturday from noon to 12:30pm; tickets (3€ adults, 2€ ages 5–18 and students) are on sale in the mornings at the post-card stand or from 11:45am at a kiosk in the south portal.

pl. de la Cathédrale. www.cathedrale-strasbourg.fr. ✆ **03-88-32-75-78** for times of services. **Cathedral:** Free admission. Mon–Sat 8:30–11:15am and 12:45–5:45pm, Sun 2–5:15pm. **Tower:** Admission 8€ adults; 5€ children 6–18; free for ages 5 and under. Apr–Sept daily 9:30am–1pm and 1:30–7:15pm; Oct–Mar daily 10am–1pm and 1:30–5:15pm.

Eglise St-Thomas ★ CHURCH   Built between 1230 and 1330, this Romanesque church was one of the first converted to Protestantism when the movement arrived in Alsace in 1524. It contains the **mausoleum** ★★ of Maréchal de Saxe, a masterpiece of French art by Pigalle (1777), and a magnificent 12th-century sarcophagus of Archbishop Aledoch.

Rue Martin-Luther (along rue St-Thomas, near pont St-Thomas). www.saint-thomas-strasbourg.fr. ✆ **03-88-32-14-46.** Free admission. Mon–Sat 10am–6pm; Sun noon–5:30pm.

Musée Alsacien ★★ MUSEUM   Housed in three mansions from the 16th and 17th centuries, this compelling museum takes visitors on a voyage through the ages of Alsatian history via its impressive collection of paintings, furniture, and other decorative arts. Be sure to pick up a copy of the English-language guide at the front as only about half of the display's wall texts are translated.

23 quai St-Nicolas. www.musees.strasbourg.eu. ✆ **03-88-52-50-01.** Admission 7.50€ adults; 3.50€ students and seniors; free for children 17 and under. Sat–Sun 10am–6pm; Mon and Wed–Fri 10am–1pm and 2–6pm.

Musée de l'Oeuvre Notre-Dame ★★★ MUSEUM   This museum, located in excellently restored buildings from the era, illustrates the art of the Middle Ages through the Renaissance and the beginnings of the Reformation, making it a perfect stop for fans of ecclesiastic art and medieval history. The collection displays many pieces that were previously displayed in the cathedral (where copies have since been substituted). The

10

ALSACE-LORRAINE

Strasbourg

An aerial view of the massive Palais de Rohan and the surrounding city.

most celebrated is a stained-glass head of Christ from about the 11th century. Other noteworthy works are the 13th-century sculpture hall with the wise and foolish virgins from 1280, the winding Renaissance staircase, and 16th- and 17th-century artifacts by Strasbourg goldsmiths.

3 pl. du Château. www.musees.strasbourg.eu. ℰ **03-88-52-50-00.** Admission (includes free audio guide) 7.50€ adults; 3.50€ students ages 24 and under and seniors; free for children 17 and under. Sat–Sun 10am–6pm; Tues–Fri 10am–1pm and 2–6pm.

Museum of Modern and Contemporary Art (MAMC) ★ MUSEUM   In the heart of La Petite France, this is Strasbourg's showcase of modern European art from 1870 to the present. While it's not quite the level of the Orsay or Pompidou in Paris, it's worth a meander for true art lovers. The collection itself was started in 1919 and has grown thanks to donations from local arts patrons. The layout of the museum starts with a historical section tracing the emergence of modern art and going forward to the 21st century, including works by Rodin, Monet, Picasso, and Kandinsky. It also has an art library, a museum shop, and a cafe-restaurant on the terrace.

1 pl. Hans-Jean-Arp. www.musees.strasbourg.eu. ℰ **03-88-23-31-31.** Admission 10€ adults; 6.50€ students 24 and under and seniors; free for children 17 and under. Sat–Sun 10am–6pm; Tues–Fri 10am–1pm and 2–6pm.

Palais de Rohan ★★ PALACE   This palace south of the cathedral was built from 1732 to 1742 for the Prince-Bishop of Strasbourg, the illegitimate son of Louis XIV. Echoing Parisian Rococo style, it is noted for its facades and sumptuous interior, making it one of the crowning design achievements in eastern France. Impressive works by Rubens, Rembrandt,

Van Dyck, Goya, and Renoir are displayed on the first-floor fine-arts museum (Musée des Beaux-Arts). On the main floor is a decorative-arts museum featuring ceramics and the original machinery of the cathedral's first astronomical clock. An archaeological museum on site has precious artifacts excavated from nearby digs, with a focus on art and utilitarian objects from the Roman and early medieval eras.

2 pl. du Château. www.musees.strasbourg.eu. ℰ **03-88-52-50-00.** Admission 7.50€ adults; 3.50€ students; free for children 17 and under. Sat–Sun 10am–6pm; Mon and Wed–Fri 10am–1pm and 2–6pm.

Where to Stay

Cour du Corbeau ★★★   Originally opening in the 17th century, this is one of the oldest hotels in all of France and certainly the most enchanting in Strasbourg. Though situated in the heart of the historic center, its traditional half-timbered architecture makes you feel like you're at a country inn. The interior has been redone and features classy contemporary furnishings; however, some rooms have wooden beams and lovely old-fashioned windows that bring out the building's heritage. In the evening you knock back cocktail at the swanky bar.

5 rue des Bouchers. www.cour-corbeau.com. ℰ **03-90-00-26-26.** 63 units. 175€–375€ double; 325€–475€ suite. **Amenities:** Babysitting; bar; free Wi-Fi.

Hôtel Gutenberg ★★   The Gutenberg is a less charming property than the other two hotels we recommend for Strasbourg, but its location, just steps from the cathedral, can't be beat, and some visitors may prefer its modernity. Guest rooms have been refurbished in sleek Scandinavian style, a surprising choice since the hotel is set in an elegant 18th-century mansion. *Tip:* Although slightly smaller, attic rooms have lovely exposed beams and rooftop views.

31 rue des Serruriers. www.hotel-gutenberg.com. ℰ **03-88-32-17-15.** 43 units. 125€–240€ double. **Amenities:** Free Wi-Fi.

Romantik Hôtel Beaucour ★★   For a restful night's sleep in the boisterous city-center, book at this peaceful hotel. Hidden away on a private street a few blocks from the cathedral, it's hard to imagine that this charming 17th-century building with timbered ceilings used to be an umbrella factory. The welcome is as warm as the foyer's toasty fireplace. Alsatian hospitality and character are sprinkled throughout, so expect a small dose of gingham and hearts. Rooms are on the large size for European hotels and another plus is the presence of whirlpool tubs. The generous breakfast buffet will prep you for your next day of touring.

6-8 rue des Couples. www.hotel-beaucour.com. ℰ **03-88-76-72-00.** 49 units. 99€–205€ double; 205€–270€ suite. Parking 16€. **Amenities:** Babysitting; free Wi-Fi.

Where to Eat

For a quick good-value meal, stop in at the **Brasserie de l'Ancienne Douane,** 6 rue de la Douane (www.anciennedouane.fr; ℰ **03-88-15-78-78**), a large brasserie serving Alsatian specialties like "sauerkraut of the Customs officers" and foie gras of Strasbourg. Alternatively, try **Maison Kammerzell,** 16 pl. de la Cathédrale (www.maison-kammerzell.com; ✆ **03-88-32-42-14**). Conveniently located on the main square, this gingerbread house is another top spot for traditional Alsatian fare.

For a *choucroute*-free lunch, track down **Bistrot et Chocolat,** 8 rue de la Râpe (www.bistrotetchocolat.fr; ✆ **03-88-36-39-60**); this cafe next to the cathedral serves tasty vegetarian, vegan, and gluten-free dishes to eat in or take away.

Au Crocodile ★★★ MODERN ALSATIAN

No, exotic meats are not a specialty here as its name might suggest, notwithstanding, this is easily the most innovative restaurant in Strasbourg. Originally a 14th-century Benedictine monastery, it was converted into an *auberge* in 1801 by a captain of Napoleon's army on his return from the Egyptian campaign (he brought the infamous crocodile, now stuffed and on display, with him). Its brilliant chefs have served major French celebrities and heads of state (notably Barack Obama). Current chef Romain Brillat's creations could include venison with cherries and almonds and local Heimbach spring trout with peas, pink ginger and cardamom.

10 rue de l'Outre. www.au-crocodile.com. ✆ **03-88-32-13-02.** Main course 46€–52€; fixed-price lunch 52€ or dinner 108€–142€. Thurs–Sat noon–1:30pm, Tues–Sat 7:30–9:30pm. Closed last 3 weeks of July and Dec 24–29.

Chez Yvonne ★★ FRENCH/ALSATIAN

Opened in 1873, this is one of the oldest and most charming *winstub* (traditional Alsatian wine tavern) in town. Located near the cathedral, it is frequented by journalists and political dignitaries. The menu features refined versions of some of the best regional cuisine such as *maennerstolz* (smoked beef and pork sausage), *Strasbourgeoise* sauerkraut with different cuts of pork, and the house specialty coq au Riesling with spaëtzle pasta.

10 rue du Sanglier. www.chez-yvonne.net. ✆ **03-88-32-84-15.** Main course 18€–30€; fixed-price menu 29€–35€. Tues–Sat noon–2:15pm and 6–10:30pm.

Le Buerehiesel ★★★ MODERN FRENCH

Also known as Le Restaurant Westermann, Buerehiesel is famous for its *cuisine moderne* and for its prime location in l'Orangerie, a park at the end of the allée de la Robertsau planned by the landscape artist Le Nôtre, which was given to Josephine during her marriage to Napoleon. The classic Alsatian building hides a swank contemporary decor which matches its dishes (like saddle of rabbit stuffed with black garlic and served with chanterelles fricassee or veal sweetbreads with caviar and roasted eggplant drizzled in Bellota chorizo jus). Reservations required.

4 parc de l'Orangerie. www.buerehiesel.fr. ✆ **03-88-45-56-65.** Main course 38€–59€; fixed-price lunch 55€ or dinner 99€–135€. Tues–Sat noon–2pm and 7–10pm. Closed Dec 24–Jan 8 and 1st 3 weeks of Aug.

Maison des Tanneurs ★★ ALSATIAN   Locals call this place "la Maison de la Choucroute," as it serves the best sauerkraut-and-pork in town. Set in a former tannery dating from 1572, this antiques-filled restaurant opened in 1949. It sits idyllically on the water, its terrace opening onto the canal. If you're not tempted by its signature dish, the chef also prepares veal kidneys with local white wine, the Belle Strabourgeoise foie gras or stuffed guineafowl on a bed of choucroute. Save room for Kougelhopf glazed with sweet Gewürztraminer liqueur.

42 rue du Bain-aux-Plantes. www.maison-des-tanneurs.com. ℭ **03-88-32-79-70.** Main course 17€–25€; fixed-price lunch 24€–26€. Tues–Sat noon–2pm and 7–10pm (also Sun noon–2pm in Dec). Closed first 2 weeks in Jan.

Winstub Le Clou ★ ALSATIAN   Warmth and hearty Alsatian goodness exude from this great-value, authentic *winstub*. Wood-paneled walls, folkloric artwork, and communal tables add to its charm. They specialize in typical regional fare, like Alsatian snails, *bibeleskas* (thick cream with garlic and herbs) with country-style potatoes, or a house favorite Pinot Noir–braised *wädele* (Alsatian sauerkraut with hearty knuckle of ham).

3 rue de Chaudron. www.le-clou.com. ℭ **03-88-32-11-67.** Main course 16€–30€. Daily 11:45am–2:00pm and 5:30pm–midnight.

Shopping

Strasbourg overflows with antiques shops, artisans, craftspeople, and beer makers. Every well-accessorized home in Alsace owns some of the napkins, aprons, tablecloths, and tea and bath towels of the Beauvillé textile mills. **Plaisirs d'Alsace,** 13 Rue des Dentelles, near Petite France (www.plaisirs-alsace.fr; ℭ **03-88-21-07-93**), has a wide selection of textiles, pottery and other quality Alsatian handicrafts.

   Bastian, 22–24 pl. de la Cathédrale (www.antiquites-bastian.com; ℭ **03-88-32-45-93**), has been a family affair since 1861. They specialize in 18th- and 19th-century ceramic tureens that Alsace produced in abundance. They also have a selection of Louis XV and Louis XVI furniture, crafted in the region during the 18th and 19th centuries following Parisian models from the same era.

   One of the most appealing shops in Strasbourg is **Arts et Collections d'Alsace,** 4 pl. du Marché aux Poissons (www.arts-collections-alsace.com; ℭ **03-88-31-20-20**), which sells copies of art objects and utilitarian ware from museums and private collections throughout Alsace in addition to upscale gift items for the home and fabric by the yard.

   A name in pottery that you're likely to encounter is **Soufflenheim,** a provincial rococo pattern—usually in blues and reds—named after the Alsatian village north of Strasbourg where the style originated. To get there, take N63 north of the center of Strasbourg for 24km (15 miles). Ceramics and pottery have been made in the village since the Bronze Age. Soufflenheim is home to at least a dozen outlets selling cake molds, tureens, saucers and cups, dinnerware, and more, usually in rustic patterns. One of the most prominent retailers is **Gérard Wehrling,** 64 rue de Haguenau (www.poterie-wehrling.fr; ☏ **03-88-86-65-25**), known for pottery that can withstand the rigors of modern ovens, microwaves, and refrigerators.

Strasbourg Nightlife

The **place de la Cathédrale** is a hub of outdoor entertainment, with an assortment of performers and artists. Dancers perform spontaneously against the illuminated cathedral. From mid-July to early August, folk dances take place in the evenings on Monday in place Gutenberg, Tuesday in place du Château, and Wednesday in place Benjamin Zix. For further information and times see https://ete.strasbourg.eu/folklore-alsacien.

THE PERFORMING ARTS   For opera and ballet, seek out the **Opéra du Rhin,** 19 pl. Broglie (www.operanationaldurhin.fr; ☏ 08-25-84-14-84); tickets cost 12€ to 90€. The **Orchestre Philharmonique de Strasbourg** performs at the Palais de la Musique et des Congrès, pl. de Bordeaux (www.philharmonique-strasbourg.com; ☏ **03-68-98-51-31**). Tickets cost 6€ to 55€. The **Théâtre National de Strasbourg** plays a busy schedule at 1 av. de la Marseillaise (www.tns.fr; ☏ **03-88-24-88-00**). Tickets cost 6€ to 30€.

BARS & CLUBS   The streets surrounding place de la Cathédrale, in particular rue des Frères, rue des Soeurs, and rue de la Croix, are bustling with cafes and bars. **Jeannette et les Cycleux,** 3 rue des Tonneliers (www.facebook.com/Jeannette.et.les.Cycleux; ☏ **03-88-23-02-71**), is a quirky retro bar filled with trendy young locals sipping on wine or nibbling at their tasty *planchettes.*

Despite being known for its white wines, Alsace is also the number-one beer-producing region of France, not surprising due to its historical links and proximity to Germany. This tradition is being maintained at the artisan brewery **Au Brasseur,** 22 rue des Veaux (www.aubrasseur.fr; ☏ **03-88-36-12-13**); additionally, a wide variety of local and international pints can be sampled at **Les Freres Berthom,** 18 rue des Tonneliers (www.lesberthom.com; ☏ **03-88-32-81-18**).

For a late night with 20-to-35 strasbourgeois, go to **Live Club,** 1 rue du Miroir (https://club-live.fr; ☏ **06-45-93-84-38**), a popular club near the cathedral playing house and electro music.

LA ROUTE DU VIN (WINE ROAD) ★★★

The fastest route between Strasbourg and Colmar, 68km (42 miles) south, is N83. But if you have time, the famous Route du Vin, the oldest "wine road" in France established in 1950, makes a rewarding experience. It rolls through 60 charming villages and is flanked by the Vosges foothills, with medieval towers and feudal ruins evoking faded pageantry. The vine-covered slopes sometimes reach a height of 435m (1,427 ft.), and an

ALSACE-LORRAINE   La Route du Vin (Wine Road)

Route du Vin, the oldest wine road in France.

estimated 20,000 hectares (49,400 acres) of vineyards line the road. Some 30,000 families earn their living tending the grapes.

Serious oenophiles will want to select specific vineyards to visit; however, the picturesque scenery and quaint towns are a highlight for any visitor to the region. The best villages are described below; charming Kaysersberg is a convenient place for lunch, while most overnights are done in the largest town, Colmar. The best time to go is for the harvest in September and October for the festivals throughout the area (especially in Ribeauvillé). Useful additional information can be found at **www.alsace-wine-route.com**; and at the website **Rue des Vignerons** (www.ruedes vignerons.com/en), which shows which wineries give tastings and tours in Alsace-Lorraine—and across France.

Mittelbergheim

The loveliness of Mittelbergheim, 43km (27 miles) from Strasbourg, has earned the town a place on the list of "most beautiful villages of France." Houses in the Renaissance style border its **place de l'Hôtel-de-Ville.** Around town are a number of medieval wells and ancient wine presses.

Andlau

This gardenlike resort, 42km (26 miles) from Strasbourg, was the site of an abbey founded in 887 by the disgraced wife of Emperor Charles the Fat. It has now faded into history, but a church remains that dates from the 12th century. In the tympanum are noteworthy Romanesque carvings. The **Office de Tourisme,** is at 5 rue du Général-de-Gaulle (www.paysdebarr. fr; ⓒ **03-88-08-33-92**).

BIKING THE wine road

A lovely way to experience the Wine Road is to leisurely breeze through the vines and villages by bicycle. This is made easy thanks to bike routes that fan out from Strasbourg into the countryside, with emphasis on cycle lanes (*les pistes cyclables* in French) that prohibit cars (see routes on www.wineroute.alsace/cycling). One of these is a 27km (17-mile) stretch that runs southwest from Strasbourg to the wine hamlet of Molsheim. It has a forest on one side, the banks of the Brûche River (a tributary of the Rhine) on the other, and little car traffic. You can rent bikes from **L'increvable,** 3, place de Zurich (https://location-velo-strasbourg.com; ✆ **09-83-52-86-44**). Their rates start at 25€ per day, and 42€ weekly. It's open Monday 2 to 7pm; Tuesday, Thursday, and Friday 7:30am to 12:30pm and 2 to 7pm; Wednesday 7:30am to 7pm; and on weekends by appointment (hours are slightly reduced in winter).

Dambach ★

One of the delights of the Wine Road, Dambach (48km/30 miles from Strasbourg) is the largest wine-producing village in Alsace. One of the finest Alsatian wines, the Grand Cru Frankstein, comes from here. The town, formally Dambach-la-Ville, has ramparts and three fortified gates and was once protected by the medieval Bernstein castle, today in ruins above the town. Its timbered houses are gabled with galleries, and many contain oriels. Wrought-iron signs still tell you if a place is a bakery or a butcher shop. A short drive from the town is the **Chapelle St-Sebastian,** with a 15th-century ossuary. The **Office de Tourisme** (www.dambach-la-ville.fr; ✆ 03-88-92-61-00) is in La Mairie (town hall), pl. du Marché.

Between Dambach and Ribeauvillé is the region's most impressive castle: **Château Haut Koenigsbourg ★★**. Clinging to the mountainside, it has a sprawling view of the whole valley. Presumed to date from the 12th century, it has typical medieval fortress features including thick defensive walls, turrets, and a tall keep. It was highly damaged and subsequently abandoned during the Thirty Years' War. It was eventually restored under German Emperor Wilhelm II in the early 20th century, although the accuracy of the restoration is somewhat dubious; nonetheless, it's a spectacular site. Entrance is 9€ adults, 5€ children 6 to 17 and free for 5 and under. It's open daily November to February 9:30am to noon and 1:15 to 5:15pm; March and October 9:30am to 5pm; April, May, and September 9:15am to 6pm; and June to August 9:15am to 6:45pm (www.haut-koenigsbourg.fr; ✆ **03-69-33-25-00**).

Ribeauvillé ★★

At the foot of vine-clad hills dotted with castle ruins, Ribeauvillé (87km/ 54 miles from Strasbourg) is picturesque, with old shop signs, pierced balconies, turrets, and flower-decorated houses. The town is noted for its Riesling and Gewürztraminer wines. See its Renaissance fountain and

Hôtel de Ville, pl. de la Mairie, which has a collection of silver-gilt medieval and Renaissance tankards known as *hanaps.* For information, go to the tourist office at 1 Grand' Rue (www.ribeauville-riquewihr.com; 📞 **03-89-73-23-23**).

Also of interest in Ribeauvillé is the **Tour des Bouchers** (Butcher's Tower), built in stages from the 13th to the 16th century.

Every year on the first weekend in September, visitors fill the town for its **Pfifferdaj** or **Jour des Menetriers (Day of the Minstrels),** the oldest festival in Alsace dating back to the Middle Ages. A medieval market, building illuminations, public dances, and other activities take place all weekend, however, the real event is Sunday at 3pm, when a parade of flute players from Alsace, the rest of France, Switzerland, and Germany, and as many as 600 parade participants make their way through town. You can stand anywhere to watch the spectacle, but seats on the medieval stone benches line each side of the parade route.

Kaysersberg ★★

Once a free city of the empire, Kaysersberg (93km/58 miles from Strasbourg) lies at the mouth of the Weiss Valley, between two vine-covered slopes; it's crowned by a castle ruined in the Thirty Years' War. From one of the many ornately carved bridges, you can see the city's medieval

Kayserberg.

fortifications along the top of one of the nearby hills. Many of the houses are Gothic and Renaissance, and most have half-timbering, wrought-iron accents, leaded windows, and multiple designs carved into reddish sandstone. Place de la Mairie hosts an **artisanal market** on Fridays from 4:30 to 7pm from mid-May to mid-September.

In the cafes, you'll hear a combination of French and Alsatian. The age of the speaker usually determines the language—the older ones remain faithful to the dialect of their grandparents.

Dr. Albert Schweitzer, who received the 1952 Nobel Peace Prize for his philosophy of "Reverence for Life," was born here in 1875; his house is near the bridge over the Weiss. You can visit the newly restored **Musée du Albert Schweitzer,** 126 rue du Général de Gaulle (https://schweitzer. org; ✆ **03-89-47-36-55**), from February to December from Tuesday to Saturday (and Sun June–Sept) from 10am to 1pm and 2 to 5pm. Admission is 7€ adults; 5.50€ for students and children 6 to 17 and free 6 and under the first Sunday of each month. The **Office de Tourisme** is at 39 rue du Général-de-Gaulle (www.kaysersberg.com; ✆ **03-89-78-22-78**).

Ammerschwihr

Ammerschwihr, 9km (5¼ miles) north of Colmar (79km/49 miles from Strasbourg), is a good stop to cap off your Wine Road tour. Once a free city of the empire, the town was almost destroyed in 1944 and has been reconstructed in the traditional style. More and more travelers visit to sample the wine, especially Käferkopf. Check out the town's gate towers, 16th-century parish church, and remains of early fortifications.

Rouffach

Rouffach is south of Colmar. One of the highest of the Vosges Mountains, Grand-Ballon shelters the town from the winds that bring rain, which makes for a dry climate and a special grape. Make a beeline for the excellent vineyard **Clos St-Landelin** (www.mure.com; ✆ **03-89-78-58-00**), on the Route du Vin, at the intersection of RN83 and route de Soultzmatt. A clerical estate from the 6th century until the Revolution, it has been celebrated over the centuries for the quality of its wine. Clos St-Landelin covers 21 hectares (52 acres) at the southern end of the Vorbourg Grand Cru area. Its steep slopes call for terrace cultivation.

The soil that produces these wines is anything but fertile. Loaded with pebbles, sand, and limestone, the high-alkaline earth produces low-yield, scraggly vines whose fruit goes into superb Rieslings, Gewürztraminers, and pinot noirs. Members of the Muré family have owned these vineyards since 1648. In their cellar is a 13th-century wine press, the oldest in Alsace, and one of only three like it in France. (The other two are in Burgundy.) The family welcomes visitors who want to tour the cellars and ask about the wine, which is for sale. It's open Monday to Friday 8am to 6:30pm, and Saturday 10am to 1pm and 2 to 6pm.

Where to Stay & Eat Along la Route du Vin

If you don't opt for one of the detailed entries below, a tasty pit stop can be made in Andlau at the unpretentious bistro **Au Boeuf Rouge,** 6 rue du Dr. Stoltz (www.andlau-restaurant.com; ✆ **03-88-08-96-26**), serving up hearty regional classics.

If you're visiting Ribeauvillé, you can satisfy hungry bellies of all ages at quaint **La Flammerie,** 9 Grand Rue (www.winstub-ribeauville.com; ✆ **03-89-73-61-08**); as the name indicates, they have excellent flammekueche tarts, in addition to a wide range of traditional dishes and even some salads, a rarity in Alsace.

The most authentic way to experience the Alsatian Wine Road is to actually sleep amongst the vines, something you can do at one of the area's many charming **B&Bs.** You can peruse an extensive list and book directly on the regional tourism website, **www.alsace-wine-route.com**.

Hostellerie Schwendi ★★   Nestled in the tiny medieval village of Kientzheim, next to popular Kaysersberg and surrounded by rolling vines, is one of most charming, excellent value inns of the Wine Route. For three generations, the Schillé-Gisie family have been running this hotel-restaurant in a completely renovated 18th-century mansion. Guest rooms are divided between the main house and an equally delightful annex. Each room features Alsatian character, exposed wooden beams, exposed stonewalls, solid wooden furniture, and colorful decorative elements. Some rooms have recently refitted bathrooms with either large showers or tubs.

The restaurant mirrors the hotel's attractive Alsatian appeal. The menu of sophisticated French and regional classics includes Munster cheese croquettes with shallot chutney or *choucroute royale,* which go perfectly with the family's own wines. On warm days, savor a leisurely lunch on their lovely terrace surrounded by bright flowers and storybook houses.

2 pl. Schwendi, Kientzheim. www.schwendi.fr. ✆ **03-89-47-30-50.** 29 units. 85€–122€ double; 108€–161€ family room. Free parking. **Amenities:** Restaurant; free Wi-Fi. **Restaurant:** Main courses 24€–32€; fixed-price menu 35€–57€. Sat–Sun noon–2pm, Thurs–Tues 7–9pm. Both restaurant and hotel closed Jan to mid-Mar.

La Cour de Bailli ★   Enjoy an authentic Alsatian *auberge* experience without breaking the bank at this historic hotel and spa. In the heart of picturesque Bergheim, this traditional half-timbered building, decked out in colorful geraniums, exudes storybook charm. Decor is simple yet comfortable in their double rooms, studios with kitchenettes, and multi-room apartments with balconies or terraces—perfect for families or travelers on a budget who might like to prepare a picnic lunch for the vineyards. That said, it would be a shame to miss out on the hotel's great value and delicious restaurant set in 16th-century wine cellars or the pretty courtyard in summer. The menu includes traditional Alsatian dishes like Munster tarte flambé or the more gourmet queen's steak with Königinpastete potato dumplings. Save room for an iced Kougelhopf with Marc de Gewurztraminer liqueur.

57 Grand Rue, Bergheim. www.cour-bailli.com. ℰ **03-89-73-73-46.** 38 units. 81€–108€ double; 123€–209€ suites. Parking 4€. **Amenities:** Restaurant; bar; indoor pool; Jacuzzi; sauna; free Wi-Fi. Annual closures first 2 weeks Jan. **Restaurant:** Main courses 7.50€–22€; fixed-price lunch 14.50€ or dinner 29€–45€; children's menu 12€. Fri–Tues noon–2pm and 6:30–9:30pm. Closed mid-Nov to Jan.

La Diligence ★★★ For a stylish stay on the Route du Vin, book at this entirely refurbished hotel in Obernai. Set on a picturesque square, once inside this typical Alsatian building, you're surrounded by modern elegance. Guest rooms have light wood furnishings, grey or brick-red toned textiles and custom Art-Deco-inspired decorative panels depicting wine country. Plush contemporary amenities include rain showers, air-conditioning, ultra-fast internet and even a telescope in the Sky suite, which also boosts a private terrace. Its **Le Comptoir** cafe serves equally refined lunch fare and tea-time snacks.

23 Place du Marché, Obernai. https://hotel-diligence.com. ℰ **03-88-95-55-69.** 33 units. 117€–270€ double; 216€–351€ suite. Parking 18€. **Amenities:** Restaurant; bar; room service; free Wi-Fi.

Le Chambard ★★★ The refined regional cuisine here is so good, it's worth planning a stop. However, with the chic two-Michelin-starred **La Table d'Olivier Nasti** and a traditional Winstub, it will be difficult to decide which one to choose. To truly tantalize your palate, opt to dine on chef Olivier Nasti's sophisticated gastronomic delights which have also earned him the prestigious title of *Meilleur Ouvrier de France.* His creative, seasonal menu could include local roebuck (venison) pie served on a bed of young greens and drizzled in truffle juice or their signature cauliflower with smoked haddock topped with Tsar Imperial caviar. Whereas over in the rustic **Winstub** you could enjoy a heartier meal of homemade game pâté, "Chambord" sauerkraut served with various pork cuts, Munster cheese from the Valley, and finally traditional Alsatian cake (*kugelhof*) with cinnamon-flavored ice cream. In either venue, the cellar is stocked with the best local vintages. Reservations are required.

Next to the restaurant is a stylish hotel annex (with an elegant spa) with 33 rooms which overlook the rooftops of town or vineyards. A double goes for 313€ to 395€, a suite from 478€.

9–13 rue du Général-de-Gaulle, Kaysersberg. www.lechambard.com. ℰ **03-89-47-10-17.** La Table d'Olivier Nasti: Main courses 92€–138€; fixed-price menu 260€–340€; Fri–Sun noon–2pm; Wed–Sun 7–9pm. La Winstub: Main courses 29€–47€; fixed-price menu 37€; daily noon–2pm and 7–9pm.

Le Sarment ★★ Located in the scenic village of Mittelbergheim, this is a good value historic inn along the Wine Road. Originally opened in 1614, the inn was taken over in 2020 by two Alsatian brothers and master restaurateurs, Laurent and Nicolas Kocher. They've added a 21st-century feel all the while keeping the auberge's historic charm, including its two-story stone staircase, classified as a historic monument. The refurbished guest rooms are each individually decorated with wooden bed frames, colorful cushions and leather armchairs; some have exposed beams and stone walls, and all have modern bathrooms with a large tub or shower. The brothers have also reinvented the inn's restaurant, now featuring a modern French bistronomic menu (set menus 16€ at lunch and 39€–44€ at dinner; restaurant closed Sun night to Tues night).

1 route du Vin, Mittelbergheim. www.le-sarment.fr. ✆ **03-88-08-91-37.** 10 units. 93€–98€ double. **Amenities:** Restaurant; free Wi-Fi. Hotel and restaurant closed Jan and from late June to early July.

COLMAR ★★★

440km (273 miles) SE of Paris; 140km (87 miles) SE of Nancy; 71km (44 miles) SW of Strasbourg

One of the most attractive towns in Alsace, Colmar is a must for any visitors to the region. Colmar has been so well restored, you'd never guess it was hard hit in two world wars. You can't help but be charmed by its medieval and early Renaissance buildings, half-timbered structures, gables, and gracious loggias. Tiny gardens and washhouses surround many of the homes. Its old quarter looks more German than French, filled with streets of unexpected twists and turns. The third-largest town in Alsace, its geographic location makes it a natural gateway to the Rhine country, near the vine-covered slopes of the southern Vosges.

Essentials

ARRIVING If you're **driving,** take N83 from Strasbourg; trip time is 1 hour. Because of the narrow streets, we suggest that you park and walk. Leave the car in the Champ-de-Mars, or in the underground place Rapp for a fee of around 1.50€ per hour, northeast of the railway station, and then walk a few blocks east to the old city; or park in the lot designated PARKING VIEILLE VILLE, accessible from rue de l'Est at the edge of the Petite Venise neighborhood, and walk a few blocks southeast to reach the old city. **Trains** link Colmar to Nancy, Strasbourg, and Mulhouse, as well as to Germany via Strasbourg, across the Rhine. There are several daily direct TGV trains from Paris's Gare de l'Est and a dozen others which involve a transfer in Strasbourg (trip time between 2 hr., 15 min. and 2 hr., 30 min.); the one-way fare is 33€ to 97€. For information, see www. sncf-connect.com or call ✆ **36-35.**

VISITOR INFORMATION The **Office de Tourisme** is at 4 rue Unterlinden (www.tourisme-colmar.com; ✆ **03-89-20-68-92**). For information on wines, vintages, and winery visits, contact the **CIVA** (Alsace Wine Committee), Maison du Vin d'Alsace, 12 av. de la Foire-aux-Vins (www.vins alsace.com; ✆ **03-89-20-16-20**). It's usually open Monday to Friday 8am to noon and 2 to 5pm. Make tour arrangements far in advance.

SPECIAL EVENTS Alsatian **folk dances** on place de l'Ancienne-Douane begin around 8pm on Tuesday from mid-May to mid-September. If you want to listen to classical music, visit during the first 2 weeks in July for the **Festival International de Musique de Colmar** (www.festival-colmar.com), which schedules 20 concerts in venues around the city, such as churches and public monuments. Tickets cost 15€ to 35€. The city also plays host to the **Colmar fête le Printemps** (www.printemps-colmar.com), a 3-week festival celebrating springtime through music, art exhibits, and a handicraft market, held late March through mid-April. The year comes to a colorful

Balcony of Maison Pfister in Colmar.

close during the city's annual **Marché de Noël,** voted one of Europe's best Christmas markets and taking place late November through the end of December (www.noel-colmar.com). You can get complete information on any of the events in town at the Office de Tourisme or by calling *℡* **03-89-20-68-92.**

[FastFACTS] COLMAR

ATMs/Banks You'll find ATMs in place de la Cathédrale or at the intersection of rue Kléber, av. de la République and rue Stanislas.

Doctors & Hospitals Hopitaux Civils de Colmar, 39 av. de la Liberté (www.ch-colmar.fr; *℡* **03-89-12-40-00**).

Mail & Postage La Poste, 34 av. de la République (*℡* **36-31**).

Pharmacies Pharmacie Lafayette des Vignes, 31 rue des Têtes (*℡* **03-89-41-30-09**).

Exploring Colmar

Colmar is rich with historic houses, many half-timbered and, in summer, accented with geranium-draped window boxes. One of the most beautiful is **Maison Pfister,** 11 rue des Marchands, at the corner of rue Mercière, a 1537 building with wooden balconies. On the ground floor is a wine boutique, **Vinum** (p. 401). If you take pont St-Pierre over the Lauch River, you'll have an excellent view of Old Colmar and can explore **Petite Venise,** which is filled with canals.

Eglise des Dominicains ★ CHURCH This deconsecrated church contains one of Colmar's most famous treasures: Martin Schongauer's painting *Virgin of the Rosebush,* or *Vierge au buisson de rose* (1473), all gold, red, and white, with fluttering birds. It's found in the choir and well worth the small entrance fee.

pl. des Dominicains. ✆ **03-89-24-46-57.** Admission 2€ adults; 1.50€ students; 1€ ages 12–16; free for children 11 and under. Tues and Thurs–Sun 10am–1pm and 3–6pm.

Eglise St-Martin ★★ CHURCH In the heart of Old Colmar is this Gothic collegiate church, considered the most beautiful in town. Begun in 1235, it was built on the site of former Carolingian and Romanesque churches. Its 70m (230-ft.) steeple beacons visitors from afar, whereas its spacious interior features soaring pointed arches, delicate medieval statuary and a choir erected by William of Marburg in 1350.

pl. de la Cathédrale. ✆ **03-89-41-27-20.** Free admission. Daily 8:15am–5:45pm. Closed to casual visitors during Mass and Sun mornings.

Musée Bartholdi ★★ MUSEUM American history buffs and New Yorkers should stop here to pay homage to Frédéric-Auguste Bartholdi, sculptor of the Statue of Liberty. This museum is located in the house where he was born in 1834. The display focuses on his masterpieces, especially the Statue of Liberty, with scale models, plans, and documents linked to its construction. A reconstruction of Bartholdi's Paris apartment, with furniture and memorabilia, gives insight into the artist's life and inspirations. Also of note are rooms dedicated to paintings of Egypt that Bartholdi amassed during his travels in 1856 and another with a fine collection of Jewish art.

30 rue des Marchands. www.musee-bartholdi.fr. ✆ **03-89-41-90-60.** Admission 5€ adults; 4€ students and seniors; free for children 17 and under. Wed–Mon 10am–noon and 2–6pm. Closed Jan and national holidays.

Musée d'Unterlinden (Under the Linden Trees) ★★★ MUSEUM This former Dominican convent (1232), the chief seat of Rhenish mysticism in the 14th and 15th centuries, became a museum around 1850, and it's been a treasure house of the art and history of Alsace ever since. An ambitious recent expansion, connects the convent to several neighboring buildings, including former municipal baths, an Art Nouveau building, and a new structure designed by Swiss architects Herzog and de Meuron. These display the museum's modern and contemporary art collections.

The jewel of its collection is the **Issenheim Altarpiece (Le Retable d'Issenheim) ★★★**, created by Würzburg-born Matthias Grünewald, "the most furious of realists," around 1515. One of the most exciting works in German art, 4 years of restoration, completed in 2022, have brought the immense altar screen back to its original glory. It consists of two-sided folding wing pieces—designed to show the Crucifixion, then the Incarnation, framed by the Annunciation and the Resurrection. The carved altar screen depicts St. Anthony visiting the hermit St. Paul; it also shows the Temptation of St. Anthony, the most beguiling part of a work that contains some ghastly birds, weird monsters, and loathsome animals. The demon of the plague is depicted with a swollen belly and purple skin, his body blotched with boils; a diabolical grin appears on his horrible face.

Other attractions include the magnificent altarpiece (dating from 1470) of Jean d'Orlier by Martin Schongauer, a large collection of religious woodcarvings and stained glass from the 14th to the 18th centuries, and Gallo-Roman lapidary collections, including funeral slabs. The armory collection contains ancient arms from the Romanesque to the Renaissance, featuring halberds and crossbows.

1 rue d'Unterlinden. www.musee-unterlinden.com. ℂ **03-89-20-15-58.** Admission 13€ adults; 8€ students under 30 and children 12–17; free for children 11 and under. Wed–Mon 9am–6pm. Closed national holidays.

Where to Stay

Rooms are also available in **La Maison des Têtes** (see "Where to Eat," below).

Hostellerie Le Maréchal ★★   Alsatian charm shines brightly at this hotel located in three 16th-century houses in the heart of la Petite Venice. Guest rooms are named after different composers and you'll discover decorative references to them throughout the hotel. Rooms are on the small side and are roughly divided between classical or modern style, some with canopy beds. Most bathrooms have been redone with contemporary fittings and tiles; the more expensive doubles and the suites have Jacuzzi tubs. The east annex is less desirable with a timbered, sloping ceiling. It's worth reserving at its gastronomic restaurant where you can enjoy duck breast with caramelized potatoes and turnips beside the fireplace or in summer, fish cooked in Riesling samosas on its canal-side terrace.

4–6 pl. des Six-Montagnes-Noires. www.hotel-le-marechal.com. ℂ **03-89-41-60-32.** 30 units. 158€–347€ double; 315€–432€ suite. Parking 20€. **Amenities:** Restaurant; room service; free Wi-Fi.

Le Colombier ★★   New York meets Colmar at this revamped historic home. The facade, old beams, and spiral staircase are virtually all that's left of the 16th century, for the rooms have all been redone with sleek contemporary furnishings and art. They come in a variety of shapes due to the age of the building; ceilings are high, but often slanted. Modern comfort is accentuated with cushy beds covered in fine linens. Bathrooms are small and mostly only have showers. Request a room with a view of the canals or the timbered courtyard.

7 rue Turenne. www.hotel-le-colombier.fr. ℂ **03-89-23-96-00.** 46 units. 187€–290€ double; 250€–340€ suite. Parking 23€. **Amenities:** Bar; room service; free Wi-Fi.

Where to Eat

La Maison des Têtes ★★★ ALSATIAN   The beauty of this historic building will capture your eye, and the chef's exceptional skills will entice your palate at one of the top restaurant/hotels in town. This 17th-century house is home to two eateries: the historic **Brasserie** and the Michelin-starred **Restaurant Girardin.** The first is ideal for a lunch break while touring Colmar. It's set in an elegant room, lit by Art Nouveau fixtures, and crossed by aged-wood beams. The fare consists of sophisticated versions of classic Alsatian dishes like *paté en croute,* and *baeckeoffe* (casserole of potatoes in a marinade of beef, pork, and lamb). Serious foodies choose dinner at **Restaurant Girardin** which has a number of inventive tasting menus, including one for vegetarians, a rarity in these parts (it's called "Journey in the Vegetable World"). It has a more contemporary ambiance.

You can also stay in one of the 21 rooms featuring crisp modern furniture juxtaposed against the charming historic features of the building—the suites even have Jacuzzis. Rates start at 250€ for a standard room and 350€ for a deluxe.

In the Hôtel des Têtes, 19 rue des Têtes. www.la-maison-des-tetes.com. ✆ **03-89-24-43-43.** Brasserie: Main courses 29€–38€; fixed-price lunch 22.50€-26.50€ or dinner 79€. Tues–Sat noon–1:30pm and 7–9:30pm. Restaurant Girardin: Fixed-price dinner menu 155€. Tues–Sat 7–9:30pm.

Le JY'S ★★★ MODERN FRENCH   Savor Colmar's most inventive cuisine at this stylish restaurant which moved to a new location within the Parc Champ de Mars in 2020. The sleek dining room, with floor-to-ceiling windows overlooking the verdant park, provides a modern and serene setting for sampling Jean-Yves Schillinger's cutting-edge French gastronomy. This talented chef combines daring and exotic flavors in his tantalizing menus, including a vegetarian option. Possibilities include king crab remoulade with papaya foam, turnip fagottini and eggplant confit with miso, roasted guinea fowl back with multicolored carrots confit with orange and coffee profiteroles with mascarpone cream infused with green cardamom.

3 allée du Champ de Mars. www.jean-yves-schillinger.com. ✆ **03-89-21-53-60.** Fixed-price menu lunch 82€ or dinner 150€–226€. Wed–Sat noon–1:45pm, Tues–Sat 7–9:45pm. Closed 3 weeks late Aug to early Sept and 1 week in mid-Nov.

Winstub Le Cygne ★★ ALSATIAN   Hidden from the tourist masses down an obscure side street, this is a best *winstub* in town. Savor authentic Alsatian specialties in the cozy wood-paneled dining room bustling with locals. You might need to bring your Alsatian dictionary to decipher the excellent value menu items such as *fleischschnackas* (regional pot-au-feu soup), *jambonneau à l'ancienne* (leg of pork), and *lawerknaepfla* (quenelle dumplings of various meats). For the less courageous, they prepare a variety of reliable and tasty *flammekueche* tarts (Alsatian flatbread with thick cream and toppings). To complete your experience, order a portion of Muster or Roquefort cheese.

17 rue Edouard Richard. www.winstublecygne.fr. © **03-89-23-76-26.** Main course 10€–20€. Mon–Fri noon–2pm, Tues–Sat 7–11pm.

Where to Stay & Eat Nearby

Die-hard gourmets flock to **Illhaeusern** to dine at the Auberge de l'Ill, one of the greatest restaurants in all of France. It's situated on a well-signposted route 18km (11 miles) from Colmar, east of the N83 highway.

Auberge de l'Ill ★★★ MODERN FRENCH   Alsatian cuisine is not all choucroute and pork, especially not at the region's best restaurant. The Haeberlin family opened their first *auberge* over a hundred years ago, gradually building up their reputation, upheld today by Marc Haeberlin and his two Michelin stars. With incredible finesse and a touch of foreign flare, Haeberlin transforms Alsatian traditions into *la grande cuisine.* His exquisite creations vary from roast rack of lamb, *kaasknepflas* (cheese pasta) with baby chanterelle shoots to spit-roasted Bresse chicken, with dainty truffle-filled *baeckaoffa* (one-pot with vegetables, potatoes, wine, and three types of marinated meat). Some dishes may require 24 hours' notice, so check when you make reservations.

To enjoy your meal without having the worry of driving back into town, stay at their **Hôtel des Berges.** It has 19 rustic but regal rooms, including an airstream, overlooking the Ill River. The splurge-worthy rates are 395€ to 420€ for a double, 495€ to 620€ for a suite or cottage and 250€ for the airstream (available May–Sept).

Rue de Collonges, Illhaeusern. www.auberge-de-l-ill.com. © **03-89-71-89-00.** Main course 61€–148€; fixed-price lunch Sat and Sun 177€, dinner 210€–235€. Wed–Mon noon–2pm, Wed–Sun 7–9pm. Closed 1st week of Jan and Feb.

Shopping

The best shopping areas are in the old town of Colmar, particularly rue de Clefs, Grand' Rue, rue des Têtes, and rue des Marchands.

ANTIQUES   Antiques abound in Colmar and shops that deserve particular attention include **Geismar Dany,** 32 rue des Marchands (© **03-89-23-30-41**), specializing in antique painted furniture, and **Antiquités Guy Caffard,** 56 rue des Marchands (www.caffard-antiquites.com; © **03-89-41-31-78**), with its mishmash of furniture, postcards, books, toys, bibelots, and the like. Also worth noting are **Lire & Chiner,** 36 rue des Marchands (© **03-89-24-16-78**), and **Antiquité Arcana,** 13 pl. l'Ancienne Douane (© **03-89-41-59-81**).

WINERIES   With Colmar being at the heart of the wine-producing Rhine country, local wine is one of the best purchases you can make here. If you don't have time to visit the vineyards along the Wine Road, stop in **Vinum** in **la Maison Pfister,** 11 rue des Marchands (www.vinum.pro; ✆ **03-89-41-33-61**), owned by a major Alsace winegrower, **Muré,** proprietor of the vineyard Clos St-Landelin. A vast selection of wines and liqueurs from the region and the rest of France is available at the **Cave du Musée,** 11 rue Kléber (✆ **03-89-23-85-29**).

You can drive to one of the most historic vineyards in Alsace-Lorraine. **Domaines Schlumberger** (www.domaines-schlumberger.com; ✆ **03-89-74-27-00**) lies 26km (16 miles) southwest of Colmar in Guebwiller. The cellars, established by the Schlumberger family in 1810, are an unusual combination of early-19th-century brickwork and modern stainless steel. These grapes become such famous wines as Rieslings, Gewürztraminers, muscats, sylvaners, and pinots (blanc, gris, and noir). Views of the vineyards and tasting rooms are available without an appointment, guided tours can be booked online or by phone. The vineyard is open to tastings Tuesday to Saturday 10am to 12:30pm and 1:30pm to 6pm. They may also have reduced hours in August and the end of December (varies each year—call for details).

LA ROUTE DES CRÊTES ★★

From Basel, Switzerland, to Mainz, Germany, a distance of some 242km (150 miles), the Vosges Mountains stretch along the west side of the Rhine Valley, bearing a similarity to the Black Forest of Germany. Many German and French families spend their summer vacation exploring the Vosges. Travelers with less time may want to settle for a quick look at the ancient mountains that once formed the boundary between France and Germany. They are filled with tall hardwood and fir trees, and a network of twisting roads with hairpin curves traverses them. The depths of the mountain forests are the closest France comes to wilderness.

Exploring the Area

You can explore the mountains by heading west from Strasbourg, but a more interesting route is from Colmar. The French High Command created **La Route des Crêtes** (Crest Road) during World War I to carry supplies over the mountains. It begins at **Col du Bonhomme,** west of Colmar, and descends south through the **Regional Natural Park of the Ballons des Vosges** (www.parc-ballons-vosges.fr) until the village of Cernay. From Col du Bonhomme, you can strike out on this magnificent road, once the object of bitter fighting but today a series of panoramic vistas, including one of the Black Forest.

ALSACE-LORRAINE FOR kids

One of the best family sites in the region is the **Ecomuseum in Ungersheim** between Colmar and Mulhouse (www.ecomusee-alsace.fr; ℂ **03-89-74-44-74**). It's a reconstructed turn-of-the-20th-century Alsatian village of over 80 buildings, including houses, farms, and traditional artisanal workshops. Kids can watch a potter at work, learn about beekeeping, poke their heads into a schoolroom or take a ride on a horse-drawn cart. Entrance is 16.50€ adults, 11€ children 4 to 17, free for children 3 and under. Open Tuesday to Sunday 10am to 6pm, though it may have alternative hours in December and is closed most of November, January, and February.

The Vosges mountains have plenty of activities for outdoor adventurers, especially the **Regional Natural Park of the Ballons des Vosges** (p. 401). You can discover this incredibly beautiful protected ecosystem by hiking, biking, canoeing, horseback riding, or at one of the park's many heritage sites from farms to former mills. For a less strenuous tour of the area, take a ride on the historic **Abreschviller train,** 2 pl. Norbert Prévot, Abreschviller (train-abreschviller.fr; ℂ **03-87-03-71-45**). Started in 1884 for logging, today old-fashioned steam or diesel trains take visitors on a 6km (4-mile) circuit around the area. The round-trip journey takes 90 minutes. It runs several times per day in July and August and less frequently April to October; check the website for a timetable. Tickets are 8€ adult one-way and 14€ round-trip, for children it's 6€ and 10.50€ respectively.

For a family break in Lorraine, stop in at the **Muséum-Aquarium de Nancy,** 34 rue Sainte-Catherine (www.museum aquariumdenancy.eu; ℂ **03-83-32-99-97**), with 57 aquariums and a display of 600 preserved animal and archaeological specimens. Open Tuesday to Sunday 9am to noon and 2 to 6pm. Admission is 5.80€ adults; 3.40€ seniors, students and children 12 to 17; free for children 11 and under and all visitors the first Sunday of the month.

By **Col de la Schlucht,** 62km (38 miles) west of Colmar, you'll have climbed 1,472m (4,828 ft.). Schlucht is a summer and winter resort and one of the most beautiful spots in the Vosges, with a panoramic view of the Valley of Münster and the slopes of Hohneck. As you skirt the edge of this glacier-carved valley, you'll be in the midst of a land of pine groves with a necklace of lakes. You may want to turn off the main road and go exploring in several directions as the scenery is that tempting. But if you're still on the Crest Road, you can circle **Hohneck,** one of the highest peaks, at 1,590m (5,215 ft.), dominating the Wildenstein Dam of the Bresse winter-sports station.

At **Markstein,** you'll come to another resort. From here, take N430 and then D10 to **Münster,** where the namesake savory cheese is made. You'll go via the Petit-Ballon, a landscape of forest and mountain meadows with grazing cows. Finally, **Grand-Ballon,** at 1,400m (4,592 ft.), is the highest point you can reach by car in the Vosges. Get out of your car and go for a walk; if it's a clear day, you'll be able to see the Jura, with the French Alps beyond.

NANCY ★★★

370km (229 miles) E of Paris; 148km (92 miles) W of Strasbourg

Nancy, in France's northeast corner, was the capital of old Lorraine. The city was built around a fortified castle on a rock in the swampland near the Meurthe River. A canal a few blocks east of the historic center connects the Marne to the Rhine.

The city is serenely beautiful, with a history, cuisine, and architecture all its own. It once rivaled Paris as the center for the design and production of Art Nouveau. Nancy has three faces: the medieval alleys and towers around the old Palais Ducal where Charles II received Joan of Arc, the rococo golden gates and fountains, and colorful Art Nouveau architecture from the turn-of-the-20th-century heyday of the Ecole de Nancy.

With a population of more than 100,000, Nancy remains the hub of commerce and politics in Lorraine. Home to a large university, it's a center of mining, engineering, metallurgy, and finance. Its 30,000 students, who have a passion for *le cool jazz,* keep Nancy jumping at night.

Essentials

ARRIVING The fast **TGV train** from Paris's Gare de l'Est arrives in Nancy after just 90 minutes, making the city a virtual commute from

Place Stanislas in the historic center of Nancy.

Paris. Many Parisians now visit for *le weekend*. The one-way fare ranges between 30€ and 85€. Trains from Strasbourg arrive in Nancy every hour, a one-way fare costing 29.30€. For information and schedules, see www. sncf-connect.com or call ☏ **36-35.** If you're **driving** to Nancy from Paris, follow N4 east (trip time: 4 hr.).

VISITOR INFORMATION The **Office de Tourisme** is at pl. Stanislas (www.nancy-tourisme.fr; ☏ **03-83-35-80-10**).

NANCY CITY PASS & PASSE-MUSÉE The Nancy City Pass is worth purchasing for travelers who want to thoroughly explore the city on foot, bike, and public transit. It's available at the tourist office or online (https://visites.nancy-tourisme.fr/en) and for 1- to 3-day durations. It costs 24€ to 35€ per person, which includes a transit pass, a city-guide app, self-guided tours via audio guide (devices must be picked up at the tourist office), free entrance to numerous museums and sites, a discount off the city's VelOstan bike-share system (see below) and other venues and services. We estimate that it will save most visitors at least 6€.

SPECIAL EVENTS Serious jazz lovers come to town for 2 weeks in October to attend **Jazz Pulsations** (www.nancyjazzpulsations.com; ☏ **03-83-35-40-86**). Some kind of performance takes place every night around sundown in a tent in the Parc de la Pépinière, a very short walk from the place Stanislas. Some performances are free, others charge varying rates from 18€ to 50€.

Getting Around

ON FOOT The train station is a 10-minute walk to the heart of the city and many main sites are within walking distance.

BY BICYCLE You can rent bikes from **VelOstan,** at the Nancy station in the Thiers entrance (www.velostanlib.fr; ☏ **06-08-05-16-43**). Their reasonable rates range from free on weekends (for usage under 30 min.) to 5€ for a full week.

BY CAR You can reach all sites of interest in Nancy on foot or by public transit. If you have a car, you can park it at the station or south of place Stanislas at the **Vinci Parking,** 6 rue Claude Charles. Car rentals are at the train station at **Avis** (www.avis.fr; ☏ **03-54-40-80-05**), or just outside the station at **Europcar** (www.europcar.fr; ☏ **03-83-37-57-24**).

BY TAXI Taxis are always outside the train station and some circulate around town. You can order one in advance from **Nancy Taxis** (www. taxis-nancy.com; ☏ **03-83-37-65-37**).

BY PUBLIC TRANSPORT Nancy has a well-serviced bus and tram system called the **Reseau Stan** (www.reseau-stan.com; ☏ **03-83-30-08-08**). A one-way ticket costs 1.40€ when purchased from automatic kiosks at a tram station or 1.60€ directly from a bus driver.

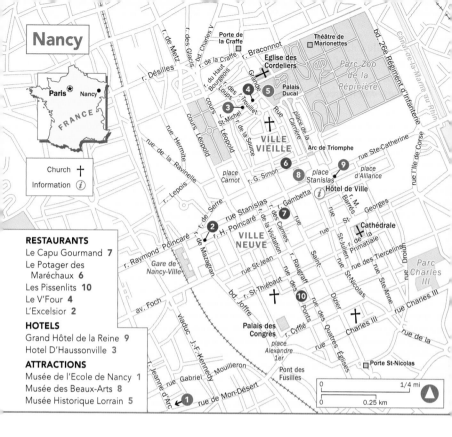

RESTAURANTS
Le Capu Gourmand **7**
Le Potager des
   Maréchaux **6**
Les Pissenlits **10**
Le V'Four **4**
L'Excelsior **2**

HOTELS
Grand Hôtel de la Reine **9**
Hotel D'Haussonville **3**

ATTRACTIONS
Musée de l'Ecole de Nancy **1**
Musée des Beaux-Arts **8**
Musée Historique Lorrain **5**

[FastFACTS] NANCY

ATMs/Banks The city center has scores of ATMs, several are along rue Saint-Jean or Saint-Dizier.

Doctors & Hospitals **Hopital Central de Nancy,** 29 av. du Maréchal de Lattre de Tassigny (www. chu-nancy.fr; ℂ **03-83-85-85-85**).

Mail & Postage **La Poste,** 10 rue Saint-Dizier (ℂ **36-31**).

Pharmacies **Pharmacie du Point Central,** 35 rue Saint-Dizier (ℂ **03-83-32-08-57**).

Exploring Nancy

The most monumental square in eastern France, and the heart of Nancy, is **place Stanislas ★★★**, named for Stanislas Leszczynski, the last of the ducs de Lorraine, ex-king of Poland, and father-in-law of Louis XV. His 18th-century building programs transformed Nancy into one of Europe's most palatial cities. It's a UNESCO World Heritage Site. The square stands between Nancy's two most notable neighborhoods: the **Ville**

Vieille (old town), in the medieval core, centered on the cathedral, Grande Rue, and the labyrinth of narrow meandering streets that funnel into it; and the **Ville Neuve,** in the southwest. Built in the 16th and 17th centuries, when streets were laid out in straight lines, Ville Neuve centers on rue St-Jean.

Place Stanislas was laid out from 1752 to 1760 according to the designs of Emmanuel Héré. Its ironwork gates are magnificent. The square is fabled for the brilliant and fanciful railings, the work of Jean Lamour. His gilded railings with flowery decorations and crests evoke Versailles. The entire plaza is an all-pedestrian zone.

The **Arc de Triomphe,** constructed by Stanislas from 1754 to 1756 to honor Louis XV, adjoins the place de la Carrière, a tree-lined promenade leading to the 1760 **Palais du Gouvernement.** This governmental palace adjoins the **Palais Ducal,** built in 1502 in the Gothic style with Flamboyant Gothic balconies.

Musée de l'Ecole de Nancy ★★ MUSEUM   In a building from the époque is a fascinating museum on the city's famous Art Nouveau movement. It features glasswork, furniture, and ceramics from the school's leading artists. Highlights include Emile Gallé's "Dawn and Dusk" bed, and "Mushroom Lamp," Eugène Vallin's oak entrance door and dining room set. Afterwards, amble through the garden in search of the intriguing stained-glass "aquarium" pavilion.

36–38 rue Sergent-Blandan. www.ecole-de-nancy.com. ✆ **03-83-40-14-86.** Admission 6€ adults; 4€ seniors; free for students, children under 17 and for all first Sun of the month. Wed–Sun 10am–6pm.

Musée des Beaux-Arts ★★ MUSEUM   Housed in an 18th-century building on place Stanislas, this outstanding regional museum dates back to the Revolution. Its collection is built on local bequeaths such as Mme. Henri Galilée's donation of 117 modern works, from Bonnard to Modigliani. On display is a remarkable Manet portrait of the wife of Napoleon III's dentist—remarkable for its intensity and luminosity. Other highlights are by Tintoretto, Caravaggio, Rubens, and Delacroix.

3 pl. Stanislas. http://mban.nancy.fr. ✆ **03-83-85-30-01.** Admission 7€ adults; 4.50€ students 12–25; free for children 11 and under and for all first Sun of the month (additional fee during exhibits). Wed–Mon 10am–6pm.

Musée Historique Lorrain ★★★ MUSEUM   *Important:* This is one of France's great museums, covering the art and history of the Lorraine region from ancient times. But at the time this book went to press the museum was closed for extensive renovations and expansion. It's scheduled to reopen in 2029. However, some works, including Georges de La Tour's *La Femme à la Puce,* will be on display at the **Musée des Beaux-Arts.** The **Eglise des Cordeliers,** a part of the museum today, will remain open and free of charge to visit. It is the burial site of the dukes of

Lorraine. The most notable of the burial monuments are those of René II (1509; attributed to the sculptor Mansuy Gauvain) and a reclining statue of his second wife, Philippa of Gueldres, by Ligier Richier. The limestone rendering of Philippa is one of Nancy's most stunning examples of Renaissance portraiture.

In the Palais Ducal, 64 Grande-Rue. www.musee-lorrain.nancy.fr. $\mathcal{C}$ **03-83-32-18-74.**

Where to Stay

Grand Hôtel de la Reine ★   As we went to press, this hotel was looking a little tired. However, it will be undergoing renovations, management says, sometime in 2024. We include it because its location, right on place Stanislas, is extraordinary. The building dates to the square's era, a former private mansion. Check in to see if the work has been done before booking. Or stop by for a drink or a meal: The lobby boasts a chichi bar serving craft cocktails, a lounge hung with portraits of local aristocrats, and an elegant restaurant.

2 pl. Stanislas. www.hoteldelareine.com. $\mathcal{C}$ **03-83-35-03-01.** 51 units. 119€–280€ double. **Amenities:** Restaurant; bar; babysitting; room service; free Wi-Fi.

Hotel D'Haussonville ★★   Set in a 15th-century classified historic mansion, this is a special find in the elegant former capital of the Duchy of Lorraine. Close to the beautiful Eglise Saint Epvre, the town house has a unique gothic balcony and a Renaissance balustrade. The wings surround a quaint courtyard adorned with flowers and a fountain. Each of the seven rooms and suites has its own international theme. Most have high ceilings, luxurious bathrooms, and the best have views of the church.

9 rue Mgr. Trouillet. www.hotel-haussonville.fr. $\mathcal{C}$ **03-83-35-85-84.** 7 units. 155€–233€ double; 197€–246€ suite. **Amenities:** Free Wi-Fi.

Where to Eat

A range of restaurants line rue des Maréchaux, nicknamed Gourmet Street. At no. 25 is **Le Potager des Maréchaux** ($\mathcal{C}$ **07-82-54-04-16**), the "vegetable patch," serving up salads, quiches or pâté Lorraine. For great market-based cuisine, walk a little farther to the tiny **Le V'Four,** 10 rue St-Michel (www.levfour.fr; $\mathcal{C}$ **03-83-32-49-48**), where you can get a fixed-price lunch menu for 24.50€ to 26.50€.

You might end your day of sightseeing by calling at the century-old brasserie **L'Excelsior,** 50 rue Henri Poincare (www.brasserie-excelsior-nancy.fr; $\mathcal{C}$ **03-83-35-24-57**), which is an amazing period piece from 1911 with stained-glass windows and polished brass chandeliers. Just a block from the rail station, it serves Lorraine specialties with fresh oysters, a delight in season.

Le Capu Gourmand ★★ MODERN FRENCH   You can taste a perfect mix of Nancy's classicism and artistic pizzazz in the town's leading restaurant, located a mere 5-minute walk from place Stanislas. The dining room has a sophisticated flair in greys and mauves with flashes of magentas and purples in the seating. The menu adds rebellious twists to traditional dishes such as foie gras flavored with black chocolate, tartare of salmon with Gewurztraminer jelly, red mullet on a salad of Granny Smith apples, pistachios drizzled with balsamic vinaigrette or the roasted pineapple with acacia honey and lavender cream.

31 rue Gambetta. www.lecapu.com. *℗* **03-83-35-26-98.** Main course 24€–34€; fixed-price weekday lunches 18€-29€ or dinner 26€–31€. Tues–Sat noon–2pm and 7:30–10pm, Sun noon–2pm (brunch only, except for July–Aug).

Les Pissenlits (The Dandelions) ★ TRADITIONAL FRENCH At this cost-conscious brasserie, the food is simple but flavorful and artfully prepared. Chef Jean-Luc Mengin's specialties are likely to include dandelion salad with fried bacon and creamy meurotte vinaigrette, veal kidneys following Grandma's recipe served with homemade späetzle noodles and matelote of freshwater zander with shallots cooked with local gris de Toule wine. The chef's wife, Danièle, is one of the few accredited female wine stewards in France. Art Nouveau antiques, many of them crafted in Nancy, fill the dining room. They also run the wine bar and cellar next door, **Vins et Tartines** (www.vins-et-tartines.com).

27 bis rue des Ponts. www.les-pissenlits.com. *℗* **03-83-37-43-97.** Main course 12.50€–25€; lunch special 13€; fixed-price menu 35€. Tues–Sat 11:45am–2pm and 7:15–10pm.

Shopping

The famous French *macaron* almond flour cookie is said to have been invented in Nancy by Benedictine nuns. **Maison des Soeurs Macarons,** 21 rue Gambetta (www.macaron-de-nancy.com; *℗* **03-83-32-24-25**), follows the original recipe. Another good place to acquire them in addition to another traditional Nancy specialty, Bergamotte candies, is at the pretty shop **Lefèvre Lemoine,** 7 rue Henri Poincaré (www.lefevre-lemoine.fr; *℗* **03-83-30-13-83**).

Though larger and more expensive, Art Nouveau antiques also make excellent souvenirs of Nancy. Visit **Denis Rugat,** 13 rue Stanislas (*℗* **03-83-35-20-79**), for the best pieces. It stocks Lalique crystal, brightly colored vases, and enameled boxes made with a technique known locally as *les émaux de Longwy,* plus an assortment of glass-shaded lamps.

You'll find more glass and crystal by **Daum,** at more reasonable prices than virtually anywhere else in France. The company's premier outlet is **Boutique Daum,** 14 pl. Stanislas (https://daum.fr; *℗* **03-83-32-21-65**), where the most perfect specimens from the Daum factory are sold at prices that are usually about 30% less than what you'd pay in other glass galleries in France. Or for savings of 30% to 40% less than what's sold in the above-mentioned boutique, you can seek out Daum's factory outlet, **Magasin d'Usine Daum,** 17 rue Cristallerie (ℰ **03-83-30-80-24**), a 5-minute walk from the place Stanislas; its pieces are slightly flawed.

Nancy Nightlife

As night approaches, most of the student population heads to the Old Town. Young *Nancéiens* start their night with a drink at **Le Pinocchio,** 9 pl. Saint-Epvre (ℰ **03-83-35-55-95**); its terrace facing the Saint Epyre church is the best place to enjoy a pint or glass of chilled wine in summer. Beer fans are camped out further along the square at Nancy's leading bar à biere **LeCh'timi,** 17 pl. Saint-Epvre (www.facebook.com/LeChtimiNancy; ℰ **03-83-32-82-76**), which stocks over 100 different types of hoppy delights.

Nancy's most popular dance club is **Les Caves,** 9 pl. Stanislas (www.facebook.com/lescavesnancy; ℰ **07-89-59-74-76**), where a techno crowd flails around in a chrome-and-metallic space. It's open Wednesday and Thursday 11:45pm to 4am and Friday and Saturday 11:45pm to 5am.

Work up a more casual sweat at **Ruin Bär** (www.facebook.com/ruinbarnancy; ℰ **06-68-56-07-09**). Inspired by the "ruin bars" of Budapest, this festive venue, decked out in street art and flea-market furnishings, attracts all ages who bust a move on the dance-floor to everything from salsa to house. It's open Tuesday to Sunday 5:30pm to 2am.

DOMRÉMY-LA-PUCELLE

443km (275 miles) SE of Paris; 10km (6¼ miles) NW of Neufchâteau

Most often visited on a day trip, Domrémy is a plain village that would have slumbered into obscurity, but for the fact that Joan of Arc was born here in 1412. Today it's a pilgrimage center attracting fans of the heroine from all over the world.

10

ALSACE-LORRAINE

Domrémy-la-Pucelle

Essentials

ARRIVING If you're **driving,** take N4 southeast of Paris to Toul, and then A31 south toward Neufchâteau/Charmes. Then take N74 southwest (signposted in the direction of Neufchâteau). At Neufchâteau, follow D164 northwest to Coussey. From there, take D53 into Domrémy.

Domrémy does not have a railway station—you must take one of four **trains** daily going to either Nancy or Toul, where you can make bus and rail connections to Neufchâteau, 9.5km (6 miles) away. You can also take a **taxi,** MBM Assistance 88 (www.mbm-assistances88.com; ✆ **03-29-06-12-13**), for about 100€ each way.

Discovering Joan's Legacy

Her four-room family's house is known as **Maison Natale de Jeanne d'Arc,** 2 rue de la Basilique (✆ **03-29-06-95-86**). Here you can see the chamber where she was born. Located beside the house, the newly renovated **Centre Johannique** is a museum dedicated to the life and times of St. Joan. The site is open July and August daily 10am to 6:30pm, April to June and September Wednesday to Monday 9:30am to 1pm and 2 to 6pm, and October to March Wednesday to Monday 10am to 1pm and 2 to 5pm. Admission is 5€ for adults, 3€ for ages 18 to 26 and free for 17 and under. The house is closed in mid-December through January.

Adjacent to the museum, on rue Principale, is **Eglise St-Rémi;** repairs and partial reconstructions from the 19th century have masked its 12th-century origins. All that remains from the age of Joan of Arc are a baptismal font and some stonework. On a slope of the Bois-Chenu 1.5km (1 mile) uphill from the village is a monument steeped in French nationalism, the **Basilique du Bois-Chenu,** built on the spot Joan is said to have heard the voices. Made of local Vosges pink granite and decorated with mosaic and monumental statues celebrating the saint, it was begun in 1881 and consecrated in 1926. To reach it, follow signs from the center and along rue de la Basilique.

VERDUN ★★

261km (162 miles) E of Paris; 66km (41 miles) W of Metz

Built on both banks of the Meuse and intersected by a series of canals, Verdun has an old section, the Ville Haute, on the east bank, which includes the cathedral and Episcopal palace. Today stone houses on narrow cobblestone streets give Verdun a medieval appearance. However, most visitors come to see the famous World War I battlefields, 3km (1¾ miles) east of the town, off N3 toward Metz.

The American cemetery at Verdun.

Essentials

ARRIVING Six **trains** arrive daily from Paris's Gare de l'Est; you'll have to change at Meuse or Metz. The one-way fare from Paris is 33€ to 52€. For train information and schedules, see www.sncf-connect.com or call ℂ **36-35. Driving** is easy; Verdun is several miles north of the Paris-Strasbourg autoroute (A4).

VISITOR INFORMATION The **Office de Tourisme** is on place de la Nation (www.tourisme-verdun.com; ℂ **03-29-84-14-18**).

Touring the Battlefields

At this garrison town in eastern France, Marshal Pétain proclaimed, "They shall not pass!" And they didn't. Verdun is where the Allies held out against a massive assault by the German army in World War I. Near the end of the war, 600,000 to 800,000 French and German soldiers died battling over a few miles along the muddy Meuse between Paris and the Rhine. Two monuments commemorate these tragic events: Rodin's *Defense* and Boucher's *To Victory and the Dead.*

The local tourist office provides maps for two tours of the brutal and bloody battlefields that helped define World War I. The "Circuit Champs de Bataille Rive Droite" encompasses the better-known battlegrounds on the River Meuse's right bank. It's a 4-hour, 32km (20-mile) route, and takes in **Fort Vaux,** where Raynal staged a heroic defense after sending his last message by carrier pigeon.

After passing a **French cemetery** of 16,000 graves—an endless field of crosses—you arrive at the **Ossuaire de Douaumont** (www.verdun-douaumont.com; ✆ **03-29-84-54-81**), where the bones of those blown to bits were embedded. Nearby, at the **Fort de Douaumont,** the "hell of Verdun" was unleashed. From the roof, you can look out at a vast field dotted by the corroded tops of the tiny "pillbox" guard posts. Then you proceed to the **Tranchée des Baïonettes (Trench of Bayonets).** Bayonets of French soldiers entombed by a shell seem to burst forth from this unique memorial.

Within a few paces of the Tranchée des Baïonettes, you'll see the **Mémorial de Verdun,** Fleury Devant Douaumont (www.memorial-de-verdun.fr; ✆ **03-29-84-35-34**). Originally built in 1967, the museum was completely redone in 2016. The sleek new exhibition space chronicles the savage battle through thematic displays of weapons, uniforms, vehicles, and archival material.

The second self-guided tour, known as **"Circuit Champs de Bataille Rive Gauche"** (or "Circuit de l'Argonne"), requires about 4 hours to cover its 97km (60 miles). The tour focuses on mostly outdoor sites. It takes in the **Butte de Montfaucon,** a hill on which Americans erected a memorial tower, and the moving **Cimetière Américain at Romagne** (www.abmc.gov/cemeteries-memorials), the largest American cemetery in Europe with over 14,000 graves. Because public transportation is inadequate, only visitors with cars should attempt to make these circuits.

BURGUNDY

By Anna E. Brooke

Bordered by the River Saône to the east and the River Loire to the west, Burgundy is an agricultural region famed for its wines: The major growing areas are Chablis, Côte de Nuits, Côte de Beaune, Côte Chalonnaise, and Mâconnais. In 2015, *Les Climats du Vignoble de Bourgogn* (Burgundy vineyards) became a UNESCO World Heritage Site. Needless to say, good food plays a large part, too. Michelin awarded stars to a whopping 30 restaurants in the region in 2023, a startlingly large number per capita.

Cistercian monasteries and medieval churches mark the landscape, along with centuries-old honey-colored villages. Several canals cross the Burgundy countryside, making it a popular destination for water-based holidays, while walkers and cyclists can explore miles of towpaths and routes through the vines. From 1032 until 1477, when it was annexed by France, the Duchy of Burgundy was an independent province whose territory included Luxembourg, Belgium, and the Netherlands; its legacy is a rich cultural heritage.

The Côte d'Or wine-growing area of Burgundy is famed for its *Premier Cru* (superior) wine appellations such as Richebourg and Vosne-Romanée, while the region's grassy agricultural plains are home to mouth-watering offerings such as Charolais beef, garlic-infused snails, and pungent Époisses cheese. Today Burgundy offers many opportunities for wine tourism, from free tastings to vineyard tours.

DIJON ★★★

312km (193 miles) SE of Paris; 320km (198 miles) NE of Lyon

Founded by the Romans, in the north of the region, this city of 155,000 residents is the capital of Burgundy—a culturally rich place of epic architecture (from a range of eras and styles), treasure-filled museums, and plenty of shops selling two of France's greatest exports: wine and mustard. Happily, most of the city's museums and major sites are free to enter, making a visit here significantly less expensive than other French cities of this scope.

On the doorstep of the illustrious Côte d'Or wine region, Dijon is a great base for exploring vineyards. But don't do that until you've sampled some of the food. The city's streets are lined with accomplished restaurants, including five with Michelin stars. Most importantly, Dijon is home

PREVIOUS PAGE: **Auxerre on the River Yonne.**

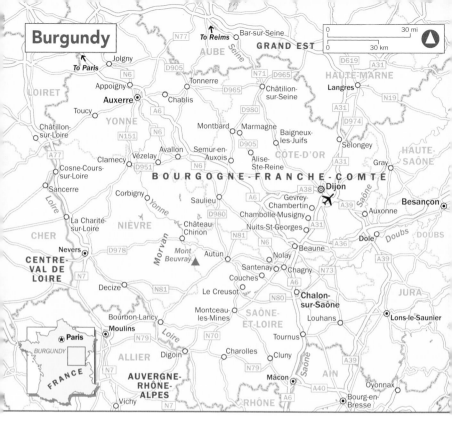

to a unique, multi-building complex created for the singular purpose of teaching the world about the proud history of French cuisine. Opened in 2022, the **Cité Internationale de la Gastronomie et du Vin ★★** (www. citedelagastronomie-dijon.fr) is a collection of foodie attractions, including: an erudite but fun, interactive museum about wine (with English-language text and audio as well as French); a cooking school; an oenology school; several restaurants; and a "gastronomic village" of shops selling local specialties from across France—and handing out lots of samples to taste. Some of the Cité's offerings are free, others incur a charge, and hours vary according to which section you're visiting, so study the website, which will also list the many culinary events the Cité sponsors each month.

Dijon sponsors a number of entertaining events throughout the year. In May, vintage motorbike fans arrive for the **Coupes Moto Légende,** Europe's biggest motorbike gathering (some 1,300 bikers) to race their two-wheeled steeds around the Prenois race track (http://coupes-moto-legende.fr). Every 2 years, the **Fêtes de la Vigne** celebrate local life

Place de la Libération in the heart of Dijon is surrounded by cafes. Stop by for a glass of wine, but dine elsewhere (the food is mediocre).

and traditions on the last weekend in August (next one 2024; fetesdela vigne.org). In November, the city hosts one of France's largest food fairs, the **Foire internationale et gastronomique de Dijon** (foirededijon.com).

Essentials

ARRIVING   If you are **driving,** from Paris follow the A6 southeast to Pouilly-en-Auxois, and then go east along A38 to turn off into central Dijon. About 15 or so TGV **trains** arrive from Paris's Gare de Lyon each day (trip time: 1 hr., 35 min.; from Gare de l'Est and Gare de Bercy in Paris too, but these trains take much longer). For information, visit www. sncf-connect.com or call ✆ **36-35.** *Important:* The high-speed trains sell out in high season, so get advance reservations.

VISITOR INFORMATION   The **Office de Tourisme** is at 11 rue des Forges (www.destinationdijon.com; ✆ **03-80-44-11-44**).

Getting Around

BY TAXI   The train station has a taxi rank. To reserve in advance, contact **Taxis Dijon** (www.taxis-dijon.fr; ✆ **03-08-41-41-12**).

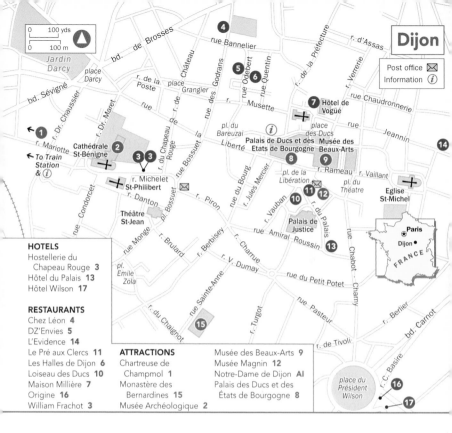

BY PUBLIC TRANSPORT   Dijon has a good network of **buses** and **trams,** although the city is easy to get around on foot. Tickets cost 1.40€, last for 1 hour, and you can buy them at machines at the bus/tram stop on the bus/tram or in the Divia office at 16 pl. Darcy (divia.fr).

BY BIKE   **DiviaVélodi** (www.divia.fr/page/diviavelodi) offers self-service and drop-off points all around town including the train station and Forges-Notre Dame by the tourist office. To use the service, you'll need a debit or credit card (and to pay a 200€ deposit, that will only be debited if you don't return the bike).

[FastFACTS] DIJON

Hospital   **CHU Dijon Bourgogne,** 14 rue Paul Gaffarel; ℰ **03-80-29-30-31.**

Pharmacy   Dijon's pharmacies take turns staying

open after hours. Ask at the police station in place Suquet (ℰ **03-80-44-55-00**). **La Pharmacie de la Liberté,** 42 rue de la

Liberté (ℰ **03-80-30-41-69;** facebook.com/pharmacie libertedijon), is open 8am to 7:30pm Monday to Saturday.

Exploring Dijon

Dijon was a backwater when the French Revolution occurred, a happy twist of fate because it meant that its churches, palaces, and mansions were largely undisturbed at a time when marauding masses were damaging and destroying historic structures in other French cities. And you'll learn a lot about the fascinating history of the city by looking at these buildings—which range from medieval half-timbered houses to palaces— if you have the right interpreter. A gent who goes by the name of Bertrand on **Airbandb/Experiences** is an excellent tour guide (at $17/person); or you can pick up the surprisingly engaging **audio walking tour** from the Tourist Board (see above; 10€).

On either tour, you'll definitely spend time at the grand **Palais des Ducs et des États de Bourgogne,** which was once seat of government for an empire that stretched all the way into today's Holland and Belgium. Its oldest section was constructed in the 14th and 15th centuries. The newer section is the **Palais des États de Bourgogne,** constructed in the 17th and 18th centuries for the Burgundian parliament; check out the **Chapelle des Élus** (free access via the tourist office), which dates from 1738 and was designed by Jacques Gabriel, Louis XV's architect. Today the palace is *la mairie* (the town hall); all of its newer section and much of its older section are reserved for the municipal government and not open to the public. However, fabulous views can be had from the top of **Tour Philippe le Bon** ★★ (316 steps; 5€ adults; days and times vary; check with the tourist office; destinationdijon.com/visites/la-montee-de-la-tour-philippe-le-bon).

Walking tours also always head into Dijon's Medieval Quarter to see the extravagant 16th- and 17th-century *hôtels particuliers* (private mansions), some of which have colorful, geometrically patterned roof tiles, a practice that dates back to the 14th century and is found throughout the region. We recommend seeking out **Hôtel Chambellan** (34 rue des Forges) and the exquisite and ornate **Maison Maillard** (38 rue des Forges); entry to the courtyard of both is free. Gothic church **Notre-Dame de Dijon** is always a stop, mostly so that participants can rub an owl gargoyle on the side of the church for luck (on Rue de la Chouette). Just across from the owl (which looks like just a lump today from all the rubbing) is **Maison Millière,** a perfectly preserved half-timbered cottage from 1483 that had a starring role in Gerard Depardieu's film version of *Cyrano de Bergerac* (1990).

The **Musée Archéologique,** 5 rue du Docteur Maret (https://archeologie.dijon.fr; ✆ **03-80-48-83-70**), housed in a medieval abbey, contains finds from the area, including the abbey itself. Admission is free, and it's open Wednesday to Monday 9am to 12:30pm and 2 to 6pm; from

November to March, the museum is open Wednesday, Saturday, and Sunday. It can be skipped if you're short on time.

A medieval nunnery, **Monastère des Bernardines,** 15–17 rue Ste-Anne (✆ **03-80-48-80-90**), is home to two museums. The chapel holds the **Musée d'Arts Sacrés** (https://art-sacre.dijon.fr), devoted to art from regional churches, and the cloister contains the **Musée de la Vie Bourguignonne** (https://vie-bourgignonne.dijon.fr), which exhibits folkloric costumes, farm implements, and some 19th- and early-20th-century storefronts from Dijon's center. Admission is free to both museums (Wed–Mon 9:30am–12:30pm and 2–6pm). If you're short on time don't feel bad about skipping these.

Chartreuse de Champmol ★★ MONASTERY

Although the fancy tombs of the dukes of Burgundy are in what is now the Musée des Beaux-Arts, their bodies are actually buried in this charterhouse at the western edge of Dijon. Now a psychiatric hospital, it's still possible to visit: The main sights are the church portal and magnificent Well of Moses, which features six prophets from the Old Testament; both were the work of influential Dutch sculptor Claus Sluter. Guided tours are available via the tourist office.

1 bd. Chanoine-Kir. ✆ **03-80-44-11-44.** Free admission. Daily 9:30am–5:30pm (Apr–Oct until 4:30pm). Bus 3 direction Fontaine d'Ouche; stop at CH La Chartreuse.

Musée des Beaux-Arts & Musée Rude ★★★ MUSEUM

One part of the ducal palace houses one of France's most important national art collections, showcasing exceptional sculpture, ducal kitchens from the mid-1400s (with great chimney pieces), and a collection of European paintings and sculptures from the 14th to the 21st centuries. Take special note of the **Salle des Gardes,** the banquet hall of the old palace built by Philip the Good (Philippe le Hardi). The tomb of Philip the Bold was created between 1385 and 1411 and is one of the best-preserved in France: A reclining figure rests on a slab of black marble, surrounded by 41 mourners. The courtyard **brasserie** is perfect for a drink or a bite on fine days (Wed–Mon 8am–8pm).

Just around the corner, at 8 rue Vaillant, don't miss the **Musée Rude ★★** (an annex of the Beaux-Arts with the same opening hours), set within the lofty transept of the decommissioned Église St-Étienne. Monumental plaster casts of works by 18th-century Dijon sculptor François Rude line the walls, including the 1792 *Marseillaise,* the colossal cast used for the **Arc de Triomphe** in Paris (p. 100).

In the Palais des Ducs et des États de Bourgogne, cour de Bar. https://beaux-arts.dijon.fr. ✆ **03-80-74-52-09.** Free admission; audio guides 6€. Wed–Mon 9:30am–6pm (June–Sept 10am–6:30pm).

Musée Magnin ★★ MUSEUM   Housed in a handsome 17th-century *hôtel particulier,* this museum boasts an impressive collection of around 2,000 artworks by lesser-known French, Italian, and Flemish artists from the 14th to the 19th centuries. Some of the paintings, like the Italian landscapes by Anne-Louis Girodet (1767–1824), a pupil of Jacques-Louis David, are exquisite. The collection was bequeathed to the state in 1938 by Maurice and Jeanne Magnin and are displayed around the house, their family home, like an amateur collector's "cabinet of curiosities" in accordance with the couple's wishes.

4 rue des Bons-Enfants. www.musee-magnin.fr. ✆ **03-80-67-11-10.** Admission 3.50€ adults; free for children 17 and under and citizens of the EU ages 26 and under. Tues–Sun 10am–12:30pm and 1:30–6pm.

Where to Stay

Like most cities, boutique-style self-catering apartments have sprung up in Dijon, including **City Loft** (cityloftdijon.fr; ✆ **03-80-54-27-54**), in the historic center from 79€ per night and **Residhome Appart Hotel Dijon Cité des Vignes** (residhome.com; ✆ **08-25-36-34-32;** from 63€/night) in a modern district near the Cité de la Gastronomie and du Vin. There is even a water-side **campsite** a 25-minute walk from the town center (www.camping-du-lac-dijon.com; ✆ **06-66-96-56-26**), open from April to mid-October. Also check **Airbnb** and **VRBO.**

Hostellerie du Chapeau Rouge ★★   "Hotel Red Hat" is our favorite luxury abode in Dijon for its style, food and friendly staff. It's only a 10-minute walk from the train station, too. Most of the rooms in this 19th-century building have had a contemporary makeover; others, notably the Initial and Superior rooms, have a more traditional style. After a hard day's sightseeing, the sauna, hammam, and hydromassage showers (all free) in the basement spa are a welcome respite, and a small range of treatments for face and body are on the menu. Speaking of menus, the hotel's restaurant, overseen by, and named for, William Frachot, is the best in town, with expertly crafted dishes that turn local produce like Bresse chicken, perch and crayfish into taste explosions.

5 rue Michelet. www.chapeau-rouge.fr. ✆ **03-80-50-88-88.** 28 units. 149€–280€ double; 280€–350€ suite or family room. Breakfast 25€. Valet parking 20€. Fixed-price menu 115€–195€. **Amenities:** Restaurant; bar; concierge; room service; spa; laundry service; free Wi-Fi.

Hôtel du Palais ★★   This utterly charming, family-run boutique offers wine-themed stays in the very center of Dijon. Set in a 19th-century town house, guests can arrange private wine tastings (35€) in the vaulted medieval cellars below the building, where the staff will tell you all about the region's Climats (wine-growing terroir) through 6 tastings. Upstairs, the 9 rooms are all named after and beautifully decorated in colors linked to the region's food and wine (the chardonnay room, for instance, is elegant gray and yellow; the *pain d'épices,* gingerbread, room is in burnt oranges).

23 rue du Palais. www.hoteldupalais-dijon.com. © **03-80-58-58-19.** 9 units. 120€–200€ double. Breakfast 14€. **Amenities:** Wine cellar; free Wi-Fi.

Hôtel Wilson ★★ This former coaching inn, dating back to the 17th century, is the ideal stop for drivers, as it's on the southeast edge of Dijon (so you won't have to brave taking your car into the historical center), yet you're just a 15-minute walk from all the action. Rooms have oodles of character with exposed beams, stone walls and Louis Philippe and Louis XIII furniture, while the bathrooms have been renovated in white contemporary style, many with pops of red. In the evening, if you're feeling flush, book ahead at the fab restaurant of chef Tomofumi Unchimura, next door (see Origine in "Where to Eat," below).

1 rue de Longvic. www.wilson-hotel.com. © **03-80-66-82-50.** 27 units. 88€–140€ double; 127€–350€ family rooms. Breakfast 14€. Parking 12€. **Amenities:** Bar; beauty treatments; room service; free Wi-Fi.

Where to Eat

In addition to the restaurants below, we heartily recommend (and so does Michelin) **Loiseau des Ducs,** 3 rue Vauban (www.bernard-loiseau.com; © **03-80-30-28-09**), where lunch menus start at 40€; and **William Frachot** at Hostellerie du Chapeau Rouge (see "Where to Stay," above). For a snack, head to 10–14 rue de la Chouette and the very quaint tearoom **Maison Millière** (www.maison-milliere.fr; © **03-80-30-99-99**) or **Les Halles de Dijon,** the city's fabulous Belle Epoque–era covered market (built in 1868) on rue Odebert, where you can grab picnic provisions galore within a structure inspired by Gustave Eiffel's designs (open 7:30am–1pm Tues and Thurs–Sat). If you find yourself there on a Sunday between June and September, reserve ahead for the Halles special **brunch** (reservation. destinationdijon.com/le-brunch-des-halles-de-dijon.html), where top chefs use the market's produce to create terrific themed meals.

Chez Léon ★★ BURGUNDIAN/FRENCH Take a step back in time, sit elbow-to-elbow with your neighbor, and savor some French dishes like *grand-mère* used to make. Chalked on the blackboard of this rustic restaurant, where family photos adorn the walls, you'll find the likes of snails, succulent homemade terrines, veal chops in Morello mushroom sauce and *tarte tatin* (apple tart). The wine list is fittingly Burgundy heavy.

20 rue des Godrans. www.restochezleon.fr. © **03-80-50-01-07.** Fixed-price lunch 16.90€–20.90€ or dinner 28€–33€. Tues–Sat noon–2pm and 7:30–10:30pm.

DZ'Envies ★★ BURGUNDIAN/FUSION   You won't find any beams or exposed stonework in this white, minimalist restaurant opposite Les Halles, but you will encounter plenty of locals. Chef David Zuddas used to have a Michelin star at his previous establishment but decided to open a new "bistrogastro" in the city center to give himself more creative freedom. The lunch menu changes daily: Expect the likes of *oeufs en meurette* (eggs in red wine and bacon sauce), beef cheeks in red Burgundy for main, followed by pain d'épices panna cotta with red fruit marmalade. In the evening you can choose from three to five *envies* ("desires," aka dishes).

12 rue Odebert. dzenvies.com. ✆ **03-80-50-09-26.** Main courses 19€–26€; fixed-price lunch 18€–25€ or dinner 37€–46€. Mon–Sat noon–2pm and 7–10pm.

Le Pré aux Clercs ★★ BURGUNDIAN FUSION   In an 18th-century house across from the Palais des Ducs, this smart restaurant, dressed in flashy red and gray, is owned by Georges Blanc, who has a small chain of upmarket hotel-restaurants in the region. Its menu fuses classic Burgundian ingredients with those from Arizona, the Caiman Islands and Thailand with surprisingly good results. If you're into steak, try the juicy Montbeliard *bavette* served Crying Tiger style. Like fish? The hake in a hazelnut and citrus crust is a must. In summertime, make sure you book a table outside on the pedestrianized crescent with its privileged view over the magnificent Palais des Duc.

13 pl. de la Libération. www.lepreauxclercs.fr. ✆ **03-80-38-05-05.** Main courses 16€–39€; fixed-price menus 25€–39€. Mon–Sat noon–1:45pm and 7–9:30pm, Sun noon–2:15pm and 7–9:30pm.

L'Evidence ★★ BURGUNDIAN/MODERN FRENCH   The stone walls are old, but everything else is modern in this delightful locals' haunt, where traditional Burgundian dishes get creative updates. Try the parsley and ham terrine in jelly with mustard cream or the slow-cooked duck, infused with smoked paprika. When in season the blue lobster in *sauce americaine* (shellfish sauce) is worth crossing town for, and desserts— think chocolate mousse with raspberries and delicate lemon meringue pie—are just as good. This is a fine example of a 21st-century "traditional" French bistro.

55 rue Jeannin. restaurant-levidence-dijon.com. ✆ **03-80-67-69-37.** Main course 26€–28€; fixed-price lunch 24€–55€; fixed-price dinner 37€–55€. Mon–Fri noon–1:30pm and 7:15–9:30pm.

Origine ★★★ BURGUNDIAN/FRENCH   This restaurant is one of the most sought-after eating places in the area, thanks to Japanese chef Tomofumi Uchimura's creative take on Burgundian cuisine. Snails come with an emulsion of yellow wine and comté cheese; foie-gras is paired with curried eel; and Charolais beef comes with carrots—but don't be fooled, *carrots* here means "fancy carrots," cooked to perfection and chopped like jewels. The weekday lunch menu is a "surprise" and depends upon what Uchimura finds in the market that day. Vegetarians are well catered-for here, with a 65€ locavore, plant-based menu. Reservations required.

10 pl. Wilson. restaurantorigine.fr. ✆ **03-80-67-74-64.** Main courses 38€–46€; fixed-price lunch 48€ and dinner 95€–125€; children's menu 25€. Wed–Sat noon–1:30pm and 7:30–9pm. Closed 1 week in Jan and 2 weeks in Aug.

Where to Eat Nearby

Auberge des Tilleuls ★★★ BURGUNDIAN/FRENCH   For a taste of Burgundian village dining, head 10 km (6 miles) north of Dijon (along D996) to this traditional little bistro—all dolled up in red and white table-cloths on the village square—where chef Nicolas Arnold serves some tre-mendously tasty classics, many cooked and served in *cocottes* (cast-iron pots). One of his signature dishes is *oeufs en meurette* (eggs poached in red wine with bacon, a traditional Burgundian dish), but the menu changes with the seasons, so might include such delights as trout with eggplant and lamb sweetbreads in wine and sage sauce. The 28€ lunch menu is good value.

Wildly varying architectural styles bump up against one another on the streets of Dijon.

8 place de l'Église, Messigny-et-Vantoux. www.restaurant-tilleuls.fr. ✆ **03-80-35-45-22.** Main courses 20€–26€; fixed-price lunch Tue–Fri 28€; dinner menus 36€–48€. Tues–Sat noon–1:30pm, Fri–Sat 7:30–9:30pm. Closed 2 weeks in Aug. Drive 10km (6 miles) north of Dijon on D903, following the signs for Troyes, then turning onto D996 towards Messigny-et-Vantoux.

Le Millésime ★★★ CONTEM-PORARY FRENCH   Remember the name Matthieu Mazoyer. He's the chef at this white table cloth-level eatery, in the itty-bitty village of Chambolle-Musigny, but we have no doubt he's headed for big-ger things. Dining here is a revela-tion: Each dish is perfectly balanced, gorgeous to look at, not overly pricey, and a tasty surprise. We have to say "surprise" because the English translations on the menu are bizarre ("monkfish in virgin sauce," "crusty seasonal vegetables"). But the menu will be the only misstep in a meal that might include such unusual dishes as sweetbreads with apple in a tonka bean sauce or crispy Ardèche trout in a wild garlic sauce. The wine list, as you might expect from a place right on the rue de Grand Crus, is superb.

1 rue Traversière, Chambolle-Musigny. www.restaurant-le-millesime.com. ℰ **03-80-62-80-37.** Main courses 24€–38€. Tues–Sat noon–2pm and 7–10pm. Take D123 to D122A. Continue on Route de Beaune/D974 and turn right onto Route de l'Ancienne Nationale/D122C. Continue right on the Route des Grands Crus/D122. Turn right onto Rue de Vergy/D122.

Shopping

Your shopping list may include regional wines, mustard, antiques, *pain d'épices* (spiced bread), and the blackcurrant liqueur, Crème de Cassis. The best shopping streets are rue de la Liberté, rue du Bourg, rue Bossuet, place Grangier for designer shops, and rue Verrerie for antiques. The aforementioned market at **Les Halles,** rue Odebert, sells fruit, vegetables, and foodstuffs on Tuesday and Thursday to Saturday 7:30am to 1pm.

Dijon has several great *fromageries* (cheese shops) including **Le Chalet Comtois,** 28 rue Musette (ollca.com/dijon/boutiques/le-chalet-comtois ℰ **03-80-30-48-61**); look out for the regionally made semi-soft Cîteaux, made by monks in the abbey of the same name, and pungent, unctuous Époisses. For bread, look no further than **Tartin'art,** 8 rue Musette (www.tartinart.com; ℰ **03-80-30-97-31**), which also offers sandwiches, quiches, and salads. For wine, we like **Dr. Wine,** 5 rue Musette (www.drwine.fr; ℰ **03-80-53-35-16**), a hybrid shop, restaurant and wine club; you can have a full-blown meal or nibble delicious platters of ham and cheese. **Les Clos Vivants,** 1 rue Musette (lesclosvivants.fr; ℰ **03-80-30-45-01**), is another brilliant wine shop that runs tastings. You won't be able to pass **Jonathan Pautet,** 2 rue de la Chouette (jonathanpautet.fr; ℰ **03-80-67-17-88**), without going in to buy some cakes or chocolates (the chocolate snails, filled with ganache, marzipan, and praline, are a must). At **La Boutique Maille,** 32 rue de la Liberté (maille.com; ℰ **03-80-30-41-02**), you can purchase many varieties of the world-famous mustard while **Mulot et Petitjean** (their ornately paneled flagship store is at 13 pl. Bossuet; www.mulotpetitjean.fr; ℰ **03-80-30-07-10**) is the place to go for homemade *pain d'épices* (a cakelike spiced bread). You can find out how the product is made at their factory at 6 bd. de l'Ouest (ℰ **03-80-53-17-10;** Tues–Sat 10am–12:30pm and 2–6:30pm; 8€ adults).

For antiques and interiors, head to the half-timbered streets around rue Verrerie. Southeast of the city center, **Le Consortium,** 37 rue de Longvic (www.leconsortium.fr; ℰ **03-80-68-45-55**), is Dijon's most interesting modern art gallery.

For the last 40 years, **Le Baldaquin,** 13 rue Verrerie (www.le-baldaquin-dijon.fr; ☎ **03-80-33-95-40**), has been a children's treasure trove of wooden toys and mobiles.

Nightlife

As well as relishing its reputation for its mustard (sorry!), Dijon is also the home of *Kir,* a mix of white Aligoté wine and Crème de Cassis blackcurrant liqueur, named after former Dijon mayor Canon Félix Kir. So be sure to raise a glass while you're here, and do so at **La Roue Libre,** 13–15 rue Auguste Comte (facebook.com/alchimiacafe; no phone; Tues–Sat 6pm–2am), a hip spot to enjoy a cocktail or craft beer, and tuck into plates of locally sourced meats and cheeses; they also have bands playing occasionally.

Popular with the young crowd, **Bam Jam,** 43 rue Auguste Comté (facebook.com/Bamjamdijon; ☎ **03-80-73-30-64**), is another small but lively music bar, with bands and DJs playing everything from Jazz to rap to techno. Opposite the Halles food market, **Gobleterie,** 1 rue Bannelier (instagram.com/lagobeleterie; ☎ **07-88-41-18-02**), is open Monday and Wednesday to Saturday 6pm to 2am (and 11am–3pm Sat) and provides an intimate setting for delicious cocktails.

To try some of the region's rarest wines, as well as surprising vintages from around the rest of France, descend into the 16th-century vaulted basement of **Caveau de Saulx,** 80 rue J-J Rousseau (lecaveaude saulx.fr; ☎ **07-63-51-17-50;** Wed–Thurs 6pm–midnight; until 2am Fri–Sat, and until 11pm Sun). You can order from the long list of wines, or opt for a blind tasting—the lot accompanied by copious pâtés, hams, snails, and cheeses.

The opera season (www.opera-dijon.fr; ☎ **03-80-48-82-82**) in Dijon stretches from October to May. Operas, dance recitals, and concerts are held in two venues: **Grand Théâtre de Dijon,** pl. du Théâtre (where you can pop by anytime Tues–Sat 11am–6pm to buy tickets), and **L'Auditorium,** pl. Jean Bouhey (that opens just 1 hr. before each performance). Although it's a good idea to buy tickets in advance online.

Several cinemas show films in their original version including **Eldorado,** 21 rue Alfred de Musset (https://cinemaeldorado.wordpress.com; ☎ **03-80-66-51-89**), and **Cinéma Olympia,** 16 av. Maréchal Foch (Tram line 1 or 2, stop Foch-Gare; www.cines-dijon.com; ☎ **03-80-43-55-99**).

AUXERRE ★★

154km (95 miles) SE of Paris; 148km (92 miles) NW of Dijon

On a hill overlooking the River Yonne, Auxerre (pronounced "Ausserre") was founded by the Gauls and enlarged by the Romans; at the bottom of rue des Pêcheurs you can see the remains of a Gallo-Roman tower

Restored half-timbered houses, Auxerre.

underneath the medieval one. Joan of Arc spent several days in the town in 1429 and Napoleon Bonaparte stopped here on his return from Elba in 1815.

Unsurprisingly (this is Burgundy, after all), Auxerre's AOC wines produced on the surrounding hills are renowned: Try Irancy and Chitry.

The city, which has around 40,000 inhabitants, is a pleasant place to spend a couple of days exploring the narrow, cobbled streets admiring the 700 or so beautifully preserved *colombage* (half-timbered) buildings. The most charming district is the **Quartier St-Nicolas,** the old fishermen's quarter. However, the main reason to visit is to see the rare crypt murals (see "Exploring Auxerre," below).

Auxerre has a full events calendar. In June, the 3-night **Catalpa** world music festival (catalpa-festival.fr) includes a food village and activities for children. In July and August, the **Garçon la note!** festival presents free music concerts daily in the city's bars and restaurants. A market takes place every Tuesday and Friday morning (7am–12:30pm) in place de l'Arquebuse.

Essentials

ARRIVING   Visitors often **drive** here because Auxerre is near A6 (the Autoroute du Soleil) motorway from Paris. About 11 TER **trains** go there from Paris (Gare de Bercy; trip time: 1 hr., 45 min.) each day. For train information, visit www.sncf-connect.com or call ✆ **36-35.**

VISITOR INFORMATION   The **Office de Tourisme** is at 7 place Hôtel de Ville (www.ot-auxerre.fr; ✆ **03-86-52-06-19**).

Getting Around

BY TAXI   If you're arriving by train you might want to book a taxi as the train station is about 1.5km (1 mile) from the main sights in the historic center. Contact ✆ **03-86-46-91-61;** there is also a taxi rank on rue Paul-Doumer at the station.

BY BIKE   You can rent bikes from **La Maison du Vélo,** pl. Achille Ribain (maison-velo.fr; ✆ **03-86-46-24-99**). Prices range from 6€ for 2 hours to 80€ for 5 days.

BY SHUTTLE   Free, pink-colored shuttle buses criss-cross the center from the outer ring roads roughly every 15 minutes. From the train station, walk 9 minutes to the stop at Quai de la République and get off at the stop Cordeliers, in the heart of the old town.

Exploring Auxerre

The railway station is at the eastern edge of town, about 1.5km (1 mile) from the historic center. Most of Auxerre is on the western bank of the Yonne. Its heart is between place du Maréchal-Leclerc (near the Hôtel de Ville [city hall]) and the Cathédrale St-Etienne. Free shuttle buses (known as *navettes;* see above) cover much of the center, so it's easy to hop on and off and get around. You could also while away quite a few hours "messing about on the river" either in your own rented electric boat, which is fun for families, or on kayaks and peddle boats (for all of these, ask at the tourist office).

Just south of the Auxerre, the Yonne River branches into the Canal du Nivernais, a 174km (108-mile) watercourse that that slices through stunning scenery, taking you past wine-making villages, limestone cliffs and even to Burgundy's biggest wine cellar, **Caves Bailly-Lapierre** (bailly-lapierre.fr; ✆ **03-86-53-77-77**), where around 7 million bottles of fizzy Crémant de Bourgogne (the region's answer to champagne) sit in vast medieval cellars, 60m (200 ft.) underground. Ask the tourist office for a list of boat hire companies, or check the website canal-du-nivernais. com. At time of writing, the town's guided cruises, by the **Bateaux Touristiques Auxerrois,** had been put on pause, though this may change, so check the website www.bateaux-auxerrois.com, if you don't fancy sailing your own boat!

Abbaye St-Germain ★★★ ABBEY This Benedictine abbey was founded in the 5th century by St-Germain, a former bishop of Auxerre, after whom it is named; he is buried here. Its school was once reputed throughout Christendom. The main reason to visit is to see the **crypt murals** depicting the stoning of St. Stephen, which date back to the 9th century and are the oldest in France. The lovely 17th-century cloister hosts art exhibitions and concerts in summer.

2 bis pl. St-Germain à Auxerre. abbayesaintgermain.fr. ℭ **03-86-18-02-90.** Guided tours of crypt 8€ adults; free for children under 16 and students 25 and under. Daily Apr–Sept 9am–noon and 2–6pm; Oct–Mar 9am–noon and 2–5pm (closed Tues). Guided tours of crypt in English daily at noon.

Cathédrale St-Etienne ★★ CATHEDRAL Dominating the River Yonne, this Gothic cathedral, the city's most emblematic sight, is also one of its most interesting. The stained-glass windows, which date from the 13th to the 16th centuries, are some of France's finest, while the crypt protects a rare 11th-century **mural** of Christ on a horse.

pl. St-Etienne. ℭ **03-86-51-29-20.** Admission to crypt 3.50€ adults; free for children 11 and under. Cathedral: daily 9am–6pm. Crypt: Apr–Oct Tues–Sat 10:15am–1pm and 2:15–5pm; Nov–Mar Sat 10am–1pm and 2:15–5pm.

Tour de l'Horloge ★★ CLOCK TOWER Built atop Gallo Roman fortifications, this 15th-century tower is a sight to behold thanks to its elegant turrets and **Astronomical Clock,** whose mechanism has been in use since 1483 and which shows the time and moon phases. The Tourist Office runs occasional guided visits, but you'll more than likely have to admire it yourself from the outside. And so take note of the clock's hands: The first is a solar hand (taking 24 hr. to go around); the second is a lunar hand. The only time the hands should align is at noon when there's a new moon and at midnight during a full moon.

pl. de l'Hôtel de Ville.

Where to Stay

Hôtel Le Maxime Auxerre ★★ This former salt storehouse on the banks of the River Yonne is our favorite hotel in town. The style is classic and elegant, mixing typical Louis XV-style furniture with modern drapes and carpets, from the public areas to the rooms; book one at the front for a view of the water. Some rooms have riverside balconies! Though it doesn't have a restaurant, plenty of eating places are nearby. Relax with a local tipple in the bar or book an in-room massage.

2 quai de la Marine. hotel-lemaxime.com. ℭ **03-86-52-14-19.** 26 units. 109€–160€ double; 145€–275€ suite. Breakfast 15€. Parking 13.50€. **Amenities:** Bar; in-room massage; laundry service; room service, free Wi-Fi.

Garden of Eden window at the Cathédrale St-Etienne.

The Originals Hôtel Normandie-Auxerre ★★   On the northern edge of town (a 5-min. walk from restaurants and the historic center), this 19th-century town house, is a good budget option, with bright and cheerful, individually decorated rooms; many with big floral prints. After a day's sightseeing, wind down in the fitness room and sauna (7€), or sip a kir with wine from a local producer in the bar. Guests also have access to free bikes.

41 boulevard Vauban. hotelnormandie.fr. 🕿 **03-86-52-57-80.** 17 units. 93€–124€ double; 144€–164€ family rooms. Breakfast 12€. Parking 8€ (including 2 Tesla charging stands). Closed Feb. **Amenities:** Restaurant; loaner bikes; free Wi-Fi.

Where to Eat

Le Noyo ★★★ MODERN BURGUNDIAN   About a 10-minute walk from the historic center, this modern little spot is the place for beautifully presented Burgundian dishes, embellished with unusual spices. This might mean local hake prepared with Spanish herbs, or curry-infused veal medallions, with shitake mushrooms and sage cream. You'll want to loosen that belt for desert: vacherin (nougat ice cream) with whipped cream and orange flower, perhaps? Or if it's on the menu, try the Cazette tart drizzled in hazelnut nectar (*Cazette* is the term for coarsely cut, roasted Burgundian hazelnuts—a real local delicacy not generally found outside the region). Delish!

26 rue du 24 Août. le-noyo-auxerre.eatbu.com. ℂ **09-87-13-26-75.** Fixed-price lunch 27€ and dinner 42€–69€. Sun–Mon and Thurs–Fri noon–1:45pm and 7–9pm; Tues noon–1:45pm; Sat 7–9pm.

Le Saint-Pèlerin ★★ BURGUNDIAN   It's well worth making a pilgrimage to "The Holy Pilgrim" for good-quality, good-value Burgundian food. The centerpiece is a wood-fired grill, where pretty much everything is cooked. The stars here are the steaks and st-jacques scallops, grilled to perfection and served with one of the house potato dishes (like creamy mash served in its skin). The cheese board is laden with regional favorites like Époisses and all dishes are homemade, including the bread and ice cream. In summer there's an outside terrace in the narrow street, a block away from the river.

56 rue Saint-Pèlerin. le-saint-pelerin-restaurant.eatbu.com. ℂ **03-86-52-77-05.** Main courses 14€–26€; fixed-price menu 30.80€. Tues–Sat noon–1:30pm and 7:15–9:30pm. Closed 1 week in May and 2 weeks at Christmas and New Year.

Where to Stay & Eat Nearby

La Côte Saint Jacques ★★★ BURGUNDIAN   The main reason to come here is for the Michelin-two-star cuisine of Jean-Michel Lorain. Each recipe is a work of art. Some have become classics: Bresse chicken steamed in champagne vapor, blood sausage with what may be the best mashed potato you've ever tasted, and rose ice cream with crystalized rose petals.

DAY TRIP TO guédelon ★★

About a 45-minute drive southwest of Auxerre on the D965 then D955 (48km/29 miles), in a disused quarry deep in the countryside, about 40 master craftsmen are building a medieval château using 13th-century tools, materials and techniques. Started in 1997, the team work closely with archaeologists and historians. Visitors to **Guédelon** (www.guedelon.com; ℂ **03-86-45-66-66;** 14€ adults, 13€ children ages 14–17, 11€ children ages 5–13, children 4 and under free; opening times vary according to the season, which runs Apr to early Nov, so please check the website) can watch the craftsmen at work in their traditional outfits and are encouraged to ask questions; you can even apply to join a 5-day working holiday to learn masonry and carpentry if you speak French. Kids can partake in hour-long stone-masonry workshops. Along with the castle-in-progress, also on site is the village where the workers and their animals live, and a working flour mill. Guided tours in English take place every day in summer. While in the area be sure to **visit St-Fargeau** (www.chateau-de-st-fargeau.com; ℂ **03-86-74-05-67),** the 17th-century Renaissance château that was the inspiration for the Guédelon castle.

When guests aren't eating they're enjoying the high life at the glamorous hotel on the banks of the River Yonne, a 30-minute drive north of Auxerre. That might mean time spent in the massive spa (spread over two floors with an indoor pool and Jacuzzi), a cooking class, a vineyard tour set up by the concierge, or just lazing in a massive, amenity-laden guest room, perhaps in the outdoor jetted tub that some rooms have on their balcony. On a budget? In a stately building linked to the main building by an underground tunnel and under the same ownership (though not affiliated with Relais & Chateaux as the main building of La Côte Saint Jacques is), you'll find 10 extra, and very nice, bedrooms that are often 100€ cheaper per night.

14 Faubourg de Paris (N6), Joigny (30km/19 miles NW of Auxerre on the D606). www.cotesaintjacques.com. © **03-86-62-09-70.** 32 units. 250€–690€. Breakfast 34€. Free parking. Main courses 95€–118€. Fixed-price lunch (from Wed–Sat) 99€ and 118€; dinner 205€–272€. Restaurant Wed 7:30–9:45pm, Thurs–Sun 12:15–2pm and 7:30–9:45pm. Hotel and restaurant closed Mon–Tues. **Amenities:** Restaurant; fitness room; indoor pool; kids' playroom; babysitting; cooking classes; wine tasting; sauna; shop; spa; free Wi-Fi.

VÉZELAY ★★

217km (135 miles) SE of Paris; 52km (32 miles) S of Auxerre

Vézelay, a living museum of French antiquity, stands frozen in time. For many, the town is the high point of a trip through Burgundy. During the 12th century, it was one of the great pilgrimage sites of the Christian world as it contained the alleged tomb of St. Mary Magdalene, that "beloved and pardoned sinner."

Today the medieval charm of Vézelay is widely known throughout France, and visitors virtually overrun the town in summer. The hordes are especially thick on July 22, the official day of homage to La Madeleine.

Essentials

ARRIVING If you're **driving** from Paris, take A6 south to Auxerre, then continue south along N6/D606 to Givry and then D951 to Vézelay. Eleven **trains** a day travel from Paris Gare de Bercy to Sermizelles, taking 2 hours, 30 minutes. For train information, visit www.sncf-connect.com or call © **36-35.** You'll need to take a taxi or the shuttle bus into town (details on tourist office website).

Alternatively, you might like to arrive on foot or by mountain bike. An 84-km (52-mile) signposted route (GR213 A) links Vézelay with the UNESCO-listed **Fontenay Abbey** (www.abbayedefontenay.com; © **03-80-92-15-00**), the world's oldest-preserved Cistercian site in Montbard.

VISITOR INFORMATION The **Office de Tourisme** is at 8 rue St-Etienne (destinationgrandvezelay.com; © **03-86-33-23-69**).

Exploring Vézelay

On a hill surrounded by countryside, Vézelay is one of France's most spiritual places as its basilica (see below) is said to house the remains of Mary Magdalene; both it and the hill are UNESCO World Heritage Sites. The town, which is known for its sculptured doorways, mullioned windows, and corbelled staircases, began as an abbey founded in 858 by Girart de Roussillon, Comté de Bourgogne. It's also classed as one of France's most beautiful villages.

On March 31, 1146, St. Bernard preached the Second Crusade here; in 1190, the town was the rendezvous point for the Third Crusade, drawing such personages as Richard the Lion-hearted and King Philippe-Auguste of France. Later, St. Louis IX came here several times on pilgrimages.

Park outside the town hall and walk through the medieval streets lined with 15th-, 16th-, and 18th-century houses and flower-filled gardens. Download a free guided tour to your smartphone from www.guidigo.com

Basilique Ste-Madeleine.

to help you better appreciate what you're seeing. **Musée Zervos** at 14 rue St-Etienne (vezelay.fr/site/le-musee-zervos; © **03-86-32-39-26;** admission 5€, free for ages 25 and under; July–Aug daily 10am–6pm, closed Tues rest of year and mid-Nov to mid-Mar), is worth a look for its fine collection of modern art, including works by Picasso.

On rue St-Etienne and rue St-Pierre are an assortment of stores selling religious books and statuary which are fascinating to browse, even if you're not a believer. For a bottle or two of Vézelay wine go to **Cave Henry de Vézelay,** 4 route de Nanchèvres, St-Père-sous-Vézelay (www. henrydevezelay.com; © **03-86-33-29-62**); they also rent electric bikes, and do winery tours and tastings (for 60€). **Brasserie de Vézelay,** on rue du Gravier (www.brasseriedevezelay.com; © **03-86-34-98-38**), about 2km (1½ miles) east of the town, makes excellent organic and gluten-free beer, and offers guided brewery tours.

Basilique Ste-Madeleine ★★★ CHURCH   Visible for miles around due to its hilltop location, the basilica was founded in the 9th century and then restored by architect Viollet-le-Duc in the 19th century, who famously also renovated Notre Dame de Paris. This Romanesque jewel is at its most atmospheric when the monks sing during the daily services (see website for details). To get the most out of your visit it's advisable to go on a guided tour led by one of the brothers. In the crypt are the supposed remains of Mary Magdalene, which attract pilgrims from around the world; many are en route to Santiago de Compostela. Most of them stay in one of the basilica's three guest houses (https://hotellerie-vezelay.fr; 17€ per person), and you could too (people of all faiths are accepted).
pl. de la Basilique. www.basiliquedevezelay.org. © **03-86-33-39-50.** Free admission; tours 6.20€ (daily 2:30pm summer; Sun only the rest of the year). Daily 7am–8pm.

Where to Stay

Hotel de la Poste et du Lion d'Or ★★   On the main square at the bottom of the hill, this former coaching inn turned hotel is our favorite in Vézelay. Rooms are calm and spacious with traditional wooden furniture; some overlook the village, while others have a view of the Morvan countryside. The onsite, and very gourmet restaurant, *L'Éternel,* serves creative Burgundian/French dishes (fixed-price menus 28€–48€) in a chic, but simple dining room. The light and airy bar, with its summer terrace, is the perfect spot to sample the local wines.
pl. du Champ de Foire. www.hplv-vezelay.com. © **03-73-53-03-20.** 39 units. 120€–248€ double; family rooms 208€–283€. Breakfast 20€. Parking nearby. Closed Jan–Feb. **Amenities:** Restaurant; bar; garden; babysitting; free Wi-Fi.

Where to Eat

A La Fortune du Pot ★★ BURGUNDIAN/FRENCH   Don't let the name "Pot Luck" turn you off. You can be sure of good-value Burgundian cooking in this old village house at the bottom of the hill: like *boeuf bourguignon,* slow-cooked lamb shank with beans and eggs poached in red wine. Everything is homemade, even the organic bread. We particularly like the *oeufs en meurette* (bacon stewed in red Burgundy wine served with a poached egg). The wine list is small but perfectly formed of regional producers. The ambiance is good too, whether in the rustic dining room or the plant-filled terrace.

6 pl. du Champ de Foire. ☏ **03-86-33-32-56.** Main courses 24€–28€. Thurs–Mon noon–2pm and 7–9pm.

AVALLON

214km (133 miles) SE of Paris; 52km (32 miles) SE of Auxerre; 96km (60 miles) NW of Dijon

This fortified town sits behind ancient ramparts, upon which you can stroll. A medieval atmosphere permeates Avallon, where you'll find many 15th- and 16th-century houses. At the town gate on Grande Rue Aristide-Briand is a 1460 clock tower. The Romanesque **Collégiale St-Lazare** dates from the 12th century and has eye-candy doorways, an artfully lit interior, and impressive woodwork. The church, open daily from 8am to 7pm, is said to have received the head of St. Lazarus in A.D. 1000, thus turning it into a pilgrimage site. Visit if you can on Saturday for the local produce market in place Général de Gaulle—it attracts foodies from miles around. While you're there, stock up on artisan tea, coffee, and hot chocolate from **Dame Jeanne,** 59 Grande Rue Aristide Briand (☏ **03-86-34-58-71**), which also has a charming tearoom.

Essentials

ARRIVING   If you're **driving,** travel south from Paris along A6 past Auxerre to Avallon. **Trains** arrive daily from Paris Gare de Bercy every 2 hours (trip time: almost 3 hr.). For train information, visit www.sncf-connect.com or call ☏ **36-35. Bus** service 49 from Dijon takes 2 hours and costs 1.50€ one-way; purchase tickets on the bus.

VISITOR INFORMATION   The **Office de Tourisme** is at 6 rue Bocquillot (www.avallon-morvan.com; ☏ **03-86-34-14-19**).

Where to Stay

Château de Vault de Lugny ★★★   This fairytale château is the place to stay if you want to feel like a king or queen for a few days. In fact, there is even a suite called "Le Roy," which was set aside for the kings of

France, complete with monumental fireplace, four-poster bed, double bath tub, and Gothic chairs; the other rooms are a bit more sedate and two are in a cottage. The grounds offer plenty to do, from exploring the parkland to taking a dip in the indoor pool, located in the vaulted cellar, or booking a wine tasting. The restaurant, which marries French cuisine with Mauritian influences (the chef was born in Mauritius) and has had a Michelin star since 2019, is housed in the 17th-century former kitchen. And, of course, the wine list is composed of the best vintages from the region.

11 rue du Château, Vault-de-Lugny (6km/4 miles west of Avallon on the D606, then D128). www.lugny.fr. © **03-86-34-07-86.** 15 units. 298€–570€ double. Breakfast 29€–36€. Free parking. Closed mid-Nov to Apr. **Amenities:** Babysitting; bar; butler; indoor pool; mountain bikes; restaurant; room service; tennis court; valet parking; free Wi-Fi.

Moulin des Ruats ★★ In a wooded valley at the gates of the Morvan Regional Natural Park, this 18th-century water mill is now a cozy hotel. The rooms, some of which have balconies overlooking either the garden or the river, are individually decorated in either contemporary or traditional style with the odd antique. The well-regarded restaurant, overlooking the forest and river, celebrates the local *terroir;* meals can be enjoyed outside in summer. Massage treatments, wine tastings and half board are also available. This is the perfect spot for a relaxing break.

23, rue des Isles Labaumes. (4km/3 miles west of Avallon on the D427). www.moulin desruats.com. © **03-86-34-97-00.** 25 units. 70€–145€ double; 250€ suite. Breakfast 17€. Free parking. Closed mid-Nov to mid-Feb. **Amenities:** Restaurant; bar; lounge; free Wi-Fi.

Where to Eat

Le Cordois Autrement ★★ MODERN BURGUNDIAN Snuggled alongside Avallon's 12th-century church, this lovely bistro has been in the same family since 1910–not that you can tell from the décor, which is resolutely modern, in slick tones of blue and yellow. The menu mixes traditional dishes with a few international ingredients—think pea risotto with mirin-infused butter, and fish of the day with saté and lime. Some classics can't be meddled with, and that's the case for the veal kidneys, served with carrot *mousseline* (purée) and cherry sauce. For dessert, the star of the show is the gooey chocolate cake.

15 rue Boquillot. http://lescordois.fr. © **03-86-33-11-79.** Main courses 16.50€–26€; Thurs–Mon noon–2pm and 7–9pm.

SAULIEU

250km (155 miles) SE of Paris; 76km (47 miles) NW of Beaune

It's the food of Saulieu that puts this town on the international map. Saulieu (pop. 2,300) has enjoyed a reputation for cooking since the 17th century and is one of France's *Sites Remarquables du Goût* for its **Fête du Charolais** (festival of Charolais cows) in August; a food festival, **Les Journées Gourmandes** (journeesgourmandessaulieu.com), also takes place here at the end of May. If you're in town on Saturday morning, take a stroll around the market then have a drink in the **Café Parisien,** 4 rue du Marché (www.cafeparisien.net), the oldest cafe in Burgundy (1832) and a historic monument.

The main sight is the 12th-century **Basilique St-Andoche,** pl. Docteur Roclore (saulieu.fr/saint-andoche-basilica), which has some interesting decorated capitals. Next door, in the **Musée François-Pompon** (saulieu. fr/musee-francois-pompon; ✆ **03-80-64-19-51;** 3€ adults, free for children 12 and under; Apr–Sept Mon 10am–12:30pm, Wed–Sat 10am–12:30pm and 2–6pm, Sun 10:30am–noon and 2:30–5pm; Oct–Dec and Mar Mon 10am–12:30pm, Wed–Sat 10am–12:30pm and 2–5:30pm, Sun 10:30am–noon and 2:30–5pm, closed Jan–Feb), you can see works by François Pompon (d. 1933), the well-known sculptor of animals; his large statue of a bull stands on a plaza off the N6 at the entrance to town. Also in the museum are archaeological remnants from the Gallo-Roman era, sacred medieval art, and a room dedicated to France's great chefs including Bernard Loiseau (see "Where to Stay & Eat," below).

Essentials

ARRIVING   If you're **driving,** head along A6 from Paris or Lyon, then take exit 22 (Avallon) to the D606 then the D906. The **train** station is northeast of the town center. Passengers coming from Paris take the TER from Paris Bercy or the TGV from Gare de Lyon, getting off in Montbard, 48km (30 miles) to the north. There are about eleven trains a day to Montbard and the journey takes about 1 hour (from 37€ one-way). From Montbard, a series of **buses** timed to the arrival of the trains carry passengers on to Saulieu (about 1 hr.) for a one-way fare of 1.50€. For bus information, contact **Mobigo** (viamobigo.fr); for rail information, visit www. sncf-connect.com or call ✆ **36-35**).

VISITOR INFORMATION   The **Office de Tourisme** is at 24 rue d'Argentine (tourisme.saulieu-morvan.fr; ✆ **03-80-64-00-21**).

Where to Stay & Eat

La Tour d'Auxois ★★   Opposite and owned by Le Relais Bernard Loiseau (see below), this handsome hotel in a 17th-century convent is a good option for those who want to experience Saulieu's foodie delights without breaking the bank. Rooms are comfortable, traditionally furnished and rustic, suites have wooden beams. As you can imagine, staying here gives you easy access to the Relais and its gastronomic delights, though you many want to opt for lower-priced spa bistro, **Loiseau des**

Sens, where you can tuck into treats like pork chops and lentils, and zucchini risotto for about 25€, and a copious lunch menu (from 28€–48€). Thankfully, the outdoor pool is inviting enough to help you work off some calories. Then you can re-tox with some wine in the vaulted-cellar bar.

2 rue d'Argentine. bernard-loiseau.com/fr/tourdauxois.html. ℰ **03-80-64-36-19.** 29 units. 110€–140€ double. Breakfast 15€. Free parking. Closed mid-Dec to mid-Feb. **Amenities:** Bar; lounge; outdoor pool; free Wi-Fi.

Le Relais Bernard Loiseau ★★★ This chichi hotel (named after the late chef who created it and part of a gastronomic empire with restaurants in Beaune, Dijon, and Besançon) is home to one of France's greatest restaurants, La Côte d'Or. Today, its Michelin-two-star cuisine is overseen by Louis-Philippe Vigilant, who inherited the reigns from Patrick Bertron, Loiseau's previous side-kick, and the restaurant's chef for over 40 years. Vigilant's cooking showcases the finest products from Brittany (Bertron's birthplace) and Burgundy. Wine connoisseurs can choose from 900 top labels. The decor throughout is "rustic luxury," with wooden beams and Burgundy-tile floors. The standard or "comfort" rooms are spacious and good value and even have their own balconies. There's an award-winning multi-sensory, hi-tech spa with a bistro showcasing local market cuisine. Children are well catered for: They have their own games room and gourmet kids' menu.

2 rue Argentine. www.bernard-loiseau.com. ℰ **03-80-90-53-53.** 34 units. 290€–385€ double; 435€–675€ suite. Breakfast 32€. Free parking. Fixed-priced lunch 95€ and dinner 210€–350€. Check website for closing times and dates. **Amenities:** Restaurant; bar; exercise room; indoor and outdoor pools; kids' playroom; pétanque; room service; sauna; shop; spa; free Wi-Fi.

AUTUN ★★

293km (182 miles) SE of Paris; 85km (53 miles) SW of Dijon; 48km (30 miles) W of Beaune; 60km (37 miles) SE of Auxerre

Autun is one of the oldest towns in France. Founded by the Romans, it was called Augustodunum: "the other Rome." Some relics still stand, including a section of its ramparts, which date from 1 B.C. Also here are the remains of the largest theater in Gaul, the Théâtre Romain (free admission). It was nearly 150m (492 ft.) in diameter and could hold some 20,000 people. In July and August, it hosts a magnificent *son et lumière* with a 1,000-strong cast recounting the turbulent relationship between the Gauls and the Romans.

Autun is a thriving provincial town of 12,800, but because it's off the beaten track, the hordes go elsewhere. Still, it has its historical associations—Napoleon Bonaparte studied here in 1779 at the military academy (today, the Lycée Bonaparte). Don't miss the Passage Balthus, a 19th-century neo-Renaissance arcade with its original features.

Essentials

ARRIVING If you're **driving,** take A6 south until reaching A38, then turn onto D981 towards Autun. Rail links to Autun are awkward. Six high-speed TGV **trains** a day from Paris's Gare de Lyon run to Le Creusot-Montceau, 40km (25 miles) south of Autun taking under 1.5 hours. From there, take a 40-minute bus connection to Autun. In Autun, **buses** (1.50€ one-way) arrive at a parking lot by the railway station on avenue de la République. For bus information, visit viamobigo.fr. For railway information, visit www.sncf-connect.com or call ☏ **36-35.**

VISITOR INFORMATION The **Office de Tourisme** is at 13 rue Général Demetz (www.autun-tourisme.com; ☏ **03-85-86-80-38**).

Exploring Autun

Autun was an important Roman link on the road from Lyon to Boulogne. A legacy of that period is the 17m (56-ft.) high **Porte d'Arroux,** once the city's northern gate, which has two archways now used for cars and smaller ones used for pedestrians. Also exceptional is the **Porte St-André (St. Andrew's Gate),** northwest of the Roman theater. Rising 20m (66 ft.), it has four doorways and is surmounted by a gallery of 10 arcades.

Cathédrale St-Lazare ★★★ CATHEDRAL   Built in the 12th century to house the relics of Lazarus (they turned out to be the remains of the bishop of Aix and not the one that rose from the dead, as was originally believed), this cathedral is one of France's finest examples of Romanesque architecture and was inspired by the famous Cluny Abbey. The steeple, however, dates from the 1460s. Its main attractions are the carving of the Last Judgment on the west tympanum, and the capitals, whose carvings depict the three Magi, the flight to Egypt, and the suicide of Judas (among others). It is fortunate that they all survived as the canons here in the 18th century covered them with plaster, thinking them ugly. At the entrance to the sacristy is *The Martyrdom of Saint Symphorian,* by Dominique Ingres. Opposite the cathedral is the **Espace Gislebertus** (free admission; daily Apr–Sept 10am–1pm and 2–6pm), an information center on the town's heritage, where you can watch a 15-minute film, *Revelation,* which explores the cathedral's *Last Judgment* tympanum in high-definition 3D.
pl. St-Louis. Free admission. Daily 9am–6pm.

Musée Rolin ★★ MUSEUM   Housed in the 15th-century birthplace of Nicolas Rolin, founder of the **Hospices de Beaune** (p. 442), this museum has a rich collection of artefacts from the Gallo-Roman era to the Middle Ages, as well as French and European paintings from the 17th to the 20th centuries. Highlights include mosaics from ancient Augustodunum; the

15th-century polychrome *Autun virgin* and paintings by Maurice Denis and Joan Miró. The building is equally as impressive as the collection.

3 rue des Bancs. museerolin.fr. ✆ **03-85-52-09-76.** Admission 6.50€ adults (1€ more during temporary exhibitions); 4.50€ students and children. Feb–Mar and mid-Oct to Nov daily 10am–noon and 2–6pm; Apr–Sept 2–6pm. Closed May 1, Nov 1 and 11, and Dec–Jan.

Where to Stay & Eat

La Tête Noire ★★   Decorated in warm tones throughout, this three-star family-run hotel offers the best value stay in Autun. From some bedrooms you can see the cathedral and from others the surrounding countryside; all have a shower or bath, and some have air conditioning. The focus of the menu, naturally, is the dishes and produce of Burgundy: Expect delicious fare like Charolais steak in pepper sauce, catch of the day (fish) in langoustine sauce and pork sauerkraut.

3 rue de l'Arquebuse. hoteltetenoire.fr. ✆ **03-85-86-59-99.** 31 units. 88€–120€ double; from 100€ family room. Breakfast 12€. Free parking nearby. Fixed-price menus 22.50€–56€. **Amenities:** Restaurant; free Wi-Fi.

BEAUNE ★★★

316km (196 miles) SE of Paris; 39km (24 miles) SW of Dijon

Beaune is the perfect base for exploring the **Côte d'Or** wine region that stretches to the north and south of the city. Burgundy's most influential wine merchants are all based here: Louis Jadot, Joseph Drouhin, and Bouchard Père et Fils, to name but a few. Beaune was a Gallic sanctuary, then a Roman town and some of its ramparts are still intact; you can even walk on them. Until the 14th century, Beaune was the residence of the ducs de Bourgogne. When the last duke, Charles the Bold, died in 1477, Louis XI annexed the town. The main sight is the **Hôtel-Dieu des Hospices Civils de Beaune** (p. 442), also known as the Hospices de Beaune. The Swiss-born Chevrolet brothers, who moved to the US and created one of the world's best-known car brands, were brought up here.

Essentials

ARRIVING   If you're **driving,** note that Beaune is a few miles from the junction of three highways—the A6, A31, and A36. Beaune has good railway connections with Dijon, Lyon, and Paris. From Paris's Gare de Lyon are several TGV **trains** per day (trip time: just over 2 hr.), most via a change in Dijon. For train information and schedules, visit www.sncf-connect.com or call ✆ **36-35.**

VISITOR INFORMATION   The **Office de Tourisme** is at 6 bd. Perpreuil (www.beaune-tourisme.fr; ✆ **03-80-26-21-30**).

wine touring **CÔTE D'OR–STYLE**

In 2015, Les Climats du vignoble de Bourgogne (Burgundy vineyards) became a UNESCO World Heritage Site, marking their importance. Beaune is the epicenter of Burgundian winemaking with many of the world's most coveted and expensive wine appellations within a 1-hour drive. To the north lies the **Côte de Nuits,** famed for its red Pinot Noir vineyards with legendary appellations such as **Romanée-Conti** and **Richebourg.** To the south lies **Côte de Beaune,** home to the great names of white chardonnay wines such as **Meursault** and **Chassagne-Montrachet.**

You may want to start your wine tour in Beaune with a visit to the **Maison des Climats** (at the tourist office; same hours; free admission; climats-bourgogne.com), a discovery center, to get an overview of the wine-producing area and find out why it got listed by UNESCO. Beaune is where many of Burgundy's *négociants* (wine merchants who process and bottle the produce of smaller winemakers and then sell under their own name) have their bases. As well as being able to simply turn up with no appointment, you'll often be able to taste a wider variety of appellations than at an individual vineyard. **Patriarche Père et Fils,** 5 to 7 rue Collège (www.patriarche.com; ✆ **03-80-24-53-78**), offers 1-hour visits to its fabulous 13th- to 14th-century vaulted tasting cellars where millions of bottles are held along 5km (3 miles) of underground cellars; it's open daily from 9:30 to 11:15am and 2 to 5:15pm; admission is 20€. **Bouchard Père et Fils,** 15 rue du Château (www.bouchard-pereetfils.com;

✆ **03-80-24-80-45**), has cellars in the 15th-century Castle of Beaune, a former royal fortress. A guided tour in English and tasting is available by reservation and costs 119€ or 239€ for the tour and the tasting of 8 premium wines (reservations required). Just opposite the celebrated Hôtel-Dieu, the **Marché aux Vins** (www.marcheauxvins.com; ✆ **03-80-25-08-20**) is housed in a former Cordeliers church. With over 100 hectares (247 acres) of vineyards, this wine *négociant* offers a wide range of appellations to taste. Tastings of five wines cost 25€ and seven wines cost 59€. It's open daily with tours leaving between 10 and 11am, and 2 to 5pm. On the northern outskirts of town on the D18, **Maison Louis Jadot** (www.louisjadot.com; ✆ **03-80-26-31-98;** reservations required) is open for a tasting and a visit to its modern cellars Monday to Friday from 3 to 7pm and Saturday from 11:30am to 5:30pm, and costs 20€.

If you fancy visiting vineyards outside Beaune, head south along D974 to

Getting Around

BY TAXI The train station is a 15-minute walk from the town center so you might want to get a taxi to your accommodation. Try **Taxi Me'Lys** (taxi-melys.fr; ✆ **06-72-50-05-00**).

BY BIKE The best way to see this vine-planted land is by bike. Near Beaune train station, **Bourgogne Randonnées,** 7 av. du 8 septembre (www.bourgogne-randonnees.fr; ✆ **03-80-22-06-03**), rents bikes for 19€ per day (39€ per day for electric bikes).

the **Château de Pommard,** 15 rue Marey Monge (www.chateaude pommard.com; ℰ **03-80-22-07-99**), the largest privately owned estate in the Côte d'Or. Built for Messire Vivant de Micault, equerry and secretary of Louis XVI in 1726, this castle was bought in 2014 by the Carabello-Baum family from San Francisco. You can pre-book one of several "experiences," from the 45-minute introduction to Burgundy's *climats* and their wine (20€) to an hour-long private tasting of six wines (95€). Next, you can head farther along the D974 to the **Château de Meursault** (www.meursault.com; ℰ **03-80-26-22-75**). This domaine owns over 60 hect-ares (148 acres) of vineyards covering appellations such as Aloxe Corton, Pommard, Puligny-Montrachet, and, of course, Meursault. You should pre-book for a visit to the cellars of this fabulous 19th-century castle, followed by a tast-ing of eight wines in the art gallery for 49€ (55€ if you just turn up). It is open daily 10am to noon and 2 to 6pm (no lunchtime closure May–Sept). For food and wine pairing opt for their *En Vigne* offer (115€), which takes place at Loiseau des Vignes back in Beaune (p. 445), another Bernard Loiseau insti-tution. Or if you'd rather stop for a wine-tasting lunch along the way, try **La Table**

d'Olivier Leflaive, 10 pl. du Monument in Puligny-Montrachet (hotel.olivier-leflaive.com/le-bistro-d-olivier; ℰ **03-80-21-95-27**), which costs 35€ and 90€ on top of the fixed-price menu (40€), depending on the accompanying wines. They also will tour you through their vineyard.

For those who'd like to visit inde-pendent, family winegrowers but don't know where to start, several excellent companies offer organized tours: **Burgundy by Request** (burgundyby request.com; ℰ **06-85-65-83-83**), run by English expat Tracy Thurling, offers enlightening personalized itineraries around five Burgundian wine-growing areas. Cristina Otel of **Burgundy Wine School** (burgundywineschool.com; contact@burgundyschool.com) is a highly qualified winemaker whose courses and tours offer an in-depth exploration of the local AOCs. A good introduction to grape varieties is also offered by **Sensation Vin,** 2A rue Paul Bouchard in Beaune (www.sensation-vin. com; ℰ **03-80-22-17-57**), during its "Essential Burgundy" session, Monday to Friday at 11am, that lasts 1 hour, 30 minutes and costs 50€. Or read the reviews, and book your own tastings, on the helpful website **Rue De Vignerons** (www.ruedesvignerons.com).

Exploring Beaune

Known as "the daughter of Cluny," the **Collégiale Notre-Dame,** pl. du Général Leclerc (paroisse-beaune.org/la-basilique-notre-dame), is a Romanesque basilica dating from 1120. Some remarkable 15th-century tapestries illustrating scenes from the life of the Virgin Mary are on dis-play in the sanctuary and you can view them from April to mid-November Sunday to Friday 2:30 to 5:30pm.

Côte d'Or vineyards.

The best **shopping** streets are rue de Lorraine, rue d'Alsace, rue Maufoux, and place de la Madeleine. For smaller boutiques, stroll down the pedestrian rue Carnot and rue Monge. You'll encounter plenty of designer labels, vintners, and antiques dealers. Just beyond the historic center, **Moutarderie Edmond Fallot,** at 31 rue Bretonnière (fallot.com; ✆ **03-80-22-10-10**), claims to be the last family-owned mustard mill in Burgundy. Open since 1840, it offers factory tours and tastings, and, of course, has a shop.

Every Saturday morning (7am–1pm), the streets around place de la Halle and place de Fleury are chock-a-block with Burgundy's liveliest market. The most serious meat and cheese producers have their stalls in Les Halles. Consider learning how to cook with all this mouth-watering produce with American expat chef Marjorie Taylor at her beautiful cooling school; **The Cook's Atelier** (www.thecooksatelier.com; ✆ **03-80-24-61-80**).

Hôtel-Dieu des Hospices Civils de Beaune ★★★ HISTORIC MONUMENT   Think "socialized medicine" is a 20th-century concept? Think again! This hospital was founded back in 1443 by Nicolas Rolin, chancellor to the Duke of Burgundy, and his wife, Guigone, for the express purpose of giving free care to indigent patients. Amazingly, it did so in this building all the way until the 1980s (the sick are now treated in a state-of-the-art building on the outskirts of town). Why Rolin and his wife undertook this monumental task, the downright weird medieval treatments that were dispensed here, and the stories of the nuns who selflessly nursed the sick, are told here in fascinating detail. Along with wall text, visitors are given excellent audio guides (they're part of the price of admission). The building also holds important works of art, including a The Last Judgment polyptych by Flemish artist Roger van der Weyden, and is known for its spectacular roof, crafted from polychromatic, geometrically patterned roof tiles.

Interestingly, the hospital is also famous for its excellent wines, produced by vineyards bequeathed to it by grateful patients over the years. Care continues to this day, supported by money earned from the hospital's annual wine auction, which takes place on the third weekend of November, the *Vente des Vins des Hospices de Beaune.*

Rue de l'Hôtel-Dieu. www.hospices-de-beaune.com. ℂ **03-80-24-45-00.** Admission 12€ adults, 8€ children ages 10–18, free for children 9 and under. Mid-Mar to mid-Nov daily 9am–7:30pm; mid-Nov to mid-Mar daily 9–11:30am and 2–5:30pm.

Musée des Beaux-Arts ★★ ART MUSEUM   This quaint museum has an eclectic collection of local history, with a rich Gallo-Roman section

and art from the 17th to 20th centuries, including pieces by Beaune-born Félix Ziem, such as *Les Flamants Roses* (Flamingoes), and lithographs by Picasso and Le Corbusier.

6 bd. Perpreuil (Porte Marie de Bourgogne). beaune.fr/culture-et-loisirs/musees/musee-des-beaux-arts. ℂ **03-80-24-56-92.** Admission 6€ adults, 4€ students and children 11–18, free for children 10 and under. June–Nov Wed–Mon 10am–1pm and 2–6pm.

Musée du Vin de Bourgogne ★ MUSEUM   To be honest, the most interesting aspects of this museum are the building itself, the former home (14th–18th c.) of the Dukes of Burgundy, and the collection of Aubusson tapestries depicting vine-yard scenes. Other than that, it's a

The famed polychromatic roofs of the Hôtel-Dieu in Beaune.

somewhat dry display of tools, bottles, presses, and wine-making life through the ages.

24 rue du Paradis. beaune.fr/culture-et-loisirs/musees/musee-du-vin-de-bourgogne. © **03-80-22-08-19.** Admission 6€ adults, 4€ students and children 11–18, free for children 10 and under. Apr–Nov Wed–Mon 10am–1pm and 2–6pm.

Where to Stay

If you'd prefer self-catering accommodation, check out **Coté Paradis,** which has two charming places to stay for up to six people (a hip duplex apartment and a modern holiday home; coteparadis.fr) from 400€ per night (min. 3 nights). Airbnb and VRBO also have a number of options, most of which are well located and in the 150€ a night range. Accommodation under 70€ per night is hard to find in Beaune, but the municipal four-star campsite, **Les Cent Vignes** (© **03-80-22-03-91**), open from Easter to October, has 116 pitches, hot showers, a tennis court, and a restaurant. Otherwise try the following:

Hôtel Le Cep ★★★ Le Cep takes its name from the roots of a vine, appropriate as it is created from several adjoining *hôtels particuliers* dating from the 16th century (Louis XIV stayed in one). The atmosphere here is of old-fashioned luxury with first-class service to match. The 32 suites, each individually designed in traditional French style and furnished with antiques, have Nespresso machines and a Night Cove (hightech lamps that emit special light frequencies), which helps guests to sleep and wake up naturally. Its spa, Marie de Bourgogne, has won international awards and the restaurant, Loiseau des Vignes (see "Where to Eat," below), is part of the famed Bernard Loiseau group.

27 rue Jean-Francois Maufoux. www.hotel-cep-beaune.com. © **03-80-22-35-48.** 65 units. 179€–600€ double. Breakfast 24€. Parking 24€. **Amenities:** Restaurant; bar; concierge; fitness room; spa; room service; free Wi-Fi.

Les Remparts ★★ Less than a 10-minute walk west of the train station, this hotel is one of the most characterful lodgings in town. The 17th-century mansion, backed up against the 5th-century ramparts, has two gorgeous inner courtyards where you can have your breakfast on warm days. Each of the rooms is individually decorated in simple, traditional style but fitted with all modern amenities; the one on the third-floor of the tower (no lift), under the rafters, is particularly charming. Original features, such as stone fireplaces and staircases, add to the bygone atmosphere. Book directly with the hotel and breakfast is free.

48 rue Thiers. www.hotel-remparts-beaune.com. © **03-80-24-94-94.** 22 units. 152€–352€ double. Breakfast 15€. Parking 15€. **Amenities:** Bar; laundry service; lounge; bike rental; babysitting; airport/train station transfers; wine tours and tastings; free Wi-Fi.

Where to Eat

La Buissonière ★★ FRENCH   This place, smack bang in the historic center, is a treat. Sit on a red banquette in the main dining room or in the picturesque inner courtyard, and the waiter will bring you a blackboard chalked up with the day's dishes: snail tart, pork in parmesan batter, beef in Cognac sauce, caramelized sweetbreads, not mention desserts like profiteroles, pineapple meringue and panna cotta—and it's all delicious! On some Saturday nights (check their Facebook page), the restaurant evolves into a lively bar where French-style street food—think mini *croque monsieurs* (cheese and ham toasties), burgers, and cordon bleus (chicken nuggets stuffed with ham and melty cheese)—are washed down with cocktails.

34 rue Maufoux. ✆ **09-50-73-21-75.** Main courses from 20€. Mon–Fri noon–1:30pm and 7–8:30pm (some Sat evenings).

Loiseau des Vignes ★★★ MODERN FRENCH   Part of Hôtel Le Cep (see "Where to Stay," above) and a satellite of the **Relais Bernard Loiseau** in Saulieu (p. 437), this wine-focused restaurant is one of our favorites in Burgundy. Sure, the food is superb, but it's all about the wine here. This was the first restaurant in Europe to serve wines solely by the glass (5€–45€). And what a choice: around 32 labels, mostly from the region, and some you won't find anywhere else. The two-course lunch menu is accessible at 28€ and features classic Burgundy dishes, designed by exciting young chef Alexandre Dutat. Come on a warm day and you'll be able to eat at a table in the gorgeous courtyard.

31 rue Maufoux. bernard-loiseau.com. ✆ **03-80-24-12-06.** Main courses 25€–34€; fixed-price lunch 28€–38€. Tues–Sat noon–2pm and 7–10pm. Closed Feb.

21 Boulevard ★★ BURGUNDIAN/FRENCH   This chic restaurant housed in a 15th-century wine cellar is the place to go if you're looking to make a night of it, as they also have an attached piano bar (Thurs–Sat) open until 2am. The menus are inspired by the seasons and naturally there's a "Menu Bourgignon" (34€) with the usual snails, *oeufs en meurette,* local cheeses, and a pudding made with *pain d'épices.* The wine list is superb, solely comprising Burgundy vintages, but also has a good selection of champagnes.

21 bd. St-Jacques. www.21boulevard.com. ✆ **03-80-21-00-21.** Main courses 24€–36€; fixed-price menus 34€–60€. Tues–Sat noon–2pm and 7–10:30pm.

Where to Stay & Eat Nearby

Hôtel Le Globe ★★   Surrounded by the vines, the wine-growing village of Meursault is a lovely spot for a break. In the heart of the village, this spanking new hotel in a grand former home offers a stylish and relaxing stay that won't break the bank. The vintage-chic rooms sport funky colors, from navy and yellow to purple and bright olive green. It sounds loud, but it works beautifully, with gold rimmed frames and mirrors, velvet headboards, and antique furniture adding a touch of class. The hotel restaurant is run by emerging chef Nicolas Marchant who serves wonderful, imaginative dishes like foie-gras with kombu seaweed and green apple, steamed lobster with seafood bisque and coriander, and chicken with girolles and crispy pasta—so eat in one day (fixed-price lunch 27€–32€ and dinner 55€–75€). Drink a Meursault wine and it may have come from the fields you can see from your bedroom window.

17 rue de Lattre de Tassigny, Meursault (9km/6 miles southwest of Beaune on the D973). hotel-globe.fr. ☏ **03-80-21-64-90.** 14 units. 115€–210€ double; from 185€–280€ suite. Breakfast 15€. Free parking. **Amenities:** Bar; reading room; room service; free Wi-Fi.

Maison Lameloise ★★★ BURGUNDIAN   Not only does it have three Michelin stars, but this gourmet eating place, housed in a coaching inn dating from the 15th century, was voted one of the world's best restaurants (in the top 40) by La Liste (www.laliste.com, which uses guidebooks, news publications, and online reviews to compile a "list" of top restaurants all over the world). Chef Eric Pras has worked in the kitchens of some of France's greatest chefs and since 2008 he's been creating exquisite dishes showcasing Burgundian produce: pigeon with plums and Burgundian beer, or Bresse chicken with Cazette (hazelnut power) and roasted chicken skin crumbs with lemon emulsion, for example. The 16 rooms are comfortably furnished but maybe not as luxurious as you'd expect, and a bit overpriced. Nonetheless, if you're a foodie, this place is one for the bucket list.

36 pl. d'Armes, Chagny (16km/10 miles southwest of Beaune on the D974). www.lameloise.fr. ☏ **03-85-87-65-65.** 16 units. 215€–380€ double. Breakfast 32€. Fixed-price lunch 105€ or dinner 205€–305€. Thurs–Mon noon–1:30pm and 7:30–9:30pm (summer lunch daily). Closed mid-Dec to mid-Jan.

MÂCON

397km (247 miles) SE of Paris; 127km (79 miles) S of Dijon; 87km (54 miles) S of Beaune.

On the banks of the River Saône, in the south of Burgundy, Mâcon is a workaday town whose historic center is a pleasant place to spend a day just strolling around the narrow streets and along the quayside. Founded by the Celts and developed by the Romans, Mâcon is famous for being the birthplace of Romantic poet and politician Alphonse de Lamartine (see "Exploring Mâcon," below). The town is particularly lively from mid-June until the end of August when the **Eté Frappé** festival takes place, featuring music concerts, open-air cinema, and children's entertainment. The surrounding area is famous for its Mâconnais and Beaujolais wines.

Essentials

ARRIVING   If you're **driving,** take A6 south past Beaune and onto Mâcon. Six direct TGV **trains** a day from Paris's Gare de Lyon run to Mâcon Loche TGV station (7km/4 miles outside Mâcon and connected to the center by shuttle bus Mon–Sat) taking 1 hour, 30 minutes. For railway information, visit www.sncf-connect.com or call ✆ **36-35.**

VISITOR INFORMATION   The **Office de Tourisme** is at 1 pl. Saint-Pierre (www.macon-tourism.com; ✆ **03-85-21-07-07**).

Exploring Mâcon

Mâcon has two churches worth a visit: the Neo-Roman Église Saint Pierre on place St-Pierre, the town's largest church, and 19th-century Cathédral Saint Vincent on Square de la Paix. The **Musée des Ursulines** at 5 rue de la Préfecture (macon.fr/vivre-et-bouger-a-macon/culture/musee-des-ursulines; ✆ **03-85-39-90-38;** 7€ adults, free for ages 26 and under; Tues–Sat 10am–12:30pm and 2–6pm, Sun 2–6pm), named after the 17th-century convent in which it is based, has archaeological finds from the area, exhibits dedicated to local life along with a space devoted to Lamartine's life and work, and, an exhibition of artworks tracing the evolution of paintings over the last 5 centuries. From May to September, you can take boat trips along the River Saône for an afternoon or a day (book at the tourist office). However, the most interesting sights are within a 30-minute drive of the town.

Where to Stay

Best Western Plus Hôtel d'Europe et d'Angleterre ★★   Dating from 1800, anyone who is anyone has stayed here over the years from Winston Churchill to Catherine Deneuve, and even the first giraffe to set foot on European soil (Zarafa, in 1827). Rooms are individually decorated in colors ranging from lemon to chic dove grey, complemented by bold floral wallpaper. Most overlook the courtyard, but we like the deluxe rooms, which have a river view (101€–169€). Breakfast features organic produce including award-winning jams, and the lobby bar has a good selection of local wines accompanied by tapas.

92–109 quai Jean Jaurès. www.hotel-europeangleterre-macon.com. ✆ **03-85-38-27-94.** 37 units. 90€–165€ double; 123€-229€ suite. Breakfast 10€–18€. Parking 12€. **Amenities:** Babysitting; bar; bikes; terrace; laundry service; packed lunches; room service; free Wi-Fi.

Where to Eat

Mâcon has a clutch of good restaurants, serving up quality French and Bourgignon cuisine. Notably **L'Ardoise,** 19 rue Franche (✆ **03-85-31-62-26;** Tues–Sat noon–1:30pm and 7–9:30pm), **Cassis,** 74 rue Joseph Dufour (www.cassisrestaurant-macon.fr; © **03-85-38-24-53;** Mon–Sat noon–1:30pm and 7:30–9pm), and **Ma Table en Ville,** 5 rue de Strasbourg (www.matableenville.fr; © **03-85-30-99-91;** Mon–Thurs noon–1:30pm and 7–9pm); all have lunch menus for less than 30€ with main courses between 18€ and 40€.

Restaurant Pierre ★★★ FRENCH   This Michelin-star restaurant is a top pick in the region. While Chef Christian Gaulin produces deftly executed French and Bourgignon dishes using seasonal produce, and his wife Isabelle takes charge in the rustic-chic dining room. Christian's twist on classic regional dishes such as Charolais beef tournedos with foie gras or pigeon cooked in two ways, is seen in his choice of imaginatively matched sauces and accompaniments. Leave room for the soufflé with glazed cherries. In summertime, nab a table on the terrace on the pedestrianized street. There's a well-priced lunch menu at 33€. Reservations required.

7-9 rue Dufour. www.restaurant-pierre.com. © **03-85-38-14-23.** Fixed-price menus 70€–135€. Wed–Sat noon–1:15pm and 7–8:30pm; Sun lunch only.

Day Trips from Mâcon

A fun way to explore the vineyards is on foot or by bike, which can be hired from the old train station (now a tourist office; www.velo-gare.com; © **03-85-21-07-14**) at Charnay-lès-Mâcon, a 10-minute drive from town on the D54. The former railway line is now a "green route." If driving, you might like to stop off at **Terres Secrètes** at 158 rue des Grandes Vignes in Prissé (www.terres-secretes.com; © **03-85-37-64-89**) to buy some wine and local produce.

Deep in Beaujolais country, the Hameau Duboeuf "wine village" created by well-known wine merchant Georges Duboeuf, is an interesting day out for the family. See p. 478 for more information. It's just 17km (11 miles) south of Mâcon on the D906.

Grand Site Solutré-Pouilly-Vergisson ★★★ NATURAL SITE Dominating the Pouilly-Fuissé vineyards, the Rock of Solutré and its environs, including the Rock of Vergisson, have been inhabited by man for 57,000 years. In 2013, the area received the label "Grand Site de France." Visitors can find out more about the site's history in the **Musée Départemental de Préhistoire,** at the base of the Rock of Solutré, before walking to the top for panoramic views (493m/1,617 ft.; takes about 30 min.). Be sure to arrive early for a car parking space in summer.

71960 Solutré-Pouilly (10km/6 miles west of Mâcon on the D54). https://rochede solutre.com. © **03-85-35-82-81.** Admission 5€ adults (audio guide included); free for children 18 and under. Museum: daily Apr–Sept 10am–6pm; Oct–Mar 10am–5pm. Closed mid-Dec to mid-Jan.

Where to Stay & Eat Nearby

Four generations of Blanc chefs have dominated the restaurant scene around Mâcon. The original Mère Blanc's Bresse chicken in a cream sauce with basmati rice is so legendary that this free-range chicken has become a Blanc trademark. The Blanc restaurant empire now extends from Lyon to its postcard-perfect hub in the village of Vonnas (www.georgesblanc.com).

Some of the gorgeous B&B accommodations in this area include **Domaine la Source des Fées** (www.lasourcedesfees.fr; ✆ 03-85-35-67-02) in Fuissé, where double rooms start at 178€; the magnificent **Château de Pierreclos** in the village of Pierreclos (www.chateaudepierreclos.com; ✆ **03-85-35-73-73**), which has rooms in both the castle and an outbuilding starting at 140€; and **Fleur de Vignes** (www.fleurdevignes.com; ✆ **03-85-35-67-41**), two sweet rooms (63€) in a wine producer's house in Loché. **Camping du Lac** (www.lac-cormoranche.com; ✆ **03-85-23-97-10**) is a four-star campsite next to a lake in Cormoranche-sur-Saône.

La Courtille de Solutré ★★   In an idyllic location in the middle of the Pouilly-Fuissé vineyards, beneath the Rock of Solutré, is this gourmet "restaurant with rooms." Contemporary and original features work well together in this old stone village inn. On the menu you'll find traditional French dishes often enhanced by Spanish flavors, such as mussels with chorizo and chestnut soup with Basque ham; and AOC Mâconnais (a hard, mild goats' cheese). The wine list has a good selection from the village and immediate area, including their own vineyard, Domaine du Chatelet in St-Amour. The six stylish rooms are each individually and tastefully decorated in whites and neutrals, with the odd antique; all but two have views over the vines.

71960 Solutré-Pouilly (10km/6 miles west of Mâcon on the D54). www.lacourtillede solutre.fr. ✆ **03-85-35-80-73.** 6 units. 90€–110€ double. Breakfast 12€. Free parking. Fixed-price lunch 25€–30€ or dinner 43.50€–59.50€. Restaurant closed Sun evening to Tues. **Amenities:** Bar; terrace; free Wi-Fi.

THE RHÔNE VALLEY

12

VALLEY

By Louise Simpson

T he Rhône Valley is the gateway connecting North and South via the popular road-trip freeway RN7— France's Route 66. Its historic roots date back to the Roman era when it served as the main trade route from the Mediterranean. Picture-perfect Beaujolais villages in the North curve towards France's third largest city, Lyon, the heartland of French gastronomy and UNESCO-classified heritage. South of Lyon, Route 86 follows the Rhône River past Roman remains in Vienne towards prehistoric cave paintings in the Ardèche and gothic architecture in Valence.

Punctuated by limestone hills and forests, the countryside brims with vineyards, chestnut orchards, lentil fields, and free-range poultry farms that bring fresh produce straight to the plates of the region's award-winning restaurants. Wine connoisseurs beat a path to prestigious Cru vineyards throughout the Rhône Valley from Côte-Rôtie and Hermitage in the Northern Rhône to Fleurie and Morgon in Beaujolais. Summer is the time for jazz festivals in Vienne and Lyon, for Segway tours around the Northern Rhône vineyards, and for canyoning in the Ardèche gorges.

LYON ★★★

431km (267 miles) SE of Paris; 311km (193 miles) N of Marseille

Lyon is the French gastronomic capital with a culinary spirit that pervades from world-class restaurants to modest *bouchons*. The forks of the rivers Saône and Rhône converge in this elegant city where Roman ruins meet UNESCO-classified medieval lanes, baroque squares, and contemporary icons such as the Musée des Confluences ethnology museum. Lyon is the perfect city break, as it's only 2 hours by train from Paris.

Essentials

ARRIVING   One of the easiest ways to reach Lyon is by train. From central London, you can take the Eurostar via Lille or Paris in under 6 hours. One-way fares from London St Pancras International start at 60€ in low season. One-way fares from Paris Gare de Lyon on the TGV start around 40€. The cheapest deals can be found online at www.thetrainline.com or at the SNCF website www.sncf.com. Make sure you book a train to the

PREVIOUS PAGE: An aerial, and angelic, view of Lyon from the top of Notre Dame de Fourviere.

451

Lyon Part-Dieu train station in central Lyon rather than **Lyon St-Exupéry** TGV station on the city outskirts as it will take another 30-minute train ride to get into the center. Depending upon where you're staying, there are connecting trains from Lyon Part-Dieu in the 3rd district to Lyon Perrache in the 2nd district (near place Bellecour). Lyon makes a good stopover en route to the Alps or the Riviera.

By **plane,** it's a 1-hour flight from Paris to Lyon-Saint Exupéry airport (www.lyonaeroports.com; ✆ **0426-007-007**), 25km (16 miles) east of the city. The 30-minute **Rhônexpress** tram link (www.rhonexpress.fr) from the airport runs every quarter of an hour to central Lyon (100m/328 ft. from TGV train station Lyon Part-Dieu) for 15.20€. **Taxis** cost 50€ to 55€ by day and 65€ to 70€ by night and take the same amount of time.

If you're **driving** from Paris, head southeast on A6 into Lyon. From Nice, head west on A8 toward Aix-en-Provence, continuing northwest toward Avignon on A7. Bypass the city and continue north along the same route into Lyon. From Grenoble or the French Alps, head northwest on A48 to A43, which will take you northwest into Lyon.

VISITOR INFORMATION   The only Lyon tourist office is on place Bellecour (www.visiterlyon.com; ✆ **04-72-77-69-69**).

Neighborhoods in Brief

Like Paris, Lyon is divided into *arrondissements* (districts). Of the nine in total, the main tourist areas are listed below.

VIEUX LYON, 5TH DISTRICT   The cheek-by-jowl cobbled lanes of the medieval town with its Renaissance *traboules* were awarded UNESCO status in 1998, helping this former slum transform into a fashionable area for artisans and antique dealers. Above the old town lies Fourvière Hill—home to Roman ruins and panoramic views towards the snowcapped Alps.

> ### Lyon City Tram
>
> Recalling the Croix-Rousse funicular that ran from 1862 to 1967, the Lyon City tram takes tourists on a 1-hour tour through La Croix Rousse district (10€ adults, 6€ children ages 4–11). Winding uphill through the narrow streets, tram-riders can enjoy views over the Gallo-Roman amphitheater and make stops at the silk workshop and *traboules*. Trams depart from 1, rue de la Martinière. For more information, visit www.lyoncitytour.fr.

PLACE BELLECOUR, 2ND DISTRICT   With its 18th-century buildings and enormous Ferris wheel, place Bellecour is Lyon's finest square. Further north, you'll find designer shops and one of France's oldest shopping arcades, **Passage de l'Argue** (p. 469). Spend an afternoon learning about Lyon's silk trade at the new **Musée des Soieries Brochier** (p. 459) or exploring science and anthropology at nearby **Musée des Confluences** (p. 461).

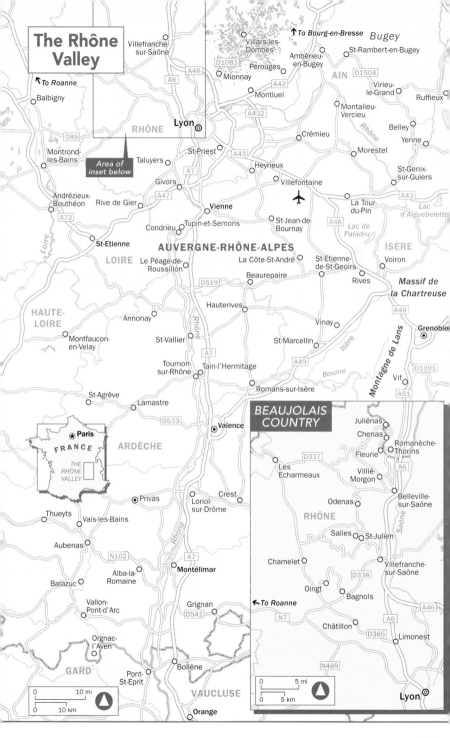

The Rhône Valley

To Roanne ←

Balbigny

Villefranche-sur-Saône

To Bourg-en-Bresse ↑   *Bugey*

Villars-les-Dombes

Ambérieu-en-Bugey   St-Rambert-en-Bugey

D1083   Pérouges   **AIN**   D1504

Mionnay   Virieu-le-Grand   Ruffieux

A46   A6   Montluel

A42   Montalieu-Vercieu

RHÔNE   A432   Belley

Lyon ◎   Yenne

D89   Crémieu

Montrond-les-Bains   St-Priest   Morestel

Area of inset below   Taluyers   A43   St-Genix-sur-Guiers

Givors   Heyrieux   A43

Andrézieux-Bouthéon   A7   Villefontaine   *Lac d'Aiguebelette*

Rive de Gier   ✈   La Tour-du-Pin

A72   Vienne   St-Jean-de-Bournay   A48   *Lac de Paladru*   **ISÈRE**

Condrieu   Tupin-et-Semons

St-Etienne   **AUVERGNE-RHÔNE-ALPES**   Voiron

LOIRE   Le Péage-de-Roussillon   La Côte-St-André   St-Etienne-de-St-Geoirs

D519   Beaurepaire   Rives   *Massif de la Chartreuse*

HAUTE-LOIRE   Hauterives   A48

Annonay   Vinay   **Grenoble** ◉

Montfaucon-en-Velay   St-Vallier   St-Marcellin

A7   A49

Tournon-sur-Rhône   Tain-l'Hermitage   *Bourne*   Vif   D1091

St-Agrève   Romans-sur-Isère   Montagne de Lans   A51

Lamastre   D533

◉ **Valence**

★ **Paris**

FRANCE

THE RHÔNE VALLEY

ARDÈCHE

Crest   Privas ◉   Loriol-sur-Drôme

Thueyts   Vais-les-Bains

Aubenas   N102

Alba-la-Romaine   A7

Balazuc   **Montélimar**

Vallon-Pont-d'Arc   Grignan   D541

Orgnac-l'Aven

GARD   Bollène

Pont-St-Esprit

VAUCLUSE

Orange

0 — 10 mi
0 — 10 km

BEAUJOLAIS COUNTRY

Juliénas   A6

Chénas   Romanèche-Thorins

Fleurie   A6

Les Echarmeaux   Villié-Morgon

D337   Belleville-sur-Saône

Odenas   *Saône*

RHÔNE

Salles   St-Julien

Chamelet   Villefranche-sur-Saône

D338

Oingt   Bagnols

To Roanne ←   N7   A46

Châtillon   D385   Limonest

A6

N489   **Lyon** ◎

0 — 5 mi
0 — 5 km

453

Place des Terreaux, Lyon.

PLACE DES TERREAUX, 1ST DISTRICT   This is the top neighborhood for *bouchons:* restaurants serving traditional Lyonnaise cuisine. It's also tops for culture vultures, what with important Matisses at the **Musée des Beaux-Arts** (p. 460), and the ancient amphitheater in Lyon's oldest park, the **Jardin des Plantes** (p. 460).

GETTING AROUND   A network of Métro lines, trams, and buses branches out to serve the city. A *plan de poche* (pocket map) is available at any office of **TCL** (www.tcl.fr; ✆ **04-26-10-12-12**), which handles all forms of mass transport. Tickets are valid on all forms of public transport, costing 2€ for the average ride or else 19€ for a *carnet* of 10 tickets. You can buy tickets from tram drivers or at machines at metro stations (the machines don't accept notes or some international credit cards, so it's best to use coins). Short-term visitors may want to purchase a 24-hour day pass for 6.50€, 12.50€ for a 48-hour pass or 17€ for a 72-hour pass. Travel is free for children under 4 years. Trams run from 5am to midnight with trams every 5 to 15 minutes, depending upon the line.

Renting and then parking a car is an expensive waste of time as Lyon has one of the most efficient city taxi services we've ever discovered: Call

Lyon

ATTRACTIONS
Amphithéâtre des Trois-Gaules 17
Basilique Notre-Dame Fourvière 3
Fresque des Lyonnais 15
Hôtel de Ville 19
L'Institut & Musée Lumière 32
Lugdunum Musée 2
Maison du Chamarier 6
Maison Thomassin 14
Musée de l'Imprimerie de Lyon 21
Musée des Confluences 30
Musée des Soieries Brochier 23
Musée des Tissus et
  des Arts-Décoratifs 28
Musée des Beaux-Arts 20
Musée d'Histoire de Lyon
  (Musée Gadagne) 13
Palais de Justice 7
Parc de la Tête d'Or 33
Primatiale St-Jean 5
Théâtres Romains 1

HOTELS
Artelit 11
Cour des Loges 12
Hôtel Bayard Bellecour 26
Hôtel Carlton 22
Hôtel des Célestins 25
Hôtel Pilo 16
InterContinental Lyon
  Hôtel Dieu 24
Le Royal Lyon 27
Mama Shelter 31
Villa Florentine 10

RESTAURANTS
Au 14 Février 9
Brasserie Georges 29
Bulle 4
Jérémy Galvan 8
L'Institut 27
Mère Brazier 18

455

Taxi Radio de Lyon (www.taxilyon.com) on ℂ 04-72-10-86-86, and you'll be surprised at the speed with which a taxi is winging its way to your door. That said, it's worth renting a car if you're planning on visiting the wine countries north and south of the city. You can rent cars at the train station Lyon Part Dieu from any of the usual the suspects. The best way to get around the narrow streets of the old town is by foot, while the easiest way to reach Fourvière Hill is by **Funicular Railway** (p. 458).

SPECIAL EVENTS Festivals take place practically every day, especially in summer. See the box **"Melody Maker"** (p. 459). For 4 days around December 8, the spectacular **Fête des Lumières** lights up Lyon's churches, monuments, and neighborhoods.

[FastFACTS] LYON

ATMs/Banks ATMs are widespread. Lyon also has several branches of international bank **HSBC,** including at 1 pl. de la Bourse (ℂ **04-72-41-28-00**) and 18 pl. Bellecour (ℂ **04-78-92-31-00**).

Dentists **Dr. Alexandre Baroud,** 74 rue Pierre Corneille (ℂ **04-78-60-36-68**). For more info, go to www.drbaroud.com.

Doctors & Hospitals For non-urgent medical attention, try **Dr. Dominique Faysse,** 25 rue Garibaldi (ℂ **04-78-93-13-25**). The central number for most hospitals in Greater

Lyon is ℂ **08-25-08-25-69,** including **Hôpital Edouard Herriot,** 5 pl. d'Arsonval, and **Hôpital de la Croix-Rousse,** Centre Livet, 103 grande rue de la Croix-Rousse. For more information, go to **www.chu-lyon.fr**.

Embassies & Consulates Lyon has an **Embassy of the United States of America** at 1 quai Jules Courmont (ℂ **01-43-12-48-60**), Monday to Friday 9:30am to 5:30pm.

Mail A branch of **La Poste** is near place

Bellecour at 10 pl. Antonin Poncet.

Pharmacies **Grande Pharmacie Lyonnaise** is on 22 rue de la République (ℂ **04-72-56-44-00**). It's open 24 hours per day. For more information, go to www.grandepharmacie -lyonnaise.fr.

Safety Lyon is a safe city. However, be aware of pickpockets around Vieux Lyon and fake charity scammers collecting money around Part-Dieu and Gare du Lyon. Expect drunken rowdiness in Rue Ste Catherine around closing time.

Exploring Lyon

If you're a determined sightseer, one who might do two museums, and a tour in a single day, the **Lyon City Card** (www.lyoncitycard.com) could be a good buy. It costs 26.90€ per day (or 35.90€ for 2 days) including transport and access to all the city's major museums, riverboats, and guided tours. Those who prefer a gentler pace, however, will just break even, or over pay, so look carefully at what interests you before purchasing.

IN VIEUX LYON

On the left bank of the Saône River lies the neo-classical **Palais de Justice,** a.k.a. the "Palace of 24 columns." Around the corner from here is the entrance to the UNESCO-certified cobbled streets of Vieux Lyon. This medieval district is the perfect place to start exploring Lyon. Try to spot Gothic facades such as 15th-century **Maison Thomassin,** 2 pl. du Change, and the 16th-century **Maison du Chamarier,** 37 rue St-Jean (✆ **04-72-10-30-30**), where Mme. de Sévigné lived. You can admire these buildings from the outside, but you are not allowed to enter.

Musée d'Histoire de Lyon (Musée Gadagne) ★ MUSEUM   The Italian banking family who resided here in the 16th century was so famed for their wealth that the Lyonnais phrase "riche comme Gadagne" was coined. Nowadays it's a museum housing 80,000 objects that chart the history of Lyon in every aspect from politics to culture. If you're short on time, skip this section and head straight to the **Musée des Arts de la Marionnette** where you'll see fun puppets by Laurent Mourguet, creator of Guignol, the best-known French marionette character. The museum has a cafe with a pretty garden overlooking the rooftops of Vieux Lyon.
1 pl. du Petit Collège. gadagne-lyon.fr. ✆ **04-78-42-03-61.** Admission to both museums 8€ adults; free for children 17 and under. Wed–Sun 10:30am–6pm.

Primatiale St-Jean ★★ CATHEDRAL   With its exterior restored to its original creamy glory, this majestic Gothic cathedral is well worth a visit. Built over the foundations of at least five former churches, the current cathedral was erected in the Middle Ages. Paintings around the cathedral belonged to Napoleon's uncle, Cardinal Fesch. A magical time to visit is towards the end of a summer afternoon when the western sun

---

Amazing Alleys

Hundreds of secret passageways connect the winding streets of Vieux Lyon. Derived from the Latin *trans-ambulare* ("to pass through"), *traboules* date back to the 4th century as a way of providing quicker access to the city's fresh water source. Forty of them are open to the public: If you wander around the old town, you'll find each one marked with an identifying bronze seal. Dirty brown doors open unexpectedly into flower-ringed courtyards with balconies perching atop medieval columns, or onto vaulted ceilings and spiral stairs. The longest is **La Longue Traboule,** running between 54 rue Saint-Jean and 27 rue du Bœuf, while one of the prettiest (featuring a six-story external staircase) lies between 9 pl. Colbert and 14 bis montée Saint-Sébastien. Alternatively, you can go on a 2-hour guided *traboules* tour with the **Tourist Board.** They occur daily most weeks of the year. See https://shop.visiterlyon.com for the range of excellent tours offered.

shines through the 14th-century rose window, bathing the nave in an ethereal white light. The most extraordinary feature is a 16th-century astronomical clock whose mechanism announces the hour daily at noon, 2, 3, and 4pm, with rooster crows and angels heralding the event.

8 pl. St-Jean. ℭ **06-60-83-53-97.** Free admission. Daily 8:15am–7pm (Mon–Fri closes at 7:45pm). The cathedral is closed to tourists for Mass during the week and on Sun mornings.

IN FOURVIÈRE HILL

A trip to Fourvière Hill will take you back to Lyon's ancient roots with Gallo-Roman remains including France's oldest theater. From Vieux Lyon, take the 19th-century **funicular railway** up to the **Colline de Fourvière** (www.fourviere.org). The funicular railway ride is priced at 3.50€ day roundtrip; the cable-driven funiculars run every 10 minutes between 6am and 10pm.

Enthroned on the hill's summit is the monumental 19th-century **Basilique Notre-Dame de Fourvière,** 8 pl. de Fourvière (ℭ **04-78-25-13-01**), rising fortresslike with four octagonal towers and crenelated walls. The interior decorations are renovated frequently to ensure that visitors enjoy the Byzantine mosaics and frescos in their brightly colored original glory. Lyonnais architect Bossan designed the basilica in eclectic styles that combine as a poem to the Virgin Mary. From the outside, spot the gold-leafed Virgin Mary that was inaugurated on December 8, 1852—a date now celebrated annually with the **Fête des Lumières.** Admission is free; open daily 7am to 8pm.

Nearby, an altar dedicated to a bull cult and a marble goddess statue is on display in the **Lugdunum Musée,** 17 rue Cléberg (ℭ **04-72-38-49-30**). With a staircase that recalls New York's Guggenheim Museum, the museum houses a fine collection of Gallo-Roman artifacts. The site is open Tuesday through Sunday 11am to 6pm (open from 10am on weekends). Admission is 7€ adults, free for ages 17 and under and for everyone on the first Sunday of the month.

The amphitheater, **Théâtres Romains** (Roman theaters) lies below at 6 rue de l'Antiquaille (ℭ **04-72-38-49-30**). You'll have a bird's eye view over this impressive Roman theater-odeum complex from a viewing point on the left of the museum. The Grand Theater is the most ancient in France, built by order of Augustus and expanded during the reign of Hadrian to seat up to over 10,000 people. Reserved for elite society, the smaller odeum seated up to 3,000 people for musical, oratory, and poetry performances. France has only two odeums like this—the other is in Vienne. Its orchestra floor still contains mosaics of marble and porphyry. The site is open from 7am until sunset, and admission is free. The most scenic way back to Vieux Lyon is by foot through the **Jardin du Rosaire,**

Melody Maker: Summer Music Festivals

Music lovers should time a trip to Lyon in June. France's **Fête de la Musique** turns the streets of Lyon into performance spaces for local bands around June 21. In June and July, **Les Nuits de Fourvière** festival combines music, theater, dance, and cinema in the Gallo-Roman theaters on Fourvière Hill and in Parc de Parilly in the suburb of Bron. Prices depend on the act and can be purchased by phone at ℰ **04-72-57-15-40** (www.nuitsdefourviere.com).

The most celebrated music festival in the Rhône Valley is **Jazz à Vienne** (www.jazzavienne.com; ℰ **04-74-78-87-87**) at the beginning of July when the Gallo-Roman town is taken over by the sounds of Jazz. Head to Vienne's **Jardin de Cybèle** for free concerts during the festival.

---

next to the Conservatoire music school where you'll often hear music trickling from the windows. In late spring, you can enjoy roses and cherry trees in bloom as well as panoramic views over Lyon.

2ND ARRONDISSEMENT

The second *arrondissement* features elegant Haussmann architecture, wide avenues and numerous shops, museums, and workshops dedicated to Lyon's industrious past in printing, silk, and decorative arts. From Vieux Lyon, walk across Bonaparte bridge to the east bank of the River Saône. Begin your tour of the 2nd district at 18th-century **place Belle-cour,** one of France's largest and most charming squares where you can take a ride on the huge Ferris wheel. Note that the **Musée des Tissus et des Arts Décoratifs** (www.mtmad.fr. ℰ **04-78-38-42-00**) on rue de la Charité is currently closed for a major renovation that is scheduled for completion by 2027.

Musée de l'Imprimerie de Lyon ★ MUSEUM Occupying a 15th-century mansion, this museum is devoted to Lyon's role in the world of printing. Exhibits include a page from a Gutenberg Bible, as well as *incunabula,* books printed before Easter 1500.

13 rue de la Poulaillerie. www.imprimerie.lyon.fr. ℰ **04-78-37-65-98.** Admission 6€ adults; 4€ students; free for children 17 and under. Wed–Sun 10:30am–6pm. Métro: Cordeliers.

Musée des Soieries Brochier ★★ MUSEUM This new museum traces the 130-year history of one Lyonnaise family's silk-making enterprises. Four generations of Brochiers have made this firm one of the biggest names in haute couture, with Givenchy, Valentino, and Yves Saint Laurent all using their fabrics. As well as viewing historic looms, you'll learn about the many uses of silk, from dresses to sleeping bags to fiber optics. It's a surprisingly fascinating attraction. The museum is situated at the back of the Brochier silk shop, under the arches of the Grand Hôtel-Dieu,

18 quai Jules Courmont. www.brochiersoieries.com. © **04-81-13-25-51.** Admission 8€ adults; 6€ students; free for children 14 and under. Mon–Sat 10am–7pm, Sun 10am–6pm. Métro: Bellecour.

1ST ARRONDISSEMENT

North of the 2nd Arrondissement and below the Croix-Rousse hill lies the 1st district with its intriguing architectural medley from Gallo-Roman remains to modern wall murals such as the **Fresque des Lyonnais** (2 rue de la Martinière) with illustrations of famous Lyonnais residents including Paul Bocuse and Antoine de Saint-Exupéry. Nearby, check out **place des Terreaux** dominated by one of Europe's most splendid city halls, the 17th-century **Hôtel de Ville,** and by the elaborate **Fontaine Bartholdi.** Designed by Frédéric Auguste Bartholdi, who also sculpted the iconic **Statue of Liberty** in New York, this historic fountain depicts France as a female on a chariot controlling four wild horses representing the four great French rivers.

Amphithéâtre des Trois-Gaules ★ RUINS   Constructed in A.D. 19 at the base of the Croix Rousse hill, this Roman amphitheater held up to 20,000 spectators. It became the site of gatherings for the 60 Gallic tribes, for gladiatorial combats and later for the Christian persecutions in 177. Classified as a historic monument in 1961, it is now integrated into Lyon's oldest park, the **Jardin des Plantes.** Although you can't wander around the grounds, you can view the amphitheater from the outside.

Rue Lucien Sportisse. Métro: Croix Paquet.

Musée des Beaux-Arts ★★★ ART MUSEUM   Fresh from being selected as France's top museum in the 2023 World Art Awards, Lyon's Fine Arts museum is more popular than ever. Housed in a former Benedictine abbey, it has an outstanding collection of paintings and sculpture including Etruscan, Egyptian, Phoenician, Sumerian, and Persian art. The top floor holds one of France's richest 19th-century collections, with works by artists from Veronese, Tintoretto, and Rubens to Matisse, Monet, and Picasso. Be sure to see Joseph Chinard's bust of *Mme. Récamier,* the Lyon beauty who charmed Napoleonic Paris by merely reclining, and the Fantin-Latour masterpiece *La Lecture* (*The Reading*).

20 pl. des Terreaux. www.mba-lyon.fr. © **04-72-10-17-40.** Admission 8€ adults; free for children 17 and under. Wed–Mon 10am–6pm (Fri from 10:30am). Métro: Hôtel de Ville-Louis Pradel.

ELSEWHERE AROUND THE CITY

L'Institut & Musée Lumière ★ HISTORIC HOME   Film buffs from all over the world head to this living museum of cinema dedicated to the

One of the ultra-contemporary buildings in the Confluence district.

famous Lumière family, who once lived in Lyon. They invented the Lumière process of color photography and produced films, including *La Sortie de L'Usine Lumière*, released in 1895 and considered the first movie. Don't miss the filmmakers' Wall of Fame further down rue du Premier Film.

25 rue du Premier Film. www.institut-lumiere.org. (Ⓒ **04-78-78-18-95.** Admission 7.50€ adults; 6€ adults over 60, students, and children ages 7–18 (with proof of age); free for children 6 and under. Tues–Sun 10am–6:30pm. Métro: Monplaisir-Lumière.

Musée des Confluences ★★★
MUSEUM   With its strategic location between the Saône and Rhône rivers, this ethnology museum is a futuristic architectural feat dreamed up by Austrian architects Coop Himmelb(l)au. It charts humanity's history and geography going all the way to the Big Bang. A hallmark of its success is that almost 1 million visitors per year from 69 countries have flocked here since its 2015 opening.

86 quai Perrache. www.museedesconfluences.fr/en. (Ⓒ **04-28-38-11-90.** Admission 9€ adults; 6€ arrival after 5pm; free for students 25 and under and for children 17 and under. Tues–Fri 11am–7pm (Thurs until 10pm); Sat–Sun 10am–7pm. Métro: Musée des Confluences.

Parc de la Tête d'Or ★★★ PARK/GARDEN   France's largest public park goes from strength to strength. On the right bank of the Rhône, this 117-hectare (289-acre) park has a magnificent lakeside setting with deer wandering freely around the grounds. The **Zoological Park** (www. zoo.lyon.fr; (Ⓒ **04-72-69-47-60;** Wed–Mon 9:30am–6:30pm) hosts some 1,000 animals, including rose-pink flamingos and Senegalese dwarf goats, while the **Botanical Garden** (Ⓒ **04-72-69-47-60;** greenhouses open daily 9am–4:30pm) features 15,000 plants including carnivorous plants and orchids. Families will be kept busy with pony rides, carousels, and pedal boats on the lake. There's a newly installed Asian forest with Cambodian temple-inspired architecture where 25 threatened species are housed.

pl. du Général Leclerc. Entrances on bd. des Belges, quai Charles de Gaulle and av. Verguin. www.loisirs-parcdelatetedor.com. Free admission. Daily 6:30am–8:30pm (until 10:30pm mid-Apr to mid-Oct). Métro: Masséna.

Where to Stay

Accommodation in Lyon needs to be chosen carefully. Staying in the heart of **Vieux Lyon** is the most convenient place for a whirlwind tour of the city's UNESCO-classified sites. However, that usually means high prices, narrow streets, and some street noise (ask for rooms facing internal courtyards). Alternatively, active guests who don't mind a steep uphill walk (or a Funicular railway ride) will be rewarded on **Fourvière Hill** with more space and panoramic city views. Another district for spacious and light-infused accommodation is across the Bonaparte Bridge from Vieux Lyon in the **2nd** *arrondissement*. Here, sought-after hotels overlook elegant squares such as place Bellecour and place des Célestins. Nearby, new luxury hotel openings along the banks of the River Rhône in the **Presqu'île** area straddle the **1st** and **2nd districts.** For travelers seeking a hipster vibe, head further north for cheap accommodation in **La Croix Rousse** area.

Note: For the sake of less-mobile visitors or those with heavy suitcases, we've noted hotels that don't have an elevator.

EXPENSIVE

Cour des Loges ★★★   Fresh from a top-to-bottom renovation, it's hard not to be impressed by this UNESCO-protected landmark. Among its lures are a magnificent loggia-ringed courtyard, a Michelin-starred restaurant, and a spa with indoor pool. Though this five-star hotel has breathtakingly lavish decor, guests should come prepared for low lighting and smaller bedrooms. The staff, Lyon's savviest, is courteous and efficient.

6 rue du Boeuf. www.courdesloges.com. 𝄐 **04-72-77-44-44.** 61 units. 200€–410€ double; 340€–520€ suite. Parking 35€. Métro: Vieux Lyon. **Amenities:** 2 restaurants; bar; room service; spa (with fitness room, indoor pool, and sauna); free Wi-Fi.

InterContinental Lyon Hôtel Dieu ★★★   Housed in an 18th-century palace topped by a dome, this former military hospital has been transformed imaginatively by designer Jean-Philippe Nuel. Expect vaulted and beamed ceilings as well as Lyonnaise silk fabrics. Mosaic-tiled bathrooms feature Parisian perfumer Frederic Malle's products; these magnolia-scented amenities echo the magnolia tree in the hotel's courtyard. A French fine-dining restaurant, with tables spilling onto a leafy outdoor terrace, completes the picture. Overlooking the River Rhône in the Presqu'île district, this luxury hotel has set new standards within Lyon, but beware of elevated private parking costs. (You'll pay less by finding parking elsewhere, or not bringing a car.)

20 quai Jules Courmont. www.intercontinental.com. ✆ **04-26-99-23-23.** 144 units. 250€–700€ double. 530€–950€ suite. Parking 42€. Métro: Bellecour. **Amenities:** Restaurant; bar; room service; spa (with fitness room, sauna, and steam room); free Wi-Fi.

Le Royal Lyon ★   Place Bellecour provides a suitably grand setting for this Haussmann-style mansion that has welcomed numerous famous faces from Sophia Loren to the Beatles. Fine fabrics by Pierre Frey and Ralph Lauren adorn every corner of this five-star hotel that is part of the Sofitel group. Decorated with *toile de jouy* wall coverings, the bedrooms vary enormously in size. It's worth upgrading from a Classic room to a Superior room as it's almost double the size. Its cooking-school restaurant, **L'Institut** (p. 467), has fast become a Lyonnaise institution.

20 pl. Bellecour. www.lyonhotel-leroyal.com. ✆ **04-78-37-57-31.** 72 units. 135€–240€ double; 230€–550€ suite. Parking 29€. Métro: Bellecour. **Amenities:** Restaurant; cooking school; bar; free Wi-Fi.

Villa Florentine ★★★   This 17th-century convent has been converted into a swank hotel and one of our favorite places to stay in Lyon. Up on Fourvière Hill, the hotel's verdant landscaped terraces offer panoramic

---

Rooms with a View

On the "praying hill" above Vieux Lyon, accommodation comes complete with panoramic city views. **Fourvière Hotel ★★★**, 23 rue Radisson (www.fourviere-hotel.com; ✆ **04-74-70-07-00**), is a former convent. This historic hotel features 36-arched cloisters, an interior garden, and a beautiful reception area created out of the 19th-century chapel. East-meets-west designer Stellar Works dreamed up the gastronomic restaurant where vintage telephones enable diners to place their order by telephone, while a second restaurant serves up Lyonnaise bistro cuisine. Nearby, **Villa Maïa ★★**, 8 rue Pierre Marion (www.villa-maia.com; ✆ **04-78-16-01-01**), is a Japanese-inspired boutique hotel designed by Jacques Grange. The best feature is the pretty courtyard garden with ancient vaults and a spa positioned over the original Roman thermal baths. For classic luxury on Fourvière Hill, it's hard to beat the long-established **Villa Florentine** (see above).

views over Vieux Lyon. The Italianate accommodations are spacious and comfortable. The annex offers modern and slightly larger rooms.

25 montée Saint Barthélémy. www.villaflorentine.com. © **04-72-56-56-56.** 28 units. 220€–530€ double; from 650€ suite. Métro: Vieux Lyon, then funicular railway to Fourvière Hill. **Amenities:** Restaurant; bar; baby-sitting; exercise room; heated outdoor pool; room service; sauna; mini spa; free Wi-Fi.

MODERATE

Artelit ★   Housed in Lyon's original **Tour de la Rose** (not to be confused with the overpriced, shabby hotel next door) in Vieux Lyon, this exceptional B&B is like an art-museum-cum-antiques-shop. Charming owner Frédéric Jean is a renowned Lyonnais photographer. This place is for art lovers who don't mind the slightly rustic approach to hospitality such as ladders to reach the bed and occasional low ceilings. *Note:* There's no elevator and no air-conditioning.

16 rue du Boeuf. www.dormiralyon.com. © **04-78-42-84-83.** 4 units. 100€–180€ double; 125€–250€ suite. Métro: Vieux Lyon. **Amenities:** Free Wi-Fi.

Hôtel Bayard Bellecour ★★   With its enviable location overlooking the majestic place Bellecour, Hôtel Bayard Bellecour offers exceptional value. This 16th-century town house has both contemporary and traditionally decorated rooms. Most of the compact bathrooms have showers and tubs. "Classic" rooms are somewhat cramped. *Note:* The hotel reception is up a flight of stairs on the first floor, and there's no elevator.

23 pl. Bellecour. www.hotelbayard.fr. © **04-78-37-39-64.** 27 units. 129€–215€ double. Parking 30€ (call ahead). Métro: Bellecour. **Amenities:** Free Wi-Fi.

Hôtel Carlton ★★   Hôtel Carlton continues to be a fail-safe place to stay in the 2nd district. Part of the Mgallery by Sofitel group, this four-star hotel combines 19th-century architecture with contemporary comfort and reliable service. Adults will appreciate the new spa by Parisian skincare

---

Private Island Living

If you've ever dreamed of sleeping on a private island, you'll love **Les Suites de l'Île Barbe** ★★★, Île Barbe, 9 Impasse Saint-Loup (www.ilebarbe.com; © **04-78-59-06-90**), After crossing the bridge onto the island, you reach the guesthouse down a winding road through two ancient gates that open onto a hamlet of private dwellings. Here, you'll find the bed and breakfast housed in the annex of a former Benedictine abbey (originally founded on the island in the 5th c.). Exposed stone pillars and vaulted ceilings combine with contemporary furnishings in three tastefully decorated suites. Modern luxuries such as air-conditioning and kitchenettes make these suites ideal for extended stays. Owner Bénédicte ensures a warm welcome.

Budget Meets Boutique: Best Backpacker Hostels

Lyon's new-generation hostels are a far cry from their threadbare predecessors. Now these backpacker hotels come complete with stencil art, designer furnishings, and healthy cuisine. As well as Hôtel Pilo (listed above), our favorites are **Slo Living Hostel ★★**, 5 rue Bonnefoi (www.slo-hostel.com; *(*04-78-59-06-90), in Saxe Gambetta with four- or six-bed dormitories as well private double rooms; **Away Hostel ★★**, 21 rue Alsace Lorraine (www.awayhostel.com; *(*04-78-98-53-20), on the slopes of Croix-Paquet in the 1st district, with dorms sleeping four to eight and private doubles with Nespresso coffee machines; and **Ho36 Hostel ★★**, 36 rue Montesquieu (www.ho36.com; *(*04-37-70-17-03), in Guillotière, offering mixed and women-only (in Lyon Opéra only) dormitories as well as private family rooms and doubles.

brand Codage, while families will like connecting rooms and cartoon TV channels.

4 rue Jussieu. www.accorhotels.com. *(*04-78-42-56-51. 80 units. 147€–324€ double; 209€–500€ suite. Métro: Cordeliers. **Amenities:** Bar; spa; hammam; room service; free Wi-Fi.

Hôtel des Célestins ★★   Seconds from the place des Célestins with its splendid 18th-century theater, this discreet hotel is a perennial favorite amongst Lyon's mid-range hotels. The secret to its success lies in its homey atmosphere, with bedrooms containing bookshelves lined with well-worn books.

4 rue des Archers. www.hotelcelestins.com. *(*04-72-56-08-98. 29 units. 99€–218€ double; 209€–418€ suite. Métro: Bellecour. **Amenities:** Breakfast room; free Wi-Fi.

Mama Shelter ★   For those who prize style above location, this hipster hotel with furnishings by Philippe Starck could be the ticket. Prices vary from fair to outrageously overpriced, depending upon how far in advance you book, so it's best to find early online deals. A big plus is the restaurant with its open kitchen, DJ stage and outdoor terrace. From this 7th-district hotel, you'll need to cross both the River Rhône and Saône to reach Lyon's Old Town.

13 rue Domer. www.mamashelter.com. *(*04-78-02-58-00. 156 units. 89€–389€ double; from 189€ family suite. Métro: Jean Macé. **Amenities:** Restaurant; business corner; indoor parking; free Wi-Fi.

INEXPENSIVE

Hôtel Pilo ★★★   This new budget hotel is a welcome addition for budget-conscious travelers. Communal (mixed and female-only) dormitories have LED-lit capsule beds designed for privacy. There are also ensuite double and twin bedrooms as well as quadruple rooms for families. Bedrooms use French linen and toiletries. Overlooking a pretty courtyard, the excellent restaurant serves locally sourced cuisine. The hotel hosts plentiful events from pop-up markets and exhibitions to live music.

10 Montée des Carmélites. www.pilohotels.com. © **04-28-01-86-00.** 200 units. 21€–30€ mixed dormitory. 78€–97€ double. Métro: Croix-Rousse. **Amenities:** Restaurant; free Wi-Fi.

Where to Eat

The Lyonnais take their cuisine seriously. Michelin stars and culinary associations abound in this gastronomic hub that produces many of France's top chefs. Vieux Lyon's **rue du Boeuf** has become the city's most Michelin-starred street with **Jérémy Galvan, La Cour des Loges'** Anthony Bonnet, and **Au 14 Février**'s Tsuyoshi Arai. Nearby, chef Guy Lassausaie has taken Fourvière Hill by storm with his new restaurant, **Bulle.**

Note that restaurants in central Lyon are often open weekdays only. Make sure you fit in a trip to a traditional Lyonnais bistro *bouchon* where you'll likely dine at a gingham-clothed table on dishes such as *quenelles de brochet* (creamed pike) and *andouillettes Lyonnaises* (course-grained pork sausages in an onion sauce). Meanwhile, excellent cheap dining can be found at the covered market, **Les Halles de Lyon Paul Bocuse** (p. 470).

EXPENSIVE

Au 14 Février ★★ FRANCO-JAPANESE   Celebrated chef Tsuyoshi Arai has gone from strength to strength with his Valentine-inspired restaurant where Raymond Peynet romantic drawings set the scene. The tasting menu is a feat of *trompe-l'oeil* Franco-Japanese cuisine that changes seasonally. A starter of Bresse free-range chicken is served in myriad ways from parsley-infused pate to *Kousyu-motuni* stew. Dessert brings a passion-fruit-and-mandarin puree served with caramel and Guinness-froth ice cream. Menus are served either with wines by the glass or with Alain Milliat's wonderful artisanal fruit juices.

36 rue du Boeuf. www.ly-au14fevrier.com. © **04-78-92-91-39.** Fixed-price menu 110€. Fri noon–1pm; Mon–Fri 7:30–8:30pm. Métro: Vieux Lyon.

Bulle ★★★ MODERN FRENCH   Chef Guy Lassausaie cut his teeth in nearby Chasselay before bringing his bistronomic cuisine to Fourvière Hill. Popular dishes include rack of Limousin lamb with crispy parmesan polenta and langoustine, spinach and mushroom ravioli with a lime-infused, shellfish broth. It's hard not to be won over by the combination of locally sourced, seasonal cuisine, and panoramic views over Lyon on the two terrasses.

9 place de Fourvière. www.bullerestaurantfourviere.fr. © **04-30-30-32-16.** Fixed-price menus 55€–75€; fixed-price lunch (Mon–Fri only) 42€. Daily 10:30am–9:30pm. Métro: Vieux Lyon.

Jérémy Galvan ★★ MODERN LYONNAISE   Jérémy Galvan showcases his culinary magic in this cozy restaurant in the heart of Vieux Lyon. His wife Nadia welcomes diners with her efficient team into two contrasting dining rooms: one brightly warm with stone walls, the other elegantly somber. With a choice of five- to seven-course menus, you may want to eat lightly before a visit here. If you want to experience his Michelin-starred cuisine for half the price, try his 4-course menu available only at Thursday lunchtime. As many as 40 wines are available by the glass.

> **Notes from South America**
>
> For award-winning, Franco-Peruvian cuisine, head to **Miraflores ★★★**, 112 boulevard des Belges (www.restaurant-miraflores.com; ✆ **04-78-24-49-71**). Chef Carlos Camino focuses on organic, seasonal produce and plentiful herbs alongside Peruvian ingredients to conjure up dishes such as ox tongue with white quinoa and drum-fish ceviche. The location near the Tête d'Or park recalls the pretty tree-lined neighborhood, Miraflores, in Lima where Camino studied.

29 rue du Boeuf. www.jeremygalvanrestaurant.com. ✆ **04-72-40-91-47.** Fixed-price menus 65€–105€. Fixed-price lunch menu (Thurs only) 75€. Thurs–Fri noon–12:45pm; Mon–Fri 7–8:30pm. Métro: Vieux Lyon.

Mère Brazier ★★★ MODERN LYONNAISE   The only two-Michelin-starred restaurant in central Lyon, Mère Brazier remains the gastronomic capital's kingpin. This legendary institution is run by the charismatic darling of French food critics, Mathieu Viannay. In a striking Art-Deco setting, you can taste Mère Brazier classics (such as Bresse chicken poached with truffles) that have been reworked by Viannay, as well as Renée Richard cheese accompanied by fine Rhône red wines.

12 rue Royale. www.lamerebrazier.fr. ✆ **04-78-23-17-20.** Main course 70€–265€; fixed-price lunch 95€; fixed-price dinner 165€–225€. Mon–Fri noon–1:15pm and 7:45–9pm. Métro: Croix Paquet.

MODERATE

Brasserie Georges ★ TRADITIONAL FRENCH   Founded in 1836, this bustling Lyonnais institution serves up to 450 diners. You can ask for a table that is identified with a plaque for hosting Ernest Hemingway or Edith Piaf. Specialties include roast beef and snails in garlic butter.

30 cours de Verdun. www.brasseriegeorges.com. ✆ **04-72-56-54-54.** Main course 18€–26€; fixed-price menus 23.50€–28.50€. Daily 11:30am–11pm (Fri–Sat until 12:15am). Closed May 1. Métro: Perrache.

L'Institut ★★ MODERN FRENCH   This stylish restaurant is run by the well-reputed catering school **L'Institut Paul Bocuse.** You can marvel at the sight of head chef Cyril Bosviel guiding future celebrity chefs in the glassed-in kitchen—part of a lavish design by Pierre-Yves Rochon. Cooking classes in English are offered at the school upstairs.

20 pl. Bellecour. www.linstitut-restaurant.fr. ✆ **04-28-31-69-06.** Main course 31€–38€. Mon–Fri noon–1pm and 7:30–9pm. Métro: Bellecour.

Mum's the Word

Lyonnaise cuisine was born through women. Generations ago, hard-working women set up low-priced bistros, known as *bouchons*, to feed the local workers with meat-oriented fare such as duck pâté and *andouillettes Lyonnaise* (coarse-grained pork sausages in an onion sauce). Nowadays these *bouchons* are so famed in Lyon that an official association has been set up to protect the 20 or so official certified *authentiques bouchons Lyonnais* from the numerous fakes that parade around the old town. Nowadays most of these gingham-clothed *bouchons* are run by men, but some pay tribute to their Lyonnais foremothers

such as the Michelin-starred **Mère Brazier** (p. 467). Our favorites include **Daniel et Denise** with three outlets around town including its original Old Town location (✆ **04-78-60-66-53**) at 156 rue de Créqui; **Les Adrets** (✆ **04-78-38-24-30**) at 30 rue du Boeuf; **Le Musée,** 2 rue des Forces (✆ **04-78-37-71-54**); long-established **Café des Fédérations** (www.lesfedeslyon.com; ✆ **04-78-28-26-00**) at 8-10 rue Major-Martin; **Le Garet,** 7 rue du Garet (✆ **04-78-28-16-94**), famously frequented by Jean Moulin, hero of *La Résistance;* and **Bouchon des Cordeliers** (www.bouchondescordeliers.com; ✆ **04-78-03-33-53**) at 15 rue Claudia.

Shopping

Each district in Lyon has different shopping hours. While shops in Vieux Lyon tend to be open on Sundays and closed on Mondays (also Tues and even Wed in low season), shops in the 2nd district tend to have more traditional Monday or Tuesday to Saturday openings with lunchtime and Sunday closures.

Vieux Lyon is home to many art galleries and one-off boutiques. With its dazzling array of *tartes au praline,* the best baker in the area is **Boulangerie du Palais,** 8 rue du Palais (✆ **04-78-37-09-43**), where you'll always find a queue of locals on weekends. **Antic Wine** is one of the best and most amusing wine shops in France, at 18 rue du Boeuf (✆ **04-78-37-08-96**).

On the pretty place Sathonay in the nearby 1st district, a new travel-inspired shop, **Hyppairs**

A *bouchon* in Lyon.

(www.hyppairs.com; ✆ **06-67-54-20-82**), blends clothes and home decor with a cozy cafe.

The wide avenues of the 2nd district focus upon designer and high-street brands. The densest concentrations of retail shops lie in the streets leading north of place Bellecour. The southern end of rue du Président Edouard Herriot is home to sought-after international brands from **Louis Vuitton** to **Mont Blanc.** Around the corner lies our favorite shopping street in Lyon: **rue des Archers.** Here you'll find chic Parisian clothes brands for adults and children, as well as two of Lyon's award-winning chocolate shops: **Bouillet** at no. 14 (www.chocolatier-bouillet.com; ✆ **04-78-42-98-40**) and **Bernard Dufoux** at no. 15 (www.chocolatsdufoux.com; ✆ **04-72-77-57-95**). Linking rue du Président Edouard Herriot with rue de la République, the historic **Passage de L'Argue,** designed by architect Farge in 1827, houses long-established merchants of hats, umbrellas, knives, and shaving brushes. Along the riverside, the newly refurbished **Grand Hôtel-Dieu,** 1 place de l'Hôpital (www.grand-hotel-dieu.com), features international brands such as Habitat and Cos.

Meanwhile, the largest shopping center in Lyon is the **Centre Commercial La Part-Dieu,** 17 rue du Dr. Bouchut, in the 3rd district (www.centrecommercial-partdieu.com; ✆ **04-72-60-60-62**), with more than 235 boutiques.

Best Workshop-Boutiques

Scattered around the city are workshop-boutiques that produce and showcase Lyon's silk industry. Our favorite workshop is **L'Atelier de Soierie**, 33 rue Romarin in the 1st district (www.brochier soieries.com; ✆ **04-72-07-97-83**), where you can watch silk carrés being printed using traditional Lyonnais techniques before browsing the scarves on display in the neighboring boutique. If you're

visiting Lyon between May and November, make sure you also drop into Brochier's sister boutique, at the foot of the Tour Rose on rue du Boeuf in Vieux Lyon, where you'll see silkworm metamorphosis in action (depending upon the availability of mulberry leaves) from hatching as caterpillars, to spinning their cocoons and transforming into moths.

Les Halles Paul Bocuse ★★★ On weekends, local gourmands crowd this covered food market to stock up on high-quality Lyonnais specialties: sausage-filled brioche, *Cervelle de Canut* cream cheese, and marzipan *coussins de Lyon* (cushions carried by the Aldermen during the 1643 Plague), as well as soups and *quenelles à brochet* (creamed pike) from **Giraudet** (p. 473). Numerous cafes offer a well-priced lunch.

102 cours Lafayette. www.halles-de-lyon-paulbocuse.com. ✆ **04-78-60-32-82.** Mon–Sat 7am–7pm; Sun 7am–1pm. Métro: Brotteaux/Part Dieu.

Lyon Nightlife

From opera to house music, Lyon has an eclectic nightlife to suit all tastes. A good start is to browse Le Petit Bulletin website (www.petit-bulletin.fr/lyon) for up-to-date listings.

The most established haunt for young Lyonnais is the mini-chain of microbreweries **Ninkasi** (www.ninkasi.fr), which has nighttime venues for live music, fresh beer, and burgers. Most live concerts are free, although there is sometimes a cover charge for well-known bands playing at the brewery headquarters, **Ninkasi Gerland,** 267 rue Marcel Mérieux ✆ **04-72-76-52-34.** To keep things simple, each venue is named after the nearest metro station. Check the website for precise opening times.

Wine lovers should head to **La Cave des Voyageurs,** 7 pl. Saint-Paul (www.lacavedesvoyageurs.fr; ✆ **04-78-28-92-28;** Tues–Sat 5pm–1am), one of the city's oldest, and most evocative, wine bars in Vieux Lyon,

If you're feeling homesick, you can head to the Anglophone pub **Smoking Dog,** 16 rue Lainerie (✆ **04-78-28-38-27**), with its bookshelf-lined walls, billiard table, and eight beers on tap. It's a popular place to watch international sports matches on T.V. Open daily from 5pm to 1am (weekends from 2pm).

Near place des Terreaux, **La Maison M.,** 21 pl. Gabriel Rambaud (www.mmlyon.com; ✆ **04-72-00-87-67;** Métro: Hôtel de Ville), has become a popular nighttime fixture. This bar and late-night club (Wed–Sat 6pm–4am) offers an eclectic musical program from soul to rock and hip-hop including live concerts. Another live music and arts venue is **Le Sucre,** 50 quai Rambaud (www.le-sucre.eu; Métro: Perrache), on the rooftop of a 1930s warehouse in the fashionable Confluence district. It's open 11pm to 5am Friday and Saturday and 6pm to midnight Sunday and Monday.

In summertime, locals flock to the quays along the Rhône. The best of the former cargo boats parked on the Rhône is **Péniche Le Sirius,** Berges du Rhône, 4 quai Victor Augagneur (www.lesirius.com; ✆ **04-78-71-78-71;** Métro: Guillotière). The ship is packed with an under-35 crowd sipping Belgian beers and dancing to the sounds of Lyon's best DJs on the lower-level floor. It's open daily from 2pm to 3am.

One of Lyon's largest nightclubs is the renamed **F&K Bistroclub,** 13/14 pl. Jules Ferry (www.f-and-k.fr; Métro: Brotteaux), whose house music and chic decor attract a young, kitten-heeled 20s to 30s crowd. Housed in the Brotteaux old railway station, the club has room for 500 people, yet you should expect a strict door policy. It's open Wednesday to Saturday from 6:30pm until 6am (closes at 4am on Wed). The restaurant is open 6:30 to 11pm. At 73 rue du Bourbonnais, the new **Sound Club** (www.thesoundclub.fr; ✆ **06-75-94-97-99**), has taken over this popular 9th district venue from Factory Club. Featuring Hip-hop, Afro-Caribbean, and Amapiano and Bouyon music, the club is open on weekends (Fri–Sat 11:30pm–6am).

Rainbow lights set the scene at **La Chapelle Café** (www.la-chapelle-cafe-lyon.eatbu.com; ✆ **04-72-56-11-92;** Mon–Thurs 4pm–1am, Fri–Sat 4pm–4am, Sun 10am–1am), 8 quai des Célestins. This riverside gay bar has a party ambience with live DJs and themed music nights. It's also a place for low-key cocktails with sunset views towards Fourvière Hill.

The oldest gay club in Lyon is **United Café** (www.united-cafe.fr; Impasse de la Pêcherie; ✆ **04-78-29-93-18**). Open Tuesday to Sunday midnight to 5am, it's busy almost every evening with themed events, drag and karaoke nights. For those who like '80s music, **It Bar** (20 bis Mnt Saint-Sébastien; ✆ **06-30-10-89-69**) is a popular gay dance club that's open weekends only 11:45pm to 4am.

Opera buffs head to the **Opéra National de Lyon,** pl. de la Comédie (www.opera-lyon.com; ✆ **04-69-85-54-54;** Métro: Hôtel de Ville-Louis Pradel; ticket office open Tues–Sat noon–7pm and Mon during performances), while **La Halle Tony Garnier,** 20 pl. des Docteurs Charles et Christophe Mérieux (www.halle-tony-garnier.com; ✆ **04-72-76-85-85;** Métro: Perrache or Debourg), is a popular venue for international pop concerts and dance shows, as it seats up to 17,000 visitors.

DAY TRIPS FROM LYON

It's worth taking time to explore the countryside around Lyon. Some places such as **Vienne,** the **Ardèche,** and the wine countries of the **Northern Rhône** and **Beaujolais** will fill several days; others such as **Bourg-en-Bresse** and **Pérouges** make ideal day trips. If you're really pressed for time, you could consider half-day trips to attractions within Greater Lyon such as Bocuse in Collonges au Mont d'Or and Mini World Lyon in Vaulx-en-Velin.

The Godfather of Lyonnaise Cuisine

International foodies continue to make the pilgrimage to Collonges au Mont d'Or to pay homage to the late Paul Bocuse (who passed away in 2018) aka the godfather of Lyonnaise cuisine. Standards remain high at **Restaurant Paul Bocuse ★★★**, 40 quai de la Plage, Collonges au Mont d'Or (www.bocuse.fr; ✆ **04-72-42-90-90;** take the N433 north of Lyon), where you can still feast on his legendary black-truffle soup. Bocuse was the only chef ever in the Lyon area to boast an unbroken run of 50 years of three Michelin stars. Be warned that you have to book months in advance to be sure of a table.

Bourg-en-Bresse ★

37km (23 miles) E of Mâcon; 425km (264 miles) SE of Paris; 61km (38 miles) NE of Lyon

There are two reasons to visit the ancient capital of Bresse: The first is to explore the intensely romantic national historic monument **Brou Monastery,** as well as arguably the best-preserved **apothecary** in France; the second is to dine on the only free-range chickens in the world to have their own *appellation d'origine contrôlée* (certificate of origin).

ESSENTIALS

GETTING THERE If you're driving down the A6 from Paris, head east out of Mâcon on the A40 towards Bourg-en-Bresse. If **driving** from Lyon, take A42 north, before turning onto A40 for the 70-minute trip. Bourg-en-Bresse is accessible by **train** from Lyon Perrache (about 1 hr.); over 20 trains arrive per day. For information, visit www.sncf-connect.com or call ✆ **36-35.**

VISITOR INFORMATION The **Office de Tourisme** is at 6 av. Alsace Lorraine (www.bourgenbressedestinations.fr; ✆ **04-74-22-49-40**).

EXPLORING BOURG-EN-BRESSE

Apothecary ★★ HISTORIC LANDMARK This 18th-century pharmacy and laboratory is chock-a-block with fascinating relics: 17th-century alembic distillers, medicine boxes filled with licorice pills and powdered deer antler, and Fleur-de-Lys pots that were hidden during the French Revolution. Visits to this hidden gem need to be organized in advance with the tourist office.

Hôtel de Dieu, 47 bd. de Brou. ✆ **04-74-22-49-40.** Guided visits every Sat afternoon; contact the tourist office for more information.

Royal Monastery of Brou ★★★ MONASTERY This huge Gothic mausoleum is France's most extravagant love token. The ill-fated Margaret of Austria built it after her husband, Philibert the Handsome, died at the age of 24 from catching a cold on a hunting expedition. You can visit the secret passageway designed for the mourning Margaret to access her chapel from her monastery residence without being seen by the public. She organized her own tomb beside her husband.

63 bd. de Brou. www.monastere-de-brou.fr. 🕐 **04-74-22-83-83.** Admission to church, cloisters, and museum 9.50€. Apr–Sept daily 9am–6pm; Oct–Mar daily 9am–5pm. Closed Jan 1, May 1, Nov 1 and 11, and Christmas.

WHERE TO EAT & SHOP

No trip to Bourg-en-Bresse is complete without visiting the **covered food market** in avenue du Champ de Foire. Every Wednesday and Saturday morning (8am–1pm), you'll be able to browse the myriad stalls for flowers, fruit, vegetables, cheese, and even live chickens. Chocoholics are catered for with no less than seven chocolate shops: One of the best is **Chocolaterie Monet,** 14 rue Bichat (🕐 **04-74-23-47-42**), where you'll find excellent truffles and seasonally themed chocolates.

Auberge Bressane ★★ TRADITIONAL FRENCH This celebrated restaurant has built up a loyal clientele of locals and tourists alike. You'll find plenty of hearty regional dishes such as Bresse chicken with cheese-and-almond gratin, frogs' legs, and pike quenelles. Summertime dining is on the terrace with views over the Brou Monastery.

166 bd de Brou. www.auberge bressane.fr. 🕐 **04-74-22-22-68.** Menus 46€–110€. Wed–Sun noon–2:30pm and 7–10pm.

> ### Gulliver's Choice
>
> A new Jurassic jungle exhibit featuring life-sized dinosaurs is now open at **Mini World Lyon,** 2 rue Jacquard (www.miniworld-lyon.com; 🕐 **04-78-52-90-88**). Situated in Vaulx-en-Velin France's largest animated miniature park explores French city, countryside, and mountain landscapes that are reproduced with miniature buildings, roads, vehicles, and characters.

Boutique Giraudet ★★ Since 1910, Giraudet's *quenelles à brochet* (creamed pike) have been the gold standard of Rhône cuisine. It is one of the last manufacturers that still produce certain quenelles by hand. This smart boutique offers over 40 different quenelles with matching sauces as well as sweet and savory soups made from classic recipes.

21 rue Maréchal Joffre. www.giraudet.fr. 🕐 **04-74-22-45-85.** Tues–Sat 9am–12:30pm and 3–7pm.

Pérouges ★★

464km (288 miles) SE of Paris; 35km (22 miles) NE of Lyon

Photogenic Pérouges sits on a hilltop throne northeast of Lyon. Ever since *The Three Musketeers* film put medieval Pérouges on the international map in 1961, this thousand-person village has attracted tourists and movie crews. Tourism has caused excessive prices in local restaurants so consider taking a picnic instead. You may also want to bring a pair of comfortable walking shoes; the cobblestone streets are slippery when it rains and from the train station, it is a 20-minute walk into central Pérouges.

Ancient house in Pérouges.

ESSENTIALS

GETTING THERE **Trains** serve **Meximeux-Pérouges** from Lyon Part Dieu taking 30 minutes; for information, visit www.sncf-connect.com or call ☎ **36-35.** If you **drive** to Pérouges, beware that the signs for the town, especially at night, are confusing. From Lyon, take A42/E611 northeast and exit near Meximeux.

VISITOR INFORMATION The **Tourist Office** is at 9 route de la Cité (www.perouges-bugey-tourisme.com; ☎ **09-67-12-70-84**).

EXPLORING PÉROUGES

Wander down the rue des Princes to place des Tilleuls where you'll find the **Arbre de la Liberté** (Tree of Liberty) planted in 1792 to commemorate the Revolution. Nearby the 14th-century **Maison des Princes de Savoie,** houses the **Musée du Comité** (☎ **04-74-61-00-88**), with its panoramic watchtower and perfectly tended 13th-century knot garden. The museum is open April to October 10am to noon and 2 to 6pm. Admission is 5€ for adults, free for children ages 10 and under.

WHERE TO STAY & EAT

Hostellerie du Vieux-Pérouges ★ REGIONAL FRENCH This slightly overpriced 13th-century timbered inn trades on its location in the picturesque town square, and the fact that its chock-a-block with antiques, from iron lanterns to dressers lined with pewter plates. With tables spilling onto the outdoor terrace, you can soak up the medieval atmosphere over an unashamedly old-fashioned lunch of Bresse chicken with creamed morels. If you do decide to stay, go all out for a *lit à* *baldaquin* (four-poster bedroom) in Le Manoir or St Georges, as Pavillion rooms lack charm.

pl. du Tilleul. www.hostelleriedeperouges.com. ℂ **04-74-61-00-88.** Main course 24€–35€; menus from 39€–67€. Fri–Tues noon–1:45pm and 7–8:45pm (closed Sun evening).

Les Terrasses de Pérouges ★★ REGIONAL FRENCH   With its pretty outdoor terrace, this reasonably priced restaurant is the perfect place for summertime dining. The menu includes French classics such as grilled sirloin steak and frogs' legs, as well as a wide choice of burgers. Try the foie gras burger with a cream sauce.

rue des Rondes Porte d'en Bas. www.terrassesdeperouges.fr. ℂ **04-74-61-38-68.** Main course 15.50€–22.50€. Thurs–Mon noon–2:30pm and 7–9pm.

BEAUJOLAIS COUNTRY ★★★

This postcard-pretty wine region punches above its diminutive size. Not only does it produce an impressive 190 million bottles of wine every year, but it also boasts more castles owned by aristocratic dynasties than Bordeaux.

Beaujolais rose to international fame through its barely fermented *vin en primeur*. The craze for **Beaujolais Nouveau** table wine started in Paris 3 decades ago. Nowadays, Beaujolais Nouveau counts for just $\frac{1}{3}$ of the annual production of Beaujolais wine. Wine drinkers are gradually becoming aware of the potential of the Gamay grape to produce red wines of finesse, yet light enough to pair with white meat and even fish.

Though wine lovers tend to include this wine-producing region as part of Greater Burgundy, geographically speaking, Beaujolais belongs to the Rhône region. From north of Lyon and to south of Mâcon, the narrow strip of Beaujolais country branches out with no defined wine route. Luckily the road signs are clear so you can branch off easily in any direction from the A6 highway. If you're in doubt, simply follow the signs to the region's capital and commercial center, Villefranche-sur-Saône.

Galettes Galore

With so much to see in these parts, you may not want to take the time for a sit-down lunch. Instead grab a galette to go. Perouge has two creperies serving savory and sweet pancakes: **La Grange aux Crêpes** (ℂ **06-09-52-18-78;** Thurs–Mon noon–2pm and 7–9pm, Sun 2–5pm), at 116 rue de la Porte d'en Haut, has a rustic farmhouse setting and **Ô Galettes de Sophie** ★ (www.o-galettes-de-sophie.business.site; Fri–Wed 11:30am–6pm; closed Oct–Feb) on rue des Rondes, is just off the town square. The latter serves delicious Peruvian savory pancakes—if you don't want the whole pancake, you can just order a slice for just €1.50.

Southern Beaujolais

With its warm-hued stone architecture, Southern Beaujolais has been dubbed "Land of the Golden Stones." It's the most attractive place to use as a base for exploring both Northern and Southern Beaujolais. Capital of Beaujolais, Villefranche-sur-Saône is a businesslike base to start, but you'll probably want to stay in one of the 39 *villages dorés*.

ESSENTIALS

GETTING THERE **Villefranche-sur-Saône** is accessible by **trains** from Lyon. It's a 25-minute journey from Lyon Part Dieu station at 5€. For information, visit www.sncf-connect.com or call ℂ **36-35.** However, the most practical way of exploring Southern Beaujolais is by car. If you're driving from Lyon, take the A6 north to Villefranche.

VISITOR INFORMATION The **Office de Tourisme** is at 96, rue de la Sous-Préfecture, Villefranche-sur-Saône (www.destination-beaujolais.com; ℂ **04-74-07-27-40;** open Mon–Sat 9:30am–12:30pm and 2:30–6pm).

EXPLORING SOUTHERN BEAUJOLAIS

Go to Villefranche-sur-Saône tourist office, not far from the marketplace for a booklet on Beaujolais country. It includes a map, itineraries, and lists the wine-tasting cellars open to the public. It also lists and details some 30 villages.

Any tour of Southern Beaujolais should include the pedestrianized, medieval village of **Oingt**—officially designated as one of the most beautiful villages in France. Only the tower remains of the medieval castle, but it's worth climbing for the panoramic views over Beaujolais. A good place to stock up on local Beaujolais wine is **Terroir des Pierres Dorées** (www.vignerons-pierres-dorees.fr; ℂ **04-78-15-91-07**), at 76 place de Presberg, on the edge of the pedestrianized center.

Another pretty village is **St-Julien-Sous-Montmelas,** 11km (6¾ miles) northwest of Villefranche (take D35). Claude Bernard, the father of physiology, was born here in 1813. His small stone house—the **Musée Claude-Bernard** (414 route du Musée; www.claude-bernard.fr; ℂ **04-74-67-51-44**)—exhibits the scholar's mementos, instruments, and books. The museum is open from April to October, Wednesday to Sunday 10am to 12:30pm and 2 to 6pm; admission is 5€ or free for children 12 and under.

If you like fairy-tale castles, you should visit **Château de Montmelas** ★★ (www.chateaudemontmelas.fr; ℂ **07-64-62-01-74**) in Montmelas-Saint-Sorlin. Known locally as Sleeping Beauty castle, it has been home to the same aristocratic family since the Middle Ages. From this hilltop castle, you'll find breathtaking views towards the distant Mont Blanc. You can telephone in advance for a 90-minute wine tasting (from 12€) in the cellars with Delphine, the charming Countess of Harcourt.

Award-winning red and white table wines, and even sparkling wines, are produced by the Comte himself. If you'd like to stay, two brightly furnished gîtes are available. For a princely sum, you can even hire out the entire castle. From St. Julien, take the D19 west and then the D44 towards the castle.

WHERE TO STAY & EAT

Château de Bagnols ★★★ Europe's best fairytale castle-hotel comes complete with a moat, landscaped gardens, a spa, and a fabulous glassed-in courtyard. Prices are competitive considering the antiques, paintings, and art that fill the mansion. Guest suites are generously sized with antique beds and period-velvet bed throws. Gastronomic dining is on offer at the hotel's **1217** restaurant. If you're staying nearby, it's worth booking a table here to enjoy the rich French fare (try roasted duck breast with saffron-and-peach gnocchi or the red-shrimp carpaccio with aloe-vera sauce and citrus sorbet) in the majestic dining room with its Gothic fireplace straight out of Hogwarts. Other dining options include the outdoor **Cuisine d'Été** for healthy summertime dining and the new **Café du Château** open for weekday snacks and for delicious spit-roast chicken on Sundays at lunch. Make time for the beautiful spa with its indoor pool and innovative Sothys treatments such as a multisensory facial using a virtual-reality headset.

118 place de la Mairie, Bagnols. www.chateaudebagnols.com. ✆ **04-74-71-40-00.** 21 units. From 200€ suite. To reach Bagnols, head west out of Villefranche on D338. **Amenities:** Restaurant; heated outdoor and indoor pools; lounge; spa; hammam; fitness room; free Wi-Fi.

La Grande ★ TRADITIONAL FRENCH This homey address has been keeping local diners happy with traditional French dishes such as Burgundy snails, Quercy foie gras and Beaujolaise *andouillettes* (blood sausage) for decades. Also available is a market-fresh fish of the day. While chef Raphaël is busy in the kitchen, cheerful owner Florence provides swift service.

322 rue de Belleville, Villefranche. www.restaurant-lagrande.com. ✆ **04-74-60-65-81.** Fixed-price menu 25€. Tues–Fri noon–1:30pm and 7–8:30pm.

La Maison Troisgros ★★★ FRENCH Four generations of Troisgros chefs have worked at this iconic restaurant/empire which has held onto three Michelin stars for over 50 years. The flagship restaurant and hotel are in Ouches within a stone farmhouse that has been cleverly converted with the addition of a wall-to-wall glass dining room that plays with the illusion of outdoor dining. Taste exceptional flavors such as caramelized rack of lamb or pineapple-infused mackerel before retiring to one of the luxurious contemporary bedrooms (from 300€). Informal dining is available at their sister property in nearby Roanne: café-épicerie, **Le Central**

(20 Cr. de la République; ℭ **04-77-67-72-72**). Farther in the countryside, Troisgros also operates **La Colline du Colombier** (Iguerande; ℭ **03-85-84-07-24**), offering farmhouse cuisine at **Le Grand Couvert** restaurant and accommodations in *cadoles* (designer cabins).

728 route de Villerest, Ouches. www.troisgros.fr. ℭ **04-77-71-66-97**. Main course 85€–210€; fixed-price menus 150€–360€. Wine-pairing menu 570€. Wed 7:30–9:30pm; Thurs–Sun noon–1:15pm and 7:30–9:30pm. Closed Jan.

Northern Beaujolais

Wine connoisseurs head straight to Northern Beaujolais where the serious Cru appellation wines are grown. Most of the 10 **Beaujolais Crus** (certified as the region's best wines that are more nuanced in flavor and capable of aging longer) are within a short drive of **Belleville,** the largest town in Northern Rhône. From Lyon or Villefranche-sur-Saône, drive north on the A6.

ESSENTIALS

GETTING THERE **Belleville-en-Beaujolais** (formerly Belleville-sur-Saône) is accessible by **trains** from Lyon. It's a 35-minute journey from Lyon Part Dieu station at 11.20€. For information, visit www.sncf-connect.com or call ℭ **36-35**. However, the most practical way of exploring Northern Beaujolais is by car. If you're **driving** from Lyon, take the A6 north to Belleville.

VISITOR INFORMATION Belleville shares the Villefranche-sur-Saône tourist office (p. 476).

EXPLORING NORTHERN BEAUJOLAIS

Caveau du Cru Morgon ★ WINERY A good place to start exploring Northern Beaujolais is at this cellar in the basement of the 18th-century Château de Fontcrenne, next to the Hôtel de Ville. Here you can taste red wines from the well-regarded Beaujolais Cru Morgon. Caveau du Cru Morgon produces and bottles wines under its own label, using grapes from local independent wine growers.

Rue du Château Fontcrenne, Villié-Morgon. ℭ **04-74-04-20-99**. From Belleville, head north on the A6, then west on the D9. Daily 10am–12:30pm and 2:30–6pm. Closed first 3 weeks of Jan.

Hameau Duboeuf ★ MUSEUM/WINERY/ADVENTURE PARK Families and wine virgins will enjoy a trip to Europe's premier wine adventure park run by the godfather of Beaujolais wine, Georges Duboeuf. The wine museum covers 2,000 years of history, while the original town train station has been converted into a wine transport exhibition. Interactive games and holograms keep the kids amused; for adults, there's a video-animated wine tour through Beaujolais. In summer, stroll around

Château de la Chaize

The much-admired, 17th-century **Château de la Chaize** (500 route de la Chaize, Odenas; www.chateaudela chaize.fr; ✆ **04-74-03-41-05**) is a fairy-tale setting to taste the sought-after wines of Brouilly. Since its recent sale to the Maïa group, new additions include more eco-friendly winemaking facilities with geothermal water systems and solar panels. The immaculate grounds come complete with a topiary garden and star-formed vegetable patch.

the Beaujolais garden, ride on the mini train, try your hand at mini golf or play on the giant chessboard. There's also an excellent cafe. Families may want to include a visit to the zoo nearby, **Touroparc** (400 rue du Parc; www.touroparc.com; ✆ **03-85-35-51-53**).

796 route de la gare, Romanèche-Thorins. www.duboeuf.com. ✆ **03-85-35-22-22**. From Belleville, head north on D906, then west on D32 to the Hameau Duboeuf. Admission to wine center, gardens, and adventure golf: 18€ adults; 6€ children ages 7–15; free for children 6 and under. Daily 10am–6pm. Closed Jan.

WHERE TO EAT

L'Auberge du Cêp ★★ GASTRONOMIC FRENCH This long-standing dining institution is today, once again, one of the must-visit addresses for gastronomes in Beaujolais. It's all thanks to the hard work of chef Aurélien Merot who has brought his own twist to traditional French fare with signature dishes such as veal sweetbread pie with foie gras and asparagus (from local farmer Jerôme Galis) with a Maltaise (blood-orange Hollandaise) sauce.

11 rue des Quatre Vents, Fleurie. www.aubergeducep.com. ✆ **04-74-04-10-77**. Fixed-price lunch 27€ or dinner 47€–70€. Tues–Sat 12:15–1:30pm and 7:45–9pm.

VIENNE ★★

A must for visitors to Vienne is **Musée Gallo-Romain** ★★, Route Départementale 502, Saint-Romain-en-Gal (www.musee-site.rhone.fr; ✆ **04-74-53-74-01**), is a must for visitors to Vienne. This 7-hectare (17-acre) archaeological site merely scratches the surface of the myriad Roman remains that still exist beneath the foundations of modern Vienne. As you take a tour around the remains of Roman houses and public baths, you'll marvel at their sophistication. Inside the museum, you'll see mosaic floors, frescos, and household items. The museum is open Tuesday to Sunday 10am to 6pm (last access 5:30pm; Nov–Mar closes at 5pm). Tickets are 6€ for adults; free for kids under 18.

Back in central Vienne, you can wonder around some Roman sites for free. In place du Palais Charles de Gaulle, you'll find one of the best-preserved Roman remains in France: the **Temple d'Auguste et de**

Livie ★★★, built on the orders of the Roman emperor Claudius and turned into a "temple of reason" during the French Revolution. Another outstanding monument is **La Pyramide ★★** (rue Fernand Point, next to the Michelin-starred restaurant) rising 16m (52 ft.) and resting on a portico with four arches. Nicknamed the "tomb of Pilate," the pyramid was allegedly built over the grave of Pontius Pilate, who was exiled to Gaul after the death of Jesus.

At the foot of Mont Pipet lies one of the town's most impressive Roman ruins: the **Théâtre Antique ★** (7 rue de Goris; ℰ **04-74-85-39-23**), where well-known bands play summertime concerts for up to 7,500 people at this Roman theater (for concert information, visit www.theatre antiquevienne.com). You can visit November to March Tuesday to Friday 9:30am to 12:30pm and 2 to 5pm, weekends 1:30 to 5:30pm; April to August daily 9:30am to 12:30pm and 1:30 to 6pm; September to October Tuesday to Sunday 9:30am to 12:30pm and 1:30 to 6pm. Admission is 3€.

Vienne also has a number of notable religious buildings. If you have to choose just one during a busy itinerary, we'd recommend the **Cloître de Saint-André-Le-Bas** (ℰ **04-74-78-71-06**) in place du Jeu-de-Paume near the river. With its Romanesque stone carvings, columns, and ornately carved capital stones, this church and cloister are all that remains of the 12th-century abbey. You can visit November to March Tuesday to Friday 9:30am to 12:30pm and 2 to 5pm, weekends 1:30 to 5:30pm; April to October Tuesday to Sunday 9:30am to 12:45pm and 1:30 to 6pm. Admission is 3€.

Temple d'Auguste et de Livie.

Where to Stay & Eat

Domaine de Clairefontaine ★★★ Surrounded by a dreamy 3-hectare (7-acre) park, this luxurious hotel is our favorite choice for Vienne and the Northern Rhône wine region. After wandering around the violet-carpeted forest and the peacock aviary, you can dine on trout from the freshwater pond in the superb restaurant run by chef/owner Philippe

The Mailman's Palace

Fit in a side trip to one of the world's strangest pieces of architecture **Palais Idéal**, 8 rue du Palais, Hauterives (south of Vienne; www.facteurcheval.com; *04-75-68-81-19*), is the lifelong work of French postman Ferdinand Cheval. Built of stone and concrete and elaborately decorated with clamshells, it's a monumental tribute to one man's whimsical imagination. The work was finished in 1912, when Cheval was 76. You can visit December to January 9:30am to 4:30pm; February, March, October, and November until 5:30pm; April to September until 6:30pm. Admission is 9.50€ adults; 5.50€ kids up to 16; free for kids 2 years and under.

Girardon. Well-priced accommodation is provided in the manor, the former stables, and Le Cottage (which also houses an informal bistro).

105 Chemin des Fontanettes, Chonas-L'Amballan. www.domaine-de-clairefontaine. fr. *04-74-58-81-52.* 35 units. 81€–195€ double; 250-280€ apartment. **Amenities:** Restaurant, bar, garden, tennis court, free Wi-Fi. Closed mid-Dec to mid-Jan.

La Pyramide ★★ MODERN FRENCH   With a *chevalier de la legion d'honneur* award and two Michelin stars under his belt, chef Patrick Henriroux's contribution to French cuisine is indisputable. La Pyramide is where Parisians-in-the-know stop over on their annual road trips to the Riviera. It was once home to the historic chef, Fernand Point, who died in 1955. Current owner-chef Patrick Henriroux has preserved many of Point's secrets, especially his sauces. Gourmands should try the lobster prepared three ways or the summer truffle, foie gras and fingerling potato pancake. Henriroux also runs the excellent and reasonably priced bistro **Espace PH3.** La Pyramide isn't just a restaurant, but also a swank hotel with 19 spacious bedrooms (doubles 200€–240€).

14 bd. Fernand Point. www.lapyramide.com. *04-74-53-01-96.* Main course 66€–105€; fixed-price menus 89€–206€. Thurs–Mon noon–1:15pm and 7:30–9:15pm (closed Mon in low season). Closed mid-Feb to mid-Mar and 1 week in mid-Aug.

L'Estancot ★ FRENCH   With its bare-stone walls and bistro-style furnishings, this fab restaurant is famed for chef Bruno Ray's *criques.* Served with a simple green salad, these grated potato *rostis* come in all guises from *Côté Mer* (seabass, red mullet, and monkfish with basil) to *Périgourdine* (foie gras escalope).

4 rue de la Table Ronde. *04-74-85-12-09.* Main courses 21.50€–39.50€. Tues 7:15–8:45pm, Wed–Sat noon–1pm and 7:15–8:45pm. Closed early Sept and early Jan.

Where to Shop

Every Saturday, the streets around central Vienne play host to one of the Rhône Valley's largest **food markets.** This is a great place to stock up on fresh fruit and vegetables as well as regional products such as pear-infused

Eau de Vie (colorless fruit brandy). Check out **rue Testé du Bailler** for art galleries and **Caire-Rougeron,** 7 rue Boson (✆ **04-74-85-20-72**), for artisanal jewelry.

NORTHERN RHÔNE WINE COUNTRY ★★★

Curving around the River Rhône from Vienne to Valence, the Northern Rhône has been growing wine since Gallo-Roman times. Sought-after reds hail from **Côte Rôtie** and **Hermitage** where steep hillsides with golden-hued stone terraces are tilled by hand with horse-drawn ploughs. This photogenic region is also home to aromatic white wines such as **Condrieu.** This must-see region can be twinned easily with a visit to the Ardèche or Vienne.

Tupin et Semons

Heading out of Vienne on the route national 86 (D386), you'll pass the legendary vineyards of Côte-Rôtie that cling to steep escarpments up to 60% gradient. The names of famous wine producers, such as Guigal and Chapoutier, are hewn into the hillside. The small village of Tupin et Semons lies at the heart of Côte-Rôtie. A little-known treasure of this appellation is **Le Domaine de Corps de Loup ★★**, 2 route de Lyon (www.corpsdeloup.com; ✆ **04-74-56-36-97**), run by the Daubrée family. You can call in advance for a tour around the vineyard and the 15th-century cellar before a tasting in the ancient chapel-turned-tasting-room. Nearby, you'll find the far grander **Maison Vidal-Fleury ★★**, RD 386, 48 route de Lyon (www.vidal-fleury.com; ✆ **04-74-56-10-18**). Founded in 1781, Vidal-Fleury is the oldest continuously operating wine producer in the Rhône Valley. Thomas Jefferson dined here in 1787. Owned by renowned wine producer Guigal, the domaine produces over 1 million bottles per year. After a tour of the bottling plant and the enormous, vaulted cellars, visitors are offered tastings of some of the 22 different wines created here.

Best Wine Markets

Seasonal wine markets bring together all the appellations of the Northern Côtes du Rhône and provide the perfect way to taste these cru wines: **Ampuis** in late January; **Tain l'Hermitage** on the last weekend in February; **Saint Péray** on the first weekend in September; and **Cornas** on the first weekend in December. For more information, contact **Tain l'Hermitage-Ardèche** tourist office, 6 place du 8 mai 1945, Tain L'Hermitage (www.ardeche-hermitage.com; ✆ **04-75-08-10-23**; open Mon–Sat 9:30am–1pm and 2–6pm; Sun 9am–1pm).

WHERE TO STAY & EAT

Hôtel Le Beau Rivage ★   This hotel in Condrieu lives up to its name: It has majestic views over the River Rhône. The best place to enjoy the riverscape is from the restaurant terrace with a glass of wine in hand. Happily meals there are fairly priced (starting at 45€ per fixed-price meal, up to 76€), and the rich French fare is served on Limoges porcelain plates. *Amuses-bouches* and a tray of chocolates bookend the meal. There's also a well-stocked wine list. Rooms are generously sized with clean, but tired furnishings—look for special deals on the hotel website.

2 rue Beau Rivage, Condrieu. www.hotel-beaurivage.com. ℂ **04-74-56-82-82.** 30 units. 155€–225€ double; 250€-330€ suite. Free parking. On southern outskirts of Condrieu, look for signs on the left. **Amenities:** Bar, restaurant; free Wi-Fi.

Tain-L'Hermitage

Drive south from Tupin et Semons along the D4 and then A7 towards Tain-L'Hermitage. A good place to start finding out about Northern Rhône

Tain l'Hermitage vineyards in Rhône Valley.

wines is at celebrated wine producer Michel Chapoutier's **wine school,** 18 av. Dr Paul Durand (www.chapoutier.fr; ℂ **04-75-08-28-65;** open daily 10am–1pm and 2–7pm; Sun closes at 6pm), which offers themed wine workshops and free wine tastings (for up to five people; prebooking at least 5 days in advance is required). Both are a great way to learn about Côtes du Rhône wines, as his expansive range covers appellations throughout the Northern and Southern Rhône Valley. Finally, gourmands of all ages will enjoy a visit to **La Cité du Chocolat,** 12 av. du Président Franklin Roosevelt (www. citeduchocolat.com; ℂ **04-75-09-27-27**). This chocolate emporium is run by commercial chocolatier, Valrhona, which has been producing chocolate for the world's finest pastry chefs since 1922. More recently, they have developed a range of consumer chocolate bars. Rather than a fact-heavy history, you're taken on a sensorial experience through the stages of chocolate making from

From Segway tours to electric bikes and 4×4, the latest vineyard tours make light of the steep hillsides of the Northern Rhône vineyards. These tours also provide an introduction to the geography and *terroir* of this prestigious wine-growing region. Our favorites are:

○ **Terres de Syrah** (www.terresdesyrah. com/en; ✆ **04-75-08-91-91** or 06-33-31-51-98), a collaboration between Les Sens Ciel and the Cave de Tain, with tours including "sur les pas de Gambert" **Hermitage walking**

trails, electric bikes, and Segway tours.

○ **Fabien Louis** (www.ausommelier-tain. com; ✆ **04-75-08-40-56** or 06-70-11-09-18), a sommelier-turned-wine-merchant whose bus and electric cycle tours of the Hermitage vineyards are followed by a visit to his shop, **Des Terrasses du Rhône** (22 rue des Bessards, Tain l'Hermitage; Mon–Fri 10am–3pm, Thurs–Fri 10am–7pm, Sat 10am), which sells more than 600 different Rhône Valley wines at vineyard prices.

collecting pods to a live factory-line replica, complete with plentiful chocolate tasting along the way. Afterwards, you can enjoy chocolate-infused savory dishes at the eco-friendly cafe.

WHERE TO STAY & EAT

Hôtel Les Deux Côteaux ★★ Fresh from a refurbishment, this spotless bed-and-breakfast is a convenient stopover for wine enthusiasts on the Rhône Valley trail. With views over the River Rhône, its 18 rooms have wooden floors and smart furnishings. Shower rooms are small. No dinner is served, but you can enjoy cheese-and-wine platters over a glass or two of wine on the riverside terrace. You'll also find excellent brasserie cuisine next door at **Brasserie Le Quai** (✆ **04-75-07-05-90**). Breakfast is copious with plentiful fresh fruit and homemade jams. Be aware that you'll need to use stairs to reach the bedrooms as there's no elevator.
18 rue Joseph Peala. www.2coteauxhotel.fr. ✆ **04-75-08-33-01.** 18 units. 90€–120€ double. **Amenities:** Terrace. Free Wi-Fi.

Le Cerisier ★★ FRENCH Located in nearby Tournon-sur-Rhône, the tiny Le Cerisier is worth a detour for its reasonably priced, hearty French fare, and its lovely outdoor terrace. Leave room for splendid desserts such as speculoos trifle with pear sorbet.
1 rue Saint-Joseph. www.lecerisier-restaurant.fr. ✆ **04-75-08-91-02.** Fixed-price menus from 25€. Tues and Thurs–Sat noon–1pm and 7:30–9pm.

Le Mangevins ★★ FRENCH The buzz of animated local diners fills this stylish, contemporary restaurant. While owner Vincent welcomes diners, his Japanese wife Keiko is busy in the kitchen. For a chef with no formal training, Keiko shows a hint of genius, cooking dishes such as yellow tuna and Iberica Bellota pork to perfection. The small menu changes daily and is excellent value, while the extensive wine list includes wines by the glass.

7 rue des Herbes, Tain-L'Hermitage. www.lemangevins.fr. ✆ **04-75-08-00-76.** Fixed-price menu 45€. Mon–Fri noon–1:30pm and 7:30–9:30pm.

VALENCE

671km (416 miles) SE of Paris; 100km (62 miles) S of Lyon

Follow the Rhône River south from Lyon and you'll reach this grey market town whose identity is now inextricably linked to its star attraction: Anne-Sophie Pic, France's only female three-star Michelin chef. A former Roman colony, it later became the capital of the Duchy of Valentinois, set up by Louis XII in 1493 for Cesare Borgia. Today Valence is a market town and distribution point for Rhône Valley fruit and vegetable producers. It's fitting that François Rabelais, who wrote of gargantuan appetites, spent time here as a student. Valence is a convenient day trip from Vienne or stopover on your way further South to Provence.

Essentials

GETTING THERE   **Trains** take 1 hour from Lyon. For information, visit www.sncf-connect.com or call ✆ **36-35.** If you're **driving** from Lyon, take A7 south. If you're travelling to Valence from Lyon by train, beware the TGV station: A 20-minute taxi ride costs around 41€. It will be quicker and cheaper to take a regional TER train straight to Valence's city center.

VISITOR INFORMATION   The **Office de Tourisme** is at 11 bd. Bancel (www.valence-romans-tourisme.com; ✆ **04-75-44-90-40;** open Mon–Sat 9:30am–12:30pm and 1:30–6pm; Sun 10am–1pm; wintertime Sun closure).

Exploring Valence

Gastronomy is the essential draw of Valence, but we'd recommend visiting the **Musée de Valence Art et Archéologie ★**, 4 place des Ormeaux (www.museedevalence.fr; ✆ **04-75-79-20-80**), that has been tastefully renovated by architect Jean-Paul Philippon. A fusion of ancient and modern architecture, the museum focuses on landscapes, with collections spanning 16th-century to contemporary art. The newest wing is topped by a 360-degree panorama over the Rhône valley towards the Vercors mountains. Open Wednesday to Sunday 10am to 6pm (10am–noon and 2–6pm low-season); admission to permanent collections is 9€ (6€ low-season) adults, and free for children under 18.

Where to Stay, Eat & Shop

It's unusual for a small market town to have a Michelin-starred restaurant, but Valence has three: the world-famous **Maison Pic** (see below), the intimate **Flaveurs,** 32 Grande Rue (✆ **04-75-56-08-40**), and the well-regarded **La Cachette,** 12 rue des Cévennes (www.lacachette-valence.fr; ✆ **04-75-55-24-13**), whose cozy sister restaurant, **Le Bac à Traille** (a couple of doors away on the same street) is also celebrated.

Maison Pic ★★★ FRENCH As one of the world's most celebrated female chefs, Pic occasionally lets fame go to her head. Luckily, you'll forget the blown-up portraits in the entranceway as soon as you reach the plush dining room. An army of staff is on hand to serve you course after course from specially commissioned cutlery. Don't miss her celebrated *berlingots* (pyramid-shaped, pasta sachets). The on-site bistro is the perfect alternative for those on a budget: **André** delivers Pic cuisine at sensible prices in a relaxed setting with an open-plan kitchen, leather banquettes, and a wood-paneled ceiling. Though this place is all about the food, there are smart double bedrooms (up to 727€ in peak season) with rosewood furnishings, leather headrests and silver-leaf screens. Prices are punchy, but there are good discounts (from 217€) in off-season. Ask for a quieter room facing the garden. There's a bijou-sized outdoor pool in the pretty garden.

> ### Spicing It Up
>
> A few doors down from the hotel-restaurant, you'll find the excellent café-deli, **L'Epicerie** ★★, 210 av. Victor Hugo (✆ **04-75-25-07-07**), where you can stock up on pantry items infused with Pic's favorite spices such as peach jam with Madras curry or Hojicha green tea leaves with Cubeb pepper.

285 av. Victor-Hugo. www.anne-sophie-pic.com. ✆ **04-75-44-15-32.** Restaurant: Fixed-price menus 110€–330€. Wed–Sun noon–1:30pm; Wed-Sat 7:30–9:30pm. Brasserie: Fixed-price menu 46€; daily noon–2pm and 7–9pm.

THE ARDÈCHE ★★

43km (27 miles) W of Montélimar; 138km (86 miles) SW of Lyon

Since the opening of the world's largest replica cave in 2015, the Ardèche has been rebranding itself as France's number-one destination for prehistoric heritage. The region is chock-a-block with history from Paleolithic caves and standing stones (dolmens and menhirs) to Troubadour castles. Of course, no visitor should miss the famous gorges, though you may want to avoid staying in tourist-swarmed Vallon Pont d'Arc.

Essentials

GETTING THERE Vallon-Pont-d'Arc is accessible by **trains** from Lyon connecting in Valence. It's a journey of 3 hours, 30 minute from Lyon at

Vallon-Pont-d'Arc, a natural bridge in the Ardèche.

about 40€ or 2 hours, 15 minutes from Valence TGV station at about 20€. For information, visit www. sncf-connect.com or call ✆ **36-35**. However, the Ardèche is best explored by car. If you're **driving** from Lyon, take the A7 south, then N7 at Montélimar Sud towards Pierrelatte. Head west on D13, then D59, and finally D4 to Vallon-Pont-d'Arc.

VISITOR   INFORMATION The **Office de Tourisme** is at Vallon-Pont-d'Arc (www.gorges-ardeche-pontdarc.fr; ✆ **04-28-91-24-10**).

Exploring the Ardèche

The Ardèche Gorges ★★

CANYON Hewn over centuries by the River Ardèche, a 60m (197-ft.) high natural limestone arch is the emblem of the Ardèche gorges. France's fastest-flowing river has carved a 30km (19-mile) path through limestone cliffs that ascend

up to 300m (984 ft.) high. Visitors have been able to canoe down the gorges since 1932. Of the dozens of kayak rental companies, we like the

L'Auberge Rouge

Balzac would laugh at this gruesome tourist attraction in the Ardèche village of Lanarce. Innkeepers Pierre and Marie Martin ran the **Auberge de Peyrebeille,** route nationale 102, Peyrebeille (✆ **04-66-69-47-51;** Mon–Wed and Fri 9am–8pm), in the 19th century, and had an unusual way of keeping food costs low. They murdered 50 guests over the years, and fed their bodies to other guests. Eponymously titled L'Auberge Rouge after Balzac's infamous novel, the inn is now a museum.

Table Wines of the Ardèche

The Ardèche is often overlooked as a wine region. Though it may not have the elite crus of the Côtes du Rhône, many well-priced table wines come from this region. A good place to start exploring the region's wines is at a wine festival: The 2-day **Festivin** in Bourg-Saint-Andéol during first week of December showcases over 30 producers with conferences and wine auctions, while wine estates open their doors for wine tastings and vineyard tours in April during the region-wide **From Farm to Farm** (www.defermeenferme.com) festival. Meanwhile, wine beginners and families can learn about wine at **Néovinum,** bd. de L'Europe Unie, Ruoms (www.neovinum.fr; ✆ **04-75-39-98-08**), a wine museum with interactive exhibits and easy-to-understand explanations.

reliable and safe **Aventure Canoës,** 1 pl. Allende Neruda (www.aventure-canoes.fr; ✆ **04-75-37-18-14**). The best time for kayaking is April to late November when the waters are green and sluggish and safer than during winter months. Alternatively, you can drive around the gorges on a well-marked route between Vallon-Pont-d'Arc and Pont St-Esprit. Watch out for careless drivers too busy taking snapshots to look where they are going. A good spot for a reliable snack in Vallon Pont d'Arc is **Le Chelsea,** 45 bd. Peschaire Alizon, Vallon-Pont-d'Arc (www.lechelsea.com; ✆ **04-75-88-01-40**), with its shaded terrace.

Vallon-Pont-d'Arc to Pont St-Esprit.

Grotte Chauvet Pont d'Arc ★ MUSEUM

Since its opening in 2015, the world's largest replica cave hasn't been without controversy. Some complain that it's an overpriced fake; the original 36,000-year-old cave, that has been awarded UNESCO World Heritage site status, sadly cannot be visited for fear of being damaged by troupes of tourists. However, this 29-hectare (71-acre) site provides an intriguing depiction of life in Upper Paleolithic times through paintings, drawings, and engravings as well as life-size fauna and interactive workshops. Guided visits are available in English. The onsite cafe has wonderful views over the Ardèche mountains.

4941 route de Bourg St Andéol, Vallon-Pont-d'Arc. www.grottechauvet2ardeche.com. ✆ **04-75-94-39-40.** Admission 18€ adults; 9€ children ages 10–17; free for children 9 and under. Daily wintertime 10:30am–5:30pm (except Jan to mid-Feb Wed–Fri noon–5pm and weekends 11am–4pm); summertime 9:30am–7:45pm. Check website for special opening hours during school and bank holiday openings.

Le Grand Site de L'Aven Orgnac ★★★ MUSEUM/CAVE

This is the perfect wet-weather attraction as the limestone caves are most beautiful when it rains. Discovered in 1939, the *grotte* is one of the largest in France with a dazzling array of stalactites and stalagmites. The adjacent archaeological museum, **Cité de la Préhistoire,** houses ancient artifacts that have been brought alive through child-friendly exhibits, 3D animations, and drawings by artist-cum-archaeologist Benoit Clarys. This imaginatively developed archaeological experience leaves visitors of all ages with palpable ideas of how prehistoric men lived in Paleolithic to Iron Age times.

Route de l'Aven, Orgnac-L'Aven. www.orgnac.com. © **04-75-38-65-10.** Admission 13€ adults; 10.40€ students and adults with 3 or more children; 8.50€ children ages 6–14; free for children 5 and under. Daily Feb 1:45–6pm; Mar 9:45am–12:30pm and 1:45–6pm; Apr–Sept 9:45am–6pm; Oct to mid-Nov 10am–1pm and 2–6pm. Check website for special opening hours during school and bank holidays.

Where to Stay & Eat

Château Clément ★★ Set within a 4-hectare (10-acre) parkland, this B&B is the place to live like a lord. Choose between garden-terrace rooms with contemporary furnishings, Jacuzzi baths and private terraces or climb the beautiful wooden staircase to sumptuous castle rooms with antiques, parquet floors and long windows. After a dip in the indoor pool, you can relax in the hammam or try a massage.

591 Mnt du Bois Vert. Vals-les-Bains. www.auchateauclement.com. © **04-75-88-33-53.** 5 units. 260€-310€ double. 375€-420€ suite. 440€–640€ apartment. **Amenities:** Spa; outdoor and indoor pools; hammam; free Wi-Fi.

Régis et Jacques Marcon ★★★ MODERN FRENCH This Relais & Châteaux eco hotel is home to a famous three-Michelin-starred restaurant run by the Marcon culinary dynasty. With its idyllic location on the hillside plateau of Saint-Bonnet-Le-Froid, this grass-roofed hotel maximizes natural light with wall-to-wall terrace windows. Its 10 large suites feature handmade wooden furniture and bathrooms with huge whirlpool tubs. The gastronomic cuisine (menus 205€–270€) focuses on local ingredients such as chestnuts and mushrooms grown in the nearby forests, while the wine list is dedicated to French wines from the 45,000-bottle cellar. The four-star hotel has a neighboring spa where guests can enjoy beauty treatments, saunas, and whirlpools while enjoying majestic mountaintop views. *Note:* Cheaper stays can be organized at the Marcon's two sister hotels, **Le Clos des Cimes** and **La Découverte** with bedrooms from 145€, while Marcon's village-center bistro, **La Coulemelle,** serves excellent, and more affordable, regional cuisine.

Larsiallas, Saint-Bonnet-Le-Froid. www.lesmaisonsmarcon.fr. © **04-71-59-93-72.** 10 units. 410€ suite (includes spa entry). **Amenities:** Restaurant; spa; cooking school; free Wi-Fi.

THE FRENCH ALPS

by Mary Novakovich

13

Part of France has more dramatic scenery than the Alps. The majestic western ramparts of the mountains and their foothills stretch along the southeastern flank of France, from the Rhône River and Lake Geneva spanning the France-Switzerland border, south to the shimmering sun of the Mediterranean. The skiing in the French Alps is truly the best in Europe. Some of the resorts are legendary, such as **Chamonix–Mont Blanc,** the capital of Alpine skiing, with its 20km (12-mile) Vallée Blanche run. Mont Blanc, at 4,810m (15,777 ft.), is the highest mountain in Western Europe. From January to April (and even into May in some resorts), skiers flock to Chamonix–Mont Blanc, Megève, Val d'Isère, and Courchevel; from July to September, spa fans head to Évian-les-Bains.

Most of this chapter covers the area known as the Savoy (La Savoie), taking in the French lake district and the largest Alpine lake, Lac Léman (Lake Geneva).

ÉVIAN-LES-BAINS ★★★

576km (357 miles) SW of Paris; 42km (26 miles) NE of Geneva

On the château-dotted southern shore of Lac Léman (Lake Geneva), Évian-les-Bains is one of the leading spa resorts in France. Its lakeside promenade, lined with trees and lawns, has been fashionable since the 19th century. Évian's waters became famous in the 18th century, and the first spa buildings were built in 1839. Bottled Evian is considered useful in everything from spa products to salt-free diets and is seen as a treatment for gout and arthritis.

In the days when Marcel Proust came to enjoy the Belle Epoque grandeur, Évian was the haunt of the very rich. Proust modeled his "Balbec baths" on Évian's. Today the spa, with its promenade and elegant casino, attracts a broader range of guests—it's no longer just for the rich. In fact, Évian, thanks to its imposing Palais Lumière conference center and numerous meetings facilities at its hotels, has earned the resort the title of "City of Conventions."

From late April to September, the lakeside **Nautical Center** (ville-evian.fr; ✆ **04-50-30-11-20**) is a popular attraction; it has a 115m (377-ft.)

Driving the Route des Grandes Alpes

Évian can be a starting point for the 741km (459-mile) drive to Nice along the **Route des Grandes Alpes ★★★**. One of Europe's great drives, it links Lake Geneva with the Riviera, crossing 35 passes along the way. Leaping from valley to valley, it's open from end to end only in summer (many passes are closed in winter).

You can make the drive in 2 days, but why hurry? The charm of this journey involves stopping at scenic highlights along the way, including Chamonix, Megève, and Val d'Isère. The most

dramatic pass is the **Galibier Pass (Col du Galibier),** at 2,645m (8,676 ft.), which marks the dividing line between the northern and southern parts of the French Alps.

En route to Nice, you'll pass to such towns as **St-Veran** (1,959m/6,426 ft.), the highest community in Europe; Entrevaux, once a fortress town marking the border between Upper Provence and the Alps; and **Touët-sur-Var,** a village filled with tall, narrow houses constructed directly against the towering rocky slope.

pool with a diving stage and water slide, solarium, restaurant, bar, and children's paddling pool. The Evian Resort Golf Club hosts the women's Amundi Évian Championship, the only Grand Slam stage in continental Europe on the LPGA tour.

Crescent-shaped Lake Geneva (Lac Léman) is the largest lake in central Europe. Covering about 362 sq. km (141 sq. miles), the lake is formed by the Rhône River and is noted for its exceptional blue color. As such, the major excursion from Évian is a boat trip on the lake offered by **CGN** (cgn.ch), a Swiss outfit whose agent is in Évian. A round-trip ticket from Évian to Lausanne in Switzerland costs 38€, 19€ for children 6 to 16. Book online, contact the company or head for the Office de Tourisme (see "Visitor Information," below) for other prices and hours. If you want to see it all, you can tour both Haut-Lac and Grand-Lac.

Essentials

GETTING THERE   The best way to approach Évian-les-Bains by **train** from the French Alps is to the gateway city of Annecy via Annemasse. (Many trains from other parts of France and Switzerland require transfers to the railway junction of Bellegarde.) The one-way fare from Annecy is 19.40€. For train information and schedules, visit sncf-connect.com or call ✆ **36-35.**

Popular **ferries (CGN)** leave Geneva from quai du Mont-Blanc, at the foot of the rue des Alpes, or from Le Jardin Anglais. Two ferries a day depart Geneva at 2:45pm and 7pm, arriving in Évian at 7:15pm and 11:20pm. Return crossings are at 10:05am, 1:15pm, and 6pm. A first-class, one-way ticket costs from 76.80€, a second-class ticket 54.70€. For

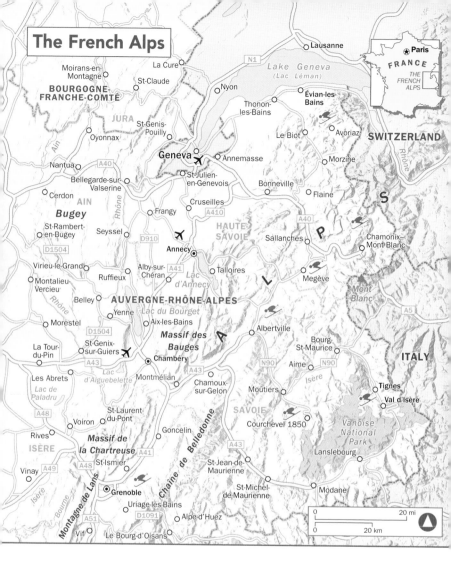

The French Alps

ferry information and schedules, visit cgn.ch or call ☎ **41-900-929-929** (calling to Switzerland).

   If you're **driving** from Geneva (trip time: 50 min.), take N5 east along the southern rim of the lake. From Paris, take A6 south. Before Mâcon, you'll see signs pointing to the turnoff for Thonon-Évian. From Thonon, N5 leads to Évian. Trip time is about 5½ hours, which can vary depending on traffic.

VISITOR INFORMATION   The **Office de Tourisme** is on place de la Porte d'Allinges (evian-tourisme.com; ☎ **04-50-75-04-26**).

An aerial shot of Évian-les-Bains.

Taking the Waters at Évian

The clear, cold waters at Évian, legendary for their health and beauty benefits, used to be the sole privilege of a clientele that possessed both the time and the money to appreciate them. Some of this hydro-grandeur is still to be found at the Évian Resort's hotels. Both **Hôtel Royal,** bd. de Royal (hotel-royal-evian.com; *Ⓣ* **04-50-26-85-00**), and **Hôtel Ermitage ★★★**, av. du Léman (hotel-ermitage-evian.com; *Ⓣ* **04-50-26-50-50**), have extensive and suitably expensive spa facilities, most of them open only to paying guests.

More reasonably priced are the spa facilities at **Les Thermes Évian,** pl. de la Libération (lesthermesevian.com; *Ⓣ* **04-50-75-02-30**). This public spa is just uphill from the edge of the lake. Hotel spas are more likely to emphasize beauty regimes and stress therapies; the public facility has a wider range of services, including massage, and skin and beauty care, plus a gym but no facilities for overnight guests.

You can indulge yourself with a day-long *thermale,* which provides access to exercise rooms and classes, saunas, steam baths, water from the Évian springs, and two massage sessions. Basic packages include a day in the pool, sauna and fitness center for 30€ or just a day in the sauna and steam room for 12€. You can also buy massage, health, and beauty regimes. The spa is open Monday to Saturday, usually from 9am to 7pm.

Where to Stay

The **Hôtel-Restaurant Le Bourgogne** (see below) also rents rooms.

Hôtel Ermitage ★★★ This grand Anglo-Normand-Savoyard-style residence is set within 19 hectares (47 acres) of private wooded grounds. Of the 80 rooms on offer, half have lake views—ask for a room with a *loggia* (enclosed balcony space) to be sure to enjoy the vistas whatever the weather. The luxury continues from the rooms to the golf course to the La Table restaurant (offering a three-course 59€ Market Menu).

1230 av. du Léman. hotel-ermitage-evian.com. ✆ **04-50-26-50-50.** 80 units. 180€– 374€ double; 428€–859€ suite. **Amenities:** Restaurant; bar; golf; indoor pool; spa; room service; free Wi-Fi.

Hôtel la Verniaz ★★★ This glamorous country house stands on a hillside with a view of woods, water (Lac Léman), and the Alps. Antiques fill the main house and the separate chalets; the chalets have their own gardens and more privacy. Throughout the hotel, you'll find comfortable, plush accommodations. Main courses in the hotel restaurant run from 21€ to 29€; fixed-price menu 39€.

1404 av. du Léman, Neuvecelle. verniaz.com. ✆ **04-50-26-94-50.** 36 units. 119€– 295€ double; 269€–370€ suite; 213€–610€ chalet. Closed mid-Nov to mid-Feb. **Amenities:** Restaurant; bar; babysitting; outdoor pool; tennis court; room service; free Wi-Fi.

Where to Eat

Hôtel Le Bourgogne ★★ TRADITIONAL FRENCH   Come here for a delectable meal, impeccable service, an attractive setting, and excellent wine. Menu choices in the restaurant are likely to include escalope of fried homemade foie gras, beef entrecôte served with morels, and a poached version of *omble chevalier* (local lake whitefish). Reservations required. The hotel also offers 30 neat, individual rooms for 135€ to 188€ for a double.

73 rue Nationale. hotelbourgogne.fr. ✆ **04-50-49-86-78.** Main course 17€–32€; fixed-price menu 19.90€–49€. Daily noon–2pm and 7–10pm.

ANNECY ★★★

538km (334 miles) SE of Paris; 56km (35 miles) SE of Geneva; 140km (87 miles) E of Lyon

Lac d'Annecy is the jewel of the Savoy Alps. The city of Annecy, which is the region's capital, makes the best base for touring the Haute-Savoie. Once a Gallo-Roman town, the seat of the comtes de Genève until the 15th century, Annecy opens onto one of the best views of lakes and mountains in the French Alps. Since the 1980s, Annecy has become a booming urban center that has managed to preserve its natural setting. Annecy's lakeside beaches are among about a dozen scattered around the lake, all of which come into their own during the summer months.

Old town of Annecy.

Essentials

GETTING THERE   If you're **driving,** Annecy is near several highways: From Paris, take A6 southeast to Beaune and connect with A6/N6 south to Mâcon-Nord. Then follow A40 southeast towards Neydens, connecting with A41 going southeast to Annecy. Allow at least 5 hours. From Geneva, follow D1201 south toward Annecy, crossing the border near Archamps. Trip time is 30 minutes.

A car is useful but not essential in the Alps. Annecy has rail links with Paris and Lyon. **Trains** arrive hourly from Lyon via Chambery (trip time: around 2 hr.), with a one-way fare from 20€. About 17 trains arrive daily from Paris's Gare de Lyon (trip time: around 4 hr.; transfer at Lyon or Aix Les Bains); the fare is from 58€ one-way. For information, visit sncf-conect.com or call ✆ **36-35.**

The nearby **airport** (annecy.aeroport.com; ✆ **04-50-27-30-06**) is in the hamlet of Meythet (Aéroport Annecy-Haute-Savoie-Mont-Blanc), with service on Air France from Paris's Orly airport.

VISITOR INFORMATION   The **Office de Tourisme du Lac d'Annecy** is at 1 rue Jean-Jaurès (lac-annecy.com; ✆ **04-50-45-00-33**).

Exploring Annecy

Built around the River Thiou, Annecy has been called the Venice of the Alps because of the canals that cut to the old part of town, **Vieil Annecy.** You can explore the arcaded streets where Jean-Jacques Rousseau arrived in 1728.

After seeing Annecy, consider a trek to the **Gorges du Fier** ★★ (gorgesdufier.com; ✆ **04-50-46-23-07**), a dramatic river gorge 9.5km (6 miles) to the west. To reach it, take a train or bus from Annecy's rail station to Poisy. From the station, go about 1.5km (1 mile), following the clearly marked signs. This striking gorge is one of the most interesting sights in the French Alps. A gangway takes you to a gully 3 to 10m (9¾–33 ft.) wide, cut through the rock by torrents of water; you'll hear the roar of the river at the bottom. Emerging from this labyrinth, you'll be greeted by a huge expanse of boulders. You can visit the gorge from June 15 to September 10 daily 9:30am to 7:15pm (last trip at 6:15pm), and from March 15 to June 14 and September 11 to October 15 daily 9:30am to 6:15pm (last trip at 5:15pm). The site is closed October 16 to March 14. A hike to its well-signposted depths takes less than 1 hour and costs 6€ for adults, 3€ for children 7 to 15; it's free for kids 6 and under.

You can also take a cruise on the ice-blue lake for which the town is famous. Tours of **Lac d'Annecy,** conducted from February to December, last 1 hour and cost 18€. An English-speaking guide points out the sights. Tours depart between one and six times a day, depending on the season. There are also crossings to the southernmost lakeside village of Doussard, as well as lunch and dinner cruises. Inquire at the

A summer day on Lake Annecy.

Office de Tourisme (see above), call the **Compagnie des Bateaux du Lac d'Annecy** or check online (bateaux-aannecy.com; ✆ **04-50-51-08-40**).

Château de Montrottier ★★ CASTLE   Within walking distance of the gorges, in the hamlet of Montrottier, is the 13th- and 14th-century Château de Montrottier. A one-time feudal citadel partially protected by the rugged geology around it, the château's tower offers a panoramic view of Mont Blanc. A small museum features the quirky items collected by a local dilettante, showcasing pottery, Asian and African costumes, armor, tapestries, lace antiques, and bronze bas-reliefs from the 16th century. Make sure to pick up the English-language guide at the front.

Lovagny. chateaudemontrottier.com. ☎ **04-50-46-23-02.** Admission 10€ adults; 8€ students; 6€ children 6–15; free for children 5 and under. Apr–June and Sept–Nov Wed–Sun 10am–5:30pm; July–Aug Mon–Fri 10am–5:30pm, Sat till 4pm, Sun till 6:30pm.

Le Palais de l'Île ★★ PALACE   This is the town's most frequently photographed symbol. Built before the 18th century and connected to the "mainland" of Annecy via a bridge, it resembles a miniature château, surrounded by water, despite its long-term use as a prison (and certainly a very cold one) for local malefactors. The ground level has insights into life during its time as a prison (sorry: French-only text), while the upper level has a fascinating collection of historical artifacts, maps and works of art.

3 passage de l'Ile. musees.annecy.fr. ☎ **04-85-46-76-80.** Admission (combined ticket with Musée Château d'Annecy) 7.20€ adults; 3.20€ ages 12–25; free for children 11 and under; admission to palais 3€ and 2€. June–Sept Wed–Mon 10:30am–6pm; Oct–May Wed–Mon 10am–noon and 2–5pm.

Musée Château d'Annecy ★ MUSEUM   This forbidding gray-stone monument, whose 12th-century pinnacle is known as the Queen's Tower, dominates the city. The château contains a museum of regional artifacts that include Alpine furniture, religious art, oil paintings, and modern works. One section is devoted to the geology and marine life of

---

The Lure of the Hills

The Office de Tourisme (see above) distributes free pamphlets that describe about a dozen easy, family-oriented hiking and biking excursions in the forests around Annecy. More experienced hikers may wish to pick up a free map with a detailed set of challenging walks.

Excursions in both categories last 2 to 6 hours. Some begin in the center of Annecy; others require a trip by car or bus from one of several towns in the area—such as **Saint-Jorioz** or **Sevrier,** to the west, or **Talloires,** to the east (see below)—to the trailhead. **Trans Dev Bassin Annecien** (annecy.transdev.com; ☎ **04-50-51-08-51**) sells bus tickets to the destinations around Annecy and Lac d'Annecy and Lac Léman. You can buy them online (which also shows timetables and routes) or at Espace Sibra at 21 pl. de la Gare. It also arranges minibus excursions to panoramic sites in July and August.

the region's deep, cold lakes. Alas, no wall text is translated into English which will make visiting a bit dull for those who don't speak French.

pl. du Château. musees.annecy.fr. ℰ **04-85-46-76-70.** Admission (combined ticket with Palais de l'Ile, valid for 48 hr.) 7.30€ adults; 4.20€ ages 12–25; free for children 11 and under; admission to château 4.30€ and 3€. June–Sept Wed–Mon 10:30am–6pm; Oct–May Wed–Mon 10am–noon and 2–5pm.

Where to Stay

Le Clos des Sens (see "Where to Eat," below) also rents rooms. And solo travelers, and real budgeteers, should check out the **Hotel du Nord** at 24 rue Sommeiller (www.annecy-hotel-du-nord.com), which has clean if forgettable-looking single rooms starting at just 75€ per night.

Best Western Plus Hotel Carlton ★   The obvious selling point of this hotel is the proximity to the train station, which is just on the other side of Square Verdun. However, each of the rooms has individual and chic decor which hits the right balance between vibrant and elegant. Some of the rooms have large balconies with castle and mountains views, and the lakeside and old town are less than a 10-minute walk away.

5 rue des Glières. bestwestern-carlton.com. ℰ **04-50-10-09-09.** 55 units. 125€–201€ double. Parking 17€. **Amenities:** Bar; room service; free Wi-Fi.

Hôtel Hébé ★★   This elegant boutique hotel is in a handy spot between the train station and the flower-fringed riverbanks of the Thiou. Its elegant rooms are a lesson in understated, contemporary style, a sort of hybrid between Scandinavian and Alpine. Even if you don't book one of the balcony rooms, you can relax in the sheltered little sun-trap terrace where they serve breakfast and drinks.

4 av. d'Aléry. hebehotel.com. ℰ **04-50-32-73-01.** 28 units. 129€–350€ double. **Amenities:** Bar; room service; bike rental; free Wi-Fi.

Where to Eat

Le Bouillon ★★ FRENCH   There's a deliberately limited menu in this buzzing little bistro, with a focus on local lake fish and seasonal produce. One fish, one meat, one vegetarian—but the food's high quality shows that you don't need a bulging menu to have a superb meal here.

9 rue de la Gare. lebouillon-annecy.com. ℰ **04-50-77-02.** Main course 23€–26€, fixed-price dinner 39€–48€. Tues–Fri noon–1:30pm and 7:30–9:30pm; Sat 12:30–2pm and 7:30–10pm.

Le Clos des Sens ★★★ MODERN FRENCH   Annecy's most acclaimed restaurant—part of the discreetly luxurious Le Clos de Sens hotel in the hilly environs of Annecy-le-Vieux just north of the old town—is a destination in itself and one you'll need to book in advance. Keeping it local is chef Franck Derouet's overriding principle in these exquisitely crafted seasonal dishes: fruit, vegetables, herbs, and flowers from the restaurant's garden; fish from Lac d'Annecy and everything else from within a 100km (62-mile) radius.

Should you wish to stay, the 11 supremely stylish rooms are beautiful places to take in views of the lake, and some have in-room hot tubs. Doubles from 370€–480€.

13 rue Jean Mermoz. closdessens.com. © **04-50-23-07-90.** Fixed-price dinner 238€–288€; fixed-price lunch 158€. Tues and Thurs 7:30–9pm; Wed and Fri–Sat noon–1pm and 7:30–9pm.

Annecy Nightlife

In the old town, you'll find bars, cafes, pubs, and (in warmer months) street dances, fairs, and carnivals. A calmer alternative is an evening of theater or dance at the **Théâtre d'Annecy,** 1 rue Jean-Jaurès (bonlieu-annecy.com; © **04-50-33-44-11**); tickets cost 10€ to 31€.

If a long day has left you thirsty, try the traditional Irish pub **Le Captain Pub,** 11 rue du Pont-Morens (captain-pub.fr; © **04-50-45-79-80**), with hearty ales on tap. Walk along Faubourg des Annonciades and take your pick from two lively neighbors: tapas at **La Verrière** (laverriere annecy.com; © **04-38-80-05-64**) and the friendly **Finn Kelly's Irish Pub** (finnkellys.com; © **04-50-51-29-40**).

For the most elegant evening on the town, head to the **Casino de l'Impérial,** Allée de l'Impérial (casino-annecy.com © **04-50-09-32-61**), part of the Belle Epoque–style Impérial Palace hotel on a peninsula jutting into Lac d'Annecy. Entrance to the gaming rooms is free; you must present a passport, and the dress code doesn't allow beachwear. The casino is open Sunday to Thursday noon to 2am, and Friday and Saturday noon to 4am.

TALLOIRES ★★

551km (342 miles) SE of Paris; 32km (20 miles) N of Albertville; 13km (8 miles) S of Annecy

The charming village of Talloires, which dates from 866, is old enough to appear on lists of territories once controlled by Lothar II, great-grandson of Charlemagne. Chalk cliffs surround a bay, and at the lower end a promontory encloses a port. An 18-hole golf course, **Golf Club du Lac d'Annecy** (golf-lacannecy.com; © **04-50-60-12-89**), and watersports such as boating, swimming, water-skiing, and fishing, make this a favorite vacation spot. Talloires also has one of France's great restaurants, Auberge du Père-Bise, and a Benedictine abbey founded in the 11th century, now the deluxe Abbaye de Talloires hotel.

Essentials

GETTING THERE   From Annecy, you can reach Talloires by **driving** south along D909 for 13km (8 miles). Regular **buses** connect Annecy to

Talloires, which take 50 minutes. In Talloires, buses stop in front of the post office. For bus information, visit Trans Dev in Annecy (annecy. transdev.com; ✆ **04-50-51-08-51**).

VISITOR INFORMATION The **Office de Tourisme,** a branch of the Lac d'Annecy tourist office, is at 28 rue André-Theuriet (lac-annecy.com; talloires.fr; ✆ **04-50-45-00-33**).

Where to Stay

Auberge du Père-Bise (see below) also rents rooms.

Abbaye de Talloires ★★ This 16th-century Benedictine monastery has been a hotel since the French Revolution, and it's one of the grand inns of the Alps. With close-up views of the lake, it doesn't equal the cuisine or the luxury of the Auberge du Père-Bise (see below), but it's a bit more affordable. The hotel is rich with beamed ceilings, antique portraits, leather chairs, gardens, and carved balustrades. The great corridors lead to converted guest rooms, of which no two are alike, and some of which have balconies with lake views. The furnishings include all the Louis periods, as well as Directoire and Empire. In summer, the restaurant expands onto a shaded lakefront terrace with a swimming area and sun loungers.

Chemin des Moines. abbaye-talloires.com. ✆ **04-50-60-77-33.** 37 units. 178€–370€ double; 339€–881€ suite. Closed mid-Nov to mid-Feb. **Amenities:** Restaurant; bar; room service; sauna; spa; free Wi-Fi.

Where to Eat

Auberge du Père-Bise ★★★ MODERN FRENCH Since the 1950s, when it attracted starlets and millionaires, Auberge du Père-Bise has radiated style and charm. A chalet built in 1901, it's one of France's most acclaimed—and expensive—restaurants. In fair weather, you can dine under a vine-covered pergola and enjoy the view of mountains and the lake. The gastronomic restaurant, helmed by chef Jean Sulpice, excels at dishes such as roe deer with beetroot and char lake fish. Reservations required. The less formal Le 1903 restaurant has floor-to-ceiling windows overlooking the lake to go with its more affordable menus from 70€–90€.

The inn also offers 23 luxurious guest rooms along with a spa, lakeside gardens and swimming area. Rates are 285€ to 800€ for a double and start at 615€ for a suite. Reserve at least 2 months in advance, especially in summer.

Rte. du Port. perebise.com. ✆ **04-50-60-72-01.** Fixed-price menu 250€–290€. Thurs–Mon noon–2:30pm and 7:30–9:30pm. Closed mid-Nov to mid-Feb.

Flora ★★ FRENCH This laid-back restaurant and bar come with an outdoor swimming pool where you can lounge around on one of the sunbeds and relax with a cocktail. When you're hungry, order some grilled lake fish, octopus, or a hearty plate of steak tartare. Talloires isn't known for being one of the cheaper places along Lac d'Annecy, but Flora does offer good value.

119 rte. du Port. flora-talloires.com; ℂ **04-50-60-71-14.** Main course 23€–38€. Sunbeds 20€. Pool open daily 11am–7pm; bar 5:30pm–1am; restaurant Mon and Wed–Fri 7–11pm, Sat–Sun noon–2:30 and 7–11pm.

GRENOBLE

567km (352 miles) SE of Paris; 55km (34 miles) S of Chambéry; 103km (64 miles) SE of Lyon

The ancient capital of the Dauphine, Grenoble is the commercial, intellectual, and tourist center of the Alps. It's a major stop for travelers, including those driving between the Riviera and Geneva.

A sports capital in winter (it hosted the 1968 Winter Olympic Games) and summer, it attracts many foreign students; its university has one of the largest summer-session programs in Europe. Founded in 1339, the University of Grenoble has a student body of some 55,000. The metropolitan area, the *agglomération grenobloise* (pop. 660,000), is also home to four other universities with a large contingent of English and American students, giving the city a cosmopolitan air.

Essentials

GETTING THERE   Grenoble is the region's gateway and lies 35 minutes by car from the Grenoble Alpes Isère airport, 40 minutes from the Lyon-Saint-Exupéry international airport, and 90 minutes from Geneva airport. Flights arrive in Grenoble from London and other airports in Britain. Airlines include **easyJet, British Airways, Ryanair, Jet2,** and **Wizz Air;** some airlines fly only during the winter season. For more information, contact **Grenoble Alpes Isère** airport (grenoble-airport.com; ℂ **04-76-65-48-48**), 41km (25 miles) northwest of the city center. The **Actibus** shuttle bus meets every flight and takes passengers to and from Grenoble's center; the cost is 17€ one-way (alps-airport-transfer.co.uk). A taxi (ℂ **06-81-51-97-12**) to the town center costs from 80€ to 110€.

For information on flying into Lyon, see chapter 12. **Flixbus** (flixbus.fr) takes passengers to Grenoble, with one-way fares from 13.99€. **BlaBlaCar** bus (blablacar.co.uk) runs the same service, with one-way fares from about 10.99€. Travel time is about 1 hour, 8 minutes.

An important rail and bus junction, Grenoble is easily accessible from Paris and all the cities in this chapter. About 24 **trains** per day arrive from Paris Gare de Lyon (trip time: 3½ hr., depending on whether it's direct or there are connections); the one-way fare starts at 35€. Trains arrive once or twice an hour from Chambéry (trip time: from 47 min.; from 13.70€ one-way). For information, visit sncf-connect.com or call ℂ **36-35.**

The city is on the Chambéry-Geneva motorway (A41) and connected to the Paris-Lyon-Marseille motorway (A6/A7) in the west via the A48. If you're **driving,** take A6 from Paris to Lyon and then continue on A48 into Grenoble. Depending on conditions, the drive should take 6 to 7 hours.

VISITOR INFORMATION The **Office de Tourisme** is at 14 rue de la République (grenoble-tourisme.com; ✆ **04-76-42-41-41**). For information about public transportation in Grenoble, contact **Transports de l'agglomération grenobloise** (TAG; tag.fr; ✆ **04-38-70-38-70**).

Exploring Grenoble

Grenoble lies near the junction of the Isère and Drac rivers. Most of the city is on the south bank of the Isère, though its most impressive monument, the **Fort de la Bastille,** stands on a rocky hilltop on the north bank. The center of Grenoble's historic section is around the **Palais de Justice;** the more modern part of town is southeast, centered on the **Hôtel de Ville** (town hall) and the nearby **Tour Perret** lookout, affectionately known as the "tower to look at the mountains."

Grenoble's cable cars.

Begin at **place Grenette,** where you can enjoy a drink or an espresso at a cafe. Don't miss the **place aux Herbes** and **place St-André,** in the very heart of the *centre ville.* Place St-André, dating from the Middle Ages, is the most evocative square in old Grenoble, with the Palais de Justice on one side and the Eglise St-André on the other. The Palace of Justice was built in many stages. The brick church went up in the 13th century. Two great streets for strolling and browsing are rue de la Poste, in the medieval core, and rue J.-J.-Rousseau, a short walk southwest of the city.

Enjoy a ride on the **Téléphérique-Grenoble-Bastille** (bastille-grenoble.fr; ✆ **04-76-44-33-65**), cable cars that take you from the south bank of the Isère River to the top of the fort (closed Jan for annual maintenance). Check the website for the cable car's operating hours. A round-trip ticket costs 9.50€ for adults and 5€ for ages 5 to 15. At the belvedere where you land, you'll have a view of the city, the mountains, and the remains of the Fort de la Bastille. Come for the view, not the fort. You can walk up in 1 hour or so if you're an athletic type; the beginning of the route is signposted to the west of place St-André. We suggest you take the *téléphérique* to the top and then stroll down along the footpath, Montée de Chalmont, that winds to Alpine gardens and past old ruins before reaching a cobblestone walk that leads to the old town.

Musée Archéologique Grenoble ★★★ MUSEUM   At the foot of the Bastille lies the former Romanesque Saint-Laurent church, built on the remains of a Gallo-Roman necropolis. The church was originally deconsecrated in 1983 to become an archaeological dig; in 1986 it became a museum. Upon entering, visitors stand on a platform high above the restored remains of the nave, with colored illuminations showing which section of the building were built during each of the many phases of construction and renovation, dating from the early Middle Ages to the 19th century. The centerpiece is the crypt which dates from the original construction of the 6th-century cruciform funerary church.

pl. Saint-Laurent. musees.isere.fr. ✆ **04-76-44-78-68.** Free admission. Wed–Mon 10am–6pm.

Musée Dauphinois ★★ MUSEUM   This place is a quick course on life in the Alps: No other museum gives such a detailed view of this culture. A collection of ethnographic and historical mementos of the Dauphine region is on show, along with folk arts and crafts, furnishings, tools, and artifacts of all sorts. Surprising highlights: the display on pop music, along with one showing how sound affects our daily lives. Housed in the original 17th-century convent Ste-Marie-d'en-Haut and enhanced by the convent's cloister, gardens, and baroque chapel, the museum lies across the Isère on the way up to La Bastille.

30 rue Maurice-Gignoux. musees.isere.fr. ✆ **04-57-58-89-01.** Free admission. Wed–Mon 10am–6pm (until 7pm Sat–Sun).

Musée de Grenoble ★★★ MUSEUM   Founded in 1796, this is one of the country's oldest art museums. It was the first French museum outside of Paris to focus on modern art, a fact appreciated by Picasso, who donated his *Femme Lisant* in 1921. The collection includes Flemish and Italian Renaissance works, but the Impressionist paintings generate the most interest, especially Matisse's *Intérieur aux aubergines* and Léger's *Le Remorqueur.* Ernst, Corot, Klee, Bonnard, Gauguin, Monet—they're all here. Visitors also see artifacts and relics from Greek, Egyptian, and Roman times, including a well-preserved mosaic. The artistic highlight is a sculpted door panel from the 1400s, depicting Jacob and his sons. A collection of 20th-century sculptures occupies the esplanade and park surrounding the museum.

5 pl. de Lavalette. museedegrenoble.fr. ✆ **04-76-63-44-44.** Admission 8€ adults; 5€ seniors and students; free for children 17 and under; free for everyone 1st Sun of each month. Wed–Mon 10am–6:30pm.

Where to Stay

Le Grand Hôtel Grenoble, BW Premier Collection ★★ In an excellent position near the Jardin de Ville, the cable car and one of Grenoble's central shopping districts, Le Grand Hôtel has sleek modern (and soundproofed) rooms that work well within this elegant 19th-century Haussmann building. You'll find a few mid-century modernist chairs to go with comfortable padded headboards, all in a pleasantly neutral palette. Some come with wrought-iron balconies where you can watch life go by down below. The hotel's bar has wonderful views to go with its range of wines and cocktails.

5 rue de la République. bestwestern.fr. ℰ **04-76-51-22-59.** 67 units. 145€–274€ double; 250€–304€ suite. **Amenities:** Bar; room service; business center; free Wi-Fi.

Okko Hotels Grenoble Jardin Hoche ★★ Okko Hotels' concept of bringing four-star chic urban design into the heart of cities continues with its Grenoble outpost, which is right by the Jardin Hoche. There's no blandness within its contemporary rooms, with stylish design details that go behind the usual cookie-cutter hotels, such as Japanese-style fold-down desks. There's more of an intimate atmosphere here, as you're welcome to help yourself to free snacks and soft drinks in the Club, a 24-hour lounge and workspace that has a terrace with fabulous views of the mountains. Drop by for the free aperitivo from 6:30 to 8:30pm or try the light menu in the Dining Cellar. There's even a compact fitness area that includes a sauna.

23 rue Hoche. okkohotels.com. ℰ **04-85-19-00-10.** 138 units. 89€–133€ double. Some rates have minimum stays of 2 or 3 nights. **Amenities:** Restaurant; bar; co-working space, fitness room, sauna; free Wi-Fi.

Park Hôtel Grenoble MGallery ★★ Overlooking Parc Paul-Mistral, this is one of the most opulent and prestigious hotels in Grenoble. On the lower floors of a mid-1960s tower mostly devoted to private condominiums, it's a short drive south of Grenoble's commercial center and close to City Hall. Each guest room is decorated differently, with a blend of dignified (sometimes antique) furniture, state-of-the-art lighting, and modern red fittings and upholstery.

10 pl. Paul-Mistral. all.accor.com. ℰ **04-76-85-81-23.** 43 units. 121€–171€ double; from 181€ suite. Parking 30€. Tram: A to Chavant. **Amenities:** Restaurant; bar; fitness center; babysitting; room service; free Wi-Fi.

Where to Eat

Auberge Napoléon ★★ FRENCH No other restaurant in France boasts as intense an association with Napoleon Bonaparte. In 1815, Napoleon spent the night here at the beginning of a 100-day reign that ended with his defeat by Wellington at the Battle of Waterloo. You'll find enough references to the history of France, from the Revolution to around 1820, to keep even a student of French history busy. The restaurant seats only about 20, and, after its former owner retired, transformed itself from a gastronomic restaurant to one offering more affordable dishes at lunchtime only. It also has become a place of training for aspiring chefs and serving staff who have learning difficulties and certain disabilities.

7 rue de Montorge. aubergenapoleon.fr. © **04-76-87-53-64.** Main course 12€–17€; fixed-price menu 17€–21€. Mon–Fri 11:30am–1pm. Closed Aug.

Café de la Table Ronde ★★ FRENCH   This is the second-oldest cafe in France, after the more famous Procope in Paris. Founded in 1739, the cafe has attracted such luminaries as Stendhal and Sarah Bernhardt. It is said to be the spot where Pierre Choderlos de Laclos conceived the plot for his 1784 novel *Les Liaisons Dangereuses.* The menu offers both regional and national cuisine—the ingredients always fresh and the portions always huge. We gravitate to *le poisson du jour* (fresh fish of the day), although the *fondue savoyarde* with charcuterie is a winter delight, as is the Alpine ham. It's always busy so book a table early and be prepared to wait.

7 pl. St-André. restaurant-tableronde-grenoble.com. © **04-76-44-51-41.** Main course 13€–39€; fixed-price menus 20€–33€. Daily noon–2:30pm and 7–10:30pm.

La Ferme à Dédé ★★★ SAVOYARDE   Owning the most popular Savoyarde restaurant in the Gateway to the Alps is a bold claim, but Dédé is able to make it with confidence. The central location and Alpine-inspired design (the cash till is situated on a traditional wooden wagon), not to mention the brilliant fondues, raclettes, enormous charcuterie platters, and good choice of local craft beer, ensure this place fills up fast even on weekdays. Try to book ahead, but if it's full try your luck at the door, as the staff—always rushed off their feet but unfalteringly happy to help—will try to squeeze you in if your group is four or less; if you're really stuck, a sister venue is near the train station.

24 rue Barnave. www.restaurantlafermeadede.com. © **04-76-54-00-33.** Main course 17.50€–24€. Daily 11:50am–2:30pm and 6:50–11:00pm.

Grenoble Nightlife

To get things started, walk to **place St-André, place aux Herbes,** or **place de Gordes.** On a good night, these squares overflow with young people, and the energy level builds in anticipation of an explosion of dancing and partying. Join fun-loving crowds of European students at **Le Couche Tard,** 1 rue du Palais (© **06-49-81-25-95**), the **London Pub,** 11 rue Brocherie (© **07-68-78-38-06**), and **Le Bukana,** 1 Quai Créqui (© **04-56-24-71-69**).

Le Vieux Manoir, 52 rue Saint-Laurent (© **04-76-42-00-68**), is often smelly and always packed. Attuned to cutting-edge music from such centers as London and Los Angeles, guests expect a mix of hip-hop, R&B, soul, and techno, but are prepared for anything.

The town's most animated LGBTQ disco is **Le Georges V,** 124 cours Berriat (✆ **06-62-06-16-23**), which is open Thursday to Saturday 10pm to 6am.

COURCHEVEL ★★

633km (392 miles) SE of Paris; 52km (32 miles) SE of Albertville; 97km (60 miles) SE of Chambéry

Courchevel has been called a resort of "high taste, high fashion, and high profile," a chic spot where multimillion-dollar chalets sit on pristine pine-covered slopes. Skiers and geographers know it as part of Les Trois Vallées, whose other resorts are Méribel, La Tania, St-Martin-de-Belleville,

A snowy view of Courchevel.

Les Menuires, Val-Thorens, and, in the "fourth valley," Orelle. The resort, with 150km (93 miles) of ski runs in Courchevel and 604km (374 miles) of ski runs in the Trois Vallées around it, employs as many workers in summer as in winter. Courchevel 1850 has excellent resorts and hotels—with price tags to match—so it draws the super-rich. Travelers on average budgets might prefer to head for more reasonably priced resorts, including La Tania, Les Menuires, and Chamonix (p. 511).

Courchevel consists of four planned ski towns, each designated by its elevation in meters. They are, in order of increasing height, prestige and price: Courchevel 1300 (Le Praz), Courchevel 1550, Courchevel 1650 (Moriond), and, crowning them all, Courchevel 1850. There's also the small resort of La Tania, which falls under Courchevel. Courchevel maintains at least nine ski schools, along with a labyrinth of chairlifts and more than 200 ski runs, which are excellent in the intermediate and advanced categories. It's also one of France's best ski resorts for beginners.

Courchevel 1850 is one of the most attractive ski resorts in the French Alps. It's also the focal point of a chair-hoist network crisscrossing the Trois Vallées region. At the eastern end of the largest ski domain in the world, Courchevel sits at the base of a soaring amphitheater whose deep snowfalls last longer than those at most other resorts because it faces north. Like ski resorts worldwide, Courcheval has had issues with snow cover in recent years, but the resort's snow-making operation is really good and goes a long way to make up for lighter natural cover. So you can still expect perfectly groomed runs, vertical cliffs, and enough wide runs to appease the intermediate skier. Experts pit themselves against the challenge of the Grand Couloir, the steepest ski run in Europe.

Essentials

GETTING THERE If you're **driving** from Paris, take A6 to Lyon, then A43 to Chambéry, and then A430 to Albertville. At Albertville, take N90 to Moûtiers and then follow the narrow roads D915 and D91A into Courchevel. Courchevel 1850 is the last stop on a steep Alpine road that dead-ends at the village center. Roads are open year-round, but driving can be treacherous during snowstorms. To go any higher, you'll have to take a cable car from the center of town. Most visitors drive here (you're legally obliged to put on snow chains from November to March), but the area has a very good **bus** network linking all four ski towns to each other and the railway junctions farther down the mountain.

The nearest **train** station is in Moûtiers (officially called Moûtiers-Salins-Brides-les-Bains). From Paris's Gare de Lyon, 10 trains per day leave for Moûtiers. The high-speed TGV trains go via Chambéry in about 3 hours (sncf-connect.com; ☎ **36-35**), while slower connections go via Lyon and Aix-les-Bains. From the station in Moûtiers, a 1-hour **bus** trip completes the journey to Courchevel. There are five buses per day Monday to Friday and 15 per day on Saturday and Sunday, costing from 10.80€ to 12€.

The nearest **airports** are in Grenoble and Geneva, although there is a limited seasonal service to Chambéry; buses are timed to coincide with flight arrivals and run to Moûtiers and Courchevel, costing from about 69€ to Moûtiers and from about 90€ to Courchevel taking around 4 hours. From the airport at Lyon, three to five buses a day go to Courchevel; the 4-hour trip costs 65€ one-way.

VISITOR INFORMATION The **Office de Tourisme,** at 9 rue de l'Eglise (courchevel.com; ☎ **04-79-08-00-29**), provides information on skiing and each of the four Courchevel ski towns, as well as La Tania.

SKI PASSES You can buy ski passes and lift tickets online in advance at skipasscourchevel.com or at one of the ski offices, located at each level (1300, 1650, and 1850) and at La Tania. A 1-day pass (lift ticket) for Courchevel costs 65€ for adults and (52€ for children ages 5–13), and a 1-day pass for all Les Trois Vallées goes for 72€ (57.60€ per child). A 3-day pass costs 195€ (156€ per child) for Courchevel, 216€ (172.80€ per child) for Les Trois Vallées. For groups, you'll need to buy a pass for at least 6 days (from 260€ for a family pass to Courchevel).

Where to Stay

Hôtel Le Strato ★★★   Not only is this one of the Alps' great hotels, but it's also one of the great hotels in all of France. This palatial property, named after the famous skis by Rossignol, features individually decorated rooms and suites including duplexes that look out over the slopes. The ostentatious luxury continues through to the enormous spa (800 sq. m/8,611 sq. ft.), the acclaimed Baumanière restaurant that serves delicately smoked trout and baby squid, and the helipad for guests' private helicopter transfers.

rue de Bellecôte. www.hotelstrato.com. ℰ **04-79-41-51-60.** 25 units. 830€ double; from 1,060€ suite. **Amenities:** Restaurant; bar; indoor pool; spa; ski rental; hair salon; room service; free Wi-Fi.

Le Chabichou ★★   This is one of the town's finest hotels, within easy walking distance of many bars and clubs, and featuring a superb restaurant of the same name (see below). Most of the guest rooms in the gingerbread-trimmed chalet are large and well furnished. Beds offer grand Alpine comfort, with quality mattresses and fine linens. The spa is the largest in Courchevel, and has an indoor pool to go with its hydrotherapy pools, steam room, sauna and treatment rooms.

90 route des Chenus. chabichou-courchevel.com. ℰ **04-79-08-00-55.** 41 units. 865€–1,083€ double; from 1,308€ suite. Rates include breakfast. Parking 30€. Closed May–June and Sept to early Dec. **Amenities:** Restaurants; bar; children's club; babysitting; exercise room; ski rental; room service; indoor pool; spa; fitness center; free Wi-Fi.

Les Monts Charvin ★★   This cozy hotel in typical Savoyard chalet style proves you don't need to spend a fortune to stay in central Courchevel. The Charvin family, which includes a former Olympic skier, has owned this friendly place since it was built in the 1950s, and it's a warm, welcoming place without any pretensions. You'll find the sort of pine interiors you expect in such a traditional place, and most of its rooms have balconies. Its lounge with a fireplace and large squashy sofas is the place to relax after a day on the slopes.

Imp. des Verdons. hotel-courchevel1850.com. ℰ **04-79-04-19-10.** 19 units. 76€–280€ double; 150€–390€ suite. **Amenities:** Ski room; room service; free Wi-Fi.

Where to Eat

Le Chabichou ★★★ MODERN FRENCH   On the second floor of the hotel of the same name, with large windows showcasing a view of the slopes, Le Chabichou's stellar cuisine by Stéphane Buron includes a number of superlative dishes that change with the seasons. Depending on the month, you might find delicately crafted plates of local lake fish, turbot, lobster and, for meat-lovers, venison. Reservations required.

In Le Chabichou hotel, 90 route des Chenus. chabichou-courchevel.com. ℂ **04-79-08-00-55.** Fixed-price lunch 45€–90€ or dinner 175€–285€. Wed–Mon noon–9:30pm. Closed May–June and Sept to early Dec.

Le Chalet de Pierres ★★★ FRENCH/SAVOYARD   This is the one of the best of the lunch restaurants scattered across the slopes. Accented with weathered planking and warmed by open hearths, it sits in the middle of Des Verdons ski slope, a few paces from the path of whizzing skiers. Lunch can be served on a terrace, but most visitors gravitate to the two-story interior, where blazing fireplaces, hunting trophies, and a hip international crowd contribute to the place's charm. Items include air-dried Alpine meat and sausages, the best french fries in Courchevel, pepper steak, and *fondue savoyarde*. Reservations required.

rue de Jardin Alpin, Piste des Verdons. chaletdepierres.com. ℂ **04-79-08-18-61.** Main course 41€–75€. Daily noon–4:30pm. Closed late Apr to mid-July and mid-Aug to early Dec.

Courchevel Nightlife

A chic but seasonal resort, Courchevel offers nightlife that roars into the wee hours in midwinter but melts away with the snow. The area around **La Croisette** (the departure point for most of the lifts) contains lots of restaurants, bars, and clubs that come and go. For guaranteed atmosphere,

---

EN ROUTE TO geneva

If you're leaving France and headed toward western Switzerland, specifically Geneva, consider a final R & R stopover at **Jiva Hill Park Hotel** ★★, route d'Harée, Crozet 01170 (jivahill.com; ℂ **04-50-28-48-48**). Set on 28 hectares (69 acres) of parkland, it's within France, but only a 10-minute drive from the Geneva airport. This frontier region of the Alpine foothills, where Voltaire was exiled by the French monarchs, seems more closely tuned to Switzerland (especially Geneva) than to the rest of France. Isolated and peaceful, with 50 rooms, the hotel bills itself as a place "where luxury meets nature."

Angular and avant garde, it has interiors by Jean-Philippe Nuel, the acclaimed French hotel designer. Each unit is accented with exposed wood and touches of wrought iron, and manages to be minimalist, stylish, and ultra-comfortable at the same time. Among the rooms and suites are the Jacuzzi Lodges, where you can book a bungalow with its own Jacuzzi on a private terrace. On the premises is a highly rated deluxe spa, decorated like the rest of the hotel with a spectacular collection of contemporary art and state-of-the-art equipment. Other amenities include a gourmet restaurant, bar, outdoor pool, heated indoor pool, two tennis courts, and nearby golf course. Rates range from 231€ to 920€ for a double or start at 437€ for a junior suite.

head to place du Tremplin, where guests can either relax to live DJs at **Polar Cafe** (ⓒ **04-79-22-63-51**), enjoy international beers and cocktails at **Prends Ta Luge et Tire Toi!, La Luge** for short (prendstalugeettiretoi. com; ⓒ **04-79-08-78-68**), or live the high life at the **Strato Bar** (hotel strato.com; ⓒ **04-79-41-51-60**).

For a big afternoon out, or a dancing break between ski sessions, **La Folie Douce** (lafoliedouce.com; ⓒ **04-79-00-58-31**) on the way to Méribel is the place to be seen just before the last lifts close.

CHAMONIX–MONT BLANC ★★★

613km (380 miles) SE of Paris; 82km (51 miles) E of Annecy

At an altitude of 1,027m (3,369 ft.), Chamonix is the historic capital of Alpine skiing. Site of the first Winter Olympic Games, in 1924, Chamonix is in a valley almost at the junction of France, Italy, and Switzerland. Skiers the world over know its 20km (12-mile) **Vallée Blanche run,** one of the most rugged, and the longest, in Europe. With exceptional equipment—gondolas, cable cars, and chairlifts—Chamonix is among Europe's major sports resorts, attracting an international crowd with lots of English and Swedish skiers. Thrill seekers also flock here for mountain climbing and

Mont Blanc.

hang gliding from late May to mid-September. An old-fashioned mountain town, Chamonix has a breathtaking backdrop, **Mont Blanc ★★★**, Western Europe's highest mountain, at 4,734m (15,528 ft.).

The 11km (6¾-mile) **Mont Blanc Tunnel** has made Chamonix a major stop along this busiest highway. The tunnel is the easiest way to the mountains to Italy; motorists stop here even if they aren't interested in skiing or mountain climbing. For vehicles originating in France, the round-trip toll for a car and its passengers is 51.50€ one-way, 64.20€ round-trip. The return half of the round-trip ticket must be used within 7 days of issue. For information, visit tunnelmb.net or call ℂ **04-50-55-55-00.**

Chamonix sprawls in a narrow strip along both banks of the Arve River. Its casino, rail, and bus stations, and most restaurants and nightlife are in the town center. Cable cars reach into the mountains from the town's edge. Locals refer to Les Praz, Les Bossons, Les Moussoux, Argentière, and Les Pélerins as satellite villages within greater Chamonix, although, technically, Chamonix refers to only a section around place de l'Eglise.

Pricewise, Chamonix-Mont Blanc is marginally less expensive than Courchevel, in that there's a bigger choice of places to eat and stay. But prices have been going insane in the French Alps over the past couple of years, so the difference is far less than it was just 5 years ago.

Essentials

GETTING THERE   Most (but not all) **trains** coming from other parts of France or Switzerland require a transfer in such nearby villages as St-Gervais (in France) or Martigny (in Switzerland). Passengers change trains in either of these villages before continuing on by train to Chamonix. Passengers from Aix-les-Bains, Annecy, Lyon, Chambéry, Paris, and Geneva pass through those villages. There are five daily connections from Paris (trip time: 6 hr.); the one-way fare is from 72.70€. From Lyon are seven rail links per day (trip time: 4½–5½ hr.): A one-way fare costs from 48.90€. For more information and schedules for trains throughout France, visit sncf-connect.com or call ℂ **36-35.**

Year-round, two to six **buses** a day run from Geneva airport; the one-way fare ranges from 19€. Buses arrive and depart from a spot adjacent to the railway station. For information, call **Cie S.A.T.** (sat-montblanc.com; ℂ **04-50-78-05-33**).

If you're **driving,** you probably won't have to worry about road conditions. Because Chamonix lies on a main road between Italy and the Mont Blanc Tunnel, conditions are excellent year-round. Even after a storm, roads are quickly cleared. From Paris, follow A6 toward Lyon, and then take A40 toward Geneva. Before Geneva, turn south along A40, which runs to Chamonix.

GETTING AROUND   Within Chamonix, small buses (*navettes*) make frequent runs from points in town to many of the *téléphériques* (cable cars) and villages up and down the valley. For information, contact **Chambus** (chamonix-bus.com; ☎ **04-50-53-05-55**).

VISITOR INFORMATION   Chamonix's **Office de Tourisme** is at 85 pl. du Triangle-de-l'Amitié (chamonix.com; ☎ **04-50-53-00-24**).

SKI PASSES   To buy passes online, go to chamonix.com, which often offers online discounts, especially early-season deals; many ski offices in the area sell same-day tickets. The ski offices are dotted around Chamonix, for example at the Brevent or Montenvers lift entrances or further afield in Les Houches. Daily ski passes cost 54€ for Les Houches only (49.50€ per child; 167.40€ for a family); 67€ for Chamonix (57€ per child; 207.80 for a family); and 83€ (70.60€ per child; 257.40€ for a family) for "Mont Blanc Unlimited."

Skiing

With the highest mountain in Western Europe, this is an area for the skilled skier. Regrettably, the five main ski areas are not connected by lifts (you must return to the resort and take a different lift to ski a different area), and lines at the most popular areas are among the longest in the Alpine world. Weather and snow conditions create crevasses and avalanches that may close sections for days and even threaten parts of the resort. However, if you have a Mont Blanc Unlimited ski pass, this gives you access to other ski areas in both Italy and Switzerland, where the weather conditions can be vastly different.

Skiing is not actually on Mont Blanc, but on the shoulders and slopes across the valley facing the giant. Vertical drops can be spectacular, with lift-serviced hills rising to as high as 3,150m (10,332 ft.). Glacier skiing begins at 3,740m (12,267 ft.), and its off-piste skiing is among the best and most challenging in Europe. It's not ideal for beginners or timid intermediate skiers, who should head for Les Houches, Balme or Le Tour. World-class skiers come here to face the challenges of the high snows of Brévent, La Flégère, and especially Les Grands Montets, a fierce north-facing wall of snow about 3 city blocks wide.

Exploring Chamonix

The belvederes (mountain viewpoints) accessible from Chamonix by cable car or mountain railway are famous. For information, contact **Compagnie du Mont-Blanc,** 35 pl. de la Mer de Glace (compagniedumont-blanc.fr; ☎ **04-50-53-22-75**).

In town, you can board a cable car for the **Aiguille du Midi ★★★** and take a ride on the highest cable car in France. It takes only 20 minutes to go from central Chamonix to the dizzying heights of 3,842m (12,605 ft.). When you reach 3,777m (12,392 ft.), you arrive on the Aiguille du Midi's terrace that gives you jaw-dropping 360-degree views of the French, Italian and Swiss Alps. Then take the elevator to reach the summit terrace and be prepared to be knocked sideways by views of Mont Blanc.

There are more thrills in store when you **Step into the Void,** a glass box that hovers thousands of meters over an open space. Then follow the **Tube,** a steel gallery that goes around the central peak of the Aiguille du Midi. You'll find places to sit in front of huge windows to take in those views, and there's also a cafeteria and the **3842m Restaurant.** Visit **Espace Vertical,** the world's highest mountaineering museum that pays tribute to all those daring souls who have scaled these mountains.

From Aiguille du Midi, expert skiers can access the **Mer de Glace** glacier and the **Valleé Blanche,** the longest ski run in the world, and certainly one of the most challenging. You can end your journey at Aiguille du Midi and return to Chamonix; this excursion takes 2 to 3 hours (longer during busy periods).

The cable cars operate year-round, subject to favorable weather: in summer daily from about 7am to 5pm, leaving every 15 to 20 minutes, and in winter daily 8:30am to 3:30pm. The round-trip from Chamonix to Aiguille du Midi is 75€ for adults and 63.80€ for children ages 5 to 14. It's not recommended for children under 5, and those under 3 aren't permitted. You can usually get online discounts when you buy your tickets at montblancnaturalresort.com. The pass for Aiguille du Midi gives you free entry to Step into the Void and Espace Vertical. The Aiguille du Midi cable car is already included if you have a Mont Blanc Unlimited pass.

The final trip on the **Panoramic Mont Blanc** cable car to **Pointe Helbronner,** Italy—at 3,407m (11,175 ft.)—does not require a passport if you want to leave the station and descend to the village of Courmayeur. The round-trip from Chamonix to Pointe Helbronner is 113€; the cable car operates from late May to late September only.

Another cableway takes you up to **Le Brévent ★★★**, at 2,525m (8,284 ft.). From here, you'll have a first-rate view of Mont Blanc and the Aiguilles de Chamonix. The round-trip excursion takes about 1½ hours. Cable cars operate year-round from 8am to 5pm every 15 minutes. A round trip costs 37€.

Another journey takes you to **Le Montenvers ★★★** (✆ **04-50-53-12-54**), at 1,883m (6,176 ft.). Access is not by cable car, but on a **rack and pinion railway** known as the **Train Montenvers–Mer de Glace.** It departs from the Gare Montenvers–Mer de Glace, behind Chamonix's Gare SNCF, near the center of town. At the end of the run, you'll have a view of the 6.5km-long (4-mile) *mer de glace* ("sea of ice," or glacier). Immediately east of the glacier, Aiguille du Dru is a rock climb notorious for its difficulty. The trip takes about 2 hours, including a return by rail, but can take longer during busy periods. Departures are 8am to 6pm in summer, until 4:30pm in the off season; service usually operates year-round. The round-trip fare is 38€.

You can also visit a cave, **La Grotte de Glace,** hollowed out of the *mer de glace;* it has 580 steps from the exit of the Montenevers-Mer de Glace gondola. It's free to visit but opening times are weather dependent.

Where to Stay

A large selection of **AirBnB** options is available in central Chamonix and Les Houches; the value for your money increases quickly as you move down the mountain. Try the picturesque villages of Combloux, Domancy, and St-Gervais-les-Bains, all less than a 30-minute drive away.

Hôtel Le Faucigny ★★   Hotel Le Faucigny sets itself apart from the rest of the herd of traditional Savoyard-style hotels with a cool, Scandinavian look. The common areas feature comfortable sofas flanking natural wood benches and tables scattered about, a chilled-out setting for the free homemade cake served every day at 4pm. Its understated yet stylish rooms have soothing muted grays, simple modern furnishings, and more natural wood accents. The compact spa is decked out on oodles of slate and the decadent terrace offers views of the Mont Blanc. Family rooms sleep up to four people and have balconies with views of Mont Blanc. In ski season and other busy periods, the hotel often requires a 2- or 3-night minimum stay.

118 pl. de l'Eglise. hotelfaucigny-chamonix.com. ✆ **04-50-53-01-17.** 28 units. 148€–310€ double; from 200€ family room. **Amenities:** Bar; spa; ski room; free Wi-Fi.

Where to Eat

La Maison Carrier ★★ FRENCH   The gastronomic restaurant at the Hameau Albert 1er hotel is excellent…but eye-wateringly expensive. Our suggestion? Head to its sister restaurant, La Maison Carrier, instead. It offers beautifully cooked traditional Alpine dishes in a trio of dining rooms, with bay windows opening onto views of Mont Blanc and walls accented by rustic artifacts and antique farm implements. Among the winners are Le Maison's menu are roast rack of lamb, slow-roasted pork and cheese fondue. Pork lovers will want to try the Menu *Tout Cochon* (55€), which makes delicious use of every edible parts of the pig.

In Hameau Albert 1er hotel, 38 rte. du Bouchet. hameaualbert.fr. ✆ **04-50-53-00-03.** Main course 25€–52€; fixed-price lunch 28€ or dinner 28€–39€. Wed–Sun noon–2pm and 7–9:30pm. Closed mid-May to early June and early Nov to early Dec.

Le Chaudron ★★ TRADITIONAL FRENCH   You'll find fancier places in town, but for good value, honest cooking, and fine mountain ingredients, Le Chaudron is near the top of our list. Chef Stéphane

Osterberger makes excellent local specialties including tartiflette, raclette, and, of course, deliciously gooey fondue as well as hefty steaks.

79 rue des Moulins. le-chaudron-chamonix.com. ☏ **04-50-53-40-34.** Main course 25€–38€; fondue savoyarde (min. 2 people) 26€ each. Closed May–June and Oct–Nov.

Le Comptoir des Alpes ★★ ITALIAN/FRENCH   The former Comptoir Nordique in the Hotel Le Morgane now serves a tasty blend of Italian and French cuisine in elegant surroundings. Try artichoke ravioli with speck and rocket, confit of lamb shoulder that's been cooking for 12 hours, or tender chargrilled Charolais beef.

15 av. de l'Aiguille du Midi. comptoir-des-alpes.com. ☏ **04-50-53-57-64.** Main course 23€–42€; fixed-price lunch 31€–39€; fixed-price dinner 55€. Daily noon–2pm and 7–9:30pm.

Chamonix Nightlife

Nightlife in Chamonix runs the gamut from classical to riotous. Check out the cluster of bars along rue des Moulins, including **Bar'd Up** (☏ **04-50-53-91-33**), a favorite among the younger crowd, plus live music at **Le Privilège** (☏ **04-50-53-29-10**). Opposite the railway station on av. Michel Croz are lively après-ski neighbors: the Swedish **Moö Bar** (☏ **04-50-55-33-42**) and the very French **Elevation 1904** (☏ **04-50-53-00-52**). The **casino,** 12 pl. H.-B.-de-Saussure (☏ **04-50-53-07-65**), has slot machines and roulette and blackjack tables. **La Folie Douce,** 823 allée Recteur Payot (☏ **04-50-55-10-00**), usually known for its afternoon slopeside après-ski parties, has raucous parties at its Chamonix hotel, with live DJs both inside and on its large terrace.

PROVENCE

By Kathryn Tomasetti

14

T he ancient Greeks left their vines, the Romans their monuments, but it was the 19th-century Impressionists who most shaped the romance of Provence today. Cézanne, Gauguin, Chagall, and countless others were drawn to the unique light and vibrant spectrum brought forth by what van Gogh called "the transparency of the air." Modern-day visitors will delight in the region's culture, colors, and world-class museums. And from the markets of the Luberon to the street-eats of buzzing Marseille, they will certainly dine well, too.

Provence, perhaps more than any other part of France, blends past and present with an impassioned pride. It has its own language and customs, and some of its festivals go back to medieval times. The region is bounded on the north by the Dauphine River, on the west by the Rhône, on the east by the Alps, and on the south by the Mediterranean. In chapter 15, we focus on the part of Provence known as the Côte d'Azur, or the French Riviera.

AVIGNON ★★★

691km (428 miles) S of Paris; 83km (51 miles) NW of Aix-en-Provence; 98km (61 miles) NW of Marseille

If Disney made a Gallic romcom set in the most French of locations, Avignon would be the movie set. This city of 95,000 has it all in one compact center: honey-colored architecture, awesome restaurants, one-of-a-kind boutiques, and a UNESCO World Heritage Site. That's the Pope's Palace, where Pope Clement V fled in 1309, when Rome was deemed too dangerous for clergymen, ushering in a 67-year golden age for Avignon (and a schism in the Catholic Church). The city even has its own vineyard that ripples against the River Rhone. It sits slap bang in the middle of Côtes du Rhône and lavender country, with hikes, tours, and tastings dedicated to both.

Today this walled city makes a perfect stop on the route from Paris to Mediterranean cities like Marseille, Cannes, and Nice. From Avignon's cute train station you can be in the thick of the city in minutes. In recent years, Avignon has become known as an arts center, thanks to its annual international music festivals, its top-drawer museums, and wealth of experimental theaters and art galleries. It's as pretty as a postcard.

PREVIOUS PAGE: **Lavender field in Valensole, Provence.**

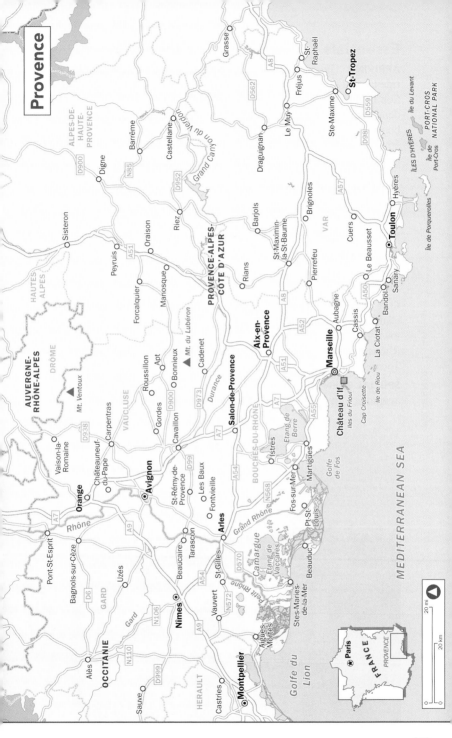

Provence

ALPES-DE-
HAUTE-
PROVENCE

Grasse

A8

St-
Raphaël

D562

Fréjus

Le Muy

St-Tropez

Ste-Maxime

ÎLE DU LEVANT

PORT-CROS
NATIONAL PARK

ÎLES D'HYÈRES

Île de
Port-Cros

Barrême

Castellane

Grand Canyon du Verdon

Digne

D900

N85

D952

Draguignan

D98

D559

Sisteron

Oraison

Riez

Barjols

Brignoles

Hyères

Toulon

Île de Porquerolles

A57

PROVENCE-ALPES-
CÔTE D'AZUR

Peyruis

A51

Forcalquier

Manosque

Rians

St-Maximin-
la-Ste-Baume

Pierrefeu

Cuers

Le Beausset

Sanary

Bandol

VAR

HAUTES-
ALPES

DRÔME

AUVERGNE-
RHÔNE-ALPES

Mt. Ventoux

Vaison-la-
Romaine

D938

Carpentras

VAUCLUSE

Apt

Roussillon

Gordes

Bonnieux

Mt. du Lubéron

Cadenet

Durance

Aix-en-
Provence

A52

Aubagne

Cassis

La Ciotat

A50

Marseille

Château d'If

Îles du Frioul

Île de Riou

Cap Croisette

Châteauneuf-
du-Pape

D900

Cavaillon

D973

Salon-de-Provence

A7

A8

A51

A7

BOUCHES-DU-RHÔNE

Orange

A7

Rhône

Avignon

D99

St-Rémy-de-
Provence

Les Baux

Fontvieille

Arles

Grand Rhône

A54

Istres

Étang de
Berre

A55

Fos-sur-Mer

Martigues

Golfe
de Fos

Pont-St-Esprit

Bagnols-sur-Cèze

Uzès

GARD

D6

Gard

N206

Beaucaire

Tarascon

St-Gilles

D570

Pt-St-
Louis

Beauduc

MEDITERRANEAN SEA

Alès

N110

Sauve

D999

OCCITANIE

HÉRAULT

Nîmes

A9

Vauvert

N572

Petit Rhône

Camargue

Étang de
Vaccarès

Castries

Montpellier

Aigues-
Mortes

Stes-Maries-
de-la-Mer

Golfe du
Lion

Paris

FRANCE

PROVENCE

0   20 km
0   20 mi

519

Essentials

ARRIVING   Frequent TGV trains depart from Paris's Gare de Lyon. The ride takes 2 hours, 40 minutes and arrives at Avignon's modern TGV station 10 minutes from town by shuttle bus. The one-way fare is around 80€ depending on the date and time, although it can also be as cheap as 25€ if booked well in advance. Regular trains arrive from Marseille (trip time: 35 min.; 32€ one-way) and Arles (trip time: 60 min.; 9.40€ one-way), arriving at either the TGV or Avignon's central station. For rail information, visit www.sncf-connect.com or call ℰ **36-35.** The regional bus routes (www.lepilote.fr; ℰ **08-21-20-22-03**) go from Avignon to Arles (trip time: 1 hr., 10 min.; 9.10€ one-way) and Aix-en-Provence (trip time: 1 hr., 30 min.; 20€ one-way). The bus station at Avignon is the Gare Routière, 5 av. Monclar (ℰ **04-90-82-07-35**). If you're driving from Paris, take A6 south to Lyon, and then A7 south to Avignon.

VISITOR INFORMATION   The **Office de Tourisme** is at 41 cours Jean-Jaurès (www.avignon-tourisme.com; ℰ **04-32-74-32-74**).

CITY LAYOUT   Avignon's picturesque Old Town is surrounded by 14th-century ramparts. Within the walls is a mix of winding roads, medieval town houses, and pedestrianized streets. To the west of the city is the Rhône River, and beyond, Villeneuve les Avignon. Just south of the Old Town sits the Gare d'Avignon Centre train station.

SPECIAL EVENTS   The international **Festival d'Avignon** (www.festival-avignon.com; ℰ **04-90-14-14-14**), held for 3 weeks in July, focuses on

An autumn view of Avignon's famous bridge.

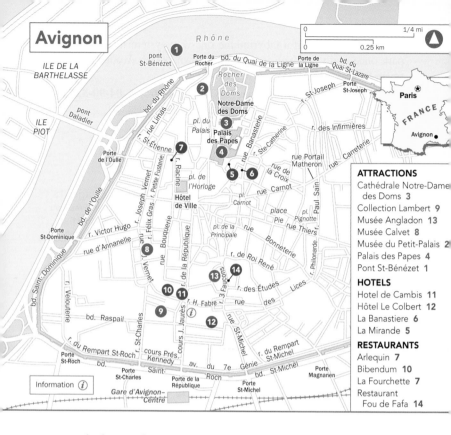

Avignon

Rhône

ILE DE LA
BARTHELASSE

ILE
PIOT

pont
St-Bénézet

pont
Daladier

Porte
de l'Oulle

Porte
St-Dominique

Porte
St-Roch

bd. du Rhône

rue Limas

r. St-Étienne

bd. de l'Oulle

r. Joseph Vernet

r. Félix Gras

r. Petite Fusterie

r. Racine

r. Victor Hugo

rue d'Annanelle

r. Bouquerie

r. Jean Vernet

r. Velouterie

St-Charles

r. du Rempart St-Roch

cours Prés.
Kennedy

bd. Raspail

rue de la République

cours J. Jaurès

Porte du
Rocher

Porte de
la Ligne

Rocher
des
Doms

Notre-Dame
des Doms

pl. du
Palais

Palais
des Papes

pl. de
l'Horloge

Hôtel
de Ville

pl.
Carnot

pl. de la
Principale

r. des Fauchons

St-Joseph

Porte
St-Joseph

bd. du Quai de la Ligne

bd. du
Quai St-Lazare

r. des Infirmières

rue Banasterie

rue Ste-Catherine

rue Portail
Matheron

rue de
la Croix

rue Carnot

place
Pie

rue Thiers

r. Bonneterie

r. de Roi René

r. des Études

rue St-Michel

Lices

r. des

av. du 7e Génie

Porte
St-Charles

Porte de la
République

cours Saint-Roch

bd.

Porte
St-Michel

Porte
Magnanen

r. du Rempart
St-Michel

bd. St-Michel

r. H. Fabre

rue

r. Carreterie

r. Paul Sain

pl.
Pignotte

rue Thiers

r. Philonarde

Information ⓘ

Gare d'Avignon–
Centre

① ② ③ ④ ⑤ ⑥ ⑦ ⑧ ⑨ ⑩ ⑪ ⑫ ⑬ ⑭ ⓘ

France / Paris / Avignon

ATTRACTIONS
Cathédrale Notre-Dame
  des Doms **3**
Collection Lambert **9**
Musée Angladon **13**
Musée Calvet **8**
Musée du Petit-Palais **2**
Palais des Papes **4**
Pont St-Bénézet **1**

HOTELS
Hotel de Cambis **11**
Hôtel Le Colbert **12**
La Banastiere **6**
La Mirande **5**

RESTAURANTS
Arlequin **7**
Bibendum **10**
La Fourchette **7**
Restaurant
  Fou de Fafa **14**

avant-garde theater, dance, and music. Tickets are 25€ to 60€. Prices for rooms skyrocket during this period, so book yours well in advance. An edgier alternative festival, the **Avignon OFF** (www.festivaloffavignon. com; ℭ **04-90-85-13-08**), takes place almost simultaneously in July, with theater performances in various improbable venues.

Getting Around

ON FOOT All of Avignon's major sights—as well as its infinitely enchanting back streets—are easily accessible on foot. The helpful tourist office's free maps show four easy walking routes, ideal for getting a feel for the city.

BY BICYCLE & MOTOR SCOOTER The Vélopop bicycle-sharing scheme (www.velopop.fr; from 1€ per day) lets registered riders borrow any of the city's 300 bikes for up to 30 minutes at a time for free. To get out of town and explore the surrounding countryside, **Provence Bike,** 7 av. St-Ruf (www.provence-bike.com; ℭ **04-90-27-92-61**), rents different models, including eBikes, from 12€ to 40€ per day. It's best to reserve a bike online in advance.

BY CAR   Traffic and a labyrinthine one-way system means it's best to park once you've arrived in Avignon's town center. Around the city are seven fee-paying parking lots and two free ones.

BY TAXI   **Taxis Avignon** (www.avignontaxis.fr; ☏ **04-90-82-20-20**). Ride apps **Bolt** and **Uber** are cheaper and easier to use.

[FastFACTS] AVIGNON

ATMs/Banks   Avignon's town center is home to banks aplenty, including three along cours Jean-Jaurès.

Doctors & Hospitals   **Hôpital Général Henri Default,** 305 rue Raoul Follereau (www.ch-avignon.fr; ☏ **04-32-75-33-33**).

Mail & Postage   **La Poste,** 4 cours Président Kennedy (☏ **36-31**).

Pharmacies   **Pharmacie des Halles,** 52 rue Bonneterie (☏ **04-90-82-54-27**).

Exploring Avignon

Avignon is undoubtedly one of the prettiest cities in France. From its impressively imposing skyline to the verdant Ile de la Barthelasse opposite, it's a delight to simply amble along aimlessly, perhaps stopping at a sidewalk cafe or two en route. Countless hidden gems crop up along the way, including the sun-dappled courtyard of the **Hôtel d'Europe** (www.heurope.com). This luxury hotel has been in operation since 1799, welcoming luminaries from Charles Dickens to Jacqueline Kennedy.

Every French child knows the ditty "Sur le pont d'Avignon, l'on y danse, l'on y danse" ("On the bridge of Avignon, we dance, we dance"). The bridge in question, **Pont St-Bénézet ★★** (www.palais-des-papes.com; ☏ **04-90-27-51-16**), was constructed between 1177 and 1185. Once spanning the Rhône and connecting Avignon with Villeneuve-lèz-Avignon, it is now a ruin, with only four of its original 22 arches remaining (half of it fell into the river in 1669). On the third pillar is the **Chapelle St-Nicolas** (www.avignon-pont.com), its first story in Romanesque style, the second in Gothic. The remains of the bridge are open daily, March to October 9am to 7pm and November to February 10am to 5pm. Admission to the bridge is 8€ for adults, 5€ for seniors and students, and free for children 8 and under. Entrance to the chapel is included.

Cathédrale Notre-Dame des Doms ★ CATHEDRAL   Near the Palais des Papes, this majestic 12th-century cathedral contains the elaborate tombs of popes Jean XXII and Benoît XII. Crowning the top is a 19th-century gilded statue of the Virgin. From the cathedral, enter the **Promenade du Rocher-des-Doms** to stroll its garden and enjoy the view across the Rhône to Villeneuve-lez-Avignon.

pl. du Palais des Papes. ☏ **04-90-82-12-21.** Free admission. Daily 8am–6pm. Hours may vary according to religious ceremonies.

Collection Lambert ★★ MUSEUM   This contemporary art space is housed within an 18th-century private home that once belonged to collector and gallery owner Yvonne Lambert. It stages three groundbreaking exhibitions each year. Works may range from video and photography to conceptual installations. Previous exhibitions have featured major artists such as Jenny Holzer, and Cy Twombly.

5 rue Violate. www.collectionlambert.fr. ℂ **04-90-16-56-20.** Admission 10€ adults; 8€ students and children ages 12–17; 2€ children ages 6–11; free for children 5 and under. July–Aug daily 10am–7pm; Sept–June Wed–Sun 1–6pm (from 11am Sat–Sun).

Musée Angladon ★ MUSEUM   Haute-couture designer Jacques Doucet (1853–1929) didn't limit himself to the appreciation of finely cut fabrics. His former home is now a showcase for the international artworks that he and his wife collected over their lifetimes—from 16th-century buddhas and Louis XVI chairs to Degas's famous dancers and canvases by Cézanne, Sisley, and Modigliani. It's a small but mighty stash that takes most visitors about 35 minutes to see. Regular temporary exhibitions showcase big art names like Bonnard and Toulouse-Lautrec.

5 rue Laboureur. www.angladon.com. ℂ **04-90-82-29-03.** Admission 8€ adults; 6.50€ students and children ages 15–17; 1.50€ children ages 4–14; free for children 3 and under. Tues–Sat 1–6pm.

Musée Calvet ★★ MUSEUM   Housed in what was formerly an 18th-century private home, the Musée Calvet is Avignon's top fine art museum. Native son Esprit Calvet bequeathed to the city upon his death a lifetime's worth of acquired art, including works by David, Corot, Manet, and Soutine, plus a collection of ancient silverware. Recent additions include a garden wing dedicated to local archaeology.

65 rue Joseph-Verne. www.musee-calvet.org. ℂ **04-90-86-33-84.** Free admission. Wed–Mon 10am–1pm and 2–6pm.

Musée du Petit-Palais ★★ MUSEUM   An ideal complement to the Palais des Papes' architectural austerity, this museum's artworks were originally part of a collection belonging to 19th-century art lover Giampietro Campania. As a quirk of history, the palace was nationalized and sold off during the French Revolution, and became a secondary school, before reopening as a museum in the 1970s. Today the museum exhibits a myriad of paintings from the Italian and Provençal schools of the 13th to 16th centuries. Botticelli's *Madonna with Child* is a highlight.

Palais des Archevêques, pl. du Palais des Papes. www.petit-palais.org. ℂ **04-90-86-44-58.** Free admission. Wed–Mon 10am–1pm and 2–6pm.

Palais des Papes ★★★ PALACE   Dominating Avignon from a hilltop is one of the most famous, or notorious, palaces in the Christian world. Headquarters of a schismatic group of cardinals who came close to destroying the authority of the popes in Rome, this fortress is the city's most popular monument. Because of its massive size, you may be tempted

Palais des Papes.

to opt for a guided tour—but these can be monotonous. The detailed audio guide, included in the price of admission, will likely suffice. The palace also offers augmented reality iPad-style tablets (included in ticket price) which reveal historic incarnations of each room you visit—in all their papal glory.

A highlight is the **Chapelle St-Jean,** known for its frescoes of John the Baptist and John the Evangelist, attributed to the school of Matteo Giovanetti and painted between 1345 and 1348. The **Grand Tinsel (Banquet Hall)** is about 41m (134 ft.) long and 9m (30 ft.) wide; the pope's table stood on the south side. The walls of the **Pope's Bedroom,** on the first floor of the Tour des Anges, are painted with foliage, birds, and squirrels. The frescoes of hunting scenes in the **Studium (Stag Room)**—the study of Clement VI—date from 1343. The **Grande Audience (Great Receiving Hall)** contains frescoes of the prophets, also attributed to Giovanetti and painted in 1352.

Note that the 12th-century **Cathédrale Notre-Dame des Doms cathedral,** just next door on the main square, contains the elaborate tombs of popes Jean XXII and Benoît XII.

pl. du Palais des Papes. www.palais-des-papes.com. ✆ **04-32-74-32-74.** Admission (including audio guide) 12€ adults; 10€ seniors and students; 6.50€ for children aged 8-17; free for children 7 and under. Daily Mar–Oct 9am–7pm, Nov–Feb 10am–5pm. Last admission 1 hr. before closing.

OUTLYING ATTRACTIONS IN VILLENEUVE-LEZ-AVIGNON ★

While the popes lived in exile, cardinals built palaces just across the Rhône in sleepy **Villeneuve-lez-Avignon.** Many visitors prefer to stay or dine here—it's quieter and less modernized, while still convenient to Avignon's major attractions. Take bus no. 5, which crosses the larger of the two relatively modern bridges, the Pont Daladier.

A local Office de Tourisme can provide further information (www.villeneuvelesavignon.fr; ℰ **04-90-25-61-33**).

Musée Pierre de Luxembourg (Musée de Villeneuve-lez-Avignon) ★★ ART MUSEUM   Villeneuve's most important museum occupies a 14th-century "urban palace" constructed for a local cardinal. Since its designation as a museum in 1986, it's been the richest repository of medieval painting and sculpture in the region. The remarkable Coronation of the Virgin, by Enguerrand Charonton, painted in 1453, depicts the denizens of hell supplicating the eternally calm mother of Christ. Equally important is a rare 14th-century ivory statue of the Virgin by an unknown sculptor; it's one of the finest of its type anywhere. For French speakers, in-depth tours courtesy of knowledgeable guides are available at 3.80€ per person.

2 rue de la République. www.villeneuvelesavignon.fr. ℰ **04-90-27-49-66.** Admission 4.50€ adults; free for children 18 and under. Mar–Oct Tues–Sun 10am–12:30pm and 2–6pm; Nov–Dec and Feb 2–5pm.

St-André Abbey Gardens ★★ GARDENS   Clustered around the 17th-century Benedictine Abbaye St-André, these spectacular gardens include a rose-trellis colonnade, fountains flecked with lily pads, and an olive orchard. They also offer unbeatable views over the Rhône Valley and Avignon's skyline beyond. Fort St-André (separate entrance fee, 5.50€), founded in 1360 by Jean-le-Bon to serve as a symbol of might to the pontifical powers across the river, is adjacent to the monastery.

Fort Saint-André, rue Montée du Fort. www.abbayesaintandre.fr. ℰ **04-90-25-55-95.** Admission 9€ adults; 7.50€ students and ages 13–18; free for children 12 and under. Mar and Oct Tues–Sun 10am–1pm and 2–5pm; Apr 10am–1pm and 2–6pm; May–Sept 10am–6pm. Closed Nov–Feb.

Val de Bénédiction Chartreuse ★ MONASTERY   France's largest Carthusian monastery, built in 1352, comprises a church, three cloisters, cells that housed the medieval monks, and a 12th-century graveyard where Pope Innocent VI is entombed. Part of the complex houses the *Centre National d'Ecritures du Spectacle,* a residence for artists and playwrights who live rent-free for up to a year to deepen their crafts. Art exhibitions, concerts, and theater are regularly held here.

58 rue de la République. www.chartreuse.org. ℰ **04-90-15-24-24.** Admission 9€ adults; 5.50€ students and under 25; free for children 17 and under. Mid-Apr to mid-Sept daily 9:30am–6:30pm; mid-Sept to mid-Apr daily 10am–1pm and 2–5pm.

Where to Stay

For travelers on a budget, the friendly **Hôtel Le Colbert** (www.avignon-hotel-colbert.com) is an excellent town center option.

Hotel de Cambis ★★★ Avignon's newest and coolest address is a skip away from the historic center, and an out-and-out charmer with unusually helpful staff. Creating by interlinking several grand apartments, it was designed by a minimalist architect high on color and Côtes du Rhône. The hotel hosts a wine bar with only-seen-here vintages, plus a breakfast salon serves local pastries and cheeses for an extra 16€ per person. A reading room is crammed with historical tomes and art books. Crisp linen meets exquisite taste in the guest rooms, some with balconies with city views.
89 Rue Joseph Vernet. www.hoteldecambis.com. ✆ **04-90-14-62-73.** 41 units. 119€–220€ double. **Amenities:** Bar; room service, free Wi-Fi.

La Banasterie ★★ This oh-so-pretty B&B is situated in a 16th-century property just opposite the Palais des Papes. It's owned by gregarious chocolate lover Tanguy—and his candy-fueled passion permeates throughout. The traditionally decorated bedrooms (exposed stone walls, sumptuous fabrics) are named for varieties of chocolate, and decadent cups of cocoa are on offer at bedtime. Don't have a sweet tooth? Guest rooms also boast Nespresso coffee machines and Missoni bath products. Four living rooms throughout the building are decked out in Hermès textiles and designer furnishings. The indulgent breakfast alone (included in the rate) makes this spot unmissable. Note that there is no elevator and all rooms require a climb up stairs.
11 rue de la Banasterie. www.labanasterie.com. ✆ **06-87-72-96-36.** 5 units. 115€–195€ double; 165€–275€ suite. Parking 10€. **Amenities:** Free Wi-Fi.

La Mirande ★★★ La Mirande was once a 14th-century cardinal's palace from the adjoining Palais des Papes. It now boasts an additional 7 centuries of fixtures and features in one gloriously palatial package. The hotel's owners are not from the hotel industry, and it shows. Guest rooms are no-expense-spared collections of locally sourced antique furniture, Carrara marble, authentic Chinoiserie, and Murano chandeliers. The courtyard chairs, for example, used to belong in the Musée d'Orsay in Paris. La Mirande is also a top pick for foodies: Chef Séverine Sagnet (who cooked for the Obamas when they visited Avignon) conducts a food tour of Les Halles market followed by a cooking course in the hotel's historic kitchen. The hotel's head chef Florent Pietravalle, purveyor of a Michelin star, showcases Avignon culinary history via a range of seasonal menus in **Le Restaurant.** An organic afternoon tea—featuring homemade madeleines, thick hot chocolate, and kombucha—is served daily on the patio or terrace.
4 pl. de l'Amirande. www.la-mirande.fr. ✆ **04-90-14-20-20.** 26 units. 393€–611€ double; suite from 811€. Parking 25€. **Amenities:** Restaurant; bar; concierge; room service; free Wi-Fi.

Where to Eat

Bibendum ★★ FRENCH Avignon's hottest address has been serving A-grade wines (from 5€ per glass) inside an ancient town house since late

2022. But you don't have to just snack at the bar on dishes like gravlax of trout to afford this unicorn of a restaurant, which offers inventive dishes on starched white tablecloths in historic surrounding for a more-than-fair price. Weekdays it's just 29€ for the three-course lunch menu!

83 rue Joseph Vernet. www.bibendumavignon.fr. ℂ **04-90-91-78-39.** Fixed-price menu 29€–50€. Mon–Sat noon–2pm and 7–9:30pm.

Harlequin ★★ PROVENÇAL   A fabulous find near the Palais des Papes with fresh, local produce prepared by head chef Corentin Roustan. Monthly menus feature a lunch special (14€) as well as seasonal items like octopus salad with tomatoes and rack of lamb with orange wine. A short, intelligent wine list accompanies dishes from 22€ per bottle. Highly recommended.

17 rue Racine. www.arlequin.restaurant. ℂ **09-50-14-94-52.** Main course 19€–27€. Mon–Fri noon–2pm and 7–11:30pm.

La Fourchette ★★ PROVENÇAL   Set a block back from the bustling place de l'Horloge, this upscale bistro has become a classic address since it opened its doors in 1982. Philippe Hilly, the sixth generation in his family's long line of chefs, dishes up a cuisine that's sophisticated yet hearty on a short no-nonsense menu: Think saffron-infused salt cod *brandied* and served with crusty bread, or ravioli of Provençal *brousse* cheese atop a saffron-spinach bed. Walls are adorned with an eclectic collection of antique cutlery (*la fourchette* translates as "the fork"), making the ambience as alluring as the food. Just don't drop by over the weekend: The restaurant is closed Saturday and Sunday.

17 rue Racine. ℂ **04-90-85-20-93.** Main course 21€; fixed-price menu 38€. Mon–Fri 12:15–1:45pm and 7:15–9:45pm. Closed 3 weeks in Aug.

Restaurant Fou de Fafa ★ FRENCH/PROVENÇAL   This cozy little restaurant dishes up authentic local cuisine—often with a contemporary twist—that truly hits its mark. Delicious combinations may include pear and Roquefort salad with caramelized walnuts, or sea bream in saffron cream paired with Camargue rice, followed by local cheeses with black olive jam. *Note:* The monthly menu is short and highly seasonal.

17 rue des Trois Falcons. ℂ **04-32-76-35-13.** Fixed-price menu 36€–41€. Thu–Mon 7–11pm. Closed Dec–Jan.

Shopping

Hervé Baume, 19 rue Petite Fusterie (ℂ **04-90-86-37-66**), is the place to buy a Provençal table—or something to put on it. A massive inventory includes French folk art and hand-blown hurricane lamps. **Jaffier-Parsi,** 42 rue des Fourbisseurs (ℂ **04-90-86-08-85**), is known for copper saucepans from the Norman town of Villedieu-les-Poêles, which has been making them since the Middle Ages. The southern French boutique chain **Souleiado,** 19 rue Joseph-Verne (ℂ **04-90-86-32-05**), sells reproductions of 18th- and 19th-century Provençal fabrics by the meter or made into clothing and linens. It also has a gorgeous selection of housewares and gifts. **Le Nid,** 7 rue Des Trois Faucons (℅ **04-90-01-70-64**), is a combination café, yoga studio, and boutique. It sells furnishings that appear borrowed from a Provençal boutique hotel as well as tableware and lighting.

In Avignon, foodie souvenirs are delightfully thick on the ground. Head over to **Le Comptoir de Mathilde,** 32 rue de la Balance (www. lecomptoirdemathilde.com; ℅ **04-90-85-44-52**), for olive tapenade, local olive oils, *Herbes de Provence* mustard, and flaky Guérande sea salt, as well as plenty of free tastings. Les Halles, pl. Pie, is a vibrant covered market with 40 different food merchants open Tuesday through Sunday (6am–1:30pm), making it a great pit stop for a picnic lunch. The photo-genic **flower market** is on place des Carmes on Saturday (8am–1pm), and the **flea market** occupies the same place each Sunday morning (6am–1pm).

Used clothing store **In' Accessible,** 36 rue Des Trois Faucons, sells vintage items purloined from a funky grandmother's wardrobe.

Nightlife

Evenings in Avignon begin in the hopping bars and pavement cafes around place des Corps-Saints. A favorite is **La Princiere** (at no. 23), which is a gelateria, but owner Camille serves drinks alongside 20 flavors of Provençal ice cream.

Beautiful people frequent **Les Ambassadeurs,** 27 rue Braincase (www. clublesambassadeurs.fr; ℅ **04-90-86-31-55**), an upscale dance club. For wine, **Le Bar à Vin,** part of the **Carré du Palais** (www.carredupalais.fr; ℅ **04-65-00-01-01**) viticulture school, is by far the best bet in town. Purchase one of 50 carefully curated wines by the glass from 4€. The stunning city center establishment hosts 700 other vintages, plus a wine-centric **Bistrot** that serves a 2-course lunch for 29€. The best place for live tunes is offbeat jazz bar **AJMI,** 4 rue des Escaliers Sainte-Anne (www.ajmi.fr; ℅ **04-13-39-07-85**), which stands for Jazz and Improvised Music Association. Behind the Hôtel d'Europe, disco-bar **L'Esclave,** 12 rue du Limas (℅ **04-90-85-14-91**), is a focal point of the city's gay scene.

DAY TRIPS FROM AVIGNON

Orange ★

31km (19 miles) N of Avignon

Antiquities-rich Orange was not named for citrus fruit, but as a dependency of the Dutch House of Orange-Nassau during the Middle Ages. It is home to two UNESCO World Heritage sites: Europe's third-largest **triumphal arch** and its best-preserved **Roman theater.** Louis XIV, who once considered moving the theater to Versailles, claimed: "It is the finest wall in my kingdom." The Théâtre Antique is now the site of **Les Choragi's d'Orange** (www.choregies.fr), a summertime opera and classical music festival.

Just 10km (6 miles) south along the D68 is **Châteauneuf-du-Pape,** a prestigious appellation known for its bold red wines. Spend an afternoon

Orange's extraordinary Roman amphitheater.

visiting the village's numerous tasting rooms, winding your way up to the ruins of a castle that served as a summer residence for Pope John XXII. A prime place to best to try a wide selection of top wines is at the **Vinothèque,** or wine library, of Vinadea (www.vinadea.com), where a union of Châteauneuf-du-Pape wines are stored. A 25€ dégustation of five wines accompanies a historical lesson about the region, all held in a cool cellar.

ESSENTIALS

Trains (trip time: 20 min.; www.sncf-connect.com; 𝄢 **36-35;** 7.10€ one-way) and **buses** (www.sudest-mobilites.fr; 𝄢 **04-32-76-00-40;** trip time: 1 hr.; 2.10€ one-way) connect Avignon and Orange. If you're driving from Avignon, take A7 north to Orange. The Office de Tourisme is at 5 cours Aristide-Briand (www.poptourisme.fr; 𝄢 **04-90-34-70-88**).

EXPLORING ORANGE & AROUND

The carefully restored **Théâtre Antique ★★★**, rue Madeleine Roch (www.theatre-antique.com; 𝄢 **04-90-51-17-60;** daily Nov–Feb 9:45am–4:30pm; Mar and Oct until 5:30pm; Apr–May and Sept 9:15am–6pm; June–Aug 9:15am–7pm), dates from the days of Augustus. Built into the side of a hill, it once held 9,000 spectators in tiered seats, and allows visitors to indulge their inner gladiator. It stands at nearly 105m (344 ft.) long and 37m (121 ft.) high. Admission (which includes a free audio guide) is 11.50€ adults, 9.50€ students and children 8 to 17, and free for children 7 and under.

Across the street, at the site of a ruined temple, the **Musée d'Art et d'Histoire d'Orange,** pl. du Théâtre-Antique (*C* **04-90-51-17-60**), displays paintings, friezes, and artifacts from local archaeological digs. A ticket to the theater also admits you to the museum. Opening hours are the same at the theater.

The imposing **Arc de Triomphe** ★, av. de l'Arc-de-Triomphe, comprises a trio of arches held up by Corinthian columns embellished with military and maritime emblems. Also built during the reign of Augustus, it was once part of the original town's fortified walls.

The **hilltop park** on the Colline St-Eutrope, accessible by stairs behind the theater, offers a panoramic view over Orange and the surrounding landscape. The scenery is awesome.

WHERE TO EAT

At **Au Petit Patio,** 58 cours Aristide Briand (*C* **04-90-29-69-27**), contemporary Provençal cuisine is served on a petite outdoor terrace. Sample dishes like smoked herrings with leeks or cod with a pistachio crust. Market-fresh menus start at 24€; open Monday to Saturday for lunch, Monday, Tuesday, Friday, and Saturday for dinner.

Vaison-la-Romaine ★★

50km (31 miles) NE of Avignon

Part medieval village, part Roman ruins, and all crowned by a 13th-century castle, Vaison-la-Romaine sits in the fertile northern reaches of Provence. Well off this region's traditional tourist trail, the combination of history and low-key allure makes for an exquisite escape. To the east of Vaison-la-Romaine towers Mont Ventoux, a monolith of a mountain (1,900m/6,300 ft.) famed for its bogeyman role in the annual Tour de France cycle race.

ESSENTIALS

Frequent **trains** (trip time: 20 min.; www.sncf-connect.com; *C* **36-35**; 7.10€ one-way) connect Avignon and Orange. From Orange, hop aboard bus no. 904 (zou.maregionsud.fr; trip time: 45 min.; 2.10€ one-way). If you're driving from Avignon, take A7 north, veering northeast onto D977.

The **Office de Tourisme** is at place du Chanoine Sauté (www.vaison-ventoux-tourisme.com; *C* **04-90-36-02-11**).

EXPLORING VAISON-LA-ROMAINE & AROUND

Ancient capital to the Voconce people, Vaison-la-Romaine is home to two important archaeological sites, **Puymin** and **La Vilasse** (www.provence romaine.com; *C* **04-90-36-50-48**). Both are peppered with ancient Roman residences, the remains of thermal baths, statues, and mosaics. The sites are open daily November, December, and February 10am to noon and 2 to 5pm; March and October 10am to 12:30pm and 2 to 5:30pm; and April to

SHOPPING FOR brocante IN PROVENCE

In France, there's a wide gap between true antiques and old knickknacks, and it's wise to know the difference. For serious purchases, stick to well-established *antiquaires*, found in almost every town and city. If you're looking for more affordable treasures and enjoy flea markets, what you really want is a *brocante*. These are usually held outside on specific days (the markets in Cannes are a good example; see chapter 15). Furniture and objects can also be found in warehouses known as *depot-ventes*.

A village that specializes in *brocante* is **Isle-sur-la-Sorgue,** situated 23km (14 miles) east of Avignon, 11km (6¾ miles) north of Cavaillon, and 42km (26 miles) south of Orange. The **Déballage Brocante** is held on Sundays; the activity starts at 9am and finishes around 6pm. From 8am to 2pm, there's also a Provençal food market. If you're driving, try for a parking space in the Parking Portalet or Parking Allele des Muriers. The *brocante* is concentrated in the southern part of town, where you'll find warehouses filled with dealers and loot—although plenty of small stalls are dotted throughout the pedestrianized town center, too.

Isle-sur-la-Sorgue's **Office de Tourisme** is at place de la Liberté (https://islesurlasorguetourisme.com; ✆ **04-90-38-04-78**).

September 9:30am to 6:30pm. In January both sites are closed. Admission (which includes a free audio guide and is valid for 24 hr.) is 9€ adults, 4€ students and children 10 to 17, and free for children 9 and under.

For more detailed information about Vaison-la-Romaine's history, visit the **Musée Archéologique Théo Desplans,** located within Puymin (entrance valid with same ticket, same opening hours), which focuses on local and regional discoveries.

The oldest part of Vaison-la-Romaine itself—the Cité Médiévale—is a medieval wonderland, crisscrossed by winding alleyways and splashed with pretty squares. To the south sits its **Roman bridge,** dating from the A.D. 1st century, which spans the Ouvèze River. If possible, time your visit to coincide with the town's superb regional market (Tues 8am–1pm, held around town).

Every 3 years, Vaison-la-Romaine holds the 10-day **Chorales,** or Choral Festival, in August (www.choralies.fr; next edition 2025). Visitors also descend on the town annually for **Vaison Dances** (www.vaison-danses.com), a prestigious dance festival held every July in the ancient Roman theater.

WHERE TO EAT

Head to **Restaurant le Bateleur,** pl. Théodore Subpanel (www.restaurant-lebateleur.com; ✆ **04-90-36-28-04;** Tues–Sat 12:15–2pm and 7:30–10pm), for an outstanding 47€ multi-course menu. The cuisine makes the most of local ingredients, from wild mushrooms and Mediterranean bonito to free-range chicken from nearby Monteux and heirloom tomatoes.

GORDES ★★★

720km (446 miles) S of Paris; 38km (24 miles) E of Avignon; 77km (48 miles) N of Aix-
en-Provence; 92km (57 miles) N of Marseille

Hilltop Gordes is a supremely chic rocky outcrop deep in Provence. From afar, this gorgeous *village perches* (perched village) is a pastiche of beiges, grays, and terra cotta that blushes golden at sunrise and sunset. The place also served as a backdrop for the love affair between Marion Cotillard and Russell Crowe in the movie *A Good Year.* So it's unbelievably pretty—but beauty has brought crowds and raised prices, making coffees and lunches in Gordes more expensive than elsewhere.

Essentials

ARRIVING Gordes is difficult to reach via public transportation. The closest train station is Cavaillon, where trains arrive from Avignon's central station (trip time: 30 min.; www.sncf-connect.com; ℰ **36-35;** 8.10€ one-way). From here, bus no. 917 departs three times daily for place du Château in Gordes (zou.maregionsud.fr; trip time: 35 min.; 2.10€ one-way). By car, Gordes is a 38km (24-mile) drive east of Avignon via D900.

VISITOR INFORMATION The **Office de Tourisme** is at Le Château (www.gordes-village.com; ℰ **04-90-72-02-75**).

[FastFACTS] GORDES

Mail & Postage **La Poste,** pl. du Jeu de Boules (ℰ **36-31**). Note that the post office also offers an ATM.

Pharmacies **Pharmacie de Gordes,** 1 rue de l'Eglise (ℰ **04-90-72-02-10**).

Exploring Gordes

Gordes is best explored on foot. Its primarily pedestrianized streets unwind downhill from the Château de Gordes, the Renaissance rehabilitation of a 12th-century fortress. Its windows still bear grooves from bows and arrows used to protect Gordes during Gallo-Roman times, when it was a border town. Today Gordes is more likely to be invaded by easels. Its austere beauty has drawn many artists, including Marc Chagall and Hungarian painter Victor Vasarely, who spent summers here gathering inspiration for his geometric abstract art.

Caves du Palais St. Firmin ★ RUINS Steep Gordes lacks an abundance of surface area, so early settlers burrowed into the rock itself, creating an underground network of crude rooms and stairways over seven levels. Over the centuries, these rooms have housed the village's production of olive oil and grain. Though the tunnels are adequately lit, children

Gordes at dusk.

are provided with a small headlamp to let them feel like true explorers. The views from the cave gardens are immense.

rue du Belvédère. www.caves-saint-firmin.com. ⓒ **04-90-72-02-75.** Admission 6€ adults; 5€ students and children ages 5–15; free for children 4 and under. Free audio guide. Apr–Oct daily 10:30am–1pm and 2:30–6pm. Closed Nov–Mar.

Château de Gordes ★ HISTORIC HOME/ART MUSEUM   Access to the ancient château, once used as a grain store and a prison, is reserved for visitors of its small museum, dedicated to contemporary Flemish painter Pol Mara (1920–98), a former resident of Gordes. More than 200 of the artist's works are on display, along with temporary shows. As one might expect, the castle grants spectacular panoramas over Gordes and the surrounding countryside.

pl. Genty Pantaly. ⓒ **04-90-72-98-64.** Admission 4€ adults; 3€ children 10–17; free for children 9 and under. Daily 10am–1pm and 2–6:30pm.

Outlying Attractions

Abbaye Nôtre Dame de Sénanque ★★★ MONASTERY   One of the prettiest sights in the Luberon—indeed, in all of Provence—is the Abbaye Nôtre Dame de Sénanque, even more so when the lavender is in bloom in late spring. Five kilometers (3 miles) down the road from Gordes, it was built by Cistercian monks in 1148. Just a handful of monks continue to live on the premises today. The structure is noted for its simple architecture and unadorned stone—though standing in a sea of lavender purple, from June to late July, it's dramatic indeed. The walk from the car park is arduous if stunningly beautiful, as it winds through lavender plants

Sénanque Abbey and lavender fields.

and plane trees. A gift shop sells items made by the resident monks, as well as lavender honey. For an extra 0.50€ per person, enjoyable tours can be had in English using a HistoPad tablet loaded with historic information available at the abbey reception desk.

D177. www.senanque.fr. ⓒ **04-90-72-05-86.** Admission 8.50€ adults; 6€ students and ages 19–25; 4€ children 6–18; free for children 5 and under. Mon–Sun 9:45–11am and 1–5pm.

Village des Bories ★ RUINS Bories are beehive-shaped dwellings made of intricately stacked stone—and not an ounce of mortar. They date back as far as the Bronze Age and as recently as the 18th century in Provence. An architectural curiosity, their thick walls and cantilevered roofs beg the question: How did they do that? The Village des Bories is the largest group of these structures in the region, comprising 30 huts grouped according to function (houses, stables, bakeries, silkworm farms, and more). Traditional tools are on display, along with an exhibit on the history of dry-stone architecture in France and around the world.

1.5km (1 mile) west of Gordes on the D15. www.levillagedesbories.com. ⓒ **04-90-72-03-48.** Admission 8€ adults; 4€ children 12–17; free for children 11 and under. Oct–Mar daily 9am–5.30pm; Apr–Sept 9am–7pm (until 8pm June–Aug).

Where to Stay

Domaine de Fontenille ★★★ A château, working vineyard, and farm-to-table dining experience par excellence. Outside nearby Lourmarin, the Domaine de Fontenille was created by the owner of Parisian fashion label Comptoir des Cotonniers—and it shows. Modern art graces the walls. The grounds are manicured to look like a Provençal photoshoot for Vogue. And best of all, guests may stroll the Domaine's 35-hectare (86-acre) all-organic vineyard and farm, then sample the goods in a gastronomic restaurant run by hot young chef Guillaume Goupil (tasting menu 125€). Oh, and there's a vineyard with tasting room on-site too. The price? This isn't St Tropez, so rates are better than you might expect.

Route de Roquefraiche, Lauris. www.domainedefontenille.com. © **04-13-98-00-00.** 17 units. 245€–445€ double; suite from 515€. Free parking. **Amenities:** 2 restaurants; bar; outdoor pool; free Wi-Fi.

Hotel Le Petit Palais d'Aglaé ★★ This timeless stone mas (Provençal farmhouse) is now a charming inn, with helpful staff. Like many establishments in this foodie corner of Provence, it offers half-board deals at its seasonal restaurants, where the ingredients are mostly sourced from the hotel's organic garden. The hotel's coolest new addition is a private cinema salon; guests can choose a movie to be screened for 20€ per person with generous snacks provided. The valley views from the infinity pool perched over a cliff face are awesome. Our only quibble? Guest rooms are a bit too 21st century, given the historic setting.

Route de Murs. www.petitpalaisdaglae-gordes.com.com. © **04-32-50-21-02.** 10 units. 141€–313€ double. Half-board available. Free parking. Closed Jan. **Amenities:** Restaurant; outdoor pool; free Wi-Fi.

THE LAST HOME OF albert camus

Author of *The Stranger*, among many other works, Algerian-born Albert Camus (1913–60) moved to France at the age of 25. Member of the French Resistance, political journalist, and philosopher, he was awarded the Nobel Prize for Literature in 1958 "for his important literary production, which with clear-sighted earnestness illuminates the problems of the human conscience in our times."

That same year, drawn by its "solemn and austere landscape despite its bewildering beauty," Camus and his wife moved to Lourmarin, 30km (18 miles) southeast of Gordes along D36. Just 2 years later, Camus was killed in a car accident near Paris. According to his wishes, he was buried in Lourmarin's cemetery.

Former French president Nicolas Sarkozy—with whom Camus would have had little in common philosophically or politically—proposed moving the writer's ashes to the Pantheon in Paris, to rest aside such literary giants as Alexander Dumas, Victor Hugo, and Emile Zola. His descendants politely declined.

La Ferme de la Huppe ★★   This combination bed-and-breakfast, and its superb Provençal restaurant (also open to non-guests), spills over a pristinely renovated 18th-century farmhouse, with a handsome swimming pool area. Country-style guest rooms are named after their former functions, such as Hay Loft or Wine Cellar, and all boast cute modern bathrooms. An abundant buffet breakfast (croissants, fresh juices, local cheeses) is served on the poolside terrace. La Ferme's location, just down the road from Gordes itself, makes it perfectly positioned for exploring the wider Luberon region, including the gorgeous villages of Bonnieux and Roussillon. In short, staying here is like lodging with your rich Provençal relatives.

R.D. 156, Les Pourquiers. www.lafermedelahuppe.com. ℂ **04-90-72-12-25.** 10 units. 160€–280€ double. Breakfast included; half-board available. Free parking. Closed Nov–Feb. **Amenities:** Restaurant; outdoor pool; free Wi-Fi.

Where to Eat

We also recommend the restaurants at the hotels listed above.

L'Outsider ★★ PROVENÇAL   In a town of many tourist traps, a leisurely meal on the al fresco terrace of L'Outsider is an experience that shouts Provence. Appetizers (all at 15€) are regional specialties like eggplant papeton. Main courses (at 28€) include French-origin fillets of beef and rosemary-seasoned lamb. A vaulted indoor dining room is available for guests on cooler days, or those too late to book a table on the outdoor terrace. Kids can choose most things from the menu; their half-portion is simply served at half price.

Rue de la Gendarmerie. www.restaurant-loutsider.com. ℂ **04-32-50-27-52.** Main course 21€–28€; fixed-price menu 49€. Thurs–Mon noon–1:30pm and 7–9pm; closed Wed lunch.

DAY TRIP FROM GORDES

Gordes is part of the **Parc Naturel Régional du Luberon** (www.parc duluberon.fr) made up of three mountain ranges and their common valley. Author Peter Mayle brought attention to the area with his *A Year in Provence* series extolling the virtues of picturesque villages such as Bonnieux, Lourmarin, and Menderes, where Mayle restored his first French home. Most of these are within 12km (7½ miles) of each other, making the Luberon well worth an afternoon's exploration. Snaps from any village will give friends back home serious Instagram envy.

For cyclists, **Vélo Loisir Provence** (www.veloloisirprovence.com) has marked hundreds of kilometers of bike routes throughout the region's vineyards and lavender fields. See the website for maps and rental agencies, as well as a great selection of bucolic dining spots en route.

Roussillon ★

10km (6 miles) E of Gordes

The remarkable town of Roussillon is perched atop undulating terrain, stained by the region's unique ochre earth. Vineyards and forests cleave the countryside, revealing stunning stripes of this natural pigment, each one ranging from amber gold to a deep scarlet. A hundred years ago, dozens of quarries mined the much-coveted Provençal ochre from the surrounding area and used it to add color to paints and textiles.

The Sentier des Ocres de Roussillon (Ochre Footpath).

ESSENTIALS

The four-times-daily no. 917 **bus** (zou.maregionsud.fr; trip time: 20 min.; 2.10€ one-way) connects Gordes and Roussillon. If you're driving from Gordes, take D2 east to Roussillon.

The **Office de Tourisme** is at rue de la Poste (www.luberon-apt. fr; ⓒ **04-90-05-60-25**).

EXPLORING ROUSSILLON

Begin with an amble through Roussillon itself. The town's compact center is trimmed by multicolored homes, each facade tinted in warm ochre hues. Every Thursday morning, **place du Pasquier** is given over to a large Provençal market. Then it's time to explore the otherworldly landscape that surrounds the town. Follow the signposts from Roussillon center about a 5-minute walk out of town to the **Sentier des Ocres de Roussillon** (Ochre Footpath), where the remains of century-old quarries expose the neon orange countryside. The footpath is open daily May through September 9:30am to 6:30pm (until 7:30pm July–Aug); March 10am to 5pm; November 10am to 4:30pm; December and February 11am to 3.30pm; closed January. Admission is 3€ and free for children 9 and under. The short walk takes around 30 minutes, and the longer walk around 60 minutes.

WHERE TO EAT

You're in prime picnic country. A take-out meal from a bakery, eaten in a lavender field, is pure Provence. For gourmet evening eats sit down at either **Le Piquebaure,** Les Estrayas (ⓒ **04-90-05-79-65;** fixed-price menu 30€ Thurs–Tues dinner) or **Restaurant David,** at Place de la Poste in Roussillon (www.leclosdelaglycine.fr/en/restaurant; main courses 30€–33€; Wed–Sun dinner), for a modern takes on Provençal classics at the first (grilled beef entrecôte, lavender crème brûlée), and more of a fusion menu at the latter. At both the seasonal ingredients are locally sourced.

ST-RÉMY-DE-PROVENCE ★

710km (440 miles) S of Paris; 24km (15 miles) NE of Arles; 19km (12 miles) S of Avignon; 10km (6¼ miles) N of Les Baux

Though the physician and astrologer Nostradamus was born here in 1503, most associate St-Rémy with Vincent van Gogh, who committed himself to a local asylum in 1889 after cutting off part of his left ear. *Starry Night* was painted during this period, as were many versions of *Olive Trees* and *Cypresses.*

Come to sleepy St-Rémy not only for its history and sights, but also for an authentic experience of daily Provençal life. The town springs into action on Wednesday mornings, when stalls bursting with the region's bounty, from wild-boar sausages to olives, elegant antiques to bolts of French country fabric, huddle between the sidewalk cafes beneath the plane trees.

Essentials

ARRIVING   Every hour the 707 regional **bus** runs from F. Mourêt, a 20-minute walk from Avignon city center, to St-Rémy (zou.maregionsud.fr; trip time: 45 min.; 2.10€ one-way). **Drivers** can head south from Avignon along D571.

VISITOR INFORMATION   The **Office de Tourisme** is on place Jean-Jaurès (www.alpillesenprovence.com; ✆ **04-90-92-05-22**).

[FastFACTS]
ST-RÉMY-DE-PROVENCE

ATMs/Banks **Société Marseillaise de Crédit,** 10 bd. Marceau (✆ **04-90-92-74-00**).

Mail & Postage **La Poste,** 5 rue Roger Selangor (✆ **36-31**).

Pharmacies **Pharmacie Cenders,** 4 bd. Mirabeau (✆ **04-32-60-16-43**).

Exploring St-Rémy

St-Rémy's pale stone Old Town is utterly charming. Scattered among its pedestrianized streets are 18th-century private mansions, art galleries, medieval church towers, bubbling fountains, and Nostradamus's birth home. Note that St-Rémy's two major sites (listed below) lie around 1km (½ mile) south of the town center. Fortify yourself French style with a stiff black coffee.

Le Site Archéologique de Galbanum ★★ RUINS Kids will love a scramble around this bucolically sited Gallo-Roman settlement, which thrived here during the final days of the Roman Empire. Its monuments include a triumphal arch (across the street and separated from the main ruins) from the time of Julius Caesar, all garlanded with sculptured fruits and flowers. Another interesting feature is the baths, which had separate chambers for hot, warm, and cold. Visitors can see entire streets and foundations of private residences from the 1st-century town, plus the remains of a Gallo-Greek town of the 2nd century B.C.

Route des Baux-de-Provence. www.site-glanum.fr. © **04-90-92-23-79.** Admission 8€; free for E.U. nationals ages 18–25 and children 17 and under. Apr–Sept daily 9:30am–6pm; Oct–Mar Tues–Sun 10am–5pm.

Saint Paul de Mausole ★ MONASTERY This former monastery and clinic is where Vincent Van Gogh was confined from 1889 to 1890. It's now a psychiatric hospital for women, which specializes in art therapy. You can't see the artist's actual cell, but there is a reconstruction of his room. The Romanesque chapel and cloisters are worth a visit in their own right, as Van Gogh depicted their circular arches and beautifully carved capitals in some of his paintings. Twenty-one reproductions of Van Gogh's paintings from the period he resided here dot a marked path between the town center and the site (east of av. Vincent Van Gogh). Interestingly, many of the reproductions are placed in the exact area where the artistic genius painted them.

Chemin Saint-Paul. www.saintpauldemausole.fr. © **04-90-92-77-00.** Admission 7€ adults; 5€ students; free for children 12 and under. Apr–Sept daily 9:30am–6:30pm; Oct–Mar daily 10:15am–4:30pm.

Where to Stay

Château des Alpilles ★★★ A rare chance to stay inside an actual castle situated at the heart of magnolia-studded parkland, Château des Alpilles was constructed by the Picot family in 1827. Françoise Bon converted the mansion in 1980, creating luxurious double rooms inside the castle itself, with additional private accommodation in the property's former chapel, farmhouse, and washhouse. Decor throughout encompasses a confident mix of antiques (plush upholstery, local artworks) and cool amenities (deep travertine-trimmed bathtubs, smartphone docks). It's 2km (1¼ miles) from the center of St-Rémy, with sprawling grounds that give it the feel of a countryside retreat.

Route de Rougadou. www.chateaudesalpilles.com. © **04-90-92-03-33.** 21 units. 350€–460€ double; 405€–670€ suite; 405€–710€ apartment. Free parking. Closed Jan to mid-Mar. **Amenities:** Restaurant; bar; outdoor pool; room service; sauna; 2 tennis courts; free Wi-Fi.

Hotel Sous les Figuiers ★★ This "hotel under the fig trees," as the name translates, resides in a quiet neighborhood a short walk from Saint-Rémy's historic center. All rooms are on the ground floor. While individually designed with local tiles and oversized beds, none are ostentatious or overly fancy, a fact reflected in the fairly priced room tariffs. Many have petite terraces where guests may reach up and pick themselves a ripe summer fig. A small swimming pool and verdant grounds top off this charming escape.

3 av. Gabriel Saint René Taillandier. www.hotelsouslesfiguiers.com. 📞 **04-32-60-15-40.** 14 units. 129€–219€ double. Free parking. Closed Oct-Apr. **Amenities:** Bar; pool; free Wi-Fi.

Where to Eat

Casa Estagnol ★★ MEDITERRANEAN   This gorgeous bar and eatery (which translates as "little pond" in the regional dialect) is strewn with mismatched chairs. It's shaded by plane trees and surrounded by pot plants. Light local cuisine ranges from Camargue bull hamburger topped with goat cheese to Provençal gazpacho with basil sorbet. A tapas selection (around 9€) includes grilled octopus and beef tataki wraps. A chalkboard advertises local wine vintages from 3.50€ per glass.

7 bl. Marceau. www.restaurant-lestagnol.com. 📞 **04-90-92-05-95.** Main course 20€–26€. Wed–Sun noon–2pm and 6:30–9:30pm.

Shopping

St-Rémy is a decorator's paradise, with many antiques shops and fabric stores on the narrow streets of the Old Town and surrounding boulevards. **Broc de Saint Ouen,** route d'Avignon (📞 **04-90-92-28-90**), is a 6,000-sq.-m (64,583-sq.-ft.) space selling everything from architectural salvage to vintage furniture. The town's famous Provençal market is held on Wednesday mornings.

LES BAUX ★★★

720km (446 miles) S of Paris; 18km (11 miles) NE of Arles; 85km (53 miles) N of Marseille

Les Baux de Provence's location and geology are extraordinary. Cardinal Richelieu called the massive, 245m (804-ft.) high rock rising from a desolate plain "a nesting place for eagles." A real eagle's-eye view of the outcropping would be part moonscape, dotted with archeological ruins and a vast plateau, with boxy stone houses stacked like cards on the rock's east side. The combination is so cinematic that it seems like a living, breathing movie set.

Baux, or *bayou* in Provençal, means "rocky spur." The power-thirsty lords who ruled the settlement took this as their surname in the 11th century, and by the Middle Ages had control of 79 other regional fiefdoms. After they were overthrown, Les Baux was annexed to France with the rest of Provence, but Louis XI ordered the fortress demolished. The settlement experienced a rebirth during the Renaissance, when structures where restored and lavish residences built, only to fall again in 1642 when, wary of rebellion, Louis XIII ordered his armies to destroy it once and for all. Today the fortress compound is nothing but ruins, but fascinating ones.

Now the bad news: Because of its dramatic beauty, plus a number of quaint shops and restaurants in the village, Les Baux is often overrun with visitors at peak times, so time your visit wisely.

Essentials

ARRIVING Les Baux is best reached by **car.** From St-Rémy, take D27 south; from Arles, D17 east. Alternatively, in July and August only, **bus** no. 707 (60 min.; 2.10€ one-way) runs from Avignon to Arles, stopping at Les Baux en route. For bus information, see zou.maregionsud.fr.

VISITOR INFORMATION The **Office de Tourisme** (www.lesbauxde provence.com; ℂ **04-90-54-34-39**) is at Maison du Roy, near the northern entrance to the old city.

FAST FACTS Note that you'll need to head to the nearby town of Maussane-les-Alpilles for access to a bank, pharmacy, or post office.

Exploring Les Baux

Les Baux's windswept ruins, **Château des Baux** ★★★ (www.chateau-baux-provence.com; ℂ **04-90-54-55-56**), cover an area of 7 hectares (17 acres), much larger than the petite hilltop village itself. Consider visiting them early in the morning before the sun gets too strong.

The medieval compound is accessed via the 15th-century **Hôtel de la Tour du Brau.** Beyond this building are replicas of wooden military

Les Baux.

equipment that would have been used in the 13th century. Built to scale—that is to say, enormous—are a battering ram and various catapults capable of firing huge boulders. From April to August, these are fired every day at 11am and 1:30pm, 3:30pm, and 5:30pm, with an extra show during July and August at 6:30pm. Medieval jousting demonstrations (noon, 2:30, and 4:30pm) are held in summer.

Other stopping points include the Chapel of St-Blaise (where you can watch a film of aerial views of Provence) include a windmill, the skeleton of a hospital built in the 16th century, and a cemetery. The Tour Sarrazin, so named because it was used to spot Saracen invaders coming from the south, yields a sweeping view. Alongside each of the major points of interest, illustrated panels show what the buildings would have originally looked like and explain how the site has evolved architecturally. A more recent addition are eleven huge panels showcasing abstract works from Dutch painter Piet Mondrian, a major figure in 20th-century art.

Admission to the Château (including audio guide) is 10€ adults and 8€ children 7 to 17. Open daily April through June and September 9am to 7pm; July and August 9am to 7:30pm; March and October 9:30am to 6pm; and November through February 10am to 5pm.

Carrières de Lumières ★★ EXHIBITION SPACE   A 10-minute stroll downhill from Les Baux, this awe-inspiring exhibition space occupies the site of a former limestone quarry. It's here that images of modern artworks (such as audiovisual exhibitions dedicated to Monet, Renoir, Van Gogh, or Gauguin) are projected against the 7 to 9m (23- to 30-ft.) columns, almost exploding in a ball of color before viewers' eyes. The museum's Cubist-style entrance featured in Jean Cocteau's final film, *The Testament of Orpheus.* An inspiring and interactive introduction to the artistic legacy of the South of France. A combined ticket offers a discount to this venue and the Château des Baux.

Route de Maillane. www.carrieres-lumieres.com. ✆ **04-90-54-47-37.** Admission 14€ adults; 12€ visitors ages 7–25; free for children 6 and under. Daily Apr–Oct 9:30am–7pm (until 7.30pm July–Aug); Nov–Mar 10am–6pm.

Where to Stay & Eat

Near the foot of Les Baux is a combo hotel/restaurant charmer that we also recommend: **Hotel Benvengudo** ★★ (https://benvengudo.com; from 220€ per night).

Baumanière ★★★ PROVENÇAL   Baumanière is the name of the cluster of fabulous inns, guesthouses, and authentically Provençal hotel accommodation dotted around the medieval town. Each section of the diverse hotel boasts kitchen gardens and swimming pools, amid scenes of pastoral bliss reminiscent of a French movie set. In terms of dining, Chef Michel Hulin of **La Cabro d'Or** (set menus 80€–120€) delivers intelligent, innovative Provençal cuisine with a lightness of touch. Diners savor the unctuousness of Mediterranean langoustines, the crispness of roasted red mullet, the froth of fresh pea velouté, and the crunch of slow-cooked suckling pig. The main **Oustau de Baumanière** (set menus 180€–330€) building has hosted the likes of Queen Elizabeth and Vanessa Paradis and also purveys an even more acclaimed (and more expensive) restaurant than the Cabro d'Or site nearby. It holds an unrivalled three Michelin stars.

Mas de Baumanière. www.baumaniere.com. ℰ **04-90-54-33-07.** 53 units. 270€–510€; 405€–895€ suite. Restaurant; bar; outdoor pool; room service; sauna; tennis courts; free Wi-Fi.

ARLES

744km (461 miles) S of Paris; 36km (22 miles) SW of Avignon; 92km (57 miles) NW of Marseille

On the banks of the Rhône River, Arles (pop. 53,000) attracts art lovers, archaeologists, gourmands, and historians. To the delight of visitors, many of the vistas van Gogh painted remain luminously present today. Here the artist was even inspired to paint his own bedroom (*Bedroom in Arles,* 1888). The newest artistic attraction is LUMA, a gigantic art space crowned with a tower designed by "starchitect" Frank Gehry.

Julius Caesar established a Roman colony here in the 1st century. Constantine the Great named Arles the second capital of his empire in A.D. 306, when it was known as "the little Rome of the Gauls." The city was incorporated into France in 1481.

Arles's ancient center is stunningly raw, with excellent restaurants and summer festivals, to the extent that every street corner could pose for an advertisement for French tourism. Its position on the river makes it a gateway to the Camargue, giving the town a healthy dose of Spanish and Roma influence.

Essentials

ARRIVING **Trains** run almost every hour between Arles and Avignon (trip time: 20 min.; www.sncf-connect.com; ℰ **36-35;** 8.70€ one-way) and Marseille (trip time: 1 hr.; 17.70€). Be sure to take local trains from city center to city center, not the TGV, which, in this case, takes more time. If driving, head south along D570N from Avignon.

VISITOR INFORMATION The **Office de Tourisme** is on bd. des Lices (www.arlestourisme.com; ℰ **04-90-18-41-20**).

SPECIAL EVENTS Arles's world-beating photographic event, **Les Recontres d'Arles** (www.rencontres-arles.com; ℰ **04-90-96-76-06**), held from early July until late September, focuses on contemporary international images from nature to warzones. Some exhibitions are free, although passes for all key shows are also available from 39€. The ticket office is located in place de la République for the duration of the festival.

[FastFACTS] ARLES

ATMs/Banks Downtown
Arles has more than a dozen
banks, including three in
place de la République.

Mail & Postage **La
Poste,** 5 bd. des Lices
(*C* **36-31**).

Pharmacies **Pharmacie
des Arènes,** 17 rue
du 4 Septembre
(*C* **04-90-96-02-77**).

Exploring Arles

The place du Forum, shaded by plane trees, stands around the old Roman forum. The Terrace du Café le Soir, immortalized by Van Gogh, is now the square's Café van Gogh. Visitors keen to follow in the footsteps of the great artist may pick up a **Van Gogh walking map** (1€; available at the tourist office), which takes in 10 important sites around the city, including the Pont Van Gogh bridge. On a corner of place du Forum sits the legendary, if charmingly faded, **Grand Hôtel Nord-Pinus** (www.nord-pinus. com): Bullfighters, artists, and A-listers have all stayed here. Three blocks south, the place de la République is dominated by a 15m (49-ft.) tall red granite obelisk.

One of the city's great classical monuments is the **Roman Théâtre Antique ★**, rue du Cloître (*C* **04-90-49-59-05**). Augustus began the theater in the 1st century; only two Corinthian columns remain. The Venus of Arles (a stunning marble statue now housed in the Louvre in Paris) was discovered here in 1651. The theater is open May through September daily 9am to 7pm; March, April, and October until 6pm; and November through February daily 10am to 5pm. Admission is 9€ adults, 7€ students, and free for children 17 and under. The same ticket admits you to the nearby **Amphitheater (Les Arènes) ★★**, rond-point des Arènes (*C* **04-90-49-59-05;** same opening hours), a UNESCO World Heritage Site, also built in the 1st century.

> ### Les Taureaux
>
> Bulls are a big part of Arlesien culture. It's not unusual to see bull steak on local menus, and **saucisson de taureau** (bull sausage) is a local specialty. The first bullfight, or **corrida,** took place in the amphitheater in 1853. Appropriately, Arles is home to a bullfighting school (the **Ecole Taurine d'Arles**). Like it or loathe it, **corridas** are still held during the Easter Ferias and in September, during the Ferias du Riz.

Sometimes called Le Cirque Romain, it seats almost 25,000. For a good view, climb the three towers that remain from medieval times, when the amphitheater was turned into a fortress.

Fondation Vincent Van Gogh Arles ★★ EXHIBITION SPACE
This permanent home for the Van Gogh Foundation is housed in the 15th-century private mansion Hôtel Léautaud de Donines. Highlighting the connection between Arles and Van Gogh, it stages a variety of temporary

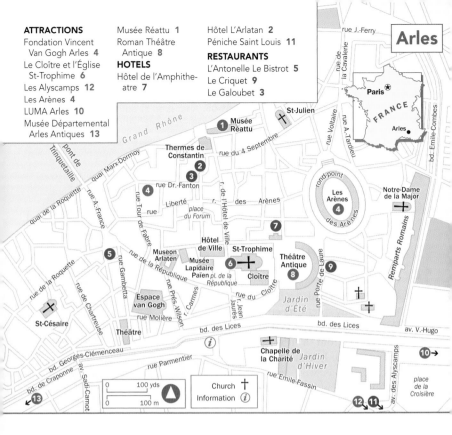

ATTRACTIONS
Fondation Vincent
  Van Gogh Arles **4**
Le Cloître et l'Église
  St-Trophime **6**
Les Alyscamps **12**
Les Arènes **4**
LUMA Arles **10**
Musée Départemental
  Arles Antiques **13**

Musée Réattu **1**
Roman Théâtre
  Antique **8**
HOTELS
Hôtel de l'Amphithe-
  atre **7**

Hôtel L'Arlatan **2**
Péniche Saint Louis **11**
RESTAURANTS
L'Antonelle Le Bistrot **5**
Le Criquet **9**
Le Galoubet **3**

Arles

exhibitions, seminars, and interactive debates. Check the website for the current program.

35 ter rue du Docteur Fanton. www.fondation-vincentvangogh-arles.org. © **04-90-93-08-08.** Admission 10€ adults; 8€ seniors; free for children 18 and under. Daily 10am–7pm.

Le Cloître et l'Eglise St-Trophime ★ CHURCH

This church is noted for its 12th-century portal, one of the finest achievements of the southern Romanesque style. Frederick Barbarossa was crowned king of Arles here in 1178. In the pediment, Christ is surrounded by the symbols of the Evangelists. The pretty cloister, in Gothic and Romanesque styles, possesses noteworthy medieval carvings: During the summer's Les Recontres d'Arles festival, contemporary photographs are also exhibited here.

East side of pl. de la République. © **04-90-49-59-05.** Free admission to church; cloister 6€ adults, 5€ students, free for children 18 and under. Church daily 10am–noon and 2–5pm; cloister May–Sept daily 9am–7pm; Mar, Apr, and Oct daily 9am–6pm; Nov–Feb daily 10am–5pm.

Les Alyscamps ★★ RUINS

Perhaps the most memorable historic sight in Arles, this once–Roman necropolis became a Christian burial ground in the 4th century. Mentioned in Dante's *Inferno*, it has been painted by both Van Gogh and Gauguin. Today it is lined with poplars and studded with ancient sarcophagi. Arlesiens escape here with a cold drink to enjoy a respite from the summer heat.

Avenue des Alyscamps. ☎ **04-90-49-59-05.** Admission 5€ adults; 4€ students; free for children 17 and under. Daily May–Sept 9am–7pm; Mar–Apr and Oct 9am–6pm; Nov–Feb 10:30am–4:30pm.

LUMA Arles ★★★ ART COMPLEX

The 15,000 square meter tower that shimmers above LUMA, Arles's newest art complex, took inspiration from the Vincent van Gogh canvas *Starry Night,* which was painted in the city. Inside there is a café, library, auditorium, and exhibition spaces. Notable recent exhibitions included a Diane Arbus photography retrospective. The Parc des Ateliers outdoor zone was converted from a former SNCF railway yard. It hosts more exhibition spaces as well as an artistic campus and landscaped gardens.

LUMA Arles.

35 av. Victor Hugo. www.luma.org. ☎ **04-65-88-10-00.** Free admission but time slots for some shows must be booked in advance. Daily 10am–7:30pm.

Musée Départemental Arles Antiques ★★ MUSEUM

Set within a sleek compound around 1km (½ mile) south of Arles' town center, this archaeological museum has finds uncovered throughout the region's rich territories. Airy rooms present Roman sarcophagi, sculptures, mosaics, and inscriptions from ancient times through the 6th century. Ancient history lovers can find glories of the Roman occupation in Arles, including muscle-clad statues and a portrait of Julius Caeser, in the vast permanent collection.

Avenue 1ere Division France Libra, presqu'île du Cirque Romain. www.arlesantique. fr. ☎ **04-13-31-51-03.** Admission 8€ adults; 5€ visitors ages 65 and over; free for children 17 and under. Wed–Mon 9.30am–6pm.

Musée Réattu ★★ ART MUSEUM

Exhibited over the labyrinthine rooms of the 15th-century Grand Priory of the Order of Malta, this museum opened in 1868 to showcase artworks previously owned by local painter Jacques Réattu. Over the past 150 years, the collection has swollen with donations and annual acquisitions—attracting prestigious visitors, including Van Gogh in 1888—and now includes dozens of Picasso drawings and close to 4,000 photographs. The building's former archives room is now dedicated to the history of the Order of the Knights Hospitaller.

10 rue du Grand-Prieuré. www.museereattu.arles.fr. © **04-90-49-37-58.** Admission 8€ adults; 6€ students; free for children 17 and under. Tues–Sun Mar–Oct 10am–6pm; Nov–Feb 10am–5pm.

Outlying Attractions

Abbaye de Montmajour ★★ MONASTERY ART SPACE This medieval monastery, founded in the leafy countryside 6km (3½ miles) northeast of Arles during the 10th century, is now an innovative exhibition venue. Temporary shows, ranging from a Christian Lacroix installation to annual photographic displays as part of Les Recontres d'Arles, which in 2023 included a 50-year retrospective of artsy newspaper Libération, are dotted throughout the atmospheric ruins. A wonderful outdoor restaurant, serviced by a food truck (dishes around 10€) is tucked under the trees.

Route de Fontvieille. www.abbaye-montmajour.fr. © **04-90-54-64-17.** Admission 6€ adults; 5€ students; free for children 17 and under. July–Sept Tues–Sun 10am–6:15pm; Oct–June Tues–Sun 10am–5pm.

Where to Stay

For an unusual but very enjoyable stay, consider booking the historic barge (built in 1931) *Péniche Saint Louis* ★, which is permanently moored on a canal painted by Van Gogh, next to rue Jean Charcot (http://penichearles.jimdo.com; © **06-19-11-81-69;** 75€ per night, including breakfast). It has only one cabin, so book early.

Hôtel de l'Amphithéâtre ★★ This delightful hotel is a firm favorite with regular visitors to Arles. Tucked into the heart of the Old Town, the main building itself was originally constructed in the 17th century and retains its historic atmosphere, with slightly more modern decor in the building opposite. Guest rooms feature reproduction Provençal furniture and some—including the bright Belvedere Suite, surrounded by windows on all four walls—offer views over the terra-cotta roofs of historic Arles. The hotel frequently proposes discounted rates out of season.

5–7 rue Diderot. www.hotelamphitheatre.fr. © **04-90-96-10-30.** 33 units. 84€–147€ double; 144€–181€ triple; 161€–212€ quadruple. Parking 10€. **Amenities:** Free Wi-Fi.

> ### Riding the New Ancient Railway Line
>
> One of Arles's zaniest family-friendly attractions is to ride a **verorail** along a disused railway track. These "bike-train" contraptions must be pedaled along one of two 8km routes through virgin countryside. The tracks themselves once hauled olive oil and minerals and were used by Vincent van Gogh. One route starts from Arles city center (www.veloraildesalpilles.fr; book online for 14€ adults, 7€ for children ages 5–17, free for children 4 and under).

A day out IN THE CAMARGUE

A marshy delta south of Arles, the Camargue is located between the Mediterranean and two arms of the Rhône. With a fragile ecosystem, it has been a nature reserve since 1970. You cannot drive into the protected parts, and some areas are accessible only to the Gardians, the local cowboys. Their ancestors may have been the first American cowboys, who sailed on French ships to the port of New Orleans, where they rode through the bayous of Louisiana and east Texas, rounding up cattle—in French, no less.

The Camargue is also cattle country. Black bulls are bred here both for their meat and for the regional bullfighting arenas. The whitewashed houses, plaited-straw roofs, plains, sandbars, and pink flamingos in the marshes make this area different, even exotic. There's no more evocative sight than the snow-white horses galloping through the marshlands, with hoofs so tough that they don't need shoes. The breed was brought here by the Arabs long ago, and it is said that their long manes and bushy tails evolved over the centuries to slap the region's omnipresent mosquitoes. Exotic flora and fauna abound. The bird-life here is among the most luxuriant in Europe. Looking much like the Florida Everglades, the area is known for its colonies of pink flamingos (*flamants roses*), which share living quarters with some 400 other bird species, including ibises, egrets, kingfishers, owls, wild ducks, swans, and ferocious birds of prey. The best place to see flamingo colonies is at the **Parc Ornithologique de Pont de Gau,** D570 (www.parcornithologique.com; ℭ **04-90-97-82-62**), 4km (3 miles), north of Camargue's capital, Stes-Maries-de-la-Mer.

You can explore the Camargue's rugged terrain by boat, bike, jeep, or horse. The latter can take you along beaches and into the interior, fording waters to places where black bulls graze and wild birds nest. Dozens of stables are located along the highway between Arles to Stes-Maries. Virtually all charge the same rate (around 50€ for 2 hr.). The rides are aimed at the neophyte, not the champion equestrian.

For details, visit Arles' Office de Tourisme (p. 543) or head to the **Office de Tourisme,** 5 av. Van Gogh, Ste-Maries-de-la-Mer (www.saintesmaries.com; ℭ **04-90-97-82-55**).

Hôtel L'Arlatan ★★ Neary 2 million fragments of tile went into the 6,000m (19,600 ft.) of brilliantly colorful mosaics that adorn many of the surfaces of this singular hotel, an establishment made up of buildings from the 15th, 18th, and 20th centuries (notably, a historic *hôtel particulier* or grand mansion). Add to this walls painted in every color of the rainbow, sculptural chandeliers, and brightly hued handmade furniture and the effect is kaleidoscopic—often dizzyingly so. Some love artist/designer Jorge Pardo's work here, others find it over the top. But with L'Arlatan's unbeatable location in the dead center of Arles, its accomplished restaurant, top quality beds, pretty miniature garden and pool, what's undeniable is that your stay will be *very* memorable.

9 rue du Sauvage. www.arlatan.fr. ℭ **04-65-88-20-20**. 35 units. 129€–295€ double; suites from 414€. **Amenities:** Restaurant; bar; outdoor pool; free Wi-Fi.

Where to Eat

L'Antonelle Le Bistrot ★★ MODERN PROVENÇAL   A classic southern bistro with a small, flavorful menu of beautifully presented dishes. Timeless starters at L'Antonelle can include chicken livers or bone marrow with crusty bread. Mains might sound inventive—like zucchini flowers stuffed with cod mousse—but they are simply Provençal classics cooked to perfection. The fragrant and fruity tartes are to die for.
9 pl. Antonelle. ℰ **06-38-62-93-32.** Fixed-price menu 37€–40€. Thurs–Mon noon–2pm and 7–9pm.

Le Criquet ★★ MODERN PROVENÇAL   Tiny, charming, and worth reserving well in advance, Le Criquet is a classic local restaurant on the back streets of Arles. It has been run by the same family for 3 decades. Friendly service meets unpretentious dishes like *bourride* of salt cod and spices, artichoke carpaccio, and stew made from local Camargue bull. Sit outside amid a romantic street setting or in the rather cramped—but with its exposed stone walls, undeniably cozy—interior.
21 rue Porte de Laure. ℰ **04-90-96-80-51.** Main course 16€–32€; fixed-price menus 24€–29€. Tues–Sat noon–1:30pm and 7–9pm.

Le Galoubet ★★ FRENCH   Occupying the ground floor of an elegant 18th-century building just off of Arles' place du Forum, this lovely little enclave boasts everything you might be seeking in an ideal Provençal bistro. Friendly owners? Check. Atmospheric dining room, leafy outdoor terrace? Check. Tasty menu? Reasonable prices? Check and Check. Depending on the season, menu may include octopus, celery, and basil salad; cod atop roasted eggplant, peppers, and black olives; or fat asparagus with poached egg and crispy fried jambon. Be sure to reserve far in advance as this place is popular.
18 rue du Docteur Fanton. ℰ **04-90-93-18-11.** Fixed-price menu 27€–40€; Tues–Sat noon–1:30pm and 7–9:30pm.

Nightlife

Because of its relatively small population, Arles doesn't offer as many nightlife options as Aix-en-Provence, Avignon, or Marseille. The town's most buzzing nightclub is **L' Esquisse,** 12 av. Victor Hugo (ℰ **04-90-97-77-98**), which spins house, lounge, and hip-hop tunes until midnight.

AIX-EN-PROVENCE ★★

760km (471 miles) S of Paris; 84km (52 miles) SE of Avignon; 34km (21 miles) N of Marseille; 185km (115 miles) W of Nice

One of the most surprising aspects of Aix is its size. Guidebooks frequently proclaim it the very heart of Provence, evoking a sleepy town filled with flowers and fountains, which it is—in certain quarters. But Aix is also a bustling university town of around 143,000 inhabitants (the Université d'Aix dates from 1413).

Founded in 122 B.C. by Roman general Caius Sextius Calvinus, who conveniently named the town Aquae Sextiae, after himself, Aix originated as a military outpost. Aix's most celebrated son, Paul Cézanne, immortalized the Aix countryside in his paintings. Just as he saw it, the **Montagne Sainte-Victoire** looms over the town today.

Time marches on, but there are still plenty of decades-old, family-run shops on the narrow streets of the Old Town. A lazy summer lunch at one of the bourgeois cafes on the **cours Mirabeau** is an experience not to be missed.

Essentials

ARRIVING Trains arrive frequently from Marseille (trip time: 40 min.; 9€ one-way) and Nice (trip time: 3 hr.; www.sncf-connect.com; ✆ **36-35; 45€** one-way). High-speed TGV trains—from Paris as well as Marseille and Nice—arrive at the modern station near Vitrolles, 18km (11 miles) west of Aix. Bus transfers to the center of Aix (www. www.lepilote.com) run every 20 minutes at peak times and cost 4.30€ one-way. If you're driving to Aix from Avignon or other points north, take A7 south to A8 and follow the signs into town. From Marseille or other points south, take A51 north.

VISITOR INFORMATION The **Office de Tourisme** is at Les Allées Provençales, 300 av. Giuseppe Verdi (www.aixenprovencetourism.com; ✆ **04-42-16-11-61**).

The Town Hall and central square of Aix-en-Provence.

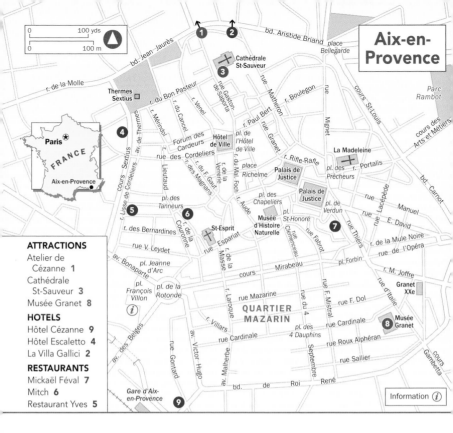

Map labels:
- bd. Aristide Briand
- place Bellegarde
- Parc Rambot
- r. de la Molle
- bd. Jean Jaurès
- Thermes Sextius
- Cathédrale St-Sauveur **3**
- r. du Bon Pasteur
- rue Gaston-de Saporta
- rue Matheron
- r. Boulegon
- cours St-Louis
- cours des Arts et Métiers
- r. du Cancel
- r. Venel
- r. Méréndol
- av. de Thermes
- Forum des Cardeurs
- Hôtel de Ville **4**
- pl. de l'Hôtel de Ville
- r. Paul Bert
- rue Granet
- Mignet
- La Madeleine
- av. Sextius
- rue des Cordeliers
- Lieutaud
- r. de la Verrerie
- r. du F. Gaut
- r. des Magnans
- r. du Mal. Foch
- r. Aude
- place Richelme
- Palais de Justice
- r. Rifle-Rafle
- pl. des Prêcheurs
- r. Portalis
- bd. Carnot
- pl. des Tanneurs
- r. Lisse de Cordeliers
- r. de la Couronne
- St-Esprit
- place des Chapeliers
- Palais de Justice
- pl. St-Honoré
- pl. de Verdun
- rue Lacépède
- Manuel
- r. E. David
- r. des Bernardines
- rue V. Leydet
- r. Espariat
- r. de la Masse
- Musée d'Histoire Naturelle
- Clemenceau
- r. Fabrot
- rue Thiers
- **7**
- r. de la Mule Noire
- rue de l'Opéra
- av. Bonaparte
- pl. Jeanne d'Arc
- pl. François Villon
- pl. de la Rotonde
- r. Villars
- cours Mirabeau
- pl. Forbin
- r. M. Joffre
- Granet XXe
- r. des Belges
- r. Laroque
- rue Mazarine
- QUARTIER MAZARIN
- rue du 4
- r. F. Mistral
- rue F. Dol
- rue Cardinale
- Musée Granet **8**
- rue Gontard
- av. Victor Hugo
- rue Cardinale
- av. Malherbe
- pl. des 4 Dauphins
- Septembre
- rue Roux Alphéran
- rue Sallier
- cours Gambetta
- Gare d'Aix-en-Provence **9**
- bd. de Roi René
- Information ⓘ

ATTRACTIONS
Atelier de
  Cézanne **1**
Cathédrale
  St-Sauveur **3**
Musée Granet **8**

HOTELS
Hôtel Cézanne **9**
Hôtel Escaletto **4**
La Villa Gallici **2**

RESTAURANTS
Mickaël Féval **7**
Mitch **6**
Restaurant Yves **5**

Paris ★
FRANCE
Aix-en-Provence

0   100 yds
0   100 m

CITY LAYOUT Aix's **Old Town** is primarily pedestrianized. To the south, it's bordered by the grand **cours Mirabeau,** flanked by a canopy of plane trees. The city was built atop thermal springs, and 40 fountains still bubble away in picturesque squares around town.

SPECIAL EVENTS The **Festival d'Aix,** created in 1948 (www.festival-aix.com; ✆ **08-20-92-29-23**), mid-June through late July, features music and opera from all over the world.

[FastFACTS]
AIX-EN-PROVENCE

ATMs/Banks Downtown Aix has scores of banks, including several along cours Mirabeau.

Mail & Postage **La Poste,** pl. de l'Hôtel de Ville (✆ **36-31**).

Pharmacies **Pharmacie des Prêcheurs,** 2 rue Peyresc (✆ **04-42-38-18-60**).

Aix Through the Eyes of Cézanne

One of the best experiences in Aix is a walk along the well-marked **route de Cézanne.** From the east end of cours Mirabeau, take rue du Maréchal-Joffre across boulevard Carnot to boulevard des Poilus, which becomes avenue des Ecoles-Militaires and D17. The stretch between Aix and the hamlet of Le Tholonet is full of twists and turns where Cézanne used to set up his easel. The route also makes a lovely 5.5km (3½-mile) stroll. Le Tholonet has a cafe or two where you can refresh yourself while waiting for one of the frequent buses back to Aix.

Exploring Aix-en-Provence

Aix's main street, **cours Mirabeau ★**, is one of the most beautiful boulevards in Europe. A double row of plane trees shades it from the Provençal sun and throws dappled daylight onto its rococo fountains. Shops and sidewalk cafes line one side; 17th- and 18th-century sandstone hôtels particuliers (private mansions) take up the other. Take a coffee in one of a dozen timeless cafes along the boulevard and you'll be in good company. The likes of Emile Zola, Cézanne, Picasso, and Sir Winston Churchill frequented Aix. Today a new range of boutiques, chocolate shops, and microbreweries dot the ancient streets of Boulevard Carnot and cours Sextius, which circle the pedestrian-only heart of the old quarter (Vieille Ville).

One fun way to check out the lay of the land is aboard an eco-friendly **Diabline** (www.la-diabline.fr; Mon–Sat 8:30am–7:30pm; 1.30€/ride, or 9.10€ for a book of 10 tickets). These vehicles operate three routes along cours Mirabeau and through most of the Old Town. We also recommend the English-language **walking tours** offered most mornings by the Tourist Board (see above for link; 12€).

In addition to the museums profiled below, serious art aficionados may want to visit **Fondation Vasarely ★** (1 av. Marcel Pagnol; www.fondationvasarely.fr; 15€ admission), a museum devoted to the work of 1960s "op-art" (optical art) master Victor Vasarely. Visitors can also view the fine 17th- and 18th-century tapestries showcased at a former Archbishop's Palace, today the **Musée des Tapisseries** (28 place des Martyrs de la Résistance; 4€).

Art and wine lovers shouldn't forget **Château la Coste ★★** (www.chateau-la-coste.com; ✆ **04-42-61-92-92**), 20km north of Aix-en-Provence, near the village of Le Puy Sainte Réparade. The vineyard's Art and Architecture Walk (25€) rambles through the bucolic Provençal countryside, taking in works by Alexander Calder, Tadao Ando, Richard Serra, Louise Bourgeois, Ai Wei Wei, Jean Nouvel and others. Allow around 2 hours to complete the full walk. On site are also several swanky restaurants, an art exhibition space, plus expansive vineyards and a winery where tastings and classes are held.

Atelier de Cézanne ★★ MUSEUM   A 10-minute (uphill) stroll north of Aix's Old Town, Cézanne's studio offers visitors a unique glimpse

Atelier de Cézanne.

into the artist's daily life. Because the building remained untouched for decades after Cézanne's death in 1906, the studio has remained perfectly preserved for close to a century. Note the furnishings, vases, and small figurines on display, all of which feature in the modern master's drawings and canvases. Cézanne aficionados will also enjoy both **Jas de Bouffan,** the artist's family manor, which is slated to reopen in 2024, and the inspirational Cubist landscape of the **Bibémus Quarries** (see website below for info on all the Cézanne sites).

9 av. Paul-Cézanne. www.cezanne-en-provence.com.   ℭ   **04-42-21-06-53.** Admission 6.50€ adults; 3.50€ students and children ages 13–25; free for children 12 and under. June–Sept daily 9:30am–6pm; Apr–May daily 9:30am–12:30pm and 2–6pm; Oct–Mar daily 9:30am–12:30pm and 2–5pm. Audio guide 3€. Closed Jan.

Cathédrale St-Sauveur ★ CATHEDRAL   The cathedral of Aix is dedicated to Christ under the title St-Sauveur (Holy Savior or Redeemer) and dates from the 4th and 5th centuries. Its pièce de résistance is a 15th-century Nicolas Froment triptych, *The Burning Bush.* One side depicts the Virgin and Child; the other, Good King René and his second wife, Jeanne de Laval.

34 pl. des Martyrs de la Résistance. ℭ **04-42-23-45-65.** Free admission. Daily 8am–noon and 2–6pm. Mass Sun 10:30am and 7pm.

Musée Granet ★★ MUSEUM   One of the South of France's top art venues, this popular museum displays a permanent collection of paintings and sculpture ranging from 15th-century French canvases to 20th-century

Giacometti sculptures. However, it's the large-scale temporary exhibitions that truly impress, such as 2023's landmark David Hockney show, operated in collaboration with the Tate museum in London.

pl. Saint Jean de Malte. www.museegranet-aixenprovence.fr. ℰ **04-42-52-88-32.** Admission 8€ adults; 6€ students and children 13–25; free for children 12 and under. Additional fee for temporary exhibitions. Tues–Sun June–Sept 10am–6pm; Oct–May noon–6pm.

Where to Stay

Hôtel Cézanne ★★ This super-chic—yet enormously friendly— boutique hotel is best suited to guests seeking a more unusual spot to snooze. Conceived by the designers behind the sophisticated (and more expensive) Villa Gallici, the Cézanne is a mélange of Baroque furnishings, and unique artworks. An honesty bar adds to the friendly atmosphere. The hotel's location—midway between the train station and Aix's Old Town—makes it ideal for visitors planning day trips farther afield. And, unusually for France, the gourmet breakfasts of truffle omelets, pancakes, and eggs benedicts are both ample and delicious.

40 av. Victor Hugo. www.boutiquehotelcezanne.com. ℰ **04-42-91-11-11.** 55 units. 126€–258€ double; 216€–560€ suite. Parking 20€. **Amenities:** Bar; free Wi-Fi.

Hôtel Escaletto ★★ In a city where expensive is the norm, try this freshly refurbished budget haven on Cours Sextius, a short walk from the Roman baths. The rooms have been upgraded with contemporary woods, cool white walls, funky mirrors, and discreet lighting. The biggest pull is the gigantic terrace where guests may gaze over the Aix-en-Provence rooftops to Montagne Sainte-Victoire. A few (tiny) single rooms for under 100€ are a great bargain for solo travelers.

74 cours Sextius. www.hotel-escaletto.com. ℰ **04-42-26-03-58.** 44 units. 112€–190€ double; quad from 144€–241€. **Amenities:** Free Wi-Fi.

La Villa Gallici ★★ This 18th-century Provençal house is one of Aix's most luxurious getaways. It also boasts a 3-hectare (7-acre) garden and a gastronomic restaurant on-site. It may be just a 5-minute stroll from the town center, yet the countrified ambience makes it feel miles away. Guest rooms are swathed in pastel-printed fabrics, while suites have their own private patios. Days may be spent lounging by the terracotta–trimmed pool; candlelit dinners are served alfresco under the stars. The villa also has a wine cellar, where guests may taste over 300 different châteaus alongside a sommelier. Note that the villa, while fancy and famous, is perhaps not the friendliest establishment in town.

Av. de la Violette. www.villagallici.com. ℰ **04-42-23-29-23.** 22 units. 360€–585€ double; from 560€ suite. Free parking. Closed Jan. **Amenities:** Restaurant; bar; babysitting; outdoor pool; room service; free Wi-Fi.

Where to Eat

Mickaël Féval ★★★ FRENCH   Chef Mickaël Féval pulls in the city's most discerning diners, and for good reason. He is a "fish whisperer" bringing out the best of anything that once swum or floated, creating innovative dishes such as seared monkfish with eggplant caviar and tarragon oil. Scallops, and giant bass from Corsica are braised in seasonal stocks of (respectively) forest fruit, oyster reduction, and mandarin—and the results are sublime. Mickaël's wife, Olivia, graciously presides over the front-of-house.

11 petite rue St Jean. www.mickaelfeval.fr. ✆ **04-42-93-29-69.** Fixed-price menu 65€–129€. Tues–Sat noon–2:30pm and 7:30–10:30pm.

Mitch ★★ FRENCH   There's a reason why Mitch isn't big on social media. Regular dinner guests are reluctant to share this gourmet homage to Southern French cuisine with anyone else. For a starter, heirloom tomatoes from France's southern shoreline might top Mediterranean scallops and red mullet. Then Mitch and his in-the-know staff, all of whom speak excellent English, deliver heftier dishes of monkfish and steaks, each paired with more fragrantly intense ingredients from Provence and the Languedoc interior. A dinnertime triumph. Reserve one of the handful of outside tables if the weather is nice.

26 rue des Tanneurs. ✆ **04-42-26-63-08.** Main course 18€–34€; fixed-price dinner 39€–58€. Mon–Sat 7:30–10pm.

Restaurant Yves ★★ ORGANIC   Christophe Buffille cheffed at the world's finest restaurants, then opened this hole-in-the-wall eatery named after his father, a vegetable gardener. Organic ingredients, vegetable-forward dishes, and carefully sourced meats crown his tiny menu. Dishes like home-made seafood ravioli and fig panna cotta are not only made by master Buffille, but served by him on the half dozen tables as well. The chef genuinely works alone, so allow ample time to dine. An inexpensive yet wondrous experience.

23 rue Lisse des Cordeliers www.yvesrestaurantaix.fr. ✆ **06-67-27-14-62.** Main courses 14€–18€. Thurs–Tues noon–2pm and 7:30–10pm.

Shopping

Opened more than a century and a half ago, **Béchard,** 12 cours Mirabeau (✆ **04-42-26-06-78**), is the most famous bakery in town. It specializes in the famous Calissons d'Aix, a candy made from ground almonds, preserved melon, and fruit syrup. Sweet-toothed Aixois also adore **Chocolaterie de Puyricard,** 7 rue Rifle-Rafle (www.puyricard.fr; ✆ **04-42-21-13-26**), which creates truly sensational chocolates filled with candied figs, walnuts, or local lavender honey.

Boutique perfumerie **Rose et Marius,** 3 rue Thiers (www.roseetmarius.com; ℭ 09-82-59-35-35), dries local flowers then distils them into fragrances and soaps in this downtown perfume bar. Public perfume-making workshops are also hosted in these floral surrounds.

Founded in 1934 on a busy boulevard just east of the center of town, **Santons Fouque,** 65 cours Gambetta (www.santons-fouque.com; ℭ **04-42-26-33-38**), stocks close to 2,000 traditional *santons* (crèche figurines).

For a range of useful souvenirs, including copper pots and pocket knives by famous French forgers such as Laguiole, try **Quincaillerie Centrale,** 21 rue de Monclar (ℭ **04-42-23-33-18**), a hardware/housewares store that's been offering a little bit of everything since 1959.

Nightlife

Aix is a major center for contemporary choreography and dance, thanks to the purpose-built dance center **Pavillon Noir** at 530 av. Mozart (www.preljocaj.org; ℭ **04-42-93-48-00;** 10€–50€ ticket). Ballets, dance shows, and public rehearsals bring performances to rapt audiences.

For raucous nightlife with a dash of history belly up to bar and café **La Rotonde,** 2A pl. Jeanne d'Arc (www.larotonde-aix.com; ℭ **04-42-91-61-70;** daily 8am–2am).

Under-30s who like big beats should head for **Le Mistral,** 3 rue Frédéric Mistral (www.mistralclub.fr; ℭ **04-42-38-16-49**), where techno and house pumps long and loud for a cover charge of around 15€ to 20€. For thumping tunes spun by a rotating roster of visiting DJs, check the Instagram feed for **Scat Club,** 11 rue de la Verrerie (ℭ **04-42-23-00-23;** Tues–Sat midnight–6am). Last but certainly not least is the **Joïa Glam Club** (ℭ **06-80-35-32-94**), chemin de l'Enfant, in the hamlet of Les Milles, 8km (5 miles) south of Aix (follow the signs to Marseille). A shuttle bus connects from La Rotonde in Aix proper. On site is a restaurant, several bars, an outdoor swimming pool, and indoor/outdoor dance floor. Be forewarned that long lines are common on Fridays (when women get in free) and Saturdays. Entrance usually costs around 20€, unless you're a star or self-confident enough to schmooze the doorman.

MARSEILLE ★★

776km (481 miles) S of Paris; 203km (126 miles) SW of Nice; 32km (20 miles) S of Aix-en-Provence

Marseille is France's electrifying second city. With nearly 2 million inhabitants in the metropolitan area, it best embodies the vibrancy, energy, and multiculturalism of modern France. The cuisine is epic too.

It's also the country's oldest metropolis, founded as a port by the Greeks in the 6th century B.C. Author Alexandre Dumas called teeming Marseille "the meeting place of the entire world." He wasn't wrong. A view from the high basilica of Notre-Dame-de-la-Garde reveals the colorful Vieux Port, with its elegant historic buildings, boat-filled harbor, and the Mediterranean beyond, from where so many arrivals originated, including one-quarter of the city's current residents all of whom are either immigrants from North Africa, or the children of those immigrants. The city is large, but it is well connected by tram, Metro, ferries, and electric scooters.

Marseille's residents do not feel overshadowed by their wealthy cousins in Paris. Nor by their neighbors in pristine, picture-book cities like Avignon and Lyon. The city, while noisy and beaten-up in places, boasts huge amounts of civic pride. This is best seen in friendly parks, al fresco restaurants, and in successful social rehabilitation schemes, including a new gourmet restaurant inside a maximum security penitentiary (p. 569).

City spirit is most prominently vocalized at the 67,000 seat Stade Vélodrome, home of ace soccer squad Olympique de Marseille. The stadium hosts matches during the 2024 Paris Olympiad, while a new Olympic marina welcomes 300 sailors competing in 10 nautical events.

One tip: Arrive hungry. Marseille is the nation's foodie go-to, with street food so good that tourism bosses regularly host TikTokers to stream the city's eats. Tuck in.

Essentials

ARRIVING **Marseille-Provence Airport** (www.marseille-airport.com; ✆ **04-42-14-14-14**), 27km (17 miles) northwest of the city center, receives international flights from all over Europe. From the airport, **shuttle buses** (*navettes;* www.navettemarseilleaeroport.com; ✆ **08-92-70-08-40**) make the trip to Marseille's St-Charles rail station, near the Vieux-Port, for 10€, 7€ passengers 12 to 26, and 5€ children 11 and under. The shuttle buses run daily every 20 minutes from 4:10am until 1.30am; the trip takes 25 minutes.

Marseille has train connections from all over Europe including Nice, Lyon, Avignon, Geneva, and Brussels. The TGV bullet train also links it

This spectacular view greets passengers at Marseille's train station.

to Paris, with departures almost every hour from the Gare de Lyon (trip time: 3 hr.; www.sncf.com; 40€–125€ one-way). Buses serve the Gare Routière, rue Honnorat (𝒞 **04-91-08-16-40**), adjacent to the St-Charles railway station. Regular fast buses run daily between Aix-en-Provence and Marseille (www.lecaraixmarseille.com; trip time: 40 min.; 7€ one-way). If you're driving from Paris, follow A6 south to Lyon, and then continue south along A7 to Marseille. The drive takes about 7 hours. From Provence, take A7 south to Marseille.

VISITOR INFORMATION　　The **Office de Tourisme** is at 11 la Canebière (www.marseille-tourisme.com; 𝒞 **08-26-50-05-00;** Métro: Vieux-Port).

CITY LAYOUT　　Marseille is a large metropolis, although most sights are concentrated around the Vieux Port. If you're keen to explore different parts of the city, you'll need to take advantage of its comprehensive public transport, have a strong set of legs, or download an app for one its eScooter rental schemes.

NEIGHBORHOODS IN BRIEF　　The major arteries divide Marseille into 16 arrondissements. Like Paris, the last two digits of a postal code tell you within which arrondissement an address is located. Visitors tend to spend

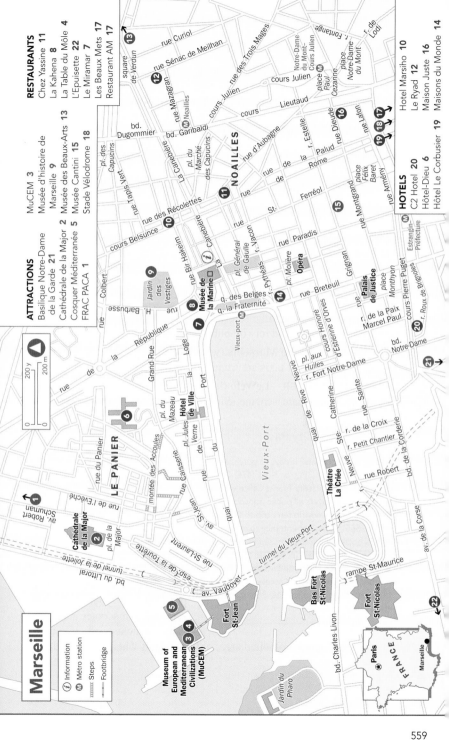

Marseille

ATTRACTIONS
Basilique Notre-Dame de la Garde **21**
Cathédrale de la Major **2**
Cosquer Méditerranée **5**
FRAC PACA **1**
MuCEM **3**
Musée d'histoire de Marseille **9**
Musée des Beaux-Arts **13**
Musée Cantini **15**
Stade Vélodrome **18**

RESTAURANTS
Chez Yassine **11**
La Kahena **8**
La Table du Môle **4**
L'Epuisette **22**
Le Miramar **7**
Les Beaux Mets **17**
Restaurant AM Vert **17**

HOTELS
C2 Hotel **20**
Hôtel-Dieu **6**
Hôtel Le Corbusier **19**
Hotel Marsiho **10**
Le Ryad **12**
Maison Juste **16**
Maisons du Monde **14**

most of their time in four main neighborhoods. The first is the **Vieux Port,** the atmospheric natural harbor that's a focal point for the city center. From here, the wide La Canebière boulevard runs eastwards, bisected by Marseille's most popular shopping avenues. To the north lies **Le Panier,** the original Old Town, crisscrossed by a pastel network of undulating alleyways. This neighborhood's western edge is trimmed by former docklands, which have been completely redeveloped over the past few years. Southeast of the Vieux Port, the alternative neighborhood around **cours Julien** is home to hipster bars, thrift stores, convivial restaurants, and one-off boutiques aplenty. And come summertime, action shifts to the **Plages du Prado,** home of the new Olympic marina, with its strip of beaches due south of the city center.

Getting Around

ON FOOT   Each of Marseille's neighborhoods is easily navigable on foot. However, unless you're an avid walker, you may want to rely on either the Métro, the tramway (see below), an eScooter, or Le Vélo public bikes, to zip around town.

BY CAR   Parking and traffic safety are so problematic that your best bet is to park in a garage and rely on public transport.

BY TAXI   **Taxis Radio Marseille** (www.taximarseille.com; ✆ **04-91-02-20-20**). Uber and Bolt taxis are frequently cheaper and friendlier.

BY BIKE OR SCOOTER   **Le Vélo** (levelo.ampmetropole.fr) is Marseille's easy-to-use bike share scheme. Simply unlock one of the 1,000 bikes from stands across the city using a credit card or sign up before you travel. The 7-day service costs just 1€ with the first 30 minutes of pedaling completely free. Equally fun are legions of electric scooters that have blossomed across the city. Simply download an app from **Lime, Bird,** or **Tier,** then unlock one for around 0.30€ per minute. Instructions will pop up on your cellphone screen. Each scooter automatically switches off if you're whizzing through a prohibited area, only to restart when it's pushed to a free riding zone.

> ### Marseille City Pass
>
> Seeing the big sights? It pays to purchase a 1-day (29€), 2-day (39€), or 3-day (47€) City Pass from the Marseille Tourist Office website. The pass covers all public transport, including the round-trip ferry trip to **Château d'If** (p. 565), as well as entrance to more than a dozen of the city's museums and a ride on the **petit-train** (p. 566) up to the **Basilique Notre-Dame-de-la-Garde** (p. 562). As the latter costs 9€ and access to MuCEM (free with the pass) costs 11€, it's easy to see the savings add up.

BY PUBLIC TRANSPORT   **Métro** lines 1 and 2 both stop at the main train station, Gare St-Charles, place Victor Hugo. Line 1 makes a U-shaped circuit from the suburbs into the city and back again; Line 2 runs north and south in the downtown area. Also with two lines, the **tramway** services the Canebière and the refurbished Joliette Docks district, as well as continuing out to the suburbs. Individual tickets are 2€; they're valid on Métro, tram, and bus lines for up to 1 hour after purchase. If you plan to take public transport several times during your stay, buy a pass journée, valid for 1 day for 5.20€. The tourism office (www.marseille-tourisme. com) has a good selection of city maps, although Google or Apple Maps could be your best friend here.

[Fast FACTS] MARSEILLE

ATMs/Banks   Marseille's banks are plentiful, including several along La Canebière.

Doctors & Hospitals   **Hopital Saint Joseph,** 26 bd. de Louvain (www. hopital-saint-joseph.fr; 📞 **04-91-80-65-00**).

Embassies & Consulates   **British Consulate Marseille,** 10 pl. de la Joliette (www.gov.uk; 📞 **04-91-15-72-10**); **Consulate General of the United States Marseille,** pl. Varian Fry (http://

marseille.usconsulate.gov; 📞 **01-43-12-48-85**).

Internet Access   Marseille's municipality hosts 50 free Wi-Fi hotspots around the city. Central locations (including Jardin du Pharo, the square outside the Hôtel de Ville, and La Vieille Charité) are indicated on the free maps distributed by the tourist office.

Mail & Postage   **La Poste,** 1 cours Jean Ballard (📞 **36-31**).

Newspapers & Magazines   Bilingual **COTE Magazine** (www.cote magazine.com) offers a good selection of tried-and-true Marseille tips, as well as local interviews and recent openings.

Pharmacies   **La Pharmacie Méditerranéenne,** 37 la Canebière (📞 **04-91-91-32-06**).

Safety   As in any big city, it's wise to keep a close eye on your belongings and avoid poorly lit areas at night.

Exploring Marseille

Immerse yourself in local life with a wander through Marseille's busy streets, including along the famous **La Canebière,** lined with hotels, shops, and restaurants. Just east is the **Nouilles** neighborhood: Think Marseille in its chaotic prime. Visitors can order food from a dozen nations in a score of languages, from a few euros up, alongside vendors of rare fruit, great coffee, and fragrant spices.

La Canebière joins the **Vieux Port** ★★, dominated at its western end by the massive neoclassical forts of St-Jean and St-Nicolas. The harbor is filled with fishing craft and yachts and ringed by seafood restaurants. For a panoramic view, head to the **Jardin du Pharo,** a promontory facing the entrance to the Vieux-Port. From the terrace of the **Château du Pharo,** built by Napoleon III, you can clearly see the city's old and new cathedrals, as well as the recently redeveloped docklands, now the **Cité de la Méditerranée,** which includes **Fort Saint-Jean** and the architectural wonders that are **Mucem** (Museum of European and Mediterranean Civilizations) and the new **Cosquer Méditerranée** museum.

North of the old port is **Le Panier,** Marseille's Old Town. Small boutiques and designer ateliers now populate these once-sketchy streets. To the south, the **corniche Président-J.-F.-Kennedy** is a 4km (2½-mile) promenade. You'll pass villas and gardens facing the Mediterranean, before reaching the popular **Plages du Prado.** Patrolled by lifeguards in the summer, these spacious sandy beaches have children's playgrounds, sun loungers, and water-

Graffiti and street art cover many buildings in Marseille.

side cafes. Serious hikers can continue south of here into the **Parc Nationale des Calanques** (www.calanques-parcnational.fr; p. 574). This series of stunning limestone cliffs, fjords, rocky promontories, and watersports opportunities stretches along the coast for 20km (12 miles) southeast of Marseille all the way to the resort of **Cassis** (p. 572).

Basilique Notre-Dame-de-la-Garde ★★ CHURCH This landmark church crowns a limestone rock overlooking the southern side of the Vieux-Port. It was built in the Romanesque-Byzantine style popular in the 19th century and topped by a 9.7m (32-ft.) gilded statue of the Virgin. Visitors come for the views (best at sunset) from its terrace. Spread out before you are the city, the islands, and the shimmering sea.

rue Fort-du-Sanctuaire. www.notredamedelagarde.com. ℂ **04-91-13-40-80.** Free admission. Daily 7am–6pm. Métro: Estrangin-Préfecture. Bus: 60.

Cathédrale de la Major ★★ CATHEDRAL One of the largest cathedrals (some 135m/443 ft. long) built in Europe during the 19th century, this massive structure has almost swallowed its 12th-century predecessor, built on the ruins of a temple of Diana. Its striped exterior is a bastardized Romanesque-Byzantine style with domes and cupolas; the intricate interiors include mosaic floors and red-and-white marble banners. The cathedral's architecture is particularly arresting now that it overlooks Marseille's redeveloped port and dockland areas. It also provides shady respite from sightseeing on a summer's day, with plenty of nearby cafés.

Esplanade de la Major. ✆ **04-91-90-53-57.** Free admission. Daily 10am–7pm. Head west of Le Panier district. Métro: Vieux-Port. Bus: 49, 60, or 82.

Cosquer Méditerranée ★★★ MUSEUM In 1985, local diver Henri Cosquer discovered a mysterious tunnel entrance 36m below the surface near the charming resort of **Cassis** (p. 572). It took him 6 years to navigate the 175m (574-ft.) tunnel. When Cosquer finally emerged, holding a diver's light, into a vast cave complex, he got the shock of his life: human handprints and spell-binding drawings of penguins, seals, and horses untouched for 20,000 years. Opened in 2022, the seafront Cosquer Méditerranée (next to MuCEM) is a near-exact replica of the cave, where multilingual headphone tours are conducted in electronic carts that move through the interactive exhibition.

Prom Robert Laffont. www.grotte-cosquer.com. No phone. Admission 16€ adults; 10€ ages 10–17; 10€ ages 6–9; free for children 5 and under. Daily 9am–9pm. Métro: Vieux-Port. Bus: 49, 60, or 82.

FRAC PACA (Fonds Régional d'Art Contemporain Provence-Alpes-Côte d'Azur) ★ MUSEUM FRAC PACA, Marseille's regional contemporary art museum anchors the hip Joliette Docks district. The museum's mosaic-like recycled glass structure was designed by Japanese architect Kengo Kuma. It's a fitting tribute to the FRAC's thousand-strong collection of artworks. Within the museum itself, exhibitions spread over two galleries. There's also a restaurant, two terraces, artists' residences, a performance hall, and a bookstore.

20 bd. de Dunkerque. www.lesfracs.com. ✆ **04-91-91-27-55.** Admission 5€ adults; 2.50€ students ages 18–25 and seniors; free for children 17 and under. Wed–Sat 10am–6pm, Sun 2–6pm. Métro: Joliette. Tram: Joliette. Bus: 35, 49, 55, or 82.

MuCEM (Museum of European and Mediterranean Civilizations) ★★★ MUSEUM Marseille's must-see museum showcases the city's crossroads history by way of 250,000 objects collected from throughout the Mediterranean region. Find also local prints, age-old photographs, and historical postcards. Temporary exhibitions focus on anything from Mediterranean football to Arabian graffiti. For some visitors, MuCEM's best part is the suspended gardens around the 12th-century **Fort Saint-Jean,** which host reclining chairs, scented herb beds, and jaw-dropping views over France's "Rebel City." A key legacy of 2,600 years of city history is food: MuCEM hosts Michelin-starred-chef Gérard

Passédat's array of eateries including **La Table du Môle** (p. 568), a petite café, and a takeaway kiosk. *Important:* MuCEM is massive, so plan your time carefully. We highly recommend the permanent exhibit on the Mediterranean diet, but feel that the other permanent exhibit on the history of the Med can be skipped if you're short on time.

1 esplanade du J4. www.mucem.org. ℰ **04-84-35-13-13.** Admission 11€ adults; 7.50€ seniors and students; 18€ family ticket, free for children 17 and under. Additional fee for temporary exhibitions. Sept–June Wed–Mon 11am–7pm (until 6pm Nov–Apr); July–Aug Wed–Mon 10am–8pm. Métro: Vieux-Port. Bus: 49, 60, or 82.

Musée Cantini ★ ART MUSEUM   This 17th-century hôtel particulier (former private mansion) organizes an outstanding modern art show. The museum houses a permanent collection, particularly strong on masterpieces (by Picasso, Dufy, de Staël, Ernst, and others) created during the first half of the 20th century. Many of the canvases, like Entrée du Port de Marseille by Paul Signac and Le port de Marseille by Oskar Kokoschka showcase city life a century ago.

19 rue Grignan. http://musees.marseille.fr/musee-cantini. ℰ **04-91-54-77-75.** Admission 6€ adults; 3€ students and seniors; free for children 17 and under. Tues–Sun 9am–6pm. Métro: Estrangin/Préfecture.

Musée des Beaux-Arts ★ MUSEUM   The 154-year-old Museum of Fine Arts is Marseille's oldest exhibition space. Its venue, the Palais Longchamp, is gloriously grand—the palace took 30 years to build. Today its high ceilings and marble floors make visitors feel like they're starring in a Netflix drama set in 19th-century France. Exhibits range from 16th-century Italian works to more modern French masterpieces, including Rodin's sculpture *La Voix Intérieure* (*The Inner Voice*). The surrounding Longchamp park is a picnic destination par excellence.

Palais Longchamp. https://musees.marseille.fr/musee-des-beaux-arts-mba. ℰ **04-91-14-59-30.** Admission 8€ adults; 4.50€ students and seniors; free for children 17 and under. Additional fee for temporary exhibitions. Tues–Sun 9am–6pm. Métro: Longchamp. Tram: Longchamp.

Musée d'histoire de Marseille ★★ HISTORY MUSEUM   Get ready for 26 centuries of history witnessed through scale models, boxes of Marseille soap, and some very old stones. The oldest reside in the museum's garden out front, discovered during the building of a shopping mall, which made up Marseille's original port. Dates entered Europe from this historic harbor, and most probably tomatoes and bananas too. If anything, France's largest urban history museum (which has inscriptions in English and French throughout) proves that locals have always loved wine, sailing, bold statues, and fine linens.

2 rue Henri Barbusse. www.musee-histoire-marseille-voie-historique.fr. ℰ **04-91-55-36-00.** Admission 6€ adults; 3€ seniors and students; free children 17 and under. Tues–Sun 9am–6pm. Métro: Noailles/Colbert.

Outlying Attractions

You can take a telegenic 25-minute ferry ride to the **Château d'If** (www.chateau-if.fr), a national monument built by François I as a fortress to defend Marseille. It was once a prison, and has graffiti dating from 400 years ago. Alexandre Dumas used the island as a setting for the fictional adventures of *The Count of Monte Cristo*. The château is open October to March 10:30am to 5pm (closed Mon); April to September daily 10:30am to 6pm. Entrance to the island is 6€ adults, free for children 17 and under. Boats leave approximately every 45 to 60 minutes, depending on the season; the round-trip transfer is 10.80€. For information, contact the Frioul If Express (www.lebateau-frioul-if.fr; *℡* **04-96-11-03-50;** Métro: Vieux-Port). The company also serves the wild hiking isle of Frioul for 16,20€; price includes a stop on Château d'If.

North of Marseille proper, **L'Estaque** was once a picturesque seaside village and it remains a chilled escape for Marseille residents. It was painted by Provence's artistic greats—including Cézanne, Renoir, and Braque—between the 1860s and 1920s. Today, visitors can tread these legendary footsteps and easel sites, following the "Painters' Path" signposted around town (strolling time around 2 hr.). L'Estaque's seafront stalls sell popular local snacks, including chichi frégi (sugar-topped fritters flavored with orange blossom water) and panisses (savory chickpea flour fritters). You can reach L'Estaque via train or bus no. 35 from Marseille's place de la Joliette (journey time: around 30 min.). Between April and September, navette ferry service runs from the Vieux Port to L'Estaque for 5€ (journey time: 40 min.).

Organized Tours

One of the easiest ways to see Marseille's centrally located monuments is aboard the fleet of open-top **Colorbus Buses** (www.colorbus.fr; *℡* **04-91-52-89-39;** Métro: Vieux-Port). You can hop off at any of 13 different stops en route and back on to the next bus in the day's sequence, usually

---

La Marseillaise

Few know that France's national anthem was actually composed in Strasbourg. Originally titled "War Song of the Army of the Rhine," it was written in a single night by army captain Claude-Joseph Rouget de Lisle in 1792. That same year, revolutionaries from Marseille (who had been given printed copies) marched into Paris singing it. In their honor, the song became known as "La Marseillaise" and was quickly adopted as the rallying cry of the French Revolution. It was officially declared the national anthem of France in 1795, only to be banned by Napoleon during the Empire, Louis XVIII in 1815, and Napoleon III in 1830. The anthem was reinstated for good in 1879.

arriving between 1 and 2 hours later, depending on the season. The buses run four to eight times a day during each month except January. A 1-day pass costs 22€; the fare for children ages 4 to 13 is 8€. Two-day passes are also available for just a few euros more.

The motorized **Trains Touristiques de Marseille** (www.petit-train-marseille.com; ✆ **04-91-25-24-69;** Métro: Vieux-Port), or **petit-trains,** make circuits around town every 20 minutes (every 40 Dec–Mar). Train no. 1 drives 75 minutes round-trip to Basilique Notre-Dame-de-la-Garde and Basilique St-Victor. From April to December, train no. 2 makes a 65-minute round-trip of old Marseille by way of the cathedral, Vieille Charité, and the Quartier du Panier. Both trains make a 30-minute stop for sightseeing en route. The trains depart from the quay just west of the Hôtel de Ville. The fare for both trains is 9€ adults and 5€ children.

Boat tours to the **Parc National des Calanques** are popular. Many tour operators with different prices and formulas (for example, three Calanques in 2 hr./26€, or eight in 3 hr./32€) can be found on the quai des Belges at the Vieux-Port. For more information about visiting the Calanques from the gorgeous nearby town of **Cassis,** see p. 572.

Airbnb/Experiences offers its usual range of locally run Marseille experiences including food tasting, urban walking tours, and becoming a bartender in a hip club.

Where to Stay

Although slightly removed from the city center, the iconic **Hôtel le Corbusier** (www.hotellecorbusier.com) is a must for architecture aficionados. The hotel's rooftop gym has astounding views and a hip contemporary art space, **MAMO** (www.mamo.fr). There's also a gourmet restaurant, **Le Ventre de l'Architecte,** overseen by talented young Ukrainian chef Andreii Bondarenko (three-course menu 37€), hidden inside the UNESCO-inscribed building.

C2 Hotel ★★★ Marseille's uber-cool option. The understatedly elegant C2 features 20 luxurious, light-filled rooms that spill over a 19th-century merchant family mansion typical of this portside quarter, each one decked out in exposed brick walls and designer furnishings. Some have a private hammam steam bath. The superb FillMed spa onsite has an indoor pool and Jacuzzi, as well as a cocktail bar. But the hotel's pièce de résistance? That would have to be C2's beach on the private Mediterranean island of Île Degaby. Pack a picnic and castaway.

48 rue Roux de Brignoles. www.c2-hotel.com. ✆ **04-95-05-13-13.** 20 units. 180€–519€ double. Free valet parking. Métro: Estrangin-Préfecture. **Amenities:** Bar; private beach; concierge; spa; free Wi-Fi.

Hôtel-Dieu ★★ The luxurious Hôtel-Dieu is perched just behind Marseille's Hôtel de Ville, overlooking the Vieux Port from Le Panier.

This five-star hotel occupies what was once an 18th-century hospital—and history oozes from every pore. It's managed by the InterContinental Group with aplomb. As well as modern, minimalist guest rooms with superb views, guests may enjoy the indoor pool and sea view bistro **Les Fenêtres.** Pick of the eateries is gastronomic restaurant **Alcyone,** where Michelin-starred superchef Lionel Levy invented the Milkshake de Bouillabaisse, a new take on the classic Marseille dish.

1 pl. Daviel. www.ihg.com. ☎ **04-13-42-42-42.** 194 units. 175€–358€ double; from 650€ suite. Parking 49€. Métro: Vieux-Port. **Amenities:** Restaurant; bar; business center; fitness center; indoor pool; room service; spa; free Wi-Fi.

Hotel Marsiho ★★   A colorful and affordable addition to Marseille's hotel scene. Marsiho sits slap-bang in the city center, a short walk from MuCEM and the Vieux Port, yet sound-proofed rooms and comfy beds give it the feeling of a calm haven amid the bustle. Attention to detail is everywhere. Staff leave hand-written notes of welcome on beds and maintain a chic common room for mingling. The hotel is particularly attractive for solo travelers with single rooms from 72€.

16 cours Belsunce. www.happyculture.fr. ☎ **04-91-47-74-54.** 51 units. 99€–143€ double; from 156€ family rooms. Métro: Noailles. **Amenities:** Free Wi-Fi.

Le Ryad ★★   Marrakech-meets-Marseille at this Moorish inspired backstreet hotel. Styled by its former Moroccan owner, the 11 rooms are now presided over by a kindly French proprietor who is a fountain of local knowledge. Breakfasts are a cornucopia of Arabian sweets, North African breads, and mint tea. From spring onwards, morning meals are served outdoors in the oasis-like garden. Rooms have a faded grandeur and less expensive ones overlook a bustling street. Family suites peek out over the garden and can comfortably sleep four.

16 rue Sénac de Meilhan. www.leryad.fr. ☎ **04-91-47-74-54.** 11 units. 81€–157€ double; from 135€ family rooms. Métro: Noailles. **Amenities:** Restaurant meals prepared by order; free Wi-Fi.

Maison Juste ★★   A tiny new hotel committed to friendliness and environmentalism (including reusing materials during construction and locally sourcing wherever possible). Each room boasts a big bed, walk-in shower, and little kitchenette with enough space to flip an omelet nature. Cash is saved by hosts Olivier and Naomi (and passed onto guests by way of low prices) by offering check-in and breakfast orders via an app. Almost everything inside the hotel is Made in France.

28 rue Dieudé. www.justejuste.com. No phone. 18 units. 115€–150€ double. Métro: Noailles. **Amenities:** Free Wi-Fi.

Maisons du Mondes ★★   This glorious new addition to Marseille's historic hotel scene is an art deco spectacular. Sixteen apart-suites are studded with funky objet d'arts that you definitely won't find in a Hilton. Four of the larger apartments (for three or four people) have terraces. Breakfast is worth staying for (rarely given in France) with a serve-yourself selection of hams, Compté cheese, seared vegetables, and further dishes made fresh by friendly wait staff.

43 quai des Belges. www.maisonsdumondehotel.com. ℭ **04-91-55-67-46.** 16 units. 130€–270€ double. Métro: Vieux Port. **Amenities:** Bar; room service; free Wi-Fi.

Where to Eat

The **Noailles** district is street food central, and feels very much like at North African *souk* (market). Stroll down rue d'Aubagne to sample Tunisian *leblebi* soup joints, Ivorian *alocco* fish grills, and stalls stocking Egyptian *mahjouba* pancakes. Bites start from 1€ apiece. Or perch on a stool for a glass of Moroccan mint tea or Syrian falafel.

Marseille's most famous recipe is bouillabaisse fish stew. In centuries past, hard-to-sell rockfish were boiled (*bouilli* in French) dockside in seawater, tomatoes, and spices. Then the heat was lowered (*abaissé*) when larger fish were lobbed in. Hence the humble bouillabaisse was born. Eat the 30€ to 40€ dish solely in portside restaurants like **Miramar** (www.lemiramar.fr), which displays the Bouillabaisse Charter and adheres to strict rules of fresh fish, virgin olive oil, and no frozen shrimps.

Chez Yassine ★ SEAFOOD   Come here for the best example of the migrant street food synonymous with the bustling Noailles neighborhood. Chez Yassine serves the unctuous Tunisian creations of three North African brothers, including spicy *lablabi* chickpea soup and *brik a l'oeuf* egg pastry. More filling dishes include seafood spaghetti, eggs in a spicy tomato sauce, and merguez lamb sausages, all served on simple tables, a few of them outside on the busy street. Pair with mint tea or the establishment's home-made lemonade.

8 rue d'Aubagne. ℭ **09-80-83-39-13.** Main courses 7€–12€. Daily 11am–9pm. Métro: Noailles.

La Kahena ★★ TUNISIAN   Among Marseille's many Tunisian restaurants, this eatery stands out from the crowd. Named for a 6th-century-B.C. Tunisian princess, La Kahena's specialty is couscous: Among the 10 varieties are versions with lamb, merguez spicy sausages, and cod. Other Tunisian classics such as mechoua salad (spicy grilled vegetables), tajines, and crispy brick pastry stuffed with shrimp are also served up in the ornate blue-tiled dining room. A solid budget choice.

2 rue de la République. www.lakahena.fr. ℭ **04-91-90-61-93.** Main course 13€–28€. Daily noon–2pm and 7–10pm. Métro: Vieux-Port

La Table du Môle ★★ MODERN MEDITERRANEAN   Triple Michelin-starred-chef Gérard Passédat's most accessible restaurant, this "chic bistro" sits atop the **MuCEM** (p. 563). Much like the MuCEM exhibits themselves, stellar dishes herald from across the Mediterranean, including seafood tart served with a creamy ginger jus, crab paired with spicy harissa, or grilled turbot with truffled potatoes. Top chef Passédat's modern take on bouillabaisse stew is gloriously inventive. All is served against a sweeping backdrop of Marseille's port and the Mediterranean Sea. Note that it's also possible to dine at Le Môle's lower-key (and cheaper) sister restaurant, **La Cuisine** (lunch only), also located at the MuCEM.

MuCEM, 1 esplanade du J4. www.passedat.fr. ✆ **04-91-19-17-80.** Reservations online only. Main course 38€; fixed-price lunch 55€ or dinner 75€. Wed–Mon 12:30–2:30pm; Wed–Sat and Mon 7:30–10:30pm. Métro: Vieux-Port. Bus: 49, 60, or 82.

L'Epuisette ★★ SEAFOOD/MEDITERRANEAN This Michelin-starred option is the premier place in Marseille to sample bouillabaisse. Bring your appetite: Fresh fish is poached in saffron-infused soup; the final product is served as two separate courses, accompanied by rouille, a mayonnaise-like sauce flavored with garlic, cayenne pepper, and saffron. Or visit during wintertime to sample the restaurant's exquisite truffle menu, a selection of courses which may feature scallops in truffle sauce, or a truffle-infused chocolate mousse (165€). The setting is as sublime as the cuisine: A seaside dining room overlooks Château d'If from the picturesque fishing port of Vallon des Auffes (where chef Guillaume Sourrieu sources his seafood), 2.5km (1½ miles) south of Marseille's Vieux Port. Make reservations well in advance.

Vallon des Auffes. www.l-epuisette.fr. ✆ **04-91-52-17-82.** Main course 23€–65€; fixed-price dinner 95€–170€. Tues–Sat noon–1:30pm and 7:30–9:30pm. Closed Thurs lunch and Aug. Bus: 83.

Les Beaux Mets ★★★ MODERN FRENCH More than just a meal, you do good when you eat here. That's because this truly gourmet restaurant, open since late 2022, is sited in the city's maximum-security

MICKY D'S goes gourmet...KINDA

In December 2022, on the site of a former McDonald's that closed shop and laid off its staff, a Marseille culinary star was born. One that flips burgers crafted by the city's most celebrated chef—the three-star-Michelin chef Gérald Passedat—and plays North African raï music through the speakers. **L'Apres M** (www.facebook.com/lapres.m), a play on the phrase "After McDonald's," is a staff-owned social project that serves locally reared fast food at budget prices. Passedat's Ovni burger costs 5.90€. It's absolutely delicious. All profits go to help neighborhoods in need of honest food. All ingredients are sustainability sourced, right down to the rosemary and thyme that grow in the fast-food joint's parking lot. L'Apres M captures Marseille's indomitable spirit in a bun.

penitentiary where some of France's longest-serving prisoners are jailed. The restaurant is a winning social project created by top chef Sandrine Sollier (a veteran of Marseille's leading kitchens) who teaches inmates cooking, service, and teamwork skills. Dishes, like slow-baked beef chef in carrot jus, are a delight. Security is obviously tight but reserving a table and entering the city's toughest jail are no harder than booking a flight and going through airport security. This is a fine dining experience you would struggle to replicate anywhere else in the world.

Baumettes Penitentiary, trav. de Rabat. www.lesbeauxmets-marseille.fr. ✆ **04-91-53-54-55.** Fixed-price menu 28€–35€. Mon–Fri noon–2:30pm. Bus: 22.

Restaurant AM ★★★ MODERN MEDITERRANEAN The city's latest must-eat won its third Michelin star in 2023. Here inspirational chef Alexandre Mazzia spins the flavors from the migrant cultures that make up Marseille—including Turkish sumac and Arabian harissa—into his award-winning cuisine. Highlights include seaweed chips layered with sweet potato jelly then topped with grated roe. Dishes are inspired by Mazzia's complex roots: In a tale typical of this melting pot city, he was born in Congo to Italian and Corsican parents, before washing up in Marseille at the age of 15. Book far in advance.

Too steep for your vacation budget? In 2022, Mazzia opened a gourmet food truck across from his restaurant. It sells delish dishes like pancakes rolled with barbecued chicken, red cabbage, and chimichurri from just 12€, including crisp fries.

9 rue Rocca. www.alexandremazzia.com. ✆ **04-91-24-83-63.** Fixed-price menus 195€–425€. Tues–Sat noon–1:30pm and 7:30–9:30pm. Closed Aug. Metro: Rond-Point du Prado. Bus: 19, 44, or 83.

Shopping

Only Paris and the French Riviera can compete with Marseille for its breadth and diversity of merchandise. Your best bet is a trip to the streets just southeast of the **Vieux-Port,** crowded with stores of all kinds. Try Made in Marseille atelier store **Marseille en Vacances,** 7 rue Bailli de Suffren (✆ **04-91-54-73-17**), for pastis jugs and branded cookware.

Rue Paradis and **rue Saint Ferréol** have many of the same upscale fashion boutiques found in Paris, as well as a **Galeries Lafayette,** France's largest chain department store. For more bohemian wear, try cours Julien, and rue de la Tour for richly brocaded and beaded items on offer in North African boutiques. **Le Panier** and Le Camas districts are home to a vibrant range of unique boutiques. In the former, try **Maison Casablanca ★**, 6 rue de la Tour (www.boutiquecasablanca.com; ✆ **04-91-33-14-27**), for cool scarves, textiles, and jewelry. For more art, try contemporary engravers **L'Atelier M,** 25 cours Estienne d'Orves (www.atelier-m.org; ✆ **04-91-33-34-45**). For unique souvenirs, head to **Ateliers Marcel**

Carbonel ★, 49 rue Neuve-Ste-Catherine (www.santonsmarcelcarbonel. com; ℭ **04-91-13-61-36**). This 80-year-old business specializes in *santons,* clay figurines meant for Christmas nativities. In addition to person-

alities you may already know, the carefully crafted pieces depict Provençal common folk such as bakers, blacksmiths, and milkmaids. The figurines sell for around 12.60€ and up.

Navettes, small cookies that resemble boats, are a Marseillaise specialty. Flavored with secret ingredients that include orange zest and orange flower water, they were invented in 1791 and are still sold at **Le Four des Navettes,** 136 rue Sainte (www.fourdesnavettes.com; ℭ **04-91-33-32-12**), for around 10€ per dozen.

One of the region's most authentic fish markets at **Quai des Belges** (daily 8am–1pm), on the old port, is partially sheltered under the Norman Foster–designed Ombrière mirrored canopy. On **cours Julien,** you'll find a market with fruits, vegetables, and other foods (Tues, Thurs, and Sat 8am–1pm); exclu-

Shoppers in a North African spice store.

sively organic produce (Wed 8am–1pm); and secondhand goods (third Sun of the month 8am–1pm). The cheapest buys are in the photogenic **Noailles** neighborhood, where stores of 50 nationalities, from Algerian to Vietnamese, sell spices, spring rolls, jewelry, and homewares. Noailles is also where **Maison Empereur ★★★** (4 rue des Récolettes; www. empereur.fr) has been selling home goods since 1827, making it one of the oldest stores in France. Along with every kitchen gadget known to man, there's a smelling room for rare perfumes, an array of Provencal clothing and décor, and an entire room devoted to the finest of the soaps manufactured in Marseille.

Nightlife

For an amusing and relatively harmless exposure to the town's saltiness, walk around the Vieux-Port, where cafes and restaurants angle their sightlines for the best view of the harbor.

L'Escale Borély, av. Pierre Mendès France, is a recreational beach spot 20 minutes south of the town center (take bus no. 83). With a dozen animated bars and cafes sited around the sand, plus restaurants of every possible background you'll be spoiled for choice, until late into the evening if you wish. For more local drinking and dining, at cheaper prices, hit the homey suburb of La Camas (ride the tram to Camas or Eugène Pierre).

What beats a rooftop party? **R2 Rooftop des Terrasses,** 9 Quai du Lazaret (www.lerooftopdesterrasses.com; © **04-91-91-79-39;** Métro: Joliette), booms from sundown most summer nights. Ride the fourth-floor elevator to **Les Réformes,** 125 La Canebière (www.lesreformes.com; © **09-71-16-35-90;** Métro: Réformés Canebière), is a bar-restaurant that lords over the Canebière boulevard.

Marseille's dance clubs are habitually packed out, especially **Trolley Bus,** 24 quai de Rive-Neuve (www.letrolley.com; © **04-91-54-30-45;** Métro: Vieux-Port), an institution known for techno, hip-hop, jazz, and salsa. Equally buzzing is **Chez Pablo,** 23 rue Saint-Saëns (© **06-47-08-44-78;** Métro: Vieux-Port), where DJs spin electro, pop, and house music classics. **The Bounce,** 35 cr. Honoré d'Estienne d'Orves (© **06-13-35-12-06;** Métro: Vieux-Port), hops until dawn with dance-hall and Latin tunes every Friday through Sunday from midnight until 5am.

For jazz right on the port, head to **La Caravelle,** 34 quai du Port (www.lacaravelle-marseille.com; © **04-91-90-36-64;** Métro: Vieux-Port), an aperitif bar with 5€ glasses of rosé and a dinner club that offers a different musical flavor almost every night, including manouche, the French Romany style most associated with guitarist Django Reinhardt.

CASSIS ★★

806km (501 miles) S of Paris; 128km (80 miles) SE of Avignon; 50km (31 miles) S of Aix-en-Provence; 32km (20 miles) E of Marseille

Cassis is inarguably the prettiest coastal town in Provence. The settlement dates from Ancient Greek times—that's as far back as both Marseille and Nice—but its fame rose in the early 20th century, when famous personalities like Virginia Woolf and Sir Winston Churchill used the resort as an artists' retreat while guzzling its crisp white wines. Cassis found a new outdoor-oriented audience as the capital of France's first mainland National Park since 1979.

Essentials

ARRIVING   Cassis Station is a cinch to reach by rail. Half-hourly **trains** arrive from Marseille (trip time: 25 min.; www.sncf-connect.com; © **36-35;** 6.90€ one-way). Sound easy? It's not, as Cassis Station is then a 3km (1¾-mile) downhill walk from Cassis town center. Walk down, grab one of the

The colorful harbor at Cassis.

waiting taxis (12€), or catch the Marcouline city bus (1.60€) every 30 minutes.

VISITOR INFORMATION The helpful Office de Tourisme is on the beachfront quai des Moulins (www.ot-cassis.com; ℭ **08-92-39-01-03**).

[FastFACTS] CASSIS

Mail & Postage **La Poste,** 3 rue Arène (ℭ **36-31**). Note that the post office also offers an ATM.

Pharmacies **Pharmacie Trossero,** 11 av. Victor Hugo (ℭ **04-42-01-70-03**).

Exploring Cassis

The deliciously beautiful center of Cassis is best explored on foot. The coastal path winds from the wide expanse of Grande Plage beach past restaurant terraces and boutiques all the way to Plage du Bestouan and the start of the Parc Nationale des Calanques. Each August the entire town comes alive for a series of literary festivals, fireworks shows, and sea jousting tournaments (yes, involving lances and motorboats).

Cassis Snorkeling Tour ★ TOUR   As you might expect from a town that borders a massive marine and land National Park, Cassis is awash with diving schools. These include **Cassis-Plongée** (www.cassis-calanques-plongee.com) and **Narval Plongée** (www.narval-plongee.com). Novice divers may also scuba or snorkel along the **Sentier Sous-Marin de Cassis,** or underwater trail. This self-guided 30-minute swim route begins on the Promenade des Lombards. Four buoys mark marine life discovery spots along the way. Be aware that a mineral water source (as in thousands of bottles of chilled Evian) seeps from the limestone cliffs into Cassis harbor, so sea temperatures are often chilly!

Cassis Wine Tour ★ WALKING TOUR   White wines from Cassis are so superb that they were protected as an AOC region in 1936 (along with **Châteauneuf-du-Pape,** outside Avignon; p. 528). Most vintages are infused with flowery Marsanne from the Rhône Valley and herby Clairette from Provence. Just a dozen small, mostly organic producers tend their ocean-facing vineyards that are planted from the port up to the Cassis train station. All can be toured (with free tasting sessions for those who wish to purchase a bottle or three) by foot or by bicycle using the free Vineyard Tour map from the Cassis Tourist Office. Alternatively, the tourist office can book visitors a 15€ tour at a specific domaine. A final fact for your friends at home: AOC Cassis is the only appellation to be entirely included within a National Park. Au natural never tasted so good.

Cassis environs. www.vinsdecassis.com.

Outlying Attractions

Cassis is the capital of the **Parc Nationale des Calanques** (www.calanques-parcnational.fr). The calanques are towering cliffs created 120 million years ago. They were then split apart by rising sea levels and bleached white by the Provençal sun. Each calanque crashes into the azure sea from heights of up to 565m (nearly 2,000 ft.). Like Norway's fjords, they surround a series of boat-only bays that stretch for 32km (20 miles) from Cassis to Marseille. So sturdy is the snow-white stone from Calanque Port-Miou, a creek within walking distance of Cassis, that it was used to build the base of the Statue of Liberty in New York.

The park occupies some 50,000 hectares (193 sq. miles) of land, coastline and sea. The cliffs are fully protected as are the wildlife, flora, and 60 species of fish that reside therein. That means scooters, jet skis, and speedboats are prohibited in the National Park, so tranquility is assured.

A hiker explores the Parc Nationale des Calanques.

The main public pathway through the park is the GR51, a long-distance hiking trail known as the "Balconies of the Mediterranean." This *grande randonnée* route links Marseille with Monaco. Those visitors without Ironman thighs (or without a spare 3 weeks of vacation) may hike along a score of shorter marked paths instead, passing lonely islands, rocky passes, secret beaches, and gaping creeks. Park maps are available from Cassis's ever-helpful Tourist Office.

A more relaxed way to tour the park is by **boat.** Head down to Cassis' harbor, where a well-signposted kiosk sells tickets for regular daily boat trips. Opt to take in three calanques (45 min.; 19€ adults, 12.50€ children 9 and under), five calanques (65 min.; 25€ adults, 18€ children) or nine calanques (2 hr.; 33€ adults, 23€ children). A particular favorite is Calanque de Sugiton, which crumbles into an island-strewn bay. The postcard-perfect **Calanque d'En Vau** is also well worth seeking out. As non-official motorboats are banned from the National Park, try paddling under the calanques by kayak or SUP instead. For equipment, contact **Cassis Sport Loisirs Nautiques** (www.cassis-kayak.com). Prices range from

15€ for a rental kayak to 40€ for a session of paddleboard yoga in a deserted bay.

Southern French travelers hoping to hike further off the beaten track are spoiled for choice. On their doorstep is the Port-Cros National Park (www.portcros-parcnational.fr; see "Exploring Ile de Port-Cros," p. 579), which covers a series of tropical-style islands. The Mercantour National Park (www.mercantour-parcnational.fr), a haven for wolves, deer, and butterflies, sits just north of Nice.

Where to Stay

Hotel La Rade ★★ The pick of Cassis's mid-range hotels, La Rade gazes out over the ocean, a 3-minute walk from the pedestrian-only quays. Its enviably tranquil position is also convenient for strolls west to plage du Bestouan and into the Calanques National Park beyond. In summer, the hotel's locally sourced breakfast—think Cassis jams and Provençal *saucisson*—is served by the swimming pool. It's not only the only sea view *piscine* in town, but heated too, which means it's open year-round. The hotel terrace is justly popular with artists. Indeed, Sir Winston Churchill honed his painting skills at the Camargo Foundation (www.camargo foundation.org) artist residency just across the street.

1 av. des Dardanelles. www.bestwestern-cassis.com. ℂ **04-42-01-02-97.** 28 units. 248€–318€ double. Breakfast 16€ per person. **Amenities:** Restaurant; outdoor pool; free Wi-Fi.

Where to Eat

Bar de la Marine ★ BISTRO This no-nonsense bar and bistro has been dishing up hearty breakfasts, *steak-frites, salade Niçoise,* and seafood salads to tired fishermen for almost a century. In season, its proximity to Cassis's working port makes it a prime spot to try sea urchins, the local delicacy. Simply order a platter from the septuagenarian street vendor to be delivered to your table. Like almost every other restaurant in Cassis, service in Bar de la Marine is slow but the result is absolutely delicious.

5 quai des Baux. ℂ **04-42-01-76-09.** Main course 12€–22€. Daily 7:30am–midnight.

Le Poisson Rouge ★★ SEAFOOD "The goldfish," as its name translates, is a small seafood kitchen in the backstreets of Cassis. Its modus operandi is to serve ingredients fresh from the fishing boats. Mains might include octopus tentacles with green beans or grilled tuna steak with pesto. Sophisticated cocktails inspired by southern French botanicals are served alongside the food. A warm and welcoming place.

Impasse Farine. ℂ **04-42-71-53-75.** Main course 25€–30€. Tues–Sun noon–1:30pm; June–Sept Tues–Sat 7:30–10pm. Closed Nov–Mar.

ILES D'HYÈRES ★★

39km (24 miles) SE of Toulon; 119km (74 miles) SW of Cannes

Bobbing off the French Riviera in the Mediterranean Sea, a small group of islands encloses the eastern boundary of Provence. During the Renaissance, they were coined the Iles d'Or (Golden Islands), named for the glow the rocks give off in sunlight. As might be expected, their location only 30 minutes from the French coast means the islands are often packed with tourists in summer—but its breathtaking beaches still have space for everyone.

If you have time for only one island, choose the beautiful, lively **Ile de Porquerolles.** In recent years it has become an artsy go-to, with a vineyard owned by Chanel and an amazing underground art foundation featuring canvases by Warhol and Picasso. The **Ile de Port-Cros** is quieter—and perhaps better for an overnight stay to take advantage of the great hiking, exploring, and snorkeling that would be too rushed for a 6-hour day trip. As for the **Ile du Levant,** 80% belongs to the French army and is used for missile testing; the remainder is a nudist colony.

View of a beach on Porquerolles Island.

Essentials

GETTING TO ILE DE PORQUEROLLES Ferries leave from several points along the Côte d'Azur. The most frequent, cheapest, and shortest trip is from the harbor of La Tour Fondue on the peninsula of Giens, a 32km (20-mile) drive east of Toulon. Depending on the season, there are 5 to 20 departures per day. The round-trip fare for the 15-minute crossing is 22€ adults and 17.70€ children ages 4 to 10 with **TLV-TVM** (www.tlv-tvm. com; ✆ **04-94-58-21-81**). **Bateliers de la Côte d'Azur** (www.bateliersde lacotedazur.com; ✆ **04-94-05-21-14**) and **Les Vedettes Ile d'Or** (www. vedettesilesdor.fr; ✆ **04-94-71-01-02**) also offer services from La Londe-les-Maures and Le Lavandou respectively.

GETTING TO ILE DE PORT-CROS The most popular ferry route to the island is the 35-minute crossing that departs from Le Lavandou 3 to 7 times daily, depending on the season (round-trip 31€ adults, 27.50€ children 4–12). For information, contact Les Vedettes Ile d'Or (see above). The TLV-TVM and Bateliers de la Côte d'Azur (see above) also service Ile de Port-Cros. Some of the former's services travel onwards to Ile de Levant.

VISITOR INFORMATION Other than temporary, summer-only kiosks that distribute brochures and advice near the ferry docks in Porquerolles and Port-Cros, the islands do not have tourist bureaus. For further information, contact the **Office de Tourisme de Hyères,** Bureau de Porquerolles (www.hyeres-tourisme.com; ✆ **04-94-01-84-50**).

MAIL/POSTAGE & MONEY The post office, **La Poste,** pl. d'Armes, Porquerolles (✆ **36-31**), also has an ATM. Even on the tiniest islands in France, Apple Pay and Google Pay are accepted in most places.

Exploring Ile de Porquerolles ★★

Ile de Porquerolles is the largest and westernmost of the Iles d'Hyères. It has a rugged south coast, but the northern strand, facing the mainland, boasts a handful of pristine white-sand beaches that could double for Thailand. The island is about 8km (5 miles) long, 2km (1¼ miles) wide, 4.8km (3 miles) from the mainland. The permanent population is only 400.

The island is said to receive 275 days of sunshine annually. The landscape is one of rocky capes, pine forests twisted by the mistral, sun-drenched vineyards, and pale ochre houses. It's best explored on foot or by bike (look for plenty of bike-rental agencies just behind the harbor). The **place d'Armes,** former site of the garrison, is home to several quaint cafes—your best bet for lunch if you're here for a day trip.

In 1971, the French government purchased a large part of the island and added it to the Port-Cros National Park (see below). Indigenous trees such as fig, mulberry, and olive are protected, as well as plants that attract butterflies.

More recently, a star-studded art collection owned by France's wealthy Carmignac family was installed under the island's surface in what looks like a Bond villain's lair. The **Villa Carmignac** (www. fondationcarmignac.com; ✆ **04-65-65-25-50**) features canvases by Roy Lichtenstein and Andy Warhol. Several are hung under an aquatic glass ceiling, which casts an eerie glow in the art below. The experience is genuinely priceless. If that wasn't enough, the villa is encircled by art-stuffed sculpture park created by the same landscape gardener who produced similar works for Christian Louboutin and Yves Saint Laurent. Visitors are encouraged to tread barefoot throughout. The estate is open from Tuesday to Sunday, May to October 10am to 6pm (until 7pm July–Aug). Closed November to April. Admission must be booked online in advance for an unguided visit, which costs 15€ for adults, 6€ for visitors aged between 12 and 26, and free for children 11 and under.

The recent purchase of biodynamic vineyard **Domaine de l'Ile** (www.domainedelile.com) by French fashion house Chanel sealed Porquerolles' fate as an A-list escape. A hiking path runs alongside the rows of vines. You can sample the wine in island restaurants.

WHERE TO STAY & EAT

Hotel Villa Saint Anne (www.sainteanne.fr) offers good value-for Porquerolles-accommodation, housed in a former abbey, in the timeless town center.

Mas du Langoustier ★★   This Provençal-style hotel is far and away Porquerolles' most luxurious accommodation. Located on the island's western tip, it's set in a 40-hectare (99-acre) park laced with bougainvillea, shaded by eucalyptus and Aleppo pines, and overlooking a lovely pine-ringed bay. Elegant rooms have a truly traditional feel and are decorated with classic local textiles; many have their own private patio. Even better, come evening time, there's no need to leave paradise. The on-site **Restaurant La Pinède** (open to non-guests) serves delicacies like peppered beef tartare and roasted nectarine salad from 28€.

www.langoustier.com. ✆ **04-94-58-30-09.** 50 units. 190€–440€ double; from 310€ suite. Closed Oct to late Apr. **Amenities:** Restaurant; bar; babysitting; outdoor pool; tennis court; free Wi-Fi.

Exploring Ile de Port-Cros ★★

The most mountainous island of the archipelago, **Port-Cros** (www.port-cros-parcnational.fr) has been France's smallest national park since 1963, although the designation now covers Porquerolles too. Port-Cros is just 5km (3 miles) long and 2km (1¼ miles) wide. The island is blanketed with beautiful beaches, pine forests, and subtropical vegetation (birders flock here to observe over 100 different species). A hiker's paradise, it also has a number of well-marked trails. The most popular and scenic is the easy, 1-hour sentier des plantes. The more adventurous and athletic take the 10km (6¼-mile) circuit de Port-Man (and pack their lunch). There is even a 274m (899-ft.) "underwater trail" along the coast where you can snorkel past laminated signs identifying the plants and fish you'll see.

WHERE TO STAY & EAT

Le Manoir de Port-Cros ★   Port-Cros's only hotel is within a white-washed building built in 1840. Accommodation may be simple—crisp white sheets, oversized copper vases, terra-cotta tiled floors—but guests (including discrete celebrities) stay here to truly switch off. Paddle in the pool, head out for a hike, or simply amble the surrounding palm and euca-lyptus-studded gardens. Plenty of day trippers visit to lunch in the restaurant's leafy gourmet restaurant (main courses from 27€), which can include monkfish medallions with kaffir lime, and grilled langoustine.

www.hotel-lemanoirportcros.com. 🕿 **04-94-05-90-52.** 21 units. 260€–400€ double; 380€–560€ bungalows for 4. Closed Oct to mid-May. **Amenities:** Restaurant; bar; outdoor pool; room service; free Wi-Fi in common areas.

THE FRENCH RIVIERA

By Tristan Rutherford

The fabled real estate known as the French Riviera, also called the Côte d'Azur (Azure Coast), ribbons for 200km (125 miles) along the sun-kissed Mediterranean. The region has long attracted artists and jetsetters alike with its clear skies, blue waters, and carefree cafe culture. Chic, sassy, and incredibly sexy, the Riviera can be explored by bus, train, boat, bike, Segway, electric surfboard, or in a dozen novel ways.

A trail of modern artists captivated by the region's light and setting has left a rich heritage: Matisse at Vence, Cocteau at Villefranche, Léger at Biot, Renoir at Cagnes, and Picasso at Antibes and seemingly everywhere in between. The finest collection of modern artworks is at the Foundation Maeght in St-Paul-de-Vence, which reopened to great fanfare in 2023. Museums dedicated to Jean Cocteau in Menton and Pierre Bonnard near Cannes also offer a vivid introduction to the Riviera's storied art scene.

A century ago, winter and spring were considered high season on the Riviera. Since then, July and August have become the most crowded months, and reservations are imperative. Summer is when global celebrity arrives en masse, and one could be sipping coffee next to Ryan Reynolds or swimming next to a yacht containing the Kardashians. Fortunately, there's always a quiet beach or National Park in which to escape the hype. The region basks in more than 300 days of sun per year, and even December and January are often pleasant and sunny.

The ribbonlike corniche roads stretch across the western Riviera from Nice to Menton are scenic stars in scores of classic films including Cary Grant's *To Catch a Thief* and Robert de Niro's *Ronin,* as well as the 2022 blockbuster *Downton Abbey: A New Era.* The lower road, the 32km (20-mile) Corniche Inférieure (often referred to as the Basse Corniche), takes in the resorts of Villefranche, Cap-Ferrat, Beaulieu, Monaco, and Cap-Martin, each a playground of the rich and famous. The 31km (19-mile) Moyenne Corniche (Middle Road) winds in and out of mountain tunnels and passes the picture-perfect village of Èze. Napoleon built the Grande Corniche—the most panoramic roadway—in 1806. La Turbie is the principal town along the 32km (20-mile) stretch, which reaches more than 480m (1,574 ft.) high at Col d'Èze.

PREVIOUS PAGE: **Beach in Nice.**

ST-TROPEZ ★★★

874km (542 miles) S of Paris; 76km (47 miles) SW of Cannes

While this sun-kissed town has a well-known air of hedonism, Tropezian style is blissfully understated—it's not in-your-face. St-Tropez attracts artists, musicians, models, writers, and an A-lister movie colony each summer to its oh-so-cute town center and epic sandy beach, with a flamboyant parade of humanity trailing behind. In winter it morphs back into a boho fishing village, albeit one with modern art galleries and some of the best restaurants along the coast.

The 1956 Brigitte Bardot movie *And God Created Woman* put St-Tropez on the tourist map. Droves of decadent tourists baring almost all on the peninsula's white-sand beaches trailed in her wake. Decades ago, Bardot pronounced St-Tropez dead, "squatted by a lot of no-goods, drugheads, and villains." But even she returned, followed in recent years by international celebrity A-listers, from David Beckham and Drake to Vanessa Paradis and Kourtney Kardashian.

A panoramic view of St-Tropez.

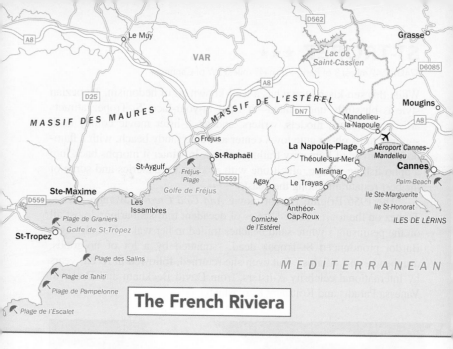

The French Riviera

Essentials

ARRIVING   The nearest rail station is in St-Raphaël, a neighboring coastal resort. **Boats** depart (www.bateauxsaintraphael.com; © **04-94-95-17-46**) from its Vieux Port for St-Tropez (trip time: 1 hr.) five times a day in high summer, reducing to once- or twice-daily sailings in winter. The one-way fare is 20€. Year-round, 10 to 15 Varlib **buses** per day leave from the Gare Routière in St-Raphaël (http://zou.maregionsud.fr; © **04-94-44-52-70**) for St-Tropez. The trip takes 1½ to 2 hours, depending on the bus and the traffic, which during midsummer is usually horrendous. A one-way ticket is 2.10€. Buses also run from Toulon train station, 56km (35 miles) away.

If you drive, note that parking in St-Tropez is tricky, especially in summer. For parking, follow the signs for **Parking des Lices** (© **04-94-97-34-46**), beneath place des Lices, or **Parking du Nouveau Port,** on waterfront avenue Charles de Gaulle (© **04-94-97-74-99**). To get here from Cannes, drive southwest along the coastal highway (D559), turning east when you see signs to St-Tropez.

VISITOR INFORMATION   The **Office de Tourisme** is on quai Jean-Jaurès (www.sainttropeztourisme.com; © **08-92-68-48-28**).

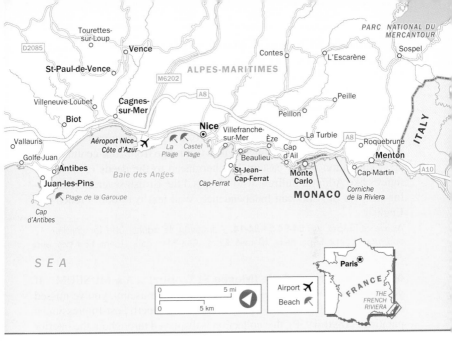

[FastFACTS] ST-TROPEZ

ATMs/Banks **Crédit Agricole,** 17 pl. des Lices (📞 **32-25**).

Mail & Postage **La Poste,** rue de la Poste (📞 **36-31**).

Pharmacies **Pharmacie du Port,** 9 quai Suffren (📞 **04-94-97-00-06**).

Exploring St-Tropez

During summertime, St-Tropez's pleasure port is trimmed with super-yachts, each one berthing stern-to after a day of excess at nearby Plage de Pampelonne. Yacht owners, their guests, and non-boaties all intermingle along the chic quays. Regular spectators can stroll the port and get an up-close look at these floating pleasure palaces, which cost from a few million to hundreds of millions of dollars.

In the Old Town, make a beeline for rue de la Miséricorde. The stone houses lining this street are now boutiques but still evoke medieval St-Tropez better than any other in town. At the corner of rue Gambetta is Chapelle de la Miséricorde, with a blue, green, and gold tile roof. Locals come to swim on **Plage de la Ponche,** an old fishing boat launching beach beyond the old town, or at **Plage des Graniers,** a longer beach 5 minutes farther east underneath the Citadelle.

Citadelle de St-Tropez & Maritime Museum ★★ MUSEUM & CASTLE   Towering above St-Tropez is the Citadelle, an early 17th-century fortified castle. It's not just the best place in town for escaping the crowds and soaking up the sun. It also boasts a hexagonal dungeon (sure to appeal to tiny travelers) and an elaborate moat system—as well as stunning views over the Bay of St-Tropez. Within the Citadelle sits the Maritime Museum, which charts the history of the city's longtime love affair with the sea. Two floors detail activities that range from 16th-century traders' exploration of the eastern Mediterranean to the deeds of maritime figures like Admiral Suffren, who whupped the British several times during the War of American Independence. Wall text is in both French and English.

Above St-Tropez. ✆ **04-94-54-84-14.** Admission 4€ adults; free for children 12 and under. Apr–Sept daily 10am–6:30pm; Oct–Mar daily 10am–12:30pm and 1:30–5:30pm.

Musée de l'Annonciade (Musée St-Tropez) ★★★ MUSEUM   If you leave town without seeing this spellbinding museum, you've missed a colorful part of St-Tropez's past. Showcasing superb post-Impressionist paintings (1890–1950), this collection is displayed throughout the interior of a 16th-century chapel just off of St-Tropez's harbor. In 1892, it was St-Tropez's adopted son, Paul Signac, who kick-started the wave of painters who flooded to this picturesque seaside town. Many of the artists featured—including Signac—painted the port of St-Tropez, a backdrop that lies right outside the building. The museum includes such masterpieces as Matisse's *La Femme à la fenètre, Nice,* as well as artworks by Bonnard, Braque, Dufy, Marquet, and Derain. Temporary shows are held on the ground floor.

pl. Grammont. ✆ **04-94-17-84-10.** Admission 6€ adults; 4€ children 11 and under. July–Sept daily 10am–7pm; Apr–June and Oct Tues–Sun 10am–6pm; Nov–Mar Tues–Sun 10am–5pm.

Outdoor Activities

BEACHES   The hottest Riviera beaches are at St-Tropez. The best for families are closest to the center, including **Plage de la Bouillabaisse** and **Plage des Salins.** More daring and infinitely more famous is the 5km (3-mile) crescent of **Plage de Pampelonne,** about 10km (6¼ miles) from town. Here, 35 expensive and hedonistic beach clubs dot the sand, often with DJ's spinning tunes for topless, and even fully nude, dartiers (day partiers). Unapogetically decadent, **Club 55** (www.club55. fr; ✆ **04-94-55-55-55**) is a former Bardot hangout, while the American-run **Nikki Beach** (www.nikkibeach.com; ✆ **04-94-79-82-04**) is younger and less overtly showy, if painfully chic. Along this stretch, old-style beach shack **Plage de 1051** (www.le1051.com; ✆ **04-94-45-36-97**) and

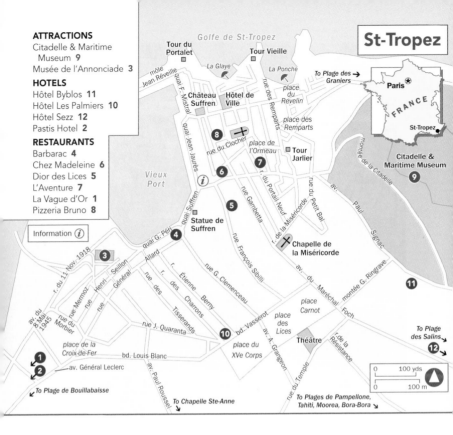

ATTRACTIONS
Citadelle & Maritime
  Museum **9**
Musée de l'Annonciade **3**

HOTELS
Hôtel Byblos **11**
Hôtel Les Palmiers **10**
Hôtel Sezz **12**
Pastis Hotel **2**

RESTAURANTS
Barbarac **4**
Chez Madeleine **6**
Dior des Lices **5**
L'Aventure **7**
La Vague d'Or **1**
Pizzeria Bruno **8**

Information ⓘ

St-Tropez

toes-in-the-sand restaurant and bar **Plage de l'Orangerie** (www.plage-orangerie.com; ✆ **04-94-79-84-74**) are less pretentious and more welcoming.

You'll need a car, bike, or scooter to get from town to Plage de Pampelonne. Parking is around 15€ for the day. More than anywhere else on the Riviera, topless bathing is the norm.

BOATING In St-Tropez port, **Octopussy** (www.octopussy.fr; ✆ **04-94-56-53-10**) rents boats 5 to 16m (16–52 ft.) long. Larger ones come with a captain at the helm. Prices begin at 550€ per day. Better rates may be available at the marketplace site **GetMyBoat.com,** where owners rent boats out when they're not in use.

DIVING Multilingual scuba training and equipment rental is available from the **European Diving School** (www.europeandiving.com; **06-07-51-15-56**), on Plage de Pampelonne. Regular dives, including all equipment, cost 45€. In 2023, two new snorkeling trails opened directly off the beaches of Pampelonne and La Croix-Valmer.

DJs, and raging daytime parties, are par for the course at many St-Tropez beach clubs.

Where to Stay

In addition to the hotels below, you won't go wrong with homey **Pastis Hotel** ★★ (75 av. Du General Leclerc; www.pastis-st-tropez.com).

Hôtel Byblos ★★★   Byblos is decked with bubbling fountains and ancient olive trees, and has been favored by rock stars and aristocrats ever since opening in 1967. Rooms range in size from medium to mega; some units have such special features as four-posters with furry spreads or sunken whirlpool tubs. The breakfast is superb: Served up around the swimming pool, it's a cornucopia of chocolate fountains, hand-baked pastries, organic granola, and unique teas from across the globe. For lunch most guests depart en masse for Pampelonne beach where **Byblos Beach** welcomes bathers with sun mattresses from 50€ per day. Back in St Tropez, dinner is inspired by Alain Ducasse, the chef with the most Michelin stars, who oversees menu items like tigelle flatbread with pistachio pesto at fun (but expensive) restaurant **Cucina.**

20 av. Paul Signac. www.byblos.com. (*) **04-94-56-68-00.** 91 units. From 510€ double; from 2,200€ suite. Breakfast 56€. Parking 40€. Pets 40€. Closed mid-Oct to mid-Apr. **Amenities:** 3 restaurants; bar; nightclub; babysitting; concierge; exercise room; massage; outdoor pool; room service; sauna; spa; free Wi-Fi.

Hôtel Les Palmiers ★★   In a town packed with pricey accommodation, this friendly, family-run hotel is a total bargain. Not only is its location fantastic—directly astride place des Lices in the center of St-Tropez—but Les Palmiers also boasts pretty Provençal-colored rooms and a top-notch contemporary courtyard garden with dark wicker furnishings, bold cushions, and sun-dappled corners, ideal for sipping a 7€ glass of pastis. Part of the hotel dates from the late 18th century, giving the place a cozy, vintage feel.

34 bd. Vasserot (pl. des Lices). www.hotel-les-palmiers.com. ℰ **04-94-97-01-61.** 25 units. 106€–226€ double. Breakfast 15€. **Amenities:** Bar; free Wi-Fi.

Hôtel Sezz ★★   Midway between St Tropez center and the golden sands of Plage de Pampelonne, Sezz sprawls like a Provençal ranch near a smaller public beach. The style is barefoot chic. Bungalows are built to incorporate inside/outside living with floor-to-ceiling sliding doors that lead to capacious terraces and al fresco showers. Public areas bathe in the sunshine with a Thai-style emphasis on minimalism and greenery. Gourmet restaurant **Colette** offers a Made in France approach to Michelin-starred cooking, pairing ingredients like squid and seaweed with local lemons.

151 route des Salins. saint-tropez.hotelsezz.com. ℰ **04-94-55-31-55.** 37 units. 200€–850€ double. Free parking. Closed Nov–Feb. **Amenities:** 3 restaurants; concierge; babysitting; bar; outdoor pool; free Wi-Fi.

Where to Eat

St-Tropez's dining scene is both expensive and exclusive, particularly during the summer season, although we've recommended some good value eats below. Reserve well in advance at top notch restaurants like **Cucina** in the Hôtel Byblos or **Colette** at Hôtel Sezz (see above) or be prepared to dine very early or very late. In addition to the suggestions below, the long-established **Chez Madeleine,** 14 pl. aux Herbes (ℰ **09-52-04-39-47**), behind the fish market, is renowned for its oyster bar, and also

---

FRENCH boules

A game of pétanque, or French boules, is seriously cool for kids. Hop to **Le Café** (www.lecafe.fr; ℰ **04-94-97-44-69**), one of many alfresco bars in place des Lices, and request a handful of pétanque boules to toss around the tree-dappled square. The game was created down the coast and is about as Provençal as it gets. Pick up some tips by watching the locals. Games begin with a toss of the jack, or bouchon. Teams then take turns to throw. Whoever is farthest away keeps trying to get closest to the *bouchon*, with any remaining balls tossed in at the end. A point is awarded for each steel ball that's closer to the jack than any balls from the opposing team.

serves stellar seafood platters; and Michelin-starred chef Yannick Alléno dishes up delights at **Dior des Lices,** 13 rue François Sibilli, the fashion house Chanel's own summertime pop-up eatery. For desserts there are two top choices: **Barbarac,** 2 rue Général Allard (www.barbarac.fr; ✆ **04-94-97-67-83**), which has been scooping up the finest artisanal ice cream in town since it opened in 1986; and **Tarte Tropézienne** (four cafes around town, including one on boulevard Vasserot). The latter's namesake pastry is a sublime and calorific rush of white sugar, white flour, and white cream.

La Vague d'Or ★★★ MODERN FRENCH   Dining at the most fabulous restaurant in St-Tropez is a rare treat. Michelin two-star chef Arnaud Donckele conducts an orchestra of 34 chefs plus an untold cast of fisherfolk, herb growers, and cheese makers. Each dish is a break-the-Internet work of art featuring edible gardens of vegetables, crayfish in various poses, and an apple tarte shaped like a rose. The downside? La Vague d'Or (which translates as "The Golden Wave") will strain the largest of bank accounts. But it will provide the memory of a lifetime.

Plage de la Bouillabaisse. www.chevalblanc.com. ✆ **04-94-55-91-00.** Fixed-price menus 360€–450€. Thurs–Tues 7:30–10pm. Closed mid-Oct to mid-Apr.

L'Aventure ★★ MODERN PROVENÇAL   A backstreet St-Tropez eatery beloved of locals and visitors alike, L'Aventure serves globally inspired market-fresh cuisine: Think classic French ingredients like snails, Provençal lamb, and harbor-fresh fish. But flavors run the gamut, from pesto and honey to ginger and preserved lemons. A typical dish is mushrooms, foraged in Provence, thrown into a searing herbal spaghetti. This venue is blessedly unpretentious, right down to the authentically battered tables on the petite terrace.

31 rue du Portail-Neuf. ✆ **04-94-97-44-01.** Main courses 28€–38€; fixed-price menu 44€. Tues–Sun 7:30–11pm.

Pizzeria Bruno ★ ITALIAN   Proving that not all good meals in St-Tropez have to break the bank, this casual joint has been turning out thin, crispy, wood-fired pizzas since 1959. Even Bardot was a regular. The menu includes a handful of creative salads, pasta dishes, and grilled meats. Note that the restaurant's copious wood-paneled and overly snug seating isn't the comfiest—and hearty eaters may find the pizzas a little on the small side—but the atmosphere is among the liveliest in town.

6 rue de l'Eglise. ✆ **04-94-97-05-18.** Main courses 14€–23€. Daily noon–2pm and 7–11pm. Closed Oct–Apr.

Shopping

St-Tropez is awash in high end shops. The merchandise is Mediterranean, breezy, and sophisticated. Dotted throughout the town's triangle d'or, the rough triangle formed by place de la Garonne, rue François Sibilli and place des Lices, labels include Hermès, Miu Miu, and Pucci. Every summer, a Chanel summer pop-up shop occupies the old Hotel la Mistralée at 1 av. du Général Leclerc. Scores of unique boutiques are around the Vieille Ville (Old Town), including **Vachon Saint-Tropez,** 33 av. Paul Roussel (✆ **04-94-97-23-90**), which has been purveying fashionable swimwear, tunics, and hats since 1919; **Titamàlà,** 53 rue Portail Neuf (www.titamala.com; ✆ **06-25-59-47-32**), an atelier and boutique that creates locally inspired bijoux jewelry; and **K. Jacques,** 25 rue Allard (www.kjacques.fr; ✆ **04-94-97-41-50**), with its iconic tropéziennes sandals. Place des Lices hosts an excellent **outdoor market,** Marché Provençal, with food, clothes, and brocante, on Tuesday and Saturday mornings.

Nightlife

On a lower level of the Hôtel Byblos' grounds, **Les Caves du Roy,** 20 av. Paul-Signac (www.lescavesduroy.com; ✆ **04-94-56-68-00**), is the most self-consciously chic nightclub in St-Tropez. Entrance is free, but drink prices are eye-wateringly high. It's open from 11:30pm until dawn Fridays and Saturdays from Easter to June, nightly from June through August, and Fridays and Saturdays from September to early October. A younger, less pretentious crowd together with a sprinkle of discreet celebrities frequents **Gaïo,** 4 av. du 11 Novembre 1918 (www.gaio.club; ✆ **04-94-97-89-98**), a combination restaurant and club with an Asian-inspired menu and similar decor.

    Tsar Folie's, 9 allée du Quai de l'Epi, and **Le Pigeonnier,** 19 rue de la Ponche (✆ **06-33-58-92-45**), welcomes a cool but friendly LGBTQ+ crowd. **L'Esquinade,** 2 rue de Four (✆ **04-94-56-26-31**), an equally buzzing venue, is the habitual sweaty follow-up club.

HEAD TO THE hills

Unfurling along the shores between St-Tropez and Cannes is a scarlet stretch of coastline known as the Esterel. It's both a regional nature reserve and a cluster of mountains (the Massif de l'Esterel), the latter renowned for their ethereal crimson hue. Hiking trails criss-cross the area and the tiny turquoise beaches are perfect for private picnics. Best of all, the Esterel receives just a fraction of the tourists that congregate along the Riviera's more popular seaside resorts. Regular trains run from Cannes to Théoule-sur-Mer, a village in the center of the park. One-way tickets cost 2.70€, and journey time is around 10 minutes. The **Théoule-sur-Mer Tourist Office,** 2 bd. de la Corniche d'Or (www.theoule-sur-mer.org; ✆ **04-93-49-28-28**), distributes walking and cycling maps of the region.

Below the Hôtel Sube in the port, **Café de Paris** (www.cafedeparis.fr; 🕽 **04-94-97-00-56**) is one of the most popular—and friendly—hangouts in town. It has 1900s-style globe lights, masses of artificial flowers, and a long zinc bar. **Café Sénéquier,** quai Jean Jaurès (www.senequier.com; 🕽 **04-94-97-20-20**), is historic, venerable, snobbish by day, and off-puttingly stylish by night.

CANNES ★★★

905km (561 miles) S of Paris; 163km (101 miles) E of Marseille; 26km (16 miles) SW of Nice

Cannes is more than a capital of cool. The little coastal city with a big reputation personifies liberal France. In a hotel lobby one can see gay couples cuddling as Gulf royals FaceTime on iPhones. Just outside on La Croisette—a hedonistic seaside promenade—billionaires frequent beach clubs while half-naked grannies zip by on rollerblades. As long as you're having a good time, anything goes.

Cannes lacks one thing: culture. Yet who needs museums (although there are two cute ones) when the rue d'Antibes fashion street is like a

Promenade de la Croisette and beach, Cannes.

living catwalk? The USPs here are sun, sea, sand, and seafood. Add Champagne if you're feeling flush. Just offshore the Iles de Lérins are bucolic islands that tempt celebrity escapees from the Cannes Film Festival. The public ferry there takes 20 minutes. With day trips to arty Vallauris and fragrant Grasse, Cannes makes a fun French Riviera base.

Essentials

ARRIVING   By train, Cannes is 10 minutes from Antibes, 30 minutes from Nice, and 45 minutes from Monaco. The TGV from Paris reaches Cannes in an incredibly scenic 5 hours. The one-way fare from Paris is around 50€ to 150€, although advance purchase bargains can be had for as low as 30€. For rail information and schedules, visit www.sncf.com or call ℂ **36-35** (.40€/min). Lignes d'Azur (www.lignesdazur.com; ℂ **08-10-06-10-06**) provides bus service from Cannes' Gare Routière (pl. Bernard Cornut Gentille) to Antibes every 20 minutes during the day (trip time: 25 min.). The one-way fare is 1.70€.

   Nice International Airport (www.nice.aeroport.fr; ℂ **08-20-42-33-33**) is a 30-minute drive east. **Bus** no. 210 (www.niceairportxpress.com) picks up passengers at the airport every 30 minutes during the day (hourly at other times) and drops them at Cannes' Gare Routière. One-way is 19€.

   By car from Marseille, take A51 north to Aix-en-Provence, continuing along A8 east to Cannes. From Nice, follow A8 or the coastal D6007 southwest to Cannes.

VISITOR INFORMATION   The **Office de Tourisme** is at 1 bd. de la Croisette (www.cannes-france.com; ℂ **04-92-99-84-22**).

SPECIAL EVENTS   Cannes is at its most frenzied in mid-May during the **International Film Festival** (www.festival-cannes.com) at the Palais des Festivals, on promenade de la Croisette. It attracts not only film stars (you can palm the cement molds of their handprints outside the Palais des Festivals), but also seemingly every photographer in the world. You have a better chance of being named prime minister of France than you do attending one of the major screenings, although if you're lucky, you may be able to swing tickets to screenings of one of the lesser films. (Hotel rooms and tables at restaurants are equally scarce during the festival.) But the people-watching is absolutely fabulous!

Getting Around

ON FOOT   Cannes' small town center is a labyrinth of one-ways and serious traffic—which makes it best explored on foot. The entire destination is shaped by La Croisette, so it's impossible to get lost.

BY BICYCLE & MOTOR SCOOTER   Despite the summertime commotion, the flat landscapes between Cannes and satellite resorts such as La

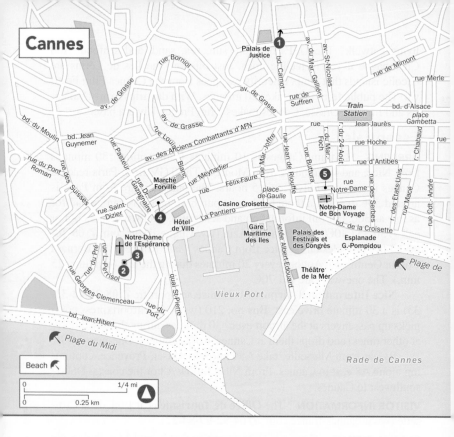

Napoule and Juan-les-Pins are well suited for bikes and motor scooters. For rentals, we recommend **Mistral Location,** 4 rue Georges Clémenceau (www.mistrallocation06.com; ☎ **04-93-39-33-60**), which charges 20€ per day for bikes, and also offers scooters and motorcycles from 30€ per day.

BY CAR   The Cannes Tourist Office website lists every public parking lot. That said, with public transport this good, hiring four wheels is a hassle.

BY TAXI   **Allô Taxi Cannes** (www.allo-taxis-cannes.com; ☎ **04-93-99-99**). **Bolt** and **Uber** might drive you to your destination more quickly and more cheaply.

BY PUBLIC TRANSPORT   **Palm Bus** (www.palmbus.fr; ☎ **08-25-82-55-99**) operates all public transport in and around Cannes. There's little need for public transport in the city center—although the open-top no. 8, which runs along the seafront from the port in the west to the Pointe Croisette peninsula in the east, makes for a fun and scenic ride. Round trip tickets on the route cost 3.20€ and must be purchased directly aboard any bus.

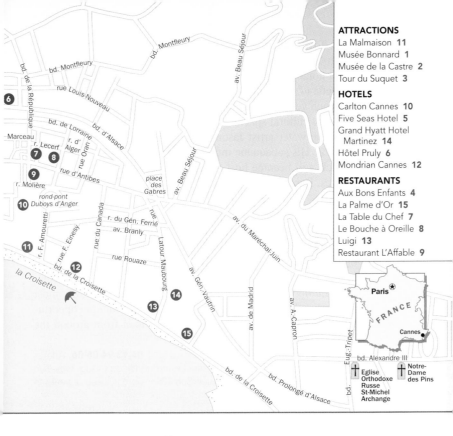

ATTRACTIONS
La Malmaison **11**
Musée Bonnard **1**
Musée de la Castre **2**
Tour du Suquet **3**

HOTELS
Carlton Cannes **10**
Five Seas Hotel **5**
Grand Hyatt Hotel
  Martinez **14**
Hôtel Pruly **6**
Mondrian Cannes **12**

RESTAURANTS
Aux Bons Enfants **4**
La Palme d'Or **15**
La Table du Chef **7**
Le Bouche à Oreille **8**
Luigi **13**
Restaurant L'Affable **9**

[FastFACTS] CANNES

ATMs/Banks Banks are dotted throughout the city, including more than a dozen along the central rue d'Antibes.

Dentists For emergency dental services, contact

SOS Dentaire opposite the train station (www.dentego.fr; ☎ **04-93-30-30-30**).

Doctors & Hospitals **Hopital de Cannes,** 15 av. Broussailles (www.ch-cannes.fr; ☎ **04-93-69-70-00**).

Mail & Postage **La Poste,** 22 rue Bivouac Napoléon (☎ **16-31**).

Pharmacies **Pharmacie Anglo-French,** 94 rue d'Antibes (☎ **04-93-38-53-79**).

Exploring Cannes

Far and away, Cannes' most famous street is the promenade de la Croisette—or simply La Croisette—which curves along the coast. It's lined by grand hotels (some dating from the 19th c.), boutiques, and exclusive beach clubs. Above the yacht-filled harbor, which makes for a fabulous stroll, the Old Town of Cannes sits on Suquet Hill, where visitors can climb the 14th-century **Tour de Suquet** near the Musée de la Castre. Cannes is also home to temporary exhibition space **La Malmaison,** 47 bd. de la Croisette (℡ **04-97-06-44-90**), which will host three major modern art shows each year when it reopens in 2025.

The best new cultural space? Snorkel offshore to the Iles de Lérins. Here British underwater artist Jason deCaires Taylor has deposited six subsea monoliths. His subaquatic museum is made from marine-friendly materials, which will become host to algae and corals, thereby creating living sculptures. Rent a kayak or solar boat (see below) then jump right in.

Musée Bonnard ★★ ART MUSEUM   The only museum in the world dedicated to the Impressionist painter Pierre Bonnard is 3km (1¾ miles) north of Cannes, in the suburb of Le Cannet. Portraits, sculptures, and sketches on display in this petite museum date from primarily between 1922 and 1947, the period during which the artist was a local resident. Temporary exhibitions, such as 2023's celebration of Bonnard's most lively canvases showing the belle époque high life, offer unique opportunities for a peek at privately owned paintings on loan from around the globe.

16 bd. Sadi Carnot, Le Cannet. www.museebonnard.fr. ℡ **04-93-94-06-06.** Admission 7€ adults; 5€ ages 12–18; free for children 11 and under. July–Aug Tues–Sun 10am–8pm (Thurs until 9pm); Sept–June Tues–Sun 10am–6pm. Closed 3 weeks in Jan. Bus no. 1 and 4 from Cannes city center.

Musée de la Castre ★ MUSEUM   Perched above Cannes' Old Town within the medieval Château de la Castre, this museum focuses primarily on ethnographic finds from around the world. Spears from the South Seas and Tibetan masks are interspersed with Sumerian cuneiform tablets and 19th-century paintings of the French Riviera. (Spoiler alert: There's a lot more hotels and villas today.) Visitors, however, will be most impressed by the astounding views from the museum's viewing tower—accessed via 109 steep steps—which offers glorious views over Cannes, the Mediterranean coastline, and the Lerins Islands beyond. The shady gardens, just outside the museum's entrance, are a welcome respite for tired sightseers.

Le Suquet. www.cannes.com. ℡ **04-89-82-26-26.** Admission 6.50€ adults; 3.50€ ages 18–25; free for children under 17. July–Aug daily 10am–7pm (Wed until 9pm); Sept and Apr–June Tues–Sun 10am–1pm and 2–6pm (June and Sept Wed until 9pm); Oct–Mar Tues–Sun 10am–1pm and 2–5pm.

Organized Tours

One of the best ways to get your bearings in Cannes is to climb aboard the **Petit Train touristique de Cannes** (www.cannes-petit-train.com;

✆ **06-22-61-25-76**). The vehicles operate daily from 10am to 8pm. The three itineraries offered are: Croisette Tour, with a ride along La Croisette and its side streets (35 min.); Historical Cannes, which weaves through the narrow streets of Le Suquet (35 min.); or the Big Tour, a combination of the two (1 hr.). All trains depart from the Palais des Festivals every 30 to 60 minutes. Shorter tours cost 9€ for adults and 5€ for children 3 to 10; the Big Tour costs 14€ for adults and 8€ for children 3 to 10.

Outdoor Activities

BEACHES   Going to the beach in Cannes has more to do with exhibitionism than actual swimming. **Plage de la Croisette** extends between the Vieux Port and the Port Canto. The beaches along this billion-dollar stretch of sand are *payante,* meaning entrance costs between 20€ to 40€. Why should you pay an entry fee at all? Well, the fee includes a full day's use of a mattress, a chaise lounge (the seafront is more pebbly than sandy), and a parasol, as well as easy access to freshwater showers. There are also outdoor restaurants and bars (some with sushi menus, others with gourmet burgers) where no one minds if you dine in your swimsuit. Every beach allows topless bathing.

Cannes has heaps of buzzy beach clubs including sassy **Plage du Festival** (www.plagedufestival.com; ✆ **04-93-39-37-37**), the town's original bathing resort, which has its own brand-new organic ice cream bar. Another favorite is freshly renovated **Plage Rado Helen** (www.rado beachhelen.com; ✆ **04-93-94-20-68**), which has its own silky-soft sand and friendly, unpretentious service.

Looking for a free public beach without chaises or parasols? Head for **Plage du Midi,** just west of the Vieux Port, or **Plage Gazagnaire,** just east of the Port Canto. Here you'll find families with children and lots of RV-type vehicles parked nearby.

BOATING   Several companies around Cannes's Vieux Port rent boats of any size, with or without a crew, for a day, a week, or even longer. A new outfit with solar-powered boats is **Solar Boat,** Port Pointe Croisette (www.bateausanspermis.fr; ✆ **06-51-05-28-02**). They can be rented, without a permit or pilot, for up to seven people, for 250€ per day.

GOLF   Ten golf courses ring Cannes and almost all are within a 20-minute drive of the city. The **Old Course,** 265 route de Golf, Mandelieu (www. golfoldcourse.com; ✆ **04-92-97-32-00**), is a leafy gem dating from 1891. Greens fees cost 130€, with big reductions for lunch deals and afternoon tee-offs. The prestigious **Royal Mougins Golf Club,** 424 av. du Roi, Mougins (www.royalmougins.fr; ✆ **04-92-92-49-69**), also boasts a gourmet restaurant and spa. Greens fees start at 220€, including cart hire; it's half-price for 9 holes. Discounts are available from mid-November through mid-April.

Sailboats at the old harbor of Cannes.

PADDLEBOARDING   Like the rest of the world, Cannes has fallen in love with kayaking and stand-up paddleboarding (SUP). Rent your own from **Cannes Standup Paddle Location,** Plage du Mouré Rouge, bd. Gazagnaire, Palm Beach (www.stand-up-paddle-kayak-cannes.com; ℂ **06-87-95-45-18**). Fees start at 15€ per hour.

TENNIS   Some resorts have their own courts. The city of Cannes also maintains 16 synthetic courts and six clay-topped courts at the **Garden Tennis Club,** 99 av. Maurice Chevalier (ℂ **04-93-47-29-33**). You'll pay 21.50€ per hour.

Where to Stay

If the hotels below are booked, know that you'll have very enjoyable stays at both the quietly chic **Five Seas Hotel** ★★ (1 rue Notre Dame; www.fiveseashotel.com) and the historic **Grand Hyatt Hotel Martinez** ★★ (73 bd. de la Croisette; http://hyatt.com).

Carlton Cannes ★★★   The Carlton is one of the world's greatest sea-side hotels. It has been a destination for celebrity and royalty since 1911, and was the primary location for the Alfred Hitchcock film *To Catch a Thief* (Grace Kelly met Prince Rainier during the filming), as well as Elton John's "I'm Still Standing" music video. In 2023, it reemerged from a pitch-perfect, top-to-bottom renovation. Today, rooms have a handsome Art Deco vibe and top-shelf amenities. But what raises the Carlton's game are huge gardens, hip bars, a state-of-the-art fitness center, and public spaces scattered with art and objets d'art. With an array of restaurants including Turkish-inspired **Rüya,** and South of France stunner **Riviera,** guests would be forgiven for never leaving the most photographed accommodation in Cannes. The **Carlton Beach Club** is the final Croisette showpiece from this grand dame hotel.

1 rue Notre Dame. www.carltoncannes.com. © **04-93-06-40-06.** 332 units. 357€–881€ double; from 890€ suite. **Amenities:** 3 restaurants; 2 bars; concierge; outdoor pool; room service; spa; fitness center; free Wi-Fi.

Hôtel Pruly ★★   Just behind Cannes' train station, this delightful hotel spills out from a renovated century-old town house. Charming rooms are decorated in bright colors and Provençal textiles; some boast traditional terra-cotta *tomette* floors or private balconies. An afternoon nap on a sun lounger in the hotel's palm-splashed private garden is a welcome respite from Cannes' summertime crowds. Depending on the season, the hotel may require a minimum stay of 3 nights.

32 bd. d'Alsace. www.hotel-pruly.com. © **04-93-38-41-28.** 14 units. 99€–290€ double. **Amenities:** Garden; free Wi-Fi.

Mondrian Cannes ★★   The Mondrian opened in 2023 in a stunning seafront location. Its décor of light wood and plush fabrics is as stylish as anything in Paris or Tokyo, yet, as this is Cannes, an aura of carefree cool pervades the entire establishment. Minimalist yet comfortable rooms offer a 1920s theme and either city or sea views. They feature wavy blue plush carpets that mirror the ocean in front of the hotel. Cannes' latest hot restaurant is **Mr Nakamoto** (daily noon–2pm and 7–11pm), which occupies the hotel's tropical garden overlooking la Croisette. It serves iconic New York dishes like steaks and seafood grills with a Japanese twist, a combination that shouldn't work but it does.

45 bd. de la Croisette. www.accor.com. © **04-93-38-15-45.** 75 units. 203€–628€ double; from 380€ suite. Parking 40€. **Amenities:** Restaurant, bar; babysitting; private beach; concierge; free Wi-Fi.

Where to Eat

Cannes' dining scene is all-encompassing: Expect to stumble across everything from Michelin-starred gastronomy to traditional Provençal cuisine. Restaurants are scattered across the city center, with a particularly heavy concentration around Le Suquet, Cannes' Old Town. A fave, beyond

15

THE FRENCH RIVIERA

Cannes

those below, is the family-run (for 3 generations!) **Aux Bons Enfants** ★★ (80 rue Meynadier; www.aux-bons-enfants.com).

EXPENSIVE

La Palme d'Or ★★★ MODERN FRENCH   Each May the Cannes Film Festival jury enjoy a special dinner at La Palme d'Or. This double-Michelin starred restaurant commands La Croisette from the iconic Martinez hotel. In 2024 the A-listers were met with a new head chef, Jean Imbert, who brought his contemporary skills (and 500k Instagram followers) from the Plaza Athénée in Paris. Expect spellbinding dishes from the most famous must-eat restaurant in Cannes.

In the Grand Hyatt Hotel Martinez, 73 bd. de la Croisette. http://cannesmartinez. grand.hyatt.com. ℰ **04-92-98-74-14.** Smart clothes recommended. Main courses 68€–84€; fixed-price menu 102€–270€. Wed–Sat 12:30–2pm and 8–10pm. Closed Jan–Mar.

MODERATE

La Table du Chef ★★ FRENCH/PROVENÇAL   Just off Cannes' premier shopping street, rue d'Antibes, this unassuming little bistro serves up some of the city's most innovative cuisine in a unique service structure. Chef Bruno Gensdarme (who spent almost 20 years working alongside superchef Guy Savoy in Paris) dishes up four plates on a "surprise menu," and you eat what you're given. Highly rated dishes can include cauliflower soup with smoked salmon, or a seared duck breast on a bed of lentils. Picky eaters beware: Waitstaff will take on any dietary requirements at the start of your meal, but from that point onwards, your taste buds are left to the whims of the chef's delectable (and surprising!) set menus.

5 rue Jean Daumas. www.latableduchefcannes. ℰ **04-93-68-27-40.** Fixed-price menu 59€. Tues–Sat 7:30–10pm.

Le Bouche à Oreille ★★ FRENCH   The motto at Bouche à Oreille is "Eat, Drink, and Share." Which makes for fun, unstuffy, yet gloriously tasty meal with sharing platters aplenty. Try the house tartine with pecorino cream and truffled ham. Or a sliced beef tenderloin with market vegetables. Every dessert, sauce, or side dish is made by hand in the open kitchen. A final bonus is a brilliant array of South of France wines served by the glass from 6€ to 8€, allowing guests a viticultural education on the French Riviera.

7 rue des Gabres. www.lebouchaoreille.com. ℰ **04-93-39-97-90.** Main courses 16€–23€; fixed-price menus 26€–32€. Tues–Sat 6:30–11pm.

Luigi ★★ ITALIAN   A few paces from La Croisette, newly opened Luigi is unashamedly glamorous. Its outdoor terrace is a place to see and be seen. While its Mad Men interior is like stepping into an upscale New York jazz club in the 1960s, with hard liqueur cocktails to match.

Musicians accompany diners on the piano most evenings. The food? It's as fancy and fabulous as Cannes itself. The linguine comes with lobster, the rigatoni with truffles, and the risotto with honking great prawns. At Luigi, it's showtime.

24 rue Latour-Maubourg. www.luigicannes.com. © **04-93-94-11-29.** Main courses 26€–56€. Daily 8pm–1am.

Restaurant L'Affable ★★ MEDITERRANEAN   Chef Jean-Paul Battaglia's menu may be petite, but his creations are as innovative and contemporary as can be. These frequently changing selections are classically French, yes…but with plenty of modern twists. Look out for pumpkin soup with foie-gras foam; ceviche "Grenoble-style," drizzled with capers and lime; or tartare of scallops and oysters served with lemon Chantilly cream. Be sure to save space for Battaglia's signature *soufflé au Grand-Marnier.* Note that the ambiance at lunch is vibrant, while evenings are more formal. The service is consistently superb—making L'Affable a good choice for a special occasion.

5 rue Lafontaine. www.restaurant-laffable.fr. © **04-93-68-02-09.** Main courses 44€–49€; fixed-price lunch 28€ or dinner 55€. Mon–Sat 12:30–2pm and 7–10pm (closed Sat lunch). Closed Aug.

Shopping

Cannes achieves a blend of resort-style leisure, glamour, and media glitz more successfully than its neighbors. You'll see every big-name designer you can think of on the living catwalk that is the rue d'Antibes, plus a legion of one-off designer boutiques and shoe stores. There are also real-people shops; resale shops for star-studded castoffs; flea markets for funky junk; and a fruit, flower, and vegetable market.

BOOKS   Autour d'un Livre, 11 rue Bivouac Napoleon (www.autour dunlivre.com; © **04-93-68-01-99**), is a combination bookshop and cafe with a small selection of English language novels and travel guides.

DESIGNER SHOPS   Most of the big fashion names line promenade de la Croisette, the main drag along the sea. Among the most pricey are **Dior,** 7 La Croisette (© **04-92-98-98-00**), and **Hermès,** 52 La Croisette (© **04-93-39-08-90**). The stores stretch from the Hôtel Carlton almost to the Palais des Festivals, with the top names closest to the **Gray d'Albion,** 38 rue des Serbes (www.lucienbarriere.com; © **04-92-99-79-79**), both a mall and a hotel (how convenient). Near the train station, department store **Galeries Lafayette** has all the big-name labels crammed into one smallish space at 6 rue du Maréchal-Foch (www.galerieslafayette.com; © **04-97-06-25-00**).

Young hipsters should try **Bathroom Graffiti,** 52 rue d'Antibes (© **04-93-39-02-32**), for sexy luggage, bikinis, and designer houseware. The rue d'Antibes is also brilliant for big-brand bargains (Zara and Max-Mara), as well as one-off boutiques like sassy colors from Tara Jarman

15

THE FRENCH RIVIERA

Cannes

(no. 61) and budget fashion at **Future** (around the corner on 10 rue Macé). If you can afford it, **JP Art** (also on rue Macé) sells sailing boats made from deconstructed Hermès luggage and pop art homages to Serge Gains-bourg and Steve McQueen.

FOOD   The Marché Forville (see below) and the surrounding streets are, unsurprisingly, the best places to search for picnic supplies. For bottles of Côtes de Provence, try **La Vinothèque,** 14 rue Marceau (✆ **04-93-99-94-02**), where knowledgeable staff can select the right bottle. **La Compagnie des Saumons,** 12 pl. Marché Forville (✆ **04-93-68-33-20**), brims with caviar, bottles of fish soup, and slabs of smoked salmon. Local cheese shop **Le Fromage Gourmet,** 8 rue des Halles (✆ **04-93-99-96-41**), is a favorite of celebrated chef Alain Ducasse.

MARKETS   The **Marché Forville,** in place Marché Forville just north of the Vieux Port, is a covered stucco structure with a few arches but no walls. From Tuesday to Sunday, 7am to 1pm, it's the fruit, vegetable, and flower market that supplies the dozens of restaurants in the area. Monday (8am–6pm) is brocante day, when the market fills with dealers selling everything from Grandmère's dishes and bone-handled carving knives to castaways from estate sales. Tuesdays to Sundays, 8am to 12:30pm, the small **Marché aux Fleurs** (Flower Market) takes place outdoors along the edges of the allée de la Liberté, across from the Palais des Festivals.

Nightlife

BARS & CLUBS   A strip of sundowner bars stretches along rue Félix Faure. Most are chic, some have happy-hour cocktails, and several have DJs after dinner. Wine bar **La Belle Époque,** 6 rue des Frères Pradignac (✆ **06-41-39-97-90**), is a late-opening gem with killer cocktails. **Happen,** 26 rue du Suquet (✆ **06-03-02-32-26**), also opens until 2am to serve Provence wines and light bites with great music. Continue the party at **Chrystie,** 22 rue Macé (www.chrystie.com; ✆ **04-93-99-66-91**), with a choice of dozens of impeccably created cocktails on offer luxurious nib-bles (try the truffle pizza), plus live pop, international DJs, and cabaret. At **Le Bâoli,** Port Pierre Canto, La Croisette (www.baolicannes.com; ✆ **04-93-43-03-43**), Europe's partying elite, from Prince Albert of Monaco to Jude Law, dance until dawn. Dress to the nines to slip past the über-tight security and into this Asian-inspired wonderland.

CASINOS   Cannes is invariably associated with easygoing permissive-ness, filmmaking glitterati, and gambling. If the latter is your thing, Cannes has world-class casinos (you must present a passport for entry) loaded with high rollers, voyeurs, and everyone in between. The most established is the **Casino Barrière Cannes Le Croisette,** in the Palais des Festivals, 1 espace Lucien Barrière (www.lucienbarriere.com; ✆ **04-92-98-78-00**).

A well-respected fixture in town since the 1950s, a collection of noisy slot machines it is most certainly not. All Cannes' casinos maintain slots that operate daily from lunchtime to around 4am. Smarter dress is expected for the *salles des grands jeux* (blackjack, roulette, craps, poker, and chemin de fer), which open nightly from 8pm to 4am.

DAY TRIPS FROM CANNES

Iles de Lérins ★★

Short boat ride from Cannes

Floating in the Mediterranean just south of Cannes' southern horizon, the Lérins Islands are an idyllic place to escape the Riviera's summertime commotion. Head for Cannes port's western quai Laubeuf, where ferryboats by **Trans-Côte d'Azur** (www.trans-cote-azur.com; ℂ **04-92-98-71-30**) offer access to Ile Ste-Marguerite. To visit Ile St-Honorat, head for the same quay, to the **Transports Planaria** (www.cannes-ilesdelerins. com; ℂ **04-92-98-71-38**) ferryboats. Both companies offer frequent service to the islands daily at intervals of between 30 and 90 minutes, depending on the season. Round-trip transport to Ile Ste-Marguerite costs 17.50€ per adult and 11€ for children 5 to 12; round-trip transport to Ile St-Honorat costs 16.50€ per adult, 15€ for children 13 to 18, 11€ for children 8 to 12, and 8€ for children 4 to 7. To preserve nature, mountain bikes, spear fishing, and drones are completely banned. As dining options on the islands are limited, pack up a picnic lunch from Cannes' Marché Forville before you set off. Feeling glamorous? Treat yourself to lunch at **Le Guérite** (www.restaurantlaguerite.com; ℂ **04-93-43-49-30**), a legendary island restaurant that has been serving charred seabream (52€) to visiting yachties since 1902.

EXPLORING ILE STE-MARGUERITE

Ile Ste-Marguerite is one big botanical garden—cars, cigarettes, and all other pollutants are banned—ringed by crystal-clear sea. From the dock, you can stroll along the island to Fort Royal, built by Spanish troops in 1637 and used as a military barracks and parade ground until World War II. The infamous *Man in the Iron Mask* was allegedly imprisoned here, and you can follow the legend back to his horribly spooky cell. The newest and most amazing addition to Ile Ste-Marguerite is France's first underwater eco-museum, where snorkel-friendly sculptures by Jason deCaires Taylor have been sunk offshore. Swim out around 100m then dive down to this subaquatic free museum.

Musée de la Mer, Fort Royal (ℂ **04-93-38-55-26**), traces the history of the island, displaying artifacts of Ligurian, Roman, and Arab civilizations, plus the remains discovered by excavations, including paintings, mosaics, and ancient pottery. The museum is open June to September

15

THE FRENCH RIVIERA

Day Trips from Cannes

An aerial shot of Abbaye de St-Honorat.

daily from 10am to 5:45pm, and Tuesday to Sunday October to May 10:30am to 1:15pm and 2:15 to 4:45pm (closing at 5:45pm Apr–May). Admission is 6.50€ for adults, 3.50€ for visitors 25 and under, and free for children 17 and under.

EXPLORING ILE ST-HONORAT ★★

Only 1.6km (1 mile) long, Ile St-Honorat is much quieter than neighboring Ste-Marguerite. But in historical terms, it's much richer than its island sibling and is the site of a monastery whose origins date from the 5th century. The **Abbaye de St-Honorat ★** (www.abbayedelerins.com; ✆ **04-92-99-54-00**) is a combination of medieval ruins and early-20th-century ecclesiastical buildings and is home to a community of about 25 Cistercian monks. Most visitors content themselves with a wander through the pine forests on the island's western side, a clamber around the ruined monastery on the island's southern edge, and a bathe on its seaweed-strewn beaches.

The monks also transform the island's herbs, vines, and honey into a wealth of organic products, including lavender oil and wine. All can be purchased in the monastery shop. There is also an excellent lunch-only restaurant, **La Tonnelle** (www.tonnelle-abbayedelerins.fr; ✆ **04-92-99-54-08**), which serves dishes like organic pasta with truffles and shaved parmesan (39€). Island wines can be ordered by the glass from 12€. It's closed from November to March. And no, it's not the monks who cook, but they can organize a wine-tasting or small island tour if arranged in advance.

Grasse ★

18km (11 miles) N of Cannes

Grasse, a 20-minute drive from Cannes, has been renowned as the capital of the world's perfume industry since the Renaissance.

Today a significant amount of the world's essences are produced here from thousands of tons of petals, including roses, violets, daffodils, wild lavender, and jasmine. The quaint medieval town, which formed the backdrop for the movie *Perfume,* has several free perfume museums where visitors can enroll in workshops to create their own scent.

ESSENTIALS

Trains run to Grasse from Cannes, depositing passengers a 10-minute walk south of town. From here, a walking trail or shuttle bus leads visitors into the center. One-way train tickets cost 4.90€ from Cannes, and journey time is around 30 minutes. For further train information, visit www.sncf-connect.com or call ✆ **36-35.**

Buses pull into town every 10 to 60 minutes daily from Cannes (trip time: 50 min.), arriving at the Gare Routière, pl. de la Buanderie (✆ **04-93-36-37-37**), a 5-minute walk north of the town center. The one-way fare is 1.70€. Visitors arriving by car may follow RN85 from Cannes. The Office de Tourisme is at 18 place aux Aires (www.paysdegrassetourisme.fr; ✆ **04-93-36-66-66**). For a guided 35-minute glide around town, ride the **Petit Train Touristique.** This electric vehicle buzzes around all the top sites daily from 11am to 6pm; tickets cost 7€ for adults, and 4.50€ for children ages 3 to 12.

EXPLORING GRASSE

Musée International de la Parfumerie ★★ MUSEUM   This comprehensive museum chronicles both Grasse's fragrant history, as well as worldwide perfume development over the past 4,000 years, is the only one of its kind in the world. Wander among raw materials, ancient flasks (including Marie Antoinette's 18th-c. toiletry set) and scented soaps, all set against a backdrop of temporary exhibitions and contemporary artworks, with explanatory inscriptions in English. Kids have their own dedicated pathway, lined with interactive exhibits to touch—and, of course, smell. An exhibition in 2023 shows how perfumiers have long commissioned the best artists, from Helmut Newton to Martin Scorsese, to help advertise this priceless industry.

2 bd. du Jeu-de-Ballon. www.museesdegrasse.com. ℰ **04-97-05-58-00.** Admission 6€ adults; 3€ students; free for children under 18. Apr–Sept daily 10am–7pm; Oct–Mar daily 10am–6pm. Closed Mon Nov–Mar.

Parfumerie Molinard ★★ FACTORY TOUR

This firm is well known in the United States, where its products are sold at Saks and Bloomingdale's. In the factory, you can witness the extraction of the essence from the flowers, understand the distillation process completed in copper tanks designed by Gustave Eiffel of tower fame, and even make your own scent. You'll also learn all the details of the process of converting flowers into essential oils. You can admire a collection of antique perfume bottle labels and see a rare collection of perfume flacons by Baccarat and Lalique. The nearby **Parfumerie Fragonard factory,** 20 bd. Fragonard, offers a similar experience.

60 bd. Victor Hugo. www.molinard.com. ℰ **04-93-36-01-62.** Free admission. Daily 10am–6pm (until 7pm July–Aug).

Villa Musée Fragonard ★ HISTORIC HOME/ART MUSEUM

The setting is an 18th-century aristocrat's town house with a magnificent, scented garden in back. The collection displayed here includes the paintings of Jean-Honoré Fragonard, who was born in Grasse in 1732; his sister-in-law, Marguerite Gérard; his son, Alexandre; and his grandson, Théophile. Alexandre decorated the grand staircase. Curiously, this is the least-visited museum in town but is surely one of the loveliest.

23 bd. Fragonard. www.museesdegrasse.com. ℰ **04-97-05-58-00.** Free admission. Daily 1–5:45pm (until 6:45pm July–Aug).

WHERE TO EAT

For light lunch or an afternoon snack, pop into **Les Delicatesses de Grasse,** 7 rue Marcel Journet (ℰ **09-81-76-59-29**), a combination restaurant with terrace, traditional food store, and charcuterie. Try the highly recommended platters of local sausage and tapenade, plus rosé wines from St-Tropez.

La Bastide St-Antoine (Restaurant Chibois) ★★★ FRENCH/PROVENÇAL

La Bastide St-Antoine offers one of the grandest farm-to-table culinary experiences along the Riviera. In a 200-year-old Provençal farmhouse, top chef Jacques Chibois sources dishes from the surrounding by 2.8 hectares (7 acres) of orchards, cottage gardens, and olive groves, which diners can stroll through before they eat. Exquisite examples include roasted pigeon smoked with girolles mushrooms. Desserts may include strawberry soup with spice wine or ice cream made with olives and a hint of olive oil. Reservations are required.

The pink umbrellas suspended above Grasse's streets (May–Oct) represent the Grasse May Rose, which is indigenous to the area and used in Dior and Chanel perfumes.

You can stay in the attached five-star accommodation of nine rooms and seven suites, decorated in upscale Provençal style. Outside there's a pool, jogging track, and boules court. Doubles cost 198€ to 530€, suites from 413€.

48 av. Henri-Dunant. www.jacques-chibois.com. ℂ **04-93-70-94-94.** Main courses 75€–98€; fixed-price lunch Mon–Sat 76€–195€ or dinner 120€–195€. Daily noon–2pm and 8–9:30pm. Closed mid-Jan to Feb.

Golfe-Juan & Vallauris ★

7km (4½ miles) NE of Cannes

Napoleon and 800 men landed at Golfe-Juan in 1815 to begin his march to Paris and famous Hundred Days in power; the pint-sized general met his Waterloo against the combined forces of Britain and Continental Europe a few months later. Today it's a family resort known for its sandy beaches and tasty seafood restaurants right on the beach; they are far cheaper than those in Cannes, a short distance away.

The 2km-long (1¼-mile) RN135 leads inland from Golfe-Juan to the typically French town of Vallauris. Once simply a stopover along the

Riviera, Vallauris's ceramics industry was in terminal decline until it was "discovered" by Picasso just after World War II. The artist's legacy lives on both in boho ceramic shops, snapshots of the master in local galleries, and in his awesome *La Paix et La Guerre* fresco.

ESSENTIALS

You can drive to Golfe-Juan or Vallauris on any of the Riviera's coastal highways. Although route numbers are not always indicated, city names are clear once you're on the highway. From Cannes or Antibes, N7 east is the fastest route. From Nice or Biot, take A8/E80 west.

Golfe-Juan's rail station, on avenue de la Gare, is linked to Cannes, Juan-les-Pins, Antibes, and Nice every 30 minutes. A one-way ticket to Cannes costs 2.20€. For railway information, visit www.sncf-connect.com or call ℂ **36-35** (.40€/min). Buses operated by Envibus (www.envibus.fr; ℂ **04-89-87-72-00**) make frequent trips from Cannes; the 20-minute trip costs 1€ each way.

EXPLORING GOLFE-JUAN & VALLAURIS

Because of its position beside the sea, Golfe-Juan long ago developed into a warm-weather resort. The town's twin strips of beach are Plage du Soleil (east of the Vieux Port and the newer Port Camille-Rayon) and Plage du Midi (west of those two). Each stretches 1km (½ mile) and charges no entry fee, with the exception of small areas administered by concessions that rent mattresses for between 25€ and 30€ for a day's use. Like everywhere else on the Riviera, Golfe-Juan indulges bathers who choose to remove their bikini tops.

In Vallauris, Picasso's *l'Homme au Mouton* (*Man and Sheep*) is the outdoor statue at place Paul Isnard. The local council had intended to enclose this statue in a museum, but Picasso insisted that it remain on the square, "where the children could climb over it and dogs piss against it." The pretty town is now backed with cool ceramics and art stores.

Musée Magnelli, Musée de la Céramique & Musée National Picasso La Guerre et La Paix ★★ ART MUSEUM   Three museums in one, this cultural center developed from a 12th-century chapel where Picasso painted *La Paix (Peace)* and *La Guerre (War)* in 1952. Visitors can physically immerse themselves in this tribute to pacifism. Images of love and peace adorn one wall; scenes of violence and conflict the other. Also on site is a permanent exposition of works by Florentine-born abstract artist Alberto Magnelli, as well as a floor dedicated to traditional and innovative ceramics from regional potters.

pl. de la Libération. www.musees-nationaux-alpesmaritimes.fr/picasso. ℂ **04-93-64-71-83.** Admission 6€ adults; 3€ for visitors 19–25; free for children 18 and under. July–Aug daily 10am–12:30pm and 2–6pm; Sept–June Wed–Mon 10am–12:15pm and 2–5pm.

WHERE TO EAT & SHOP

Join the locals for lunch at **Le Clos Cosette,** 1 av. du Tapis Vert (www.leclos cosette.com; ✆ **04-93-64-30-64**). The restaurant's menu proposes an excellent home-made steak tartare (22€), plus a daily 21€ three-course lunchtime set menu. For souvenirs, head around the corner to avenue Georges-Clemenceau, lined with small shops selling brightly glazed, locally made ceramics. These include **Les Petites Porcelaines** at no. 39 and the **Salle Arias-Picasso** at no. 35. The latter, housed in the former barbershop frequented by Picasso, exhibits works from the local pottery guild as well as linocuts that Picasso gifted to the association. Picasso's former ceramics studio, **Galerie Madoura,** rue Georges et Suzanne Ramié, is open to well-dressed tourists (the sort that look interested in buying some pricey pottery at the same time). The **Musée de la Poterie,** 21 rue Sicard (✆ **04-93-64-66-51**), run by a private enthusiast, offers free tours of a working ceramics factory. It's closed at weekends.

Le Bistrot du Port ★★ SEAFOOD Amid the line of fabulous sea-food restaurants in Golfe-Juan, visiting celebrities in search of fresh fish book tables at this particular ocean-front eatery. The Allinei brothers, Thomas and Mathieu, serve simple, modern creations including tuna tar-tare, and John Dory seared on a hot stone. The restaurant purveys a superb array of rosé wines, including Le Clos Saint Joseph from the hills above Nice. The 3-course weekday lunchtime menu for 35€ is a particular steal.
53 av. des Frères-Roustan, Golfe-Juan. www.bistrotduport.com. ✆ **04-93-63-70-64**. Main courses 27€–45€; fixed-price lunch menu 35€. Tues–Sun noon–2pm and 7–10pm.

Mougins ★★
7km (4½ miles) N of Cannes

A fortified hill town, Mougins preserves the quiet life in a postcard-perfect manner. The town's artsy legacy—Picasso, Jean Cocteau, Paul Eluard, Fernand Léger, Isadora Duncan, and Christian Dior were all previous resi-dents—has blessed the town with must-see galleries and two amazing new museums, opened in 2021 and 2024 respectively. Real estate prices are among the highest on the Riviera, and the wealthy residents support a dining scene that also punches well above its weight. The **Etoile des Mougins food festival** (www.lesetoilesdemougins.com), held each Sep-tember, is a gastronomic love-in featuring Michelin-starred chefs from across the globe.

ESSENTIALS

From Cannes, the best way to get to Mougins is to drive north of the city along D6285. By bus, **ZOU** (zou.maregionsud.fr) runs bus no. 663 from Cannes to Saint-Basile, a 20-minute walk from the center of

Mougins. One-way fares cost 2.10€. The **Office de Tourisme** is at 18 bd. Courteline (www.mougins-tourisme.fr; ℂ **04-93-75-87-67**).

EXPLORING MOUGINS

Picasso discovered Mougins' tranquil maze of flower-filled lanes in the company of his muse, Dora Marr, and photographer Man Ray, in 1935. The Vieux Village's pedestrianized cobblestone streets—each corner prettier than the last—have changed little over the decades since. The setting is so romantic that, according to locals, former French President François Hollande wined and dined his former first lady, Valérie Trierweiler, in one of the restaurants listed below. He then proceeded to indulge his mistress, Julie Gayet, in the same establishment. Classy guy.

Chefs explaining a recipe at the Etoile des Mougins food festival.

Centre de la Photographie de Mougins ★★ PHOTOGRAPHY

MUSEUM   Picasso's close friend, photographer André Villers, chronicled the artist's Mougins years in black-and-white photos. Some are hilarious, such as the photo showing Picasso sitting down for breakfast in his trademark Breton shirt, pretending he has croissants for fingers. From 2021 this archive has been exhibited at the new photography center, alongside Villers' portraits of personalities like Salvador Dalí and Edith Piaf. Harder hitting temporary exhibitions, like the recent *Amexica,* which detailed politics and tragedy on the Mexican/United States border, are also part of the experience here.

43 rue de l'Église. www.centrephotographiemougins.com. ℂ **04-22-21-52-12.** Admission 6€ adults; 3€ students; free for children 18 and under. Apr–Sept Wed–Mon 11am–7pm; Oct–Mar Wed–Sun 1–6pm.

Chapelle Notre-Dame de Vie ★ RELIGIOUS SITE   The most romantic site in Mougins is surely this medieval chapel. It lies 1.5km (1 mile) southeast of Mougins. It was built in the 12th century and reconstructed in 1646. Its tree-dappled grounds inspired local resident Picasso and were once painted by Sir Winston Churchill. More importantly, the priory next door was once Picasso's studio and private residence for the

last 12 years of his life. On his death in 1973, the art collection inside was worth in excess of $1 billion.

Chemin de la Chapelle. Free admission.

FAMM: Femmes Artistes du Musée de Mougins ★★ FEMALE ART MUSEUM   In spring 2024, Europe's first museum dedicated to female artists opened in a gorgeous Mougins town house. It showcases a revolving selection of contemporary art from the likes of Tracey Emin, Barbara Hepworth, and Elaine de Kooning, among others. The museum owner, former trader Christian Levett, owns a nonpareil collection of female Abstract Expressionism works, many of which are shown here.

32 rue Commandeur. www.mouginsmusee.com. ✆ **04-93-75-18-22.** Admission 14€ adults; 7€ students and seniors; 6€ children 10–17; free for children 9 and under. Daily 10am–6pm (July–Sept until 8pm).

WHERE TO EAT

Mougins is a global dining capital so you can't go far wrong, wherever you choose to dine. Pick of a good bunch is **L'Amandier de Mougins** ★★, 48 av. Jean-Charles-Mallet (www.amandier.fr; ✆ **04-93-90-00-91;** menus 27€–65€). It serves daily specials, included in the lunch formula, like cod and aïoli on Tuesday, and confit of rabbit on Sunday.

For a more budget-friendly option, try the traditional bistro **Le Resto des Arts** ★, 2 rue Maréchal Foch (www.restodesarts.com; ✆ **04-93-75-60-03**), which dishes up hearty specials like basil-spiked *soupe au pistou,* red mullet doused in tomato sauce, or seared steak with morel mushrooms.

JUAN-LES-PINS ★★

913km (566 miles) S of Paris; 9.5km (6 miles) S of Cannes

Just west of the Cap d'Antibes, this Art Deco resort burst onto the South of France scene during the 1920s, under the auspices of American property developer Frank Jay Gould. A decade later, Juan-les-Pins was already drawing a chic summer crowd, as the Riviera "season" flipped from winter respites to the hedonistic pursuit of summer sun, sea, and sensuality. It has been attracting the young and the young-at-heart from across Europe and the U.S. ever since. F. Scott Fitzgerald decried Juan-les-Pins as a "constant carnival." His words ring true each and every summer's day.

Essentials

ARRIVING   Juan-les-Pins is connected by rail to most nearby coastal resorts, including Nice (trip time: 30 min.; 5.70€ one-way), Antibes, and Cannes. For further **train information,** visit www.sncf.com or call ✆ **36-35.** A **bus** (www.envibus.fr; ✆ **04-89-87-72-00**) leaves for Juan-les-Pins from Antibes' Pôle d'Echanges (bd. Vautrin) daily every 20 minutes and costs 1€ one-way (trip time: 10 min.). To drive to Juan-les-Pins from

Nice, travel along coastal D6007 south; from Cannes, follow the D6007 north.

VISITOR INFORMATION   The **Office de Tourisme** is at Palais des Congrès, 60 chemin des Sables (www.antibesjuanlespins.com; ✆ **04-22-10-60-01**).

SPECIAL EVENTS   The town offers some of the best nightlife on the Riviera. The action reaches its peak during the annual 10-day **Festival International de Jazz** (www.jazzajuan.com) in mid-July. It attracts jazz, blues, reggae, and world music artists who play nightly on the beachfront Parc de la Pinède. Recent performers have included George Benson, Lenny Kravitz, Norah Jones and Cory Wong. Tickets cost 25€ to 120€ and can be purchased at the Office de Tourisme in both Antibes and Juan-les-Pins, as well as online.

[FastFACTS] JUAN-LES-PINS

ATMs/Banks **BNP Paribas,** 14 av. Maréchal Joffre (✆ **34-77**).

Mail & Postage **La Poste,** 1 av. Maréchal Joffre (✆ **36-31**).

Pharmacies **Pharmacie Provençale,** 144 bd. Président Wilson (✆ **04-93-61-09-23**).

Exploring Juan-les-Pins

Spilling over from Antibes' more residential quarter, Juan-les-Pins is petite—which makes it best navigated on foot. Be sure to swing by the shady square known as **La Pinède** (square Frank Jay Gould) to check out the legions of local *pétanque* players. Nearby, the ultra-contemporary **Antipolis Palais des Congrès,** or Convention Center (www.antipolis-events.com), hosts both year-round international conferences as well as the town's friendly Tourist Office.

Most of us, however, would prefer to give business events a miss in favor of a stroll along the sweeping beachside promenade to Golfe-Juan instead. It was here that Napoleon kicked off his march to Paris and famous Hundred Days in power in 1815. Alternatively, pick a beach bar, order a glass of rosé, and watch the sun drop over the Iles de Lérins.

Outdoor Activities

BEACHES   Part of the reason people flock to Juan-les-Pins is for its wealth of sandy beaches, all lapped by calm waters. The town also basks in a unique microclimate, making it one of the warmest places on the Riviera to soak up the sun, even in winter. **Plage de Juan-les-Pins** is the most central beach, although quieter stretches of sand wrap around the Cap d'Antibes and include family-friendly **Plage de la Salis** and chic **Plage de**

15

THE FRENCH RIVIERA | Fast Facts: Juan-les-Pins

612

la Garoupe. If you do want to stretch out on a sun lounger, go to any of the beach-bar concessions that line the bay, where you can rent a mattress for around 20€ (although prices can stretch up to 135€ for the most exclusive waterfront spots, depending on the venue). Topless sunbathing and overt shows of cosmetic surgery are the norm.

WATERSPORTS If you're interested in scuba diving, try **Easy Dive** (www.easydive.fr; © **04-93-61-26-07**). A one-tank dive costs 50€ to 75€, including all equipment. Sea kayaking, pedalos, and paddleboarding are available at virtually every beach in Juan-les-Pins but are best booked at **Blue Drop** (www.blue-drop.fr; © **06-31-48-30-90**), a friendly establishment that knows all the secret ocean spots. Or explore the coast with Sea-Zen (www.seazen.fr), who offer private tours of Juan-les-Pins aboard solar-powered catamarans, as well as boat rentals. Tours cost from 143€ per hour for up to five people. Waterskiing was invented at the Hôtel Belles-Rives in the 1920s, and it's still a great place to try out the sport.

Where to Stay

Hôtel Belles-Rives ★★★ This luxurious hotel is one of the Riviera's most fabled addresses. It started life in 1925 as a holiday villa rented by Zelda and F. Scott Fitzgerald (as depicted in Fitzgerald's semi-autobiographical novel *Tender Is the Night*). Today, almost a century after her grandparents first opened the Belles-Rives' doors, the elegant Madame Estène-Chauvin owns and oversees this waterside gem. Guest rooms are sumptuous yet eclectic—each one its own unique size and shape. The lower terraces hold garden dining rooms, an elegant bar and lounge, as well as a private jetty. Also on site is the Michelin-starred **La Passagère** restaurant run by superb chef Aurélien Véquaud, who was poached from St-Tropez's three-star eatery La Vague d'Or. Dinner overlooking the shimmering Mediterranean costs from 155€ for five courses. If you're daring, you can even try waterskiing at the waterside Le Belles Rives Ski Nautique Club where, almost a century ago, the sport was invented.

33 bd. Edouard Baudoin. www.bellesrives.com. © **04-93-61-02-79.** 43 units. 160€– 780€ double; from 650€ suite; from 270€ family room; from 330€ cottage. Parking 15€. Closed Jan–early Mar. **Amenities:** 2 summer restaurants; winter restaurant; 2 bars; private beach; room service; free Wi-Fi.

Le 1932 Hotel & Spa Cap d'Antibes—MGallery ★★ Nestled in an unbeatable location between the base of the Cap d'Antibes and Juan-les-Pins' center, this Art Deco edifice is just a 2-minute walk to the beach. The elegant building has been recently restored, returning it to its Golden Age glory. Many guest rooms possess private balconies and sea views, plus original herringbone parquet floors and funky black and white bathrooms. Sun-seekers can ride the elevator to the rooftop Quinto Cielo restaurant, pool and bar, all of which have fabulous views over the annual Festival International de Jazz in the neighboring park.

5 av. Saramartel. www.accor.com. ✆ **04-92-93-54-54.** 64 units. 298€–390€ double; 424€–673€ suite. Parking 29€. **Amenities:** Bar; restaurant; room service; free Wi-Fi.

Where to Eat

La Passagère (see above) offers one of the town's most memorable meals.

Cap Riviera ★★ FRENCH   One of Juan-les-Pins' most appealing attributes is its endless ripple of beachside restaurants, all peering out over the picturesque Iles de Lérins. And Cap Riviera is undoubtedly one of this resort town's finest. Cuisine is seafood-based with a squeeze of French sophistication. Think shrimp flambéed in pastis, lemon-infused sardine rillettes, or sole meunière; staff are charming and attentive. It's well worth popping by in advance to select your own special sea-facing table. Lunchtime diners can also indulge in a 38€ set menu, which may include local specialties like rockfish soup and filet of John Dory.

13 bd. Edouard Baudoin. www.cap-riviera.fr. ✆ **04-93-61-22-30.** Main courses 27€–29€; fixed-price lunch 38€ or dinner 56€. Daily noon–3pm and 8–10pm. Closed Nov to mid–Dec and Jan.

Le Perroquet ★★ PROVENÇAL   One of the best restaurants in Juan-les-Pins, Le Perroquet attracts both casual visitors and longtime locals. The assortiment de poissons grillés—grilled sea bream, John Dory, giant prawns, and red mullet—is an excellent introduction to the best of the Mediterranean; a good-value fixed-price lunch changes daily. The pretty sidewalk seating looks out over La Pinède's Aleppo pines.

9 av. Georges-Gallice. www.restaurantleperroquet.fr. ✆ **04-93-61-02-20.** Main courses 16€–32€; fixed-price lunch 18€ or dinner 37€–45€. Daily noon–2pm and 7–10:30pm. Closed Nov–Dec.

Le Potager ★★ MEDITERRANEAN   Chef Michaël Linlaud creates a delicious mix of pan-Mediterranean delights—each one with a southern French twist—at this friendly restaurant. The menu is seasonal, and dishes range may from gnocchi in arugula pesto to truffled burrata cheese served with a classic local medley of zucchini, eggplant and artichokes. There's an extensive wine list too, with a special selection from chef Michaël's personal cellar. Restaurant décor may be simple, but it allows the cuisine to truly shine.

6 square du Lys. www.restaurant-juan-les-pins.fr. ✆ **09-52-19-48-06.** Main courses 18€–24€; fixed-price menu 37€. June–Sept Wed–Mon 11am–2pm and 6:30–10pm, Tues 6:30–10pm; Oct–May Wed–Sun 11am–2pm and 6:30–10pm.

Nightlife

Embrace the faux-tropical-island experience at **Le Pam Pam,** 137 bd. Wilson (www.pampam.fr; ℐ **04-93-61-11-05**), a time-honored "rhumerie" where guests sip rum and people-watch while reggae beats drift around the bar. More modern is **La Réserve,** 1 bd. de la Pinède (ℐ **04-93-61-20-07**), where a younger crowd sips rosé on leopard-print seats.

If you prefer high-energy partying, you're in the right place. The entire Riviera descends upon Juan-les-Pins' discos every night in summer, and it's best to follow the crowds to the latest hotspot. **Le Village,** 1 bd. de la Pinède (ℐ **04-92-93-90-90**), is one of the more established clubs and boasts an action-packed dance floor with DJs spinning summer sounds from salsa to soul. The cover charge is usually 20€ including one drink; more for themed evenings. For top jazz, head to **Le New Orleans,** 9 av. Georges Gallice (ℐ **04-93-65-53-63**), a buzzing spot with a regular selection of live music.

ANTIBES & CAP D'ANTIBES ★★

913km (566 miles) S of Paris; 21km (13 miles) SW of Nice; 11km (6¾ miles) NE of Cannes

Antibes has a quiet charm unique to the Côte d'Azur. Fishing boats and pleasure yachts fill its harbor. The likes of Picasso and Monet painted its oh-so-pretty streets, today thronged with promenading locals and well-dressed visitors. A pedestrianized town center makes it a family-friendly destination as well, and a perfect place for an evening stroll. An excellent covered market is also located near the harbor, open every morning except Mondays.

Spiritually, Antibes is totally divorced from Cap d'Antibes, a peninsula studded with the villas of the super-rich. But the less affluent are welcome to peek at paradise, and a lovely 6km (3¾ miles) coastal path rings the headland, passing picnic and diving spots en route.

Essentials

ARRIVING   Trains from Cannes arrive at the rail station, pl. Pierre-Semard, every 20 minutes (trip time: 15 min.); the one-way fare is 3.30€. Around 25 trains arrive from Nice daily (trip time: 20 min.); the one-way fare is 5.20€. For further train information, visit www.sncf-connect.com or call ℐ **36-35.** The **Pôle d'Echanges d'Antibes,** bd. Vautrin (www.envibus.fr; ℐ **04-89-87-72-00**), offers bus service throughout the region.

To drive to Antibes from Nice, travel along coastal D6007 south; from Cannes, follow the D6007 north. The Cap d'Antibes is clearly visible from most parts of the Riviera. To drive here from Antibes, follow the coastal road south—you can't miss it.

VISITOR INFORMATION The **Office de Tourisme** is at Place Guynemer (www.antibesjuanlespins.com; ☏ **04-22-10-60-01**).

[FastFACTS] ANTIBES

ATMs/Banks Among others, there are half a dozen banks dotted along av. Robert Soleau.

Mail & Postage **La Poste,** 2 av. Paul Doumer (☏ **36-31**).

Pharmacies **Grande Pharmacie d'Antibes,** 2 pl. Guynemer (☏ **04-93-34-16-12**).

Exploring Antibes

Antibes' largely pedestrianized Old Town—all pale stone homes, weaving lanes, and window boxes of colorful flowers—is easily explored on foot. The highlights are undoubtedly a dip into Picasso's former home, now a museum, and a stroll along the bling-tastic pleasure port, where artist Jaume Plensa's giant *Nomad* sculpture shimmers in the night.

The town is also skirted by wonderful walking trails. It's an easy stroll around the ancient walls of the 16th-century **Fort Carré,** just north of Antibes's port. Alternatively, like all of the prominent peninsulas on the French Riviera, the Cap d'Antibes boasts a scenic hiking trail around its perimeter. Highlights include the rustic coastal path south of Plage de la Garoupe, as well as a stop—if you can time it correctly—at the **Villa Eilenroc,** 460 av. L.D. Beaumont (☏ **04-93-67-74-33**). The latter is where Woody Allen directed *Magic in the Moonlight,* the Riviera romp starring Emma Stone and Colin Firth. The garden and villa are currently open to the public on Wednesdays and Saturdays from 10am to 4pm, but check the tourism office website before you visit. Admission is 2€, free for children 11 and under.

Musée Picasso ★★ ART MUSEUM Perched on the Old Town's ramparts, the 14th-century Château Grimaldi was home to Picasso in 1946, when the Spanish artist lived and worked here at the invitation of the municipality. Upon his departure, he gifted all the work he'd completed to the château museum: 44 drawings and 23 paintings, including the famous La Joie de Vivre. In addition to this permanent collection inside the kooky building, contemporary artworks by Joan Miró, Arman, and Modigliani, among many others, are also on display. In 2023, the museum's exhibition *Picasso 1969–1972: The End of the Beginning* was one of 50 international Picasso shows that celebrated the 50th anniversary of the artist's death.

Château Grimaldi, pl. Mariejol. ☏ **04-92-90-54-28.** Admission 8€ adults; 6€ students and seniors; free for children 17 and under. Mid-June to mid-Sept Tues–Sun 10am–6pm; mid-Sept to mid-June Tues–Sun 10am–1pm and 2–6pm.

Artworks and an ocean view atop the Musée Picasso.

Posidonia-Espace Mer et Littoral ★ MARITIME CENTER
Located within this stone-sided fort and tower on the Cap d'Antibes, built
in stages as a coastal gunnery battery the 17th and 18th centuries, is a
child-friendly space focusing on the coastal flora and fauna of the region.
A permanent exhibition covers Mediterranean habitats, an aquarium and
the miliary history of the fort. Visitors keen to escape the crowds will revel
in the center's seaside park (which overlooks the grounds of the ultra-
exclusive Hôtel du Cap–Eden-Roc!). The center also organizes fun, scientific **snorkeling trips** (25€ per adult; 15€ per child up to 16 years old; plus
an additional 6€ per person payable at the entrance to the Espace Mer et
Littoral to access the site; www.graillon-aquarando.com) around the pristine Cap d'Antibes.
Rampe du Graillon, 175 bd. J.F. Kennedy. ℂ **04-93-61-45-32.** Admission 12€ adults;
6€ for children ages 7–17; free for children 6 and under. June–Sept Tues–Sun 10am–
7pm; Apr–May and Oct Tues–Sun 10am–5pm; Nov–Mar Tues–Sat 10am–5pm.

Where to Stay

Hôtel du Cap–Eden-Roc ★★★ This legendary hotel debuted in
1887, serving as a Mediterranean getaway for visitors seeking winter sunshine. Over the intervening years, it's played host to the world's most

famous clientele, from the Duke and Duchess of Windsor (who escaped here after the former king's abdication) to the Hollywood superstars who cavort at the Vanity Fair Cannes Film Festival party, which welcomed Robert De Niro, Storm Reid, Bryan Cranston and Naomi Campbell in 2023. Surrounded by a maze of manicured gardens, accommodation is among the most sumptuous on the Riviera. The hotel's suites were renovated in 2023, and now boast a light and airy seaside theme, while the Villa Sainte-Anne, complete with private swimming pool, is the largest of the hotel's accommodation options. Guests lounge by the seawater swimming pool, carved from natural basalt rock, and evenings are spent at the panoramic **Restaurant Eden-Roc** or the **Bellini Bar** (don't miss the signature Eden-Roc Splash cocktail, a heady mix of rosé Champagne, cognac, and raspberries). Signature treatments at the onsite spa come courtesy of Dior.

Bd. J.F. Kennedy. www.hotel-du-cap-eden-roc.com. ✆ **04-93-61-39-01.** 118 units. From 680€ double. Closed mid-Oct to mid-Apr. **Amenities:** 2 restaurants; 3 bars; babysitting; exercise room; massage; outdoor pool; room service; spa; tennis, free Wi-Fi.

La Villa Fabulite ★★ A fabulously friendly hotel a 5-minute stroll from the Hôtel du Cap–Eden-Roc…without the 1,000€ price tag. This leafy estate with wild gardens and naturally heated pool is housed on the site of a former diving school. That means it's close to all the Cap d'Antibes' elite—yet publicly accessible—beaches. Rooms aren't large but they are chic and functional, with a private terrace apiece. Better still is wide range of activities, including mountain biking and paddleboarding around the peninsula.

150 Traverse des Nielles, Cap d'Antibes. www.fabulite.com. ✆ **04-93-61-47-45.** 12 units. 200€–256€ double; 342€–629€ suite. Closed Nov to mid-Apr. Parking 25€. **Amenities:** Garden; bar; massage; restaurant; free Wi-Fi.

Where to Eat

The Zelda and Scott Fitzgeralds of today head for the **Restaurant Eden-Roc** at the Hôtel du Cap-Eden-Roc for grand service and grand cuisine. Alternatively, the excellent **Restaurant de Bacon,** bd. de Bacon (www.maisondebacon.fr; ✆ **04-93-61-50-02**), has served the best seafood around for more than 7 decades. For light bites and unusual local wines, stop into **Entre 2 Vins,** 2 rue James Close (✆ **04-93-34-46-93**).

La Closerie ★★ FRENCH A top-notch pâtisserie and lunchtime restaurant with a sun-dappled courtyard tucked alongside, Le Closerie turns out the tastiest éclairs, macarons and millefeuilles in town. Lunchtime ingredients, including zucchini flowers, Cavaillon melon and cœur de bœuf tomatoes, are all local, and everything in the restaurant and on the pâtisserie menu is made in house. An idyllic spot for an early morning café crème and pastry, or an unhurried, market-fresh meal.

8 bd. Dugommier. www.lacloserieantibes.com. ℰ **04-93-34-09-92.** Main courses 14€–29€; desserts 7.50€–9.50€. Pâtisserie Mon–Sat 8am–6pm. Restaurant Mon–Sat noon–3pm.

Le Vauban ★★ FRENCH   Chef Thierry Aix describes his restaurant as "semi-gourmet." Which means diners enjoy the extravagant flavors and presentation of an exclusive gastronomic eatery—but at affordable prices. The cuisine is seasonal, contemporary and very creative. The menu may include fine de claire oysters and poached quail eggs on a bed of cucumber jelly, or veal tartare with tuna sauce served alongside chickpea panisse fries. Staff are friendly, and the restaurant is extremely popular, so be sure to book in advance.

7 bis rue Thuret. www.levauban.fr. ℰ **04-93-34-33-05.** Main courses 22€–42€; lunch menu 27€; dinner menu 47€–55€. Wed–Sun 12:15–1:45pm and 7:15–9:30pm.

DAY TRIP FROM ANTIBES

Biot ★

6.5km (4 miles) NW of Antibes

Biot has been famous for its pottery since merchants began to ship earthenware jars to Phoenicia and throughout the Mediterranean. It's also where Fernand Léger painted until the day he died, leaving a magnificent collection of his work on display just outside town.

ESSENTIALS

Bus no. 10 from Antibes's pl. Guynemer (www.envibus.fr; ℰ **04-89-87-72-00**) runs to Biot's town center. Tickets cost 1€. To drive to Biot from Antibes, follow D6007 east, then head west on the D4.

Biot's **Office de Tourisme** is at 4 chemin Neuf (www.biot-tourisme. com; ℰ **04-93-65-78-00**).

EXPLORING BIOT

Exploration of Biot's small historic center begins at place des Arcades, where you can see the 16th-century gates and the remains of the town's ramparts. The **Musée d'Histoire et Céramique Biotoise,** 9 rue St-Sebastien (www.musee-de-biot.fr; ℰ **04-93-65-54-54**), has assembled the best works from local artists, potters, ceramists, painters, and silver- and goldsmiths. Hours are July to September Wednesday to Sunday 10am to 6pm, and October to June Wednesday to Sunday 2 to 6pm. Admission is 4€, 2€ for seniors and students, and free for children 16 and under.

Outside of town, the excellent **Musée National Fernand Léger** ★★, 255 chemin du Val de Pôme (www.musees-nationaux-alpesmaritimes.fr/fleger; ℰ **04-93-53-87-20**), displays a comprehensive collection of the artist's colorful creations, from 1930s Cubist ladies to circus scenes of the 1950s. Some 400 sq. m (4,305 sq. ft.) of mosaics, while modernistic stained-glass windows pour light inside. Hours are Wednesday to Monday May to October 10am to 6pm, November to April 10am to 5pm. Admission is 5.50€, 4€ for students and seniors, and free for ages 25 and under. Also on site are temporary exhibitions and a cafe garden.

In the late 1940s, local glassmakers created a hand-blown, bubble-flecked glass known as verre rustique. You'll easily spot its brilliant cobalts and emeralds while window shopping in town. To learn how it is made, head to La Verrerie de Biot and its **Écomusée du Verre** (www.verreriebiot.com; ℂ **04-93-65-03-00**). Throughout summer, it's open Monday to Saturday 10am to 7pm, and Sundays 10.30am to 1.30pm, and 2.30pm to 7pm. During the rest of the year, it opens Monday to Saturday 10am to 1pm and 2 to 6pm, and Sundays 10:30am to 1:30pm and 2:30 to 6pm. The museum displays both traditional tools and outlines modern glassblowing techniques, and there are frequent demonstrations. Entry is free, while workshops start at 4€ per person.

The famed verre rustic glassware of Biot.

WHERE TO EAT

For a Provençal take on crêpes—such as summery tomato, olive tapenade with basil or the house specialty, crêpe-pizza—stop in to **Crêperie Auberge du Village,** 29 rue St-Sébastien (ℂ **04-93-65-72-73**). This low-key lunch spot sits at the northern end of Biot's main shopping street.

ESPECIALLY FOR KIDS

Just south of Biot sits a kid-tastic complex of theme parks. **Aquasplash** (www.aquasplash.fr) has more than 2km (1¼ miles) of waterslides, including toboggan-style Rainbow Cannon and the Side Winder. **Adventure Golf** (www.marineland.fr) is criss-crossed by two dinosaur-dotted miniature golf courses. And, newest of the bunch, **Kid's Island** (www.marineland.fr) caters to animal-loving little ones, with pony rides and a petting zoo, plus plenty of jungle gyms and a Magic River. Admission is as follows: Aquasplash 32.90€, 26.90€ children between 3 and 12; Adventure Golf 11.50€, 10€ children between 3 and 12; and Kid's Island 14€, 11€ children between 3 and 12. All are free for children 2 and under. Aquasplash, Adventure Golf, and Kid's Island all have varying opening hours, which stretch right into the evening in summer. In all cases, booking a ticket online before you visit saves around 30% on the same day ticket.

ST-PAUL-DE-VENCE ★★

926km (574 miles) S of Paris; 23km (14 miles) E of Grasse; 28km (17 miles) E of Cannes; 31km (19 miles) N of Nice

Of all the hilltop villages of the Riviera, St-Paul-de-Vence is by far the most famous. It gained popularity in the 1940s and '50s, when artists including Picasso, Chagall, and Matisse frequented the town, trading their paintings for hospitality at the Colombe d'Or inn. Art is now the town's principal attraction, and the winding streets are studded with artists' ateliers, contemporary galleries, and museums. Circling the town are magnificent old ramparts that overlook flowers and olive and orange trees.

A narrow street of shops and art galleries in St-Paul-de-Vence.

Allow about 30 minutes to an hour to walk the full loop, including the new **Henri Layet Fortifications Discovery Walk** at the base of the western ramparts, which details St-Paul's history, architecture, and agricultural heritage with multi-lingual plaques on the walls of the ancient town.

Essentials

ARRIVING   The nearest rail station is in Cagnes-sur-Mer. From here, **buses** (no. 655) depart every 30 minutes, dropping passengers off in St-Paul-de-Vence (1.70€ one-way, trip time: 30 min.), then in Vence 10 minutes later. Bus (no. 9) also leaves from Nice every 15 minutes, dropping passengers off in Vence (1.70€ one-way, trip time: 1 hr.), from where you can hop aboard bus no. 655 down to St-Paul-de-Vence (trip time: 10 min.). For information, contact **Lignes d'Azur** (www.lignesdazur.com; *C* **08-10-06-10-06**). If you're driving from Nice, take either the A8 highway or the coastal route du Bord du Mer west, turn inland at Cagnes-sur-Mer, and follow signs north to St-Paul-de-Vence.

VISITOR INFORMATION   The **Office de Tourisme** is at 2 rue Grande (www.saint-pauldevence.com; *C* **04-93-32-86-95**).

Getting Around

St-Paul's Old Town is entirely pedestrianized, and most of the narrow streets are paved in cobblestones. Since driving a car here is prohibited, except to drop off luggage at an Old Town hotel by prior arrangement only. The Fondation Maeght is around half a mile out of town.

[FastFACTS]
ST-PAUL-DE-VENCE

ATMs/Banks **BNP Paribas,** rd-pt Sainte Claire (*C* **34-77**).

Mail & Postage **La Poste,** rd-pt Sainte Claire (*C* **36-31**).

Pharmacies **Pharmacie Saint Paul,** rd-pt Sainte Claire (*C* **04-93-32-80-78**).

Exploring St-Paul

Perched at the top of the village, the **Collégiale de la Conversion de St-Paul** ★ was constructed in the 12th and 13th centuries and has been much altered over the years. The Romanesque choir is the oldest part, containing some remarkable stalls carved in walnut in the 17th century. Look to the left as you enter: You'll see the painting Ste-Cathérine d'Alexandrie, which has been attributed to Tintoretto. The Trésor de l'Eglise is one of the most beautiful in the Alpes-Maritimes, with a spectacular ciborium.

Look also for a low relief of the Martyrdom of St-Clément on the last altar on the right. It's open Monday to Friday 8:15am to 4:15pm, Saturday and Sunday 10am to 6pm. Admission is free.

Just around the corner is the light-flooded **Chapelle des Pénitents Blanc ★★ (📞 04-93-32-41-13)**. The artist Jean-Michel Folon, who worked on this masterpiece until his death in 2005, decorated the church with modern stained-glass windows, shimmering mosaics, and rainbow-hued frescos—the 17th century meets the 21st. It's open mid-April to mid-October daily 10am to 12:30pm and 2 to 6pm, and mid-October to mid-November and December to April daily from 10am to 12:30pm and 2 to 5pm. Admission is 3€ adults, 9€ for a family ticket (two adults and two children over 12 years), and free for children 12 and under.

Fondation Maeght ★★★ ART MUSEUM   A museum you would travel thousands of miles to visit. Established by Parisian art dealers Aimé and Marguerite Maeght in 1964, this avant-garde building houses one of the most impressive modern art collections in Europe. It was Spanish architect José Luis Sert who designed the pagoda-like exhibition space, ensuring the artwork it displays sits in perfect harmony with the surrounding pine-studded woods. In the gardens, colorful Alexander Calder installations are clustered with skinny bronze sculptures by Alberto Giacometti. A rotating selection of artworks is displayed over the various levels inside, showcasing key pieces by artists like Matisse, Chagall, Bonnard, and Léger. Each year the museum stages a large seasonal show, including *Jean Paul Riopelle—Essence of Studios* in 2023, part of the "Riopelle 100" celebrations, with exclusive artworks loaned from around the world to coincide with the centenary of the abstract impressionist's birth. In celebration of the Fondation's 60th anniversary, summer 2024 will see the inauguration of two brand-new galleries, designed by architect Silvio d'Ascia and overlooking the surrounding pine forests.

623 chemin des Gardettes, outside the town walls. www.fondation-maeght.com. 📞 **04-93-32-81-63.** Admission 16€ adults; 11€ students and ages 10–18; free for children 9 and under. July–Aug daily 10am–7pm; Sept–June daily 10am–6pm.

Organized Tours

With advance booking, the local tourist office offers 8 different walking tours of the town's historic core and outskirts. Themed tours (8.50€–20€, free for children under 12 or under 6, depending on the tour) last around 1 hour. They include following in the footsteps of former resident Marc Chagall, trying your hand at the beloved Provençal pastime of pétanque (also known as boules) under the instruction of accomplished locals, or the brand-new back in time, virtual reality tour. Almost all tours are given in both English and French.

Where to Stay

La Colombe d'Or rents deluxe rooms (see "Where to Eat," below). Note that Vence's hotels are less expensive than those on the coast, a short bus ride away, while the town makes an accessible base for exploring St-Paul-de-Vence, too.

Domaine du Mas de Pierre ★★ The most relaxed hotel on the St-Paul scene is a vision of Provençal elegance, surrounded by manicured grounds studded with contemporary art, orchids, roses, and the hotel's own vegetable garden. It's about 2km (1¼ miles) from the village center—walkable but a taxi home after a night of rosé and fine dining is recommended. Completely revamped in 2021, this luxury hotel boasts a family-friendly vibe: eating in jeans and a jacket inside the superb Table de Pierre restaurant, or outside on its poolside terrace, is completely acceptable. The Mediterranean gardens loop around the hotel, extensive spa and three outdoor swimming pools. The latter range from the thatched huts and playful sands of the Lagoon (with adjacent Kids' Club) to a chic, adults-only space.

2320 route de Serres. www.lemasdepierre.com. ✆ **04-93-59-00-10.** 76 units. 195€–1,250€ double; from 342€ suite. Free parking. **Amenities:** 2 restaurants; bar; 3 outdoor pools; spa; free Wi-Fi.

La Vague de Saint-Paul ★★★ La Vague filled a glaring gap in the St-Paul accommodations market when it opened just over a decade ago: an affordable hotel for art lovers seeking country tranquility and wow-factor design. The wavelike main hotel building was originally conceived by far-out architect André Minangoy in the 1960s. Color-coded guest rooms look out onto a vast garden complete with pétanque run, tennis court, bar, and pool. During the summer, private yoga lessons are offered among the olive trees in the surrounding gardens. The attached restaurant is overseen by accomplished Chef Akhara Chay, who delivers a mix of French and Asian flavors on his seasonal set menus (39€–90€). The complex sits a short walk from the Fondation Maeght contemporary art museum—and a longer stroll through the forest to St-Paul-de-Vence village via a secret trail. Check the website for fabulous low season offers, with rates for 3 nights for the price of 2.

Chemin des Salettes. www.vaguesaintpaul.com. ✆ **04-920-11-20-00.** 37 units. 170€–240€ double; from 290€ suite. Free parking. **Amenities:** Restaurant; bar; concierge; outdoor pool; room service; spa; tennis; free Wi-Fi.

Where to Eat

St-Paul's petite size means that dining options are limited and may also be pricey. That said, the views and the ambience of pretty much any local eatery often make up for these shortcomings.

La Brouette ★★ SCANDINAVIAN   This Scandinavian restaurant has become an institution in St-Paul-de-Vence. For over 4 decades, La Brouette has been cooking local ingredients, especially seafood and mushrooms, in true Danish style. That means fish comes smoked not grilled, and though wine is served, *bien sur,* many patrons choose to sip jam jar smoothies containing lavender honey and kefir instead. Also notable: bargain prices (a rarity in this historic village), a lovely outdoor terrace in summer, and a raging fire in winter. *Note:* For those with allergies, they serve gluten-free breads.

830 route de Cagnes. www.la-brouette.fr. ✆ **04-93-58-67-16.** Main courses 10€–20€. Fixed-price lunch 17€ or dinner 25€–35€. June–Sept daily noon–2pm and 7:30–10pm; Oct–May Tues–Sun noon–2pm and 7:30–10pm.

La Colombe d'Or ★★ PROVENÇAL   This celebrated restaurant opened its doors in 1920. At the time it was little more than a scattering of tables overlooking an overgrown artichoke patch. It was Paul Roux, the restaurant's art-adoring owner, who encouraged the era's struggling artists, such as Raoul Dufy, Paul Signac, and Chaime Soutine, to swap a canvas or two for generous room and board. Picasso, Braque, and Miró followed—and today La Colombe d'Or's private art collection is one of the finest in the world. For a peek at these masterpieces, you'll need to dine here, either indoors beneath works by the likes of Signac, Matisse, and Braque or outdoors on the fig-trimmed terrace. The colorful handwritten menu, which has barely changed in a century, is famous for its selection of fresh starters (such as crudités with anchoïade, a traditional anchovy dip), and crispy roast chicken. It also offers 25 luxurious accommodations in the original 16th-century stone house and the two 1950s wings. Prices are 385€ for a double, 530€ for a suite.

1 pl. du Général-de-Gaulle. www.la-colombe-dor.com. ✆ **04-93-32-80-02.** Main courses 20€–65€. Daily noon–2pm and 7:30–10pm. Closed late Oct to 3rd week of Dec and 10 days in Jan.

Shopping

The pedestrian-only rue Grande is St-Paul's most evocative street, running the length of the town. Most of the stone houses along it are from the 16th and 17th centuries, and several still bear the coats of arms placed there by the original builders. Today many of the houses are antiques shops, arts-and-crafts galleries, and souvenir and gift shops; some are still artists' studios.

   Galerie du Vieux Saint-Paul, 16 rue Grande (www.galeries-bartoux. com; ✆ **04-93-32-74-50**), is the place to pick up serious art, from sculptures by local artist Arman to bronze works by Salvador Dalí. Just down the road, **Galerie Capricorne,** 64 rue Grande (www.galeriecapricorne. com; ✆ **04-93-58-34-42**), offers a colorful array of prints, including a selection by Marc Chagall. Nearby **Atelier Silvia B,** 11 pl. de la Mairie (www.silviabertini.com; ✆ **06-75-21-68-85**), is packed with bright collages of St-Paul. Tasty souvenirs include herb, spice, and Camargue salt blends from **L'Herbier en Provence - Florence Tholance,** 7 descente de la Castre (✆ **04-93-32-91-51**), and organic olive oils and honeys, plus Provencal linens, from **Le Goût du Soleil,** 63 rue Grande (✆ **04-23-20-85-60**).

VENCE ★

926km (574 miles) S of Paris; 31km (19 miles) N of Cannes; 24km (15 miles) NW of Nice

Often bypassed in favor of nearby St-Paul-de-Vence, the pretty village of Vence is well worth a detour. Its pale stone Old Town is atmospheric yet untouristy, splashed with shady squares and pavement cafes. The highlight is undoubtedly Matisse's Chapelle du Rosaire, set among a countryside studded with cypresses, olive trees, and oleanders.

Essentials

ARRIVING   Frequent buses (no. 09) originating near Nice Airport take 50 minutes to reach Vence, passing the nearest rail station in Cagnes-sur-Mer, about 10km (6¼ miles) southwest from Vence, en route. The one-way fare is 1.70€. For bus information, contact **Lignes d'Azur** (www.lignesdazur.com; ✆ **08-10-06-10-06**). For train information, visit www.sncf-connect.com or call ✆ **36-35.** To drive to Vence from Nice, take D6007 west to Cagnes-sur-Mer, and then D36 north to Vence. Visitors with sturdy legs can also hike mostly downhill from Vence to St-Paul-de-Vence; but it's tough going in the opposite direction.

VISITOR INFORMATION   The **Office de Tourisme** is on place due Grand-Jardin (www.vence-tourisme.com; ✆ **04-93-58-06-38**).

[FastFACTS] VENCE

ATMs/Banks   Vence has many banks, including **BNP Paribas,** 28 pl. du Grand-Jardin (✆ **08-20-82-00-01**).

Mail & Postage   **La Poste,** pl. Clemenceau (✆ **36-31**).

Pharmacies   **Pharmacie du Grand-Jardin,** 30 pl. du Grand-Jardin (✆ **04-93-58-00-39**).

Exploring Vence

Vence's medieval *Vieille Ville* (Old Town) is compact, making it easy to explore on foot. A poke around its picturesque squares reveals place du

Peyra's bubbling *Vieille Fontaine* (Old Fountain), while nearby the **Châ-teau de Villeneuve/Fondation Emile Hugues,** 2 pl. du Frêne (www.museedevence.fr; ☏ **04-93-58-15-78**), is a temporary exhibition space dedicated to 20th-century art. Also inside sits a **permanent Matisse collection** of items owned by city hall including lithographs and plates from his "Jazz" series. Hours are Tuesday to Sunday 11am to 6pm. Admission is 6€ for adults, 3€ for students, and free for children under 12. Also in the Old Town is **place Godeau,** where the **mosaic** *Moses Saved from the Nile* by Marc Chagall adorns the 11th-century **cathedral**'s baptistery (free).

Vence's main draw, however, lies just outside the fortified main town. The Chapelle du Rosaire represents one of Matisse's most remarkable achievements.

Chapelle du Rosaire ★★ RELIGIOUS SITE   From the age of 47, Henri Matisse made Nice his home. But Vence held a special place in the artist's heart: It was his place of residence during World War II, as well as home to Dominican nun Sister Jacques-Marie, Matisse's former nurse and muse. So in 1947, when Matisse discovered that the sisters were planning the construction of a new chapel, he offered not only to design it, but fund the project as well. Matisse was 77 at the time. Not to mention an atheist too.

The Chapelle du Rosaire was completed in 1951. A beautifully bright space, it offers the exceptional possibility of stepping into a three-dimensional artwork. As Sir Nicholas Serota, former director of London's Tate gallery claimed: "It has to be one of the great works made anywhere at any time. Sistine Ceiling or Vence Chapel? I wouldn't want to choose between the two." Truly, visit to commune with one of the leading works from one of the greatest artists of all time.

From the front of the chapel, you may find the structure unremarkable and pass it by—until you spot a 12m (39-ft.) crescent-adorned cross rising from a blue-tile roof. Within, dozens of stained-glass windows shimmer cobalt blue (symbolizing the sea), sapphire green (the landscape), and golden yellow (the sun). Most remarkable are the 14 black-and-white-tile Stations of the Cross, featuring Matisse's self-styled "tormented and passionate" figures.

The bishop of Nice came to bless the chapel in the late spring of 1951; Matisse died 3 years later.

466 av. Henri-Matisse. www.chapellematisse.com. ☏ **04-93-58-03-26.** Admission 7€ adults; contributions to maintain the chapel are welcome; free for children ages 12 and under. Mar–Oct Tues and Thurs–Fri 10–11:30am and 2–5:30pm, Wed and Sat 2–5:30pm; Nov–Feb Tues and Thurs–Fri 10–11:30am and 2–4:30pm, Wed and Sat 2–4:30pm. Closed late Nov to mid-Dec.

15

THE FRENCH RIVIERA

Vence

Where to Stay

Note that St-Paul-de-Vence's hotels also make an excellent base for exploring Vence, and vice versa.

Cantermerle Hotel ★★   Just south of Vence's Old Town, this hotel, restaurant, and spa is set within 1.2 hectares (3 acres) of lush gardens. Spacious guest rooms feature terra-cotta tile floors and Provençal fabrics; many also boast their own private terrace. At the gourmet restaurant **La Table du Cantemerle,** chef Benjamin Bourgoin, who has a keen focus on locally sourced ingredients, dishes up grilled Aveyron lamb in a parsley crust and lobster ravioli in the elegant dining room or outdoors alongside the pool. Best value is the 33€ two-course weekday lunch menu (more expensive in the evening and on weekends). Use of the spa's heated indoor pool, mosaic Turkish baths, and fitness area is complimentary for guests.
258 chemin Cantemerle. www.cantemerle-hotel-vence.com. ℰ **04-93-58-08-18.** 27 units. 190€–295€ double; 291€–785€ suite. Closed Nov–Mar. **Amenities:** Restaurant; 2 bars; outdoor pool; spa; free Wi-Fi.

La Victoire ★★   Slap bang on Vence's main square, La Victoire is a hop away from every site and transport link. It wins top marks for friendliness and local advice—staff can source a driver, an airport journey, or tickets to a concert. Of course, room sizes are reflective of the bargain price but all are clean and comfortable if simply furnished, with a desk and air conditioning in each. And it's more fun to eat breakfast in the buzzing boulevard outside rather than pay 9.50€ for the indoor dining room experience. In short, a rare Riviera bargain and a great base from which to explore the area.
4 place du Grand Jardin. www.hotel-victoire.com. ℰ **04-93-24-15-54.** 15 units. 78€–121€ double. **Amenities:** Bar; free Wi-Fi.

Where to Eat

Vence's unpretentious attitude is also evident in the local cuisine. It tends to be traditional, tasty, dished up in a sublime setting (often), and frequently cheaper than on the coast. Fancier Michelin-starred eats are also available.

Auberge des Seigneurs ★★ PROVENÇAL   A generations-old restaurant housed in a former post office that sings with rural cooking. Within a medieval interior salon (imagine Louis XVI is coming to dinner) find a large fireplace, where hunks of meat are charred from autumn through spring. Summer dishes are lighter, like zucchini flowers stuffed with scallops. The sensational order is a saddle of lamb (27€), seasonally served with asparagus and a skewer of potatoes. A timeless country classic since 1916. The hotel also has six rural-chic **guest rooms** from 75€ to 110€.
1 rue du Docteur Binet. www.auberge-seigneurs.fr. ℰ **04-93-58-04-24.** Main courses 17€–27€; fixed-price menu dinner 28€-39€. Tues–Sat noon–2pm and 7–10pm.

NICE ★★★

929km (576 miles) S of Paris; 32km (20 miles) NE of Cannes

Nice is known as the "Queen of the Riviera" and is the largest city on this fabled stretch of coast. It's also one of the most ancient, founded by the Greeks, who called it Nike (Victory). By the 19th century, Russian aristocrats and the British upper class—led by Queen Victoria herself—were sojourning here. These days Nice is not as chichi as Cannes or St-Tropez. But it does have more global dining and high culture than its neighbors, with many free-to-enter historic sites. In fact, the city has more museums than any other French city outside Paris.

It's also the most economical place to base yourself on the Riviera, especially if you're dependent on public transportation. Getting around is now easier than ever. From 2020 a new tram whizzed from Nice Airport right into the city center and Port. Also from the airport, which is the second busiest in France, you can travel by train or bus along the entire coast to resorts such as Cannes, Antibes, Juan-les-Pins, and Monaco. It's also possible to catch a train to San Remo, a glamorous town over the Italian border, have lunch, then return to Nice by nightfall.

A typically colorful street in Nice.

Because of its brilliant sunshine and liberal attitude, Nice has long attracted notable thinkers and artists, among them Friedrich Nietzsche, Gustave Flaubert, and Elton John. Henri Matisse, who made his home in Nice, said, "Though the light is intense, it's also soft and tender." The city averages 300 sunny days a year.

Essentials

ARRIVING Trains arrive at the city's main station, Gare Nice-Ville, avenue Thiers. From here you can take trains to Cannes for 7.90€, Monaco for 4.40€, and Antibes for 5.20€, with easy connections to Paris, Marseille, and anywhere else along the Mediterranean coast. For more information, visit www.sncf-connect.com or call 𝄐 **36-35.**

Buses (www.lignesdazur.com; 𝄐 **08-10-06-10-06**) to towns east, including Monaco (no. 100) depart from place Garibaldi; to towns west, including Cannes (no. 200) from Jardin Albert I. Tickets to all French Riviera destinations under 74 minutes away (which may include a change of buses) cost 1.70€.

Intercontinental, European, and domestic flights land at **Aéroport Nice–Côte d'Azur** (www.nice.aeroport.fr; 𝄐 **08-20-42-33-33**). From there, tram lines (no. 2) departs at 20-minute intervals for the city center and Port, passing near most of Nice's hotels enroute; the one-way fare is 1.70€. Trip time is about 25 minutes. Official taxis are not cheap. A ride from the airport to the city center costs around 50€; **Uber taxis** are less than half the price. Drive time is about 20 minutes.

Ferryboats operated by **Trans-Côte d'Azur** (www.trans-cote-azur. com; 𝄐 **04-92-00-42-30**), on quai Lunel on Nice's port, link the city with Ile Ste-Marguerite (p. 603; 45€) and St-Tropez (74€) from May to September.

VISITOR INFORMATION Nice maintains four **tourist offices.** The largest is at 5 promenade des Anglais, near place Masséna (www.nice tourisme.com; 𝄐 **08-92-70-74-07**). Additional offices are in the Promenade du Paillon city center park, in the arrivals hall of the Aéroport Nice–Côte d'Azur, and outside the railway station on avenue Thiers.

CITY LAYOUT The city is divided into five main neighborhoods: the **Italianate Old Town;** the **vintage port;** the **commercial city center** between place Masséna and the main train station; the affluent residential quarter known as the **Carre d'Or,** just inland from the promenade des Anglais; and **hilltop Cimiez,** where several museums are located. All are easy to navigate on foot, with the exception of Cimiez. For more, see "Exploring Nice," p. 633.

SPECIAL EVENTS The **Nice Carnaval** (www.nicecarnaval.com), known as the "Mardi Gras of the Riviera," runs from mid-February to early

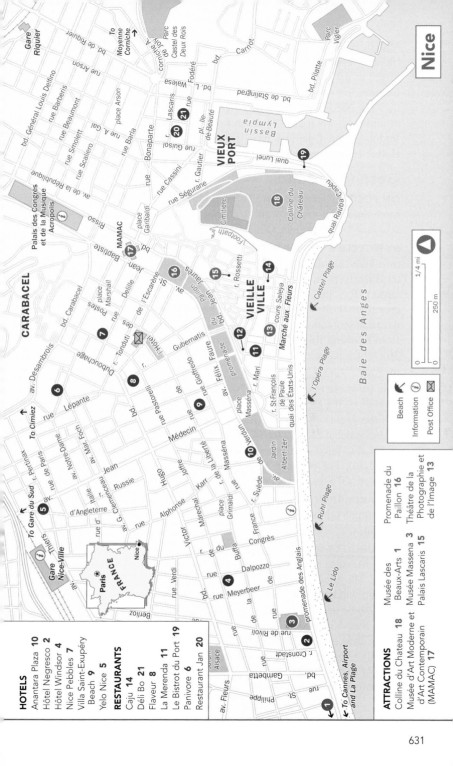

Nice

HOTELS
Anantara Plaza **10**
Hôtel Negresco **2**
Hôtel Windsor **4**
Nice Pebbles **7**
Villa Saint-Exupéry
  Beach **9**
Yelo Nice **5**

RESTAURANTS
Caju **14**
Déli Bo **21**
Flaveur **8**
La Merenda **11**
Le Bistrot du Port **19**
Panivore **6**
Restaurant Jan **20**

ATTRACTIONS
Colline du Chateau **18**
Musée d'Art Moderne et
  d'Art Contemporain
  (MAMAC) **17**
Musée des
  Beaux-Arts **1**
Musée Massena **3**
Palais Lascaris **15**
Promenade du
  Paillon **16**
Théâtre de la
  Photographie et
  de l'Image **13**

Beach ⚓
Information ⓘ
Post Office ⊠

1/4 mi
250 m

Baie des Anges

VIEUX PORT

VIEILLE VILLE

CARABACEL

Marché aux Fleurs

March, celebrating the return of spring with 3 weeks of parades, corsi (floats), veglioni (masked balls), confetti, and battles in which flowers are tossed at the audience. The theme for the 2024 event was "King of Pop Culture."

The **Nice Festival du Jazz** (www.nicejazzfestival.fr) runs for a week in mid-July, when jazz, funk, and reggae artists perform al fresco in the Jardins Albert I gardens near the seafront. Recent performers included Herbie Hancock and Sir Tom Jones.

Getting Around

ON FOOT Nice is very walkable, and no point of interest downtown is more than a 10-minute walk from place Massena, including the seafront promenade des Anglais, Old Town, and yacht-filled harbor.

BY BICYCLE & MOTOR SCOOTER Like many French cities, Nice has its own bike-sharing scheme, **Vélo Bleu** (www.velobleu.org). You can register directly at one of Nice's 161 bike stands (difficult) or online (much easier); fees range from free (for the first hour) with a 3€ registration charge to 7€ for a week. Alternatively, you can rent bikes (from 18€ per day) and scooters (from 26€ per day; driver's license and deposit required) from **Booking Bikes,** 6 rue Massenet (www.loca-bike.fr; © 04-93-04-15-36), which has additional rental offices in Cannes and Antibes.

BY CAR Rental agencies for gas and electric cars are sited around Nice. **Sixt** (www.sixt.fr; © 01-70-97-61-11) ranks among the most centrally located, on the ground floor of Le Méridien hotel. Cooler cats may rent an E Type Jaguar or vintage Chevrolet from **Rent A Classic Car** (www. rentaclassiccar.com; © 09-54-00-29-33) from 529€ per day. The funkiest addition to Nice's car hire scene is **NiceCar** (www.nice-car.fr; © 04-93-16-90-36). For 40€ per 2 hours, visitors can drive one of their three-wheeled, GPS-guided cabriolet cars.

BY TAXI **Taxis Nice** (www.taxis-nice.fr; © 04-93-13-78-78) will pick up within 5 minutes across town, although most locals book cabs via Uber or Bolt.

BY PUBLIC TRANSPORT Most local buses leave from the streets around place Masséna. Municipal **buses** charge 1.70€ for rides within the entire Alpes-Maritime province, even as far as Monaco or Cannes, within a 74-min window, which can include several bus changes. The same ticket can also be used on Nice's **tramway,** which connects the Old Town with Gare Nice-Ville, Nice Airport, the Allianz Riviera stadium, and northern Nice. Tickets, day passes (5€), and week passes (15€) can be bought directly onboard buses (although not trams) or at electronic kiosks around the city (where 10€ carnets of 10 tickets can also be purchased). For further information, see www.lignesdazur.com.

[FastFACTS] NICE

ATMs/Banks Nice is home to dozens of banks; **LCL Banque,** 15 av. Jean Médecin (𝄐 **04-93-82-84-61**), is one of the most central.

Dentists **SOS Dentaire** (www.ordre-chirurgiens-dentistes-06.com; 𝄐 **04-93-01-14-14**).

Doctors & Hospitals **Hôpital Lenval,** 57 av. de la Californie (www.lenval.org; 𝄐 **04-92-03-03-92**).

Local Information **Nice-Matin** (www.nice matin.com) has covered local news and events since 194. Google will translate the entire newspaper into English. **Riviera Buzz** (www.riviera-buzz.com) covers news, art, culture, and events in and around Nice.

Mail & Postage **La Poste,** 6 rue Louis Gassin (𝄐 **36-31**).

Pharmacies **Pharmacie Masséna,** 7 rue Masséna (𝄐 **04-93-87-78-94**).

Safety Nice is generally a very safe place. However, as in any big city, it's important to keep an eye on your valuables, in particular anywhere that's crowded. Avoid poorly lit streets at night, including in Nice's Old Town. Short-changing in shops across Nice is commonplace, so be sure to count your change.

Exploring Nice

In 1822, Nice's orange crop had an awful year. The workers faced a lean time, so the English residents employed them to build the **Promenade des Anglais ★★**, today a wide boulevard fronting the bay that stretches for 7km (4¼ miles), all the way to the airport. Along the beach are rows of grand cafes, the Musée Masséna, and the city's most glamorous hotels.

Crossing this boulevard in the tiniest bikinis are some of the world's most attractive bronzed bodies. They're all heading for the beach. Tough on tender feet, *le plage* is made not of sand, but of pebbles (and not small ones, either).

Rising sharply on a rock at the eastern end of the promenade is the Colline du Château. Once a fortified bastion, the hill has since been turned into a wonderful public park complete with a waterfall, cafes, and a giant children's play area, as well as an incredibly ornate cemetery. Head up aboard an elevator from the quai des Etats-Unis; more athletic visitors can walk up one of five sets of steep steps. The park is open daily from 8.30am to dusk.

Continuing east of the Colline, you reach the **Vieux Port,** or harbor, where locals fill the restaurants. While lingering over a drink at a sidewalk cafe, you can watch the ferries depart for Corsica and the yachts for St-Tropez. Just inland, the neighborhood around **rue Bonaparte** and **place Garibaldi** has become one of the hippest in town: Head here for authentic eateries, hip bars, and the superb **MAMAC** (Museum of Contemporary Art; see below).

The **Vieille Ville ★★**, or Old Town, begins at the foot of the Colline and stretches to place Masséna. Sheltered by red-tiled roofs, many of the Italianate facades suggest 17th-century Genoese palaces, including the free museum **Palais Lascaris** (see below). The Old Town is a maze of narrow streets teeming with local life, flower-strewn squares, and traditional *boulangeries:* Sample a Niçois-style onion pizza (pissaladière) here. Many of the buildings are painted a faded Roman gold, and their banners are laundry flapping in the sea breeze.

From Tuesday through Sunday (8am–1pm), the Old Town's main pedestrianized thoroughfare, the **cours Saleya,** is crowded with local producers selling seasonal fruits and vegetables, cured meats, and artisanal cheeses. At the market's western end is the **Marché aux Fleurs.** A rainbow of violets, lilies, and roses, the market operates Tuesday to Sunday from 8am to around 6pm. On Monday (8am–6pm) the cours Saleya is occupied by a superb **antiques market,** with vendors carting wares in from across France and Italy.

Nice's centerpiece is **place Masséna,** with rococo buildings and bubbling fountains, as well as the **Promenade du Paillon** parkway that stretches from the MAMAC down to the Jardin Albert-1er and seafront. With palms and exotic flowers, this pedestrian-only zone is one of the prettiest places in town.

At the other end of town, above the airport where jets swoop in direct from New York and Dubai, sits the **Musee International d'Art Naif Anatole-Jakovsky ★** (✆ **04-93-71-78-33**). Housed in a fabulous pink chateau, it features so-called naive art from self-taught painters including Henri Rousseau and Grandma Moses.

Musée d'Art Moderne et d'Art Contemporain ★★ MUSEUM

Nice's Modern and Contemporary Art Museum (or MAMAC) is a visionary display of art, architecture, and color. The building itself is boldness personified. It comprises 2 stone blocks clad in shimmering Carrera marble, with a glass walkway winding around the top. Stride around in winter to see snow on the Alps to the north as sunshine glitters on the Mediterranean to the south. Of the 10 main salons, three permanent collections stand out. The first is the American Pop Art display featuring Tom Wesselmann, Robert Indiana, and Andy Warhol, which includes the latter artist's rejection letters from the New York MoMA. The second is the European New Realist display of César, Arman, and Niki de Saint Phalle. The third unique collection is the School of Nice room of locally acclaimed artists including Sacha Sosno and Ben.

pl. Yves Klein (adjoining pl. Garibaldi). www.mamac-nice.org. ✆ **04-97-13-42-01.** Admission 10€ adults; free for children aged 18 and under. Tues–Sun 10am–6pm (from 11am Nov–May).

Musée des Beaux-Arts ★★ ART MUSEUM

Housed in the fabulous former residence of the Ukrainian Princess Kotchubey, this fine collection of 19th- and 20th-century art includes works by Rodin and Dufy, as well as works by a dynasty of painters, the Dutch Vanloo family. One of its best-known members, Carle Vanloo, born in Nice in 1705, was

Louis XV's premier peintre. High drama hit the museum in 2007, when armed robbers broke into the museum on a quiet summer Sunday, stealing priceless canvases by Monet and Sisley. The artworks were recovered less than a year later in Marseille.

33 av. des Baumettes. www.musee-beaux-arts-nice.org. ℰ **04-92-15-28-28.** Admission 10€ adults; free for children aged 13 and under. Tues–Sun 10am–6pm. Bus: 3, 9, 10, 22, or 38.

Musée Masséna ★★★ MUSEUM   Riviera aficionados will adore this astounding history museum. Located within an imposing Belle Epoque villa, it exhibits a quirky range of objects charting local life in Nice and its surrounds, from the first Victorian visitors through the roaring 1920s. Elegantly printed menus, train tickets from London to Nice, period maps, and snapshots of the promenading rich on vacation bring the past to life. Of additional note are the paintings and *objets d'art* donated by the Masséna family, a noble set of locals who constructed the villa. Botanist Edouard Ardre, who also designed the verdant greenery in front of the Casino de Monte-Carlo, landscaped the museum's neatly manicured gardens, which make a fine venue for a picnic.

65 rue de France or 35 promenade des Anglais. ℰ **04-93-91-19-10.** Admission 10€ adults; free for children aged 16 and under. Wed–Mon 10am–6pm (from 11am Nov–May).

Palais Lascaris.

Palais Lascaris ★★ PALACE   The baroque Palais Lascaris in the city's historic old town is associated with the Lascaris-Vintimille family, whose recorded history dates back over 7 centuries. Built in the 17th century, it contains elaborately detailed ornaments and suits of armor. An intensive restoration by the city of Nice in 1946 brought back its original beauty, and the palace is now classified as a historic monument. The venue also hosts contemporary art exhibitions within the baroque setting. The most elaborate floor, the étage noble, retains many of its 18th-century panels and plaster embellishments.

15 rue Droite. www.palais-lascaris-nice.org. ℰ **04-93-62-72-40.** Entrance with Pass Musées de Nice; 5€ adults; free for children aged 18 and under. Wed–Mon 10am–6pm.

OGC nice football club

In recent years **Olympique Gymnaste Club Nice Côte d'Azur,** the city's soccer club, have enjoyed a run of success. Ownership by Britain's richest person, Sir Jim Ratcliffe, has introduced star players including Danish goalkeeper Kasper Schmeichel and Welsh winger Aaron Ramsey. The team's shiny new stadium, Allianz Riviera, was chosen to host football matches during the 2024 Olympic Games.

Théâtre de la Photographie et de l'Image ★★ PHOTOGRAPHY MUSEUM Nice's brand-new photography exhibition space houses world-beating photography displays. Spectacles have included homages to Riviera photographer Jean Gilletta, Paris chronicler Brassaï, as well as images from Nice in the roaring 1920s. The Théâtre also held an acclaimed retrospective of National Geographic photographer Steve McCurry, whose most captivating image was of a green-eyed Afghan refugee girl taken in 1984.

1 pl. Pierre Gautier. www.tpi-nice.org. ℰ **04-97-13-42-20.** Free admission. Wed–Mon 10am–6pm).

Outlying Attractions in Cimiez

In the once-aristocratic hilltop quarter of Cimiez, 5km (3 miles) north of Nice, Queen Victoria wintered at the Hôtel Excelsior. Half the English court traveled down from Calais with her on a luxurious private train. To reach this suburb and its attractions, take bus no. 15 from bd. Dubouchage.

Monastère de Cimiez (Cimiez Convent) ★ CONVENT The convent includes a church that owns three of the most important works by the locally prominent Bréa brothers, who painted in the late 15th century. In a restored part of the convent where some Franciscan friars still live, 17th-century frescoes decorate the Musée Franciscain. Some 350 documents and works of art from the 15th to the 18th centuries are on display. The magnificent gardens are a photographer's dream, and there's rarely a tourist in sight. Panoramic views pan over Nice and the Baie des Anges. Artists Matisse and Dufy are buried in the cemetery nearby, and their graves are modern day pilgrimage spots; Matisse's in particular is scattered with flowers and letters from aspiring artists.

pl. du Monastère. ℰ **04-93-81-00-04.** Free admission. Museum Mon–Fri 10am–12:30pm and 3–5:30pm. Church daily 7:30am–6:30pm.

Musée Matisse ★★ ART MUSEUM In 1963, this beautiful old Italian villa was transformed into a museum honoring Henri Matisse, one of the 20th century's greatest painters. Matisse came to Nice for the light and made the city his home, living in the Hotel Beau Rivage and on the cours Saleya, and dying in Cimiez in 1954. Most of the pieces in the museum's permanent collection—including *Nude in an Armchair with a Green Plant* (1937) and *Blue Nude IV* (1952)—were created in Nice. Artworks are interspersed with Matisse's personal possessions, such as ceramic vases and antique furniture, as well as scale models of his architectural masterpiece, Vence's **Chapelle du Rosaire** (p. 627).

164 av. des Arènes de Cimiez. www.musee-matisse-nice.org. © **04-93-81-08-08.** Admission 10€ adults; free for children aged 18 and under. Wed–Mon 10am–6pm (from 11am Oct–June).

Musée National Marc Chagall ★★★ ART MUSEUM Surrounded by pools and a garden, this handsome museum is devoted to Marc Cha-gall's treatment of biblical themes. Born in Russia in 1887, Chagall became a French citizen in 1937 and painted with astonishing light and color until his death in St-Paul-de-Vence in 1985. This museum's focal set of artworks—12 large paintings, illustrating the first two books of the Old Testament—was originally created to adorn the central cathedral in Vence. The church's high humidity nixed the artist's original plans, and Chagall assisted in planning this purpose-built space instead.

Av. du Dr. Ménard. www.musee-chagall. fr. © **04-93-53-87-20.** Admission 10€ adults. May–Oct Wed–Mon 10am–6pm; Nov–Apr Wed–Mon 10am–5pm.

Visitors admire the art at the Musée National Marc Chagall.

Organized Tours

One of the most enjoyable ways to quickly gain an overview of Nice is aboard a **Nice Open Top Bus** (www.nicelegrandtour.fr; © **04-92-29-17-00**). Between 10am and 5:30pm year-round, one of a flotilla of this company's buses departs from a position adjacent to the Jardin Albert I. The panoramic 90-minute tour takes in the harbor, the museums of Cimiez, the Russian church, and the promenade. Per-person rates for the experience are 23€ adults and 8€ for children 4 to 11. Participants can get off at any of 12 stops en route and re-board any other buses, which follow at 45-minute intervals. Advance reservations aren't necessary, and commentary is piped through to headsets in nine different languages. For just 3€ more, visitors can purchase a 2-day pass.

Another easy way to see the city is by the small **Train Touristique de Nice** (www.francevoguette.com), which also departs from the promenade des Anglais, opposite Jardin Albert I. The 45-minute ride passes many of Nice's most-heralded sites, including place Masséna, the Old Town, and the Colline du Château. Departing every hour., the train operates daily 9:30am to 5:30pm (from 10:30am to 4:30pm Oct–Apr). The round-trip price is 10€ adults and 5€ children 4 to 12.

For a 2-hour **walking tour of Nice** (www.freewalkingtournice.com), meet at the fountain on Place Massena, every day, year-round, at 10:55am. The guide will be carrying a red umbrella. The tour is advertised as "free," but it's expected that participants tip the guide 10€ to 20€. For offbeat, artsy tours **Botox(s)** (www.botoxs.fr), founded by the funky Hotel Windsor, operates guided visits to small private galleries.

Possibly the coolest way to get around Nice is by Segway, the two-wheeled electronic scooters. **Mobilboard,** 2 rue Halévy (www.mobil board.com; ✆ **04-93-80-21-27**) runs tours. Children 14 (minimum age) to

FRENCH RIVIERA & NICE museum & travel passes

Visitors who aim to hit the sights hard can save with three great value travel cards.

Those visiting more than one cultural attraction in Nice, a city with more museums than any French city outside Paris, should purchase the **Pass Musées de Nice** (www.nice.fr), which can be bought at any museum or cultural site. For 15€ pass holders are granted 4 days of complimentary access to all 12 of Nice's public museums. Under 18s require no pass for free entry.

The **French Riviera Pass** (www.french rivierapass.com) is best for hardcore culture vultures who plan to sightsee across the Riviera. It costs 26€ for 24 hours, 38€ for 48 hours, or 56€ for 72 hours and offers access to over 60 choice sights. These include the **Villa Kerylos** on Cap-Ferrat (usually 10€), the **Musée Chagall** in Nice (normally 10€), and the

Oceanographic Museum in Monaco (a whopping 16€). City tours like the **Mobilboard Segway** ride (17€) and the **snorkeling boat trip to Villefranche** (25€) are also included.

The **Cote d'Azur Card** (www.cote dazur-card.com) costs 45€, or 25€ for children. Holders can visit all the sights featured on the French Riviera Pass and get bus tours and seaside activities too. A more relaxed adventure, it allows for unlimited usage for 3 days out of 6, so you don't have to kill yourself with culture during a 72-hour window. Highlights include Nice's hop-on hop-off **Open Top Bus Tour** (normally 22€), plus **paddleboard trips** and **island boat rides** from Cannes.

NICE'S grand new HIKING LOOP

A newly marked Grande Randonnée hiking trail loops around Nice for 42km, passing by art museums and chestnut forests. The **Camin Nissart** is easy to follow. It rises from Nice Port to the Roman fort on Mont Boron, then the Nice Observatory, before passing the art museums in the ritzy suburb of Cimiez.

The most rural part of the region's only GR de Pays trail runs along abandoned rail lines to AOC Bellet, one of France's smallest wine appellations, 400m above sea level, near Nice Airport.

Some 8,500 volunteers of the Fédération Française de la Randonnée used pruners, paintbrushes, and GPS trackers to create this fab hiking trail.

17 must be accompanied by an adult. A 1-hour tour of Nice costs 32€ per person. More energetic guests may join **Nice Cycle Tours** (www.nicecycletours.com; ✆ **06-19-99-95-22**) 3-hour bike voyages around the city. Tours cost 35€ per person, and the friendly team also run food tours and eBike expeditions. The hottest Cervélo racing bikes are available to rent from **Café de Cycliste,** 10 quai de Docks (www.cafeducycliste.com; ✆ **09-67-02-04-17**), a hipster café frequented by Tour de France pros, from 85€ per day. Staff are great for repairs and bike route advice. Nice's newest tour is an aerial speedboat parascend from the friendly team at **SuperFly** (www.superfly-watersport.com), where guests rise 100m into the air for fabulous panoramas. Rides cost 100€ for two guests.

Outdoor Activities

BEACHES Along Nice's seafront, beaches extend uninterrupted for more than 7km (4¼ miles), going from the edge of Vieux-Port (the old port, or harbor) to the international airport. Tucked between the public areas are several rather chic private beaches. Many of these beach bars provide mattresses and parasols for around 30€ per day. The coolest club, **Castel Plage** (www.castelplage.com; ✆ **04-93-85-22-66**), is a celebrity hangout in summer. In 2023, new beach club **La Plage** (www.hotel-negresco-nice.com; ✆ **04-93-16-64-00**), from hotel Le Negresco, staked its claim by offering lobster rolls from a Michelin-starred chef, with mattresses plus parasol for 45€.

SCUBA DIVING Of the many diving outfits in Nice harbor, **Nice Diving,** 13 quai des Deux Emmanuel (www.nicediving.com; ✆ **06-14-46-04-06**), offers bilingual instruction and *baptêmes* (dives for first-timers) around Nice and Cap-Ferrat. A dive for experienced divers, equipment included, costs around 50€; diver's certification is required.

Where to Stay

EXPENSIVE

Anantara Plaza ★★   Opened in 2023 alongside the seafront Jardins Albert Ier, Anantara splices the style of an Asian spa with a tech zillionaire's private escape. Each light-filled room and suite, most with a magnificent Mediterranean view, is styled in a 1920s-themed decor. There's an ultra-modern basement spa too, with hammam, massage suites, and enough Technogym equipment to tone the entire French soccer squad. Arrive hungry. Because the restaurant **SEEN** (which looks like a UFO has landed on the top floor of the hotel) has upgraded Niçois classics like petits farcis stuffed vegetables (served here atop an unctuous marrow bone) and rolls locally caught seafood into sushi. Breakfast is also served in this modernistic space. At the very least stop in for a cocktail. The views are, in a word, epic.

12 avenue de Verdun. www.anantara.com. ✆ **04-93-16-75-75.** 151 units. 285€–720€ double; from 555€ suite. **Amenities:** 2 restaurants; bar; babysitting; exercise room; massage; room service; free Wi-Fi.

Hôtel Negresco ★★   For more than a century, the Negresco has been Nice's most iconic hotel. Its flamingo-pink dome crowns the promenade des Anglais, its Belle Epoque facade turned towards the sea. Guest rooms—a mix of Louis XIV antiques and state-of-the-art bathrooms—have hosted each era's most noted celebrities, from the Beatles and Salvador Dalí to Leonardo Di Caprio. An exceptional collection of private art decorates the public areas. Dining includes the exquisite **Chantecler,** which holds a Michelin star under the direction of young female chef Virginie Basselot. Basselot is known to tour France on her Triumph motorbike, selecting the best Cancale oysters and Pierlas poultry for her tasting menus (from 175€). She also presides over the less formal **La Rotonde** bistro (set lunch 39€) and new **La Plage** beach club.

37 promenade des Anglais. www.hotel-negresco-nice.com. ✆ **04-93-16-64-00.** 117 units. 330€–830€ double; from 650€ suite. Parking 28€. **Amenities:** 2 restaurants; bar; beach club; babysitting; exercise room; massage; room service; free Wi-Fi.

A night shot of the elegant Hôtel Negresco.

MODERATE

Hôtel Windsor ★★ The coolest, funkiest, and most friendly hotel in Nice is also one of its best-value lodgings. This *maison bourgeoise* was built by disciples of Gustav Eiffel in the 1890s and has remained a family-run hotel for three generations. Current owner Mme. Payen-Redolfi has ushered in an artsy era where a different acclaimed artist decorates another guest room each year. The hotel currently has over 30 contemporary-art rooms, including one painted entirely in gold leaf by Claudio Parmigiani. Art and color stream outside into the **WiJungle** bamboo garden—location for the alfresco breakfast as well. Back indoors, **WiLounge** serves dinner and chilled rosé. **WiZen** is the fifth-floor health club, hammam, sauna, and meditation zone.

11 rue Dalpozzo. www.hotelwindsornice.com. ℰ **04-93-88-59-35.** 57 units. 105€– 310€ double. Parking 20€. **Amenities:** Restaurant; bar; babysitting; health club; outdoor pool; room service; sauna; free Wi-Fi.

INEXPENSIVE

Villa Saint Exupéry Beach ★ Welcome to what has been voted the best hostel accommodation in France. Travelers of all ages adore the dormitory-style beds (some mixed, some female-only) and private twin rooms, which are painted in homage to great French artists. For an extra 8€, guests may graze on an abundant buffet breakfast; use of a communal kitchen and gym with sauna is free. Finds also include daily happy hour drinks prices (large beers are 4€) and quality meals at backpacker prices. A popular free addition is the daily art tour, which meanders past Matisse's old house in Cimiez. Also expect weekly communal activities including canyoning, beach yoga and sailing.

6 rue Sacha Guitry. www.villahostels.com. ℰ **04-93-16-13-45.** 60 units. 30€–80€ per person in a single or twin-bedded room; 18€–45€ per person for dormitory bed. Rates include sheets, and towels. **Amenities:** Bar; cooking facilities; computers; luggage room; TV lounge; free Wi-Fi.

Yelo Nice ★★ Open since 2022, Yelo resides on Nice's grandest boulevard. Minimalist bedrooms are blessed with fine linen, natural light, and ultra-fast Wi-Fi, while some overlook the buzzing street below. And there's a big sofa-filled communal lounge full of co-working guests. The 16€ breakfast is worth it. Help yourself to organic eggs, smoked trout, vegetable juices, and croissants from the local bakery; under 12s eat half price; under 5s breakfast for free.

47 av. Jean Médécin. www.yelohotelcollection.com. ℰ **04-91-65-85-05.** 54 units. 71€–210€ double. **Amenities:** Bar; free Wi-Fi.

ALTERNATE ACCOMMODATIONS

Nice Pebbles ★★★ A short-term rental of one of these holiday apartments allows you time to truly immerse yourself in local life, from cooking up morning-market bounty to sipping sunset aperitifs on your private terrace. More than 100 carefully selected properties (from studios to four-bedroom homes) are dotted throughout the city's central neighborhoods, including the Old Town and harbor and along the promenade des Anglais. Apartments boast first-class amenities (Netflix and designer bathrooms are common) yet weigh in at just a fraction of the price of a hotel room, for a much larger space. Demand is high, so book well in advance.

32 rue Tonduti de l'Escarene. www.nicepebbles.com. © **04-97-20-27-30.** 90€–350€ per apartment per night. **Amenities:** Free Wi-Fi.

Where to Eat

The combined regions of Provence and the Riviera boast almost 100 Michelin stars across 78 restaurants (as of 2023)—that's an incredible statistic only trumped by city destinations like Tokyo and Paris. The Riviera's regional capital of Nice teems with exquisite restaurants, from the high end to the downright local. Excellent eateries are scattered across the city—although beware of many of the Old Town's careless offerings, keen to lure in tourists for a single dinner only. In addition to the suggestions below, the portside **Le Bistrot du Port,** 28 quai Lunel (© **04-93-55-21-70;** closed Tue–Wed), is where the Orsini family has been dishing up top-quality fish and creative seafood concoctions for over 30 years. After a quick bite? **Deli Bo,** 5 rue Bonaparte (© **04-93-56-33-04**), is a top spot for café au lait, juices and patisserie.

EXPENSIVE

Flaveur ★★★ MODERN FRENCH   Flaveur is Nice's most highly rated restaurant—and rightly so. Brothers Mickaël and Gaël Tourteaux (whose last name, almost unbelievably, translates as "cake"), a pair of fabulously talented chefs, hold two Michelin stars. Both brothers, now in their forties, spent decades in the kitchens of the Riviera's top restaurants. A childhood growing up on the tropical islands of Réunion and Guadeloupe means their contemporary cuisine is laced with exotic flavors: plump scallops seasoned with Japanese gomasio; artistically displayed lemongrass and bubbles of lemon caviar sit atop risotto. Meals are variations on fixed-price menus only; there's no ordering à la carte. Simply let the Tourteauxs take you on a voyage gastronomique.

25 rue Gubernatis. www.flaveur.net © **04-93-62-53-95.** Fixed-price lunch 150€ or dinner 180€–220€. Tues–Fri noon–2pm and 7:30–11pm; Sat 7:30–11pm. Closed early Jan.

Restaurant Jan ★★★ MODERN MEDITERRANEAN   This extraordinary restaurant is situated in the city's hottest dining district a block behind Nice Port. The inventive cuisine of South African chef Jan

Hendrik van der Westhuizen blends regional ingredients (line-caught sea-bass, Charolais beef) with African spice (Madagascar vanilla, rooibos jelly) and Italian style (Parmesan shavings, prosciutto chips). Foodies may also book Jan's new "tour du fromage" cheese-tasting room, named Maria, across the street. Dining with Jan is a once-in-a-lifetime treat.

12 rue Lascaris. www.restaurantjan.com. ℰ **04-97-19-32-23.** Main courses 28€–43€; fixed-price menu 165€-195€. Fri–Sat noon–2pm and Tues–Sat 7:30–10pm.

MODERATE

La Merenda ★★ NIÇOIS   Top chef Dominique Le Stanc left the world of *haute cuisine* far behind to take over this tiny, traditional, family-run bistro. And how lucky we all are. La Merenda is now one of the most authentic and unpretentious eateries along the French Riviera. Market-fresh specials scribbled on a small chalkboard depend on the season and may include stuffed sardines, tagliatelle drenched in delicious basil pesto, or a delectable *tarte au citron.*

4 rue Raoul Bosio. www.lamerenda.net. No phone. Main courses 17€–31€. Mon–Fri noon–2pm and 7:30–10pm.

INEXPENSIVE

Caju ★★ VEGAN   A vegan restaurant so good it makes you embarrassed that you're still eating meat and dairy. Their "Beauty and the Beets" burger with "slaw lights up the palate with texture, flavor, and zing." Homemade potato chips with nut mayo make for an easy snack, alongside a freshly pressed juice (all 5.50€). As long as you like hemp seeds, cocoa, and unaffectedly enthusiastic service, you're in the right place.

1 rue Jules Gilly. www.cajuvegan.fr. ℰ **06-09-10-62-49.** Main courses 12€–17€. Tues–Sat noon–3pm and 5:15–7:15pm, Sun noon–3:30pm.

Panivore ★ SANDWICHES   The concept of hole-in-the-wall diner Panivore is simple: Fresh, local, and organic ingredients are piled on top-drawer French bread, then served for a song on an outdoor terrace. Sandwiches contain a meal in themselves including the "Tristan": stuffed with pickles, eggs and smoked herrings. For a few euros extra, guests can add a soup starter, small dessert and natural juice to their order.

14 avenue du Maréchal Foch. www.panivore.fr. No phone. Sandwiches from 7€. Mon–Sat 8am–3pm.

Type 55 ★★ NIÇOIS   A game-changing addition to Nice's dining scene, Type 55 raises pizza to hitherto unattained heights. The same for the dish's associated cocktails and desserts. Don't believe us? Just try their black flour pizza with tuna tataki and jellied passion fruit, or seafood pizza with sautéed squid and garlic rouille. Informal, fun and highly recommended, especially for large groups.

1 rue de la Préfecture. www.instagram.com/type.55.nice ℰ **09-73-60-49-82.** Pizzas 15€. Tues–Sat noon–2pm and 7–10pm.

Place Masséna.

Shopping

CLOTHING Clustered around **rue Masséna** and **avenue Jean-Médecin** is Nice's densest concentration of fashionable French labels. For more high-end couture, the streets around **place Magenta**, including **rue de Verdun, rue Paradis,** and **rue Alphonse Karr** are Apple Pay's worst nightmare. A shop of note is **Cotelac,** 12 rue Alphonse Karr (✆ **04-93-87-31-59**), which sells chic women's clothing. Men should try **Façonnable,** 7–9 rue Paradis (www.faconnable.com; ✆ **04-93-88-06-97**). This boutique is the original site of a chain with several hundred branches worldwide; the look is conservatively stylish. For more unusual apparel, **Lucien Chasseur,** 2 rue Bonaparte (✆ **04-93-55-52-14**), is the city's coolest spot for Italian-designed shoes, scarves, and soft leather satchels. In the Old Town, rue de la Prefecture is home to far-out stores including **WeMood** (no. 17), for vintage French Riviera posters, and **Antic Boutik** (no. 19), for men's fashion. Also try nearby **Harrison,** 10 rue Alexandre Mari (www.harrison-opticien.com; ✆ **04-93-01-69-25**), for a decade-by-decade presentation of designer sunglasses, including 1980s Top Gun aviators.

FOOD The winding streets of Nice's Old Town are the best place to find local crafts, ceramics, gifts, and foodie purchases. If you're thinking of indulging in a Provençale pique-nique, **Nicola Alziari,** 14 rue St François de Paule (www.alziari.com.fr; ☎ **04-93-62-94-03**), will provide everything from olives, anchovies, and pistous to aiolis and tapenades. For an olive-oil tasting session—and the opportunity to buy the goods afterward—check out **Oliviera,** 2 rue Benoit Bunico (www.oliviera.com; ☎ **04-93-11-06-45**), run by the amiable Nadim Beyrouti. **Caves Caprioglio,** 16 rue de la Préfecture (☎ **04-93-85-66-57**), is the go-to place for rare Provençal wines and big-name Bordeaux vintages. In the port, **Confiserie Florian,** 14 quai Papacino (www.confiserieflorian.com; ☎ **04-93-55-43-50**), has been candying fruit, chocolate-dipping roasted nuts, and crystalizing edible flowers since 1949. The tastiest take-home treats for self-catering guests are pastas from **Maison Barale,** 7 rue Sainte-Reparate (www.maison-barale.fr; ☎ **04-93-85-63-08**), which has been stuffing Niçoise stew and candied lemon into fresh ravioli for decades.

SOUVENIRS The best selection of Provençal fabrics is at **Le Chandelier,** 7 rue de la Boucherie (☎ **04-93-85-85-19**), where you'll see designs by two of the region's best-known producers of cloth, Les Olivades and Valdrôme. Nearby, seek out **L'Atelier des Cigales,** 17 rue du Collet (☎ **04-93-85-70-62**), for Provençal platters and smart local handicrafts. For antiquarian books, contemporary art, kitsch, and comic books, wander north of place Garibaldi to **rue Delille** and **rue Defly,** just past the MAMAC modern art gallery. For art deco *objets d'art* from the 1930s to 1960s, hit **Harter,** 36 rue Ségurane (☎ **04-93-07-10-29**)—prices are not cheap but the items are museum-quality.

Nightlife

Nice has some of the most active nightlife and cultural offerings along the Riviera. Big evenings out usually begin at a cafe or bar, take in a restaurant, opera, or film, and finish in a club near Nice Old Town. You have the choice of many cinemas, most of which show films in English with French subtitles, with the art house **Cinéma Jean-Paul Belmondo,** 16 place Garibaldi (☎ **04-89-04-52-00**), particularly recommended for cult version originale films.

The major cultural center on the Riviera is the **Opéra de Nice,** 4 rue St-François-de-Paule (www.opera-nice.org; ☎ **04-92-17-40-00**), built in 1885 by Charles Garnier, fabled architect of the Paris Opéra. It presents a full repertoire, with emphasis on serious, often large-scale operas, such as *Tristan and Isolde* and *La Bohème,* as well as a saison symphonique dominated by the Orchestre Philharmonique de Nice. The opera hall is also the major venue for concerts and recitals. Tickets are available right up until the day of performance. You can show up at the box office (Tues–Sat 11am–5pm) or, more easily, buy tickets in advance online. Tickets run from 12€ to 90€.

A chic gaming spot is the **Casino in the Palais de Mediterranée,** 15 promenade des Anglais (www.casinomediterranee.com; ℰ **04-92-14-68-00**), which offers an elegant gambling experience daily from 10am for slot machines, 8pm for gaming tables.

Within the cool-kitsch decor of a former garage in the port area, talented staff serves up fruity cocktails and pétanque (French boules) on its own indoor court at **La Boulisterie,** 16 rue Lascaris (ℰ **04-93-89-34-96**). Around the corner, LGBTQ+-friendly **Comptoir Central Electrique,** 10 rue Bonaparte (ℰ **04-93-14-09-62**), is the place in Garibaldi neighborhood's epicenter of cool.

The party spirit is best lapped up in the alfresco bars on the **cours Saleya.** Otherwise, head a block inland to **Wayne's Bar,** 15 rue de la Préfecture (www.waynesbar-restaurant.com; ℰ **04-93-13-46-99**), where dancing on the tables to raucous cover bands is the norm. For excellent house tunes, nonstop dancing, and heaps of understated cool, head to **High Club,** 45 promenade des Anglais (ℰ **07-81-88-42-04**).

Day Trips from Nice

CAGNES-SUR-MER ★

7km (4½ miles) W of Nice

The orange groves and fields of carnations of the upper village of **Haut-de-Cagnes** provide a beautiful setting for the narrow flower-filled streets and 17th- and 18th-century homes. Head to the top, where you can enjoy the view from place du Château and have lunch or a drink at a pavement cafe. The old fishing port and beach resort of Cros-de-Cagnes is known for its 4km (2½ miles) of pebbly beach. For years Cagnes-sur-Mer attracted the French literati, such as Simone de Beauvoir. Great Impressionist painter Renoir said the village was "the place where I want to paint until the last day of my life." His former home (see below) is the highlight of a visit here.

Frequent no. 200 **buses** (1.70€) and **trains** (3.10€) zip along the coast between Nice and Cagnes-sur-Mer. The climb to hilltop Haut-de-Cagnes is strenuous; a free minibus runs daily about every 15 minutes year-round from place du Général-de-Gaulle in the center of Cagnes-sur-Mer to Haut-de-Cagnes. Cagnes' **Office de Tourisme** is at 6 bd. Maréchal Juin, Cagnes-sur-Mer (www.cagnes-tourisme.com; ℰ **04-93-20-61-64**).

In Haut-de-Cagnes, the ever-popular **Josy-Jo,** 2 rue du Planastel (www.josy-jo.com; ℰ **04-93-20-68-76**), was the home and studio of painters Modigliani and Soutine during their hungriest years. The menu features Niçois specialty petits farcis (tiny stuffed vegetables), grilled lamb from the Hautes-Alpes, and a variety of homemade desserts. In Cros-de-Cagnes, chef Jacques Maximin dishes up fresh fish at the seafront **Bistrot de la Marine,** 96 promenade de la Plage (www.lebistrotdelamarine.fr;

C **04-93-26-43-46**). The best seafood deal is their daily lunchtime three-course special for 29€.

Château-Musée Grimaldi (Musée de l'Olivier & Musée d'Art Moderne Méditerranéen) ★ HISTORIC HOME/MUSEUMS   Château-Musée was a fortress built in 1301 by Rainier Grimaldi I, a lord of Monaco and a French admiral (his portrait is in the museum). In the early 17th century, the castle was converted into a gracious Louis XIII château, which now contains two museums. The Museum of the Olive Tree shows the steps involved in cultivating and processing the olive. The Museum of Mediterranean Modern Art displays works by Kisling, Carzou, Dufy,

ROYA VALLEY & THE mercantour national park

The timeless Roya Valley and the Mercantour forests (one of only seven National Parks in mainland France) are a train hop away from Nice. The entire area was once the private hunting ground of Italy's Turin-based kings. It only became part of France in 1947, and the Italianate train stations and tumbling hill villages remain. Thankfully, a lot of wildlife is left, too, in the form of wolves, marmots, ibex, eagles, and deer.

The **Train de Merveilles** (www.menton-riviera-merveilles.fr), climbs up into the Roya Valley from Nice-Ville station up to six times daily. A stunning stop is Sospel, 45 minutes from Nice. This age-old village is sliced in two by a raging river, and is a center for mountain biking, horseback riding, and alpine hikes.

Further north up the valley, the village of **Breil-sur-Roya** has stolen a few hearts, too. It lies at the nexus of several hiking paths, one of them leading downhill to Sospel.

The large ex-Italian town of Tende, 2 hours from Nice, is the train's final stop. The names above its stores, on its churches, and in its rococo graveyard are distinctly non-French. It's also the gateway to the **Mercantour National Park** (www.mercantour-parcnational.fr). Before partaking in the park's 100 hiking routes, make a visit to Tende's **Musée des Merveilles,** which highlights the area's prehistory, cave paintings, and fairytale geography.

Lovers of *la bella italia* may continue on to Cuneo in Italy using a locals-only train that runs from Tende towards Turin several times each day.

Mercantour National Park.

Cocteau, and Seyssaud, plus temporary exhibits. In one salon is an interesting trompe l'oeil fresco, La Chute de Phaeton. The tower affords a view of the Côte d'Azur.

7 pl. Grimaldi, Haut-de-Cagnes. ✆ **04-92-02-47-30.** Admission to both museums 4€ adults and free for visitors 26 and under; double ticket to museum plus the Musée Renoir 8€. July–Aug Wed–Mon 10am–1pm and 2–6pm; Apr–June and Sept Wed–Mon 10am–noon and 2–6pm; Oct–Mar Wed–Mon 10am–noon and 2–5pm.

Musée Renoir & Les Collettes ★★ HISTORIC HOME/MUSEUM
Built in 1907 in an orange grove, this was the Impressionist master's home for 12 years. The terrace of Mme. Renoir's bedroom faces stunning views over Cap d'Antibes and Haut-de-Cagnes. On a wall hangs a photograph of one of Renoir's sons, Pierre, as he appeared in the 1932 film *Madame Bovary*. Although Renoir is best remembered for his paintings, in Cagnes he began experimenting with sculpture, a form he found easier to manage, given his growing arthritis. The museum has 20 portrait busts and portrait medallions, most of which depict his wife and children. For many, the orange groves, olive plantation, and unkempt gardens that so inspired the artist are a definite highlight. Be aware the museum is poorly signposted. Following a cellphone marker on Google Maps is strongly advised.

19 chemin des Collettes. ✆ **04-93-20-61-07.** Admission (includes admission to Château-Musée Grimaldi) 6€ adults; free for ages 26 and under. July–Aug Wed–Mon 10am–1pm and 2–6pm; Apr–June and Sept Wed–Mon 10am–noon and 2–6pm; Oct–Mar Wed–Mon 10am–noon and 2–5pm.

VILLEFRANCHE-SUR-MER ★★

935km (580 miles) S of Paris; 6.5km (4 miles) E of Nice

Just east of Nice, the coastal Lower Corniche sweeps inland to reveal Villefranche, its medieval Old Town tumbling downhill into the shimmering sea. Paired with a dazzling sheltered bay set against picturesque Cap-Ferrat beyond, it's little wonder that countless artists made this beachy getaway their home—or that it's served as the cinematic backdrop for numerous movies including *Dirty Rotten Scoundrels,* hit TV crime drama *Riviera,* and sassy Netflix showpiece *Emily in Paris.* In short, it's a perfect sandy escape, with an oh-so-cute village attached, just minutes from Nice.

Essentials

ARRIVING Trains arrive from all the Côte d'Azur's coastal resorts from Cannes to Monaco every 30 minutes or so. For rail schedules, visit www.sncf-connect.com or call ✆ **36-35. Lignes d'Azur** (www.lignesdazur.com; ✆ **08-10-06-10-06**) maintains a bus service at 5- to 15-minute intervals aboard line no. 100 from Nice to Monte Carlo via Villefranche. One-way fares cost 1.70€. Buses deposit passengers just above the Old Town, almost directly opposite the tourist information office. Many visitors drive via the Basse Corniche (Lower Corniche).

VISITOR INFORMATION   The **Office de Tourisme** is on Jardin François-Binon (www.villefranche-sur-mer.com; ✆ **04-93-01-73-68**).

[Fast FACTS] VILLEFRANCHE

ATMs/Banks   **Caisse Nationale d'Epargne,** 1 esc. Baptistin Saliva (✆ **08-26-08-36-15**).

Mail & Postage   **La Poste,** 6 av. Albert 1er (✆ **36-31**).

Pharmacies   **Pharmacie du Tahiti,** 4 av. du Maréchal Joffre (✆ **04-89-24-60-51**).

Exploring Villefranche

Villefranche's long arc of golden sand, **plage des Marinières,** is the principal attraction for most visitors. From here, **quai Courbet** runs along the sea to the colorful Old Town past scores of bobbing boats; it's lined with waterside restaurants, all with fabulous sea views. Visitors can dive into the sea anywhere they please.

Old-town action revolves around **place Amélie Pollonnais,** a delightful square shaded by palms and spread with the tables of six easygoing restaurants. These include **Le Cosmo** (✆ **04-93-01-84-05**), which serves big salads, great cocktails, and a fantastic selection of ice creams. The square is also the site of a Sunday antiques market, where people from across the Riviera come to root through vintage tourism posters, silverware, 1930s jewelry, and ex-hotel linens.

The painter, writer, and filmmaker Jean Cocteau left a fine memorial to the town's inhabitants. He spent a year (1956–57) painting frescoes on the 14th-century walls of the **Romanesque Chapelle St-Pierre,** quai Courbet (✆ **04-93-76-90-70**). He presented it to "the fishermen of Villefranche in homage to the Prince of Apostles, the patron of fishermen." In the apse is a depiction of the miracle of St. Peter walking on the water, not knowing that an angel supports him. Villefranche's busty local women, in their regional costumes, are honored on the left side of the narthex. Admission is 4€ for adults, free for children 14 and under. It is open Wednesday to Sunday 9:30am to 6pm. Annual closure from mid-November to mid-December.

A short coastal path leads from the car park below place Amélie Pollonnais to the 16th-century citadelle. This castle dominates the bay, and its ramparts are open for leisurely wandering and letting kids run around to play pirates. Inside the citadel sits a cluster of small, locally focused **museums** including the **Fondation Musée-Volti,** a collection of voluptuous female sculptures by Villefranche artist Volti (Antoniucci Voltigero) and **Le Musée Goetz-Boumeester,** featuring around 50 artworks by Dutch artist Christine Boumeester, both of which reopen in 2025.

Where to Stay

Along with the hotels below, **Hôtel de la Darse,** at 32 avenue du Général de Gaulle (www.hoteldeladarse.com), offers affordable rooms with forgettable decor but lovely balconies.

Hotel Villa Patricia ★   This petite seaside hotel really does offer some of the Riviera's cheapest double rooms during the height of summer. A 5-minute stroll from the water, it also boasts a shared garden sheltered by lemon trees. As one might expect for the price, some rooms are small, while others are oddly shaped, but all are stylish, smart, and exceptionally clean, and share a large lounge area complete with book swap, outdoor sofas, and a piano. It's a gentle 10-minute stroll from Villefranche, Beaulieu, and Cap-Ferrat.

310 av. de l'Ange Gardien. www.hotel-patricia.riviera.fr. ℰ **04-93-01-06-70.** 10 units. 92€–125€ double; 120€–150€ triple; 130€–170€ suite. Free parking. Closed Dec–Jan. **Amenities:** Free Wi-Fi.

Hôtel Welcome ★★   Villefranche's most prestigious hotel, the Welcome sits in the center of town and has been home to Riviera artists since the 1920s, including author and filmmaker Jean Cocteau (in room 22). Every one of the modern hotel's midsize-to-spacious rooms possesses a balcony and sea views. The wine bar spills out onto the quay in warm weather. The Welcome offers a *petit déjeuner famille* option for breakfast: 48€ for all the family instead of 20€ per person. Staff can also organize rental or a kayak, paddleboard, or motorboat.

3 quai Amiral Courbet. www.welcomehotel.com. ℰ **04-93-76-27-62.** 35 units. 149€–415€ double; 229€–908€ suite. **Amenities:** Bar; babysitting; room service; free Wi-Fi.

Where to Eat

Le Cosmo, mentioned above, is another nice dining option.

Le Mayssa ★ MEDITERRANEAN   A little-known rooftop restaurant overlooking the yachts in the Bay of Villefranche? Yes, please. On linen-covered tables a sea-sourced cornucopia of crab salads and scallop risottos are served in style. Daily specials might include a carpaccio of scallops and mozzarella-burrata salad. The establishment sits atop the town's Gare Maritime boat office and is owned by the family behind **Paloma Plage** (www.paloma-beach.com; ℰ **04-93-01-64-71**), the coolest beach club on Cap-Ferrat.

pl. Wilson. www.mayssabeach.fr. ℰ **04-93-01-75-08.** Main courses 14€–25€. Daily noon–2:30pm and 7–11pm.

ST-JEAN-CAP-FERRAT ★★

942km (584 miles) S of Paris; 9.5km (6 miles) E of Nice

Of all the oases along the Côte d'Azur, no other place has the snob appeal of Cap-Ferrat. It's a 15km (9¼-mile) promontory sprinkled with luxurious villas and outlined by sheltered bays, beaches, and sun-kissed coves that can occupy a full day on the sand. In the stroll-friendly port of St-Jean, the harbor accommodates yachts, fishing boats, and a dozen exclusive eateries.

It's worth mentioning that Cap-Ferrat is seriously wealthy. As in seriously, seriously rich. Stars like David Niven and Gregory Peck called "Le Cap" home before a new generation of Russian oligarchs and Hollywood A-listers bargained for homes that cost 100-million-plus euros. It's all very hush-hush, but we can tell you that Madonna is a regular visitor and Brad Pitt enjoys dinner on Paloma Plage, the best of St-Jean-Cap-Ferrat's beach clubs. The world's most expensive property, Villa Leopolda, went on sale here a few years back for a cool half-billion dollars. The BBC recently confirmed that the peninsula is the second most expensive location in the world (since you ask, Monaco came first). A wonderful (and

St-Jean-Cap-Ferrat.

completely free) coastal path loops past many of the world's richest residents' private homes.

Essentials

ARRIVING   Trains connect Beaulieu with Nice, Monaco, and the rest of the Côte d'Azur every 30 minutes. Many visitors then take a taxi to St-Jean from Beaulieu's rail station; alternatively, it's a 30-minute walk along Cap-Ferrat's promenade Maurice Rouvier to St-Jean village. For rail information, visit www.sncf-connect.com or call ✆ **36-35.** Bus line no. 81 connects Nice with St-Jean every hour. One-way fares costs 1.70€. For bus information and schedules, contact **Lignes d'Azur** (www.lignes dazur.com; ✆ **08-10-06-10-06**). By car from Nice, take D6098 (the basse corniche) east.

VISITOR INFORMATION   St-Jean's **Office de Tourisme** is on 59 av. Denis-Séméria (www.saintjeancapferrat-tourisme.fr; ✆ **04-93-76-08-90**).

[FastFACTS] ST-JEAN

| ATMs/Banks **Banque Populaire Côte d'Azur,** 5 av. Claude Vignon, St-Jean 06230 (✆ **04-89-81-11-42**). | Mail & Postage **La Poste,** 51 av. Denis Séméria, St-Jean 06230 (✆ **36-31**). | Pharmacies **Pharmacie Pont Saint Jean,** 57 bd. Dominique Durandy, St-Jean 06230 (✆ **04-93-01-62-50**). |

Exploring St-Jean

One way to enjoy the area's beautiful backdrop is to stroll the public pathway that loops around Cap-Ferrat from Beaulieu all the way to Villefranche. The most scenic section runs from **plage de Paloma,** near Cap-Ferrat's southernmost tip, to **pointe St-Hospice,** where a panoramic view of the Riviera landscape unfolds. Allow around 3 hours to hike from St-Jean to family-friendly plage Passable, on the northwestern "neck" of the peninsula. Visitors can also explore the cap's crystal-clear waters from two locales in the old port. Ride on top of the waves on a rental kayak for 20€, or efoil for 225€, with **Cap Ferrat Watersports** (www.capferrat watersports.com; ✆ **06-16-67-78-28**). Or dip under with snorkel kit or scuba tanks from **Cap Ferrat Diving** (www.capferratwatersports.com; ✆ **06-89-26-95-25**).

Villa Ephrussi de Rothschild ★★ HISTORIC HOME/MUSEUM   If Jay-Z and Beyoncé had been born a century earlier, this is where they would live. The winter residence of Baronne Béatrice Ephrussi de Rothschild, this Italianate villa was completed in 1912 according to the finicky

CAP-FERRAT'S HOMES OF THE rich & famous

The global aristocratic, business, and cultural elite have long favored Cap-Ferrat. As you wander around keep your eyes out for these four key villas. **Lo Scoglietto** is a rococo pink edifice looking out towards Monaco from the promenade Maurice Rouvier coastal path. Once owned by Charlie Chaplin, it later passed to fellow British actor David Niven. More famous still is **Villa Mauresque** at the Cap's southern tip. In 1928 it was acquired by British author Somerset Maugham. The writer took up residence again after World War II to find that the liberating Allies had bombed his ornamental garden and the occupying Italians had raided his wine cellar. More modernist is **Villa La Voile.** This yacht-shaped mansion has "sails" that draw across the property each day to diffuse the Riviera sun. To lend an idea of Cap-Ferrat's worth, that particular project was overseen by Lord Norman Foster, the architect responsible for the world's biggest airport (in Beijing). Peek over the fence between Villefranche and Cap-Ferrat at the **Villa Nelcotte.** Once owned by Count Ernst de Brulatour, a secretary of the American embassy in France, then by Samuel Goldenberg, a wealthy American survivor of the Titanic, it was rented in 1971 by reprobate rocker Keith Richards. That summer the Rolling Stones recorded the album *Exile on Main Street* in the villa's sweaty basement. John Lennon dropped by, as did half the personalities of the Riviera underworld.

15

specifications of its ultra-rich owner. Today the pink edifice preserves an eclectic collection, gathered over her lifetime: 18th-century furniture, Tiepolo ceilings, tapestries from Gobelin, a games table gifted from Marie-Antoinette (Ephrussi's hero) to a friend, and tiny seats for her beloved poodles. The nine themed gardens, from Florentine to Japanese, are a particular delight. The attractive tea salon, which overlooks the Bay of Villefranche, is run by Aude Filipowski, a chef who learnt her trade at the Grand Hôtel du Cap-Ferrat. Try her large main courses for 24€ including Le Coquelicot, a salad of Crimean tomatoes, burrata, red fruits, and hand-made pesto.

1 av. Ephrussi de Rothschild. www.villa-ephrussi.com. ℂ **04-93-01-33-09.** Admission 14€ adults; 10€ students and children 7–17; free for children 6 and under. Family ticket (2 adults, 2 kids) 45€. July–Aug daily 10am–7pm; Mar–June and Sept–Oct daily 10am–6pm; Nov–Feb Mon–Fri 2–6pm and Sat–Sun 10am–6pm.

Where to Stay

Four Seasons Resort: Grand Hôtel du Cap-Ferrat ★★★   Put simply, this grande dame of a hotel is the greatest building on Europe's richest peninsula. It's sumptuous, stylish, and incredibly sexy. Set on nearly 7 hectares (17 acres) of tropical trees and manicured lawns, it's been the exclusive retreat of the international elite since 1908. The **Le Spa**

wellness center spills outside into curtained cabanas, where you can indulge in massages and other treatments. Aside from the modernist guest rooms, the coolest place to hang out is the seaside **Club Dauphin** beach club (nonguests can gain access for 110€ per day). It's reached by a funicular rail pod that descends from the hotel. The children of many visiting celebrities, including the Kennedys and Paul McCartney, have learned to swim in the Olympic-size infinity pool.

71 bd. du Général-de-Gaulle. www.fourseasons.com/capferrat. ✆ **04-93-76-50-50.** 73 units. From 676€ double; from 1,191€ suite. Closed mid-Nov–Feb. **Amenities:** 3 restaurants; bar; babysitting; beach club; bikes; Olympic-size heated outdoor pool; room service; spa; tennis; free Wi-Fi.

Hôtel Brise Marine ★ An Italianate villa constructed in 1878, the Brise Marine is tucked into a quiet residential neighborhood south of St-Jean. Rooms are simply furnished and sunny, with enchanting sea views. During breakfast on the rose-twined terrace, you can almost imagine you're aboard one of the luxury superyachts bobbing off Paloma Plage.

58 av. Jean-Mermoz. www.hotel-brisemarine.com. ✆ **04-93-76-04-36.** 16 units. 168€–246€ double; 203€–264€ triple. Parking 18€. Closed Nov–Mar. **Amenities:** Bar; room service; free Wi-Fi.

Where to Eat

Capitaine Cook ★★ PROVENÇAL/SEAFOOD Perhaps the peninsula's most beloved eatery, Capitaine Cook is run by husband-and-wife team Lionel and Nelly Pelletier. Dine outdoors on the leafy terrace or indoors within the ruggedly maritime dining room. The menu is particularly strong on hearty yet imaginative fish dishes, from Cap-Ferrat style bisque to salmon ravioli, with a strawberry and raspberry soup for dessert. A timeless classic.

11 av. Jean-Mermoz. ✆ **04-93-76-02-66.** Main courses 23€–31€; fixed-price menu 37€. Fri–Tues 12:30–2pm, Thurs–Tues 7:30–10:30pm. Closed mid-Nov to Dec.

BEAULIEU-SUR-MER ★

941km (583 miles) S of Paris; 9.5km (6 miles) E of Nice

Cradled on the mainland just east of Cap-Ferrat, the Belle Epoque resort of Beaulieu-sur-Mer has long attracted *bons vivants* with its casino and fine restaurants. Its palm-backed beaches and alfresco restaurants now welcome discreet celebrities from Bono to Kate Moss. A prime destination for a sunny afternoon in one of France's richest seaside resorts.

Essentials

ARRIVING Trains connect Beaulieu with Nice, Monaco, and the rest of the Côte d'Azur every 30 minutes. For rail information, visit www.sncf-connect.com or call ✆ **36-35.** Bus line no. 100 from Nice to Monte Carlo passes through Beaulieu. One-way fares cost 1.70€. For bus information and schedules, contact **Lignes d'Azur** (www.lignesdazur.com; ℂ **08-10-06-10-06**). By car from Nice, take D6098 (the basse corniche) east.

VISITOR INFORMATION Beaulieu's **Office de Tourisme** is on place Georges Clémenceau (www.otbeaulieusurmer.com; ℂ **04-93-01-02-21**), adjacent to the train station.

[FastFACTS] BEAULIEU

ATMs/Banks **Banque Populaire Côte d'Azur,** 40 bd. Marinoni (ℂ **04-89-81-10-56**).

Mail & Postage **La Poste,** pl. Georges Clemenceau (ℂ **36-31**).

Pharmacies **Pharmacie Anglaise,** 45 bd. Marinoni (ℂ **04-93-01-00-35**).

Exploring Beaulieu

Beaulieu has popular public beaches at both ends of town. The beaches aren't as rocky as those in Nice or other nearby resorts. The longer of the two is **Petite Afrique,** just past the yacht harbor. It has a submerged diving platform, a beach bar, and a family-friendly atmosphere. The shorter is **Baie des Fourmis,** which lies beneath the casino at the foot of Cap Ferrat. It's fun to stroll between the two and soak up the tony vibe.

The town is home to an important church, the late-19th-century **Église de Sacré-Cœur,** a quasi-Byzantine, quasi-Gothic mishmash at 13 bd. du Maréchal-Leclerc (ℂ **04-93-01-01-46**). It's open daily 8am to 7pm and provides calming shade on a sunny day.

For a memorable 90-minute walk, start north of boulevard Edouard-VII, where a path leads up the Riviera escarpment to **Sentier du Plateau St-Michel.** A belvedere here offers panoramic views from Cap d'Ail to the Estérel. A 1-hour alternative is the stroll along **promenade Maurice-Rouvier** past a dozen Belle Epoque mansions. The promenade runs parallel to the water, stretching from Beaulieu to St-Jean. On one side, you'll see the most elegant mansions in well-landscaped gardens, including the pink palace of former resident David Niven on place Niven; on the other, views of the Riviera landscape and the peninsular point of St-Hospice.

Villa Kérylos ★★ HISTORIC HOME/MUSEUM This replica ancient Greek residence, constructed between 1902 and 1908, was painstakingly designed by archaeologist and devoted Hellenophile Theodore Reinach. Both indoors and out, the villa is a fastidiously flawless copy of a 2nd-century Greek home. The bucolic waterside gardens, dotted with olive and pomegranate trees, offer sweeping vistas over nearby Cap-Ferrat. Little wonder the ritzy site doubles as a wedding venue for ultra-high net worth individuals, aided by the villa's proximity to five-star hotels like the Royal Riviera and Grand Hôtel du Cap-Ferrat. A calming escape from the Ferraris roaring past on the road behind.

Impasse Gustave Eiffel. www.villakerylos.fr. © **04-93-01-01-44.** Admission 11.50€ adults; free for children 18 and under. May–Aug daily 10am–6pm; Sept–Apr daily 10am–5pm.

Where to Stay

Le Havre Bleu ★★   You could spend a fortune on a luxury hotel. Or you could check into this Riviera stalwart that underwent a recent design overhaul, and blow your money in boutiques and beach clubs instead. Le Havre Bleu has a variety of comfy and modern (if tiny) accommodation options, including triples and family rooms, some with terraces and patios, that rarely rise above 100€ per night. Breakfast (8€) is served on the sunny communal terrace, where guests may sip a rosé or a café au lait any time of day. The train station, Villa Kérylos, and Villa Ephrussi de Rothschild are all within strolling distance.

29 bd. Maréchal Joffre. www.lehavrebleu.com. © **04-93-01-01-40.** 19 units. 80€–110€ double. Parking 12€. **Amenities:** Bar; free Wi-Fi.

Royal Riviera ★★   A bona-fide Riviera luxury hotel with all the trappings, yet none of the pretention. Opened in 1904, the hotel has a palatial look from outside, with airy, contemporary guest rooms within. They're prized for their plush, oversized beds, vibrant furnishings (they vary by room) and fabulous sea views. The hotel's low-key friendliness extends to kids, too, who will enjoy treasure hunts on the hotel's private beach, waterskiing lessons, and pottery workshops. The gigantic swimming pool is heated in autumn and spring, and surrounded by verdant gardens.

3 av. Jean Monnet. www.royal-riviera.com. © **04-93-76-31-00.** 94 units. 250€–715€ double; from 765€ suite. Parking 25€. **Amenities:** 2 restaurants; bar; babysitting; concierge; exercise room; indoor pool; private beach; room service; spa; free Wi-Fi. Closed mid Nov–Jan.

Where to Eat

The African Queen ★★ FRENCH/INTERNATIONAL   A lively mix of yachties and excellent cuisine makes this portside restaurant perennially popular. Wood-fired pizzas are superb; the finely chopped *salade Niçoise* is dressed at your table; the sole *meunière* is a buttery classic. Service can be erratic, but both the menu and the marina-side atmosphere are a delight. Celebrity-spotting opportunities abound all summer long here and yachts bob just a few feet from the dining tables. (The rental price tag on most of them starts at around 100,000€ per week.)

Port de Plaisance. www.africanqueen.fr. © **04-93-01-10-85.** Pizzas 16€; main courses 18€–40€. Daily noon–midnight. Closed some holidays.

Baia Bella ★★ MEDITERRANEAN   Beaulieu's newest restaurant is a carbon-neutral beach bar and eatery operated by passionate environmentalist Agathe Vanini. That means wooden furniture, returnable glasses, and recycled shower water. Beach mattresses cost 27€ per day. Beyond the beach club, most patrons come here for the cool restaurant area which serves tasty char-grilled swordfish steaks and clam linguine. Sunset cocktails are a delight.

Petite-Afrique plage. www.baiabella.fr. ✆ **04-93-01-11-00.** Main courses 17€–36€. Apr–Sept daily noon–3pm and 7–10pm.

ÈZE & LA TURBIE ★★

942km (584 miles) S of Paris; 11km (6¾ miles) NE of Nice

The hamlets of Èze and La Turbie, 6.5km (4 miles) apart, are picture-perfect hill villages that literally cling to the mountains. Both have fortified medieval cores overlooking the coast, and both were built during the early Middle Ages to stave off raids from Saracen pirates on the coast

below. In Èze's case, it's now tour buses that make daily invasions into town. Impossibly cute streets contain galleries, boutiques, and artisans' shops. La Turbie is much quieter, offering a welcome respite from the summertime heat.

Essentials

ARRIVING   Trains connect Èze-sur-Mer with Nice, Monaco, and the rest of the Côte d'Azur every 30 minutes. You may take a taxi from here up 427m (1,400 ft.) to Èze; alternatively, bus no. 83 connects the rail station with the hilltop village. For rail information, visit www.sncf-connect.com or call ✆ **36-35. Bus** line no. 82 runs between Nice and Èze around every 90 minutes, with a journey time of 40 minutes, while several daily buses (no. 605) connect Èze with La Turbie, a journey of around 20 minutes. For all bus

The hilltop village of Èze.

information and schedules, contact **Lignes d'Azur** (www.lignesdazur.com; ✆ **08-10-06-10-06**). By **car** from Nice, take the spellbindingly pretty D6007 (the *moyenne corniche*) east.

Èze's **Office de Tourisme** is on place du Général-de-Gaulle, Èze-Village (www.eze-tourisme.com; ☎ **04-93-41-26-00**). La Turbie's small **tourist information point** is at 2 pl. Detras, La Turbie (www.menton-riviera-merveilles.fr; ☎ **04-93-41-21-15**).

[FastFACTS] ÈZE & LA TURBIE

ATMs/Banks **Société Générale,** pl. de Gaulle, Eze (☎ **39-33**); **Banque Postal,** pl. Nueve, La Turbie (☎ **09-69-39-99-98**)

Mail & Postage **La Poste,** av. du Jardin Exotique, Èze; **La Poste,** pl. Neuve, La Turbie 06360; both ☎ **36-31**.

Pharmacies **Pharmacie de l'Aigle,** pl. de Gaulle, Èze (☎ **04-93-41-06-17**); **Pharmacie de La Turbie,** 6 av. Général de Gaulle, La Turbie 06360 (☎ **04-93-41-16-50**).

Exploring Èze & La Turbie

Aside from its pretty lanes, the leading attraction in Èze is the **Jardin d'Èze ★**, 20 rue du Château (☎ **04-93-41-10-30**). Here exotic plants are interspersed with feminine sculptures by Jean Philippe Richard, all perched atop the town at 427m (1,400 ft.; 7€ adults, 4€ students and ages 12–25, and free for children 11 and under). In July and August, it's open daily 9am to 7:30pm; until 6.30pm in April, May, June, and October; and until 4:30pm from November to March.

La Turbie boasts an impressive monument erected by Roman emperor Augustus in 6 B.C., the **Trophée des Alps (Trophy of the Alps) ★**. Still partially intact today, it was created to celebrate the subjugation of the French Alpine tribes by the Roman armies, and appears straight out of a Hollywood blockbuster. The nearby **Musée du Trophée d'Auguste,** cours Albert-1er de Monaco (www.trophee-auguste.fr; ☎ **04-93-41-20-84**), is an interactive mini-museum containing finds from digs nearby, a historical 3D film, and details about the monument's restoration. Both the ruins and the museum are open daily May to August 10am to 6pm, and September to April 10am to 1pm and 2 to 5pm. Admission to both sites is 6€ adults and free for children 17 and under.

Where to Stay

Château de la Chèvre d'Or ★★★ No hotel better sums up the glamour and grace of the French Riviera than La Chèvre d'Or. The resort hotel is built into and around the elegant hilltop town of Èze. Each sumptuously decorated suite is a grand apartment with a panoramic view of the coastline. It's a habitual favorite of royalty and A-listers, who adore its privacy, and the extremely personal service: There's a ratio of three staff members to each room or suite. The outdoor spaces are as grand as the indoor ones, thanks to 38 terraced gardens that drip down the hill towards the Mediterranean. But the best thing about La Chèvre d'Or is its eponymous double-Michelin-starred **restaurant** overseen by chef Arnaud Faye (fixed-price menus 140€–220€). Experimental dishes include a vegan square decorated with an edible garden of herbs and flowers; San Remo shrimp wrapped in oyster-infused gossamer-thin pasta; and roast lamb served with chickpea pancakes and lemon leaves.

Rue du Barri. www.chevredor.com. © **04-92-10-66-66.** 37 units. 277€–409€ double; from 790€ suite. Parking 20€. Closed Dec–Feb. **Amenities:** 4 restaurants; bar; babysitting; exercise room; outdoor pool; room service; sauna; free Wi-Fi.

Where to Eat

Top dining experience in these parts is at La Chèvre d'Or (see above).

La Table de Patrick Raingeard ★★ MODERN FRENCH   Cap Estel hides one of most discreet, and insanely pricey, Riviera hotels, a place where older A-listers stay. We're not recommending it as a hotel, but we *do* like chef Patrick Raingeard's Michelin-starred restaurant within, set in glorious, seafront gardens. Food becomes theater by way of zucchini flowers on verbena ice cream and crayfish atop Gewürztraminer wine jelly. Raingeard is big on local produce, sourcing carrots from above Nice, girolles mushrooms from Provence forests, and red mullet from the local coast. Just beware the initial offer of Champagne, which clocks in at 30€ or more per glass.

Inside the Hotel Cap Estel, 1312 av.Raymond-Poincaré. www.capestel.com.© **04-93-76-29-29.** Fixed-price menus 155€–250€. Tues–Sat 7:30–10pm. Closed Oct–Apr.

Le Nid d'Aigle ★ FRENCH   The "Eagle's Nest" is just that: a restaurant perched high above the ocean in Èze village with staggering views from some outdoor tables. Ambience is casual with plastic chairs on the

EXPLORING local history

On the western side of Monaco, reachable by a picturesque coastal trail cut into the coastline's rocks, is the **Villa les Camélias,** 17 av. Raymond Gramaglia, Cap d'Ail (www.villalescamelias.com; © **04-93-98-36-57**). A local history museum, albeit one with astounding sea views and a private swimming pool, the villa charts the history of this Monaco suburb by way of photographs, handwritten notes from regular visitor Sir Winston Churchill, and even a calling card from a glamorous local bordello. It's open from April to November Tuesday to Friday 9:30am to 12:30pm and 2 to 6pm, and Sunday 11am to 6pm; and from December to March Tuesday to Friday 9:30am to noon and 1:30 to 4:30pm, and Sunday 10am to 4pm. Admission is 9€ adults, 5€ for children aged 12 to 18, and free for children 11 and under.

al fresco terrace. The focus is on the family-run kitchen that serves up no-nonsense classics like tagliatelle alla carbonara and beef bourguignon with gnocchi. The wooden tables inside offer a cozy retreat in winter.

1 rue du Chateau. www.leniddaigle-eze.com. ✆ **04-93-41-19-08.** Main courses 16€–24€. July–Aug Sun–Thurs noon–9pm; Sept–June Sun–Thurs noon–5pm.

MONACO ★★

939km (582 miles) S of Paris; 18km (11 miles) E of Nice

This sunny stretch of coast became the property of the Grimaldi clan in 1297. The dynasty has maintained something resembling independence ever since. In recent decades the family has turned Monaco into the world's chicest city-state with its own mini-airport (with direct helicopter links to Nice and St-Tropez, no less).

Hemmed in by France on three sides and the Mediterranean on the fourth, this feudal anomaly harbors the world's greatest number of billionaires per capita. And as almost everybody knows, the Monégasques do not pay taxes. The tax regime attracts celebrity exiles as well—including racing driver Lewis Hamilton and tennis legend Novak Djokovic. Nearly all of Monaco's revenue comes from banking, tourism, and gambling. Better still, in an astute feat of cunning, local residents aren't allowed to gamble away their inheritance, so visitors must bring a passport to play in the Principality's famed casino.

The yacht-filled harbor of Monte Carlo.

Monaco, or, more precisely, its capital of Monte Carlo, has for a century been a symbol of glamor. The 1956 marriage of Prince Rainier III to actress Grace Kelly enhanced its status. She met the prince while in Cannes to promote *To Catch a Thief.* Their daughter, Caroline, was born in 1957; a son, Albert, in 1958; and a second daughter, Stephanie, in 1965. The next generation of Grimaldis, personified by socialite and philanthropist Andrea Casiraghi, born in 1984, the eldest grandchild of Prince Rainier, have stepped up to carry the royal flag.

Prince Rainier was nicknamed the "Builder Prince" as he expanded Monaco by building into the Mediterranean. Prince Albert took over from his late father in 2005 and burnishes his "Eco-Prince" credentials with pride. Newer, more environmentally conscious land-reclamation schemes near the Fairmont Hotel involve transporting hundreds of thousands of tons of sand from Sicily to create an extra 6 hectares (15 acres) of land. The entirely new seafront quartier, known as Mareterra, will open in 2025. The Principality also has its own green car manufacturer, Venturi—although this marquee specializes in a typically Monégasque market for all-electric supercars.

Fortunately for the Grimaldi line, Albert married his girlfriend, South African swimmer Charlene Wittstock, in 2011, now Her Serene Highness The Princess of Monaco. Despite rumors of a strained relationship, the royal couple are honored in the Principality. Their twins, Jacques and Gabriella, will celebrate their 10th birthday in 2024. The royal family's official portrait has pride of place in every bar, hotel, and bakery in the land.

Essentials

ARRIVING   Monaco has rail, bus, highway—and helicopter—connections from other coastal cities, particularly Nice. There are no border formalities when entering Monaco from France. The 19km (12-mile) drive from Nice takes around 30 minutes and runs along the N7 Moyenne Corniche. The pretty D6098 coast road takes a little longer. **Lignes d'Azur** (www.lignes dazur.com; ✆ **08-10-06-10-06**) runs a bus service at 15-minute intervals aboard line no. 100 from Nice to Monte Carlo. One-way bus transit from Nice costs 1.70€. Trains arrive every 30 minutes from Cannes, Nice, Menton, and Antibes (www.sncf-connect.com; ✆ **36-35.** Monaco's underground railway station (*gare*) is on place St. Devote. A system of pedestrian tunnels, escalators, and elevators riddle the Principality, and such an underground walkway links the train station to Monte Carlo. The scheduled **chopper** service to Nice Airport costs 195€ via **Heli Air Monaco** (www.heli airmonaco.com; ✆ **92-05-00-50**). The company also offer tandem parachute jumps, by helicopter, high above the Principality. By **bus** it's just 19.40€ (www.niceairportxpress.com; ✆ **04-97-00-07-00**) to Nice Airport.

> ### Phoning Monaco
>
> To call Monaco from within France, dial 00 (the access code for all international long-distance calls from France); followed by the country code, 377; and then the eight-digit local phone number. (Don't dial 33; that's the country code for France.)

VISITOR INFORMATION   The **Direction du Tourisme et des Congrés tourist office** is at 2A bd. des Moulins (www.visitmonaco.com; ✆ **92-16-61-16**).

CITY LAYOUT   The second-smallest state in the world (Vatican City is the tiniest), Monaco consists of four parts. The Old Town, **Monaco-Ville,** is on a rocky promontory 60m (197 ft.) high. It's the seat of the Prince's Palace and the government building, as well as the Oceanographic Museum. To the west, **La Condamine** is at the foot of the Old Town, forming its ritzy harbor and port sector. This area also has an open-air daily market. Up from the port (Monaco is seriously steep) is **Monte**

Carlo, the playground of royalty and celebrity, and the setting for the casino, the Tourist Office, and various luxurious hotels. The fourth part, **Fontvieille,** is an industrial suburb housing the Monaco Football club.

SPECIAL EVENTS   Two of the most-watched car-racing events in the world take place here in January (**Le Rallye**) and May (the **Grand Prix**); see www.acm.mc and www.formula1monaco.com. The **Monte-Carlo Masters ATP** tennis tournament (www.montecarlotennismasters.com) takes place in April. The Monte-Carlo International Fireworks Festival lasts all summer long. The skies above the harbor light up several times a week as millions of euros go up in smoke, courtesy of those who can assuredly afford it.

[Fast FACTS] MONACO

ATMs/Banks   Among many others, several banks are along boulevard Albert 1er behind the Port of Monaco.

Mail & Postage   **La Poste,** pl. de la Mairie in Monte-Carlo (𝄢 **36-31**).

Pharmacies   **Pharmacie Internationale,** 22 rue Grimaldi (𝄢 **04-93-50-35-99**).

Getting Around

BY FOOT   Aside from two very steep hills, the world's second-smallest country is **pedestrian-friendly.**

BY TAXI   Taxis wait outside Monaco train station, or call 𝄢 **08-20-20-98-98.** Expect to pay 20€ for a journey within Monaco. Brace yourself: Uber doesn't work here.

BY ELECTRIC BIKE   **MonaBike** (www.monabike.mc) lets guests unlock 350 electric bikes from 35 docking stations around the city-state. Pay 1€ per ride or 3€ for a 24-hour stint.

BY PUBLIC TRANSPORT   **CAM** (www.cam.mc; 𝄢 **97-70-22-22**) runs buses inside the Principality. Line nos. 1 and 2 link Monaco-Ville with the casino area. CAM's **solar-powered shuttle boat** hops between the banks of Monaco's port every 20 minutes. The ride is great for kids and connects the casino area with the foot of Monaco-Ville. All CAM tickets cost 2€.

BY OPEN-TOP BUS   **Monaco–Le Grand Tour** (www.monacolegrand tour.com; 𝄢 **97-70-26-36**) open-top minibuses allow visitors to hop on and hop off at the Principality's 12 main sights. Day passes cost 23€ adults; 8€ children between 4 and 11; free for children 3 and under.

BY ELECTRIC CAR   It may be the land of the gas-guzzling Grand Prix, but Monaco is a global pioneer in green technology and is justly proud of its eco-credentials. Join the club with **Mobee** (www.mobee.mc), Monaco's sexy car-sharing service based around the **Renault Twizy,** a super-tiny electric car. Prices are around 20€ per hour or 40€ for 4 hours—enough time to whiz to some secret beaches and all the Monaco sights. These electric cars enjoy complimentary parking in 14 public spaces across Monaco, with distribution points highlighted on an app.

Exploring Monaco

Monaco's main sights—including its glamorous port, casino, and hotels—are clustered around the pedestrianized place du Casino. Its principal museums, including the Prince's Palace and Oceanographic Museum, are situated on the history-laden rock of Monaco-Ville.

Erudite local Jean-Marc Ferrie at **Monaco Rando** (www.monaco-rando.com; © **06-30-12-57-03**) organizes guided hikes in French around his hometown from 15€ per person with an interpreter in-tow.

Casino de Monte-Carlo ★★★ CASINO   Founder François Blanc developed the Casino de Monte-Carlo into the most famous in the world, attracting the exiled aristocracy of Russia, Sarah Bernhardt, Mata Hari, King Farouk, and Aly Khan. The architect of Paris's Opéra Garnier,

Casino de Monte-Carlo.

Charles Garnier, built the oldest part of the casino, and it remains an example of the 19th century's most opulent architecture. Casino de Monte-Carlo, which has been the subject of countless legends and the setting for many films (remember poor Lucy Ricardo and the chip she found lying on the casino floor?). Depending on the era, you might have seen Mata Hari shooting a tsarist colonel with a jewel-encrusted revolver when he tried to slip his hand inside her bra to discover her secrets—military, not mammary. The late King Farouk, known as "the Swine," used to devour as many as eight roast guinea hens and 50 oysters before losing thousands at the table. Richard Burton presented Elizabeth Taylor with the obscenely huge Kohinoor diamond here.

The casino's marble-floored Atrium is open to all (with the presentation of a valid passport). Gamers can shoot slots or play blackjack in the hallowed Salle des Amériques or try their luck at roulette in the Salle Europe. For roulette, trente et quarante, and Texas Hold'em visit the private areas of rococo Salon Touzet and Salon Médecin. Entrance to Les Salons Supers Privés is by invitation only (heh, they've got our number!) and requires smart dress and nerves of steel. In warm weather head to the alfresco terrace. Here visitors may play roulette and poker overlooking the moonlit Mediterranean.

Place du Casino. www.montecarlosbm.com. ℂ **377-98-06-21-21.** Entry 18€. Daily 2pm on.

Collection des Voitures Anciennes de S.A.S. le Prince de Monaco ★★ CAR MUSEUM   This massive showcase of the Princes' private collection exhibits more than 200 vintage autos, including the 1956 Rolls-Royce Silver Cloud that carried the prince and princess on their wedding day. Other highlights include a 2009 Mercedes McLaren SLR, a 1986 Lamborghini Countach. A Toyota Lexus with a bulletproof glass roof served as the royal wedding car for the marriage of Prince Albert and Charlene Wittstock.

Les Terrasses de Fontvieille. www.mtcc.mc. ℂ **92-05-28-56.** Admission 10€ adults, 5€ students and children 6–17, free for children 5 and under. Daily 10am–6pm. Closed Christmas.

Les Grands Appartements du Palais ★★ PALACE   The home of Monaco's royal family, the Palais du Prince dominates the Principality from the Rock. A tour of the Grands Appartements—with audio tour recorded by none other than Prince Albert himself—allows visitors to glimpse the Throne Room and artworks by Bruegel and Holbein. The palace was built in the 13th century, and some of it dates from the Renaissance. The ideal time to arrive is 11:55am, so you can watch the 10-minute Relève de la Garde (Changing of the Guard). Summer concerts by the Monte-Carlo Philharmonic Orchestra are held outside in the courtyard.

Fancy a Facebook post? Forget it—taking photos inside the Prince's palace is strictly prohibited.

pl. du Palais. www.palais.mc. ℂ **93-25-18-31.** Admission 10€ adults; 5€ children 6–17; free for children 5 and under. Daily Apr–Oct 10am–6pm. Closed Nov–Mar.

Musée Océanographique de Monaco ★★ AQUARIUM This mammoth oceanfront museum was founded by Albert I, great-grandfather of the present prince, in 1910. It's now a living, breathing science lesson covering the world's oceans by way of a Mediterranean aquarium, tropical tanks, and a shark reserve. A delight for budding marine scientists is the 18m-long (60-ft.) whale skeleton that washed up on a local beach a century ago. Equally as compelling are the scientific specimens brought up from the ocean depths over the past 100 years. The restaurant and bar on the museum roof have brilliant views.

The Musée Océanographique de Monaco.

Av. St-Martin. www.oceano.mc. ℂ **93-15-36-00.** Admission 19€ adults; 12€ children 4–17; free for children 3 and under. Daily Apr–June and Sept 10am–7pm; July–Aug 9:30am–8pm; Oct–Mar 10am–6pm.

Nouveau Musée National de Monaco ★★ ART MUSEUM The Villa Sauber and Villa Paloma museums are two stunning art spaces set in palatial former homes across the city from one another. Both bring in global culture vultures by way of contemporary-art exhibitions and shows covering sculpture, architecture, photography, and the French Riviera's glamorous history. The villas are amazing in themselves; the Sauber is a belle époque home built by the developers of the Casino de Monte-Carlo, while Villa Paloma was constructed by an American, Edward N. Dickerson, who adored the view across the Bay of Monaco. In 2023, the Villa Sauber dedicated a show to the zany former Riviera home of artist Jean Cocteau, who "tattooed" the walls with frescoes with the help of friend Pablo Picasso.

Villa Sauber, 17 av. Princess Grace; Villa Paloma, 56 bd. du Jardin Exotique. www.nmnm.mc. ℂ **98-98-16-82.** Admission to both 6€ adults; free for visitors 26 and under. June–Aug daily 11am–7pm; Sept–May daily 8am–6pm.

Opéra de Monte-Carlo ★ OPERA HOUSE   Monaco takes music seriously. The Principality's lavish Opera House sits next to the casino, where its Salle Garnier hosts rock, pop, classical, and opera events—and even hosted the wedding reception of Prince Albert and Charlene Wittstock. Naturally, when guests attend the Opera House for events like 2024's performance of Brahms' *Requiem,* they dress to impress. For big-hitting pop, orchestral, and DJ events, head to the **Grimaldi Forum,** 10 av. Princesse-Grace (www.grimaldiforum.com; ✆ **99-99-20-00**).

pl. du Casino. www.opera.mc. ✆ **98-06-28-28.** Year-round admission prices 40€–180€ adults; reduced entrance for visitors 26 and under.

Thermes Marins ★★   This century-old institution embodies wellness at its most chic. It hosts a gigantic modernist swimming pool, gym room overlooking Monaco, and sunbathing terrace perched above the Formula One Grand Prix circuit. Spread over four floors are a Turkish hammam (steam bath), healthy restaurant, juice bar, tanning booths, fitness center, beauty center, and private treatment rooms. Get a day pass for access to all the facilities. Therapies go beyond the usual, including cryotherapy (intense cold) and lymphatic drainage.

2 av. de Monte-Carlo. www.thermesmarinsmontecarlo.com. ✆ **98-06-69-00.** Day pass 195€, pricing varies on other therapies.

Outdoor Activities

BEACHES   Just outside the border on French soil, the Monte-Carlo Beach Club adjoins the **Monte-Carlo Beach Hotel,** 22 av. Princesse-Grace (www.monte-carlo-beach.com; ✆ **93-28-66-66**), a five-star sister

---

MONACO glamour

Museums are all well and good, but to survey the soul of Monaco you need a credit card, a suntan, and a late-morning wake-up call. Early-evening glamour revolves around the bars that surround the historic port. Here, locally based luxury yacht agencies like **Y.CO** (www.y.co; ✆ **93-50-12-12**) charter 50m-long (262-ft.-) sailing craft for around $400,000 per week. At lunchtime, **Odyssey** (www.metropole.com; ✆ **93-15-15-56**), a pool lounge inside the Hôtel Metropole designed by Karl Lagerfeld, is the place to see-and-be-seen.

At sundown the action moves uphill to place du Casino, where **Buddha Bar** (✆ **98-06-19-19**) is bedecked with chinoiserie, Asian statues, and a raised DJ booth. **Le Bar Américain** (✆ **98-06-38-38**), in the Hôtel de Paris, is far more raucous, with chillingly expensive cocktails and nightly jazz. Near Plage du Larvotto, the timeless superclub **Jimmy'z** (✆ **98-06-36-36**), open Wednesday to Saturday 11:30pm until dawn, has attracted stars from Farrah Fawcett to George Clooney.

But it's the iconic **Casino de Monte-Carlo** (see above) that's still the biggest player in Monaco's raging nightlife scene.

establishment of the ultra-elegant Hôtel de Paris. Princess Grace used to frolic here, and today it's an integral part of Monaco social life. It has an Olympic-size swimming pool, a La Prairie spa, cabanas, a poolside fine dining restaurant, and a low-key Mediterranean restaurant. Beach activities include inner tubes, jet skis, and parachute rides. As the temperature drops in late October, the beach closes for the winter. The admission charge of 80€ to 170€, depending on the season, grants you access to changing rooms, toilets, restaurants, and bar, along with use of a mattress for sunbathing.

More low-key swimming and sunbathing is at **Plage du Larvotto,** off avenue Princesse-Grace. Part of this popular strip of sand is public. The other part contains private beach clubs with bars, snacks, and showers, plus a kids' club. A jogging track runs behind the beach.

SWIMMING   Overlooking the yacht-studded harbor, the **Stade Nautique Rainier-III,** quai Albert-1er, at La Condamine (✆ **93-30-64-83**), a pool filled with warm filtered seawater frequented by the Monégasques, was a gift from Prince Rainier to his subjects. There are multiple diving platforms and a slide. It's open May to October daily 9am to 6pm (June–Aug until 8pm). Admission costs 12€ per adult, or 9€ for children aged between 3 and 17. Between November and March, it's an ice-skating rink.

Where to Stay

Fairmont Monte Carlo ★★   This five-star hotel is easily Monaco's most fun. It combines fine-dining restaurants, a spa, and a rooftop pool with an unstuffy attitude; albeit one backed by a legion of ever-smiling, mostly Italian, staff. Of course, this vision of modern opulence is also one of the most valuable pieces of real estate on the Côte d'Azur. It dips into the Mediterranean from behind the Casino de Monte-Carlo—indeed, a private passageway runs to the casino's rear entrance—and guests may combine the endless breakfast with the best sea views in the Principality. Formula 1 fans should also note that the fastest part of the Monaco Grand Prix zips right beneath the basement. Post-race, winning drivers traditionally leap into the rooftop pool full clothed. The Fairmont also has a partnership with several local beach clubs, where guests are dropped off with towels, mineral water, and sun spray, then picked up on demand.
12 av. des Spélugues. www.fairmont-montecarlo.com. ✆ **93-50-65-00.** 602 units. 257€–1,034€ double; from 432€ suite. Parking 60€. **Amenities:** 3 restaurants; 2 bars; babysitting; concierge; health club; outdoor pool; room service; spa; free Wi-Fi.

Hôtel de Paris ★★★   Never has so much history and glamour been suffused into 158 effortlessly chic guest rooms. Sir Winston Churchill was also a regular. Accommodation culminates in a series of super suites, including the Princess Grace suite, which has a price tag of over 40,000€ per night. The former British Prime Minister used to sneak along a secret rooftop passageway from his suite to restaurant **Le Grill,** which has a special 85€ three-course lunch menu—a relative bargain in Monaco. It's one of three award-winning restaurants in the hotel (see also the Louis XV, below). If that isn't enough, the Hôtel de Paris boasts several sister hotels, including the five-star family friendly **Monte-Carlo Beach Hotel** (www.monte-carlo-beach.com; ✆ **93-28-66-66**)—where received the region's first 100% organic certificate—and the imposingly elegant **Hôtel Hermitage** (www.hotelhermitagemontecarlo.com; ✆ **98-06-40-00**), just around the corner, which is more intimate and less showy as the Hôtel de Paris, but just as luxurious.

pl. du Casino. www.montecarlosbm.com. ✆ **98-06-30-00.** 115 units. From 750€ double; from 1,850€ suite. Valet parking 60€. **Amenities:** 3 restaurants (see Le Louis XV, p. 670); bar; babysitting; concierge; exercise room; large indoor pool; room service; sauna; Thermes Marins spa offering thalassotherapy; free Wi-Fi.

Hôtel Miramar ★★   Open since 2022, every room at Monaco's cutest—and usually least expensive—hotel has a sea view. Regular double rooms aren't large (but the entire country occupies 202 hectares/less than 1 sq. mile, so little wonder). But they do come with king sized beds, free coffee at reception, and the priceless harbor panorama. Nine of the rooms have private terraces, which would cost a thousand dollars anywhere else. Breakfast is served on the top floor terrace.

1 av. JF Kennedy. www.hotelmiramar.com. ✆ **97-97-96-96.** 14 units. 160€–270€ double. Breakfast included. Parking 10€. **Amenities:** Bar; free Wi-Fi.

Where to Eat

This postcard-sized Principality boasts a total of nine Michelin stars and includes one of the most celebrated restaurants on planet earth, Le Louis XV. For several others, see the hotel listings above.

Conscientiae ★★ MEDITERRANEAN   In body-beautiful Monaco, this hot new restaurant (open since summer 2023) focuses on environmentally conscious cuisine using the freshest and most sustainable vegetables, fish, and meats. The principality's cool crowd sips homemade lemonade and kombucha on sofas overlooking the port, or dine inside in the Bali-style interior on the bargain set lunch, which can include a starter of artichoke salad and goat cheese, followed by a main course of raw seafood ceviche, plus dessert. Other specialties include a triple hummus (colored by chickpeas, beets, and lentils) and a V-bowl of quinoa, tomatoes, and spirulina.

6 quai Antoine 1er. www.conscientiae.com. ✆ **97-97-95-95.** Main courses 26€–46€; fixed-price lunch 28€. Mon–Sat noon–3pm and 7–10:30pm (coffee and juices served all day from 8am).

Il Terrazzino ★★ Italian   This locals-only restaurant, serving food like mamma used to make, has won the respect of the many Italians living in Monaco. The lunchtime set menu of a daily pasta, a dessert, and a Neapolitan coffee at 19€ ranks among the best value in the entire Principality.

Meat dishes served amid the southern Italian décor include Napoli-style meatballs with pasta, and tuna fillet in a pistachio crust. As proof of how small Monaco is, diners can walk 20 second north straight into France.

26 rue des Iris. www.il-terrazzino.com. ⓒ **93-50-24-27.** Main courses 13€–28€; fixed-price lunch 19€ or dinner 38€. Mon–Sat noon–2pm and 7:30–10pm.

Le Café de Paris ★ MODERN FRENCH   Celebrities regularly sip morning *café au lait* (6€) at this Place du Casino beauty spot. So though it is pricey, and service can be pretentious, this could be a pitstop to write home about. Later in the day, its classic bistro menu includes simple start-ers like garlic escargot and *croque-monsieur* plus more innovative main courses, like filet of plaice (a North Sea fish) with pumpkin purée. Best value is the bistro-style weekday dish of the day, which may include braised beef cheeks with polenta or scallop risotto.

pl. du Casino. ⓒ **98-06-76-23.** Main courses 30€–61€. Daily 8am–midnight.

Le Louis XV ★★★ MEDITERRANEAN   The Louis XV offers one of the finest dining experiences on the Riviera, and thus the world. Superstar chef Alain Ducasse oversees the refined but not overly adorned cuisine that has won three Michelin stars. Head chef Emmanuel Pilon presides over the painstakingly sourced yet awesomely executed starters like San Remo shrimp on a bed of rockfish jelly with caviar. Everything is light and attuned to the seasons, with intelligent, modern interpretations of Pro-vençal and northern Italian dishes. The old-school service, decor (the fres-coed ceiling includes the portraits of Louis XV's six mistresses), and the sheer amount of cutlery used, makes for a memorable evening.

In the Hôtel de Paris, pl. du Casino. www.montecarlosbm.com/en. ⓒ **98-06-88-64.** Jacket and tie recommended for men. Main courses 130€–145€; fixed-price lunch 210€ or dinner 280€–420€. Sat–Sun 12:15–1:45pm and 8–9:45pm; Thurs–Fri and Mon 8–9:45pm. Closed first 2 weeks Mar.

Shopping

Pricey duds from Hermès, Gucci, Lanvin, and the like can be found cheek by jowl near the Hôtel de Paris and the Casino de Monte-Carlo. To pick up the latest canvas from Damien Hirst, which sell for hundreds of thou-sands of dollars, try **Maison d'Art,** 27 av.de Costa (ⓒ **97-97-11-60**). **Chocolaterie de Monaco,** 20 rue Princesse Marie de Lorraine (ⓒ **97-97-88-88**), is the official chocolate supplier to the Prince of Monaco and offers more affordable treats. Just west of place du Casino, **Pretty You,** 5 av. Princesse Alice (ⓒ **97-70-48-08**), sells Oscar de la Renta and Elie Saab. Just east of this piazza, **Galeries du Métropole** is packed with high fashion and specialty stores. As well as Marina Rinaldi and Sonia Rykiel, try **Etro** for types of blingy fashions best worn in Monte Carlo. **Fnac** (ⓒ **08-25-02-00-20**) is recommended for English-language novels, Monaco his-tory books, and the latest electronics. Heading east from place du Casino,

boulevard de Moulins sells "everyday" Monaco labels. We're talking **Baby Dior,** no. 31 (✆ **97-25-72-12**), and swimwear-to-the-stars brand **Erès,** also at no. 31 (✆ **97-70-76-50**). For Repetto ballet slippers and Michael Kors satchels try **La Botterie,** no. 14 (✆ **97-25-80-55**). For real-people shopping, stroll **rue Grimaldi,** the Principality's most commercial street, near the fruit, flower, and food market at place des Armes, which is open daily from 7:30am until noon.

ROQUEBRUNE & CAP-MARTIN ★★

Roquebrune: 953km (591 miles) S of Paris, 7km (4½ miles) W of Menton, 58km (36 miles) NE of Cannes, 3km (1¾ miles) E of Monaco. Cap-Martin: 4km (2½ miles) W of Menton, 2.5km (1½ miles) W of Roquebrune.

Roquebrune, along the Grande Corniche, is a charming mountain village with vaulted streets. The views over the Mediterranean rival the village of Èze and are equally immense. Artists' workshops and boutiques with pricey merchandise line rue Moncollet. In 2022, an architecturally dazzling hotel and restaurant complex called Maybourne Riviera debuted, bringing with it a number of new visitors in search of the high life.

Down the hill from Roquebrune, Cap-Martin is a pine-covered peninsula, long associated with the rich and famous since the empress Eugénie wintered here in the 19th century. In time, the resort was honored by the presence of Sir Winston Churchill, who came here often in his final years. The long, pebbly plage de la Buse lies underneath Roquebrune-Cap-Martin train station. Its tranquility is disturbed only by the odd paraglider looping down to the beach from Roquebrune village.

Essentials

GETTING THERE   To drive to Roquebrune and Cap-Martin from Nice, follow N7 east for 26km (16 miles). Cap-Martin has train and bus connections from the other cities on the coast, including Nice and Menton. For railway information and schedules, www.sncf-connect.com or call ✆ **36-35.** To reach Roquebrune, you'll have to take a taxi or follow the hiking signs for 30 minutes uphill. For **bus information,** contact the Gare Routière in Menton (www.zestbus.fr; ✆ **04-93-28-43-27**).

ROQUEBRUNE

Exploring Roquebrune (www.menton-riviera-merveilles.fr) will take about 1 hour. You can stroll through its colorful streets, which retain their authentic feel. **Château de Roquebrune** (✆ **04-93-35-07-22**) was originally a 10th-century Carolingian castle; the present structure dates in part from the 13th century, although it was jazzed up by its wealthy British owner, Sir William Ingram, nearly a century ago. From the towers is a panoramic view along the coast. The interior is open in February to May

LE CORBUSIER & EILEEN GRAY on
cap-martin

Cap-Martin is the fabulously rich spit of land between Monaco and Menton. Not as glitzy as Cap-Ferrat nor as fabled as Cap d'Antibes, its beauty lies in a 2-hour coastal trail that loops past the gardens of countless billionaires.

This seaside path is as historical as it is beautiful. It was named after Le Corbusier, the zany French architect who built an urban utopia in Marseille before constructing a coastal retreat here. Pride of place goes to Le Corbusier's **Cabanon** log cabin. It was created by the architect to showcase his love of low-impact prefabricated living spaces. This ecologically conscious space was decades ahead of its time.

Even more fun is the row of five teeny-tiny **Holiday Cabins** nearby. Le Corbusier designed these 9-sq.-m (97-sq.-ft.) seaview escapes to prove that vacations should be about simplicity, not all-out luxury. Each one fits two beds, windows, storage, and sinks. Best of all is **Villa E-1027,** designed by Le Corbusier's sometime rival, the furniture designer Eileen Gray. Splashed with frescoes and beset with period furnishings, it's among the world's finest visions of art deco design. The rooftop garden is pretty special too. All the structures are now part of a (stunningly located) UNESCO World Heritage Site.

Guided visits to all three sites are compulsory for all visitors. Contact **Cap Moderne** (capmoderne.monuments-nationaux.fr; admission 18€ adults, 10€ children ages 7–17, 2€ for children ages 6 and under).

The **Sentier le Corbusier** path extends between Pointe du Cap-Martin to the eastern frontier of Monaco. If you have a car, you can park it in the lot at av. Winston-Churchill and begin your stroll. A sign labeled PROMENADE LE CORBUSIER marks the path. As you hike along, you'll take in a view of Monaco set in a natural amphitheater. In the distance, you'll see Cap-Ferrat and, high above, Roquebrune village.

The scenic path ends at Monte-Carlo Beach and passes several secret sandy coves en route. Walkers may then take the line no. 100 bus back to their rough starting point. An alternative is to return on foot from either Monte-Carlo Beach or Roquebrune-Cap-Martin train station, following the walking signs back through the Parc des Oliviers, which occupies the central spine of Cap-Martin.

daily 10am to 12:30pm and 2 to 6pm; June to September daily 10:30am to 6.30pm; and October to January daily 10am to 12:30pm and 2 to 5pm. Admission is 5€ for adults, 4€ for seniors, 3€ students and children 7 to 11, and free for children 6 and under.

Rue du Château leads to place William-Ingram. Cross this square to rue de la Fontaine and take a left. This leads you to the **Olivier millénaire** (millenary olive tree), the oldest tree in France—it's around 2,000 years old.

CAP-MARTIN

Once the exclusive domain of Belgian despot King Leopold II, Cap-Martin is still a fabulously rich peninsula of land. At its base, you can see the ruins of the Basilique St-Martin, a ruined priory constructed by the monks of the Lérins Islands in the 11th century.

You can also take one of the most scenic walks along the Riviera here, lasting about 2 hours. The coastal path, **Sentier Le Corbusier ★**, extends between Pointe du Cap-Martin to the eastern (meaning, the closest) frontier of Monaco. If you have a car, you can park it in the lot at avenue Winston-Churchill and begin your stroll. A sign labeled PROMENADE LE CORBUSIER marks the path. See the box on p. 672.

Where to Stay

Maybourne Riviera ★★   The newest grand hotel on the French Riviera is a razor-sharp triangle of glass set on an olive-scented mountaintop with epic views. Décor in the suites, many with tiny pools, is inspired by former local residents Le Corbusier and Coco Chanel. All share a photogenic infinity pool that appears suspended above the Monaco coastline. With its Michelin-starred restaurant **Ceto** (one of six dining establishments), which makes smart use of raw seafood and fresh fruit, there's little incentive to leave this lofty paradise. For an extra 40€ per day, guests can hit the new Maybourne La Plage beach club at the very tip of Cap Martin (150€ for nonguests). The seaside locale has sun loungers and local seafood dishes prepared by Mirazur's Mauro Colagreco, a previous winner of the best restaurant in the world.

1551 rte. de la Turbie. http://maybourneriviera.com. ⓒ **93-37-00-00.** 69 units. 608€–2,100€ double; from 1,460€ suite. Parking 50€. **Amenities:** 5 restaurants; 2 bars; babysitting; concierge; health club; outdoor pool; room service; spa; free Wi-Fi. Closed Jan-Mar.

MENTON ★★

963km (559 miles) S of Paris; 30km (19 miles) E of Nice

Pack your shades, for the Belle Époque resort of Menton is the sunniest place in all France. It's no surprise that this balmy locale hosts both a winter lemon festival and the finest botanical gardens in the country. Liberal sprinklings of sun, sand, and citrus also attracted artists by the dozens, among them Picasso, Matisse, and Jean Cocteau, who installed several artistic sights around town.

The aptly named Promenade du Soleil runs in front of Menton's Old City, port, and casino. Game guests may follow this seaside boulevard all the way into Monaco—provided they have a spare 90 minutes and a sturdy set of legs.

Essentials

ARRIVING   Trains run to Menton from Nice, Monaco, the rest of the Côte d'Azur en route, and right into Italy every 30 minutes. For rail information, visit www.sncf-connect.com or call ⓒ **36-35** (.40€/min.). Bus line no. 100 to Nice runs every 30 minutes until 8pm. One-way fares cost 1.70€. For bus information and schedules, contact **Lignes d'Azur** (www. lignesdazur.com; *C* **08-10-06-10-06**). By car from Nice, take D6098 (the basse corniche) east.

VISITOR INFORMATION   The **Office de Tourisme** occupies a magnificent Belle Époque building near the train station at 8 av. Boyer (www. menton-riviera-merveilles.fr; *C* **04-92-41-76-76**).

[FastFACTS] MENTON

ATMs/Banks   **Crédit Mutuel,** 24 rue de la République (*C* **32-25**).

Mail & Postage   **La Poste,** 2 cours George V (*C* **36-31**).

Pharmacies   **Grande Pharmacie Mentonnaise,** 32 rue de la République (*C* **04-93-57-57-79**).

Exploring Menton

Mentonnaise are lucky devils. They can choose to hang out in the historic Old Town, on a very long beach, or on the seaside boulevard (the Promenade du Soleil). The resort's world-famous gardens all lie just behind this ocean walk. Meanwhile, Jean Cocteau's artist legacy is spread out along the seafront.

Jardin Val Rahmeh ★★ GARDEN   Even if you loathe botanical gardens, and even if you only visit one in Menton, we beg you to come here. Menton's microclimate has reared a leafy wonderland within its protective walls. Fragrant paths weave past giant Amazon water lilies, Buddha's Hand citruses from Thailand, and flowering *toromiro* trees from Easter Island. The scene is most magical within the black bamboo plantation, where sunlight dapples a babbling brook. Menton's other botanical gardens include **Serre de la Madone.** They were designed and owned by American heir Lawrence Johnston, whose family made their fortune in the Klondike gold rush.

Route St Jacques. www.jardinbotaniquevalrahmehmenton.fr. *C* **04-93-35-86-72**. Admission 7€ adults; 5€ for children 16 and under. Apr–Oct Wed–Mon 9:30am–6pm; Nov–Mar Wed–Mon 9:30am–5pm.

Outdoor Activities

BEACHES   The all-public Plage du Soleil pans west from Menton to Cap Martin. Private beach clubs are on Plage du Garavan just east of town. All-day sun loungers at **Plage Les Sablettes** (www.sablettesbeach.com; *C* **07-76-14-18-32**) cost around 23€ per day.

BIKING   The verdant hills around Menton are the training ground for several Tour de France cyclists. Lesser mortals may still peddle along the

CHASING COCTEAU in menton

When not judging the Cannes Film Festival or chasing ballet dancers from the Monaco stage, *bon viveur* Jean Cocteau turned his artistic hand to painting on a grand scale. Cocteau's life-size love scenes inside Menton's **Salle des Marriages** (marriage office, pl. Ardoïno; adults 2€, free to children 17 and under; Mon–Fri 8:30am–noon and 2–4:30pm) earned him honorary citizenship of the town in 1958. Three years after Cocteau's death in 1963, the **Musée du Bastion** (Tues–Sun 10am–6pm) opened on Menton's seafront to showcase his final period of work. Sadly the grand **Musée Jean Cocteau** in the town center is closed until further notice due to flooding.

seafront from Italy to Monaco on a rented mountain bike (from 16€/day) or electric bike (from 25€/day) from **Bike Trip,** 1 av. Carnot (www.rent-bike.fr; ℂ **04-94-96-48-93**), which also offers self-guided tour maps of the Menton Riviera.

HIKING Three breathtakingly beautiful *villages perchés* (or perched villages) hover high above Menton. Each one is linked to the French Riviera by a winding mountain road. Better still, precipitous hiking trails run between each settlement.

- At 360m (1,181 ft.) in altitude, **Gorbio** is the lowest of the three. Beloved of artists seeking sanctuary from the coastal bustle, it boasts several colorful churches and a panoramic sea view.

- At 750m (2,461 ft.) high, **Sainte-Agnès** is the loftiest. Cobbled streets and country restaurants set the scene. The village once formed part of the Maginot Line fortifications built to protect France from Nazi Germany (not that it did much good). Remnants of the military bastion remain.

- Around 6km (4 miles) from **Menton,** Castellar perches above the Mediterranean like a fairytale redoubt. It's cute, quiet, and both the GR51 and GR52 walking trails pass through its medieval streets.

SAILING From the end of April until October visitors may bob around the Bay of Menton on a paddleboard, kayak, or sailing dinghy available for rent from the **Centre Nautique de Menton** (www.voile-menton.fr; ℂ **04-93-35-49-70**), beside beach bar La Pergola.

Where to Stay

Hôtel Napoléon ★★★ Is this the perfect French Riviera hotel? It comes pretty close. Guest rooms at this Cocteau-themed delight were designed by Jean-Philippe Noel, an artist usually found creating 7-star hotels in Dubai. Yet prices at the Napoléon couldn't be fairer for such a stunning beachfront location. The hotel also boasts a private beach club, a solar-powered heated swimming pool, and a leafy garden. Leaving such a cocoon of fine linen and original art for real life can be a painful experience.

29 porte de France. www.napoleon-menton.com. ℂ **04-93-35-89-50.** 44 units. 101€–372€ double. Parking 12€. **Amenities:** Bar; concierge; outdoor pool; free Wi-Fi.

Hôtel Palm Garavan ★★

The prize for the friendliest hotel in Menton goes to the Palm Garavan. Superior rooms boast cracking views over the resort's botanical gardens, while guests may also gaze at Italy in their bathrobes. The spotless modern accommodation boasts touch-sensitive lights and ice-white decor. A top touch is the 3.50€ express breakfast, offering early-bird guests a croissant and cappuccino before they hit the resort's gardens, art museums, and beach. Sometimes simple is best.

3 porte de France. www.hotelpalm.fr. ℂ **04-93-78-80-67.** 19 units. 90€–190€ double. Parking 10€. **Amenities:** Bar; free Wi-Fi.

Hôtel Royal Westminster ★

A grand hotel without the grand prices, the venerable Westminster has a plum emplacement, facing due south towards the shimmering Mediterranean in the center of town. Attracting an older clientele, guests may relax in the genteel front gardens or in the various lobby bars. Yes, the rooms are a little dated, but the sea views from its privilege rooms are a delight. On permanent display in the hotel are works by 150 different artists, many inspired by the sun-kissed climate of Menton. The hotel boasts a library and billiards room, too.

28 av. Félix Faure. www.hotel-royal-westminster.com. ℂ **04-93-28-69-69.** 92 units. 92€–218€ double. Parking 15€. **Amenities:** 2 restaurants; bar; concierge; library; free Wi-Fi.

Where to Eat

A mere mile from the Italian border, Menton does pizza and pasta with aplomb. For more exotic fare laced with Menton lemons and offerings from the Ligurian fishing fleet, sail in to one of the eateries below.

Al Vecchio Forno ★★ ITALIAN

As authentic as a Neapolitan scooter, this established eatery serves Menton's Italian neighbors from just across the border. If the dress and dialect of its patrons shout *The Godfather,* the pizza is just as genuine. Seasonal artichokes and *funghi* come from Italy, as does the mozzarella and sea bream. The latter is seared crisp alongside the pizzas in the wood-fired oven.

39 quai Bonaparte. ℂ **04-92-10-04-78.** Main courses 10€–22€. Daily 7–11pm.

Le Galion ★★ ITALIAN SEAFOOD

A guaranteed winner of a seafood restaurant that has hooked the same, mostly Italian, clientele for 5 decades. Dishes are served inside what looks like a historic galleon, decorated like the 1930s Moulin Rouge. Many ingredients come from the markets just across the Italian border. On starched white tablecloths find dishes like seabass baked in a salt crust and seared tuna coated with black sesame seeds.

Menton port. www.le-galion-restaurant-menton.fr. © **04-93-35-89-73.** Main courses 13€–36€. Thurs–Mon noon–2pm and 7–10pm.

Restaurant Mirazur ★★★ MODERN MEDITERRANEAN   The awards have rolled in for Mirazur's Argentine chef Mauro Colagreco, not least of all first place on San Pellegrino's World's 50 Best Restaurants list. The restaurant also held three stars in 2023's Michelin Guide. The watchword on Colagreco's single fixed-price menu (you'll pay dearly for this once-in-a-lifetime experience) is élan, not experimentation. This is sleepy Menton after all. Expect tuna carpaccio with raspberries and almonds, and langoustine decorated with edible flowers picked from the on-site vegetable garden, which is central to Colagreco's cuisine. Graceful service and a panoramic sea view over Menton Port complete this priceless picture. Oh, and book as far in advance as you possibly can.

30 av. Aristide Briand. www.mirazur.fr. © **04-92-41-86-86.** Fixed-price menu 450€. Wed–Sun noon–2pm and 7:30–10pm, Tues 7:30–10pm.

Shopping

Menton has an Italian heart, with the taste buds to match. The best place to start food shopping is the pedestrian-only **rue Saint Michel.** Try **Famille Mary** at no. 10 (© **04-92-09-19-43**) for flowery honey; or Menton-based **Oliviers & Co** at no. 5 (© **04-89-74-19-76**) for olive oil tastings. The town's most venerated product, its home-grown lemons, are sold by two rival stores at no. 22 and no. 27. From the former, **Au Pays du Citron** (www.aupaysducitron.fr, © **04-92-09-22-85**), purchase lemon soap and citrus liqueur. From the latter, **Coté Citron** (© **04-89-74-19-76**), find limoncello and marmalade. **Pasta Piemonte,** 34 rue Partouneaux (© **04-93-57-26-21**), sells fabulous fresh Italian ravioli, as well as cheeses, salamis, and truffles wrapped for the airplane home. One of Menton's most charming stores is **Maison Herbin,** 2 rue Vieux Collège (www.confitures-herbin.com, © **04-93-57-20-29**). Visitors can see local citrus turned into jams, chutneys, and candies in their adjoining sweet factory.

Nightlife

Sunny Menton hosts the highest number of retirees in France, so the resort doesn't exactly dance until dawn. However, the town buzzes all August during the **Menton Music Festival** (www.festival-musique-menton.fr), where evening classical concerts occupy almost every Old Town square. Gamblers may also test their luck at the **Menton Casino,** at 2 av. Félix Faure (www.casinosbarriere.com; © **04-92-10-16-16**). It boasts a traditional poker room as well as a vast seaview gaming terrace.

16

OCCITANIE

by Lily Heise

Occitanie in the south of France includes the cities of Montpellier, Nîmes, Toulouse, and Carcassonne. One of the leading wine-producing areas of the world, it's also known for its impressive Roman heritage and the 240km (149-mile) Canal du Midi.

Occitanie comprises two old provinces of France, Languedoc-Roussillon and Midi-Pyrénées, and is bordered by Provence-Alpes-Côte d'Azur to the east, Nouvelle-Aquitaine to the west and Spain to the south. Its name comes from the language (Occitan) previously spoken by its occupants. It roughly covers the former fiefdom of the Counts of Toulouse, who ruled it in the 12th and 13th centuries and whose eponymous city is now the regional capital.

The coast of this region, from Montpellier to the Spanish frontier, might be called France's "second Riviera" (after the Côte d'Azur). This land of ancient cities has an almost continuous strip of sand stretching west from the Rhône toward the Pyrénées, adored by sun lovers in July and August. But it's a far more relaxed region than its eastern rival, particularly out of season when the beaches empty, the cities return to their inhabitants and the crowds disappear.

The area around Perpignan is French Catalonia. From the 13th to the 17th centuries, it passed between the kings of Aragón, Majorca, and France. In 1659, it became part of Louis XIV's centralized kingdom. Though officially French today, cultural links with Spain are strong, and the high-speed rail link to Barcelona has brought the two Catalan cities even closer.

As for wine, Hérault, Aude, and Garde, all located in Occitanie, are some of the largest wine producers in the world. Huge investment over the years has led to a new reputation for the region's wines. It's become an area to discover small, boutique producers, biodynamic and organic experts, unknown labels and the local co-operatives. Look for Fitou in the Hautes-Corbières district near Narbonne, Minervois, north of Carcassonne, Gaillace west of Albi, and Blanquette de Limoux, south of Carcassonne.

NÎMES ★★★

713km (443 miles) S of Paris; 43km (27 miles) W of Avignon

Nîmes, originally Nemausus, is an extraordinarily rich city for Roman relics, with one of the best-preserved Roman amphitheaters in the world plus a near-perfect Roman temple. During the reign of Caesar Augustus (27

PREVIOUS PAGE: **Visitors walk between the two outer ramparts of Carcassonne, one of the most impressive fortified cities in Europe.**

679

B.C.–A.D. 14) Nîmes became an important city on the vital chariot route between Spain and Rome.

Like many cities, its fortunes waxed and waned, particularly after Arles took over as the local capital. By 1860, the togas of Nîmes' Roman citizenry had long given way to denim, the cloth *de Nîmes*. An Austrian immigrant to Nîmes, Levi Strauss, exported the heavy fabric to California to make into work pants for gold-rush prospectors. The rest, as they say, is history.

The city is more like Provence than Occitanie in feel. You might notice a touch of Pamplona, Spain, in the festivals of the *corridas* (bull-fights) at the arena and the flamenco festivals. But Nîmes has also championed modern architecture; the most innovative contemporary building is the Musée de la Romanité, which opened in June 2018.

Essentials

GETTING THERE   Nîmes has bus and train services from the rest of France and is near several autoroutes. It lies on the main rail line between Marseille and Bordeaux. Regular TGV trains arrive daily from Paris's Gare de Lyon; the one-way fare is from 24€ and the journey takes 2 hours, 51 minutes. The station is a 5-minute walk from the old center. Train information and schedules are on www.sncf-connect.com or call ✆ **36-35.** If you're driving, take A7 south from Lyon to Orange and connect to A9 into Nîmes.

VISITOR INFORMATION   The **Office de Tourisme** is at 6 rue Auguste (www.ot-nimes.fr; ✆ **04-66-58-38-00**).

CITY LAYOUT   All the main attractions, both ancient and modern are in a small central area, originally the Roman city.

Jardin de la Fontaine.

Occitanie

FRANCE

Paris

LANGUEDOC-ROUSSILLON

20 mi

20 km

GETTING AROUND   The center of Nîmes is traffic free, but five car parks surround the center, so park and walk.

Exploring Nîmes

It's worth getting the **Nîmes romaine** combined ticket, valid for 1 month and sold online and at the ticket counter of each site. It covers the three main ancient sites that are all close together: Maison Carrée, les Arènes de Nîmes, and Tour Magne. The fee is 13€ for adults, 11€ for students and 6€ for children aged 7 to 17, and free for children 6 and under. More information is available from **Culturespaces** (www.arenes-nimes.com; ✆ **04-66-21-82-56**). *Tip:* Admission to all of following attractions is free on the first Sunday of each month.

The pride of Nîmes is the **Maison Carrée ★★★**, pl. de la Maison Carrée (www.arenes-nimes.com; ✆ **04-66-21-82-56**). Founded around A.D. 3 by the Emperor Augustus, it's the only completely preserved ancient Roman temple in Europe. It may be small but it's perfectly proportioned: 26m (85 ft.) long by 15m (49 ft.) wide and 15m (49 ft.) high. It inspired the builders of La Madeleine in Paris, and Thomas Jefferson's Virginia Capitol building. It makes a perfect start to a Nîmes visit with a film showing the founding of the city from its Celtic roots through the fortunes of a fictional family from 55 B.C. to A.D. 90. Admission is 6€ for adults or 5€ for students and children, free for ages 7 and under. It's open daily (hours vary seasonally; see site).

Across the square stands its modern-day twin, the **Carré d'Art ★★**, whose understated design by Norman Foster was inspired by (but doesn't overpower) the ancient monument. Inside, the **Musée d'Art Contemporain** (www.carreartmusee.com; ✆ **04-66-76-35-70**; 8€ adults, 6€ students, free for kids 17 and under; Tues–Sun 10am–6pm) has a permanent collection of art from 1960 to the present day as well as temporary exhibitions that take in both past masters like Picasso and the work of contemporaries like photographer Wolfgang Tillmans.

Scholars call it **Amphithéâtre Romain de Nîmes ★★★**; locals refer to it as **Les Arènes.** No matter what you call it, the monument at place des Arènes is spectacular (www.arenes-nimes.com; ✆ **04-66-21-82-56**; 10€

NÎMES events

The Roman Games in the ancient Arena in April take you back to the city's Roman roots with battles, gladiators, and chariot races. At Pentecost (Whitsun and 7 weeks after Easter), the 5-day **Féria de Pentecôte** is one of Europe's most popular festivals. Along with the bull fights, the city hosts plenty of street entertainment, while the bodegas offer plenty of drinking, dancing, and Spanish food. A second *féria*, **Féria des Vendanges,** celebrating the grape harvest, takes place the third weekend of September. Every **Thursday night during July and August,** Nîmes' squares fill with jazz and rock, classic and salsa musicians and stalls selling books, crafts, works of art, and bric-a-brac.

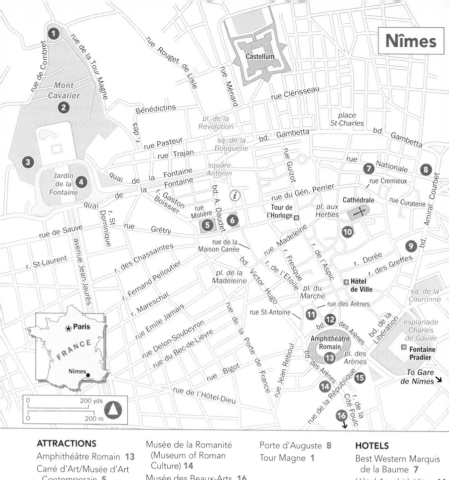

Nîmes

Castellum

ATTRACTIONS

Amphithéâtre Romain 13
Carré d'Art/Musée d'Art
Contemporain 5
Jardin de la Fontaine 4
Le Temple de Diane 3
Maison Carrée 6
Mont Cavalier 2

Musée de la Romanité
(Museum of Roman
Culture) 14
Musée des Beaux-Arts 16
Musée d'Histoire
Naturelle 9
Musée du Vieux-
Nîmes 10

Porte d'Auguste 8
Tour Magne 1

RESTAURANTS

Le Lisita 12
Wine Bar le Cheval
Blanc 15

HOTELS

Best Western Marquis
de la Baume 7
Hôtel Amphithéâtre 11

adults, 8€ for students and children 7–17 years, free for visitors 6 years old and under). It's a better-preserved twin of the one at Arles, and far more complete than Rome's Colosseum. Two stories high—each floor has 60 arches—it was built by master Roman engineers who fitted the huge stones together without mortar. It once held over 20,000 spectators who entered through arched entrances (*vomitaria,* coming from the Latin for "to spew") ringing the building to see gladiatorial combat and chariot races. Today it's used for everything from ballet to bullfights. Open daily (hours change seasonally; see website).

One of the most beautiful gardens in France, the **Jardin de la Fontaine ★★**, at the end of quai de la Fontaine, was laid out in the 18th century around a centerpiece of ruins of a Roman shrine. It was France's first public park and is a godsend on a baking hot summer's day with its shady paths and fountains. The garden is open daily (Apr–Aug 7:30am–10pm, Mar and Sept 7:30am–8pm, Oct–Feb 7:30am–6:30pm). Within the formal garden is the ruined **Le Temple de Diane ★** and the remains of some Roman baths. Make your way through the wooded paths to **Mont Cavalier ★**, a low, rocky hill topped by the sturdy bulk of the **Tour Magne ★** (*☎ 04-66-21-82-56*), the city's oldest Roman monument. You can climb it for 3.50€ for adults and 3€ for students and children 7 to 17, free for children 6 and under. It's open daily (hours vary seasonally; see website).

Nîmes has a good variety of museums, augmented by the opening in 2018 of the **Musée de la Romanité (Museum of Roman Culture) ★★★**, 16 bd. des Arènes (www.museeromanite.com; *☎ 06-19-61-56-58;* free admission plus charges for special exhibits). The futuristic building opposite Les Arènes is clad in a translucent glass facade that sinuously covers the museum. A remarkable and wide collection of art and artifacts fills the galleries, while interactive displays lead you through ancient Rome. Open daily from April to October (10am–7pm) and from Tuesday to Sunday November to March (10am–6pm).

The **Musée des Beaux-Arts ★★**, rue Cité Foulc (www.nimes.fr; *☎ 04-66-28-18-32;* Tues–Sun 10am–6pm; 5€ adults, 3€ students, free for children 17 and under), contains French paintings and sculptures from the 17th to the 20th centuries, as well as Flemish, Dutch, and Italian works from the 16th to the 18th centuries. Some unexpected masterpieces here include Rubens' *Portrait of a Monk* and the masterpiece of G. B. Moroni, *La Calomnie d'Apelle.* With the opening of the Museum of Roman Culture in this ancient city, the first thing to see should be the huge Gallo-Roman mosaic showing the mythical marriage of Admetus.

If time allows, visit the **Musée du Vieux-Nîmes ★**, pl. aux Herbes (www.nimes.fr; *☎ 04-66-76-73-70;* Tues–Sun 10am–6pm; 5€ adults, 3€ students and children), to the north of Les Arènes and housed in an Episcopal palace from the 1700s. It covers the all-important textile industry here, from the silk shawls that were must-have items in the 18th century to the story of denim. Also on display: antiques, antique porcelain, and workday objects from the 18th and 19th centuries.

About 45m (148 ft.) east, you come to the **Musée d'Histoire Naturelle ★**, 13 bis bd. l'Amiral-Courbet (www.nimes.fr; *☎ 04-66-76-73-45;* Tues–Sun 10am–6pm; 5€ adults, 3€ students and children). It's a strange and quirky collection of masks, spears, and taxidermy animals. From here, you can walk north along one of the city's busiest thoroughfares, **boulevard de l'Amiral-Courbet,** to the **Porte d'Auguste (Porte d'Arles)**— the remains of a gate built by the Romans during the reign of Augustus.

Outlying Attractions

Outside the city, 27km (16 miles) northeast, the great **Pont du Gard ★★★** spans the Gardon River. The great bridge with its huge stones, fitted together without mortar, stands as one of France's most vivid reminders of ancient glory. The top tier of the three tiers of arches in graceful symmetrical patterns carried water to the growing city of Nîmes. Probably constructed in the 1st century, this masterpiece of engineering stands 50m (164 ft.) high and measures 360m (1,181 ft.) at its longest point. If you can, tour the upper tier and the water canal giving panoramic views over the countryside.

The Site du Pont du Gard visitors' complex gives the best introduction to the monument. The interactive museum, **Le Musée** ★★ (www.pontdugard.fr; ✆ **04-66-37-50-99**), shows ancient building techniques and the complex construction of the Pont du Gard, how it worked during the Middle Ages, and its status through the centuries as a symbol of the architectural savvy of ancient Rome. Working models, films, and interactive displays are centered around different themes, with the all-precious water taking center stage. A film takes you through the history. You can wander through the **Mémoires de Garrigue** garden of nature trails and take the children to the interactive Ludo center. The large site also has a restaurant, cafe, and gift shop. The car park is open year-round 8am to midnight, the cultural sites are open daily (July–Aug 9am–8pm, Apr–June and Sept 9am–7pm, Mar–Oct 9am–6pm, Nov–Feb 9am–5pm). Parking is 9€. Discovery Pass of the main sites is 6.50€ adults, 5€ students and free for children 17 and under.

To get here, take the highway D6086 from Nîmes to a point 3km (1¼ miles) from the village of Remoulins, then follow signs to the site.

During July and August, artificial beaches and small shelters are installed on the right bank of the Gardon near the bridge for **"Rendez-vous à la Rivière,"** with lifeguards overseeing river swimming.

Where to Stay

Best Western Marquis de La Baume ★★   Originally built for the de la Baume family in the 17th century, this central hotel happily mixes old and new. The old comes in the form of a magnificent stone staircase with columns (in the interior courtyard), stone-flagged floors, wooden beamed ceilings, and chandeliers. The new are bang up-to-date bedrooms with contemporary fittings, padded headboards above the large comfortable beds, and pastel or grey toned textiles. Tiled bathrooms are well designed with lighted mirrors, though some come with a bathtub only. Ask for a room at the back to avoid street noise.

21 rue Nationale. www.hotel-marquis-de-la-baume-nimes.com. ✆ **04-66-76-28-42.** 34 units. 99€–264€ double; 167€–364€ jr. suite. **Amenities:** Bar; room service; free Wi-Fi.

Hôtel Amphithéâtre ★★   Perfectly placed in a small square across from Les Arènes, this unpretentious, comfortable three-star hotel offers great value. Entirely renovated in 2020, it has good-sized bedrooms decorated in a soft palette paired with white wooden furnishings. Ask for a room looking onto the square to watch the action at the bars and restaurants (which are not noisy). Friendly staff ready to help with any questions or assistance.

4 rue des Arènes. www.hoteldelamphitheatre.com. ✆ **04-66-67-28-51.** 11 units. 97€–100€ double. **Amenities:** Free Wi-Fi.

Where to Eat

Le Lisita ★★ FRENCH/FUSION   With views over the Roman Arena from the open-air terrace, the cooking here doesn't have to be as good as it is. But the owners—a chef and sommelier (Olivier Douet and Stéphane Debaille) who met at the famed Le Gavroche in London—have serious culinary cred. They emphasize local products (rice from the Camargue, truffles from Uzès, fab local wines) and use it in inventive preparations, like a green lentil soup with duck foie gras foam, or honey-marinated duck with Cajun spices. A find!

2 bis bd. des Arènes. www.lelisita.com. © **04-66-67-29-15.** Main courses 19€–25€; fixed-price menus 29€–58€. Wed–Sun noon–2pm and 7–10pm.

Wine Bar le Cheval Blanc ★★ FRENCH   Owner Michel Hermet knows his wines; he comes from a family of winemakers and keeps 300 varieties in stock, with 13 to 15 available by the glass each day. But this historic wine bar (vaulted ceilings, waiters carrying loaded trays above their heads, a ham ready for carving on the bar) isn't just a place to tipple and eat light snacks. It's where many locals choose to lunch and after you've sampled some of that Mont Pilat ham atop *pan con tomate* or the grilled fish special, you'll understand why.

1 pl. des Arènes. www.winebar-lechevalblanc.com. © **04-66-76-19-59.** Main courses 14€–29€; fixed-price lunch 16€; dinner menu 25€–31€. Mon–Sat noon–2pm and 7–11pm (Fri–Sat until midnight).

Shopping

Tops shopping streets are **rue du Général-Perrier, rue des Marchands, rue du Chapître,** and the pedestrian **rue de l'Aspic** and **rue de la Madeleine.** A Friday **flea market** (8am–1pm) is held on boulevard Jean Jaurès; the daily food market is **Les Halles.**

If you have a sweet tooth, go to any pastry shop and ask for the regional almond-based cookies called *croquants,* or visit **Maison Villaret,** 13 Rue de la Madeleine (www.maison-villaret.com), specialists in croquants since 1775. A wide range of other local specialties, from Camargue salt to handcrafted knives, can be procured at **La Boutique Nîmoise,** 5 Rue de la République (https://epicerie-fine-nimes.fr; © **04-66-08-36-61**).

Nîmes Nightlife

In the warm weather, the arena hosts many events, including open-air concerts and theater. The Office de Tourisme has a complete listing.

For nightlife with the locals, head to the famous **Café Le Napoleon,** 46 bd. Victor-Hugo (https://le-napo.fr; © **04-66-67-20-23**). **O'Flaherty's,** 26 bd. Amiral-Courbet (https://pub-oflahertys.com; © **04-66-67-22-63**), is also a hot spot. It serves British beer (seven on tap), and has live Irish, country, and bluegrass music on Thursdays.

The dance floor of **Le Club Kafé Fashion-CKF,** 20 rue de l'Etoile (✆ **04-66-21-59-22**), attracts a young crowd of Nîmois with techno DJs and theme nights from Thursday to Saturday starting at 11pm. **Lulu Club,** 10 impasse de la Curaterie (www.lulu-club.com; ✆ **04-66-36-28-20**), is the gay and lesbian stronghold in Nîmes with a straight following as well. It's open Friday and Saturday. Streets to explore on virtually any night of the week include **place de la Maison Carrée** and **boulevard Victor-Hugo.** For nightlife try **rue Fresque, rue Saint-Antoine,** and **rue de l'Etoile.**

AIGUES-MORTES ★★

750km (465 miles) SW of Paris; 53km (33 miles) NE of Séte; 44km (27 miles) E of Nîmes; 43km (26 miles) SW of Arles

South of Nîmes in Provence lies the Camargue with its marshes and great saltwater lagoons. To the west of this great nature reserve you come across Aigues-Mortes, the city of the "dead waters." This is France's most perfectly preserved walled town, impossibly romantic but also horribly crowded during the high season. In the 13th century, Louis IX and his crusaders set forth from Aigues-Mortes, then a thriving port. Alas, then the Rhône silted up, leaving the city 6.5km (4 miles) inland from the sea. The **ramparts ★★**, which still enclose the town, were constructed between 1272 and 1300. The **Tour de Constance ★★** (www.aigues-mortes-monument.fr; ✆ **04-66-53-61-55**) is a model castle of the Middle Ages. Take the lift to the top for panoramic view of the marshes. Admission is 8€ for adults and free for children 17 and under. The monument is open May to August daily 10am to 7pm, and September to April daily 10am to 5:30pm.

Aigues-Mortes main appeal is the medieval atmosphere that permeates virtually every building, rampart, and cobble-covered street. The city's religious centerpiece is the **Eglise Notre-Dame des Sablons ★**, rue Jean-Jaurès. Constructed of wood in 1183, it was rebuilt in stone in 1246. The church is open May to September daily 8:30am to 6pm, and October to April daily 10am to 5pm.

The waterways and wetlands of the Petite Camargue can be explored in many ways: You can join a jeep safari, canoe, kayak, cycle, ride on a paddle steamer, or just put your hiking boots on and wander along the trails that are inaccessible by car. Your reward is the sight of flocks of flamingoes and other birdlife, white Camargue horses, and herds of Camargue bulls. Just make sure to cover yourself with plenty of mosquito repellent. Jeep safaris and bike excursions can be organized by **Camargue Autrement** (www.camargue-autrement.com; ✆ **04-30-08-52-91**). Other activities can be arranged through the tourist office.

Essentials

GETTING THERE   Six **trains** per day connect Aigues-Mortes and Nîmes. Trip time is from 40 minutes, costing 8€. The station is a 5-minute walk to the old town. **Taxis:** ℰ **06-11-56-20-12** or 04-66-53-40-04. Train information and schedules are on www.sncf-connect.com or call ℰ **36-35.** If you're **driving** to Aigues-Mortes, take D979 south from Gallargues, or A9 from Montpellier or Nîmes.

VISITOR INFORMATION The **Office de Tourisme** is at place St-Louis (www.ot-aiguesmortes.com; ℰ **04-66-53-73-00**).

Where to Stay

Hôtel Les Templiers ★★ This 18th-century former merchant's house by the medieval ramparts offers a peaceful stay at reasonable rates. The ambience is redolent of times past, with stone-flagged floors, antique furnishings, and wood-beamed high ceilings in the common area. Bedrooms are comfy, decorated in country style with modern pictures on the walls and shelves of books, Provençal pottery, and colorful textiles in each room (some with fireplaces). A pool is hidden from the street by a high wall and tall cypress trees. The hotel's restaurant serves regional food. *Two warnings:* Because the hotel is within the city walls, parking isn't nearby, so you'll need to drag your suitcase over cobblestones. You'll also have to lug it upstairs: no elevator here.

23 rue de la République. www.hotellestempliers.fr. ℰ **04-66-53-66-56.** 14 units. 127€–192€ double. **Amenities:** Restaurant; bar; pool; room service; free Wi-Fi.

Yelloh! Village La Petite Camargue ★ This friendly campsite is just 3.7km (2½ miles) outside Aigues-Mortes and 3.5km (2⅓ miles) from the sea. You can rent a mobile home or take your own caravan or tent. With a bar, restaurant, food market, swimming pool, water slides, sports and even horse-riding available on site you might find it difficult to move the kids away.

Rte de Cacharel. www.yellohvillage.co.uk. ℰ **04-66-53-98-98.** 553 sites. 40€–322€ mobile home; 21€ tent. **Amenities:** Bar, restaurant; outdoor pool; free Wi-Fi (for 1 device; fee for additional devices); free Internet area.

Where to Eat

Hôtel Les Templiers (see above) is also a good choice for dining.

L'Atelier de Nicolas ★★ MODERN FRENCH Hidden down a side street, this is a place that mostly locals know about. The building is nearly as old as the nearby fortifications, but inside it's a modern, industrial-style space. The combines classic French traditions with Asian touches that subtly enhance the flavors. Start with heritage tomato *tarte tatin* topped with cucumber and wasabi sorbet, then move on to pan-fried tuna with Chimichurri sauce. The chef uses organic products when possible. Reservations are recommended in high season.

28 Rue Alsace Lorraine. https://restaurant-latelierdenicolas.fr. ℰ **04-34-28-04-84.** Main course 29€; fixed-price menu 48€–68€. Mon–Tues and Fri–Sat noon–1:30pm and 7–9pm. Closed June 30–July 11, Aug 22–25, and first 2 weeks in Jan.

MONTPELLIER ★★

750km (466 miles) SW of Paris; 170km (105 miles) NW of Marseille; 56km (34 miles) SW of Nîmes

Montpellier is one of France's most exciting cities with architecture that mixes old and new and a university that brings a dynamic edge to daily life. Its renowned medical school was founded in the 13th century. Nostradamus qualified as a doctor here, and Rabelais studied at the school. A medieval, not a Roman city, its oldest buildings date back to the 15th century. Today Montpellier is a bustling metropolis with a population of 277,000, one of southern France's fastest-growing cities.

Cars are banned from the center, which is the largest pedestrianized area in France; the excellent public transport system is great for getting around outside this area. The city has a handsome core, with tree-flanked promenades, broad avenues, and historic monuments.

Essentials

GETTING THERE   The fastest way to get to Montpellier is to fly from Paris's Orly or Charles de Gaulle airports to **Aéroport Montpellier Méditerranée** (www.montpellier.aeroport.fr; ℂ **04-67-20-85-00**), 8km (5 miles) southeast of Montpellier (trip time: 1 hr., 17 min.). **Taxis** (ℂ **04-30-96-60-60**) from the airport to the center cost from approximately 25€. The airport shuttle no. 120 goes to place Europe and costs 1.60€. Trains arrive regularly daily from Avignon (trip time: from 1 hr., 8 min.; one-way fare from 18.60€), from Marseille (trip time: 1.5 hr.; one-way fare from 13.90€), from Toulouse (trip time: 2 hr., 12 min.; one-way fare from 21€), and from Perpignan (trip time: 1½ hr.; one-way fare from 10€). Fourteen TGV trains arrive daily from Paris Gare de Lyon, taking less than 3½ hours. The one-way fare is from 65€. Train information and schedules are on www.sncf-connect.com or call ℂ **36-35.**

If you're **driving,** Montpellier lies off A9.

VISITOR INFORMATION   The **Office de Tourisme** is at 30 Allée Jean de L. de Tassigny (www.montpellier-tourisme.fr; ℂ **04-67-60-60-60**).

LAYOUT OF THE CITY   The compact, pedestrianized old town lies north and west of the heart of Montpellier, the place de la Comédie.

SPECIAL EVENTS   From June 20 to July 4 (approximately), classical and modern dancers leap into town for the **Festival International Montpellier Danse.** Tickets for performances range from free to 35€ and are available from the box office, 18 rue Ste-Ursule (www.montpellierdanse.com; ℂ **04-67-60-83-60**).

Exploring Montpellier

The expansive **place de la Comédie** is the living room of Montpellier, a square full of bars and cafes where the 18th-century "Fountain of the

Three Graces" takes pride of place in front of the 19th-century opera. The former military parade ground, champ du Mars is where you'll find the **Tourist Office, Musée Fabre,** and **Le Corum** convention and arts venue. Head up **rue de la Loge** to explore the old town.

Walk west along the **rue Foch** past the Arc de Triomphe and into the park. The formal arch was erected in 1691 to celebrate the victories of Louis XIV whose equestrian statue you pass on your way up to the 17th-century **promenade du Peyrou ★★** with views of the Cévennes and the Mediterranean. The lofty classical-style pavilion, **Château d'Eau ★** is a monument

One of Montpellier's many medieval streets.

to 18th-century classicism, built as the terminus of an aqueduct carrying water to the city from a nearby source. Just to the northeast lie the cathedral and botanical gardens.

Cathédrale St-Pierre ★ CATHEDRAL   Originally a monastery church founded in 1364, it was rebuilt in the 17th-century after the Wars of Religion. You enter through an odd structure: a projecting porch held up by two towers into a light-filled nave. If you're lucky, you might hear the splendid 18th-century organ being played.

pl. St-Pierre. www.cathedrale-montpellier.fr. *℗* **04-67-66-04-12.** Free admission. Mon–Fri 10:30am–11:45am and 2:30–6pm; Sat 2:30–6pm

Le Jardin des Plantes ★ PARK/GARDEN   Paul Valéry met André Gide in the Jardin des Plantes, the oldest such garden in France. The botanical garden, filled with exotic plants and a handful of greenhouses, opened in 1593.

163 rue Auguste-Broussonnet (enter from 1 bd. Henri-IV). *℗* **04-67-63-43-22.** Free admission. Jun–Sept Tues–Sun noon–8pm; Oct–May Tues–Sun noon–6pm.

Musée Fabre ★★★ MUSEUM   One of France's great art galleries, the museum occupies the splendid former Hôtel de Massilian. The collection has over 800 works from the Renaissance to the 20th century and includes art by Rubens, Reynolds, Delacroix, David, and Dufy. It began when Napoleon sent Montpellier an exhibition from the Académie Royale in 1803 then expanded with a donation of its most important works from François Fabre, a Montpellier painter, in 1828. One of its highlights is Poussin's *Venus and Adonis.* An entire wing is devoted to abstract expressionist Pierre Soulages. Opposite it, the **Hôtel Cabrières** displays ornate furniture, luxurious textiles and other 18th and 19th century decorative objects. One ticket works for both museums.

39 bd. Bonne Nouvelle. www.museefabre.fr. ℂ **04-67-14-83-00.** Admission 9€ adults; 6€ students 18–25; free for children 17 and under and for all 1st Sun of the month (additional fee for special exhibits). Tues–Sun 10am–6pm; Hôtel Cabrières Tues and Sat–Sun 2–5pm.

Where to Stay

Best Western Hôtel Le Guilhem ★   Two former residences in the Old Town have been converted into this comfortable hotel. It's well located on a street that leads to the charming Jardin des Plantes and just a 10-minute walk from the station. Rooms are all individually decorated, running from pretty country chintz, to a stark stone-vaulted room. Some look towards the cathedral, others onto small gardens. The location in the old town makes it an ideal base for sightseeing.

18 rue Jean-Jacques-Rousseau. www.leguilhem.com. ℂ **04-67-52-90-90.** 35 units. 125€–180€ double. Nearby parking 14€. **Amenities:** Room service; free Wi-Fi.

Grand Hôtel du Midi ★★★   If you want the best, book this aptly named, three-story lodging opposite the Opera House. Built in 1876 in Second Empire style it retains much of the original stained glass, molded ceilings and columns. The unusually spacious guest rooms have a contemporary look—boldly patterned wallpapers, fan shaped headboards on the beds— and each gets a small balcony. There's a bar and an outside terrace for watching the world go by. Staff are friendly and very helpful and efficient.

22 bd. Victor-Hugo. www.grandhoteldumidimontpellier.com. ℂ **04-67-92-69-61.** 44 units. 134€–254€ double; 234€–304€ suite. Public parking nearby at reduced rate. **Amenities:** Bar; business center; room service; free Wi-Fi.

Hôtel du Palais ★★   Built in the late 18th century at the top of the old town in a delightful neighborhood, this three-star hotel is housed in a warm stone building with wrought-iron balconies. It's a real find: good value for the money and charming as well. Different sized bedrooms have traditional furniture and pastel curtains and bed coverings. The bathrooms are old-fashioned rather than state-of-the-art but have everything you need. Enjoy your breakfast either in the pretty downstairs cafe or out on the terrace in front of the hotel.

3 rue du Palais des-Guilhem. www.hoteldupalais-montpellier.fr. ℂ **04-67-60-47-38.** 26 units. 115€–135€ double. Public parking nearby. **Amenities:** Room service; free Wi-Fi.

Where to Eat

La Réserve Rimbaud ★★ FRENCH   The oldest restaurant in Montpellier, founded in 1835, has a lovely riverside position on the banks of the Lez. It is light and spacious inside with pale grey and white furnishings and has a large terrace for summer dining directly overlooking the gently flowing river. Passionate about local ingredients, chef Charles Fontès produces imaginative cooking. Start with the likes of roast scallops with beetroot carpaccio then take in sole meunière with cauliflower in curry sauce.

Desserts are superb; try the lemon ice cream scented with rosemary coming in a lemon shell.

820 av. Saint-Maur. www.reserve-rimbaud.com. ℭ **04-67-72-52-53.** Main courses 24€–48€; fixed-price lunch 38€–47€ or gourmet menu 95€–120€. Mon–Fri noon–2pm and 7:30–8:30pm.

Le Grillardin ★★ FRENCH   Located in a busy, shaded square where restaurant tables spill out into the surrounding terraces, it's difficult to know which to choose. Go for Le Grillardin where chef Mickaël Diore makes the most of local seasonal ingredients, changing his dishes daily. Grilled meat and fish are specialties here, although free-range chicken and filet de boeuf may also be on offer. The restaurant has a bistro decor of wooden tables and chairs but harks back to the past with its stone walls and wood ceiling.

2 pl. de la Chapelle Neuve. www.facebook.com/legrillardinrestaurant. ℭ **04-67-66-24-33.** Main courses 22€–26€; lunch special (weekdays) 14€. Daily noon–2pm and 7–11pm (Fri–Sat until 10:30pm).

Le Petit Jardin ★★★ FRENCH   In the historic old town, with a view of the cathedral from the spacious garden, this pretty restaurant makes you feel you've made a discovery, even though it's a favorite of locals and visitors in the know. In 2022, chef Clément Gueudré took over the reins of the 100-year-old establishment, which includes both a gastronomic restaurant and a bistro. At the former, the menu might include smoked eggplant cannelloni topped with spicy tomato jam or meagre fish from the Mediterranean with beluga lentil risotto. The bistro's more casual dishes come in an excellent set lunch menu of one course plus a café gourmand (espresso with mini desserts) for 29€.

20 rue Jean-Jacques Rousseau. www.petit-jardin.com. ℭ **04-67-60-78-78.** Main course 47€–82€; fixed-price menu 48€–55€. Tues–Sat noon–1:30pm and 7:30–9:30pm. Closed last week of Dec and 1st week of Jan.

Les Vignes ★★ PROVENÇAL/LANGUEDOCIENNE   This restaurant in the old town champions regional and local ingredients and cuisine. Only open at lunch, you can opt to sit in either a 13th-century arched dining room or an interior courtyard. Bull from the Camargue, sweet lamb from Provence, veal from the Aveyron, and fish from the Mediterranean appear on a monthly changing menu of classic dishes. The wine list is similarly regional with wines from Collioure to Provence and a good selection from Languedoc vineyards.

2 rue Bonnier d'Alco. www.lesvignesrestaurant.com. ℭ **04-67-60-48-42.** Main courses 16€–18€; fixed-price lunch 18€–22€. Mon–Sat noon–1:30pm.

Montpellier Nightlife

After the sun sets, locals congregate in the bars and cafes of **place Jean-Jaurès, rue des Ecoles Laïques, place St Ravy,** or the more sophisticated area around **rue du Palais de Guilhems.** The large student population means Montpellier has its fair share of great bars. **Fitzpatricks,** 5 pl.

St-Côme (www.fitzpatricksirishpub.com; ℰ **04-67-60-58-30**), serves Irish beer and has an Irish music evening on Fridays. It's open daily noon to 1am. **La FaBRik,** 12 rue Boussairolles (www.facebook.com/lafabrik34; ℰ **09-60-37-86-45**), is friendly, crowded, and noisy, showing TV sports and live music during the week. **Rockstore,** 20 rue de Verdun (www.rock store.fr; ℰ **04-67-06-80-00**), has 1950s rock memorabilia, a Cadillac embedded in its front entrance, live concerts of all music genres, several bars, and a disco. No cover, but charges for music nights. For the best jazz and blues in town, check out **JAM,** 100 rue Ferdinand-de-Lesseps (www. lejam.com; ℰ **04-67-58-30-30**). Regular concerts in the noisy, industrial-style space average 10€ to 25€.

    Le Coxx, 5 rue Jules Latreilhe (www.facebook.com/lecoxx34; ℰ **04-99-66-77-61**), is one of the most popular hangouts for mainly gay men. Good bar plus karaoke nights and dancing are the main attractions.

    For a drink, casual bite and possibly some dancing, hop in a taxi to **Le Marché de Lez,** 1348 av. de la Mer-Raymond Dugrand (https:// marchedulez.com), a resurrected industrial area in southern Montpellier now home to funky boutiques, street food stands and a few lively bars.

NARBONNE ★

787km (489 miles) SW of Paris; 61km (38 miles) E of Carcassonne; 93km (58 miles) S of Montpellier

In 118 B.C., Narbonne was the first town outside Italy to be colonized by the Romans. At that time, it was a busy port, and the largest town in Gaul after Lyon. It remained a hub for more than a millennium (in the A.D. 12th and 13th c., it had a prestigious Jewish university), and even today you can see evidence of its former wealth. But in the 14th century the river silted up and Narbonne became a backwater.

    It's still a wonderful place to come to dig deep into history (see below). Visitors also do tastings and tours in the surrounding vineyards (the website RueDesVignerons.com lists those open to the public); or head to nearby beaches. The latter can be found a hop away in the village of **Gruisson** and its adjoining beach, Gruisson-Plage; and in the suburb of **St-Pierre la Mer** and its adjoining beach, Narbonne-Plage. Both are 15km (9¼ miles) south of Narbonne. Buses from the town are frequent, each marked with its destination.

Essentials

GETTING THERE   Narbonne has rail, bus, and highway connections with other cities on the Mediterranean coast and with Toulouse. Rail travel is the best way to get here, with regular daily **trains** from Perpignan (trip time: 35 min.; one-way from 6.20€), 13 per day from Toulouse (trip time: 1¼ hr.; one-way fare from 12€), and 42 per day from Montpellier (trip time: from 58 min.; one-way fare is 12.30€). From Paris, the TGV runs directly to Narbonne (trip time: 4½ hr.; one-way from 49€). Train info and schedules are on www.sncf-connect.com or call ⓒ **36-35.** If you're **driving,** Narbonne is at the junction of A61 and A9, easily accessible from either Toulouse or the Riviera.

VISITOR INFORMATION The **Office de Tourisme** is at 31 rue Jean Jaurès (www.cotedumidi.com; ⓒ **04-68-65-15-60**).

GETTING AROUND La Citadine is a free shuttle around the town center. Taxi: ⓒ **06-73-22-33-78.**

Exploring Narbonne

The **Canal de la Robine,** which connects to the **Canal du Midi,** bisects the town. The old town, which contains all the sights, is compact and easy to navigate.

Start at the oldest site, the **Horreum ★**, 7 rue Rouget de Lisle (ⓒ **04-68-32-45-30**), an underground warren of granaries and grain chutes

A view of the cathedral in Narbonne.

built by the Romans in the 1st century B.C. It's in the restored medieval quarter, which is now full of attractive shops and restaurants. In the center of town, dominating the main place de l'Hôtel-de-Ville, the huge palace and cathedral complex, built from the 12th to the 14th centuries, reveals vaunting ecclesiastical ambitions. The **Cathédrale de St-Just et St-Pasteur ★★**, rue Armand Gautier (ⓒ **04-68-32-09-52;** free admission; daily June–Sept 9am–6pm and Oct–Apr 10am–12:45pm and 2–6pm), is just a section of the original cathedral plan which was never completed, but it is still magnificent, decorated with 14th-century statues, stained glass, and Aubusson tapestries. Cloisters join it to the **Palais des Archevêques** (Archbishops' Palace), which contains the **Archaeology Museum ★** with an impressive collection of Roman artifacts and mosaics, and the **Museum of Art and History ★** (for all: ⓒ **04-68-90-30-54**).

Additional sights include the **Donjon Gilles-Aycelin ★**, pl. de l'Hôtel-de-Ville (ⓒ **04-68-90-30-65**), a watchtower and prison from the late 13th century, where an observation platform looks out at the cathedral, the plain, and the Pyrénées; and the **Maison Charles Trenet ★**, 13 av. Charles Trenet (ⓒ **04-68-90-30-66**), birthplace of the singer/songwriter. There are pleasant walks by the canal, which is lined with 18th-century houses and *chais* (wine warehouses).

All Narbonne museums and the Horreum have the same opening hours and prices. Admission to one museum is 6€ adults and 4€ students and children ages 10 to 17 (children 9 and under are free); a pass for all museums (the Pass Monuments & Musées), plus the Donjon Gilles-Aycelin, the Cathedral treasure, and Charles Trenet's birthplace is 10€ (6€ students and children ages 10–17, free for children 9 and under). Attractions are open June to September daily 10am to 6pm, May Wednesday to Sunday 10am to noon and 2 to 5pm.

Where to Stay

La Résidence ★★   Ideally placed on a quiet street near the Cathédrale St-Just, La Résidence is housed in a former 19th-century house. The reception area is gracious, lit by chandeliers with a large sweeping staircase. Bedrooms are comfortably furnished with traditional fixtures and pretty textiles and bathrooms are a good size and well equipped. Some have a separate bath. Book a superior room if you want a larger room and larger bed.

6 rue du 1er-Mai. www.hotelresidence.fr. ✆ **04-68-32-19-41.** 26 units. 80€–165€ double. Parking 9€. **Amenities:** Free Wi-Fi.

---

touring **CATHAR COUNTRY**

In the early 13th century, Occitanie experienced its darkest moment: the Cathar Cusade, also called the Albigensian Crusade. A religious movement widely practiced in Occitanie, Catharism diverged from traditional Christianity in its belief in two deities, a good one and his evil adversary. Priests lived very humbly (unlike some of their Catholic counterparts), and women were also allowed to serve as spiritual leaders.

Branded heretical by the Roman Catholic Church, in 1209, Pope Innocent III led a bloody 20-year war, with the help of the French King, to eradicate Catharism. The gruesome conflict resulted in the death of at least 200,000 Cathars, as well as Catholics who tolerated or protected the Cathars in their fortresses and castles. It also led to the previously independent County of Toulouse falling under French rule.

While there are sites linked to the Cathars throughout the region, there are especially evocative venues between Narbonne and Carcassonne. Fifteen kilometers southwest of Narbonne is the **Abbaye de Fontfroide** (www.fontfroide.com; ✆ **04-68-45-11-08**). One of the largest Cistercian abbeys in France, it played an important role in the Albigensian Crusade. Privately owned today, visitors can join guided tours of the

Abbey, sample the estate's wines in the cellar or have a meal at its notable restaurant.

Sitting precariously on a rocky outcrop northwest of Narbonne is **Minerve.** The magnificent Medieval town hasn't changed much since it underwent a 6-week-long siege led by Simon de Montfort in 1210. Nods to the heroes—and villains—of the Crusade can be spotted in its charming streets, boutiques and cafes.

Time was less kind to **Lastours,** an archaeological site containing the remains of four hilltop Cathar castles. An undulating trail connects the craggy fortifications, and offers spectacular views (although this is only recommended for seasoned hikers).

For further information on these and other Cathar sites, see www.payscathare.org.

Will's ★ Conveniently right by the station, Will's occupies a 19th-century town house. The hotel changed hands in 2021, yet its friendly ambiance remains the same. It's a good value option with neutral-colored rooms furnished with new queen-sized beds, patchwork quilts and a desk in each room. Bathrooms are up to date and a good size for the price. Due to its low rates it's a popular option, so book in advance.

23 av. Pierre-Semard. www.willshotelnarbonne.fr. ℂ **06-45-98-18-80.** 14 units. 93€–113€ double; 163€ family room. **Amenities:** Free Wi-Fi.

Where to Eat

La Table Saint Crescent ★★★ FRENCH/LANGUEDOCIENNE It's well worth making the excursion just south of the canal to this white-washed, terracotta-tiled two-Michelin-starred restaurant. It's part of the local wine producers' Palais des Vins which promotes and sells the wines of Languedoc-Roussillon. Chef Lionel Giraud produces carefully sourced and beautifully presented dishes using top seasonal ingredients. The freshest fish from the coasts of France goes into dishes like lobster cooked on pine cones with ravioli and an Armganac sauce; free range chicken might come cooked in clay with fresh verbena; and there's always Wagyu beef matured for 60 days. Wines are, as you would expect, exemplary and the sommelier is particularly knowledgeable about local varieties. This is not a cheap option, but it will be a meal to remember. Alternatively, you can sample a less fussy version of Giraud's cuisine at his wine bar where a three-course menu goes for 35€.

In the Palais des Vins, 68 av. Général Leclerc, rte. de Perpignan. www.la-table-saint-crescent.com. ℂ **04-68-41-37-37.** Fixed-price menu 120€–220€. Tues–Sat noon–1pm and 7–9pm (closed Wed night Oct–May).

COLLIOURE ★★

882km (548 miles) SW of Paris; 28km (17 miles) SE of Perpignan

A port established by the Greeks in 6000 B.C. and later owned by the kings of Majorca, Collioure is best known as the home of a colony of artists known as the Fauvists, who included Derain, Dufy, Picasso, and Matisse. Attracting art lovers from all over the world, it has some of the charm of a pre-Bardot St-Tropez.

Essentials

GETTING THERE Collioure has frequent **train** and **bus** service, especially from Perpignan (trip time: 22 min.). Train info and schedules are on www.sncf-connect.com or call ℂ **36-35.** There's a good **drive** along the coastal road (RN114) leading to the Spanish border.

VISITOR INFORMATION The **Office de Tourisme** is on place du 18-Juin (www.collioure.com; ℂ **04-68-82-15-47**).

GETTING AROUND In high season, park your car for free at Cap Dourats (2km/1¼ miles to the east) and take the free shuttle bus into town.

Shopping in the narrow streets of Collioure.

Exploring Collioure

Two beaches sit on either side of the 13th-century **Château Royal ★**, pl. de 8-Mai-1945 (𝄐 **04-68-82-06-43;** 7€ adults, free for children 17 and under). Originally built for the Templars, it was later used by the Kings of Mallorca and Aragon. It's a huge building with formidable medieval fortifications that hark back to its past. In summer it hosts changing exhibitions by contemporary artists. Open daily (May–June and Sept–Oct 10am–6pm, July–Aug 9:30am–6:30pm, Nov–Mar 10am–5pm).

The **Eglise Notre-Dame-des-Anges ★**, rue de l'Eglise (𝄐 **04-68-88-33-49**), is the town's most famous monument. The church with a tower that once acted as the lighthouse, looks austere from the outside, but inside features a floor-to-ceiling altarpiece dripping with gilt. The church is undergoing renovations in 2024, but remains open daily from 9am to noon and 2 to 6pm. Also try to visit the **Modern Art Museum ★**, founded by Jean-Peské in the Villa Pams, rue de Port-Vendres (https://museecollioure. com; 𝄐 **04-68-82-10-19;** 3€ adults, 2€ children 12–16 and students, free for children 11 and under). It's home to works by artists who painted in Collioure. It's open daily June to September 10am to noon and 2 to 6pm and from October to May it has the same hours but is closed on Tuesdays. The **Chemin du Fauvisme** is a walking trail with 19 stops where you can see reproductions of paintings by Matisse, Dérain, and other Fauvists beside the actual scene they painted. Maps are for sale at the tourist office.

Where to Stay

Casa Païral ★★ This pleasant family-run hotel is rightly popular. A short walk to the port and the beach, the 150-year-old house has delightful, well-sized rooms furnished in different styles. Loft rooms have high ceilings and wooden beams while the best rooms come with a small

sitting room and balcony with typical south of France views over red-tiled rooftops and the sea. There's a delightful swimming pool for hot days.
Impasse des Palmiers. www.hotel-casa-pairal.com. ⓒ **04-68-82-05-81.** 27 units. 166€–433€ double. Parking 19€. **Amenities:** Outdoor pool; room service; free Wi-Fi. Closed Dec–Jan.

Relais des 3 Mas ★★ Collioure's best hotel and restaurant has wonderful harbor views and rooms that are simple but elegant with red Provençal tiled floors, pale wood, colorful bedding, and white painted furniture. Deluxe rooms have balconies, one has a pretty grass terrace or take the suite with a garden. Bathrooms are large and have Jacuzzis. La Balette restaurant has a Michelin star. Fixed-price menus run from 65€ at lunch on weekdays to a gastronomic feast at 95€ to 150€.
Rte. de Port-Vendres. www.relaisdestroismas.com. ⓒ **04-68-82-05-07.** 23 units. 120€–355€ double; 195€–485€ suite. Free parking. Closed mid-Nov to mid-Feb. **Amenities:** Restaurant; babysitting; outdoor pool; Jacuzzi; room service; sauna; free Wi-Fi.

Where to Eat

Restaurant La Balette, at the Relais des 3 Mas (see above), is the best restaurant in town.

Le Neptune ★★ FRENCH/CATALAN This is a place for toying with a dozen oysters and drinking the local sparkling wine while looking out over the deep blue Mediterranean. Set in a tiered garden just above the beach, with views over to the port to the castle, this little gem is a seafood specialist and crafts paellas, and simple roasted fish dishes, from whatever is freshest at the market. A good wine list contains some notable organic varieties.
9 rte. de Porte-Vendres. www.leneptune-collioure.com. ⓒ **04-68-82-02-27.** Main courses 28€–69€; fixed-price lunch 32€; other fixed-price menus (including vegetarian menu) 42€–120€. Wed–Sun noon–2pm and 7–9pm.

PERPIGNAN ★★

849km (527 miles) SW of Paris; 318km (197 miles) NW of Marseille; 64km (40 miles) S of Narbonne

The former capital of the kingdom of Majorca and second city of Catalonia is just 45 minutes from Barcelona, making it a Catalan cultural and business hub and confirming its multi-cultural status. Perpignan's new Espace Méditerranée neighborhood around the Théâtre de l'Archipel arts complex was designed by France's favorite architect, Jean Nouvel. It's just one of the major building projects that's transformed the city in the last decade.

This is one of the sunniest places in France, but during summer afternoons in July and August, it's a cauldron. That's when many locals catch the 9.5km (6-mile) ride to the beach resort of Canet-en-Roussillon. Bus no. 3 runs from the center of Perpignan every 30 minutes in the summer and costs 1.30€.

A young scene brings energy to Perpignan, especially along the flower-decked quays of the Basse River, site of impromptu nighttime concerts, beer drinking, and tapas eating, a tradition adopted from nearby Barcelona. The city has a raging nightlife scene.

Essentials

GETTING THERE   Regular TGV **trains** per day arrive from Paris mostly from Gare de Lyon and some from Austerlitz (trip time: from 5 hr.); others change at Montpellier; the one-way fare starts at 29€. Trains run regularly from Marseille (trip time: from 3 hr., 5 min., depending on the route; from 21€ one-way). Train information and schedules are on www.sncf-connect.com or call ✆ **36-35.** If you're **driving** from the French Riviera, take the A9 west to Perpignan.

VISITOR INFORMATION   The **Office Municipal du Tourisme** is in place Francois-Arago (www.perpignantourisme.com; ✆ **04-68-66-30-30**).

GETTING AROUND   The free shuttle **P'tit Bus** runs around the old town and to the station. Taxis: ✆ **04-68-35-15-15** or 04-68-83-83-83.

Exploring the City

Most of Perpignan's major sites are concentrated in the compact, pedestrianized old town. The huge Palais des Rois de Majorque (see below) dominates the southern side of town. West of the river lies the new town.

Place de la République is at the heart of the pedestrianized city center. Off it, inviting streets are lined with shops, many carrying Catalan textiles, pottery and regional food items. You can pick from a good selection of Catalan wares at the **Visca Perpinya,** 16 rue Lazare Escarguel (https://viscaweb.net/botigaweb1; ✆ **04-68-57-23-29**). For a wide selection of Catalan ceramics by several makers, visit **Centre Sant-Vicens,** 40 rue Sant-Vicens (www.santvicens.fr; ✆ **04-68-50-02-18**). It's 4km (2½ miles) south of the town center; follow signs to Enne and Collioure.

Processions & Parties in Perpignan

Perpignan is the only city in France to celebrate Holy Week in the same way as Spain: with remarkable processions of penitents dressed in hooded gowns. The **Procession de la Sanch** leaves from Eglise St-Jacques on Good Friday morning and moves through the city center, accompanied by chants and the beating of drums. In summer the city puts on many festivals, including **Les Soirées Rayonnantes** (www.perpignantourisme.com; ✆ **04-68-66-30-30**), a series of free concerts and sound and light shows held on Tuesday and Thursday evenings from mid-July to mid-August.

During the first 2 weeks of September, Perpignan is host to the most famous celebration of photojournalism in the industry, **Visa pour l'Image** (www.visapourlimage.com; ✆ **04-68-62-38-00**). Photographs are exhibited in at least 10 sites of historical (usually medieval) interest. Entrance to the shows is free, and an international committee awards prizes.

At place Cassanyes is a daily, outdoor market (**Marché Cassanyes**) for fruits, vegetables, preserves and cheap clothes. The city's covered market, **Halles Vauban,** houses a number of eateries (perfect places for a snack or light lunch), along with vendors selling organic produce, fish, meats and other regional delicacies. It's at Quai Vauban and is open Tuesday to Saturday 8am to 8pm and Sunday from 8am to 3pm.

Cathédrale St-Jean ★ CATHEDRAL

The city's cathedral began construction in 1324 but was not completed until the late 16th century. Its built in a Catalan gothic style which is very different from classic French gothic. The impressive columned nave is wide, with side chapels retaining ornate 16th and 17th-century retables (altarpieces). Leave through the south door to see the chapel with the polychrome wooden *Devost-Christ* (Devout Christ), a magnificent 14th-century woodcarving depicting the suffering of Jesus on the cross.

pl. Gambetta/rue de l'Horloge. ℰ **04-68-51-33-72.** Free admission. June–Sept daily 8am–7pm; Oct–May daily 8am–6pm.

Le Castillet ★ MONUMENT/MUSEUM

This crenelated red-brick building is a combination gateway and fortress and the only surviving fortification from the 14th-century town walls. Climb its bulky tower for a view of the town and the surrounding narrow streets. It houses the **Musée des Arts et Traditions Populaires Catalans** (also known as La Casa Païral), with exhibitions of Catalan regional artifacts and folkloric items, including typical dress.

pl. de Verdun. ℰ **04-68-35-42-05.** Admission 2€ adults; free for children 18 and under. June–Sept daily 10:30am–6:30pm; Oct–May Tues–Sun 11am–5:30pm.

Musée d'Art Hyacinthe Rigaud ★★ MUSEUM

A huge recent expansion has given this museum a new look and tons of new space. Housed in two 18th-century *hôtels particuliers,* just off the cafe-lined place Arago, the museum displays the history of art from the 15th to 20th centuries, concentrating on those artists who lived or passed through Perpignan. The original collection was from native son Hyacinthe Rigaud, the official court artist of Versailles who painted Louis XIV and Louis XV. The collection, and temporary exhibitions, show works from the likes of Aristide Maillol, Picasso, Dufy, Jean Lurçat, and Miró as well as Catalan ceramics and contemporary artists.

16 rue Mailly. www.musee-rigaud. ℰ **04-68-66-19-83.** Admission 8€ adults; 6€ students and children ages 12–18; free for children 11 and under (additional fee for exhibits). June–Sept daily 10:30am–7pm; Oct–May Tues–Sun 11am–5:30pm.

Palais des Rois de Majorque (Palace of the Kings of Majorca) ★★ CASTLE

At the southern end of the old city, the massive Spanish citadel encloses the now restored former Palace of the Kings of Majorca. Built in the 13th and 14th centuries around a 2-story courtyard encircled by arcades, this is Perpignan's most famous building. Entering via a huge ramp wide enough to take several horsemen side by side, you walk into a park with the castle ahead. From the courtyard you climb to the first-floor king's and queen's apartments. The square tower with its double gallery gives panoramic views of the Pyrénées. A free guided tour, in French only, departs at 11am and 3pm.

Rue des Archers. ⓒ **04-68-34-96-29.** Admission 7€ adults; free for visitors 25 and under. July–Aug daily 9:30am–6:30pm; Apr–June and Sept–Oct daily 10am–6pm; Nov–Mar daily 10am–5pm.

Where to Stay

Hotel de la Loge ★★   In the center of the old town, this excellent-value hotel's biggest selling point is its location: It's tucked away on a car-free, very quiet street, in a lovely 16th-century building. A wrought-iron staircase leads up to the bedrooms (there is an elevator as well) and a small bar and breakfast room are on the ground floor. Bedrooms range from surprisingly spacious to quite small, and some have eccentric decor (oddly patterned wallpaper, mostly). Bathrooms have tubs and some rooms have small terraces overlooking place de la Loge. There's a pretty courtyard and prices include a light breakfast.

1 rue Fabrique d'en Nabot. www.hoteldelaloge.com. ⓒ **04-68-34-41-02.** 22 units. 68€–87€ double. **Amenities:** Bar; room service; free Wi-Fi.

La Villa Duflot ★★★   This is the area's finest hotel, yet its prices are reasonable for the luxury it offers. Located in a suburb 4km (2½ miles) from Perpignan, the Mediterranean-style dwelling is surrounded by gardens of orange and olive trees, mimosa, and eucalyptus. Under the trees are an outdoor bar and pool. The good-size guest rooms are spacious and soundproof, with stylish Art Deco interiors. All have king-size beds and good bathrooms. The restaurant is reason enough to stay, using ingredients from regional suppliers (minutely detailed on the menu) for dishes like foie gras with smoked eel, salmon candied in citrus fruits and Orgues olives with pea mousse and duck stuffed with lobster with zucchini cannelloni. It's open daily noon to 2pm and 8 to 11pm, with main courses from 36€ to 39€, and fixed-price menus at 55€ and 82€.

Rond-Point Albert Donnezan, Perpignan. www.villa-duflot.com. ⓒ **04-68-56-67-67.** 52 units. 161€–292€ double; 277€–384€ suite. From central Perpignan, follow signs to Perthus–Le Belou and A9, 3km (1¾ miles) south. Just before you reach A9, you'll see the hotel. **Amenities:** Restaurant; 2 bars; outdoor pool; spa; room service, free Wi-Fi.

Where to Eat

La Villa Duflot (see above) has an excellent restaurant.

Le Divil ★★ CATALAN   Near Le Castillet, this bull-themed restaurant fits perfectly into Perpignan's love affair with all things bovine. There are brick walls, stone floors, decorative bulls' heads on the walls, and a cold meat store full of steaks. The popular outside terrace fills up quickly in summer. It's fun, full of locals, and laid back. Starters include truffled eggs, and fish options, but this is a beef restaurant so you'd do best to order their grilled beef fillet, burgers or steaks, all of which come with perfect fries. Set menus are devised with a nutritionist and dietician.

9 rue Fabriques d'En Nabot. www.restaurant-le-divil-66.com. ℂ **04-68-34-57-73.** Main courses 16€–32€; fixed-price lunch 21€–26€. Mon–Sat noon–2pm and 7–10pm.

Le 17 ★★ MODERN FRENCH   The perfect blend of classic and modern cuisine is served up at this inventive restaurant next to Saint-Jean Cathedral. From its charming courtyard terrace, gaze up at the cathedral's flying buttresses while nibbling on chef Frédéric Marchand's creative daily-changing dishes. He uses mainly local organic ingredients in his salmon confit with coconut milk foam, roasted hazelnuts and fried seaweed and grilled squid with pattypan squash, figs and crunchy dried fruit. If you've arrived too late for lunch, the restaurant also doubles as a tea salon in the afternoon serving equally original cakes.

1 rue cité Bartissol. www.facebook.com/fredle17. ℂ **04-68-38-56-82.** Main courses 25€–32€; fixed-price lunch 29€. Tues–Sat noon–2pm and 7:30–10pm.

Perpignan Nightlife

Perpignan's cultural life is centered around the **Théâtre de l'Archipel,** av. Maréchal Leclerc (www.theatredelarchipel.org; ℂ **04-68-62-62-00**), which presents plays, concerts and children's shows year-round.

Perpignan shows its Spanish and Catalan side at night, getting lively after other cities have gone to bed. Nightclubs in Perpignan open around 11pm. The streets around **place de la Loge** and **avenue Maréchal Leclerc** buzz after dark with bars and clubs.

Begin at **Le Habana Bodeguita,** 5 rue Grande-des-Fabriques (www. lahabanabodeguita.com; ℂ **04-68-34-11-00**), where salsa and merengue play and Cuban cocktails flow. **Le O'Flaherty's,** 27 av. Marechal Leclerc (www.oflahertys-perpignan.com), is a good Irish bar with Irish beer on draft and DJs to keep you dancing from 5pm onward. **Le Cosy Club,** 4 rue du Théâtre (www.facebook.com/lecosyclub; ℂ **04-68-66-02-57**), is a discotheque which rings the changes with jazz, electro, and soul on different nights washed down with cocktails.

During summer, the beachfront strip at the nearby resort of **Canet-Plage,** 12km (7½ miles) east of Perpignan's historic core, lights up with seasonal bars and dance clubs that come and go with the tourist tides.

CARCASSONNE ★★★

770km (479 miles) SW of Paris; 94km (59 miles) SE of Toulouse; 105km (65 miles) S of Albi

The greatest fortress city of Europe stands out against the background of the Pyrénées. Seen from afar, this glorious citadel surrounded by fortified walls suggests fairy-tale magic, but in its heyday in the Middle Ages, it was very different. Shattering the peace and quiet were battering rams, grapnels, a mobile tower (inspired by the Trojan horse), catapults, flaming arrows, and the mangonel (a type of catapult) as the forces of the French King fought the heretical Cathars (p. 695).

Today, the city is used for movies (most notably the 1991 movie *Robin Hood, Prince of Thieves*) and is overrun with visitors. But the elusive charm of Carcassonne emerges in the evening, when the day-trippers have departed and floodlights bathe the ancient monuments.

Carcassonne is also a major stop along the **Canal du Midi,** that marvel of engineering that runs for 240km (150 miles) from the Garonne River at Toulouse all the way to the Mediterranean Sea at Sète. A 17th-century minor noble, Pierre-Paul Riquet, became obsessed with the idea of linking the Atlantic and the Mediterranean and devoted decades of his life and all of his fortune to make his plan a reality. Unfortunately, he died just months before the canal was officially opened in 1681. Although the arrival of the railways in the 19th century eroded much of the canal traffic, nowadays it is one of the most pleasurable ways of exploring this part of France. Barge companies run independent or skippered cruises along the full length of the canal (p. 817), or you can just take short circular jaunts from ports in Carcassonne and other towns along the route. Its wide towpaths make it popular for cyclists and walkers who appreciate the combination of flat terrain and plenty of scenic restaurant stops along the way.

Essentials

GETTING THERE   Carcassonne is a major stop for **trains** between Toulouse and destinations south and east. Seventeen trains per day arrive from Toulouse (trip time from 48 min.; 15€ one-way), 16 per day from Montpellier (trip time: 1½ hr.; from 10€ one-way), and 10 per day from Marseille (trip time: from 3 hr.; from 26€ one-way). Train info and schedules are on www.sncf-connect.com or call ℂ **36-35.** If you're **driving,** Carcassonne is on A61 south of Toulouse.

VISITOR INFORMATION   The **Office de Tourisme** has locations: 28 rue de Verdun (www.carcassonne-tourisme.com; ℂ **04-68-10-24-30**) and in the medieval town at Porte Narbonnaise.

SPECIAL EVENTS   The town's nightlife sparkles during its summer festivals. Concerts, modern and classical dance, operas, and theater fill the city for the **Festival de Carcassonne** (www.festivaldecarcassonne.com; ℂ **04-68-11-59-15**) from mid-July to mid-August, with international stars appearing at the **Théâtre Jean Deschamps,** an amphitheater seating 5,000 in La Cité. Tickets run 9€ to 85€. On July 14, **Bastille Day,** one of the best fireworks spectacles in France lights up the skies at 10:30pm. Over 6 weeks in July and August, the merriment and raucousness of the Middle Ages take over the city during the **Spectacles Medievaux,** in the form of jousts, food fairs, and street festivals. For info, contact the **Office de Tourisme** (see above).

Exploring Carcassonne

Carcassonne consists of two towns: the **Bastide St-Louis** ★★ (also known as Ville Basse, or "Lower City") and the UNESCO World Heritage Site upper town, or medieval **Cité** ★★★, which is among the top attractions in all of France. The impressive fortifications here consist of inner and outer walls, a double line of ramparts with walkways between them called *les lices*. The city began in the 6th century B.C., was later settled by the Romans and Visigoths, then became the main city of the Languedocian family, the Trencavels and its prosperity was ensured.

The epic medieval poems "Chansons de Geste" tell how the city got its name. During a siege by Charlemagne when the city was under Muslim rule, the starving populace was near surrender until a local noblewoman, Dame Carcas, reputedly gathered up the last of their grain, fed it to a sow, and tossed the pig over the ramparts. The pig burst, scattering the grain. Dame Carcas then demanded a parley and cried, *"Carcas te sonne!"* ("Carcas is calling you!") The Franks, concluding that Carcassonne must have unlimited food supplies, ended their siege. Like all such stories, it is not checkable and almost certainly apocryphal.

Carcassonne's walls were further fortified by the *vicomtes* de Trencavel in the 12th century but the town was taken during the Albigensian Crusade by anti-Cathar troops under Simon de Montfort. In 1249 the city passed to Louis IX who laid out the *ville basse*. It was razed to the ground in 1355 by the English Black Prince during the Hundred Years War, then rebuilt by the citizens. By the mid-17th century, the city had lost its position as a strategic frontier, and the ramparts were quarried for their stones. But interest in the Middle Ages revived in the mid-19th century, and the

An aerial shot of the old city of Carcassonne.

government ordered Viollet-le-Duc (the restorer of Notre-Dame in Paris) to repair and, where necessary, rebuild the walls. He took considerable license when rebuilding the citadel to incorporate various very un-medieval features. In addition, the city today has an overabundance of souvenir shops, and silly attractions like virtual reality "tours" and torture museums. But what does that matter? Carcassonne casts its spell on all who come here.

To learn more about the city's history—and it really *is* fascinating—you'll want to visit the Chateau Comtal (see below) and also take a **guided walking tour** ★★★ of the Cité. The Tourist Board hosts excellent 1½-hour daily tours in English for 12€ per adult (7€ for children) at times that vary by season. In the course of the tour you'll learn about a medieval Duke's tragic betrayal, how World War II resistance fighters II used Cathedral passageways to spy on German officers, and stories of the residents who still live in the castle. Note that there are some steep areas to hike up during the tour. There's also a **tourist train** that circles the ramparts of the old city, and a **horse and carriage tour,** but their narration is only in French (info at tourist board website; see above).

Pair the walking tour with a visit to the **Château Comtal** ★★★, pl. du Château (www.remparts-carcassonne.fr; ✆ **04-68-11-70-72;** 9.50€ adults, free for children 17 and under; Apr–Sept daily 10am–6:15pm, Oct–Mar daily 9:30am–4:45pm), the restored 12th-century fortress defended by Raymond Trencavel then surrendered to the Crusaders in 1209. Though there is wall text in places, you'll better understand what you're seeing if you ante up the 5€ for an audio guide. It's a bit goofy in parts (actors play the historic characters) but overall is quite informative. You'll see the archaeological remnants discovered on-site, view works of art in the small museum, and learn about daily life in the Middle Ages and 19th-century restorations. The entrance to the castle/fortress is in the highest part of the Cité, on rue Cros Mayrevielle.

The major church of the Old City, **Basilique St-Nazaire** ★★, pl. de l'Eglise (✆ **04-68-25-27-65**), dates from the 11th to the 14th centuries and contains some beautiful stained-glass windows including two exceptional rose windows. It has other attractions: a soaring Romanesque nave, a gothic choir and transept, and the original tombstone of Simon de Montfort, the leader of the Crusade against the Cathars. The 16th-century organ is one of the oldest in southwestern France. The basilica is open Monday through Saturday 9am to noon and 2 to 7pm, Sunday 9am to 10:45am and 2 to 5pm. It closes slightly earlier in winter. Mass is celebrated on Sunday at 11am. Admission is free.

In the lower city are two worthwhile museums: the **Musee des Beaux Arts** ★★, 15 bd. Camille Pelletan (free admission; daily 9:45am–12:30pm and 1:30–6:15pm), which has contemporary art and important pieces by Corot and Courbet; and the **Musée De L'école** ★, 3 rue de Plo (4€ admission; Tues–Sat 9:30am–12:30pm and 1:30–6pm), set in a former elementary school, with exhibits exploring what it was like to be a student in 1880 and 1960.

More info on all the sites discussed above can be found at www.
tourisme-carcassonne.fr.

Where to Stay

IN THE CITÉ

Hôtel de la Cité ★★★   The best hotel in Carcassonne was originally a
palace for the ruling bishops before it was turned into a hotel in 1909. This
is where you can escape the crowds, safe behind an enclosed courtyard in
the old city. The best bedrooms are straight out of a fairy tale book with paneled walls, wooden or tiled floors; some have friezes running around the top
of the walls while others have fireplaces or a four-poster bed. Many rooms
look out onto the ramparts or the garden and certain suites have private
terraces. The hotel is renowned for its restaurant, **La Barbacane** (p. 707).
pl. Auguste Pierre Pont. www.hoteldelacite.com. ☎ **04-68-71-98-71.** 59 units. 264€–
522€ double; 470€–935€ suite. Parking 28€. **Amenities:** Restaurant; bar; babysitting;
outdoor pool; spa; room service; free Wi-Fi.

AT THE ENTRANCE TO THE CITÉ

Hôtel Le Donjon ★★   The second hotel within the city walls is big on
charm and offers the best value in the moderate price range. The main
building has a honey-colored stone exterior with iron bars on the windows. The lobby is cozy with suits of armor and elaborate Louis XIII–
style furniture. Bedrooms are modern and very comfortably furnished;
some have old exposed stone walls or views of the ramparts. At the end of
the garden a second building has the family rooms and suites, all with a
terrace. Bathrooms here have both a tub and a shower. The hotel also runs
the adjacent restaurant, **Chez Christine** (see below). In summer, the garden is the perfect breakfast spot.
2 rue du Comte-Roger. www.hotel-donjon.fr. ☎ **04-68-11-23-00.** 46 units. 134€–
261€ double; 194€–290€ suite. Parking 20€. **Amenities:** Restaurant; bar; room service; free Wi-Fi.

IN VILLE-BASSE

Hôtel du Pont Vieux ★★   Near the old bridge (*le vieux pont*) and a
10-minute walk to the citadel, this friendly, family-run hotel is on a lively
street of bars, restaurants, and shops. It occupies an 18th-century building,
which has the advantage of a large courtyard, an internal garden, and a terrace which gives panoramic views of the citadel. The recently renovated
bedrooms are simply furnished but pretty with bright fabrics. Pale tiled
bathrooms are a good standard; some have rain showerheads. Pick a room on
the upper floor for a splendid view. Triple and family rooms are available.
32 rue Trivalle. www.hotelpontvieux.com. ☎ **04-68-25-24-99.** 19 units. 69€– 155€
double. Parking 10€. **Amenities:** Lounge; free Wi-Fi.

Where to Eat

Chez Christine ★★, run by Le Donjon hotel and with a menu designed by
La Barbacane's renowned chef Jérôme Ryon, is also highly recommended.

As is **Comte Roger ★★**, at 14 rue Saint-Louis in the Cite (www.comte roger.com), an indoor/outdoor restaurant with a lovely patio shaded by grape vines. If you want to try *cassoulet*—the rich and very comforting stew of beans with several types of meat that's an Occitanie specialty—this is where to do so in Carcassonne.

La Barbacane ★★ FRENCH   You'll find this baronial-style restaurant in the Hotel de la Cité. Start with a drink in the majestic Library Bar looking out to the castle. The setting might be medieval but the cooking is bang up to date. Chef Jérôme Ryon uses local ingredients as a base for innovative Michelin-starred dishes. His gourmet menu, with health-conscious and vegetarian options, could feature grilled red tuna with zucchini carpaccio and zucchini flower tempura; filet of Aubrac beef with truffled potato *dauphinoise;* or Roussilon apricot *tarte tatin* with pine nut ice-cream. This is the place for a special meal in a grand setting, with crisp linen on the large tables and a welcoming and knowledgeable staff.

In the Hôtel de la Cité, pl. de l'Eglise. www.hoteldelacite.com. ℂ **04-68-71-98-71.** Main courses 50€; fixed-price lunch 49€ or gourmet menu 84€–130€. Daily 12:30–2pm and 7:30–9:30pm. Closed Feb to early Mar.

Le Jardin en Ville ★★ FRENCH/CATALAN   How's this for an unusual restaurant concept: an eatery within a shop selling modern and fairly hip items and occasional exhibition space? Eat inside where the funky interior features mismatched furniture and the likes of a hanging bicycle; or dine on the pretty shaded terrace. Share a platter of Catalan tapas then enjoy sliced duck breast with roast potatoes and spiced vegetables or red mullet with tomato compote and fresh pesto. Vegetables are picked each morning from the garden; meat comes from local southwest suppliers.

5 rue des Framboisiers. www.lejardinenville.fr. ℂ **04-68-47-80-91.** Main courses 14€–22€; fixed-price lunch 23€. Tues–Wed noon–2pm; Thurs–Sat noon–2pm and 7–9pm; July and Aug Tues–Sat noon–2pm and 7–9pm.

L'Escargot ★★ CATALAN   This popular tapas and wine bar is first rate for a light lunch or casual meal. Inside it has stone walls, a big-beamed ceiling and wooden floors and tables; the outside terrace tables fill up quickly. Tapas range from six snails at 6€ to top Iberico ham at 15€. Other dishes include large salads and the excellent value three-course menus include beef on skewers with roast potatoes, salad, and vegetables. Service is fast, fun, and efficient; its central location couldn't be better.

7 rue Viollet-le-Duc. www.restaurant-lescargot.com. ℂ **04-68-47-12-55.** Fixed-price menus 18.50€–28.50€. Thurs–Tues noon–2:30pm and 7–9:30pm.

Shopping

Carcassonne has two distinct shopping areas. In the Lower City, the major streets for shopping, particularly for clothing, are **rue Clemenceau** and **rue de Verdun.** In the walled medieval city, the streets are chock-full of tiny stores and boutiques; many sell gift items such as antiques and local arts and crafts, others sell souvenirs like plastic swords, and lavender sachets.

In the Cité, visit **Comptoir des Vins,** 3 rue du Conte Roger (✆ **04-68-26-44-76**), for its wide selection of regional wines. Find a wide range of regional foods at **La Ferme,** 55 Rue de Verdun (✆ **04-68-25-02-15**). Antiques stores of merit include **Antiquités Safi,** 26 rue Trivalle (✆ **04-68-25-60-51**), for paintings and art objects; and **Maison du Sud,** 13 porte d'Aude (✆ **04-68-47-13-72**), for home decoration.

Carcassonne Nightlife

Carcassonne nightlife centers on **boulevard Omer-Sarraut** in La Bastide and **place Marcou** in La Cité. For a wonderful nighttime view of La Cité, live music and events, walk up to **La Métairie,** 3 chemin de Montlegun (www.facebook.com/lametairie.carcassonne; ✆ **04-68-26-80-38**). It's open daily 6pm to 2am.

For some late-night dancing, get sparkled up and saunter to **Le Café de Nuit,** 31 bd. Omer Sarraut (www.facebook.com/lecafedenuit carcassonne; ✆ **04-68-72-43-38**), with DJs spinning Electro, House, and Techno music until dawn. It's open Thursday 11pm to 4am and Friday and Saturday 11pm to 6am.

CASTRES ★

721km (448 miles) SW of Paris; 42km (26 miles) S of Albi; 78km (43½ miles) E of Toulouse

On the bank of the Agout River, Castres is a delightful small town and the gateway for trips to the odd rock formations of the Sidobre granite massif and the mountains of Lacaune. Once a Roman military town, it became a religious center and stop on the pilgrim route to Santiago de Compostela after Benedictine monks arrived with the remains of St. Vincent of Saragossa. Caught up in the Cathar heresy (p. 695), the first Albigensian martyrs were burnt here in 1209 and it continued its anti-Catholic church stance in the wars of religion in the late 16th century. The Eglise St-Benoît in French baroque style was started in 1677 on the Benedictine site but never finished. Echoes of Castres as a wool-producing town in the 14th century are found in the brightly colored old tanners' and weavers' houses by the river.

Essentials

GETTING THERE From Toulouse, there are regular **trains** each day (trip time: around 1 hr., 21 min.; one-way fare is 16.10€). Train information and schedules are on www.sncf-connect.com or call ✆ **36-35.** Shuttle bus no. 2 runs between the station and the center. If you're **driving,** Castres is on N126 east of Toulouse and N112 south of Albi.

VISITOR INFORMATION The **Office de Tourisme** is at 2 pl. de la République (www.tourisme-castres.fr; ✆ **05-63-62-63-62**).

Exploring Castres

Jean-Jaurès Museum ★ MUSEUM   Jean-Jaurès, born in Castres, was one of France's most liberal political activists. He supported Dreyfus, founded the communist newspaper *L'Humanité* (still in print today), was leader of the socialist party, and campaigned for causes like abolishing the death penalty. His pacifist beliefs led to his assassination in Paris in July 1914. Though the documentation is in French, the large collection of satirical cartoons and lithographs gives a good picture of political life in France in the 1900s. Temporary exhibitions focus on life in all its aspects—cultural, economic, and social—between 1880 and 1914.

2 pl. Pélisson. ✆ **05-63-62-41-83.** Admission 3€ adults, 1.50€ students, free for children 17 and under. July–Aug daily 10am–noon and 2–6pm; May–June and Sept Tues–Sun 10am–noon and 2–5pm; Oct–Mar Tues–Sat 10am–noon and 2–5pm.

Musée Goya ★★ MUSEUM   Located in the town hall, once the archbishop's palace, designed by Louis XIV's chief architect in 1669, this museum reopened in 2023 after 3 years of extensive renovations. The new displays showcase France's second largest collection of Spanish art, after the Louvre, spanning from antiquity to the 20th century. The museum also houses 16th-century tapestries, some outstanding sculpture, and paintings by Spanish artists from the 15th to the 20th centuries including works by Velázquez and Murillo. Despite the museum's name, only a few works by Francisco Goya are on display. Pierre Briguiboul, son of the Castres-born artist Marcel Briguiboul, donated these to the town in 1894. On show are portraits, including the famous *Self-Portrait with Glasses.* Before leaving, don't miss the beautiful formal garden designed by Le Nôtre, principal gardener to Louis XIV.

In the Jardin de l'Evêché. www.museegoya.fr. ✆ **05-63-71-59-27.** Admission 9€ adults, 6€ students, free for children 17 and under. July–Aug daily 10am–7pm; Oct–May Tues–Sun 10am–6pm.

Where to Stay

Hôtel Renaissance ★   This charming lodging in the old town is housed in a red-brick, half-timbered 17-century building that started life as a grand family home. Bedrooms are decorated with differing styles: Couples may like the Medieval room with a canopy bed and wooden beamed ceiling. Families can surprise the kids with the Harry Potter themed room. It's not for those with minimalist tastes but it's great fun if you like something different. Public rooms are equally exuberant in decor, plus there's a cozy bar. Although the hotel doesn't have a restaurant, room service is available.

17 rue Victor-Hugo. www.hotel-renaissance.fr. ✆ **05-63-59-30-42.** 20 units. 80€–130€ double; 116€–145€ suite. Parking 14€. **Amenities:** Bar; room service; free Wi-Fi.

Where to Eat

La Part des Anges ★★ MODERN FRENCH   Enjoy a heavenly meal in Castres at La Part des Anges, or "the angel's share." Located across the

Agout River from the Goya Museum, the restaurant's airy dining room is decorated in light wood furniture and cloudlike lighting. The seasonal *bistronomie* menu might include pan-fried foie gras with pear and tonka bean chutney, or filet mignon with parsnips, black olives and red piquillo sauce.

5 bd. Raymond-Vittoz. www.lapartdesangescastres.fr. *©* **05-63-51-65-25.** Main courses 20€–24€; fixed-price weekday lunch menu 22€; other fixed-price menus 36€–44€. Tues noon–1:45pm; Wed–Sat noon–1:45pm and 7:30–9:45pm.

Le Bistrot des Saveurs ★★ FRENCH   Englishman Simon Scott worked in the kitchens of the Ritz and Savoy hotels in London before moving to France with his French wife and opening this Michelin-rated restaurant. It's a smart, modern restaurant with comfortable leather chairs, wooden floor and stone vaults. Like the decor, the classically based cooking has a chic contemporary touch. The menu changes weekly or every 10 days according to the seasons and the markets. A typical menu might include black pudding with squash foam and apple chutney followed by grilled beef with carrots fresh from the garden. At lunch a glass of wine and coffee comes at a mere 4€ extra. Beautiful desserts, a good wine list and charming staff complete the package.

5 rue Sainte-Foy. http://bistrot-saveurs-81.fr. *©* **05-63-50-11-45.** Fixed-price lunch 19€–25€ or dinner 35€–50€; tasting menu 90€. Mon–Fri noon–2:30pm and 7:30–9:15pm. Closed 2 weeks in Aug.

ALBI ★★★

697km (432 miles) SW of Paris; 76km (47 miles) NE of Toulouse

Albi straddles both banks of the Tarn River and is dominated by its 13th-century cathedral, the heart of the remarkable Episcopal city. The whole of this medieval city center was added to UNESCO's World Heritage List in 2010. Albi is known as the "red city," its major remarkable buildings constructed from red bricks. Toulouse-Lautrec was born in the Hôtel Bosc in Albi; it's still a private home and not open to visitors, but a plaque is on the wall of the building, on rue Toulouse-Lautrec in the town center. Naturally, one of the town's major attractions is the Toulouse-Lautrec museum with a world-class collection of the artist's work.

Essentials

GETTING THERE   Sixteen **trains** per day link Toulouse with Albi (trip time: from 1 hr.; the one-way fare is 14.40€). Train info and schedules are on www.sncf-connect.com or call *©* **36-35.** If you're **driving** from Toulouse, take A68 northeast.

VISITOR INFORMATION   The **Office de Tourisme** is in place Ste-Cécile (www.albi-tourisme.fr; *©* **05-63-36-36-00**).

Exploring Albi

The old town is a delightful mix of narrow streets near the cathedral and south of the river Tarn. Lovers of fashion should dive into the **Musée de la**

Mode ★, 17 rue de la Souque (www.musee-mode.com; ☏ **05-63-43-15-90;** 6€ adults, 4€ students and children 9–14, free for children 8 and under), for its annual exhibitions of clothes and accessories through history from its 1,000-strong collection. It's open Wednesday to Sunday from 10:30am to noon and 2:30 to 6pm. The old town is also a good area for shops.

Cathédrale Ste-Cécile ★★★ CATHEDRAL   Fortified with ramparts and parapets, this extraordinary 13th-century cathedral dominates the city. It was started as a building to strike fear into the hearts of the Albigensian heretics, 50 years after their defeat (p. 695), but it took 200 years to complete. It holds three records: It is the largest brick-built cathedral in the world, it has the oldest medieval depiction of the Last Judgment (complete with devils and grimacing souls), and it has the largest surface area of Italian Renaissance frescos in France. It also has an exceptional restored 15th-century rood screen with unique polychromatic statues from the Old and New Testaments. It's worth getting to the cathedral on Wednesdays and Sundays at 4pm in July and August for a free organ recital.

Place Ste-Cecile. https://cathedrale-albi.com. ☏ **05-63-43-23-43.** Cathédrale: Free admission. Choir and Treasury: 6€ including audio guide; free for children 12 and under. Daily 10am–6:30pm.

Musée Lapérouse ★★ MUSEUM   On the opposite bank of the Tarn from the bulk of Albi's medieval core (take the Pont-Vieux), this museum tells the story of the Albigeois Jean-François de Lapérouse. Louis XVI was so impressed by the sea-faring captain that he sent him on a mission with two frigates and 225 sailors and scientists to map and chart the coastlines of Alaska, California, and China at a time of commercial rivalry with

Construction began on Albi's "Old Bridge" in 1020, making it one of France's oldest still-in-use bridges.

England over overseas colonies. In 1788 they reached the Salomon Islands, then vanished without a trace. The museum tries to unravel the mystery.

Square Botany Bay. ✆ **05-63-49-15-55.** Admission 4€ adults, 2.50€ students and ages 13–25, free for children 12 and under. July–Aug daily 9am–12:30pm and 2–6:30pm; Sept Tues–Sun 10am–12:30pm and 2–6:30pm; Mar–June and Oct Tues–Sun 9am–noon and 2–6pm; Nov–Feb Tues–Sun 10am–noon and 2–5pm.

Palais de la Berbie: Musée Toulouse-Lautrec ★★★ MUSEUM
The Palais de la Berbie dating from the 13th century was the fortified residence of the Archbishops. Today it houses the Toulouse-Lautrec museum containing the world's most important collection of the 19th-century artist's paintings and works, more than 1,000 in all. It follows the life of the aristocratic Albigeois from his teenage years to those famous drawings (563 of them), 219 oil paintings, 183 lithographs, and 31 posters depicting the raffish demi-monde of turn-of-the-century Paris. For an art buff or Toulouse-Lautrec fan, this is a must-see museum. The top floor displays work by other French artists: Degas, Bonnard, Matisse, Utrillo, and Rouault. Another gallery focuses on Albi's Episcopal city. The grand garden here is also worth a visit.

pl. Ste-Cécile. www.musee-toulouse-lautrec.com. ✆ **05-63-49-48-70.** Admission 10€ adults, 5€ students, free for children 17 and under. Daily June–Sept 10am–6pm; Oct–May Tues–Sun 10am–12:30pm and 2–6pm. Closed Jan 1, May 1, Nov 1, and Dec 25.

Where to Stay

Alchimy ★★★   This is the sort of spectacular boutique hotel that you'd expect to find in central Paris—not Albi. The inspiration of two professional interior designers, every room is individually decorated with panache. Furnishings are super comfortable with armchairs, matching fabrics and colors and one-off accessories carefully sourced. Public areas are equally sophisticated, including an elegant outdoor terrace. The onsite brasserie is another must-experience venue with columns, mirrors, a glass roof, and modern chandelier. A la carte main dishes range from 18€ to 30€ but order the fixed-price menus for great food superbly cooked. Menus are 20€ for lunch and 29€ to 39€ for dinner.

50 rue Séré-de-Rivières. www.alchimyalbi.fr. ✆ **05-63-76-18-18.** 10 units. 160€–190€ double; 180€–270€ suite. Parking 10€. **Amenities:** Restaurant; bar; room service; free Wi-Fi.

Hôtel Chiffre ★   Originally a coaching inn, this city-center hotel remains a good choice for travelers. Today's renovated version offers good-sized rooms with fabric-covered or wall-papered walls and old-fashioned, comfortable furniture; some overlook the inner courtyard where you can enjoy your breakfast. It's a good-value option with super friendly staff on a quiet street just 10 minutes from the cathedral.

50 rue Séré-de-Rivières. www.hotelchiffre.com. ✆ **05-63-48-58-48.** 36 units. 72€–135€ double. Parking 15€. **Amenities:** Bar; room service; free Wi-Fi.

Hotel St-Antoine ★★   One of the oldest hotels in France, this former monastery was rebuilt as an inn in 1734. The same family has owned it for five generations; today Caroline Rieux manages the hotel just a 10-minute walk from the Episcopal City. Most bedrooms have been recently refurbished with colorful modern drapes and fabrics, although some still feature antique furniture and lamps. Ask for a room with a view over the garden where you can sit on a balmy day.

17 rue St-Antoine. www.hotel-saint-antoine-albi.com. © **05-63-54-04-04.** 44 units. 96€–158€ double; 165€–198€ suite. Parking 15€. **Amenities:** Free Wi-Fi. Closed Nov–Mar.

Where to Eat

For a gourmet meal in chic surroundings book at **Alchimy.** Both **La Hostellerie St-Antoine** and the **Hôtel Chiffre** also have good eateries. See "Where to Stay," above.

Jardin des Quatre Saisons ★★ MODERN FRENCH   As its name suggests, this restaurant highlights seasonal garden ingredients. For almost 50 years the restaurant's cuisine, now supervised by chef Alexandre Bravi, keeps local gastronomes coming back. Depending on what's freshest at the market, the good-value menu might have *millefeuille* of crawfish and eggplant, seafood *pot au feu* and saddle of lamb with thyme. The small brick-walled restaurant is full of everyday objects and has a fireplace that gives it a homely feel.

5 rue de la Pompe. www.le-jardin-des-quatre-saisons.fr. © **05-63-60-77-76.** Main courses 17€–23€; fixed-price weekday lunch 18€ and dinner 33€. Tues–Fri noon–1:30pm and 7:30–9:30pm; Sat 7:30–10pm

La Planque de l'Evêque ★★ MODERN FRENCH   All the dishes that you would hope to find in a restaurant where modern touches have revitalized traditional French cooking are found here. Try the likes of cod ceviche with ginger and citrus fruits followed by deboned chicken stuffed with ricotta and spinach served with chorizo jus. But an equally compelling reason to cross the river is the spectacular view you get of the cathedral complex from the summer terrace. It's far enough off the main tourist track that you'll likely be eating with locals only.

1 rue de Lamothe. www.laplanquedeleveque.com. © **05-63-56-89-49.** Main courses 18€–22€; fixed-price lunch 16€–19€; other fixed-price menus 26€–34€. Wed–Sat noon–1:30pm and 7:30–9:15pm; Sun noon–1:30pm. Closed 3 weeks in Jan.

CORDES-SUR-CIEL ★★

651km (404 miles) SW of Paris; 25km (16 miles) NW of Albi

This remarkable site is like an eagle's nest on a hilltop looking out onto the Cérou valley. The fortified town, or bastide, circled by several medieval walls, looks especially spectacular at sunrise. Stand on the ramparts when the air is soft and the colors muted before the crowds arrive to swell a population of under 1,000 to 10,000.

Founded in 1222 by Count Raymond VII of Toulouse during the war between his Cathar subjects and the French king, its prosperity came from its leather, textile, and silk industries. Today, it's an arts-and-crafts city with artisans occupying many of the old houses on the narrow streets—blacksmiths, enamellers, graphic artists, weavers, engravers, sculptors, and painters. In days gone by, intellectual celebrities like Jean-Paul Sartre and Albert Camus made this town a favorite hideaway.

Essentials

GETTING THERE　If you're **driving,** take A68 northeast from Toulouse to Gaillac, turning north at exit 9 on D922 to Cordes-sur-Ciel. Park outside and then pass under an arch leading to the old town. If you're coming by **train,** get off in Cordes-Vindrac and walk, rent a bicycle, or take a taxi the remaining 5km (3 miles) to Cordes. Train info and schedules are on www.sncf-connect.com or call 🕿 **36-35.** For taxis or a **minibus,** call **Taxi Barrois** (🕿 **05-63-56-14-80**). A few times daily, bus 707 travels between Albi and Cordes, see **www.lio-occitanie.fr**.

VISITOR INFORMATION　The **Office de Tourisme** is at Maison Gaugrin, 38-42 Grand-Rue (www.cordessurciel.fr; 🕿 **05-63-56-00-52**).

Exploring Cordes-sur-Ciel

Sometimes called "the city of a hundred Gothic arches," the winding narrow streets are full of *maisons gothiques* ★★ of pink sandstone. The **Grande Rue Raymond VII,** also called **rue Droite,** is lined with houses, distinguished by 13th- and 14th-century pointed arches over the doors and windows. The old citadel or "upper town" runs along the ridge; the "lower town" hugs the eastern end of the old town.

You get to the upper town via the steep Grand-Rue de l'Horloge from the **Maison de Pays** (8 pl. Jeanne Ramels-Cals), which organizes the Saturday morning **market** in place de la Bouteillerie and sells regional products. Walk along the Rue St-Michel past the **St-Michel Church,** dating from the 13th century but much modified in the intervening centuries. Its organ was brought from Notre-Dame in Paris in 1842.

Musée Charles-Portal ★ MUSEUM　Small and quirky, this somewhat sleepy museum is near a pass-through (Painted Gate) in the fortifications surrounding the city's medieval center. Inside reveals the story of Cordes and the surroundings with photographs, films, local textiles and embroidery, and medieval artifacts. Climb to the top-floor terrace for stunning views.
Porte des Ormeaux. https://museecharlesportal.fr. 🕿 **09-72-87-07-95.** Admission 3€ adults, 2.50€ ages 12–25, free for children 11 and under. July–Aug Wed–Mon 2:30–6:30pm; Sept to mid-Nov and Apr–June Fri–Sun 2:30–6pm.

Where to Stay & Eat

Au Jardin des Saveurs ★ MODERN FRENCH　Just outside Cordes and set in its own park, this 19th-century mansion is a restaurant with rooms.

Run by husband-and-wife team Léa and Joffrey Morgallet since 2023, it features a pretty wood-paneled dining room with a baronial fireplace, though in good weather some opt to dine in the shaded garden surrounded by tall trees. Top dishes include a starter of *pissaladière*-style tart with confit tomatoes, a main of pollack cooked in a Thai bouillon and a dessert of poached pear with Roquefort cheese. The hotel offers 5 comfortable and well-furnished rooms, some with terraces; a double costs 90€ to 110€.

Les Cabannes. www.aujardindessaveurs81.fr. ☏ **05-63-56-02-59.** From the town center, take rte. de St-Antonin (D600) for about 1km (½ mile) west. Main courses 28€; fixed-price menu 36€–60€. Tues 7–9pm, Wed–Sun noon–2pm. **Amenities:** Bar; restaurant; room service; free Wi-Fi.

Hôtel Raymond VII ★★ Found in a 13th-century building, this small hotel is your best bet for overnighting in the heart of Cordes. Stepping into its stone, brick and half-timbered courtyard, you'll instantly fall under its Medieval charm. Standard doubles have simple wooden furniture and cream or grey walls; the additional fee for a Superior Room is small and buys you lovely digs with wooden-beamed ceilings, chandeliers and soaring views over the Cerou valley.

19 Grand rue Raimond VII. http://raymond7.fr. ☏ **05-63-60-02-80.** 7 units. 85€–120€ double; 95€–110€ suites. **Amenities:** Free Wi-Fi.

TOULOUSE ★★★

677km (420 miles) SW of Paris; 245km (152 miles) SE of Bordeaux; 94km (59 miles) W of Carcassonne

The old capital of Languedoc, and now the capital of the new Occitanie region, Toulouse (known as *La Ville Rose*), is France's fourth-largest city. It's lively and cosmopolitan and filled with spacious squares and gardens. Most of Toulouse's fine old mansions date from the Renaissance, when this was one of the richest cities in Europe. Today Toulouse is an artistic and cultural hub and a high-tech center, home to two huge aircraft makers—Airbus and Aerospatiale. Also making the city tick is its large student population: The university is France's third largest.

A city with a distinguished past, Toulouse is also a city of the future with the National Center for Space Research making its headquarters here since 1968. The first regularly scheduled airline flights from France took off from the local airport in the 1920s. Today Airbus planes are assembled in a gargantuan hangar in the suburb of Colombiers.

Essentials

GETTING THERE The Toulouse-Blagnac international **airport** lies in the city's northwestern suburbs, 10km (6 miles) from the center; for flight information, go to www.toulouse.aeroport.fr or call ☏ **00-8-25-38-00-00** from abroad or 08-25-38-00-00 in France. **Air France** (www.airfrance.fr; ☏ **09-69-39-02-15**) has about 25 flights a day from Paris and flies to Toulouse from London twice a day in high season. easyJet flies from the UK

Place du Capitole.

to Toulouse. The regular shuttle bus from the airport to the bus station takes 20 minutes and costs 9€ one-way.

Seven TGV **trains** per day arrive from Paris Montparnasse (trip time: from 4¼ hr.; from 25€ one-way), 18 trains (TGV and local) from Bordeaux (trip time from 2 hr.; from 16€ one-way), and eight from Marseille (trip time: from 3 hr., 42 min.; from 20€ one-way). Train info and schedules are on www.sncf-connect.com or call ✆ **36-35.** The **drive** from Paris takes 6 to 7 hours. Take A10 south to Bordeaux, connecting to A62 to Toulouse. The **Canal du Midi** links many of the region's cities with Toulouse by waterway.

VISITOR INFORMATION   The **Office de Tourisme** is in the Donjon du Capitole in the Square de Gaulle (www.toulouse-tourisme.com; ✆ **05-17-42-31-31**). *Note:* The tourist board offers an excellent 6€ **audio walking tour,** available on all smart phones.

LAYOUT OF THE CITY   The old town contains the main sights, encircled by large boulevards which follow the city's former defensive walls.

GETTING AROUND   Toulouse has the most efficient public transportation system of any city in southwestern France. The heart of the city, the historic core of most interest to visitors, is served by a modern and efficient **Métro (subway)** system administered by TISSEO Réseau urbain (✆ **05-61-41-70-70;** www.tisseo.fr). The service operates daily from 5:15am to midnight (until 3am Fri–Sat), and tickets and maps are available at ticket booths. The average Métro fare is 1.60€ per ticket (tourist passes and multiple-trip tickets are also available). The most useful stops, which are within walking distance of all the main attractions, are Capitole, Jean Jaurès, and Esquirole.

Exploring Toulouse

Start at the impressive place du Capitole, the heart of the old town. Cafes on the west side offer great views over the square that fills with market

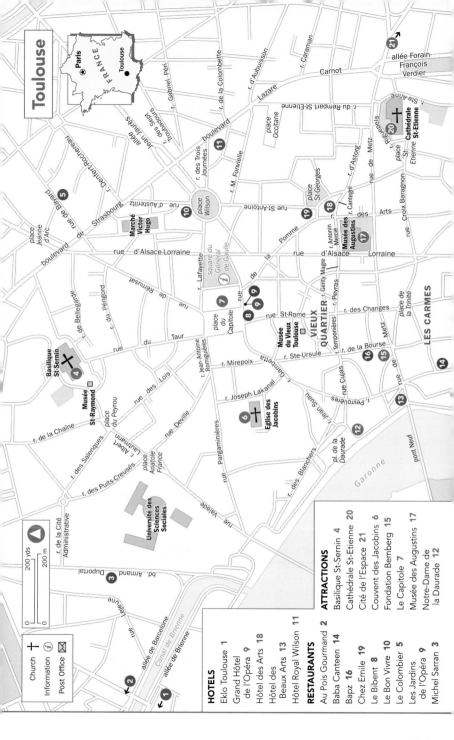

Toulouse

HOTELS

Eklo Toulouse 1
Grand Hôtel
de l'Opéra 9
Hôtel des Arts 18
Hôtel des
Beaux Arts 13
Hôtel Royal Wilson 11

RESTAURANTS

Au Pois Gourmand 2
Baba Canteen 14
Bapz 16
Chez Emile 19
Le Bibent 8
Le Bon Vivre 10
Le Colombier 5
Les Jardins
de l'Opéra 9
Michel Sarran 3

ATTRACTIONS

Basilique St-Sernin 4
Cathédrale St-Etienne 20
Cité de l'Espace 21
Couvent des Jacobins 6
Fondation Bemberg 15
Le Capitole 7
Musée des Augustins 17
Notre-Dame de
la Daurade 12

717

stalls daily. **Le Capitole ★**, pl. du Capitole (☏ **05-61-22-34-12**), is an outstanding achievement of civic architecture with its columns of pink marble and brickwork. Built in baroque style in 1753, it houses the **Hôtel de Ville** (City Hall) as well as the **Théâtre National du Capitole** (☏ **05-61-63-13-13**), which presents operas and ballets. Admission is free; group tours allow access to the theater (held Oct–June). It is open Tuesday through Saturday 11am to 6pm.

The gothic brick **Couvent des Jacobins ★★**, parvis des Jacobins (www.jacobins.toulouse.fr; ☏ **05-61-22-23-82**), west of the place du Capitole in the narrow streets of the old town, dominates its surroundings. Founded in 1230 by the Dominicans to fight the Cathar heresy (p. 695), the convent and church formed the center of a powerful monastery complex that includes a peaceful cloister, sacristy, chapter house, and refectory. Inside the 13th century church, look up at its "palm tree" ceiling of delicate fan vaults supported by seven huge columns. The chapelle de la Vierge contains richly embroidered ceremonial robes. The old refectory now houses temporary exhibitions. The complex is open Tuesday to Sunday 10am to 6pm, admission to the church and chapelle is free; the rest costs 5€ from June to September and 4€ October to May, free for those 17 years and under and free on first Sunday of the month.

Small and dating mostly from the 18th century, **Notre-Dame de la Daurade ★**, 1 pl. de la Daurade (☏ **05-61-21-38-32**), sits to the west of the place du Capitole beside a riverside park from where you can take a boat cruise. Built on the site of a pagan temple, it was once covered in gilding. Its main possession is a statue of the Black Virgin, about 1m (3¼ ft.) tall, believed to cure ailments. The present *Vierge noire,* made in 1807, is a replica of the original destroyed during the French Revolution. Admission is free, and it is open daily 9am to 6pm.

Basilique St-Sernin ★★★ BASILICA   Walk north from the place du Capitole to reach the St-Sernin district. Consecrated in 1096, the basilica is the largest, finest, and purest Romanesque church in Europe, topped by a wedding-cake style bell tower. An important stop on the pilgrimage route to Santiago de Compostela, it was also the burial place of the Counts of Toulouse. The interior may be plain but it impresses with its enormous size. The old baroque *retables* (altarpieces) and shrine in the ambulatory around the church have been reset; the relics here are those of the apostles and the first bishops of Toulouse. In the crypt are the body parts of more major Catholic saints, plus a thorn said to be from the Crown of Thorns.

pl. St-Sernin. www.basilique-saint-sernin.fr. ☏ **05-61-21-80-45.** Free admission to church; combined admission to the crypt and ambulatory 2.50€. Church June–Sept Mon–Sat 8:30am–7pm, Sun 8:30am–7:30pm; Oct–May Mon–Sat 8:30am–6pm, Sun 8:30am–7:30pm. Crypt and ambulatory June–Sept Mon–Sat 10am–6pm, Sun 11:30am–6pm; Oct–May Mon–Sat 10am–noon and 2–5:30pm, Sun 2–5:30pm.

Cathédrale St-Etienne ★ CATHEDRAL   Because it took so long to build, from the 13th to the 17th centuries, and is smaller than the original plan, this cathedral is an odd mix of proportions and architectural styles. Inside are Renaissance tapestries along the nave and stained-glass windows that go back to the 15th century.

pl. St-Etienne. No phone. Free admission. Mon–Sat 8am–7pm; Sun 9am–7pm.

Fondation Bemberg ★★★ MUSEUM   Housed in the magnificent Hôtel Assézat built in 1555, the museum, which opened in 1955, provides an overview of 5 centuries of world-class European art. The first floor displays Renaissance furniture and works by old masters like Van der Weyden and Lucas Cranach plus Boucher's 18th-century landscapes. The 2nd floor offers a wonderful overview of the 19th century with rooms dedicated to the Impressionists, the Fauvists, and Pointillists. German-French collector *extraordinaire* Georges Bemberg started the collection, donating 331 works including works by Pissarro, Matisse, and Monet. Pierre Bonnard's gift of his 28 paintings includes his Moulin Rouge. *Important:* The museum was closed for renovations as we went to press but is expected to reopen some time in 2024. Check the website before heading over.

pl. d'Assézat, rue de Metz. www.fondation-bemberg.fr. ℂ **05-61-12-06-89.** Admission 10€ adults, 8€ students and children ages 8–26, free for children 7 and under. Tues–Sun 10am–12:30pm and 1:30–6pm (Thurs until 9pm).

La Cité de l'Espace ★★★ MUSEUM/PLANETARIUM   It may be out of the center, but with Toulouse being the center of European space exploration, this high-tech attraction is very popular. Hands-on experiences teach visitors how to program a satellite launch and what life is like on board the Soyuz spacecraft. The IMAX cinema and Planetarium have spectacular shows, and the MIR Space Station demonstrates what it's like to be a real astronaut with a disturbed sense of direction. It's a great place for kids, with special play areas and their own planetarium. In summer on Thursday evenings, the museum stays open late so guests can peer through massive telescopes before watching fireworks arch into the sky next to the Ariane 5 rocket.

av. Jean Gonord. https://en.cite-espace.com. ℂ **05-67-22-23-24.** Admission 21.50€–24.50€ adults, 16€ ages 5–18, free for children 4 and under. Open 9:30am/10am–5pm/6pm/7pm/11pm, depending on the season and day of the week. Check the website. Closed Jan. Bus: 37 from Ramonville metro station. Follow N126 from the center of town to the E. Peripheral route and take exit 17.

Musée des Augustins ★★ MUSEUM   Originally built for the powerful Augustinians in 1309, the monastery became a museum in 1793, shortly after the French Revolution and is the 2nd oldest in France after the Louvre. The two main collections are in the monastery buildings and the refectory built in the 19th century by Viollet-le-Duc: 17th-to-19th-century paintings and a striking collection of medieval sculpture. The original French gothic cloisters contain the world's most valuable collection of beautifully carved Romanesque capitals. On the upper floors the large painting collection includes works by Rodin, Brueghel, Gérard,

Guest room at the Grand Hôtel de l'Opéra.

Delacroix, Ingres, and others. The museum also contains several portraits by Antoine Rivalz, a local artist and major talent. ***Important:*** As we went to press, the majority of the museum was closed for renovations; it is scheduled to reopen in 2025. The church and cloisters are still open to the public, however, with worthwhile art exhibits in the church (free entry).
21 rue de Metz. www.augustins.org. ✆ **05-61-22-21-82.** Wed 10am–9pm; Thurs–Tues 10am–6pm. Closed public holidays.

Where to Stay

MODERATE

Grand Hôtel de l'Opéra ★★ If you're after a great location, kicky decor, and friendly service, this is the answer. The hotel looks out over the main square and is just a 2-minute walk from the metro. Guest rooms are painted in strong reds, oranges, and blues with painterly headboards behind many of the comfortable beds (each room has different decor, but they all have high-quality mattresses). If you want a view of the famous square, be sure to ask; many bedrooms overlook the interior courtyard (on the plus side, these are quieter). The hotel restaurant, Michelin-starred **Les Jardins de l'Opéra ★★** is one of the top Toulouse restaurants so it's expensive, though it has a good value 37€ weekday lunch menu. More modest meals are at the **Grand Café de l'Opéra** brasserie, also on-site.
1 pl. du Capitole. www.grand-hotel-opera.com. ✆ **05-61-21-82-66.** 55 units. 120€–190€ double; 210€–280€ suite. Public parking 19€–22€. Métro: Capitole. **Amenities:** Restaurant; brasserie; bar; room service; free Wi-Fi.

Hôtel des Arts ★★ This charming hotel is on a quiet street just behind the Musée des Augustins, a 5-minute walk from the place du

Capitole. The decor combines old and new: Think exposed red-brick walls with smart contemporary furniture. Each room evokes a different art form from music to photography; each has a glass-topped desk, bright colored cushions and throws on comfortable beds, colored lighting you can control, and good modern tiled bathrooms. The bilingual staff are welcoming and will carry your luggage (all rooms are on the second floor and above, and alas, there's no elevator).

1 bis rue Cantegril. www.hoteldesartstoulouse.fr. ℂ **05-61-23-36-21.** 12 units. 99€–259€ double; 149€–179€ family room for 4. **Amenities:** Room service; free Wi-Fi.

Hôtel des Beaux-Arts ★★

Despite the fact that its set in a charming 18th-century red brick building, this hotel is far from conventional. Each bedroom was designed by a different artist, and each contains a startling piece of art. Choose from relatively classic rooms to those with swirling patterns on the walls, punchy murals, and oddball furniture (like a side table in the shape of an orange teddy bear). Such daring has to be done well to work, and this hotel has perfected it. Our favorite? The "Chamber Only You" for its terrace and top floor view, though all rooms do look over the Garonne River. The independently run Brasserie Les Beaux-Arts is in the same building and offers both traditional and contemporary dishes, including vegetarian options.

1 pl. du Pont-Neuf. www.hoteldesbeauxarts.com. ℂ **05-34-45-42-42.** 19 units. 80€–240€ double; 145€–220€ jr. suite. Nearby parking 18€. Métro: Esquirol. **Amenities:** Restaurant; bar; free Wi-Fi.

INEXPENSIVE

Eklo Toulouse ★★   Save money without compromising style at this hip eco-friendly hostel-hotel in Toulouse's up-and-coming Cartoucherie neighborhood. Only 15 minutes by public transit from place du Capitole, this former industrial area is being converted into an avant-garde green district and Eklo fits in perfectly. In addition to the hotel's energy-efficient design, only regional products are sourced for the restaurant and shop. The large lounge has urban art, colorful sofas, a foosball table and digital nomads busy at their laptops. After sipping cocktails and making new friends on the terrace, guests retreat to their comfortable dorm, single or double rooms (or small apartments), which are smartly decked out in leafy wallpaper, light wood furniture and well-designed bunks.

181 av. de Grande Bretagne. www.eklohotels.com/toulouse. ℂ **05-82-95-92-31.** 100 units. 28€–40€ dorm; 52€–75€ single; 51€–80€ double; 83€–120€ family room and apt. **Amenities:** Restaurant; bar; grocery shop; free Wi-Fi.

Hôtel Royal Wilson ★★   Just off Rue d'Aubuisson and a 2-minute walk to the place Wilson, this hotel is a real find. Bedrooms vary in size, from single rooms to a six-person dorm. Each one is comfortable, decorated in pleasant colors with either a contemporary feel or with antiques. Some look over the theater and have balconies; others open onto a pretty Moorish-style interior courtyard. The bi-lingual staff are welcoming and helpful. The hotel caters also for bicyclists with an "Acceuil Vélo" (Cyclists Welcome) label and a secure garage for bicycles.

6 rue Labéda. www.hotelroyalwilson-toulouse.com. ☎ **05-61-12-41-41.** 27 units. 28€ 6-bed shared dorm; 80€–99€ double; 109€–124€ quad. Parking 15€. **Amenities:** Breakfast room; room service; free Wi-Fi.

Where to Eat

Brunch is a big deal in Toulouse, and one of the best places to get it (as well as breakfast and lunch) is **Baba Canteen ★★★** (http://babacanteen. com; 26 rue de Couteliers; Mon–Fri 8:30am–4:30pm, Sat–Sun 10am–4pm). Among its offerings are different types of house-baked breads topped with the freshest of veggies, labneh, smoked meats, or house-fermented pickles; delicious *pain perdue* (French toast to us); and salads straight from the garden. There will be a line out front, but it's worth the wait. For a glam evening out, we also highly recommend the restaurant in the **Grand Hotel de l'Opera** (p. 720).

EXPENSIVE

Au Pois Gourmand ★★ FRENCH   Set in a mansion with the types of wooden carvings and balconies that might have covered a colonial house in a far-flung corner of the world, Au Pois Gourmand goes well beyond "snow peas" ("pois gourmand"). Menu offerings are usually sumptuous, along the lines of lobster *liégeois,* piccata of roe deer from the Pyrénées, and smartly curated arrays of local cheeses. Guests have the choice of dining in the elegant, grey-toned dining room or on the large terrace that overlooks the river (it's partially closed and heated, so it remains open on chilly evenings). Lunch is an excellent value.

3 rue Emile Heybrard. https://pois-gourmand.fr. ☎ **05-34-36-42-00.** Fixed-price lunch 32€ or dinner 55€–89€. Mon–Fri noon–2pm; Mon–Sat 8–10pm. Closed 2 weeks in Aug and 2 weeks around Christmas.

Michel Sarran ★★★ MODERN FRENCH   Regarded as the top restaurant in Toulouse, a meal here is worth the slight journey west to the University district. Master chef Michel Sarran produces dishes that challenge the norm of modern French cooking using imaginative Asian and Middle Eastern spicing: A starter of foie gras, for example, is marinated in seaweed and saké, followed by Aveyron lamb cooked in a couscous bouillon and dates plus a chickpea and almond puree. This is complex cooking done with great skill. Sarran's wife, Françoise, oversees the main dining room which is decorated with a touch of whimsy (purple and green chairs, lamps hanging off branches, sculptural flower arrangements). Sophisticated dining in a sophisticated setting.

21 bd. Armand Duportal. www.michel-sarran.com. ☎ **05-61-12-32-32.** Main courses 55€–85€; fixed-price lunch 75€; other fixed-price menus 145€–195€. Mon–Fri noon–1:45pm and 8–9:45pm (closed Mon and Wed for lunch). Closed Aug and 1 week around Christmas. Métro: Capitole.

MODERATE

Chez Emile ★★ TOULOUSIAN   You'll see far more locals than tourists at Chez Emile, a place as homey as its name. Set in a traditional red-brick house on a busy square, it has a pleasant small-town look. Chef Christophe Fasan's dishes are all Southwestern French—lamb from the Pyrénées, Catalan seafood stew with mussels, freshwater calamari, and prawns—but if you're hungry, order the *cassoulet* made from the recipe of the original chef. Cooked in duck fat, with the traditional crackly crust, it's what locals have been order here for 50 years. It gives Le Colombier, below, a run for the money (although that restaurant gets the blue ribbon for this dish). There's a good wine list, too.

13 pl. St-Georges. www.restaurant-emile.com. ✆ **05-61-21-05-56.** Telephone reservations only. Main courses 25€–36€; fixed-price lunch 25€; other fixed-price menus 35€–60€. Tues–Sat noon–2pm and 7:30–10pm. Closed Dec 23–Jan 9. Métro: Capitole or Esquirol.

Le Bibent ★★ MODERN FRENCH   Originally opened in 1861, right in the heart of Toulouse in the place du Capitole, Le Bibent is a glorious example of a classic brasserie. The huge room has a vaulted ceiling, painted panels, gilding galore, mirrors, and chandeliers. Taken over by star chef Christian Constant in 2011, in 2021 he passed the reins to his second, Yann Ghazal, who is not yet as accomplished a chef (our last meal had many hits, but a few dishes were simply pedestrian). Still, the ambiance alone here makes it worth a visit, and we can heartily recommend Le Bibent's copious breakfasts, its Caesar du Bibent salads (a good lunch), and the excellent grilled squid with ratatouille.

5 pl. du Capitole. www.bibent.fr. ✆ **06-48-71-73-65.** Main courses 22€–48€. Daily 8am–midnight. Métro: Capitole.

Le Colombier ★★ TOULOUSIAN   Walls of alternating red brick and stone and a wood-beamed ceiling take you back to the origins of this popular restaurant. You're in the former stables of the Capitole, where Alain Lacoste has been delighting locals and visitors since 2007 with his robust southwest France-inspired dishes. But the greatest of these, as every Toulousian will tell you, is his cassoulet, slow cooked for 8 hours. This is a dish for the hearty: It's made of white beans, pork, Toulouse sausage, and confit goose leg. Yum!

14 rue Bayard. www.restaurant-lecolombier.com. ✆ **05-61-62-40-05.** Main courses 20€–29€; fixed-price lunch 18€–20€ or dinner 29.50€–42€. Tues–Fri noon–2pm and Mon–Sat 7:15–10pm. Métro: Jeanne d'Arc.

INEXPENSIVE

Bapz ★★ CAFE/TEA ROOM   Dainty china, silver teapots that your grandmother might have used, and a collection of odd artifacts suggest an English tea room but undeniable French influences are palpable here. (*Note:* Tea at 5pm is 1 hr. late for the true enthusiast.) But try brunch and the generous quiches and salads, and you can forgive any lapse of etiquette at this pretty, welcoming place.

13 rue de la Bourse. www.bapz.fr. ℰ **05-61-23-06-63.** Brunch 18€; lunch 12€. Tues–Sat noon–7pm. Metro: Esquirol.

Le Bon Vivre ★ SOUTHWESTERN FRENCH   This popular, welcoming and bustling bistro is also known as Café Cantine du Bon Vivre. Locals simply call this place Huguette after the founder, Huguette Meliet, who now runs it with her daughter, Cathy. The 18th-century mansion features a simple, modern decor where its good, honest, southwest France food shines. Ingredients come from the Midi-Pyrénées and particularly from Gers in Gascony. Choose the Toulousain sausage with fried potatoes and seasonal veggies or free-range chicken fricassee with sauteed mushrooms.

15 bis pl. Wilson. www.lebonvivre.com. ℰ **05-61-23-07-17.** Main courses 16€–33€; fixed-price lunch 16€–19€. Daily 11am–11pm. Métro: Capitol.

Shopping

Head for the streets north and west of **place St-Etienne** for sophisticated clothing and houseware shops. You'll find more boutiques in the **rue Croix-Baragnon, rue des Arts,** and rue **St-Antoine de T** (including The Kooples, originally from Toulouse). The **Reflets Compans** shopping center (www.reflets-compans.com), to the north of the old town, offers mid-range French and international brands. Antique lovers head for **rue Fermat.** More downmarket antiques spread out each Saturday 6am to 1pm during the weekly **flea market** by the place Saint-Aubin. The Square Charles

The pink stone buildings of Toulouse.

De Gaulle holds an **organic market** on Tuesday and Saturday mornings and around Eglise St-Aubin on Sunday mornings. The three main covered markets, all filled with food stalls, restaurants, and cafes, are the 126-year-old **Les Carmes** (pl. des Carmes), the large **Victor Hugo** (pl. Victor Hugo) with 100 stalls, and **Saint-Cyprien** at place Rouguet. They all have late night openings (check times with the Tourist Office). For superb chocolates and cakes, try **Maison Pillon,** 2 rue Ozenne and 2 rue d'Austerlitz.

Violets grow in abundance in meadows near Toulouse. Two shops selling items like violet-scented perfume and patterned-violet clothes and accessories include **Violettes & Pastels,** 10 rue St-Pantaléon (ℰ **05-61-22-14-22**), and **La Maison de la Violette,** a boat on the Canal du Midi opposite 2 bd. Bonrepos (www.lamaisondelaviolette.com; ℰ **05-61-99-01-30**).

Toulouse Nightlife

Toulouse's theater, dance, and opera are often on a par with those found in Paris. It's also a city of festivals throughout the year from a world-famous **Piano aux Jacobins** in the cloister of the Jacobins to rock and world music. Contact the Tourist Office for detailed information.

PERFORMING ARTS

The city's most notable theaters are **Théâtre du Capitole,** pl. du Capitole (www.theatreducapitole.fr; ☎ **05-61-63-13-13**), which specializes in operas, operettas, and works from the classical French repertoire; and **Halle aux Grains,** 1 pl. Dupuy (www. onct.toulouse.fr; ☎ **05-61-63-13-13**), home of the Orchestre National du Capitole de Toulouse and the venue for mostly classical concerts. **Théâtre Garonne,** 1 av. du Château d'Eau (www.theatregaronne.com; ☎ **05-62-48-56-56**), stages plays, dance from classic to flamenco, and a wide variety of music. **Zénith de Toulouse,** 11 av. Raymond-Badiou (www.zenith-toulousemetropole.com; ☎ **05-34-31-10-00**), is one of France's biggest rock music venues with variety acts and musical comedies from other European cities as well. Another venue, with a roughly equivalent mix of music, theater, and entertainment, is **Théâtre National de Toulouse,** 1 rue Pierre Baudis (www.tnt-cite.com; ☎ **05-34-45-05-05**).

BARS & CLUBS

The liveliest squares to wander after dark are **place du Capitole, place St-Georges, place St-Pierre,** and **place Wilson.**

Oenophiles shouldn't miss the renowned **N5 Wine Bar,** 5 rue de la Bourse (www.n5winebar.com; ☎ **05-61-38-44-51**), which has over 3,600 bottles to choose from. For bars and pubs, **La Tantina de Burgos,** 27 rue de la Garonette (www.la-tantina-de-burgos-bodega.com; ☎ **05-61-55-59-29**), has a Latin flair popular with students. The busiest English-style pub in town, **Le Frog & Le Roast Beef,** 14 rue de l'Industrie (www.facebook.com/FrogPubsToulouse; ☎ **05-61-99-28-57**), has its own microbrewery, hosts quiz nights, shows football, and is usually crowded with the city's English-speaking community. **The iBar,** 3 rue Gabrielle-Peri (www.i-bar.fr; ☎ **05-61-62-08-07**), with restaurant, bar, and club lounge, is the smart place for tapas and cocktails before dancing to the DJs' tunes.

L'Ubu Club, 16 rue Saint Rome (☎ **05-61-23-26-75**), in the heart of town, is a series of cellars with a restaurant and a discotheque that notches up the beat later.

For dancing in a LGBTQ+ friendly setting, dress your best and head to **Limelight,** 23 Bis Boulevard Riquet (www.limelight-club.com; ☎ **05-61-23-37-80**). It's open nightly from midnight to 7am, entrance is free during the week and cover on weekends is around 10€.

THE BASQUE COUNTRY

17

by Mary Novakovich

land rich in folklore, the Basque Country extends to the Spanish border in southwest France. The Basque capital, Bayonne, and the resorts of Biarritz and St-Jean-de-Luz are on the coast, while Pau and Lourdes are the gateway to the Pyrénées.

The vast Pyrenean region is a land of glaciers, summits, thermal baths, subterranean grottoes and caverns, winter-sports centers, and trout-filled mountain streams. **Pau** is a good base for excursions to the western Pyrénées with its many hiking opportunities.

PAU ★★★

768km (476 miles) SW of Paris; 196km (122 miles) SW of Toulouse

High above the banks of the Gave de Pau River, Pau is the capital of the Pyrénées-Atlantiques *département* (administrative region). It was once the land of the kings of Navarre, the most famous and beloved of whom was Henri IV, who was born in Pau. The British discovered Pau in the early 19th century, bringing fox hunting, which lingers on in the form of the Pau Hunt. British soldiers—Scottish, to be more precise—also founded continental Europe's oldest golf club. Even if you're just passing through, follow boulevard des Pyrénées, an esplanade erected on Napoleon's orders, for a panoramic view.

Essentials

GETTING THERE **Pau-Pyrénées airport** is 12km (7½ miles) north of town. There are good **train** connections from Biarritz (about 12, some direct, per day, taking 1 hr., 40 min., and the same again via Bayonne); the one-way fare starts at 21.80€. For train information, visit sncf-connect.com or call ✆ **36-35. Driving** to Pau is relatively easy because the A65 motorway has dramatically speeded up access times from the north. From Paris, take A10 south to Bordeaux, the N230 ring road around Bordeaux, the A62 Autoroute des Deux Mers, until joining the new A65 motorway at Langon just south of Bordeaux, which runs all the way to Pau. Alternatively, from Toulouse, the smaller N117 runs to Pau.

VISITOR INFORMATION The **Office de Tourisme** is on place Royale (pau-pyrenees.com; ✆ **05-59-27-27-08**).

SPECIAL EVENTS In late May and early June, during the **Grand Prix de Pau** (grandprixdepau.fr; ✆ **05-59-98-60-70**), race cars compete for speed records in what may remind you of a small-scale and slightly less glamorous Monaco Grand Prix.

PREVIOUS PAGE: The colorful harbor of St-Jean-de-Luz.

Exploring Pau

The city center is 30m (98 ft.) up from the river and the railway station, and if you arrive by train, you'll have the pleasure of ascending in its historic **Funicular** from near the station to place Royale. More than a century old, it runs Monday to Saturday from 6:45am to 9:40pm and on Sundays from 1:30 to 8:50pm; admission is free. **Place Royale** is in the center of the 2km (1¼-mile) **boulevard des Pyrénées,** a popular promenade since the 19th century for its views over palm-landscaped slopes to the distant mountains. At the eastern end is Parc Beaumont, where the **Palais Beaumont** (pau-congres.com; ✆ **05-59-11-20-00**), built as a casino and winter garden, now hosts concerts, theater performances, and exhibitions; and at the western end is the **Château de Pau ★**, 2 rue du Château (chateau-pau. fr; ✆ **05-59-82-38-00**), dating from the 12th century and steeped in the Renaissance spirit of the bold Marguerite de Navarre, who wrote the bawdy novel *Heptaméron* at age 60. Inside that castle are many relics from the age, including a crib made of a single tortoiseshell for Henri de Navarre, who was born here, and a splendid array of Flemish and Gobelin tapestries. The great rectangular tower, **Tour de Gaston Phoebus,** is from the 14th century. The château is open daily for visits from 9:30am to 11:45am and 2pm to 4:45pm. The gardens are also open for walking from 8am most days until nightfall. Guided tours (conducted only in French) depart at 15-minute intervals during open hours. Admission is 7€ for adults, 5.50€ for students 18 to 25, and free for ages 17 and under.

The **Musée des Beaux-Arts ★**, 1 rue Mathieu-Lalanne (✆ **05-59-27-33-02**), displays a collection of European paintings, including Spanish, Flemish, Dutch, English, and French masters such as El Greco, Zurbarán, Degas, and Boudin. It's open Tuesday to Sunday 11am to 6pm. Admission is free. Pau is also famous for its **Haras National de Gelos** (National Stud), created by Napoléon, which is no longer open to the public but does hold some wonderful race and jumping events throughout the year that are worth attending if you are in the area. It's situated south of the Gave de Pau at 1 rue du Maréchal Leclerc (http://ifce.fr; ✆ **05-59-06-98-37**).

A little further out of town, heading towards the foothills of the Pyrénées, the **Zoo d'Asson** is an excellent place for children, with more than 500 species of animals, kept in large, open spaces and carefully maintained enclosures. Of particular interest are the white

An elegant walkway in Pau.

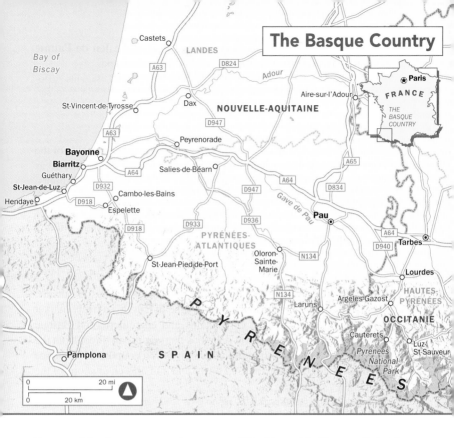

tigers and the kangaroo sanctuary, one of the biggest in Europe. In total, the zoo covers 5 hectares (12 acres); the entrance is at 6 Chemin du Brouquet, Asson (zoo-asson.org; © **05-59-71-03-34**). It's open daily April to September 10am to 7pm, and the rest of year from 10am to 6pm. Admission is 16€ adults, 10€ children ages 3 to 11, and free for tots 2 and under.

Where to Stay

Hotel Bristol ★★   This handsome 19th-century town house is very well located, with a friendly, helpful staff. Its 21 rooms are a homey mingling of mid-century furnishings with original features such as ornate fireplaces; views are either of the courtyard garden or the mountains. After a long day of sightseeing, the leather sofas in front of the fire in the cozy lounge bar are the perfect place to kick back.

3 rue Gambetta. hotelbristol-pau.com. © **05-59-27-72-98.** 21 units. 91€–175€ double. **Amenities:** Breakfast room; bar; free parking; free Wi-Fi.

Hotel Parc Beaumont ★★   This MGallery hotel offers some of the best accommodations in the city. All of the rooms have balconies, with views over either lovely Parc Beaumont or the upmarket residential area of Trespoey (worth a wander around if you have time). Rooms are oversized, with high quality beds and strong Wi-Fi. The **Jeu de Paume** restaurant is particularly recommended, as is the on-site spa.

1 av. Edouard VII. hotel-parc-beaumont.com. © **05-59-11-84-00.** 75 units. 187€– 255€ double. Free parking. **Amenities:** Bar; restaurant; indoor pool; spa; room service; free Wi-Fi.

Where to Eat

Au Dali ★★ TAPAS   Taking its culinary cues from the other side of the Pyrénées, Au Dali offers superior tapas and the Basque version known as pintxos, all in a rustic setting of exposed stone walls and terracotta floors. These include tasty morsels of stuffed baby bell peppers or mini Spanish tortillas, followed by larger tapas of ham croquettes and calamari. Surprisingly, the hearty burgers and fries are also winners here (and more filling, if you need more than just tapas).

16 rue Latapie. www.audalipau.fr. © **06-82-07-04-49.** Pintxos 3€; tapas 8€–14.50€; main courses 17.50€–24€. Tues–Fri 11:45am–1:45pm and 6pm–1am, Sat 5pm–1am.

Les Halles ★★ FOOD MARKET   Fairly discreet from the outside, this is one of the most enjoyable places to dine in Pau. It's a lively market full of local foodstuffs, from cured hams and charcuterie and Basque cheeses, to fruits, vegetables, and delicious patisseries, all direct from the producers. Buy a **Pass Gourmand** which gives you coupons to exchange for food (also in other shops around town) and pull up a chair at one of the market's many counters.

pl. de la République. hallesdepau.fr. Tasting pass 15€. Tues–Sat 7am–1pm or 3pm, 9am–1pm or 3pm Sun, and a night market last Fri of the month 5–11pm.

Omnivore ★★ FRENCH   The typical bistro interior (warm wooden paneling and leather banquettes) provides a cozy backdrop for Omnivore's generous, creative cuisine. It relies heavily on fresh market produce and whatever the seasons bring. You'll find a few Asian-inspired flavors to go with the Pyrenean ingredients, but the cheese is firmly French.

1 place Gramont. www.omnivore-restaurant-pau.com. © **05-59-27-09-08.** Main courses 23€—25€. Tues–Fri noon–1:30pm and 7:30–9pm; Sat 7:30–9pm.

Shopping

Pau's shopping doesn't quite live up to its surrounding scenery and cultural attractions, but it does offer regional specialties such as chocolates, sweet jams, and Basque antiques. The pedestrian **rue Serviez** and **rue des Cordeliers** harbor an array of boutiques and shops that carry these items, as do **rue Louis-Barthou** and **rue du Maréchal-Foch,** which are all around the central **place Georges Clemenceau.**

Pau has some of the region's best antiques shops, such as **Delan Antiquaire,** 4 rue Gassion (delan-antiquaire.com; © **05-59-27-45-62**).

One of the best-known shops in Pau is **Maison Francis Miot and Salon de Thé** ★★★, 46-48 rue du Maréchal Joffre (francis-miot.com; © **05-59-27-69-51**). The owner, M. Francis Miot, has been voted best jam and candy maker in France several times. If you're interested in seeing where his confections are made, head for the suburbs of Pau, about 1.5km (1 mile) southeast of the center, to the residential hamlet of Uzos. Here you'll find **Féerie Gourmande Musée et Boutique** (✆ **05-59-35-05-56**), where the factory also features exhibits displaying the history of jams from medieval times to the present, as well as offering numerous workshops and tastings detailing his techniques. It's open Monday to Saturday 10am to noon and 2 to 4pm; admission is 4.60€ adults and 3€ ages 3 to 12; closed in December. It has a special price of 3€ adults, 2€ ages 3 to 12 during July and August.

Pau Nightlife

Nightlife in Pau has always centered on **Le Triangle,** an area in the town center that's flanked by the rue Emile Garet, rue Lespy, and rue Castetnau. In recent years, a few new bars along **boulevard des Pyrénées** near place Clemenceau have augmented Pau's nightlife.

Within the borders of Le Triangle, **Le Garage Bar,** at 47 rue Emile Garet (le-garage-bar.com; ✆ **05-59-83-75-17**), has been going strong since 1993. Set within an old auto repair shop, it retains many of its original industrial-looking fixtures, plus a collection of antique traffic lights, road signs, and mopeds hanging from chains in the ceiling. It's open Monday to Friday 11am to 2am, Saturday 3pm to 2am and Sunday 3pm to 1am. Top wine bar, open nightly, is **Au Grain de Raisin,** 11 rue Sully, right in the center (http://au-grain-de-raisin.business.site).

Near Parc Beaumont is **L'Adresse,** 20 rue des Orphelines (✆ **06-03-88-52-44**), offers tapas, cocktails, and music that goes late. It's open Tuesday to Friday 6pm to 2am and Saturday 6pm to midnight.

BAYONNE ★★

770km (477 miles) SW of Paris; 184km (114 miles) SW of Bordeaux

Bayonne is the leading port and pleasure-yacht basin of the Côte Basque, divided by the Nive and Adour rivers. A cathedral city and the capital of the Pays Basque, it's characterized by narrow streets, quays, and ramparts. Enlivening the scene are bullfights (although there are protests against them in France and Spain), *pelota* (jai alai), and street dancing at annual fiestas. You may want to buy some of Bayonne's famous chocolate at one of the arcaded shops along rue du Port-Neuf, and then enjoy coffee at a cafe along place de la Liberté, the hub of town.

Essentials

GETTING THERE   Six TGV **trains** per day link Bayonne and Paris (trip time: 3 hr., 55 min.; from 82€ one-way). Fourteen trains per day arrive from Bordeaux (average trip time: 1 hr., 50 min.; 28€ one-way). For train information and schedules, visit sncf-connect.com or call ✆ **36-35.**

A **bus** service connects to Biarritz, 25 minutes away. Buses depart from Biarritz throughout the day, depositing passengers on place de la

Mairie in Bayonne; the one-way fare is 1.20€, and tickets can be bought on the bus. Bus service also connects Bayonne and outlying towns and villages not serviced by train. For bus information in Bayonne, call ☏ **05-59-59-04-61** or visit http://txiktxak.eu.

Bayonne is near the end of the N117 roadway, easily accessible by **car** from Toulouse and other cities in the south of France. From Paris, take A10 south to Bordeaux, and then the N10 and A63 down the Atlantic coast towards Bayonne.

Fête de Bayonne.

VISITOR INFORMATION The **Office de Tourisme** is on place des Basques (visitbayonne.com; ☏ **05-59-46-09-00**).

SPECIAL EVENTS During the 5-day **Fêtes de Bayonne,** the last week in July, a frenzy of outdoor concerts and dancing fills the streets. The celebration is intense. Bayonne's two major contributions to France's culinary scene, namely chocolate and ham, have their own festivals. Come in April for the 4-day Foire au Jambon when the center of town is overtaken by concerts, food competitions and family events. In October, things turn sweeter with Chocolate Days, when local chocolate makers bring their tasty treats to town.

Exploring Bayonne

Vieux Bayonne, the old town, is inside the ramparts, on the left bank of the Nive. The early-13th-century **Cathédrale Ste-Marie** (☏ **05-59-59-17-82**) dominates this part of town on rue d'Espagne and rue des Gouverneurs. The spiny 19th-century steeples are the best-known landmarks in Bayonne. The cathedral is worth 30 minutes of your time and is a good retreat on a hot day. It was begun in 1258 when Bayonne was under English rule; it fell to the French in 1451. Don't miss the gorgeous 14th-century cloisters. They're like a secret garden from the Middle Ages. The cathedral is open Monday to Saturday 8am to 7pm (Sun until 8pm); admission is free.

Atelier du Chocolat ★★ FACTORY TOUR   Bayonne's chocolate tradition began with the Jewish community that fled here from the Spanish Inquisition. Come to this always-popular place, which includes the Musée du Chocolat, for an insight into the history and ingredients for one of the world's most sought-after confections, followed, of course, by a tasting. Expect to spend around 1½ hours.

7 allée de Gibéléou, Zone Artisanale Sainte-Croix. atelierduchocolat.fr. ☏ **05-59-55-70-23.** Entrance 6.80€ adults; 4.80€ children 3–10. Mon–Sat 9:30–11:30am and 2–4pm. Chocolate makers work only Mon–Fri.

Jardin Botanique ★★ PARK   After stocking up on information and maps at the tourist office, wander through these lovely Japanese-style gardens next door.

Allée de Tardies. ☏ **05-59-46-60-93.** Free admission. Apr 15–Oct 15 Tues–Sat 9:30am–noon and 2–6pm.

Musée Basque ★★ MUSEUM   You don't have to spend long in the Basque region to realize how proud the locals are of their culture—and quite rightly so. This is the place to find out more about the origins of the region's distinctive architecture, music, textiles, and local crafts. It's also had major internal renovations over recent years, making it a beautiful place to visit, with the exhibits clearly and carefully laid out, and plenty of interactive displays. Although the text is in French, there's a free audio guide in English you can download on the museum's app.

37 quai des Corsaires. musee-basque.com. ☏ **05-59-59-08-98.** Admission 8€ adults; free for visitors 26 and under; free for all 1st Sun of each month. Tues–Wed and Fri–Sun 10am–6pm, Thurs 1–8pm (free admission 6–8pm).

Musée Bonnat-Helleu ★★ MUSEUM   The city's modern art museum has been closed for renovations since 2011 and is due to open in 2025 with more than double the current floor space—and poised to transform the art scene in the city.

5 rue Jacques Lafitte. mbh.bayonne.fr. ☏ **05-59-46-63-60.** See website for opening details.

Plaine d'Ansot et Musée d'Histoire Naturelle ★★ MUSEUM   Set in a conservation area just outside of the city, this is a rare example of a museum that is located in the heart of a protected area. You can head off along the walking and bike paths, all laid out around lakes, open spaces and rivers over 89 hectares (220 acres) of parkland. The Maison des Barthes is the official museum space set at the entrance to the park, with information on activities, as well as temporary exhibits. A traditional Natural History museum forms a separate building.

Plaine d'Ansot. http://bayonne.fr. ☏ **05-59-42-22-61.** Free admission. Maison des Barthes mid-Apr to mid-Oct Tues–Sun 10:30am–12:30pm and 1:30–6pm, rest of year 1:30–5pm. Museum Tues–Sun 10:30am–12:30pm and 1:30pm–6pm (Thurs morning during term time for school groups only); rest of park 9am–7pm. Rest of the year: Museum Tues and Thurs–Fri 1:30–5pm, Wed and Sat–Sun 10:30am–12:30pm and 1:30–5pm; park Tues–Fri 9am–5pm, Sat–Sun from 9:30am.

Where to Stay

Hotel des Basses Pyrénées ★   The oldest in Bayonne, this hotel on the Vauban ramparts is only a few minutes from the cathedral and the pedestrianized old town. Two suites (at a higher price) are in the turret and feature exposed stone walls, while the other rooms have soothing color palettes in neutral tones. The hotel's excellent restaurant offers creative local food, and its cozy bar has a wide range of wines. Downside? Some noise between rooms due to thin walls.

1 pl. des Victoires (pedestrian access) and 13 rue Tour de Sault. hotel-basses pyrenees-bayonne.com. ℂ **05-25-70-88-00.** 27 units. 110€–300€ double. Parking 12€. **Amenities:** Restaurant; bar; room service; free Wi-Fi.

Villa La Renaissance Hotel ★★★   If you can manage to get a room here, you'll enjoy a dreamy setting and the owners' personal touch. On a hill overlooking the Nive River, 900m (¼ mile) from the town center, this lovely 1905 villa, entirely renovated in 2021, is surrounded by an Italianate garden that also features a pool. The brightly colored rooms have individual décor (one with a balcony), and are divided between the main villa and a converted garden outbuilding by the pool.

12 Chemin de Jacquette. villa-larenaissance.com. ℂ **09-79-99-88-42.** 10 units. 130€–250€ double. Free parking. **Amenities:** Pool; free Wi-Fi.

Where to Eat

Bistrot Itsaski ★★ BASQUE   Head to this relaxed, contemporary-styled bistro for delicious local Basque products matched to a wide array of wines from around the world. The menu changes regularly, depending on the season and what the chef found in the market that morning, but you're certain to find typically Basque flavors including the local chili pepper known as piment d'espelette and Pyrenean cheeses.

43 quai Amiral Jaureguiberry. lebistrotitsaski.fr. ℂ **05-59-03-80-21.** Main courses 19.50€–23€; fixed-price menu 18.50€–28€. Thurs–Mon 11am–3pm and 7–11pm.

La Table Sébastien Gravé ★★ BASQUE   Just down the road from Bistrot Itsaski is this utterly gorgeous restaurant that is worth the travel to Bayonne alone. Chef Sébastien Gravé uses only seasonal, local ingredients, beautifully and imaginatively presented in an industrial-chic setting. Gravé makes a point of showcasing his local suppliers, including fresh fish caught in St-Jean-de-Luz.

21 Quai Amiral Dubourdieu. latable-sebastiengrave.fr. ℂ **05-59-46-14-94.** Main courses 25€; fixed-price menu 45€; tasting menu 60€. Tues–Sun noon–2pm and 7–10pm (closed Wed for lunch).

Shopping

Most of Bayonne's specialty shops and boutiques lie inside the ramparts of the old town, Grand Bayonne. The pedestrian streets of **rue Port Neuf** (aptly nicknamed the "street of chocolate shops"), **rue Victor-Hugo,** and **rue de la Salié** are major shopping destinations. For antiques, walk along the **rue des Faures** and the edges of **place Montaut,** behind the cathedral. Most of the modern shops and French chain stores are on **rue Thiers** and **quai de la Nive,** outside the old town. Visit the **Maison Jean Vier** ★★ shop, carrefour Cinq Cantons (jean-vier.com; ℂ **05-24-33-05-05**), to get your Basque bathroom, kitchen, and bed linens. Do not miss a visit to **Chocolat Cazenave** ★★★, 19 rue Port Neuf (chocolats-bayonne-cazenave.fr; ℂ **05-59-59-03-16**), pretty much the only place left that still works directly with cacao in its raw form and specializes in turning it into *chocolats de Bayonne.* Stop in the tearoom here for a warm chocolate mousse, one of the richest you'll taste.

Take a tour of **Les Halles** ★★, quai Dominque Roquebert (✆ **05-59-46-60-60**), Bayonne's covered market overlooking the Nive River, and get a flavor of Basque produce from its 21 traders and indoor and outdoor cafes. Unlike many French markets, this one is open daily.

The accessories of one Basque tradition have become something of a fine art. In olden days, the *makhila* was used as a walking stick, a cudgel, or—when equipped with a hidden blade—a knife. Today carved *makhilas* are sold as collectors' items and souvenirs. For safety's sake, they almost never come with a blade. One of the best outlets in town is **Makilas-Leoncini,** 37 rue Vieille Boucherie (https://makhila.com; ✆ **05-59-59-18-20**). Another famous product of the Basque country is *jambon de Bayonne,* cured hams, which taste best shaved into paper-thin slices and consumed with one of the region's heady red wines. **Pierre Ibaïalde** ★★★, 41 rue des Cordeliers (pierre-ibaialde.com; ✆ **05-59-25-65-30**), prepares and sells these hams either whole or in thin slices. Also available: an impressive roster of sausages, pâtés, and terrines.

Bayonne Nightlife

Nightlife centers on the neighborhood known as Petit Bayonne, the town's historic core. **Rue des Tonneliers, rue Pannecau,** and **rue des Cordeliers** are the liveliest areas after dark. For an interesting taste of local color and traditional music, head to **La Luna Negra Café-Théâtre,** also on rue des Augustins (lunanegra.fr; ✆ **05-59-25-78-05**). The 11€-to-18€ cover charge includes cabaret, jazz, or blues performances and popular French songs.

BIARRITZ ★★★

779km (483 miles) SW of Paris; 193km (120 miles) SW of Bordeaux

One of the world's most famous seaside resorts, Biarritz was once a fishing village. Empress Eugénie and her husband, Napoléon III, put it on the map and started a constant stream of royal visitors. In the 1930s, the Prince of Wales (before and after his brief reign as Edward VIII) and Wallis Simpson did much to make Biarritz more fashionable as they headed south with these instructions: "Chill the champagne, pack the pearls, and tune up the Bugatti." These days, the resort has kept its fashionable edge and has since become France's surf capital, giving it an agreeable blend of chicness and a laid-back vibe.

Essentials

GETTING THERE   About 15 **trains** arrive daily from Bayonne (trip time: 8 min.), which has rail links with Paris and other cities in the south of France. The one-way fare is 3€. The rail station is 3km (1¾ miles) south of the town center, in La Négresse. For information, visit sncf-connect.

com or call ✆ **36-35.** Bus no. 2 carries passengers from the station to the center of Biarritz; the one-way fare is 1€. You can also take a cab for around 15€ to 20€. If you're **driving,** Biarritz is at the end of the N117 roadway, the major thoroughfare for the Basque country. From Paris, take A10 south to Vierzon, and then N20 south to Limoges. Continue on N21 south to Tarbes, and then head west on N117.

VISITOR INFORMATION   The **Office de Tourisme** is on square d'Ixelles (biarritz.fr; ✆ **05-59-22-37-10**).

SPECIAL EVENTS   If you're in town in mid-September, check out the modern dance and ballet performances during the 9-day festival **Le Temps d'Aimer** (letempsdaimer.com). Tickets range from 12€ to 40€ for performances, with reduced rates for children, students, and families. Buy a 12€ pass for a 30% discount. At the end of September, the **Festival Biarritz Amérique Latine** (festivaldebiarritz.com) is the world's most important Latin American film festival. It's much more laid-back than Cannes—you'll find yourself rubbing shoulders or even doing the salsa with top Latin directors in the casino, where most events are held. Entry to the whole week's films is 75€, or buy a day pass for 20€.

Biarritz is the surfing capital of France, and each year dozens of competitions are held through the summer months, usually centered on the waves offshore from Plage de la Côte des Basque. For more information, contact the tourist office.

Biarritz also has 10 golf courses within a short drive of the town. A good practice setting is the **Centre d'Entraînement d'Ilbarritz-Bidart,** av. du Château, Bidart 64210 (golfilbarritz.com; ✆ **05-59-43-81-30**); you can play 9 holes for 34€ to 44€. The **Biarritz Cup** is a nationwide competition attended by mostly French golfers in the third week in July at the Golf du Phare, av. Edith-Cavell (biarritz-cup.com; ✆ **05-59-03-41-08**). Information on both festivals is available from the tourist office.

Exploring Biarritz

Eglise St-Martin, rue St-Martin (paroisse-biarritz.fr; ✆ **05-59-23-08-36**), is one of the few vestiges of the port's early boom days. In the 12th century, Biarritz grew prosperous as a whaling center. The mammals' departure from the Bay of Biscay marked a decline in the port's fortunes. The church dates from the 1100s and was restored in 1541 with a flamboyant Gothic chancel. It's in the town center between two of Biarritz's major arteries, rue d'Espagne and avenue de Gramont, and is open daily 8am to 7pm. Admission is free.

Biarritz's turning point came with the arrival of Queen Hortense, who spent lazy summers here with her two daughters. One of them, Eugénie, married Napoléon III in 1853 and prevailed on him to visit Biarritz the next year. The emperor fell under its spell and ordered the construction of the **Hôtel du Palais.** The hotel remains the town's most enduring landmark. When Biarritz's star started to wane in the 1950s, the municipality

The iconic stone bridge to the Rocher du Basta.

showed a great deal of foresight in buying the hotel and the equally monumental casino, the essence of Biarritz's fading glamour. In a commanding
spot on Grande Plage, the hotel is worth a visit even if you're not a guest.
Grab a drink in one of the bars or even head over for breakfast after you
have stayed somewhere a little less pricey.

Across from the Hôtel du Palais, the **Eglise Orthodoxe Russe,** 8 av.
de l'Impératrice (eglise-orthodoxe-biarritz.com; ✆ **05-59-24-16-74**), was
built in 1892 so that wintering Russian aristocrats could worship when
they weren't enjoying champagne and caviar. It's noted for its gilded
dome, the interior of which is the color of a blue sky on a sunny day. It can
be visited only Thursday and Saturday 3:30 to 5:30pm and Sunday 2 to
4pm. After you pass the Hôtel du Palais, the walkway widens into **quai de
la Grande Plage,** Biarritz's principal promenade. This walkway continues to the opposite end of the resort, where a final belvedere opens onto
the southernmost stretch of beach. This whole walk takes about 3 hours.
At the southern edge of Grande Plage, steps will take you to **place Ste-
Eugénie,** Biarritz's most gracious old square. Right below place Ste-
Eugénie is the colorful **Port des Pêcheurs** (fishers' port). Crowded with
fishing boats, it has old wooden houses and shacks backed up against a
cliff, along with small harborfront restaurants and cafés.

The rocky **plateau de l'Atalaye** forms one side of the Port des Pêcheurs. Carved on orders of Napoléon III, a tunnel leads from the plateau to
an esplanade. Here a footbridge stretches over the sea to a rocky islet that
takes its name, **Rocher de la Vierge (Rock of the Virgin),** from the statue
crowning it. Alexandre-Gustave Eiffel (designer of the tower) directed
construction of the footbridge. The walk out onto the edge of the rock, with
crashing surf on both sides, is the most dramatic in Biarritz. You can see all
the way to the mountains of the Spanish Basque country, far to the south.

Here you can visit the **Biarritz Aquarium,** 14 plateau de l'Atalaye
(aquariumbiarritz.com; ✆ **05-59-22-75-40**), and wander past about 50
tanks with giant rays, sharks, barracudas and other vivid marine life. The

seals steal the show at their daily 10:30am and 5pm feedings. Admission is 16.50€ adults, 14€ students, 12€ children 4 to 12, and free for children 3 and under. It's open 9:30am to 7pm, and from August 1 to 25, it's open from 9am to 10pm and from 2pm to 7pm on New Year's Day. Closed Christmas Day. Don't miss the other space in Biarritz dedicated to the sea: the **Cité de L'Océan,** at 1 av. de la Plage, La Milady (citedelocean.com; ✆ **05-59-22-75-40**), which you can reach by the free shuttle bus that runs through Biarritz. It's a spectacularly designed building that—of course— overlooks the Atlantic and explains pretty much everything you might want to know about the seas and oceans of the world. You can even take a virtual surfing class. Admission is 14€ adults, 12€ for children ages 13 to 17 and students, 9.90€ children ages 6 to 12. Or combine both the aquarium and the Cité de l'Océan for 26€ adults, 17.50€ children 6 to 12, and 22€ students. Opening hours vary throughout the year, but it's closed from January 9-31.

A Day at the Beach

Along the seafront facing the Casino is the **Grande Plage.** During the Belle Epoque, this was where Victorian ladies promenaded under parasols and wide-brimmed veiled hats. Today's bathers are more likely to be in wetsuits or surfy combos.

Walk along the **Quai de la Grande Plage,** whose sections have been designed as rock gardens with flowers, turning the area into a public park. From here, you can head north to **Pointe St-Martin,** where you'll find more gardens and a staircase (look for the sign DESCENTE DE L'OCEAN) leading you to allée Winston-Churchill, a paved path going along **Plage Miramar.**

La Perspective de la Côte des Basques, a walk that goes up to another plateau, leads to one of the wildest beaches in France: **Plage de la Côte des Basques,** with breakers crashing at the base of the cliffs. This is where serious surfers head. It's easy to hire a surfboard for a few hours or to get a lesson, but if you don't want to surf yourself, find a café and enjoy a few hours people watching. Check the tide times, though, because the beach completely disappears at high tide.

If you like calmer beaches, the safest is the small, horseshoe-shaped **Plage du Port-Vieux,** along the path from plateau de l'Atalaye. Its tranquil waters, protected by rocks, make it a favorite with families. Carry on further south to **Plage Marbella,** another surfing hotspot, or the laid-back **Plage de la Milady.**

Where to Stay

Biarritz has a lot of holiday rentals and summer houses, as well as options available through AirBnB, so it's always worth comparing prices.

Hotel de Silhouette ★★   The Les Halles district of Biarritz is great for eating and drinking, making this hotel a particularly good choice. Fully restored, this is actually one of the oldest buildings in the city, but it

The Grande Plage in Biarritz.

manages to pull off that difficult trick of retaining period features while delivering a luxury, contemporary and often funky feel. It regularly hosts art exhibitions, and its landscaped garden is a beauty.

30 rue Gambetta, Quartier des Halles. hotel-silhouette-biarritz.com. *C* **05-59-24-93-82.** 20 units. 185€–395€ double. Parking 19€. **Amenities:** Restaurant; bar room service; free Wi-Fi.

Le Beaumanoir ★★★ It is hard not to love this converted traditional Basque house set in around 1.25 hectares (around 3 acres) of grounds just over a mile from the Grande Plage in downtown Biarritz. Views over the Atlantic coast and surrounding countryside, a lovely snug bar, marble bathrooms, crystal chandeliers—this is Baroque-style luxury delivered with a tongue-in-cheek charm. You can even indulge in a free Rolls-Royce transfer from the airport.

10 av. de Tamamès. lebeaumanoir.com. *C* **05-59-24-89-29.** 8 units. 495€–600€ double; from 850€ suite. Closed mid-Nov to mid-Apr. Free parking. **Amenities:** Bar; spa; butler service; outdoor pool; free Wi-Fi.

Maison Garnier ★★ A good value and well-located hotel converted from a spacious 1870s villa. The hotel does not offer suites, but the largest room is 35 sq. m (376 sq. ft.), and feels wonderfully airy. Though there is no parking, you can easily get around downtown on foot, so this is handy if you are traveling without a car.

1 av. de l'Impératrice. hotel-biarritz.com. *C* **05-59-01-60-70.** 7 units. 90€–160€ double. **Amenities:** Tea tray with kettle; electric bike rental (charge); free Wi-Fi.

Where to Eat

Restaurant Léonie ★★ FRENCH/BASQUE This Biarritz institution is slightly out of the center, but it's worth the walk. Although Léonie has been around in some form since the 1940s, its current chefs have made it a convivial, fresh place with a constantly changing menu. Léonie today is creatively French but with a few spicy Basque flavors seeping in: Think roast hake with piquant piperade sauce.

7 av. Larochefoucauld. restaurant-biarritz-leonie.com. ☎ **05-59-41-01-26.** Main courses 23€; fixed-price menu 40€. Thurs–Mon noon–1:30pm and 7:30–9:30pm.

Saline Ceviche Bar ★★ SOUTH AMERICAN   You're going to love this place for its laid-back beach vibe and its brilliant food. Thankfully, it is in a particularly good spot along rue Gambetta where you can find dozens of tiny restaurants with their own atmosphere, so don't worry too much if you haven't booked ahead. As the name suggests, the specialty is super fresh ceviche and poke dishes made with local fish. True to their Peruvian roots, you can even get a Pisco sour.

62 rue Gambetta. ☎ **05-59-443-65-98.** Main courses 16€–22€. Daily noon–2pm and 7–10pm.

Shopping

The major boutiques, with all the big designer names from Paris, are on **place Clemenceau** in the heart of Biarritz. From this square, fan out to **rue Gambetta, rue Mazagran, avenue Victor-Hugo, avenue Edouard-VII, avenue du Maréchal-Foch,** and **avenue de Verdun.** Look for the exceptional Biarritz chocolates and confections, and textiles from the Basque country.

The finest chocolatiers are **Pariès,** 1 pl. Bellevue (paries.fr; ☎ **05-59-22-07-52**), where you can choose from seven kinds of *tourons* (nougats), ranging from raspberry to coffee; and **Henriet,** pl. Clemenceau (chocolaterie-henriet. com; ☎ **05-59-24-24-15**), where the house specialty is *rochers de Biarritz* (morsels of candied orange peel and roasted almonds covered in dark chocolate). At the other end of the gastronomic spectrum, try **1001 Fromages,** 8 rue Victor Hugo (1001fromages.com; ☎ **05-59-24-67-88**), specializing in, as the name suggests, French cheeses, as well as a host of hearty wines to accompany them. They also have a stall in Les Halles food market.

Virtually every souvenir shop and department store in the region sells **espadrilles,** the canvas-topped, rope-bottomed slippers which originate from the Pyrénées. Check out the large and varied selection at **Art of Soule,** 28 rue Gambetta (artofsoule.com; ☎ **05-59-47-42-24**).

Biarritz Nightlife

Start the night with a stroll around **Port des Pêcheurs,** an ideal spot for people-watching, with its sport fishermen, restaurants, and fascinating crowds. Especially lively will be the area around Les Halles market. The wine bar **L'Art Dit Vin,** 15 av. de Verdun (☎ **05-59-23-73-74**), which stays open till at last midnight gets a particularly buzzy crowd. Tapas-style food is on offer also, but the real draw is the 300-strong wine list at extremely good prices, with a particular focus on Spain. Another perfect mid- to late-evening hangout is **The Beach House,** a little further up the road in Anglet but worth the trip. At 26 av. des Dauphins (beachhouseanglet.com; ☎ **05-59-15-27-17**), it is a bar and restaurant right on the beach. It is open

April to December, but at its height in July and August the aperitifs start at 6pm and things can go pretty late.

Fortunes have been made and lost at **Casino Barrière,** 1 av. Edouard-VII (*©* **05-59-22-77-77**). The less formal section, containing only slot machines, is open daily 9am to 3am (until 4am in high season, and all year Sat until 4am). Entrance is free and no ID is required. The more elegant section (for *les jeux de table,* or table games) is open Sunday to Friday 8pm to 3am, Saturday and daily in high season 8pm to 4am. This section requires a passport or photo ID, and both sections ask that you don't wear shorts or beach attire.

ST-JEAN-DE-LUZ ★★

791km (490 miles) SW of Paris; 15km (9¼ miles) S of Biarritz

This tuna-fishing port and beach resort is ideal for a seaside vacation. St-Jean-de-Luz lies at the mouth of the Nivelle, opening onto the Bay of Biscay, with the Pyrénées in the background. Tourists have been flocking here since the 1920s, when H. G. Wells, Aldous Huxley, and friends "discovered" the town.

Essentials

GETTING THERE Fifteen daily **trains** arrive from Biarritz (trip time: 14 min.; from 3.70€ one-way), and eight per day arrive from Paris (trip time: 5 hr., 40 min.; from 45€ one-way). For train information and schedules, visit sncf-connect.com or call *©* **36-35. Buses** pulling into town from other parts of the Basque country arrive at the Gare Routière (*©* **05-59-26-06-99**), in front of the railway station. St-Jean-de-Luz is a short **drive** from Biarritz along N10 south.

VISITOR INFORMATION The **Office de Tourisme** is on 20 bd. Victor Hugo (saint-jean-de-luz.com; *©* **05-59-26-03-16**).

SPECIAL EVENTS In July and August on Wednesday after 10:30pm and Sunday after 10:30pm, people pile into place Louis-XIV to take part in **Toro de Fuego,** a celebration of the bull. Revelers take to the streets to dance and watch fireworks. The highlight of the festivities is a snorting papier-mâché bull carried around place Louis-XIV. During the second half of June, the city celebrates the **Festival of St-Jean (***Fêtes Patronales de la Saint-Jean***)** with concerts and a series of food kiosks along the harborfront. For 4 days during the first half of October, the **Festival International du Film** (fifsaintjeandeluz.com; *©* **05-59-85-80-81**) has grown more ambitious over recent years. For information about festivals, contact the Office de Tourisme (see above).

Fun on & off the Beach

The major draw here is the gracefully curving stretch of the white-sand **Grande Plage St-Jean-de-Luz;** it's one of the best beaches in France and, consequently, very crowded in July and August. The beach lies in a half-moon-shaped bay between the ocean and the source of the Nivelle River. Lifeguards are on duty daily in July and August from 11am to 7:30pm and from 12:30pm to 6:30pm in June and September. You can also hire parasols and deck chairs. All of St-Jean-de-Luz's other beaches have lifeguards from 11am to 7pm in July and August only.

St-Jean-de-Luz is also a **working port,** where colorfully painted fishing boats jut right up to the shopping streets. Eating seafood recently plucked from the sea is one of the reasons to visit, especially when Basque chefs transform the big catch into intriguing platters. This port's many narrow streets flanked by old houses are great for strolling. For one of the best views, climb the **Colline de Sainte-Barbe,** a large hill at one end of the waterfront. It has a walking path and lovely views over the city.

Exploring St-Jean-de-Luz

In the town's principal church, the 13th-century **Eglise St-Jean-Baptiste ★★**, at the corner of rue Gambetta and rue Garat (℗ **05-59-26-08-81**), Louis XIV and the Spanish Infanta, Maria Theresa, were married in 1660. The interior is stunning: Look out for the altar with its statue-studded gilded *retable* (altarpiece). The interior is open to visitors daily from 8:30am to 6:30pm.

Two houses are associated with the couple. **La Maison Louis XIV** (also known as **Lohobiague Enea**), place Louis XIV (maison-louis-xiv. fr; ℗ **05-59-26-27-58**), was the scene of the royal wedding night. Built of chiseled gray stone between 1644 and 1648 beside the port, it is richly furnished with antiques and mementos. It's open daily for guided tours in July and August from 10:30am to 12:30 and 2:30 to 6:30pm; and generally from April to June and September to October from 11:30am to 3pm and 4pm to 5pm. Entrance is 7€. **La Maison de l'Infante,** 1 rue de l'Infante, is where the Infanta lived at the time of her marriage. It was designed and built by wealthy weapons merchant Johannot de Haraneder. It used to be open to the public, but has since become a private house.

St-Jean-de-Luz.

Where to Stay

A wide range of options are available here, from the **Camping Ferme Erromardie** on the Erromardie breach, 40 Erromardie (camping-erromardie.com; ℗ **05-59-26-34-26**) with its cabins and lodges as well as pitching spots, to a number of good AirBnB listings.

Hotel Les Goélands ★★ Two handsome Basque villas dating from the early 20th century make up this laid-back hotel just a 5-minute walk from the beach but in a pleasantly residential neighborhood. Many of its brightly colored rooms come with balconies, and some with a sea view. The gardens are a delight, with plenty of space to lounge around. There's also a play area for children as well as table tennis.

4/6 av. Etcheverry. hotel-lesgoelands.com. ☎ **05-59-26-10-05.** 28 units. Closed mid-Nov to late Mar. 86€–205€ double. Parking 12€. **Amenities:** Electric bike rental; gardens; laundry room; children's play area; free Wi-Fi.

La Réserve ★★ Palm trees, wide lawns, and blue skies (more often than not) all set off the lovely white walls and tiled roof of this hotel, complete with an outdoor pool and a gorgeous view of the ocean. The Residence has studios and apartments for rent, with terraces overlooking the Atlantic, which are a good option for larger families. But the main hotel's rooms and suites have a similar breezy and airy style, with many featuring balconies or patios. Its Restaurant Ilura specializes in fresh seafood and has superb views that match the cuisine. The beaches of St.-Jean-de-Luz are accessible by a (fairly steep) coastal path.

1 rue Gaëtan de Bernoville. hotel-lareserve.com. ☎ **05-59-51-32-00.** 47 hotel units, 44 residence units. Closed Nov–Mar. 172€–392€ double; 325€–578€ suite; 162€–586€ residence apt. for 2–6 people. Free parking. **Amenities:** Restaurant; bar; outdoor pool; spa; tennis court; free Wi-Fi.

Where to Eat

Kako Etxea ★★ BASQUE An oldie but a goodie. This is a St-Jean-de-Luz institution but manages to keep on delivering, so we keep on recommending. It's well located in Les Halles also, so even if every table here is full (and that happens fairly often), plenty of other places stacked with the fresh Basque produce are just around the corner. But book a table ahead if you don't want to risk losing out. Take your pick of the choice selection of wines and ciders also.

18 rue du Maréchal Harispe at the pl. des Halles. restaurant-kako-saintjeandeluz. com. ☎ **05-59-85-10-70.** Main courses 19€–70€. Tues–Sat 9:30am–2:30pm and 7:30–10pm (Fri–Sat until 10:30pm). Closed Sun evening and Mon.

La Guinguette d'Erromardie ★★ BASQUE Follow the surfing crowd to this lunch spot that turns into a tapas and cocktail bar at night. You'll get good fresh seafood, with dishes such as oysters, mussels, and breaded calamari, topped off by fabulous views, DJ sets and some of the best sunsets along the coast. You can book ahead for lunch.

Plage Erromardie. ☎ **05-59-43-97-66.** Main courses 10€–22€. Daily 10am–1am. Closed Nov–Mar.

Ostalamer ★★ BASQUE/FRENCH Awe-inspiring views and brilliant food make this place hard to beat. Just outside town overlooking Lafitenia beach, the best thing to order here is shellfish or fresh fish and lots of it. The *chipirones à la plancha,* one of the most traditional Basque

exploring BASQUE VILLAGES

The entire Basque region is dotted with atmospheric, beautifully preserved villages. From Saint-Jean-de-Luz, the most easily reached is **Guéthary,** 3km (2 miles) away either on the main N10 road to Biarritz, or along the pretty coastal backroads. A traditional fishing village which has become something of a gourmet center and artistic refuge, the old town is laid out around the lovely church and fishing port, and a walk takes you along the headland, past some dramatic coves. Heading the other way from Saint-Jean-de-Luz, along the D932 up into the hills of the Pyrénées, both **Saint-Jean-Pied-de-Port** and **Espelette** are unmissable. They epitomize the traditional Basque village—classic half-timbered houses in red and white or white and green, shops offering local cheeses and hams, Irouléguy wines, and other specialties, all with the mountains rising dramatically behind. Espelette is known for its tiny red peppers, often seen strung outside the houses around the main square like cheerful garlands, while Saint-Jean-Pied-de-Port has a 17th-century citadel along banks of the pretty Nive River.

ways of serving squid, aren't to be missed. This place also has a sister restaurant-farm-BnB called **Ostalapia** (ostalapia.fr) a little further into the Pyrénées mountains.

160 route des Plages. ostalamer.com. © **05-59-85-84-71.** Main courses 25€–66€. Wed–Sun noon–2:30pm and 7:30–10pm. Closed Jan.

Shopping

You'll find the best shopping along pedestrian **rue Gambetta** and around the Eglise St-Jean-de-Luz. You can find anything here from clothes and leather handbags to books and chocolates, dishes and linens.

You can also ramble around the port, sip pastis in a harborfront cafe, and debate the virtues of the beret. Then scout out **Maison Adam,** 49 rue Gambetta (maisonadam.fr; © **05-59-26-03-54**), which has sold almond-based confections from this boutique since 1660. For quality tablecloths, throws, bedding, and other gorgeous linen, the traditional **Mendiburutegia Tissus,** 3 rue Renau-d'Elissagaray (mendiburutegia.fr; © **05-59-26-02-63**), is worth a visit.

St-Jean-de-Luz Nightlife

Start by taking a walk along the promenade to watch the sunset. Around place Louis-XIV, you'll find a hotbed of activity at the cafes and bars, whose terraces crowd the square. Then continue towards rue de la République, which is packed with places to eat and drink. Look out for the lively **Pub du Corsaire** at 16 rue de la République (© **05-59-26-10-74**), which carries on serving drinks daily from 5pm to 2am both in its cozy galleon-like interior and on its buzzing terrace. Come between 6:30pm and 10:30pm for a delicious spread of tapas to go with your cocktails and a sophisticated jazzy soundtrack. They also have a huge selection of gins and whiskies as well as beers from around the world.

BORDEAUX & THE ATLANTIC COAST

by Mary Novakovich

From La Rochelle to the Bordeaux wine district, the southwest of France is often just a quick stopover for visitors driving from Paris to Spain. However, this area is well worth a more in-depth visit for its Atlantic beaches, medieval and Renaissance ruins, Romanesque and Gothic churches, vineyards, and the dynamic and beautiful city of Bordeaux. The high-speed rail link from Paris to Bordeaux makes its considerably easier to get to know this corner of France.

This intriguing region also merits a detour inland to sample cognac in Cognac and to visit nearby art cities, such as Poitiers and Angoulême. If you can manage it, allow a week here—enough time to sample the wine, savor the cuisine, and see some of the sights.

BORDEAUX ★★★

578km (358 miles) SW of Paris; 549km (340 miles) W of Lyon

No longer called *La Belle Endormie* ("Sleeping Beauty"), today Bordeaux is one of the most vibrant cities in France, with property prices overtaking Lyon and often listed as the city that most French people would like to move to. Its renaissance started soon after the arrival of mayor Alain Juppé in 1995. First the **historic city center** was cleaned up, revealing the splendors of its harmonious 18th-century architecture. Then a sleek tramway (streetcar) system was installed, and cars were banished from most of the historic center. Finally, the **quays of the Garonne River** were given an extensive overhaul and are now lined with public gardens, fountains, and playgrounds. The city has reconnected with the river, as best symbolized by the stunning 18th-century **place de la Bourse,** which opens directly on the banks and is now scrubbed down and bedecked with a "water mirror," a long, shallow fountain that you can walk and splash around in on sunny days.

As you move away from the center, elegant streets give way to narrow cobbled streets, ancient churches, and a more youthful, funky Bordeaux. More than 50,000 students go to the University of Bordeaux, bringing the average age of the population down sharply when class is in session, and they also fuel a lively nightlife scene. The urban overhaul has bled into former working-class neighborhoods like **Chartrons,** where you can find galleries, bars, and restaurants. Other districts have been completely revamped, such as the cool **Darwin** complex on the other side of the Garonne, where old army barracks have been converted into bars, organic food shops, skate parks, workspaces, studios and live music venues.

PREVIOUS PAGE: **St-Emilion.**

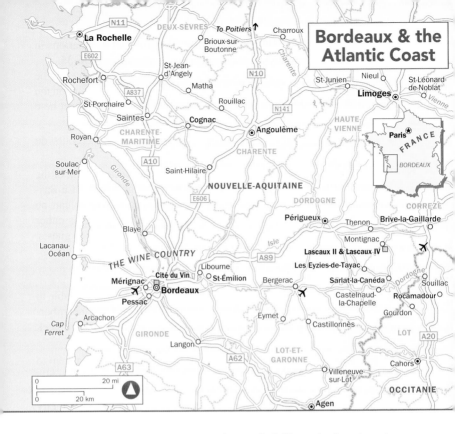

Bordeaux, of course, is also a wine capital. Not only does it make a great base for exploring **thousands of wine estates,** you can also taste many of the region's wares right here, particularly if you stop in at the **Ecole du Vin de Bordeaux** (p. 760) or at the **Cité du Vin** (p. 754), or one of the dozens of wine bars that have opened in recent years.

Essentials

ARRIVING   Bordeaux–Mérignac **airport** (bordeaux.aeroport.fr; ℂ **05-56-34-50-50** for flight information) is 15km (9¼ miles) west of the city in Mérignac and is one of easyJet's French hubs, increasing the number of flights to here from around Europe. A **shuttle bus** (30'Direct) runs from the airport to the train station every 30 minutes (trip time: 30 min.). The one-way trip is 8€ adults, 7€ for passengers 25 and under, free children under 5. The tramway line A runs between the airport and downtown and departs every 10 minutes (trip time: 35 min.). A single ticket costs 1.70€. A **taxi** (ℂ **05-56-96-00-34**) from the airport to the train station costs about 30€ during the day and 45€ at night.

Some 15 to 30 high-speed TGV **trains** arrive from Paris each day; the trip takes 2 hours, 7 minutes if you take the high-speed link, which costs from 45€ one-way. Cheaper fares exist if you are booking in advance. Other rail connections include Toulouse, Avignon, Biarritz, and destinations in Spain. For train information, visit sncf-connect.com or call ☎ **36-35**.

While Bordeaux is easy to reach by **car** (about a 6-hr. drive on the A10 autoroute from Paris; 2 hr. via the A62 from Toulouse; 15 min. on the A63 from the Spanish border), you won't use it much once you get here as most of the historic center is closed to motorized traffic.

VISITOR INFORMATION The **Office de Tourisme** is at 12 cours du 30-Juillet (bordeaux-tourisme.com; ☎ **05-56-00-66-00**).

CITY LAYOUT Bordeaux lays almost entirely on the western bank of the **Garonne River,** though the small up-and-coming neighborhood La Bastide and the Darwin complex are on the eastern bank, which can be accessed by the **Pont de Pierre** or the ferry. The historic center is rather compact and clusters near the river. Most hotels offer city maps to guests; you can also pick up a map at the tourist office.

Getting Around

ON FOOT With a good pair of comfortable shoes, you should be able to visit most sites on foot. If you want to explore more far-flung neighborhoods, or are just plain tired, you can easily get around town on the sleek tram system.

BY PUBLIC TRANSPORTATION The **tram** (streetcar) makes it a snap to get around the city. Three lines (A, B, and C) crisscross the town, while line D goes northwest from downtown to the suburb of Cantinolle. The tram runs daily from 5am to 1am. Tickets are good on the tram, the **city**

Modern tram on the place de la Comédie, Bordeaux.

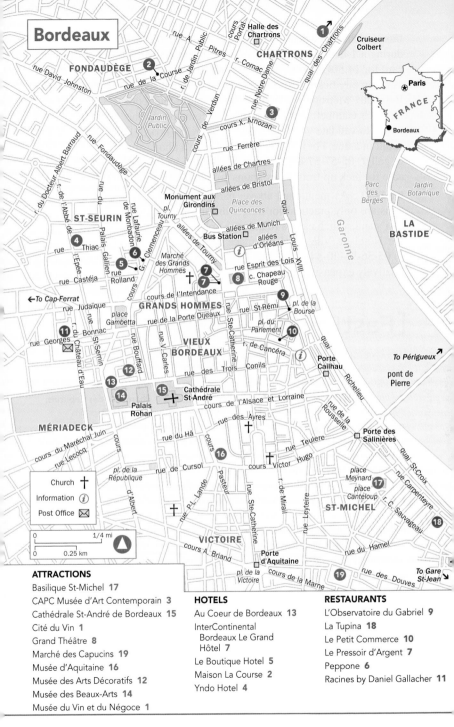

Bordeaux

FONDAUDÈGE

CHARTRONS

Cruiseur Colbert

Paris

FRANCE

Bordeaux

Jardin Public

ST-SEURIN

Monument aux Girondins

Place des Quinconces

Bus Station

Parc des Berges

Jardin Botanique

LA BASTIDE

Garonne

Marché des Grands Hommes

GRANDS HOMMES

pl. de la Bourse

pl. du Parlement

VIEUX BORDEAUX

Porte Cailhau

To Périgueux

pont de Pierre

←To Cap-Ferrat

place Gambetta

MÉRIADECK

Cathédrale St-André

Palais Rohan

Porte des Salinières

pl. de la République

place Meynard

place Canteloup

ST-MICHEL

Church ✝
Information ⓘ
Post Office ✉

0   1/4 mi
0   0.25 km

VICTOIRE

Porte d'Aquitaine

pl. de la Victoire

To Gare St-Jean

bus, and the **ferry** that crosses the river, and cost 1.80€, transfers included during a 1-hour period. You can get a 2-ticket card for 3.20€, a 10-ticket card for 14.50€, as well as 1-day pass for 5€ and a 7-day pass for 14.20€. You can buy tickets from the driver; at the tram stops or at the Transport Bordeaux Métropole (TBM) outlets at place Quinconces, Gare St. Jean, or place Gambetta; online at infotbm.com; or via the TBM app. Don't forget to validate your ticket once you are on board; failure to do so can result in a fine. For information, maps, and a phone app, visit infotbc.com or call ✆ **05-57-57-88-88. Bicycles** for hire by the hour or day are available for pick up from 179 stations around the city (infotbm.com/en/v3).

BY TAXI As mentioned above, parts of the city center are car-free, so taxis are only practical for longer distances. You must hail a taxi from a taxi stand, which can be found at the place Gambetta, the Grand Théâtre, the Hôtel de Ville, and the place de la Victoire. Or call **Taxi-Télé** at ✆ **05-56-96-00-34.** Uber is also an option and, since traditional taxis are relatively expensive, can save money depending on the time of day.

[FastFACTS] BORDEAUX

ATMs/Banks The historic center has plenty of banks, including several ATMs on the cours de l'Intendance.

Doctors & Hospitals Groupe Hospitalier Pellegrin, pl. Amélie Raba-Léon (chu-bordeaux.fr; ✆ 05-56-79-56-79).

Embassies & Consulates American

Consulate, 89 quai des Chartrons (fr.usembassy.gov; ✆ 01-43-12-48-65); **British Consulate Bordeaux,** 14 rue Montesquieu (gov.uk; ✆ 05-57-22-21-10).

Mail & Postage La Poste, 6 pl. Saint-Projet (✆ 36-31).

Pharmacies Pharmacie des Grands Hommes, 1 pl.

des Grands Hommes (✆ 05-56-81-70-90). Pharmacy open 24/7: **Pharmacie des Capucins,** 30 pl. des Capucins (✆ 05-56-91-62-66).

Safety The area around the Gare Saint-Jean train station and place des Victoires can get a little seedy at night.

Exploring Bordeaux

THE HISTORIC CENTER ★★★

At first sight, the 18th-century grandeur of Bordeaux is almost overwhelming. At the very center is the supremely sophisticated "**Golden Triangle,**" defined by three boulevards: Cours Georges Clemenceau, Cours de l'Intendance, perhaps the grandest street in the city, and Allées de Tourny. This last street leads down the **place de la Comédie,** the unofficial heart of the city, a large square that is dominated by the **Grand Théâtre,** a colonnaded masterpiece by 18th-century architect Victor Louis, who also designed the Comédie Française.

A quick walk east towards the river brings you to the splendid **place de la Bourse,** a creation of Ange-Jacques Gabriel, King Louis XV's architect. Considered the *ne plus ultra* of French 18th-century architecture, the

Place de la Bourse, Bordeaux.

two wings of the plaza open onto the Garonne River like a giant bird. On warm days, the Bordelais (particularly the youngest ones) come here to splash through the 3,500 sq. m (37,000 sq. ft.) 1-in. deep water, known as the **Miroir d'Eau** (Water Mirror), that lies between the square and the river.

Those suffering from elegance overload will be relieved to find a younger, more accessible version of Bordeaux hiding just behind the grandiose plaza. A warren of small streets and pretty squares extends from **place du Parlement** south-ish to **place Saint-Pierre, place du Palais,** and **place Camille-Jullien.** The farther you get from place du Parlement, the less touristy it is, and the better the restaurants get. That amazingly turreted gateway at place du Palais is the **Porte Caihau,** left over from the days when the city was surrounded by ramparts.

Heading back westward, you will no doubt cross **rue Saint-Catherine,** which is hyped as the longest pedestrian street in Europe, but you'll find better shopping on **rue du Pas-Saint-Georges** and **Saint-James.** Further on are the spires of the imposing **Cathedral Saint-André** and its separated bell tower, the **Tour Pey-Berland.** Just behind the cathedral are two of the city's best-known museums: the **Musée des Beaux Arts** and the **Musée des Arts Décoratifs** (which is being refurbished and should reopen in 2025). A little farther to the south lies the **Musée d'Aquitaine,** a regional history museum (p. 752).

Cathédrale Saint-André de Bordeaux ★★ CHURCH   This towering edifice, originally built in the early 12th century, was where Eleanor of Aquitaine celebrated her first (and ill-fated) marriage to Louis VII. While there have been additions and subtractions over the centuries (during the French Revolution, it was used for storing animal feed), the main

751

attraction is the soaring heights of the nave, with its 12th-century Planta-genet Gothic arches that reach as high as 29m (95 ft.). The church is also known for its stunning organ, whose sculpted wood case has been declared a historic monument. Outside, are two beautifully sculpted portals: The North Portal, dating from 1250, shows the Judgment of Christ, while the Royal Portal (c. 1330) details the Ascension. Next to the church is the 15th-century **Tour Pey-Berland,** the cathedral's belfry, which is separate because the vibrations from the huge bells could have damaged the cathedral if the tower had been attached. If you can handle climbing the 232 stairs, the belfry offers a terrific view from the top.

pl. Pey Berland. cathedrale-bordeaux.fr; pey-berland.fr. 🕐 **05-56-52-68-10.** Free admission to the cathedral. Admission to the Tour Pey-Berland: adults 6€; free for children 17 and under, and on the 1st Sun of the month Nov–Mar. Church: Mon 2–7pm (3–7pm July–Aug), Tues–Sat 10am–noon and 2–6pm (10:30am–1:30pm July–Aug), Sun 9:30am–noon (until 1:30pm July–Aug) and 2–6pm (3–8:15pm July–Aug). Tower: May 29–Oct 1 daily 10am–6pm, Oct 2–Mar 31 Tues–Sun 10am–12:30pm and 2–5:30pm. Tram A or B: Hôtel de Ville.

Grand Théâtre ★★ THEATER   As soon as it was inaugurated in 1780, everybody who was anybody in the performing arts wanted to per-form in this gorgeous theater. Then, as now, top names in opera, classical music, and dance grace the stage here. If you don't have time for a show, you can still take a tour you can book through the Bordeaux tourism web-site for (10€ adults, 7.50€ for children 13–17, 5€ for children 5–12). You can also choose specific times for tours in French, English or Spanish. At the very least, try to pop in and check out the magnificent staircase.

pl. de la Comédie. opera-bordeaux.com. 🕐 **05-56-00-85-95.** Tram B: Grand Théâtre.

Musée d'Aquitaine ★★ HISTORY MUSEUM   This museum offers a fascinating look at the growth of Bordeaux from its Gallo-Roman begin-nings right up to the outbreak of World War II, passing by its explosive growth as a global port in the 17th, 18th, and 19th centuries. The sections devoted to the 20th and 21st centuries take you on an immersive walking tour of how the city has changed in recent decades. However, the real draw here is the unflinching permanent exhibition looking at the role that slavery played in the growth of Bordeaux.

20 cours Pasteur. musee-aquitaine-bordeaux.fr. 🕐 **05-56-01-51-00.** Permanent collections 8€ adults, 2€ students under 26, free for visitors under 18. Tues–Sun 11am–6pm. Tram B: Musée d'Aquitaine.

Musée des Beaux-Arts ★★ MUSEUM   Bordeaux's oldest public museum houses an impressive collection of artworks from the 15th to the 20th centuries in an elegant space. Look out for works by Caravaggio, Rubens, Delacroix and Morisot as well as works by Symbolism pioneer and Bordeaux-born Odilon Redon.

20 cours d'Albret. musba-bordeaux.fr. 🕐 **05-56-10-20-56.** Admission 5€. Wed–Mon 11am–6pm. Tram A: Palais du Justice.

THE QUAYS ★★★

In the 18th century, the banks of the Garonne were just as elegant as the rest of the city, and wealthy wine merchants lived in limestone mansions on the edge of the river. However, time was not kind to the quays, which became known as a messy array of warehouses, gritty bars, and traffic jams. Fortunately, the city came to the rescue, and after a multi-year overhaul, the banks of the Garonne River have been given a superb makeover. Today, a **stroll along the quays** is Bordeaux's favorite weekend activity. You can start your walk at the vast **Esplanade des Quinconces,** just north of the place de la Bourse. Laid out in the early 1800s, this gargantuan esplanade covers 12 hectares (30 acres). Be sure to admire the huge **Monument to the Girondins.** During the French Revolution, this relatively moderate local faction tried to put the brakes on a revolution that was getting out of hand. They butted heads with the radical Montagnards, who came out on top, resulting in the mass execution of the Girondins and the beginning of the Reign of Terror.

Now stroll northwards along the river, and enjoy the gardens, skateboard park, and playgrounds that line the **quai Louis XVIII** and the **quai des Chartrons.** At the **quai de Bacalan,** just before the space-age **Pont Jacques-Chaban-Delmas** bridge, a few old warehouses were left intact and transformed into a giant outlet center, but one where you can both shop and relax. Among the bargains are spiffy cafes, restaurants, and bars with terraces overlooking the water, as well as plenty of benches to plunk yourself down on. Just beyond the bridge is the **Cité du Vin** museum (p. 754).

THE CHARTRONS QUARTER ★★

Once the beating heart of the Bordeaux wine trade, where every wine broker worth a cork set up shop, today Chartrons is the hot spot for young and enterprising creative types, especially those with some money to throw around. The neighborhood's hub is the refurbished **Halle des Chartrons,** an erstwhile covered market that is now a cultural center. A block east is **rue Notre Dame,** lined with cafes, clothes shops, antiques dealers, and interior design boutiques. If you're here on a Sunday morning, make your way to the **Quai des Chartrons** where a food market offers some of the finest seafood from the Aquitaine region. The neighborhood is also home to two good museums: on the southern end, the enormous **CAPC Musée d'Art Contemporain;** and up near the skateboard park, the small, but fascinating wine-history museum **Musée du Vin et du Négoce,** 41 rue Borie (museeduvinbordeaux.com; ✆ **05-56-90-19-13;** 10€ adults, 5€ students, including two wine tastings, free for children under 18; daily 10am–6pm; closed Dec 25 and Jan 1; tram B: Chartrons).

CAPC Musée d'Art Contemporain ★★ CONTEMPORARY ART MUSEUM   Back in the 19th century, this vast building was a customs depot, where goods from the French colonies were held before being sold off in Northern Europe. Those crusty civil servants would probably faint

at the sight of today's holdings, a compendium of avant-garde art from the 1950s up until today. Director María Inés Rodríguez has overseen recent exhibitions from, among others, Beatriz Gonzalez, Daniel Buren, and Judy Chicago. If you are hungry, stop in at the museum's chic cafe, by design maven Andrée Putman.

7 rue Ferrère. capc-bordeaux.fr. ✆ **05-56-00-81-50.** Admission 7€ adults, 4€ students, free for children 17 and under. Tues–Sun 11am–6pm. Tram B: CAPC station.

Cité du Vin ★★ MUSEUM   The designers of this cleverly constructed museum would say it's more a cross between a cultural space, a gallery, and a theme park, with interactive exhibits showcasing the entire world of wine. Cafes, a restaurant, and a panoramic bar (where wine tastings are held) complete the picture, so allow yourself a good few hours to explore. Oh, and the wine shop also stocks bottles from more than 80 countries, as well as holding regular tastings.

134 quai de Bacalan. laciteduvin.com. ✆ **05-56-16-20-20.** Admission 22€ (including a tasting), 9€ children 6–17, free for children 5 and under. Early Apr to early Sept daily 10am–7pm, Sept–Dec 31 Mon–Fri 10am–6pm and until 7pm weekends and French school holidays. Tram C: Cité du Vin.

SAINT-MICHEL QUARTER ★

This neighborhood revolves around its church, the **Basilica of Saint-Michel.** This lively, working-class quarter is home to Arab, Portuguese, and African immigrants, as well as a good sprinkling of the city's artists and *bobos* (bourgeois bohemians). The main draw here is the wide plaza (**place Duburg**) surrounding the church where the open-air food, clothes and bric-a-brac **market,** known as the Marché Royale, takes place on Saturdays (8am–2pm). The market also invades the nearby quai des Salinières. A drink at one of the cafes on the edge of the square is a post-shopping must. The whole area has been fully renovated in recent years.

Basilique Saint-Michel ★★ CHURCH   The most stunning thing about this church is its bell tower, which is not even attached to the building. Like the **Cathedral of Saint André** (p. 751), the vibrations of the bells and the weight of the tower were deemed too much for a church built on marshy land. At 114m (374 ft.), *la flèche* (the arrow) can be seen for miles around. The church itself is nothing to sniff at either. Built between the 14th and 16th centuries, it is lauded for its architectural harmony, its Flamboyant Gothic style, and its organ, which was recently restored. A fantastic view can be had from the top of the tower, which is being restored and is scheduled to reopen in 2026.

pl. Canteloup et Meynard. bordeaux-tourisme.com. ✆ **05-56-94-30-50.** Free admission to church. Daily 9am–7pm. Tram C: Saint-Michel.

Organized Tours & Boat Rides

The **Bordeaux Tourist Office** (p. 748) organizes a variety of guided tours in both French and English. The most popular is the 1½-hour **walking tour** of the city center, which leaves the tourist office at 10:30am (arrive

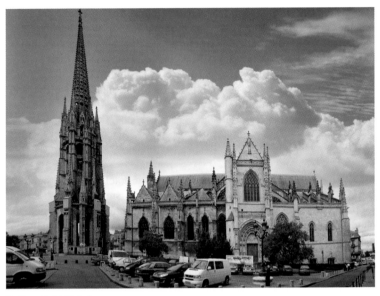

Basilique Saint-Michel.

at least 10 min. before), daily (12€ adults, 9€ ages 13–17, 6€ ages 5–12, free for children 4 and under). They also offer several **day trips to nearby wineries.** For a complete list of tours, visit the website.

You can also get a riverside view of Bordeaux on a **boat cruise** on the Garonne. You can taste wine, eat, or just gaze at the view, depending on the cruise and your budget. The two best cruise companies are **Crosières Burdigala,** 7 quai de Queyries (croisieresburdigala.fr; ✆ **05-56-49-36-88**), which offers a 1½-hour cruise of Bordeaux for 15€ Monday through Saturday, and **Bordeaux River Cruise,** quai des Chartrons (lesbateaux bordelais.com; ✆ **05-56-39-27-66**), which has a 2-hour Bordeaux cruise with a winemaker and onboard tasting for 21€. Both also offer much more elaborate tours of Bordeaux and the wine country. The **Bat3** (known as the BatCub; use your public transit ticket) is a boat-bus that ferries locals and tourists from one side of the Garonne to the other, between La Bastide, Jean-Jaurès, Les Hangars, and Lormont. These run Monday to Friday from 7am to 7:30pm and Saturday and Sunday from 9am to 7:30pm (although times may vary, depending on how busy things are; infotbm. com should have up-to-date times).

Where to Stay

EXPENSIVE

InterContinental Bordeaux Le Grand Hôtel ★★★   The majestic 18th-century Grand Hôtel is as much of an institution as the equally opulent Grand Théâtre directly opposite. Taking inspiration from its highly theatrical neighbor, the lush decoration by celebrated designer Jacques

Garcia hints at 19th-century theater trimmings, and the unusual color schemes gracefully blend the old and the new. The top-floor spa goes even farther into the past—ancient Rome, to be exact—with red columns, black trim, and a mosaic pool with a ceiling that opens to the sky. The rooftop bar has a terrific view and is a popular nightspot in the warmer months. There is a bistro as well as a gourmet restaurant, **Le Pressoir d'Argent,** run by Gordon Ramsay (p. 757).

2–5 pl. de la Comédie. bordeaux.intercontinental.com. ✆ **05-57-30-44-44.** 130 units. 322€–770€ double; from 484€ suite. Parking 45€. **Amenities:** 2 restaurants; 2 bars; indoor and outdoor pools; spa; fitness center; business center, concierge; room service; tea room; free Wi-Fi.

Le Boutique Hotel ★★   This well-located hotel, right on the doorstep of the Golden Triangle of chic shops, has small but high-design rooms named after local châteaux. Once a 17th-century mansion (note the handsome neo-Renaissance façade), the building's rough stone walls and parquet floors contrast nicely with furnishings by Philippe Starck, Kartell and Eichholtz. Many rooms have peek-a-boo bathrooms (you'll see into the shower), so keep that in mind when booking. The inner courtyard garden/wine bar gets fairly busy with locals in the summer months. Parking is available at an underground public car park around the corner.

3 rue Lafaurie de Monbadon. hotelbordeauxcentre.com. ✆ **05-56-48-80-40.** 27 units. 275€–966€ double. Breakfast 28€. Nearby public parking 20€. **Amenities:** Babysitting; wine bar; dry-cleaning; free Wi-Fi.

Yndo Hotel ★★★   What do you get when you combine an owner with a penchant for contemporary art and design, with an exquisite 19th-century *hotel particulier* (mansion)? That would be the Yndo. And because owner Agnès Guiot du Doignon has such good taste, the mash up of molded ceilings and exposed beams with vibrant Murano chandeliers, bold contemporary furnishings (like whale-tail chairs by trendsetting designer Huber Le Gall) and dozens of paintings, works. Guest rooms have unique touches, too, like round showers that follow the curve of the building's tower, bathtubs lit by skylights, and modern four poster beds. There are several categories of rooms, from more sedate (but wonderfully woodsy) "cozy" ones, to "crazy" rooms and suites that are a riot of colors. The Yndo is on a quiet side road only a few minutes' stroll from place Gambetta and the lovely shops on rue Judaïque.

108 rue de l'Abbée de l'Epée. yndohotelbordeaux.fr. ✆ **05-56-23-88-88.** 12 units. 250€–600€ double; 780€ suite. Breakfast 18€. Parking 28€. **Amenities:** Restaurant (for hotel guests only); wine tastings; winery tours; free Wi-Fi.

MODERATE

Maison La Course ★★   Right opposite the Jardin public park, this beautifully appointed *chambre d'hotes* offers friendly service, a wine-tasting cellar, and easy access to the shops of Chartrons. The style here is eclectic—from a rustic cabin-style room to ones with gilded mirrors and traditional fireplaces. If you want to push the boat out, the "Under the

Stars" suite has a glass roof and private terrace with a small pool (around 5 sq. m/54 sq. ft., so don't get too excited).

69 rue de la Course. lacourse-bordeaux.fr. ✆ **05-56-52-28-07.** 5 units. 200€–260€ double; 265€–650€ suite. Breakfast included. **Amenities:** Free Wi-Fi.

INEXPENSIVE

Au Coeur de Bordeaux ★★   This charming chambre d'hôtes near the Jardin Public suits its name—it really is in the heart of Bordeaux. Its five pleasingly traditional rooms occupy a 19th-century town house, with elegant antiques giving the rooms a warm look. The family suite offers good value, with an extra set of twin beds to go with its queen bed and a balcony. For an enjoyable crash course in wine, book one of the evening tastings in the atmospheric wine cellar.

28 rue Boulan. aucoeurdebordeaux.fr. ✆ **06-89-65-84-21.** 5 units. 109€–150€ double; 150€–160€ suite. Breakfast included. **Amenities:** Free Wi-Fi.

Where to Eat

Eating is serious business in Bordeaux, where tantalizing restaurants seem to line every street. Vegetarians rejoice: You'll find today's Bordeaux increasingly caters to your tastes. If you aren't ready for a full meal, fear not. Tapas are all the rage; you can even tapas-hop from bar to bar on rue du Parlement-Saint-Pierre. Keep an eye out for tearooms, too—a great option for breakfast or a quick snack.

EXPENSIVE

Le Pressoir d'Argent ★★★ CLASSIC FRENCH/SEAFOOD   The gourmet restaurant in the Grand Hotel has Gordon Ramsay installed as head chef (or, rather, overseeing the restaurant from his base in London, with Gilad Peled as full-time head chef in Bordeaux). Named after its rare silver lobster press, this gastronomic palace honors seafood from the Atlantic coast but also the best-quality produce from around southwest France, such as the celebrated chicken from Les Landes, organic vegetables from the Pays Basque, and many more, depending on the season. Reservations essential.

2-5 pl. de la Comédie. bordeaux.intercontinental.com. ✆ **05-57-30-44-44.** Tasting menu 155€–235€. Tues–Sat 7–9:30pm.

L'Observatoire du Gabriel ★★★ MODERN FRENCH/SEAFOOD   The setting is as spectacular as the cuisine at this immensely stylish gastronomic restaurant. Within the 18th-century splendor of the main building of Place de la Bourse, you'll taste exquisite things done to all sorts of seafood, on a menu that changes with the seasons. Budgeteers take note: You can try the restaurant's slightly less expensive bistro version at Le 1544 on the first floor of La Bourse.

10 pl. de la Bourse. le-gabriel-bordeaux.fr. ✆ **05-56-30-00-80.** Fixed-price lunch 57€; tasting menu 125€–175€. Mon–Fri 7:30–9:15pm and Tues–Fri noon–1:45pm. Closed late July to late Aug.

La Tupinia ★★ FRENCH   This is the place for good solid comfort food from southwest France. Bring a big appetite to devour plates of Basque chicken, Charolais beef, grilled duck breast and Bigorre pork. Happily, among the meat feasts, there are vegetarian options that show some creativity.

6 rue Porte de la Monnaie. latupina.com. ℂ **05-56-91-56-37.** Main courses 19€–47€; fixed-price lunch 21€ or dinner 64€. Tues–Sun noon–2pm and 7–10pm; Mon 7–10pm.

Le Petit Commerce ★★ TRADITIONAL FRENCH/SEAFOOD   This unassuming restaurant is so successful it had to open a second dining room across the narrow street. Fish, fish, and more fish is the motto here, though a steak or veal roast can be found on the menu as well. Book ahead, as this is just as popular as ever.

22 rue du Parlement-Saint-Pierre. ℂ **05-56-79-76-58.** Main courses 16€–36€. Daily noon–2:30 and 7–10:30pm.

Racines by Daniel Gallacher ★★★ MODERN FRENCH   Scottish chef Daniel Gallacher planted new roots (*racines*) in Bordeaux in 2015, and hasn't looked back. He deliberately keeps the seasonal menu short and sweet, with classy and creative dishes that make the most of local seafood and produce. While the focus is French, Gallacher spices things up with flavors from around the world. For food of this quality, the prices are remarkably good value.

59 rue Georges Bonnac. racines-bordeaux.com. ℂ **05-56-98-43-08.** Fixed-price menus 38€–58€; lunch menus 25€–32€. Tues–Sat 7:30–9:30pm; Thurs–Sat also noon–1:30pm.

A terrific taste OF ANOTHER BORDEAUX

Out in a working-class quarter just east of the place de la Victoire lies Bordeaux's best and largest covered market, **Marché des Capucins** at place des Capucins (Tues–Fri 6am–2pm, Sat–Sun 5:30am–2:30pm; tram B: place de la Victoire; tram C: Sainte Croix). The city's chefs head here as soon as it opens, and all food fans will go nuts when they see the vast selection of goodies before them: fresh vegetables, fruits, meats, fish, cheese, bread, *charcuterie*—not to mention all the delicious prepared foods waiting for you to pounce on. You can buy dried sausage, pastries, olives, and salads to take away, or you can treat yourself to one of the dozen or so food stands that serve from their bars or seating areas. On Saturdays, tapas are everywhere and everyone seems to be selling them, from the charcutier to the cheese guy. Other stands serve their treats on a daily basis. Crepes, couscous, and steamed mussels are all on hand. **La Maison de Pata Negra** (maisondupatanegra.com; ℂ 06-32-22-74-20), specializes in the famous Spanish ham but also terrific tapas, technically, *pintxos* (served on slices of bread), made with various smoked meat combos as well as grilled bonito, or even sautéed foie gras. Other favorites include **Chez Jean-Mi** (www.facebook.com/chez.jean.mi; ℂ 06-81-20-24-49), where if you stand too close to the bar, you'll suddenly find yourself savoring a plate of six sparkling fresh oysters with a cold glass of white wine, and **Bistro Poulette** (ℂ 06-25-56-17-97), which keeps things simple: a plate of mussels and fries, plus a tiramisu and a glass of wine for 20€.

INEXPENSIVE

Peppone ★ ITALIAN   You might think you don't come to Bordeaux for Italian food, but there's a reason a queue forms outside this restaurant pretty much every evening—it's one of the liveliest and most enjoyable restaurants in town. Take your pick of wood-fired pizza and freshly made pasta, all beautifully done and served by the friendly staff. A personal favorite pizza is the Saint Pierre de Roma with fresh basil and mozzarella. The same owners run **Ragazzi da Peppone** on Quai Richelieu on the waterfront with the same menu and an outside terrace.

31 cours Georges Clemenceau. ✆ **05-56-44-91-05.** Main courses 13€–25€. Sun–Thurs noon–2:15pm and 7–10:30pm; Fri–Sat noon–2:30pm and 7–11pm.

Shopping

For chic clothing and designer shops, go to the couture quarter around **place des Grands Hommes** and **cours de l'Intendance.** More high-end goodies, including wine and chocolates, can be found on the **Allées de Tourny.** For shopping that is easier on the budget, stroll down **rue Ste-Catherine,** which claims to be the longest pedestrian street in Europe. On either side of this road are two other good finds: Promenade Saint-Catherine and the quirky boutique-style shops on rue du Pas-St-Georges and rue Saint-James. Another good budget option is the pleasant riverside **outlet shops** at the Hangars (also known as the **Quai des Marques,** quai des Chartrons; quaidesmarques.com).

Antiques hunters will want to head to **rue Notre-Dame** in the Chartrons quarter, which harbors the **Village Notre-Dame** (✆ **06-84-69-69-02**), an indoor antiques market with dozens of stands.

Food hounds can find lots of yummy things at the **Marché des Capucins** (p. 758) as well as **Le Comptoir Bordelais,** 1 bis rue des Piliers de Tutelle (✆ **05-56-79-22-61**), a terrific gourmet grocery. Chocoholics will feel compelled to pay their respects at **Cadiot-Badie,** 26 Allées de Tourny (cadiot-badie.com; ✆ **05-56-44-24-22**), considered the best in the city.

Bordeaux Nightlife

Starting at **place du Parlement,** the tiny nearby streets are filled with nightspots and tapas bars, particularly as you approach **place St-Pierre** and **place Camille-Jullian. Place Gambetta** and **place de la Victoire** swarm with students. Night owls in Bordeaux gravitate toward **quai du Paludate** where restaurants, bars, and discos remain open until the wee hours.

One of the most fun drinking spots in Bordeaux remains **Le Calle Ocho,** 24 rue des Piliers de Tutelle (✆ **05-56-48-08-68**), a red-and-black enclave of Cuban music, photographs, mojitos, and salsa. If you're into cocktails, try the creative concoctions at **L'Alchimiste Nomade Bar à Cocktails,** 16 rue Parlement Saint-Pierre (✆ **06-35-52-55-77**), and **Pointe Rouge,** 1 quai de Paludate (pointrouge-bdx.com; ✆ **05-56-94-94-40**).

Buying Bordeaux in Bordeaux

Not surprisingly, wine stores are on just about every corner of the city, many staffed with knowing initiates of the mysteries of the vine. If you want to sigh over rare bottles and legendary vintages, take a spin around **Badie,** 62 allées de Tourny (badie.com; ✆ **05-56-52-23-72**), or **La Vinothèque de Bordeaux,** 8 cours du 30-Juillet (vinotheque-bordeaux.com; ✆ **05-57-10-41-41**). For a more educational approach, you can join one of the classes offered by the **Ecole du Vin** (Wine School) at the Conseil Interprofessionnel du Vin de Bordeaux (**CIVB**), an industry association representing some 8,000 Bordeaux wine producers and growers. It offers beginners' classes that will give you a good introduction to the aromas of wine for about 30€. It's easy to find the distinctive flat-iron building at 3 cours du 30-Juillet (bordeaux.com; ✆ **05-56-00-22-66**). The CIVB is also home to **Le Bar à Vin,** a chic wine-tasting bar where you can sample the local wares from at least half of the region's 65 appellations, along with a plate of local cheeses and charcuterie.

For a more laidback night on the town, **Café Populaire,** 1 rue Kléber (cafepop.fr; ✆ **05-56-94-39-06**), is a fun place to have a drink and mix with the locals, as is **Aux 4 Coins du Vin,** 8 rue de la Devise (aux4coins duvin.com; ✆ **05-57-34-37-29**), which has an enormous selection of wine by the glass.

Day Trips from Bordeaux
ST-EMILION ★★
40km (25 miles) E of Bordeaux

Surrounded by vineyards, the village of St-Emilion sits on a ridge overlooking the Dordogne Valley. Aside from its famous wine, the town is a treasure in itself: Ancient alleyways lined with centuries-old limestone buildings, half-timbered homes from the Renaissance era, and pleasant cobblestoned plazas draw visitors from all over the world. Sometimes too many—the town can get clogged with tourists in the summer months. Since most come for the day, the best time to visit is in the late afternoon when they are all leaving, and you can enjoy an early-evening glass of red in relative peace.

Essentials
Trains from Bordeaux make the 35-mi. trip to St-Emilion at least 15 times per day; the one-way fare is 10.40€. Trains from elsewhere in France require transfers in either Bordeaux or Libourne, a 10-minute train ride from St-Emilion. For train schedules visit sncf-connect.com or call ✆ **36-35.**

The **Office de Tourisme** is on place des Créneaux (saint-emilion-tourisme.com; ✆ **05-57-55-28-28**).

Exploring St-Emilion
At the town's heart is the medieval **place de l'Eglise Monolithe,** which is brimming with outdoor cafes. From here, a knot of cobbled streets and stone houses beckon with gift shops, wine-tasting rooms, and boutiques.

The **Eglise Monolithe** ★★, pl. de l'Eglise Monolithe (✆ **05-57-55-28-28**), was carved into the limestone side of a small hill sometime around the beginning of the 12th century. The largest underground church in Europe, it is dedicated to a saintly hermit named Emilion who frequented the neighborhood in the 8th century. To get in, you'll have to take a tour, which also gets you into the **catacombs,** the 13th-century Chapelle de la Trinité, and its underground grotto—where St-Emilion sequestered himself during the latter part of his life. The 45-minute tour costs 15€ for adults, 12€ for students, 8€ for children ages 6–17, and free for children 6 and under. The tour is in French but there are written translations in English.

St-Emilion.

For a splendid view of the town and its vine-covered environs, climb the 196 steps to the top of the **bell tower** (*clocher*) of the Eglise Monolithe. Access to the tower depends on the opening hours of the tourist office, so check there first. More views can be had from the top of the **Tour du Roy** (✆ 05-57-55-28-28), a 13th-century castle keep (2€ adults, free for children under 6). Open afternoons from February to November, this moody tower offers views of the surrounding countryside—on a clear day you can see the Dordogne River. The tourist office will have the latest opening hours. For more medieval thrills, take a stroll around the crenellated **ramparts.**

Where to Stay & Eat

Enjoy serene vineyard and countryside views yet be only a 15-minute walk from the center of St-Emilion when you book one of the elegant rooms at **Clos 1906** ★★, 14 La Gaffelière (clos1906.com; ✆ **06-76-69-15-11**). Within this handsome 18th-century manor house are four stylish guest rooms, plus an apartment, and all seamlessly combine 19th-century decor with modern furnishings. The gardens are a wonderfully calm place to relax, especially in the outdoor pool. The house also includes an antiques shop, so don't hesitate to browse around. Doubles from 189€, and there's free parking and an honesty bar. For lunch or dinner, book ahead at **L'Envers du Décor,** 11 rue du Clocher (envers-dudecor.com; ✆ **05-57-74-48-31;** daily noon–2pm and 7–9pm; main courses 25€–45€), a popular restaurant and wine bar with a courtyard terrace. Also worth trying is **Le Terrasse Rouge,** 1 Château La Dominique (laterrasserouge.

com; ☎ **05-57-24-47-05;** Mon–Sun noon–2:30pm, Tues–Sat 7:30–9:30pm; main courses 32–37€; fixed-price lunch and dinner 50€), just 5 minutes out of town at Château la Dominique, this laid-back bistro has stunning views over the vineyards.

ARCACHON & CAP FERRET ★★★
40km (25 miles) W of Bordeaux

Arcachon and Cap Ferret are situated at either end of the Arcachon Bay, almost touching each other from either side of the opening to the Atlantic Ocean, but completely different in atmosphere. Arcachon is a delightfully old-fashioned coastal resort that comes with a casino, an excellent food market, plenty of spa hotels and an increasingly smart pocket of hotels based around the town of **Pyla** (where you can climb Europe's largest sand dune). Cap Ferret, on the other hand, is all about understated chic, like a dollop of Cape Cod in Western France. While the whole peninsula is called Cap Ferret, the village of the same name at its southern tip is the one that comes to mind for visitors looking for a stylish retreat. Bordeaux châteaux owners and Parisian bankers have their second homes here, but you'd never know, as the dress code is strictly casual. A lovely shaded bike path runs for 200km (125 miles) between the two, tracing the shoreline of the bay and passing through beaches, pine forests, and over a dozen small fishing villages along the way, each one loaded with waterside oyster huts where you can refuel on fresh seafood. Bike hire is also available at pretty much every village, although it gets busy in the summer.

Where to Stay & Eat
Just a few minutes' walk from the main beach in Cap Ferret village is **La Maison du Bassin,** 5 rue des Pionniers (lamaisondubassin.com; ☎ **05-56-60-60-63;** 165€–310€ double), a charming, laidback hotel and restaurant with 11 understated, rustic-chic rooms, some with little patios. Feast on fresh local seafood (main courses 23€–45€) on the lively terrace or in the cozy dining room. Rooms start at 165€.

THE WINE COUNTRY ★★

Certainly France has so many wonderful vineyards that the entire country could be considered "the wine country." Still, when it comes to mystique, nothing says wine like the **Bordelais,** the world's most famous wine-growing region. **Pomerol, St-Emilion, Margaux, St-Estèphe**—this is where you'll find the greatest stars, a sort of oenological Beverly Hills. However, not all of the wine estates are grandiose affairs with names like Mouton-Rothschild and Château d'Yquem. The region has literally thousands of wineries, and many are relatively approachable family affairs where, if you call ahead, you can drop in for a *dégustation* (wine tasting). But here's the rub. Your hard-working vintners are not always available to show off their estate to tourists. For some of them you will need to book in advance, but increasingly even the most prestigious châteaux offer

Vine-covered chateau with vineyard. Ah!

excellent visits and wine shops, some catering for the smaller members of your party with picnics or brunch (**Château Kirwan** in Margaux for example; chateau-kirwan.com) and adventure trails (**Château d'Agassac** in Haut-Médoc; agassac.com). To find wineries that accept visitors, beyond the ones in this book, we highly recommend the website **Rue de Vignerons** (www.ruedesvignerons.com/en/), which lists a wide range of wine experience across this region and across France.

You'll have several ways to enjoy this beautiful region, whether you are a wine fanatic or just someone who likes wine and would like to learn (and taste) more. The major areas of Bordeaux are the Médoc, Bourg and Blaye, Entre-Deux-Mers, Saint Emilion, Castillon, and Graves and Sauternes. The **Médoc** and **Bourg/Blaye** are both fairly flat, stretching out towards either side of the Gironde estuary. Both are pretty, but you don't come here to sightsee: These are some of the most high-rent vineyards in the country. **Graves** and **Sauternes** is more scenic, but for rolling hills, adorable villages, and photo opportunities, **Entre-Deux-Mers, Saint Emilion,** and **Castillon** are where it's at. The beautiful towns of St-Emilion and Castillon are packed full of medieval treasures, while the Entre-Deux-Mers harbors *bastides* (neatly ordered towns around a central square—strategic urban planning left over from the Hundred Years' War) like **Sauveterre-de-Guyenne** and **Cadillac.**

Visiting the Grand Crus

If you are a serious wine fan, you will no doubt be aching to visit the famous châteaux. You can visit these estates, but in general, you must reserve a visit well in advance. Below are a few of the *grand crus;* for a more complete listing visit the tourist websites of the individual areas or bordeaux.com.

Château Margaux ★ WINE ESTATE   Known as the Versailles of the Médoc, this stately Empire-style château was built in the 19th century. This

763

estate has had an extension by Sir Norman Foster, and there is an interesting architecture exhibition about the old and new building. You can visit the cellars, but tastings are for professionals only, and you can't buy bottles on-site. On D2, Margaux. chateau-margaux.com. ☎ **05-57-88-83-83.** Free admission, by appointment only Mon–Fri. Closed Aug. Tours in English on request.

Château Pichon Baron ★★ WINE ESTATE   A little further north in Pauillac, this 19th-century wonder includes turrets, a reflecting pool, and an excellent onsite wine shop. Pauillac. pichonbaron.com. ☎ **05-56-73-17-17.** 15€ with tasting. Tours in English on request. By appointment only.

Château Prieuré Lichine ★★ WINE ESTATE   Although you should make an appointment in advance for the full tour, there is a well-stocked boutique that you can drop into as you drive past. 34 av. de la 5ième Répubiique, Margaux-Cantenac. prieure-lichine.fr. ☎ **05-57-88-36-28.** Discovery tour including tasting from 12€, as well as picnics and electric bike rental to explore the grounds. Mon–Sat 9am–12:30pm and 2–6pm. Closed Aug.

Visiting Smaller Estates

As noted above, the Bordelais has thousands of wine estates, and the smaller, less-hyped wineries are becoming increasingly visitor-friendly.

Bed & Breakfasting in Wine Country

While you can easily fit your wine country excursion into a day trip from Bordeaux, you could also use it as an excuse to get away from it all. There aren't a lot of hotels to choose from, but there are loads of charming *gîtes* (vacation cottages) and bed-and-breakfasts. Even more intriguing, many wine producers have **onsite bed-and-breakfasts** and offer their overnight guests tours and tastings. Your best bet is to visit the **Gîtes de France** website: gites-de-france.com. This vast network has been around for decades and has very strict standards about cleanliness and comfort. If you want to stay at a vineyard, just search for "Oenotourism" under the "themed holidays" heading on the site's English version. If you can surf in French, go to the **Gîtes de France Gironde** site (gites-de-france-gironde.com, look under "vacances en vignobles"), which will give you plenty of options in the Bordeaux region. Aside from vineyards, both sites list restored ancient outbuildings, and country castles, as well as humbler farms and homes.

Rates for a double with breakfast vary hugely, but can run from 65€ to 120€ per night, depending on comfort levels. Many bed-and-breakfasts offer a *table d'hôte*, a dinner with other guests for 25€ to 50€.

For an enjoyable lunch while out in the vines, stop off at **Café Lavinal** in the small village of Bages just south of Pauillac. This small hamlet has been renovated by Château Lynch Bages, which offers guided tours and tastings in its enormous, hi-tech and "resolutely modern" (as its owners describes it) winery that was recently built on the extensive grounds of the chateau that overlook the Gironde. It's open Mon–Sat 9am–12:30pm and 2–6pm by appointment only. Tours last 90 minutes and cost 25€. There is also an upscale hotel-restaurant in the village, the **Cordeillan-Bages** (cordeillanbages.com).

Where to Find the Château of Your Dreams

Each area has its own wine associations that function as information clearing-houses. To find out more about a particular wine area and listings for wine estates, visit the following websites:

○ **Conseil des Vins de Medoc**
(medoc-bordeaux.com)

○ **Conseil du Vin de Saint-Emilion**
(vins-saint-emilion.com)

○ **Maison du Vin de Blaye**
(vin-blaye.com)

○ **Maison du Vin de Entre-Deux-Mers**
(vins-entre-deux-mers.com)

○ **Maison du Vin de Graves**
(vins-graves.com)

○ **Maison du Sauternes** (maisondu sauternes.com)

Some have joined up with labels or listings publications. One of the most comprehensive is a booklet titled **"Les Bordeaux Itinéraires,"** which also has a terrific website (where you can download the booklet): itineraires-vignobles.fr. They have a huge list of wine estates, including many smaller operations where you can actually drop in (although even they prefer that you call ahead to let them know you are coming). The listings include hours, websites, if they speak English, whether or not you need to reserve—in short, everything you need to know to plan your own wine trip.

Another good strategy is to contact the area's wine association (see "Where to Find the Château of Your Dreams").

Going on a Wine Tour

If you'd like to know more about wine, but are not sure where to begin, or are strapped for time and not up for adventure, an organized tour is a good option. Nonetheless, you could visit the website for **Bordeaux Wine Trip** (bordeauxwinetrip.com), which helps you navigate the wine country, with maps and listings for wineries, restaurants, accommodations, and information on upcoming events. The site also publishes an online magazine, Pulpe, which has English-language features about the food and lifestyle in the region.

A La Française ★★ TOURS Specializing in wine tours, this well-established company works to open up the sometimes-intimidating Bordeaux wine world to non-expert wine fans. A wide variety of tour configurations include a day-long "wine and bike" tour of St-Emilion and two châteaux (169€ per person), and a day spent in a classic Citroën 2CV along the wine routes with a tour guide and visits and tastings in selected châteaux (300€).
3 rue Enghien, Bordeaux. alafrancaise.fr. ✆ **05-57-30-04-27.**

Bordeaux Tourist Office Tours ★★ TOURS Led by guides with ample wine expertise, these tours cover a broad range of experiences. Start with a 5-hour exploration one of the nearby wine regions for 50€, which includes transport, English-language tours, winery visits, and tastings.

Depending on the day of the week, you can visit St-Emilion (which includes a tour of the town and a visit to the underground church), Médoc, Graves and Sauternes, Blaye and Bourge, or Entre-Deux-Mers. Or spend a whole day in St-Emilion for 145€, which includes lunch as well as châteaux visits, wine tastings, tours of the village and the underground church. For a complete list of tours, click on the Bordeaux Vineyards and Wines heading on the website. 12 cours du 30-Juillet, Bordeaux. bordeaux-tourisme.com. ℰ **05-56-00-66-00.**

Uncorked Wine Tours ★★ TOURS   One of the friendliest options for regional wine tours comes care of Caroline Matthews, who does fully tailored tours for a minimum of 1 day. Prices are flexible, but usually start at 950€ for a day's private bespoke tour. www.uncorkedwinetours.com. ℰ **06-50-04-28-84.**

POITIERS ★★

333km (206 miles) SW of Paris; 177km (110 miles) SE of Nantes

Poitiers stands on a hill overlooking the Clain and Boivre rivers—a strategic location that tempted many conquerors. Everybody has passed through here—from Joan of Arc to Richard the Lion-Heart. Charles Martel chased out the Muslims in A.D. 732 and altered the course of European civilization. Poitiers was the chief city of Eleanor of Aquitaine, who had her marriage to pious Louis VII annulled, so she could wed England's Henry II (a marriage that effectively launched the modern Bordeaux wine trade).

For history buffs, this is one of the most fascinating towns in France. The Battle of Poitiers, fought on September 19, 1356, between the armies of Edward the Black Prince and King John of France, was one of the three great English victories in the Hundred Years' War, distinguished by the use of the longbow in the skilled hands of English archers.

The lures here aren't just historic. **Futuroscope** theme park now gets upward of 3 million visitors per year. The thriving student population (25,000 of Poitiers's 92,000 residents are students) adds vitality as well.

Essentials

GETTING THERE   Frequent **rail** service is available from Paris, Bordeaux, and La Rochelle. Around 18 high-speed TGV trains arrive daily from Paris's Gare Montparnasse (average trip time: 90 min.; 39€ one-way), with the high-speed rail link cutting times by 20 minutes. Another 15 TGVs arrive daily from Bordeaux (trip time: 1¾ hr.; 16€ one-way), and 16 regular trains arrive from La Rochelle (trip time: 1¾ hr.; 17€ one-way). For train information, visit sncf-connect.com or call ℰ **36-35. Bus** service from Poitiers is so badly scheduled that it's virtually nonexistent. If you're **driving,** Poitiers is located on the A10 highway; from Paris, follow A10 south through Orléans and Tours, and on to Poitiers.

VISITOR INFORMATION   The **Office de Tourisme** is at 45 pl. Charles de Gaulle (visitpoitiers.fr; ℰ **05-49-41-21-24**).

SPECIAL EVENTS   The liveliest time to visit is from mid-June to mid-September during **Poitiers l'Eté,** a festival of free live jazz, theater, opera, rock, and fireworks. Free concerts and theater pieces, both in and out of the streets, take place at various parks and churches around the city. Check with the tourist office for schedules.

Exploring Poitiers

The **International Greeters Association** (https://internationalgreeter. org) has volunteers in Poitiers who lead excellent and free tours for visitors. Visit the website above for info.

Baptistère St-Jean ★★ RELIGIOUS SITE   From the cathedral, you can walk to the most ancient Christian monument in France. It was built as a baptistery in the early 4th century on Roman foundations and extended in the 7th century. It contains frescoes from the 11th to the 13th centuries and a collection of funerary sculpture.

Rue Jean-Jaurès. ✆ **05-49-41-21-24.** Admission 2€ adults; 1€ children 11 and under. June 21–Sept 30 daily 10:30am–12:30pm and 2–6pm; Apr–June 20 Tues–Sun 2–6pm; Nov–Mar Tues–Sun 2–4pm; Oct Tues–Sun 2–5pm.

Cathédrale St-Pierre ★★ CATHEDRAL   In the eastern sector of Poitiers is the twin-towered Cathédrale St-Pierre, begun in 1162 by Henry II of England and Eleanor of Aquitaine on the ruins of a Roman basilica. The architecturally undistinguished cathedral was completed much later. The interior, 89m (292 ft.) long, contains some admirable 12th- and 13th-century stained glass.

pl. de la Cathédrale. ✆ **05-49-41-23-76.** Free admission. Daily 9am–7:30pm (until 6pm in winter).

Place Charles de Gaulle, Poitiers.

Eglise Notre-Dame-la-Grande ★★ CHURCH   This church, built in the Romanesque-Byzantine style and richly decorated, is from the late 11th century. See in particular its western front, dating from the mid–12th century. Surrounded by an open-air market, the facade, carved like an ivory casket, is characterized by pine cone-shaped towers. Rising majestically behind the choir stalls' Renaissance splendor is the modern yet sympathetically designed organ that was created by master organ-builder Yves Sévère. Carvings on the doorway represent biblical scenes.

pl. Charles de Gaulle. ✆ **05-49-41-22-56.** Free admission. Daily 9am–7pm.

Futuroscope ★★ AMUSEMENT PARK   This multimedia amusement park in a suburb of Poitiers is a wonderland of technology that lets you experience sounds, images, and sensations with the world's most advanced film-projection techniques and largest screens. The architecture is extraordinary—take a peek at the **Kinémax,** a 400-seat cinema shaped like a rock crystal covered with mirrors, or the **Cité du Numérique** (Digital City), a giant glass triangle with a huge white globe sitting in the middle. The site has six IMAX theaters, as well as attractions that use 3D technology, motion simulators, and sophisticated lighting effects. Attractions let you rocket deep into space, dive under the ocean, or fly up in the air for a virtual sky tour. Recent additions include *Chasseurs de Tornades* (Tornado Chasers), a thrilling adventure in the Dynamic Motion Theater that makes you feel as if you've been whisked away by a tornado. Every evening, *les nocturnes* are staged with illuminated fountains, lights, and recorded music.

The park's success is such that it has its own TGV train station with direct connections to Bordeaux, Paris, and other major cities, as well as a selection of hotels and restaurants (detailed on the website). Book your tickets in advance to get up to 10€ off the admission.

Jaunay-Clan. futuroscope.com. ✆ **05-49-49-30-80.** Admission from 56€ adults, 47€ children ages 5–12, free for children 4 and under. Daily 9am–11:30pm, with slightly shorter hours in winter. Bus: Lines 1 and 21 direct from Poitiers Centre train station. Driving: From Poitiers, take D910 or A10 autoroute about 12km (7½ miles) north. Closed Jan to mid-Feb and weekdays in Nov and most of Dec.

Musée Ste-Croix ★★ MUSEUM   On the site of the old abbey of Ste-Croix, this museum has extensive art and archeology collections. Exhibits date right back to the Gallo-Roman times, but the really unmissable part for is the fine art section that covers paintings and sculpture from 14th century right up to contemporary art. Works by Bonnard, Sisley, Mondrian, and Moreau are on display, as well as an impressive collection of sculptures, including Maillol, Rodin, and seven statues by Camille Claudel.

61 rue St-Simplicien. poitiers.fr. ✆ **05-49-41-07-53.** Admission 5€ adults, 2.50€ Sun, free for children ages 17 and under. Tues–Fri 10am–6pm; Sat–Sun 1–6pm.

Where to Stay

Hôtel de l'Europe ★★   Composed of several buildings, one of which dates from the 19th century, this family-owned hotel successfully manages

Futuroscope.

to combine contemporary and fin-de-siècle style. The breakfast room features curlicue moldings and a grand fireplace, while the rooms are modern and sleek. Not all of the rooms have air-conditioning, so ask for one specifically if you visit during hot weather. You can eat or enjoy an aperitif outside in the lovely garden complete with a boules court.

39 rue Carnot. hotel-europe-poitiers. com. ✆ **05-49-88-12-00.** 87 units. 87€– 110€ double. Parking 9€. **Amenities:** Room service; Wi-Fi.

Hôtel Mercure Poitiers ★★ If you think you don't want to stay in a Mercure, you haven't been to this one. In one of the city's most attractive old buildings, a former Jesuit chapel, with the brilliant Les Archives restaurant directly underneath, this is both inexpensive and well located. Inside you get Gothic windows, vaulted ceilings, pure character everywhere you look, with almost nothing to say you are in a chain hotel.

14 Edouard-Grimaux. all.accor.com. ✆ **05-49-50-50-60.** 20 units. 117€–162€ double; 217€–285€ suite. **Amenities:** Restaurant; bar; free Wi-Fi.

La Maison de Marc ★★ Small, cozy, and super welcoming, this *chambres d'hôtes* makes an excellent alternative to the bigger hotels in town. Well-thought-out details abound, from luxurious throws on the bed to double sinks in all the bathrooms, and there's also a two-bedroom apartment to rent. Book ahead if you are coming during the summer.

12 rue Bourbeau. lamaisondemarc.com. ✆ **06-18-54-68-99.** 4 units. 95€–120€ double; from 125€ for the apartment. Breakfast included. **Amenities:** Free Wi-Fi.

Where to Eat

Les Archives ★★ MODERN FRENCH   Just below the Hotel Mercure, this is one of the best places to eat in Poitiers, hands down. Set in a beautiful large space with a mezzanine level, this was once the Jesuit chapel, and today is a restaurant, bar, tea-room, and sometimes live music space. The food is excellent, with an emphasis on updating French classics with whatever is in season. A good range of vegetarian options is also available, including a set vegetarian menu.

14 rue Edouard-Grimaux. lesarchives.fr. ✆ **05-49-30-53-00.** Main courses 15€–29€; fixed-price lunch 17.90€–21.90€ or dinner 35€–65€. Daily noon–2pm and 7–10pm (Fri–Sat until 10:30pm).

Oh! Le Bistro ★★ FRENCH   You can't book ahead at this convivial bistro, but it's worth the effort to grab a table either inside its brick-lined interior or on its lively terrace. Owners Sylvie and Manu make a point of sourcing high-quality ingredients from trusted local suppliers. It's hearty bistro fare here: steak tartare with or without truffles, generous steaks and lamb dishes, plus vegetarian options and fish specials. And all very good value for money.

31 rue Carnot. ohlebistro.fr. ☎ **05-49-03-37-02.** Main courses 16.90€; fixed-price lunch 14.90€–16.90€; fixed-price dinner 25.50€–39.90€. Daily noon–1:45pm and 7–10pm (10:30pm Fri–Sat).

Day Trip from Poitiers
ANGOULÊME ★★
443km (275 miles) SW of Paris; 116km (72 miles) NE of Bordeaux

The old town of Angoulême hugs a hilltop between the Charente and Aguienne rivers. You can visit it on the same day you visit Cognac or take your time and do both separately. The town has been a center for the French paper industry since the 17th century, a tradition that carries on today in the city's remaining paper mills. These days, Angoulême (pop. 43,000) is probably best known for something that gets printed on that paper: comics. Authors, artists, and fans come from all over the world to attend the **Festival International de la Bande Dessinée,** one of the largest comic book/graphic novel gatherings on earth. The festival takes over the town for 4 days in January, when the latest books are presented, prizes awarded, and contracts signed. For more information, contact the festival (bdangouleme.com; ☎ **05-45-97-86-50**) or the tourist office (see below). If you miss the festival, you can still explore this graphic world at the **Cité Internationale de la Bande Dessinée et de l'Image (CNBDI)** also known as the **Musée de la Bande Dessinée;** see "Exploring the Town," below.

GETTING THERE About two TGV **trains** per hour (trip time: 55 min.) and a handful of regular trains (trip time: 1½ hr. or 1 hr. high speed) arrive every day from Bordeaux; the one-way fare is 16€. Frequent train service also arrives from Saintes (trip time: 1 hr.) and Poitiers (trip time: 45 min.). From Paris's Montparnasse Station, some 15 TGV trains make the trip daily (trip time: 1 hr., 47 min.); one-way fares from 19€. For train information and schedules, visit sncf-connect.com or call ☎ **36-35. Bus Line No15** runs about 10 buses per day between Cognac and Angoulême. The trip

Statue of Princess Margaret of Valoise in front of the town hall.

takes 1 hour and costs 2.30€ each way. If you're **driving** from Bordeaux, take N10 northeast to Angoulême.

VISITOR INFORMATION   The **Office de Tourisme** is at place des Halles (angouleme-tourisme.com; ℰ **05-45-95-16-84**).

Exploring the Town

The hub of the town is **place de l'Hôtel-de-Ville.** The town hall was erected from 1858 to 1866 on the site of the palace of the ducs d'Angoulême, where Marguerite de Navarre, sister of François I, was born. All that remains of the palace are the 15th-century Tour de Valois and 13th-century Tour de Lusignan.

Cathédrale St-Pierre ★, 4 pl. St-Pierre, was built in the 11th and 12th centuries and restored in the 19th. Flanked by towers, its facade has 75 statues, each in a separate niche, representing the Last Judgment. This is one of France's most startling examples of Romanesque-Byzantine style. The 19th-century architect Abadie (designer of Sacré-Coeur in Paris) tore down the north tower and then rebuilt it with the original materials in the same style. In the interior, you can wander under a four-domed ceiling. It's open daily 9am to 6pm (from 9:30am Fri).

As the European capital of comic book art, the city is home of the **Cité Internationale de la Bande Dessinée et de l'Image,** Quai de Charente (citebd.org; ℰ **05-45-38-65-65;** July–Aug Tues–Sat 10am–7pm and Sun 2–7pm; Sept–June Tues–Sat 10am–6pm and Sun 2–6pm), which might just be the best resource for graphic art lovers in Europe. The **Musée de la Bande Dessinée ★** offers a complete history of French and American comics, with more than 12,000 original drawings in an exhibition space that also shows audiovisual sequences of the artists drawing their works. There's a book shop on site, and across the Charente River at 121 rue de Bordeaux there's giant library and research center, and, nearby at 60 av. de Cognac, the **Cinéma de la Cité** complete the picture. Entrance to the museum is 10€ for adults, 6€ for students under 26, free for children under 18.

To get out into the city itself, you can walk along the panoramic **promenade des Remparts ★**, a path that flanks the site of the long-gone fortifications that once surrounded the historic core of Angoulême. The most appealing section of the 3km (1¾-mile) walkway is the 1km (½-mile) section that connects the cathedral with Les Halles (the covered market). Views from here stretch over the hills that flank the Charente River almost 75m (246 ft.) below. Or stroll the **Circuit des Murs Peints ★** (Murals Walk). Famous graphic artists such as Florence Cestac and Marc-Antoine Mathieu have created more than 20 commissioned pieces of street art at various public spots around the city; the tourist office has a walking tour map.

Where to Eat

L'Agape ★★ FRENCH   This classic French restaurant with a contemporary feel has an ever-changing menu from an inventive young chef and a wide-ranging wine list. L'Agape represents great value for this quality of cooking; plenty of vegetarian options are available as well. Reservations recommended.

16 pl. du Palet. l-agape.com. ✆ **05-45-95-18-13.** Main courses 20€–27€, fixed-price lunch menu 17.50€–20€; dinner menu 46€–58€. Thurs–Mon noon–1:30pm and 7–9:30pm (until 9pm Sun–Mon).

Les Halles Market ★ MARKET As in most French cities, the daily market is one of the best places to eat. You'll find plenty of stalls with bars and high stools offering a range of local products.

pl. des Halles. Tues–Sun 7am–2pm.

LA ROCHELLE ★★★

467km (290 miles) SW of Paris; 145km (90 miles) SE of Nantes; 183km (113 miles) N of Bordeaux; 142km (88 miles) NW of Angoulême

La Rochelle is a historic port and ancient sailors' city, formerly the stronghold of the Huguenots. It was founded as a fishing village in the 10th century on a rocky platform in the center of a marshland. Eleanor of Aquitaine gave La Rochelle a charter in 1199, freeing it from feudal dues. After becoming an independent city-state, the port capitalized on the wars between France and England. It was the departure point for the founders of Montreal. From the 14th to the 16th century, La Rochelle was one of France's great maritime cities. It became the principal port between France and the colony of Canada, but France's loss of Canada ruined its Atlantic trade.

As a hotbed of Protestant factions, it armed privateers to prey on Catholic vessels but was eventually besieged by Catholic troops, led by Cardinal Richelieu (with his Musketeers) and Jean Guiton. When Richelieu blockaded the port, La Rochelle bravely resisted. It took 15 months to

La Rochelle.

During the French Wars of Religion that raged off and on for much of the 17th century, a large number of both Huguenots and Catholics emigrated from La Rochelle to North America, especially Canada. It is thought that as many as 14,000 emigrants landed in New France (the term referred to French colonies across north America, including Québec, Newfoundland, Nova Scotia, and parts of the Great Lakes) in the century up to 1760. Besides the **Musée du Nouveau-Monde** (p. 776), you will also see a sculpture in the Vieux-Port called Globe de la Francophonie by artist Bruce Krebs, celebrating this global spread of French culture and language.

If you are tracing your own roots here, you could start with the **Unicaen Project** run by Caen University (no longer active, but the information gathered in a research project from 2001–2006 is searchable on unicaen.fr/mrsh/prefen/index.php). The **Musée Rochelais d'Histoire Protestante,** 2 rue Saint-Michel (protestantisme-museelarochelle.fr; ✆ **05-46-50-88-03;** 5€ adults, 2.50€ students and visitors 24–18, free for children 17 and under), has some potentially useful archives. It's open Monday through Saturday 2:30 to 6pm from mid-June to mid-Sept, and by request at other times of the year.

starve the city into submission, during which time 25,000 citizens perished from hunger. On October 30, 1628, Richelieu entered the city and found only 5,000 survivors.

Today La Rochelle, a city of 77,000, is the cultural and administrative center of the Charente-Maritime *département* (administrative region, now part of the larger Nouvelle Aquitaine). While many of La Rochelle's sights are old, the city is riddled with high-rise condos and home to the largest pleasure-boat basin in Europe. In summer, the city gets extremely busy with visitors.

Essentials

GETTING THERE The La Rochelle–Ile-de-Ré **airport** (larochelle.aeroport.fr; ✆ **08-92-23-01-03**) is on the coast, 4km (2½ miles) north of the city. Take Illico bus 1b to reach it; one-way ticket 1.30€ bought on the bus. For information and schedules, visit yelo-agglo-larochelle.fr or call ✆ **08-10-17-18-17**. Six to nine **trains** from Bordeaux and Nantes arrive daily (trip time: 2 hr.; from 26€ one-way). A few direct TGVs arrive from Paris's Gare Montparnasse, although some require a transfer at Nantes (trip time: 3 hr., although this also benefits from the high-speed rail link if you work out the connection times well); the one-way fare is from 35€. For train information, visit sncf-connect.com or call ✆ **36-35**. The main **bus** lines in, out, and around the city leave from place de Verdun (✆ **05-46-00-95-15** for information). If you're **driving,** follow A10 south from Poitiers to exit 33 toward La Rochelle/Niort/St-Maixent, and then take N11 west to the coast and La Rochelle.

VISITOR INFORMATION The **Office de Tourisme** is on Quai Georges Simenon, Le Gabut (larochelle-tourisme.com; ✆ **05-46-41-14-68**).

SPECIAL EVENTS   The busiest month is July because the **Festival La Rochelle Cinéma (Fema)** rolls in at the beginning of the month. It attracts a huge following of fans, press, actors, directors, and, of course, paparazzi. Screenings are held around town; a pass for 10 screenings costs 55€. For information, contact the festival office, at 10 Quai Georges Simenon (festival-larochelle.org; ℂ **05-46-52-28-96** or 01-48-06-16-66). For a week in mid-July, **Les Francofolies,** a festival of French-language music, features big names as well as not-so-famous groups, many of them international musicians. The town is overrun with fans, and a party atmosphere prevails. Tickets range from 17€ to 70€. Call ℂ **05-46-28-28-28** for details (francofolies.fr).

La Rochelle is also the site of the biggest showcase of boats and yachts in Europe, **Le Grand Pavois–Salon Nautique.** It's a 6-day extravaganza in late-September attracting some 80,000 visitors. The action is based in and around La Rochelle's Port de Plaisance (better known as the Bassin des Yachts, or Yacht Basin). Sellers and buyers of boats and marine hardware, as well as weekend sailors from everywhere, usually attend. For information about dates and venues, check grand-pavois.com or call ℂ **05-46-44-46-39**.

Exploring La Rochelle

La Rochelle has two sides: the old and unspoiled town inside the Vauban defenses and the modern and industrial suburbs. The city's **fortifications** have a circuit of 5.5km (3½ miles), with a total of seven gates. It's an easy city to walk around, or you can use the yellow bicycles (or electric cars), called **Yélo** (yelo.agglo-larochelle.fr), that are available for hire from stations around the city. There are even solar-powered boats called **Yélo bateaux** that chug across the harbor. This *passeur*, as it's also known, crosses La Rochelle's channel from Cours des Dames to La Médiathèque and are called by pressing a button on the quayside. A single ride is 1€.

The town, with its streets covered in arcades that keep out the intense sun (and occasionally the rain), is great for strolling. The port is a fishing harbor and one of Europe's major sailing centers. If you are here during the summer, try to schedule a visit in time to attend a **fish auction** (called *La Criée aux Poissons*) at the Marché Central de la Rochelle, starting at 4:45am every Thursday in July and August (8.50€ per person booked through the tourist office or online; see above). The 19th-century covered food market, **Les Halles de la Rochelle**, has a superb selection of seafood from the region along with other specialties of Charente-Maritime. If you're here in July or August, join one of the Tuesday guided tours of the best food stalls to get a sense of what the region has to offer. Tours last 2½ hours, start at 10am and 12:30pm, cost 14€, and include a tasting. Book either at the tourist office or online. The best streets for strolling, each with a 17th-century arcade, are **rue du Palais, rue du Temple, rue Chaudrier,** and **rue des Merciers,** with its ancient wooden houses (seek out the ones at nos. 3, 5, 8, and 17).

The town's 14th-century showcase **Hôtel de Ville (City Hall)** ★ is built in flamboyant Gothic style with battlements. It was heavily damaged in a 2013 fire, but many of its treasures were saved and the building reopened in 2019 after extensive restoration. Step inside for a look at its wonderfully ornate public rooms. Open Monday to Friday 8am to 6pm and Saturday 10am to 12:30pm and 1:30 to 6pm.

Aquarium de La Rochelle ★★★ AQUARIUM   La Rochelle's block-buster crowd pleaser, this is one of the biggest aquariums in Europe. It rises from a portside position near the Port des Minimes, north of the old city. Inside are guided walkways stretching over several floors of massive seawater tanks loaded with some 10,000 species of flora and fauna from the oceans of the world, living in what look like natural habitats. Its exhibits look at the ocean's deepest depths, with five large tanks employing light shows and interactive high-definition images to illuminate these little-known corners of the earth, along with the ecosystem of the Atlantic coastline and the stunning array of sea life carried by the Gulf Stream. The jelly fish exhibition remains as beautiful and popular as ever.

Quai Louis Prunier, Le Vieux Port. aquarium-larochelle.com. ✆ **05-46-34-00-00.** Admission 17.50€ adults, 15.50€ students, 12.50€ children ages 3–17, free for children 2 and under. Audio guides in English 2€ for children 3–17 and 2.50€ for adults. July–Aug daily 9am–11pm; Apr–June and Sept daily 9am–8pm; Oct–Dec daily 10am–8pm; Jan daily 10am–7pm.

Musée des Beaux-Arts ★ ART MUSEUM   **Important:** *Since 2018 the museum has been undergoing a major renovation, and a date for reopening has yet to be set, so check online before heading over.* This museum is in an Episcopal palace built in the mid–17th century. The 900-strong art collection spans the 15th to the 20th centuries but focuses mainly on 19th-century art with works by Gustave Doré, Brossard de Beaulieu, Camille Corot, and Paul Huet, as well as local artists William Bouguereau and Eugène Fromentin.

28 rue Gargoulleau. museedesbeauxarts.larochelle.fr. ✆ **05-46-41-64-65.**

Sightseeing Pass: Yes or No?

If you plan to do a *lot* sightseeing, and we mean a LOT, you should buy a **La Rochelle Océan Pass** (larochelleocean pass.com), which gives you admission to more than 30 attractions plus public transport (but not Yélo bicycles). It's valid over 48 hours, 72 hours and 7 days, and extends into the Charente-Maritime region. Sites include La Rochelle's towers, Musée Maritime, Musée du Nouveau-Monde, Musée d'Histoire Naturelle, boat rides and a trip to Ile-de-Ré, among others. A 48-hour pass costs 44€ adults, 22€ for children 12–17 and 11€ for

children 6–11 (free for children under 6). You have to be a dedicated sightseer to get the most out of this, though. A more realistic option might be to buy the single ticket that gives you admission to all three historic towers of La Rochelle, which costs 9.50€ adults and is free for children under 18. If you want to combine the towers with a museum visit, a ticket costing 13€ gets you into the three towers as well as one of the following: Musée du Nouveau-Monde, Musée Maritime, and Muséum d'Histoire Naturelle.

Musée du Nouveau-Monde ★ MUSEUM   In an 18th-century town house named after the Fleuriau family who lived there from 1772 to 1974, this is one of La Rochelle's most intriguing museums—if you speak French. It vividly shows how the city played such a prominent role in the colonization of Canada, with La Rochelle being the primary port in France for voyages to New France (as Québec was known). Exhibits start with LaSalle's discovery of the Mississippi Delta in 1682 and end with the settling of the Louisiana territory. Alas none of this is translated into English. You'll find other examples of the link between La Rochelle and Canada around the city, with many on the walking path "Les Chemins du Québec" (map available in the tourist office).

10 rue Fleuriau. museedunouveaumonde.larochelle.fr ✆ **05-46-41-46-50.** Admission 8€ adults, free for children 18 and under. Mid-June to mid-Sept Mon, Wed–Fri, Sun 10am–6pm and Sat 2–6pm; mid-Sept to mid-June Mon, Wed–Fri, Sun 10am–12:30pm and 1:30–5:30pm and Sat 1:30–5:30pm.

Musée Maritime ★★ MUSEUM   This museum comprises eight permanently docked boats, two of which can be visited: a weather ship that was used in the North Atlantic until the 1980s, and an antique *chalutier de pêche* (fishing trawler). The vintage yachts evoke the grand days of La Rochelle as a maritime power and its New World commerce.

Pl. Bernard Moitessier. museemaritimelarochelle.fr. ✆ **05-46-28-03-00.** Admission 8€ adults, free for students under 26 and children under 18. Mid-June to mid-Sept Wed–Sun 10am–6pm (Sat 2–6pm); mid-Sept to mid-June Tues–Sun 10am–12:30pm and 1:30–5:30pm (Sat 1:30–5:30pm only).

Muséum d'Histoire Naturelle ★★ MUSEUM   One of the hidden treasures of La Rochelle, this lovely museum is set within an enormous (2,500-sq.-m/26,910-sq.-ft.) mansion in the heart of town and surrounded by colorful botanical gardens. This is truly a museum to get lost in. Expect an array of taxidermied animals, African masks, maps of prehistoric migration patterns, and more. They are all part of the 10,000 or so objects, brought back by La Rochelle's 17th-century traders on their ships. The gardens outside are part of the exhibition, with plants from many of the same far-flung locations.

28 rue Albert 1er. museum.larochelle.fr. ✆ **05-46-41-18-25.** Admission 8€, free for students under 26 and children 17 and under. Mid-June to mid-Sept Tues–Sun 10am–6pm (Sat 2–6pm); mid-Sept to mid-June Tues–Sun 10am–12:30pm and 1:30–5:30pm (Sat 1:30–5:30pm only).

Tour de la Chaîne ★★ HISTORIC SITE   During the 1300s, this tower was built as an anchor piece for the large forged-iron chain that stretched across the harbor, closing it against hostile warships. The exhibits focus on the history of the first migration to Canada.

Quai du Gabut. tours-la-rochelle.fr. ✆ **05-46-34-11-81.** Admission, see sightseeing pass box above. Apr–June and Sept daily 10am–1pm and 2:15–6:30pm; Oct–Mar daily 10am–1pm and 2:15–5:30pm. Closed 1st Mon morning of the month.

Tour de la Lanterne ★★ HISTORIC SITE   Built between 1445 and 1476, this was once a lighthouse but was used mainly as a jail as late as the 19th century. A low rampart connects the cylindrical tower to the Tour de la Chaîne. During the Wars of Religion, 13 priests were tossed from its summit. You climb 162 steps to the top hold; in clear weather, the panoramic view extends all the way to Ile d'Oléron. On the way up, you can still see graffiti scrawled by former prisoners.

Opposite Tour St-Nicolas, quai du Gabut. © **05-46-41-56-04.** Admission, see box. Apr–June and Sept daily 10am–1pm and 2:15–6:30pm; Oct–Mar daily 10am–1pm and 2:15–5:30pm. Closed 1st Mon morning of the month.

Tour St-Nicolas ★★ HISTORIC SITE   The oldest tower in La Rochelle, Tour St-Nicolas was built between 1371 and 1382. It originally guarded the town against surprise attacks. From its second floor, you can enjoy a view of the town and harbor; from the top, you can see only the old town and Ile d'Oléron.

Admission, see box. Apr–June and Sept daily 10am–1pm and 2:15–6:30pm; Oct–Mar daily 10am–1pm and 2:15–5:30pm. Closed 1st Mon morning of the month.

Where to Stay

Hôtel La Monnaie ★★   This hotel near the Tour de la Lanterne is in a 17th-century building that has been tastefully restored in a luxurious, contemporary style. Some rooms have rococo touches such as elaborate chandeliers and gilt mirrors, but the normal doubles can be a little small and plain. There's also a compact spa with a fitness center, and a beautiful garden where you can relax with a cocktail.

3 rue de la Monnaie. hotelmonnaie.com. © **05-46-50-65-65.** 41 units. 129€–204€ double; 249€–475€ suite. Parking 20€ reserved in advance. **Amenities:** Bar; spa; room service; free Wi-Fi.

Un Hôtel en Ville ★★   This good-value option stands out because of its roof terrace with sun loungers and amazing views over the city, as well as its friendly welcome. It's centrally located close to the port with its bars and restaurants, and every element has been recently redone, introducing welcome touches such as high-quality bedding and hearty breakfasts. You can snag an excellent deal during the winter months, so do check with them directly.

20 pl. du Maréchal Foch. unhotelenville.fr. © **05-46-41-15-75.** 11 units. 88€–200€ double. **Amenities:** Room service; free Wi-Fi.

Where to Eat

Christopher Coutanceau ★★★ MODERN FRENCH   This is not only the city's most glamorous and prestigious restaurant, but also among the Atlantic coast's finest. It is worth the expense for a special evening. With stunning views over Concurrence beach and the bay beyond, the restaurant is contemporary in feel with luxurious touches everywhere. Christopher Coutanceau is owner and chef (and, as he likes to underline, a fisherman), and so very much aware of the importance of sustainability in what he catches and serves. For example, no fish on the menu here will

La Rochelle

be served during its breeding season. If you book far enough ahead, you could bag a place at the Chef's Table and watch the masters at work. The insanely comprehensive wine list has more than 2,400 wines listed from a cellar with 22,000 bottles. Reservations required.

Plage de la Concurrence. christophercoutanceau.com. © **05-46-41-48-19.** Main courses 105€–120€; fixed-price menus 260€–310€. Tues–Sat 12:15–1:15pm and 7:30–9pm.

Les 4 Sergents ★★ MODERN FRENCH/SEAFOOD This classy place stands out among the busy throng along the car-free rue St-Jean du Pérot, not just for its extensive seafood menu and superb meat dishes, but also for its wonderful interior. Its glass and metal atrium was designed by Gustave Eiffel's workshop and is filled with soothing greenery. The kitchen isn't afraid to add a few Asian flavors to its incredibly fresh seafood and fish dishes.

49 rue St-Jean du Pérot. les4sergents.com. © **05-46-41-35-80.** Fixed-price menus 34€–39€; seafood platters 39€–45€; fixed-price lunch 26.90€–29.90€. Daily noon–2:30pm and 7–10:30pm (until 10pm Thurs and 11pm Fri–Sat).

Prao Resto ★★ MODERN FRENCH Named for the simple wooden *prao* boats with triangular sails that you find in the Indian Ocean, Prao Resto is part of the slow food movement. Its menu focuses on local foodstuffs, from oysters to fish to locally sourced meats; it also has topnotch vegetarian options. As for the ambiance: The exposed stone walls and heating pipes give the interior an industrial but creative feel.

10 rue Saint-Nicolas. prao.biz. © **05-46-37-85-46.** Main courses 19.50€; fixed-price lunch 18€–20€; fixed-price dinner 28€–36€. Mon–Sat noon–2pm and 7:30–10pm.

La Rochelle Nightlife

From July to September, head for **quai Duperré, cours des Dames,** and **cours des Templiers.** Once the sun starts to set, this becomes one big pedestrian zone peppered with street performers. It's a fun, almost magical area that sets the tone for the rest of the night. Your early evening should include an aperitif at **La Cave de Guignette,** 8 rue St-Nicolas (la-guignette.fr; © **05-56-41-05-75**), which looks pretty much unchanged since it opened in the 1930s and has on tap *la guignette*, a blend of white wine, sparkling water, and syrup rarely found outside of La Rochelle (and possibly this bar).

Day Trip from La Rochelle
COGNAC

478km (296 miles) SW of Paris; 37km (23 miles) NW of Angoulême; 113km (70 miles) SE of La Rochelle

The world enjoys 163 million bottles a year of the nectar known as cognac, which Victor Hugo called "the drink of the gods." It's worth a detour to visit one of the château warehouses of the bottlers. Martell, Hennessy, and Otard welcome visits from the public, as well as other worthy *maisons de*

sailing THE PORTS OF LA ROCHELLE

La Rochelle has always earned its living from the sea and the ships that make its harbor their home. Four distinct harbors have grown up over the centuries, each a world unto itself, rich with local nuance and lore. They include the historic **Vieux-Port**, the **Port de Plaisance** (a modern yacht marina), the **Port de Pêche** (the fishing port), and the **Port de Commerce**, mostly used by large container ships.

The best way to appreciate them is to take a boat tour. Visit the tourist office (see "Essentials," earlier in this chapter), which acts as a clearinghouse for the tour companies (most prominently Croisières Inter-Iles and Navipromer). Tours combine a look at the modern facilities with a waterside view of the historic ramparts—which, despite their girth and height, did not protect the city's 17th-century Protestants from starvation and eventual annihilation.

The company with the most frequent departures is the **Croisières Inter-Iles** (inter-iles.com; ✆ **05-46-50-55-54**). Every day from April to October, about a half-dozen cruises glide into each of the six ports. In winter, they're offered less frequently, usually only on school vacations. Tours last about 1 hour, 45 minutes each; are conducted in French; and average 20€.

Another excellent waterborne outing—but only during the warmer months—involves taking a **ferry** from the Vieux-Port of La Rochelle to **Ile de Ré**. The island, 26km (16 miles) off the coast of La Rochelle and ringed with 69km (43 miles) of sandy beaches, holds nature preserves crisscrossed with biking and hiking paths, and a number of excellent restaurants in the island's main town, St-Martin-de-Ré. Croisières Inter-Iles (see above) serves the island. If you want to get here during July or August, and if you don't have a car, we recommend taking the ferry for a round-trip fare of 22€. It's worth spending a few days on the island if you have time, joining the many Parisians who escape here during the summer months. The island has many bike rental shops and more than 100km (62 miles) of excellent bike paths. Since the island is fairly flat (the highest point only 19m/62 ft.) you can easily do the trip without a car.

You can also drive your car across the bridge that connects the Ile de Ré to the French mainland. It's accessible from a point 3km (1¾ miles) south of La Rochelle. The toll is 16€ in summer, 8€ in winter. By bus, **Transports Nouvelle Aquitaine** (transports.nouvelle-aquitaine. fr; ✆ **09-70-87-08-87**) offers up to 15 round-trips per day year-round (line 3) and charges 2.30€ one-way or 4.10€ round-trip from La Rochelle to several stops along the island.

négoce; visits usually include free tastings, although increasingly the big houses are charging for visits but making them more interesting in return.

GETTING THERE Eleven trains per day arrive from Angoulême (trip time: 40 min., ticket price from 11.30€ one-way), and 10 trains pull in from Saintes (trip time: 20 min., ticket price from 5€ one-way). For train information and schedules, visit sncf.connect.com or call ✆ **36-35**. Limited **bus** service arrives from Angoulême; the trip takes 50 minutes and costs 2.30€; visit thorin-vriet.com or call ✆ **05-45-62-09-36** for schedules. If you're **driving** to Cognac, the best route from Saintes (which lies along the major route A10) is N141 east.

Exploring the Town

Many visitors don't realize that this unassuming town of some 20,000 people is about more than just a drink. Though the air is perfumed with the sweet scent from the distilleries, business goes on as usual in the cobbled streets, some of which still sport a few half-timbered houses from the Renaissance.

If you'd like to visit a distillery, go to its main office during regular business hours and request a tour, or visit the tourist office for assistance. On a tour, you'll see some brandies that have aged for as long as 50 or even 100 years. You can have a free taste and then purchase a bottle or two. As far as we're concerned, **Baron Otard** offers the most informative and insightful tours, partly because of the sheer majesty of its headquarters, in the late-medieval **Château de Cognac,** 127 bd. Denfert-Rochereau (chateaudecognac.com; ✆ **05-45-36-88-86**). The tour is half historical overview of the castle, half technical explanation of cognac production. Parts of the château are appropriately baronial (King François I was born here). Tours last about 1 hour, 15 minutes, include tastings and cost from 18€ for adults, 5€ for students 12 to 18, and are free for children 12 and under. From April to October, tours depart at frequent intervals daily. During November to March, you need to contact them in advance to arrange the tour. Call the tourist office or the company several days in advance for exact schedules.

Other distilleries that conduct tours include **Hennessy,** 1 quai Hennessy (hennessy.com; ✆ **05-45-35-06-44; 29€** for an immersive tour and via an innovative art installation and a tasting; opening hours vary, but usually from

Cognac at Hennessy.

10am–7pm); **Camus,** 21 rue de Cagouillet (camus.fr; ℂ **05-45-32-70-14;** tastings from 25€ to a master sommelier class where you blend your own cognac 190€; selected days of the week throughout the year at 10am, 2pm, and 4pm, booked via the website); and **Rémy Martin,** 20 rue de la Société Vinicole (visitesremymartin.com; ℂ **05-45-35-76-66**). Here, you can take a variety of tours of the estate, the cellars, a combination of the two, by train or by bike, or enjoy various themed tastings. Priced from 25€, the most elaborate package costs 1,500€ for a gastronomic lunch, visit of the cellars and the Grollet estate, a walk through the Grande Champagne vineyards and two tastings of the top-flight Louis XIII cognac. For all tours, call in advance for reservations or book a slot online.

If you're short on time, a good retail outlet is **La Cognathèque,** 8 pl. Jean-Monnet (cognatheque.com; ℂ **05-45-82-43-31**), which prides itself on having the widest selection from all the region's distilleries, large and small (some 150 different cognacs).

The **Musée des Savoir-Faire de Cognac** is in the town center at place de la Salle Verte (les-distillateurs-culturels.fr; ℂ **05-45-36-03-65;** July–Aug daily 10:30–6:30pm; Sept–June Tues–Sun 2–6pm). This takes you through the history of the trade coupled with modern and immersive exhibitions, often incorporating local artists. The museum also has a good boutique. Entrance is 5€ for adults, 3€ for ages 13–25. Admission is free for anyone 12 and under.

Within a 15-minute walk is the **Musée d'Art et l'Histoire de Cognac,** 48 bd. Denfert-Rochereau (les-distillateurs-culturels.fr; ℂ **05-45-32-07-25**). Located in a gorgeous building classified as a historic monument, it has exhibits on popular arts and traditions, and a fine art collection. It's currently closed while it's undergoing renovations.

Cognac has two beautiful parks: the **Parc François-1er** and the **Parc de l'Hôtel-de-Ville**. The Romanesque-Gothic Eglise St-Léger, rue de Monseigneur LaCroix, is from the 12th century, and its bell tower is from the 15th. Admission is free.

Where to Eat

In downtown Cognac, **Le Bistro de Claude,** 15 rue Grande (bistro-de-claude.com; ℂ **05-45-82-60-32;** main courses 24€–39€; fixed-price menus 24€–39€; Mon–Fri noon–2pm and 7:30–10pm), serves carefully prepared, well-presented classic French fare along with an excellent cognac list.

La Ribaudière ★★★ MODERN FRENCH   Set 10km (6 miles) east of Cognac, this is perhaps the area's best restaurant, certainly the most acclaimed. Chef Thierry Verrat has been producing the best of the region's cuisine for more than 30 years, and has been joined by his son, Julien. Reservations recommended.

2 pl. du Port, Bourg-Charente. laribaudiere.com. ℂ **05-45-81-30-54.** Main courses 42€–68€; fixed-price menus 60€–140€. Wed–Sat noon–2pm and 7:30–9pm; Sun noon–2pm.

THE DORDOGNE & THE LOT

by Anna E. Brooke

19

Hilltop villages, medieval castles, prehistoric sites and glorious food—truffles, foie-gras, duck, lamb, veal, cheese, walnuts, strawberries, melons and plums—make the Dordogne and Périgord much loved travel destinations. In this region, we can find Cro-Magnon artwork drawn on the walls of caves, softly sigh at the beauty of the Dordogne River's valley, explore the lofty heights of Rocamadour and, finally, visit Cahors, the ancient capital of Quercy, well known for its robust, deep purple wines made from the Malbec grape.

Though the larger towns are inviting, the countryside is the main attraction here. Villages, carved into the limestone cliffs, overlook the Dordogne River; medieval fortresses peer down from craggy bluffs; and breathtaking cave paintings offer a glimpse of daily, prehistoric life. Allow several days to explore, eat, and simply gaze.

PÉRIGUEUX ★★

485km (301 miles) SW of Paris; 85km (53 miles) SE of Angoulême; 113km (70 miles) NE of Bordeaux; 101km (63 miles) SW of Limoges

Capital of the old province of Périgord, Périgueux stands on the Isle River. In addition to its food products (foie gras and truffles reign supreme here), the town is known for its medieval and Renaissance architecture and its Gallo-Roman ruins. The city is divided into three sections: Le Puy St-Front (the medieval town), on the slope of the hill; the Cité (the old Roman town); and, to the west, the modern town.

Though Périgueux (pop. 30,000) is very pretty, it is basically a sleepy provincial town. Its attractions probably won't hold your interest for more than a day, but you'll likely pass through on your way to the Dordogne Valley and the cave paintings at Les Eyzies.

Essentials

GETTING THERE   At least a dozen **trains** per day arrive from Paris from either Montparnasse or Gare d'Austerlitz (trip time: 3½–4½ hr.; 50€–145€ one-way), around 18 direct trains from Bordeaux (trip time: 1½ hr.; 10€–25€ one-way), and five or six direct trains from Limoges (trip time: 1 hr.; 10€–32€ one-way). For train information, visit sncf-connect.com or call ✆ **36-35.** If you're **driving** from Paris, take A10 south to Orléans and then A20 south to just north of Brive-la-Gaillarde, where you'll pick up the A89 to Périgueux.

The **Office du Tourisme** is at 9 bis pl. du Coderc (tourisme-grandperigueux.fr; ℂ **05-53-53-10-63**). You may want to rent a bike and explore the countryside; a map is available to download on the tourist office website.

Electric bikes can be found at **3ABikes,** 22 Cr. Montaigne (ℂ **05-53-53-15-62**); prices start at 15€ for an hour up to 45€ a day and 175€ week.

Exploring Périgueux & Environs

Give yourself the time to amble through the **Puy St-Front,** Périgueux's well-preserved medieval quarter, rich with ancient houses, cobbled alleyways, and Renaissance facades. It's hard to miss the imposing **Tour Mataguerre,** a 15th-century tower that is all that's left of the city's fortifications. Follow the winding streets up to the **Cathedral St-Front** (see below) and the **place de Coderc,** once a literal pigsty, and later the administrative center of the medieval town. Both a covered market and an outdoor market take place here each day from 7am to 1pm (2pm in summer), the outdoor part of which snakes down to place de la Cautre and the Hôtel de Ville on Wednesdays and Saturdays (7am–1pm).

Périgueux is a treasure trove of Gallo-Roman antiquities. The most visible is the **Tour de Vésone,** a partially ruined site that stands 26m (85 ft.) tall, just southwest of town beyond the railway station. Here you'll see the remains of a Roman temple dedicated to the goddess Vesuna, surrounded by a pleasant garden. The remains of a large 1st-century Gallo-Roman villa were discovered next to the temple, spurring the creation of a sleek new museum, **Musée Gallo Romain Vesunna,** dedicated to everyday Roman life (see below).

Nearby is the **Jardin des Arènes,** a public garden that holds a few remains of an amphitheater that held as many as 22,000 spectators back in the 2nd century. Near the arena are the ruins of the **Château Barrière,** rue Turenne, built in the 11th or 12th century on Roman foundations.

Gastronomy reigns supreme in Périgueux, especially when it comes to foie gras, or "fat liver," which comes from force-fed geese and ducks. (Vegans may want to skip directly to truffles below.) Stores that sell what some call a delicacy (and others animal cruelty) abound. One is **L'Espace Du Sixième Sens,** 6 pl. Saint-Silain (ℂ **05-53-09-24-29**). If you want an adventure, and to see an example of less industrial production methods, head for a goose farm that makes its own foie gras, such as **La Ferme de Puygauthier,** about 15 minutes south of town in Marsaneix (ferme puygauthier.com; ℂ **05-53-08-87-07;** take the D2 and follow signs to Brive). The ducks here are free-range and only fed non-genetically modified corn. There's a shop, of course, selling pâtés and tins of preserved duck, but the really interesting part is the free farm visit (reserve ahead), which shows you where and how the ducks are raised.

Black truffles are another local specialty, and many fans of the delectable mushroom come to the area with only one aim: to eat as many as possible, in as many forms as possible, especially during the **Truffle**

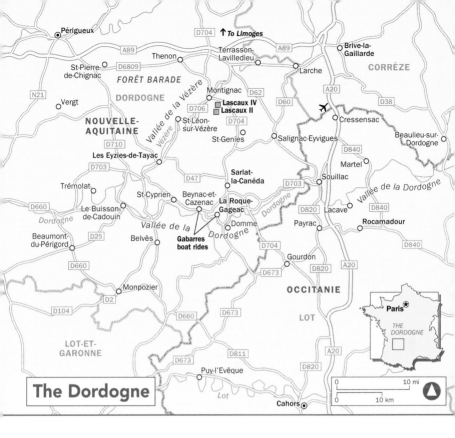

The Dordogne

Festival (Fête de la Truffe) in mid-December. Truffle markets are held during November to March in place St Louis in Périgueux (Wed and Sat), and in a few local villages, most notably in Saint Genies and Brantome.

Cathédrale St-Front ★★★ CATHEDRAL This 12th-century cathedral is one of the rare Byzantine-style churches to be found in France. Left in ruins after the Wars of Religion, it was restored with more than a few 19th-century flourishes by Paul Abadie, who, thus inspired, went on to design the Sacre-Coeur in Paris. With its five white domes and colonnaded turrets, St-Front evokes Constantinople. The cathedral's bell tower is one of the only authentic vestiges of the original church. The interior is built on the plan of a Greek cross, unusual for a French cathedral. The recently restored cloisters, which date from the 9th century, can be visited for a fee of 1.50€.
pl. de la Clautre. amiscathedralesaintfront.fr. ℭ **05-53-53-10-63.** Free admission. Daily 8:30am–7pm (July–Aug until 7:30pm; in winter until 6pm).

Eglise St-Etienne-de-la-Cité ★★ CHURCH Périgueux's other remarkable church—this one in the Cité area—was a cathedral until 1669, when it lost its position to St-Front. The church was built in the 12th century but has been much damaged since. It contains a 12th-century

785

Cathédrale St-Front.

bishop's tomb and a carved 17th-century wooden reredos depicting the Assumption of the Madonna.

10 av. Cavaignac. ℰ **05-53-06-48-10.** Free admission. Mon–Sat 9am–6pm (closed most Sun).

Musée d'Art et d'Archéologie du Périgord (MAAP) ★★ MUSEUM   Built on the site of an Augustinian monastery, this museum has one of the most extensive collections of prehistoric relics in France and is an excellent introduction to the wealth of the Périgord region (as most were found from local digs). A smaller collection of medieval and Renaissance treasures is also on offer.

22 cours Tourny. perigueux-maap.fr. ℰ **05-53-06-40-70.** Admission 6€ adults, 4€ students, free for children 5 and under. Apr–Sept Mon and Wed–Fri 10:30am–5:30pm, Sat–Sun 1–6pm; Oct–Mar Mon and Wed–Fri 10am–5pm, Sat–Sun 1–6pm.

Musée Militaire ★ MUSEUM   You don't have to be a military buff to enjoy this small museum. Its collections of medals, insignia, flags, military uniforms, helmets, badges, and weaponry (from medieval times to today) are well-worth browsing.

32 Rue des Farges. museemilitaire-perigord.fr. ℰ **05-53-53-47-36.** Admission 6€ adults, 3€ students, free for children 17 and under. Daily Mon–Sat 2–6pm.

Vesunna, Site-Musée Gallo Romain ★★★ MUSEUM   This fascinating museum presents extensive vignettes of Roman life based on the ruins of a villa, replete with mosaics and many of the workaday artifacts of everyday life in the ancient Roman provinces. The mainly glass-fronted building was designed by renowned architect Jean Nouvel. A short walk from the center of Périgueux, the site also features several interactive displays, including a 3D movie, and an escape game where players are given 1 hour to unlock an archaeological mystery (over 13s only). Joint tickets for the MAAP (above) can be bought here for 9€ (6€ students).

Rue du 26e Régiment d'Infanterie. perigueux-vesunna.fr. ℭ **05-53-53-00-92.** Admission 6€ adults, 4€ students and children ages 6–25, free for children 5 and under. Oct–Mar Tues–Fri 9:30am–12:30pm and 1:30–5pm, Sat–Sun 10am–12:30pm and 2:30–6pm; Apr–June and Sept Tues–Fri 9:30am–5:30pm, Sat–Sun 10am–12:30pm and 2:30–6pm; July–Aug daily 10am–7pm. Closed 1st and 2nd week of Jan; closed Mon except July and Aug; closed Nov 1 and 11, Dec 25.

Where to Stay

Périgueux does not have a huge amount of choice for places to stay, but there's the decent chain lodging, **Mercure** Périgueux Centre Hotel (all. accor.com; double 118€). The **Château des Reynats** (www.chateau-hotel-perigord.com; double from 94€; also see "Where to Eat," below) also has rooms. Otherwise, try these two places:

Hôtel Bristol ★★   It's not a looker but this place is a good bet if you want to stay central. Fully updated over the past few years, it has comfortable rooms with small but workable bathrooms. It's only a 5-minute walk to the town's best restaurants and major points of interest.

37–39 rue Antoine Gadaud. bristolfrance.com. ℭ **05-53-08-75-90.** 29 units. 74€–102€ double. Free parking. Closed btw. Christmas and New Year's Day. **Amenities:** Room service; free Wi-Fi.

Villa Marguerite ★★   A 10-minute walk from the center, this is a lovely little spot: an early-20th-century family mansion with a linden tree-shaded garden (perfect for al fresco *petit-dejeuner*) and just five bright, vintage inspired bedrooms. It feels as though you're staying in someone's home, and that's what makes it so enjoyable.

7 rue du Parc. chambres-hotes-perigueux.com. ℭ **06-13-76-55-32.** 5 units. 115€–200€ double. **Amenities:** Garden; free Wi-Fi.

Where to Eat

Eating is a major occupation in Périgueux. Stores that sell truffles and foie gras abound, but one of the best known is **L'Espace du Sixième Sens,** 6 pl. Saint Silain (ℭ **05-53-09-24-29**), where visitors can also eat. Fans of the delectable mushroom come from far and wide, especially during the **Truffle Festival** (Fête de la Truffe; perigueux-city.com/fete-de-la-truffe-a-perigueux.html), held 1 day in January.

Au Bien Bon Tome II ★★ TRADITIONAL FRENCH   The name roughly means "at the place that is really good," and this homey restaurant (which has closed and reopened a few times, hence the name Tome II) doesn't disappoint. Hearty portions of *magret de canard* (duck breast in

BIKING & CANOEING DOWN THE dordogne

The Dordogne's rivers meander through countryside that's among the most verdant and historic in France. This area is underpopulated but dotted with monuments, châteaux, 12th-century villages, and charming churches.

As you bike around, the rural character of the area unfolds before you. No château, hotel, or inn treats you disdainfully if you show up on two rather than four wheels. (*Au contraire,* the staff will probably offer advice on suitable bike routes.) If you're ever in doubt about where your handlebars should lead you, know that you'll rarely go wrong if your route parallels the riverbanks of the Lot, the Vézère, the Dordogne, or any of their tributaries. Architects and builders since the 11th century have added greatly to the visual allure of their watersides.

France's national train service, SNCF, makes it easy to transport a bike on the nation's railways. However, if you don't want to bring your own wheels on the train, the region has plenty of rental shops. (Recommended rentals are in this chapter's sections on Périgueux and Les Eyzies-de-Tayac.)

Exploring the rivers by canoe is another option. Every summer, a flotilla of bathing-suited visitors can be seen paddling down the Dordogne; the Lot and the Vézère get less traffic and are also beautiful. The rivers tend to be shallow and lazy, perfect for a family outing.

Le Comité Départemental du Tourism, 25 rue du Président Wilson (dordogne-perigord-tourisme.fr), provides information about all the towns in the *département* and will help you organize biking, hiking, kayaking, and canoeing trips. A popular route to look out for is La Flow Vélo, a 290-km route across Périgord from Thiviers to the Atlantic coast (en.francevelotourisme.com/cycle-route/la-flow-velo).

Two of the best outdoors outfitters are **Canoë Loisir,** Vitrac (canoes-loisirs.com; *☎* **05-53-28-23-43**), and **Canoë Vézère,** St-Léon sur Vézère (canoevezere.com; *☎* **05-53-50-67-71**), or just head to the town of Brantôme, which has several places to pick up canoes.

wine sauce), *andouillette* sausage, duck *confit,* and other regional specialties are on the menu, which changes according to what's good at the market that day. Wash it all down with a glass of the local Bergerac wine and you've had a true southwestern experience.

2 rue Montaigne. facebook.com/aubienbon. *☎* **09-83-85-09-35.** Main courses 13€–18€; fixed-price lunch 15€–18€ or dinner 28€. Tues–Sat noon–1:30pm, Fri 7:30–9:30pm, Sat 7–9:30pm.

Château des Reynats ★★ MODERN FRENCH   This slate-roofed spa hotel, set in a 19th-century manor, has a soft-gray Empire dining room and a bright, bustling glass-roofed conservatory in which you can enjoy consistently excellent regional *cuisine du marché* (dishes cooked with fresh market fare). The place has an interesting history, dating from France's disastrous exit from its former department of Algeria, in 1962, when it functioned as a kind of refugee center for French citizens booted off their estates. You can also stay in the château or l'Orangerie, a comfortable space but less grand than the château. Doubles in the château

Kayaking on the Dordogne River.

range from 113€ to 220€, suites 240€ to 460€, whereas doubles in the guesthouse go for 110€ to 135€.

15 av. des Reynats, Chancelade. www.chateau-hotel-perigord.com. ✆ **05-53-03-53-59.** Main courses 20€–28€. Daily noon–2pm and 7–10pm. Restaurant closed 1st 3 weeks in Jan.

Le Clos Saint Front ★★ MODERN FRENCH Still going strong and delivering innovative takes on local market food, this makes a good choice if you are just a little tired of duck and truffles and want to find a more contemporary (although almost always still rich) menu. It has a lovely garden for summer months, but this is a year-round destination.

5-7 rue de la Vertu. leclossaintfront.com. ✆ **05-53-46-78-58.** Main courses 26€; fixed-price menu lunch 35€ or dinner 42€–78€. Tues and Thurs–Sun 12:30–1:30pm; Tues–Sat 7:30–9:30pm.

L'Essentiel ★★ MODERN FRENCH Book ahead for a chance to dine at Périgueux's one-star Michelin restaurant. The wine list alone is worth the trip, and the food in this family-run establishment is equally good. Service is attentive, ingredients top quality, and food carefully prepared. Diners can start with a dozen oysters in vegetable jelly with creamed crab and a langoustine tartare, followed by a stuffed, roasted half pigeon with caramelized sugar almonds and artichoke, and finish up with a dark chocolate tart with raspberries and almond ice-cream.

8 rue de la Clarté. restaurant-perigueux.com. ✆ **05-53-35-15-15.** Fixed-price lunch and dinner menu 65€–130€; a la carte main courses 31€–53€. Tues–Fri noon–1:15pm and 7:15–9pm; Sat 7:15–9pm.

Périgueux Nightlife

There are a few dance clubs and bars, but alas, none worth mentioning here. So begin your evening with a stroll in the streets and alleyways

789

surrounding **place St-Silain, place St-Louis,** and **place du Marché.** Then do as the locals do and hit a wine bar: **Le Petit Caviste,** 12 rue Saint Front (✆ **06-64-28-97-72**), is open until midnight (Wed–Sat) and serves an eclectic range of wines and gut-busting platters of cheese and charcuterie, while **Le Chai Bordin,** 8 rue de la Sagesse (lechaibordin.com; open until 10pm Thurs–Sat), is known for its excellent organic wines.

LASCAUX (MONTIGNAC) ★★

496km (308 miles) SW of Paris; 47km (29 miles) SE of Périgueux

The **Caves at Lascaux,** 2km (1¼ miles) from the Vézère River town of Montignac in the Dordogne region, contain the most beautiful and most famous cave paintings in the world. Unfortunately, you can't view the actual paintings (the caves have been closed to the public to prevent deterioration), but a precise replica gives you a clear picture of the remarkable works.

Four boys looking for a dog called Robot discovered the caves in 1940. They opened to the public in 1948, quickly becoming one of France's major attractions and drawing 125,000 visitors annually. However, the hordes of tourists caused atmospheric changes in the caves, endangering the paintings. Scientists went to work to halt the destructive fungus plaguing the paintings, known as "the green sickness," and a detailed facsimile was constructed nearby for visitors. The town of Montignac where the Lascaux caves are situated is worth a stop in itself, for its well-preserved medieval streets and houses.

Essentials

GETTING THERE   By far, the easiest way to reach Montignac is to **drive** northeast from Les Eyzies on D706 for 19km (12 miles).

Rail service is to neighboring Condat-Le-Lardin, 9.5km (6 miles) northeast. From there, **taxis** (✆ **05-53-51-80-46**) take visitors to Montignac for 25€. If no taxis are waiting, a railway station employee will call one. For train info, visit sncf-connect.com or call ✆ **36-35.**

VISITOR INFORMATION   For information on Lascaux, visit the website lascaux.fr/en or call ✆ **05-53-50-99-10;** the **Office de Tourisme** in Montignac, on place Bertrand-de-Born (lascaux-dordogne.com; ✆ **05-53-51-82-60**), can also assist. The tourist office does not sell tickets for Lascaux. Online booking is recommended, although for same-day reservations it is best to call Lascaux directly.

Exploring the Caves & Other Attractions

Public visits to the original Lascaux caves ceased in 1963. Permission to visit for research purposes is given only to qualified archaeologists, so unless you've got an advanced degree and good connections, you will have to make do with the replica. That said, Lascaux II is nothing to sniff at. Years of painstaking artistic and scientific labor went into re-creating the cave, including the use of prehistoric painting techniques and natural

Lascaux cave paintings.

colorants. While some of the magic is lost, what you see is virtually identical to the real thing. For more virtual reality, you can visit the original cave online at an extensive site set up by the French government (archeologie.culture.gouv.fr/lascaux/en). More recently, the new Lascaux IV has opened (with Lascaux III being a touring exhibit). Somewhat confusingly, the Lascaux website refers to Lascaux IV as The International Centre For Cave Art, something to bear in mind when buying tickets online. You can also buy combined tickets for both Lascaux sites and Le Thot (check the websites for details).

Lascaux II ★★★ HISTORIC SITE   A short walk downhill from the real cave is the first reproduction of the original, duplicated and molded in concrete to look and feel like the original stone. The 39m (128-ft.) tunnel faithfully reproduces the section of the cave harboring 90% of the famous paintings, so you will get a good idea of what the "Sistine Chapel of Prehistory" looks like. You'll see majestic bulls, ibex, stags, horses, and deer, the originals of which were painted by Cro-Magnon peoples 15,000 to 20,000 years ago. No one has yet figured out exactly what purpose these paintings served, but the artistry of these prehistoric painters is startling. Picnic tables abound in the woods outside, so pack some snacks and soak up the pretty setting. Check online for options on combined tickets with Le Thot.

2km (1¼ miles) from Montignac, off D706. lascaux-ii.fr/en. ✆ **05-53-51-95-03.** Admission 15.40€ adults, 10€ children ages 5–12, free for children ages 4 and under. Daily Apr 8–July 9 10am–1pm and 2–6pm; July 10–Aug 27 9am–7pm; Aug 25–Nov 5 10am–1pm and 2–5pm. Closed Nov 5 to early Apr.

Lascaux IV or the International Centre for Cave Art ★★★

HISTORIC SITE   Open since January 2018 and still very much in demand, the home of the latest replica reveals far more of the cave than previous versions and uses a range of technology to take visitors back 20,000 years. Sections cover the cave's discovery and its position in relation to cave art more generally. The center took 3 years to create and has been integrated into the surrounding landscape. From the outside, Lascaux IV is a clever fissure in the landscape—an angular bunkerlike block carved into the ground. In an interview with design website "designcurial," one of the exhibit's designers, Roger Mann, of Casson Mann (the same scenographers that designed Bordeaux's Cité du Vin), said he wanted visitors to feel as though they were entering the original cave—something that he has achieved. Check online for options on combined tickets with Le Thot (see below).

2km (1¼ miles) from Montignac, off D706. www.lascaux.fr/en/. © **05-53-50-99-10.** Admission 21€ adults, 13.50€ children ages 6–13, free for children ages 5 and under. Daily Jan 23–Apr 7 10am–5pm; Apr 8–July 9 9am–7pm; July 10–Aug 27 8am–10pm; Aug 28–Nov 5 10am–7pm; Nov 6–Dec 31 10am–5pm. Closed 1st 3 weeks in Jan.

Le Thot ★★ ZOO/MUSEUM

This attraction focuses on the ice-age, including Cro-Magnon's hunting techniques and the climatic changes that led to the extinction of species like mammoths. A major part of the attraction is a zoo with animals that look just like those depicted on the walls of Lascaux, such as Przewalski horses and European bison. Young children particularly love seeing the real-life version after their Lascaux visit. Projection rooms show short films on the discovery of cave art at Lascaux. After your visit, walk out on the terrace for a view of the Vézère Valley and the Lascaux hills.

Thonac, 7km (4¼ miles) southwest of Montignac along D706 (follow the signs for Les Eyzies). parc-thot.fr/en/. © **05-53-50-70-44.** Admission 11.50€ adults, 7.20€ children 5–12, free for children 4 and under. Daily Nov 6–Dec 31 and Feb 4–Apr 7 10am–5pm; Apr 8–July 9 and Aug 28–Nov 5 10am–6pm; July 10–Aug 27 9:30am–7pm. Closed Jan. Check online for combined tickets with either Lascaux II or Lascaux IV.

Préhisto Parc ★★ MUSEUM

Around 15km (9 miles) from Lascaux but well worth the detour, this is a child-friendly overview of how Neanderthal and Cro-Magnon man lived. The exhibits are set around a wooded walkway through a 5-hectare (12-acre) park, with recreations of scenes from daily life, such as a Wooly Mammoth hunt, and a family making tools and cooking around an open fire that really bring history to life. Workshops during school holidays and the summer months teach skills such as fire-making, flint-cutting and spear-throwing. **La Madeleine,** a riverside cave village just a few minutes' drive away, also makes an excellent visit.

La Faure Reignac, Tursac. prehistoparc.fr. © **05-53-50-73-19.** Admission 8.50€ adults, 7.50€ students, 4.80€ children 5–13, free for children 4 and under. July–Aug daily 10am–7:30pm. Check with the site directly for openings the rest of the year.

Site Préhistorique de Regourdou ★★ MUSEUM   About 450m (1,476 ft.) uphill from Lascaux, a minor road branches off and runs through a forest until it reaches this site, discovered in 1954 by Roger Constant when he conducted an archeological dig in front of his house. Among the treasures here is a skeleton of a Neanderthal man and several bear skeletons. The house has been made into an archaeological museum; nearby, four semi-wild bears roam around a naturalized and barricaded habitat. Depending on the time of year, you may be required to take a guided tour (available in English and French, at no extra cost).

24290 Montignac-Lascaux. regourdou.fr. ℂ **05-53-51-81-23.** Admission 7€ adults, 4€ children 6–12, free for children 5 and under. July–Aug daily 10am–7pm; Apr 10– June 30, Sept, and Oct 23–Nov 6 11am–6pm; Feb 5–Apr 9, Oct 1–22, and Nov 7–15 1–6pm. Closed late Nov to Jan.

Where to Stay & Eat

Aux Berges de la Vézère ★★ MODERN FRENCH/ITALIAN   This is easily one of the best restaurants in the area, without being fussy or over-polished. It sits right on the banks of the river, with views over the medieval streets on the far banks of the Vézère and a large terrace for the summer months. The bistro-style French menu offers a good range of freshly caught river fish, and a few local surprises such as Périgord bison. Their Italian pizza menu may seem odd, but it is expertly done, with quality touches such as 36-month aged parmesan and 24-month aged Prosciutto ham. Loaner books for children add to the relaxed feeling. In a town where restaurants can be tourist traps in the summer, this is a great choice.

pl. Tourny, Montignac. restaurant-montignac.fr. ℂ **05-53-50-56-31.** Main courses 13€–21€. Sept–June Mon and Thurs–Sat noon–2pm and 7–9pm, Sun and Tues noon–2pm; July–Aug Thurs–Mon noon–2pm and 7–9pm.

Hostellerie la Roseraie ★★   In the heart of the medieval village, this little charmer is both affordable and cozy, complete with a rose garden out back. It was converted from a comfortable home built for a local merchant in the 17th century on the banks of the Vézère. The bedrooms have individual character and well-kept bathrooms with either a tub or shower. There is a pleasant rose terrace to enjoy in summer. The restaurant serves traditional French cuisine (evenings and Sun lunch only; closed Thurs); fixed-price menus cost 32€ to 62€.

11 pl. d'Armes, Montignac. laroseraie-hotel.com. ℂ **05-53-50-53-92.** 14 units. 96€– 128€ double; 155€–245€ family apt. Parking 10€. **Amenities:** Restaurant; bar; outdoor pool; free Wi-Fi. Closed Nov–Apr 8.

Restaurant and Hotel de Bouilhac ★★★   This wonderful hotel occupies a stunning historic chateau from the 17th century, typical of the Périgord Noir style, with an excellent restaurant, right in the heart of town. Gaze over the village rooftops from your rustic-chic room, take a post-massage plunge in the indoor pool, but above all else tuck into exciting regional cuisine by chef Cécile Gallouédec: artichoke with poached egg, quail with peas and feta, and red-fruit mille-feuille, perhaps. Main courses range from 25€ to 33€. It really is a lovely place.

av. du Professeur Faurel, Montignac. hoteldebouilhac-montignac.fr. ⓒ **05-53-51-21-46.** 10 units. From 175€ double; up to 320€ for 4-person room. Free parking. **Amenities:** Restaurant; bar; spa; free Wi-Fi.

LES EYZIES-DE-TAYAC ★★★

533km (330 miles) SW of Paris; 45km (28 miles) SE of Périgueux

When prehistoric skeletons were unearthed here in 1868, the market town of Les Eyzies-de-Tayac (known as Les Eyzies) suddenly became an archaeologist's dream. This area in the Dordogne Valley was found to be one of the richest in the world in ancient sites and deposits. Some of the caves contain primitive drawings made 30,000 years ago. The most beautiful and most famous are at Lascaux (see above), but many caves around Les Eyzies are open to the public.

Essentials

GETTING THERE   **Trains** run from Périgueux (1 hr.). For info, see sncf-connect.com or ⓒ **36-35.** To **drive** from Périgueux, start along D710 southeast to Le Bugue, and then follow the signs to Les Eyzies-de-Tayac.

VISITOR INFORMATION   The **Office de Tourisme** (tourisme-vezere. com; ⓒ **05-53-51-82-60**) is open year-round at 19 av. la Préhistoire (pl. de la Mairie).

Exploring the Area

Many of the caves in this area limit the number of daily visitors they admit; you should therefore try to reserve tickets online several weeks before your visit—especially if you plan to visit in summer. You can hire both classic bikes and electric bikes (if you want to save your legs; some roads get can get hilly) from the snack bar **O'Bison,** at 1 route Sorcier, Les Eyzies (https://sandwicherie-obison.business.site/), for 20€ per day (pedal bike) and 35€ electric. Or you'll find electric bicycles (they don't offer regular bikes) at a self-service stand on place de la Mairie (mobility-parc.net; you'll need to register online beforehand). The first 30 minutes are free, then it's 2€ or 3€ per hour, according to the season. You can also book a tour with **Canoe Loisirs Evasion** (ⓒ **06-33-00-29-19**), open from April to September (canoe24.com/en/welcome/). They offer sightseeing paddles along the Vezère river, past castles and caves, lasting 2 to 6 hours (you can actually see a lot from the water).

　　Whether you're biking or driving, the loveliest villages in the **Dordogne Valley ★★★** include **Sarlat-la-Canéda,** 17km (11 miles) southeast of Les Eyzies, and **La Roque-Gageac,** 14 km (8¾ miles) south of Sarlat. Smaller villages, including **Beynac-et-Cazenac, Castelnaud, Domme,** and **Montfort,** lie beside the road that meanders through the Dordogne

Valley. Throughout the region, routes are country roads marked only with signs leading to the above-mentioned destinations.

Make a special effort to stand in the shadow of the foreboding **Château de Beynac ★★**, Beynac-et-Cazenac (chateau-beynac.com; ✆ **05-53-29-50-40;** daily 9am–8pm; 11.50€ adults, 7€ ages 11–16, ages 10 and under free), a remarkably intact 12th-century fortress that peers out over the Dordogne Valley from a rocky crag. The fortress played an important role in the 100 Years War and at one point was seized by Richard the Lionheart. Today it belongs to Alberic and Audrey de Mongolfier; and has served as a backdrop in several movies, including Luc Besson's *Jean d'Arc*. The view alone is worth the hike up hill; fans of knights in shining armor will surely appreciate the visit, which includes period rooms and a glimpse at truly breathtaking medieval architecture. A free phone app (available when you buy your tickets) serves as an audio guide. Most convenient dining is at the nearby **Hôtel Restaurant du Château** (hotel duchateau.fr; ✆ **05-53-29-19-20).**

Grotte de Font-de-Gaume ★★ HISTORIC SITE   This is one of the last caves with multicolored prehistoric paintings still open to the public (although there are rumors that this, too, will be closed within a few years, so move fast). Only a limited number of visitors are allowed per day, so make sure you reserve online in advance (reservations open 2 weeks before visit date). Or turn up early and be prepared to change your plans. You will be on a 45-minute guided tour (12 per tour; request one in English when you reserve) through a rather narrow cave (claustrophobes beware). Discovered in 1901, the paintings and etchings in the cave date from the Magdalenian period (17,000–9,000 B.C.). While the paintings are not as spectacular as those at Lascaux, here you are seeing the real thing, including depictions of bison, mammoths, horses, and other animals. The knowledgeable guides will point out how prehistoric artists used the shape of the cave walls to make their paintings more lifelike. They may also show some eerie prehistoric hand prints.

On D47, 1.5km (1 mile) outside Les Eyzies. eyzies.monuments-nationaux.fr/en. ✆ **05-53-06-86-00.** Admission 11.50€ adults, free for visitors 18 and under. May 15–Sept 15 Sun–Fri 9:30am–5:30pm; Sept 16–May 14 9:30am–12:30pm and 2–5:30pm.

Grotte des Combarelles ★ HISTORIC SITE   Discovered at the turn of the 20th century, this wide cave on the southeast edge of town is also one of the only caves with visible etchings—over 400 animals, including musk oxen, horses, bison, and aurochs (prehistoric oxen). Think of it as a gallery of Magdalenian art. Advanced reservations required; reservations open 2 weeks before visit date. Daily visits are limited to 60 people.

On D47, 17km (11 miles) north of Bergerac. eyzies.monuments-nationaux.fr/en. ✆ **05-53-06-97-72.** Admission prices and time same as Font-de-Gaume.

Grotte du Grand-Roc ★ NATURAL ATTRACTION   The artistic marvels here are all created by nature, not man; this cave is a geological wonder of crystals, stalagmites, and stalactites. The cave is about 1.5km (1 mile) northwest of Les Eyzies on the left bank of the Vézère (signs point the way on D47). While the venue does not limit visitor numbers, you might still get stuck in a queue in the summer. Ensure you have a sweater, as it gets chilly underground.

Grotte du Grand-Roc, Les Eyzies. semitour.com. ℰ **05-53-06-92-70.** Admission 8.60€ adults, 5.90€ children 5–12, free for children 4 and under. Daily Feb 4–Apr 7 and Nov 6–Dec 31 10am–1pm and 2–5pm; Apr 8–July 9 and Aug 28–Nov 5 10am–1pm and 2–6pm; July 10–Aug 27 10am–7pm. Closed Jan.

Musée National de la Préhistoire ★★ MUSEUM   In the shadow of the limestone cliff that hovers above the village, this museum had a major overhaul and is now set in a modern limestone building next to a fortress-castle from the 16th century.

One of the largest collections of prehistoric artifacts in Europe ("only" 18,000 of its 5 million objects are on display), this museum traces 400,000 years of human history, from the origins to the end of the Ice Age (around 10,000 B.C.). Highlights include the 15,000-year-old bone **etching of a bison** licking its flank★, **tools** dating back 150,000 years and replicas of the **first-known human footprints,** thought to date back about 3.6 million years, as well as a very lifelike statue of a Neanderthal man. Teaching workshops are available for children, but these also need booking an advance.

Musée National de la Préhistoire.

1 rue du Musée, Les Eyzies. musee-prehistoire-eyzies.fr. ℰ **05-53-06-45-45.** Admission 6€ adults, free for ages 18 and under (and for visitors 24 under and from the EU); free to all 1st Sun of month. July–Aug daily 9:30am–6pm; June and Sept Wed–Mon 9:30am–6pm; Oct–May Wed–Mon 9:30am–12:30pm and 2–5:30pm.

Where to Stay & Eat

Hôtel Le Moulin de la Beune ★★   What a lovely spot this is: an ivy-clad 17th-century mill just off the main street, with a tree-shaded garden and a waterwheel fed by a babbling stream. The simple but cozy rooms are nicely decorated with homey touches. In good weather, you can have breakfast on a shaded terrace or just laze in a lounge chair next to the water. The hotel no longer has an on-site restaurant, but its Italian eatery just up the road—the Don Camillo—is a homey spot for pizza.

2 rue du Moulin Bas, Les Eyzies-de-Tayac. moulindelabeune.com. ℰ **05-53-06-94-33.** 20 units. 96€–140€ double. Closed Nov–Apr. **Amenities:** Free Wi-Fi.

Hôtel Les Glycines ★★★ This looker of a hotel has beautiful gardens set among the trappings of the 19th-century building. You get top quality cuisine (courtesy of a bistro and a chic restaurant), comfortable accommodation, and drinks on a veranda with a grape arbor. Rooms are painted in relaxing neutral shades, combining regional charm with designer style. Some rooms look out over the ample, tree-filled grounds. You'll also find a beautiful spa, replete with a sauna and an indoor pool.

The Scoop on Cave Tickets

To prevent deterioration of the art, a limited number of visitors are allowed into **Les Eyzies-de-Tayac** caves each day (specifically Font-de-Gaume and Combarelles), which are now managed by the same ticket office. You can only buy online tickets 2 weeks in advance of your visit, so check the websites. If you do want to try without a ticket, arrive early and have a plan B.

Dishes at the bistro might include pan-fried snails, veal with asparagus and caramel rice pudding (main courses 29€; fixed-price lunch 39€), while the one-star Michelin restaurant ups the game with modern twists on foie gras, cèpes, and truffles (fixed-price menus 75€–135€). Many ingredients come from the hotel's impressive kitchen garden.

Rte. de Périgueux (D47), Les Eyzies-Tayac-Sireuil. les-glycines-dordogne.com. ✆ **05-53-06-97-07.** 25 units. 144€–250€ double; 315€–545€ suite. Closed mid-Nov and Dec. **Amenities:** Restaurant; bar; spa; babysitting; room service; free Wi-Fi.

Restaurant de Laugerie Basse ★ REGIONAL This picturesque, large family restaurant is tucked in an interesting setting just under the troglodyte cliff, close to the Grotte du Grand Roc. It offers local basic Périgueux-style food and also welcomes large groups.

Les Eyzies-Tayac-Sireuil. laugerie-basse.com. ✆ **05-53-06-97-91.** Main courses 16€–19€; fixed-price menus 18€–29€. Closed weekends Halloween to Easter.

SARLAT-LA-CANÉDA ★★★

9.5km (6 miles) E of Les Eyzies-de-Tayac; 530km (329 miles) SW of Paris; 60km (37 miles) NW of Cahors

If Sarlat looks like it could be a movie set, that's because it is so picture perfect that it actually has starred in a dozen or so films, including Luc Besson's *Jean d'Arc,* Robert Hossein's *Les Misérables* in 1982, and Peter Hyams' *D'Artagnan.* You can't come to the Dordogne and not at least take a quick stroll through its narrow streets, a pristine collection of medieval architecture and delightful squares. Unfortunately, you won't be alone, especially if you come in high season. Traffic can snarl as you enter the town, so try to plan your arrival for early morning, or better yet, late afternoon, when everyone is leaving.

Sarlat grew up around a Benedictine abbey back in the 8th century, but its glory days were in the 14th, when it bustled with artisans, painters, and students. Many of the buildings from that era survived, along with other jewels from the Renaissance and subsequent periods, and the town's beauty was such that it was the first to be officially preserved by French law in the 1960s. The **Old Town (Vieille Ville)** ★★★, which has been carefully restored, is as romantic and historic as ever—if anything, it's been overly cleaned up, giving it a slightly Disney-esque feel. If you ignore the tourist traps and wander off down the tiny medieval streets, you will still fall under the spell of this beautiful place.

Essentials

GETTING THERE   About five direct **train** connections arrive daily from Bordeaux (trip time: 2½ hr.; 31€). Trains from Paris take between 5 and 6 hours and pass via Bordeaux. For train info and schedules, visit sncf-connect.com or call ✆ **36-35.** The terminus in Sarlat lies 1km (½ mile) south of the old town. You can walk it in 15 minutes or else take a taxi.

To reach Sarlat from Paris, motorists **drive** the A10 autoroute to Orléans, then the A71 to Vierzon, followed by the A20 to Brive-la-Gaillarde, after which the smaller D roads (1089, 60, 56, and 47) get you to Sarlat's *centre-ville.* Or you can take the A89 from Bordeaux (turning off for the D704 at La Bachellerie). Sarlat lies 180km (112 miles) east of Bordeaux, which takes about 2½ hours.

VISITOR INFORMATION   The **Office de Tourisme,** 3 rue Tourny (sarlat-tourisme.com; ✆ **05-53-31-45-45**), has area maps and offers English-language tours from May to October.

SPECIAL EVENTS   In the summer, the streets of Sarlat are bustling with people, many of whom come to attend the **Féstival des Jeux de Théâtre de Sarlat** (festival-theatre-sarlat.com; ✆ **05-53-31-10-83**), a theater festival that runs from mid-July to the first week of August. During the month of August and into the first week of September, Sarlat also hosts the **Féstival de Musique du Périgord Noir** (festivalduperigordnoir.fr; ✆ **05-53-51-61-61**). The November film festival, **Le Féstival de Film de Sarlat** (festivaldufilmdesarlat.com), is the biggest such event in France after Cannes and Deauville.

Exploring Sarlat-la-Canéda

Start your tour of Old Sarlat at **place du Peyrou** ★★ and allow at least 2 hours to wander around. Opening onto place du Peyrou is the **Cathédral de Saint Sacerdos,** which enjoyed its greatest prestige when it was an Episcopal seat between 1317 and 1790. The cathedral has a Romanesque bell tower, but most of the structure dates from the 16th and 17th centuries with the interior in the late Gothic style. The structure is to the right of the tourist office (see above). Leave by the south doorway.

Behind the cathedral is **Lanterne des Morts** ★★, or "Lantern to the Dead," which was reputedly built in the 1100s to honor St. Bernard's pilgrimage to Sarlat and a fine example of early medieval sepulchral architecture.

The Watcher statue in Sarlat-la-Canéda.

Also opening on place du Peyrou, **Maison de la Boétie ★★** stands opposite the cathedral. You can admire its facade, as it's the most charming Renaissance house in Sarlat. Dating from 1525, the house has mullioned windows and a painted gable. It was once inhabited by the town's most famous son, Etienne de la Boétie, who was born about the time the house was completed. A criminal magistrate, he had a lifelong friendship with Montaigne, who was at La Boétie's bedside when he died in 1563. That death inspired Montaigne's famous essay "Friendship."

The second square to visit is **place du Marché aux Oies ★★**, known for its bronze statue of three geese by Lalanne. For centuries, this market sold live fowl, and the statue commemorates that long-ago role. The most stunning Renaissance facade on this square belongs to Hotel Chassaing.

One of Sarlat's most colorful medieval streets is **rue des Consuls ★★**, whose greatest buildings include **Hôtel Plamon,** its Gothic windows making it look like a church. Beyond the doorway of Plamon is a series of five arcades on the ground floor opening onto a covered market. A trio of Gothic bay windows on the second floor has been restored to its original appearance.

If you follow **Jardin des Enfeus** (behind the cathedral), you reach **rue Montaigne ★★**, where the great 16th-century philosopher was born and once lived. The buildings along this street are extremely photogenic.

Feel free to roam the back streets of Sarlat. You can allow yourself to get lost, as you'll invariably wind up back at **place de la Liberté,** in the center of town, and the 18th-century Hotel de Ville, or City Hall.

Sarlat is celebrated by French gastronomes for its truffle market, **Le Marché aux Truffes,** held December to mid-March at the bottom of rue Fénelon, Saturdays from 9am to noon and on Place de la Liberté Wednesdays after 2:30pm December to February. The first weekend of March honors Sarlat's other specialty: goose, with its raucous **Fest'Oie** festival, which involves demonstrations of goose taming, goose plume calligraphy and goose carving, and plenty of goose eating in all its forms, from foie gras to carcass soup. Sarlat is also known for its wines, and the best selection is found at **Julien de Savignac,** pl. Pasteur (julien-de-savignac.com; ℰ **05-53-31-29-20**).

Château des Milandes ★★★ MUSEUM   Although very impressive, this château is outshone by the star-power of its former owner, the internationally renowned singer and entertainer, Josephine Baker. Born Freda Josephine McDonald in St. Louis, Missouri, Baker rented the château from 1940 and eventually bought it in 1947. Famous for many things, her active role in the French Resistance (for which she was later honored by the nation) is probably the least well-known part of her history. Able to move freely, thanks to her international reputation, she helped refugees leave the country and acted as an informant and courier. Her musical acts at the time also contained coded messages. The home is worth a visit for the history, architecture, gardens, fencing lessons, and birds of prey demonstrations. It is about 30 minutes south of Sarlat-la-Canéda. Allow about 2 hours minimum for a visit.
On D53, Castelnaud-la-Chapelle. milandes.com/en. ℰ **05-53-59-31-21.** Opening times are many, detailed, and changeable; check the website for specifics.

Gabarres de Benac ★★ RIVER RIDE   *Gabarres* are the traditional flat-bottomed boats that used to ply up and down the shallow Dordogne, taking goods from one town to the next. Today they are used for guided river cruises and offer visitors a unique, highly enjoyable way to experience this unspoiled waterway and dramatic landscape. Children go free here on the morning sailings (one child per adult), up to 11:30am and dogs are allowed on board. The departure point is at the end of the car park, opposite the Post Office. A wide range of sailings (up to every 30 min. in high season) are available but much depends on the time of year. Call or check the website for sailing times. This dock is about 20 minutes south of Sarlat-la-Canéda, in the village of Beynac-et-Cazenacbout.
On D46, Beynac-et-Cazenac. www.gabarre-beynac.com. ℰ **05-53-28-51-15.** Admission 9.50€ adults, 5.50€ children 12 and under. Group rates available.

A Side Trip to Gorodka

After a few days exploring the prehistoric and medieval riches of the Dordogne, a trip to **Gorodka, village of modern art** ★★ (gorodka.com; ℰ **05-53-31-02-00** or 06-83-36-77-96), 4km (2 miles) from Sarlat in La Canéda, is a refreshing change. The brainchild of late artist Pierre Shasmoukine, it's all about the now, with exhibits by artists-in-residence, live theater shows, or sculptures and multimedia exhibits, either dotted around a forest with three separate walkways or within eight art galleries displaying over 500 works. Gorodka is only open at night—and many of the works of art start glowing and moving when you least expect them to. The site seems to be constantly threatened by local opposition, but it remains for now one of the most unusual and inspiring sites in the region. Gorodka can be visited daily July and August from 7pm to 11pm and in winter by appointment. Admission 10€ adults, free for children ages 15 and under.

Les Gabarres Norbert ★★ RIVER RIDE   Another top *gabarre* option is Gabarres Norbert, about 20 minutes south of Sarlat-la-Canéda in La Roque-Gageac. It offers three different itineraries (two taking about 50 min. and one that's 1½ hr.), all gliding past several impressive châteaux and chocolate-box landscapes. Audio guides in English provide a historical context to the surrounding landscape.

On D57, La Roque-Gageac. pl. du 8 Mai. www.gabarres.com. ✆ **05-53-29-40-44.** Admission 11.50€ adults, 9€ children 12 and under (for 50 min.), 17€ adults, 13€ children for 1½ hr. Apr–Nov 1 from 9:30am, with last boat departing at 6pm; check ahead to confirm availability and sailings.

Where to Stay

Manoir de la Malartrie ★★★   The most sumptuous way to live in and around Sarlat is at this 19th-century châteaulike mansion in Vézac, filled with antiques and surrounded by glorious cliff-top gardens and rocky terraces that overlook the Dordogne and La Roque-Gageac village. The five rooms all have plush furnishings in reds, creams and beiges, and overlook gardens, river or cliffs. The two apartments almost feel like minilofts, with ample living space, and kitchens for preparing all that lovely produce you'll inevitably bring back from nearby Sarlat. Breakfast is organic and served in either a stately lounge (complete with beamed ceilings and a huge fireplace) or in the garden alongside the heated outdoor pool. Meals and massages are available on request.

Vézac 24220. D57, 12km (7½ miles) from Sarlat on the outskirts of La Roque-Gageac. chambresdhotes-lamalartrie.com. ✆ **05-53-29-03-51.** 7 units. 170€–240€ double; 215€–285€ apt; communicating room for 4 people 340€–395€. **Amenities:** Pool; massage services; evening meals on request; free Wi-Fi.

Naâd Boutique Hôtel ★★   This is one of those well-appreciated, highly central hotels that are incredibly useful when returning for forgotten items, children who need a break, or if you just for a nap. The rooms are comfortable, air-conditioned, and funkily decorated in deep blues and reds with pops of bright art and vintage-inspired furniture. The staff is helpful and the place is LBGTQ friendly too.

48 av. Gambetta. naad-hotel.com. ✆ **05-53-59-40-00.** 25 units. 65€–140€ double. Closed Dec to mid-Mar. **Amenities:** Bar; free Wi-Fi.

Noreli B&B ★★   You're going to be popular with your family if you choose this place—especially if they love ice cream. Well located on the pedestrianized place de la Liberté, this *chambres d'hotes* is housed in an 18th-century building and is full of character. The well-sized bedrooms have slightly old-fashioned private bathrooms. A brasserie and ice cream parlor are on the ground floor, making plans easy with children in the evenings.

9 pl. de la Liberte, Sarlat. ✆ **05-53-29-99-99.** 4 units. From 95€ double; 145€ 4-person suite. **Amenities:** Restaurant; ice-cream parlor; free Wi-Fi.

Where to Eat

Le Bistrot ★★ FRENCH   Just in front of the cathedral, in a pretty stone building, Le Bistrot has a simple menu of IGP products (officially labeled as coming from geographically recognized areas known for their production of this particular product, such as the IGP foie gras du Périgord). Other options include beef tartare, fresh fish, and handmade ice cream. Helpfully the restaurant has opened a sister establishment, Le Petit Bistrot (lepetitbistrot-sarlat.com) about a 5-minute walk from this one, in case it's overbooked for the night.

14 pl. du Peyrou, Sarlat. le-bistrot-sarlat.com. ✆ **05-53-28-28-40.** Fixed-price menus 26€–36.50€; main courses 17€–20€. Mid-Mar to mid-Nov daily 9am–2:30pm and 6:45–9:30pm.

Le Grand Bleu ★★   If you've taken the train to Sarlat, you can tumble out of the station and right into this wonderful restaurant. This might not sound like the best location, but the food here is excellent, with the emphasis, as you would expect, on the many local Périgord ingredients, but given imaginative twists from spices like coriander or ginger, or from techniques like smoking rather than roasting the duck. The 29€ lunch menu (served Thurs–Sat) is an exceptionally good value.

43 av. de la Gare, Sarlat. legrandbleu.eu. ✆ **05-53-31-08-48.** Fixed-price lunch 29€–84€, dinner 39€–84€. Wed 7:30–9pm, Tues and Thurs–Sat 12:30–1:30pm and 7:30–9pm, Sun 12:30–1:30pm. Closed Jan.

ROCAMADOUR ★★★

541km (335 miles) SW of Paris; 66km (41 miles) SE of Sarlat-la-Canéda; 55km (34 miles) S of Brive; 63km (39 miles) NE of Cahors

Rocamadour reached the zenith of its fame and prosperity in the 13th century, when it was one of the most famous pilgrimage sites in Christendom. Countless miracles were said to have taken place here, thanks to the sacred aura of the Chapel of Notre Dame and, specifically, the statue of the Black Madonna. Pilgrims still come (in significantly smaller numbers), but most visitors are secular tourists who come to admire this spectacular village that seems to be carved into sheer rock. It's definitely worth a detour, even if it's out of your way. The setting is one of the most unusual in Europe: Towers, churches, and oratories rise in stages up the side of a cliff above the usually dry gorge of Alzou.

Only around 600 people live in the village year-round, but in the summer that numbers skyrockets during the day, when crowds of tourists arrive. For obvious logistical reasons, vehicles are prohibited in the town; you'll have a lot of stair climbing to do. The faint of heart or the mobility-impaired can take an elevator from the village at the base of the cliff up to the religious sanctuary, and from the religious sanctuary to the château. There's also a tourist train (see below). It's a short walk from the parking lot to the village.

Rocamadour.

Essentials

GETTING THERE   The best way to reach Rocamadour is by **car.** From Bordeaux, travel east along A89 autoroute to Brive-la-Gaillarde, then take the A20 to exit 54 toward Gramat. Then continue on D840 and take the D673 south to Rocamadour.

Rocamadour and neighboring Padirac share a **train** station, Gare de Rocamadour-Padirac, that isn't convenient to either—it's 4km (2½ miles) east of Rocamadour on N140. Trains arrive about three times a day from Brive in the north and six times Capdenac in the south; for transport from the station, your only option is to call a **taxi** (phone numbers posted at the station). For train info, visit sncf-connect.com or call ✆ **36-35.**

VISITOR INFORMATION   The **tourist office** is found on rue Roland-le-Preux (vallee-dordogne.com; ✆ **05-65-33-22-00**).

Exploring Rocamadour

This gravity-defying **village ★★★** rises abruptly across the landscape. Its single street, lined with souvenir shops, runs along the side of a steep hill. It's best seen when approached from the road coming in from the tiny village of L'Hospitalet. Once in Rocamadour, you will want to get from the lower town (Basse Ville) to the **Cité Réligieuse,** a cluster of chapels and churches halfway up the cliff. The main way of getting from bottom to top is a narrow street/staircase that loops and twists its way upward. Called the *Chemin de la Croix,* or the Stations of Christ, it was the route medieval penitents used to make their way to the sacred chapel—the most penitent did it on their knees.

For the unrepentant, and others who are loath to negotiate the town's steep inclines, the town maintains two elevators. One goes from Basse

Ville to Cité Réligieuse, midway up the rocky heights of Rocamadour. The ride costs 2.20€ one-way, 3.20€ round-trip (free for ages 8 and under). It can be combined with tickets from Cité Réligieuse to the panoramic medieval ramparts near the hill's summit for 4.30€ one-way, 6.30€ round-trip. **Le Petit Train de Rocamadour,** a tourist train, also trundles up and down at regular intervals from April to September (10:30am–7pm), for 4€ round-trip adult and 2.50€ ages 5 to 9 (free 4 and under). It's touristy, but it will save your legs.

For a superb **view,** head toward the **Château de Rocamadour,** on a rock spur high above the town center. You can reach it by way of Chemin de la Croix or take the elevator. It was built in the 14th century and restored by the local bishops in the 19th century. Its interior is off-limits, except for guests of the church officials who live and work here. You can, however, walk along its panoramic **ramparts ★★**, which open at 8am daily year-round. Closing times vary, usually just before sunset and no later than 9pm in the summer. Admission to the ramparts costs 2€. *Note:* You must buy your entrance ticket at a machine; be sure to have exact change, or you will have made the trip up for nothing. If possible, try an evening visit when the crowds should have thinned a little.

CITÉ RÉLIGIEUSE ★★★

This cluster of chapels and churches is the town's religious centerpiece, visited by both casual tourists and devoted pilgrims. Site of many conversions, with mystical connotations that date to the Middle Ages, it's accessible from the town on the **Grand Escalier,** a stairway of 216 steps. Climbing the weathered steps will lead you to the **parvis des Eglises,** place St-Amadour, with seven chapels. Volunteers conduct free tours; schedules change frequently, according to holidays and church schedules. Two to five 1-hour tours take place each day (depending on the season); times are prominently posted at the entrance. Guided tours are also available organized by the tourist office over Easter, and July and August from 6.50€ (free for ages 18 and under). The most important churches are detailed below.

Basilique St-Sauveur ★★ RELIGIOUS SITE   Set against the cliff, this small basilica was built in the Romanesque-Gothic style from the 11th to the 13th centuries. It's decorated with paintings and inscriptions recalling visits of celebrated persons, including Philippe the Handsome. sanctuairerocamadour.com. ✆ **05-65-14-10-59.** Free admission; donations appreciated. Suggested donation for tour 6€ adults, 3.50€ children 8–18. Daily winter 8am–6:30pm; spring and autumn 8am–8pm; summer 7am–10pm. Crypt year-round daily 11am–6:30pm.

Chapelle Notre-Dame ★★ RELIGIOUS SITE   This is the *chapelle miraculeuse,* the holy of holies, where St. Amadour is said to have carved out an oratory in the rock (who exactly St. Amadour was, however, is subject of debate). After caving in during the 15th century, it was rebuilt in flamboyant Gothic style, and it underwent various alterations in the 19th century, when it was restored. It shelters the venerated **Black Madonna,** a small sculpture carved out of wood that dates from the 12th century, depicting the Virgin seated with a small Jesus on her knee. Hanging from the roof is a 9th-century **bell** that was rung when a miracle occurred. Outside, above the door leading to the chapel, is an iron sword stuck in the rock that is said to be **Durandal,** the sword of Roland, the legendary 8th-century knight.

sanctuairerocamadour.com. ✆ **05-65-14-10-59.** Daily winter 8am–6:30pm; spring and autumn 8am–8pm; summer 7am–10pm.

Chapelle St-Michel, Chapelle St. Jean-Baptiste, Chapelle St. Anne ★ RELIGIOUS SITE   Sheltered by an overhanging rock on the outside of this Romanesque chapel are two impressive **12th-century frescoes** representing the Annunciation and the Visitation. More frescoes are inside, though many are damaged.

sanctuairerocamadour.com. ✆ **05-65-14-10-59.** Daily winter 8am–6:30pm; spring and autumn 8am–8pm; summer 7am–10pm.

Where to Stay & Eat

Hôtel Le Bellaroc ★★   This is a good option and a good value, well located with views over Rocamadour from across the valley, which are particularly beautiful when illuminated at night. Air-conditioned rooms have simple, tasteful, vintage-inspired décor. Many of then have views—as does the Italian restaurant, which serves pizza and pasta in a modern space with a vast panoramic terrace, a fab spot for dinner on a summer evening. There's also an outdoor pool for a dip after a long day's sightseeing. The owners also have another charming hotel and restaurant, Le Belvedere, just down the road, though its rooms aren't air-conditioned (68€–71€ double).

Route de la Corniche 46500. www.hotel-bellaroc.com. ✆ **05-65-33-63-06.** 12 units. 54€–71€ double. Free parking. Closed Dec–Mar. **Amenities:** Restaurant; bar; outdoor pool; free Wi-Fi.

Le Beau-Site ★★   Smack bang in the middle of the medieval town, with terraces overlooking the verdant valley, this hotel's location is pretty unbeatable. The stone walls were built in the 15th century by an Order of Malta commander, Jehan de Valon (1440–1516). Today the rear terrace provides a view of the Val d'Alzou. The reception area has heavy beams and a cavernous fireplace. Rooms are comfortable, air-conditioned and tastefully decorated; many have beautiful views, and some have bathtubs. Family rooms for up to four people have a small staircase, leading to a mezzanine sleeping area. The restaurant affords breathtaking views and serves regional cuisine prepared by chef Xavier Menot, whose family has owned the place for generations. Fixed-price menus cost 40€ at lunch and dinner, with main courses ranging from 19.50€ to 33€. The kids' menu costs 14€.

Cité Médiévale. beausite-rocamadour.com. ✆ **05-65-33-63-08.** 32 units. 90€–135€ double; 113€–165€ family room. Free parking. Pets stay for free. Breakfast 14€. Closed mid-Nov to mid-Feb. **Amenities:** Restaurant; bar; free Wi-Fi.

Where to Stay & Eat Nearby

Hotel Château de La Treyne ★★★   With sections dating from the 14th and 17th centuries, this splendid château sits on the edge of a particularly tranquil bend of the Dordogne River. The owner points out that this is one of the cleanest rivers in France and is itself a UNESCO World Heritage Site. It's open for dry and wet fly fishing; typical catches include pike and trout. The hotel is blessed with lush grounds of about 120 hectares (300 acres) of forest for hiking and truffle hunting, and a classic French garden. River kayaking, canoeing, and tennis are on offer. There's also a heated outdoor pool. The spacious rooms and even larger suites, which can sleep up to five people, feature plush fabrics, antiques, and exposed beams; the more luxurious ones feel like private apartments from another era. The restaurant (Sun–Mon lunch; dinner available Thurs–Tue) has been awarded a Michelin star for chef Andrieux's delectable creations. Set menus from 128€ to 182€.

Lacave. chateaudelatreyne.com. ☏ **05-65-27-60-60.** 17 units. 396€–585€ double; from 600€ suite. Closed mid-Nov to Christmas and Jan to mid-Mar. Take the D43 from Rocamadour to Souillac, and you will find Lacave. **Amenities:** Restaurant; bar; heated outdoor pool; tennis court; free Wi-Fi.

Hôtel Troubadour ★★★   In a handsome converted farmhouse surrounded by rolling hills, this quaint hotel, just 3km (2 miles) from Rocamadour, is the perfect spot to escape the crowds. The rooms are spotless and fresh, with simple country-style wood furnishings and modern bathrooms. There are apartments for 4 or 5 people in an annex in the surrounding gardens, which also house a *gariotte,* a circular stone hut once used by shepherds watching their sheep. The owners recently planted *truffiers* (oak trees that allow truffles to grow), and offer morning truffle hunting demonstrations with their shaggy brown dog, Toupie. If you're lucky, they'll even add a few home-grown truffles to your breakfast eggs! Or you pick some up (along with other local produce, like foie gras, soap, walnuts, wine…) in the hotel shop.

3km (2 miles) from Rocamadour on the D32, then off the D673. hotel-troubadour. com. ☏ **05-65-33-70-27.** 14 units. 69€–155€ double; 145€–350€ apt. Closed mid-Nov to late March. **Amenities:** Bar; Outdoor pool; billiards; free Wi-Fi.

CAHORS ★★

541km (335 miles) SW of Paris; 217km (135 miles) SE of Bordeaux; 89km (55 miles) N of Toulouse

The ancient capital of Quercy, Cahors was a thriving university city in the Middle Ages, and many antiquities from its illustrious past remain. Today Cahors is best known for the red wine that's made principally from the Malbec grapes grown in vineyards around this old city. Firm but not harsh, Cahors is one of the most deeply colored fine French wines.

Since the mid-1990s, the city of Cahors has funded the redesign and replanting of at least **20 municipal gardens** laid out in medieval patterns, using historically appropriate plants. The most spectacular of these lie immediately adjacent to Town Hall. Together they function as a magnet for horticultural societies throughout France.

Essentials

GETTING THERE   To **drive** to Cahors from Toulouse, follow the A62 autoroute north to the junction with A20 and continue on A20 north into Cahors. **Trains** serve Cahors from Toulouse, Brive, and Montauban. For train information and schedules, visit sncf-connect.com or call ✆ **36-35.** Infrequent **bus** service connects some of the outlying villages, several of which are of historical interest, but it's vastly easier to drive.

VISITOR INFORMATION   The **Office de Tourisme** is on place François-Mitterrand (cahorsvalleedulot.com; ✆ **05-65-53-20-65**).

SPECIAL EVENTS   The **Festival du Blues** turns this town upside down for a week in mid-July, when blues groups descend. Most of the performances are free outdoor affairs along boulevard Gambetta. Main concerts are usually at the open-air **Théâtre des Verdures,** a courtyard in the heart of the medieval city. Ticket prices vary, but the average is about 40€. For exact dates and information, contact the Office de Tourisme (see above) or visit the site of **Cahors Blues Festival** (cahorsbluesfestival.com). You can buy tickets on the website or at any Fnac bookstore (www.fnac.fr). Every year at the end of June and early July the **Lot of Saveurs** festival turns the city into a whopper of a gourmet hub, with food events, markets and an outdoor banquet for over 2,000 people. Info and meal tickets can be found at lotofsaveurs.fr.

Exploring the Area

The town is on a rocky peninsula almost entirely surrounded by a loop of the Lot River. It grew near a sacred spring that still supplies the city with

water. At the source of the spring, the **Fontaine des Chartreux** stands by the side of **Pont Valentré ★★** (also called Pont du Diable), a bridge with a trio of towers. It's a magnificent example of medieval defensive design erected between 1308 and 1380 and restored in the 19th century. The pont, the first medieval fortified bridge in France, is the most eye-catching site in Cahors, with crenelated parapets, battlements, and pointed arches.

Dominating the old town, the **Cathédrale St-Etienne ★★**, 30 rue de la Chantrerie (✆ **05-65-35-27-80**),

Pont Valentré.

was begun in 1119 and reconstructed between 1285 and 1500. It was the first cathedral in the country to have cupolas, giving it a Romanesque-Byzantine look. One remarkable feature is its sculptured Romanesque north portal, carved around 1135 in the Languedoc style. It's open daily from 9am to 7pm; in winter the cathedral is closed Sunday mornings.

> ### Tasting Cahors Wine
>
> You cannot come to Cahors and not sample its most famous export: Malbec red wine! Nicknamed the "black wine" after the deep, blackish red color it gets from its Malbec grapes, the wines are suave and full-bodied, with notes of red fruit and spices, and constitute some of the southwest's best vintages, along with Bordeaux. One of the loveliest places to try it, is at **Château Lagrezette** (chateau-lagrezette.com; ✆ **05-65-20-07-42**), a stunning stone castle and vineyard, 11km (7 miles) west of Cahors. It's open daily July and August from 10am to 7pm for tastings and offers tours of the *chai* (cellars). Or it has its own shop, right by the Pont Valentré (Allée des Soupirs).

Adjoining the cathedral are the remains of a Gothic cloister from the late 15th century.

The **Musée de Cahors Henri-Martin,** 792 rue Emile Zola (www.museehenrimartin.fr; ✆ **05-65-20-88-88**), is also worth an hour of browsing with its extensive range of 18th- and 19th-century art.

The Romans left their mark on Cahors too, with parts of an amphitheater visible in a parking lot under allée Fenélon and the more impressive **L'Arc de Diane,** the vestiges of a thermal baths and a frigidarium on rue Emile Zola. Other fine buildings to seek out include **La Halle,** a 19th-century covered market (place St. Maurcie) dripping with delectable food stalls, and the medieval houses that lines the narrow streets of Rue du **Docteur Bergougnoux** and Rue du **Château du Roi.** Ask at the tourist office for their suggested walking itineraries.

Where to Stay

Brit Hôtel Le Valentré ★ Hotel choices are limited in Cahors, although the stock has grown recently. The Brit Hotel is a chain offering in the historic center, only about 200m (656 ft.) from the train station, with simple, but comfortable rooms and a handy parking lot 8€ per day.

252 av. Jean-Jaurès. cahors-valentre.brithotel.fr. ✆ **05-65-35-16-76.** 70 units. 70€–117€ double. Parking 8€. **Amenities:** Baby cots (5€); free Wi-Fi.

Hôtel Chartreuse ★★ This hotel on the banks of the River Lot about 5 minutes from the town center gives you the choice of hill or river views. Traditional Quercy and French cooking is available in the restaurant (fixed-price menus 22€–32€, main courses 15€). Pilgrim's Packages are available for those on the Saint-Jacques-de-Compostelle route and have a Pilgrim's Passport.

130 chemin de la Chartreuse. la-chartreuse.com. ✆ **05-65-35-17-37.** 50 units. 75€–162€ double. **Amenities:** Restaurant; free Wi-Fi.

Hôtel Terminus ★★ On the avenue leading from the railway station into the heart of town, this hotel oozes turn-of-the-20th-century character with its original stone construction and a fabulous 1920s-style bar. Rooms are conservative yet tasteful, with floral prints, fresh flowers, and firm beds. On the premises is an excellent bistro specializing in regional dishes from the surrounding Périgord-Quercy district. Fixed-price menus are 29€.

5 av. Charles de Freycinet. terminus-1911.fr. ✆ **05-65-53-32-00.** 21 units. 65€–110€ double; 105€–140€ suite. Free courtyard parking, 9€ in garage. Closed last 2 weeks in Nov. **Amenities:** Restaurant; bar; room service; free Wi-Fi.

Where to Eat

La Petite Auberge ★★ TRADITIONAL FRENCH   Sophisticated regional food is served here, in an old brick and stone work building, on the outskirts of the old town, with a small terrace for summer dining. The atmosphere is warm and welcoming and generally busy but accommodating. The wine list focuses on regional wines and (rare for the region) there are vegetarian dishes on the menu. Open Monday nights, which is very useful in a country where many places can be closed.

134 rue Saint-Urcisse. lapetiteaubergecahors.com. ✆ **05-65-35-06-05.** Fixed-price menu 30€ and 40€; main courses 17€–25€. Daily noon–2pm and 7–9pm.

Le Coin des Halles ★★ TRADITIONAL FRENCH   Just a few steps from the main market, right in the center of town, this is one of the less pricey options. The good food here often comes directly from the nearby market with the signature dish being the DropBurger (a rugby ball-shaped burger sponsored by famed French chef Thierry Marx), a nod to one of the restaurant's most faithful clients, a local figure of the rugby world. Above the restaurant are also 17 hotel rooms. They are clean and basic and cost 50€ to 87€ for a two- or four-person room.

30 pl. St. Maurice. coin-des-halles.com; ✆ **05-65-30-24-27.** Fixed-price menus 13€–25€. Mon–Sat noon–1:30pm, Wed–Sat 7:30–9:30pm.

L'O à la Bouche ★★★ MODERN FRENCH   One of Cahors's best brasseries is in a restored mansion from the turn of the 20th century in the center of town. Meals at this popular spot might include fresh trout from the Pyrénées served with leeks in vinaigrette, and Quercy lamb flavored with walnuts and Esplette peppers, all depending on what chef Jean-Francois Dive has found locally. The wine list includes an excellent sampling of Cahors vintages but also draws its bottles from further afield in France. Reservations recommended.

56 allée Fénelon. loalabouche-restaurant.com. ✆ **05-65-35-65-69.** Fixed-price menu 23€–30€ lunch and 30€–65€ dinner. Tues–Sat noon–1:30pm and 7–9:30pm.

LIMOGES ★★

396km (246 miles) S of Paris; 311km (193 miles) N of Toulouse; 93km (58 miles) NE of Périgueux

Limoges, the ancient capital of Limousin in west-central France, is world famous for its exquisite porcelain and enamel works. Enamel production is a medieval industry revived in the 19th century and still going strong. In fact, Limoges is the economic capital of western France. Occupying the Vienne's right bank, the town has historically consisted of two parts: La Cité (aka Vieux Limoges), with its narrow streets and old *maisons* on the lower slope, and La Ville Haute (aka "Le Château," although no castle remains), at the summit.

Essentials

GETTING THERE Limoges has good **train** service from most regional cities, with direct trains from Toulouse, Poitiers, and Paris. Twelve or so trains depart daily from Paris's Gare d'Austerlitz for Limoges (trip time: 3½ hr.; prices vary, but from about 60€ one-way). About 14 trains a day arrive from Périgueux (trip time: 1 hr.; from about 17€ one-way). For complete train information, sncf-connect.com or call ✆ **36-35.** If you're **driving** from Périgueux, take N21 north for the 1½-hour trip. If driving from Cahors, take A20 north for the 2-hour trip.

VISITOR INFORMATION The **Office de Tourisme** is at 12 bd. de Fleurus (destination-limoges.com; ✆ **05-55-34-46-87**).

Exploring Limoges

Don't be put off by the outskirts of Limoges, which are frankly gray and dismal. In the town center you'll find lovely half-timbered districts (seek out the Quartier de la Boucherie, the former medieval butcher area around Rue de la Boucherie), buzzing with shops and restaurants, quaint old churches, top-notch museums and the refurbished 19th-century **Halles** (covered food market; leshallescentraleslimoges.fr), easily one of the best

Limoges.

in the region. Sadly, the porcelain workshops no longer offer opportunities for the public to make their own porcelain. However, you can still admire the result of the rich deposits of kaolin clay (known locally as "white gold") found near Limoges in the 18th century. More than 30 porcelain manufacturers have set up operations here through the years. Many of the most famous maintain shops that offer good-quality seconds at reduced prices, as well as items from out-of-date collections, and, of course, the new collections. One of the best is the **Fondation Bernardaud,** 27 av. Albert-Thomas (bernardaud.com; ℂ **05-55-10-21-86**), where as well as the ceramics, regularly changing exhibitions of "super super contemporary" (as the director said) artistic porcelain are on display. Guided visits are available all year (reserve in advance online). Other options are the **Magasin d'usine Raynaud,** 14 ancienne rte. d'Aixe (www.raynaud.fr; ℂ **05-55-01-77-65**), and **Porcelaines Philippe Deshoulières-Lafarge,** 21 rue de la Mauvendière (www.deshoulieres.com; ℂ **05-55-50-33-43**), which highlights the eco-friendly nature of its raw materials and production processes.

Basilique St-Michel-des-Lions ★★ CHURCH   Two stone lions guard the entrance to this church (which Rome gave basilica status in 2023). Constructed between the 14th and 16th centuries, it features a typically Limousin bell tower surmounted by a strange copper globe and splendid vaulting supported by slender pillars. Despite its name, the church is the center of the cult of St-Martial, a Limoges hometown bishop who died in the 3rd century. The church is the home of what's reputed to be his skull, stored in an elaborately enameled reliquary. Les Ostensions is a religious pilgrimage, established in 994, that occurs every 7 years from February to November. The skull, La Châsse de St-Martial—which some believers credit with healing powers—is removed from storage and exhibited as part of religious processions (which take place all over France, although this is the only one in Limoges) that attract tens of thousands of devout adherents. The next such procession is scheduled for 2030. A smaller ceremony, when the skull is brought out into the church, also takes place every year on the day of St-Martial.

pl. St-Michel. ℂ **05-55-34-46-87** (Tourist Office) or 05-55-34-18-13 (church). Free admission. Daily 9am–7pm.

Cathédrale St-Etienne ★★★ CATHEDRAL   The cathedral was begun in 1273 and took years to complete. The choir was finished in 1327, but work continued in the nave until almost 1890. The cathedral is the only one in the old province of Limousin built entirely in the Gothic style. The main entrance is through Porte St-Jean, which has carved wooden doors from the 16th century (constructed at the peak of the Flamboyant Gothic style). Inside, the nave appears so harmonious it's hard to imagine that its construction took 6 centuries. The rood screen is of particular interest, built in 1533 in the ornate style of the Italian Renaissance. The cathedral also contains some bishops' tombs from the 14th to the 16th centuries.

pl. de l'Evêché. cathedrale-limoges.fr. ✆ **05-55-34-46-87.** Free admission. Daily Nov–Mar 9am–5pm; Apr–Oct 9am–6pm.

Centre de la Mémoire, Oradour-sur-Glane ★★★ MUSEUM

It's well worth the 22km (13-mile) drive north of Limoges to see this hard-hitting WWII place of remembrance—part museum, part village left exactly as it was found after the Nazis decimated both its population and buildings on June 10, 1944. The unique, fully preserved settlement—chilling and moving in equal measures—is where 642 people (247 of which were children) were massacred in the worst Nazi killings of civilians recorded in France. The museum carefully documents the rise of Nazism and France's role under the Vichy Regime, before linking events to what happened in Oradour. Not for the faint-hearted, but it's an incredibly important place to see.

L'Auze, Oradour-sur-Glane, 87520. oradour.org. ✆ **05-55-43-04-30.** Admission 7.80€ adults, 5.20€ ages 10–18, free for children ages 9 and under. Daily Nov–Feb 9am–4pm; Mar–May and Sept–Oct 9am–5pm; May–Sept 9am–6pm.

Musée des Beaux-Arts de Limoges ★★ MUSEUM

This museum has an outstanding collection of spectacularly colored enamels (said to be the best in Europe outside those in the Hermitage in St. Petersburg, Russia) and a range of Limoges porcelain from the 12th century to the present day. Other attractions include a 2,000-piece Egyptian collection; archeology finds; and sculptures and fine art, including works by Auguste Renoir, the impressionist painter who was born in Limoges in 1841. The main part of the museum is housed in the 18th-century archbishops' palace with luminous modern galleries for temporary exhibitions. The Jardins de l'Evêché (botanical gardens), which offer a view of the Vienne and the 13th-century pont St-Etienne, surround the museum. See the website for an events calendar.

1 pl. de l'Evêché. beauxarts.limoges.fr. ✆ **05-55-45-98-10.** 5€ adults, free for visitors 26 and under, jobseekers, disabled, and other categories with special dispensations; free to all 1st Sun of every month. Mon and Thurs–Fri 9:30am–noon and 1:30–5:30pm; Sat–Sun 1:30–5:30pm. Check website for annual closures.

Musée National de la Porcelaine Adrien-Dubouché ★★ MUSEUM

This is the largest museum in Europe for Limoges porcelain, and the largest in in the world on global ceramic history. It has 18,000 pieces, 5,000 of which are on display, which illustrate the history of glassmaking and ceramics (porcelain, earthenware, stoneware, and terra cotta) throughout the ages, starting with Ancient History and moving toward the present. In France, its porcelain collection is second in quantity only to that of Sèvres. The modern building of glass, metal, and porcelain, sits alongside the traditional 19th-century space to offer a vast exhibition area of 7,200 sq. m (77,500 sq. ft.). For English-speaking visitors, the museum has iPads with exhibit explanations in English (free). There's also an app for personal download. The museum shop (no ticket required) sells a lovely range of souvenirs, from books to porcelain jewelry. The website details a range of temporary exhibitions and events.

8 bis pl. Winston-Churchill. musee-adriendubouche.fr/en. ℂ **05-55-33-08-50.** Admission 7€ adults, free for visitors 25. Wed–Mon 10am–12:30pm and 2–5:45pm. Closed Dec 25 and Jan 1.

Where to Eat & Stay

Les Échoppes Gogaille ★★ FRENCH   This smart bistro close to the Halles food market is full of locals and a warm and convivial atmosphere. Choices are classic: sausage with potato purée, steak tartare, and matured ribs of beef. If you don't fancy a blow-out meal, come for wine and platters of locally sourced cheese and charcuterie. **La Loge Gogaille** is a brilliant boutique hotel, with 13 vintage-inspired rooms and 4 apartments in an apartment building, a 2-minute walk from the restaurant (prices start at 96€ double). The bonus? Gogaille also owns one of Limoges' best bakeries, so the breakfast croissants are to die for.

8 rue Adrien Duboucher. gogaille.fr. ℂ **09-74-99-32-32.** Fixed-price lunch 19€; main courses 17€–23€. Tues–Sat 10am–11pm (until 1am Fri–Sat).

La Tables du Couvent ★★ FRENCH   In a former convent, this restaurant is known for its bistro food including veal, terrines, various egg dishes, and a range of Limousin beef cooked on an open fire. It also offers cooking courses every Wednesday and Saturday, from 3pm to 5pm; an on-site shop sells freshly made pasta, olive oil, and other goodies including kitchen accessories. Weekly menus depend on seasonal produce, but expect fresh local ingredients put together with imagination and a delicate touch.

15 Rue Neuve des Carmes. www.latableducouvent.com. ℂ **05-55-32-30-66.** Main courses 11€–40€. Tues 7–10pm, Wed–Sat noon–2pm and 7–10pm, Sun noon–2pm.

PLANNING YOUR TRIP & USEFUL PHRASES

By Tristan Rutherford & Kathryn Tomasetti

20

Of almost any destination in the world, flying into France is one of the most effortless undertakings in global travel. There are no immunizations to get and no particular safety precautions, and more and more French people now speak English. With your passport, airline or train ticket, and enough money, you just go. In the pages that follow, you'll find everything you need to know to plan your trip: getting around the country, deciding when to go, and much, much more.

GETTING THERE

By Plane

The two Paris airports—**Orly** (airport code: ORY) and **Charles de Gaulle** (airport code: CDG)—are about even in terms of convenience to the city's center. Orly, the older of the two, is 13km (8 miles) south of the center; Charles de Gaulle is 22km (14 miles) northeast. Air France serves Charles de Gaulle (Terminal 2E) from North America. Direct flights from the land at both airports. Flight status and transport information for both airports can be found online (www.aeroportsdeparis.fr). If you're heading to the South of France, **Nice Côte d'Azur** (airport code: NCE; www.nice.aeroport.fr) is served seasonally by direct flights from Atlanta and New York.

Most airlines charge their lowest fares between November and mid-March. The shoulder season (Oct and mid-Mar to May) is a bit more expensive, but we think it's the ideal time to visit France. For inexpensive fares year-round from the United States, look into two relatively new upstart airlines: French Bee (www.frenchbee.com) and **Norse Atlantic Airways** (https://flynorse.com). Alternatively, Icelandic carrier **PLAY Airlines** (www.flyplay.com) also offers cheap flights, although it makes a short stop in Reykjavik en route.

By Train

Paris is one of Europe's busiest rail junctions, with trains departing from its seven major stations every few minutes. If you are in the U.K., Germany, Holland, Italy, or Spain, our recommendation is to travel to the country by train.

Eurostar (www.eurostar.com; ✆ **44 (0)3432 186 186** from the U.S.) links London directly with Paris Gare du Nord station from as little as $65 one-way; trip time just over 2 hours. It also runs a direct route to Disneyland Paris. (In the past, there have been direct trains from the London to Lyon, Avignon, Marseille, and Aix-en-Provence. Although these routes were "temporarily" suspended at the time of writing—a holdover from the pandemic—it would be well worth checking if they've been reinstated.) Trips from London can be booked online to any major station in France. For the best deals, book as tickets become available exactly 6 months in advance (although tickets between London and Paris are available up to 11 months in advance).

By Bus

Paris is a major arrival and departure point for Europe's largest bus operator, **Flixbus** (www.flixbus.com). Its buses leave from various points around the city, including the Gare Routière de Bercy-Seine (Métro: Bercy or Dugommier). Standard singles to London start around $35; trip time is approximately 8 to 9 hours. Long-haul buses are equipped with toilets, and they stop at mealtimes for rest and refreshment. Tickets must be purchased online before you travel.

By Car

The major highways into Paris are A1 from the north (Great Britain and Benelux); A13 from Rouen, Normandy, and northwest France; A11 from Nantes and the Loire valley; and the A6 from Lyon, Provence, the Riviera, and Italy.

By Boat from England

Ferries and hydrofoils operate day and night from the English Channel ports to Normandy. The major routes include at least 12 trips a day between Dover or Folkestone and Calais or Boulogne. Ferries often drop passengers off by the rail junction of each port.

Various ferry operators cross the channel for multiple ports in France. **P&O Ferries** (www.poferries.com; ✆ 03-66-74-03-25) operate car and passenger ferries between Dover, England and Calais, France. **Brittany Ferries** (www.brittanyferries.com; ✆ 0330/159-7000) operates ferry services from Portsmouth to Cherbourg, Caen, Le Havre or St. Malo, France; from Poole, England to Cherbourg, France; and from Plymouth, England to Roscoff, France. **DFDS Seaways** (www.dfds.co.uk; ✆ 0871/574-7235 in the U.K.) sail three times daily between Newhaven and Dieppe; and dozens of times daily between Dover and Calais and Dover and Dunkirk.

SPECIAL-INTEREST TRIPS & TOURS

Language Classes

The **Alliance Française,** 101 bd. Raspail, Paris 75006 (www.alliancefr. org; ✆ 01-42-84-90-00), is a nonprofit French-language teaching organization with a network of 800 establishments in 133 countries. Its school in Paris is open all year; courses range from 2 weeks (6 hr./week; 190€) to an intensive 4-week (18 hr./week; 1,350€).

Just outside Nice, the **Institut de Francais,** 23 av. Général-Leclerc, Villefranche-sur-Mer 06230 (www.institutdefrancais.com; ✆ 04-93-01-88-44), offers highly acclaimed month-long French immersion courses. Each day includes 8 hours of lessons, plus breakfast and lunch taken together with professors, and cost 5,800€.

A clearinghouse for information on French-language schools is **Lingua Service Worldwide** (www.linguaserviceworldwide.com; ☎ **800/394-5327**). Its programs are available in many cities throughout France. Cost ranges from around $200 to $2,500 per week, depending on the city, the school, and number of lessons per week.

Adventure Trips

ACTIVE VACATIONS Headwater (www.headwater.com; ☎ **44 (0)1606 720 199** from the U.S.) offers family-friendly, self-guided canoeing holidays on the Dordogne River. Participants paddle past postcard-perfect perched villages and troglodyte cave dwellings. Prices start at $2,879 per person for 8 days, including all accommodation and some meals.

For serious cycling enthusiasts, **Sports Tours International** (www.sportstoursinternational.co.uk; ☎ **06-47-97-97-75**) organizes Ride & Watch packages during the world's most exciting cycling race, the annual Tour de France.

Exodus Travels (www.exodustravels.com; ☎ **844/227-9087**) also offer adventure travel around France, from white water rafting to Alpine hiking. Their 1-week tour, "Wine, Walks & Chateaux of the Loire Valley," costs $3,600.

BARGE CRUISES Before the advent of rail, many crops, building supplies, raw materials, and finished products were barged through France on a series of rivers, canals, and estuaries. Many of these waterways retain their old-fashioned locks and pumps, allowing shallow-draft boats easy access through idyllic countryside.

European Waterways (www.europeanwaterways.com; ☎ **800/394-8630**) operates cruises departing from all around France, as well as the possibility of privately chartering an entire barge for your group (6–20 passengers). Trips include a 7-night tour from Marseille up the Canal du Midi to rural Provence. Fares start for this voyage start around 4,400€ per person (based on double occupancy) including bike tours, vineyards visits, and all meals and drinks.

It's also possible to captain your own boat on rivers around France. **Le Boat** (www.leboat.com) is the leading company for these types of adventures, renting boats that can sleep up to 8 people, starting at $1389 per week for a couple, and going up for larger boats. Boats include full kitchens, and multiple bedrooms and bathrooms. No experience is necessary: A 1- to 2-hour lesson in steering, boat maintenance, and navigating locks is included in the cost of a rental.

A number of France's rivers are also plied by luxury river cruises from such companies as **Ama Waterways, Avalon Waterways, Croisi River Cruises, Viking River Cruises, Tauck, Uniworld River Cruises,** and other companies. To compare all the options—and this form of travel *is* pricey, often starting at $500 a day per person—look at a cruise marketplace site such as **CruisesOnly.com** or **CruiseCritic.com.** Frommer's also has an excellent guide to river cruising.

Food & Wine Trips

The famous/infamous Georges Auguste Escoffier (1846–1935) taught the Edwardians how to eat. Today the Hôtel Ritz maintains the **Ecole Ritz Escoffier,** 15 pl. Vendôme, Paris 75001 (www.ritzescoffier.com; ✆ **01-43-16-30-50**), with culinary, cocktail, and pastry workshops, as well as professional-level courses and lessons for kids.

Established in 1895, **Le Cordon Bleu,** 13-15 Quai André Citroën, Paris 75015 (www.cordonbleu.edu; ✆ **01-85-65-15-00**), is the most famous French cooking school, where Julia Child learned to perfect her *pâté brisée* and *mousse au chocolat.* The best-known courses last 9 months and cost 33,400€, including equipment and uniform, after which you are awarded a certificate. Many enthusiasts prefer a less intense immersion, opting for a 2-day bread-making workshop (from 510€) or a 1- to 2-hour cooking demonstration (from 60€).

Less formal but equally enjoyable are the cooking classes offered by **La Cuisine Paris,** 80 quai de l'Hôtel de Ville, 75004 (www.lacuisineparis. com; ✆ **01-40-51-78-18**), a friendly school set up by a Franco-American team. It organizes small classes by professional chefs in both French and English, including the popular French Macaron Class (79€). Other courses include French Bistrot Lunches and Le Croissant & Breakfast Pastries (both 109€). Alternatively, **Les Caves du Louvre** (www.cavesdulouvre. com; ✆ **01-40-28-13-11**) offers English guided tours of former royal wine cellars (50€, including a *dégustation* of three wines). Plus, serious oenophiles can create their own wines in one of the workshops (85€).

On Rue Tatin (www.onruetatin.com) is a Paris-based cooking school taught by award-winning author Susan Herrmann Loomis. Her extremely popular classes focus on different French regions such as Normandy or the French Mediterranean, and cost from $575 per person per day.

Les Petits Farcis (www.petitsfarcis.com), run by Cordon Bleu–trained Canadian chef Rosa Jackson, offers tours of Nice's colorful produce market, followed by daylong gourmet cooking sessions. Prices begin at 200€ per person and include a four-course lunch with wine.

In Burgundy, **L'Ecole des Vins de Bourgogne** (www.ecoledes vins-bourgogne.com; ✆ **03-80-26-35-10**) in Beaune has courses ranging from 3 hours to 3 days for both novices and experts to learn about the region's wines. Or explore Beaune's traditional cuisine with American chef Marjorie Taylor and her daughter Kendall Smith Franchini at **The Cook's Atelier** (www.thecooksatelier.com; ✆ **03-80-24-61-80**). Classes range from A Day in Burgundy (495€) to the 5-day Burgundy Master Class (5,500€, not including accommodations).

In Bordeaux, **Wine Cab** (www.wine-cab.com) conducts behind-the-scenes tours around the city's top vineyards from the back of a decommissioned London black cab. The fleet former taxis ply the narrow lanes of the Médoc and around St-Emilion, with tasting tours starting at 280€ for two persons. (Or book a tour in one of their "deudeuche" instead, a classic Citroën 2CV.) **Uncorked Wine Tours** (www.uncorkedwinetours.com; ✆ 06-50-04-28-84) offers a wide range of options for getting the inside route into Bordeaux châteaux, courtesy of friendly Irish owner Caroline Matthews. **Grape Escapes** (www.grapeescapes.net; ✆ **44 (0) 1920 46 86 66** from the U.S.) offers a range of guided tours throughout many of France's most famous wine regions. Champagne enthusiasts can opt for the whirlwind "24 Champagnes in 24 Hours," priced from around $585 per person.

Last but not least, it's possible to join locals in their homes for meals and, sometimes, cooking demonstrations, through the web marketplace **EatWith.com.** It offers dozens of these experiences in every major city in France, but most especially in Paris. **Airbandb.com/Experiences** also has a number of food based tours and classes, but you'll want to read the reviews of them carefully before booking, as no entity is vetting these offerings for quality. On the plus side, these experiences tend to be significantly less expensive, and shorter in duration, than many of the ones we've listed above.

Guided Tours

BIKE TOURS Independent travelers can make use of a host of websites set up by the French government to encourage bicycle tourism, including **Loire à Vélo** (www.loireavelo.fr) and **La Provence à Vélo** (www.provence-a-velo.fr), as well as the more general **France Vélo Tourisme** (www.francevelotourisme.com). These websites give cyclists information on bike routes and rental options, as well as services that carry luggage, bike-friendly lodgings, and places to charge e-bikes. In general, independent bike tours will be less pricey than those listed below (but just as much fun!).

Some of the best guided cycling tours of France are offered by **Butterfield & Robinson** (www.butterfield.com; ✆ **866/551-9090**), which offers some 20 different trips through most scenic parts of France. Rides range from a gentle pedal among the Loire's châteaux or skirting Burgundy's legendary vineyards, to a more challenging exploration of the D-Day beaches. Prices start at $4,995 per person, with luxury accommodation and some gourmet meals thrown in.

Cycling for Softies (www.cycling-for-softies.co.uk; ✆ **020-3813-9204** in the U.K.) is ideal for easygoing travelers with little cycling experience. Tours—most of which are self-guided—cover much of France. Prices start at £895 per person for 4 nights; luxury accommodation, breakfasts, and a few gourmet dinners are included.

Fat Tire Bike Tours (http://paris.fattirebiketours.com; ✆ **01-82-88-80-96**) offers a 4-hour day or night tour of Paris by bike; adult tickets cost 39€. It also organizes cycling tours of Versailles.

SHOPPING TOURS   Paris is a dream come true for shopaholics. From flea markets and vintage threads to African fashion in the city or shopping with a stylist, **Airbnb Experiences** (www.airbnb.com/s/Paris-France/experiences) is your best bet for tours that fit your personal style. Tours are normally 2 to 3 hours and start around 45€ per person.

GETTING AROUND

Within most major cities—including Paris, Lyon, and Marseille—public transportation is efficient, comprehensive, and cheap. In smaller towns, such as Rouen, Arles, or Antibes, it's easy to navigate the city center on foot. Alternatively, download the Uber app to your phone for easy access to taxis. It works in many, but not all, cities throughout France.

By Plane

Air France (www.airfrance.com; ☎ **800/237-2747** in the U.S.), with its low-cost offshoot **Air France Hop,** is the country's primary carrier, serving around 30 cities in France and 30 more destinations throughout Europe. Air travel time from Paris to almost anywhere in France is about 1 hour. In 2023, to reduce carbon emissions, the French government banned any internal flights where train travel exists, and the journey takes less than 2 hours and 30 minutes. Few routes have been affected to date.

British Airways (www.ba.com) links London with Paris, Bordeaux, Chambery, Grenoble, Lyon, Marseille, Montpellier, Nantes, Strasbourg, Toulouse, and Nice. Low-cost airline **easyJet** (www.easyjet.com) also links London with a dozen French cities. The budget airline offers additional internal flights between Paris, Nantes, Toulouse, and Nice, and connects French cities to dozens of other European destinations.

By Car

The most charming châteaux and country hotels always seem to lie away from the main cities and train stations. Renting a car is a good way to travel around the French countryside, especially along the Normandy beaches, the Loire Valley, the vineyards of Bordeaux, and in rural Provence. Day car hire is inexpensive, so visitors may want to rent a vehicle just for a day en route if they wish.

Driving schedules in Europe are largely a matter of conjecture, urgency, and how much sightseeing you do along the way. Driving time is 2½ hours from Paris to Rouen, 3½ hours to Nantes, and 7 hours to anywhere in Provence.

RENTALS   To rent a car, you'll need to present a passport, a driver's license, and a credit card. You will also have to meet the company's minimum-age requirement: 21 or above at most rental agents. The biggest agencies have pickup spots all over France, including **Budget** (www.budget.com; ☎ **800/472-3325**), **Hertz** (www.hertz.com; ☎ **800/654-3001**), and **Europcar** (www.europcar.com; ☎ **877/940-6900**). We highly recommend **AutoSlash.com** over other online car rental services. It applies every available coupon on the market to the booking, yielding surprisingly low daily rates. If the cost of a rental drops, it automatically rebooks, again lowering the price.

Note: The best deals are always booked online, in advance. Though the rental company won't usually mind if you drive your car into, say, Germany, Switzerland, Italy, or Spain, it's often forbidden to transport your car by ferry, including across the Channel to England.

In France, **collision damage waiver (CDW)** is usually factored into the overall rate quoted, but you should always verify this before taking a car on the road. At most companies, the CDW provision won't protect you against theft, so if this is the case, ask about purchasing extra theft protection. Automatic transmission is a luxury in Europe. If you prefer it to stick-shift, you must specifically request it—and you'll pay a little extra for it.

GASOLINE   Known in France as *essence,* gas is expensive for those accustomed to North American prices, although the smaller cars common in Europe use far less gas. Depending on your car, you'll need either leaded (*avec plomb*) or unleaded (*sans plomb*).

Note: Sometimes you can drive for miles in rural France without encountering a gas station; don't let your tank get dangerously low.

DRIVING RULES   Everyone in the car, in both the front and the back seats, must wear seat belts. Children 10 and under must ride in the back seat.

In France, you drive on the right. Drivers are supposed to yield to the car on their right (*priorité a droite*), except where signs indicate otherwise, as at traffic circles. If you violate the speed limit, expect a big fine. Limits are 130kmph (80 mph) on expressways, 110kmph (68 mph) on major national highways, and 90kmph (55 mph) on country roads. In towns, don't exceed 50kmph (31 mph).

Note: It's illegal to use a cellphone while you're driving in France; you will be ticketed if you're stopped.

MAPS   While most French drivers are happy with Google Maps and to a lesser extent, Waze, traditional motorists opt for the large **Michelin maps** of the country and regions (www.viamichelin.com) on sale at all gas stations. GPS navigation devices can be rented at rental car agencies.

BREAKDOWNS/ASSISTANCE   A breakdown is called *une panne* in France. Call the police at ☎ **17** (if calling from a landline) or ☎ **112** (if calling from a mobile phone) anywhere in France to be put in touch with the nearest garage. Most local garages offer towing.

By Train

The world's fastest trains—known as *Train à Grande Vitesse,* or TGVs—link some 50 French cities, allowing you to travel from Paris to just about anywhere else in the country within hours. With 32,000km (20,000 miles) of track and 3,000 stations, **SNCF** (French National Railroads;

www.sncf.com or call ℭ **36-35**) is fabled for its on-time performance and comfy trains. You can travel in first or second class by day and couchette by night. Most trains have light dining facilities.

For information or reservations, go online (www.sncf-connect.com). You can also use your credit card to buy your ticket at the easy-to-use *billetteries* (ticket machines with an English-menu option) in every train station.

> ## OUIGO for Cheaper Train Tickets
>
> **OUIGO** (www.ouigo.com) is a subsidiary of SNCF that offers cheap TGV travel to 16 major cities, as well as a myriad of smaller destinations, throughout France. Flat-rate tickets start at 16€ per adult and 5€ per child. Taking a cue from Europe's low-cost airlines, OUIGO charges 5€ per piece of baggage larger than an airline carry on.

RAIL PASSES Rail passes as well as individual rail tickets are available from **Rail Europe** (www.raileurope.com). Options include a 5-day rail pass usable for a 1-month period in Second Class for $324. **Eurail** (www.eurail.com) offers regional rail passes throughout Europe, including a France pass for $198, allowing 4 days of travel within a 1-month period in Second Class. With advance planning of your route, these rail passes offer great savings as compared with booking individual tickets, especially for longer distances. Note that if you are traveling during high season, it's often worth paying that little bit more (around $10–$20 extra per travel day) to journey in the far less-crowded environs of First Class.

[FastFACTS] FRANCE

Business Hours Business hours in France can be erratic. Most banks are open Monday through Friday from 9:30am to 4:30pm. Many, particularly in small towns, take a long lunch break. Hours are usually posted on the door. Most museums close 1 day a week (often Tues), and they're generally closed on national holidays. Usual hours are from 9:30am to 5pm. In Paris or other big French cities, stores are open from around 10am to 6 or 7pm, with or without a lunch break (up to 2 hr.). Some shops, delis, cafes, and newsstands open at 8am and close at 8 or 9pm; restaurants often have two seatings, one for lunch (noon–2pm) and a second for dinner (usually 7–9pm), and close in between. Beware seasonal closings for many businesses in regions dependent on seasonal tourism, such as the coastal resorts and Alpine ski areas.

Customs & Etiquette French value pleasantries and take manners seriously: Say "Bonjour, Madame/Monsieur" when entering an establishment and "Au revoir" when you depart. Always say "Pardon" when you accidentally bump into someone. With strangers, people who are older than you and professional contacts use *vous* rather than *tu* (*vous* is the polite form of the pronoun *you*).

Disabled Travelers Facilities for travelers in France, and nearly all new or modern hotels, provide disabled access. The TGVs (high-speed trains) are wheelchair accessible; older trains have compartments for wheelchair boarding. If you visit the Paris tourist office website (www.paris jetaime.com) and click on "Accessible Paris," this section includes links to a number of websites dedicated to travelers with disabilities. There's also an extensive section detailing disabled-access to Paris public transport.

Doctors   Doctors are listed in the Pages Jaunes (Yellow Pages; www.pages jaunes.fr) under "Médecins: Médecins généralistes." The minimum fee for a consultation is about 35€—for this rate, look for a doctor who is described as "secteur 1." The higher the "secteur," the higher the fee. **SOS Médecins** (www.sosmedecins.fr; ☏ **36-24**) can make house calls. See also "Emergencies" and "Health," later in this section.

Drinking Laws   As well as bars and restaurants, supermarkets, and cafes sell alcoholic beverages. The legal drinking age is 18, but persons under that age can be served alcohol if accompanied by a parent or guardian. Drinking and driving is illegal and incurs a heavy fine. You can drink in public, but you cannot be drunk in public. Local laws may prohibit drinking at certain times or in certain places.

Electricity   Electricity in France runs on 220 volts AC (60 cycles). Adapters or transformers are needed to fit sockets, which you can buy in branches of Darty or Fnac.

Emergencies   In an emergency while at a hotel, contact the front desk. If the emergency involves theft, go to the police station in person. Otherwise, call ☏ **112**

from a cellphone. The fire brigade can be reached at ☏ **18.** For an ambulance, call ☏ **15.** For the police, call ☏ **17.** SOS Help is a hotline for English-speaking callers in crisis ☏ **01-46-21-46-46** (www.soshelpline. org; open 3–11pm daily).

Health   For travel abroad, non-E.U. nationals should consider buying medical travel insurance. For U.S. citizens, Medicare and Medicaid do not provide coverage for medical costs incurred abroad; check your health insurance before leaving home. France offers some of the best healthcare on the planet, so you won't need evacuation insurance. To compare policies, go to an insurance marketplace site like **TravelInsurance. com** or **SquareMouth.com.** U.K. nationals need a **European Health Insurance Card** (**EHIC;** www.ehic.org. uk) to receive free or reduced-cost medical care during a visit to France. If you take regular medication, pack it in its original pharmacy containers, along with a copy of your prescription.

Holidays   Major public holidays are New Year's Day (Jan 1), Easter Sunday and Monday (late Mar/Apr), Labor Day (May 1), VE Day (May 8), Ascension Thursday (40 days after Easter), Pentecost/Whit Sunday and Whit Monday (seventh Sun/Mon after Easter), Bastille Day (July 14), Assumption Day (Aug 15), All Saints' Day (Nov 1), Armistice Day (Nov 11), and Christmas Day (Dec 25).

Hospitals   Dial ☏ **15** for medical emergencies.

LGBTQ+ Travelers   In general, France is a welcoming place for LGBTQ+ travelers. Bear in mind that occasionally you may find that small towns foster a small-town mentality, but this is not the case for the majority of the country. Most cities in France—in particular Paris and Nice—boast a large LGBTQ+ population, with various club nights, restaurants, organizations, and services. For books and local information in Paris, visit **Les Mots à la Bouche,** 37 rue Saint-Ambroise, 11e (www.motsbouche.com; ☏ **01-42-78-88-30;** Métro: Rue Saint Maur). The Paris Tourist Office (www.paris jetaime.com) also hosts a dedicated list of perennially popular LGBTQ+ bars and clubs on their website, while www.gayvox.fr has updated listings about LGBTQ+ issues throughout France.

Mail   Most post offices in France are open Monday to Friday from 8am to 5pm and every Saturday from 8am to noon. A **24-hour post office** is located in Paris at 52 rue du Louvre 1e (☏ **36-31**). Allow 5 to 8 days to send or receive mail from home. Stamps are also sold in *tabacs* (tobacconists). For more information, see www.laposte.fr.

Mobile Phones   You can use your mobile phone in France, provided it is **GSM** (Global System for Mobile Communications) and triband or quad-band;

just confirm with your operator before you leave.

Using your phone abroad can be expensive. Check with your provider before travelling for a clear idea as to what your roaming package includes. Alternatively, it may be a good idea to get your phone "unlocked" before you leave. This means you can buy a French SIM card from one of the three main French providers, **Bouygues Télécom** (www.bouygues telecom.fr), **Orange** (www.orange.fr), or **SFR** (www.sfr.fr). Or do like the locals do and use **WhatsApp** (www.whatsapp.com) for long-distance calls.

Money & Costs
Frommer's lists exact prices in the local currency. The currency conversions quoted here were correct at press time. However, rates fluctuate, so before departing, consult a currency exchange website such as www.xe.com to check current rates.

It's always advisable to bring a mix of cash and credit cards on vacation. Before you leave home, exchange enough petty cash to cover airport incidentals, tipping, and transportation to your hotel. In many international destinations, ATMs offer the best exchange rates. Avoid exchanging money at commercial exchange bureaus, airports, and hotels, which often have the highest transaction fees and terrible exchange rates. ATMs are widely available in France.

Newspapers
The most popular French newspapers are **Le Monde** (www.le monde.fr), **Le Figaro** (www.lefigaro.fr), and left-leaning **Libération** (www.liberation.fr).

The **International New York Times** (www.nytimes.com) has a key office in Paris. Published from Monday to Saturday, it is distributed all over France.

Pharmacies
Spot French *pharmacies* by the green neon cross above the door. If your local pharmacy is closed, a sign on the door should indicate the nearest one open. Alternatively, **Pharmacies de Garde** (www.pharmaciedegarde.co or www.3237.fr; ✆ **32-37**) can direct you to the nearest open pharmacy.

Police
In an emergency, call ✆ **17** (from a land-line) or **112** (from a cell phone) anywhere in France.

Safety
The most common menace, especially in large cities, is the plague of *pickpockets*. Take precautions and be vigilant at all times: Don't take more money with you than necessary, keep your passport in a concealed pouch or leave it at your hotel, and ensure that your bag is firmly closed at all times. In cafes, bars, and restaurants, it's best not to leave your bag under the table, on the back of your chair, or on an empty chair beside you. Keep it between your legs or on your lap. Never leave valuables or luggage in a car, and never travel with your car unlocked.

In general, the major cities of France are safe, and it's safe to use public transportation in them at night, though it is always best to not drawn attention to the fact you are foreign by speaking loudly in English. Use common sense when taking public transport at night.

Although there is a significant level of discrimination against West and North African immigrants, there has been almost no harassment of African-American tourists to Paris or France itself in recent decades. However, **S.O.S. Racisme,** 51 av. de Flandre, 19e (www.sos-racisme.org; ✆ **01-40-35-36-55**), offers legal advice to victims of prejudice and will even intervene to help with the police.

Female travelers should not expect any more hassle than in other countries, and the same precautions apply.

THE VALUE OF THE EURO VS. OTHER POPULAR CURRENCIES

Euro (€)	US$	C$	UK£	A$	NZ$
1	1.08	1.47	0.86	1.67	1.81

Avoid walking alone at night and never get into an unmarked taxi. If you are approached in the street or on public transportation, it's best to avoid entering into conversation, and walk into a well-lit, populated area.

Senior Travel Many discounts are available to adults over 65. Visiting senior citizens do not get a discount for traveling on public transport in most major cities, but national trains have senior discounts. Check out www.sncf-connect.com for more information. From-mers.com also offers more information and resources on travel for seniors.

Smoking Smoking is banned in all public places in France, including cafes, restaurants, and nightclubs. It's permitted on outdoor and semi-enclosed terraces.

Student Travel Student discounts are less common in France than in other countries, simply because young people under 26 are usually offered reduced rates. Be on the lookout for the **Navigo Jeunes Week-end** when using the Métro in Paris. It can be used on a Saturday, Sunday, or bank holiday, and provides unlimited travel in zones 1 to 3 for 4.60€. SNCF also offer discounts for under-26-year-olds traveling on national trains (www.sncf-connect.com).

Taxes As a member of the European Union, France routinely imposes a value-added tax (VAT in English; TVA in French) on most goods. The standard VAT is 20%, and prices that include

it are often marked TTC (*toutes taxes comprises,* "all taxes included"). If you're not an E.U. resident, you can get a VAT refund if you're spending less than 6 months in France, you purchase goods worth more than 100€, purchased at a single shop on the same day, the goods fit into your luggage, and the shop offers *vente en détaxe* (duty-free sales or tax-free shopping). Give them your passport and ask for a *bordereau de détaxe* (export sales invoice). When you leave the country, you need to get this invoice validated by France's Customs officials. Present this document plus your passport at the tax refund desk (whether at the airport, train station, or port) for an immediate VAT refund.

Telephones The country code for France is **33.** To make a local or long-distance call within France, dial the person or place's 10-digit number. If you're calling from outside of France, drop the initial 0 (zero).

Mobile numbers begin with 06 or 07. Numbers beginning with 0-800, 0-804, 0-805, and 0-809 are free in France; other numbers beginning with 8 are not. Most four-digit numbers starting with 10, 30, and 31 are free of charge.

Time France is on Central European Time, which is 1 hour ahead of Greenwich Mean Time. French daylight savings time lasts from the last Sunday in March to the last Sunday in October, when clocks are set 1 hour ahead of the standard time.

France uses the 24-hour clock (so 13h is 1pm, 14h15 is 2:15pm, and so on).

Tipping By law, all bills in **cafes, bars,** and **restaurants** say *service compris,* which means the service charge is included. However, it is customary to leave 1€ or 2€, depending on the quality of the service; in more upscale restaurants leave 5€ to 10€. **Taxi drivers** usually expect a 5% to 10% tip, or for the fare to be rounded up to the next euro. The French tip **hairdressers** around 15%, and if you go to the theater, you're expected to tip the **usher** about 2€.

Toilets If you're in dire need, duck into a cafe or brasserie to use the lavatory. It's customary to make a small purchase if you do so. Paris is full of gray-colored automatic street toilets, some of which are free to use, and are washed and disinfected after each use. France still has some hole-in-the-ground squat toilets. Try not to lose your change down the pan!

Visitor Information Before you go, your best source of information is the **French Government Tourist Office** (www.france.fr/en).

Water Drinking water is generally safe. If you ask for water in a restaurant, it'll be served bottled (for which you'll pay), unless you specifically request *une carafe d'eau* or *l'eau du robinet* (tap water). Your waiter may ask if you'd like your water *avec gas* (carbonated) or *sans gas* (without bubbles).

TURNING TO THE internet or apps FOR A HOTEL DISCOUNT

It's not impossible to get a good deal by calling a hotel, but you're more likely to snag a discount online and with an app. Here are some strategies:

1. Browse extreme discounts on sites where you reserve or bid for lodgings without knowing which hotel you'll get. You'll find these on **Priceline. com** and **Hotwire.com,** and they can be money-savers, particularly if you're booking within a week of travel (that's when the hotels get nervous and resort to deep discounts). These feature major chains, so it's unlikely you'll book a dump.

2. Review discounts on the hotel's website. Hotels often give the lowest rates to those who book through their sites rather than through a third party. But you'll only find these truly deep discounts in the loyalty section of these sites—so join the club.

3. Use the right hotel search engine. They're not all equal, as we

at Frommers.com learned after putting the top 20 sites to the test in 20 destinations around the globe. We discovered that **HotelsCombined. com** listed the lowest rates for hotels in the city center, and in the under $200 range, 16 out of 20 times—the best record, by far, of all the sites we tested. And Booking.com includes all taxes and fees in its initial results (not all do, which can make for a frustrating shopping experience).

4. Consider joining a travel club for very deep discounts. Some, like the one run by **Travel + Leisure** have a hefty membership fee, but since the discounts start at 25%, and regularly go as high as 50%, you may be able to make back your initial investment. **@Hotel** is a private club without membership fee, that can be accessed on Instagram. It, too, has remarkably deep discounts.

GLOSSARY OF FRENCH-LANGUAGE TERMS

A word or two of halting French will often change your hosts' dispositions in their home country. Try to learn at least a few numbers, basic greetings, and—above all—the life raft, *"Parlez-vous anglais?"* Many French speak passable English and will use it liberally if you demonstrate the basic courtesy of greeting them in their language. Go on, try our glossary, and don't be bashful. *Bonne chance!*

BASICS

English	French	Pronunciation
Yes/No	Oui/Non	**wee/nohn**
Okay	D'accord	**dah-*core***
Please	S'il vous plaît	**seel voo *play***
Thank you	Merci	**mair-*see***

English	French	Pronunciation
You're welcome	De rien	**duh ree-*ehn***
Hello (during daylight hours)	Bonjour	**bohn-*jhoor***
Good evening	Bonsoir	**bohn-*swahr***
Goodbye	Au revoir	**o ruh-*vwahr***
What's your name?	Comment vous appellez-vous?	**ko-*mahn* voo za-pell-ay-*voo*?**
My name is . . .	Je m'appelle . . .	**jhuh ma-*pell* . . .**
Happy to meet you	Enchanté(e)	**ohn-shahn-*tay***
Miss	Mademoiselle	**mad-mwa-*zel***
Mr.	Monsieur	**muh-*syuh***
Mrs.	Madame	**ma-*dam***
How are you?	Comment allez-vous?	**ko-mahn tahl-ay-*voo*?**
Fine, thank you, and you?	Très bien, merci, et vous?	**tray bee-*ehn*, mair-*see*, ay voo?**
Very well, thank you	Très bien, merci	**tray bee-*ehn*, mair-*see***
So-so	Comme ci, comme ça	**kum-*see*, kum-*sah***
I'm sorry/excuse me	Pardon	**pahr-*dohn***
I'm so very sorry	Désolé(e)	**day-zoh-*lay***
That's all right	Il n'y a pas de quoi	**eel nee ah pah duh kwah**

GETTING AROUND/STREET SMARTS

English	French	Pronunciation
Do you speak English?	Parlez-vous anglais?	**par-lay-voo ahn-*glay*?**
I don't speak French	Je ne parle pas français	**jhuh ne parl pah frahn-*say***
I don't understand	Je ne comprends pas	**jhuh ne kohm-*prahn* pas**
Could you speak more loudly/more slowly?	Pouvez-vous parler un peu plus fort/plus lentement?	**poo-vay-voo par-lay un puh ploo for/ploo lan-te-*ment*?**
Could you repeat that?	Répetez, s'il vous plaît?	**ray-pay-*tay*, seel voo *play***
What is it?	Qu'est-ce que c'est?	**kess kuh *say*?**
What time is it?	Qu'elle heure est-il?	**kel uhr eh-*teel*?**
What?	Quoi?	**kwah?**
How? or What did you say?	Comment?	**ko-*mahn*?**
When?	Quand?	**kahn?**
Where is . . . ?	Où est . . . ?	**ooh eh . . . ?**
Who?	Qui?	**kee?**
Why?	Pourquoi?	**poor-*kwah*?**
Here/there	ici/là	**ee-*see*/lah**
Left/right	à gauche/à droite	**a goash/a drwaht**
Straight ahead	tout droit	**too drwah**
I'm American/Canadian/British	Je suis américain(e)/canadien(e)/anglais(e)	**jhe sweez a-may-ree-*kehn*/can-ah-dee-*en*/ahn-glay (*glaise*)**

English	French	Pronunciation
Fill the tank (of a car), please	Le plein, s'il vous plait	**luh plan, seel voo play**
I'm going to . . .	Je vais à . . .	**jhe vay ah . . .**
I want to get off at . . .	Je voudrais descendre à . . .	**jhe voo-dray day-son-drah ah**
I'm sick	Je suis malade	**jhuh swee mal-ahd**
airport	l'aéroport	**lair-o-por**
bank	la banque	**lah bahnk**
bridge	pont	**pohn**
bus station	la gare routière	**lah gar roo-tee-air**
bus stop	l'arrêt de bus	**lah-ray duh boohss**
by means of a bicycle	en vélo/par bicyclette	**ahn vay-low/par bee-see-clet**
by means of a car	en voiture	**ahn vwa-toor**
cashier	la caisse	**lah kess**
cathedral	cathédral	**ka-tay-dral**
church	église	**ay-gleez**
dead end	une impasse	**ewn am-pass**
driver's license	permis de conduire	**per-mee duh con-dweer**
elevator	l'ascenseur	**lah-sahn-seuhr**
stairs	l'escalier	**les-kal-yay**
entrance (to a building or a city)	une porte	**ewn port**
exit (from a building or a freeway)	une sortie	**ewn sor-tee**
fortified castle or palace	château	**sha-tow**
garden	jardin	**jhar-dehn**
gasoline	du pétrol/de l'essence	**duh pay-trol/de lay-sahns**
highway to . . .	la route pour	**la root por**
hospital	l'hôpital	**low-pee-tahl**
museum	le musée	**luh mew-zay**
no entry	sens interdit	**sehns ahn-ter-dee**
no smoking	défense de fumer	**day-fahns de fu-may**
on foot	à pied	**ah pee-ay**
one-day pass	ticket journalier	**tee-kay jhoor-nall-ee-ay**
one-way ticket	aller simple	**ah-lay sam-pluh**
police	la police	**lah po-lees**
rented car	voiture de location	**vwa-toor de low-ka-see-on**
round-trip ticket	aller-retour	**ah-lay-re-toor**
slow down	ralentir	**rah-lahn-teer**
store	le magasin	**luh ma-ga-zehn**
street	rue	**roo**
subway	le Métro	**le may-tro**
telephone	le téléphone	**luh tay-lay-phone**
ticket	un billet	**uh bee-yay**
ticket office	vente de billets	**vahnt duh bee-yay**
toilets	les toilettes/les WC	**lay twa-lets/lay vay-say**

BASICS

English	French	Pronunciation
I'd like . . .	Je voudrais . . .	**jhe voo-*dray* . . .**
a room	une chambre	**ewn *shahm*-bruh**
the key	la clé (la clef)	**la *clay***
I'd like to buy . . .	Je voudrais acheter . . .	**jhe voo-dray ahsh-*tay* . . .**
aspirin	des aspirines/des aspros	**deyz ahs-peer-*eens*/ deyz ahs-*prohs***
condoms	des préservatifs	**day pray-ser-va-*teefs***
dictionary	un dictionnaire	**uh deek-see-oh-*nare***
dress	une robe	**ewn robe**
envelopes	des envelopes	**days ahn-veh-*lope***
gift (for someone)	un cadeau	**uh kah-*doe***
handbag	un sac	**uh sahk**
hat	un chapeau	**uh shah-*poh***
magazine	une revue	**ewn reh-*vu***
map of the city	un plan de ville	**unh plahn de *veel***
matches	des allumettes	**dayz a-loo-*met***
necktie	une cravate	**eun cra-*vaht***
newspaper	un journal	**uh jhoor-*nahl***
postcard	une carte postale	**ewn carte pos-*tahl***
road map	une carte routière	**ewn cart roo-tee-*air***
shirt	une chemise	**ewn che-*meez***
shoes	des chaussures	**day show-*suhr***
skirt	une jupe	**ewn jhoop**
soap	du savon	**dew sah-*vohn***
socks	des chaussettes	**day show-*set***
stamp	un timbre	**uh *tam*-bruh**
trousers	un pantalon	**uh pan-tah-*lohn***
writing paper	du papier à lettres	**dew pap-pee-ay a *let*-ruh**
How much does it cost?	C'est combien?/Ça coûte combien?	**say comb-bee-*ehn*?/sah coot comb-bee-*ehn*?**
Do you take credit cards?	Est-ce que vous acceptez les cartes de credit?	**es-kuh voo zaksep-*tay* lay kart duh creh-*dee*?**

NUMBERS & ORDINALS

English	French	Pronunciation
zero	zéro	**zare-*oh***
one	un	**uh**
two	deux	**duh**
three	trois	**twah**
four	quatre	***kaht*-ruh**
five	cinq	**sank**

English	French	Pronunciation
six	six	**seess**
seven	sept	**set**
eight	huit	**wheat**
nine	neuf	**nuf**
ten	dix	**deess**
eleven	onze	**ohnz**
twelve	douze	**dooz**
thirteen	treize	**trehz**
fourteen	quatorze	**kah-*torz***
fifteen	quinze	**kanz**
sixteen	seize	**sez**
seventeen	dix-sept	**deez-*set***
eighteen	dix-huit	**deez-*wheat***
nineteen	dix-neuf	**deez-*nuf***
twenty	vingt	**vehn**
twenty-one	vingt-et-un	**vehnt-ay-*uh***
twenty-two	vingt-deux	**vehnt-*duh***
thirty	trente	**trahnt**
forty	quarante	**ka-*rahnt***
fifty	cinquante	**sang-*kahnt***
sixty	soixante	**swa-*sahnt***
sixty-one	soixante-et-un	**swa-*sahnt*-et-*uh***
seventy	soixante-dix	**swa-sahnt-*deess***
seventy-one	soixante-et-onze	**swa-sahnt-et-*ohnze***
eighty	quatre-vingts	**kaht-ruh-*vehn***
eighty-one	quatre-vingt-un	**kaht-ruh-vehn-*uh***
ninety	quatre-vingt-dix	**kaht-ruh-venh-*deess***
ninety-one	quatre-vingt-onze	**kaht-ruh-venh-*ohnze***
one hundred	cent	**sahn**
one thousand	mille	**meel**
one hundred thousand	cent mille	**sahn meel**
first	premier	***preh*-mee-ay**
second	deuxième	***duhz*-zee-em**
third	troisième	***twa*-zee-em**
tenth	dixième	***dees*-ee-em**
twentieth	vingtième	***vehnt*-ee-em**
thirtieth	trentième	***trahnt*-ee-em**
one-hundredth	centième	***sant*-ee-em**

THE CALENDAR

English	French	Pronunciation
Sunday	dimanche	**dee-*mahnsh***
Monday	lundi	***luhn*-dee**
Tuesday	mardi	***mahr*-dee**
Wednesday	mercredi	***mair*-kruh-dee**
Thursday	jeudi	***jheu*-dee**
Friday	vendredi	***vawn*-druh-dee**
Saturday	samedi	***sahm*-dee**
yesterday	hier	**ee-*air***
today	aujourd'hui	**o-jhord-*dwee***
this morning/this afternoon	ce matin/cet après-midi	**suh ma-*tan*/set ah-preh-mee-*dee***
tonight	ce soir	**suh *swahr***
tomorrow	demain	**de-*man***

GLOSSARY OF BASIC MENU TERMS

Note: To order any of these items from a waiter, simply preface the French-language name with the phrase *"Je voudrais"* (jhe voo-*dray*), which means "I would like. . . ." *Bon appétit!*

MEATS

English	French	Pronunciation
beef stew	du pot au feu	**dew poht o *fhe***
beef braised with red wine	du boeuf à la mode	**dew bewf ah lah *mhowd***
chicken	du poulet	***dew poo*-lay**
chicken, veal, or fish rolls	des quenelles	**day ke-*nelle***
chicken with mushrooms and wine	du coq au vin	**dew cock o vhin**
frogs' legs	des cuisses de grenouilles	**day cweess duh gre-*noo*-yuh**
ham	du jambon	**dew jham-bohn**
kidneys	des rognons	**day *row*-nyon**
lamb	de l'agneau	**duh lahn-*nyo***
rabbit	du lapin	**dew lah-pan**
sirloin	de l'aloyau	**duh lahl-why-*yo***
steak	du bifteck	**dew beef-*tek***
pepper steak	un steak au poivre	**uh stake o *pwah*-vruh**
beef tenderloin	du chateaubriand	**dew *sha*-tow-bree-ahn**
sweetbreads	des ris de veau	**day *ree* duh voh**
veal	du veau	**dew *voh***

FRUITS/VEGETABLES

English	French	Pronunciation
cabbage	du choux	**dew *shoe***
eggplant	de l'aubergine	**duh loh-ber-*jheen***
grapefruit	un pamplemousse	**uh *pahm*-pluh-moose**
grapes	du raisin	**dew ray-*zhan***
green beans	des haricots verts	**day ahr-ee-coh *vaire***
green peas	des petits pois	**day puh-tee *pwah***
lemon/lime	du citron/du citron vert	**dew cee-*tron*/dew cee-tron *vaire***
orange	une orange	**ewn o-*rahnj***
pineapple	de l'ananas	**duh lah-na-*nas***
potatoes	des pommes de terre	**day puhm duh *tehr***
french fried potatoes	des pommes frites	**day puhm *freet***
spinach	des épinards	**dayz ay-pin-*ards***
strawberries	des fraises	**day *frez***

BEVERAGES

English	French	Pronunciation
beer	de la bière	**duh lah bee-*aire***
milk	du lait	**dew *lay***
orange juice	du jus d'orange	**dew joo d'or-*ahn*-jhe**
water	de l'eau	**duh *lo***
red wine	du vin rouge	**dew vhin *rooj***
white wine	du vin blanc	**dew vhin *blahn***
coffee	un café	**uh ka-*fay***
coffee (black)	un café noir	**uh ka-fay *nwahr***
coffee (with cream)	un café crème	**uh ka-fay *krem***
coffee (with milk)	un café au lait	**uh ka-fay o *lay***
coffee (decaf)	un café décaféiné (slang: un déca)	**un ka-fay day-kah-fay-*nay* (uh *day*-kah)**
coffee (espresso)	un café espresso (un express)	**uh ka-fay e-*sprehss*-o (un ek-*sprehss*)**
tea	du thé	**dew *tay***

Index

Restaurants

PHOTO CREDITS